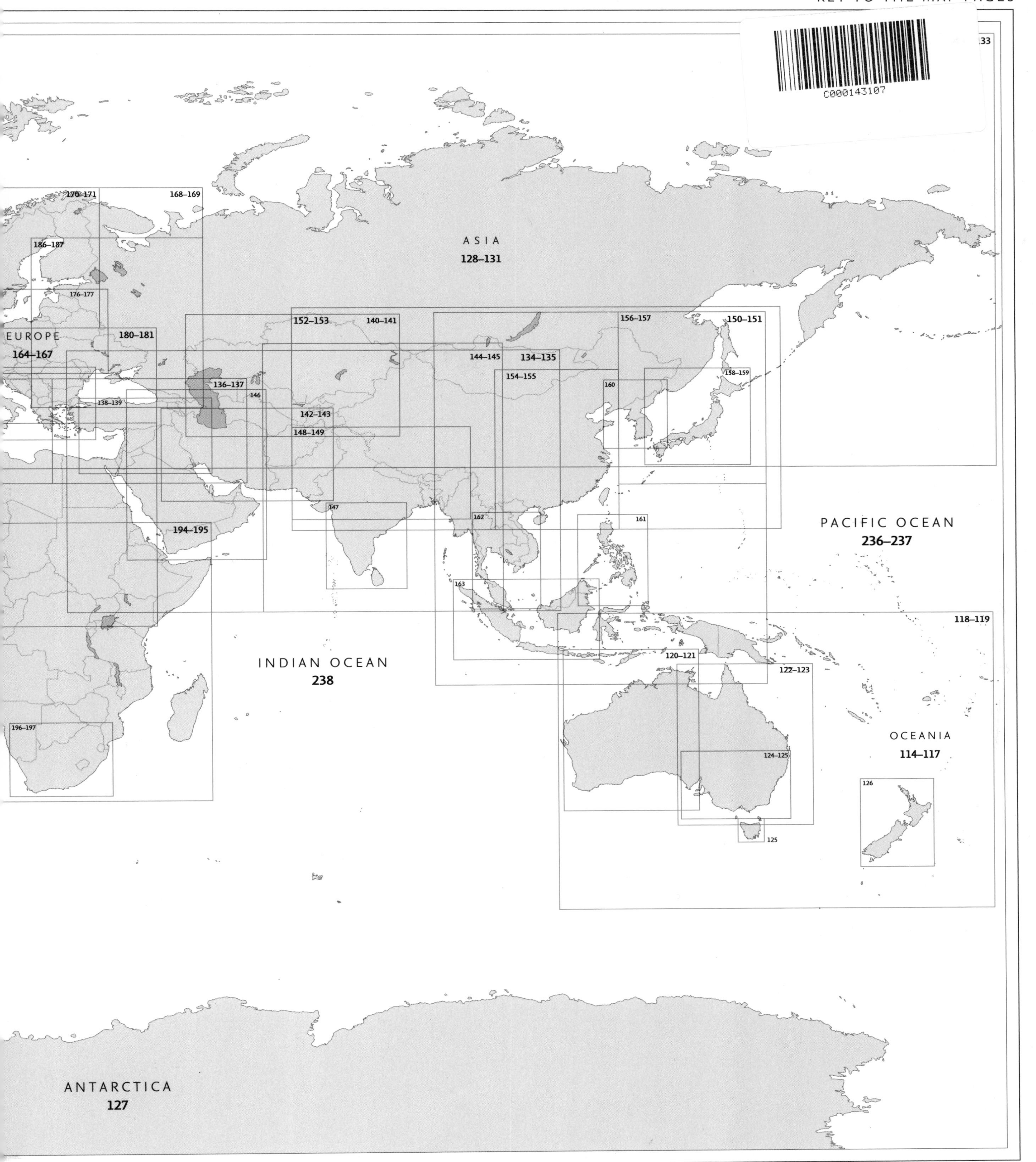

33

ASIA
128–131

170–171   168–169

186–187

176–177

EUROPE   180–181   152–153   140–141   156–157   150–151
164–167
                                            144–145   134–135   158–159
                        136–137   154–155
138–139   146   160
                              142–143
                              148–149

                                            147   162   161

                        194–195   PACIFIC OCEAN
                                                                                                    236–237

                                                                                            118–119

        INDIAN OCEAN   120–121
            238   122–123

                                                                                        OCEANIA
196–197   114–117

                                                                        124–125   126

                                                                        125

ANTARCTICA
    127

To, My big cousin myles

Love from, Ethan

I thought you could see where
we could go on holiday when
we are older
x x

Traveller's World Atlas

Collins Traveller's World Atlas

Collins
An imprint of HarperCollins Publishers
77-85 Fulham Palace Road London W6 8JB

First Published 2010

Copyright © HarperCollins Publishers 2010
Maps © Collins Bartholomew Ltd 2010

Collins ® is a registered trademark of
HarperCollins Publishers Ltd

Printed in Thailand by Imago

British Library Cataloguing in Publication Data
A catalogue record for this book is available from the British Library

ISBN 978 0 00 737184 6

Imp 001

All mapping in this atlas is generated from
Collins Bartholomew digital databases.

Collins Bartholomew, the UK's leading independent geographical
information supplier, can provide a digital, custom,
and premium mapping service to a variety of markets.
For further information:
Tel: +44 (0) 141 306 3752

e-mail: collinsbartholomew@harpercollins.co.uk
or visit our website at: www.collinsbartholomew.com

Cover image: © Philip and Karen Smith / Getty

More mapping online at
www.collinsmaps.com

Collins
Traveller's World Atlas

DISCOVER THE WORLD THROUGH MAPS

Contents

Oceania

The continent of Oceania comprises Australia, New Guinea, New Zealand and the islands of the Pacific Ocean. The main Pacific island groups of Melanesia, Micronesia and Polynesia sit among the complex of ridges and troughs which make up the Pacific sea floor. Notable among these, and visible extending northwards from New Zealand, are the Kermadec and Tonga trenches – the latter reaching a depth of 10 800 m at Horizon Deep. Australia itself appears largely dry and barren, its vast interior consisting of several deserts, with brighter salt lakes in the low artesian basin of the east central area. The east coast of Australia, separated from the interior by the Great Dividing Range – the source of the continent's longest rivers the Murray and the Darling – is more densely vegetated. New Guinea is covered by dense tropical forest, while New Zealand displays a great variety of land cover types, most prominent being the snow-capped Southern Alps on South Island.

Ring of Fire

This image shows the western portion of the 'Ring of Fire' – the 35 000 km boundary between the Pacific oceanic crustal plate and its neighbouring continental plates which is characterized by the frequent occurrence of earthquakes and volcanoes. Approximately 70 per cent of historically recorded active volcanoes have occurred within this belt. The ocean floor topography reveals the plate boundaries running north from New Zealand, through the islands of the West Pacific, eastern Indonesia, the Philippines and Japan. In the far northeast of the image, the remarkable Hawaiian-Emperor chain of volcanic islands is visible. Over 5800 km long, this chain of islands has formed over the last 70 million years as the Pacific plate has moved across an area of high volcanic activity known as a hotspot. This has created a chain of volcanoes which get progressively younger and higher in elevation towards the southeast. The island of Hawaii is the most recent addition to the chain with active volcanoes Mauna Loa and Kilauea.

Australian Deserts

Australia is the driest inhabited continent on earth, 70 per cent of it is arid or semi-arid. Deserts occupy 30 per cent of land, mainly on the western plateau and the interior lowlands. The orange area near the centre of the country is the Simpson Desert where the world's longest parallel sand dunes run for hundreds of kilometres. The light yellow area to the southeast of this is the inhospitable area of the Tirari, Strzelecki and Sturt Stony Deserts. Salt lakes occur in many lowland areas. The largest is Lake Eyre, its dry lake bed appearing white on the image. Until recently, Lake Eyre was thought to be permanently dry. In the last forty years, however, it has been spectacularly filled several times, becoming, temporarily, Australia's largest lake.

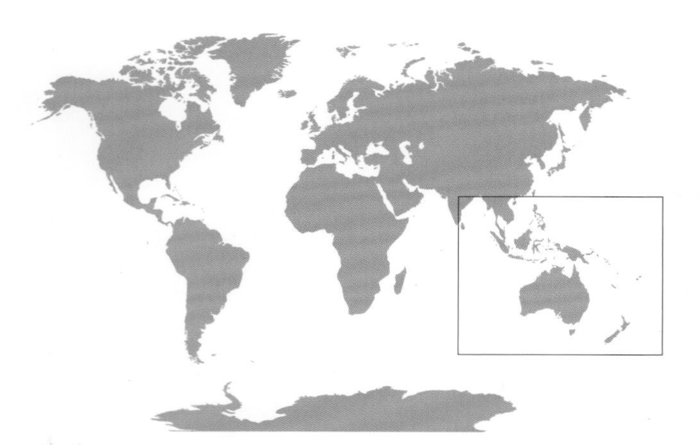

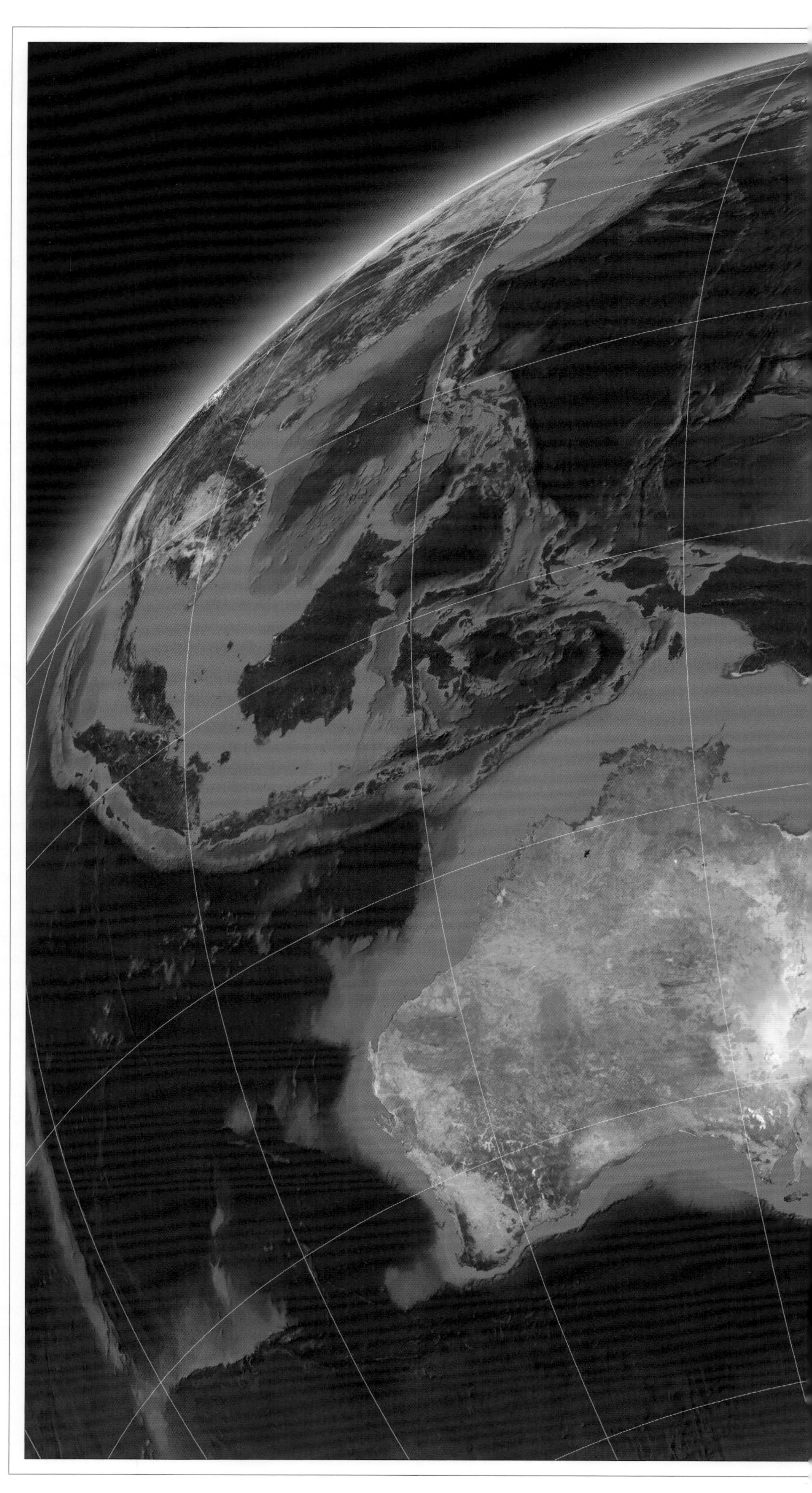

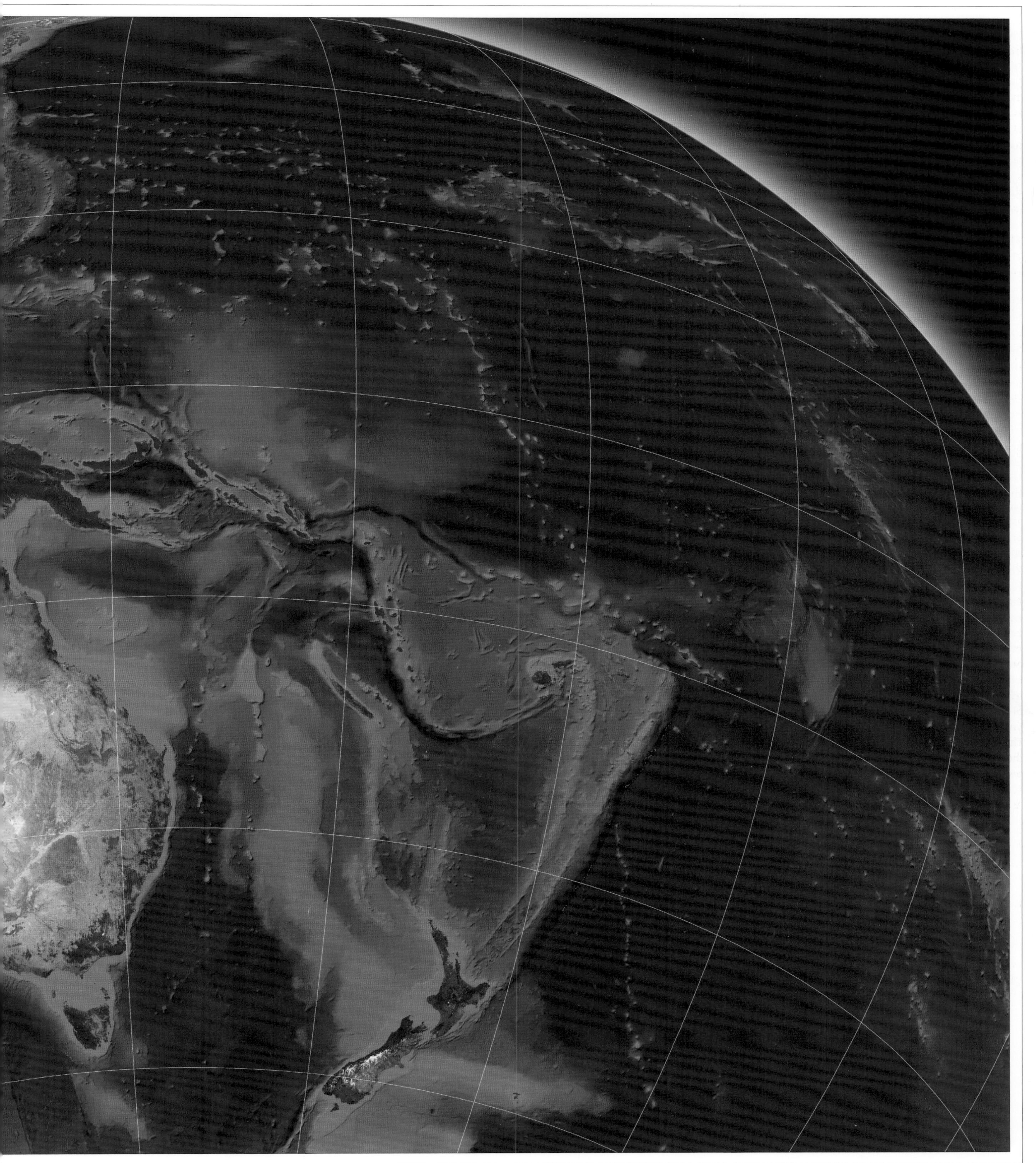

7

Asia

This vast continent – the world's largest – covers an enormous area and contains a great variety of landscapes, evident on this image. It stretches from the Mediterranean Sea in the west to the far east of the Russian Federation and Japan, and from arctic Siberia in the north to the tropical islands of Indonesia. The Caspian Sea – the world's largest lake – is prominent in the west. The snow-capped Caucasus mountains stretching from the Caspian Sea to the Black Sea clearly mark the divide between Asia and Europe. Just east of the Caspian Sea lies the complex shape of the Aral Sea. This was once the world's fourth largest lake, but is now drastically reduced in size because of climate change and the extraction of water for irrigation.

The Himalaya

The great Asian mountain system of the Himalaya can be seen as a snow-covered arc on the image as it stretches for over 2000 km in a series of parallel ridges from the Ganges basin in the east to the Plateau of Tibet in the west. Formed 25–70 million years ago, as the earth's crust folded due to the northward push of the Indian subcontinent, the system is still growing and is subject to severe earthquakes. All fourteen of the world's peaks above 8000 m are found in the Himalaya and adjoining ranges. The main range, in which the highest peaks are found, is permanently snow-covered and there are extensive glaciers which give rise to the Indian subcontinent's major rivers. The image clearly shows the contrast between the aridity of the Plateau of Tibet and the Tarim Basin to the north, shown in yellow tones in this image, and the more vegetated land to the south, appearing green-brown. This is a result of the interception of the moisture-laden monsoon weather system by the south-facing slopes of the Himalaya.

Rivers of Bangladesh

The courses and confluence of the Ganges and Brahmaputra Rivers can be seen in the centre of the image. Bangladesh, the country in which they meet, is dominated by rivers and, as most of the country lies less than 110 m above sea level, is prone to flooding. Many of India's largest cities lie in the valley of the Ganges where its flood plains support over 8 per cent of the world's population. The Ganges, considered sacred by Hindus, discharges into the Bay of Bengal, nearly 2500 km downstream from its source in the Gangotri Glacier in the Himalaya. It carries with it 2 billion tons of sediment every year which has led to the formation of the world's largest river delta. Dense wetland forests, known as the Sundarbans, grow along the coast and appear as a dark green strip on this image.

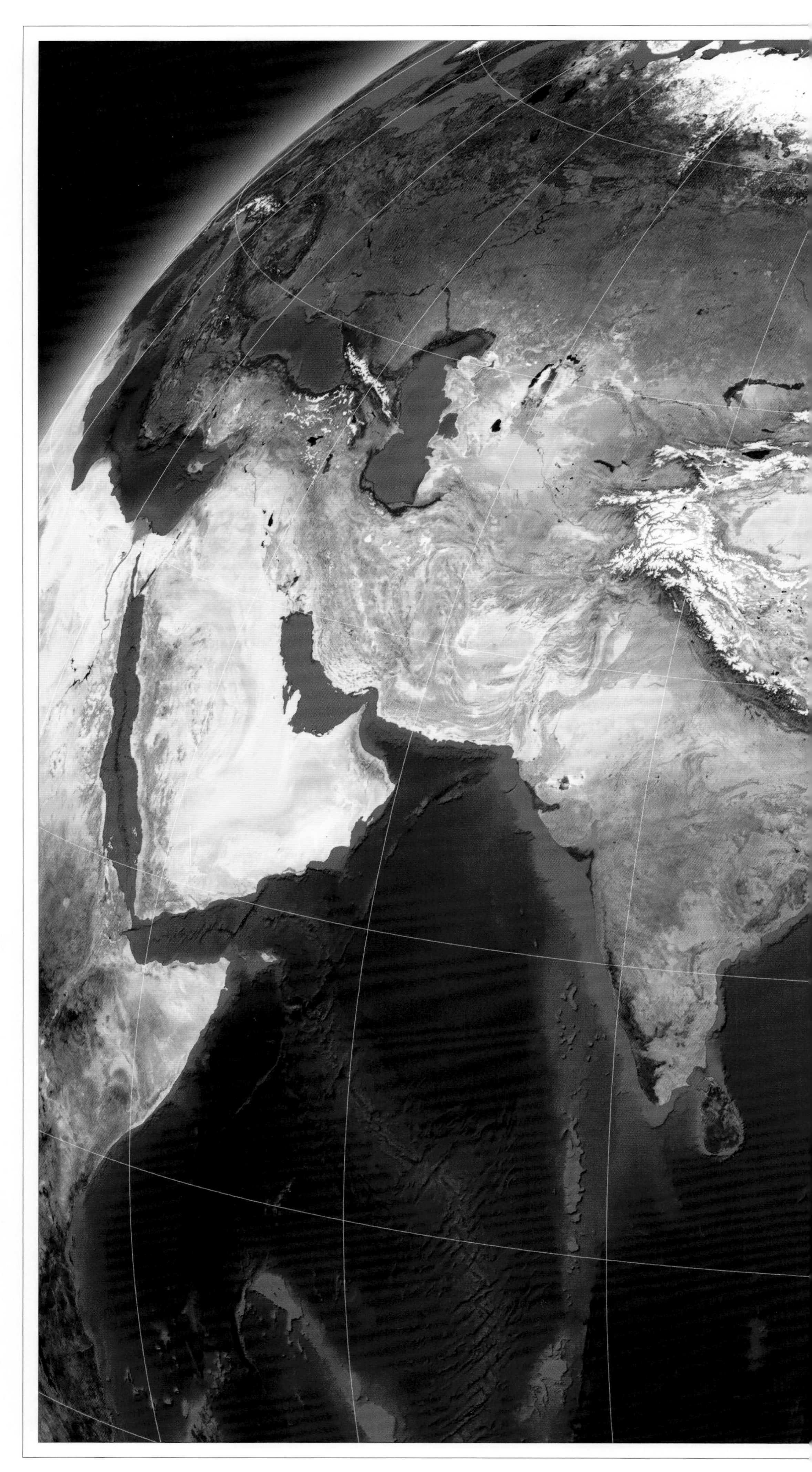

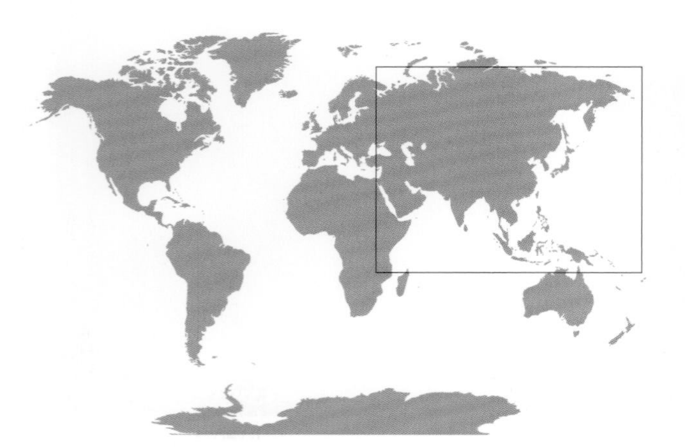

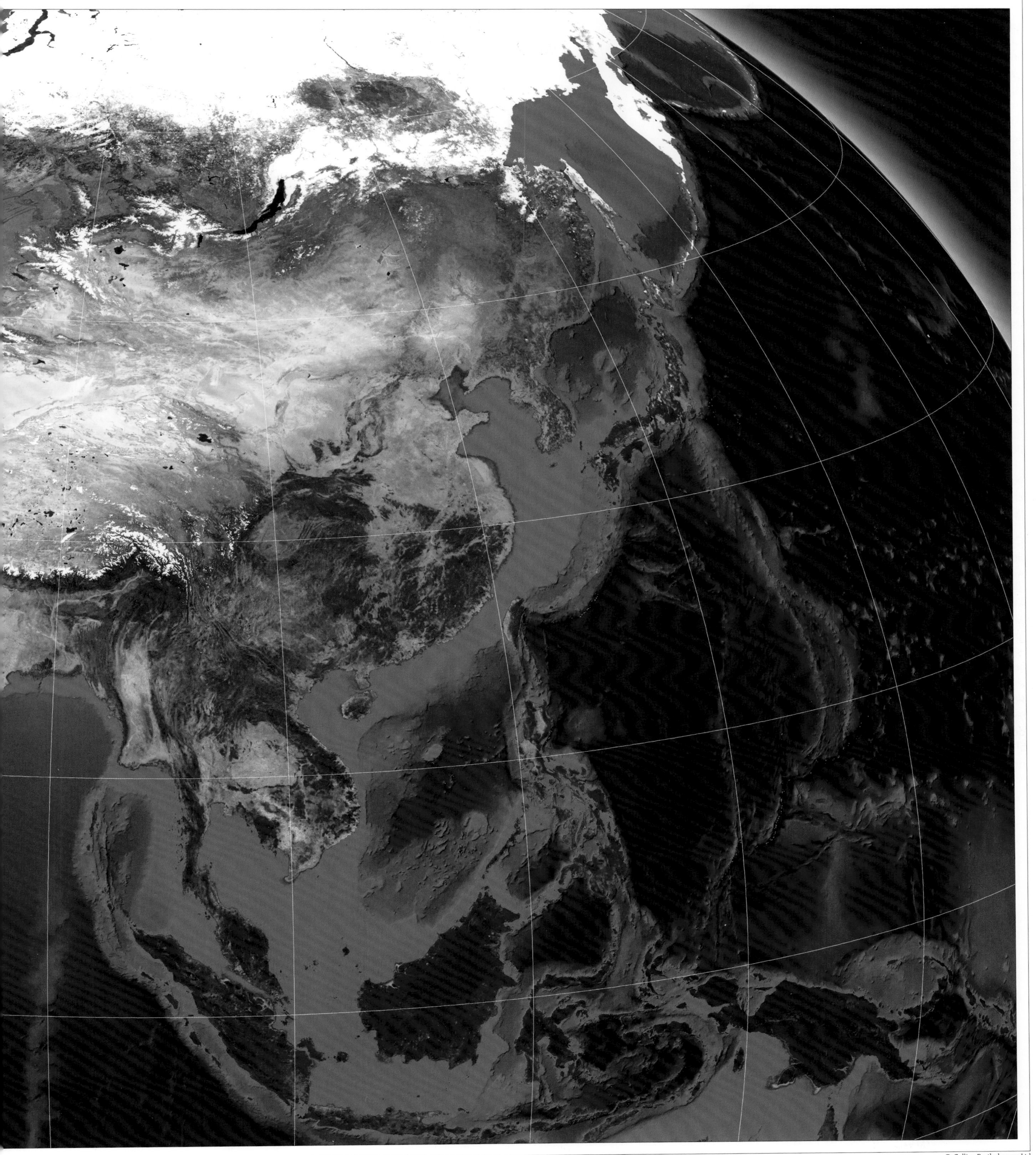

Europe

The generally densely vegetated continent of Europe contains some dramatic geographical features. The complex coastlines of Iceland, Scandinavia and northwestern Russian Federation mark its northern and western limits, while the British Isles sit on the flat, wide continental shelf. Europe's mountain ranges divide the continent – in the southwest, the Pyrenees separate France from the drier Iberian Peninsula; the wide arc of the Alps separates Italy from the rest of western Europe; the Carpathian Mountains, appearing as a dark curve between the Alps and the Black Sea, mark the edge of the vast European plains; and the Caucasus, stretching between the Black Sea and the Caspian Sea, create a prominent barrier between Europe and Asia. Two of Europe's greatest rivers are also clearly visible on this image – the Volga, Europe's longest river, flowing south from the Ural Mountains into the Caspian Sea and the Dnieper flowing across the plains into the northern Black Sea.

The Alps

Highlighted by snow cover on this image, this 800-km-long mountain system in south central Europe has been formed in the last 55 million years by the northward movement of the African landmass crumpling up the rocks of the Eurasian landmass. This squeezing action formed huge folds in the rock many kilometres in size. The folds would often break and slide over one another to form huge thrust faults as they pushed northwards. The resultant mountain range has Mont Blanc (4808 m) as its highest peak, and is the source of several of Europe's major rivers, including the Rhine, the Rhone and the Po. The highest peaks are permanently snow-capped and there are numerous glaciers. Glaciation was more extensive in the past and carved a unique Alpine mountain landscape characterized by U-shaped valleys and long, moraine-blocked lakes, several of which appear black on this image.

Caspian Sea

Seen near the eastern edge of this image is the Caspian Sea – the world's largest body of inland water. Like the much smaller Aral Sea, to its northeast, the Caspian Sea was once connected to the Mediterranean before falling sea levels during the ice age cut it off. The Volga river supplies over 75 per cent of its inflow. Water levels have fluctuated greatly as a result of dam construction and water extraction from the Volga. Rapid lowering of its level was seen between 1929 and 1978 but since then levels have risen by 2.5 m, pushing the Volga delta (the dark area on the northwest shore of the sea) 100 km inland. The Caspian Sea has no outflow and salinity levels vary across it. Highest levels of 20 per cent are found in the very shallow Garabogazköl Aýlagy – the prominent grey inlet on the eastern shoreline – which is exploited for salt.

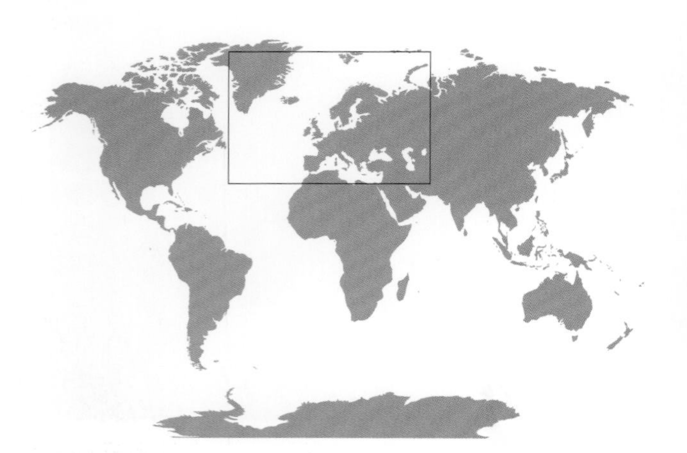

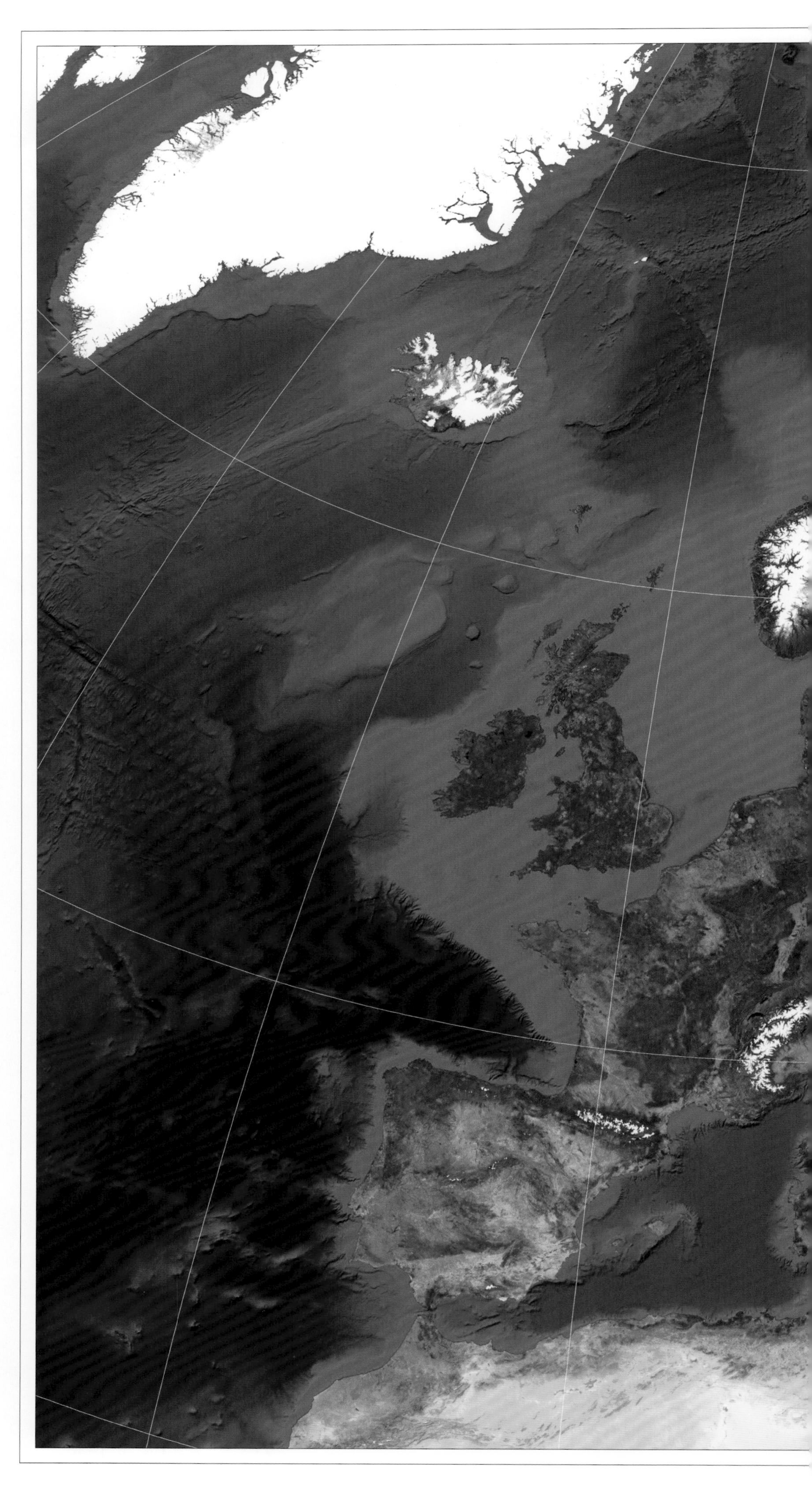

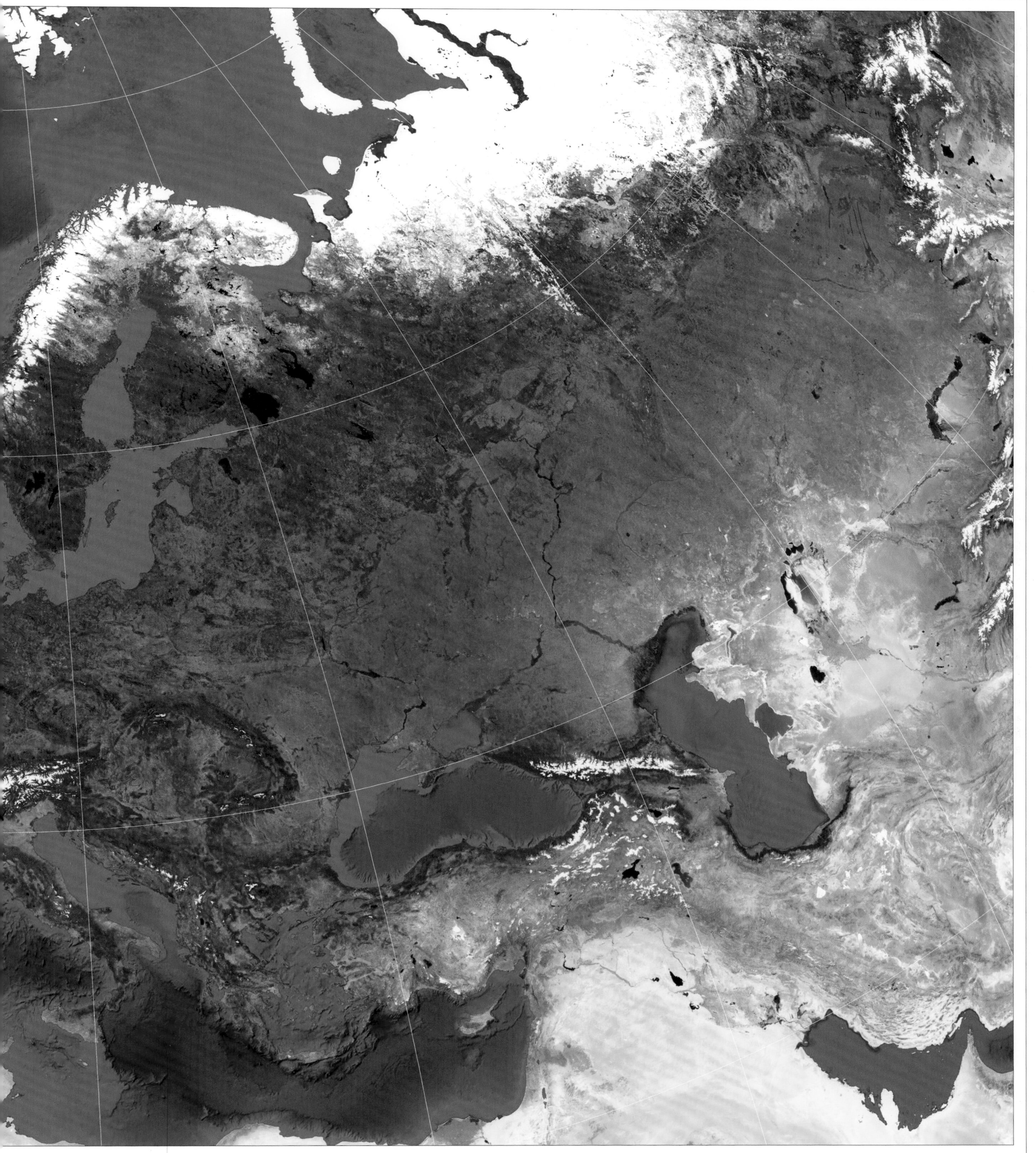

Africa

This image of Africa clearly shows the change in vegetation through the equatorial regions from the vast, dry Sahara desert covering much of the north of the continent, through the rich forests of the Congo basin – the second largest drainage basin in the world – to the high plateau of southern Africa. Lake Victoria dominates central east Africa and the Nile and its delta create a distinctive feature in the desert in the northeast. The path of the Great Rift Valley can be traced by the pattern of linear lakes in east Africa, to Ethiopia, and along the Red Sea. The small, dark fan-shaped feature in central southern Africa is the Okavango Delta in Botswana – one of the world's most ecologically sensitive areas. To the east of the continent lies Madagascar, and in the Indian Ocean northeast of this is the Mascarene Ridge sea feature stretching from the Seychelles in the north to Mauritius and Réunion in the south.

East Africa Rift Valley

More than 6700 km long, the East African Rift was formed 30 million years ago when the African and Arabian continental plates separated. The two branches of the Rift, each of which is about 50 km wide, are visible on this image. The western branch is dominated by larger lakes, including Lake Albert in the north and Lake Tanganyika in the south, while the eastern branch is dotted with smaller lakes including Lake Natron. The land here is mostly 1000 m above sea level, and drier and less densely vegetated than west Africa. Lake Victoria, the third largest lake in the world, lies on the equatorial plain between the two branches of the Rift. One of the main headwater reservoirs of the River Nile, its lake basin is heavily populated and intensely cultivated. Mount Kilimanjaro and Mount Kenya – the two highest mountains in Africa – lie to the east of Lake Victoria.

Sahel

The Sahel is a thin band of dry savanna grassland stretching 5000 km from Senegal and Mauritania in northwest Africa to the Red Sea coast of Sudan and Eritrea in the northeast. It appears on this image as a light green and tan strip running across the continent between the yellow desert sands of the Sahara, and the dark green densely vegetated area of equatorial Africa. The Sahel region is one of Africa's most productive crop areas but it has a history of famine due to highly erratic rainfall. A dry period from the early 1970s to the mid 1990s left many wondering if the Sahara was creeping south. Satellite images are being used to study the area over time and, although the area is not becoming a desert on a large scale, areas of land degradation are being identified.

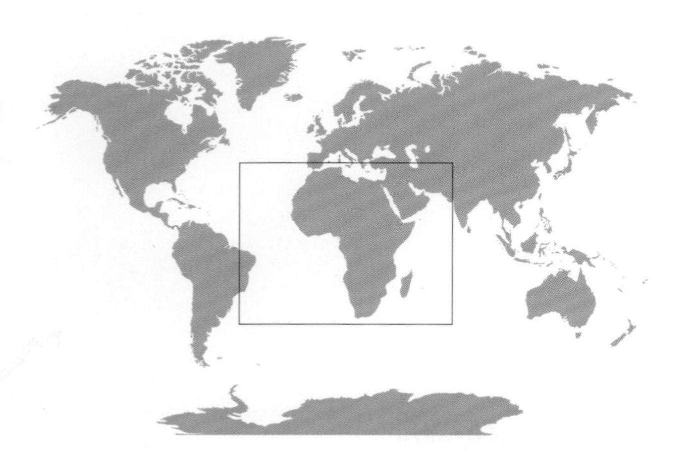

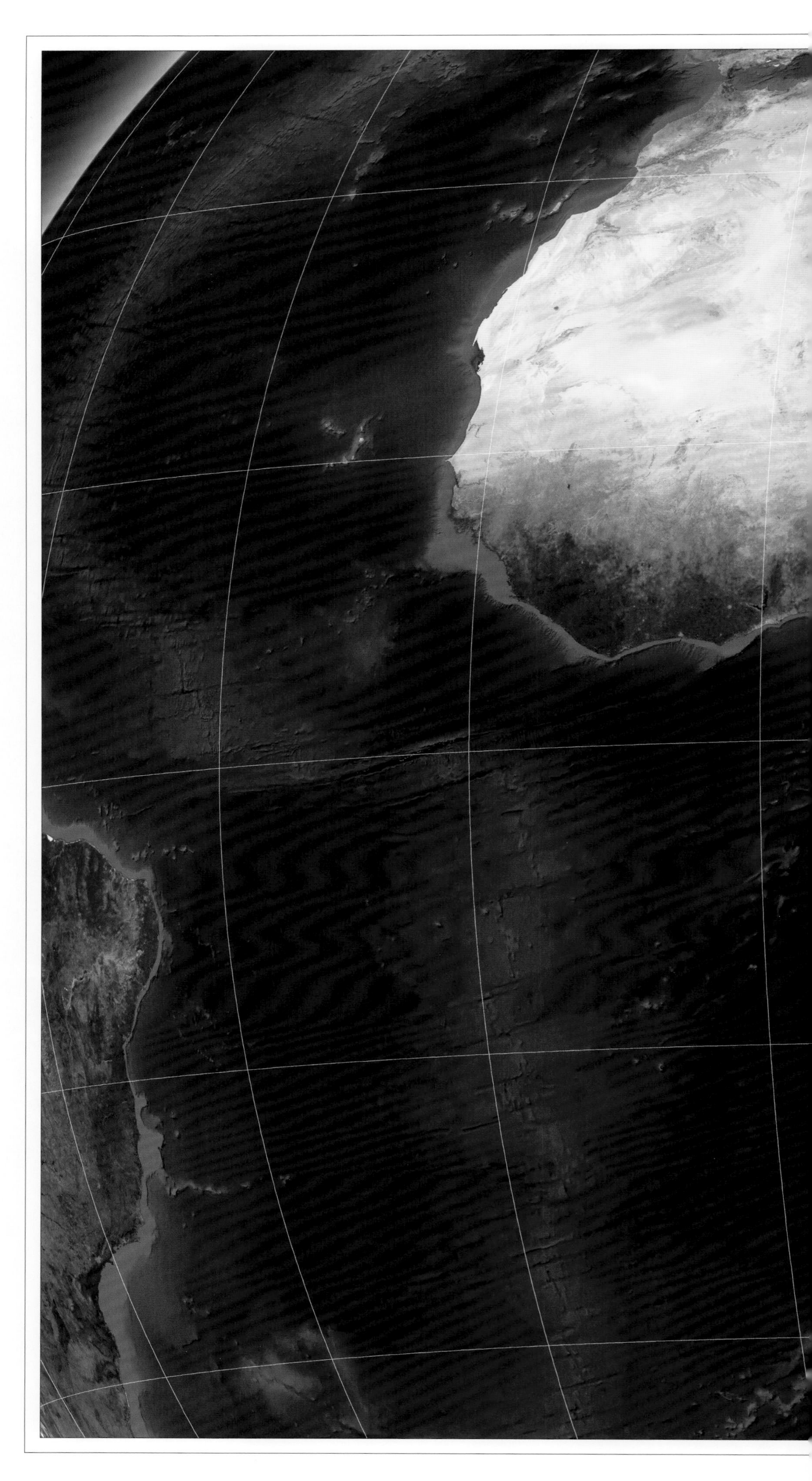

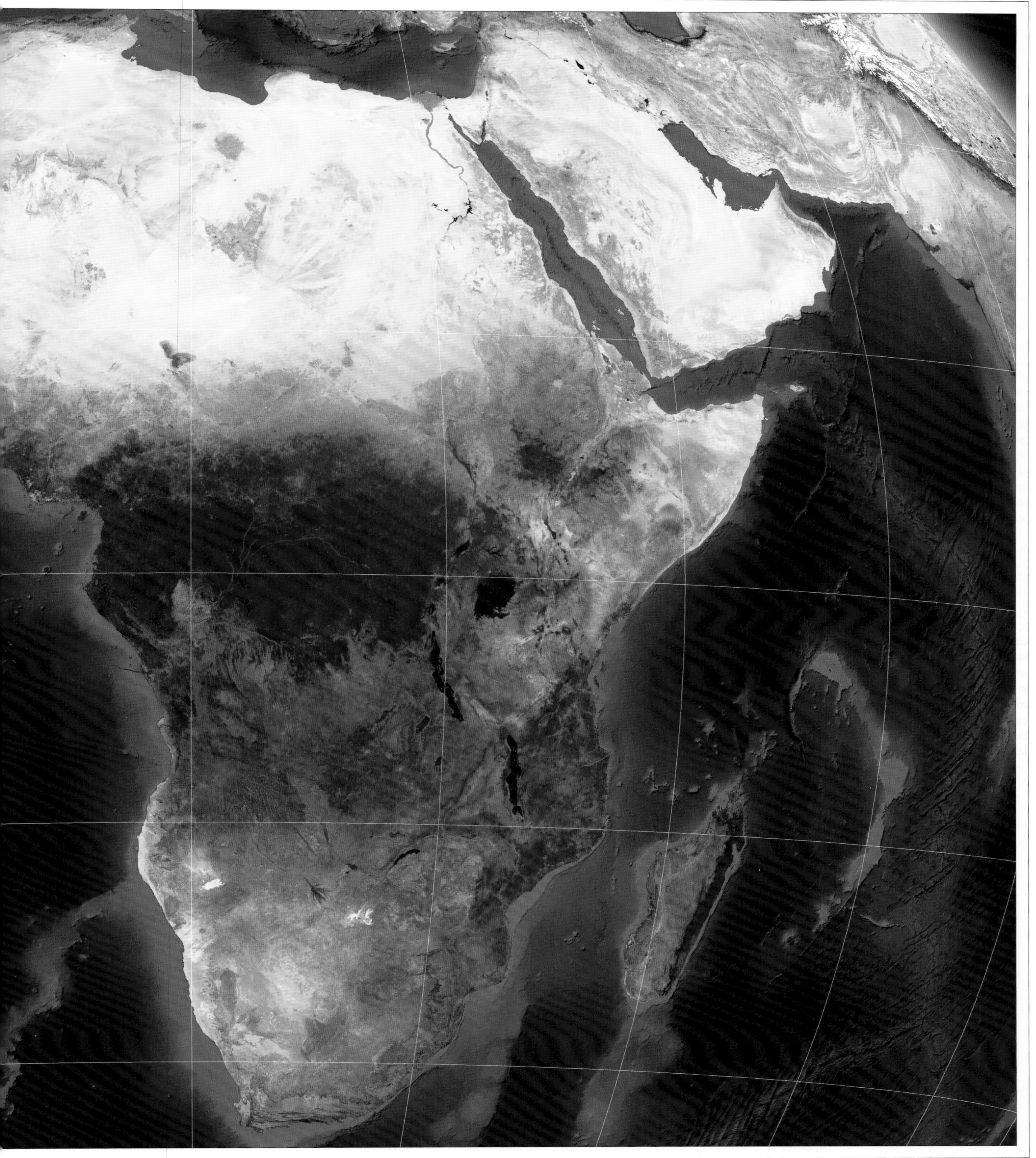

13

North America

Many well-known geographical features are identifiable on this image of North America, which also illustrates the contrasts in landscapes across the continent. Greenland – the world's largest island – sits off the northeast coast while the dramatic chain of the Aleutian Islands in the northwest stretches from Alaska across the Bering Sea to the Kamchatka Peninsula in the Russian Federation. Further south in the Pacific Ocean, at the far left of the image, lie the Hawai'ian Islands and their very distinctive ocean ridge. There is a strong west-east contrast across the continent. The west is dominated by the Rocky Mountains which give way to the Great Plains. In the east, the Great Lakes, the largest of which, Lake Superior, is second in size only to the Caspian Sea in Asia, the valley of the Mississippi and the Coastal Plain are prominent. In the southeast the complex floor of the Caribbean Sea is visible, particularly the dramatic Cayman Trench, stretching from the Gulf of Honduras to southern Cuba.

Great Lakes

During a succession of ice ages in the last 2 million years, much of Canada was covered by a vast ice sheet. When it melted, a huge volume of water was released southwards and some of this remains trapped in the glacier-carved lake basins of the Great Lakes and numerous smaller lakes on the Canadian Shield – a plateau in eastern Canada and the northeast USA. Four of the five Great Lakes mark the boundary between the USA and Canada. The lakes are connected by canals and short rivers creating a 1867 km waterway from the western end of Lake Superior to the St Lawrence river outflow at the eastern end of Lake Ontario. The St Lawrence Seaway, opened in 1959, allowed deep-draught shipping direct access to the lakes from the Atlantic Ocean. The height above sea level of the lake surfaces varies. The greatest height difference, of 51 m, occurs between Lakes Erie and Ontario at Niagara Falls.

Greenland Ice sheet

The ice sheet which covers more than 80 per cent of Greenland is the northern hemisphere's largest remaining relic of the last ice age. The ice sheet has shrunk noticeably since 1978. Studies of satellite data reveal that it has lost 20 per cent more mass than it received in recent years due to melting and iceberg calving. There are fears that the rate of melting is increasing due to global warming, and that this could have serious implications for world sea levels, ocean currents and weather patterns. If the Greenland ice sheet were to melt completely, the sea level would rise by more than 7 m. In 2007, a new island Uunartoq Qeqertoq (Warming Island) was discovered. This was previously thought to be part of mainland Greenland, but as ice melted it was revealed as an island.

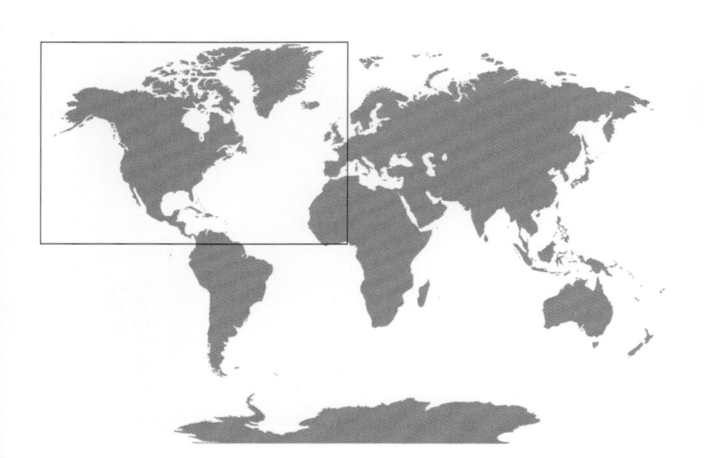

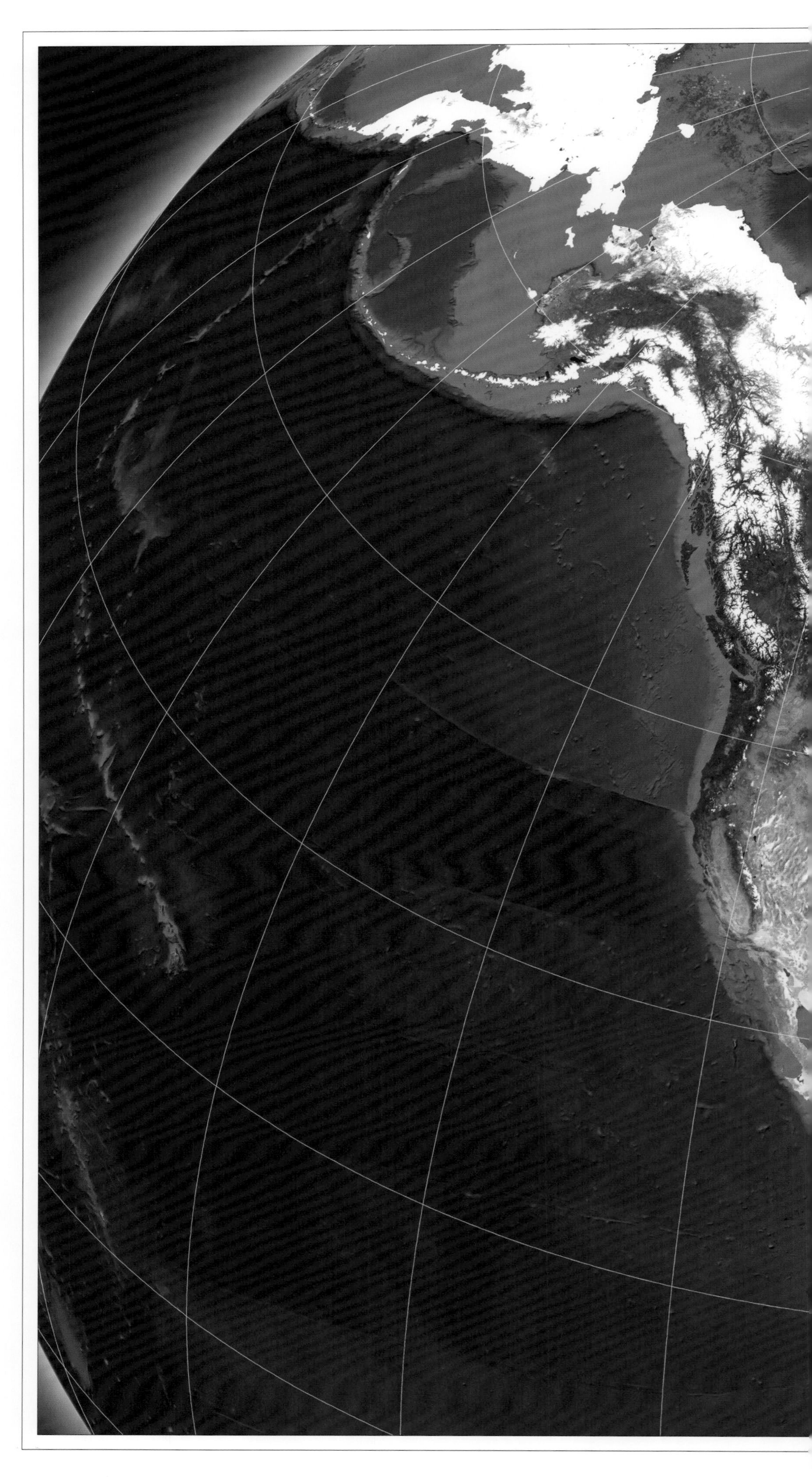

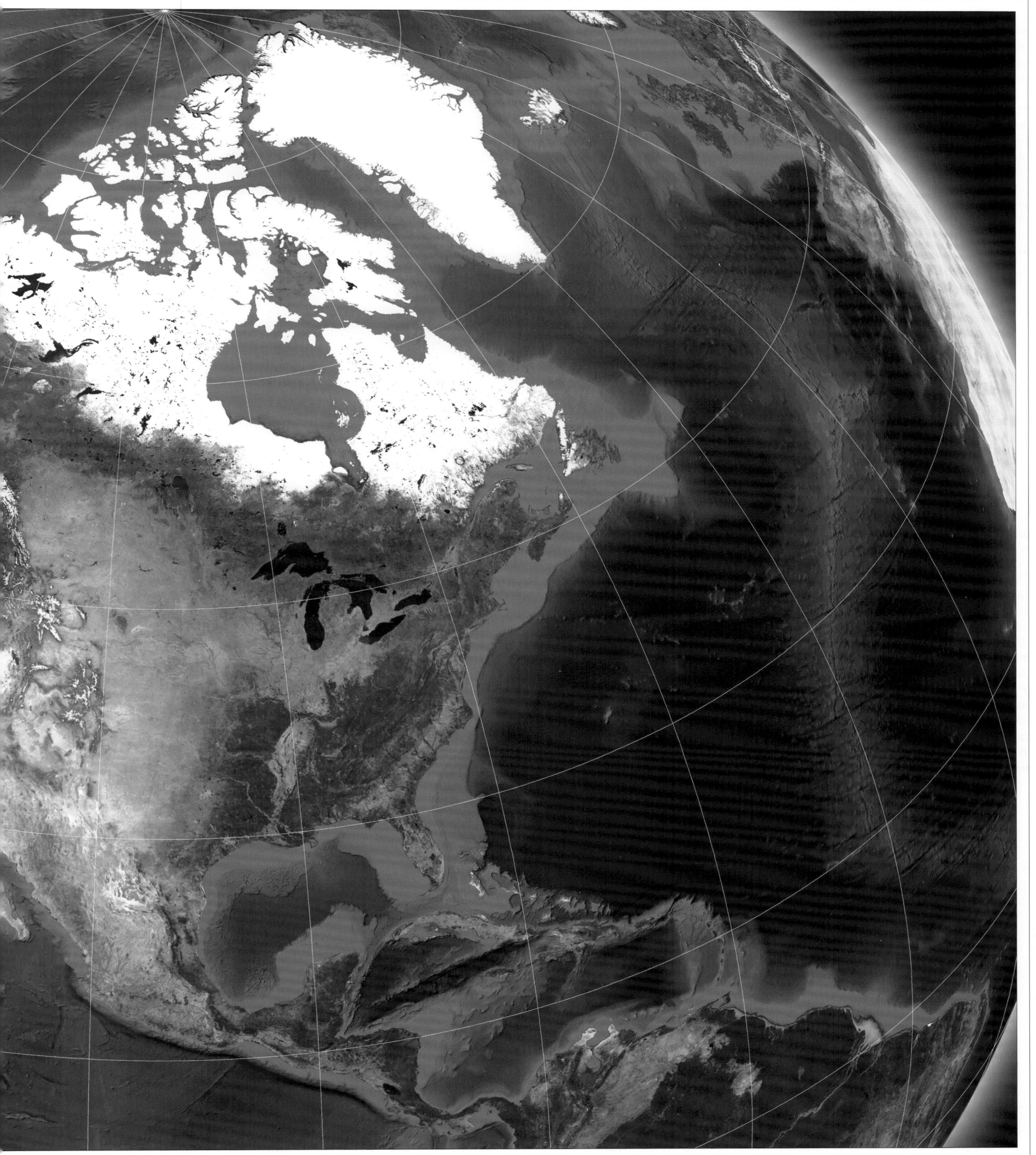

15

South America

The Andes mountains stretch along the whole length of the west coast of South America, widening into the high plains of the Altiplano in Bolivia and Peru in the centre of the continent. Lake Titicaca, the world's highest large navigable lake, lies on the Altiplano, straddling the Bolivia-Peru border. Running parallel to the Andes, just off the west coast, is the Peru-Chile Trench which marks the active boundary between the Nazca and South American tectonic plates. Movement between these plates gives rise to numerous volcanoes in the Andes. The Amazon river runs across almost the whole width of the continent in the north, meeting the Atlantic Ocean in its wide delta on the northeast coast. The vast Amazon basin is one of the most ecologically diverse areas of the Earth. In the south, the wide continental shelf stretches eastwards from the tip of the continent to the Falkland Islands and South Georgia on the bottom edge of the image.

Amazon

The world's second longest river, the 6516 km long Amazon, discharges one-fifth of the total fresh water entering the world's oceans. The enormous Amazon Basin covers most of northern Brazil, as well as parts of five other South American countries and supports the world's largest rainforest, its rich plant life shown in dark green tones on this image. The Andes define the western rim of the Basin and supply the headwaters of many of the Amazon's 500 tributaries. The confluence of the Rio Negro (appearing black on the image) and the Amazon (appearing yellow) is visible near the centre of the Basin. The difference in appearance between the rivers is a result of the low sediment content of the Rio Negro. In contrast, the Amazon empties approximately 1.3 million tons of sediment into the Atlantic Ocean every day. The vast delta which has formed from this sediment is seen as a bright yellow area on the image.

Andes

The world's longest mountain range, the Andes, stretches more than 8000 km from Venezuela to Chile. Higher than any other mountains, with the exception of the Himalaya, they are home to many areas of volcanic activity. Earthquakes, mudflows and landslides present additional hazards. The bright area in the centre of the image, near the west coast of the continent, is the driest place on earth – the Atacama Desert. This is a large area of saltpans and bare rock, some parts of which have not had rain for more than a century. Other, smaller salt flats are also visible as light areas. These are remnants of a vast inland sea which once covered the area. White areas on the southern part of the image are glaciers in the southern Andes.

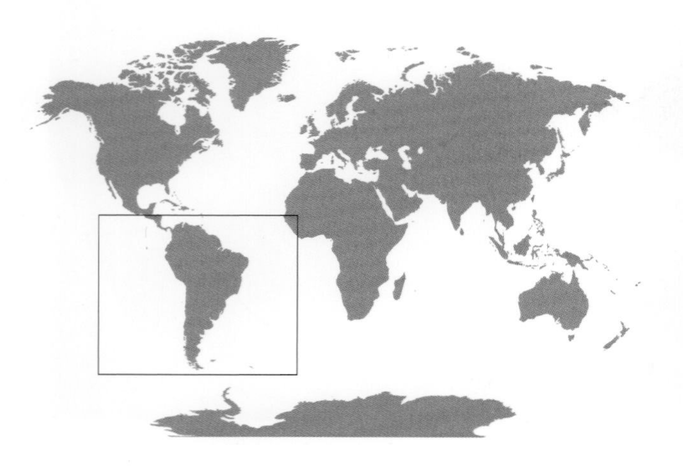

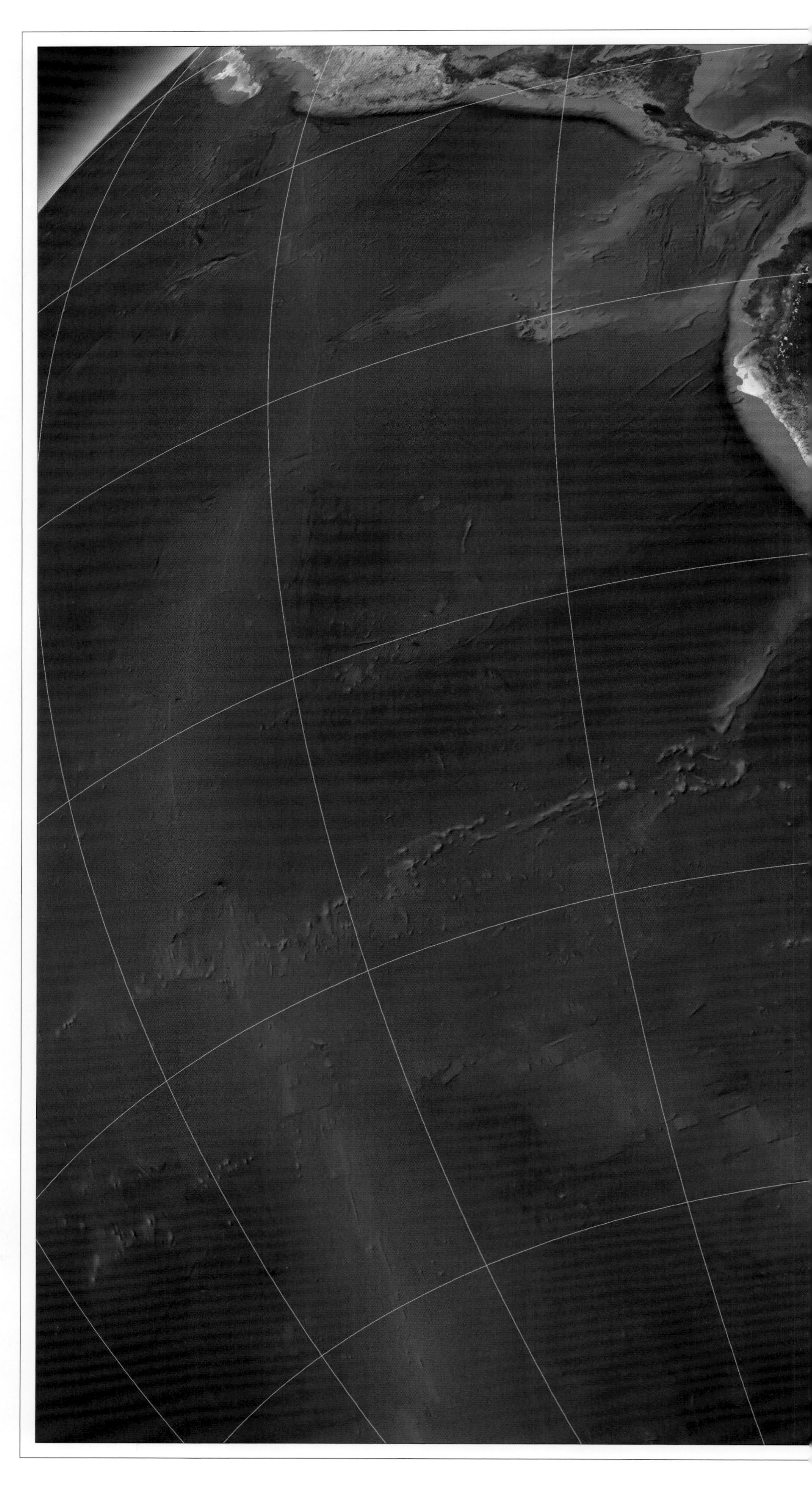

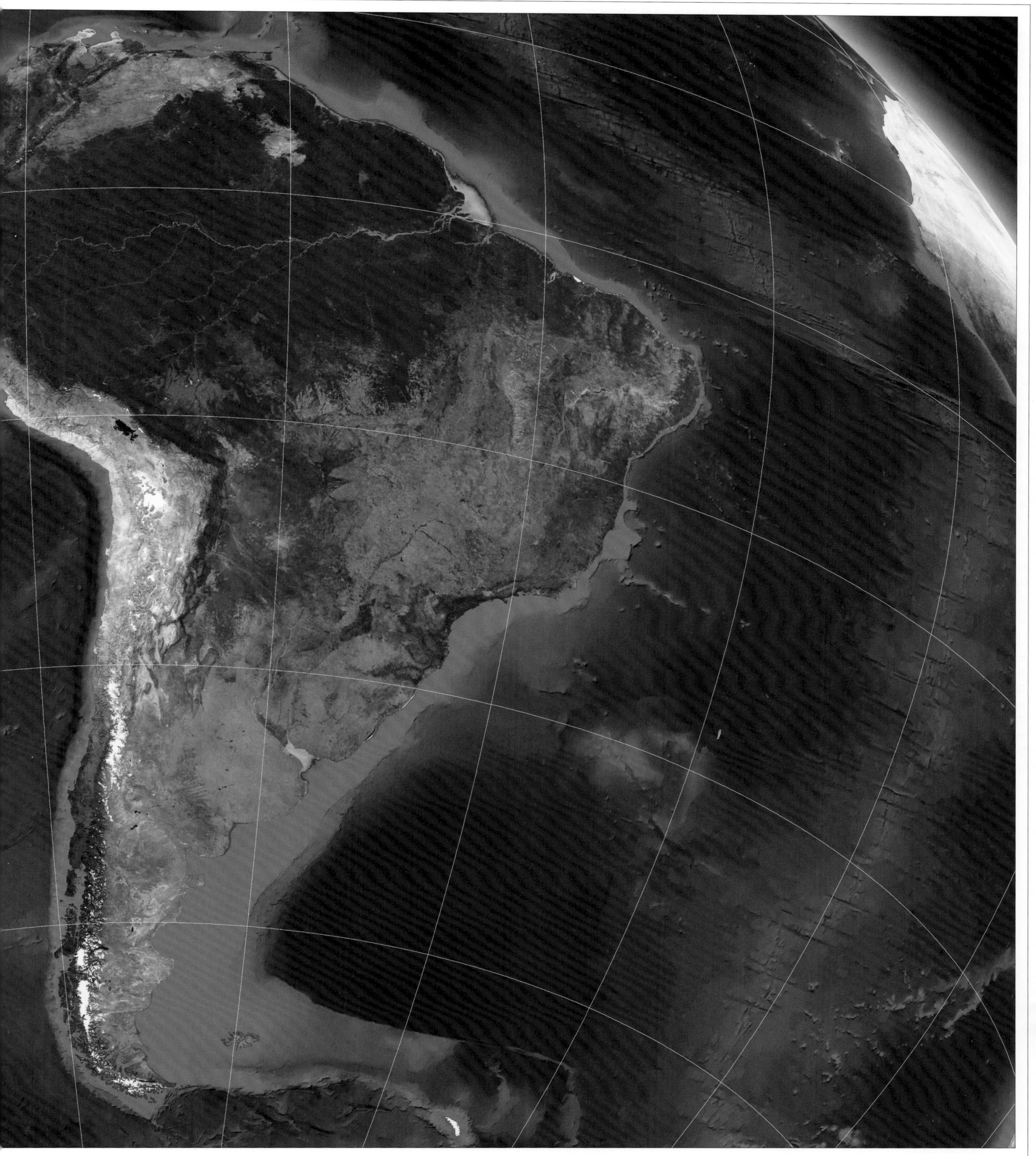

17

Antarctica

Protected by the Antarctic Treaty, implemented in 1959, from commercial exploitation and from the realization of territorial claims, Antarctica is perhaps the world's greatest unspoilt, and relatively unexplored, wilderness. This image combines bathymetric data (incomplete in some black areas) with satellite images to show the extent of the continental ice sheet in an austral summer. Floating sea ice is not shown. The Antarctic Peninsula – home to numerous scientific research stations – in the top left of the image reaching towards South America, the huge Ronne and Ross ice shelves, and the Transantarctic Mountains – dividing the continent into West and East Antarctica – are the dominant physical features.

Antarctica Ice Sheet Under Threat

The largest mass of ice on earth, the Antarctic ice sheet contains over 70 per cent of the earth's fresh water. On Antarctica's high inland plateau the ice sheet is up to 4.5 km thick and feeds massive ice shelves which float out onto the surrounding seas. This particular image does not show floating sea ice but the analysis of satellite images (commonly known as the science of remote sensing) provides valuable data for scientists studying the extent and characteristics of the ice. The stability of the ice sheet is being threatened by global warming and in the 1990s it was predicted that the ice shelves that surround Antarctica were in danger of becoming unstable.

Studies of the extent of seven ice shelves along the Antarctic Peninsula, in the top left of this image, reveal a decline of 13 500 sq km since 1974. In 1998, over only thirty-one days, the Larsen B ice shelf disintegrated into thousands of icebergs and it is now a mere 40 per cent of its previous extent. After analyzing twenty years of satellite data of the continent as a whole, scientists have concluded that persistent melting of the ice has been occurring further inland and at higher altitudes over the past two decades. These changes are attributed to a steady warming of the climate in the region. The rate of warming is approximately 0.5 Centigrade degrees (C°) per decade and the trend has been present since the late 1940s.

McMurdo Dry Valleys

A few parts of Antarctica have little or no snow or ice cover and the 4800 sq km McMurdo Dry Valleys, near the bottom of the image at the southern end of the Transantarctic Mountains, is the largest of these areas. The bare rock here is representative of the ancient rocky continent beneath the continental ice sheet. Valley floors are covered with gravel and the 19-km-long Onyx River flows during the brief summer. Endolithic plants – plants growing within rocks – have been found here but the area is extremely barren and is described as one of the world's most extreme deserts.

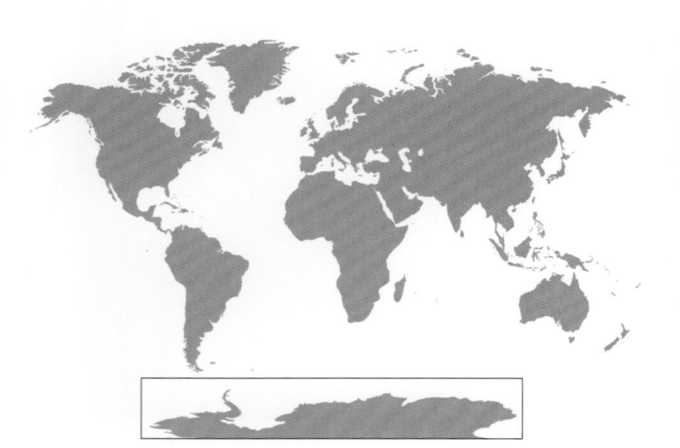

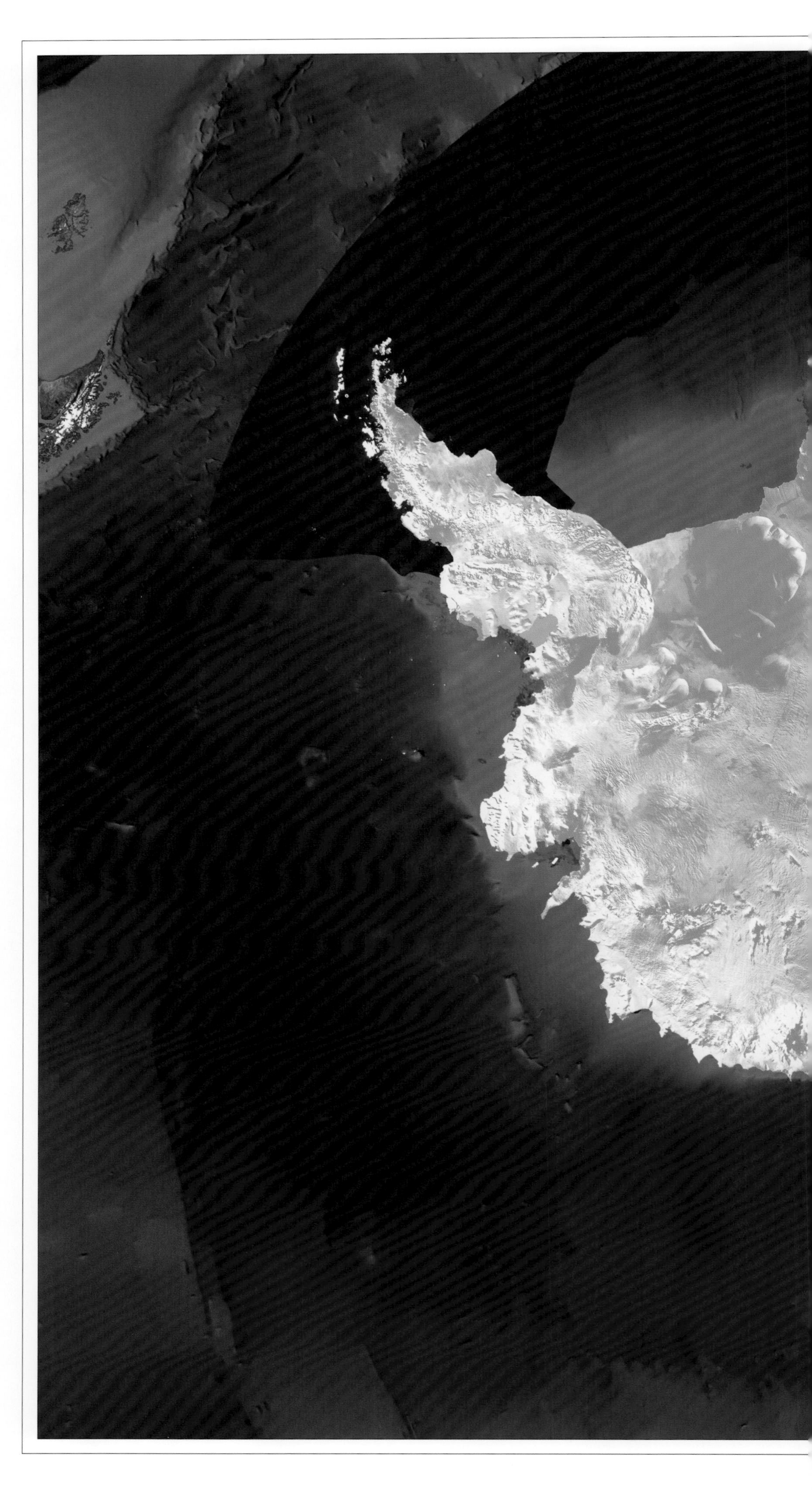

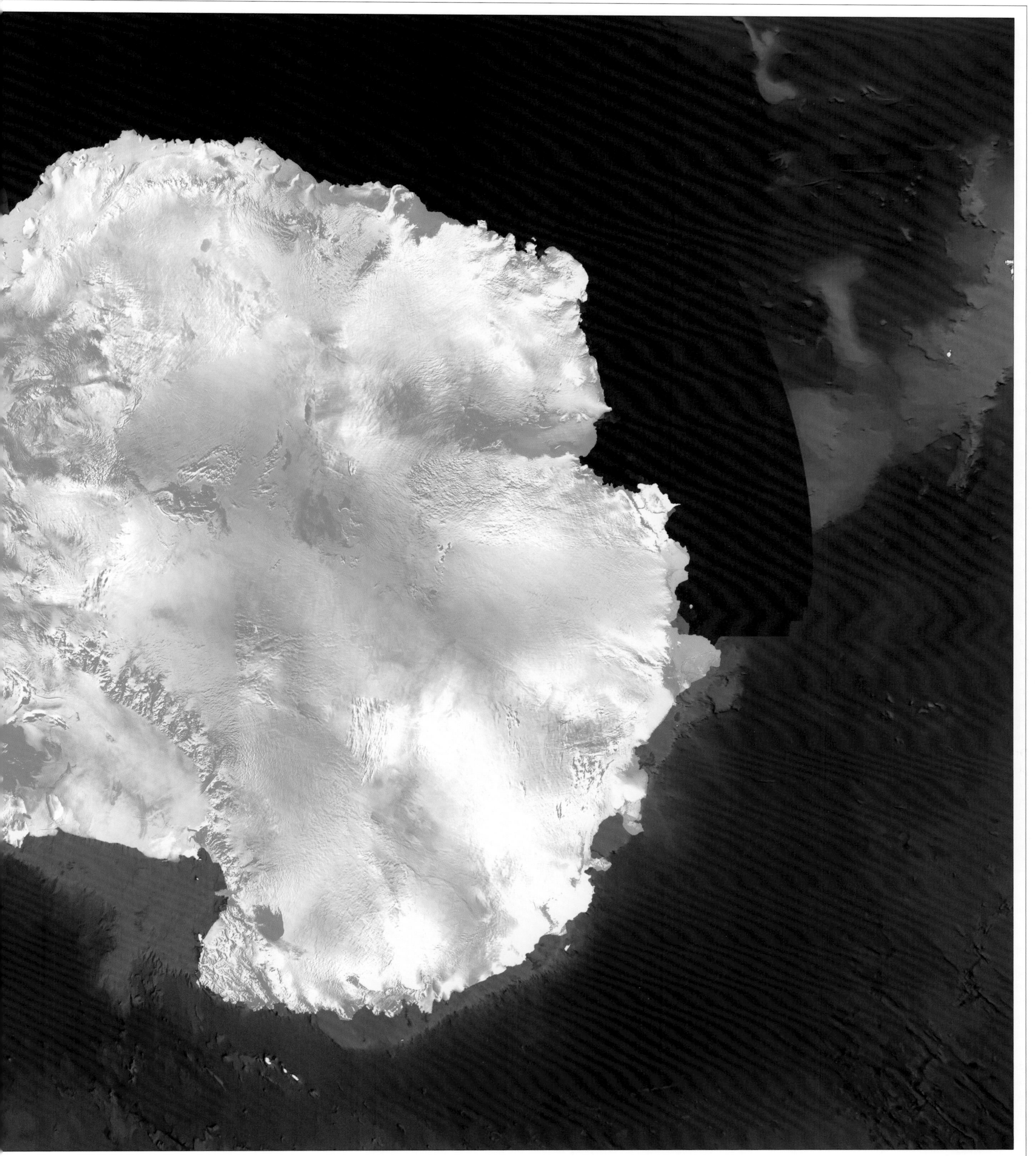

The Earth

Before the end of the 19th century, earth scientists had no way of discovering the composition of the interior of the Earth. Ideas about the internal structure were therefore based almost entirely on speculation. The only evidence related to phenomena apparent at the Earth's surface, but which seemed to arise from within. These consisted of earthquakes, volcanoes, and geysers. To early thinkers, earthquakes indicated that the Earth could not be made entirely of solid rock, but might contain underground caverns full of air. Geysers and springs also suggested that the interior of the Earth was partly, or largely, made up of water. On the other hand, volcanic eruptions seemed to indicate that fire existed underground. For a long time, debate continued between the neptunists who favoured a watery interior and the volcanists favouring a fiery one. With the development of instrumental seismology and worldwide seismic monitoring, starting around 1900, a more soundly based answer began to appear. Careful study of the time differences of different earthquake waves showed that features of the Earth's structure could be deduced by analysing the way in which waves travel through it. Boundaries between different layers within the Earth were identified by the way waves were reflected or refracted by them. It was also possible to tell which parts of the Earth's interior must be liquid, since some types of wave can only travel through solid regions. As a result, the basic internal structure of the Earth became known.

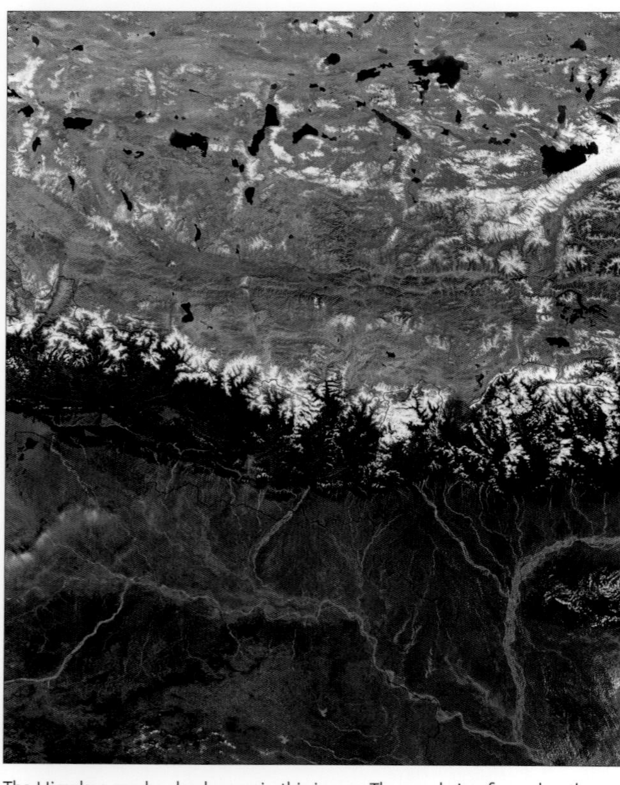

The Himalaya can be clearly seen in this image. They are being formed as the Indian continental plate to the south collides with the Asian plate to the north. This is an example of a continental destructive plate boundary.

Plate Tectonics

Over the course of geological time the Earth's crust has broken up into large fragments, which are known as lithospheric or tectonic plates. These plates are slowly moving relative to one another at rates of a few centimetres per year. This process – originally described as continental drift, a term coined by the meteorologist Alfred Wegener who first proposed the idea in the 1920s – is known as plate tectonics. The interaction of plates along their boundaries causes volcanic and seismic activity. The fact that the shapes of South America and Africa dovetail neatly into one another was noticed as early as the 17th century, and this has proved to be no coincidence.

The Earth's Internal Structure

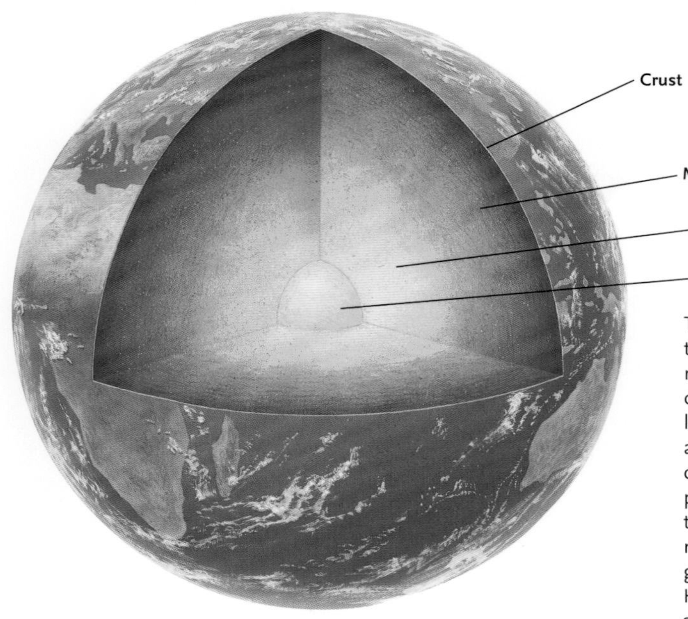

The interior of the Earth can be divided into three principal regions. The outermost region is the crust which is extremely thin compared to the Earth as a whole. The next layer down is known as the mantle. This is about 2850 km thick and is believed to consist mostly of the minerals olivine, pyroxene and garnet. Below the mantle is the Earth's core, which is about 3470 km in radius, and is mainly made up of iron. The greater part of the core is completely liquid. However, there is an inner core which is solid, and about 1220 km in radius.

Mass	5.974 x 10²¹ tonnes
Total area	509 450 000 sq km / 196 698 645 sq miles
Land area	149 450 000 sq km / 57 702 645 sq miles
Water area	360 000 000 sq km / 138 996 000 sq miles
Volume	1 083 207 x 10⁶ cubic km / 259 911 x 10⁶ cubic miles
Equatorial diameter	12 756 km / 7 927 miles
Polar diameter	12 714 km / 7 901 miles
Equatorial circumference	40 075 km / 24 903 miles
Meridional circumference	40 008 km / 24 861 miles

Plate Tectonics

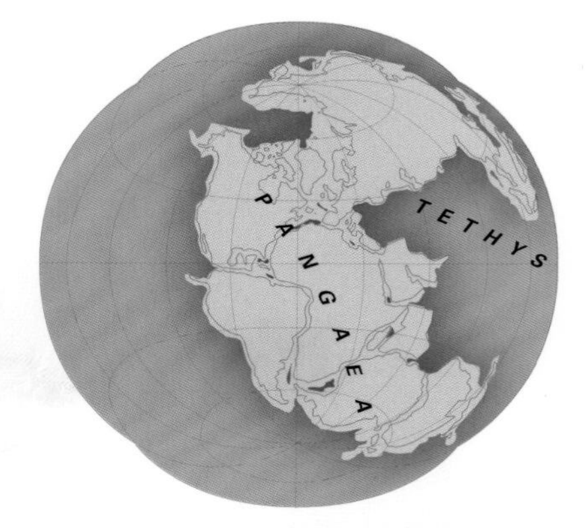

The Earth looked very different 200 million years ago. All the continents were at one time joined together in a great landmass called Pangaea.

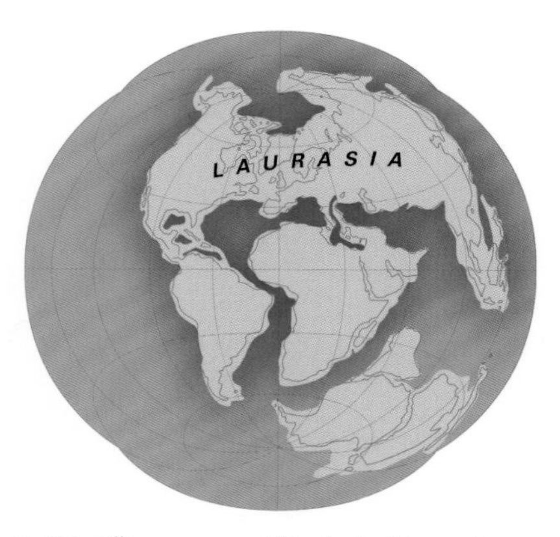

By 100 million years ago Africa had split away from the Americas, Antarctica and Australia then broke away from Africa and subsequently from each other.

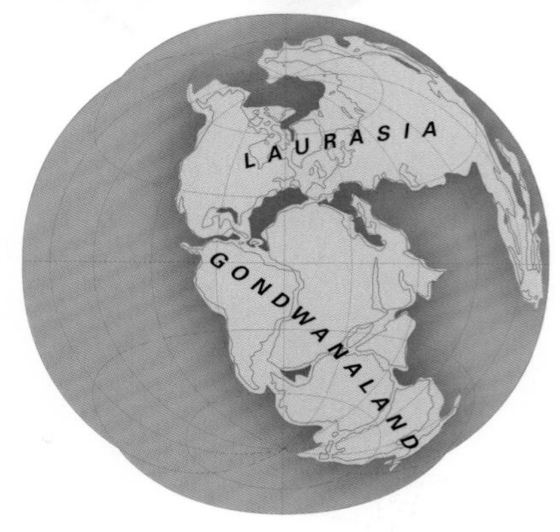

About 165 million years ago this super-continent began to break up.

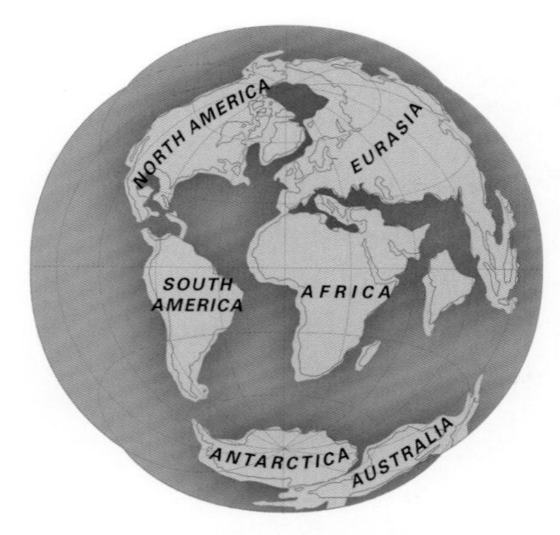

Around 50 million years ago, North America and Europe separated, and India, which was formerly attached to Antarctica, moved northwards to collide with Asia.

Types of Plate Boundary

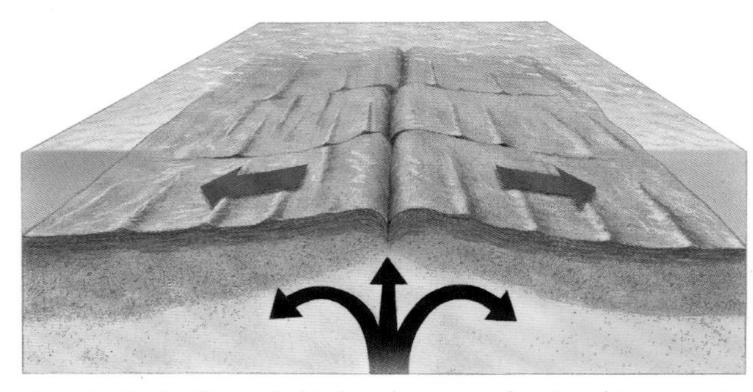

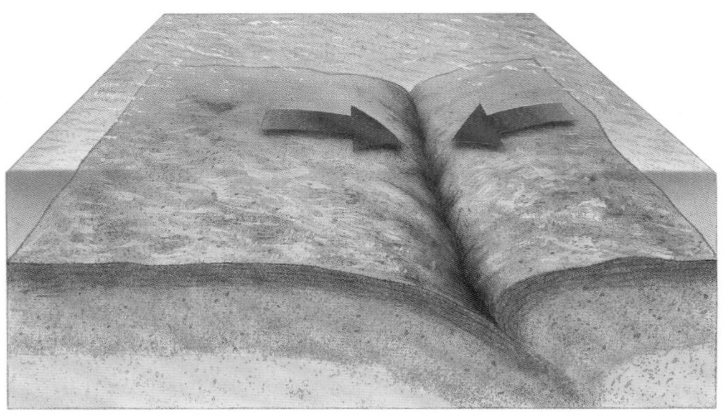

A constructive (or divergent) plate boundary occurs where two plates are moving away from each other, with new crust being formed along the ridge between them. One place where such a boundary occurs on land is in Iceland. Here the mid-Atlantic ridge creates a dramatic rift in the landscape at Thingvellir, the site of the old Icelandic parliament.

With a destructive (or convergent), boundary two plates are colliding. When an oceanic crust meets another piece of oceanic crust it sinks under it, creating a subduction zone (usually accompanied by a deep ocean trench) as it does so.

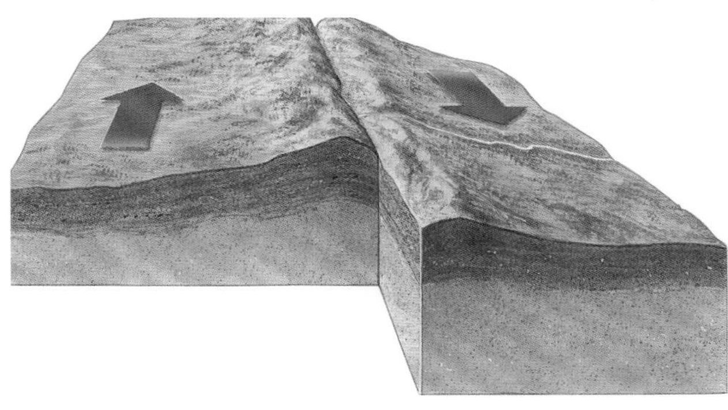

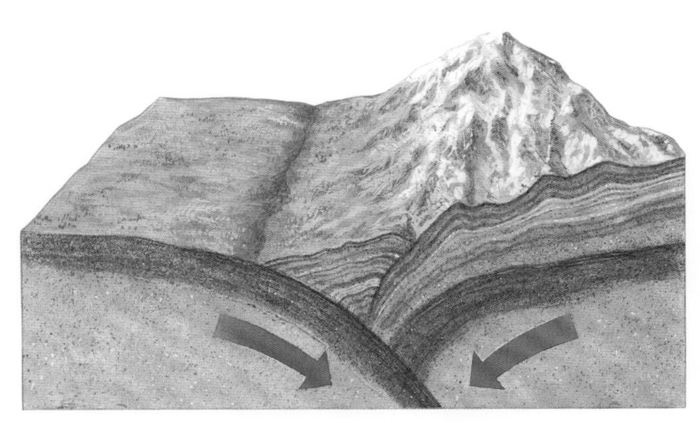

In some places, two plates slide past one another, with neither being destroyed. This is known as a conservative (or transform) boundary. The classic example is in California, where the Pacific Plate is sliding northwest relative to the North American Plate, along the line of the San Andreas Fault.

Occasionally, with a destructive (or convergent) boundary a continental crust meets another continental crust, and the two crumple up, one eventually being forced under the other. This is what is happening between India and Asia, with the Himalaya being formed as a result.

Tectonic Plate Boundaries

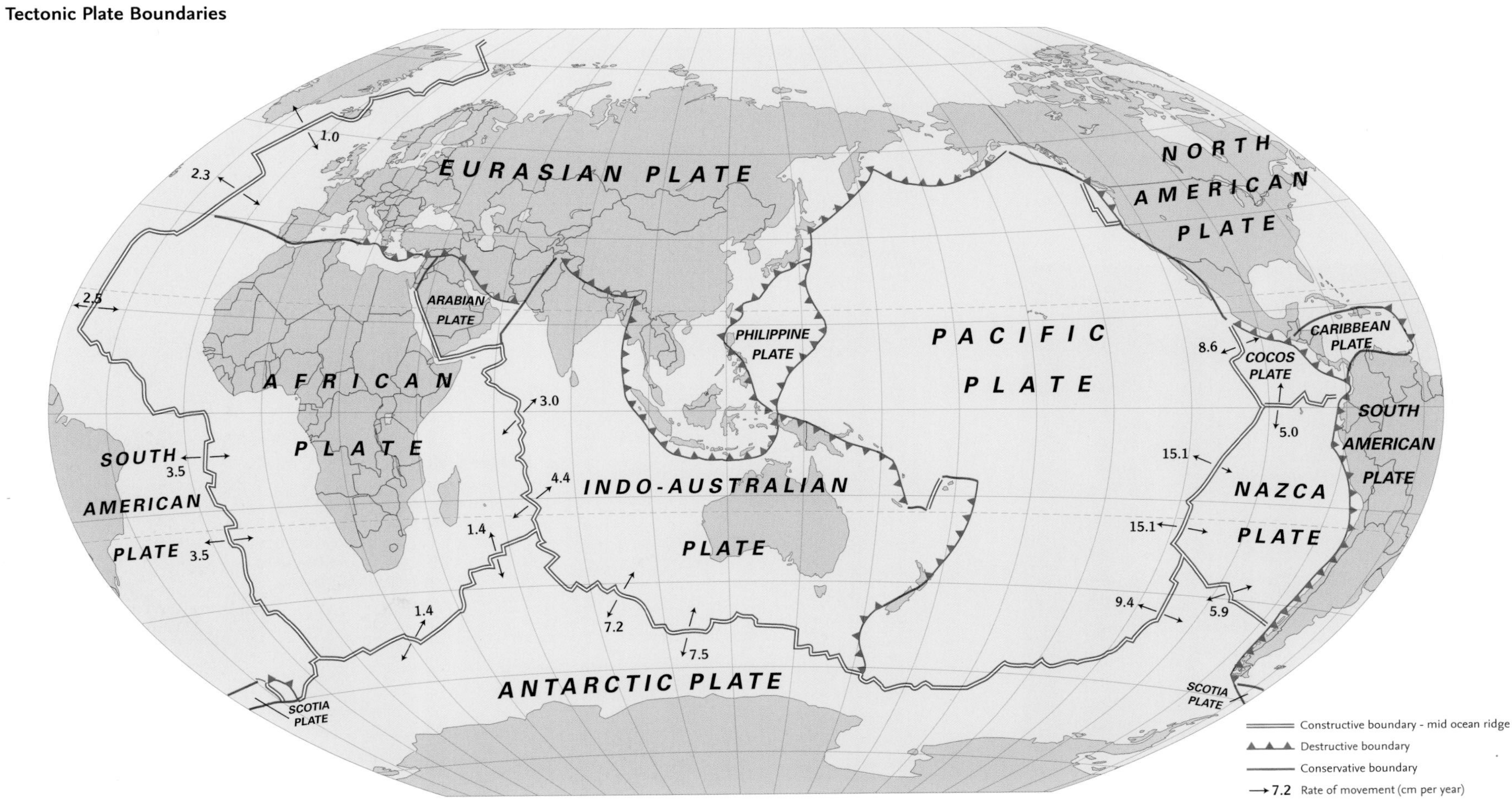

Constructive boundary - mid ocean ridge
Destructive boundary
Conservative boundary
→ 7.2 Rate of movement (cm per year)

Earthquakes and Volcanoes

Any map showing the distribution of earthquakes and volcanoes will inevitably look very similar to a map showing the boundaries of the tectonic plates. This is because both phenomena are largely controlled by the processes of plate tectonics. The vast majority of the world's earthquakes occur at plate boundaries as a result of one plate pushing past, or under, another. Even those earthquakes which occur away from plate margins are still mostly due to stresses in the rocks which result indirectly from plate movements.

Tsunamis

Earthquakes can sometimes give rise to another phenomenon which can cause even more destruction and loss of life – the tsunami. Tsunami is a Japanese word, meaning 'harbour wave', and is used today in preference to the expression 'tidal wave' (tides are not involved). When an earthquake occurs offshore, it may cause a sudden change in the shape of the ocean floor, as a result of submarine landslides or vertical fault movement. This causes a massive displacement of water, which in turn produces a powerful wave or series of waves, able to travel over huge distances.

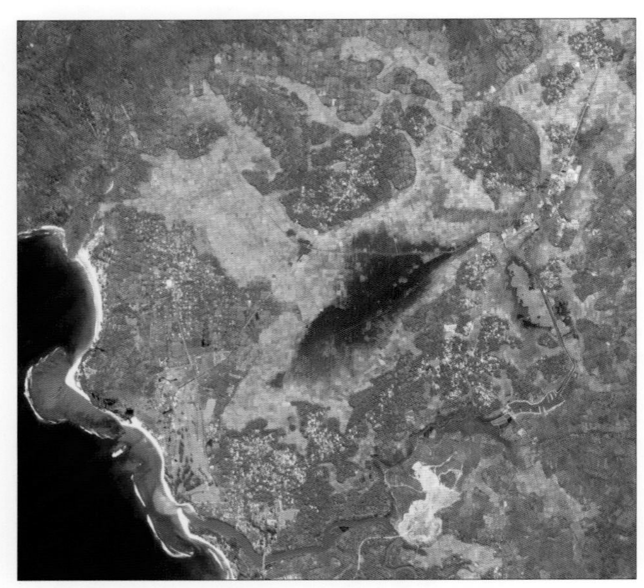

This satellite image of Lhoknga near the provincial capital of Banda Aceh, Sumatra was taken in January 2003 and shows lush and well-cultivated land, with woodland and several villages. The darker area in the centre is water. The coast has sandy beaches, some with barrier islands or reefs protecting them.

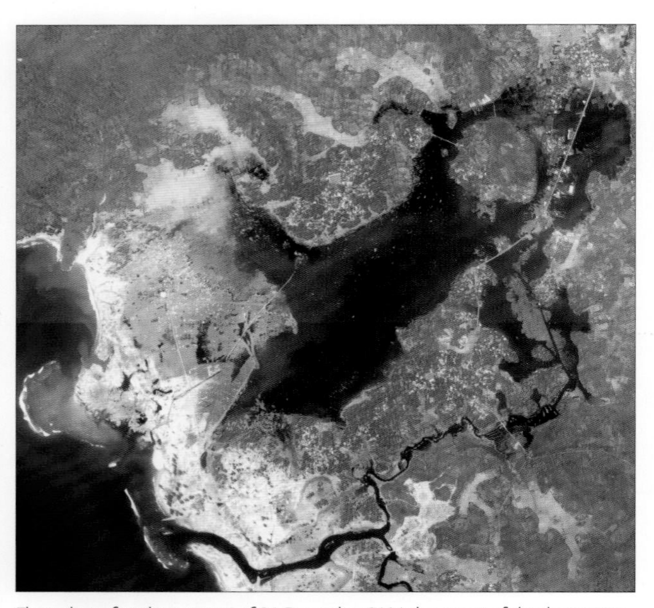

Three days after the tsunami of 26 December 2004 the extent of the destructive force of the waves can be seen. The coastal area has been stripped bare of vegetation and buildings. Inland, the low-lying areas are now filled with salt water and it is only the slightly higher level of the roads which keeps them visible.

Distribution of Earthquakes and Volcanoes

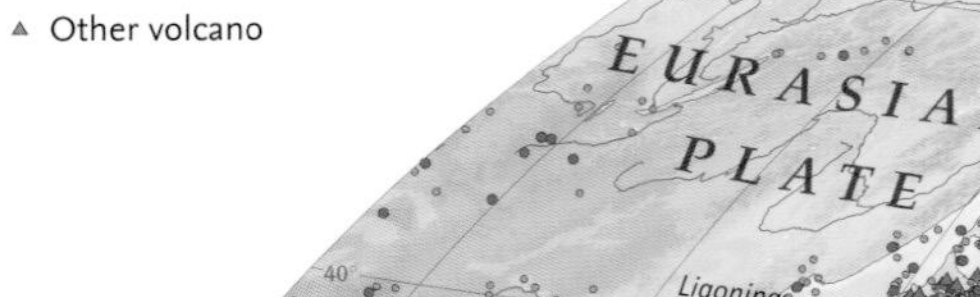

- ● Deadliest earthquake
- • Earthquake of magnitude >=7.5
- ◦ Earthquake of magnitude 5.5 – 7.5
- ▲ Major volcano
- ▴ Other volcano

Deadliest Earthquakes 1900–2008

Year	Location	Deaths
1905	Kangra, India	19 000
1907	west of Dushanbe, Tajikistan	12 000
1908	Messina, Italy	110 000
1915	Abruzzo, Italy	35 000
1917	Bali, Indonesia	15 000
1920	Ningxia Province, China	200 000
1923	Tōkyō, Japan	142 807
1927	Qinghai Province, China	200 000
1932	Gansu Province, China	70 000
1933	Sichuan Province, China	10 000
1934	Nepal/India	10 700
1935	Quetta, Pakistan	30 000
1939	Chillán, Chile	28 000
1939	Erzincan, Turkey	32 700
1948	Aşgabat, Turkmenistan	19 800
1962	northwest Iran	12 225
1970	Huánuco Province, Peru	66 794
1974	Yunnan and Sichuan Provinces, China	20 000
1975	Liaoning Province, China	10 000
1976	central Guatemala	22 778
1976	Tangshan, Hebei Province, China	255 000
1978	Khorāsān Province, Iran	20 000
1980	Chlef, Algeria	11 000
1988	Spitak, Armenia	25 000
1990	Manjil, Iran	50 000
1999	İzmit (Kocaeli), Turkey	17 000
2001	Gujarat, India	20 000
2003	Bam, Iran	26 271
2004	Sumatra, Indonesia/Indian Ocean	>225 000
2005	northwest Pakistan	74 648
2008	Sichuan Province, China	>40 000

Richter Scale

The scale measures the energy released by an earthquake. The scale is logarithmic – a quake measuring 4 is 30 times more powerful than one measuring 3, and a quake measuring 6 is 27 000 times more powerful than one measuring 3.

Not recorded
Recorded, tremor felt
Quake easily felt, local damage caused
Destructive earthquake
Major earthquake
Most powerful earthquake recorded – 8.9

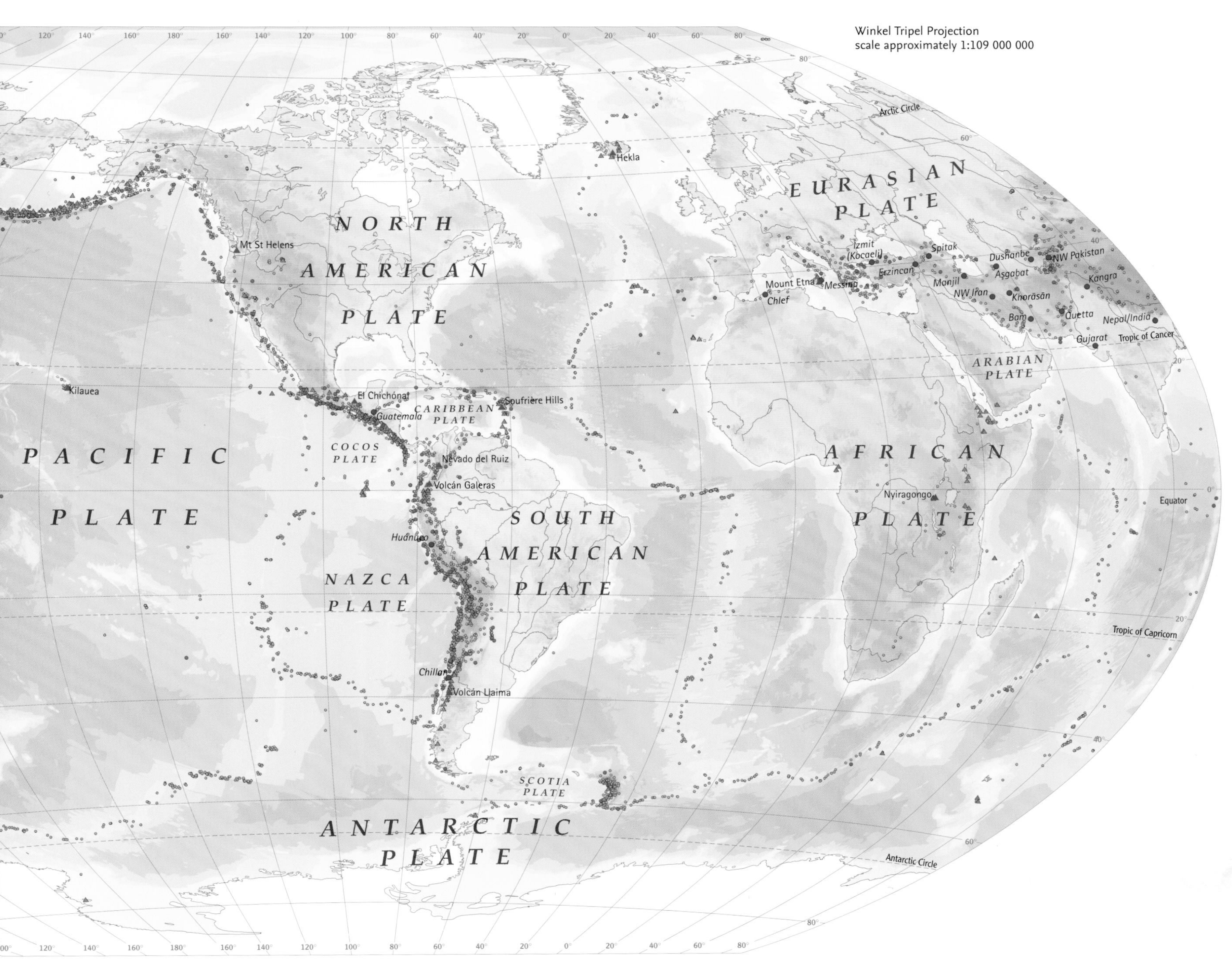

Winkel Tripel Projection
scale approximately 1:109 000 000

EURASIAN PLATE

Hekla

Izmit
(Kocaeli)
Spitak
Dushanbe
NW Pakistan
Erzincan
Aşgabat
Kangra
Mount Etna
Messina
Manjil
NW Iran
Khorāsān
Chlef
Bam
Quetta
Nepal/India
Gujarat
Tropic of Cancer

NORTH AMERICAN PLATE

Mt St Helens

Arctic Circle

60°

40°

20°

ARABIAN PLATE

Kilauea

El Chichónal
CARIBBEAN PLATE
Soufrière Hills
Guatemala

AFRICAN PLATE

COCOS PLATE

Nevado del Ruiz

Volcán Galeras

Nyiragongo

Equator

PACIFIC PLATE

SOUTH AMERICAN PLATE

Huánuco

NAZCA PLATE

Tropic of Capricorn

Chillán

Volcán Llaima

SCOTIA PLATE

ANTARCTIC PLATE

Antarctic Circle

Major Volcanic Eruptions 1980–2007

Year	Volcano	Country
1980	Mt St Helens	USA
1982	El Chichónal	Mexico
1982	Gunung Galunggung	Indonesia
1983	Kilauea	Hawaii, USA
1983	Ō-yama	Japan
1985	Nevado del Ruiz	Colombia
1991	Mt Pinatubo	Philippines
1991	Unzen-dake	Japan
1993	Mayon	Philippines
1993	Volcán Galeras	Colombia
1994	Volcán Llaima	Chile
1994	Rabaul	Papua New Guinea
1997	Soufrière Hills	Montserrat
2000	Hekla	Iceland
2001	Mount Etna	Italy
2002	Nyiragongo	Democratic Republic of the Congo

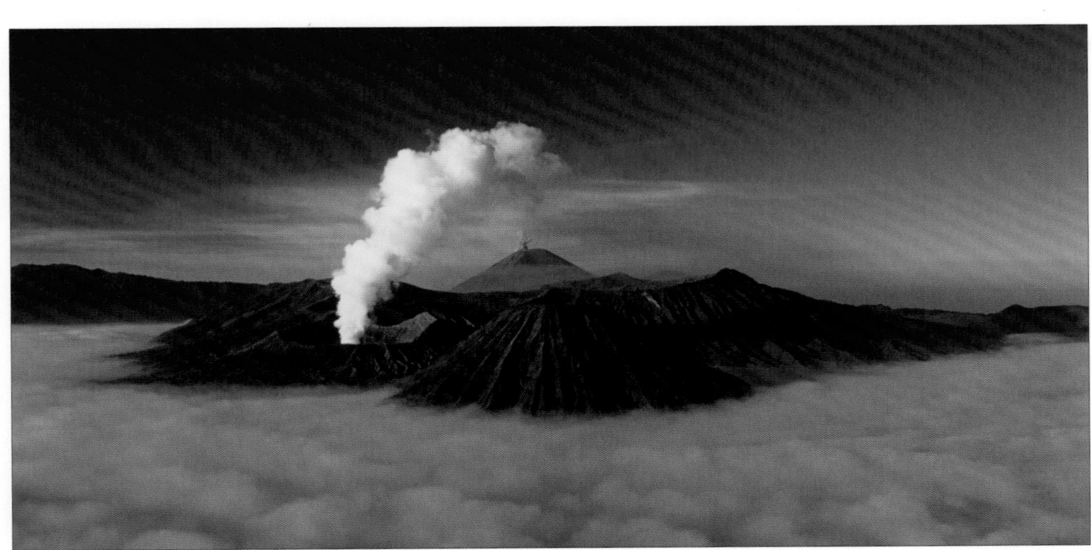

Mount Bromo, Java, Indonesia, is one of the many active volcanoes that have formed around the edge of the Pacific Ocean. It is unique in having seven eruptive centres in the caldera and is also a great location to see spectacular sunrises.

Climate

The climate classification shown on the main map is a simplified version of the system developed by W. Köppen. It is based on the relationship between temperature and precipitation data, and on vegetation characteristics. Extremes of climate, particularly tropical storms and tornadoes, are significant because of their destructive power. Increasing knowledge of these phenomena – particularly through the use of satellite imagery – will help in their prediction and will allow action to minimize their destructive effects.

Tornadoes

A tornado is a violent rotating column of air extending from a thunderstorm to the ground. The most violent tornadoes can cause massive destruction with wind speeds of 400 km per hr (249 miles per hr) or more. Although tornadoes occur in many parts of the world, they are found most frequently in the USA east of the Rocky Mountains and west of the Appalachian Mountains. They occur during the spring and summer months. In the USA in an average year 800 tornadoes are reported.

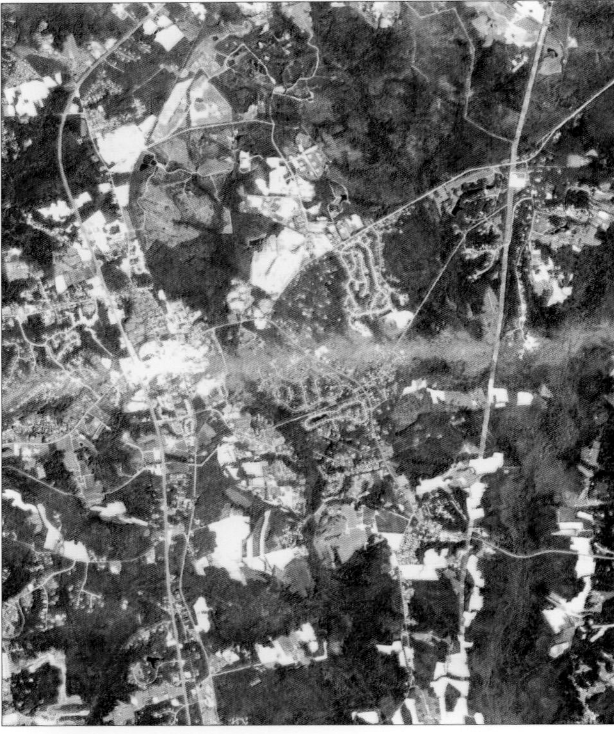

In April 2007 intense storms in northeast USA created a powerful tornado which touched down in southern Maryland destroying the historic centre of La Plata before moving east, flattening vegetation as it passed.

Tropical Storms

Tropical storms have different names in different parts of the world: hurricanes in the north Atlantic and east Pacific; typhoons in the northwest Pacific; and cyclones in the Indian Ocean region. There are also many other local names for these often catastrophic events. Tropical storms are among the most powerful and destructive weather systems on Earth. Of the eighty to one hundred which develop annually over the tropical oceans, many make landfall and cause considerable damage to property and loss of life as a result of high winds and heavy rain.

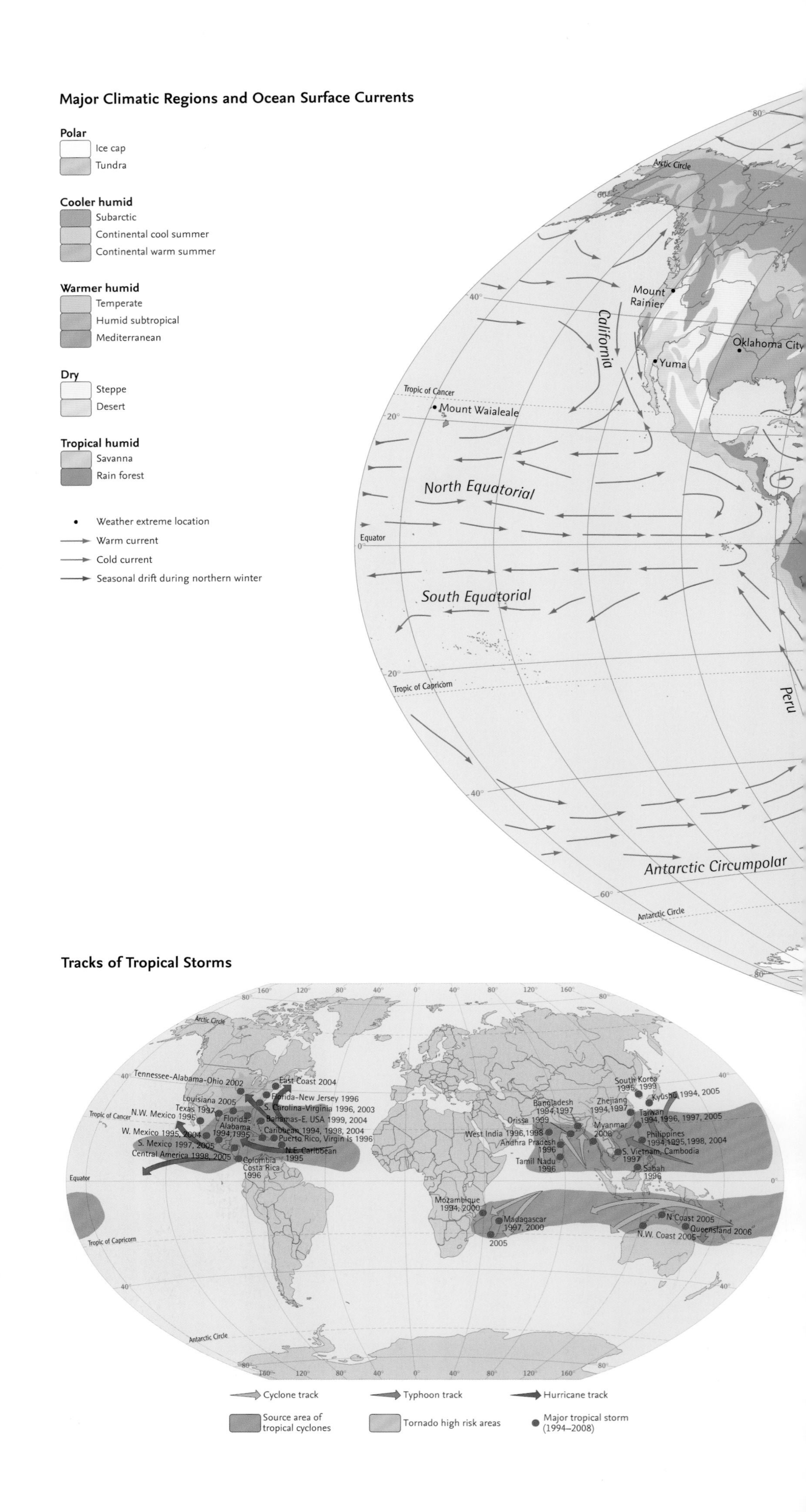

Major Climatic Regions and Ocean Surface Currents

Polar
- Ice cap
- Tundra

Cooler humid
- Subarctic
- Continental cool summer
- Continental warm summer

Warmer humid
- Temperate
- Humid subtropical
- Mediterranean

Dry
- Steppe
- Desert

Tropical humid
- Savanna
- Rain forest

- Weather extreme location
- Warm current
- Cold current
- Seasonal drift during northern winter

Tracks of Tropical Storms

- Cyclone track
- Typhoon track
- Hurricane track
- Source area of tropical cyclones
- Tornado high risk areas
- Major tropical storm (1994–2008)

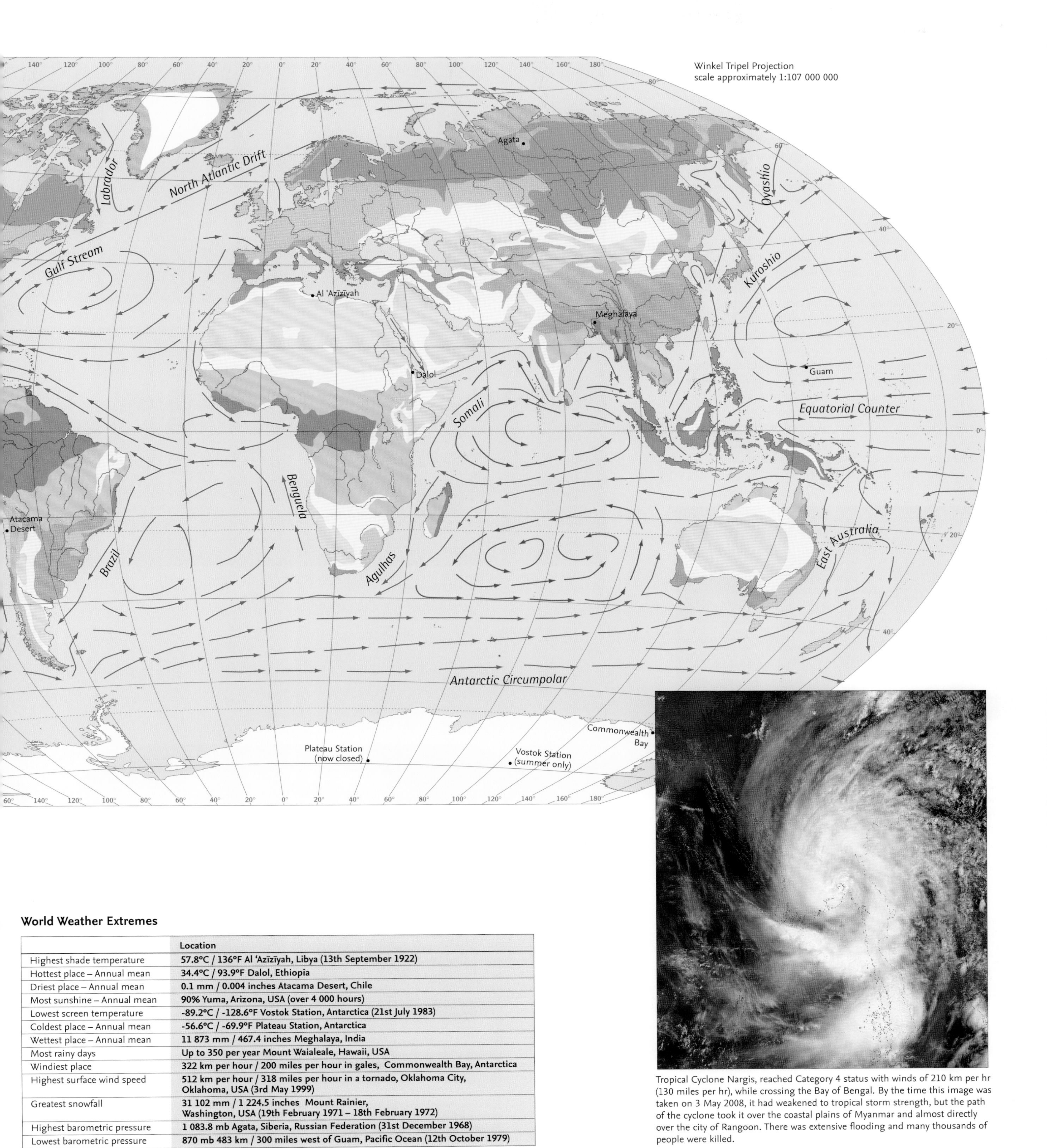

Winkel Tripel Projection
scale approximately 1:107 000 000

World Weather Extremes

	Location
Highest shade temperature	57.8°C / 136°F Al 'Azīzīyah, Libya (13th September 1922)
Hottest place – Annual mean	34.4°C / 93.9°F Dalol, Ethiopia
Driest place – Annual mean	0.1 mm / 0.004 inches Atacama Desert, Chile
Most sunshine – Annual mean	90% Yuma, Arizona, USA (over 4 000 hours)
Lowest screen temperature	-89.2°C / -128.6°F Vostok Station, Antarctica (21st July 1983)
Coldest place – Annual mean	-56.6°C / -69.9°F Plateau Station, Antarctica
Wettest place – Annual mean	11 873 mm / 467.4 inches Meghalaya, India
Most rainy days	Up to 350 per year Mount Waialeale, Hawaii, USA
Windiest place	322 km per hour / 200 miles per hour in gales, Commonwealth Bay, Antarctica
Highest surface wind speed	512 km per hour / 318 miles per hour in a tornado, Oklahoma City, Oklahoma, USA (3rd May 1999)
Greatest snowfall	31 102 mm / 1 224.5 inches Mount Rainier, Washington, USA (19th February 1971 – 18th February 1972)
Highest barometric pressure	1 083.8 mb Agata, Siberia, Russian Federation (31st December 1968)
Lowest barometric pressure	870 mb 483 km / 300 miles west of Guam, Pacific Ocean (12th October 1979)

Tropical Cyclone Nargis, reached Category 4 status with winds of 210 km per hr (130 miles per hr), while crossing the Bay of Bengal. By the time this image was taken on 3 May 2008, it had weakened to tropical storm strength, but the path of the cyclone took it over the coastal plains of Myanmar and almost directly over the city of Rangoon. There was extensive flooding and many thousands of people were killed.

Climate Change

The global average temperature can be established for approximately the last 150 years from the worldwide network of weather stations on land and observations made on board ships. Eleven of the last twelve years rank among the twelve warmest years on record, so the world has been warmer over the last decade than at any time since measurements began. This warming is observed over the oceans as well as over land, suggesting that it is a truly global phenomenon and not a conglomeration of 'local' increases in temperature caused by some small-scale process such as the urban heat island effect.

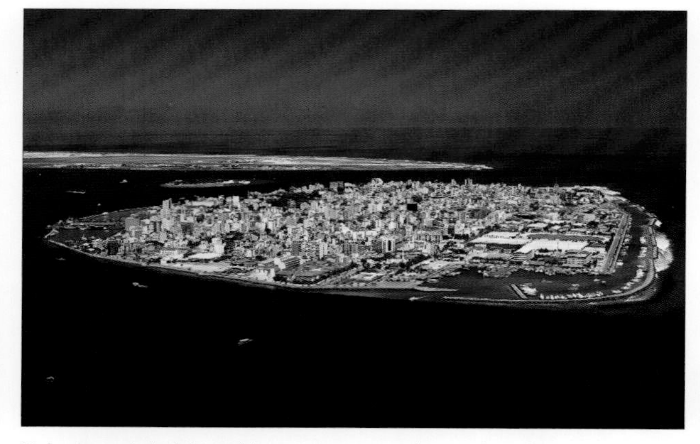

Observing Climate Change

Changes have also been seen in various areas of the climate system. Snow cover and mountain glaciers have shrunk, and some melting of the Greenland and Antarctic ice sheets has been measured. Global average sea level rose by approximately 17 cm through the 20th century, partly because of the additional water in the ocean basins resulting from the melting of ice on land, and partly because water expands when it heats up. Patterns of precipitation (rainfall and snowfall) have also changed, with parts of North and South America, Europe and northern and central Asia becoming wetter while the Sahel region of central Africa, southern Africa, the Mediterranean and southern Asia have become drier. Intense rainfall events have become more frequent. In Europe, Asia and North America, growing seasons have extended, with flowers emerging and trees coming into leaf several days earlier in the year than in the mid-twentieth century.

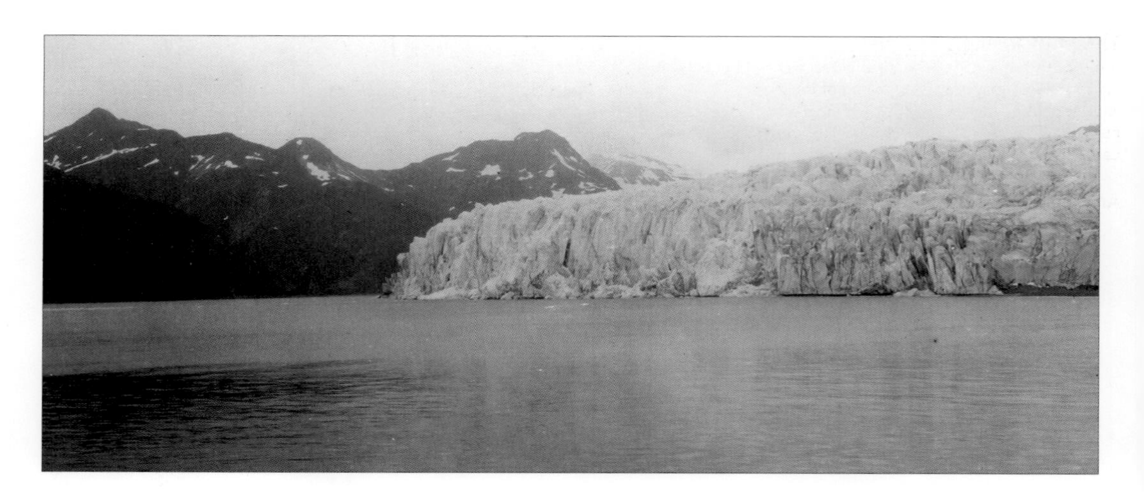

The McCarty Glacier in the Kenai Peninsula in Alaska is a tidewater glacier which has retreated around 16 km between 1909 (top) and 2004 (bottom).

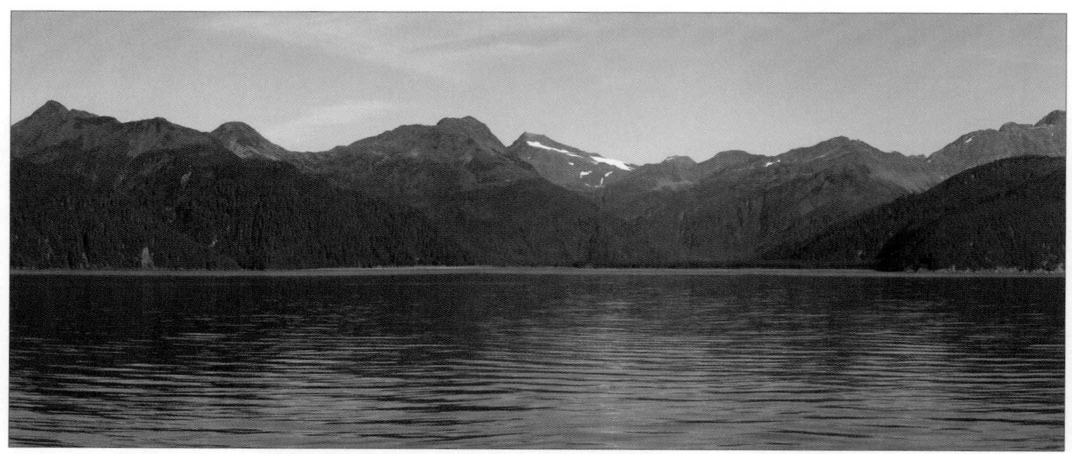

Male, the capital of the Maldives, is approximately 2 m above the sea, but its reclaimed land is lower leaving it very vulnerable to a sustained rise in sea level.

The Causes of Climate Change

Climate can change naturally, but over the last century the industrial and agricultural activities of humans have become additional causes of climate change. Changes in the concentration of 'greenhouse gases' can also result in climate change. The most important greenhouse gas is water vapour, followed by carbon dioxide. While many of these gases occur naturally in the atmosphere, humans are responsible for increasing the concentration of many of them through the burning of fossil fuels, deforestation and other industrial and agricultural processes. We have also introduced new greenhouse gases, the 'halocarbons' such as chlorofluorocarbons (CFCs) which have damaged the ozone layer in the stratosphere.

Projection of Global Temperatures 2090–2099
Based on IPCC scenario A1B. Change relative to 1980–1999.

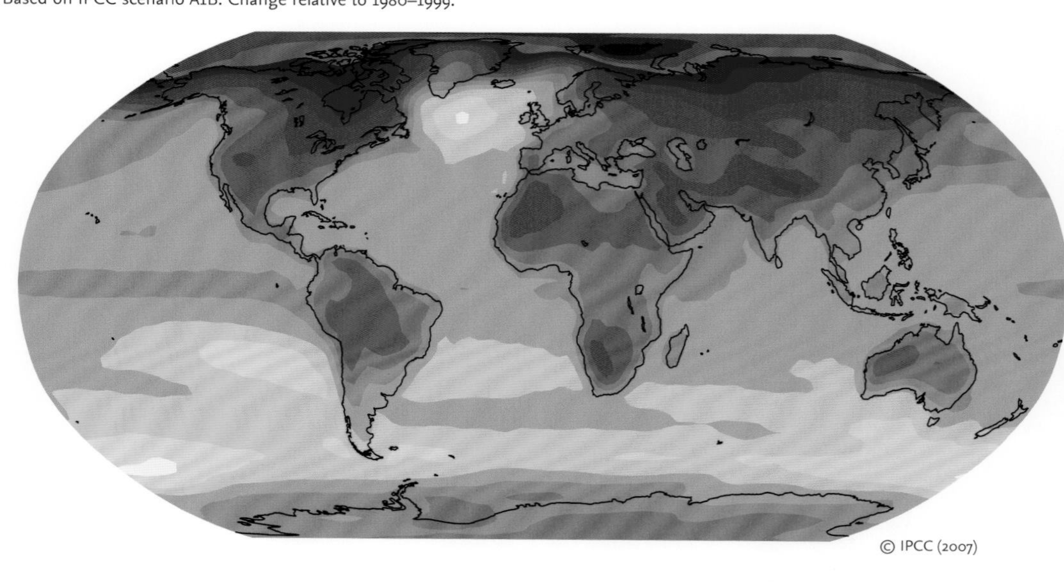

© IPCC (2007)

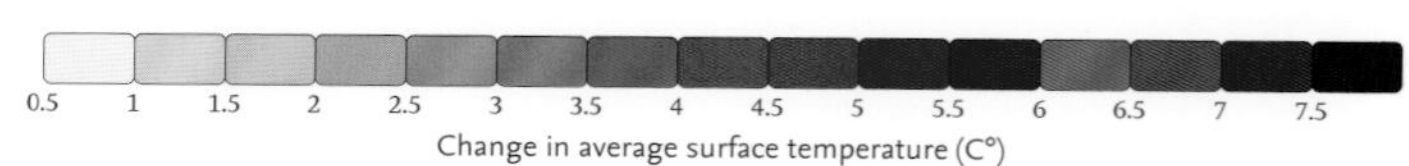

0.5   1   1.5   2   2.5   3   3.5   4   4.5   5   5.5   6   6.5   7   7.5

Change in average surface temperature (C°)

Faster warming is expected near the poles, as the melting snow and sea ice exposes the darker underlying land and ocean surfaces which then absorb more of the sun's radiation instead of reflecting it back to space in the way that brighter ice and snow do.

Threat of Rising Sea Level

It has been suggested that further global warming of between 1.0 and 6.4 C° may occur by the end of the 21st century. Sea level is projected to rise by between 28 cm and 58 cm, threatening a number of coastal cities, low-lying deltas and small islands. Larger rises are predicted in some locations than others.

Areas at Risk of Submersion

- ○ Major cities
- Coastal areas at greatest risk
- Islands and archipelagos
- Areas of low-lying islands

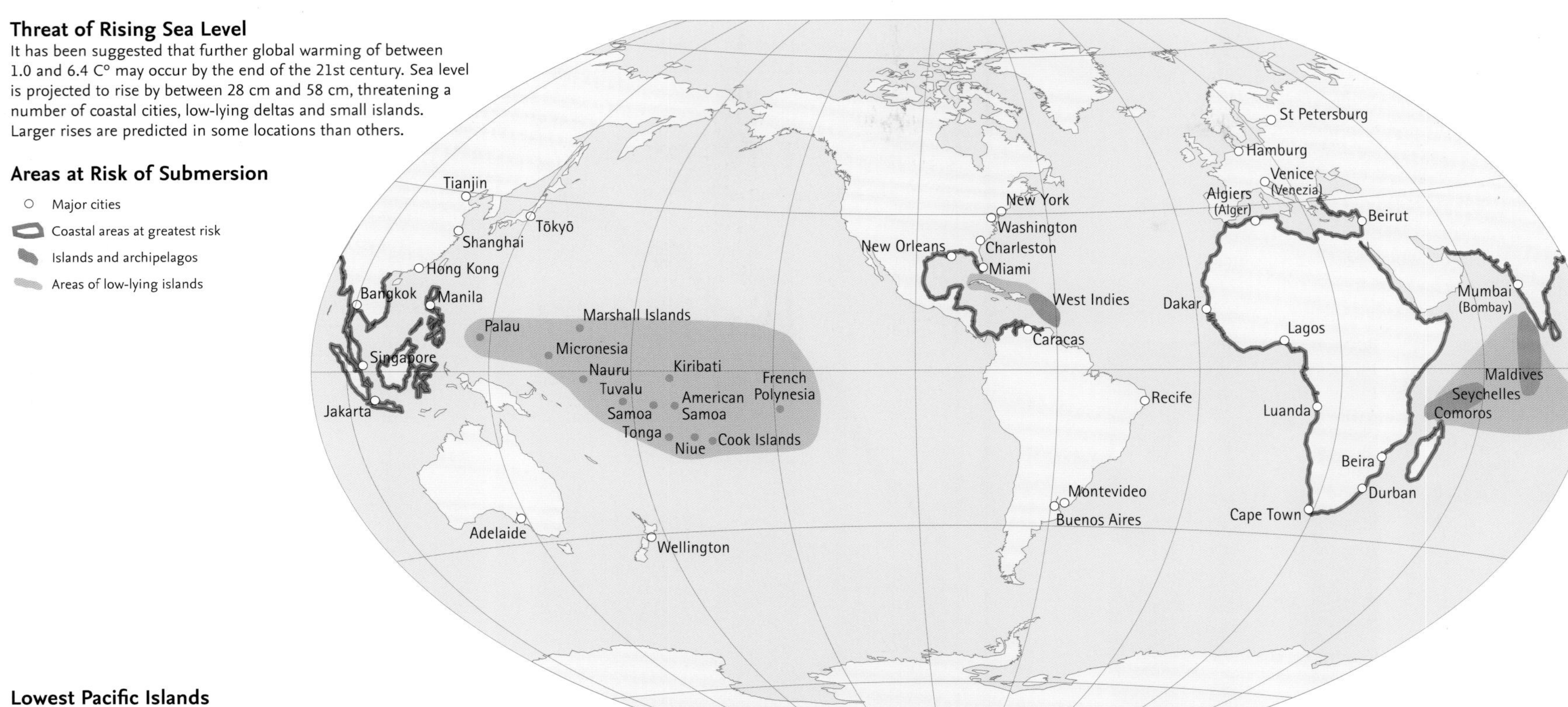

Lowest Pacific Islands

Location	Maximum height above sea level	Land area sq km	sq miles	Population
Kingman Reef	1 m (3 ft)	1	0.4	0
Palmyra Atoll	2 m (7 ft)	12	5	0
Ashmore and Cartier Islands	3 m (10 ft)	5	2	0
Howland Island	3 m (10 ft)	2	1	0
Johnston Atoll	5 m (16 ft)	3	1	0
Tokelau	5 m (16 ft)	10	4	1 000
Tuvalu	5 m (16 ft)	25	10	10 000
Coral Sea Islands Territory	6 m (20 ft)	22	8	0
Wake Island	6 m (20 ft)	7	3	0
Jarvis Island	7 m (23 ft)	5	2	0

Projection of Global Precipitation 2090–2099

Based on IPCC scenario A1B. Change relative to 1980–1999.

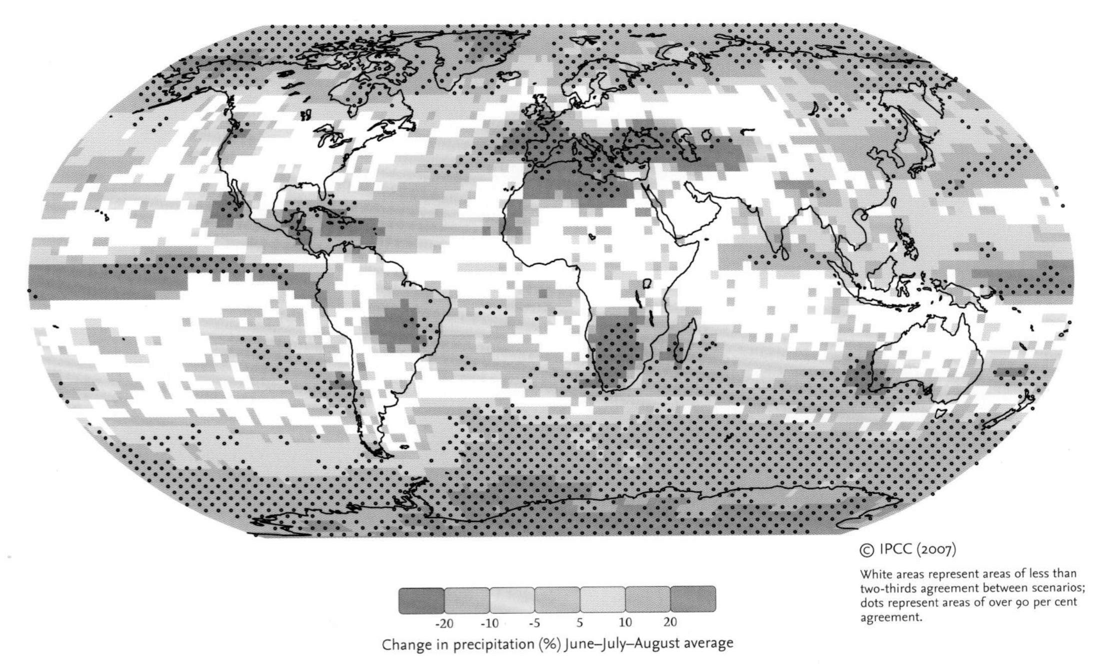

© IPCC (2007)

White areas represent areas of less than two-thirds agreement between scenarios; dots represent areas of over 90 per cent agreement.

-20 -10 -5 5 10 20
Change in precipitation (%) June–July–August average

In the high-latitude regions (central and northern Europe, Asia and North America) the year-round average precipitation is projected to increase, while in most sub-tropical land regions it is projected to decrease by as much as 20 per cent. This would increase the risk of drought and, in combination with higher temperatures, threaten agricultural productivity.

Historical Climate Records

Changes relative to 1961–1990 averages

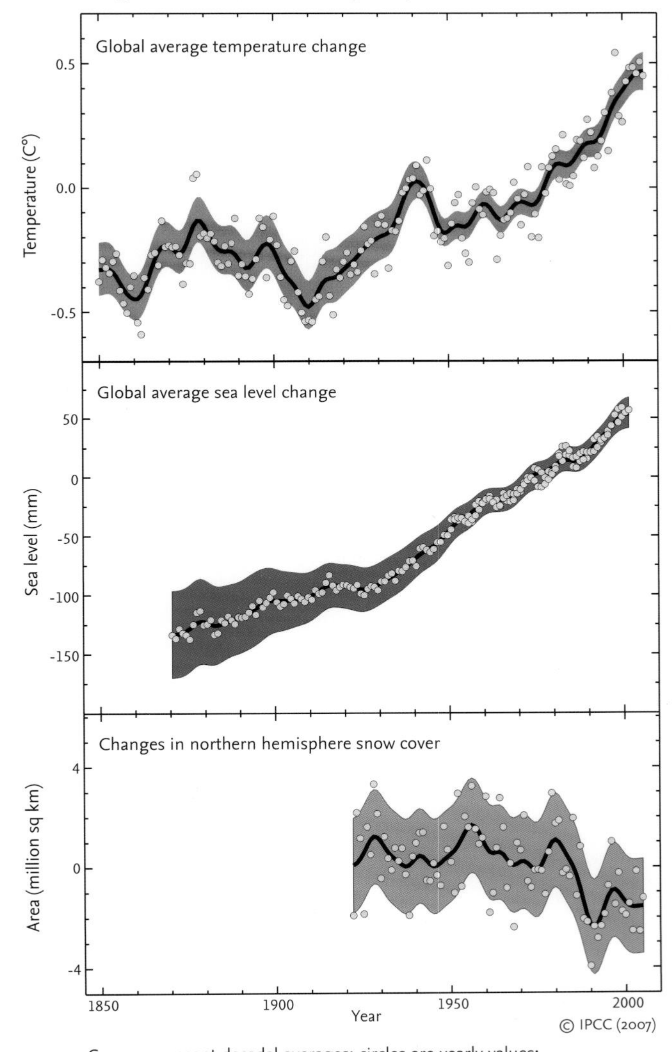

Curves represent decadal averages; circles are yearly values; shaded areas are uncertainty intervals.

Environment and Biodiversity

Throughout history people have altered the natural environment, influencing landscapes, land cover, biodiversity, and the chemical composition of air, land, and water. The rate of change has accelerated dramatically since the industrial revolution, as a result of advances in technology, changing lifestyles and associated patterns of production and consumption, and the rapidly growing global population. As the human population has increased, so too has demand for the Earth's natural resources, leading in many areas to environmental degradation which has had significant impacts on people's lives in many parts of the world.

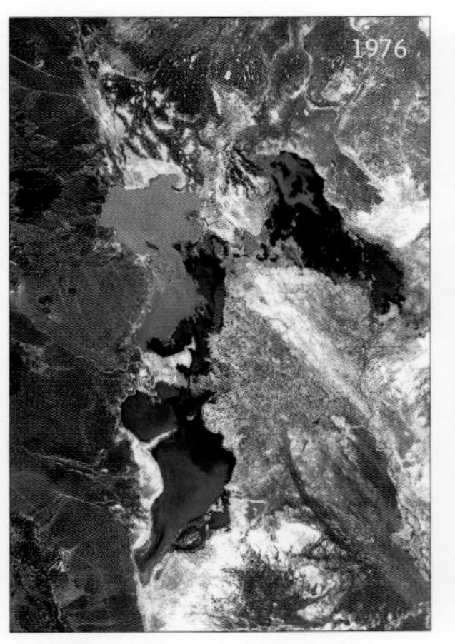 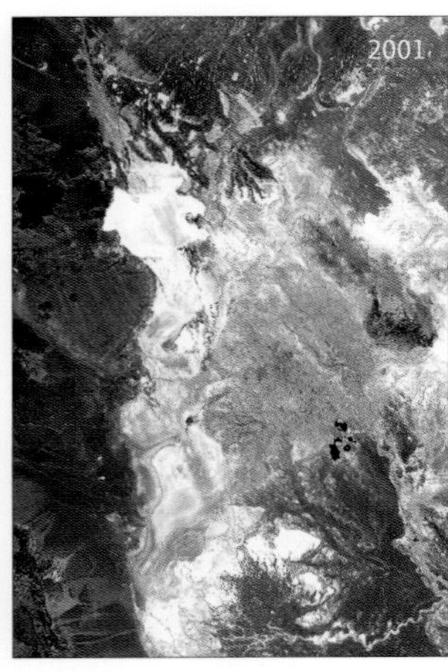

For many thousands of years the Hamoun wetlands have been a major source of food and shelter in the middle of vast arid plains in central Asia. From the mid 1990s however, the Helmand river was increasingly used for irrigation and diverted into dams leaving the area vulnerable to a prolonged drought. These false colour images of 1976 and 2001 show the extent of the devastation.

Environmental Change

Land cover has changed more over the past fifty years than at any time in human history. Much of this change has been due to the conversion of natural ecosystems to agricultural land to help meet demand for food production. Wetlands and other freshwater environments have been dramatically affected by changes in land cover and use. It is speculated that approximately one-third of all mangroves and half of all inland wetlands were converted during the 20th century. Fragmentation and the modification of river flow have resulted from the construction of dams and other structures along rivers, affecting almost 60 per cent of the large river systems in the world.

Biodiversity

Biodiversity, derived from the term 'biological diversity', is the name given to the variety and processes of all life on Earth, including individual living organisms, their genes, and the habitats or ecosystems of which they are part, whether terrestrial, freshwater or marine. The diversity of life is not evenly distributed around the world, and based on the number of species in a location, or 'species richness', a general pattern emerges of considerably more biodiversity in the tropics than at higher latitudes. To date approximately two million species have been identified and described.

Ecological Footprint
Humanity's ecological footprint by component 1961–2003.

Legend:
- Built-up land
- Energy
- Fishing grounds
- Forest
- Grazing land
- Cropland

Total footprint of humanity in 'number of Earths used'

'Number of Earths' available

Number of Earths (y-axis)
Year (x-axis)

World Land Cover
Winkel Tripel Projection
scale approximately 1:112 000 000

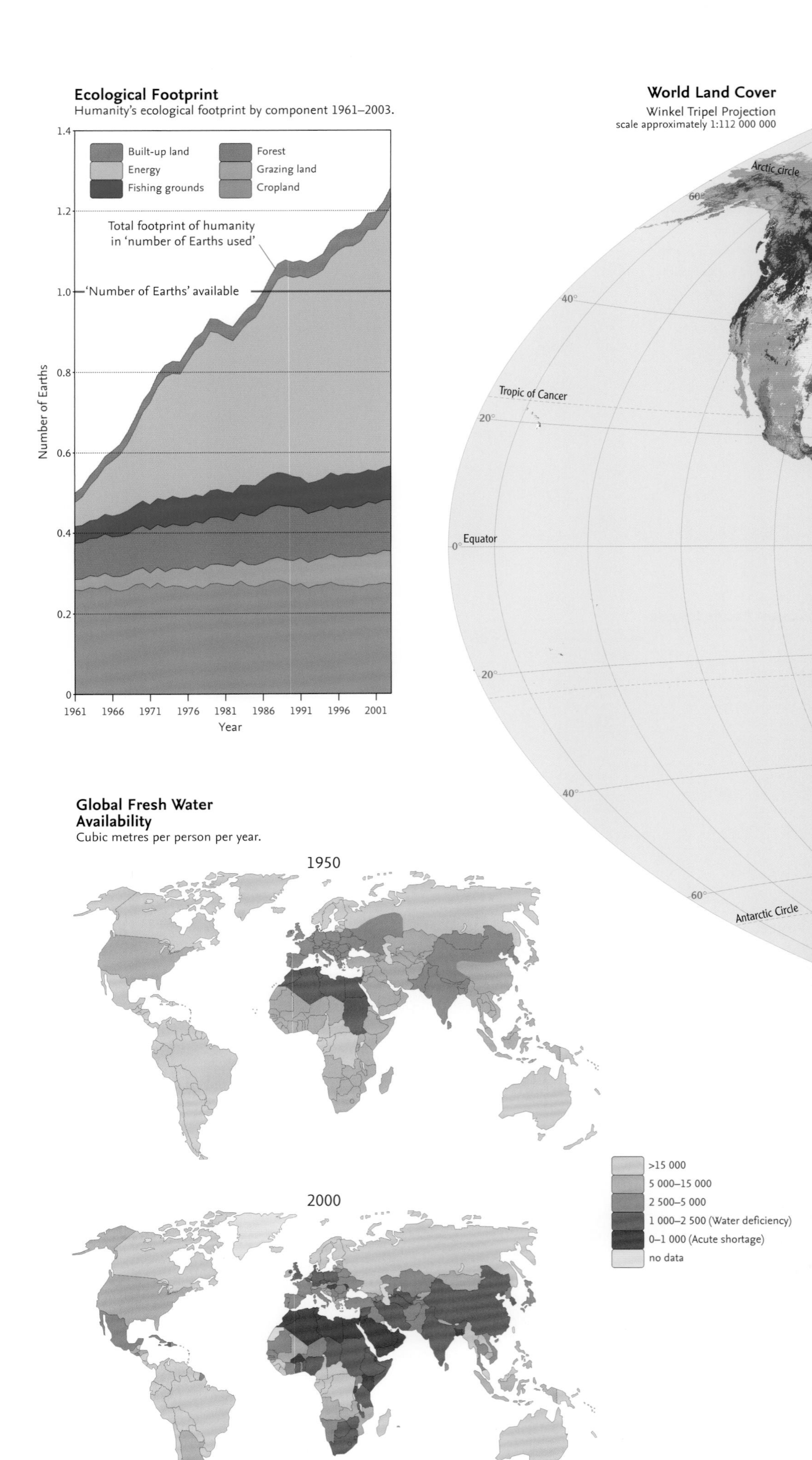

Global Fresh Water Availability
Cubic metres per person per year.

1950

2000

- >15 000
- 5 000–15 000
- 2 500–5 000
- 1 000–2 500 (Water deficiency)
- 0–1 000 (Acute shortage)
- no data

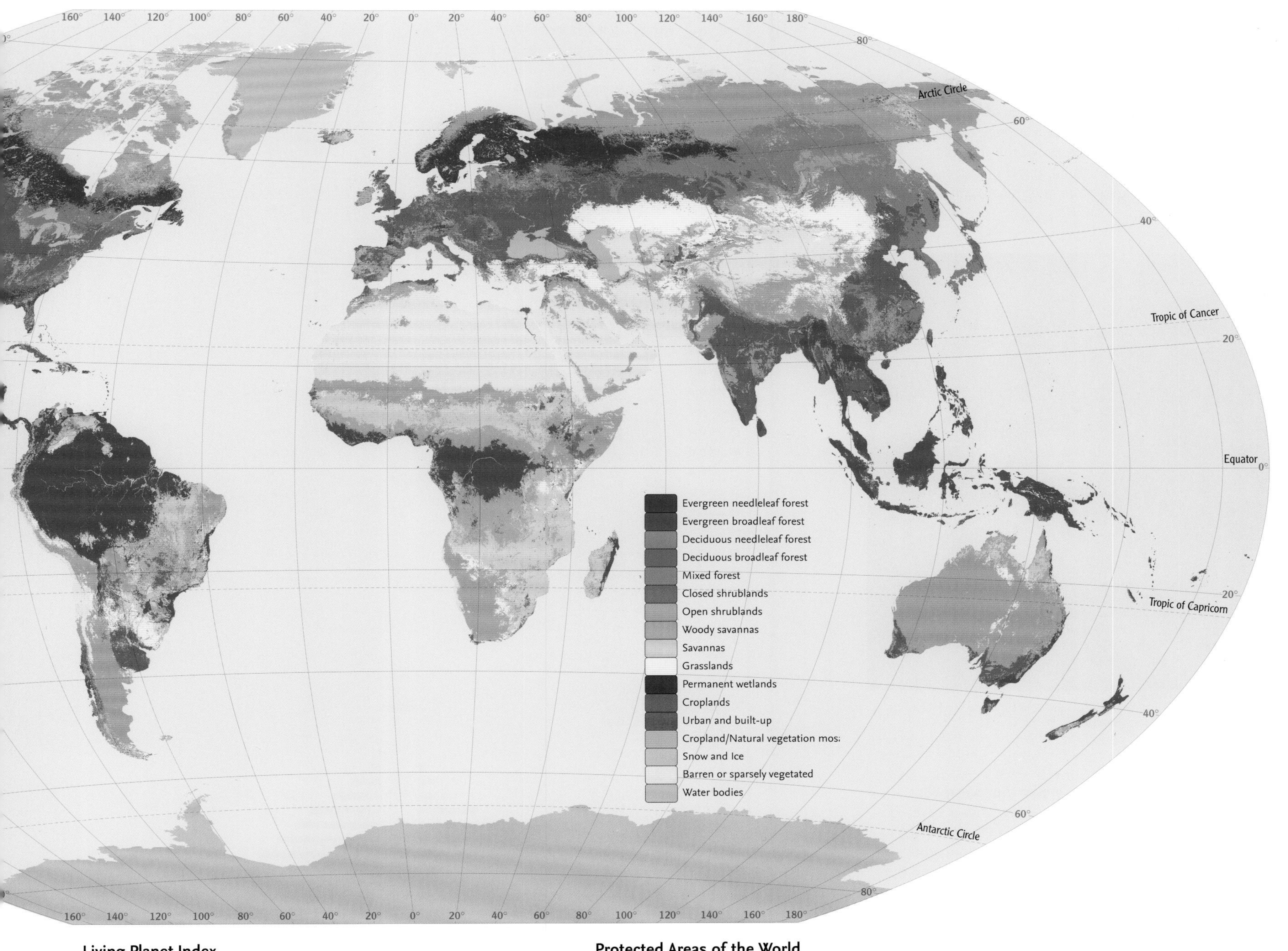

	Evergreen needleleaf forest
	Evergreen broadleaf forest
	Deciduous needleleaf forest
	Deciduous broadleaf forest
	Mixed forest
	Closed shrublands
	Open shrublands
	Woody savannas
	Savannas
	Grasslands
	Permanent wetlands
	Croplands
	Urban and built-up
	Cropland/Natural vegetation mos:
	Snow and Ice
	Barren or sparsely vegetated
	Water bodies

Living Planet Index

Trends in population of terrestrial, freshwater and marine species 1970–2003.

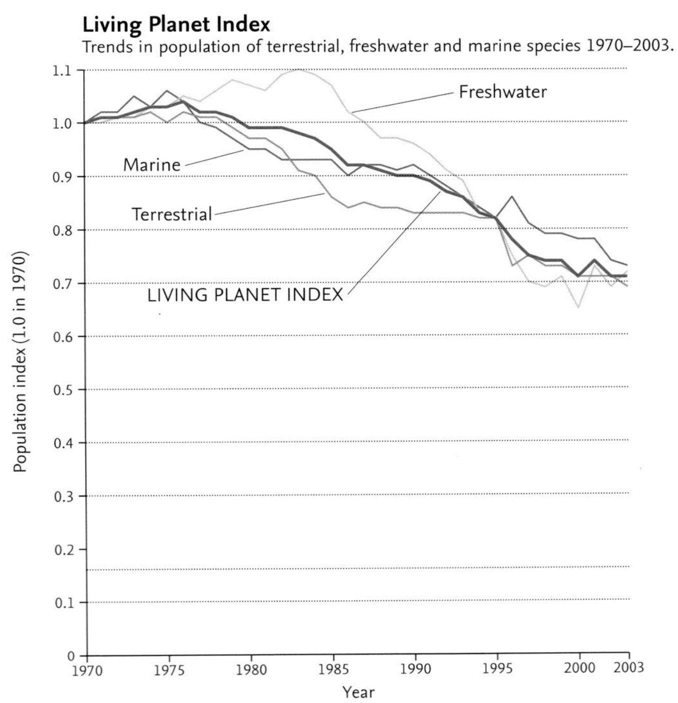

Protected Areas of the World

Proportion of large marine ecosystems and terrestrial ecoregions under protection.

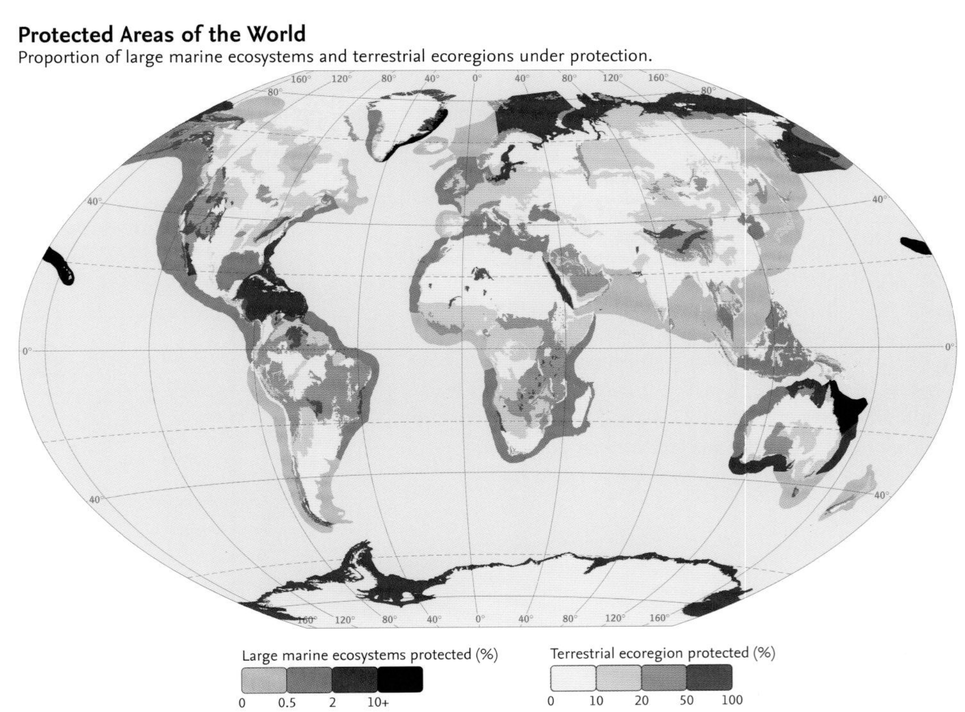

Large marine ecosystems protected (%)

0   0.5   2   10+

Terrestrial ecoregion protected (%)

0   10   20   50   100

Population

World population is currently undergoing the biggest transformation that it has ever seen, but this process is impacting very unevenly. While overall numbers have been growing extremely rapidly since 1950, almost nine-tenths of the increase has taken place in the less developed regions, especially southern and eastern Asia, while Europe's population is now estimated to be in overall decline and ageing rapidly. India and China alone are responsible for over one-third of current growth, but most of the highest percentage rates of growth are to be found in Sub-Saharan Africa, where the demographic transition process is still at a relatively early stage.

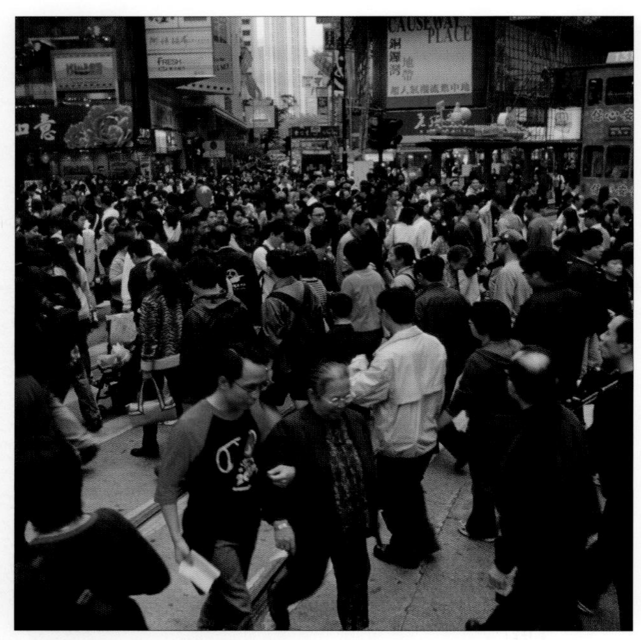

Population growth in the 20th century was rapid and continued growth could carry the world's population past seven billion by 2015.

Population Distribution

People are distributed very unevenly over the face of the planet, even after allowing for the two-thirds that is covered by water. As shown on the main map, over a quarter of the land area is uninhabited or has extremely low population density, notably the polar regions, the Amazon basin and the dry deserts of Saharan Africa, southwest and central Asia, and Australia.

Population Growth

Over the past half century world population has been growing faster than it has ever done before. While world population did not pass the one billion mark until 1804 and took another 123 years to reach two billion, it then added the third billion in 33 years, the fourth in 14 years and the fifth in 13 years, with the addition of the 6 billionth person being celebrated by the UN 12 years after this on 12 October 1999. The latest trends in population growth at country level emphasize the continuing contrast between the more and less developed regions. Annual growth rates of 1.5 per cent or more remain common in Latin America, Africa and southern Asia. A number of countries have rates in excess of 3.0 per cent, which if continued would lead to the doubling of population in 23 years or less. Ten countries account for 60 per cent of the world's current population growth, with India and China responsible for over half.

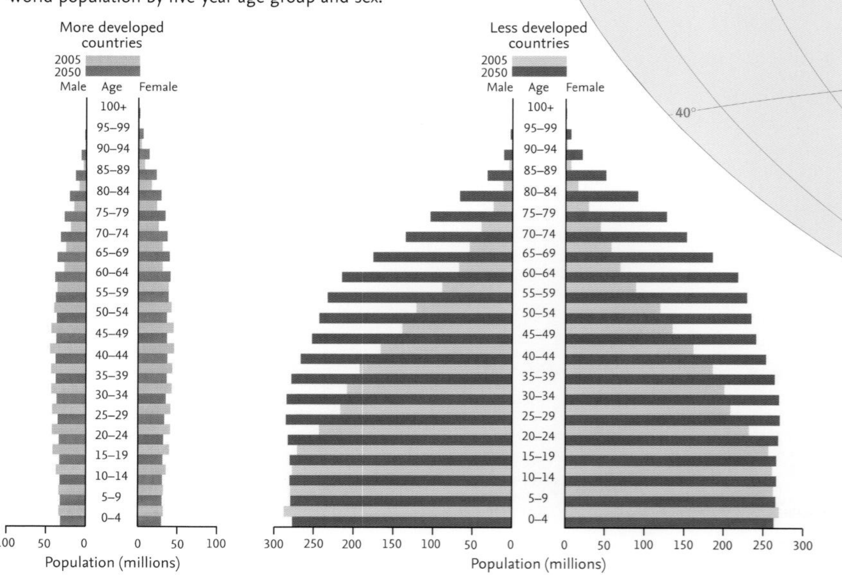

Top Twenty Countries by Population and Population Density 2007

Total population	Country	Rank	Country*	Inhabitants per sq mile	Inhabitants per sq km
1 313 437 000	China	1	Bangladesh	2 854	1 102
1 169 016 000	India	2	Taiwan	1 638	632
305 826 000	United States of America	3	South Korea	1 258	486
231 627 000	Indonesia	4	Netherlands	1 024	395
191 791 000	Brazil	5	India	988	381
163 902 000	Pakistan	6	Belgium	887	343
158 665 000	Bangladesh	7	Japan	877	339
148 093 000	Nigeria	8	Sri Lanka	762	294
142 499 000	Russian Federation	9	Philippines	759	293
127 967 000	Japan	10	Vietnam	687	265
106 535 000	Mexico	11	United Kingdom	646	249
87 960 000	Philippines	12	Germany	599	231
87 375 000	Vietnam	13	Pakistan	528	204
83 099 000	Ethiopia	14	North Korea	511	197
82 599 000	Germany	15	Italy	506	195
75 498 000	Egypt	16	Nepal	496	192
74 877 000	Turkey	17	Nigeria	415	160
71 208 000	Iran	18	China	355	137
63 884 000	Thailand	19	Czech Republic	335	129
62 636 000	Democratic Republic of the Congo	20	Uganda	332	128

*Only countries with a population of over 10 million are considered.

Age Pyramids

World population by five-year age group and sex.

More developed countries
2005
2050
Male Age Female

Less developed countries
2005
2050
Male Age Female

Population (millions)

Key Population Statistics for Major Regions

	Population 2007 (millions)	Growth (per cent)	Infant mortality rate	Total fertility rate	Life expectancy (years)	% aged 60 and over 2005	% aged 60 and over 2050
World	6 671	1.2	49	2.6	67	10	22
More developed regions[1]	1 223	0.3	7	1.6	77	20	33
Less developed regions[2]	5 448	1.4	54	2.8	65	8	20
Africa	965	2.3	87	4.7	53	5	10
Asia	4 030	1.1	43	2.3	69	9	24
Europe[3]	731	0.0	8	1.5	75	21	35
Latin America and the Caribbean[4]	572	1.2	22	2.4	73	9	24
North America	339	1.0	6	2	79	17	27
Oceania	34	1.2	26	2.3	75	14	25

Except for population and % aged 60 and over figures, the data are annual averages projected for the period 2005–2010.

1. Europe, North America, Australia, New Zealand and Japan.
2. Africa, Asia (excluding Japan), Latin America and the Caribbean, and Oceania (excluding Australia and New Zealand).
3. Includes Russian Federation.
4. South America, Central America (including Mexico) and all Caribbean Islands.

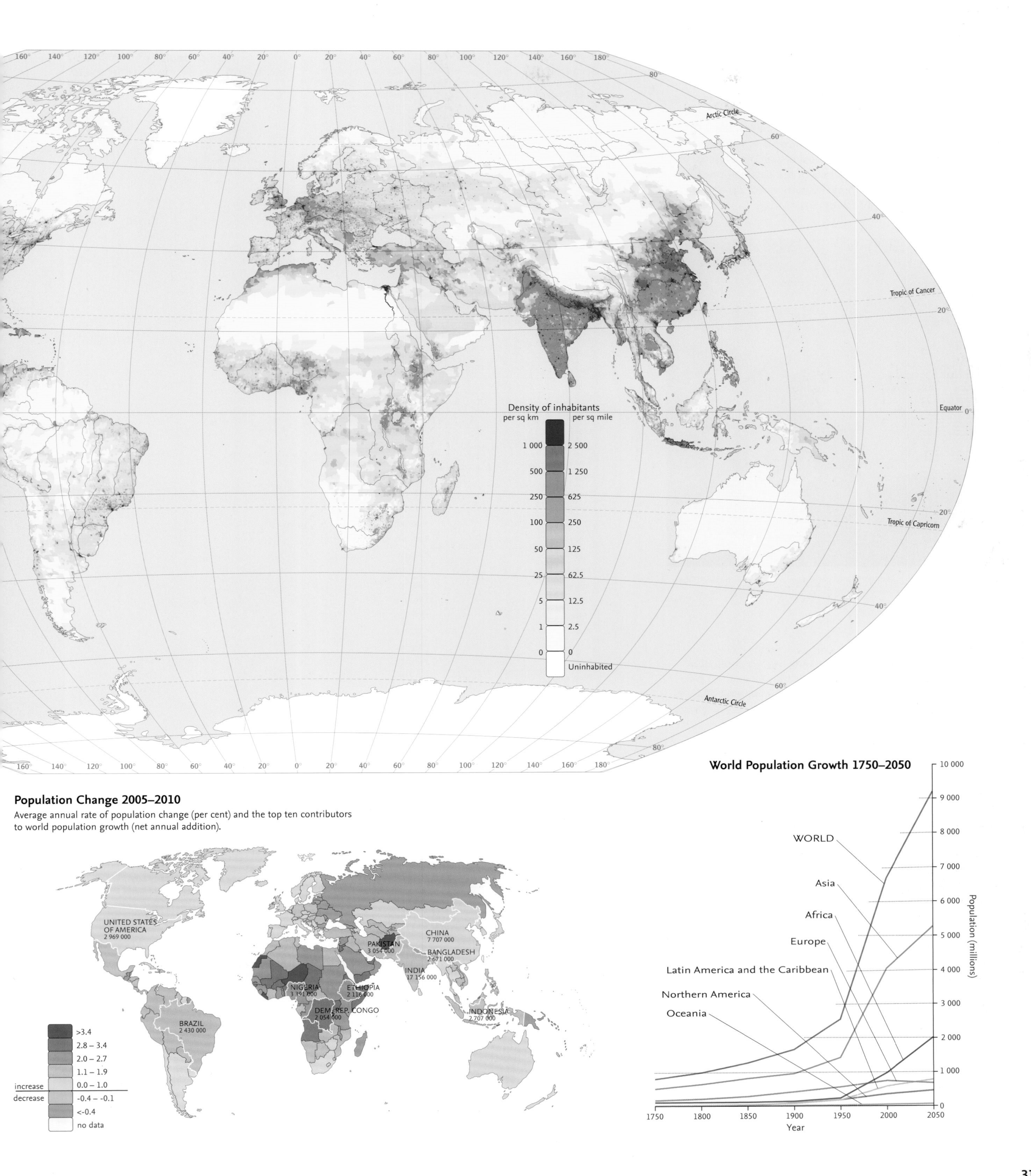

Density of inhabitants

per sq km		per sq mile
1 000		2 500
500		1 250
250		625
100		250
50		125
25		62.5
5		12.5
1		2.5
0		0
	Uninhabited	

Population Change 2005–2010

Average annual rate of population change (per cent) and the top ten contributors to world population growth (net annual addition).

UNITED STATES OF AMERICA 2 969 000

CHINA 7 707 000

PAKISTAN 3 054 000

BANGLADESH 2 671 000

INDIA 17 156 000

NIGERIA 3 391 000

ETHIOPIA 2 116 000

DEM. REP. CONGO 2 054 000

INDONESIA 2 707 000

BRAZIL 2 430 000

	>3.4
	2.8 – 3.4
	2.0 – 2.7
	1.1 – 1.9
increase	0.0 – 1.0
decrease	-0.4 – -0.1
	<-0.4
	no data

World Population Growth 1750–2050

WORLD
Asia
Africa
Europe
Latin America and the Caribbean
Northern America
Oceania

Population (millions)

Year

Urbanization

World population is urbanizing rapidly and, in this respect, 2008 is a momentous point in world history. In 2008, for the first time urban dwellers will outnumber those living in traditionally rural areas. But the current level of urbanization varies greatly across the world, as too does its rate of increase. In the hundred years up to 1950 the greatest changes took place in Europe and North America. Relatively few large cities developed elsewhere and most of these were in coastal locations with good trading connections with the imperial and industrial nations. The main feature of the past half century has been the massive growth in the numbers of urban dwellers in the less developed regions.

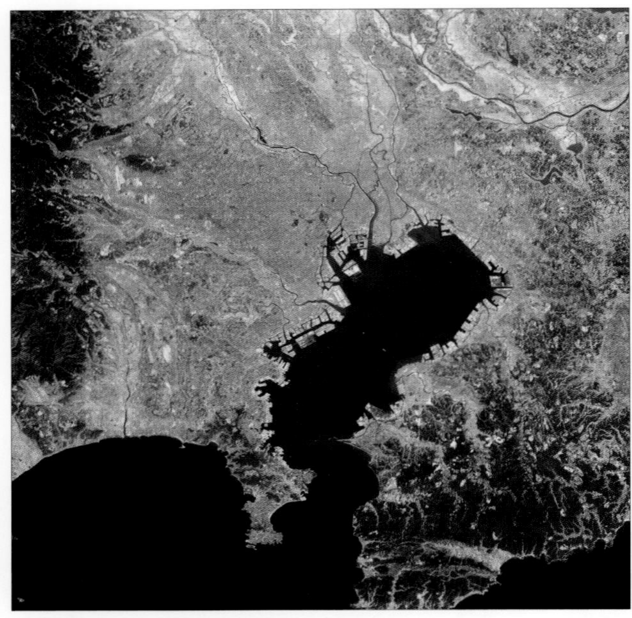

Tōkyō is the largest city in the world and more than a quarter of the population of Japan live here. The city was established in 1603 and has been growing steadily ever since then.

Towards an Urbanized World

The annual rise in the percentage of the world's population living in cities has been accelerating steadily since the 1970s and it will be running at very high levels until at least 2030. As a result, by then, 3 in 5 people (59.9 per cent) will be urbanites compared to 35.9 per cent in 1970 and 50.8 per cent in 2010. In absolute terms, the global urban population more than doubled between 1970 and 2000, adding 1.5 billion to its 1970 total of 1.33 billion, and it is expected to grow by a further 2.07 billion by 2030. There is a broad contrast in the level of urbanization between the more and less developed regions, but also a great deal of variation within them. In the more developed regions as a whole, three-quarters of the population now live in urban areas.

The Growth of Large Cities

Alongside the rise in the world's urban population has occurred a massive increase in the number and size of cities, especially of the very large cities or 'megacities'. In 1950, New York was the only agglomeration with over 10 million inhabitants, and there were still only three cities of this size by 1975 – New York, Tōkyō and Mexico City. By 2000, there were eighteen and there are expected to be twenty-two by 2015. Urban areas are also becoming more diffuse and polycentric, making the task of defining separate cities on the ground even more difficult.

World's Largest Cities 2010

Figures are for the urban agglomeration, defined as the population contained within the contours of a contiguous territory inhabited at urban levels without regard to administrative boundaries. They incorporate the population within a city plus the suburban fringe lying outside of, but adjacent to, the city boundaries.

City	Country	Population
Tōkyō	Japan	35 467 000
Mexico City	Mexico	20 688 000
Mumbai	India	20 036 000
São Paulo	Brazil	19 582 000
New York	USA	19 388 000
Delhi	India	16 983 000
Shanghai	China	15 790 000
Kolkata	India	15 548 000
Jakarta	Indonesia	15 206 000
Dhaka	Bangladesh	14 625 000
Lagos	Nigeria	13 717 000
Karachi	Pakistan	13 252 000
Buenos Aires	Argentina	13 067 000
Los Angeles	USA	12 738 000
Rio de Janeiro	Brazil	12 170 000
Cairo	Egypt	12 041 000
Manila	Philippines	11 799 000
Beijing	China	11 741 000
Ōsaka	Japan	11 305 000
Moscow	Russian Federation	10 967 000
İstanbul	Turkey	10 546 000
Paris	France	9 856 000
Seoul	South Korea	9 554 000
Guangzhou	China	9 447 000
Chicago	USA	9 186 000
London	United Kingdom	8 607 000
Bogotá	Colombia	8 416 000
Shenzhen	China	8 114 000
Tehrān	Iran	7 807 000
Lima	Peru	7 590 000
Chennai	India	7 545 000
Wuhan	China	7 542 000
Kinshasa	Dem. Rep. Congo	7 526 000
Tianjin	China	7 468 000
Hong Kong	China	7 416 000
Bangalore	India	7 216 000
Lahore	Pakistan	7 201 000
Bangkok	Thailand	6 963 000
Hyderabad	India	6 749 000
Chongqing	China	6 690 000
Baghdād	Iraq	6 593 000

World's Major Cities

Urban agglomerations with over 2.5 million inhabitants.

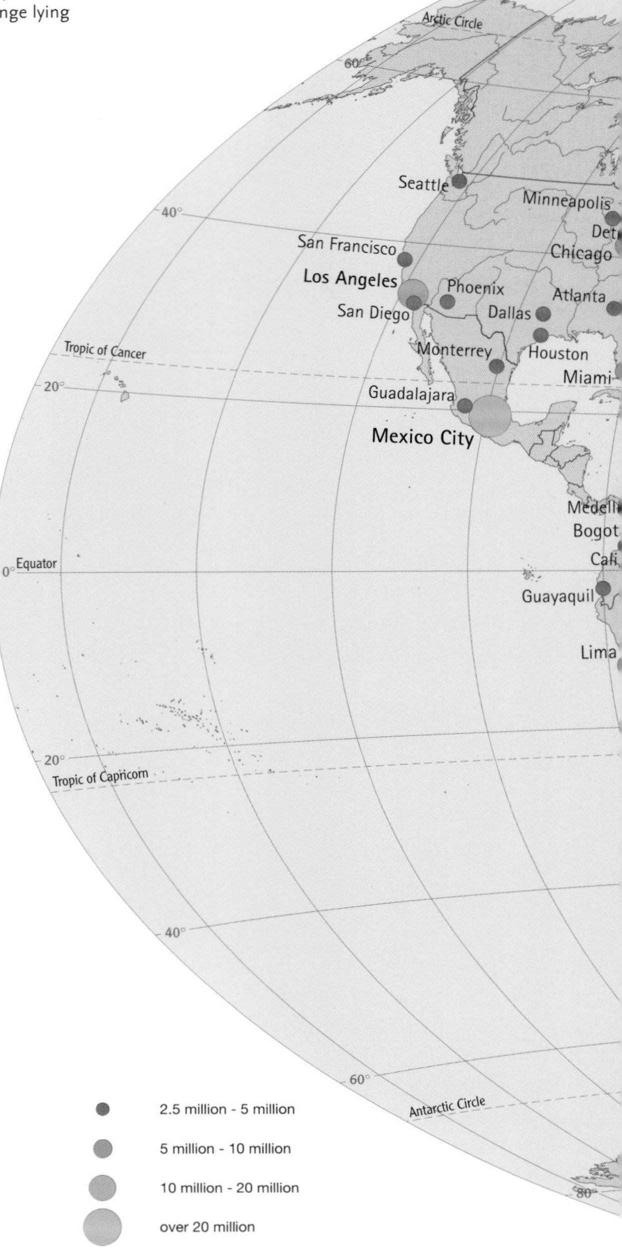

- 2.5 million - 5 million
- 5 million - 10 million
- 10 million - 20 million
- over 20 million

Level of Urbanization

Percentage of total population living in urban areas 2005. The world's urban population is expected to reach 50 per cent of the total population during 2008.

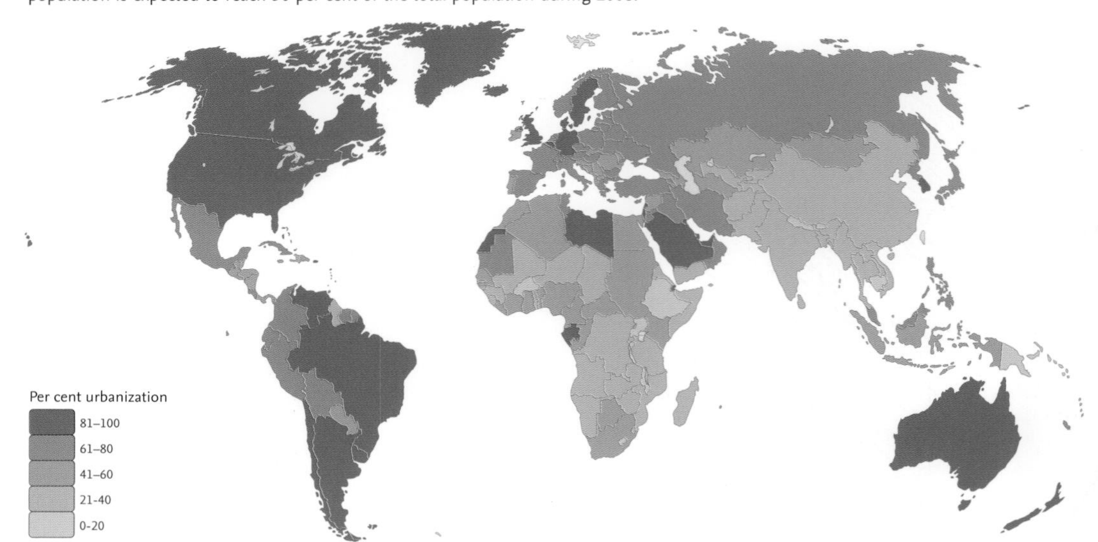

Per cent urbanization
- 81–100
- 61–80
- 41–60
- 21–40
- 0–20

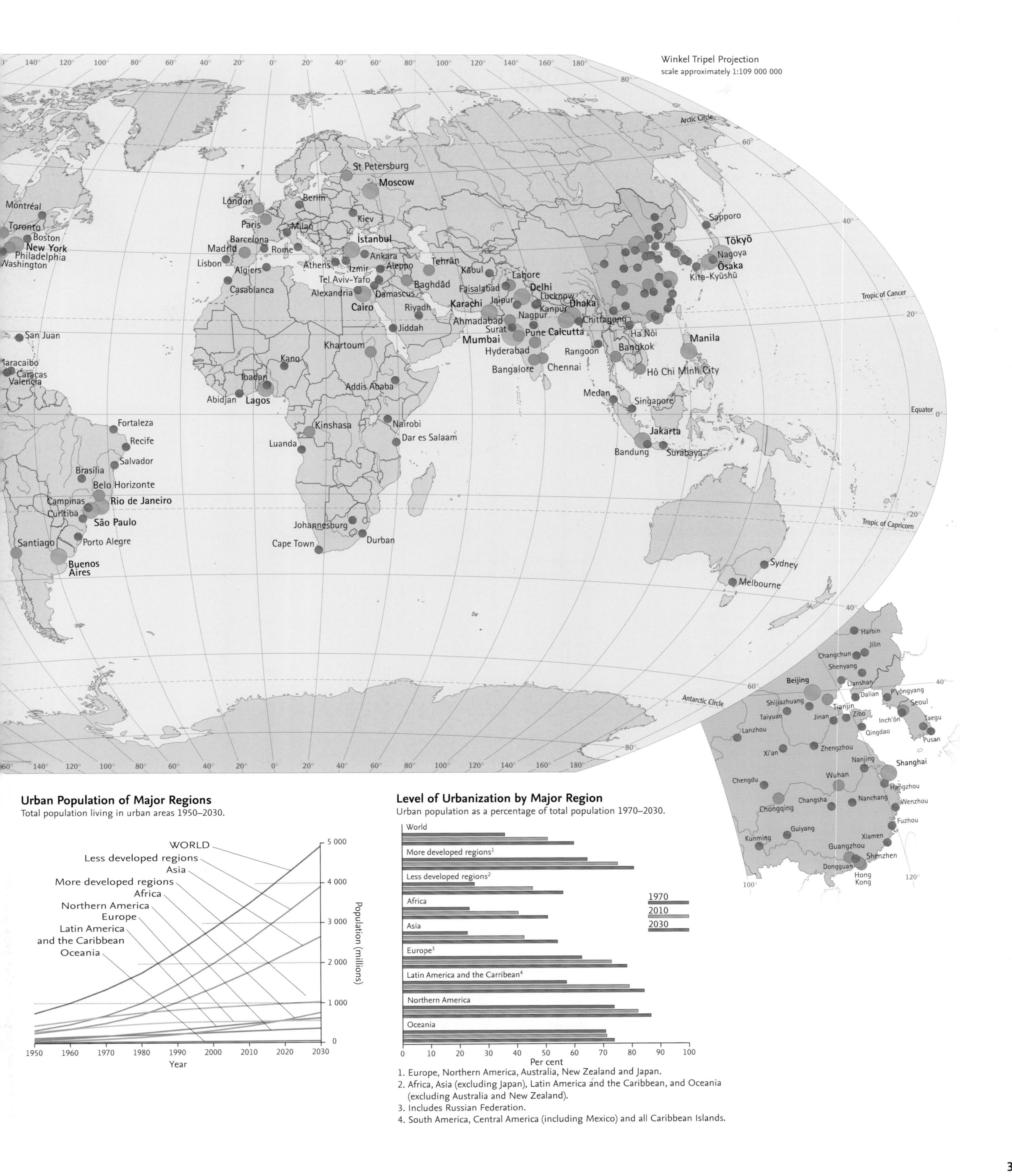

Winkel Tripel Projection
scale approximately 1:109 000 000

Urban Population of Major Regions
Total population living in urban areas 1950–2030.

WORLD
Less developed regions
Asia
More developed regions
Africa
Northern America
Europe
Latin America
and the Caribbean
Oceania

Population (millions)

Year

Level of Urbanization by Major Region
Urban population as a percentage of total population 1970–2030.

World
More developed regions[1]
Less developed regions[2]
Africa
Asia
Europe[3]
Latin America and the Carribean[4]
Northern America
Oceania

1970
2010
2030

Per cent

1. Europe, Northern America, Australia, New Zealand and Japan.
2. Africa, Asia (excluding Japan), Latin America and the Caribbean, and Oceania
   (excluding Australia and New Zealand).
3. Includes Russian Federation.
4. South America, Central America (including Mexico) and all Caribbean Islands.

Wealth, Poverty and Trade

The globalization of the economy is making the world appear a smaller place. However, this shrinkage is an uneven process. Countries are being included and excluded to differing degrees in the global economy. The world economy remains divided between the richer (core) and relatively poorer (peripheral) countries. A common method of defining these groups uses Gross National Income (GNI) per capita as a measure of average income in each country. The fates of core and peripheral countries are closely related. Economic success and prosperity for one country can often be at the expense of others. Some newly industrializing countries have attempted to grow fast enough to cross the divide between core and periphery. Economic inequalities exist between and within countries, as well as between and within social groups in countries. These inequalities are evident in terms of wealth, growth, and debt. Increasingly large and dominant transnational corporations are driving and, in turn, being driven by the process of globalization.

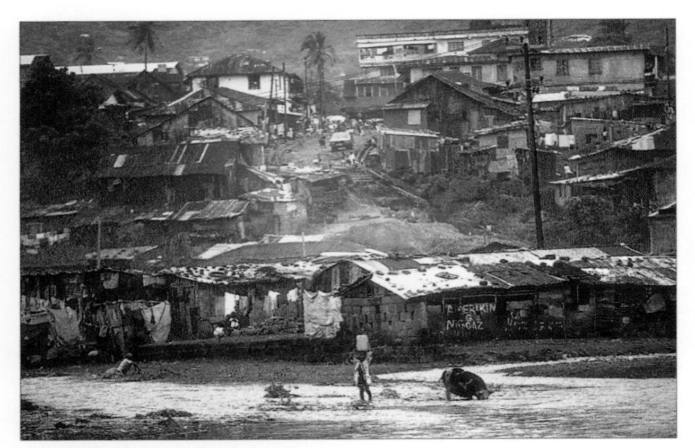

Poverty, hunger, and environmental degradation are problems experienced in areas such as this in Freetown, capital of Sierra Leone, one of the world's poorest countries.

Trade, Debt and Aid

Different countries and regions are participating in the global economy to different degrees. The value of merchandise exports, for instance, illustrates the extent to which countries are engaged in cross-border trading. Global trade is concentrated among the developed countries, in particular North America, the European Union, and the Asia-Pacific region. The USA, Germany, and Japan stand out as the world's largest exporters. Since exports earn hard currency, it is no coincidence that the weakest exporters are among the world's poorest countries, including Burundi and the Democratic Republic of the Congo in Africa. The developed countries with the higher values of exports are more closely integrated into the core of the global economy. The weak exporters remain reliant upon imports and stay on the periphery of the global trading system. Foreign direct investment (FDI) is another motor of the global economy. FDI inflows in 2004 were dominated by the developed countries, in particular western Europe, and, to a lesser degree, the Asia-Pacific region among the developing nations.

Globalization means the poorest countries find it particularly hard to develop and attract economic activity, resulting in an inability to repay loans or stimulate their own economies. Therefore their debts become greater and more loans are taken out to cover them. International efforts are ongoing in trying to suspend or write off some of these debts but meanwhile overseas aid is essential for the survival of some of the poorest countries.

Inequalities in Wealth Distribution

Gross National Income (GNI) per capita, 2005 and Gini Index (latest available figures).

The Gini Index reveals the degree of inequality in the internal distribution of income . When the figure is higher, national income is more concentrated in the hands of fewer people.

Gini Index

US dollars

core countries	>10 725
	3 466 – 10 725
peripheral countries	876 – 3 465
	0 – 875
	no data

Winkel Tripel Projection
scale 1 : 107 000 000

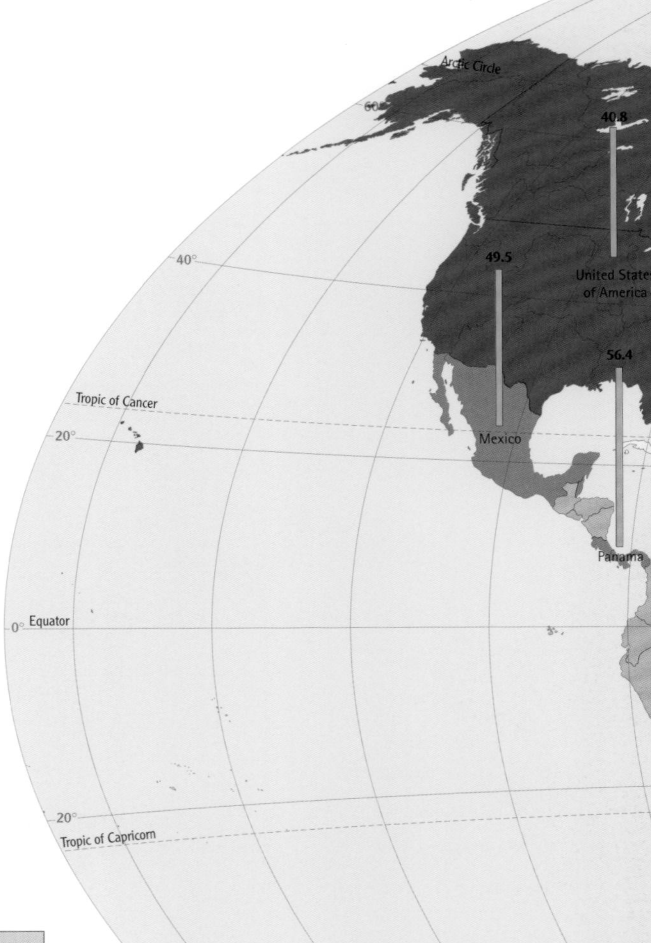

Foreign Direct Investment
Host Economies 2004

	Country	US$ (millions)
Developed countries	United States	106 831
	Luxembourg	78 678
	United Kingdom	72 561
	Australia	42 469
	Belgium	40 080
Developing countries	China	54 937
	Hong Kong	34 035
	Brazil	18 166
	Mexico	17 377
	Singapore	16 032

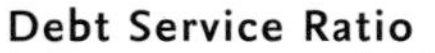

Debt Service Ratio

Debt as a percentage of GNI and top 5 total debt service, 2004.

	100 – 800
	70 – 99.9
	50 – 69.9
	30 – 49.9
	20 – 29.9
	0 – 19.9
	no data

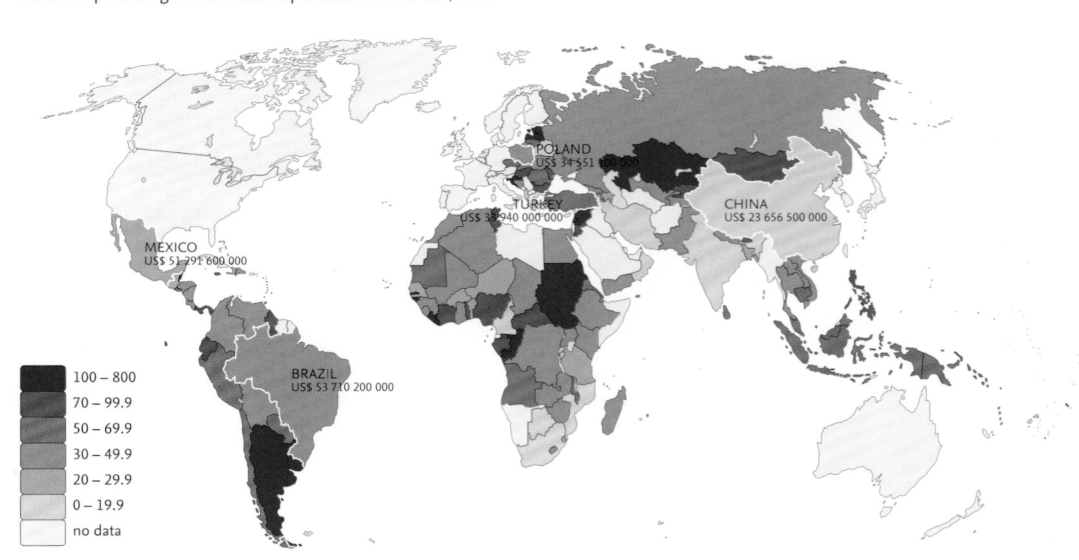

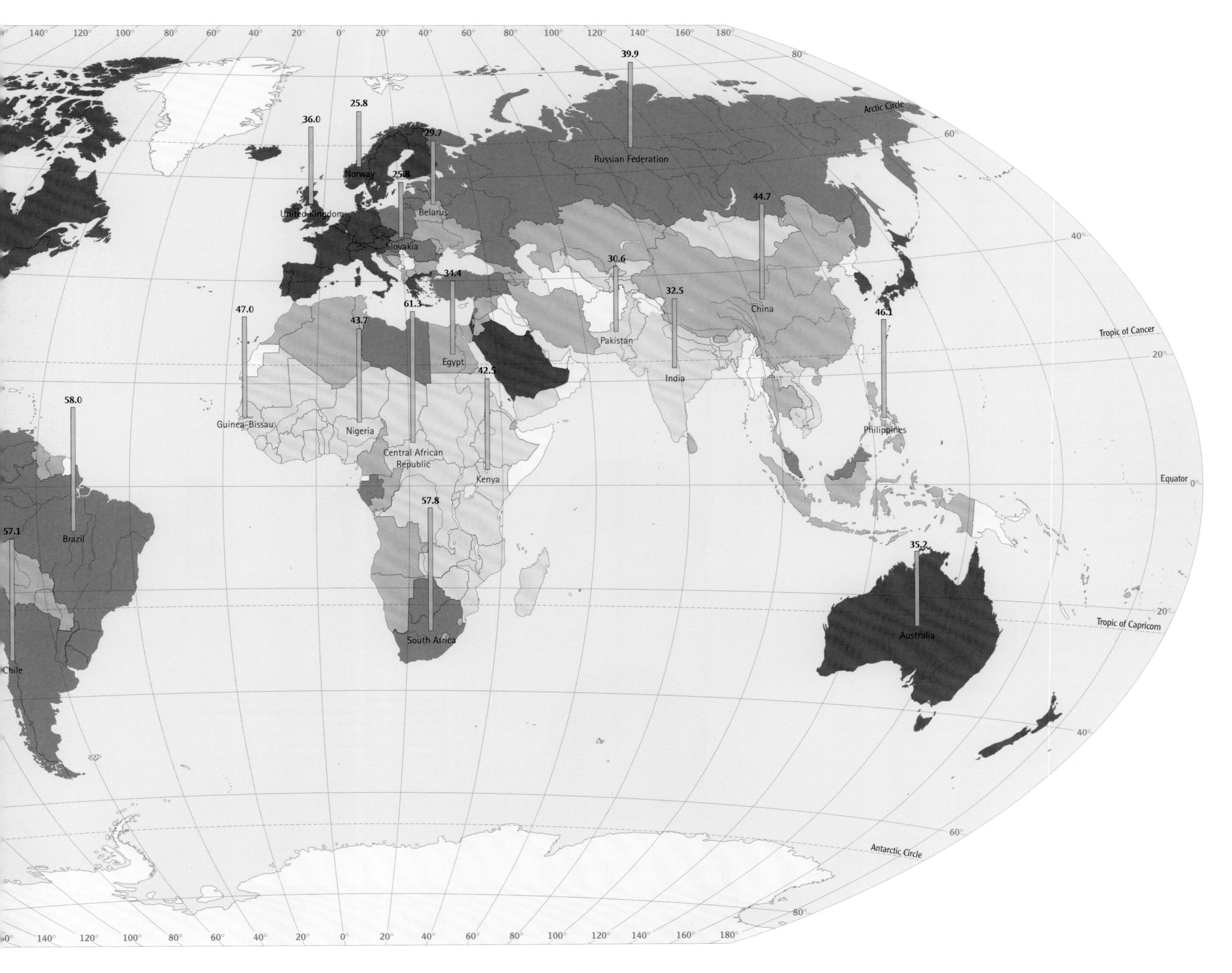

39.9 Russian Federation

Arctic Circle

25.8

36.0 United Kingdom

29.7

Norway

25.8

Belarus

Slovakia

44.7

34.4

61.3

30.6

Pakistan

China

46.1

Egypt

India

Philippines

47.0

43.7

42.5

Guinea-Bissau

Nigeria

Central African
Republic

Kenya

Tropic of Cancer

58.0

Equator

57.8

57.1

Brazil

35.2

Chile

South Africa

Australia

Tropic of Capricorn

Antarctic Circle

Value of Exports 2004

	US$ (millions)
World	9 145 028
Developed Countries	6 138 451
Developing Countries	2 837 539
High Income Countries	6 490 100
Low Income Countries	212 769
Middle Income Countries	2 259 406
Asia (excluding Middle East)	2 374 267
Central America and Caribbean	223 513
Europe	4 197 378
Middle East and North Africa	534 350
North America	1 135 732
Oceania	111 638
South America	241 703
Sub-Saharan Africa	143 693

Overseas Aid

Donations as a percentage of GNI, 2005.

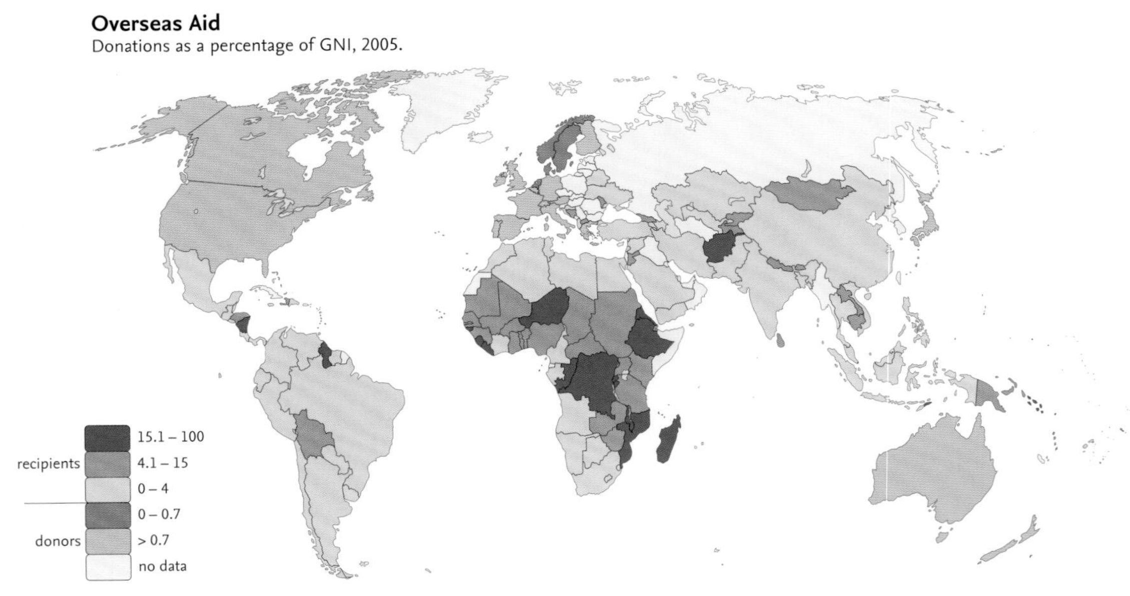

recipients

- 15.1 – 100
- 4.1 – 15
- 0 – 4

donors

- 0 – 0.7
- > 0.7
- no data

Communications

The rapid growth of the telecommunications industry over the last two decades, has contributed to the 'death of distance' by linking different parts of the world ever more cheaply and reliably due to improvements in technology. This process has meant that millions of virtual places, identified by telephone numbers, e-mail addresses, and World Wide Web sites, have become an essential part of the world's social and economic landscape. The huge demand for mobile and satellite telephones has contributed to satellite demand and to the building of ground stations. The parallel demand for electronic addresses has also triggered a building boom for international submarine cables as well as adding to the demand for satellites. Initially, most of these networks served an information belt running from western Europe across North America to eastern Asia, but now the rest of the world is gradually becoming connected.

Internet Communications

Internet users have been increasing rapidly, especially in the last ten years. However, access levels vary, with approximately thirty countries still with less than 1 per cent internet penetration. In the G8 countries, with 15 per cent of the world's population, there are almost 50 per cent of total internet users while the entire continent of Africa, with over fifty countries, has fewer internet users than France. Constraints include the high costs of international bandwidth to developing countries if they have to pay for a link to a hub in a developed country. International bandwidth is a critical part of the infrastructure as it is the most important factor in the speed of access to websites in other countries.

Satellite Communications

Communications satellites are important for person-to-person communication, including cellular telephones, and for broadcasting. Unlike submarine cables, which must connect at fixed points, satellites can transmit information between Earth stations located anywhere within a satellite's radio beam, or 'footprint'. Geostationary satellites, which orbit at 36 000 kilometres (22 370 miles) above the Earth may have footprints spanning over 1000 kilometres (620 miles), thus providing a broad service area for point-to-multi-point voice, video and data communications. The positions of communications satellites are critical to their use, and reflect the demand for such communications in each part of the world. While satellites are historically most important for international telephone calls they have since developed for the provision of television, radio and to provide broadband internet services.

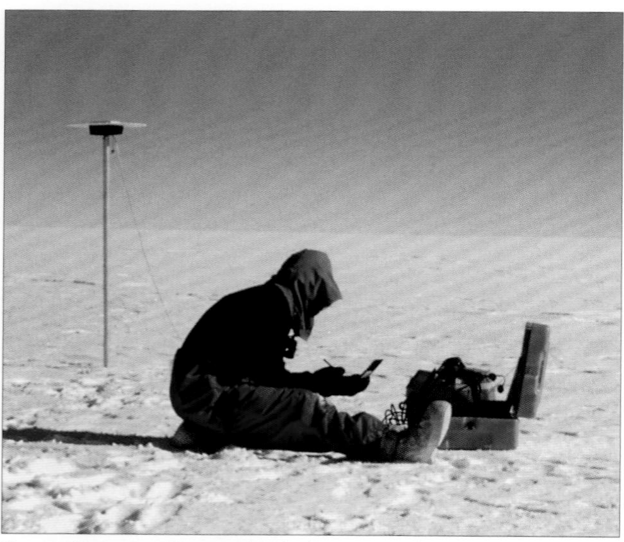

Communications satellites are placed in 'geostationary' orbit above the equator. This means that they move at the same speed as the earth and remain fixed above a single point on the earth's surface. The Global Positioning System (GPS) – seen in use here in Antarctica for monitoring glacier movement – allows accurate position fixing and navigation. Originally developed by the US military, the signals from the satellites now serve hand-held personal and in-car navigation uses, as well as more sophisticated surveying and mapping applications.

World Communication Equipment 1991–2006

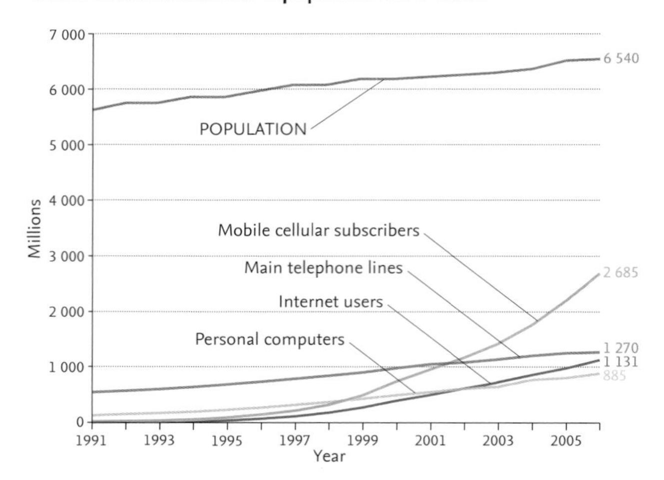

International Telecommunications Indicators by Region 2006

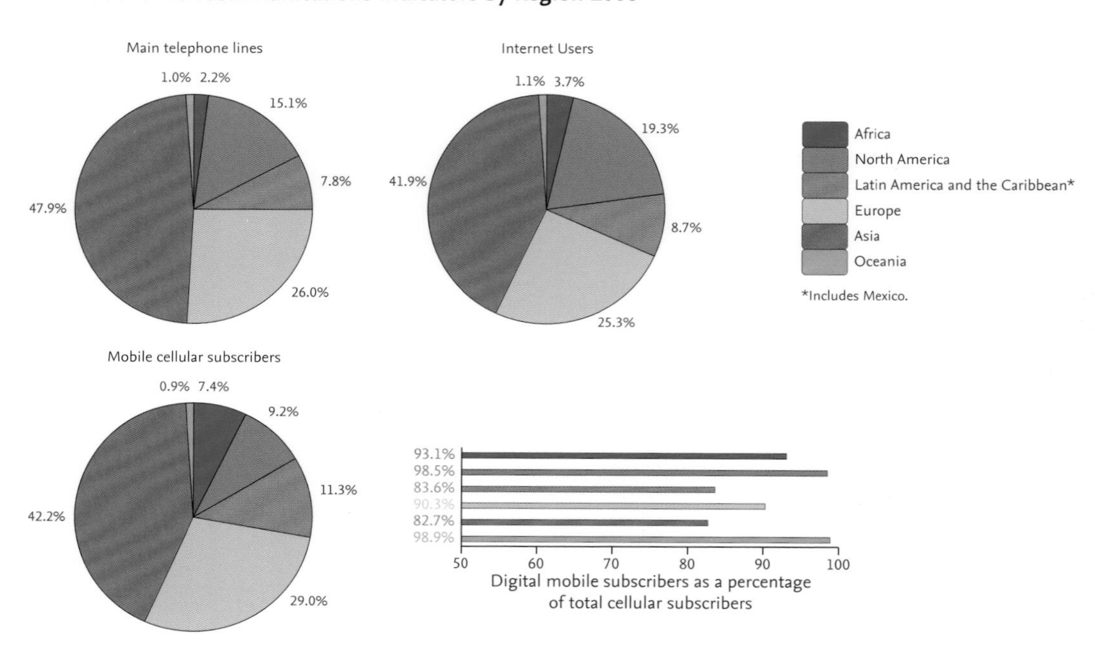

Main telephone lines

1.0% 2.2% 15.1% 7.8% 26.0% 47.9%

Internet Users

1.1% 3.7% 19.3% 8.7% 25.3% 41.9%

Mobile cellular subscribers

0.9% 7.4% 9.2% 11.3% 29.0% 42.2%

Africa
North America
Latin America and the Caribbean*
Europe
Asia
Oceania

*Includes Mexico.

93.1%
98.5%
83.6%
90.3%
82.7%
98.9%

Digital mobile subscribers as a percentage of total cellular subscribers

Internet Users and Capacity

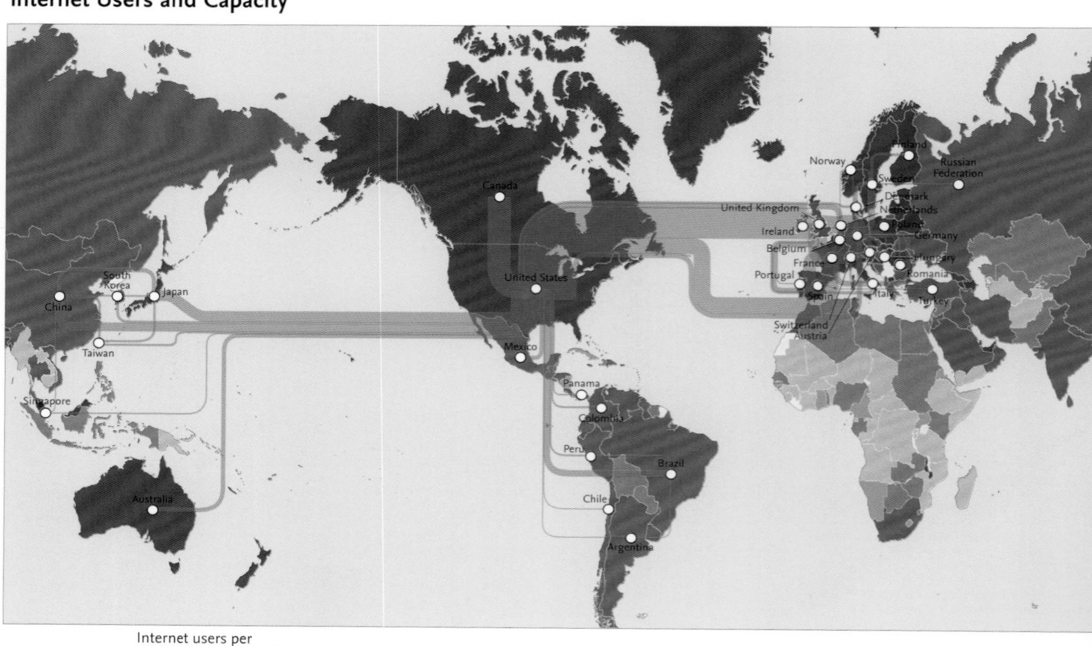

Internet users per
10 000 inhabitants 2006

3 000–11 000
1 000–2 999
400–999
200–399
0–199
no data

Aggregate international internet capacity 2007

150   50   15

Gigabytes per second

© TeleGeography Research   www.telegeography.com

International Telecommunications Traffic 2006

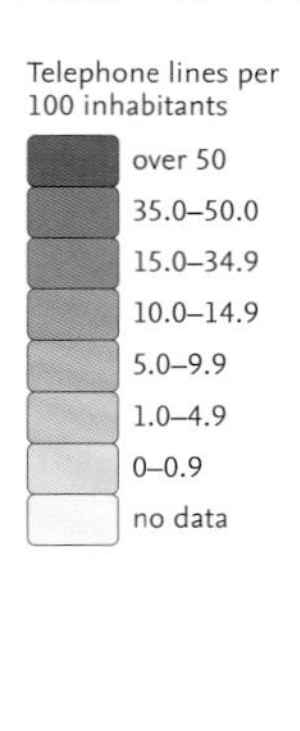

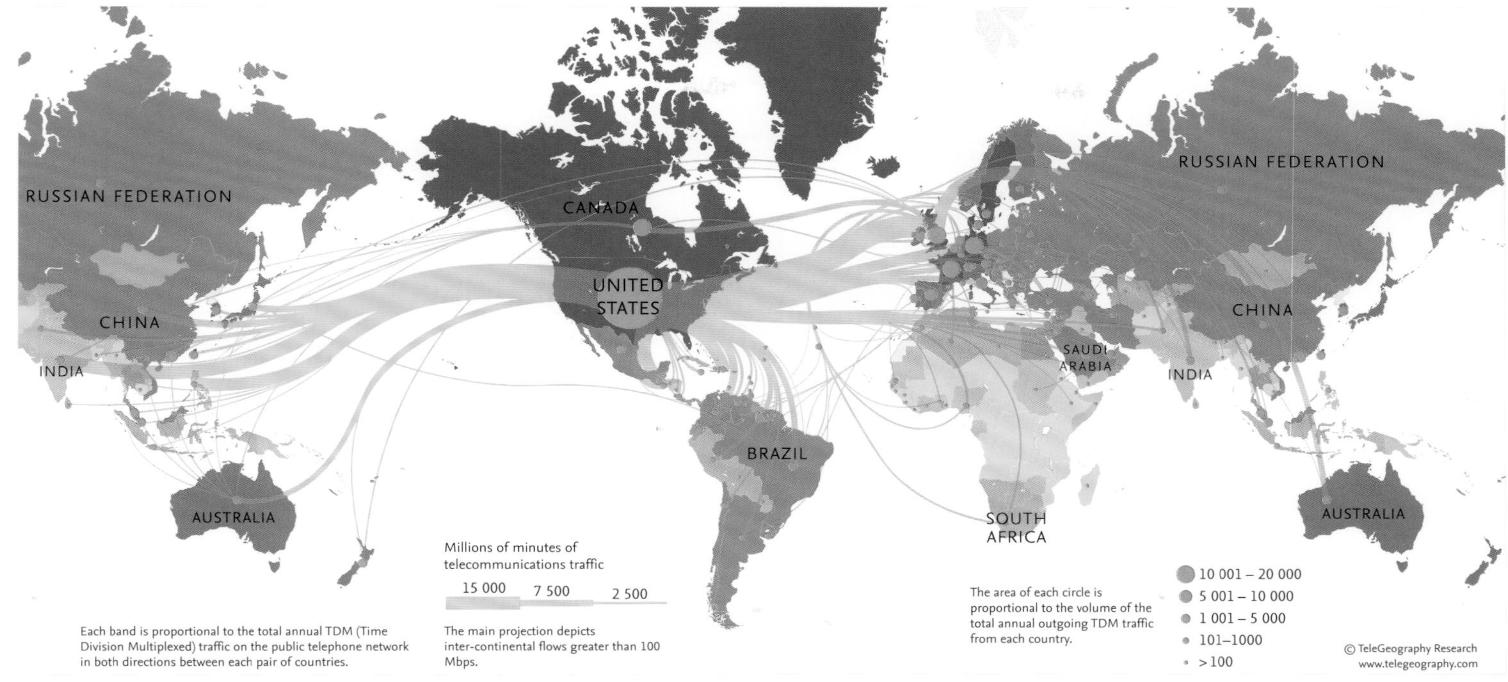

Telephone lines per
100 inhabitants

- over 50
- 35.0–50.0
- 15.0–34.9
- 10.0–14.9
- 5.0–9.9
- 1.0–4.9
- 0–0.9
- no data

RUSSIAN FEDERATION

CANADA

RUSSIAN FEDERATION

CHINA

UNITED STATES

SAUDI ARABIA

CHINA

INDIA

INDIA

BRAZIL

SOUTH AFRICA

AUSTRALIA

AUSTRALIA

Millions of minutes of
telecommunications traffic

15 000   7 500   2 500

The main projection depicts
inter-continental flows greater than 100
Mbps.

Each band is proportional to the total annual TDM (Time
Division Multiplexed) traffic on the public telephone network
in both directions between each pair of countries.

The area of each circle is
proportional to the volume of the
total annual outgoing TDM traffic
from each country.

- 10 001 – 20 000
- 5 001 – 10 000
- 1 001 – 5 000
- 101–1000
- >100

Geostationary Communications Satellites and Cellular Mobile Subscribers

Geostationary
communication
satellites

- In service
- Inclined orbit
- Planned

Cellular mobile subscribers
per 100 inhabitants 2006

- over 100
- 80–100
- 60–79.9
- 40–59.9
- 20–39.9
- 0–19.9
- no data

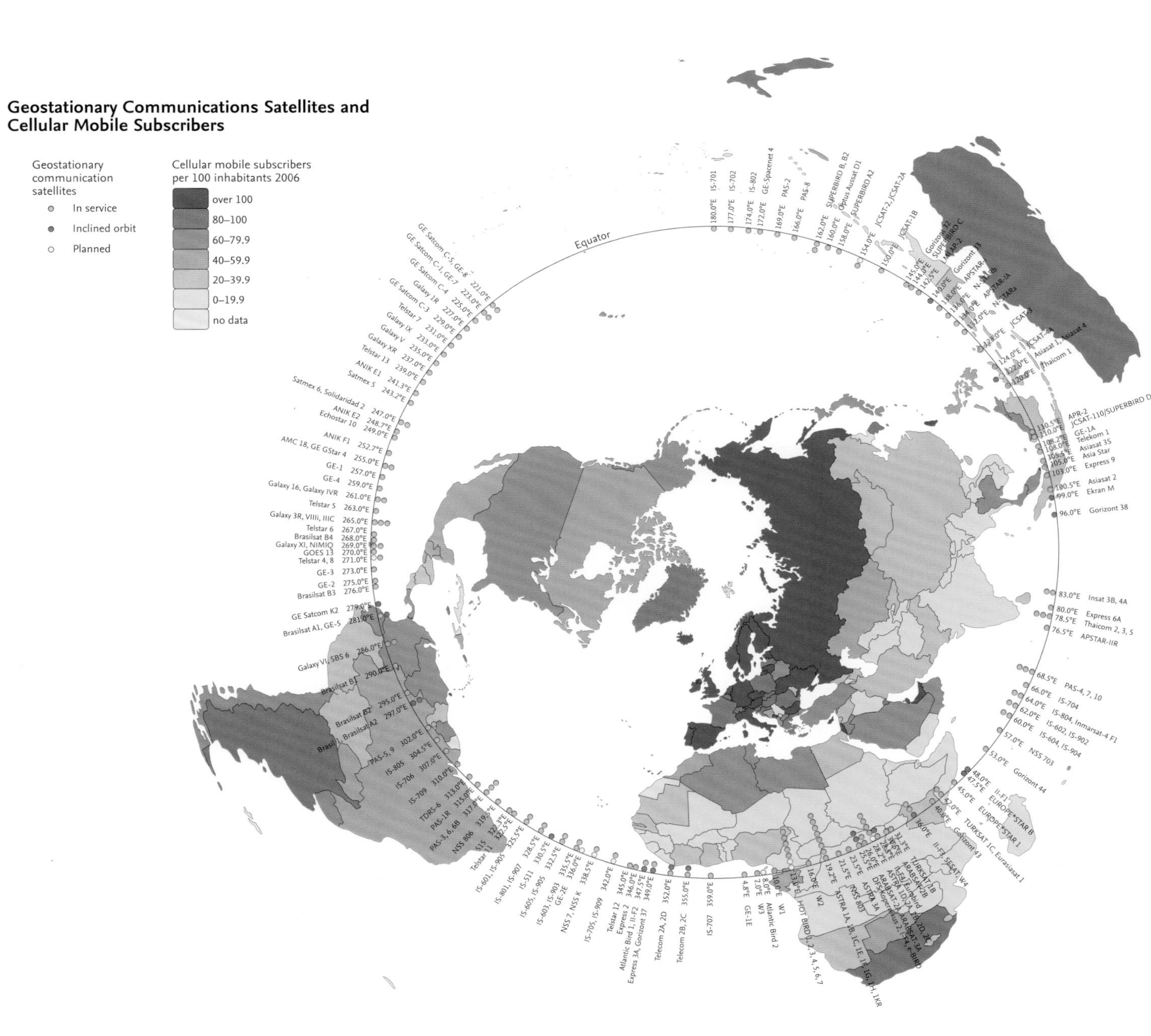

Physical Features

The images below illustrate some of the major physical features of Australasia, Asia, Europe and Africa.

Australasia

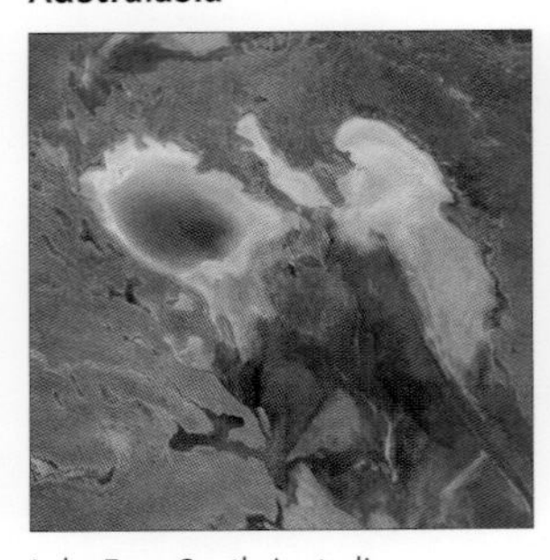

Lake Eyre, South Australia

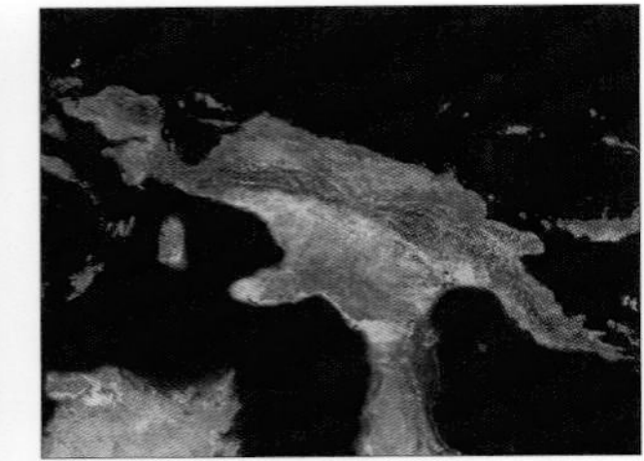

The island of New Guinea

Asia

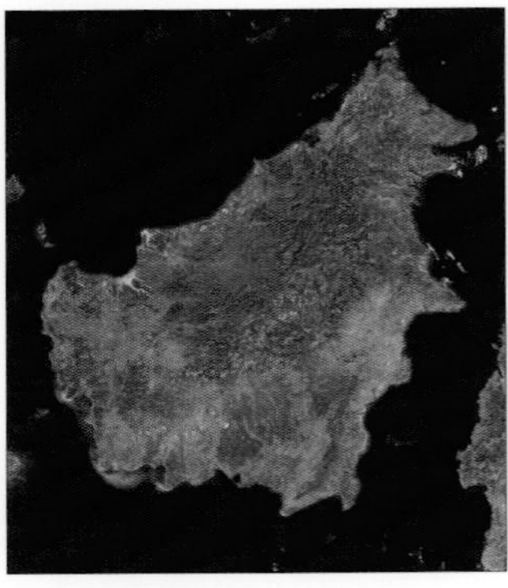

The island of Borneo

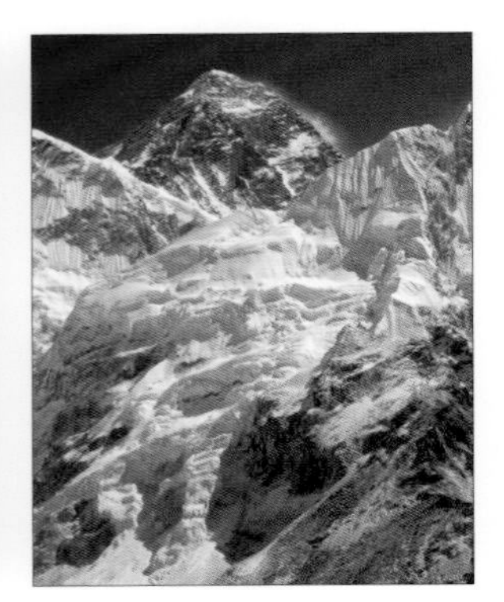

Mt Everest, China/Nepal

Europe

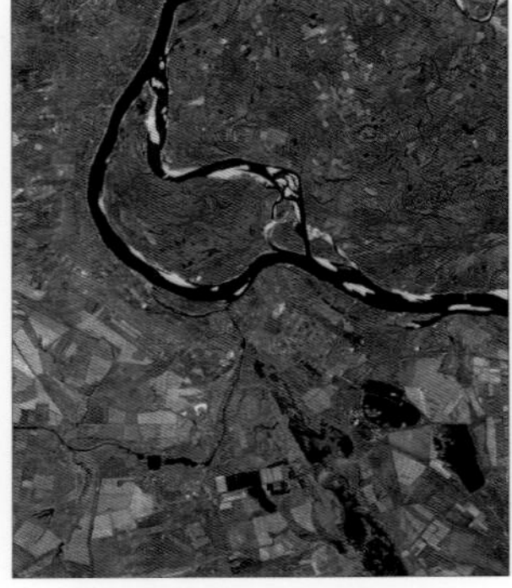

The river Volga, Russian Federation

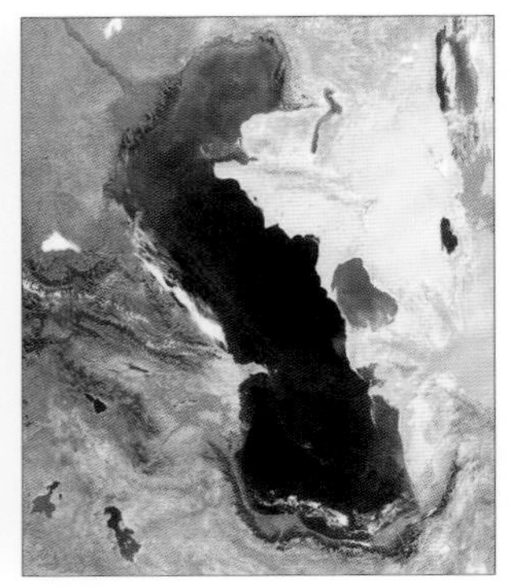

The Caspian Sea

Africa

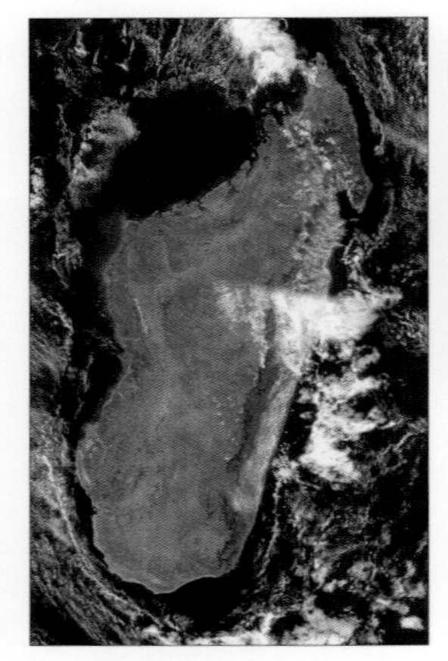

The island of Madagascar

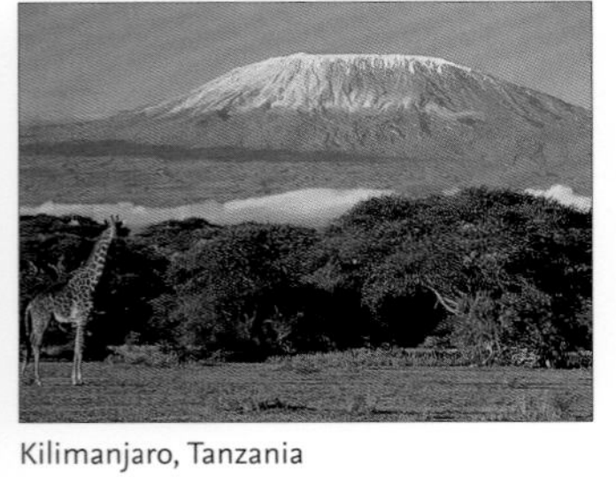

Kilimanjaro, Tanzania

Australasia Total Land Area 8 844 516 sq km / 3 414 887 sq miles (includes New Guinea and Pacific Island nations)

HIGHEST MOUNTAINS	metres	feet
Puncak Jaya, Indonesia	5 030	16 502
Puncak Trikora, Indonesia	4 730	15 518
Puncak Mandala, Indonesia	4 700	15 420
Puncak Yamin, Indonesia	4 595	15 075
Mt Wilhelm, Papua New Guinea	4 509	14 793
Mt Kubor, Papua New Guinea	4 359	14 301

LARGEST ISLANDS	sq km	sq miles
New Guinea	808 510	312 167
South Island, New Zealand	151 215	58 384
North Island, New Zealand	115 777	44 701
Tasmania	67 800	26 178

HIGHEST MOUNTAIN
Puncak Jaya

LARGEST ISLAND
New Guinea

LARGEST LAKE AND
LOWEST POINT
Lake Eyre

Asia Total Land Area 45 036 492 sq km / 17 388 686 sq miles

HIGHEST MOUNTAINS	metres	feet
Mt Everest (Sagarmatha/ Qomolangma Feng), China/Nepal	8 848	29 028
K2 (Qogir Feng), China/Pakistan	8 611	28 251
Kangchenjunga, India/Nepal	8 586	28 169
Lhotse, China/Nepal	8 516	27 939
Makalu, China/Nepal	8 463	27 765
Cho Oyu, China/Nepal	8 201	26 906

LARGEST ISLANDS	sq km	sq miles
Borneo	745 561	287 861
Sumatra (Sumatera)	473 606	182 859
Honshū	227 414	87 805
Celebes (Sulawesi)	189 216	73 056
Java (Jawa)	132 188	51 038
Luzon	104 690	40 421

LARGEST LAKE
Caspian Sea

LARGEST DRAINAGE
BASIN
Ob'-Irtysh

LOWEST POINT
Dead Sea

HIGHEST MOUNTAIN
Mt Everest

LONGEST RIVERS	km	miles
Murray-Darling	3 750	2 330
Darling	2 739	1 702
Murray	2 589	1 609
Murrumbidgee	1 690	1 050
Lachlan	1 480	920
Macquarie	950	590

LARGEST LAKES	sq km	sq miles
Lake Eyre	0–8 900	0–3 436
Lake Torrens	0–5 780	0–2 232

LONGEST RIVER AND LARGEST DRAINAGE BASIN
Murray-Darling

HIGHEST MOUNTAINS	metres	feet
El'brus, Russian Federation	5 642	18 510
Gora Dykh-Tau, Russian Federation	5 204	17 073
Shkhara, Georgia/Russian Federation	5 201	17 063
Kazbek, Georgia/Russian Federation	5 047	16 558
Mont Blanc, France/Italy	4 808	15 774
Dufourspitze, Italy/Switzerland	4 634	15 203

LARGEST ISLANDS	sq km	sq miles
Great Britain	218 476	84 354
Iceland	102 820	39 699
Novaya Zemlya	90 650	35 000
Ireland	83 045	32 064
Spitsbergen	37 814	14 600
Sicily (Sicilia)	25 426	9 817

LONGEST RIVERS	km	miles
Volga	3 688	2 292
Danube	2 850	1 771
Dnieper	2 285	1 420
Kama	2 028	1 260
Don	1 931	1 200
Pechora	1 802	1 120

LARGEST LAKES	sq km	sq miles
Caspian Sea	371 000	143 243
Lake Ladoga (Ladozhskoye Ozero)	18 390	7 100
Lake Onega (Onezhskoye Ozero)	9 600	3 707
Vänern	5 585	2 156
Rybinskoye Vodokhranilishche	5 180	2 000

LARGEST ISLAND
Great Britain

LONGEST RIVER AND LARGEST DRAINAGE BASIN
Volga

HIGHEST MOUNTAIN
El'brus

LARGEST LAKE AND LOWEST POINT
Caspian Sea

LONGEST RIVERS	km	miles
Yangtze (Chang Jiang)	6 380	3 965
Ob'-Irtysh	5 568	3 460
Yenisey-Angara-Selenga	5 550	3 449
Yellow (Huang He)	5 464	3 395
Irtysh	4 440	2 759
Mekong	4 425	2 750

LARGEST LAKES	sq km	sq miles
Caspian Sea	371 000	143 243
Lake Baikal (Ozero Baykal)	30 500	11 776
Lake Balkhash (Ozero Balkhash)	17 400	6 718
Aral Sea (Aral'skoye More)	17 158	6 625
Ysyk-Köl	6 200	2 394

LONGEST RIVER
Yangtze (Chang Jiang)

LARGEST ISLAND
Borneo

HIGHEST MOUNTAINS	metres	feet
Kilimanjaro, Tanzania	5 892	19 330
Mt Kenya (Kirinyaga), Kenya	5 199	17 057
Margherita Peak, Democratic Republic of the Congo/Uganda	5 110	16 765
Meru, Tanzania	4 565	14 977
Ras Dejen, Ethiopia	4 533	14 872
Mt Karisimbi, Rwanda	4 510	14 796

LARGEST LAKES	sq km	sq miles
Lake Victoria	68 870	26 591
Lake Tanganyika	32 600	12 587
Lake Nyasa (Lake Malawi)	29 500	11 390
Lake Volta	8 482	3 275
Lake Turkana	6 500	2 510
Lake Albert	5 600	2 162

LONGEST RIVERS	km	miles
Nile	6 695	4 160
Congo	4 667	2 900
Niger	4 184	2 600
Zambezi	2 736	1 700
Webi Shabeelle	2 490	1 547
Ubangi	2 250	1 398

LARGEST ISLANDS	sq km	sq miles
Madagascar	587 040	226 656

LONGEST RIVER
Nile

LOWEST POINT
Lake Assal

LARGEST DRAINAGE BASIN
Congo

HIGHEST MOUNTAIN
Kilimanjaro

LARGEST LAKE
Lake Victoria

LARGEST ISLAND
Madagascar

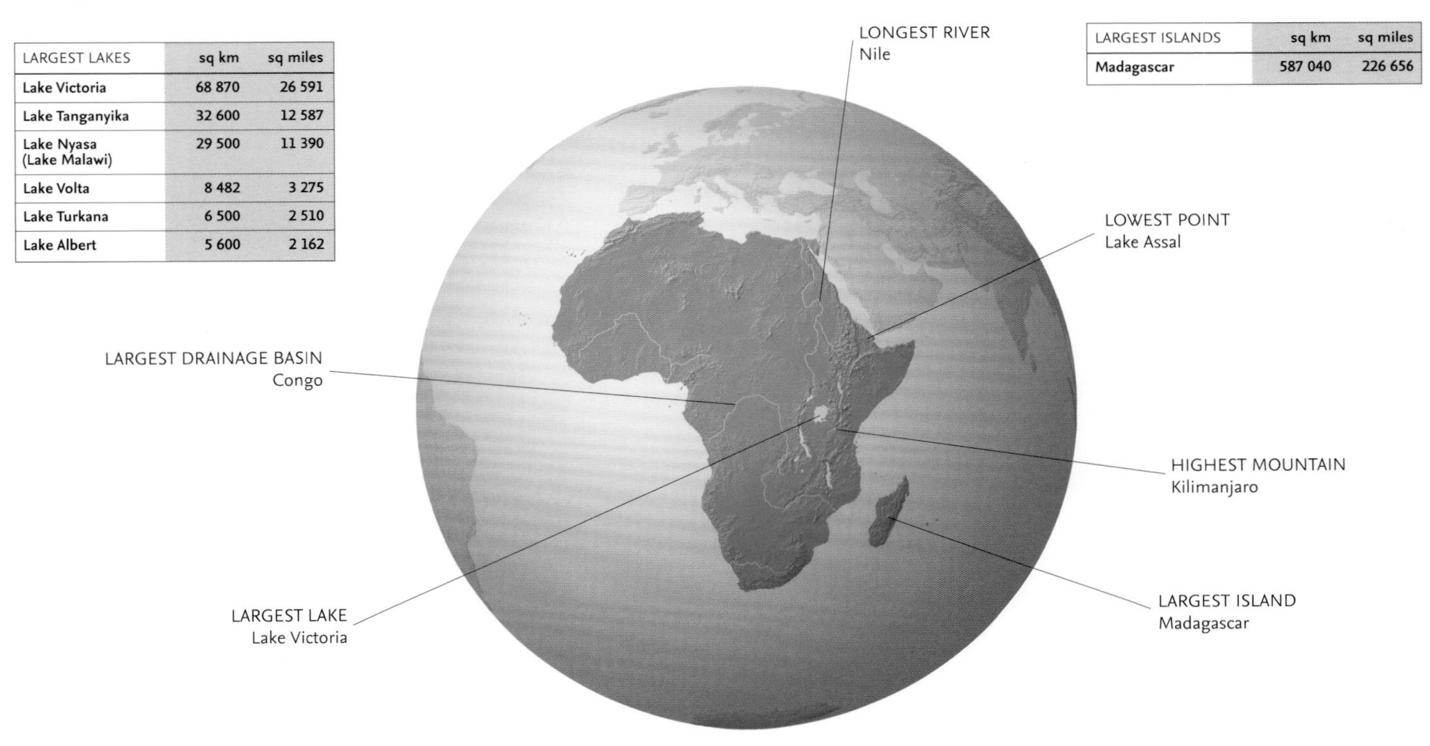

Physical Features

The images below illustrate some of the major physical features of North America, South America, and Antarctica.

North America

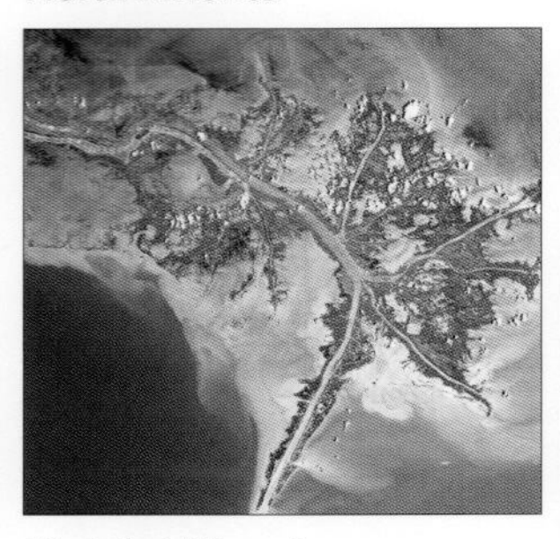

Mississippi-Missouri,
United States of America

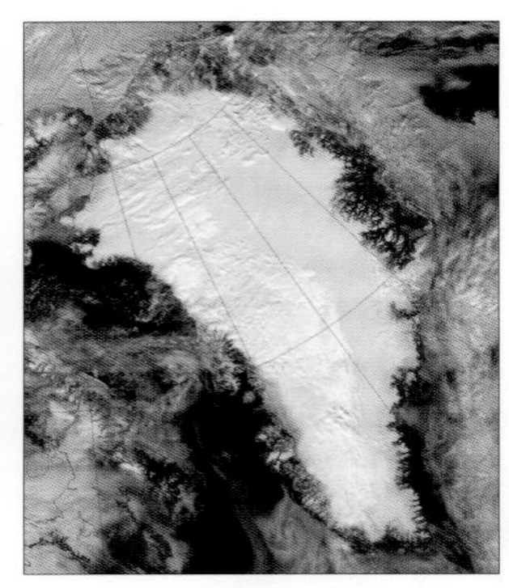

The island of Greenland

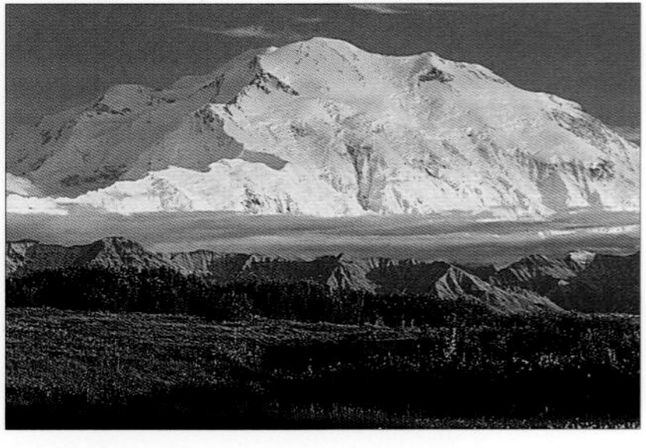

Mt McKinley, United States of America

South America

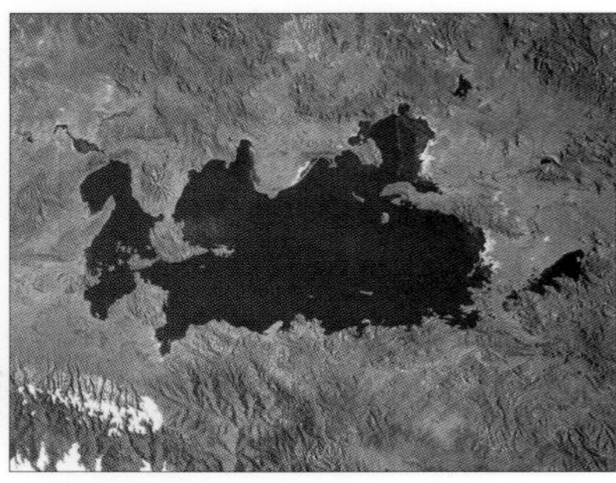

Lake Titicaca, Bolivia/Peru

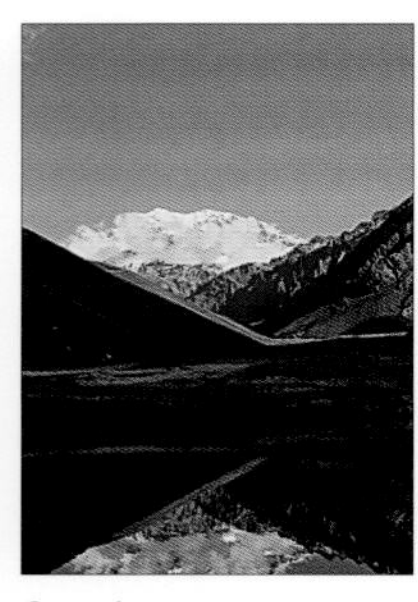

Cerro Aconcagua,
Argentina

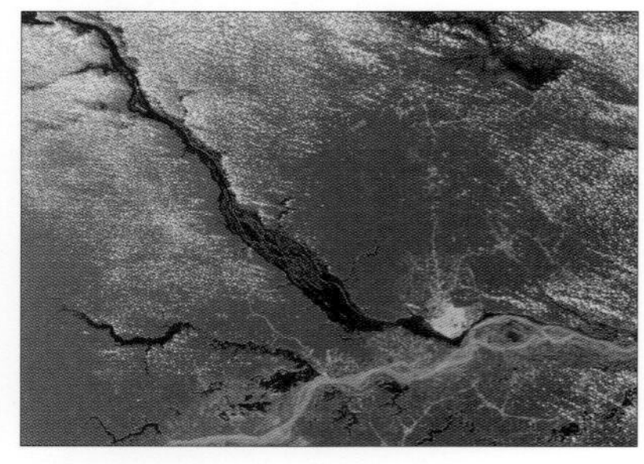

The river Amazon

Antarctica

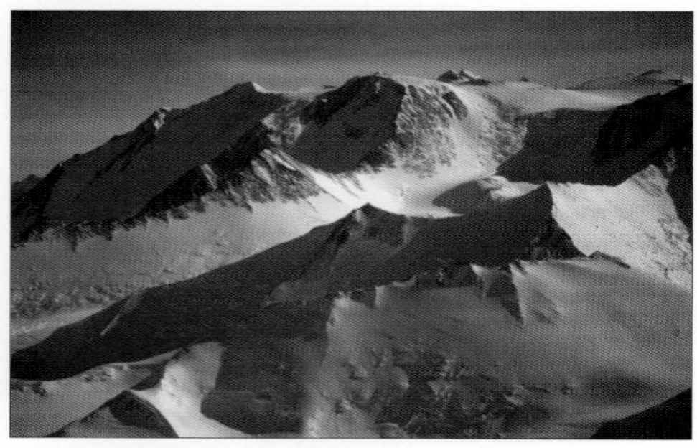

Vinson Massif, West Antarctica

North America Total Land Area 24 680 331 sq km / 9 529 129 sq miles (including Hawaiian Islands)

HIGHEST MOUNTAINS	metres	feet
Mt McKinley, USA	6 194	20 321
Mt Logan, Canada	5 959	19 550
Pico de Orizaba, Mexico	5 610	18 405
Mt St Elias, USA	5 489	18 008
Volcán Popocatépetl, Mexico	5 452	17 887
Mt Foraker, USA	5 303	17 398

LARGEST ISLANDS	sq km	sq miles
Greenland	2 175 600	839 999
Baffin Island	507 451	195 927
Victoria Island	217 291	83 896
Ellesmere Island	196 236	75 767
Cuba	110 860	42 803
Newfoundland	108 860	42 031
Hispaniola	76 192	29 418

HIGHEST MOUNTAIN
Mt McKinley

LARGEST ISLAND
Greenland

LOWEST POINT
Death Valley

South America Total Land Area 17 815 420 sq km / 6 878 572 sq miles

HIGHEST MOUNTAINS	metres	feet
Cerro Aconcagua, Argentina	6 959	22 831
Nevado Ojos del Salado, Argentina/Chile	6 908	22 664
Cerro Bonete, Argentina	6 872	22 546
Cerro Pissis, Argentina	6 858	22 500
Cerro Tupungato, Argentina/Chile	6 800	22 309
Cerro Mercedario, Argentina	6 770	22 211

LARGEST ISLANDS	sq km	sq miles
Isla Grande de Tierra del Fuego	47 000	18 147
Isla de Chiloé	8 394	3 241
East Falkland	6 760	2 610
West Falkland	5 413	2 090

LONGEST RIVER AND
LARGEST DRAINAGE BASIN
Amazon (Amazonas)

LARGEST LAKE
Lake Titicaca

HIGHEST MOUNTAIN
Cerro Aconcagua

LARGEST LAKES	sq km	sq miles
Lake Superior	82 100	31 699
Lake Huron	59 600	23 012
Lake Michigan	57 800	22 317
Great Bear Lake	31 328	12 096
Great Slave Lake	28 568	11 030
Lake Erie	25 700	9 923
Lake Winnipeg	24 387	9 416
Lake Ontario	18 960	7 320

LARGEST LAKE
Lake Superior

LONGEST RIVER AND
LARGEST DRAINAGE BASIN
Mississippi-Missouri

LONGEST RIVERS	km	miles
Amazon (Amazonas)	6 516	4 049
Río de la Plata-Paraná	4 500	2 796
Purus	3 218	2 000
Madeira	3 200	1 988
São Francisco	2 900	1 802
Tocantins	2 750	1 709

LARGEST LAKES	sq km	sq miles
Lake Titicaca	8 340	3 220

LOWEST POINT
Laguna del Carbón

LARGEST ISLAND
Isla Grande de Tierra del Fuego

HIGHEST MOUNTAIN
Vinson Massif

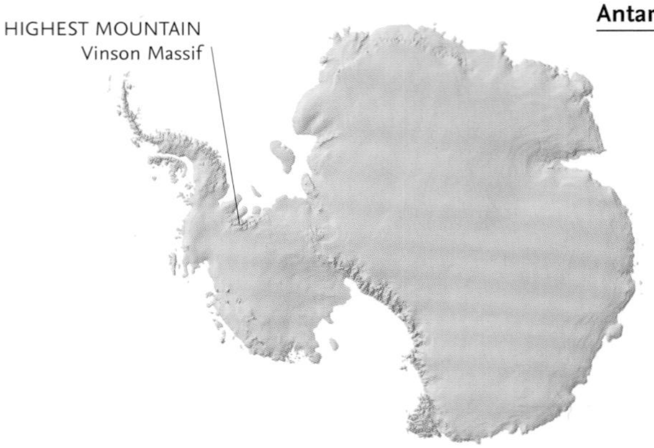

Antarctica Total Land Area 12 093 000 sq km / 4 669 133 sq miles (excluding ice shelves)

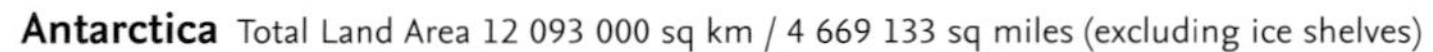

HIGHEST MOUNTAINS	metres	feet
Vinson Massif	4 897	16 066
Mt Tyree	4 852	15 918
Mt Kirkpatrick	4 528	14 855
Mt Markham	4 351	14 275
Mt Jackson	4 190	13 747
Mt Sidley	4 181	13 717

Atlantic Ocean Total Area 86 557 000 sq km / 33 420 000 sq miles

ATLANTIC OCEAN	Area square km	square miles	Deepest Point metres	feet
Extent	86 557 000	33 420 000	8 605	28 231
Arctic Ocean	9 485 000	3 662 000	5 450	17 880
Caribbean Sea	2 512 000	970 000	7 680	25 196
Mediterranean Sea	2 510 000	969 000	5 121	16 800
Gulf of Mexico	1 544 000	596 000	3 504	11 495
Hudson Bay	1 233 000	476 000	259	849
North Sea	575 000	222 000	661	2 168
Black Sea	508 000	196 000	2 245	7 365
Baltic Sea	382 000	147 000	460	1 509

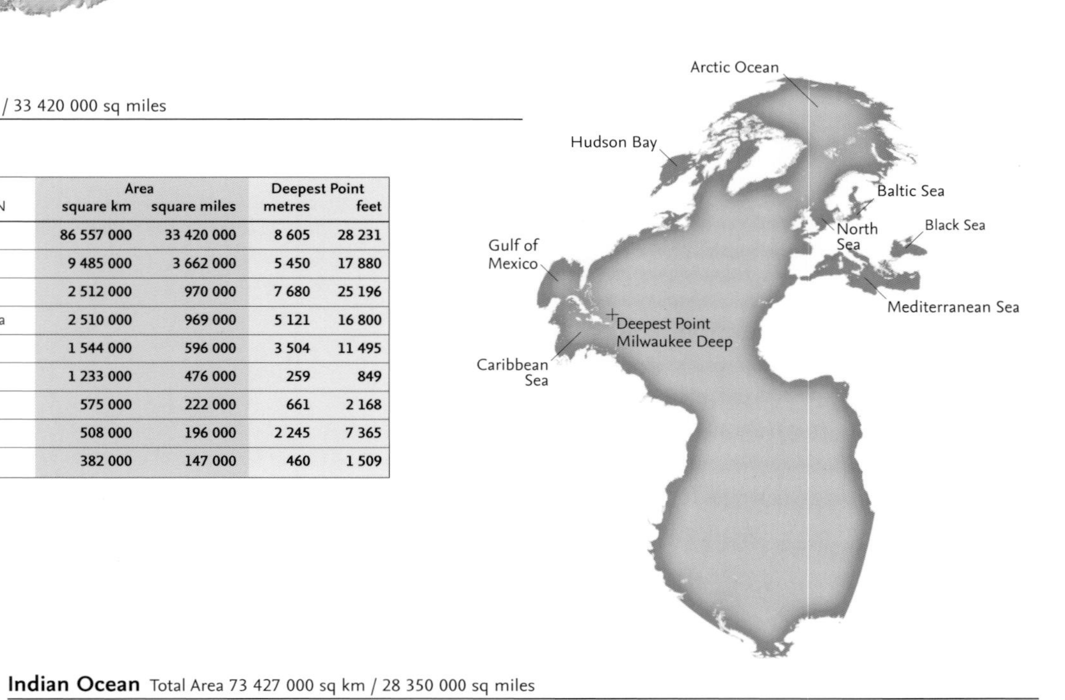

Arctic Ocean

Hudson Bay

Baltic Sea

North Sea

Black Sea

Gulf of Mexico

Mediterranean Sea

Deepest Point
Milwaukee Deep

Caribbean Sea

Red Sea

The Gulf

Bay of Bengal

Indian Ocean Total Area 73 427 000 sq km / 28 350 000 sq miles

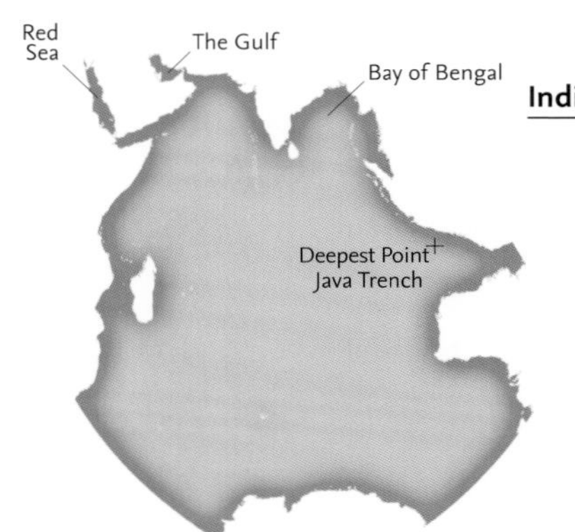

Deepest Point
Java Trench

INDIAN OCEAN	Area square km	square miles	Deepest Point metres	feet
Extent	73 427 000	28 350 000	7 125	23 376
Bay of Bengal	2 172 000	839 000	4 500	14 763
Red Sea	453 000	175 000	3 040	9 973
The Gulf	238 000	92 000	73	239

Pacific Ocean Total Area 166 241 000 sq km / 64 186 000 sq miles

PACIFIC OCEAN	Area square km	square miles	Deepest Point metres	feet
Extent	166 241 000	64 186 000	10 920	35 826
South China Sea	2 590 000	1 000 000	5 514	18 090
Bering Sea	2 261 000	873 000	4 150	13 615
Sea of Okhotsk	1 392 000	537 000	3 363	11 033
Sea of Japan (East Sea)	1 013 000	391 000	3 743	12 280
East China Sea and Yellow Sea	1 202 000	464 000	2 717	8 913

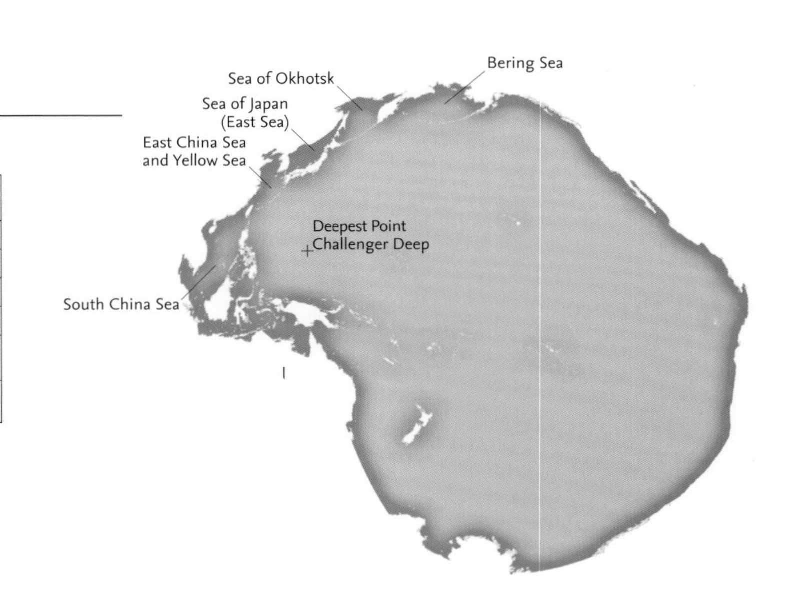

Sea of Okhotsk

Bering Sea

Sea of Japan (East Sea)

East China Sea and Yellow Sea

Deepest Point
Challenger Deep

South China Sea

World Tourism

The growth of low-cost air transport opened up the world for global tourism, making air travel accessible to an increasing share of the world's population. More recently, the widespread use of the Internet has accelerated the direct selling of travel and accommodation options, broadening the possibilities for researching and booking holidays, and increasing the scope to search for discounted deals. Since the early 1990s world tourism, measured by international tourist arrivals, has nearly doubled.

Global economic difficulties combined with an increasing awareness of the environmental cost of long distance destinations has led to a slight decline in this upward trend in more recent years, but the general forecast is still for growth. Global policies increasingly support the sustainable development of tourism, and the individual is finding ways to reconcile and adapt beliefs and circumstances with the irresistible longing to experience the wonders of our world.

Europe and the Americas retain a long-standing and steady attraction to tourists but emerging destinations in Asia, the Pacific, Africa and the Middle East are showing the greatest increase in tourism. Speciality travel is also emerging as a growth industry, fulfilling such needs as the ecological and social consciousness of ecotourism and the adrenaline rush of extreme tourism. Yet, remaining at the heart of world tourism is a desire to see and experience lands and cultures outside the realm of our everyday life, and so the world's great natural wonders and iconic landmarks remain in the list of the world's most visited places.

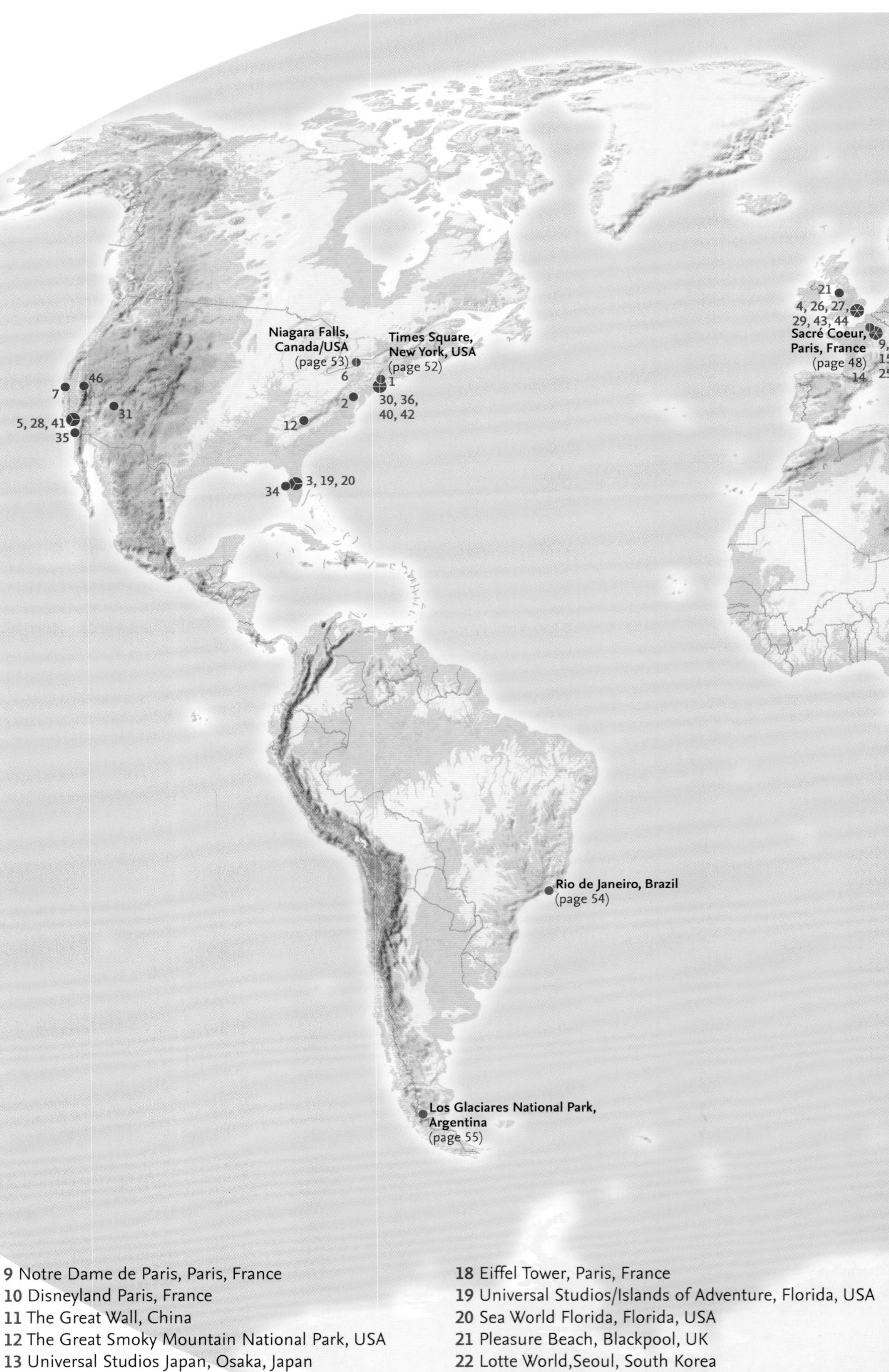

● Highlighted tourist sites (page numbers)

44 Sydney, Australia
45 Fiordland, New Zealand
46 Beijing, China
47 Bali, Indonesia
48 Sacré Coeur, Paris, France
49 Colosseum, Rome, Italy
50 Luxor, Egypt
51 Masai Mara, Kenya
52 Times Square, New York, USA
53 Niagara Falls, Canada/USA
54 Rio de Janeiro, Brazil
55 Los Glaciares National Park, Argentina

● Top 50 tourist attractions

1 Times Square, New York, USA
2 National Mall & Memorial Parks, Washington D.C., USA
3 Disney World's Magic Kingdom, Florida, USA
4 Trafalgar Square, London, UK
5 Disneyland Park, California, USA
6 Niagara Falls, Canada/USA
7 Fisherman's Wharf/Golden Gate National Recreation Area, San Francisco,
8 Tokyo Disneyland/Disney Sea, Tokyo, Japan

9 Notre Dame de Paris, Paris, France
10 Disneyland Paris, France
11 The Great Wall, China
12 The Great Smoky Mountain National Park, USA
13 Universal Studios Japan, Osaka, Japan
14 Basilique du Sacré Coeur de Montmartre, Paris, France
15 Musée du Louvre, Paris, France
16 Everland, South Korea
17 The Forbidden City/Tiananmen Square, Beijing, China

18 Eiffel Tower, Paris, France
19 Universal Studios/Islands of Adventure, Florida, USA
20 Sea World Florida, Florida, USA
21 Pleasure Beach, Blackpool, UK
22 Lotte World, Seoul, South Korea
23 Yokohama Hakkeijima Sea Paradise, Japan
24 Hong Kong Disneyland, China
25 Centre Pompidou, Paris, France
26 Tate Modern, London, UK
27 British Museum, London, UK

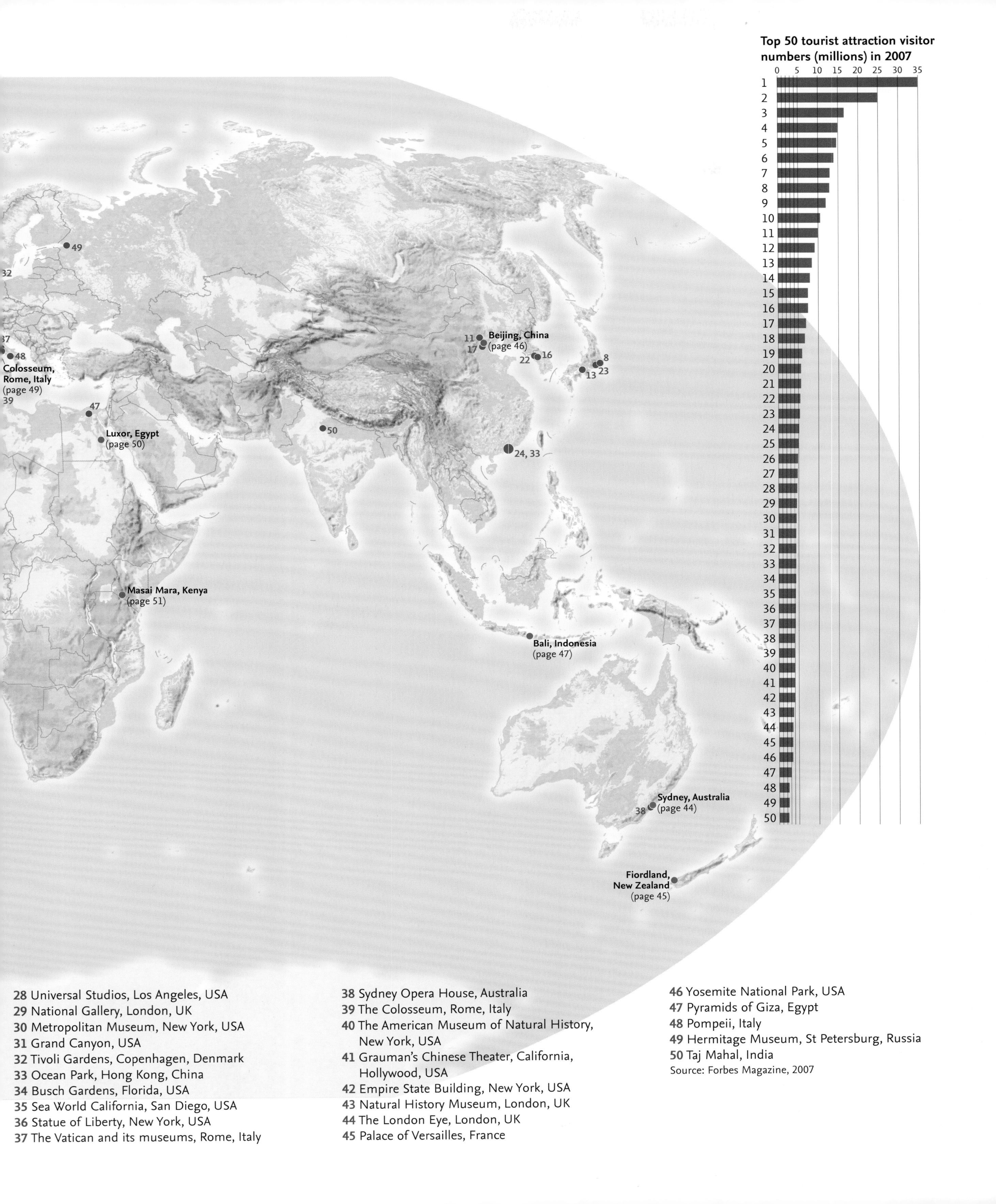

Top 50 tourist attraction visitor numbers (millions) in 2007

Colosseum,
Rome, Italy
(page 49)

Luxor, Egypt
(page 50)

Beijing, China
(page 46)

Masai Mara, Kenya
(page 51)

Bali, Indonesia
(page 47)

Sydney, Australia
(page 44)

Fiordland,
New Zealand
(page 45)

28 Universal Studios, Los Angeles, USA
29 National Gallery, London, UK
30 Metropolitan Museum, New York, USA
31 Grand Canyon, USA
32 Tivoli Gardens, Copenhagen, Denmark
33 Ocean Park, Hong Kong, China
34 Busch Gardens, Florida, USA
35 Sea World California, San Diego, USA
36 Statue of Liberty, New York, USA
37 The Vatican and its museums, Rome, Italy

38 Sydney Opera House, Australia
39 The Colosseum, Rome, Italy
40 The American Museum of Natural History, New York, USA
41 Grauman's Chinese Theater, California, Hollywood, USA
42 Empire State Building, New York, USA
43 Natural History Museum, London, UK
44 The London Eye, London, UK
45 Palace of Versailles, France

46 Yosemite National Park, USA
47 Pyramids of Giza, Egypt
48 Pompeii, Italy
49 Hermitage Museum, St Petersburg, Russia
50 Taj Mahal, India
Source: Forbes Magazine, 2007

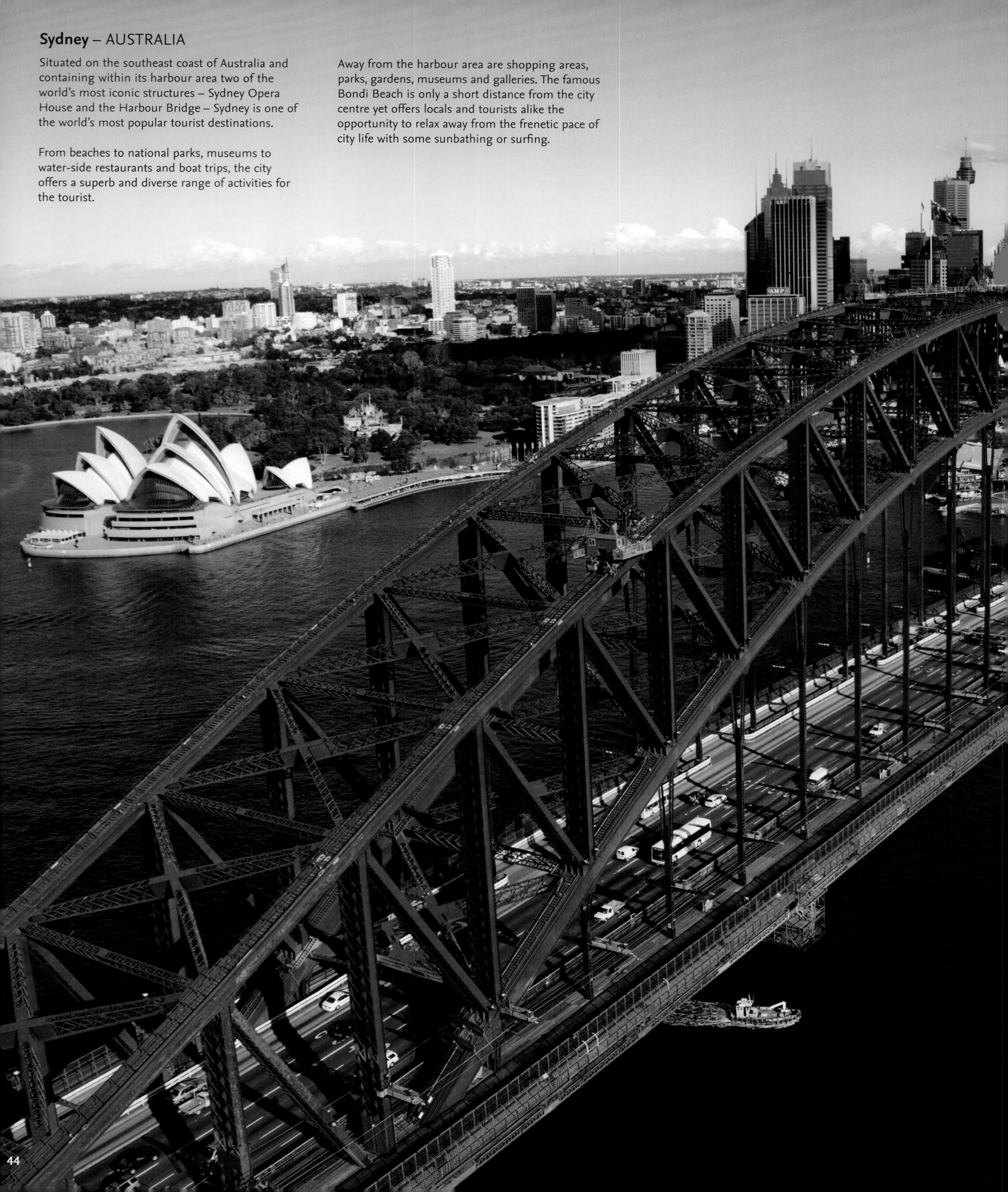

Sydney – AUSTRALIA

Situated on the southeast coast of Australia and containing within its harbour area two of the world's most iconic structures – Sydney Opera House and the Harbour Bridge – Sydney is one of the world's most popular tourist destinations.

From beaches to national parks, museums to water-side restaurants and boat trips, the city offers a superb and diverse range of activities for the tourist.

Away from the harbour area are shopping areas, parks, gardens, museums and galleries. The famous Bondi Beach is only a short distance from the city centre yet offers locals and tourists alike the opportunity to relax away from the frenetic pace of city life with some sunbathing or surfing.

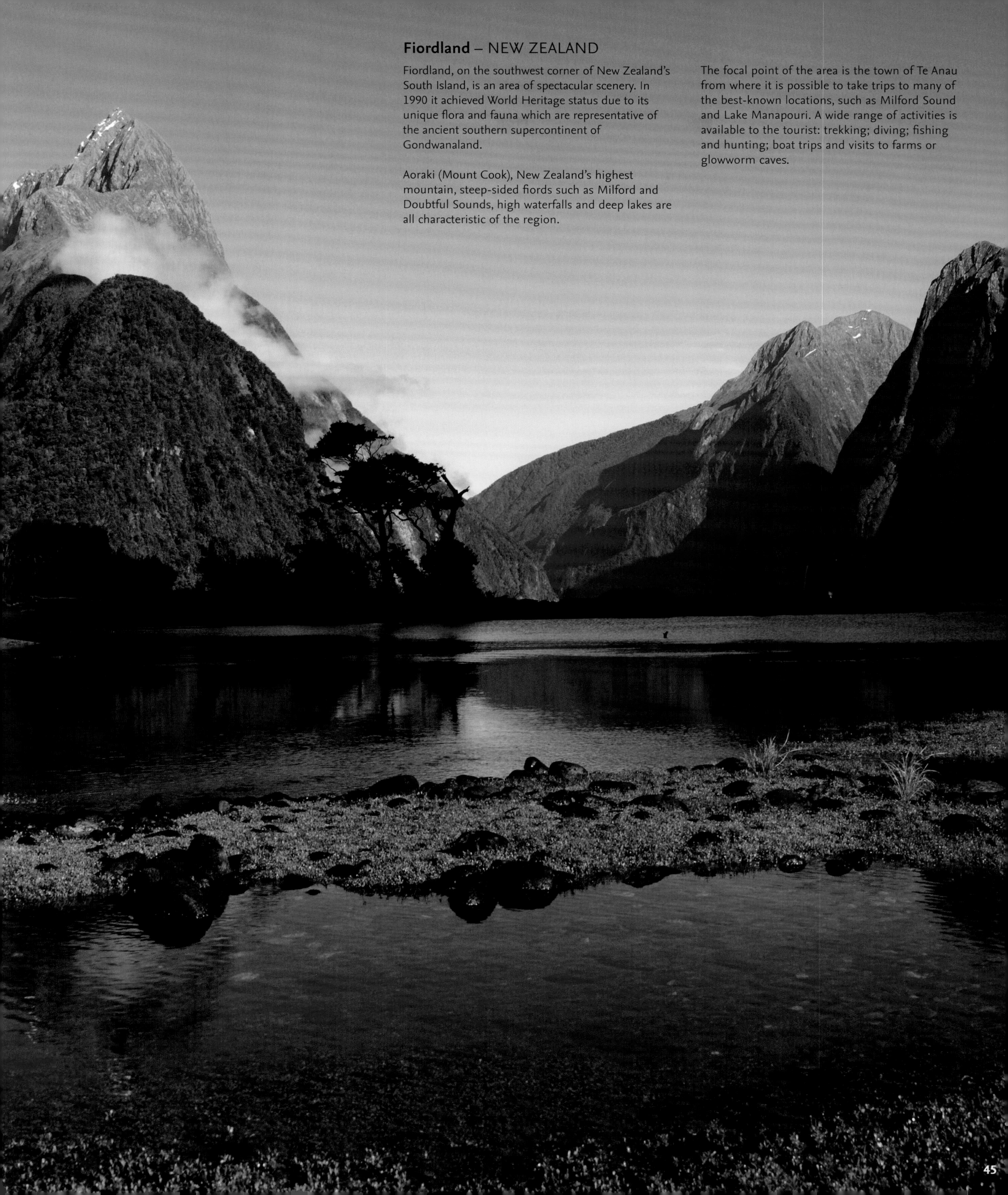

Fiordland – NEW ZEALAND

Fiordland, on the southwest corner of New Zealand's South Island, is an area of spectacular scenery. In 1990 it achieved World Heritage status due to its unique flora and fauna which are representative of the ancient southern supercontinent of Gondwanaland.

Aoraki (Mount Cook), New Zealand's highest mountain, steep-sided fiords such as Milford and Doubtful Sounds, high waterfalls and deep lakes are all characteristic of the region.

The focal point of the area is the town of Te Anau from where it is possible to take trips to many of the best-known locations, such as Milford Sound and Lake Manapouri. A wide range of activities is available to the tourist: trekking; diving; fishing and hunting; boat trips and visits to farms or glowworm caves.

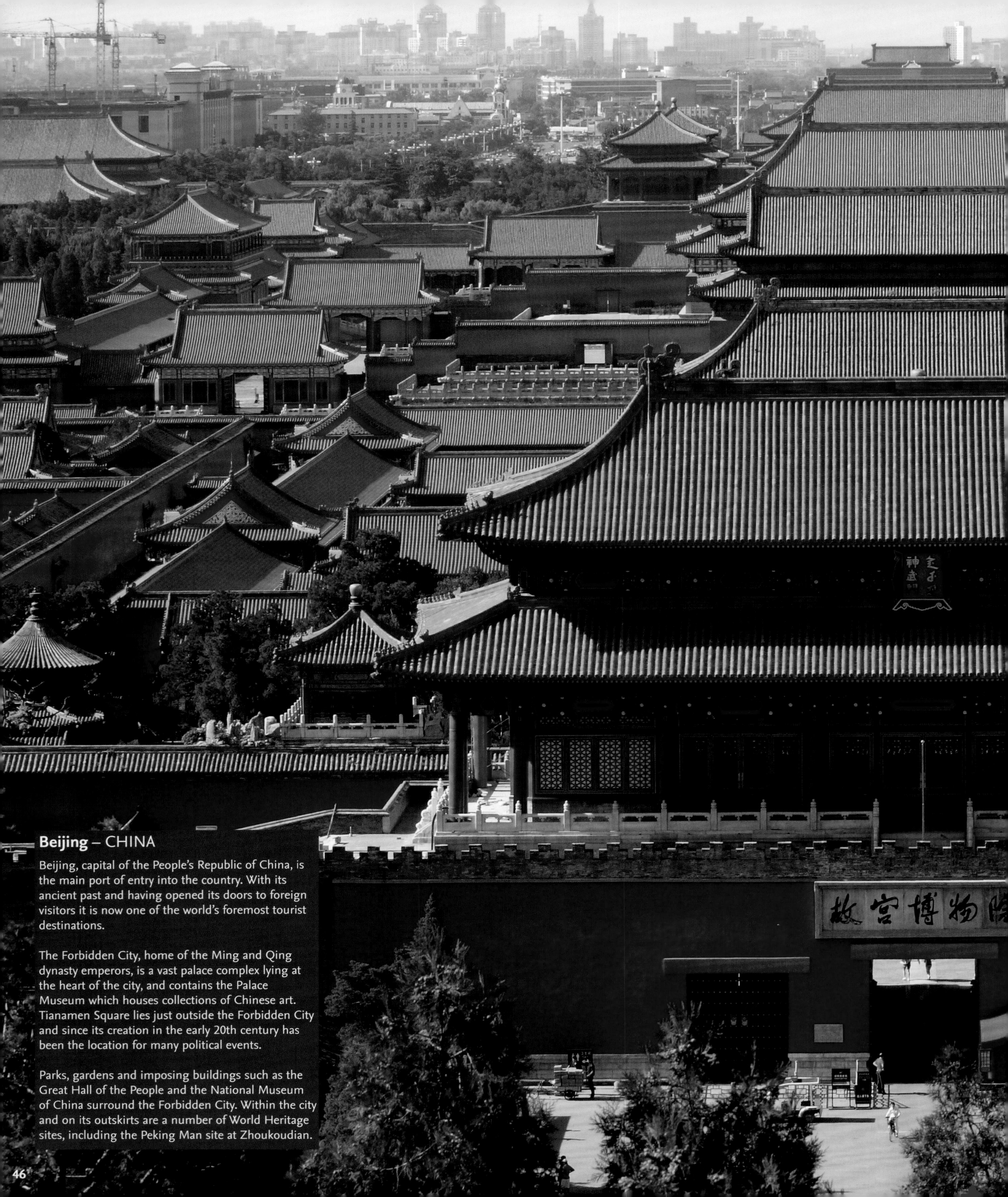

Beijing – CHINA

Beijing, capital of the People's Republic of China, is the main port of entry into the country. With its ancient past and having opened its doors to foreign visitors it is now one of the world's foremost tourist destinations.

The Forbidden City, home of the Ming and Qing dynasty emperors, is a vast palace complex lying at the heart of the city, and contains the Palace Museum which houses collections of Chinese art. Tianamen Square lies just outside the Forbidden City and since its creation in the early 20th century has been the location for many political events.

Parks, gardens and imposing buildings such as the Great Hall of the People and the National Museum of China surround the Forbidden City. Within the city and on its outskirts are a number of World Heritage sites, including the Peking Man site at Zhoukoudian.

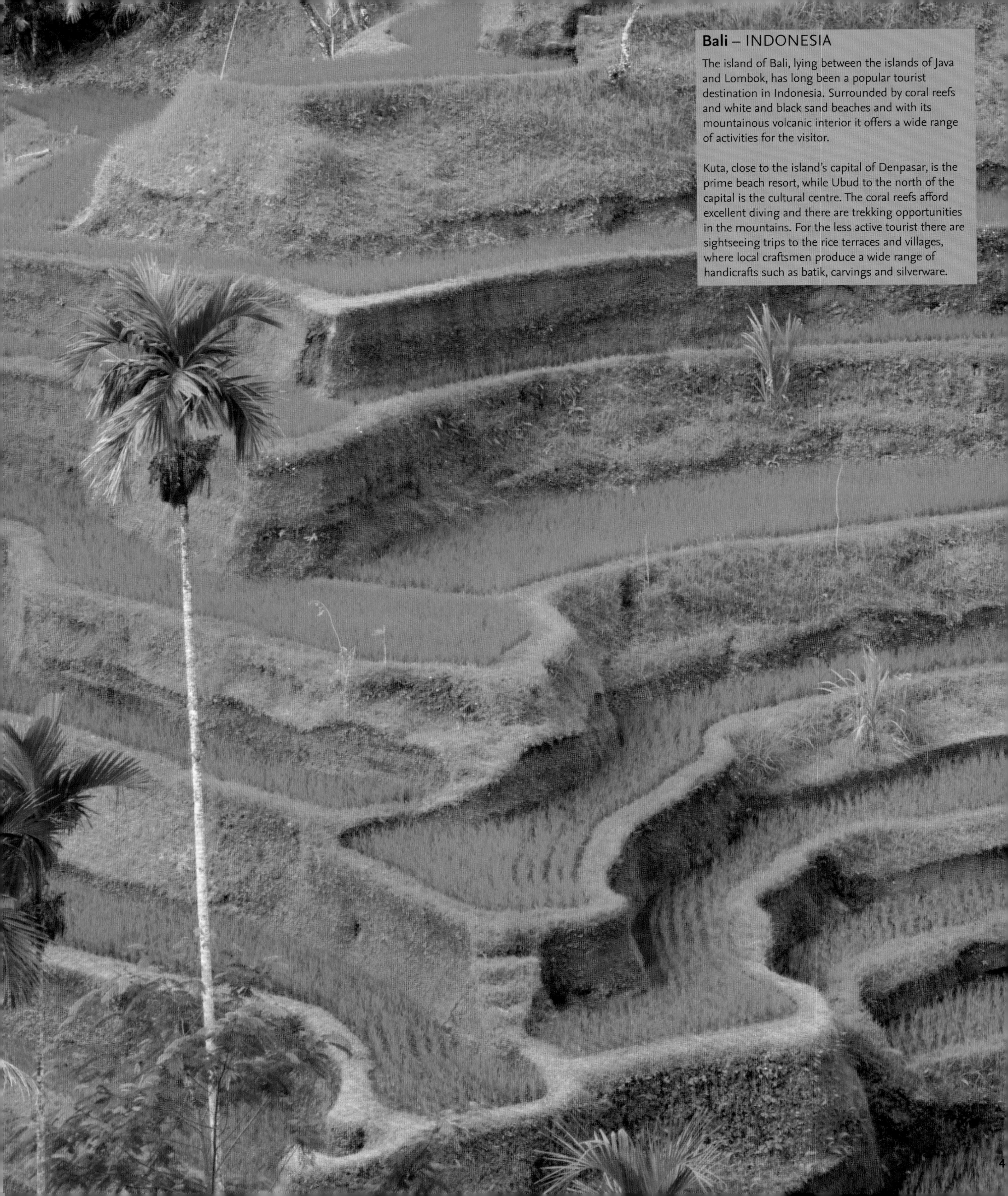

Bali – INDONESIA

The island of Bali, lying between the islands of Java and Lombok, has long been a popular tourist destination in Indonesia. Surrounded by coral reefs and white and black sand beaches and with its mountainous volcanic interior it offers a wide range of activities for the visitor.

Kuta, close to the island's capital of Denpasar, is the prime beach resort, while Ubud to the north of the capital is the cultural centre. The coral reefs afford excellent diving and there are trekking opportunities in the mountains. For the less active tourist there are sightseeing trips to the rice terraces and villages, where local craftsmen produce a wide range of handicrafts such as batik, carvings and silverware.

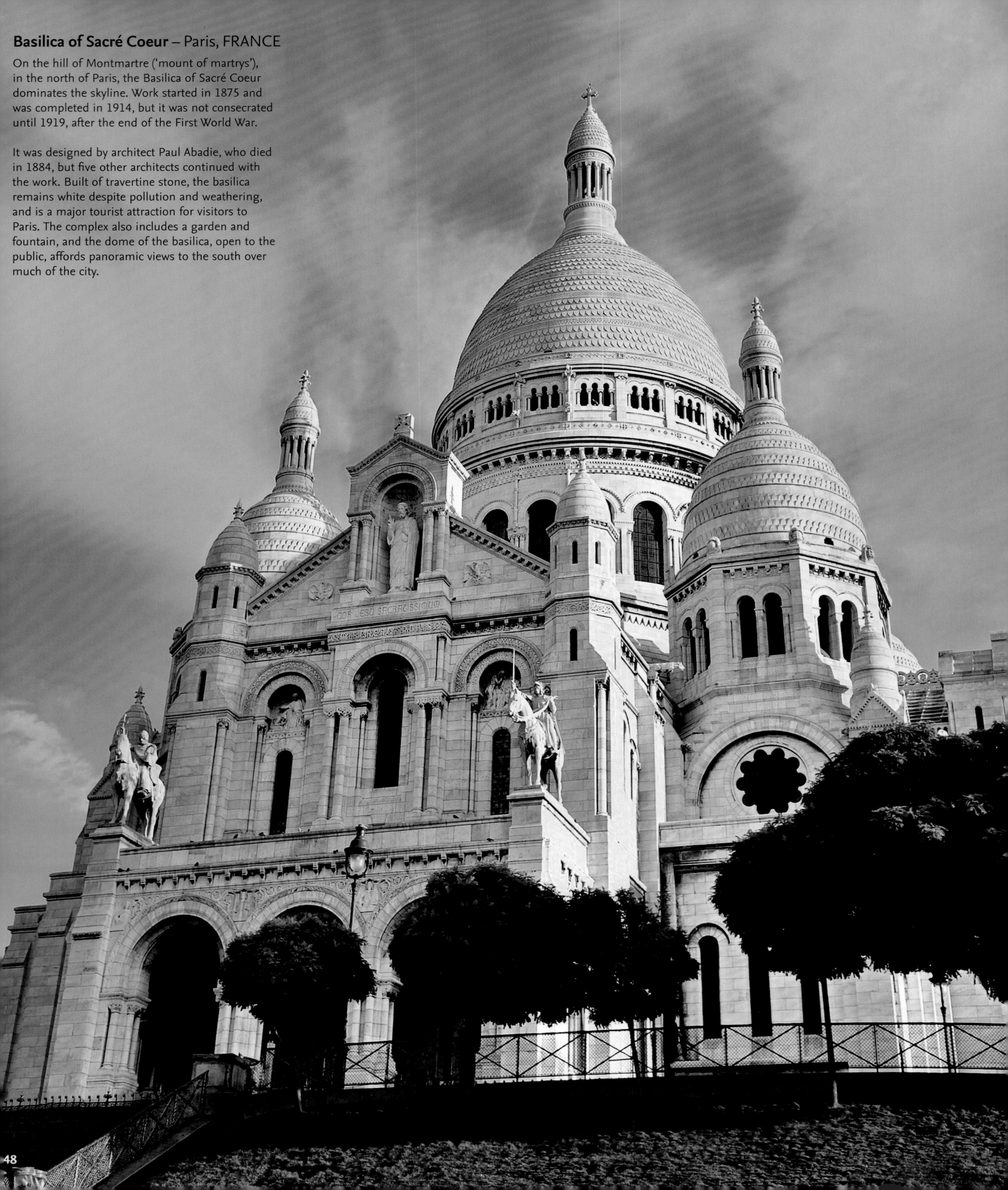

Basilica of Sacré Coeur – Paris, FRANCE

On the hill of Montmartre ('mount of martrys'), in the north of Paris, the Basilica of Sacré Coeur dominates the skyline. Work started in 1875 and was completed in 1914, but it was not consecrated until 1919, after the end of the First World War.

It was designed by architect Paul Abadie, who died in 1884, but five other architects continued with the work. Built of travertine stone, the basilica remains white despite pollution and weathering, and is a major tourist attraction for visitors to Paris. The complex also includes a garden and fountain, and the dome of the basilica, open to the public, affords panoramic views to the south over much of the city.

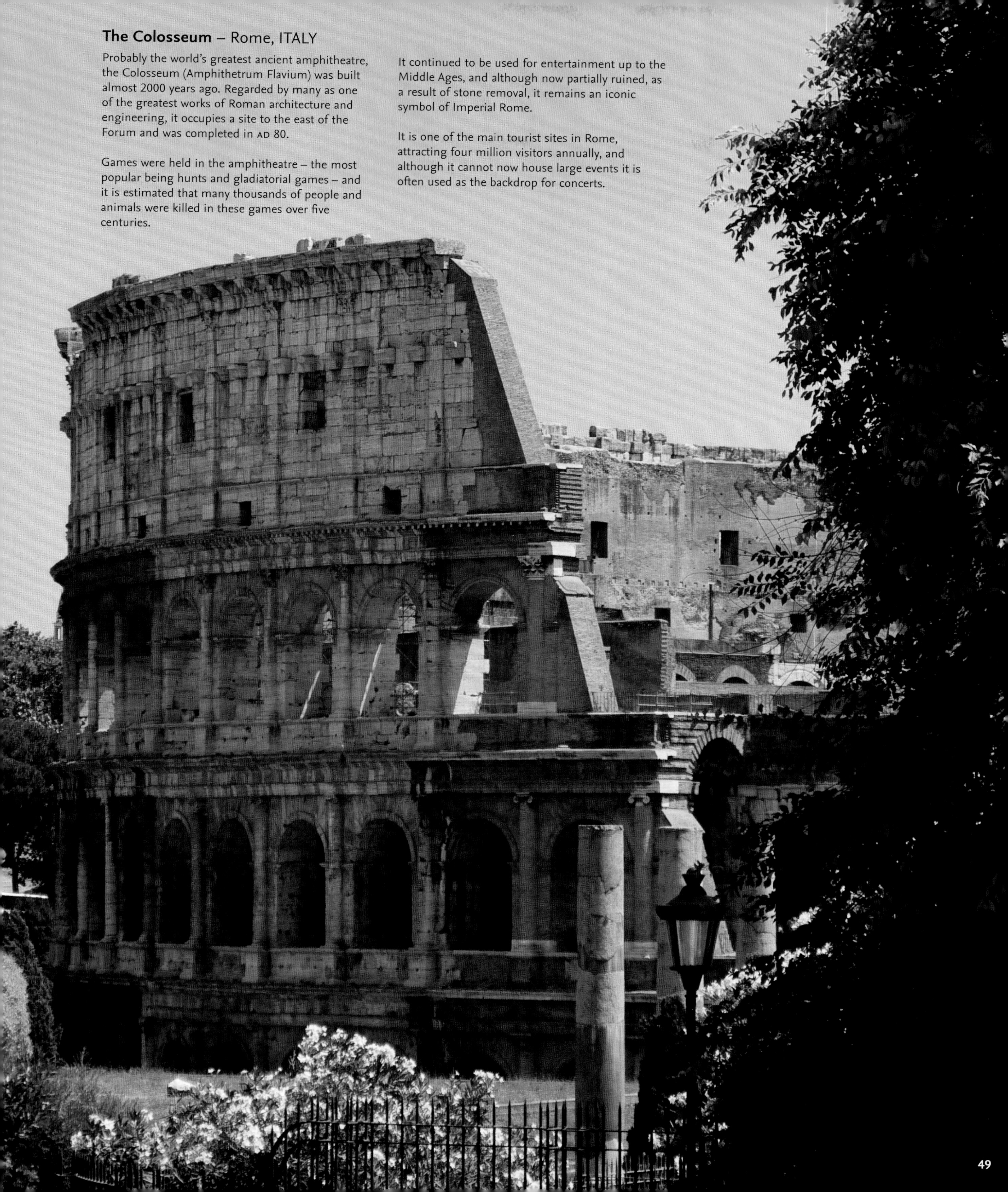

The Colosseum – Rome, ITALY

Probably the world's greatest ancient amphitheatre, the Colosseum (Amphithetrum Flavium) was built almost 2000 years ago. Regarded by many as one of the greatest works of Roman architecture and engineering, it occupies a site to the east of the Forum and was completed in AD 80.

Games were held in the amphitheatre – the most popular being hunts and gladiatorial games – and it is estimated that many thousands of people and animals were killed in these games over five centuries.

It continued to be used for entertainment up to the Middle Ages, and although now partially ruined, as a result of stone removal, it remains an iconic symbol of Imperial Rome.

It is one of the main tourist sites in Rome, attracting four million visitors annually, and although it cannot now house large events it is often used as the backdrop for concerts.

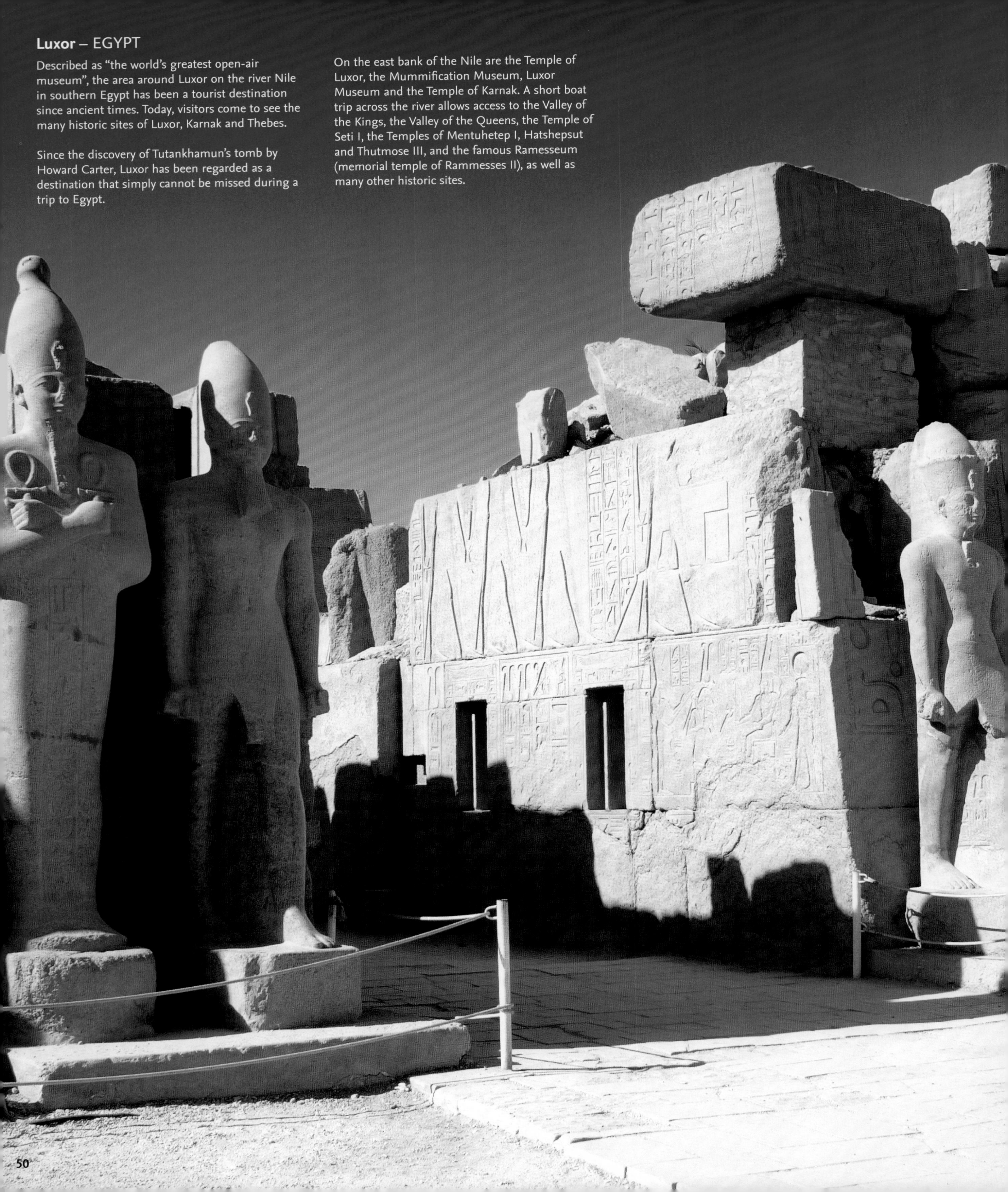

Luxor – EGYPT

Described as "the world's greatest open-air museum", the area around Luxor on the river Nile in southern Egypt has been a tourist destination since ancient times. Today, visitors come to see the many historic sites of Luxor, Karnak and Thebes.

Since the discovery of Tutankhamun's tomb by Howard Carter, Luxor has been regarded as a destination that simply cannot be missed during a trip to Egypt.

On the east bank of the Nile are the Temple of Luxor, the Mummification Museum, Luxor Museum and the Temple of Karnak. A short boat trip across the river allows access to the Valley of the Kings, the Valley of the Queens, the Temple of Seti I, the Temples of Mentuhetep I, Hatshepsut and Thutmose III, and the famous Ramesseum (memorial temple of Rammesses II), as well as many other historic sites.

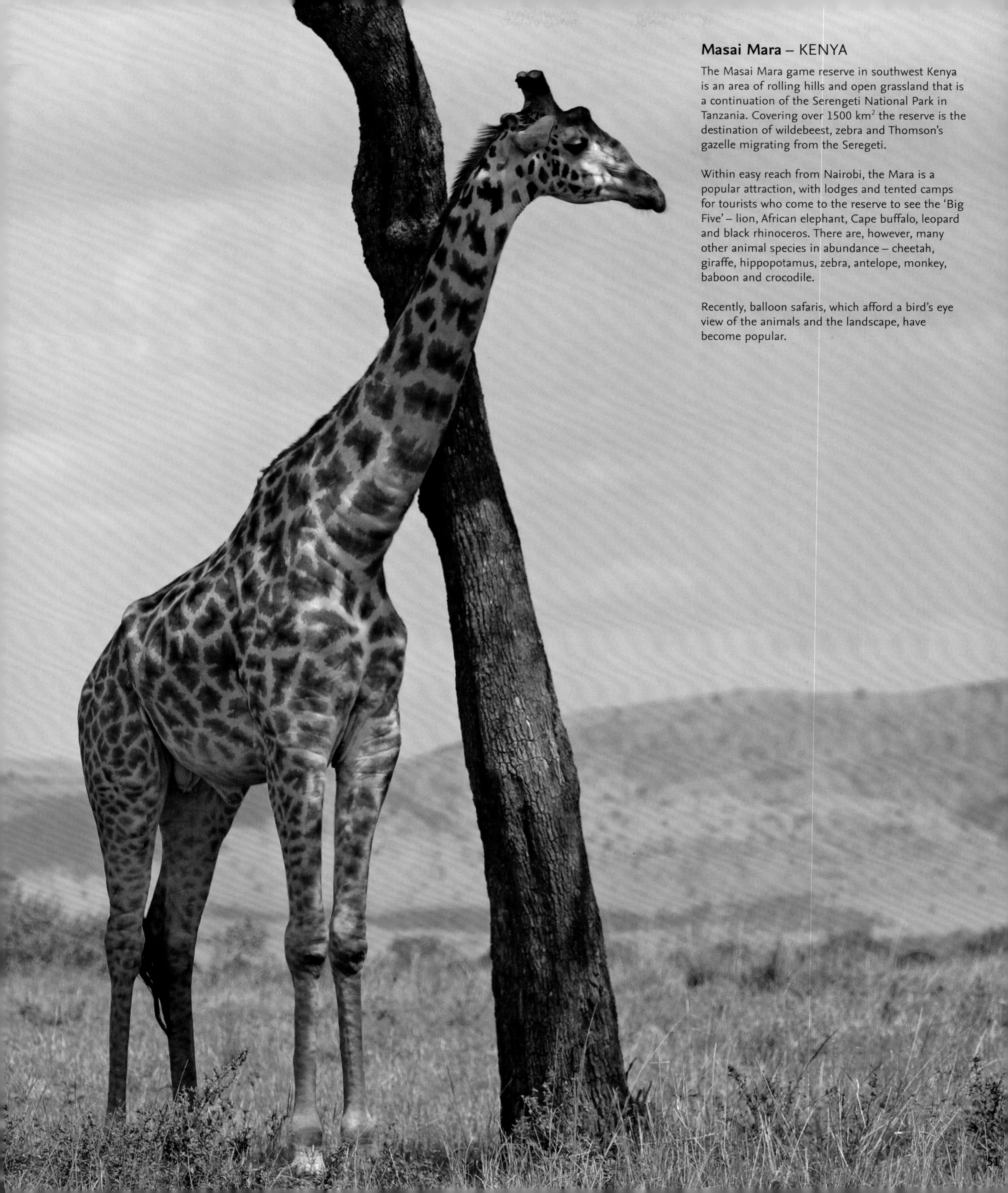

Masai Mara – KENYA

The Masai Mara game reserve in southwest Kenya is an area of rolling hills and open grassland that is a continuation of the Serengeti National Park in Tanzania. Covering over 1500 km^2 the reserve is the destination of wildebeest, zebra and Thomson's gazelle migrating from the Seregeti.

Within easy reach from Nairobi, the Mara is a popular attraction, with lodges and tented camps for tourists who come to the reserve to see the 'Big Five' – lion, African elephant, Cape buffalo, leopard and black rhinoceros. There are, however, many other animal species in abundance – cheetah, giraffe, hippopotamus, zebra, antelope, monkey, baboon and crocodile.

Recently, balloon safaris, which afford a bird's eye view of the animals and the landscape, have become popular.

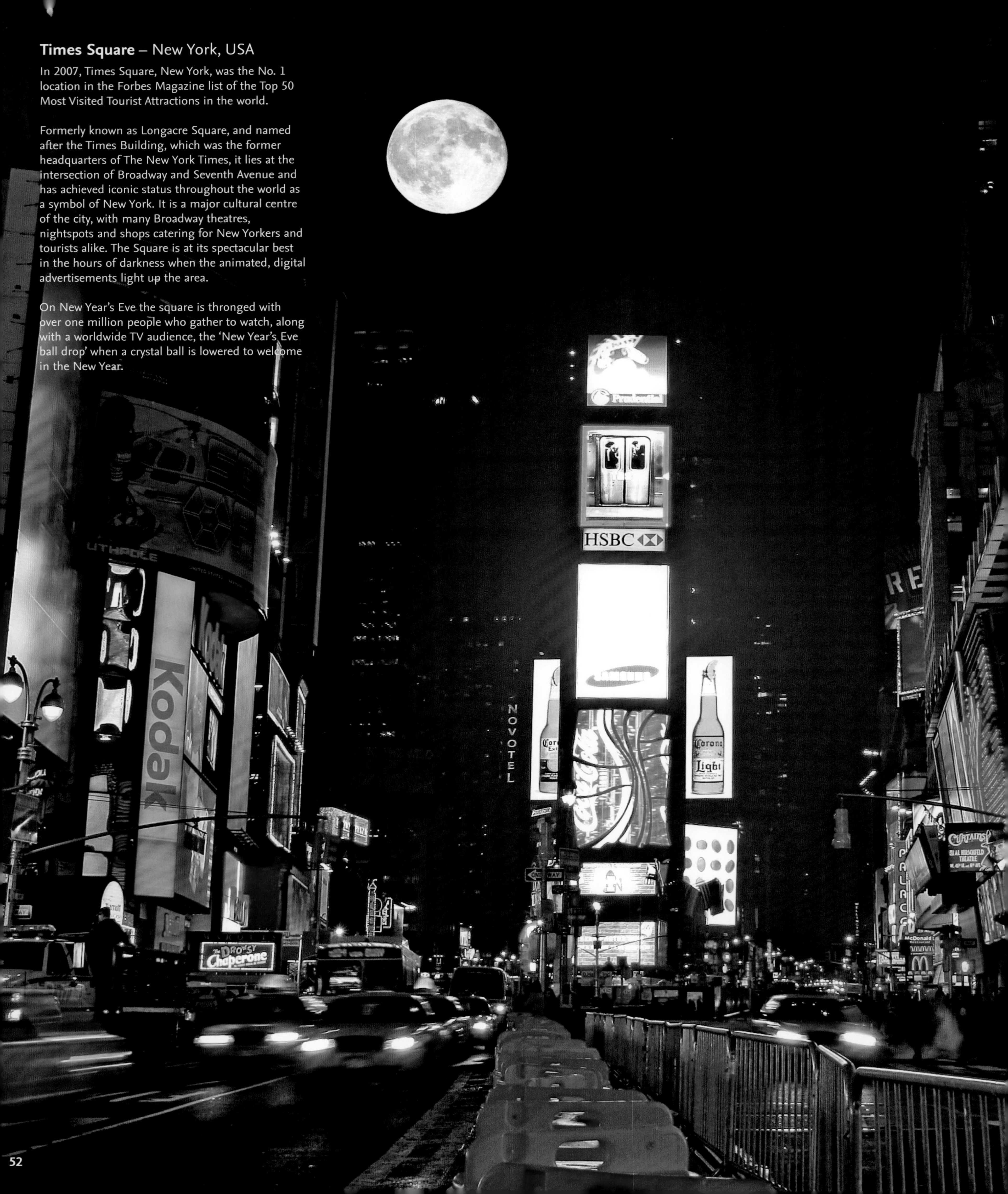

Times Square – New York, USA

In 2007, Times Square, New York, was the No. 1 location in the Forbes Magazine list of the Top 50 Most Visited Tourist Attractions in the world.

Formerly known as Longacre Square, and named after the Times Building, which was the former headquarters of The New York Times, it lies at the intersection of Broadway and Seventh Avenue and has achieved iconic status throughout the world as a symbol of New York. It is a major cultural centre of the city, with many Broadway theatres, nightspots and shops catering for New Yorkers and tourists alike. The Square is at its spectacular best in the hours of darkness when the animated, digital advertisements light up the area.

On New Year's Eve the square is thronged with over one million people who gather to watch, along with a worldwide TV audience, the 'New Year's Eve ball drop' when a crystal ball is lowered to welcome in the New Year.

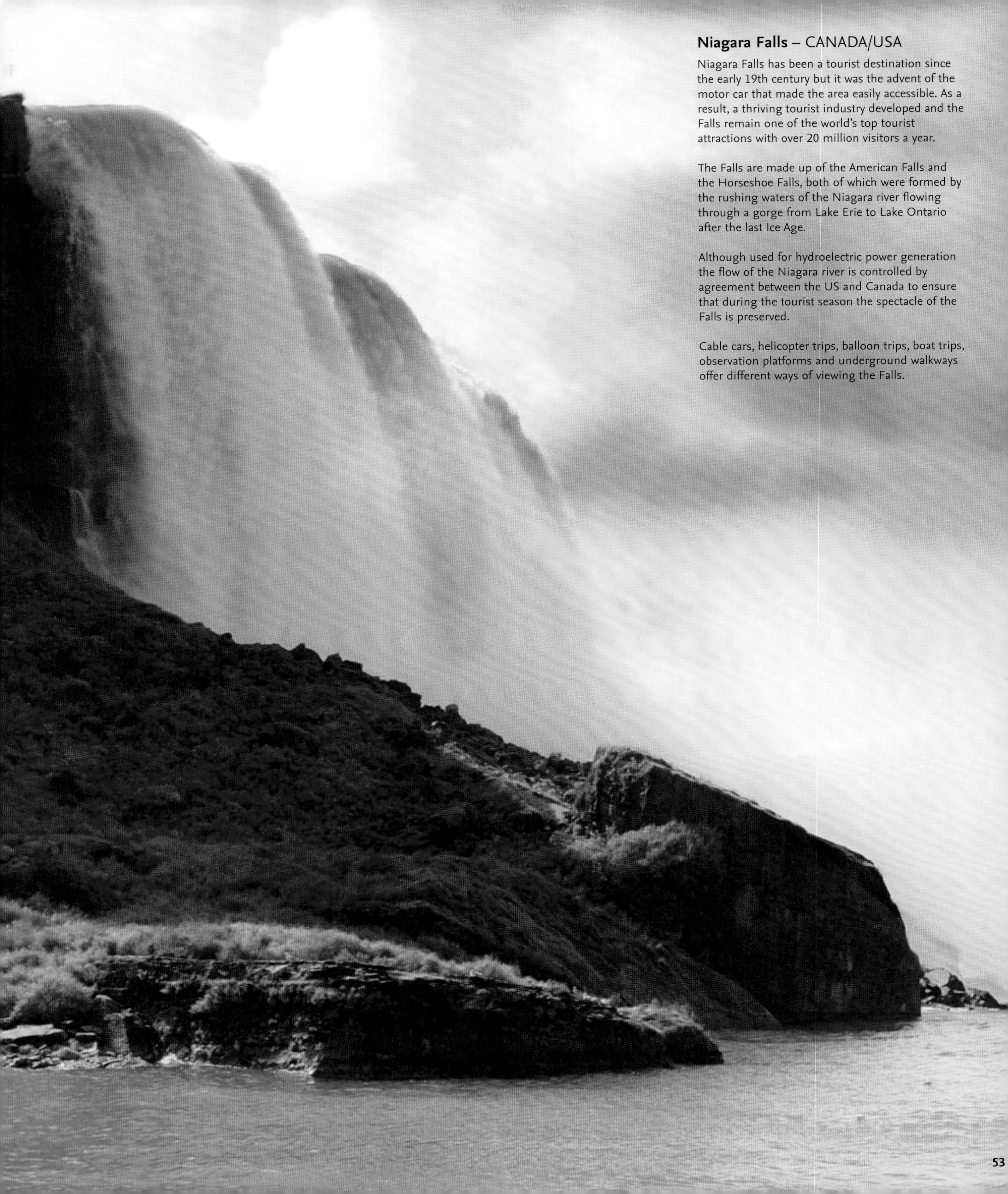

Niagara Falls – CANADA/USA

Niagara Falls has been a tourist destination since the early 19th century but it was the advent of the motor car that made the area easily accessible. As a result, a thriving tourist industry developed and the Falls remain one of the world's top tourist attractions with over 20 million visitors a year.

The Falls are made up of the American Falls and the Horseshoe Falls, both of which were formed by the rushing waters of the Niagara river flowing through a gorge from Lake Erie to Lake Ontario after the last Ice Age.

Although used for hydroelectric power generation the flow of the Niagara river is controlled by agreement between the US and Canada to ensure that during the tourist season the spectacle of the Falls is preserved.

Cable cars, helicopter trips, balloon trips, boat trips, observation platforms and underground walkways offer different ways of viewing the Falls.

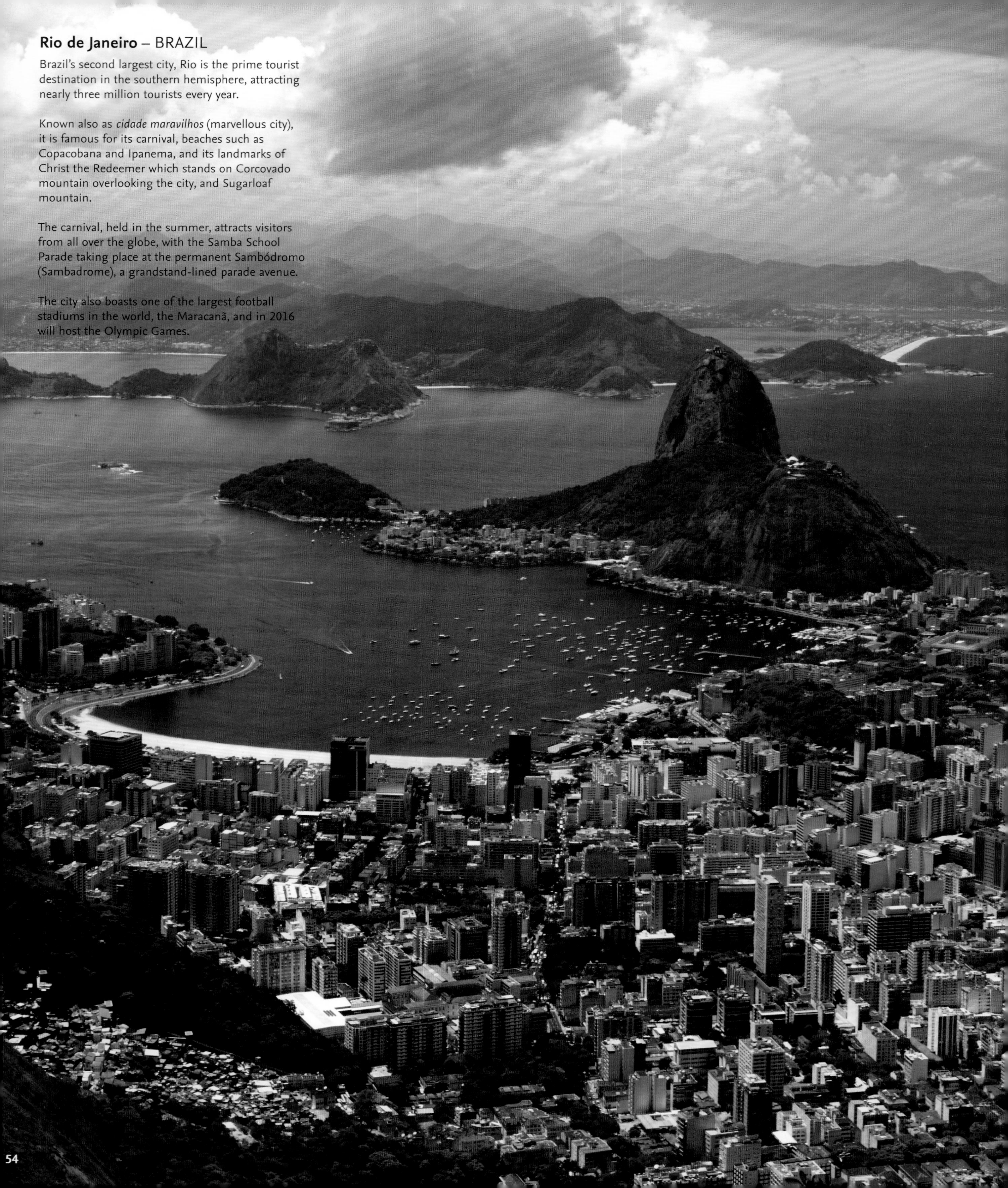

Rio de Janeiro – BRAZIL

Brazil's second largest city, Rio is the prime tourist destination in the southern hemisphere, attracting nearly three million tourists every year.

Known also as *cidade maravilhos* (marvellous city), it is famous for its carnival, beaches such as Copacobana and Ipanema, and its landmarks of Christ the Redeemer which stands on Corcovado mountain overlooking the city, and Sugarloaf mountain.

The carnival, held in the summer, attracts visitors from all over the globe, with the Samba School Parade taking place at the permanent Sambódromo (Sambadrome), a grandstand-lined parade avenue.

The city also boasts one of the largest football stadiums in the world, the Maracanã, and in 2016 will host the Olympic Games.

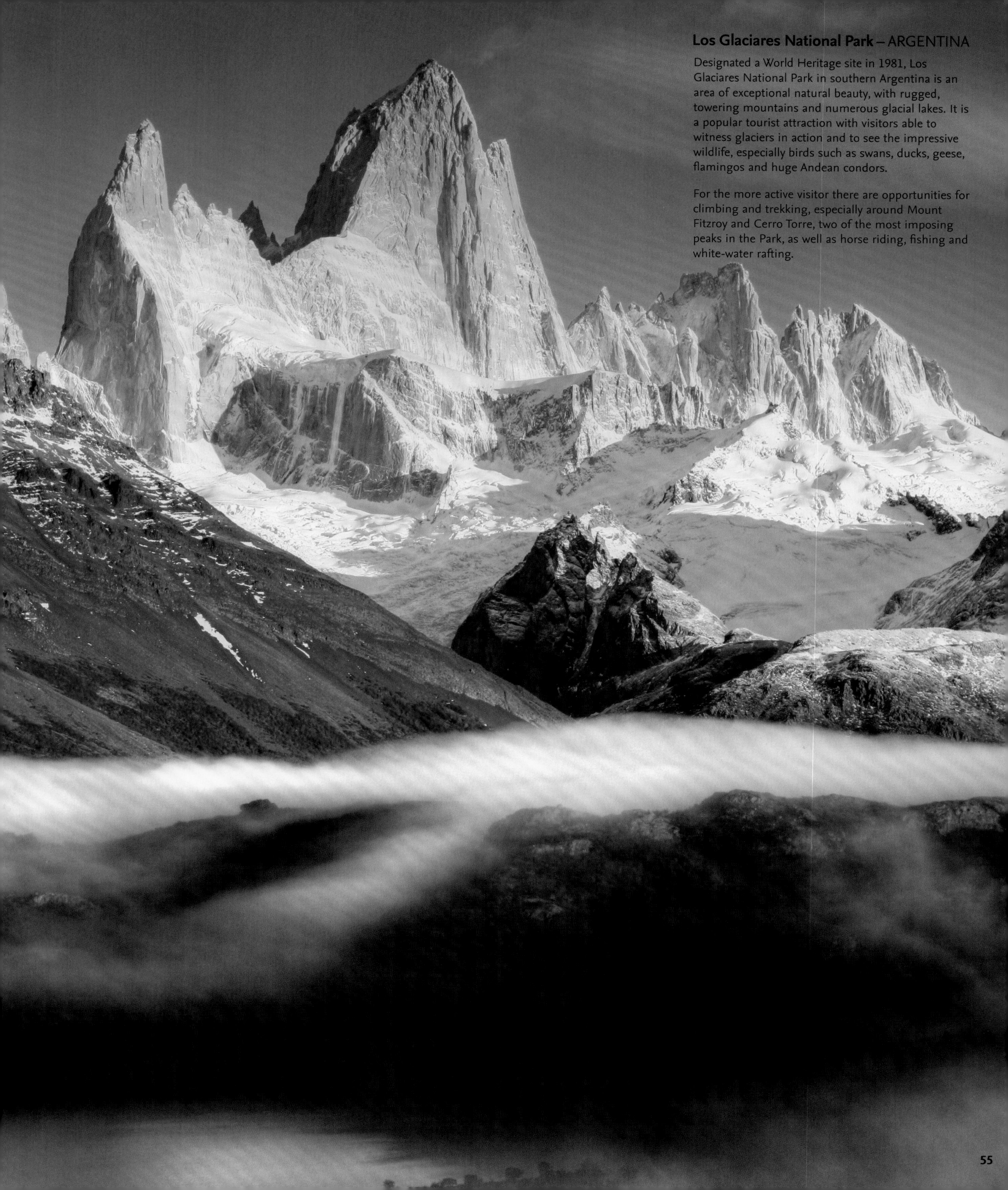

Los Glaciares National Park – ARGENTINA

Designated a World Heritage site in 1981, Los Glaciares National Park in southern Argentina is an area of exceptional natural beauty, with rugged, towering mountains and numerous glacial lakes. It is a popular tourist attraction with visitors able to witness glaciers in action and to see the impressive wildlife, especially birds such as swans, ducks, geese, flamingos and huge Andean condors.

For the more active visitor there are opportunities for climbing and trekking, especially around Mount Fitzroy and Cerro Torre, two of the most imposing peaks in the Park, as well as horse riding, fishing and white-water rafting.

World Heritage and UNESCO's World Heritage Mission

A visit to a World Heritage site is often an activity in a tourist's itinerary. On the reference maps in this atlas the locations of World Heritage sites are shown, and in the following pages selected ones are described in detail. The sites are those submitted by various countries to the UNESCO World Heritage Committee and approved by it for inclusion on the World Heritage List. To be accepted for inclusion various criteria, as explained below, have to be met.

Heritage is our legacy from the past, what we live with today, and what we pass on to future generations. Our cultural and natural heritage are both irreplaceable sources of life and inspiration. Places as unique and diverse as the wilds of East Africa's Serengeti, the Pyramids of Egypt, the Great Barrier Reef in Australia and the Baroque cathedrals of Latin America make up our world's heritage.

The United Nations Educational, Scientific and Cultural Organization (UNESCO) seeks to encourage the identification, protection and preservation of cultural and natural heritage around the world considered to be of outstanding universal value to humanity. This is embodied in a unique international treaty, called the Convention Concerning the Protection of the World Cultural and Natural Heritage adopted by UNESCO in 1972 (see http://whc.unesco.org/en/conventiontext).

One of the world's most successful conservation instruments, the World Heritage Convention is exceptional in that it links together in a single document the concepts of nature conservation and the preservation of cultural properties. It is also significant in its universal application – World Heritage sites belong to all the peoples of the world, irrespective of the territory on which they are located. By regarding heritage as both cultural and natural, the Convention recognizes the ways in which people interact with nature, and of the fundamental need to preserve the balance between the two.

UNESCO's World Heritage mission is to:
- encourage countries to sign the World Heritage Convention and to ensure the protection of their natural and cultural heritage;
- encourage States Parties to the Convention to nominate sites within their national territory for inclusion on the World Heritage List;
- encourage States Parties to establish management plans and set up reporting systems on the state of conservation of their World Heritage sites;
- help States Parties safeguard World Heritage properties by providing technical assistance and professional training;
- provide emergency assistance for World Heritage sites in immediate danger;
- support States Parties' public awareness-building activities for World Heritage conservation;
- encourage participation of the local population in the preservation of their cultural and natural heritage;
- encourage international cooperation in the conservation of our world's cultural and natural heritage.

THE CRITERIA FOR SELECTION
The World Heritage Convention stipulates the creation of a World Heritage List. In a detailed process, properties are inscribed by an intergovernmental twenty-one member elected Committee, only after a preselection, nomination, and evaluation process. Two leading international Non-Governmental Organizations, the International Union for the Conservation of Nature (IUCN) and the International Council on Monuments and Sites (ICOMOS), review and advise on the natural and cultural nominations respectively. The International Centre for the Study of the Preservation and Restoration of Cultural Property provides the Committee with expert advice on conservation of cultural sites. To be included, sites must be of outstanding universal value and meet at least one out of ten selection criteria:

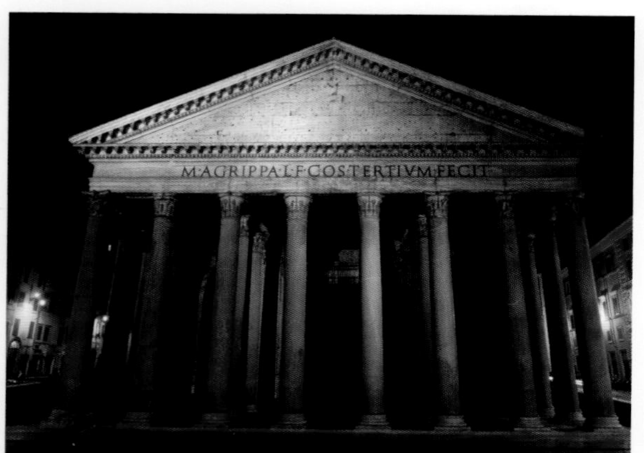

Historic Centre of Rome, Italy

Human creative genius
i. to represent a masterpiece of human creative genius;

Testimony to cultural tradition
iii. to bear a unique or at least exceptional testimony to a cultural tradition or to a civilization which is living or which has disappeared;

Interchange of values
ii. to exhibit an important interchange of human values, over a span of time or within a cultural area of the world, on developments in architecture or technology, monumental arts, town-planning or landscape design;

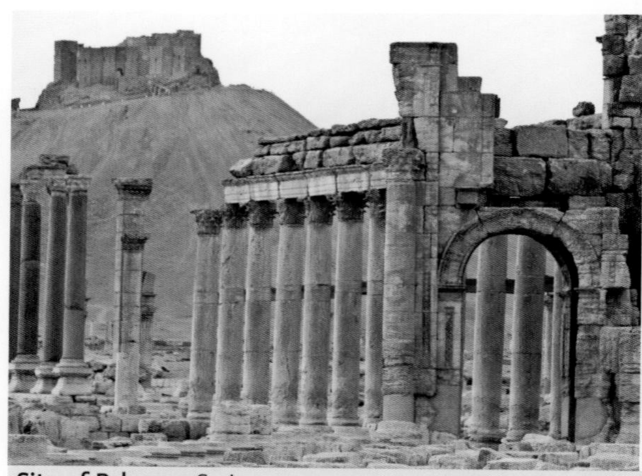

Site of Palmyra, Syria

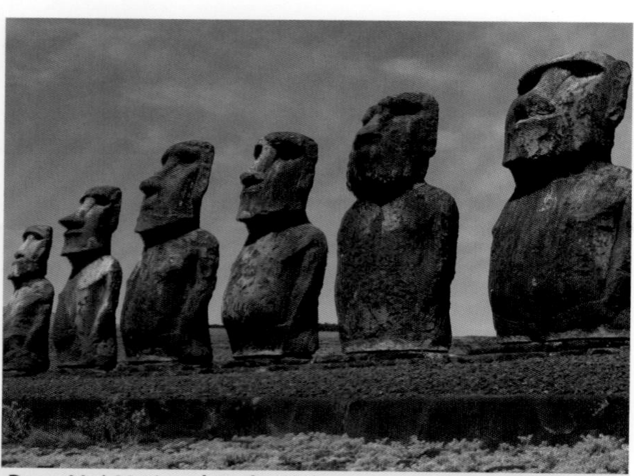

Rapa Nui National Park, Chile

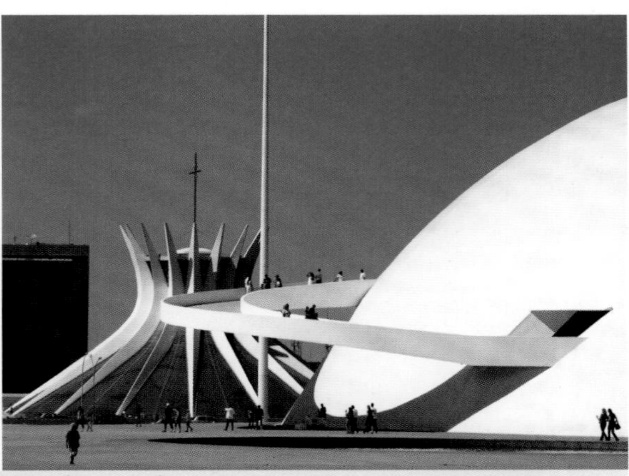

Brasilia, Brazil

Significance in human history
iv. to be an outstanding example of a type of building, architectural or technological ensemble or landscape which illustrates (a) significant stage(s) in human history;

Traditional human settlement
v. to be an outstanding example of a traditional human settlement, land-use, or sea-use which is representative of a culture (or cultures), or human interaction with the environment especially when it has become vulnerable under the impact of irreversible change;

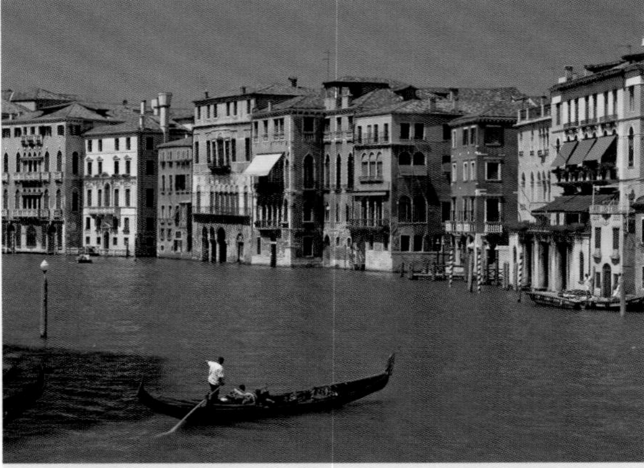

Venice and its Lagoon, Italy

Heritage associated with events of universal significance
vi. to be directly or tangibly associated with events or living traditions, with ideas, or with beliefs, with artistic and literary works of outstanding universal significance. (The Committee considers that this criterion should preferably be used in conjunction with other criteria);

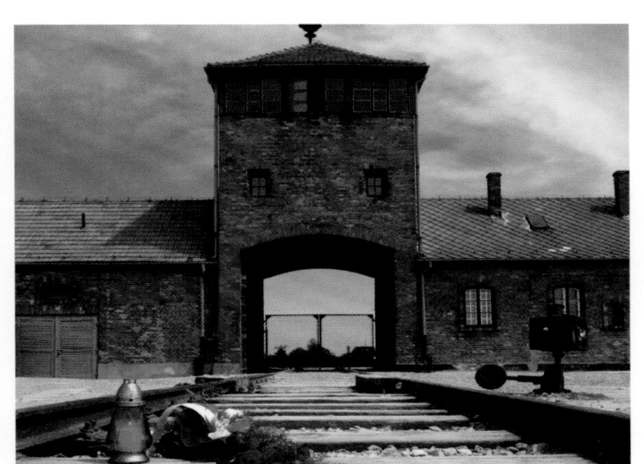

Auschwitz Birkenau, Poland

Natural phenomena or beauty
vii. to contain superlative natural phenomena or areas of exceptional natural beauty and aesthetic importance;

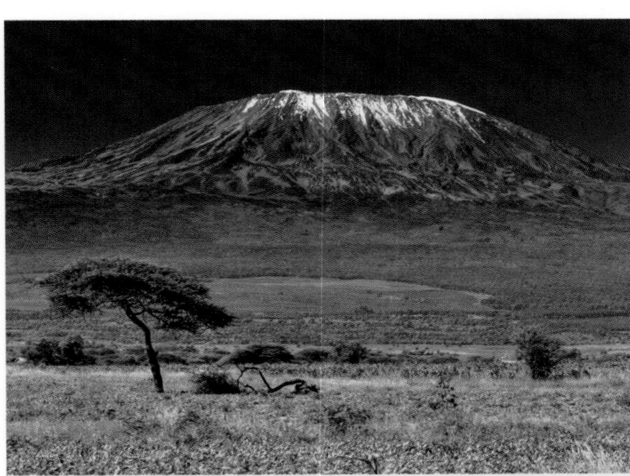

Kilimanjaro National Park, Tanzania

Major stages of Earth's history
viii. to be outstanding examples representing major stages of Earth's history, including the record of life, significant on-going geological processes in the development of landforms, or significant geomorphic or physiographic features;

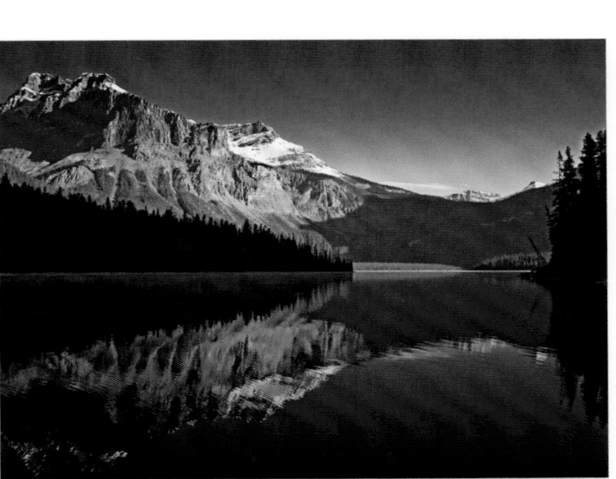

Emerald Lake, Yoho National Park, Canada

Significant ecological and biological processes
ix. to be outstanding examples representing significant on-going ecological and biological processes in the evolution and development of terrestrial, fresh water, coastal and marine ecosystems and communities of plants and animals;

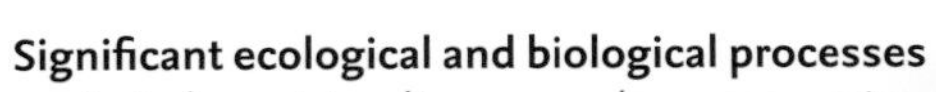

Everglades National Park, USA

Significant natural habitat for biodiversity
x. to contain the most important and significant natural habitats for in-situ conservation of biological diversity, including those containing threatened species of outstanding universal value from the point of view of science or conservation.

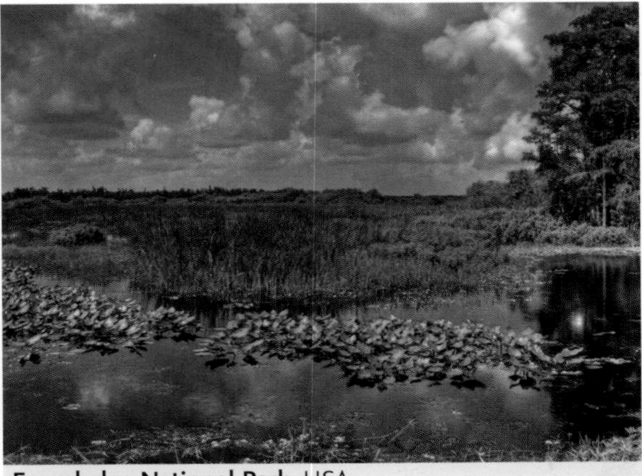

Virunga National Park, Dem. Rep. of the Congo

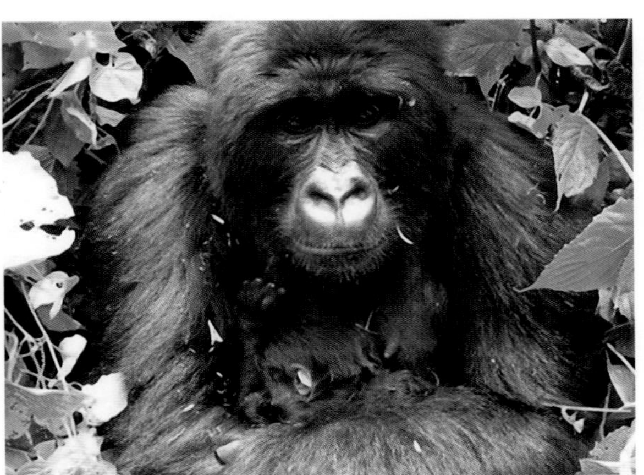

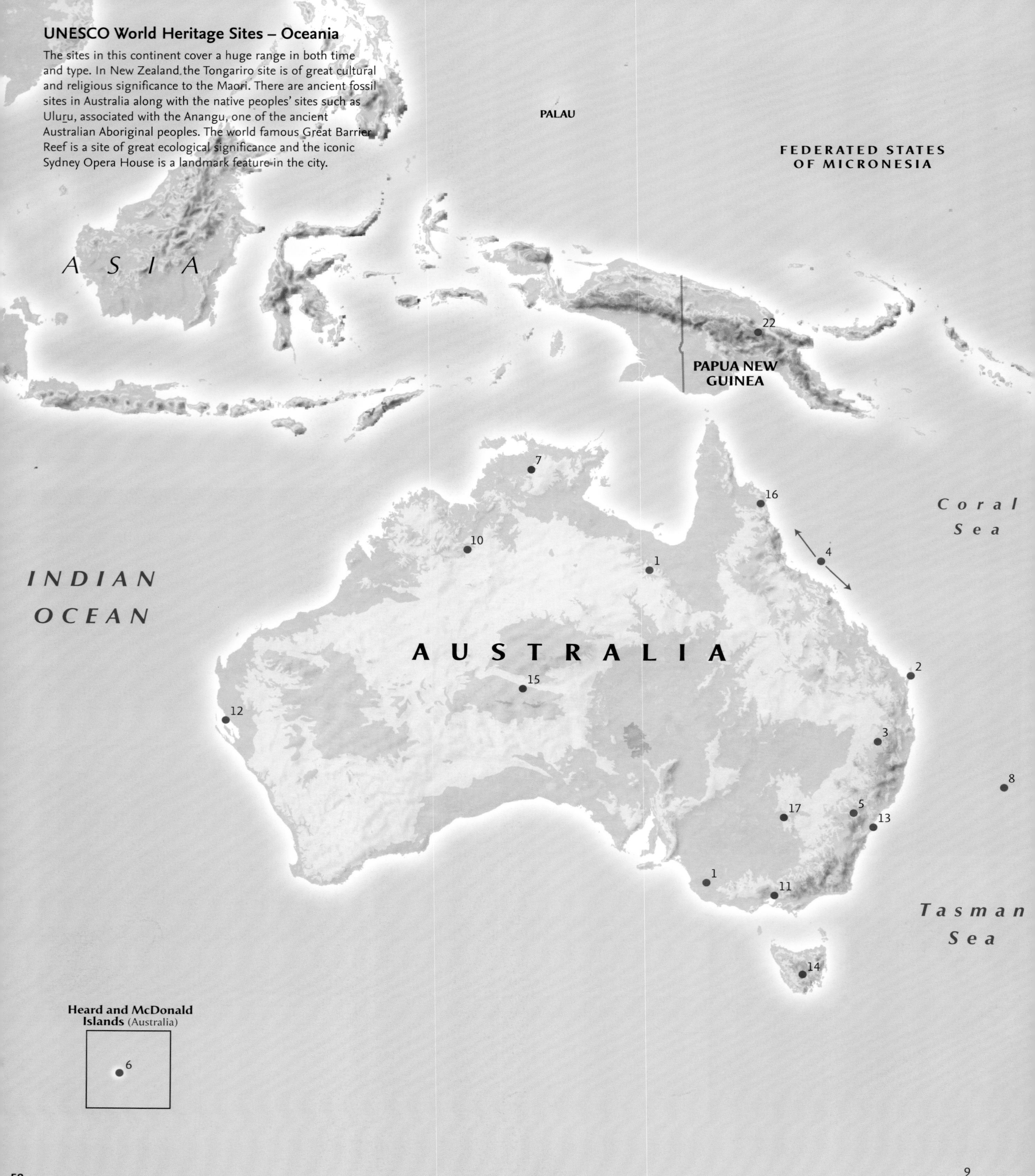

UNESCO World Heritage Sites – Oceania

The sites in this continent cover a huge range in both time and type. In New Zealand, the Tongariro site is of great cultural and religious significance to the Maori. There are ancient fossil sites in Australia along with the native peoples' sites such as Uluru, associated with the Anangu, one of the ancient Australian Aboriginal peoples. The world famous Great Barrier Reef is a site of great ecological significance and the iconic Sydney Opera House is a landmark feature in the city.

PALAU

FEDERATED STATES
OF MICRONESIA

ASIA

PAPUA NEW
GUINEA

22

INDIAN
OCEAN

Coral
Sea

7

16

10

4

1

AUSTRALIA

2

15

3

12

8

17   5

13

1

11

Tasman
Sea

14

**Heard and McDonald
Islands** (Australia)

6

9

MARSHALL
ISLANDS

NAURU

PACIFIC

KIRIBATI

SOLOMON
ISLANDS

TUVALU

4

VANUATU

25

SAMOA

FIJI

18

New
Caledonia
(France)

Niue
(N.Z.)

TONGA

OCEAN

Cook
Islands
(N.Z.)

Pitcairn Islands (U.K.)

23

NEW
ZEALAND

21

20

20
20

20

19

19

19

19

Australia
1. Australian Fossil Mammal Sites
   (Riversleigh/Naracoorte)
2. Fraser Island
3. Gondwana Rainforests of Australia
4. Great Barrier Reef
5. Greater Blue Mountains Area
6. Heard and McDonald Islands
7. Kakadu National Park
8. Lord Howe Island Group
9. Macquarie Island
10. Purnululu National Park
11. Royal Exhibition Building and Carlton
    Gardens
12. Shark Bay, Western Australia
13. Sydney Opera House
14. Tasmanian Wilderness
15. Uluru-Kata Tjuta National Park
16. Wet Tropics of Queensland
17. Willandra Lakes Region

New Caledonia
18. Lagoons of New Caledonia:
    Reef Diversity and Associated Ecosystems
    (France)

New Zealand
19. New Zealand Sub-Antarctic Islands
20. Te Wahipounamu – South West
    New Zealand
21. Tongariro National Park

Papua New Guinea
22. Kuk Early Agricultural Site

Pitcairn Islands
23. Henderson Island (U.K.)

Solomon Islands
24. East Rennell

Vanuatu
25. Chief Roi Mata's Domain

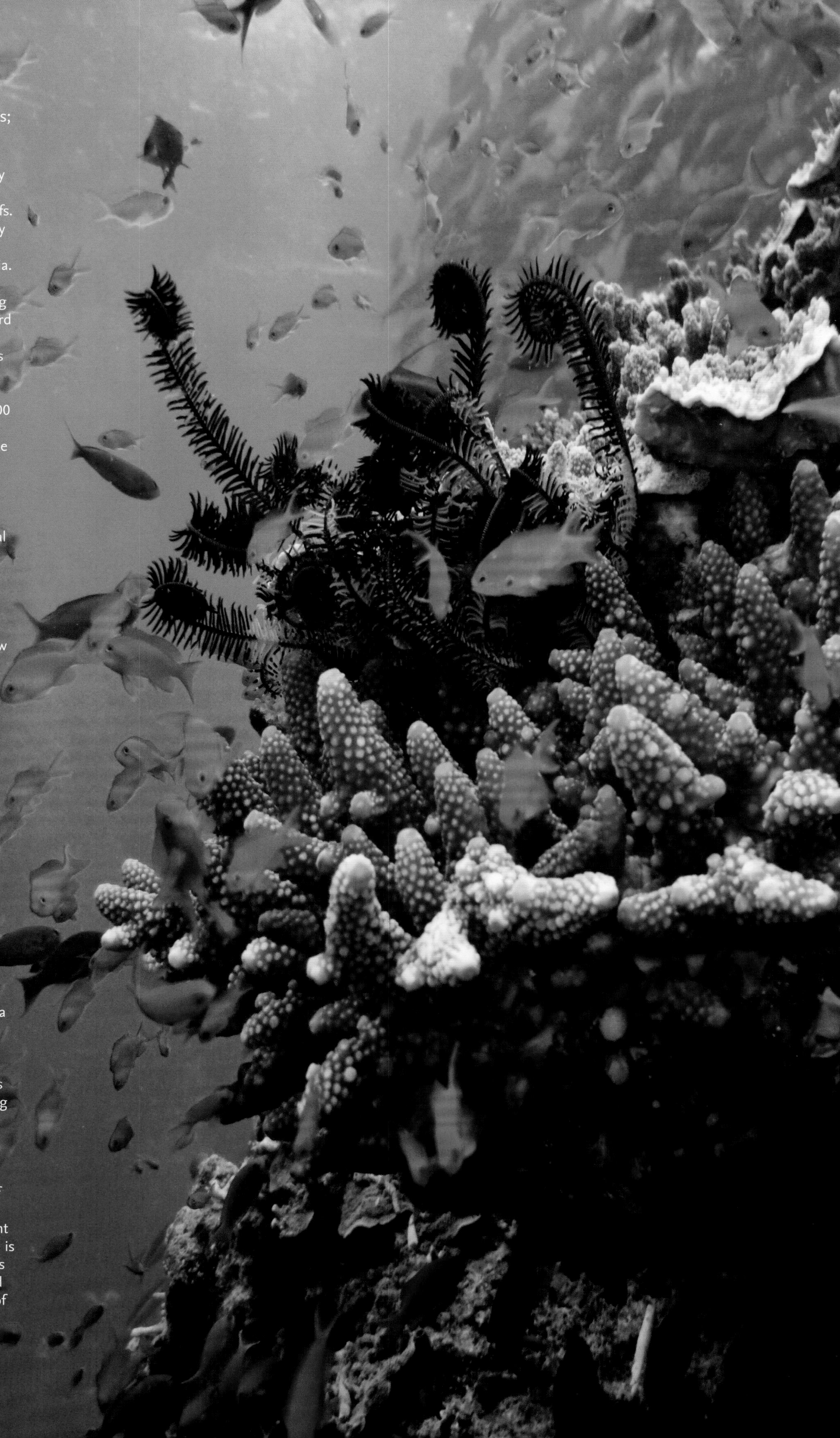

Great Barrier Reef – AUSTRALIA

Inscribed 1981 – Natural phenomena or beauty; Major stages of Earth's history; Significant ecological and biological processes; Significant natural habitat for biodiversity.

The Great Barrier Reef is a site of remarkable variety and beauty on the northeast coast of Australia. It is the world's most extensive stretch of coral reefs. The great diversity of its fauna reflects the maturity of an ecosystem that has evolved over millions of years on the northeast continental shelf of Australia.

The site contains a huge range of species including over 1 500 species of fish, about 360 species of hard coral and 5 000 species of mollusc, plus a great diversity of sponges, sea anemones, marine worms and crustaceans. About 215 species of birds are found in its islands and cays. Extending to Papua New Guinea, the reef system comprises some 2 900 individual reefs covering more than 20 000 km², including 760 fringing reefs. The reefs range in size from under 0.01 km² to over 100 km² and vary in shape to provide the most spectacular marine scenery on Earth. There are approximately 600 continental islands including many with towering forests and freshwater streams, and some 300 coral cays and unvegetated sand cays. A rich variety of landscapes and seascapes, including rugged mountains with dense and diverse vegetation, provide spectacular scenery.

The form and structure of the individual reefs show great variety. There are two main classes: platform or patch reefs, resulting from radial growth; and wall reefs, resulting from elongated growth, often in areas of strong currents. There are also the many fringing reefs where growth is established on subtidal rock of the mainland coast or continental islands.

The site includes major feeding grounds for the endangered dugong and nesting grounds of world significance for four species of marine turtle including the endangered loggerhead turtle. Given the severe pressures on these species elsewhere, the Great Barrier Reef may be a last stronghold. It is also an important breeding area for humpback and other whale species.

A wide range of fleshy algae occurs, often small and inconspicuous but highly productive and heavily grazed by turtles, fish, molluscs and sea urchins. In addition, calcareous algae are an important component of reef building processes. Fifteen species of seagrass grow throughout the area, forming over 3 000 km² of seagrass meadows and providing an important food source for grazing animals, such as dugongs and turtles.

The Great Barrier Reef is important in the historic and contemporary culture of the Aboriginal and Torres Strait Islander groups of the coastal areas of northeast Australia. The contemporary use of and association with the Marine Park plays an important role in the maintenance of their cultures and there is a strong spiritual connection with the ocean and its inhabitants. New species continue to be discovered throughout the Great Barrier Reef. A new species of dolphin, the Australian snub-nose dolphin, was discovered in 2005 within inshore areas.

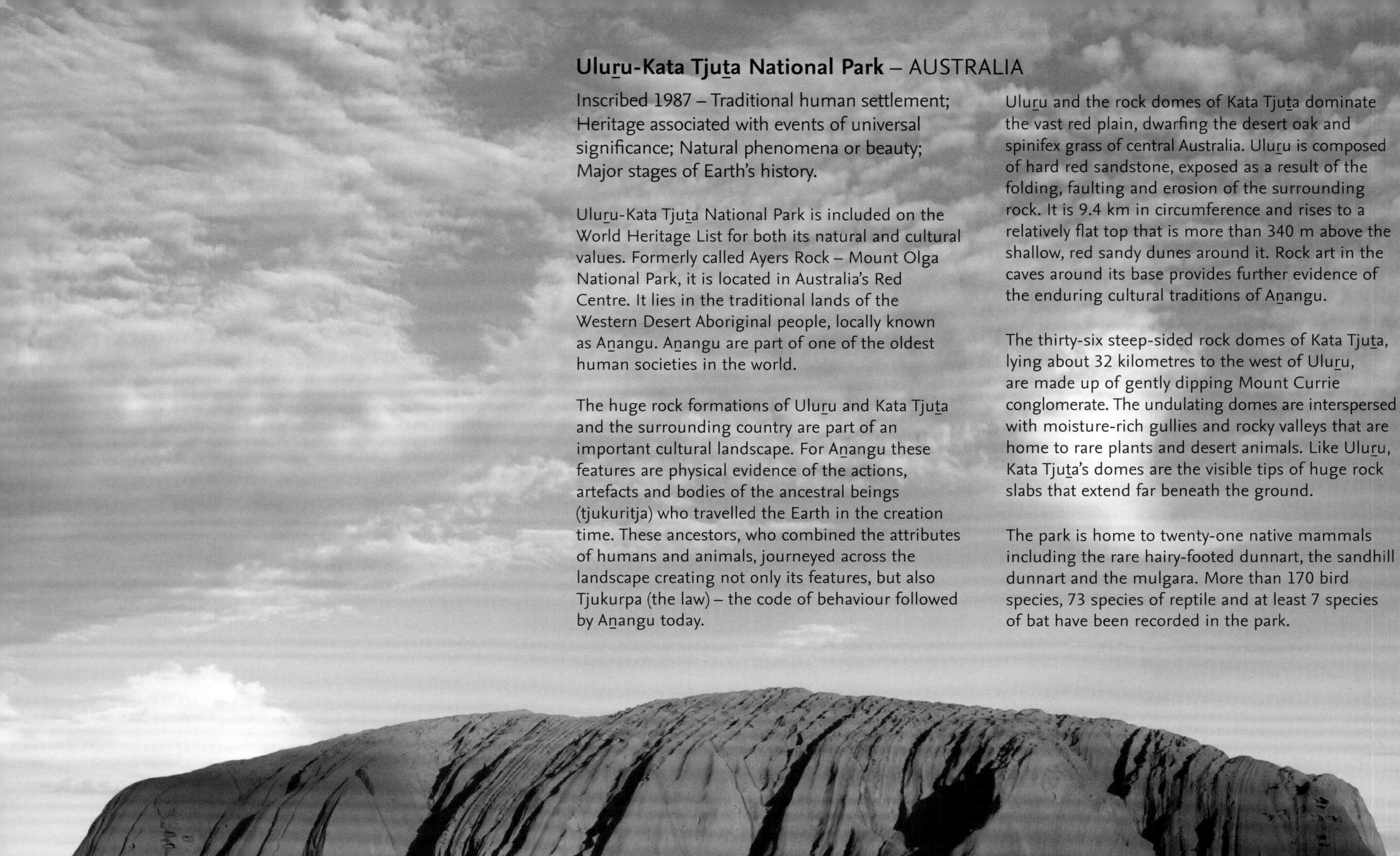

Uluru-Kata Tjuta National Park – AUSTRALIA

Inscribed 1987 – Traditional human settlement; Heritage associated with events of universal significance; Natural phenomena or beauty; Major stages of Earth's history.

Uluru-Kata Tjuta National Park is included on the World Heritage List for both its natural and cultural values. Formerly called Ayers Rock – Mount Olga National Park, it is located in Australia's Red Centre. It lies in the traditional lands of the Western Desert Aboriginal people, locally known as Anangu. Anangu are part of one of the oldest human societies in the world.

The huge rock formations of Uluru and Kata Tjuta and the surrounding country are part of an important cultural landscape. For Anangu these features are physical evidence of the actions, artefacts and bodies of the ancestral beings (tjukuritja) who travelled the Earth in the creation time. These ancestors, who combined the attributes of humans and animals, journeyed across the landscape creating not only its features, but also Tjukurpa (the law) – the code of behaviour followed by Anangu today.

Uluru and the rock domes of Kata Tjuta dominate the vast red plain, dwarfing the desert oak and spinifex grass of central Australia. Uluru is composed of hard red sandstone, exposed as a result of the folding, faulting and erosion of the surrounding rock. It is 9.4 km in circumference and rises to a relatively flat top that is more than 340 m above the shallow, red sandy dunes around it. Rock art in the caves around its base provides further evidence of the enduring cultural traditions of Anangu.

The thirty-six steep-sided rock domes of Kata Tjuta, lying about 32 kilometres to the west of Uluru, are made up of gently dipping Mount Currie conglomerate. The undulating domes are interspersed with moisture-rich gullies and rocky valleys that are home to rare plants and desert animals. Like Uluru, Kata Tjuta's domes are the visible tips of huge rock slabs that extend far beneath the ground.

The park is home to twenty-one native mammals including the rare hairy-footed dunnart, the sandhill dunnart and the mulgara. More than 170 bird species, 73 species of reptile and at least 7 species of bat have been recorded in the park.

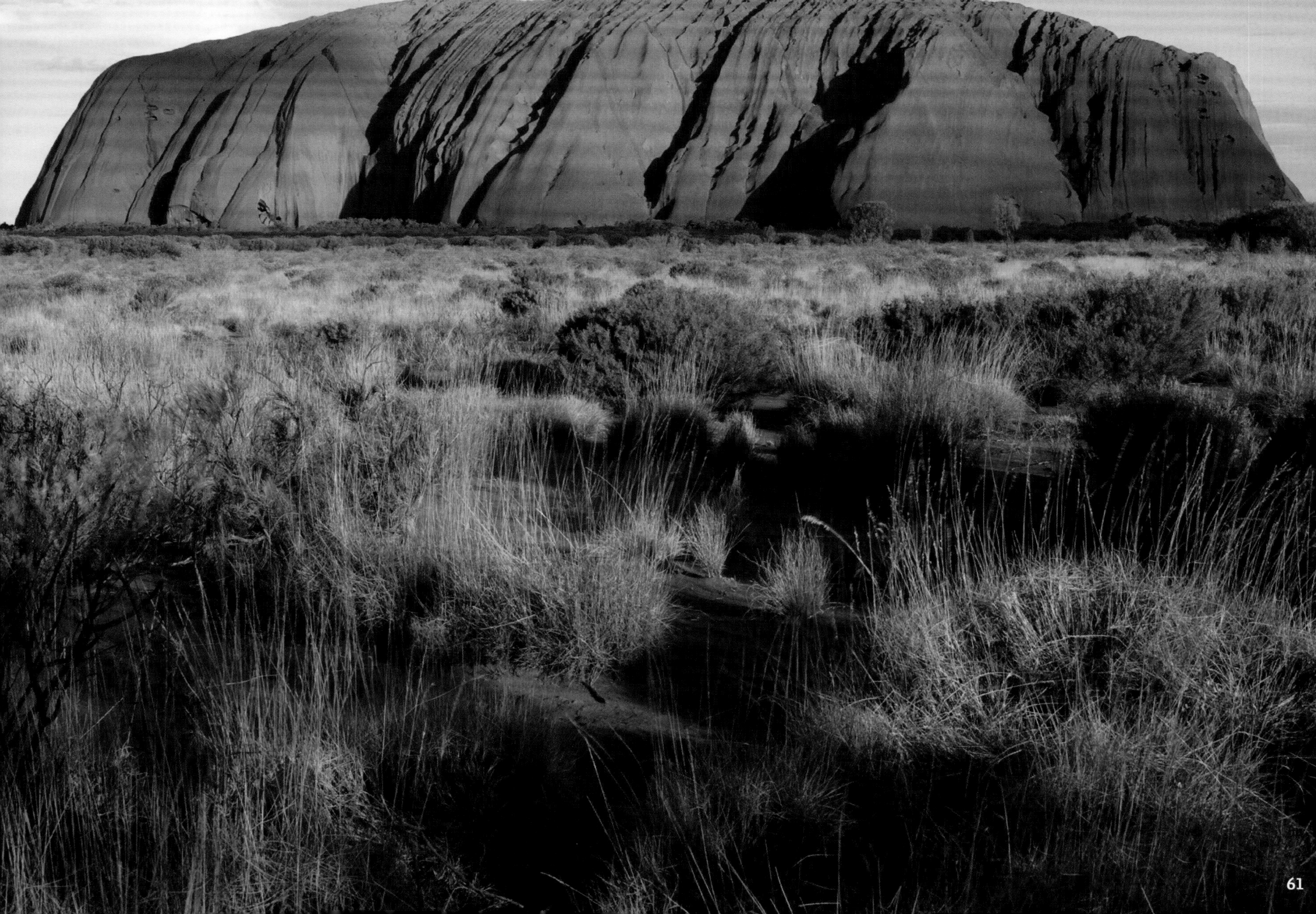

UNESCO World Heritage Sites – Asia

This vast continent contains some of the world's most spectacular sites. The Great Wall of China, the terracotta warriors in the Tomb of the First Qin Emperor, the temple of Angkor and the Taj Mahal are all well known, but smaller yet equally important sites are also on the World Heritage List.

- ● Cultural site
- ● Natural site
- ● Mixed site

Afghanistan
1. Cultural Landscape and Archaeological Remains of the Bamiyan Valley
2. Minaret and Archaeological Remains of Jam

Armenia
3. Cathedral and Churches of Echmiatsin and the Archaeological Site of Zvartnots
4. Monasteries of Haghpat and Sanahin
5. Monastery of Geghard and the Upper Azat Valley

Azerbaijan
6. Gobustan Rock Art Cultural Landscape
7. Walled City of Baku with the Shirvanshah's Palace and Maiden Tower

Bahrain
8. Qal'at al-Bahrain – Ancient Harbour and Capital of Dilmun

Bangladesh
9. Historic Mosque City of Bagerhat
10. Ruins of the Buddhist Vihara at Paharpur
11. The Sundarbans

Cambodia
12. Angkor
13. Temple of Preah Vihear

China
14. Ancient Building Complex in the Wudang Mountains
15. Ancient City of Ping Yao
16. Ancient Villages in Southern Anhui – Xidi and Hongcun
17. Capital Cities and Tombs of the Ancient Koguryo Kingdom
18. Classical Gardens of Suzhou
19. Dazu Rock Carvings
20. Fujian Tulou
21. Historic Centre of Macao
22. Historic Ensemble of the Potala Palace, Lhasa
23. Huanglong Scenic and Historic Interest Area
24. Imperial Palaces of the Ming and Qing Dynasties in Beijing and Shenyang
25. Imperial Tombs of the Ming and Qing Dynasties
26. Jiuzhaigou Valley Scenic and Historic Interest Area
27. Kaiping Diaolou and Villages
28. Longmen Grottoes
29. Lushan National Park
30. Mausoleum of the First Qin Emperor
31. Mogao Caves
32. Mount Emei Scenic Area, including Leshan Giant Buddha Scenic Area
33. Mount Huangshan
34. Mount Qingcheng and the Dujiangyan Irrigation System
35. Mount Sanqingshan National Park

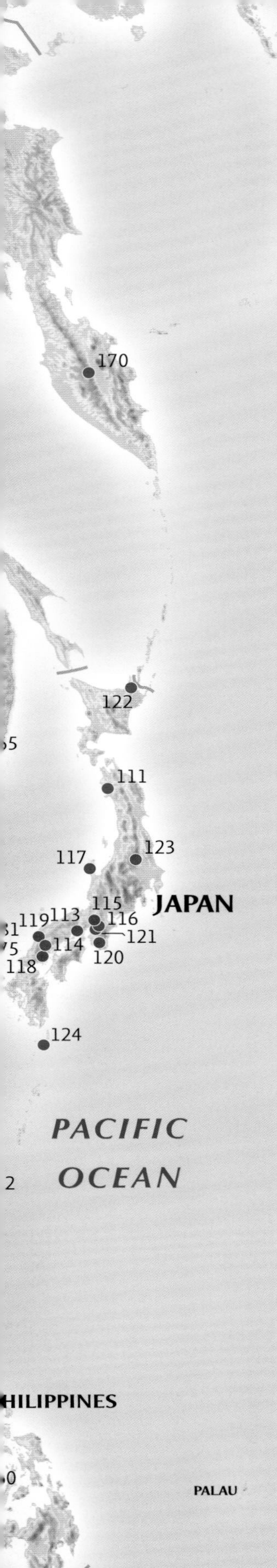

36. Mount Taishan
37. Mount Wutai
38. Mount Wuyi
39. Mountain Resort and its Outlying Temples, Chengde
40. Old Town of Lijiang
41. Peking Man Site at Zhoukoudian
42. Sichuan Giant Panda Sanctuaries – Wolong, Mt Siguniang and Jiajin Mountains
43. South China Karst
44. Summer Palace and Imperial Garden in Beijing
45. Temple and Cemetery of Confucius and the Kong Family Mansion in Qufu
46. Temple of Heaven: an Imperial Sacrificial Altar in Beijing
47. The Great Wall
48. Three Parallel Rivers of Yunnan Protected Areas
49. Wulingyuan Scenic and Historic Interest Area
50. Yin Xu
51. Yungang Grottoes

Cyprus
52. Choirokoitia
53. Painted Churches in the Troodos Region
54. Paphos

Georgia
55. Bagrati Cathedral and Gelati Monastery
56. Historical Monuments of Mtskheta
57. Upper Svaneti

India
58. Agra Fort
59. Ajanta Caves
60. Buddhist Monuments at Sanchi
61. Champaner-Pavagadh Archaeological Park
62. Chhatrapati Shivaji Terminus (formerly Victoria Terminus)
63. Churches and Convents of Goa
64. Elephanta Caves
65. Ellora Caves
66. Fatehpur Sikri
67. Great Living Chola Temples
68. Group of Monuments at Hampi
69. Group of Monuments at Mahabalipuram
70. Group of Monuments at Pattadakal
71. Humayun's Tomb, Delhi
72. Kaziranga National Park
73. Keoladeo National Park
74. Khajuraho Group of Monuments
75. Mahabodhi Temple Complex at Bodh Gaya
76. Manas Wildlife Sanctuary
77. Mountain Railways of India
78. Nanda Devi and Valley of Flowers National Parks
79. Qutb Minar and its Monuments, Delhi
80. Red Fort Complex
81. Rock Shelters of Bhimbetka
82. Sun Temple, Konârak
83. Sundarbans National Park
84. Taj Mahal

Indonesia
85. Borobudur Temple Compounds
86. Komodo National Park
87. Lorentz National Park
88. Prambanan Temple Compounds
89. Sangiran Early Man Site
90. Tropical Rainforest Heritage of Sumatra
91. Ujung Kulon National Park

Iran
92. Armenian Monastic Ensembles of Iran
93. Bam and its Cultural Landscape
94. Bisotun
95. Meidan Emam, Esfahan
96. Pasargadae
97. Persepolis
98. Shushtar Historical Hydraulic System
99. Soltaniyeh
100. Takht-e Soleyman
101. Tchogha Zanbil

Iraq
102. Ashur (Qal'at Sherqat)
103. Hatra
104. Samarra Archaeological City

Israel
105. Bahá'í Holy Places in Haifa and the Western Galilee
106. Biblical Tels – Megiddo, Hazor, Beer Sheba
107. Incense Route – Desert Cities in the Negev
108. Masada
109. Old City of Acre
110. The White City of Tel-Aviv – The Modern Movement

Japan
111. Buddhist Monuments in the Horyu-ji Area
112. Gusuku Sites and Related Properties of the Kingdom of Ryukyu
113. Himeji-jo
114. Hiroshima Peace Memorial (Genbaku Dome)
115. Historic Monuments of Ancient Kyoto (Kyoto, Uji and Otsu Cities)
116. Historic Monuments of Ancient Nara
117. Historic Villages of Shirakawa-go and Gokayama
118. Itsukushima Shinto Shrine
119. Iwami Ginzan Silver Mine and its Cultural Landscape
120. Sacred Sites and Pilgrimage Routes in the Kii Mountain Range
121. Shirakami-Sanchi
122. Shiretoko
123. Shrines and Temples of Nikko
124. Yakushima

Jerusalem (Site proposed by Jordan)
125. Old City of Jerusalem and its Walls

Jordan
126. Petra
127. Quseir Amra
128. Um er-Rasas (Kastrom Mefa'a)

Kazakhstan
129. Mausoleum of Khoja Ahmed Yasawi
130. Petroglyphs within the Archaeological Landscape of Tamgaly
131. Saryarka – Steppe and Lakes of Northern Kazakhstan

Kyrgyzstan
132. Sulaiman-Too Sacred Mountain

Laos
133. Town of Luang Prabang
134. Vat Phou and Associated Ancient Settlements within the Champasak Cultural Landscape

Lebanon
135. Anjar
136. Baalbek
137. Byblos
138. Ouadi Qadisha (the Holy Valley) and the Forest of the Cedars of God (Horsh Arz el-Rab)
139. Tyre

Malaysia
140. Gunung Mulu National Park
141. Kinabalu Park
142. Melaka and George Town, Historic Cities of the Straits of Malacca

Mongolia
143. Orkhon Valley Cultural Landscape
144. Uvs Nuur Basin

Nepal
145. Kathmandu Valley
146. Lumbini, the Birthplace of the Lord Buddha
147. Royal Chitwan National Park
148. Sagarmatha National Park

North Korea
149. Complex of Koguryo Tombs

Oman
150. Aflaj Irrigation Systems of Oman
151. Archaeological sites of Bat, Al-Khutm and Al-Ayn
152. Bahla Fort
153. Land of Frankincense

Pakistan
154. Archaeological Ruins at Moenjodaro
155. Buddhist Ruins of Takht-i-Bahi and Neighbouring City Remains at Sahr-i-Bahlol
156. Fort and Shalamar Gardens in Lahore
157. Historical Monuments at Makli, Thatta
158. Rohtas Fort
159. Taxila

Philippines
160. Baroque Churches of the Philippines
161. Historic Town of Vigan
162. Puerto-Princesa Subterranean River National Park
163. Rice Terraces of the Philippine Cordilleras
164. Tubbataha Reefs Natural Park

Russian Federation (see also page 68)
165. Central Sikhote-Alin
166. Citadel, Ancient City and Fortress Buildings of Derbent
167. Golden Mountains of Altai
168. Lake Baikal
169. Natural System of Wrangel Island Reserve
144. Uvs Nuur Basin
170. Volcanoes of Kamchatka
171. Western Caucasus

Saudi Arabia
172. Al-Hijr Archaeological Site (Madâin Sâlih)

South Korea
173. Changdeokgung Palace Complex
174. Gochang, Hwasun and Ganghwa Dolmen Sites
175. Gyeongju Historic Areas
176. Haeinsa Temple Janggyeong Panjeon, the Depositories for the Tripitaka Koreana Woodblocks
177. Hwaseong Fortress
178. Jeju Volcanic Island and Lava Tubes
179. Jongmyo Shrine
180. Royal Tombs of the Joseon Dynasty
181. Seokguram Grotto and Bulguksa Temple

Sri Lanka
182. Ancient City of Polonnaruwa
183. Ancient City of Sigiriya
184. Golden Temple of Dambulla
185. Old Town of Galle and its Fortifications
186. Sacred City of Anuradhapura
187. Sacred City of Kandy
188. Sinharaja Forest Reserve

Syria
189. Ancient City of Aleppo
190. Ancient City of Bosra
191. Ancient City of Damascus
192. Crac des Chevaliers and Qal'at Salah El-Din
193. Site of Palmyra

Thailand
194. Ban Chiang Archaeological Site
195. Dong Phayayen-Khao Yai Forest Complex
196. Historic City of Ayutthaya
197. Historic Town of Sukhothai and Associated Historic Towns
198. Thungyai-Huai Kha Khaeng Wildlife Sanctuaries

Turkey
199. Archaeological Site of Troy
200. City of Safranbolu
201. Göreme National Park and the Rock Sites of Cappadocia
202. Great Mosque and Hospital of Divriği
203. Hattusha: the Hittite Capital
204. Hierapolis-Pamukkale
205. Historic Areas of Istanbul
206. Nemrut Dağ
207. Xanthos-Letoon

Turkmenistan
208. Kunya-Urgench
209. Parthian Fortresses of Nisa
210. State Historical and Cultural Park 'Ancient Merv'

Uzbekistan
211. Historic Centre of Bukhara
212. Historic Centre of Shakhrisyabz
213. Itchan Kala
214. Samarkand – Crossroads of Cultures

Vietnam
215. Complex of Hué Monuments
216. Ha Long Bay
217. Hoi An Ancient Town
218. My Son Sanctuary
219. Phong Nha-Ke Bang National Park

Yemen
220. Historic Town of Zabid
221. Old City of Sana'a
222. Old Walled City of Shibam
223. Socotra Archipelago

JAPAN

PACIFIC

OCEAN

PHILIPPINES

PALAU

EAST TIMOR

I A

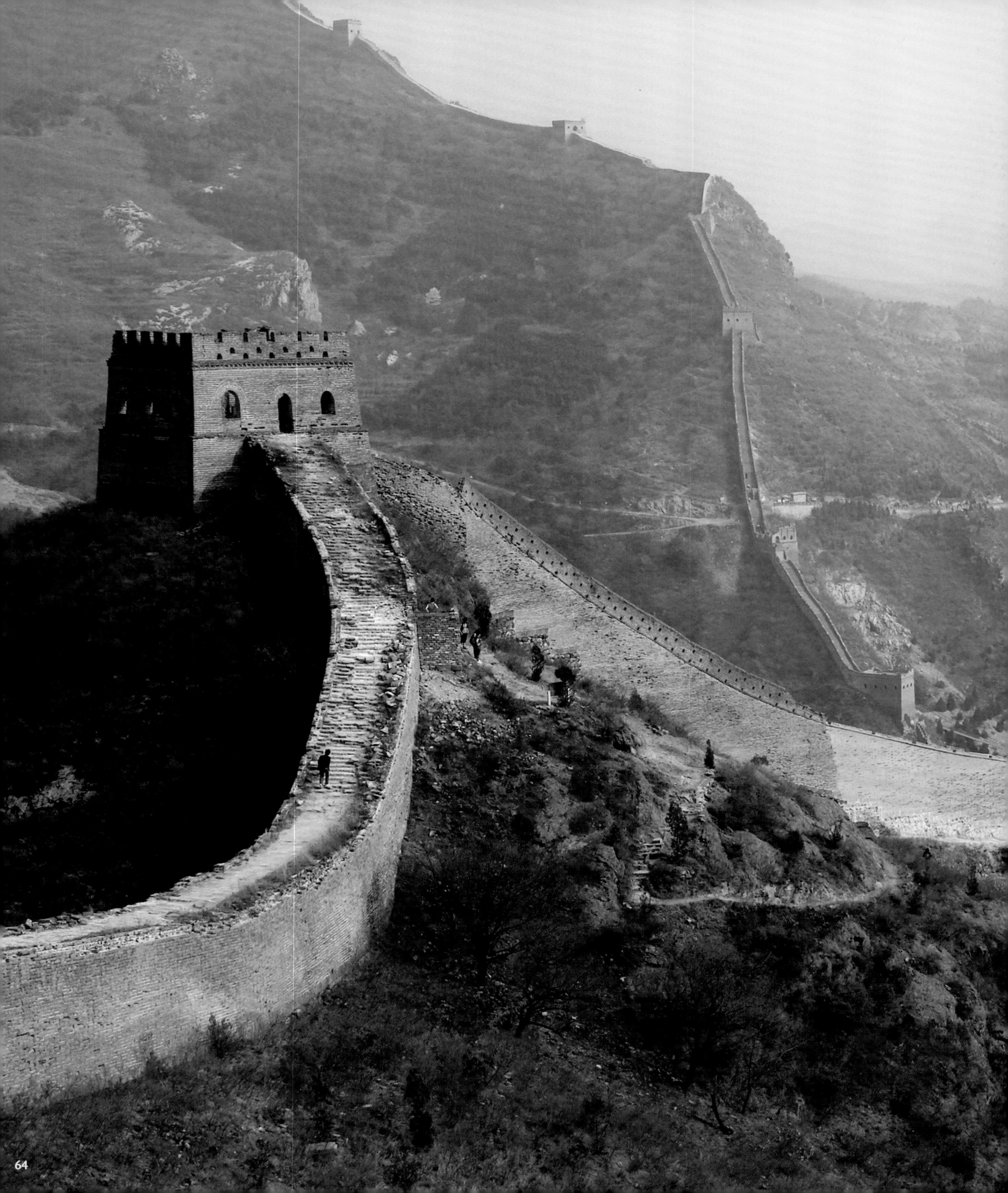

The Great Wall – CHINA

Inscribed 1987 – Human creative genius; Interchange of values; Testimony to cultural tradition; Significance in human history; Heritage associated with events of universal significance.

Known to the Chinese as the 'Long Wall of Ten Thousand Li', the formidable defensive structures built to ward off invasion is more commonly known as the Great Wall of China. At the end of its nineteen-century-long construction, the Great Wall was the world's largest military structure. Its historic and strategic importance is matched only by its architectural significance.

The building of defensive walls was a common strategy against potential invasion and several were built in China from the eighth century BC onwards. From 220 BC Qin Shi Huang, the first emperor of a unified China, undertook to restore and link the separate sections of the Great Wall which stretched from the region of the Ordos to Manchuria. These were to form the first cohesive defence system against invasions from the north, and by the first century BC, ongoing extensions meant the Wall spanned approximately 6 000 km between Dunhuang in the west and the Bohai Sea in the east.

After the downfall of the Han dynasty in AD 220, construction and maintenance works on the Great Wall were halted: China at that time enjoyed such great military power that the need for a defence policy was no longer felt.

It was the Ming emperors (1368–1644) who, after a long period of conflict that ended with the expulsion of the Mongols, revived the principles of Qin Shi Huang's defence policy and during these centuries 5 650 km of wall were built.

To defend the northern frontier, the Wall was divided into nine *zhen*, or military districts, and fortresses were built at strategically important points such as passes or fords. Passageways running along the top of the wall made it possible to move troops rapidly and for imperial couriers to travel.

The Great Wall of the Ming is a masterpiece, not only because of the ambition of the

undertaking but also the perfection of its construction. The wall constitutes, on the vast scale of a continent, a perfect example of architecture integrated into the landscape.

This complex, diachronic cultural property is a unique example of a military architectural ensemble serving a single strategic purpose for 2 000 years. Its construction history illustrates advances in defence techniques and adaptation to changing political contexts. The Wall's testimony to the civilizations of ancient China is illustrated as much by the earlier, tamped-earth sections in Gansu Province as by the famed masonry of the Ming period.

The purpose of the Great Wall was to protect China from military aggression and cultural ingression, and it remains an essential reference in Chinese literature.

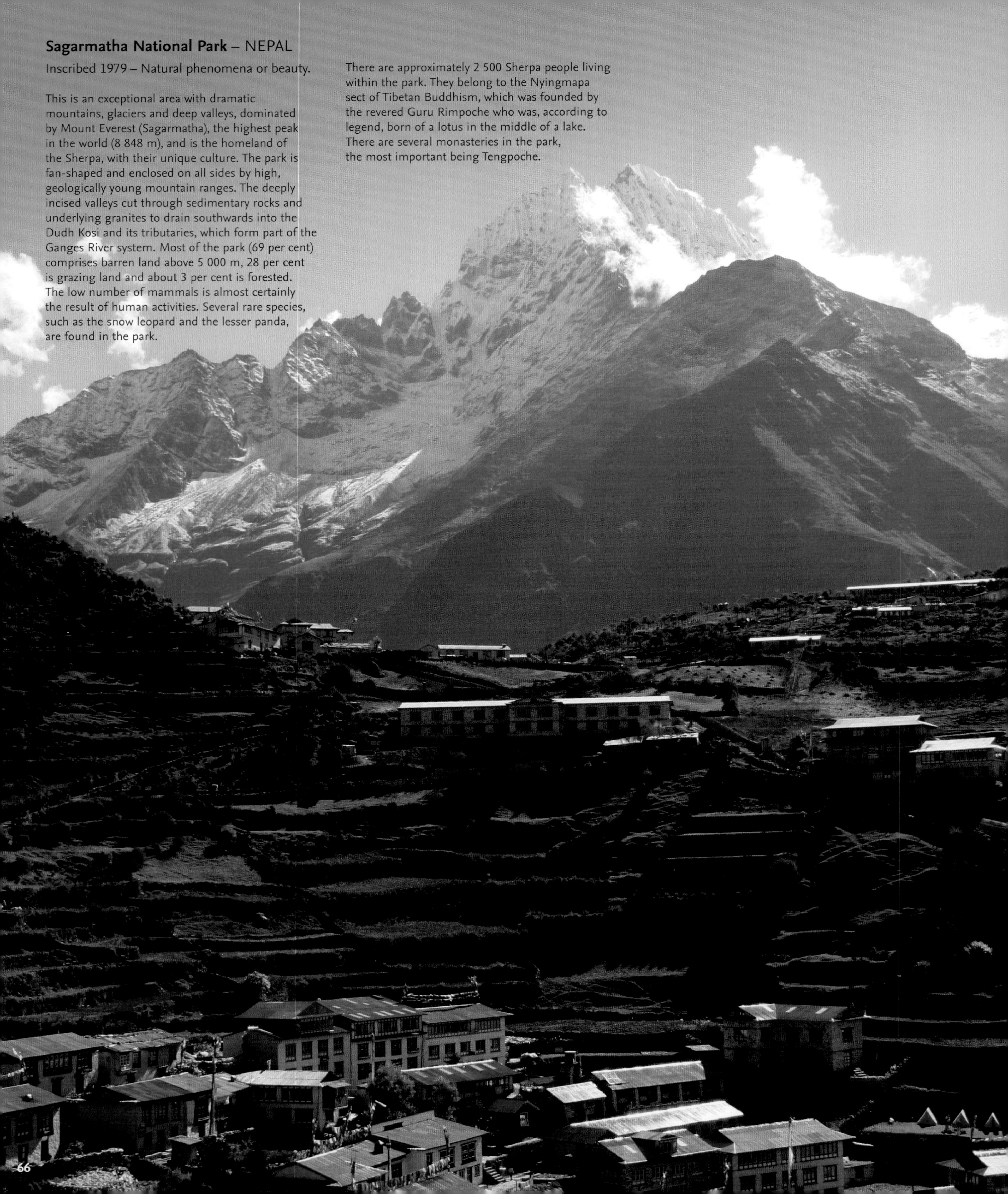

Sagarmatha National Park – NEPAL

Inscribed 1979 – Natural phenomena or beauty.

This is an exceptional area with dramatic mountains, glaciers and deep valleys, dominated by Mount Everest (Sagarmatha), the highest peak in the world (8 848 m), and is the homeland of the Sherpa, with their unique culture. The park is fan-shaped and enclosed on all sides by high, geologically young mountain ranges. The deeply incised valleys cut through sedimentary rocks and underlying granites to drain southwards into the Dudh Kosi and its tributaries, which form part of the Ganges River system. Most of the park (69 per cent) comprises barren land above 5 000 m, 28 per cent is grazing land and about 3 per cent is forested. The low number of mammals is almost certainly the result of human activities. Several rare species, such as the snow leopard and the lesser panda, are found in the park.

There are approximately 2 500 Sherpa people living within the park. They belong to the Nyingmapa sect of Tibetan Buddhism, which was founded by the revered Guru Rimpoche who was, according to legend, born of a lotus in the middle of a lake. There are several monasteries in the park, the most important being Tengpoche.

Angkor – CAMBODIA

Inscribed 1992 – Human creative genius; Interchange of values; Testimony to cultural tradition; Significance in human history.

Angkor is one of the most important archaeological sites in southeast Asia. Stretching over some 400km², Angkor Archaeological Park contains the magnificent remains of the different capitals of the Khmer Empire, from the ninth to the fifteenth century. It includes the famous Temple of Angkor Wat and the Bayon Temple with its countless sculptural decorations at Angkor Thom. In total, there are over a hundred temples throughout the site.

In the early ninth century, Jayavarman II united the two states that covered the territory of modern Cambodia, laying the foundations of the Khmer Empire that was to be the major power in southeast Asia for five centuries. Jayavarman's son Yashovarman established Yashodapura (later called Angkor), permanent capital of the Khmer Empire until the fifteenth century.

The first city had the fundamental elements of a Khmer capital: a defensive bank and ditch; a brick- or stone-built state temple at the centre; and a wooden palace. A large reservoir was another essential feature of a Khmer capital and this, now known as the Eastern Baray, was added a decade later with a third temple built in its centre.

In the 960s, Rajendravarman built a second capital at Angkor; the state temple was situated at Pre Rup. He also built the Eastern Mebon temple on an artificial island in the Eastern Baray, and the exquisite temple of Banteay Srei. Rajendravarman's son Jayavarman V abandoned Pre Rup in favour of a new location with its state temple at Ta Kev, which was consecrated around 1000. Shortly afterwards he was overthrown by Suryavarman I, who was responsible for erecting the formidable fortifications around his Royal Palace and state temple, the Phimeanakas, and also for the construction of the great Western Baray. In 1050 his successor created a new and more impressive state temple, the Baphuon.

The accession of Suryavarman II in 1113 brought the next great phase of building. He was responsible for the greatest Khmer monument, Angkor Wat, set within an extensive enclosure and dedicated to Vishnu.

A period of internal instability after Suryavarman's death was ended in the 1180s by Jayavarman VII who celebrated his military success by creating yet another capital at Angkor Thom and launching an unprecedented building campaign. His state temple was the towering Bayon, dedicated to Buddha.

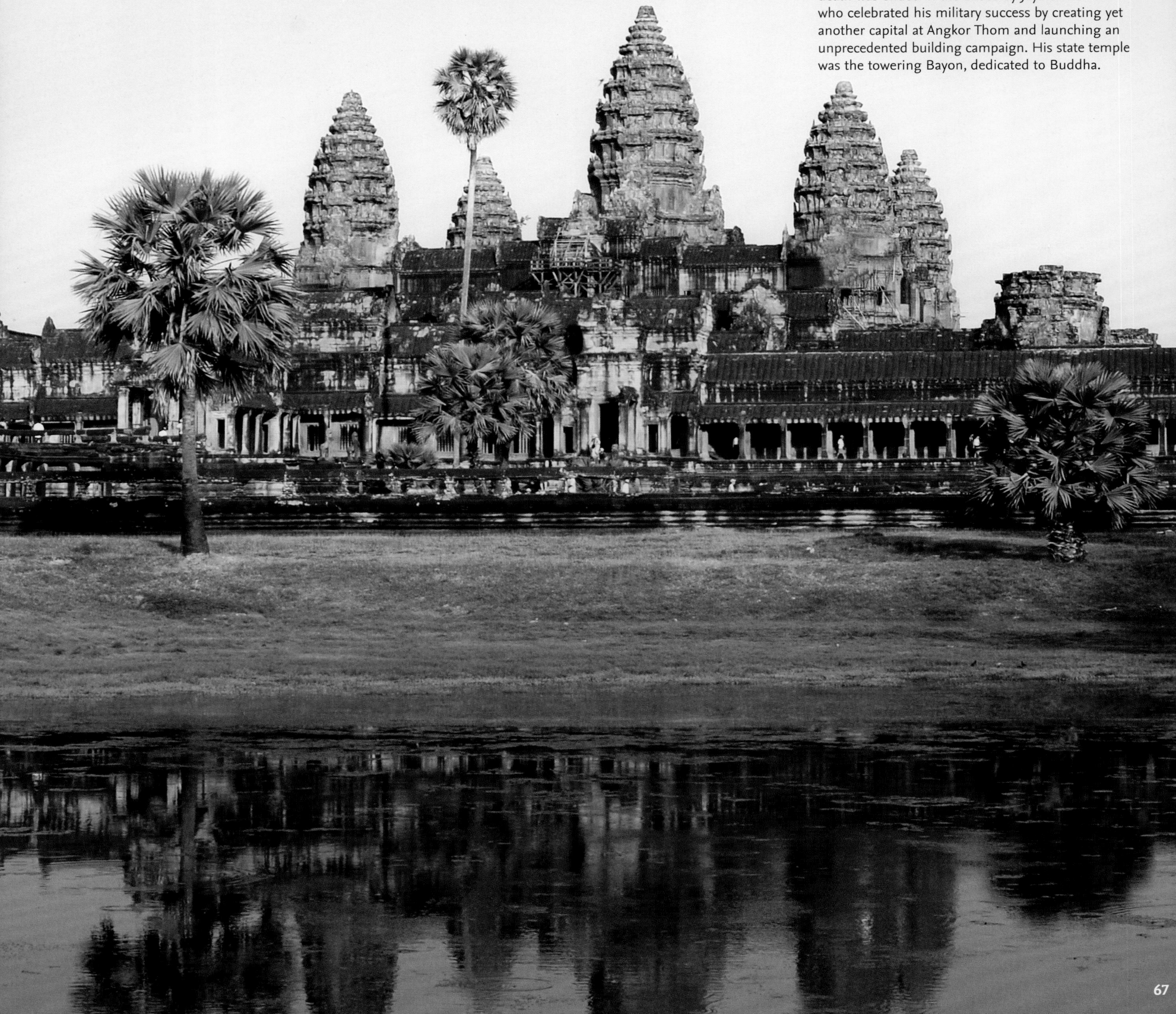

UNESCO World Heritage Sites – Europe

World Heritage sites in Europe are found across the continent, from the far north of Scandinavia to the extreme south of Sicily. They span the whole of Earth's human history – from Neolithic Orkney and Stonehenge, through the Acropolis and Pompeii, to twentieth century Auschwitz and the Works of Gaudi.

● Cultural site   ● Natural site   ● Mixed site

Belarus
1. Architectural, Residential and Cultural Complex of the Radziwill Family at Nesvizh
2. Belovezhskaya Pushcha/Białowieża Forest
3. Mir Castle Complex
4. Struve Geodetic Arc

Denmark
5. Jelling Mounds, Runic Stones and Church
6. Kronborg Castle
7. Roskilde Cathedral
   Ilulissat Icefjord (see map on pages 80-81)

Estonia
8. Historic Centre (Old Town) of Tallinn
4. Struve Geodetic Arc

Finland
9. Bronze Age Burial Site of Sammallahdenmäki
10. Fortress of Suomenlinna
11. High Coast/Kvarken Archipelago
12. Old Rauma
13. Petäjävesi Old Church
4. Struve Geodetic Arc
14. Verla Groundwood and Board Mill

Germany
15. Aachen Cathedral
16. Abbey and Altenmünster of Lorsch
17. Bauhaus and its Sites in Weimar and Dessau
18. Berlin Modernism Housing Estates
19. Castles of Augustusburg and Falkenlust at Brühl
20. Classical Weimar
21. Collegiate Church, Castle and Old Town of Quedlinburg
22. Cologne Cathedral
23. Frontiers of the Roman Empire: Upper German-Raetian Limes
24. Garden Kingdom of Dessau-Wörlitz
25. Hanseatic City of Lübeck
26. Historic Centres of Stralsund and Wismar
27. Luther Memorials in Eisleben and Wittenberg
28. Maulbronn Monastery Complex
29. Messel Pit Fossil Site
30. Mines of Rammelsberg and Historic Town of Goslar
31. Monastic Island of Reichenau
32. Museumsinsel (Museum Island), Berlin
33. Muskauer Park/Park Muzakowski
34. Old town of Regensburg with Stadtamhof
35. Palaces and Parks of Potsdam and Berlin
36. Pilgrimage Church of Wies
37. Roman Monuments, Cathedral of St Peter and Church of Our Lady in Trier
38. Speyer Cathedral
39. St Mary's Cathedral and St Michael's Church at Hildesheim
40. The Wadden Sea
41. Town Hall and Roland on the Marketplace of Bremen
42. Town of Bamberg
43. Upper Middle Rhine Valley
44. Völklingen Ironworks
45. Wartburg Castle
46. Würzburg Residence with the Court Gardens and Residence Square
47. Zollverein Coal Mine Industrial Complex in Essen

Iceland
48. Surtsey
49. Þingvellir National Park

Ireland
50. Archaeological Ensemble of the Bend of the Boyne
51. Skellig Michael

Latvia
52. Historic Centre of Riga
4. Struve Geodetic Arc

Lithuania
53. Curonian Spit
54. Kernavė Archaeological Site (Cultural Reserve of Kernavė)
4. Struve Geodetic Arc
55. Vilnius Historic Centre

Netherlands
56. Defence Line of Amsterdam
57. Droogmakerij de Beemster (Beemster Polder)
58. Ir. D.F. Woudagemaal (D.F. Wouda Steam Pumping Station)
59. Mill Network at Kinderdijk-Elshout
60. Rietveld Schröderhuis (Rietveld Schröder House)
61. Schokland and Surroundings
40. The Wadden Sea
   Historic Area of Willemstad, Inner City and Harbour, Netherlands Antilles (see map on pages 86-87)

Norway
62. Bryggen
63. Rock Art of Alta
64. Røros Mining Town
4. Struve Geodetic Arc
65. Urnes Stave Church
66. Vegaøyan – the Vega Archipelago
67. West Norwegian Fjords – Geirangerfjord and Nærøyfjord

Poland
68. Auschwitz Birkenau German Nazi Concentration and Extermination Camp (1940–1945)
69. Castle of the Teutonic Order in Malbork
70. Centennial Hall in Wroclaw
2. Belovezhskaya Pushcha/Białowieża Forest
71. Churches of Peace in Jawor and Swidnica
72. Cracow's Historic Centre
73. Historic Centre of Warsaw
74. Kalwaria Zebrzydowska: the Mannerist Architectural and Park Landscape Complex and Pilgrimage Park
75. Medieval Town of Toruń
33. Muskauer Park/Park Muzakowski
76. Old City of Zamość
77. Wieliczka Salt Mine
78. Wooden Churches of Southern Little Poland

Portugal
79. Alto Douro Wine Region
80. Central Zone of the Town of Angra do Heroismo in the Azores
81. Convent of Christ in Tomar
82. Cultural Landscape of Sintra
83. Historic Centre of Évora
84. Historic Centre of Guimarães
85. Historic Centre of Oporto
86. Landscape of the Pico Island Vineyard Culture
87. Laurisilva of Madeira
88. Monastery of Alcobaça
89. Monastery of Batalha
90. Monastery of the Hieronymites and Tower of Belém in Lisbon
91. Prehistoric Rock-Art Sites in the Côa Valley

Russian Federation (see also page 62)
92. Architectural Ensemble of the Trinity Sergius Lavra in Sergiev Posad
93. Church of the Ascension, Kolomenskoye
94. Cultural and Historic Ensemble of the Solovetsky Islands
53. Curonian Spit
95. Ensemble of the Ferrapontov Monastery
96. Ensemble of the Novodevichy Convent
97. Historic and Architectural Complex of the Kazan Kremlin
98. Historic Centre of Saint Petersburg and Related Groups of Monuments
99. Historic Monuments of Novgorod and Surroundings
100. Historical Centre of the City of Yaroslavl
101. Kizhi Pogost
102. Kremlin and Red Square, Moscow
4. Struve Geodetic Arc
103. Virgin Komi Forests
104. White Monuments of Vladimir and Suzdal

Spain
105. Alhambra, Generalife and Albayzín, Granada
106. Aranjuez Cultural Landscape
107. Archaeological Ensemble of Mérida
108. Archaeological Ensemble of Tárraco
109. Archaeological Site of Atapuerca
110. Burgos Cathedral
111. Catalan Romanesque Churches of the Vall de Boí
112. Cathedral, Alcázar and Archivo de Indias in Seville
113. Cave of Altamira and Paleolithic Cave Art of Northern Spain
114. Doñana National Park
115. Garajonay National Park
116. Historic Centre of Cordoba
117. Historic City of Toledo
118. Historic Walled Town of Cuenca
119. Ibiza, Biodiversity and Culture
120. La Lonja de la Seda de Valencia
121. Las Médulas
122. Monastery and Site of the Escurial, Madrid
123. Monuments of Oviedo and the Kingdom of the Asturias
124. Mudéjar Architecture of Aragon
125. Old City of Salamanca
126. Old Town of Ávila with its Extra-Muros Churches
127. Old Town of Cáceres
128. Old Town of Segovia and its Aqueduct
129. Palau de la Música Catalana and Hospital de Sant Pau, Barcelona
130. Palmeral of Elche
131. Poblet Monastery
132. Pyrénées - Mont Perdu
133. Renaissance Monumental Ensembles of Úbeda and Baeza
134. Rock Art of the Mediterranean Basin on the Iberian Peninsula
135. Roman Walls of Lugo
136. Route of Santiago de Compostela
137. Royal Monastery of Santa María de Guadalupe
138. San Cristóbal de La Laguna
139. San Millán Yuso and Suso Monasteries
140. Santiago de Compostela (Old Town)
141. Teide National Park
142. University and Historic Precinct of Alcalá de Henares
143. Tower of Hercules
144. Vizcaya Bridge
145. Works of Antoni Gaudí

IC
49
48

IRELAN
51

ATLANTIC

OCEAN

Bay
Bisca

86
80
Azores
(Portugal)

87
Madeira
(Portugal)

143
140   135   123
136   121   113
85   84   79
110   109
PORTUGAL   91   125
88   89   128
90   82   81   126   122
83   127   117   142   118
107   137   106
S P A I N
112   120
116   133
114   105

138   **Canary Islands**
115   (Spain)
141

A F

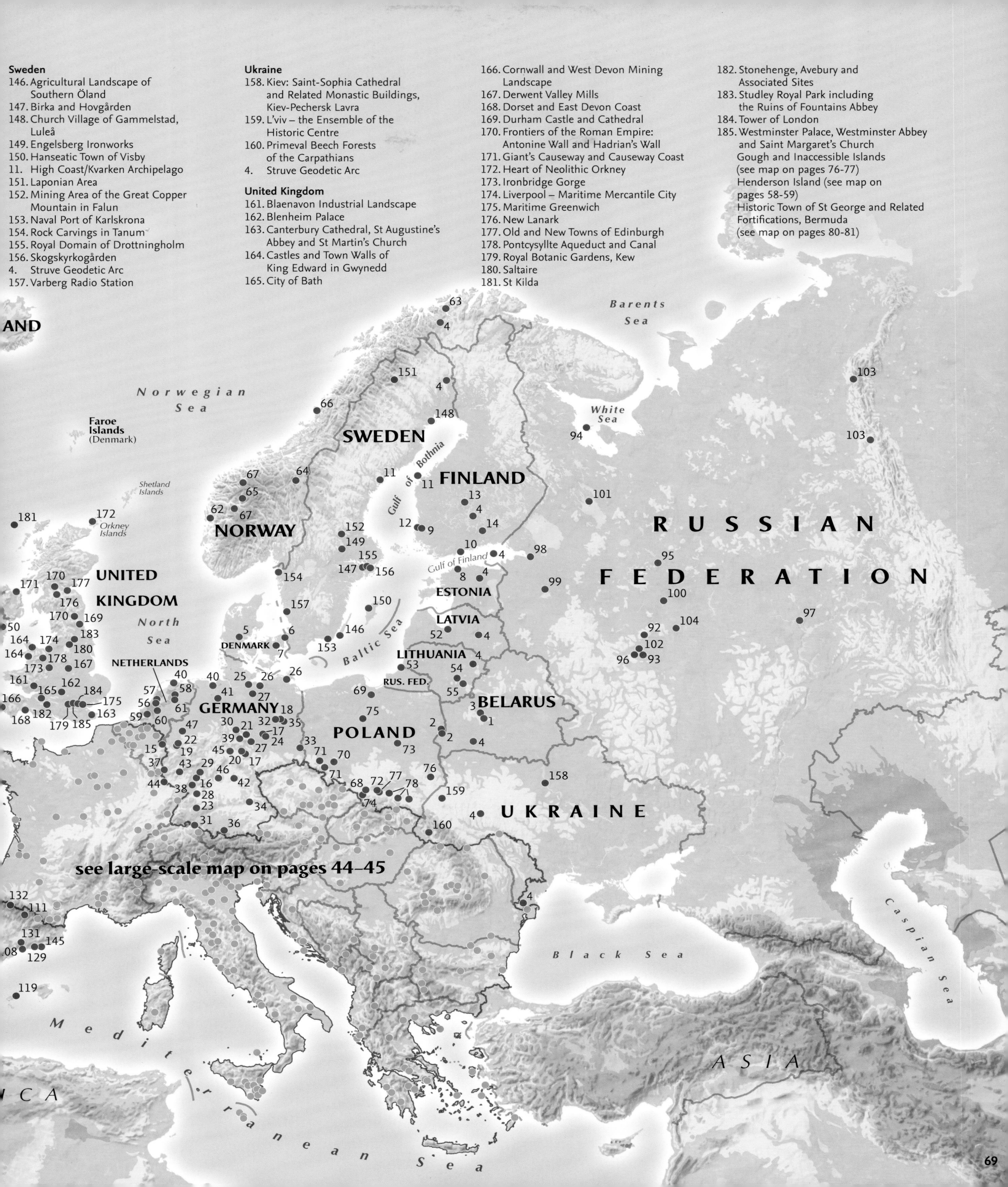

see large-scale map on pages 44–45

69

Sweden
146. Agricultural Landscape of Southern Öland
147. Birka and Hovgården
148. Church Village of Gammelstad, Luleå
149. Engelsberg Ironworks
150. Hanseatic Town of Visby
11. High Coast/Kvarken Archipelago
151. Laponian Area
152. Mining Area of the Great Copper Mountain in Falun
153. Naval Port of Karlskrona
154. Rock Carvings in Tanum
155. Royal Domain of Drottningholm
156. Skogskyrkogården
4. Struve Geodetic Arc
157. Varberg Radio Station
Ukraine
158. Kiev: Saint-Sophia Cathedral and Related Monastic Buildings, Kiev-Pechersk Lavra
159. L'viv – the Ensemble of the Historic Centre
160. Primeval Beech Forests of the Carpathians
4. Struve Geodetic Arc
United Kingdom
161. Blaenavon Industrial Landscape
162. Blenheim Palace
163. Canterbury Cathedral, St Augustine's Abbey and St Martin's Church
164. Castles and Town Walls of King Edward in Gwynedd
165. City of Bath
166. Cornwall and West Devon Mining Landscape
167. Derwent Valley Mills
168. Dorset and East Devon Coast
169. Durham Castle and Cathedral
170. Frontiers of the Roman Empire: Antonine Wall and Hadrian's Wall
171. Giant's Causeway and Causeway Coast
172. Heart of Neolithic Orkney
173. Ironbridge Gorge
174. Liverpool – Maritime Mercantile City
175. Maritime Greenwich
176. New Lanark
177. Old and New Towns of Edinburgh
178. Pontcysyllte Aqueduct and Canal
179. Royal Botanic Gardens, Kew
180. Saltaire
181. St Kilda
182. Stonehenge, Avebury and Associated Sites
183. Studley Royal Park including the Ruins of Fountains Abbey
184. Tower of London
185. Westminster Palace, Westminster Abbey and Saint Margaret's Church
Gough and Inaccessible Islands (see map on pages 76-77)
Henderson Island (see map on pages 58-59)
Historic Town of St George and Related Fortifications, Bermuda (see map on pages 80-81)

UNESCO World Heritage Sites – Europe

● Cultural site   ● Natural site   ● Mixed site

Albania
1. Butrint
2. Historic Centres of Berat and Gjirokastra

Andorra
3. Madriu-Perafita-Claror Valley

Austria
4. City of Graz – Historic Centre
5. Fertö/Neusiedlersee Cultural Landscape
6. Hallstatt-Dachstein/Salzkammergut Cultural Landscape
7. Historic Centre of the City of Salzburg
8. Historic Centre of Vienna
9. Palace and Gardens of Schönbrunn
10. Semmering Railway
11. Wachau Cultural Landscape

Belgium
12. Belfries of Belgium and France
13. Flemish Béguinages
14. Historic Centre of Brugge
15. La Grand-Place, Brussels
16. Major Town Houses of the Architect Victor Horta (Brussels)
17. Neolithic Flint Mines at Spiennes (Mons)
18. Notre-Dame Cathedral in Tournai
19. Plantin-Moretus House-Workshops-Museum Complex
20. Stoclet House
21. The Four Lifts on the Canal du Centre and their Environs, La Louvière and Le Roeulx (Hainault)

Bosnia-Herzegovina
22. Mehmed Paša Sokolović Bridge in Višegrad
23. Old Bridge Area of the Old City of Mostar

Bulgaria
24. Ancient City of Nessebar
25. Boyana Church
26. Madara Rider
27. Pirin National Park
28. Rila Monastery
29. Rock-Hewn Churches of Ivanovo
30. Srebarna Nature Reserve
31. Thracian Tomb of Kazanlak
32. Thracian Tomb of Sveshtari

Croatia
33. Cathedral of St James in Šibenik
34. Episcopal Complex of the Euphrasian Basilica in the Historic Centre of Poreč
35. Historic City of Trogir
36. Historical Complex of Split with the Palace of Diocletian
37. Old City of Dubrovnik
38. Plitvice Lakes National Park
39. Stari Grad Plain

Czech Republic
40. Gardens and Castle at Kroměříž
41. Historic Centre of Český Krumlov
42. Historic Centre of Prague
43. Historic Centre of Telč
44. Holašovice Historical Village Reservation
45. Holy Trinity Column in Olomouc
46. Jewish Quarter and St Procopius' Basilica in Třebíč
47. Kutná Hora: Historical Town Centre with the Church of St Barbara and the Cathedral of Our Lady at Sedlec
48. Lednice-Valtice Cultural Landscape
49. Litomyšl Castle
50. Pilgrimage Church of St John of Nepomuk at Zelená Hora
51. Tugendhat Villa in Brno

France
52. Abbey Church of Saint-Savin sur Gartempe
53. Amiens Cathedral
54. Arles, Roman and Romanesque Monuments
12. Belfries of Belgium and France
55. Bordeaux, Port of the Moon
56. Bourges Cathedral
57. Canal du Midi
58. Cathedral of Notre-Dame, Former Abbey of Saint-Rémi and Palace of Tau, Reims
59. Chartres Cathedral
60. Cistercian Abbey of Fontenay
61. Fortifications of Vauban
62. From the Great Saltworks of Salins-les-Bains to the Royal Saltworks of Arc-et-Senans, the production of open-pan salt
63. Gulf of Porto: Calanche of Piana, Gulf of Girolata, Scandola Reserve
64. Historic Centre of Avignon: Papal Palace, Episcopal Ensemble and Avignon Bridge
65. Historic Fortified City of Carcassonne
66. Historic Site of Lyons
67. Jurisdiction of Saint-Emilion
68. Le Havre, the city rebuilt by Auguste Perret
69. Mont-Saint-Michel and its Bay
70. Palace and Park of Fontainebleau
71. Palace and Park of Versailles
72. Paris, Banks of the Seine
73. Place Stanislas, Place de la Carrière and Place d'Alliance in Nancy
74. Pont du Gard (Roman Aqueduct)
75. Prehistoric Sites and Decorated Caves of the Vézère Valley
76. Provins, Town of Medieval Fairs
77. Pyrénées – Mont Perdu
78. Roman Theatre and its Surroundings and the 'Triumphal Arch' of Orange
79. Routes of Santiago de Compostela in France
80. Strasbourg – Grande Île
81. The Loire Valley between Sully-sur-Loire and Chalonnes
82. Vézelay, Church and Hill
Lagoons of New Caledonia: Reef Diversity and Associated Ecosystems (see map on 58-59)

Greece
83. Acropolis, Athens
84. Archaeological Site of Aigai (modern name Vergina)
85. Archaeological Site of Delphi
86. Archaeological Site of Mystras
87. Archaeological Site of Olympia
88. Archaeological Sites of Mycenae and Tiryns
89. Delos
90. Historic Centre (Chorá) with the Monastery of Saint John, the Theologian, and the Cave of the Apocalypse on the Island of Pátmos
91. Medieval City of Rhodes
92. Meteora
93. Monasteries of Daphni, Hosios Loukas and Nea Moni of Chios
94. Mount Athos
95. Old Town of Corfu
96. Paleochristian and Byzantine Monuments of Thessalonika
97. Pythagoreion and Heraion of Samos
98. Sanctuary of Asklepios at Epidaurus
99. Temple of Apollo Epicurius at Bassae

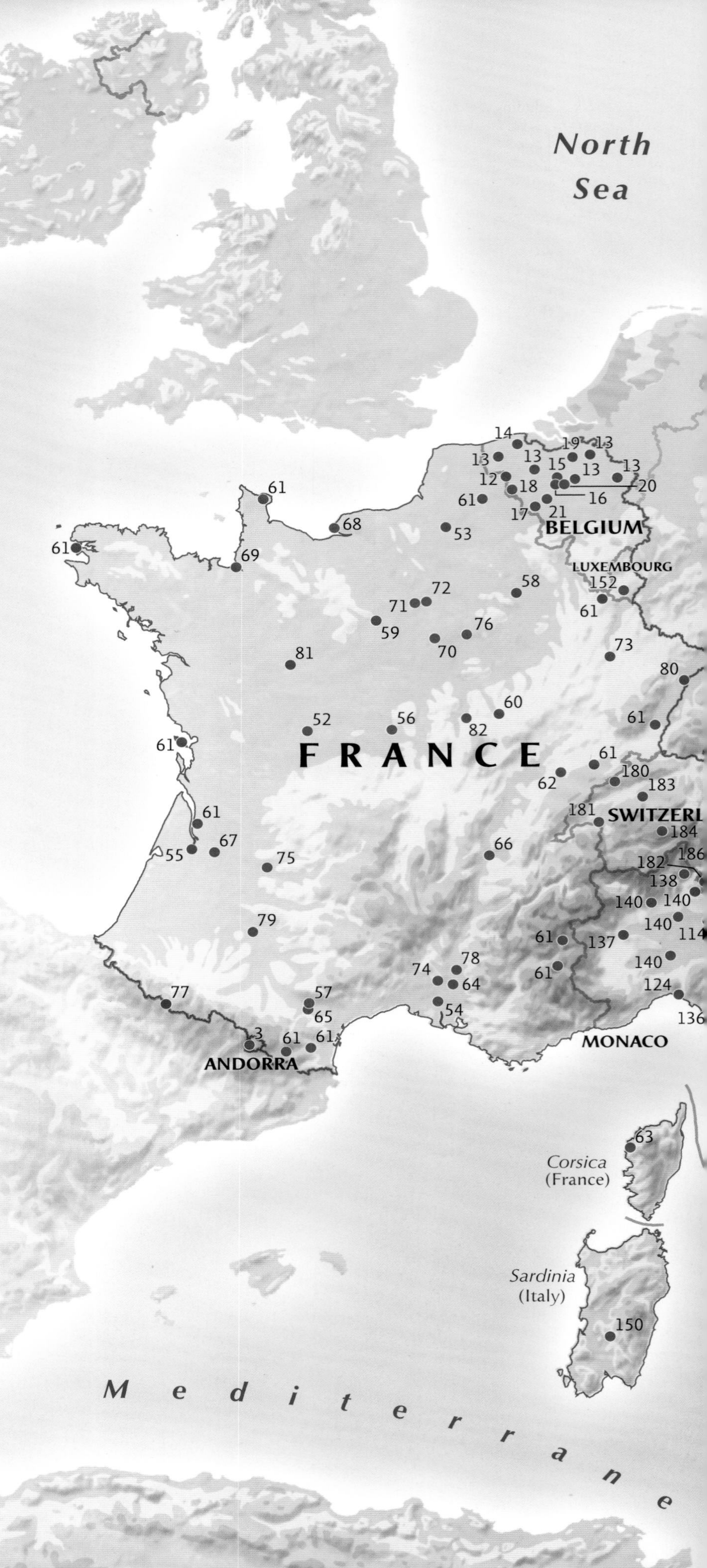

Hungary
100. Budapest, including the Banks of the Danube, the Buda Castle Quarter and Andrássy Avenue
101. Caves of Aggtelek Karst and Slovak Karst
102. Early Christian Necropolis of Pécs (Sopianae)
5. Fertö/Neusiedlersee Cultural Landscape
103. Hortobágy National Park – the Puszta
104. Millenary Benedictine Abbey of Pannonhalma and its Natural Environment
105. Old Village of Hollókő and its Surroundings
106. Tokaj Wine Region Historic Cultural Landscape

Italy
107. Archaeological Area and the Patriarchal Basilica of Aquileia
108. Archaeological Area of Agrigento
109. Archaeological Areas of Pompei, Herculaneum and Torre Annunziata
110. Assisi, the Basilica of San Francesco and Other Franciscan Sites
111. Botanical Garden (Orto Botanico), Padua
112. Castel del Monte
113. Cathedral, Torre Civica and Piazza Grande, Modena
114. Church and Dominican Convent of Santa Maria delle Grazie with 'The Last Supper' by Leonardo da Vinci
115. Cilento and Vallo di Diano National Park with the Archeological sites of Paestum and Velia, and the Certosa di Padula
116. City of Verona
117. City of Vicenza and the Palladian Villas of the Veneto
118. Costiera Amalfitana
119. Crespi d'Adda
120. Early Christian Monuments of Ravenna
121. Eighteenth-Century Royal Palace at Caserta with the Park, the Aqueduct of Vanvitelli, and the San Leucio Complex
122. Etruscan Necropolises of Cerveteri and Tarquinia
123. Ferrara, City of the Renaissance, and its Po Delta
124. Genoa: Le Strade Nuove and the system of the Palazzi dei Rolli
125. Historic Centre of Florence
126. Historic Centre of Naples
127. Historic Centre of Rome, the Properties of the Holy See in that City Enjoying Extraterritorial Rights and San Paolo Fuori le Mura
128. Historic Centre of San Gimignano
129. Historic Centre of Siena
130. Historic Centre of the City of Pienza
131. Historic Centre of Urbino
132. Isole Eolie (Aeolian Islands)
133. Late Baroque Towns of the Val di Noto (South-Eastern Sicily)
134. Mantua and Sabbioneta
135. Piazza del Duomo, Pisa
136. Portovenere, Cinque Terre, and the Islands (Palmaria, Tino and Tinetto)
137. Residences of the Royal House of Savoy
138. Rhaetian Railway in the Albula/Bernina Landscapes
139. Rock Drawings in Valcamonica
140. Sacri Monti of Piedmont and Lombardy
141. Su Nuraxi di Barumini
142. Syracuse and the Rocky Necropolis of Pantalica
143. The Dolomites
144. The Sassi and the park of the Rupestrian Churches of Matera
145. The Trulli of Alberobello
146. Val d'Orcia
147. Venice and its Lagoon
148. Villa Adriana (Tivoli)
149. Villa d'Este, Tivoli
150. Villa Romana del Casale

Kosovo
151. Medieval Monuments in Kosovo

Luxembourg
152. City of Luxembourg: its Old Quarters and Fortifications

Macedonia (F.Y.R.O.M.)
153. Natural and Cultural Heritage of the Ohrid Region

Malta
154. City of Valletta
155. Hal Saflieni Hypogeum
156. Megalithic Temples of Malta

Moldova
157. Struve Geodetic Arc

Montenegro
158. Durmitor National Park
159. Natural and Culturo-Historical Region of Kotor

Romania
160. Churches of Moldavia
161. Dacian Fortresses of the Orastie Mountains
162. Danube Delta
163. Historic Centre of Sighişoara
164. Monastery of Horezu
165. Villages with Fortified Churches in Transylvania
166. Wooden Churches of Maramureş

San Marino
167. San Marino Historic Centre and Mount Titano

Serbia
168. Gamzigrad-Romuliana, Palace of Galerius
169. Stari Ras and Sopoćani
170. Studenica Monastery

Slovakia
171. Bardejov Town Conservation Reserve
101. Caves of Aggtelek Karst and Slovak Karst
172. Historic Town of Banská Štiavnica and the Technical Monuments in its Vicinity
173. Levoča, Spišský Hrad and the Associated Cultural Monuments
174. Primeval Beech Forests of the Carpathians
175. Vlkolínec
176. Wooden Churches of the Slovak part of the Carpathian Mountain Area

Slovenia
177. Škocjan Caves

Switzerland
178. Benedictine Convent of St John at Müstair
179. Convent of St Gall
180. La Chaux-de-Fonds/Le Locle, watchmaking town planning
181. Lavaux, Vineyard Terraces
182. Monte San Giorgio
183. Old City of Berne
138. Rhaetian Railway in the Albula/Bernina Landscapes
184. Swiss Alps Jungfrau-Aletsch
185. Swiss Tectonic Arena Sardona
186. Three Castles, Defensive Wall and Ramparts of the Market-Town of Bellinzone

Vatican City
127. Historic Centre of Rome, the Properties of the Holy See in that City Enjoying Extraterritorial Rights and San Paolo Fuori le Mura
187. Vatican City

Stonehenge, Avebury and Associated Sites –
UNITED KINGDOM

Inscribed 1986 – Human creative genius; Interchange of values; Testimony to cultural tradition.

Stonehenge and Avebury are among the most famous groups of megaliths in the world. Together with their associated sites, they represent a masterpiece of human creative genius of the Neolithic age.

The megalithic sites of Stonehenge and Avebury consist of circles of menhirs arranged in a pattern of obvious astronomical significance which is still being explored. However, a number of satellite sites make it possible to better understand the more famous sites by examining them in a broader context.

Stonehenge was built in several distinct phases from 3100–1100 BC and its size, height and perfection make it one of the most impressive megalithic monuments in the world. Its plan was based on a series of concentric circles and the menhirs used are huge: from the third phase of construction onwards, large lintels were placed upon the vertical blocks, thereby creating a type of bonded entablature. The Avenue, an earthwork cut into the chalk soil, runs straight into the northeast corner of Stonehenge.

Avebury lies about 30 km to the north of Stonehenge, and although less well known, it is nevertheless Europe's largest circular megalithic ensemble: its exterior circle comprises some 100 menhirs. In all, 180 standing stones were put into place here before the beginning of the third millennium BC, as demonstrated by abundant ceramic samples found on the site.

There are four avenues at Avebury of which only the southern one, West Kennet Avenue, is still lined with megaliths; the avenues lead to the four cardinal points of the circle.

West Kennet Avenue leads to the site of The Sanctuary at Overton Hill 2.5 km away. The Sanctuary was a series of concentric timber and stone circles; their purpose remains unknown. There are several other Neolithic satellite sites around Avebury, including Silbury Hill, the largest known man-made earthen mound in Europe. As with The Sanctuary, its purpose is not known.

Windmill Hill, a Neolithic causewayed enclosure, is 2 km northwest of Avebury and West Kennet chambered long barrow lies to the south.

Although the ritual function of Stonehenge is not known in detail, the cosmic references of its structure appear essential. An old theory is that the site was a sanctuary for worship of the sun. Although there is no unanimous agreement among prehistorians on the subject, Stonehenge nevertheless attracts a folkloric gathering at dawn each Midsummer Day.

Two different materials were used for the Stonehenge constructions: irregular sandstone blocks, known as sarsens, which were quarried in a plain near Salisbury; and bluestones, quarried about 200 km away in Pembrokeshire in Wales.

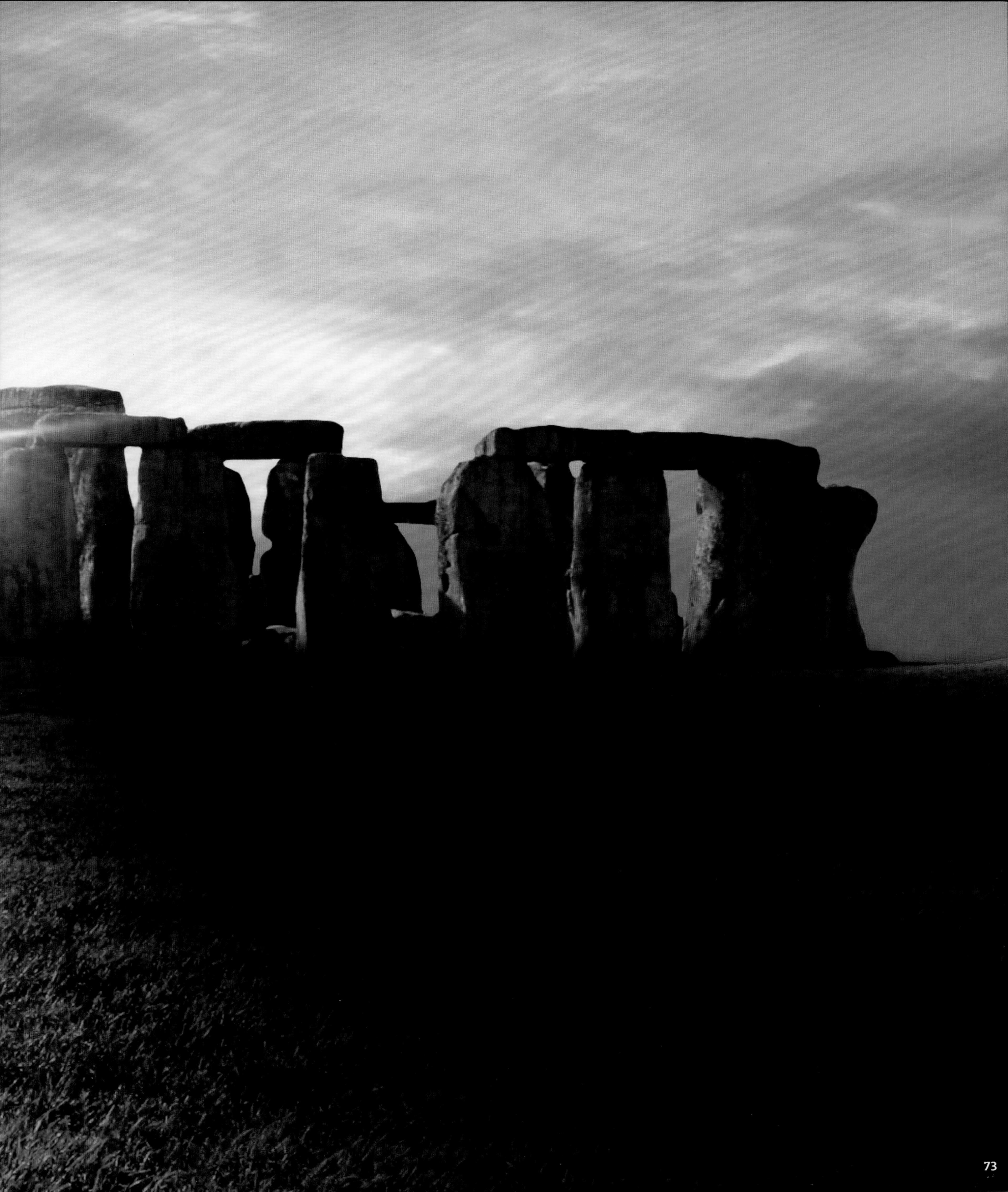

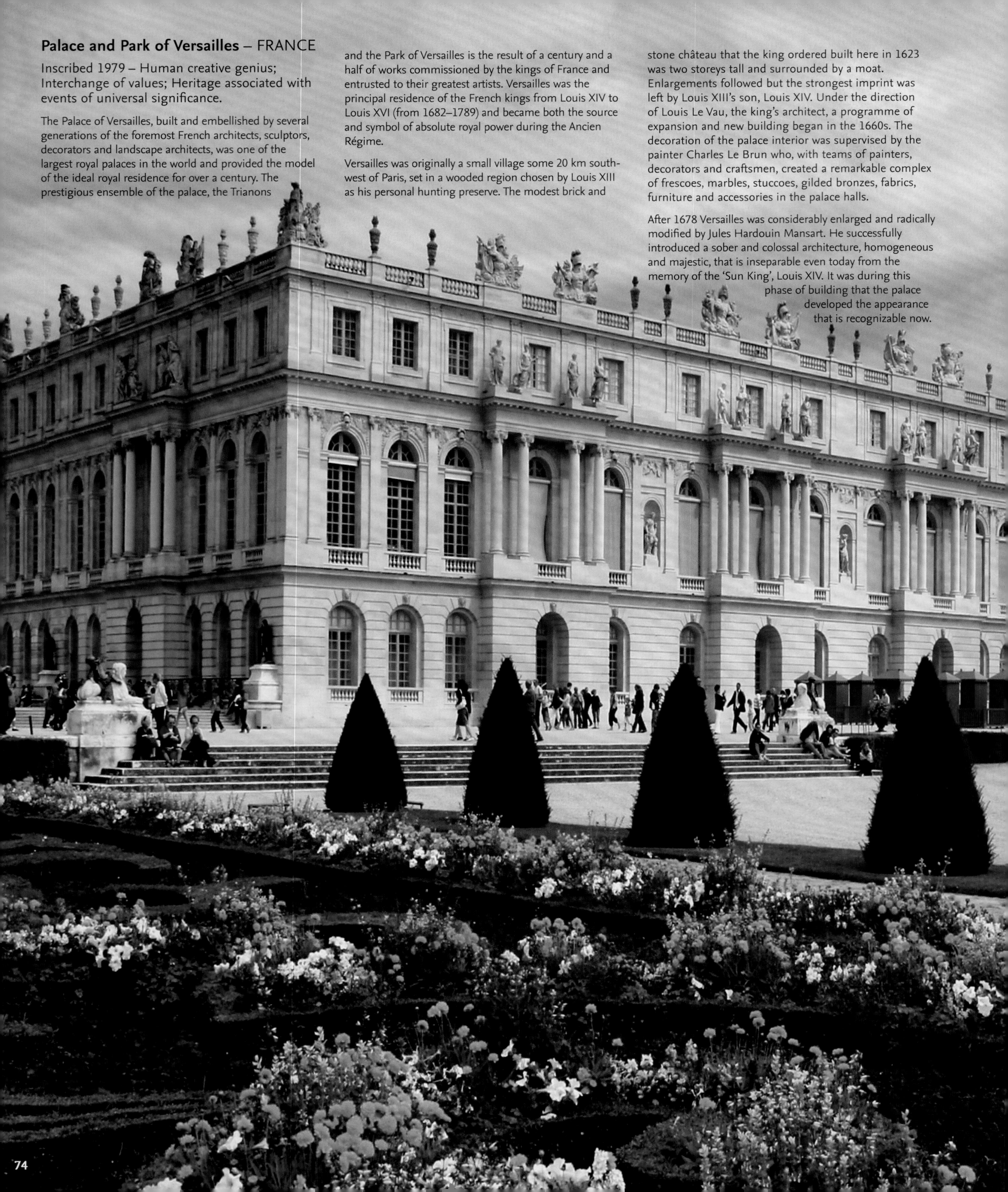

Palace and Park of Versailles – FRANCE

Inscribed 1979 – Human creative genius; Interchange of values; Heritage associated with events of universal significance.

The Palace of Versailles, built and embellished by several generations of the foremost French architects, sculptors, decorators and landscape architects, was one of the largest royal palaces in the world and provided the model of the ideal royal residence for over a century. The prestigious ensemble of the palace, the Trianons and the Park of Versailles is the result of a century and a half of works commissioned by the kings of France and entrusted to their greatest artists. Versailles was the principal residence of the French kings from Louis XIV to Louis XVI (from 1682–1789) and became both the source and symbol of absolute royal power during the Ancien Régime.

Versailles was originally a small village some 20 km south-west of Paris, set in a wooded region chosen by Louis XIII as his personal hunting preserve. The modest brick and stone château that the king ordered built here in 1623 was two storeys tall and surrounded by a moat. Enlargements followed but the strongest imprint was left by Louis XIII's son, Louis XIV. Under the direction of Louis Le Vau, the king's architect, a programme of expansion and new building began in the 1660s. The decoration of the palace interior was supervised by the painter Charles Le Brun who, with teams of painters, decorators and craftsmen, created a remarkable complex of frescoes, marbles, stuccoes, gilded bronzes, fabrics, furniture and accessories in the palace halls.

After 1678 Versailles was considerably enlarged and radically modified by Jules Hardouin Mansart. He successfully introduced a sober and colossal architecture, homogeneous and majestic, that is inseparable even today from the memory of the 'Sun King', Louis XIV. It was during this phase of building that the palace developed the appearance that is recognizable now.

Acropolis, Athens – GREECE

Inscribed 1987 – Human creative genius; Interchange of values; Testimony to cultural tradition; Significance in human history; Heritage associated with events of universal significance.

The Athenian Acropolis is the supreme expression of the adaptation of architecture to a natural site, a unique series of public monuments built and conserved in one of the densest spaces of the Mediterranean. This grand composition of perfectly balanced massive structures creates a monumental landscape of unique beauty consisting of a complete series of masterpieces of the fifth century BC. The monuments of the Acropolis have exerted an exceptional influence, not only in Graeco-Roman antiquity, a time in the Mediterranean world when they were considered exemplary models, but also in contemporary times.

In the later fifth century BC, Athens followed its victory against the Persians and the establishment of democracy by taking a leading position among the other city-states of the ancient world. In the age that followed, as philosophy and art flourished, an exceptional group of artists put into effect the ambitious plans of Athenian statesman Pericles and, under the inspired guidance of the sculptor Pheidias, transformed the rocky hill of the Acropolis into a unique monument of thought and the arts.

The years from 447–406 BC saw the successive building of the Parthenon, the main temple dedicated to Athena; the Propylaea, the monumental entrance to the Acropolis built on the site of one of the entrances to the Citadel of the Ancient Kings; the temple of Athena Nike; and the Erechtheion – the four masterpieces of classical Greek art.

The sacred hill of Athens was protected throughout the period of Roman domination until the Herulian raid in AD 267. Since then and despite long periods of relative calm, the monuments and site have been damaged many times.

The Byzantines converted the temples into churches and removed their art treasures to Constantinople. After the Byzantine Empire fell in 1204, Athens was put into the hands of Frankish lords who had little respect for its ruins. When the Turks took the city in 1456, it became a mosque and the Erechtheion was the occasional harem of the Turkish governor. In 1687 the siege of the Acropolis by Venetian armies resulted in the explosion of the Parthenon, used as the Turks' powder magazine. Finally in the nineteenth century, the British ambassador Lord Elgin pillaged the marble sections which since 1815 have been in the British Museum.

The Acropolis of Athens and its monuments are universal symbols of the classical spirit and civilization, and form the greatest architectural and artistic complex of Greek antiquity.

It stands on a rocky promontory 156 m above the Ilissos valley and covers an area of less than 30 000 m^2. From the third millennium BC it was a fortress protecting places of worship and royal palaces.

The Acropolis is now a testing ground for innovative open-air conservation techniques aimed at safeguarding the marble sections which are being affected by pollution.

UNESCO World Heritage Sites – Africa

Famous archaeological sites such as the Pyramids of Giza and Abu Simbel, Egypt and the wildlife reserves of the Serengeti and Selous in Tanzania have been on the World Heritage List for a number of years. However more recently Robben Island, where Nelson Mandela was imprisoned, and the rainforests of Madagascar, their biodiversity under threat from development, have been included as representative of Africa's culture and environment.

● Cultural site   ● Natural site   ● Mixed site

Algeria
1. Al Qal'a of Beni Hammad
2. Djémila
3. Kasbah of Algiers
4. M'Zab Valley
5. Tassili n'Ajjer
6. Timgad
7. Tipasa

Benin
8. Royal Palaces of Abomey

Botswana
9. Tsodilo

Burkina
10. The Ruins of Loropéni

Cameroon
11. Dja Faunal Reserve

Cape Verde
12. Cidade Velha, Historic Centre of Ribeira Grande

Central African Republic
13. Manovo-Gounda St Floris National Park

Congo, Democratic Republic of the
14. Garamba National Park
15. Kahuzi-Biega National Park
16. Okapi Wildlife Reserve
17. Salonga National Park
18. Virunga National Park

Côte d'Ivoire
19. Comoé National Park
20. Mount Nimba Strict Nature Reserve
21. Taï National Park

Egypt
22. Abu Mena
23. Ancient Thebes with its Necropolis
24. Historic Cairo
25. Memphis and its Necropolis – the Pyramid Fields from Giza to Dahshur
26. Nubian Monuments from Abu Simbel to Philae
27. Saint Catherine Area
28. Wadi Al-Hitan (Whale Valley)

Ethiopia
29. Aksum
30. Fasil Ghebbi, Gondar Region
31. Harar Jugol, the Fortified Historic Town
32. Lower Valley of the Awash
33. Lower Valley of the Omo
34. Rock-Hewn Churches, Lalibela
35. Simien National Park
36. Tiya

Gabon
37. Ecosystem and Relict Cultural Landscape of Lopé-Okanda

Gambia, The
38. James Island and Related Sites
39. Stone Circles of Senegambia

Ghana
40. Asante Traditional Buildings
41. Forts and Castles, Volta, Greater Accra, Central and Western Regions

Gough Island
42. Gough and Inaccessible Islands (U.K.)

Guinea
20. Mount Nimba Strict Nature Reserve

Kenya
43. Lake Turkana National Parks
44. Lamu Old Town
45. Mount Kenya National Park/ Natural Forest
46. Sacred Mijikenda Kaya Forests

Libya
47. Archaeological Site of Cyrene
48. Archaeological Site of Leptis Magna
49. Archaeological Site of Sabratha
50. Old Town of Ghadamès
51. Rock-Art Sites of Tadrart Acacus

Madagascar
52. Rainforests of the Atsinanana
53. The Royal Hill of Ambohimanga
54. Tsingy de Bemaraha Strict Nature Reserve

Malawi
55. Chongoni Rock-Art Area
56. Lake Malawi National Park

Mali
57. Cliff of Bandiagara (Land of the Dogons)
58. Old Towns of Djenné
59. Timbuktu
60. Tomb of Askia

Mauritania
61. Ancient Ksour of Ouadane, Chinguetti, Tichitt and Oualata
62. Banc d'Arguin National Park

Mauritius
63. Aapravasi Ghat
64. Le Morne Cultural Landscape

Morocco
65. Archaeological Site of Volubilis
66. Historic City of Meknes
67. Ksar of Ait-Ben-Haddou
68. Medina of Essaouira (formerly Mogador)
69. Medina of Fez
70. Medina of Marrakesh
71. Medina of Tétouan (formerly known as Titawin)
72. Portuguese City of Mazagan (El Jadida)

Mozambique
73. Island of Mozambique

Namibia
74. Twyfelfontein or /Ui-//aes

Niger
75. Aïr and Ténéré Natural Reserves
76. W National Park of Niger

Nigeria
77. Osun-Osogbo Sacred Grove
78. Sukur Cultural Landscape

Senegal
79. Djoudj National Bird Sanctuary
80. Island of Gorée
81. Island of Saint-Louis
82. Niokolo-Koba National Park
39. Stone Circles of Senegambia

Seychelles
83. Aldabra Atoll
84. Vallée de Mai Nature Reserve

South Africa, Republic of
85. Cape Floral Region Protected Areas
86. Fossil Hominid Sites of Sterkfontein, Swartkrans, Kromdraai, and Environs
87. iSimangaliso Wetland Park
88. Mapungubwe Cultural Landscape
89. Richtersveld Cultural and Botanical Landscape
90. Robben Island
91. uKhahlamba/Drakensberg Park
92. Vredefort Dome

Sudan
93. Gebel Barkal and the Sites of the Napatan Region

Tanzania
94. Kilimanjaro National Park
95. Kondoa Rock-Art Sites
96. Ngorongoro Conservation Area
97. Ruins of Kilwa Kisiwani and Ruins of Songo Mnara
98. Selous Game Reserve
99. Serengeti National Park
100. Stone Town of Zanzibar

Togo
101. Koutammakou, the Land of the Batammariba

Tunisia
102. Amphitheatre of El Jem
103. Dougga/Thugga
104. Ichkeul National Park
105. Kairouan
106. Medina of Sousse
107. Medina of Tunis
108. Punic Town of Kerkuane and its Necropolis
109. Site of Carthage

Uganda
110. Bwindi Impenetrable National Park
111. Rwenzori Mountains National Park
112. Tombs of Buganda Kings at Kasubi

Zambia
113. Mosi-oa-Tunya/Victoria Falls

Zimbabwe
114. Great Zimbabwe National Monument
115. Khami Ruins National Monument
116. Mana Pools National Park, Sapi and Chewore Safari Areas
113. Mosi-oa-Tunya/Victoria Falls
117. Matobo Hills

WESTERN SAHARA

CAPE VERDE 12

SENEGAL
81 79
80 39
38
THE GAMBIA

GUINEA-BISSAU

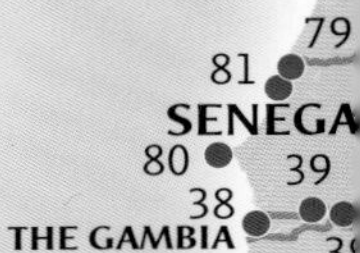

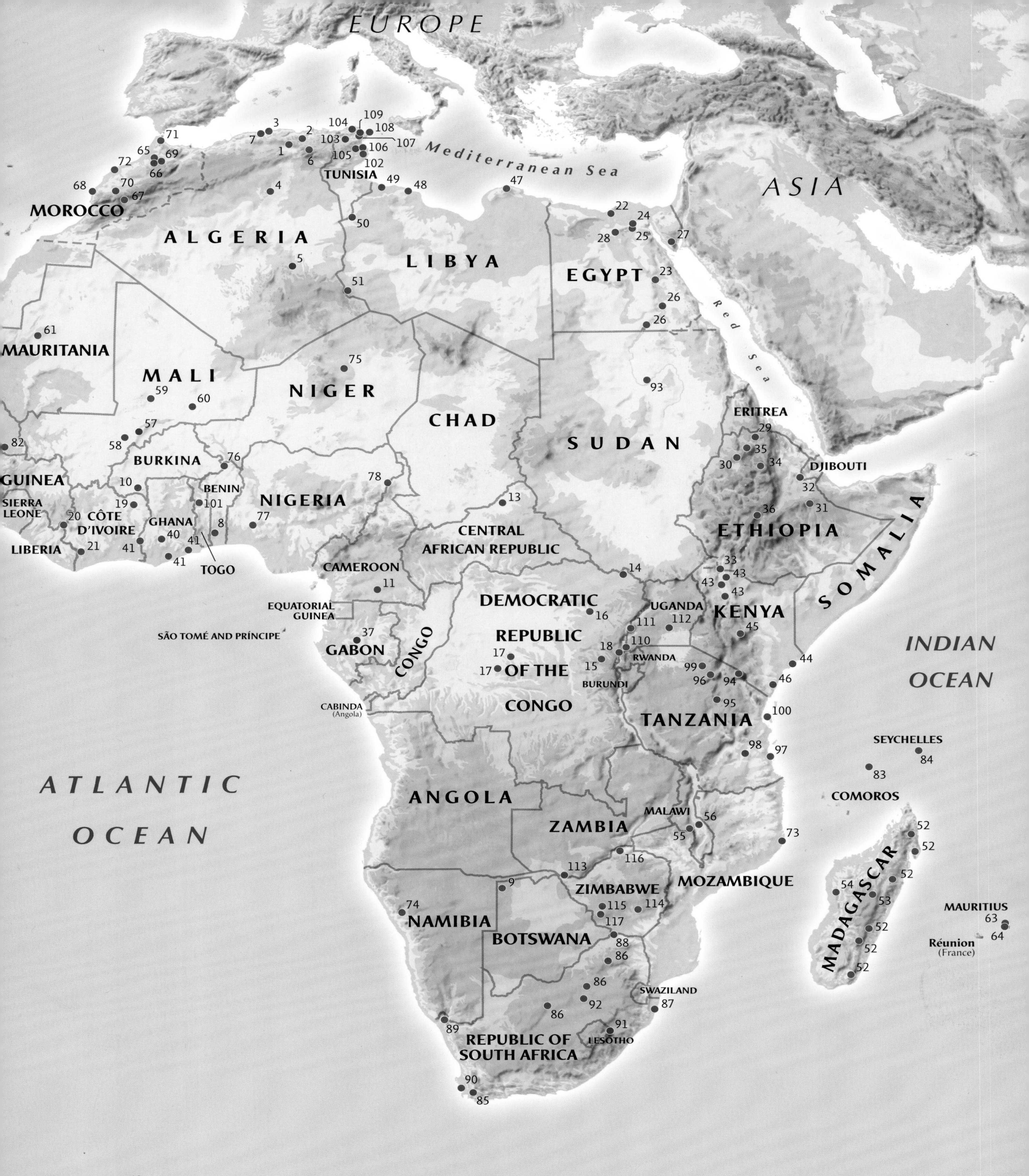

EUROPE

Mediterranean Sea

ASIA

MOROCCO

ALGERIA

LIBYA

EGYPT

Red Sea

TUNISIA

MAURITANIA

MALI

NIGER

CHAD

SUDAN

ERITREA

DJIBOUTI

BURKINA

GUINEA

SIERRA
LEONE

CÔTE
D'IVOIRE

LIBERIA

GHANA

BENIN

NIGERIA

TOGO

CAMEROON

EQUATORIAL
GUINEA

SÃO TOMÉ AND PRÍNCIPE

GABON

CONGO

CENTRAL
AFRICAN REPUBLIC

DEMOCRATIC

REPUBLIC

OF THE

CONGO

CABINDA
(Angola)

ETHIOPIA

SOMALIA

UGANDA

KENYA

RWANDA

BURUNDI

TANZANIA

INDIAN

OCEAN

SEYCHELLES

ATLANTIC

OCEAN

ANGOLA

ZAMBIA

MALAWI

MOZAMBIQUE

COMOROS

NAMIBIA

BOTSWANA

ZIMBABWE

MADAGASCAR

MAURITIUS

Réunion
(France)

SWAZILAND

REPUBLIC OF
SOUTH AFRICA

LESOTHO

Gough Island
(U.K.)

77

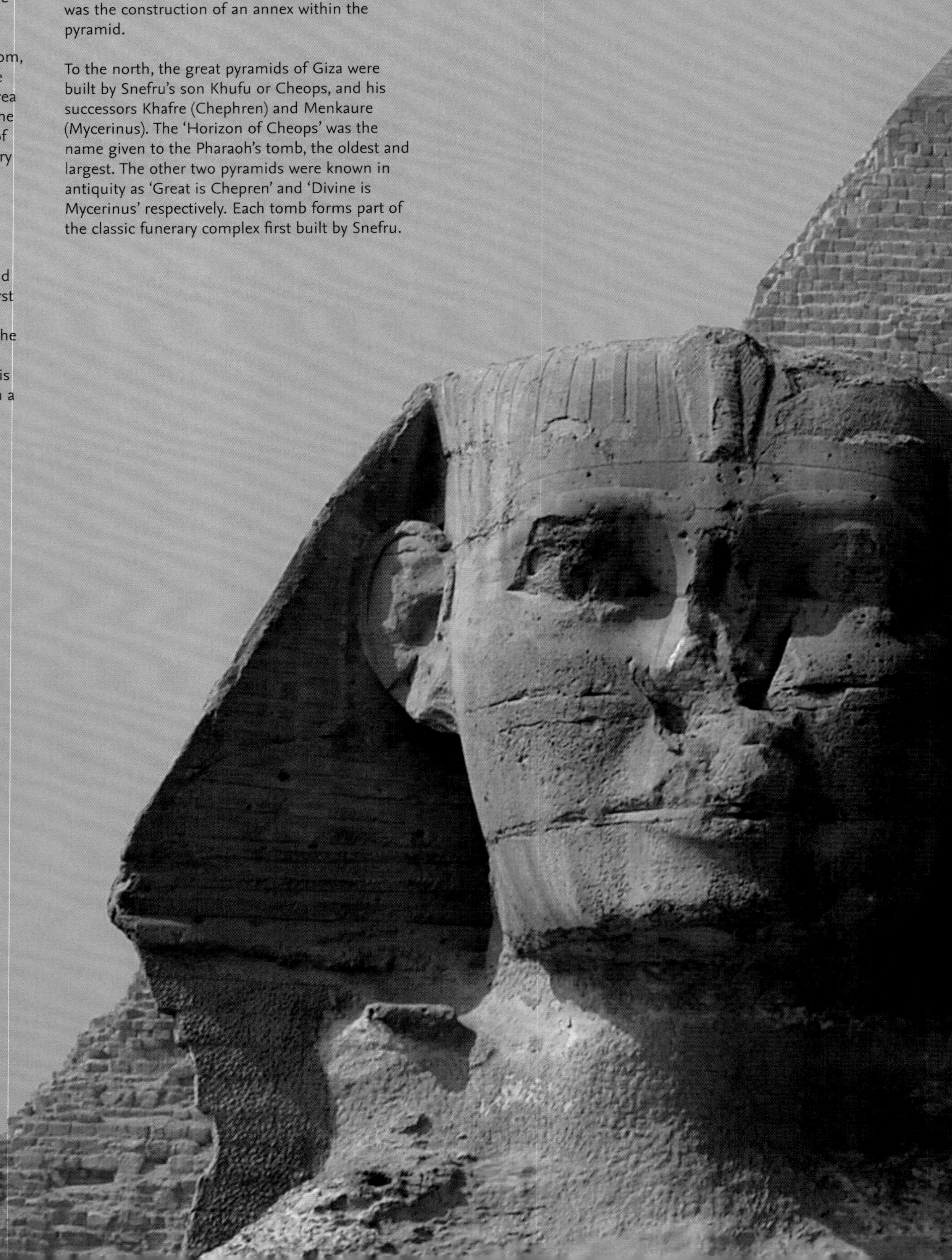

Memphis and its Necropolis – the Pyramid Fields from Giza to Dahshur – EGYPT

Inscribed 1979 – Human creative genius; Testimony to cultural tradition; Heritage associated with events of universal significance.

The capital of the Old Kingdom of Egypt in the third millennium BC, Memphis was one of the Seven Wonders of the Ancient World. The area of pyramid fields that served as the its necropolis contains a number of exceptional monuments that bear witness to the status of Ancient Egypt as one of the most brilliant civilizations of this planet.

The first sovereign of the unified Egyptian kingdom, Menes (or Narmer), was said to have ordered the construction of a new capital in the Nile Delta area around 3100 BC. It was from Menes that the name of Mennufer (City of Menes) came. The temple of Ptah built there was the most important sanctuary dedicated to this primary god of Creative Force, and its ruins are all that survive today of the grandeur of Memphis, as it was known to the ancient Greeks.

Nearby Saqqara was the necropolis of the city and the largest in the land, and it is the site of the first great stone pyramid. The pyramid was built as a mausoleum for the pharaoh Djoser, founder of the Third Dynasty, who ruled from around 2668 BC. Designed by his architect and vizier, Imhotep, it is the oldest step pyramid in the world. It stands in a funerary complex enclosed by a 10-m-high wall.

To the south lies the necropolis of Dahshur. The founder of the Fourth Dynasty, Snefru, who reigned from around 2613 BC, built here. During his twenty-nine year reign he transformed the structure of Egyptian royal tombs: he chose the now familiar pyramid shape with a square base. He built both the Red Pyramid, named after its reddish-coloured limestone, and the Rhomboid (or Bent) Pyramid, with its double-angled slope on each of the four faces; this was apparently an intermediate form. Another innovation of Snefru was the construction of an annex within the pyramid.

To the north, the great pyramids of Giza were built by Snefru's son Khufu or Cheops, and his successors Khafre (Chephren) and Menkaure (Mycerinus). The 'Horizon of Cheops' was the name given to the Pharaoh's tomb, the oldest and largest. The other two pyramids were known in antiquity as 'Great is Chepren' and 'Divine is Mycerinus' respectively. Each tomb forms part of the classic funerary complex first built by Snefru.

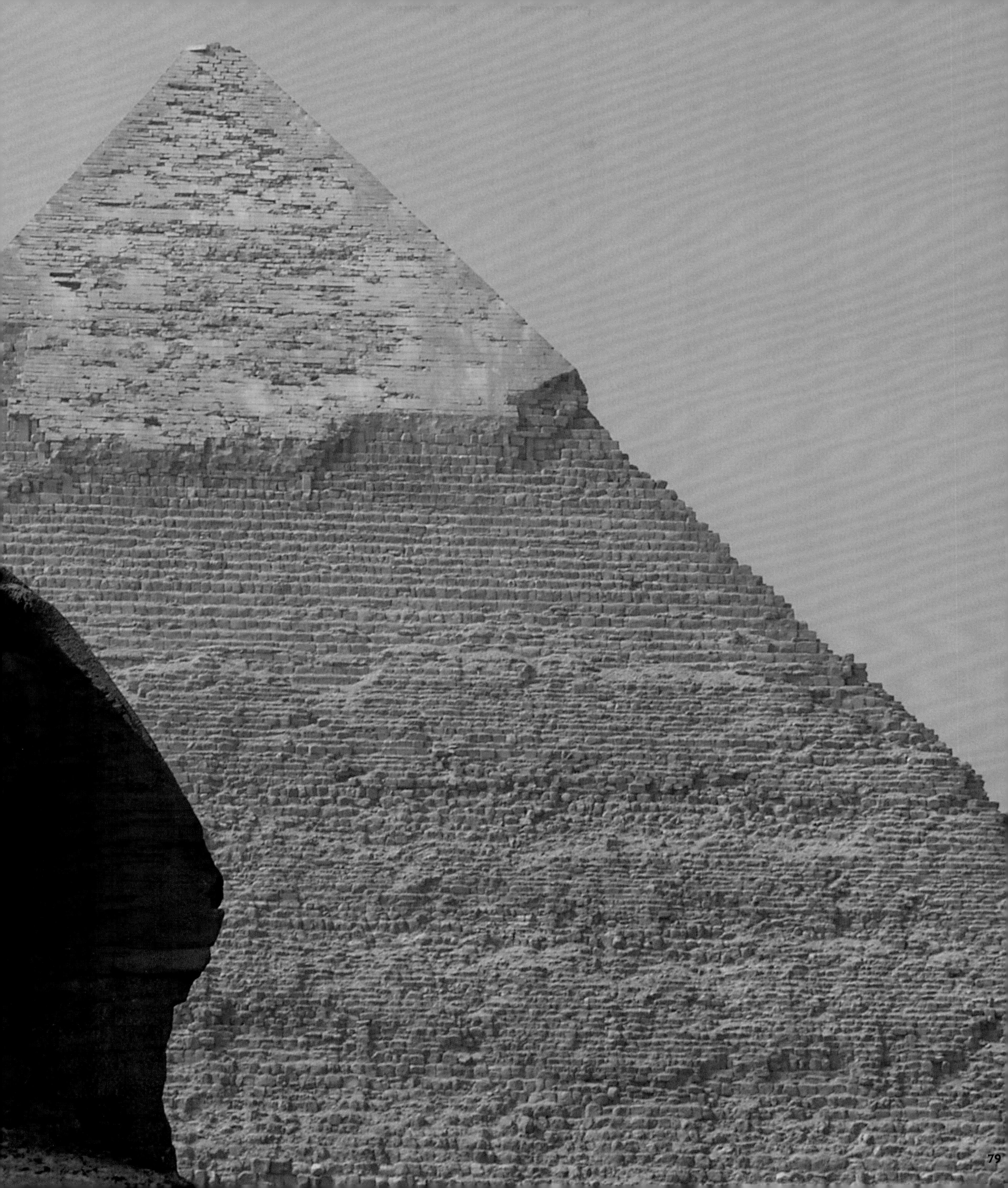

UNESCO World Heritage Sites – North America

The New World has relatively few sites compared to Europe or Asia. However the sites represent significant stages in Earth's formation and human history. Ancient geological processes are preserved in Gros Morne National Park in Canada, early civilizations are represented in Central America and evidence of the slave trade and plantations is found in the islands of the Caribbean.

● Cultural site   ● Natural site   ● Mixed site

Belize
1. Belize Barrier Reef Reserve System

Bermuda
2. Historic Town of St George and Related Fortifications (UK)

Canada
3. Canadian Rocky Mountain Parks
4. Dinosaur Provincial Park
5. Gros Morne National Park
6. Head-Smashed-In Buffalo Jump
7. Historic District of Old Québec
8. Joggins Fossil Cliffs
9. Kluane/Wrangell-St Elias/Glacier Bay/ Tatshenshini-Alsek
10. L'Anse aux Meadows National Historic Site
11. Miguasha National Park
12. Nahanni National Park
13. Old Town Lunenburg
14. Rideau Canal
15. SGang Gwaay
16. Waterton Glacier International Peace Park
17. Wood Buffalo National Park

Costa Rica
18. Area de Conservación Guanacaste
19. Cocos Island National Park
20. Talamanca Range-La Amistad Reserves/La Amistad National Park

Cuba
21. Alejandro de Humboldt National Park
22. Archaeological Landscape of the First Coffee Plantations in the South-East of Cuba
23. Desembarco del Granma National Park
24. Historic Centre of Camagüey
25. Old Havana and its Fortifications
26. San Pedro de la Roca Castle, Santiago de Cuba
27. Trinidad and the Valley de los Ingenios
28. Urban Historic Centre of Cienfuegos
29. Viñales Valley

Dominica
30. Morne Trois Pitons National Park

Dominican Republic
31. Colonial City of Santo Domingo

El Salvador
32. Joya de Cerén Archaeological Site

Greenland
33. Ilulissat Icefjord (Denmark)

Guatemala
34. Antigua Guatemala
35. Archaeological Park and Ruins of Quirigua
36. Tikal National Park

Honduras
37. Maya Site of Copán
38. Río Plátano Biosphere Reserve

Haiti
39. National History Park – Citadel, Sans Souci, Ramiers

Mexico
40. Agave Landscape and Ancient Industrial Facilities of Tequila
41. Ancient Maya City of Calakmul, Campeche
42. Archaeological Monuments Zone of Xochicalco
43. Archeological Zone of Paquimé, Casas Grandes
44. Central University City Campus of the Universidad Nacional Autónoma de México (UNAM)
45. Earliest 16th-Century Monasteries on the Slopes of Popocatepetl
46. El Tajin, Pre-Hispanic City
47. Franciscan Missions in the Sierra Gorda of Querétaro
48. Historic Centre of Mexico City and Xochimilco
49. Historic Centre of Morelia
50. Historic Centre of Oaxaca and Archaeological Site of Monte Albán
51. Historic Centre of Puebla
52. Historic Centre of Zacatecas
53. Historic Fortified Town of Campeche
54. Historic Monuments Zone of Querétaro
55. Historic Monuments Zone of Tlacotalpan
56. Historic Town of Guanajuato and Adjacent Mines
57. Hospicio Cabañas, Guadalajara
58. Islands and Protected Areas of the Gulf of California
59. Luis Barragán House and Studio
60. Monarch Butterfly Biosphere Reserve
61. Pre-Hispanic City and National Park of Palenque
62. Pre-Hispanic City of Chichen-Itza
63. Pre-Hispanic City of Teotihuacan
64. Pre-Hispanic Town of Uxmal

65. Protective town of San Miguel and the Sanctuary of Jesús Nazareno de Atotonilco
66. Rock Paintings of the Sierra de San Francisco
67. Sian Ka'an
68. Whale Sanctuary of El Vizcaino

Nicaragua
69. Ruins of León Viejo

Panama
70. Archaeological Site of Panamá Viejo and Historic District of Panamá
71. Coiba National Park and its Special Zone of Marine Protection
72. Darien National Park
73. Fortifications on the Caribbean Side of Panama: Portobelo-San Lorenzo
20. Talamanca Range-La Amistad Reserves/La Amistad National Park

Saint Kitts and Nevis
74. Brimstone Hill Fortress National Park

Saint Lucia
75. Pitons Management Area

United States of America
76. Cahokia Mounds State Historic Site
77. Carlsbad Caverns National Park
78. Chaco Culture
79. Everglades National Park
80. Grand Canyon National Park
81. Great Smoky Mountains National Park
82. Hawaii Volcanoes National Park
83. Independence Hall
84. La Fortaleza and San Juan National Historic Site in Puerto Rico
9. Kluane/Wrangell-St Elias/Glacier Bay/ Tatshenshini-Alsek
85. Mammoth Cave National Park
86. Mesa Verde National Park
87. Monticello and the University of Virginia in Charlottesville
88. Olympic National Park
89. Pueblo de Taos
90. Redwood National Park
91. Statue of Liberty
16. Waterton Glacier International Peace Park
92. Yellowstone National Park
93. Yosemite National Park

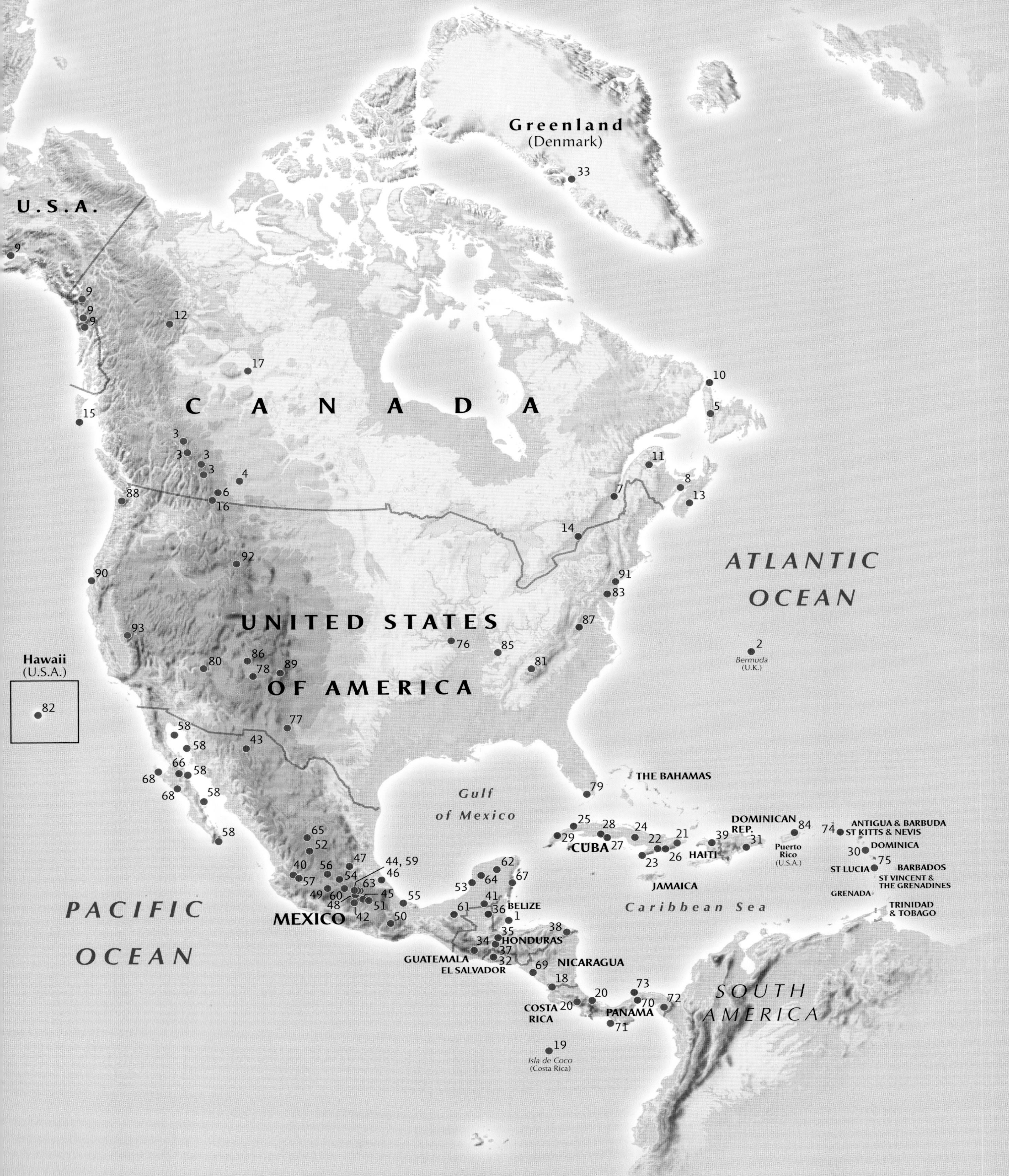

Greenland
(Denmark)

33

U.S.A.

9

9
9
9

12

17

C A N A D A

15

10

5

3
3   3
3
4
6
16

88

11

7
8
13

14

92

ATLANTIC
OCEAN

90

UNITED STATES

91
83

93

87

Hawaii
(U.S.A.)

80   86
78 89

OF AMERICA

76   85

2
Bermuda
(U.K.)

81

82

77

58

43

58

THE BAHAMAS

79

66 58
68

25   28   24
29   22   21
CUBA 27

DOMINICAN
REP.   84   74   **ANTIGUA & BARBUDA**
39   **ST KITTS & NEVIS**
31 Puerto   30 **DOMINICA**
Rico
(U.S.A.) **ST LUCIA** 75 **BARBADOS**
ST VINCENT &
THE GRENADINES

68

58

58

65
52

40   56   47   44, 59
57   54   46
49 60 63   45   55
48 51
42   50

62
64   67
53
41
61   36   **BELIZE**
1

23   26   **HAITI**

JAMAICA

Caribbean Sea

GRENADA

TRINIDAD
& TOBAGO

MEXICO

Gulf

of Mexico

38
35
HONDURAS
34   37
32   69   **NICARAGUA**
GUATEMALA   18
EL SALVADOR   20   73
20   70   72
COSTA   **PANAMA**
RICA   71

PACIFIC

OCEAN

19

Isla de Coco
(Costa Rica)

SOUTH

AMERICA

Grand Canyon National Park – USA

Inscribed 1979 – Natural phenomena or beauty; Major stages of Earth's history; Significant ecological and biological processes; Significant natural habitat for biodiversity.

The Grand Canyon, carved nearly 1 500 m deep into the rock by the Colorado River, is the most spectacular gorge in the world. Its horizontal strata retrace the geological history of the past two billion years as it cuts across the Grand Canyon National Park. It also contains prehistoric traces of human adaptation to a particularly harsh environment.

The Grand Canyon dominates the national park, which was created in 1919 by an act of Congress and was one of the first national parks in the United States. The steep, twisting gorge, 1.5 km deep and 445.8 km long, was formed during some 6 million years of geological activity and erosion by the Colorado River on the raised Earth's crust (2.5 km above sea level). The gorge, which ranges from 200 m–30 km wide, divides the park into the North Rim and South Rim: the buttes, spires, mesas and temples in the canyon are in fact mountains, looked down upon from the rims.

Erosion is ongoing and seasonal and permanent rivers produce impressive waterfalls and rapids of washed-down boulders along the length of the canyon and its tributaries. The horizontal geological strata that erosion has exposed span some 2 000 million years of geological history, providing evidence of the four major geological eras: early and late Precambrian, Palaeozoic, Mesozoic and Cenozoic.

The canyon is also a vast biological museum in which there are five different life and vegetation

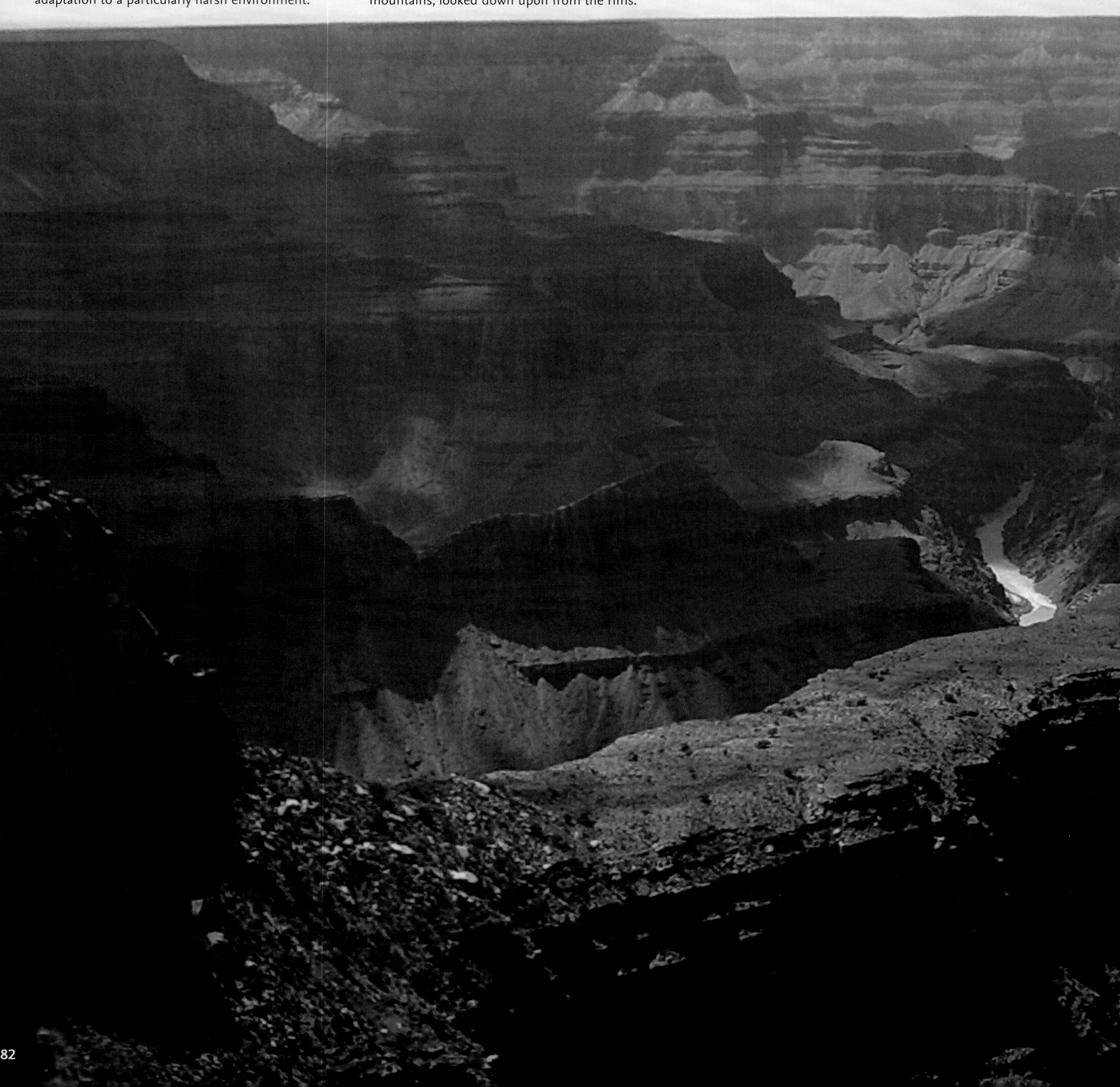

zones. Over 1 000 plant species have so far been identified including several officially listed as threatened. The park is also home to 76 mammal, 299 bird and 41 reptile and amphibian species, and some 16 fish species inhabit the Colorado River and its tributaries.

Archaeological remains show the adaptation of human societies to the area's severe climate and landscape, with evidence of settlement. The park contains more than 2 600 documented prehistoric ruins, including evidence of Archaic cultures (the earliest known inhabitants), Cohonina Indians along the South Rim, and Anasazi Indians on both the South Rim, North Rim, and within the Inner Canyon. Hualapai and Havasupai Indians moved into the canyons at this time, remaining undisturbed until the arrival of the Anglo-Americans in 1860.

The Grand Canyon area was first protected in 1893 as a forest reserve in which mining, lumbering and hunting continued to be allowed. It was upgraded to a game reserve in 1906, giving protection to the wildlife, and redesignated a National Monument in 1908.

Altitudinal range provides a variety of climates and habitats, ranging from desert to mountain conditions. Fossil remains found in the park include early plants, marine and terrestrial specimens, early reptiles and some mammals.

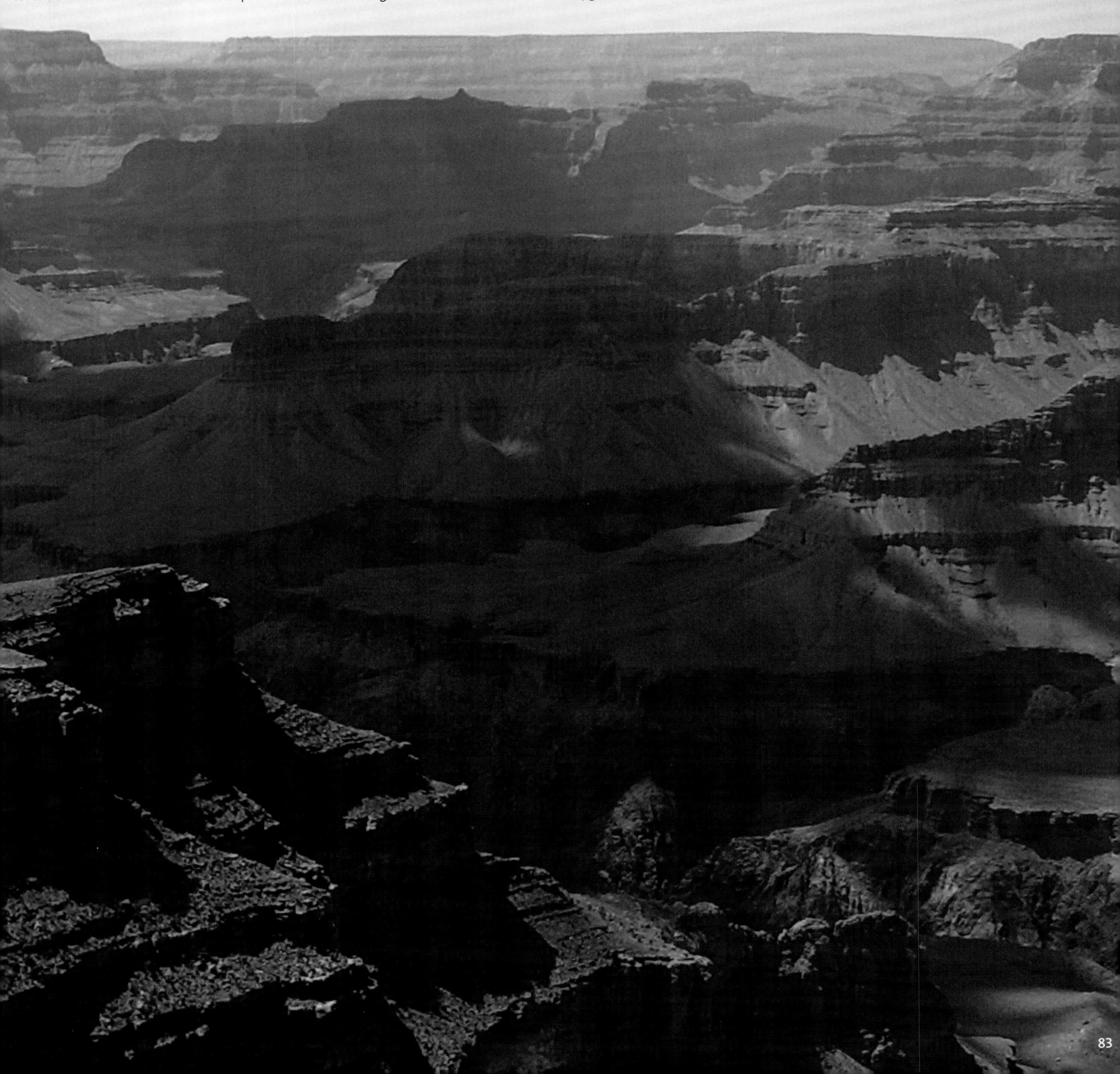

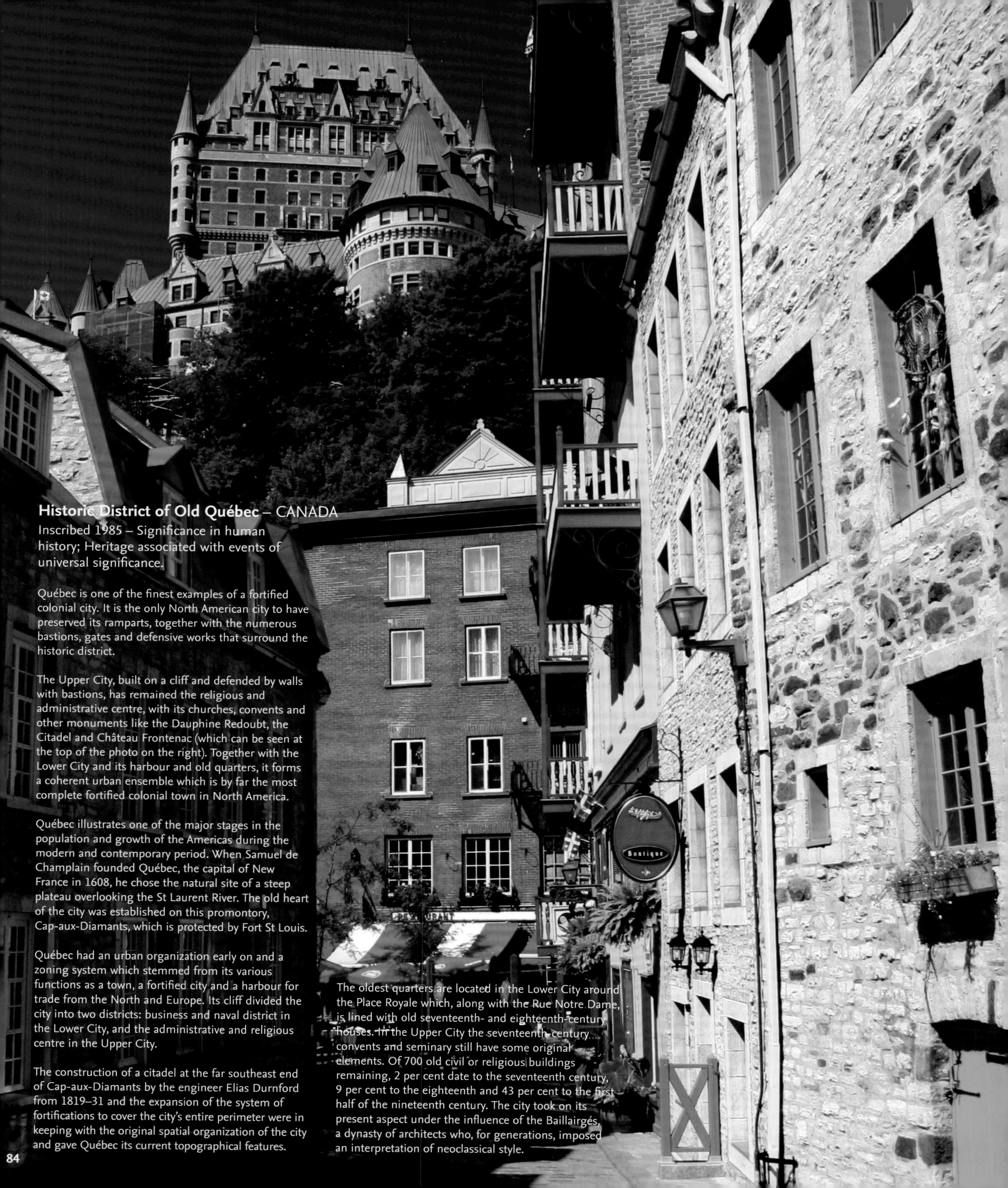

Historic District of Old Québec – CANADA

Inscribed 1985 – Significance in human
history; Heritage associated with events of
universal significance.

Québec is one of the finest examples of a fortified
colonial city. It is the only North American city to have
preserved its ramparts, together with the numerous
bastions, gates and defensive works that surround the
historic district.

The Upper City, built on a cliff and defended by walls
with bastions, has remained the religious and
administrative centre, with its churches, convents and
other monuments like the Dauphine Redoubt, the
Citadel and Château Frontenac (which can be seen at
the top of the photo on the right). Together with the
Lower City and its harbour and old quarters, it forms
a coherent urban ensemble which is by far the most
complete fortified colonial town in North America.

Québec illustrates one of the major stages in the
population and growth of the Americas during the
modern and contemporary period. When Samuel de
Champlain founded Québec, the capital of New
France in 1608, he chose the natural site of a steep
plateau overlooking the St Laurent River. The old heart
of the city was established on this promontory,
Cap-aux-Diamants, which is protected by Fort St Louis.

Québec had an urban organization early on and a
zoning system which stemmed from its various
functions as a town, a fortified city and a harbour for
trade from the North and Europe. Its cliff divided the
city into two districts: business and naval district in
the Lower City, and the administrative and religious
centre in the Upper City.

The construction of a citadel at the far southeast end
of Cap-aux-Diamants by the engineer Elias Durnford
from 1819–31 and the expansion of the system of
fortifications to cover the city's entire perimeter were in
keeping with the original spatial organization of the city
and gave Québec its current topographical features.

The oldest quarters are located in the Lower City around
the Place Royale which, along with the Rue Notre Dame,
is lined with old seventeenth- and eighteenth-century
houses. In the Upper City the seventeenth-century
convents and seminary still have some original
elements. Of 700 old civil or religious buildings
remaining, 2 per cent date to the seventeenth century,
9 per cent to the eighteenth and 43 per cent to the first
half of the nineteenth century. The city took on its
present aspect under the influence of the Baillairgés,
a dynasty of architects who, for generations, imposed
an interpretation of neoclassical style.

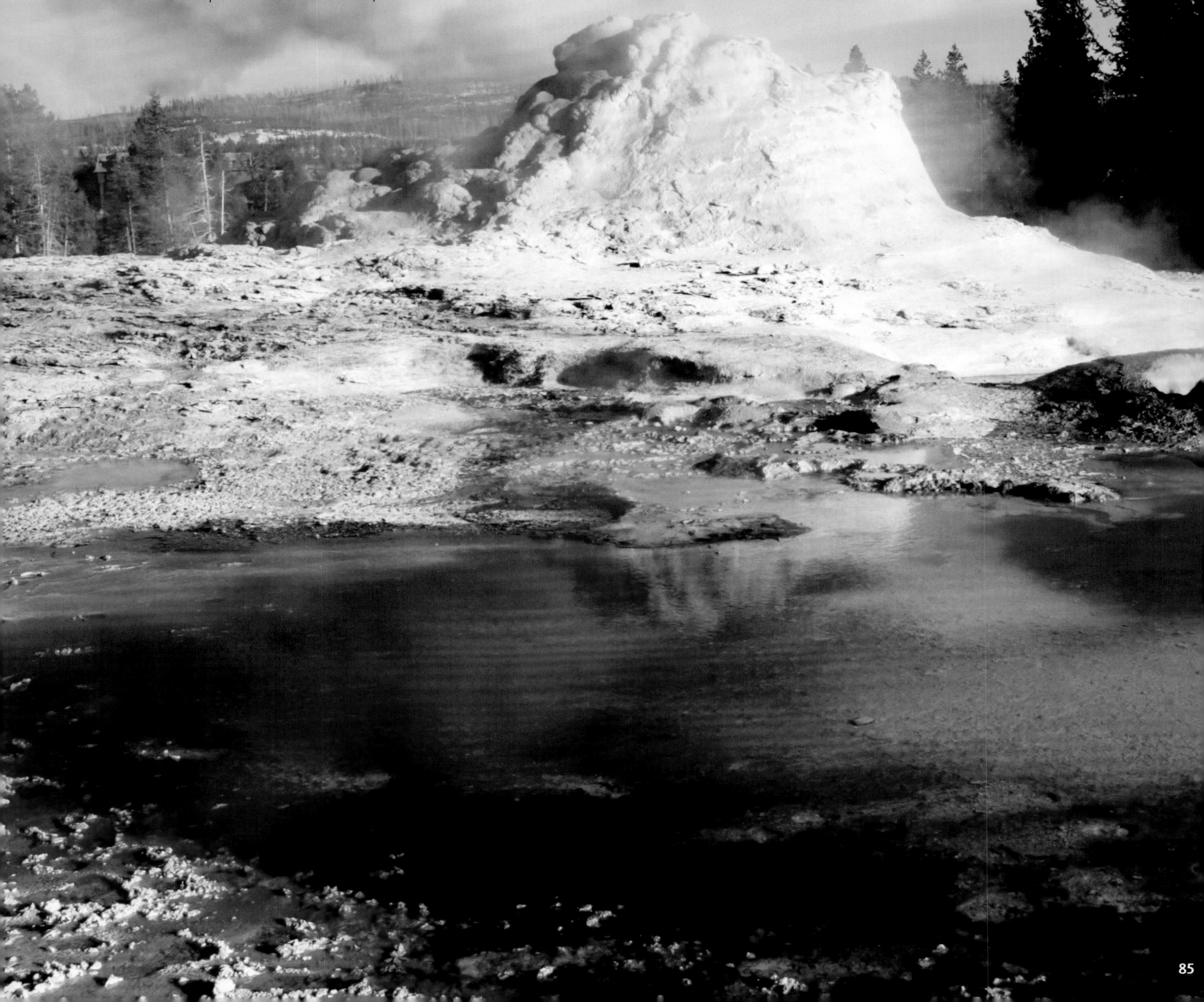

Yellowstone National Park – USA

Inscribed 1978 – Natural phenomena or beauty; Major stages of Earth's history; Significant ecological and biological processes; Significant natural habitat for biodiversity.

Yellowstone National Park covers 9 000 km² of a vast natural forest of the southern Rocky Mountains in the North American west. The park holds half of the world's known geothermal features, with over 10 000 examples, and is equally renowned for its wildlife which includes grizzly bears, wolves, bison and wapitis.

Established as America's first national park in 1872, Yellowstone boasts an impressive array of geothermal phenomena, with geysers, lava formations, fumaroles, hot springs and waterfalls, lakes and canyons. There are more than 580 geysers – the world's largest concentration, and two-thirds of all those on the planet. The source of these phenomena lies under the ground in the area's geological origins: Yellowstone is part of the most seismically active region of the Rocky Mountains, a volcanic 'hot spot'.

Crustal uplifts 65 million years ago formed the southern Rocky Mountains and volcanic outflows were common until around 40 million years ago. A more recent period of volcanism began in the region about 2 million years ago, when thousands of cubic kilometres of magma filled immense chambers under the plateau and then erupted to the surface. Three cycles of eruption produced huge explosive outbursts of ash. The latest cycle formed a caldera 45 km wide and 75 km long when the active magma chambers erupted and collapsed. The crystallizing magma is the source of heat for hydrothermal features such as geysers, hot springs, mud pots and fumaroles.

Most of the area was glaciated during the Pleistocene (from 1.8 million to 10 000 years ago, when the last ice age ended) and many glacial features remain. The park lies at the headwaters of three major rivers – Yellowstone, Madison and Snake. Lower Yellowstone Falls is the highest of more than forty named waterfalls in the park.

Great elevational differences produce a range of plant communities, from semi-arid steppe to alpine tundra. The park has seven species of coniferous tree, especially lodgepole pine, and 1 100 species of vascular plant, including an endemic grass. Thermal areas have unique assemblages of thermal algae and bacteria.

UNESCO World Heritage Sites – South America

The first World Heritage site to be listed in 1978 was the Gálapagos Islands off the coast of South America. Famous for its association with Darwin and its giant tortoises it was followed on to the List by sites representing ancient civilizations, European invaders and the continent's rich and diverse physical and natural environment.

● Cultural site   ● Natural site   ● Mixed site

Argentina
1. Cueva de las Manos, Río Pinturas
2. Iguazu National Park
3. Ischigualasto/Talampaya Natural Parks
4. Jesuit Block and Estancias of Córdoba
5. Jesuit Missions of the Guaranis: San Ignacio Miní, Santa Ana, Nuestra Señora de Loreto and Santa María Mayor (Argentina), Ruins of Saõ Miguel das Missões (Brazil)
6. Los Glaciares
7. Península Valdés
8. Quebrada de Humahuaca

Bolivia
9. City of Potosí
10. Fuerte de Samaipata
11. Historic City of Sucre
12. Jesuit Missions of the Chiquitos
13. Noel Kempff Mercado National Park
14. Tiwanaku: Spiritual and Political Centre of the Tiwanaku Culture

Brazil
15. Atlantic Forest South-East Reserves
16. Brasilia
17. Brazilian Atlantic Islands: Fernando de Noronha and Atol das Rocas Reserves
18. Central Amazon Conservation Complex
19. Cerrado Protected Areas: Chapada dos Veadeiros and Emas National Parks
20. Discovery Coast Atlantic Forest Reserves
21. Historic Centre of Salvador de Bahia
22. Historic Centre of São Luís
23. Historic Centre of the Town of Diamantina
24. Historic Centre of the Town of Goiás
25. Historic Centre of the Town of Olinda
26. Historic Town of Ouro Preto
27. Iguaçu National Park
5. Jesuit Missions of the Guaranis: San Ignacio Miní, Santa Ana, Nuestra Señora de Loreto and Santa María Mayor (Argentina), Ruins of Saõ Miguel das Missões (Brazil)
28. Pantanal Conservation Area
29. Sanctuary of Bom Jesus do Congonhas
30. Serra da Capivara National Park

Chile
31. Churches of Chiloé
32. Historic Quarter of the Seaport City of Valparaíso
33. Humberstone and Santa Laura Saltpeter Works
34. Rapa Nui National Park
35. Sewell Mining Town

Colombia
36. Historic Centre of Santa Cruz de Mompox
37. Los Katíos National Park
38. Malpelo Fauna and Flora Sanctuary
39. National Archeological Park of Tierradentro
40. Port, Fortresses and Group of Monuments, Cartagena
41. San Agustín Archeological Park

Curaçao
42. Historic Area of Willemstad, Inner City and Harbour, Netherlands Antilles (Netherlands)

Ecuador
43. City of Quito
44. Galápagos Islands
45. Historic Centre of Santa Ana de los Ríos de Cuenca
46. Sangay National Park

Paraguay
47. Jesuit Missions of La Santísima Trinidad de Paraná and Jesús de Tavarangue

Peru
48. Chan Chan Archaeological Zone
49. Chavín (Archaeological site)
50. City of Cuzco
51. Historic Centre of Lima
52. Historic Sanctuary of Machu Picchu
53. Historical Centre of the City of Arequipa
54. Huascarán National Park
55. Lines and Geoglyphs of Nasca and Pampas de Jumana
56. Manú National Park
57. Río Abiseo National Park
58. Sacred City of Caral-Supe

Suriname
59. Central Suriname Nature Reserve
60. Historic Inner City of Paramaribo

Uruguay
61. Historic Quarter of the City of Colonia del Sacramento

Venezuela
62. Canaima National Park
63. Ciudad Universitaria de Caracas
64. Coro and its Port

● 34
Easter Island
(Chile)

Caribbean Sea

Curaçao
(Netherlands)

42
40   64   63
36

VENEZUELA

37

62   GUYANA

COLOMBIA   60
SURINAME   French
59   Guiana

38

39

41

18   22

43

ECUADOR   46   17

44   45
Galápagos Islands
(Ecuador)

57   25

48   54   30

49   PERU   BRAZIL

58   51   56

52   50   19

55   20   21

53   14   24   16

BOLIVIA   23

10   12   28   19

11   20

9   33   26

8   15   29

PARAGUAY   15

47   27

5   2

URUGUAY   5

3   4

3   61

32

35

ARGENTINA

CHILE

31   7

ATLANTIC
OCEAN

PACIFIC
OCEAN

1

6

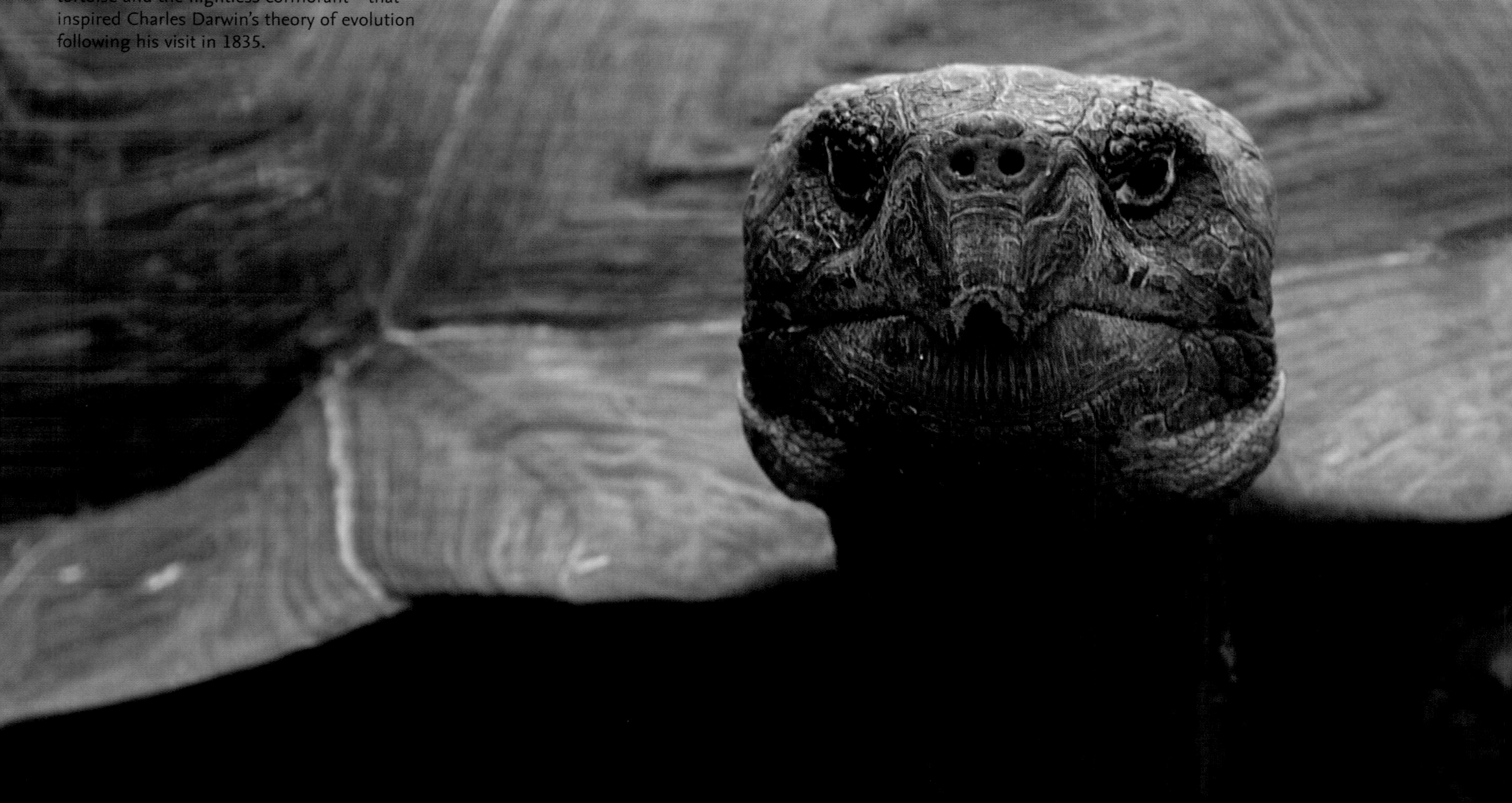

Galápagos Islands – ECUADOR

Inscribed 1978 – Natural phenomena or beauty; Major stages of Earth's history; Significant ecological and biological processes; Significant natural habitat for biodiversity.

Situated in the Pacific Ocean approximately 1 000 km from the South American mainland, the Galápagos Archipelago of nineteen major islands and their marine reserve have been called a unique 'living museum and showcase of evolution'. Located at the confluence of three ocean currents, the Galápagos are a 'tossed salad' of marine species.

Volcanic processes formed the islands, most of which are volcanic summits, some rising over 3 000 m from the Pacific floor. They vary greatly in altitude, area and orientation and these differences, combined with their physical separation, contributed towards the species diversity and endemism on particular islands. Ongoing seismic and volcanic activity reflects the processes that formed the islands and it was these processes, together with the islands' extreme isolation, that led to the development of unusual animal life – such as the marine iguana, the giant tortoise and the flightless cormorant – that inspired Charles Darwin's theory of evolution following his visit in 1835.

The western part of the archipelago experiences intense volcanic and seismic activity. The larger islands typically comprise at least one gently sloping shield volcano, culminating in collapsed craters or calderas. Long stretches of shoreline are only slightly eroded, but in many places faulting and marine erosion have produced steep cliffs and lava, coral or shell sand beaches.

There is coastal vegetation along beaches, salt-water lagoons and low, broken, boulder-strewn shores, and mangrove swamps dominate protected coves and lagoons.

The arid zone that lies immediately inland dominates the Galápagos landscape. The humid zone emerges above the arid zone through a transition belt in which elements of the two are combined. It is very damp and is maintained in the dry season by thick, *garua* fogs. A fern-grass-sedge zone covers the summit areas of the larger islands where moisture is retained in temporary pools.

The endemic fauna includes invertebrate, reptile, marine and bird species. There are a few indigenous mammals. All the reptiles, except for two marine turtles, are endemic.

Marine environments are highly varied and are associated with water temperature regimes reflecting differences in nutrient and light levels. These range from warm temperate conditions brought on by vigorous upwelling (Cromwell Current) and a moderately cool, warm temperate-subtropical influence (Peru Flow)

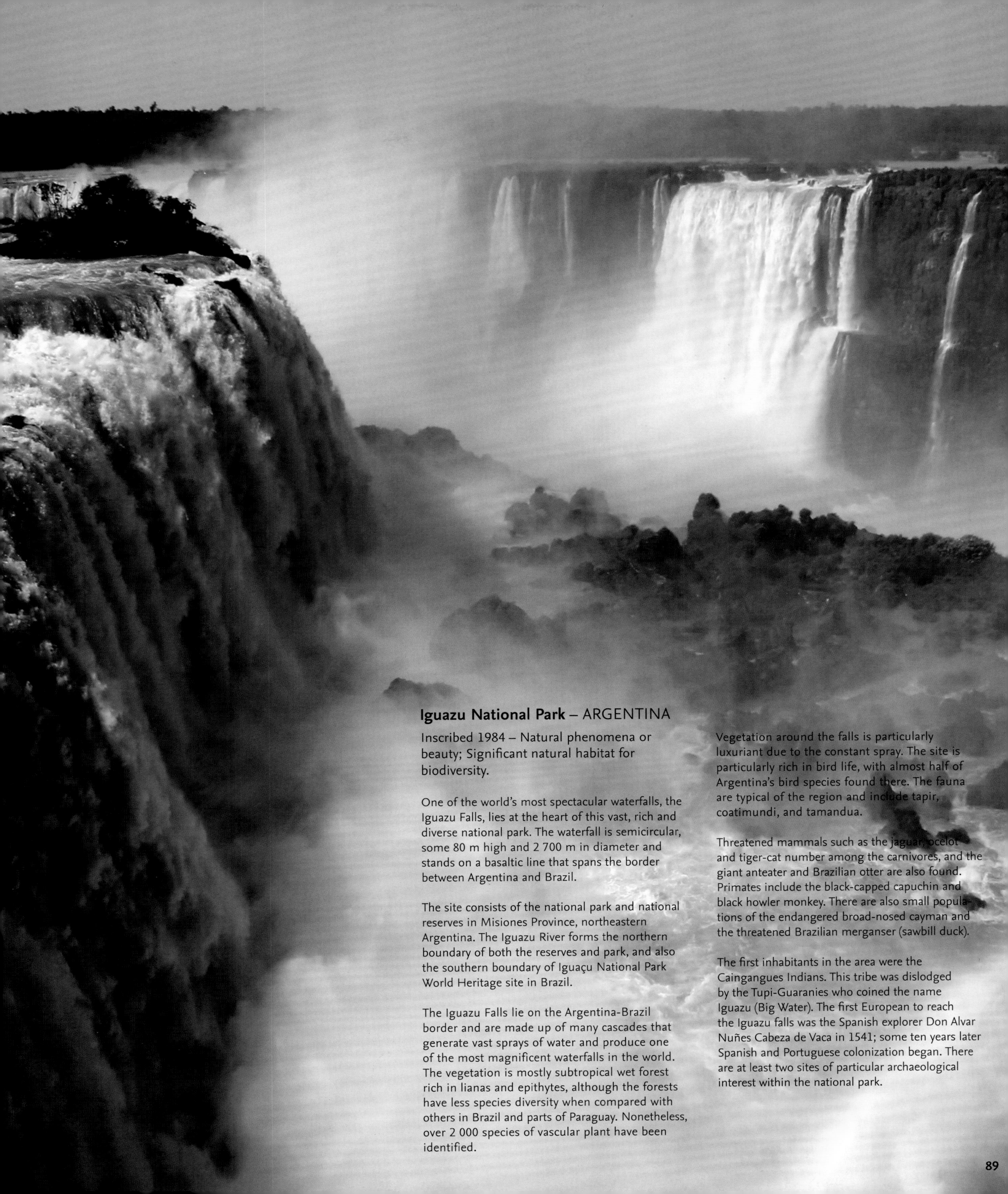

Iguazu National Park – ARGENTINA

Inscribed 1984 – Natural phenomena or beauty; Significant natural habitat for biodiversity.

One of the world's most spectacular waterfalls, the Iguazu Falls, lies at the heart of this vast, rich and diverse national park. The waterfall is semicircular, some 80 m high and 2 700 m in diameter and stands on a basaltic line that spans the border between Argentina and Brazil.

The site consists of the national park and national reserves in Misiones Province, northeastern Argentina. The Iguazu River forms the northern boundary of both the reserves and park, and also the southern boundary of Iguaçu National Park World Heritage site in Brazil.

The Iguazu Falls lie on the Argentina-Brazil border and are made up of many cascades that generate vast sprays of water and produce one of the most magnificent waterfalls in the world. The vegetation is mostly subtropical wet forest rich in lianas and epithytes, although the forests have less species diversity when compared with others in Brazil and parts of Paraguay. Nonetheless, over 2 000 species of vascular plant have been identified.

Vegetation around the falls is particularly luxuriant due to the constant spray. The site is particularly rich in bird life, with almost half of Argentina's bird species found there. The fauna are typical of the region and include tapir, coatimundi, and tamandua.

Threatened mammals such as the jaguar, ocelot and tiger-cat number among the carnivores, and the giant anteater and Brazilian otter are also found. Primates include the black-capped capuchin and black howler monkey. There are also small populations of the endangered broad-nosed cayman and the threatened Brazilian merganser (sawbill duck).

The first inhabitants in the area were the Caingangues Indians. This tribe was dislodged by the Tupi-Guaranies who coined the name Iguazu (Big Water). The first European to reach the Iguazu falls was the Spanish explorer Don Alvar Nuñes Cabeza de Vaca in 1541; some ten years later Spanish and Portuguese colonization began. There are at least two sites of particular archaeological interest within the national park.

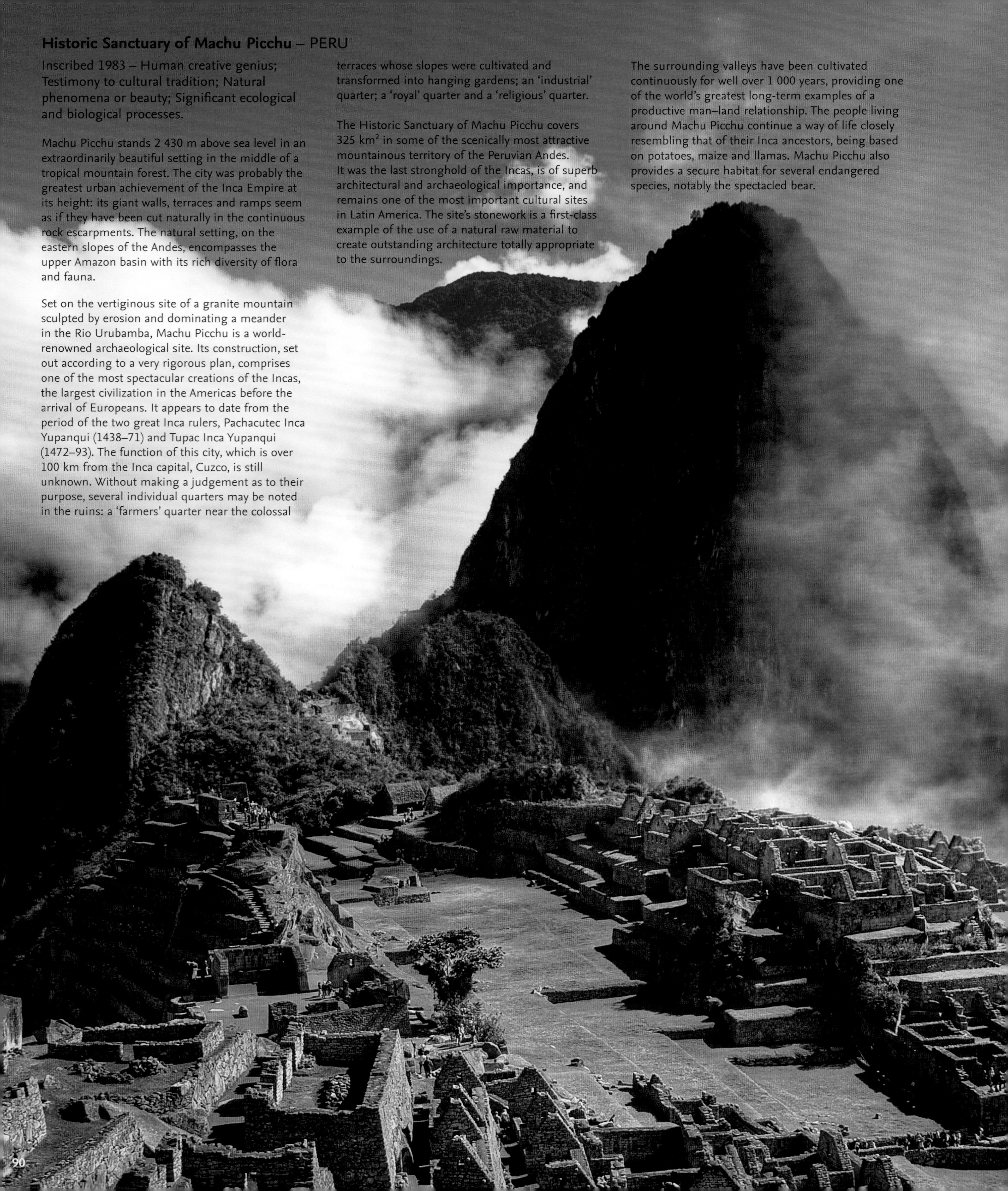

Historic Sanctuary of Machu Picchu – PERU

Inscribed 1983 – Human creative genius; Testimony to cultural tradition; Natural phenomena or beauty; Significant ecological and biological processes.

Machu Picchu stands 2 430 m above sea level in an extraordinarily beautiful setting in the middle of a tropical mountain forest. The city was probably the greatest urban achievement of the Inca Empire at its height: its giant walls, terraces and ramps seem as if they have been cut naturally in the continuous rock escarpments. The natural setting, on the eastern slopes of the Andes, encompasses the upper Amazon basin with its rich diversity of flora and fauna.

Set on the vertiginous site of a granite mountain sculpted by erosion and dominating a meander in the Rio Urubamba, Machu Picchu is a world-renowned archaeological site. Its construction, set out according to a very rigorous plan, comprises one of the most spectacular creations of the Incas, the largest civilization in the Americas before the arrival of Europeans. It appears to date from the period of the two great Inca rulers, Pachacutec Inca Yupanqui (1438–71) and Tupac Inca Yupanqui (1472–93). The function of this city, which is over 100 km from the Inca capital, Cuzco, is still unknown. Without making a judgement as to their purpose, several individual quarters may be noted in the ruins: a 'farmers' quarter near the colossal

terraces whose slopes were cultivated and transformed into hanging gardens; an 'industrial' quarter; a 'royal' quarter and a 'religious' quarter.

The Historic Sanctuary of Machu Picchu covers 325 km² in some of the scenically most attractive mountainous territory of the Peruvian Andes. It was the last stronghold of the Incas, is of superb architectural and archaeological importance, and remains one of the most important cultural sites in Latin America. The site's stonework is a first-class example of the use of a natural raw material to create outstanding architecture totally appropriate to the surroundings.

The surrounding valleys have been cultivated continuously for well over 1 000 years, providing one of the world's greatest long-term examples of a productive man–land relationship. The people living around Machu Picchu continue a way of life closely resembling that of their Inca ancestors, being based on potatoes, maize and llamas. Machu Picchu also provides a secure habitat for several endangered species, notably the spectacled bear.

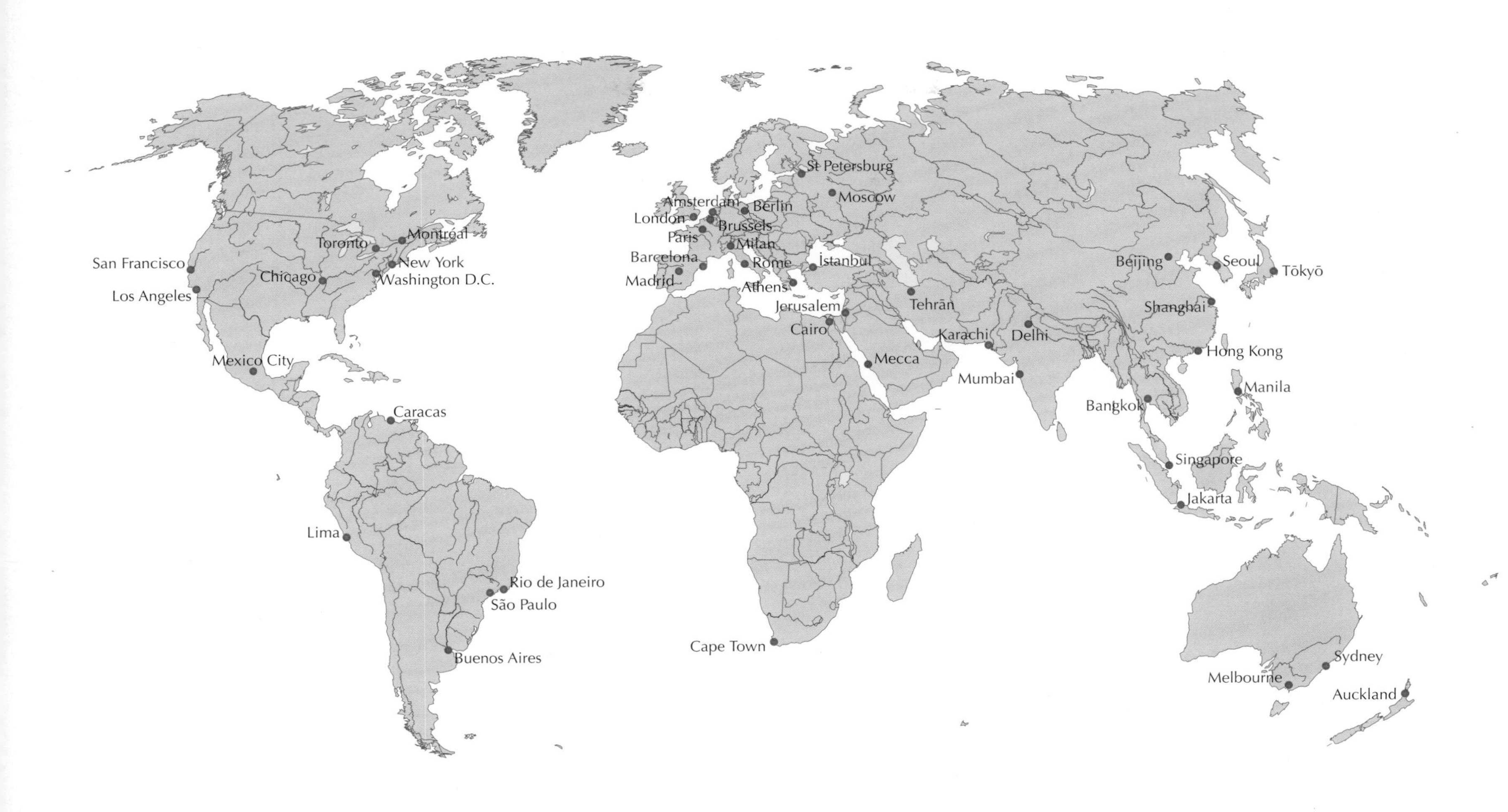

City	Page	City	Page	City	Page
AMSTERDAM Netherlands	97	İSTANBUL Turkey	96	MUMBAI India	96
ATHENS Greece	97	JAKARTA Indonesia	92	NEW YORK U.S.A.	104–105
AUCKLAND New Zealand	92	JERUSALEM Israel	96	PARIS France	100–101
BANGKOK Thailand	93	KARACHI Pakistan	93	RIO DE JANEIRO Brazil	106
BARCELONA Spain	102	LIMA Peru	106	ROME Italy	102
BEIJING China	93	LONDON United Kingdom	98–99	ST PETERSBURG Russia	97
BERLIN Germany	97	LOS ANGELES U.S.A.	103	SAN FRANCISCO U.S.A.	103
BRUSSELS Belgium	97	MADRID Spain	102	SÃO PAULO Brazil	106
BUENOS AIRES Argentina	106	MANILA Philippines	92	SEOUL South Korea	93
CAIRO Egypt	102	MECCA Saudi Arabia	96	SHANGHAI China	93
CAPE TOWN South Africa	102	MELBOURNE Australia	92	SINGAPORE	92
CARACAS Venezuela	106	MEXICO CITY Mexico	106	SYDNEY Australia	92
CHICAGO U.S.A.	103	MILAN Italy	102	TEHRĀN Iran	96
DELHI India	96	MONTRÉAL Canada	103	TŌKYŌ Japan	94–95
HONG KONG China	93	MOSCOW Russia	97	TORONTO Canada	103
				WASHINGTON D.C. U.S.A.	103

Key to City Plans

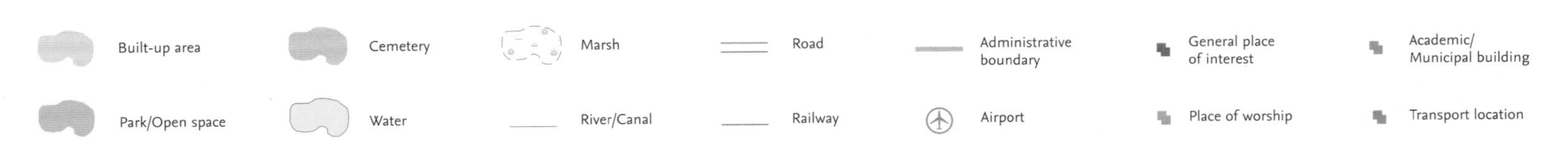

Built-up area	Cemetery	Marsh	Road
Park/Open space	Water	River/Canal	Railway

Administrative boundary	General place of interest	Academic/Municipal building
Airport	Place of worship	Transport location

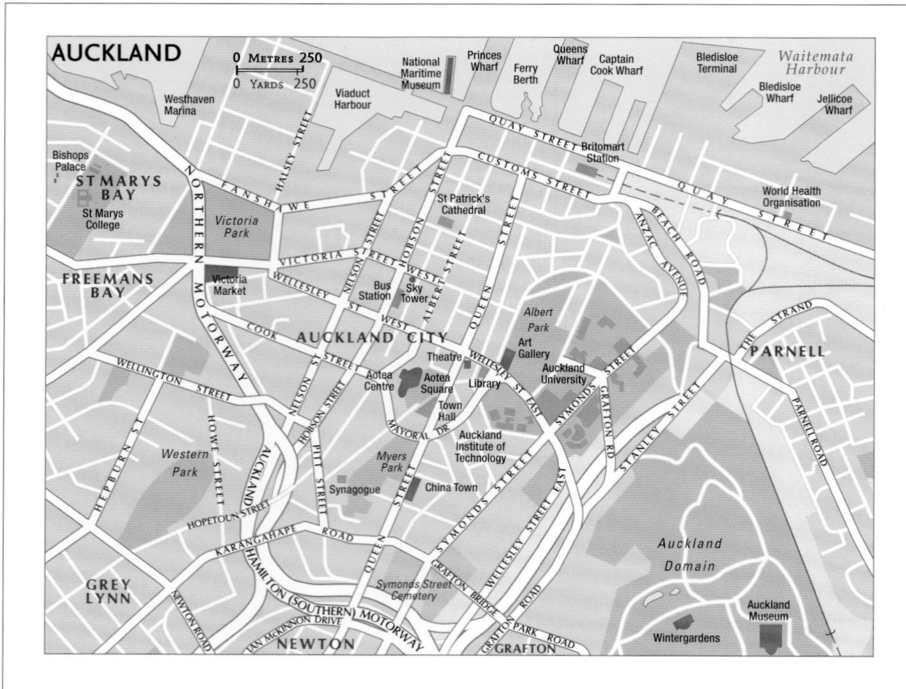
AUCKLAND
0 Metres 250
0 Yards 250
Westhaven Marina
Viaduct Harbour
National Maritime Museum
Princes Wharf
Ferry Berth
Queens Wharf
Captain Cook Wharf
Bledisloe Terminal
Waitemata Harbour
Bledisloe Wharf
Jellicoe Wharf
Bishops Palace
ST MARYS BAY
St Marys College
FREEMANS BAY
Victoria Park
Victoria Market
Britomart Station
St Patrick's Cathedral
World Health Organisation
Bus Station
Sky Tower
AUCKLAND CITY
Albert Park
Art Gallery
Auckland University
Theatre
Aotea Centre
Aotea Square
Library
Town Hall
Auckland Institute of Technology
Myers Park
Synagogue
China Town
PARNELL
Western Park
Auckland Domain
Symonds Street Cemetery
Auckland Museum
Wintergardens
GREY LYNN
NEWTON
GRAFTON
QUAY STREET
CUSTOMS STREET
FANSHAWE STREET
VICTORIA STREET
WELLESLEY STREET
COOK STREET
WELLINGTON STREET
NORTHERN MOTORWAY
HOPETOUN STREET
KARANGAHAPE ROAD
HAMILTON (SOUTHERN) MOTORWAY
IAN McKINNON DRIVE
NEWTON ROAD
PARK ROAD
GRAFTON BRIDGE
SYMONDS STREET
STANLEY STREET
PARNELL ROAD
STRAND
BEACH ROAD

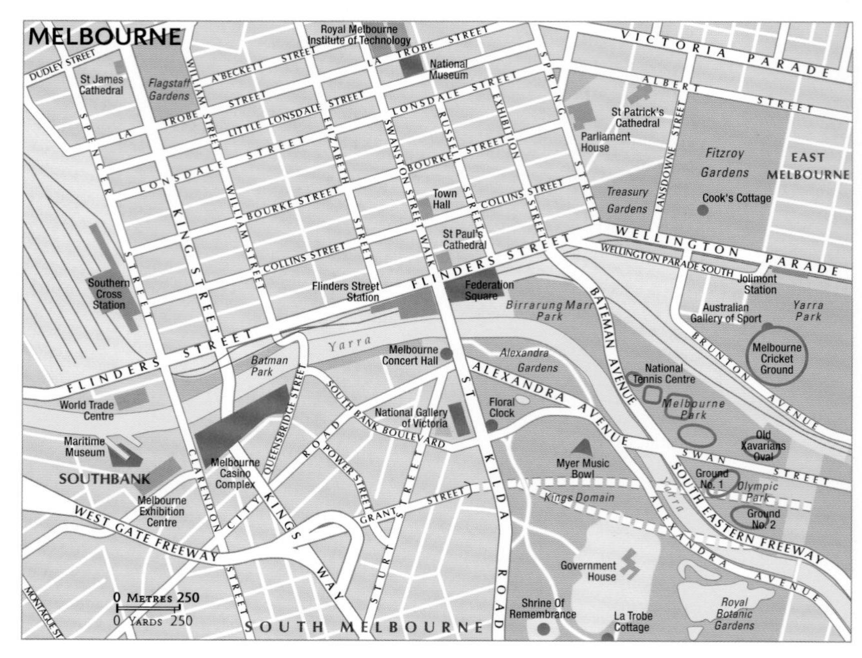
MELBOURNE
Royal Melbourne Institute of Technology
National Museum
St James Cathedral
Flagstaff Gardens
St Patrick's Cathedral
Parliament House
Fitzroy Gardens
EAST MELBOURNE
Treasury Gardens
Cook's Cottage
Town Hall
St Paul's Cathedral
Southern Cross Station
Flinders Street Station
Federation Square
Birrarung Marr Park
Jolimont Station
Australian Gallery of Sport
Yarra Park
Melbourne Cricket Ground
Yarra
Batman Park
Melbourne Concert Hall
Alexandra Gardens
National Tennis Centre
Melbourne Park
Old Kavanians Oval
World Trade Centre
National Gallery of Victoria
Floral Clock
Maritime Museum
Melbourne Casino Complex
Myer Music Bowl
SOUTHBANK
Ground No. 1
Olympic Park
Ground No. 2
Kings Domain
Melbourne Exhibition Centre
Government House
Shrine Of Remembrance
La Trobe Cottage
Royal Botanic Gardens
SOUTH MELBOURNE
0 Metres 250
0 Yards 250
VICTORIA PARADE
WELLINGTON PARADE
FLINDERS STREET
KING STREET
COLLINS STREET
BOURKE STREET
LONSDALE STREET
LA TROBE STREET
SPENCER STREET
WILLIAM STREET
ALEXANDRA AVENUE
BATEMAN AVENUE
BRUNTON AVENUE
SWAN STREET
SOUTH EASTERN FREEWAY
WEST GATE FREEWAY
KINGS WAY
ST KILDA ROAD
CITY ROAD
SOUTHBANK BOULEVARD

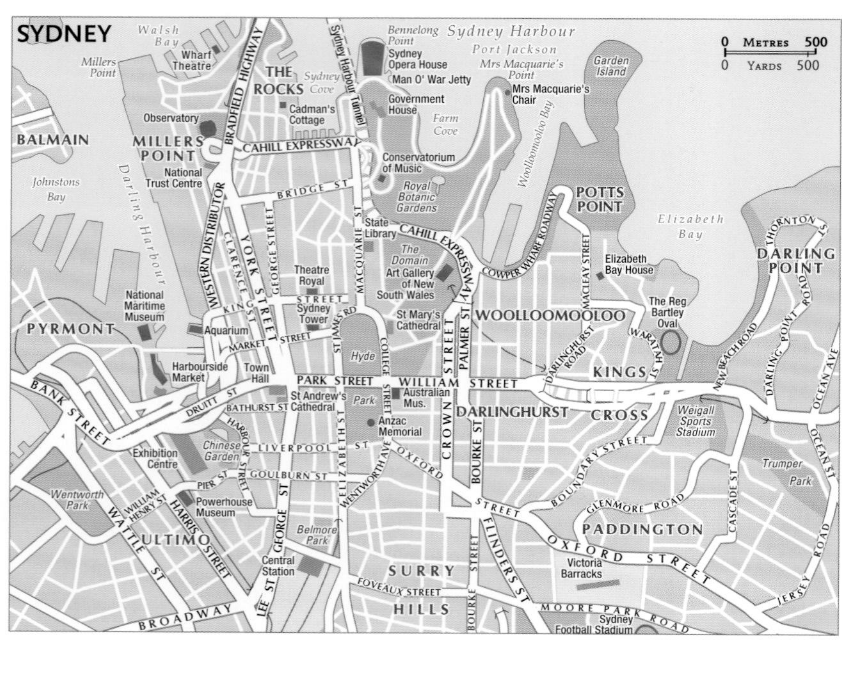
SYDNEY
Walsh Bay
Millers Point
Wharf Theatre
Bennelong Point
Sydney Harbour
Sydney Opera House
Port Jackson
Mrs Macquarie's Point
Man O' War Jetty
Garden Island
Mrs Macquarie's Chair
THE ROCKS
Sydney Cove
Cadman's Cottage
Government House
Farm Cove
Woolloomooloo Bay
0 Metres 500
0 Yards 500
BALMAIN
Observatory
MILLERS POINT
CAHILL EXPRESSWAY
Conservatorium of Music
Royal Botanic Gardens
National Trust Centre
Johnstons Bay
Darling Harbour
POTTS POINT
Elizabeth Bay
State Library
The Domain
Art Gallery of New South Wales
Elizabeth Bay House
DARLING POINT
Theatre Royal
Sydney Tower
National Maritime Museum
St Mary's Cathedral
WOOLLOOMOOLOO
The Reg Bartley Oval
PYRMONT
Aquarium
Hyde Park
Harbourside Market
Town Hall
KINGS CROSS
St Andrew's Cathedral
Australian Mus.
DARLINGHURST
Anzac Memorial
Weigall Sports Stadium
Exhibition Centre
Chinese Garden
Trumper Park
Wentworth Park
Powerhouse Museum
PADDINGTON
ULTIMO
Belmore Park
Central Station
SURRY HILLS
Victoria Barracks
Sydney Football Stadium
BRADFIELD HIGHWAY
WESTERN DISTRIBUTOR
YORK STREET
GEORGE STREET
PARK STREET
WILLIAM STREET
LIVERPOOL STREET
OXFORD STREET
CROWN STREET
BOURKE STREET
FLINDERS STREET
MOORE PARK ROAD
BROADWAY
HARRIS STREET
WATTLE STREET
BANK STREET

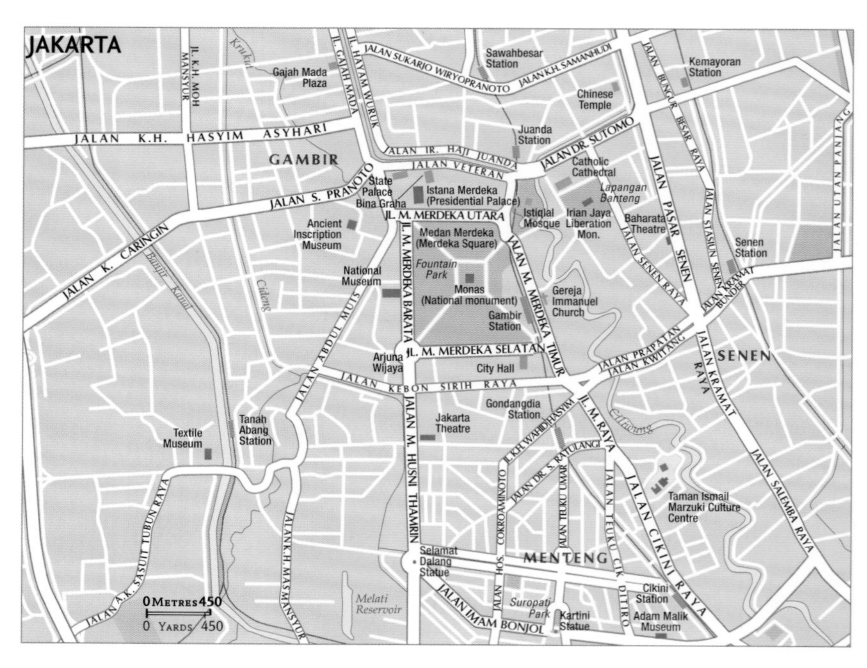
JAKARTA
Sawahbesar Station
Gajah Mada Plaza
Kemayoran Station
Chinese Temple
Juanda Station
JALAN K.H. HASYIM ASYHARI
GAMBIR
Catholic Cathedral
State Palace
Bina Graha
Istana Merdeka (Presidential Palace)
Lapangan Banteng
Ancient Inscription Museum
Istiqlal Mosque
Irian Jaya Liberation Mon.
Baharata Theatre
Medan Merdeka (Merdeka Square)
Senen Station
National Museum
Fountain Park
Monas (National monument)
Gereja Immanuel Church
Gambir Station
JALAN K. CARINGIN
Arjuna Wijaya
City Hall
SENEN
Textile Museum
Tanah Abang Station
Jakarta Theatre
Gondangdia Station
Taman Ismail Marzuki Culture Centre
MENTENG
Selamat Datang Statue
Melati Reservoir
Suropati Park
Kartini Statue
Cikini Station
Adam Malik Museum
0 Metres 450
0 Yards 450
JALAN M. H. THAMRIN
JALAN IMAM BONJOL
JALAN CIKINI RAYA
JALAN PASAR SENEN
JALAN S. PRANOTO
JALAN KEBON SIRIH RAYA

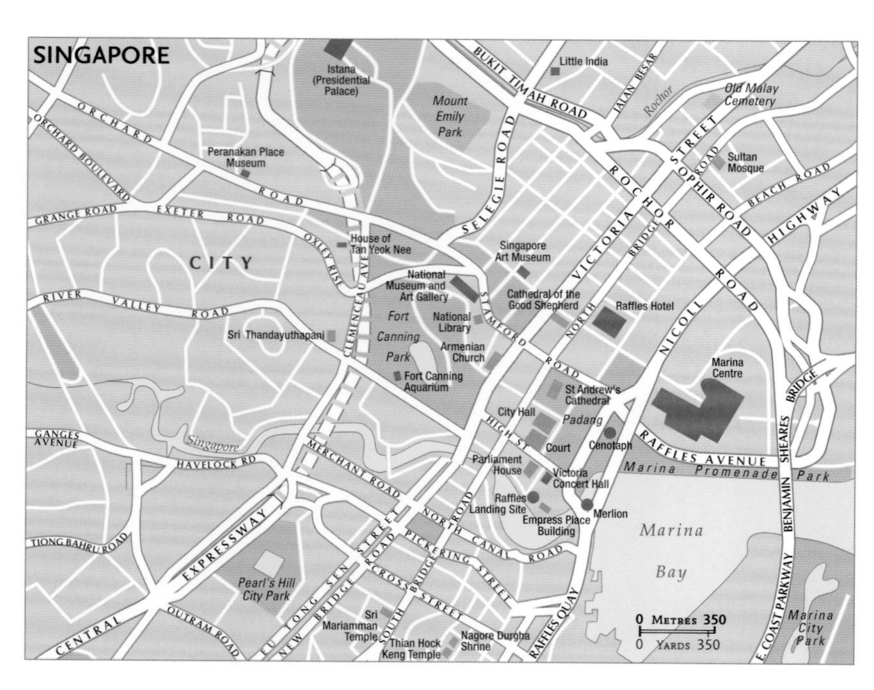
SINGAPORE
Istana (Presidential Palace)
Little India
Mount Emily Park
Old Malay Cemetery
Peranakan Place Museum
Sultan Mosque
House of Tan Yeok Nee
CITY
Singapore Art Museum
National Museum and Art Gallery
Cathedral of the Good Shepherd
Raffles Hotel
Fort Canning Park
National Library
Armenian Church
Sri Thandayuthapani
Fort Canning Aquarium
Marina Centre
City Hall
St Andrew's Cathedral
Padang
Court
Cenotaph
Parliament House
Victoria Concert Hall
Raffles Landing Site
Merlion
Empress Place Building
Marina Promenade Park
Marina Bay
Pearl's Hill City Park
Sri Mariamman Temple
Thian Hock Keng Temple
Nagore Durgha Shrine
Marina City Park
0 Metres 350
0 Yards 350
ORCHARD ROAD
BUKIT TIMAH ROAD
SELEGIE ROAD
ROCHOR ROAD
VICTORIA STREET
NICOLL HIGHWAY
RAFFLES AVENUE
HAVELOCK RD
CENTRAL EXPRESSWAY
RIVER VALLEY ROAD
NORTH CANAL ROAD
E. COAST PARKWAY
BENJAMIN SHEARES BRIDGE
RAFFLES QUAY

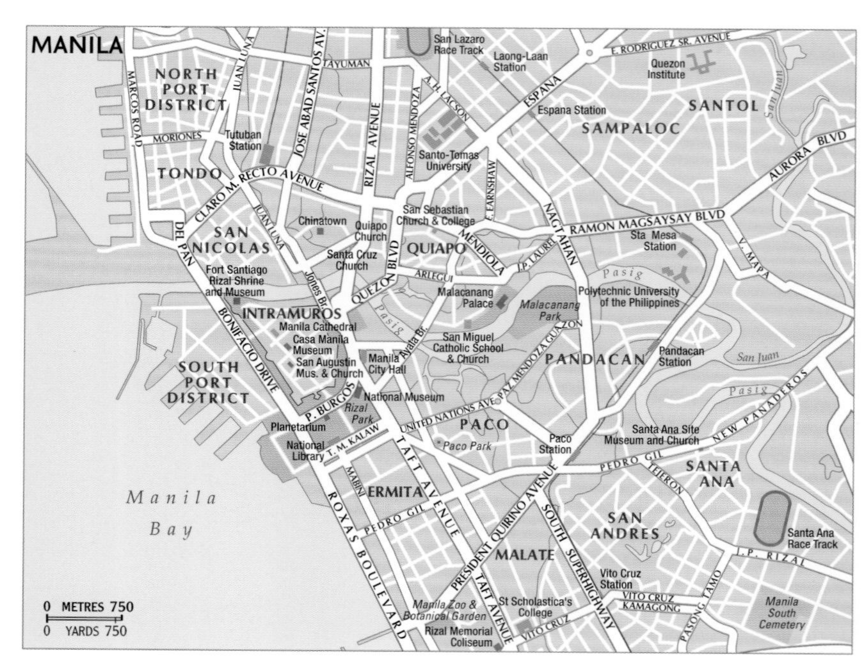
MANILA
NORTH PORT DISTRICT
San Lazaro Race Track
Laong-Laan Station
Quezon Institute
SANTOL
Espana Station
SAMPALOC
Tutuban Station
Santo Tomas University
TONDO
Chinatown
San Sebastian Church & College
SAN NICOLAS
Quiapo Church
QUIAPO
Sta Mesa Station
Santa Cruz Church
Fort Santiago Rizal Shrine and Museum
Malacanang Palace
Malacanang Park
Polytechnic University of the Philippines
INTRAMUROS
Manila Cathedral
Casa Manila Museum
San Augustin Mus. & Church
Manila City Hall
San Miguel Catholic School & Church
PANDACAN
Pandacan Station
SOUTH PORT DISTRICT
Rizal Park
National Museum
Planetarium
National Library
PACO
Paco Park
Paco Station
Santa Ana Site Museum and Church
SANTA ANA
Manila Bay
ERMITA
SAN ANDRES
Santa Ana Race Track
MALATE
Vito Cruz Station
Manila Zoo & Botanical Garden
St Scholastica's College
Rizal Memorial Coliseum
Manila South Cemetery
0 Metres 750
0 Yards 750
RIZAL AVENUE
ESPANA
QUEZON BLVD
CLARO M. RECTO AVENUE
RAMON MAGSAYSAY BLVD
AURORA BLVD
ROXAS BOULEVARD
TAFT AVENUE
UNITED NATIONS AVE
PRESIDENT QUIRINO AVENUE
SOUTH SUPERHIGHWAY
PEDRO GIL
VITO CRUZ
BONIFACIO DRIVE
NAGTAHAN

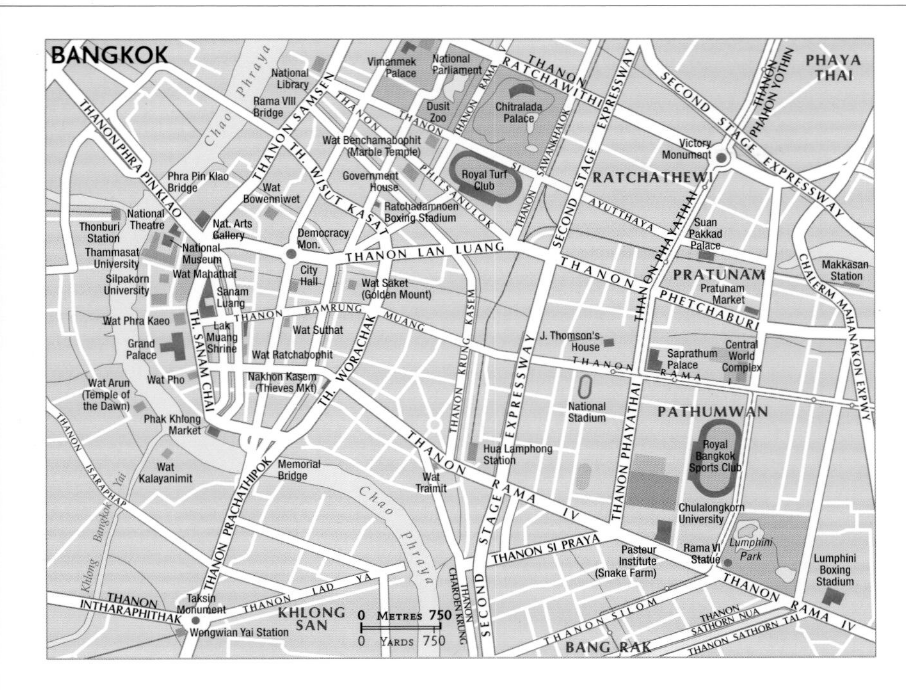
BANGKOK
Vimanmek Palace
National Parliament
National Library
Rama VIII Bridge
Dusit Zoo
Chitralada Palace
Wat Benchamabophit (Marble Temple)
Victory Monument
RATCHATHEWI
PHAYA THAI
Royal Turf Club
Phra Pin Klao Bridge
Wat Bowonniwet
Government House
Ratchadamnoen Boxing Stadium
Thonburi Station
National Theatre
Nat. Arts Gallery
Democracy Mon.
Thammasat University
National Museum
Wat Mahathat
City Hall
Wat Saket (Golden Mount)
Suan Pakkad Palace
PRATUNAM
Pratunam Market
Makkasan Station
Silpakorn University
Sanam Luang
Wat Phra Kaeo
Lak Muang Shrine
Wat Suthat
J. Thomson's House
Saprathum Palace
Central World Complex
Grand Palace
Wat Ratchabophit
Wat Pho
Nakhon Kasem (Thieves Mkt)
Wat Arun (Temple of the Dawn)
National Stadium
PATHUMWAN
Phak Khlong Market
Royal Bangkok Sports Club
Wat Kalayanimit
Memorial Bridge
Hua Lamphong Station
Wat Traimit
Chulalongkorn University
Pasteur Institute (Snake Farm)
Rama VI Statue
Lumphini Park
Lumphini Boxing Stadium
Taksin Monument
Wongwian Yai Station
KHLONG SAN
BANG RAK
THANON RATCHAWITHI
SECOND STAGE EXPRESSWAY
THANON LAN LUANG
THANON PHETCHABURI
THANON RAMA I
THANON RAMA IV
THANON SI PRAYA
THANON SILOM
THANON SATHORN NUA
THANON SATHORN TAI
THANON INTHARAPHITHAK
THANON PRACHATHIPOK
THANON PHAYATHAI
Chao Phraya
0 METRES 750
0 YARDS 750

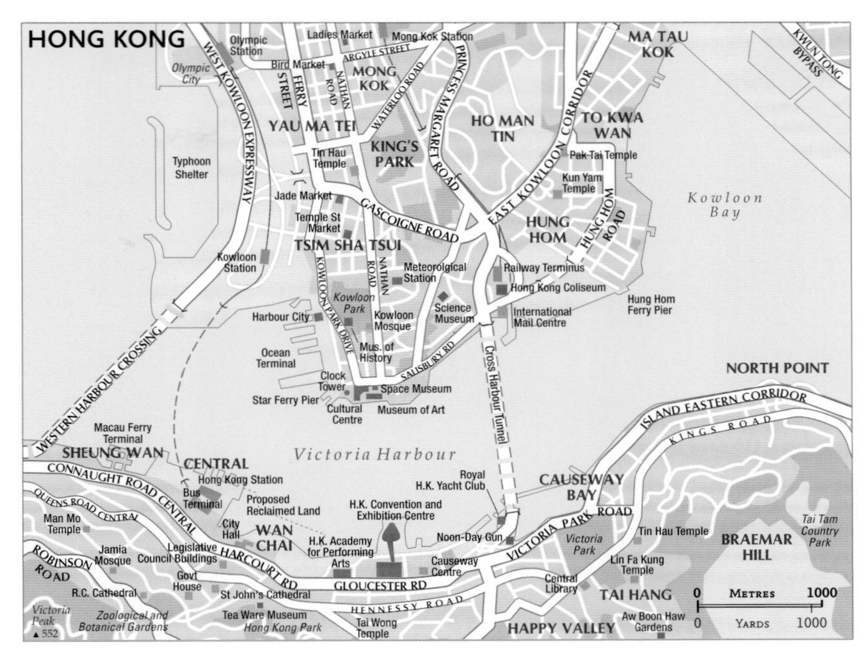
HONG KONG
Olympic Station
Ladies Market
Mong Kok Station
MONG KOK
MA TAU KOK
KWUN TONG BYPASS
YAU MA TEI
KING'S PARK
HO MAN TIN
TO KWA WAN
Typhoon Shelter
Tin Hau Temple
Pak Tai Temple
Kun Yam Temple
Jade Market
Temple St Market
GASCOIGNE ROAD
EAST KOWLOON CORRIDOR
HUNG HOM
Kowloon Bay
TSIM SHA TSUI
Kowloon Station
Meteorological Station
Railway Terminus
Hong Kong Coliseum
Kowloon Park
Harbour City
Kowloon Mosque
Science Museum
International Mail Centre
Hung Hom Ferry Pier
Ocean Terminal
Mus. of History
Clock Tower
Space Museum
Star Ferry Pier
Cultural Centre
Museum of Art
NORTH POINT
ISLAND EASTERN CORRIDOR
Cross Harbour Tunnel
WESTERN HARBOUR CROSSING
WEST KOWLOON EXPRESSWAY
Macau Ferry Terminal
Victoria Harbour
SHEUNG WAN
CENTRAL
CONNAUGHT ROAD CENTRAL
Hong Kong Station
Royal H.K. Yacht Club
CAUSEWAY BAY
Bus Terminal
Proposed Reclaimed Land
H.K. Convention and Exhibition Centre
Man Mo Temple
City Hall
WAN CHAI
Noon-Day Gun
Tin Hau Temple
BRAEMAR HILL
H.K. Academy for Performing Arts
Victoria Park
Tai Tam Country Park
Jamia Mosque
Legislative Council Buildings
HARCOURT RD
Causeway Centre
Lin Fa Kung Temple
ROBINSON ROAD
R.C. Cathedral
Govt House
St John's Cathedral
GLOUCESTER RD
Central Library
TAI HANG
Victoria Peak ▲552
Zoological and Botanical Gardens
Tea Ware Museum
Hong Kong Park
HENNESSY ROAD
Tai Wong Temple
HAPPY VALLEY
Aw Boon Haw Gardens
0 METRES 1000
0 YARDS 1000

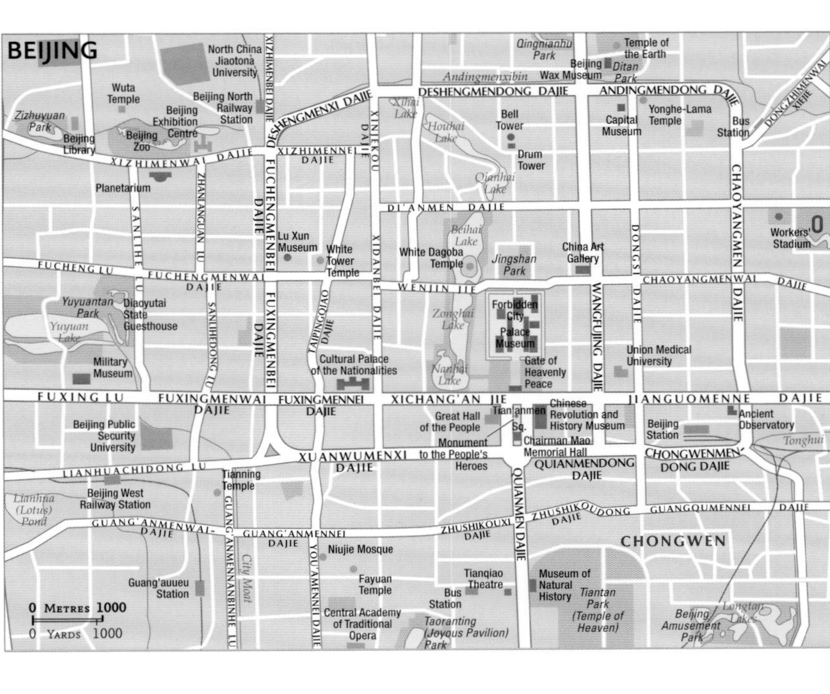
BEIJING
North China Jiaotona University
Qingnianhu Park
Temple of the Earth
Beijing Ditan Park
Wax Museum
Wuta Temple
Beijing North Railway Station
Beijing Exhibition Centre
Zizhuyuan Park
Beijing Library
Beijing Zoo
DESHENGMENDONG DAJIE
ANDINGMENDONG DAJIE
Bell Tower
Drum Tower
Yonghe-Lama Temple
Capital Museum
Bus Station
XIZHIMENWAI DAJIE
Planetarium
DI'ANMEN DAJIE
Lu Xun Museum
White Tower Temple
White Dagoba Temple
Beihai Lake
Jingshan Park
China Art Gallery
Workers' Stadium
FUCHENG LU
FUCHENGMENWAI DAJIE
WENJIN JIE
CHAOYANGMENWAI DAJIE
Yuyuantan Park
Diaoyutai State Guesthouse
Forbidden City Palace Museum
Cultural Palace of the Nationalities
Union Medical University
Military Museum
Gate of Heavenly Peace
FUXING LU
FUXINGMENWAI DAJIE
FUXINGMENNEI DAJIE
XICHANG'AN JIE
JIANGUOMENNEI DAJIE
Ancient Observatory
Beijing Public Security University
Great Hall of the People
Tiananmen Sq.
Chinese Revolution and History Museum
Beijing Station
Chairman Mao Memorial Hall
Monument to the People's Heroes
XUANWUMENXI DAJIE
QIANMENDONG DAJIE
CHONGWENMEN DONG DAJIE
LIANHUACHIDONG LU
Tianning Temple
Beijing West Railway Station
Lianhua (Lotus) Pond
ZHUSHIKOUXI DAJIE
GUANGQUMENNEI DAJIE
CHONGWEN
Niujie Mosque
Fayuan Temple
Tianqiao Theatre
Museum of Natural History
Tiantan Park (Temple of Heaven)
Guang'aueeu Station
Bus Station
Central Academy of Traditional Opera
Taoranting (Joyous Pavilion) Park
Beijing Amusement Park
0 METRES 1000
0 YARDS 1000

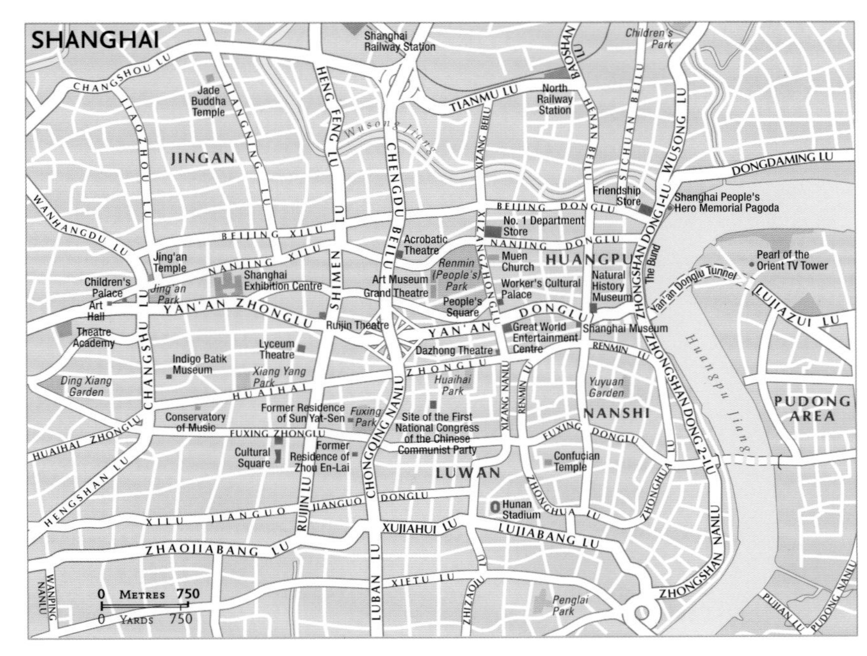
SHANGHAI
Shanghai Railway Station
Children's Park
CHANGSHOU LU
Jade Buddha Temple
TIANMU LU
North Railway Station
JINGAN
DONGDAMING LU
Friendship Store
Shanghai People's Hero Memorial Pagoda
BEIJING DONGLU
No. 1 Department Store
Acrobatic Theatre
Jing'an Temple
Shanghai Exhibition Centre
Renmin (People's) Park
Muen Church
HUANGPU
Pearl of the Orient TV Tower
Children's Palace
Art Museum
Grand Theatre
Worker's Cultural Palace
Natural History Museum
The Bund
Yan'an Dong Lu Tunnel
LUJIAZUI LU
Art Hall
YAN'AN ZHONGLU
People's Square
Theatre Academy
Ruijin Theatre
Great World Entertainment Centre
Shanghai Museum
Indigo Batik Museum
Lyceum Theatre
Dazhong Theatre
Xiang Yang Park
Huaihai Park
Yuyuan Garden
Ding Xiang Garden
HUAIHAI ZHONGLU
Former Residence of Sun Yat-Sen
Fuxing Park
Site of the First National Congress of the Chinese Communist Party
NANSHI
PUDONG AREA
Conservatory of Music
Huangpu Jiang
Cultural Square
Former Residence of Zhou En-Lai
Confucian Temple
LUWAN
HENGSHAN LU
Hunan Stadium
XUJIAHUI LU
LUJIABANG LU
ZHAOJIABANG LU
Penglai Park
ZHONGSHAN NANLU
0 METRES 750
0 YARDS 750

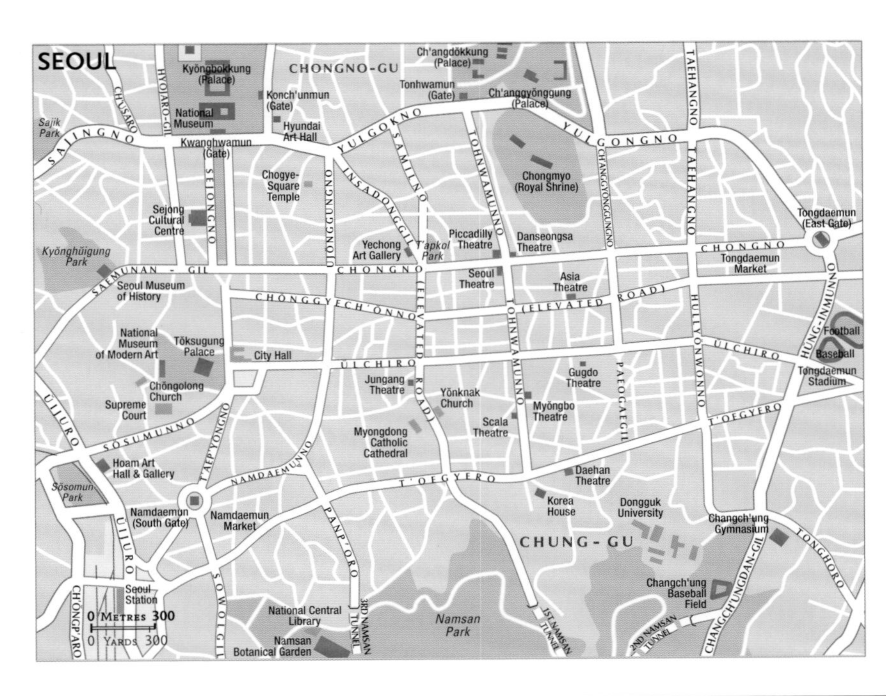
SEOUL
Kyŏngbokkung (Palace)
CHONGNO-GU
Ch'angdŏkkung (Palace)
Tonhwamun (Gate)
Ch'anggyŏnggung (Palace)
National Museum
Konch'unmun (Gate)
Hyundai Art Hall
Sajik Park
Kwanghwamun (Gate)
YULGONGNO
Chongmyo (Royal Shrine)
Chogye-Square Temple
Tongdaemun (East Gate)
Sejong Cultural Centre
Piccadilly Theatre
Danseongsa Theatre
Yechong Art Gallery
Tapkol Park
Kyŏnghŭigung Park
CHONGNO
Tongdaemun Market
Seoul Museum of History
Seoul Theatre
Asia Theatre
National Museum of Modern Art
Tŏksugung Palace
City Hall
Football
Baseball
Tongdaemun Stadium
Chŏngolong Church
Jungang Theatre
Gugdo Theatre
ULCHIRO
Supreme Court
Yŏnknak Church
Myŏngbo Theatre
Scala Theatre
Myongdong Catholic Cathedral
Hoam Art Hall & Gallery
Daehan Theatre
Sosomun Park
Namdaemun (South Gate)
Namdaemun Market
Korea House
Dongguk University
T'OEGYERO
CHUNG-GU
Changch'ung Gymnasium
Seoul Station
Changch'ung Baseball Field
Namsan Park
National Central Library
Namsan Botanical Garden
0 METRES 300
0 YARDS 300

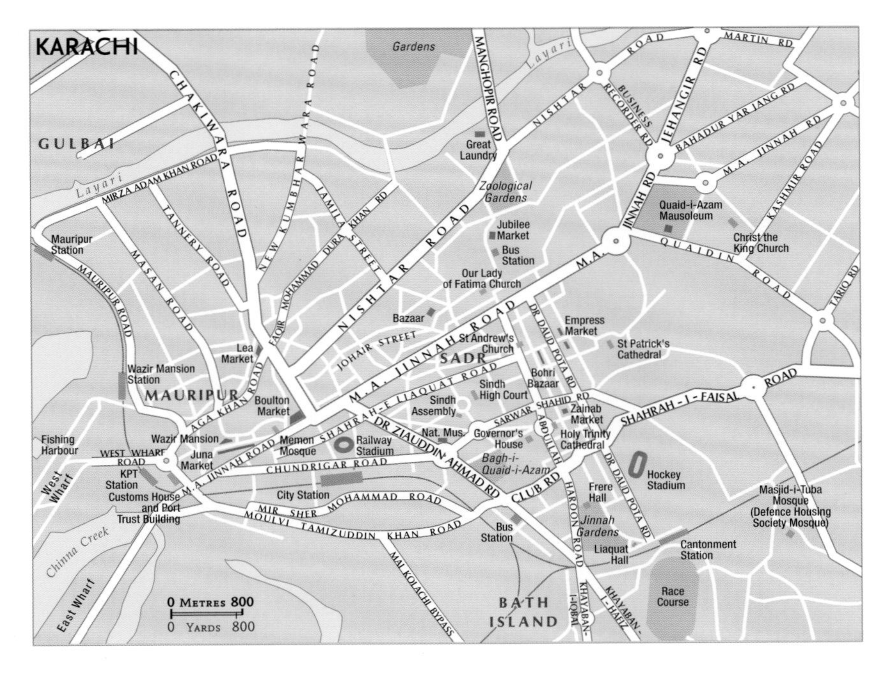
KARACHI
Gardens
MARTIN RD
GULBAI
Lyari
Great Laundry
Zoological Gardens
Quaid-i-Azam Mausoleum
Mauripur Station
Jubilee Market
Bus Station
Christ the King Church
Our Lady of Fatima Church
NISHTAR ROAD
M.A. JINNAH RD
Empress Market
St Patrick's Cathedral
Bazaar
St Andrew's Church
SADR
Lea Market
Bohri Bazaar
Sindh High Court
Wazir Mansion Station
MAURIPUR
Sindh Assembly
Zainab Market
Boulton Market
SHAHRAH-I-FAISAL
Fishing Harbour
Wazir Mansion
Juna Market
Memon Mosque
Railway Stadium
Nat. Mus.
Governor's House
Holy Trinity Cathedral
Bagh-i-Quaid-i-Azam
KPT Station
Customs House and Port Trust Building
CHUNDRIGAR ROAD
City Station
Hockey Stadium
West Wharf
Frere Hall
Masjid-i-Tuba Mosque (Defence Housing Society Mosque)
Chinna Creek
Bus Station
Jinnah Gardens
Liaquat Hall
Cantonment Station
East Wharf
Race Course
BATH ISLAND
0 METRES 800
0 YARDS 800

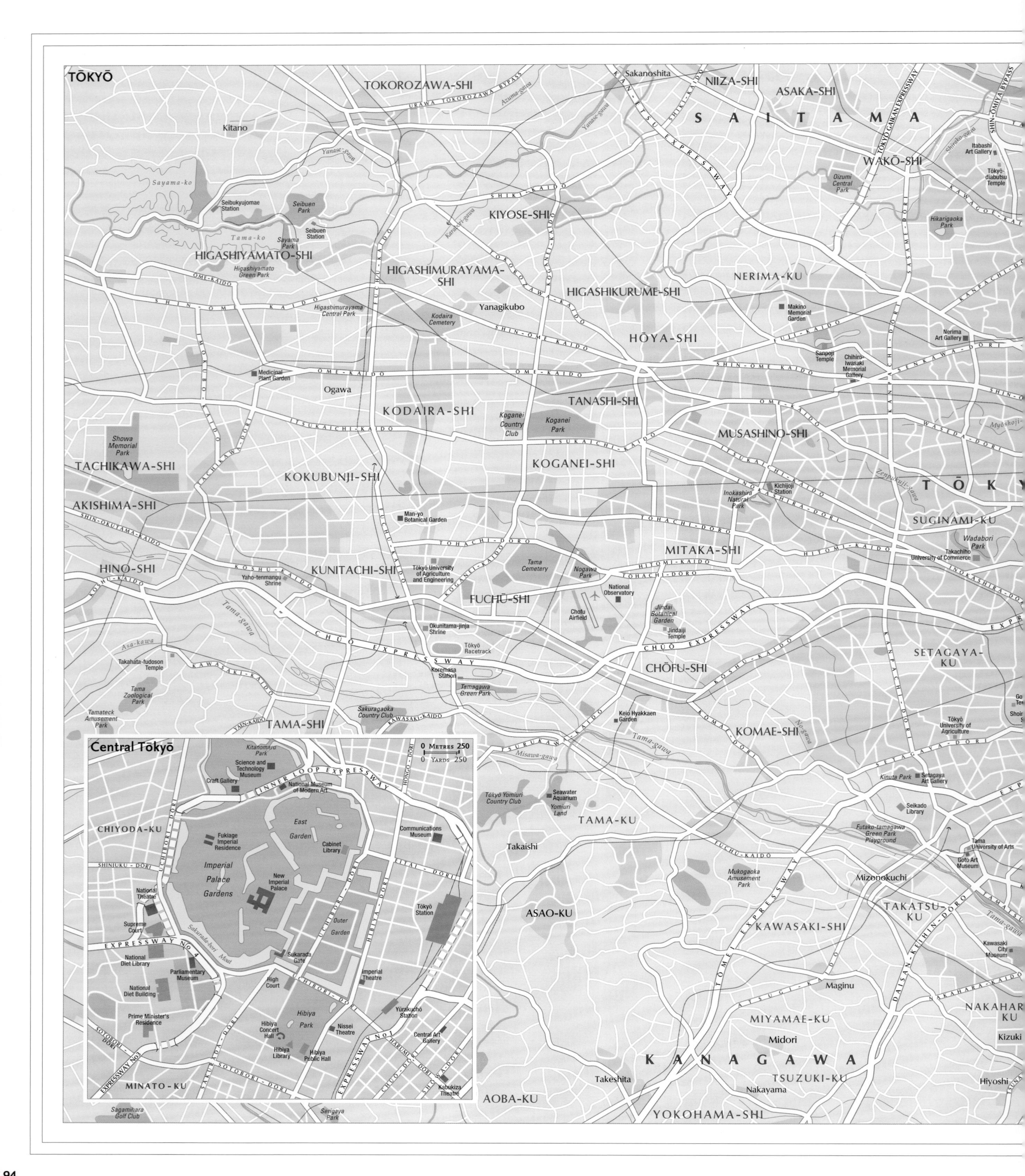

TŌKYŌ

TOKOROZAWA-SHI

Kitano

Sayama-ko

Seibukyujomae
Station

*Seibuen
Park*

Tama-ko

*Sayama
Park*

Seibuen
Station

HIGASHIYAMATO-SHI

*Higashiyamato
Green Park*

Ogawa

Medicinal
Plant Garden

*Showa
Memorial
Park*

TACHIKAWA-SHI

AKISHIMA-SHI

HINO-SHI

Tama-gawa

Takahata-fudoson Temple

*Tama
Zoological
Park*

*Tamateck
Amusement
Park*

TAMA-SHI

*Sagamihara
Golf Club*

SAITAMA

Sakanoshita

NIIZA-SHI

ASAKA-SHI

WAKŌ-SHI

Oizumi
Central
Park

Itabashi
Art Gallery

Tōkyō-
diabutsu
Temple

Hikarigaoka
Park

KIYOSE-SHI

HIGASHIMURAYAMA-
SHI

Yanagikubo

NERIMA-KU

Makino
Memorial
Garden

Nerima
Art Gallery

HIGASHIKURUME-SHI

HŌYA-SHI

Sanpoji
Temple

Chihiro-
Iwasaki
Memorial
Gallery

*Higashimurayama
Central Park*

*Kodaira
Cemetery*

KODAIRA-SHI

*Koganei
Country
Club*

*Koganei
Park*

TANASHI-SHI

SHIN-OME-KAIDO

MUSASHINO-SHI

KOGANEI-SHI

Kichijoji
Station

*Inokashira
Natural
Park*

TŌKY

SUGINAMI-KU

*Wadabori
Park*

Takachiho
University of Commerce

KOKUBUNJI-SHI

Man-yo
Botanical Garden

TOHACHI-DORO

MITAKA-SHI

KUNITACHI-SHI

Yaho-tenmangu
Shrine

Tōkyō University
of Agriculture
and Engineering

*Tama
Cemetery*

*Nogawa
Park*

National
Observatory

FUCHŪ-SHI

Okunitama-jinja
Shrine

Chōfu
Airfield

*Jindai
Botanical
Garden*

Jindaiji
Temple

CHŪŌ EXPRESSWAY

CHŪŌ EXPRESSWAY

Tōkyō
Racetrack

CHŌFU-SHI

SETAGAYA-
KU

Keio Hyakkaen
Garden

KOMAE-SHI

Koremasa
Station

*Tamagawa
Green Park*

*Sakuragaoka
Country Club*

Tama-gawa

KAWASAKI-SHI

Misawa-gawa

Tōkyō Yomiuri
Country Club

Seawater
Aquarium

*Yomiuri
Land*

TAMA-KU

Takaishi

ASAO-KU

*Mukogaoka
Amusement
Park*

Kinuta Park

Setagaya
Art Gallery

*Futako-tamagawa
Green Park
Playground*

Seikado
Library

Goto Art
Museum

Tama
University of Arts

Mizonokuchi

TAKATSU-
KU

Kawasaki
City
Museum

Maginu

MIYAMAE-KU

Midori

NAKAHAR
KU

Kizuki

KANAGAWA

Takeshita

TSUZUKI-KU

Nakayama

AOBA-KU

YOKOHAMA-SHI

Hiyoshi

Central Tōkyō

*Kitanomaru
Park*

Science and
Technology
Museum

Craft Gallery

National Museum
of Modern Art

*East
Garden*

Cabinet
Library

Communications
Museum

INNER LOOP EXPRESSWAY

CHIYODA-KU

Fukiage
Imperial
Residence

*Imperial
Palace
Gardens*

New
Imperial
Palace

SHINJUKU-DORI

National
Theatre

Supreme
Court

*Outer
Garden*

Tōkyō
Station

National
Diet Library

Parliamentary
Museum

High
Court

Imperial
Theatre

National
Diet Building

Prime Minister's
Residence

Hibiya
Concert
Hall

*Hibiya
Park*

Nissei
Theatre

Yūrakuchō
Station

Central Art
Gallery

Hibiya
Library

Hibiya
Public Hall

Sakurada
Gate

Sukarada
Gate

Kabukiza
Theatre

MINATO-KU

*Serigaya
Park*

0 METRES 250
0 YARDS 250

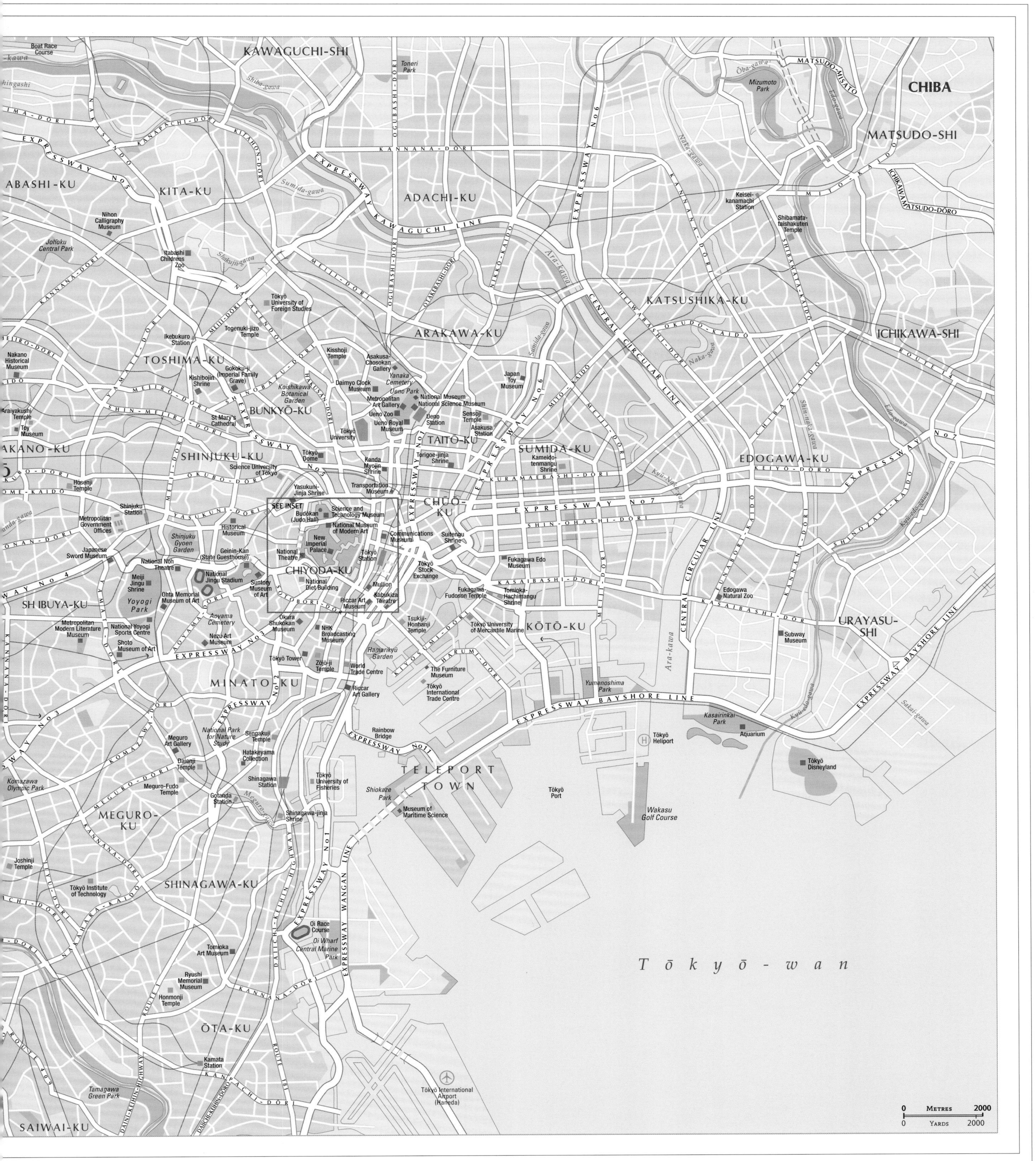

KAWAGUCHI-SHI

CHIBA

MATSUDO-SHI

Boat Race
Course

Toneri
Park

Mizumoto
Park

ABASHI-KU

KITA-KU

ADACHI-KU

KATSUSHIKA-KU

Keisei-
kanamachi
Station

ICHIKAWA-SHI

Nihon
Calligraphy
Museum

Shibamata-
taishakuten
Temple

Joōhoku
Central Park

Itabashi
Childrens
Zoo

Tōkyō
University of
Foreign Studies

Kisshoji
Temple

Asakusa-
Chosokan
Gallery

Japan
Toy
Museum

TOSHIMA-KU

Nakano
Historical
Museum

Gokoku-ji
(Imperial Family
Grave)

Yanaka
Cemetery

Ikebukuro
Station

Togenuki-jizo
Temple

Daimyo Clock
Museum

Ueno Park

National Museum

SUMIDA-KU

Kishibojin
Shrine

Koishikawa
Botanical
Garden

Metropolitan
Art Gallery.

National Science Museum

Araiyakushi
Temple

St Mary's
Cathedral

BUNKYŌ-KU

Ueno Zoo

Ueno Royal
Museum

Sensōji
Temple

EDOGAWA-KU

Toy
Museum

Ueno
Station

Asakusa
Station

AKANO-KU

Tōkyō
University

TAITŌ-KU

SHINJUKU-KU

Tōkyō
Dome

Kanda
Myojin
Shrine

Torigoe-jinja
Shrine

Kameido-
tenmangu
Shrine

Hosenji
Temple

Science University
of Tōkyō

Transportation
Museum

Shinjuku
Station

Yasukuni-
Jinja Shrine

SEE INSET

Science and
Technology Museum

Metropolitan
Government
Offices

Historical
Museum

Budōkan
(Judo Hall)

National Museum
of Modern Art

CHUŌ-
KU

Communications
Museum

Suitengu
Shrine

Japanese
Sword Museum

Shinjuku
Gyoen
Garden

Geinin-Kan
(State Guesthouse)

New Imperial
Palace

National
Theatre

Tōkyō
Station

Fukagawa Edo
Museum

National Noh
Theatre

National Jingu Stadium

Suntory
Museum
of Art

CHIYODA-KU

Tōkyō
Stock
Exchange

Meiji
Jingu
Shrine

Mullion

SHIBUYA-KU

Yoyogi
Park

Ohta Memorial
Museum of Art

National
Diet Building

Riccar Art
Museum

Kabukiza
Theatre

Fukagawa-
Fudoson Temple

Tomioka-
Hachimangu
Shrine

Edogawa
Natural Zoo

KŌTŌ-KU

URAYASU-
SHI

Metropolitan
Modern Literature
Museum

National Yoyogi
Sports Centre

Aoyama
Cemetery

Okura
Shukokan
Museum

NHK
Broadcasting
Museum

Tsukiji-
Honhanji
Temple

Tōkyō University
of Mercantile Marine

Subway
Museum

Shoto
Museum of Art

Nezu Art
Museum

Hamarikyu
Garden

Tōkyō Tower

Zojo-ji
Temple

World
Trade Centre

The Furniture
Museum

Kasairinkai-
Park

Aquarium

MINATO-KU

Riccar
Art Gallery

Tōkyō
International
Trade Centre

Yumenoshima
Park

Meguro
Art Gallery

National Park
for Nature Study

Sengakuji
Temple

Rainbow
Bridge

Tōkyō
Heliport

Tōkyō
Disneyland

Komazawa
Olympic Park

Daianji
Temple

Hatakeyama
Collection

TELEPORT
TOWN

MEGURO-
KU

Meguro-Fudo
Temple

Shinagawa
Station

Shiokaze
Park

Tōkyō
Port

Wakasu
Golf Course

Gotanda
Station

Tōkyō University
of Fisheries

Joshinji
Temple

Shinagawa-jinja
Shrine

Museum of
Maritime Science

Tōkyō Institute
of Technology

SHINAGAWA-KU

Tomoka
Art Museum

Oi Race
Course

Ryushi
Memorial
Museum

Oi Wharf
Central Marine
Park

Tōkyō-wan

Honmonji
Temple

Kamata
Station

ŌTA-KU

Tamagawa
Green Park

Tōkyō International
Airport
(Haneda)

SAIWAI-KU

0   METRES   2000

0   YARDS   2000

© Collins Bartholomew Ltd

95

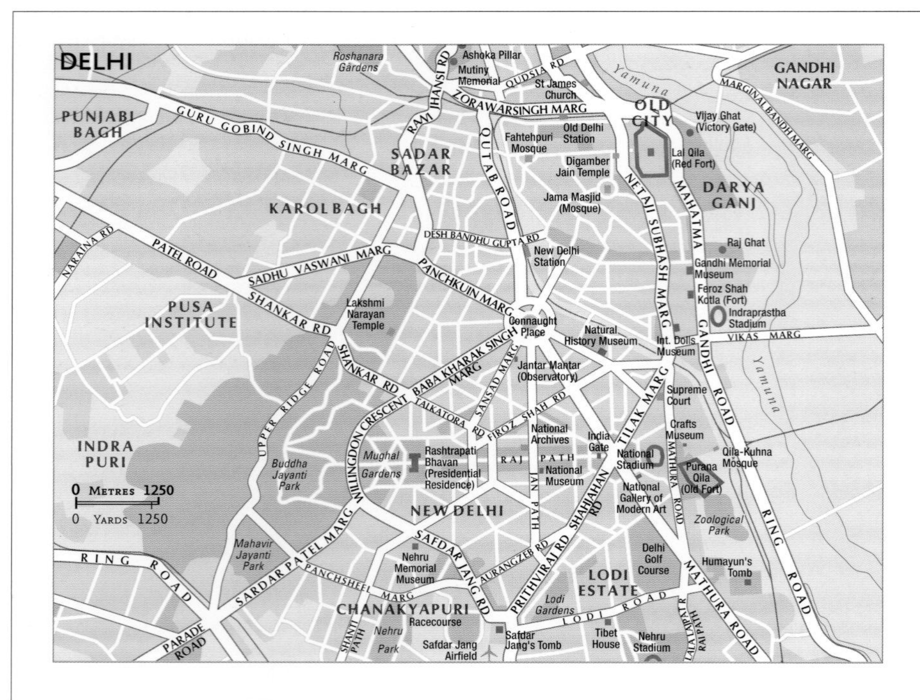
DELHI
Roshanara Gardens
Ashoka Pillar
Mutiny Memorial
St James Church
GANDHI NAGAR
PUNJABI BAGH
OLD CITY
Vijay Ghat (Victory Gate)
Old Delhi Station
Fahtehpuri Mosque
Digamber Jain Temple
Lal Qila (Red Fort)
SADAR BAZAR
DARYA GANJ
Jama Masjid (Mosque)
KAROL BAGH
New Delhi Station
Raj Ghat
Gandhi Memorial Museum
Feroz Shah Kotla (Fort)
Indraprastha Stadium
PUSA INSTITUTE
Lakshmi Narayan Temple
Connaught Place
Natural History Museum
Int. Dolls Museum
Jantar Mantar (Observatory)
Supreme Court
Crafts Museum
National Archives
India Gate
National Stadium
Rashtrapati Bhavan (Presidential Residence)
Purana Qila (Old Fort)
Qila-Kuhna Mosque
National Museum
National Gallery of Modern Art
INDRA PURI
Buddha Jayanti Park
Mughal Gardens
NEW DELHI
Zoological Park
Mahavir Jayanti Park
Nehru Memorial Museum
Delhi Golf Course
Humayun's Tomb
LODI ESTATE
CHANAKYAPURI
Racecourse
Lodi Gardens
Nehru Park
Safdar Jang Airfield
Safdar Jang's Tomb
Tibet House
Nehru Stadium
RING ROAD
0 Metres 1250
0 Yards 1250

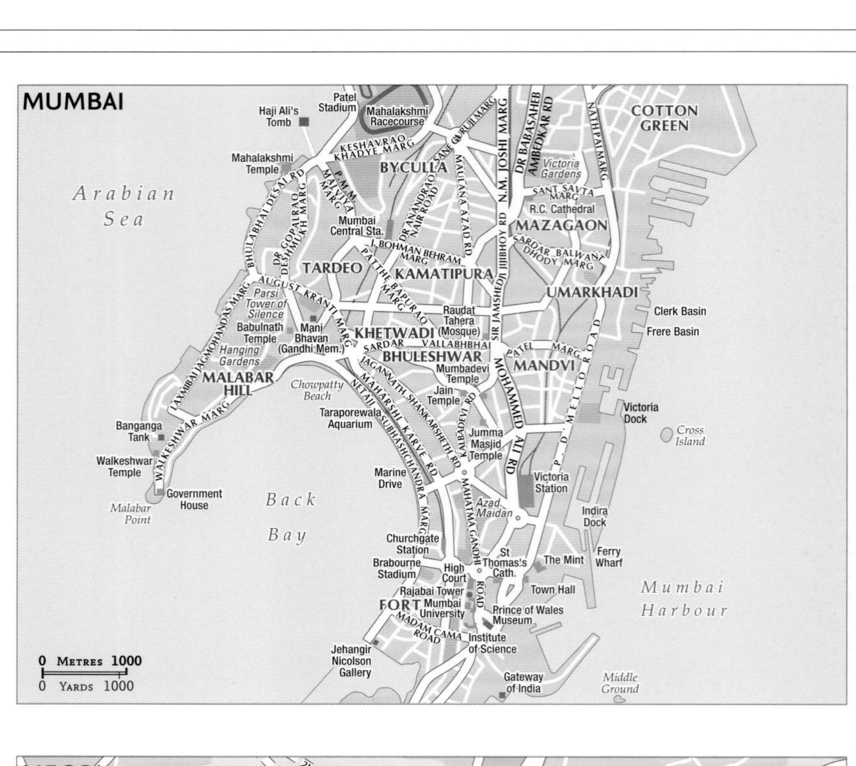
MUMBAI
Patel Stadium
Haji Ali's Tomb
Mahalakshmi Racecourse
COTTON GREEN
Mahalakshmi Temple
BYCULLA
Victoria Gardens
Arabian Sea
R.C. Cathedral
Mumbai Central Sta.
MAZAGAON
TARDEO
KAMATIPURA
UMARKHADI
Parsi Tower of Silence
Babulnath Temple
KHETWADI
Raudat Tahera (Mosque)
Clerk Basin
Frere Basin
Hanging Gardens
Mani Bhavan (Gandhi Mem.)
BHULESHWAR
Mumbadevi Temple
MANDVI
MALABAR HILL
Chowpatty Beach
Jain Temple
Taraporewala Aquarium
Victoria Dock
Cross Island
Banganga Tank
Jumma Masjid
Walkeshwar Temple
Marine Drive
Victoria Station
Malabar Point
Government House
Back Bay
Azad Maidan
Indira Dock
Churchgate Station
Brabourne Stadium
St Thomas's Cath.
The Mint
Ferry Wharf
High Court
Rajabai Tower
Town Hall
Mumbai Harbour
FORT
Mumbai University
Prince of Wales Museum
Institute of Science
Jehangir Nicolson Gallery
Gateway of India
Middle Ground
0 Metres 1000
0 Yards 1000

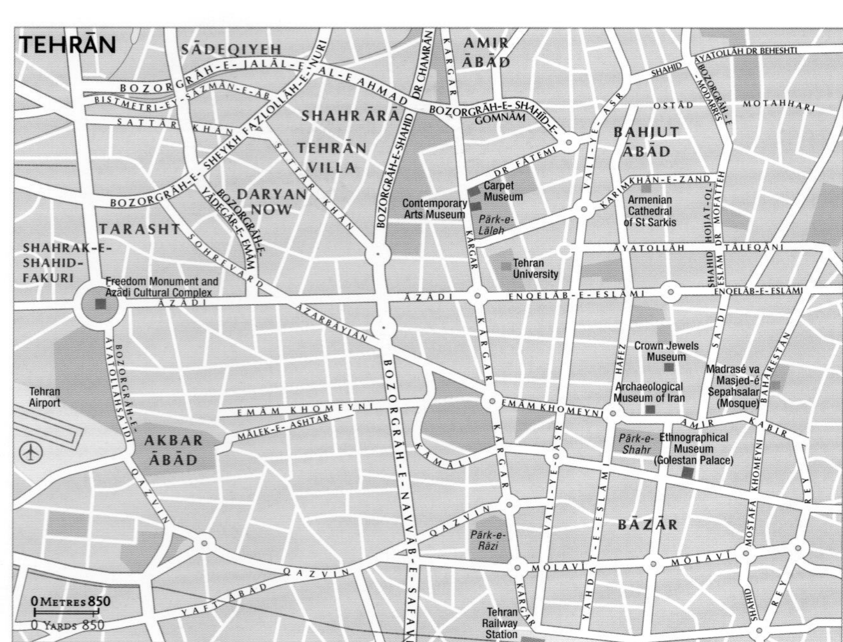
TEHRĀN
SĀDEQIYEH
AMĪR ĀBĀD
SHAHRĀRĀ
TEHRĀN VILLA
BAHJUT ĀBĀD
DARYAN NOW
Contemporary Arts Museum
Carpet Museum
Armenian Cathedral of St Sarkis
TARASHT
Pārk-e-Lāleh
SHAHRAK-E-SHAHID-FAKURI
Tehran University
Freedom Monument and Āzādī Cultural Complex
Crown Jewels Museum
Tehran Airport
Archaeological Museum of Iran
Madrasé va Masjed-e-Sepahsalar (Mosque)
AKBAR ĀBĀD
Pārk-e-Shahr
Ethnographical Museum (Golestan Palace)
BĀZĀR
Pārk-e-Rāzi
Tehran Railway Station
0 Metres 850
0 Yards 850

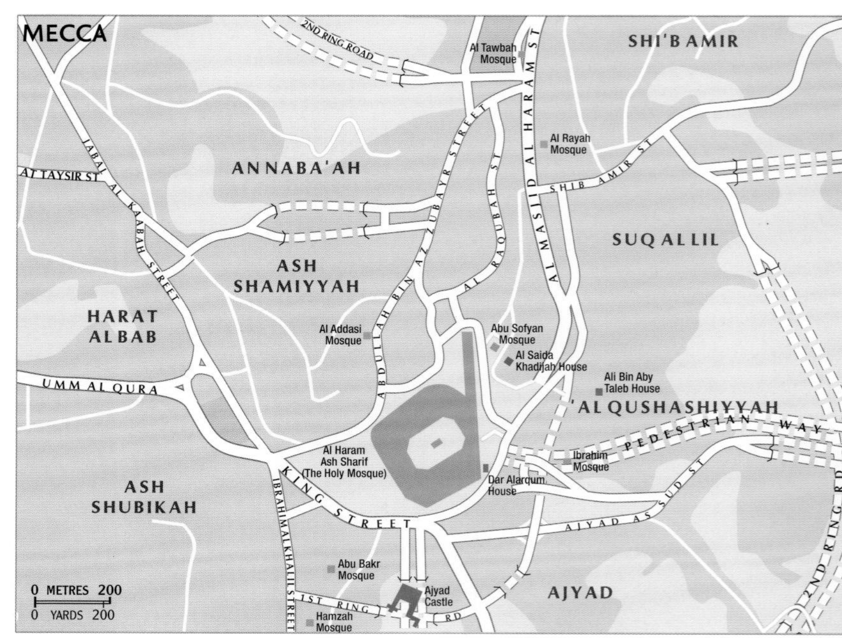
MECCA
2ND RING ROAD
Al Tawbah Mosque
SHI'B AMIR
Al Rayah Mosque
AT TAYSIR ST
ANNABA'AH
SUQ AL LIL
ASH SHAMIYYAH
HARAT AL BAB
Al Addasi Mosque
Abu Sofyan Mosque
Al Saida Khadijah House
Ali Bin Aby Taleb House
UMM AL QURA
'AL QUSHASHIYYAH
PEDESTRIAN WAY
Al Haram Ash Sharif (The Holy Mosque)
Ibrahim Mosque
Dar Alarqum House
ASH SHUBIKAH
KING STREET
AJYAD AS SUD ST
Abu Bakr Mosque
AJYAD
Ajyad Castle
Hamzah Mosque
0 Metres 200
0 Yards 200

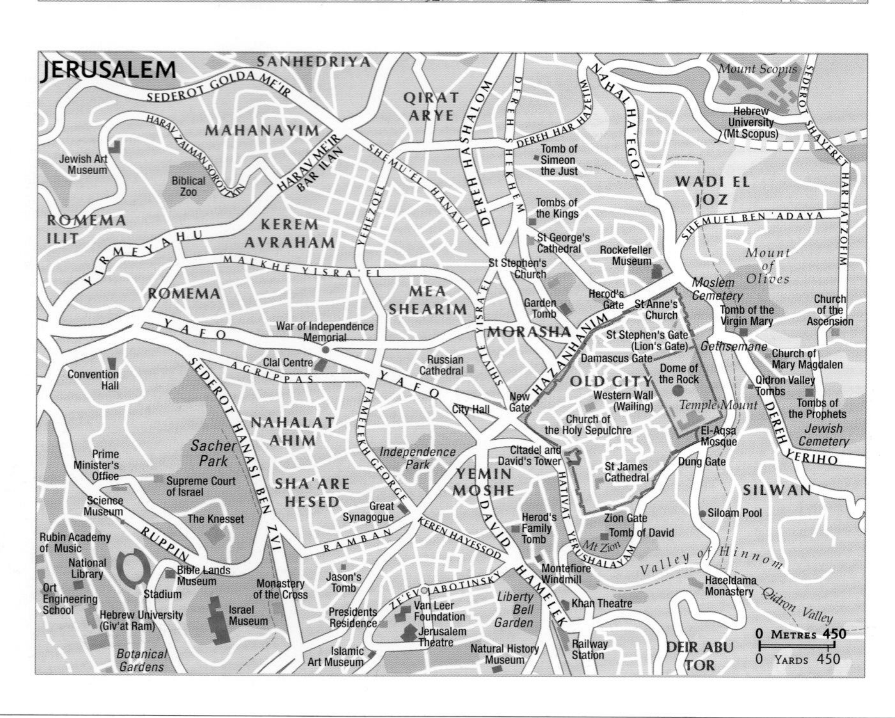
JERUSALEM
SANHEDRIYA
Mount Scopus
QIRYAT ARYE
Hebrew University (Mt Scopus)
MAHANAYIM
Jewish Art Museum
Tomb of Simeon the Just
Biblical Zoo
WADI EL JOZ
Tombs of the Kings
ROMEMA ILIT
KEREM AVRAHAM
St George's Cathedral
Rockefeller Museum
Mount of Olives
St Stephen's Church
ROMEMA
MEA SHEARIM
Herod's Gate
St Anne's Church
Moslem Cemetery
Church of the Ascension
Garden Tomb
Tomb of the Virgin Mary
War of Independence Memorial
MORASHA
St Stephen's Gate (Lion's Gate)
Gethsemane
Clal Centre
Damascus Gate
Church of Mary Magdalen
Convention Hall
Russian Cathedral
OLD CITY
Dome of the Rock
Qidron Valley Tombs
City Hall
Western Wall (Wailing)
Temple Mount
Tombs of the Prophets
NAHALAT AHIM
Church of the Holy Sepulchre
Jewish Cemetery
Sacher Park
Independence Park
Citadel and David's Tower
El-Aqsa Mosque
Prime Minister's Office
YEMIN MOSHE
St James Cathedral
Dung Gate
Supreme Court of Israel
SHA'ARE HESED
SILWAN
Science Museum
Great Synagogue
Siloam Pool
The Knesset
Herod's Family Tomb
Zion Gate
Rubin Academy of Music
Tomb of David
National Library
Mt Zion
Bible Lands Museum
Monastery of the Cross
Jason's Tomb
Montefiore Windmill
Valley of Hinnom
Ort Engineering School
Stadium
Hebrew University (Giv'at Ram)
Israel Museum
Van Leer Foundation
Liberty Bell Garden
Haceldama Monastery
Presidents Residence
Jerusalem Theatre
Khan Theatre
Qidron Valley
Botanical Gardens
Islamic Art Museum
Natural History Museum
Railway Station
DEIR ABU TOR
0 Metres 450
0 Yards 450

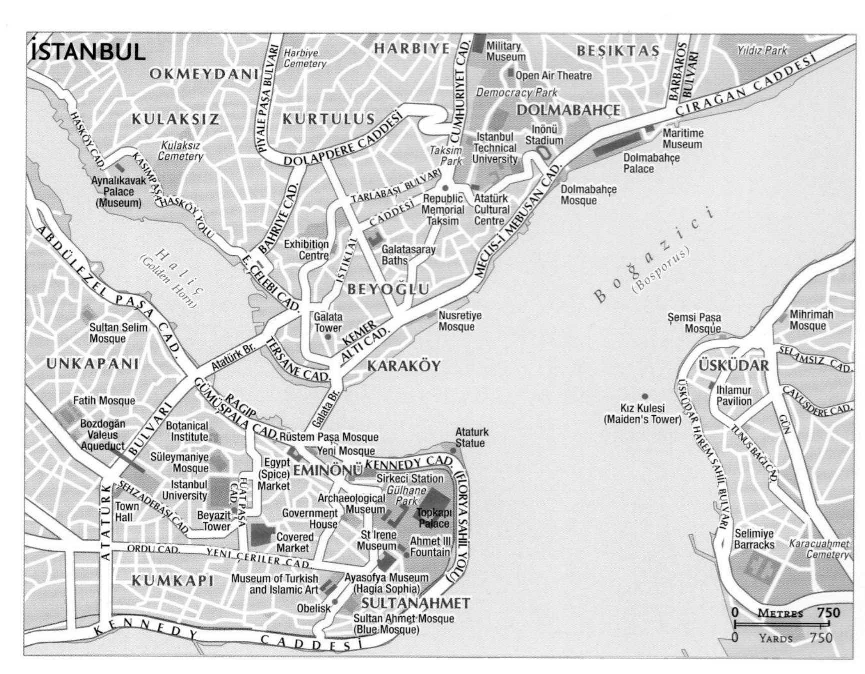
İSTANBUL
HARBIYE
Military Museum
BEŞIKTAŞ
Yıldız Park
OKMEYDANI
Harbiye Cemetery
Open Air Theatre
Democracy Park
DOLMABAHCE
ÇIRAĞAN CADDESI
KULAKSIZ
KURTULUŞ
İnönü Stadium
Maritime Museum
Kulaksız Cemetery
Istanbul Technical University
Dolmabahçe Palace
Taksim Park
Aynalıkavak Palace (Museum)
Republic Memorial Taksim
Atatürk Cultural Centre
Dolmabahçe Mosque
Exhibition Centre
Galatasaray Baths
Haliç (Golden Horn)
BEYOĞLU
Boğaziçi (Bosporus)
Galata Tower
Nusretiye Mosque
Sultan Selim Mosque
Şemsi Paşa Mosque
Mihrimah Mosque
UNKAPANI
KARAKÖY
ÜSKÜDAR
Fatih Mosque
Kız Kulesi (Maiden's Tower)
Ihlamur Pavilion
Bozdoğan Valeus Aqueduct
Botanical Institute
Rüstem Paşa Mosque
Ataturk Statue
Süleymaniye Mosque
Yeni Mosque
EMINÖNÜ
KENNEDY CAD.
Istanbul University
Egypt (Spice) Market
Sirkeci Station
Gülhane Park
Archaeological Museum
Topkapı Palace
Town Hall
Beyazit Tower
Government House
Covered Market
St Irene Museum
Ahmet III Fountain
Selimiye Barracks
Karacaahmet Cemetery
KUMKAPI
Museum of Turkish and Islamic Art
Ayasofya Museum (Hagia Sophia)
SULTANAHMET
Obelisk
Sultan Ahmet Mosque (Blue Mosque)
KENNEDY CADDESI
0 Metres 750
0 Yards 750

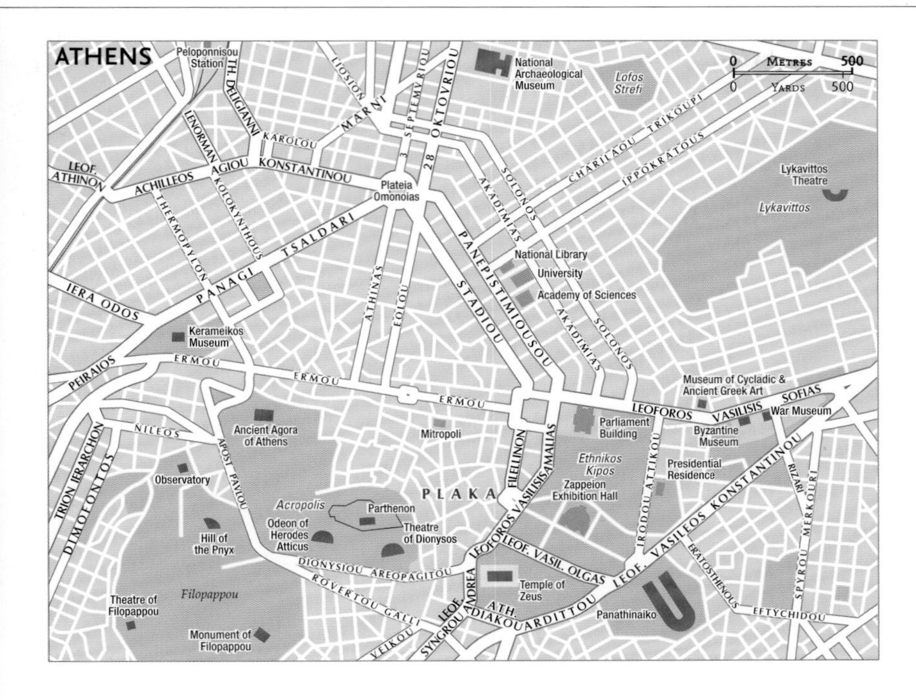
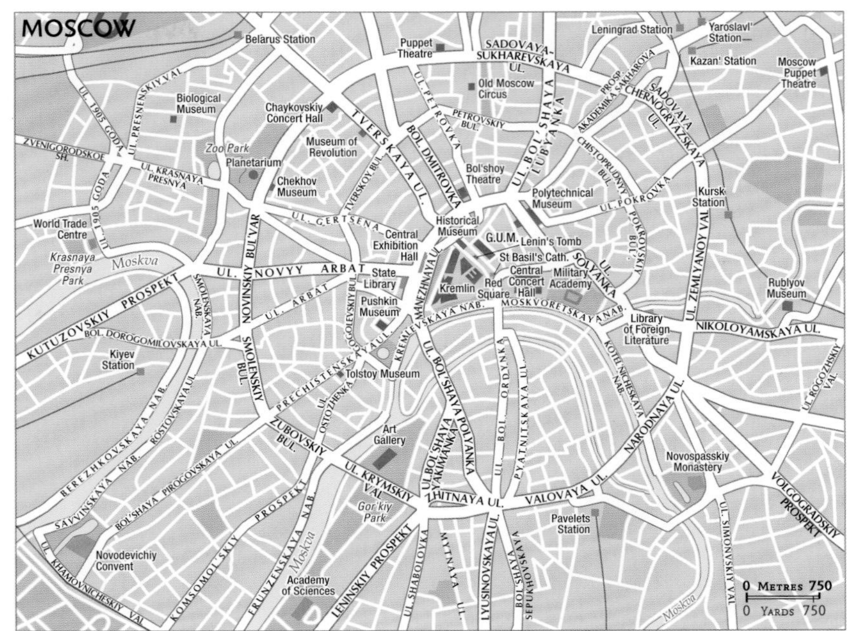
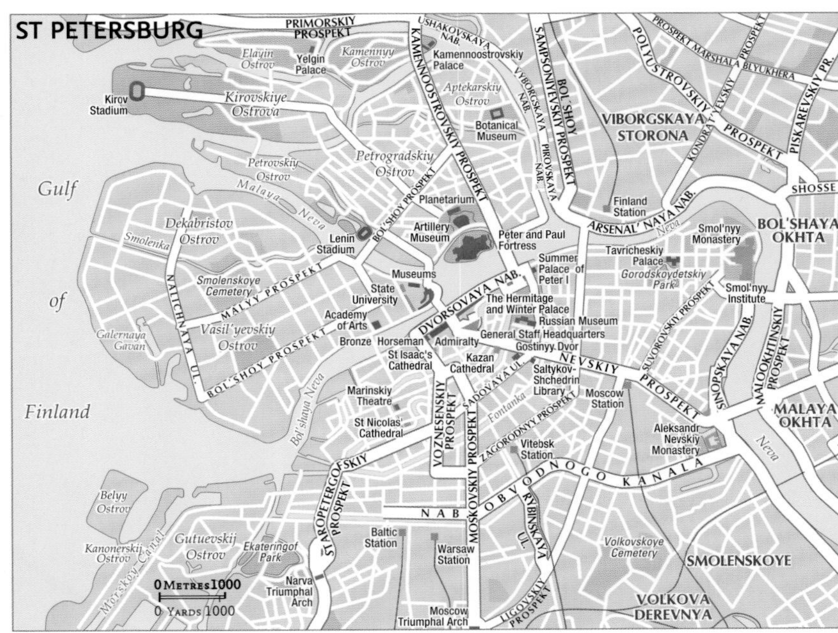
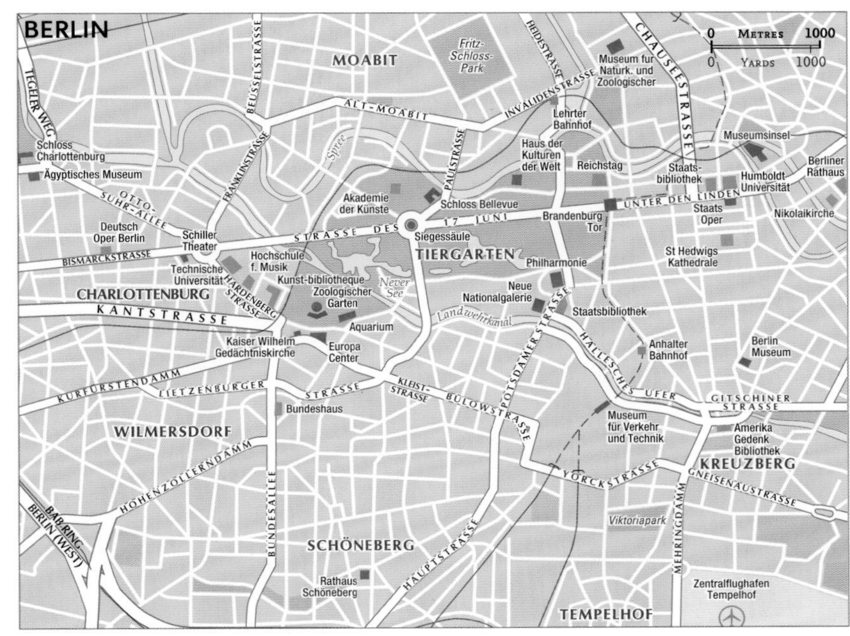
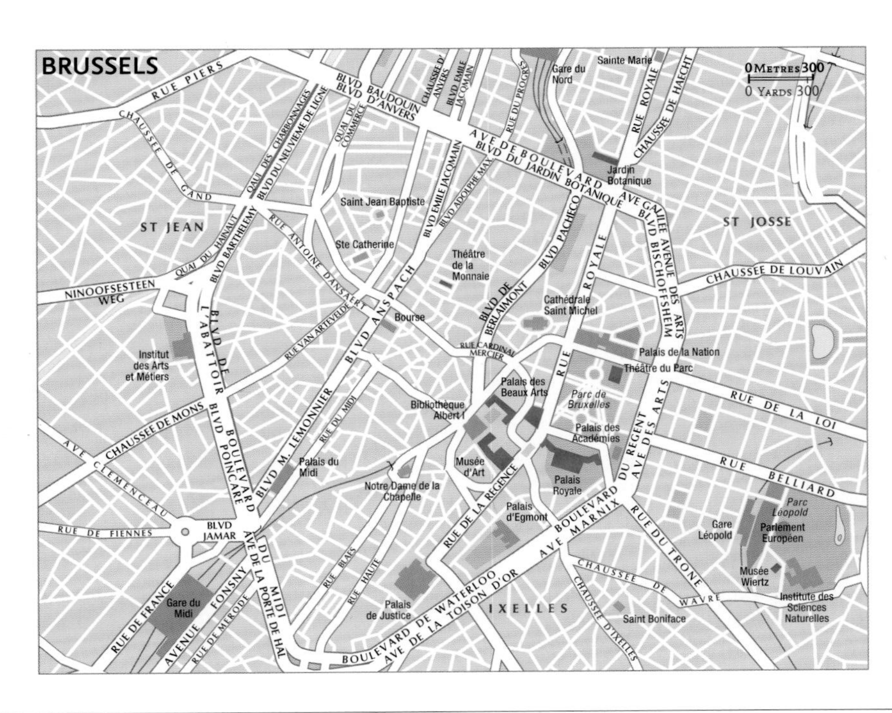
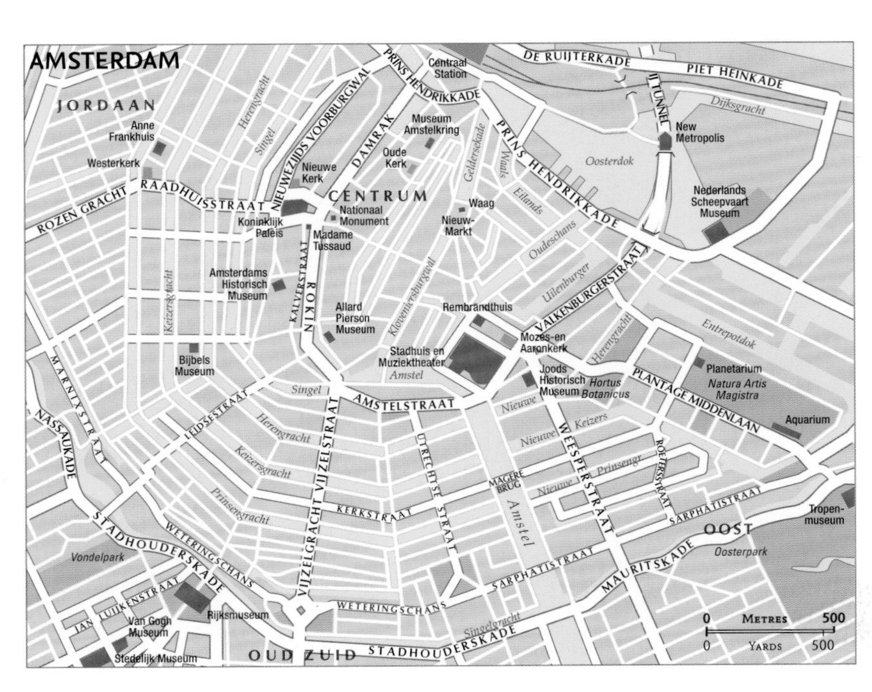

© Collins Bartholomew Ltd

ATHENS
Metres 500
Yards 500
Peloponnisou Station
National Archaeological Museum
Lofos Strefi
Lykavittos Theatre
Lykavittos
Plateia Omonoias
National Library
University
Academy of Sciences
Kerameikos Museum
Museum of Cycladic & Ancient Greek Art
Parliament Building
Byzantine Museum
War Museum
Ancient Agora of Athens
Mitropoli
Ethnikos Kipos
Zappeion Exhibition Hall
Presidential Residence
Observatory
PLAKA
Acropolis
Parthenon
Odeon of Herodes Atticus
Theatre of Dionysos
Hill of the Pnyx
Temple of Zeus
Filopappou
Theatre of Filopappou
Monument of Filopappou
Panathinaiko
KONSTANTINOU
ACHILLEOS
PANAGI TSALDARI
IERA ODOS
PEIRAIOS
ERMOU
STADIOU
PANEPISTIMIOU
LEOFOROS VASILISIS SOFIAS
DIONYSIOU AREOPAGITOU
MOSCOW
Belarus Station
Puppet Theatre
SADOVAYA-SUKHAREVSKAYA UL.
Old Moscow Circus
Leningrad Station
Yaroslavl' Station
Kazan' Station
Moscow Puppet Theatre
Biological Museum
Chaykovskiy Concert Hall
Zoo Park
Planetarium
Museum of Revolution
Chekhov Museum
Bol'shoy Theatre
Polytechnical Museum
World Trade Centre
Krasnaya Presnya Park
Moskva
Historical Museum
Central Exhibition Hall
G.U.M.
Lenin's Tomb
St Basil's Cath.
State Library
Kremlin
Red Square
Central Concert Hall
Military Academy
Pushkin Museum
Kursk Station
Rublyov Museum
Library of Foreign Literature
NIKOLOYAMSKAYA UL.
Kiyev Station
Tolstoy Museum
Art Gallery
Gor'kiy Park
Novospasskiy Monastery
Pavelets Station
Novodevichiy Convent
Academy of Sciences
NOVYY ARBAT
KUTUZOVSKIY PROSPEKT
LENINSKIY PROSPEKT
VALOVAYA UL.
Metres 750
Yards 750
ST PETERSBURG
PRIMORSKIY PROSPEKT
Elagin Ostrov
Yelgin Palace
Kamennyy Ostrov
Kamennoostrovskiy Palace
Kirov Stadium
Kirovskiye Ostrova
Aptekarskiy Ostrov
Botanical Museum
VIBORGSKAYA STORONA
Petrogradskiy Ostrov
Gulf of Finland
Dekabristov Ostrov
Planetarium
Artillery Museum
Lenin Stadium
Peter and Paul Fortress
Finland Station
ARSENAL'NAYA NAB.
Smol'nyy Monastery
BOL'SHAYA OKHTA
Tavricheskiy Palace
Summer Palace of Peter I
Smolenskoye Cemetery
Vasil'yevskiy Ostrov
Museums
State University
Academy of Arts
The Hermitage and Winter Palace
Russian Museum
General Staff Headquarters
Smol'nyy Institute
Bronze Horseman
Admiralty
St Isaac's Cathedral
Kazan Cathedral
Gostinyy Dvor
Saltykov-Shchedrin Library
NEVSKIY PROSPEKT
Moscow Station
Marinskiy Theatre
St Nicolas' Cathedral
Aleksandr Nevskiy Monastery
MALAYA OKHTA
Vitebsk Station
Belyy Ostrov
Gutuevskij Ostrov
Ekateringof Park
Baltic Station
Warsaw Station
Volkovskoye Cemetery
SMOLENSKOYE
Narva Triumphal Arch
Moscow Triumphal Arch
VOLKOVA DEREVNYA
Metres 1000
Yards 1000
BERLIN
MOABIT
Fritz-Schloss-Park
Museum für Naturk. und Zoologischer
Metres 1000
Yards 1000
ALT-MOABIT
Lehrter Bahnhof
Haus der Kulturen der Welt
Reichstag
Museumsinsel
Berliner Rathaus
Schloss Charlottenburg
Ägyptisches Museum
Akademie der Künste
Schloss Bellevue
Brandenburg Tor
UNTER DEN LINDEN
Staatsbibliothek
Humboldt Universität
Staats Oper
Nikolaikirche
Deutsch Oper Berlin
Schiller Theater
Siegessäule
STRASSE DES 17 JUNI
TIERGARTEN
St Hedwigs Kathedrale
Technische Universität
Hochschule f. Musik
Kunst-bibliothek
Zoologischer Garten
Philharmonie
CHARLOTTENBURG
KANTSTRASSE
Neue Nationalgalerie
Staatsbibliothek
Aquarium
Kaiser Wilhelm Gedächtniskirche
Europa Center
Anhalter Bahnhof
Berlin Museum
KURFÜRSTENDAMM
Bundeshaus
WILMERSDORF
Museum für Verkehr und Technik
Amerika Gedenk Bibliothek
KREUZBERG
Viktoriapark
SCHÖNEBERG
Rathaus Schöneberg
TEMPELHOF
Zentralflughafen Tempelhof
BRUSSELS
RUE PIERS
Gare du Nord
Sainte Marie
Metres 300
Yards 300
BLVD D'ANVERS
BLVD BAUDOUIN
AVE DE BOULEVARD
BLVD DU JARDIN BOTANIQUE
Jardin Botanique
Saint Jean Baptiste
ST JEAN
ST JOSSE
Ste Catherine
Théâtre de la Monnaie
CHAUSSÉE DE LOUVAIN
NINOOFSESTEEN WEG
Cathédrale Saint Michel
Bourse
Institut des Arts et Metiers
Palais de la Nation
Théâtre du Parc
Palais des Beaux Arts
Parc de Bruxelles
Bibliothèque Albert I
RUE DE LA LOI
Palais des Académies
Palais du Midi
Musée d'Art
Palais Royale
RUE BELLIARD
Notre Dame de la Chapelle
Palais d'Egmont
Gare Leopold
Parc Leopold
Parlement Europeen
BLVD JAMAR
Gare du Midi
Musée Wiertz
Palais de Justice
IXELLES
Saint Boniface
Institute des Sciences Naturelles
BOULEVARD DE WATERLOO
AVE DE LA TOISON D'OR
AMSTERDAM
JORDAAN
Centraal Station
DE RUIJTERKADE
PIET HEINKADE
PRINS HENDRIKKADE
Anne Frankhuis
Westerkerk
Museum Amstelkring
Oude Kerk
New Metropolis
Oosterdok
Nieuwe Kerk
CENTRUM
Koninklijk Paleis
Nationaal Monument
Madame Tussaud
Waag
Nieuw-Markt
Nederlands Scheepvaart Museum
RAADHUISSTRAAT
ROZENGRACHT
DAMRAK
Amsterdams Historisch Museum
Allard Pierson Museum
Rembrandthuis
Stadhuis en Muziektheater
Mozes-en Aaronkerk
Joods Historisch Museum
Hortus Botanicus
Planetarium
Natura Artis Magistra
Aquarium
Bijbels Museum
AMSTELSTRAAT
VALKENBURGERSTRAAT
PLANTAGE MIDDENLAAN
VIJZELGRACHT
Amstel
Tropen-museum
OOST
Oosterpark
Vondelpark
STADHOUDERSKADE
Rijksmuseum
Van Gogh Museum
Stedelijk Museum
OUD ZUID
MAURITSKADE
Metres 500
Yards 500

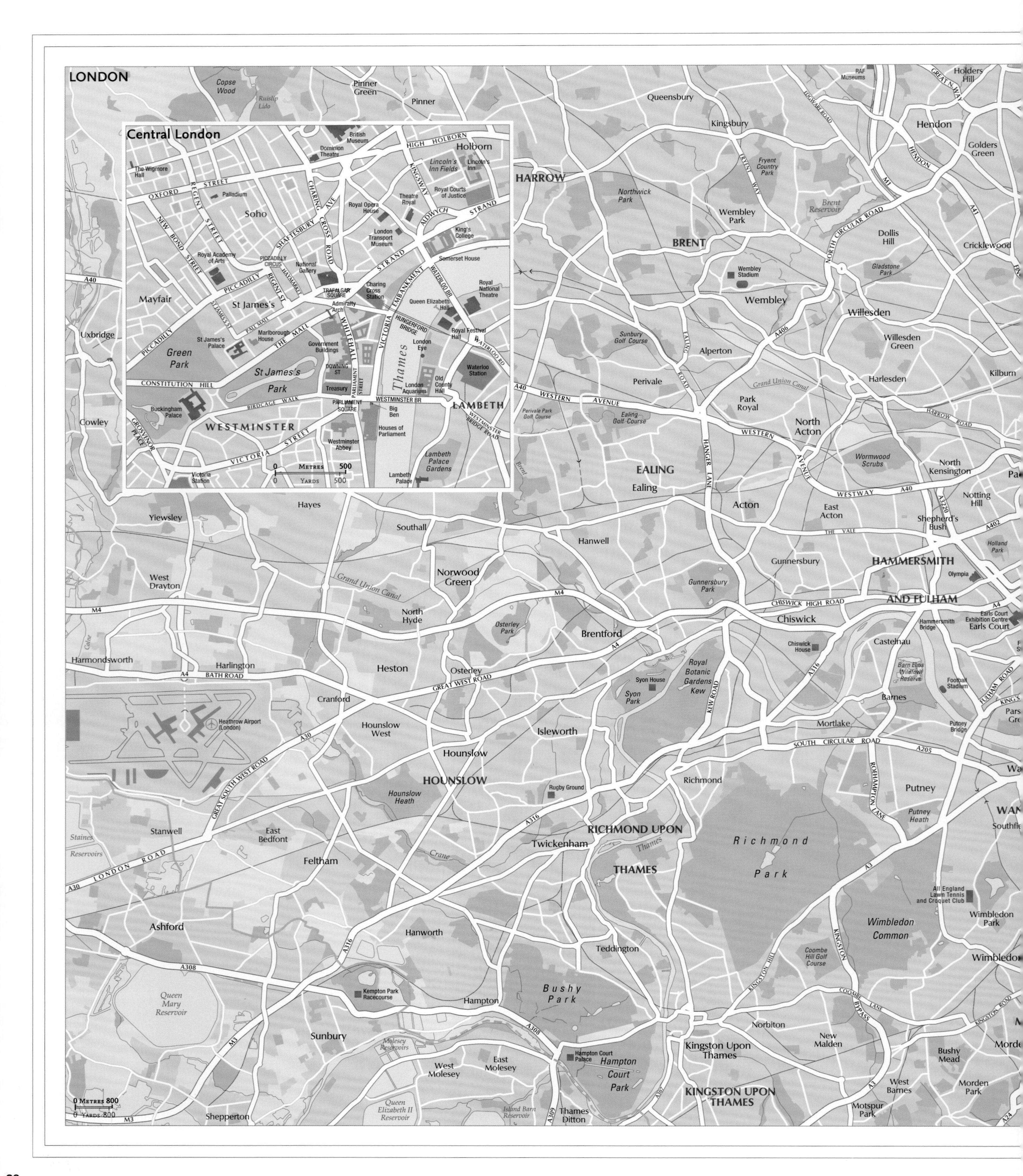

LONDON

Central London

The Wigmore Hall · Dominion Theatre · British Museum · HIGH HOLBORN · Holborn

OXFORD STREET · REGENT STREET · Palladium · CHARING CROSS ROAD · Lincoln's Inn Fields · Lincoln's Inn

Soho · SHAFTESBURY AVENUE · KINGSWAY · Royal Courts of Justice · STRAND · ALDWYCH

NEW BOND STREET · Royal Opera House · Theatre Royal · King's College · London Transport Museum · Somerset House · Royal National Theatre

Royal Academy of Arts · PICCADILLY CIRCUS · National Gallery · Charing Cross Station · Queen Elizabeth Hall

Mayfair · PICCADILLY · HAYMARKET · REGENT STREET · TRAFALGAR SQUARE · Admiralty Arch · HUNGERFORD BRIDGE · London Eye · Royal Festival Hall · WATERLOO RD

St James's · PALL MALL · Marlborough House · Government Buildings · WHITEHALL · VICTORIA EMBANKMENT · Thames · London Aquarium · Old County Hall · Waterloo Station

Green Park · St James's Palace · THE MALL · DOWNING ST · St James's Park · Treasury · PARLIAMENT STREET · Old County Hall

CONSTITUTION HILL · BIRDCAGE WALK · Buckingham Palace · Big Ben

CROSVENOR PLACE · WESTMINSTER · PARLIAMENT SQUARE · Houses of Parliament · WESTMINSTER BR · WESTMINSTER BRIDGE ROAD · LAMBETH

Victoria Station · VICTORIA STREET · Westminster Abbey · Lambeth Palace Gardens · Lambeth Palace

METRES 500 / YARDS 500

Outer areas

HARROW · Queensbury · Kingsbury · Hendon · Holders Hill · Golders Green · Cricklewood

Northwick Park · Wembley Park · BRENT · Dollis Hill · Gladstone Park

Uxbridge · Wembley Stadium · Wembley · Willesden · Willesden Green · Harlesden · Kilburn

Cowley · Sunbury Golf Course · Alperton · Perivale · Park Royal · North Acton · Wormwood Scrubs · North Kensington · Pa[]

Perivale Park Golf Course · Ealing Golf Course · EALING · Ealing · Acton · East Acton · WESTWAY · Notting Hill · Holland Park

Yiewsley · Hayes · Southall · Hanwell · Gunnersbury · HAMMERSMITH · Olympia

West Drayton · Grand Union Canal · Norwood Green · Gunnersbury Park · CHISWICK HIGH ROAD · AND FULHAM · Earls Court Exhibition Centre · Earls Court

North Hyde · Osterley Park · Brentford · Chiswick · Chiswick House · Hammersmith Bridge · Castelnau · Barn Elms Wildfowl Reserve · Football Stadium

Harmondsworth · Harlington · BATH ROAD · Heston · Osterley · GREAT WEST ROAD · Royal Botanic Gardens Kew · Syon House · Syon Park · Mortlake · Barnes · Putney Bridge · Pars[] Gre[]

Heathrow Airport (London) · Cranford · Hounslow West · Hounslow · Isleworth · SOUTH CIRCULAR ROAD · Putney · WAN[]

Stanwell · East Bedfont · HOUNSLOW · Hounslow Heath · Rugby Ground · Richmond · Putney Heath · Southfie[]

Staines Reservoirs · Feltham · Crane · RICHMOND UPON · Twickenham · Richmond Park · All England Lawn Tennis and Croquet Club · Wimbledon Park

Ashford · Hanworth · Teddington · THAMES · Thames · Wimbledon Common · Wimbledo[]

Queen Mary Reservoir · Kempton Park Racecourse · Bushy Park · Coombe Hill Golf Course

Sunbury · Molesey Reservoirs · Hampton · Norbiton · New Malden · Bushy Mead · Morde[]

West Molesey · East Molesey · Hampton Court Palace · Hampton Court Park · KINGSTON UPON THAMES · Kingston Upon Thames · West Barnes · Morden Park

Shepperton · Queen Elizabeth II Reservoir · Island Barn Reservoir · Thames Ditton · Motspur Park

0 Metres 800 / 0 Yards 800

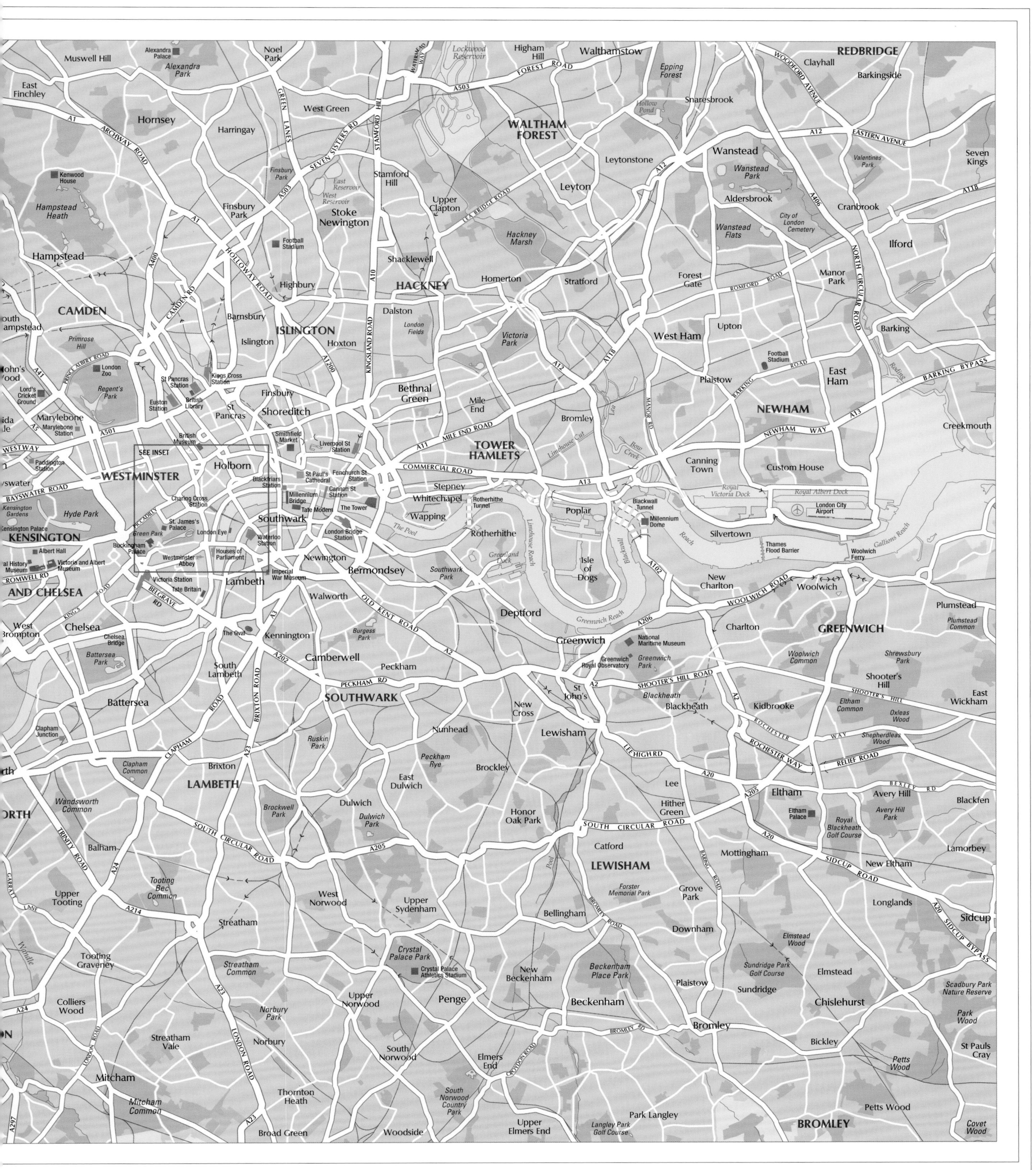
Muswell Hill
Alexandra Palace
Alexandra Park
Noel Park
Lockwood Reservoir
Higham Hill
Walthamstow
REDBRIDGE
Clayhall
Barkingside
East Finchley
Hornsey
West Green
Harringay
Epping Forest
Snaresbrook
Hollow Pond
WALTHAM FOREST
Wanstead
Seven Kings
Leytonstone
Kenwood House
Hampstead Heath
Finsbury Park
East Reservoir
West Reservoir
Stamford Hill
Upper Clapton
Leyton
Wanstead Park
Valentines Park
Aldersbrook
Cranbrook
Stoke Newington
Wanstead Flats
City of London Cemetery
Ilford
Hackney Marsh
Football Stadium
Hampstead
Shacklewell
Homerton
Stratford
Forest Gate
Manor Park
Highbury
HACKNEY
CAMDEN
Barnsbury
Dalston
Islington
ISLINGTON
Hoxton
London Fields
Victoria Park
West Ham
Upton
Barking
Primrose Hill
London Zoo
Regent's Park
Lord's Cricket Ground
St Pancras Station
Kings Cross Station
Euston Station
British Library
Finsbury
Bethnal Green
Mile End
Plaistow
East Ham
NEWHAM
Marylebone
Marylebone Station
St Pancras
Shoreditch
Bromley
Creekmouth
British Museum
Smithfield Market
Liverpool St Station
TOWER HAMLETS
WESTWAY
Paddington Station
SEE INSET
Holborn
Canning Town
Custom House
WESTMINSTER
Blackfriars Station
St Paul's Cathedral
Fenchurch St Station
Stepney
BAYSWATER ROAD
Charing Cross Station
Millennium Bridge
Cannon St Station
Whitechapel
Rotherhithe Tunnel
Poplar
Royal Victoria Dock
Royal Albert Dock
Kensington Gardens
Hyde Park
Tate Modern
The Tower
Wapping
Blackwall Tunnel
London City Airport
Kensington Palace
Green Park
St. James's Palace
London Eye
Southwark
Millennium Dome
KENSINGTON
London Bridge Station
The Pool
Rotherhithe
Silvertown
Albert Hall
Buckingham Palace
Waterloo Station
Greenland Dock
Limehouse Reach
Thames Flood Barrier
Woolwich Ferry
Gallions Reach
Natural History Museum
Victoria and Albert Museum
Westminster Abbey
Houses of Parliament
Newington
Isle of Dogs
Blackwall
Bermondsey
Southwark Park
Victoria Station
Lambeth
Imperial War Museum
New Charlton
Woolwich
AND CHELSEA
Tate Britain
Walworth
Deptford
Plumstead
Plumstead Common
West Brompton
Chelsea
Greenwich Reach
Charlton
GREENWICH
Chelsea Bridge
The Oval
Kennington
Burgess Park
Battersea Park
Greenwich
National Maritime Museum
Camberwell
Peckham
Greenwich Royal Observatory
Greenwich Park
Woolwich Common
Shrewsbury Park
South Lambeth
Shooter's Hill
St John's
East Wickham
SOUTHWARK
Blackheath
Battersea
New Cross
Kidbrooke
Eltham Common
Oxleas Wood
Clapham Junction
Ruskin Park
Nunhead
Lewisham
Shepherdleas Wood
Peckham Rye
Clapham Common
Brixton
Brockley
East Dulwich
LAMBETH
Lee
Eltham
Avery Hill
Blackfen
Wandsworth Common
Brockwell Park
Dulwich
Hither Green
Eltham Palace
Avery Hill Park
Dulwich Park
Honor Oak Park
Royal Blackheath Golf Course
Balham
Catford
Mottingham
Lamorbey
LEWISHAM
New Eltham
Tooting Bec Common
Upper Tooting
West Norwood
Upper Sydenham
Forster Memorial Park
Grove Park
Longlands
Sidcup
Streatham
Bellingham
Downham
Elmstead Wood
Crystal Palace Park
Crystal Palace Athletics Stadium
Tooting Graveney
Streatham Common
Beckenham Place Park
New Beckenham
Sundridge Park Golf Course
Elmstead
Scadbury Park Nature Reserve
Plaistow
Sundridge
Upper Norwood
Penge
Beckenham
Chislehurst
Colliers Wood
Norbury Park
Park Wood
Streatham Vale
Norbury
Bromley
Bickley
St Pauls Cray
South Norwood
Elmers End
Petts Wood
Mitcham
Thornton Heath
Mitcham Common
South Norwood Country Park
Park Langley
Petts Wood
Upper Elmers End
BROMLEY
Covet Wood
Broad Green
Woodside
Langley Park Golf Course
A1
ARCHWAY ROAD
HOLLOWAY ROAD
CAMDEN RD
PRINCE ALBERT ROAD
GREEN LANES
SEVEN SISTERS RD
STAMFORD HILL
KINGSLAND ROAD
A10
FOREST ROAD
A503
LEA BRIDGE ROAD
WOODFORD AVENUE
EASTERN AVENUE
A12
A406
NORTH CIRCULAR ROAD
ROMFORD ROAD
A118
BARKING BYPASS
BARKING ROAD
NEWHAM WAY
A13
MILE END ROAD
A11
COMMERCIAL ROAD
A1200
A400
A501
A41
A5
A102
A206
WOOLWICH ROAD
OLD KENT ROAD
A2
A202
PECKHAM RD
SHOOTER'S HILL ROAD
ROCHESTER WAY
ROCHESTER WAY RELIEF ROAD
LEE HIGH RD
A20
A205
BEXLEY RD
SOUTH CIRCULAR ROAD
SIDCUP ROAD
SIDCUP BYPASS
BROMLEY ROAD
BROMLEY RD
CROYDON ROAD
CLAPHAM ROAD
BRIXTON ROAD
A23
LONDON ROAD
A3
BELGRAVE RD
KING'S ROAD
TRINITY ROAD
A24
A214
A297
A217
GARRATT LANE
Wandle
Limehouse Cut
Bow Creek
Lea
MANOR RD
Roding
PICCADILLY
WATERWORKS WAY

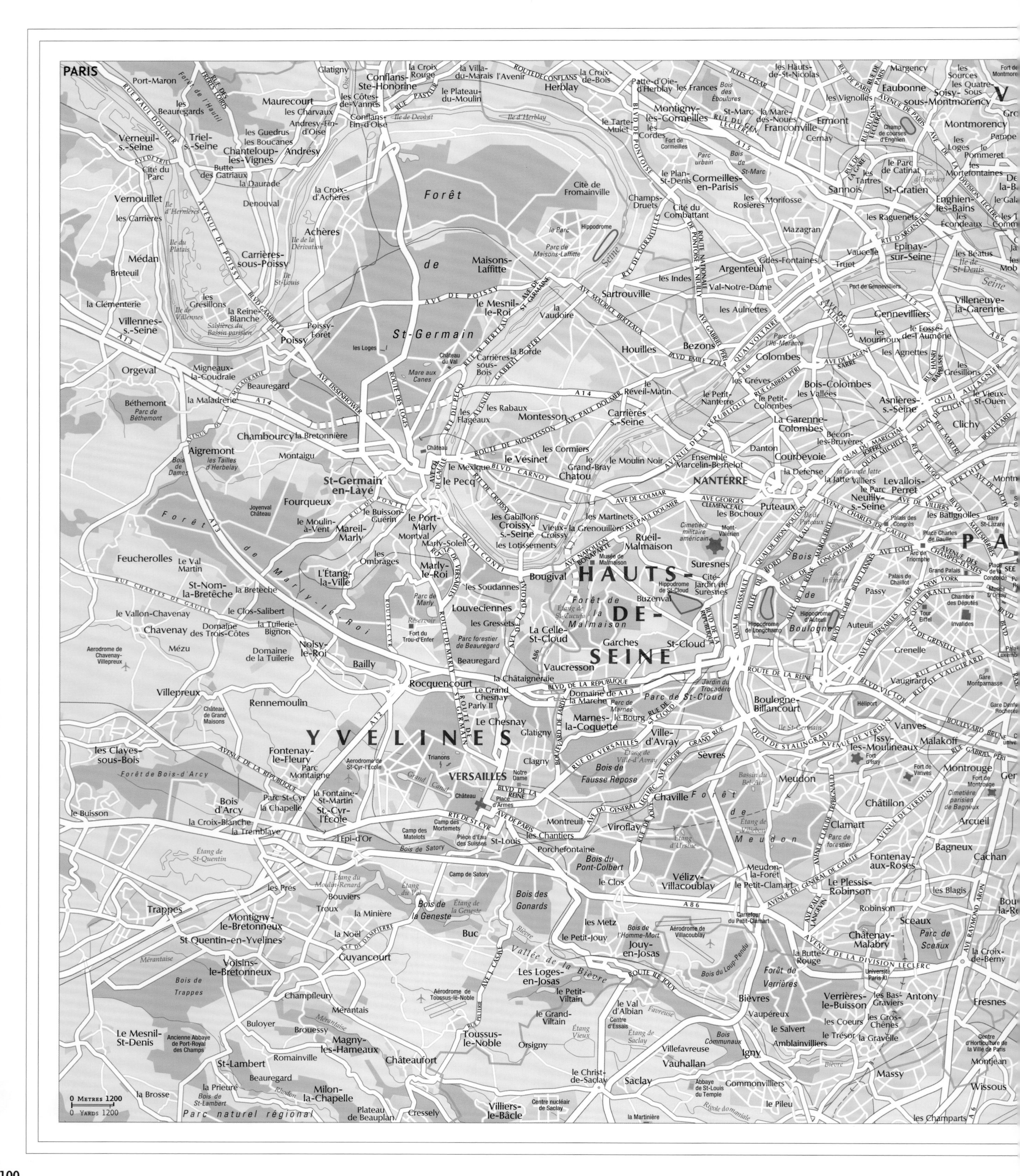
PARIS
Port-Maron
Glatigny
Conflans-
Ste-Honorine
la Croix
Rouge
la Villa-
du-Marais
l'Avenir
Herblay
la Croix-
de-Bois
Patte-d'Oie-
d'Herblay
les France
les Hauts-
de-St-Nicolas
Margency
Eaubonne
Soisy-
sous-Montmorency
Montmorency
Maurecourt
les Charvaux
Andresy-Fin-
d'Oise
les Côtes-
de-Vannes
Conflans-
Fin-d'Oise
le Plateau-
du-Moulin
les
Beauregards
Verneuil-
s.-Seine
Triel-
s.-Seine
les Guedrus
les Boucanes
Chanteloup-
les-Vignes
Andrésy
Montigny-
les-Cormeilles
les
Cordes
le Tarte-
Mulet
St-Marc
la Mare-
des-Noues
Franconville
Ermont
Cernay
Sannois
St-Gratien
Enghien-
les-Bains
Cité du
Parc
Butte
des Gatriaux
la Daurade
Vernouillet
Denouval
la Croix-
d'Achères
Forêt
Cité de
Fromainville
le Plan-
St-Denis
Cormeilles-
en-Parisis
les Rosières
Morifosse
les Carrières
Achères
Champs-
Druets
Cité du
Combattant
Mazagran
les Raguenets
Médan
Breteuil
Carrières-
sous-Poissy
de
Maisons-
Laffitte
Argenteuil
Gdes-Fontaines
Vaucelle
Epinay-
sur-Seine
les Indes
Val-Notre-Dame
la Clémenterie
les
Grésillons
la Reine-
Blanche
le Mesnil-
le-Roi
la
Vaudoire
Sartrouville
Villeneuve-
la-Garenne
Villennes-
s.-Seine
Poissy
Poissy-
Forêt
St-Germain
les Aulnettes
Gennevilliers
les Loges
Château
du Val
Carrières-
sous-
Bois
la Borde
Houilles
Bezons
Colombes
les Agnettes
Orgeval
Migneaux-
la-Coudraie
Mare aux
Canes
Beauregard
le
Réveil-Matin
les Grèves
Bois-Colombes
les Vallées
Asnières-
s.-Seine
Béthemont
Parc de
Béthemont
la Maladrerie
les Rabaux
Montesson
les
Flageaux
Carrières-
s.-Seine
le Petit-
Nanterre
le Petit-
Colombes
La Garenne-
Colombes
Clichy
Chambourcy
la Bretonnière
Aigremont
Montaigu
Château
les Cormiers
le Vésinet
le Mexique
le Pecq
le
Grand-Bray
Chatou
le Moulin Noir
Ensemble
Marcelin-Berthelot
Danton
Courbevoie
Bécon-
les-Bruyères
la Défense
la Jatte
Villiers
Levallois-
Perret
le Parc
Neuilly-
s.-Seine
NANTERRE
Puteaux
St-Germain
en-Laye
Fourqueux
Joyenval
Château
le Buisson-
Guérin
le Port-
Marly
le Moulin-
à-Vent
Mareil-
Marly
Montval
les Gabillons
Croissy-
s.-Seine
les Lotissements
Vieux-
Croissy
la Grenouillère
les Martinets
Rueil-
Malmaison
les Bochoux
Cimetière
militaire
américain
Mont-
Valérien
Suresnes
les Batignolles
Place Charles
de Gaulle
Arc de
Triomphe
Feucherolles
le Val
Martin
les
Ombrages
L'Étang-
la-Ville
Marly-Soleil
Marly-
le-Roi
Bougival
Musée de
Malmaison
HAUTS-
DE-
SEINE
Cité-
Jardin de
Suresnes
Hippodrome
de St-Cloud
Bois
de
Boulogne
Hippodrome
d'Auteuil
Hippodrome
de Longchamp
Passy
Auteuil
Palais de
Chaillot
Tour
Eiffel
Invalides
Chambre
des Députés
St-Nom-
la-Bretêche
la Bretêche
le Vallon-Chavenay
le Clos-Salibert
Chavenay
Domaine
des Trois-Côtes
la Tuilerie-
Bignon
Mézu
Parc de
Marly
Réservoir
Fort du
Trou-d'Enfer
les Soudannes
Louveciennes
les Gressets
Parc forestier
de Beauregard
Forêt de
la Malmaison
La Celle-
St-Cloud
Buzenval
Garches
St-Cloud
Grenelle
Aerodrome de
Chavenay-
Villepreux
Domaine
de la Tuilerie
Noisy-
le-Roi
Bailly
Beauregard
Vaucresson
la Châtaigneraie
Villepreux
Rocquencourt
Le Grand
Chesnay
Parly II
Domaine de
la Marche
Parc de St-Cloud
Jardin du
Trocadéro
Boulogne-
Billancourt
Vaugirard
Héliport
Rennemoulin
Château
de Grand
Maisons
Le Chesnay
Glatigny
Marnes-
la-Coquette
le Bourg
Ville-
d'Avray
Vanves
Malakoff
Issy-
les-Moulineaux
YVELINES
les Clayes-
sous-Bois
Fontenay-
le-Fleury
Parc
Montaigne
Aerodrome de
St-Cyr-l'Ecole
Trianons
VERSAILLES
Notre
Dame
Clagny
Bois de
Fausse Repose
Sèvres
Meudon
Montrouge
Forêt de Bois-d'Arcy
Bois
d'Arcy
Parc St-Cyr
la Chapelle
la Fontaine-
St-Martin
St.-Cyr-
l'École
Château
Place
d'Armes
Chaville
Châtillon
le Buisson
la Croix-Blanche
la Tremblaye
Camp des
Matelots
Camp des
Mortemets
Montreuil
Viroflay
Clamart
Arcueil
l'Epi-d'Or
St-Louis
les Chantiers
Porchefontaine
Bagneux
Étang de
St-Quentin
Bois de Satory
Camp de Satory
Bois du
Pont-Colbert
le Clos
Fontenay-
aux-Roses
Cachan
Meudon-
la-Forêt
le Petit-Clamart
Vélizy-
Villacoublay
Le Plessis-
Robinson
les Blagis
les Prés
Bouviers
Troux
la Minière
Bois de
la Geneste
Bois des
Gonards
Robinson
Sceaux
Trappes
Montigny-
le-Bretonneux
St Quentin-en-Yvelines
la Noël
Buc
les Metz
le Petit-Jouy
Bois de
l'Homme-Mort
Aérodrome de
Villacoublay
Carrefour
du Petit-Clamart
Châtenay-
Malabry
Parc de
Sceaux
Guyancourt
Voisins-
le-Bretonneux
Vallée de la Bièvre
Jouy-
en-Josas
la Butte-
Rouge
la Croix-
de-Berny
Bois de
Trappes
Champfleury
Aérodrome de
Toussus-le-Noble
Les Loges-
en-Josas
le Petit-
Viltain
Forêt de
Verrières
Université
Paris XI
Mérantais
le Grand-
Viltain
le Val
d'Albian
Bièvres
Verrières-
le-Buisson
les Bas-
Graviers
Antony
Fresnes
Le Mesnil-
St-Denis
Ancienne Abbaye
de Port-Royal
des Champs
Buloyer
Brouessy
Magny-
les-Hameaux
Toussus-
le-Noble
Orsigny
Centre
d'Essais
Vaupéreux
le Salvert
Amblainvilliers
les Coeurs
les Gros-
Chênes
le Trésor
la Gravelle
Centre
d'Horticulture de
la Ville de Paris
St-Lambert
Romainville
Châteaufort
Villefavreuse
Vauhallan
Igny
Montjean
Massy
Beauregard
le Christ-
de-Saclay
Saclay
Abbaye
de St-Louis
du Temple
Commonvilliers
Wissous
la Brosse
la Prieuré
Milon-
la-Chapelle
Plateau
de Beauplan
Cressely
Villiers-
le-Bâcle
Centre nucléaire
de Saclay
le Pileu
la Martinière
les Champarts
Parc naturel régional
0 Metres 1200
0 Yards 1200

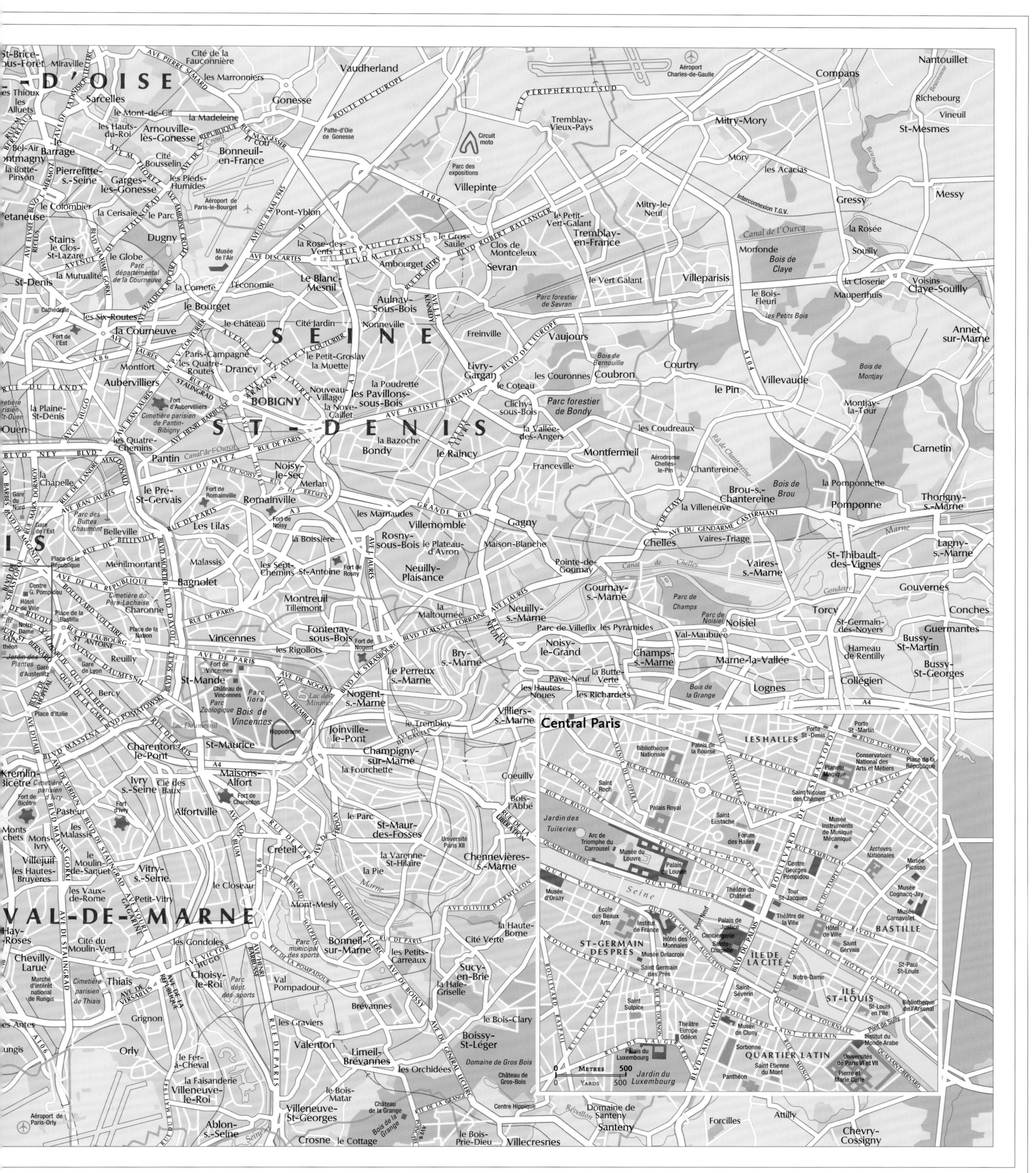

D'OISE

St-Brice-sous-Forêt · Miraville
les-Thioux
les Allouets · Sarcelles
le Mont-de-Gif
Bel-Air · le Barrage
ntmagny · la Butte-Pinson
Pierrefitte-s-Seine
Garges-lès-Gonesse
les Pieds-Humides
taneuse · le Colombier
la Cerisaie · le Parc
Stains · le Clos-St-Lazare
la Mutualité
St-Denis
Cathédrale
Fort de l'Est
la Courneuve
Montfort
Aubervilliers
la Plaine-St-Denis
Ouen
les Quatre-Chemins
la Chapelle
Gare du Nord
Pantin
la Villette
Belleville
Ménilmontant
Place de la République
Centre G. Pompidou
Notre Dame
Place de la Bastille
Reuilly
Gare de Lyon
Bercy
Place d'Italie
Kremlin-Bicêtre
Monts chets · Mons
Ivry
Villejuif
les Hautes-Bruyères
les Vaux-de-Rome
Hay-Roses
Chevilly-Larue
Thiais
Grignon
Orly

Cité de la Fauconnière
Vaudherland
AVE PIERRE SEMARD
les Marronniers
Gonesse
la Madeleine
Arnouville-lès-Gonesse
les Hauts-du-Roi
Cité Bousselin
Dugny
Musée de l'Air
Patte-d'Oie de Gonesse
Aéroport de Paris-le-Bourget
Pont-Yblon
le Blanc-Mesnil
le Bourget
le Château
Cité-Jardin
Nonneville
SEINE
Paris-Campagne
les Quatre-Routes
Drancy
le Petit-Groslay la Muette
BOBIGNY
Nouveau-Village la Nove-Caillet
la Poudrette
les Pavillons-sous-Bois
ST-DENIS
la Bazoche
Bondy
le Raincy
Noisy-le-Sec
Merlan
Romainville
Fort de Noisy
les Marnaudes
Villemomble
Gagny
Rosny-sous-Bois
le Plateau-d'Avron
Maison-Blanche
Neuilly-Plaisance
Fontenay-sous-Bois
la Maltournée
Neuilly-s-Marne
les Rigollots
Bry-s-Marne
Nogent-s-Marne
Le Perreux-s-Marne
Villiers-s-Marne
Joinville-le-Pont
le Tremblay
Champigny-sur-Marne
la Fourchette
Coeuilly
St-Maur-des-Fossés
Université Paris XII
la Varenne-St-Hilaire
la Pie
Chennevières-s-Marne
le Closeau
Mont-Mesly
Créteil
Bonneuil-sur-Marne
Cité Verte
la Haute-Borne
Sucy-en-Brie
la Haie-Griselle
le Bois-Clary
Boissy-St-Léger
le Bois-Matar
Villeneuve-St-Georges
Ablon-s-Seine
Crosne
Villecresnes

Aéroport Charles-de-Gaulle
PÉRIPHÉRIQUE SUD
Tremblay-Vieux-Pays
Mitry-Mory
Mory
Mitry-le-Neuf
Parc des expositions
Villepinte
le Petit-Vert-Galant
Tremblay-en-France
Villeparisis
le Vert Galant
Parc forestier de Sevran
Aulnay-sous-Bois
Sevran
Livry-Gargan
le Coteau
Clichy-sous-Bois
Franceville
Montfermeil
Parc forestier de Bondy
la Vallée-des-Angers
les Coudreaux
Aérodrome Chelles-le-Pin
Chantereine
Brou-s-Chantereine
la Villeneuve
Chelles
Vaires-Triage
Gournay-s-Marne
Pointe-de-Gournay
Parc de Villeflix les Pyramides
Noisy-le-Grand
Champs-s-Marne
Val-Maubuée
le Pave-Neuf la Butte-Verte
les Hautes-Noues
les Richardets
Bois de la Grange
Lognes
Marne-la-Vallée

Compans
Richebourg
Vineuil
St-Mesmes
les Acacias
Gressy
Messy
la Rosée
Canal de l'Ourcq
Bois de Claye
Souilly
Morfonde
la Closerie
Voisins Claye-Souilly
le Bois-Fleuri
les Petits Bois
Mauperthuis
Annet-sur-Marne
Bois de Montjay
Villevaude
le Pin
Montjay-la-Tour
Carnetin
la Pomponnette
Pompone
Thorigny-s-Marne
Lagny-s-Marne
St-Thibault-des-Vignes
Gouvernes
Conches
St-Germain-des-Noyers
Guermantes
Bussy-St-Martin
Hameau de Rentilly
Noisiel
Torcy
Bussy-St-Georges
Collégien

IS

VAL-DE-MARNE
Cité du Moulin-Vert
Marché d'intérêt national de Rungis
Cimetière parisien de Thiais
Parc dépt. des sports
les Gondoles
les Petits-Carreaux
Val Pompadour
Parc municipal des sports
Choisy-le-Roi
Vitry-s-Seine
Petit-Vitry
Valenton
Limeil-Brévannes
les Orchidées
Domaine de Gros Bois
Château de Gros-Bois
Centre Hippique
Domaine de Santeny
Santeny
Forcilles
Attilly
Chevry-Cossigny

Central Paris

LES HALLES
Porte St-Denis
Porte St-Martin
Bibliothèque Nationale
Palais de la Bourse
RUE REAUMUR
Conservatoire National des Arts et Métiers
Place de la République
Planète Magique
Saint Roch
Saint Eustache
Saint Nicolas des Champs
Musée Instruments de Musique Mécanique
Palais Royal
Forum des Halles
Archives Nationales
Jardin des Tuileries
Arc de Triomphe du Carrousel
Musée du Louvre
Palais du Louvre
Centre Georges Pompidou
Musée Picasso
Théâtre du Châtelet
Tour St-Jacques
Musée Cognacq-Jay
Musée d'Orsay
Théâtre de la Ville
Musée Carnavalet
Seine
BASTILLE
École des Beaux Arts
Institut de France
Palais de Justice
Conciergerie
Sainte-Chapelle
Hôtel de Ville
Saint Gervais
ST-GERMAIN DES PRÉS
Hôtel des Monnaies
Musée Delacroix
Saint Germain des Prés
ÎLE DE LA CITÉ
St-Paul St-Louis
Notre-Dame
Saint Séverin
ÎLE ST-LOUIS
St-Louis en l'Île
Bibliothèque de l'Arsenal
Saint Sulpice
Théâtre Europe Odéon
Musée de Cluny
Pont de Sully
Institut du Monde Arabe
Palais du Luxembourg
Sorbonne
QUARTIER LATIN
Saint Etienne du Mont
Universités de Paris VI et VII Pierre et Marie Curie
Panthéon
Jardin du Luxembourg
Domaine de Santeny

0 MÈTRES 500
0 YARDS 500

© Collins Bartholomew Ltd

101

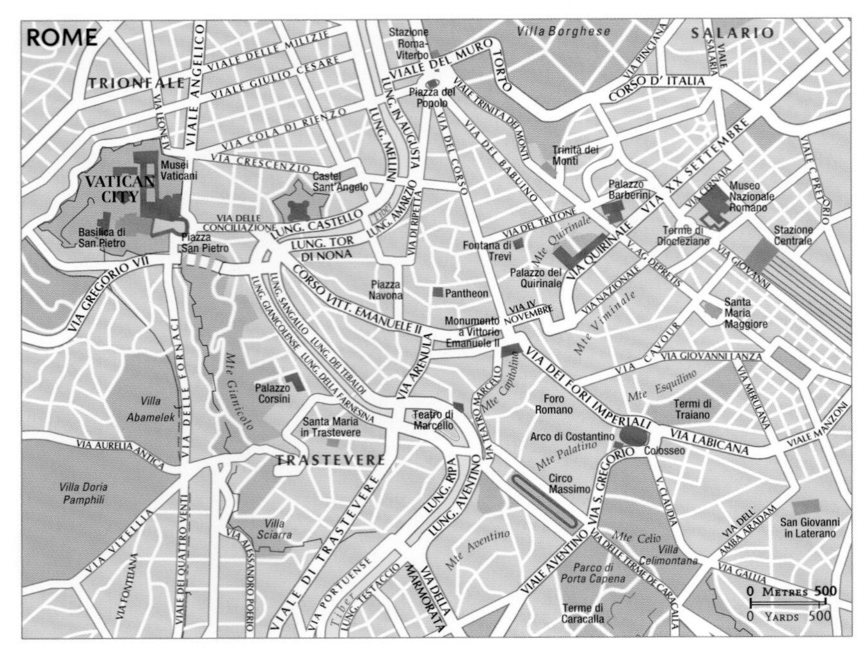

ROME
TRIONFALE
VATICAN CITY
Musei Vaticani
Basilica di San Pietro
Piazza San Pietro
Castel Sant'Angelo
Villa Borghese
SALARIO
Stazione Roma-Viterbo
Piazza del Popolo
Trinità dei Monti
Palazzo Barberini
Museo Nazionale Romano
Stazione Centrale
Fontana di Trevi
Palazzo del Quirinale
Terme di Diocleziano
Piazza Navona
Pantheon
Monumento a Vittorio Emanuele II
Santa Maria Maggiore
Palazzo Corsini
Santa Maria in Trastevere
Teatro di Marcello
Foro Romano
Arco di Costantino
Colosseo
Termi di Traiano
Villa Abamelek
TRASTEVERE
Villa Doria Pamphili
Villa Sciarra
Circo Massimo
Mte Aventino
Mte Celio
Villa Celimontana
Parco di Porta Capena
Terme di Caracalla
San Giovanni in Laterano
Mte Gianicolo
Mte Palatino
Mte Capitolino
Mte Quirinale
Mte Viminale
Mte Esquilino
VIALE DEL MURO TORTO
CORSO D' ITALIA
VIA XX SETTEMBRE
VIA CAVOUR
VIA DEI FORI IMPERIALI
VIA LABICANA
CORSO VITT. EMANUELE II
VIA GREGORIO VII
VIALE DI TRASTEVERE
VIA AURELIA ANTICA
0 METRES 500
0 YARDS 500

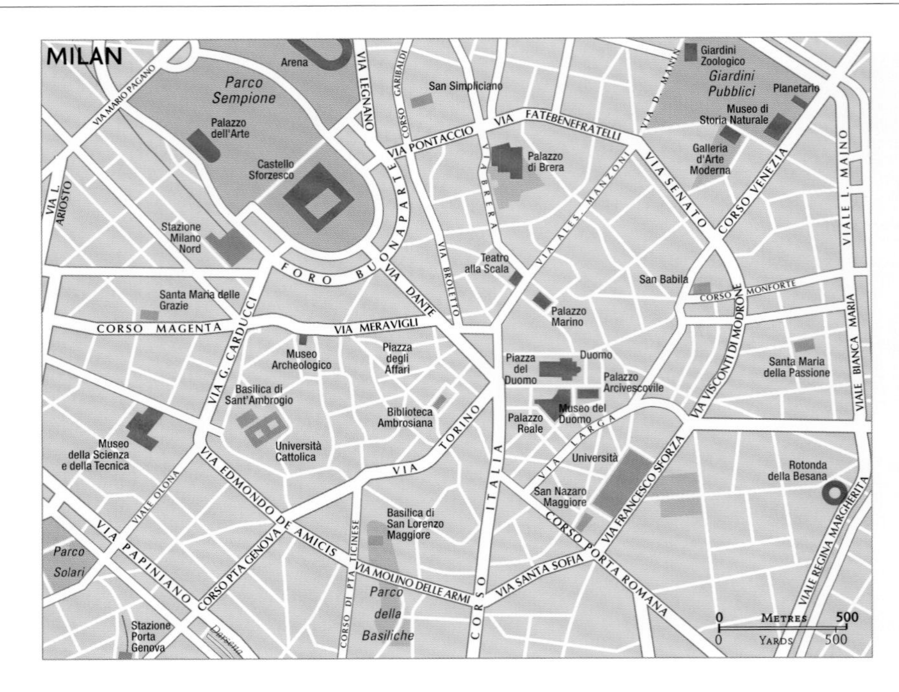

MILAN
Arena
Parco Sempione
Palazzo dell'Arte
Castello Sforzesco
Stazione Milano Nord
San Simpliciano
Palazzo di Brera
Giardini Zoologico
Giardini Pubblici
Planetario
Museo di Storia Naturale
Galleria d'Arte Moderna
Teatro alla Scala
San Babila
Santa Maria delle Grazie
CORSO MAGENTA
VIA MERAVIGLI
Museo Archeologico
Piazza degli Affari
Palazzo Marino
Piazza del Duomo
Duomo
Palazzo Arcivescovile
Santa Maria della Passione
Basilica di Sant'Ambrogio
Biblioteca Ambrosiana
Palazzo Reale
Museo del Duomo
Università Cattolica
Università
Museo della Scienza e della Tecnica
Rotonda della Besana
San Nazaro Maggiore
Basilica di San Lorenzo Maggiore
Parco Solari
Parco della Basiliche
Stazione Porta Genova
FORO BUONAPARTE
CORSO VENEZIA
VIA SENATO
CORSO PORTA ROMANA
VIALE REGINA MARGHERITA
0 METRES 500
0 YARDS 500

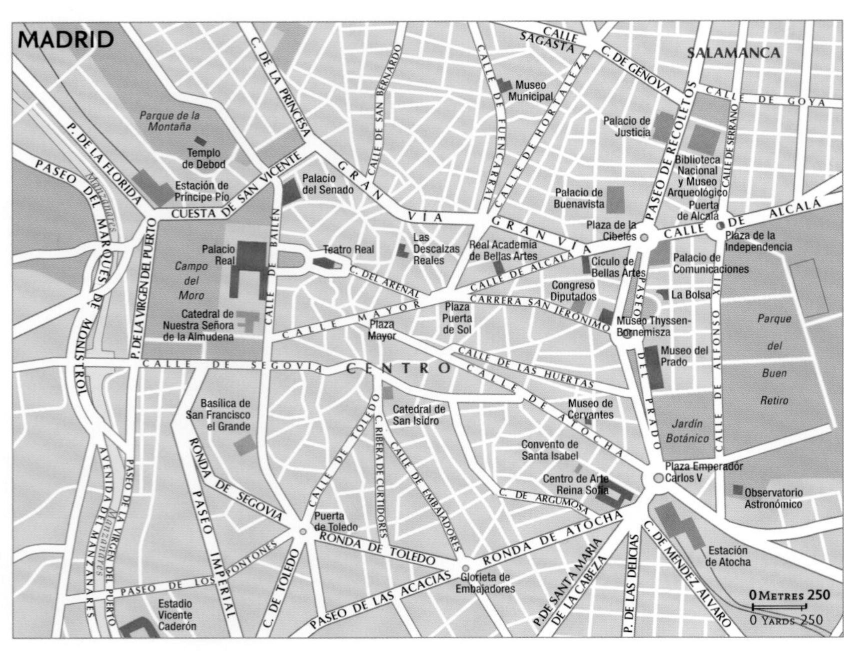

MADRID
Parque de la Montaña
Templo de Debod
Estación de Principe Pío
Palacio del Senado
SALAMANCA
Museo Municipal
Palacio de Justicia
Biblioteca Nacional y Museo Arqueológico
Puerta de Alcalá
Palacio de Buenavista
Plaza de la Cibeles
Plaza de la Independencia
Palacio de Comunicaciones
Teatro Real
Palacio Real
Campo del Moro
Las Descalzas Reales
Real Academia de Bellas Artes
Círculo de Bellas Artes
Catedral de Nuestra Señora de la Almudena
Congreso Diputados
La Bolsa
Plaza Puerta de Sol
Plaza Mayor
Museo Thyssen-Bornemisza
Museo del Prado
Parque del Buen Retiro
CENTRO
Basilica de San Francisco el Grande
Catedral de San Isidro
Museo de Cervantes
Jardín Botánico
Convento de Santa Isabel
Centro de Arte Reina Sofía
Plaza Emperador Carlos V
Observatorio Astronómico
Puerta de Toledo
Glorieta de Embajadores
Estación de Atocha
Estadio Vicente Calderón
GRAN VIA
CALLE DE ALCALÁ
RONDA DE ATOCHA
PASEO DE LAS ACACIAS
0 METRES 250
0 YARDS 250

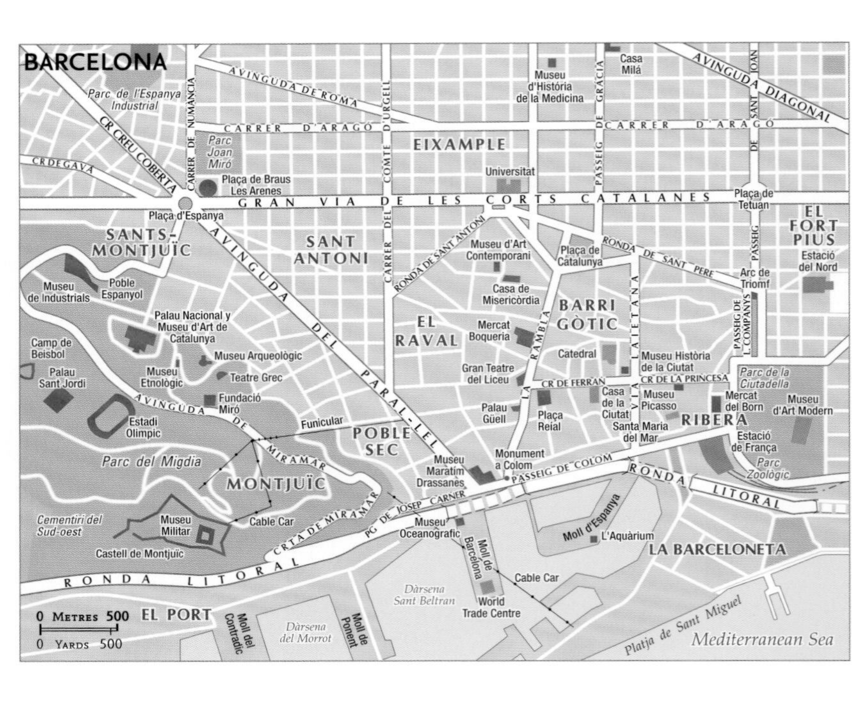

BARCELONA
Parc de l'Espanya Industrial
Parc Joan Miró
Plaça de Braus Les Arenes
Plaça d'Espanya
EIXAMPLE
Universitat
Museu d'Història de la Medicina
Casa Milà
AVINGUDA DIAGONAL
GRAN VIA DE LES CORTS CATALANES
Plaça de Tetuan
SANTS-MONTJUÏC
SANT ANTONI
Museu d'Art Contemporani
Plaça de Catalunya
EL FORT PIUS
Estació del Nord
Arc de Triomf
Museu de Industrials
Poble Espanyol
Palau Nacional y Museu d'Art de Catalunya
Casa de Misericòrdia
BARRI GÒTIC
Mercat Boqueria
EL RAVAL
Catedral
Museu Història de la Ciutat
Camp de Beisbol
Palau Sant Jordi
Museu Arqueològic
Teatre Grec
Museu Etnològic
Gran Teatre del Liceu
Casa de la Ciutat
Museu Picasso
Mercat del Born
Parc de la Ciutadella
Museu d'Art Modern
RIBERA
Fundació Miró
Estadi Olímpic
Palau Güell
Plaça Reial
Santa Maria del Mar
Funicular
POBLE SEC
Parc del Migdia
MONTJUÏC
Museu Marítim Drassanes
Monument a Colom
Estació de França
Parc Zoològic
Cementiri del Sud-oest
Museu Militar
Castell de Montjuïc
Cable Car
Museu Oceanogràfic
Museu de Barcelona
Moll d'Espanya
L'Aquàrium
LA BARCELONETA
RONDA LITORAL
Dàrsena Sant Beltran
World Trade Centre
EL PORT
Moll del Contradic
Dàrsena del Morrot
Moll de Ponent
Platja de Sant Miguel
Mediterranean Sea
0 METRES 500
0 YARDS 500

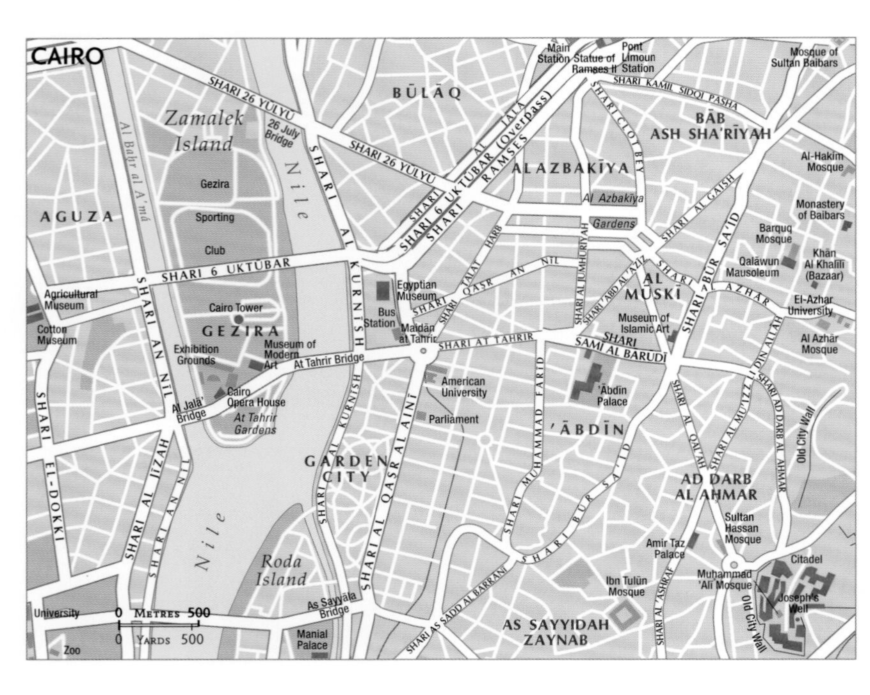

CAIRO
Main Station
Statue of Ramses II
Pont Limoun Station
Mosque of Sultan Baibars
BŪLĀQ
BĀB ASH SHA'RĪYAH
Zamalek Island
26 July Bridge
Nile
AL AZBAKĪYA
Al Azbakiya Gardens
Al-Hakim Mosque
Gezira
Sporting Club
AGUZA
Monastery of Baibars
Barquq Mosque
Qalāwun Mausoleum
Khān Al Khalīlī (Bazaar)
SHARI 6 UKTUBAR
Agricultural Museum
Cotton Museum
Cairo Tower
GEZIRA
Egyptian Museum
Bus Station
Maidān at Tahrīr
AL MUSKI
El-Azhar University
Museum of Islamic Art
Al Azhar Mosque
Exhibition Grounds
Museum of Modern Art
At Tahrir Bridge
Al Jalā' Bridge
Cairo Opera House
At Tahrir Gardens
American University
Parliament
'Ābdīn Palace
'ĀBDĪN
GARDEN CITY
AD DARB AL AHMAR
Sultan Hassan Mosque
Amir Taz Palace
Citadel
Ibn Tulūn Mosque
Muhammad 'Alī Mosque
Joseph's Well
Old City Wall
Roda Island
University
Zoo
As Sayyala Bridge
Manial Palace
AS SAYYIDAH ZAYNAB
0 METRES 500
0 YARDS 500

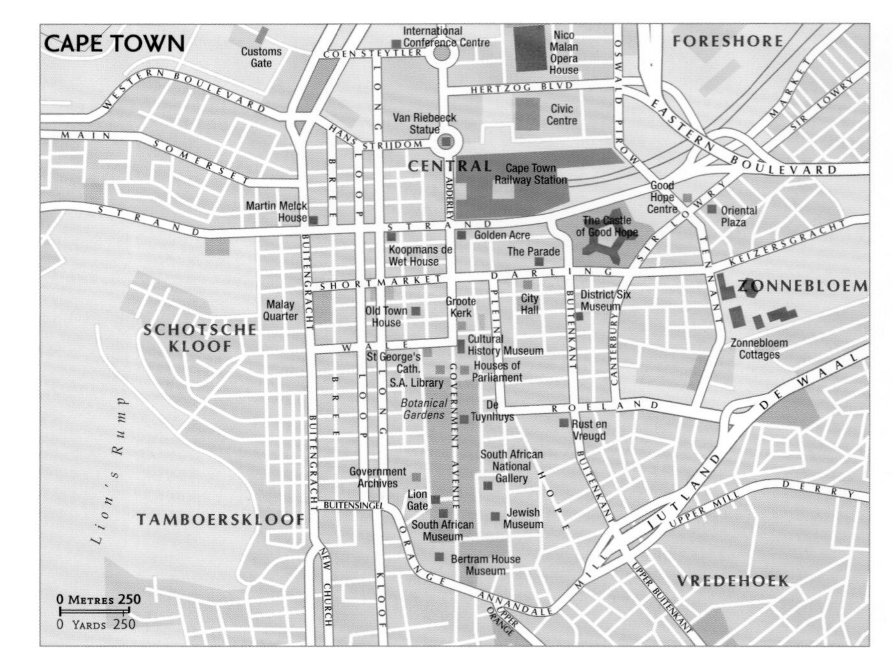

CAPE TOWN
Customs Gate
International Conference Centre
Nico Malan Opera House
FORESHORE
WESTERN BOULEVARD
HERTZOG BLVD
Civic Centre
Van Riebeeck Statue
EASTERN BOULEVARD
CENTRAL
Cape Town Railway Station
Good Hope Centre
Oriental Plaza
Martin Melck House
The Castle of Good Hope
Golden Acre
The Parade
Koopmans de Wet House
ZONNEBLOEM
District Six Museum
City Hall
Groote Kerk
Old Town House
Malay Quarter
SCHOTSCHE KLOOF
Cultural History Museum
St George's Cath.
S.A. Library
Houses of Parliament
Zonnebloem Cottages
Botanical Gardens
De Tuynhuys
Rust en Vreugd
South African National Gallery
Government Archives
Lion Gate
Jewish Museum
South African Museum
Lion's Rump
TAMBOERSKLOOF
Bertram House Museum
VREDEHOEK
0 METRES 250
0 YARDS 250

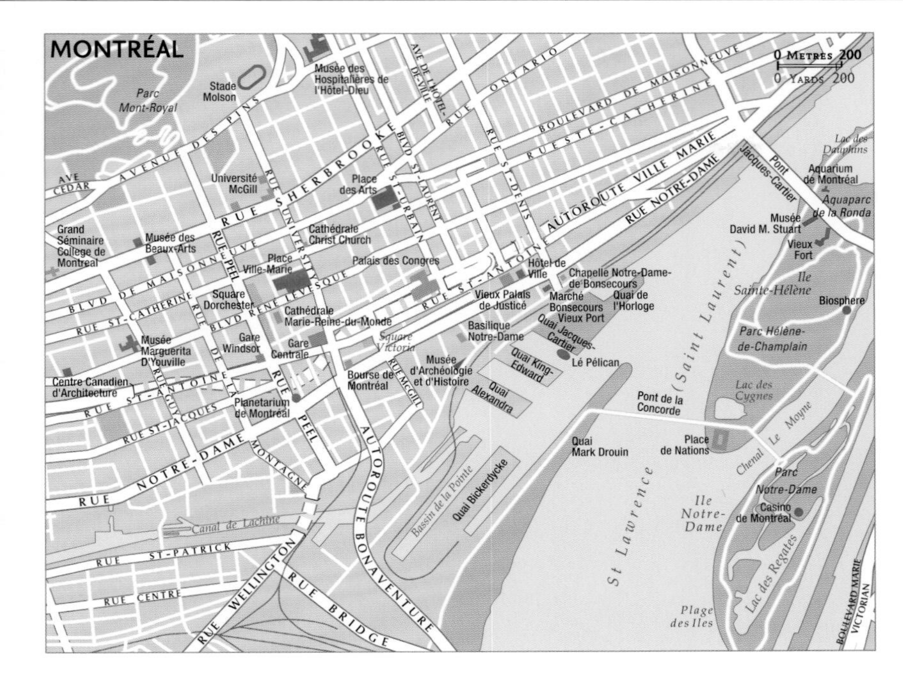
MONTRÉAL
0 Metres 200
0 Yards 200
Parc Mont-Royal
Stade Molson
Musée des Hospitalières de l'Hôtel-Dieu
Université McGill
Place des Arts
Aquarium de Montréal
Aquaparc de la Ronda
Lac des Dauphins
Pont Jacques-Cartier
Grand Séminaire Collège de Montréal
Musée des Beaux-Arts
Cathédrale Christ Church
Palais des Congrès
Place Ville-Marie
Square Dorchester
Cathédrale Marie-Reine-du-Monde
Musée Marguerita D'Youville
Gare Windsor
Gare Centrale
Square Victoria
Centre Canadien d'Architecture
Planetarium de Montréal
Bourse de Montréal
Musée d'Archéologie et d'Histoire
Hôtel de Ville
Chapelle Notre-Dame-de Bonsecours
Marché Bonsecours
Quai de l'Horloge
Vieux Port
Vieux Palais de Justice
Basilique Notre-Dame
Quai Jacques-Cartier
Quai King-Edward
Quai Alexandra
Le Pélican
Musée David M. Stuart
Vieux Fort
Ile Sainte-Hélène
Biosphère
Parc Hélène-de-Champlain
Lac des Cygnes
Pont de la Concorde
Place de Nations
Quai Mark Drouin
Quai Bickerdycke
Bassin de la Pointe
Canal de Lachine
Chenal Le Moyne
Parc Notre-Dame
Casino de Montréal
Ile Notre-Dame
Lac des Regates
Plage des Iles
St Lawrence
(Saint Laurent)
Autoroute Ville Marie
Autoroute Bonaventure
Rue Sherbrooke
Rue Notre-Dame
Rue St-Antoine
Rue St-Jacques
Rue St-Patrick
Rue Centre
Rue Wellington
Rue Bridge
Rue Peel
Rue Ontario
Rue Ste-Catherine
Boulevard de Maisonneuve
Avenue des Pins
Ave Cedar
Boulevard Marie Victorian

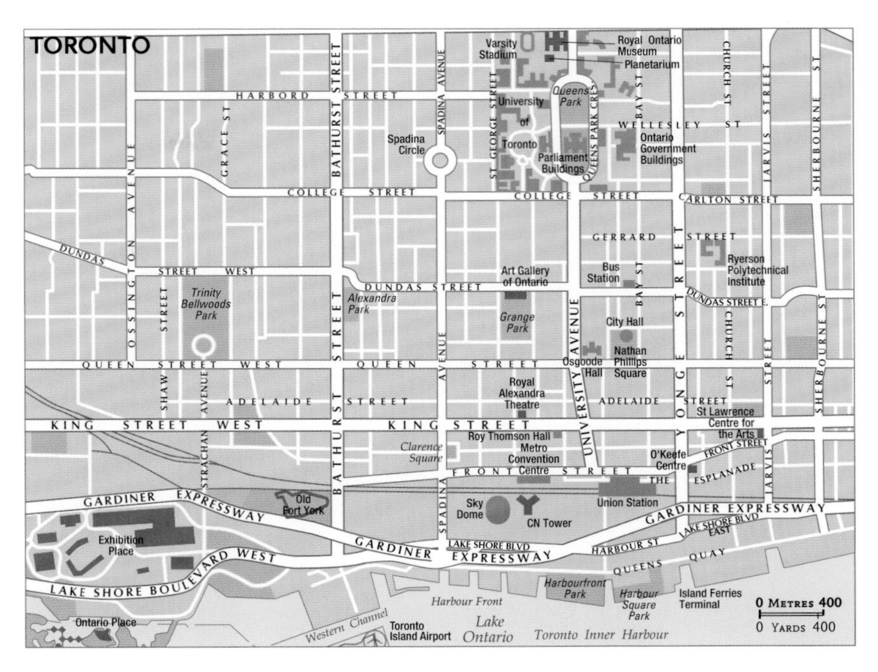
TORONTO
Varsity Stadium
Royal Ontario Museum
Planetarium
Queens Park
University of Toronto
Spadina Circle
Parliament Buildings
Ontario Government Buildings
Harbord Street
Wellesley St
College Street
Carlton Street
Gerrard Street
Dundas Street
Dundas Street East
Queen Street West
Queen Street
Adelaide Street
King Street West
King Street
Front Street
Gardiner Expressway
Lake Shore Boulevard West
Lake Shore Blvd
Harbour St
Queens Quay
Ryerson Polytechnical Institute
Bus Station
Art Gallery of Ontario
Alexandra Park
Trinity Bellwoods Park
Grange Park
City Hall
Nathan Phillips Square
Osgoode Hall
Royal Alexandra Theatre
St Lawrence Centre for the Arts
Roy Thomson Hall
Metro Convention Centre
Clarence Square
O'Keefe Centre
Esplanade
Sky Dome
CN Tower
Union Station
Old Fort York
Exhibition Place
Ontario Place
Harbourfront Park
Harbour Square Park
Harbour Front
Island Ferries Terminal
Toronto Island Airport
Western Channel
Lake Ontario
Toronto Inner Harbour
Ossington Avenue
Shaw Street
Strachan Avenue
Grace St
Bathurst Street
Spadina Avenue
St George Street
University Avenue
Bay St
Yonge Street
Church St
Jarvis Street
Sherbourne St
0 Metres 400
0 Yards 400

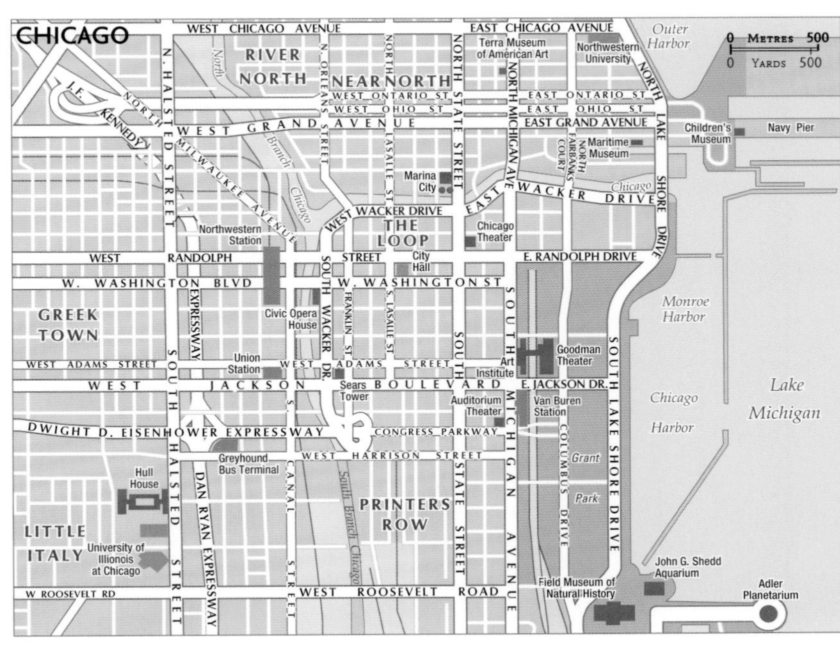
CHICAGO
0 Metres 500
0 Yards 500
West Chicago Avenue
East Chicago Avenue
Outer Harbor
Terra Museum of American Art
Northwestern University
River North
Near North
East Ontario St
East Ohio St
West Ohio St
East Grand Avenue
West Grand Avenue
Navy Pier
Children's Museum
Maritime Museum
Marina City
Wacker Drive
The Loop
Chicago Theater
Northwestern Station
Randolph
City Hall
E. Randolph Drive
W. Washington Blvd
W. Washington St
Greek Town
Civic Opera House
Monroe Harbor
West Adams Street
Union Station
Goodman Theater
Art Institute
Jackson Boulevard
E. Jackson Dr
Sears Tower
Auditorium Theater
Van Buren Station
Lake Michigan
Chicago Harbor
Dwight D. Eisenhower Expressway
Congress Parkway
West Harrison Street
Greyhound Bus Terminal
Hull House
Printers Row
Grant Park
Little Italy
University of Illinois at Chicago
John G. Shedd Aquarium
Field Museum of Natural History
Adler Planetarium
West Roosevelt Road
W Roosevelt Rd
N. Halsted Street
South Halsted Street
Kennedy Expressway
Dan Ryan Expressway
South Wacker Dr
South State Street
North Michigan Ave
South Michigan Avenue
Columbus Drive
Lake Shore Drive
South Lake Shore Drive
South Branch Chicago

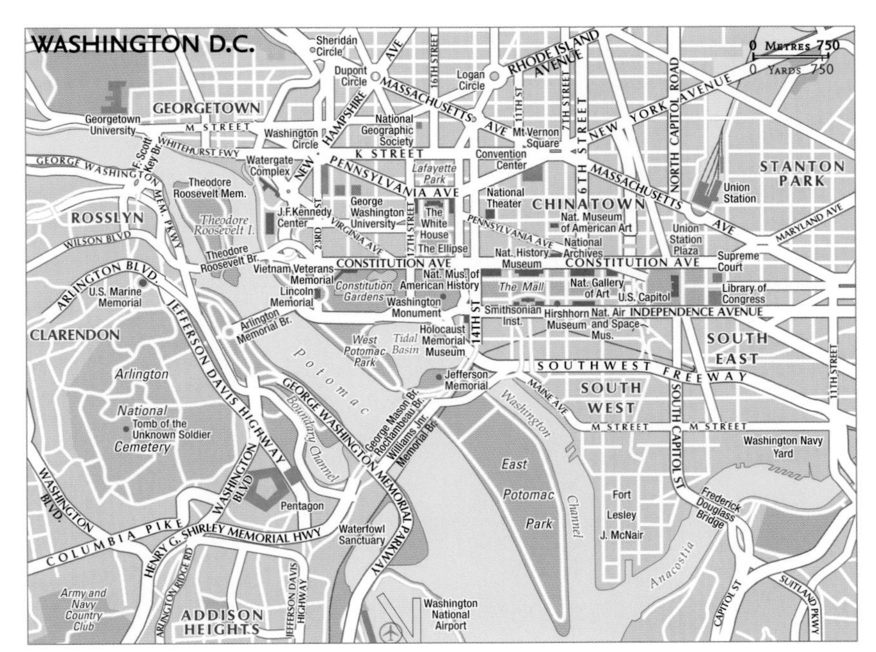
WASHINGTON D.C.
0 Metres 750
0 Yards 750
Sheridan Circle
Dupont Circle
Logan Circle
Rhode Island Avenue
Massachusetts Ave
Georgetown
Georgetown University
M Street
National Geographic Society
Washington Circle
Mt Vernon Square
New York Avenue
K Street
Convention Center
Stanton Park
Watergate Complex
Whitehurst Fwy
Lafayette Park
Union Station
Theodore Roosevelt Mem.
Pennsylvania Ave
National Theater
Chinatown
Rosslyn
J.F.Kennedy Center
George Washington University
The White House
Nat. Museum of American Art
Wilson Blvd
Theodore Roosevelt I.
The Ellipse
National Archives
Union Station Plaza
Maryland Ave
Theodore Roosevelt Br.
Vietnam Veterans Memorial
Constitution Ave
Nat. History Museum
Supreme Court
Arlington Blvd
Lincoln Memorial
Constitution Gardens
Nat. Mus. of American History
The Mall
Nat. Gallery of Art
U.S. Capitol
Library of Congress
U.S. Marine Memorial
Washington Monument
Smithsonian Inst.
Hirshhorn Museum
Nat. Air and Space Mus.
Independence Avenue
Clarendon
Arlington Memorial Br.
West Potomac Park
Tidal Basin
Holocaust Memorial Museum
South East
Southwest Freeway
Arlington
Jefferson Memorial
South West
Potomac
National Tomb of the Unknown Soldier Cemetery
George Mason Br.
Rochambeau Br.
Williams Jr. Memorial Br.
Washington Navy Yard
East Potomac Park
Washington Channel
Fort Lesley J. McNair
Frederick Douglass Bridge
Pentagon
Boundary Channel
Waterfowl Sanctuary
Anacostia
Columbia Pike
Shirley Memorial Hwy
Henry G. Shirley Memorial Hwy
Jefferson Davis Highway
George Washington Memorial Parkway
Washington Blvd
Army and Navy Country Club
Addison Heights
Washington National Airport
North Capitol Road
South Capitol St
Suitland Pkwy

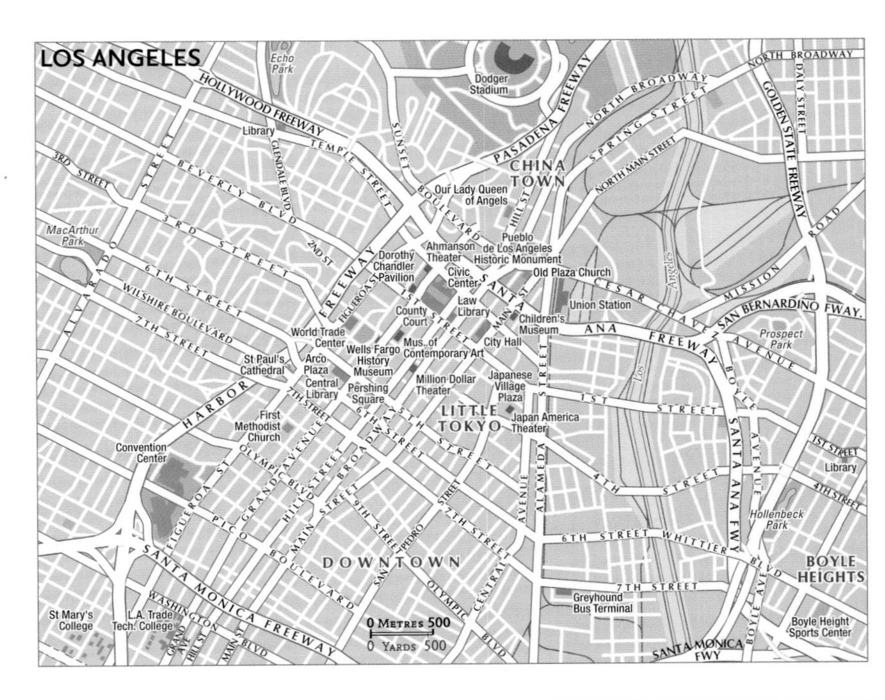
LOS ANGELES
Echo Park
Dodger Stadium
North Broadway
Hollywood Freeway
Library
Temple Street
Pasadena Freeway
Golden State Freeway
China Town
North Main Street
Our Lady Queen of Angels
Pueblo de Los Angeles Historic Monument
Ahmanson Theater
Dorothy Chandler Pavilion
MacArthur Park
Civic Center
Old Plaza Church
Union Station
Law Library
County Court Library
Children's Museum
San Bernardino Fwy.
Santa Ana Freeway
World Trade Center
Wells Fargo History Museum
City Hall
Mus. of Contemporary Art
Prospect Park
St Paul's Cathedral
Arco Plaza
Central Library
Pershing Square
Million Dollar Theater
Japanese Village Plaza
Little Tokyo
Japan America Theater
First Methodist Church
Harbor Freeway
Convention Center
1st Street
Library
4th Street
6th Street
7th Street
Whittier Blvd
Hollenbeck Park
Downtown
Boyle Heights
Greyhound Bus Terminal
Boyle Height Sports Center
St Mary's College
L.A. Trade Tech. College
Santa Monica Freeway
Santa Monica Fwy
Santa Ana Fwy
Wilshire Boulevard
Olympic Blvd
Pico Boulevard
Grand Ave
Figueroa St
0 Metres 500
0 Yards 500

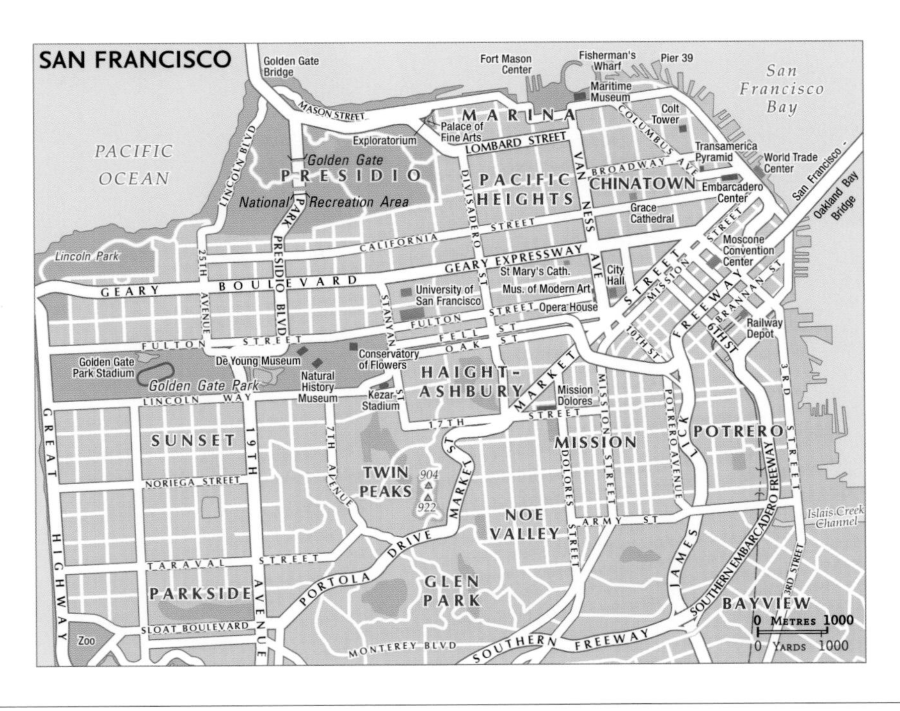
SAN FRANCISCO
Golden Gate Bridge
Fort Mason Center
Fisherman's Wharf
Pier 39
San Francisco Bay
Maritime Museum
Mason Street
Marina
Palace of Fine Arts
Exploratorium
Lombard Street
Colt Tower
Transamerica Pyramid
World Trade Center
Pacific Ocean
Golden Gate
Presidio
National Recreation Area
Pacific Heights
Chinatown
Embarcadero Center
San Francisco-Oakland Bay Bridge
Grace Cathedral
California
Lincoln Park
Geary Expressway
Geary Boulevard
St Mary's Cath.
City Hall
Moscone Convention Center
University of San Francisco
Mus. of Modern Art
Opera House
Railway Depot
Fulton Street
Golden Gate Park Stadium
De Young Museum
Conservatory of Flowers
Golden Gate Park
Natural History Museum
Kezar Stadium
Haight-Ashbury
Lincoln Way
Mission Dolores
Sunset
Mission
Potrero
Twin Peaks
Noriega Street
Noe Valley
Army St
Islais Creek Channel
Taraval Street
Parkside
Portola Drive
Glen Park
Sloat Boulevard
Zoo
Monterey Blvd
Southern Freeway
Southern Embarcadero Freeway
Bayview
Great Highway
19th Avenue
Presidio Blvd
Market
Van Ness Ave
Divisadero
Dolores
James
0 Metres 1000
0 Yards 1000

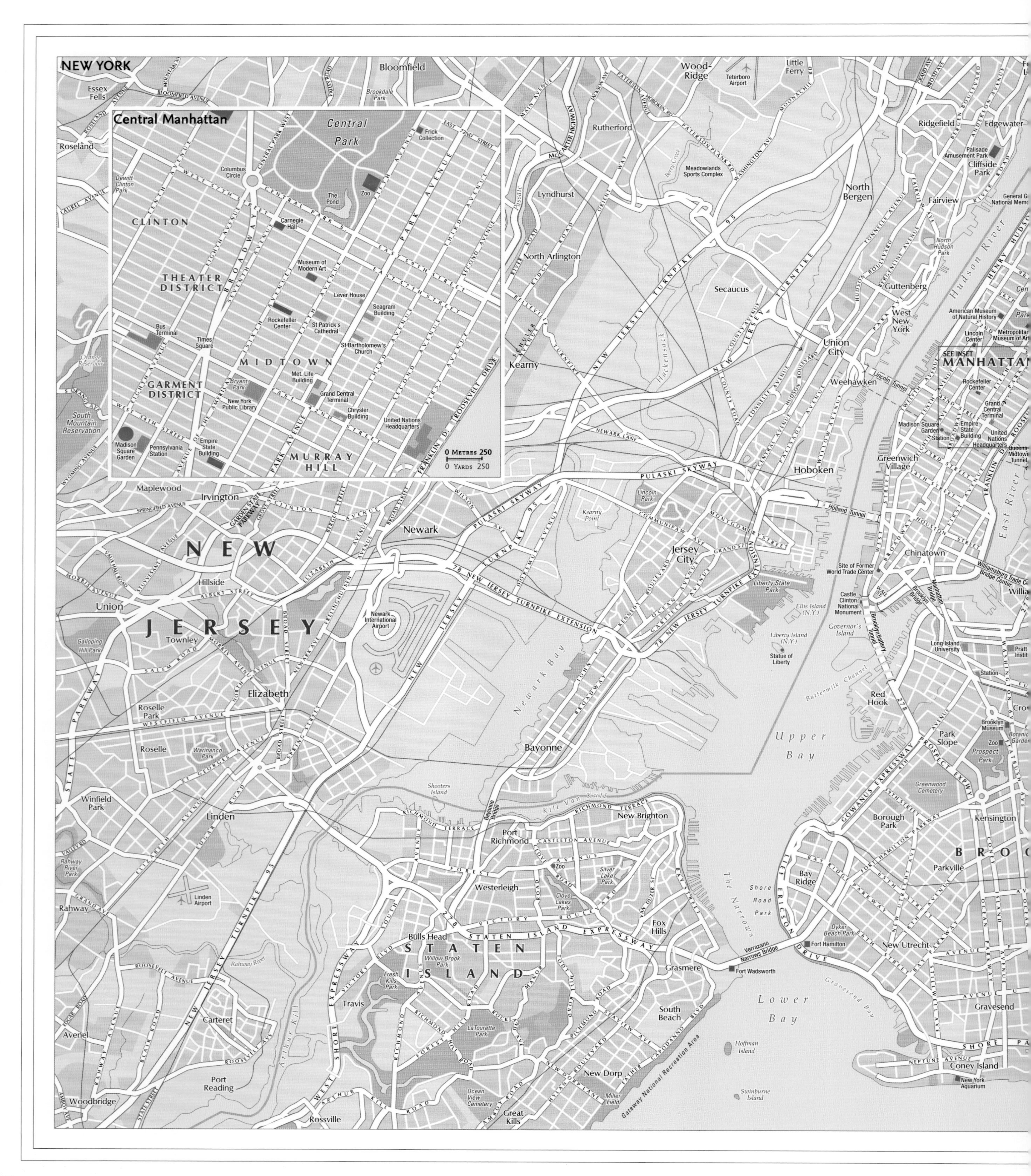
NEW YORK
Central Manhattan
Central Park
Frick Collection
Columbus Circle
The Pond
Zoo
Dewitt Clinton Park
CLINTON
Carnegie Hall
Museum of Modern Art
THEATER DISTRICT
Lever House
Seagram Building
Rockefeller Center
St Patrick's Cathedral
St Bartholomew's Church
Bus Terminal
Times Square
MIDTOWN
Met. Life Building
Grand Central Terminal
Chrysler Building
GARMENT DISTRICT
Bryant Park
New York Public Library
United Nations Headquarters
Madison Square Garden
Pennsylvania Station
Empire State Building
MURRAY HILL
0 Metres 250
0 Yards 250
BROADWAY
PARK AVENUE
FIFTH AVENUE
SECOND AVENUE
FIRST AVENUE
FRANKLIN D. ROOSEVELT DRIVE
Essex Fells
Roseland
Bloomfield
Brookdale Park
Wood-Ridge
Teterboro Airport
Little Ferry
Rutherford
Meadowlands Sports Complex
Lyndhurst
North Arlington
North Bergen
Ridgefield
Edgewater
Palisade Amusement Park
Cliffside Park
Fairview
Guttenberg
West New York
Secaucus
Kearny
Union City
Weehawken
Lincoln Tunnel
Hoboken
Holland Tunnel
Hudson River
Greenwich Village
Chinatown
East River
SEE INSET MANHATTAN
American Museum of Natural History
Lincoln Center
Metropolitan Museum of Art
Orange Reservoir
South Mountain Reservation
Maplewood
Irvington
Newark
NEW JERSEY
Hillside
Union
Townley
Galloping Hill Park
Elizabeth
Roselle Park
Roselle
Warinanco Park
Winfield Park
Linden
Rahway River Park
Rahway
Linden Airport
Newark International Airport
Lincoln Park
Kearny Point
Jersey City
Liberty State Park
Ellis Island (N.Y.)
Liberty Island (N.Y.)
Statue of Liberty
Governor's Island
Site of Former World Trade Center
Castle Clinton National Monument
Brooklyn-Battery Tunnel
Long Island University
Red Hook
Buttermilk Channel
Newark Bay
Bayonne
Bayonne Bridge
Upper Bay
Shooters Island
Kill Van Kull
New Brighton
Port Richmond
Westerleigh
Zoo
Silver Lake Park
Clove Lakes Park
Bulls Head
STATEN ISLAND
Willow Brook Park
Fresh Kills Park
Travis
Fox Hills
Grasmere
Fort Wadsworth
Verrazano Narrows Bridge
Fort Hamilton
The Narrows
Shore Road Park
Bay Ridge
Dyker Beach Park
New Utrecht
Borough Park
Kensington
Parkville
Park Slope
Prospect Park
Brooklyn Museum
Botanic Garden
Greenwood Cemetery
GOWANUS EXPRESSWAY
PROSPECT EXPY
Gravesend
Gravesend Bay
Coney Island
New York Aquarium
Lower Bay
Hoffman Island
Swinburne Island
Gateway National Recreation Area
South Beach
New Dorp
Miller Field
Great Kills
Ocean View Cemetery
LaTourette Park
Rossville
Carteret
Port Reading
Avenel
Woodbridge
Rahway River
Arthur Kill
NEW JERSEY TURNPIKE
PULASKI SKYWAY
STATEN ISLAND EXPRESSWAY
WEST SHORE EXPRESSWAY
GARDEN STATE PARKWAY

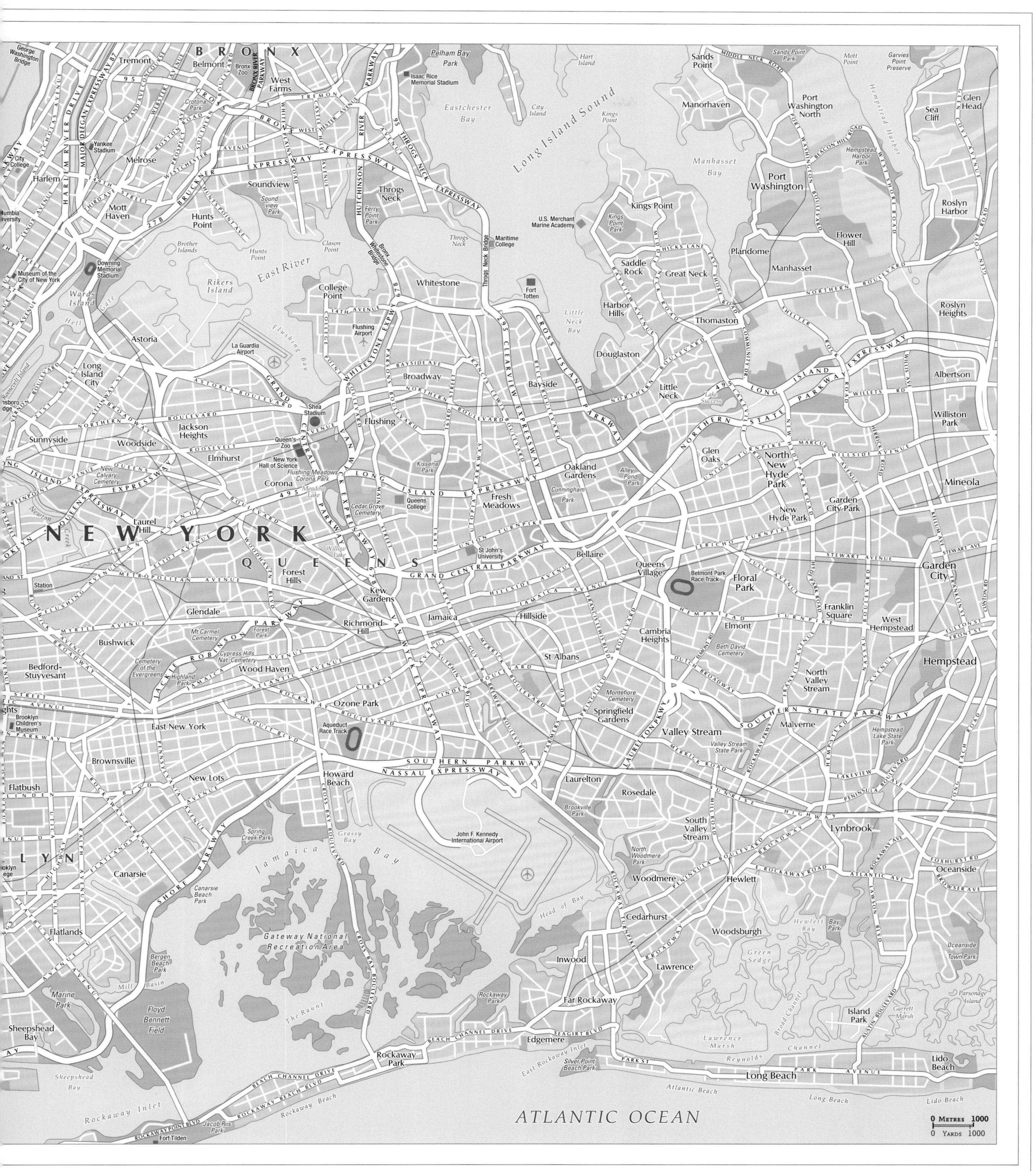

ATLANTIC OCEAN

0 Metres 1000
0 Yards 1000

© Collins Bartholomew Ltd

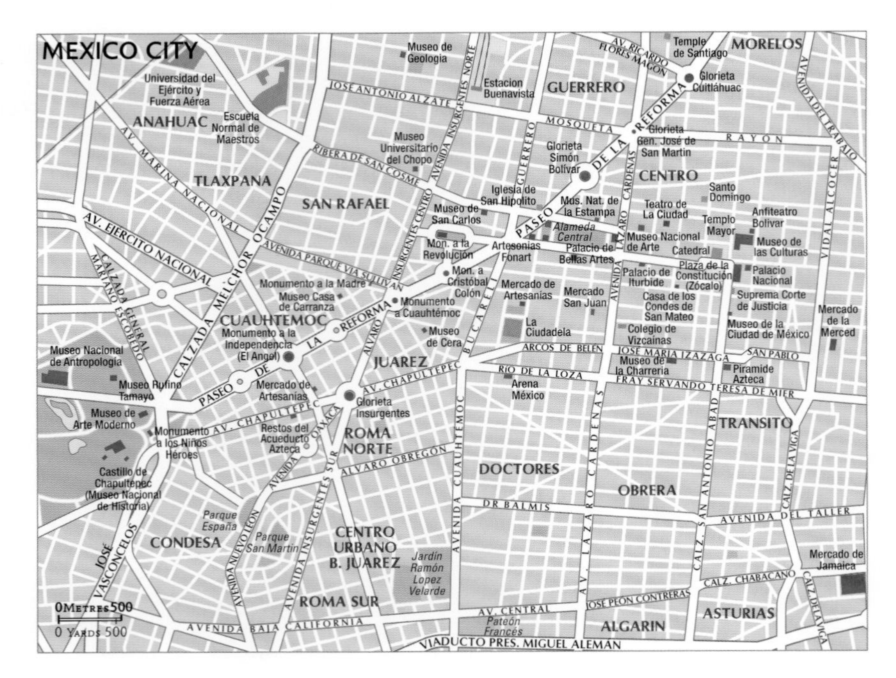
MEXICO CITY
GUERRERO
MORELOS
ANAHUAC
TLAXPANA
SAN RAFAEL
CENTRO
CUAUHTEMOC
JUAREZ
ROMA NORTE
DOCTORES
OBRERA
TRANSITO
CONDESA
CENTRO URBANO B. JUAREZ
ROMA SUR
ALGARIN
ASTURIAS
Museo Nacional de Antropologia
Castillo de Chapultepec (Museo Nacional de Historia)
Palacio de Bellas Artes
Catedral
Palacio Nacional
Templo Mayor
Monumento a la Independencia (El Angel)
Monumento a la Revolución
Museo de Arte Moderno
Viaducto Pres. Miguel Alemán
0 Metres 500
0 Yards 500

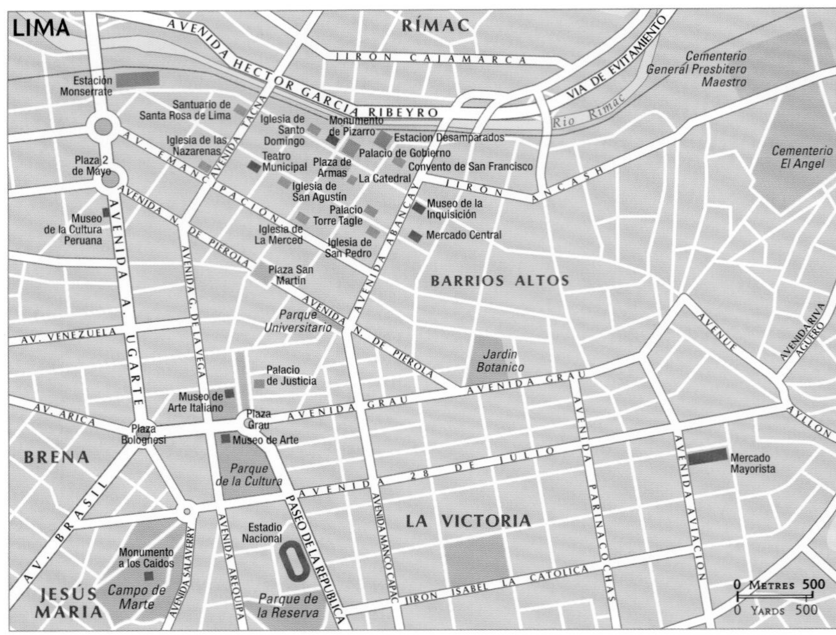
LIMA
RÍMAC
BARRIOS ALTOS
BREÑA
LA VICTORIA
JESÚS MARÍA
Cementerio General Presbitero Maestro
Cementerio El Angel
Estación Monserrate
Plaza de Armas
Palacio de Gobierno
Catedral
Convento de San Francisco
Plaza San Martín
Parque Universitario
Palacio de Justicia
Museo de Arte Italiano
Museo de Arte
Parque de la Cultura
Estadio Nacional
Campo de Marte
Parque de la Reserva
Mercado Central
Mercado Mayorista
Jardín Botanico
0 Metres 500
0 Yards 500

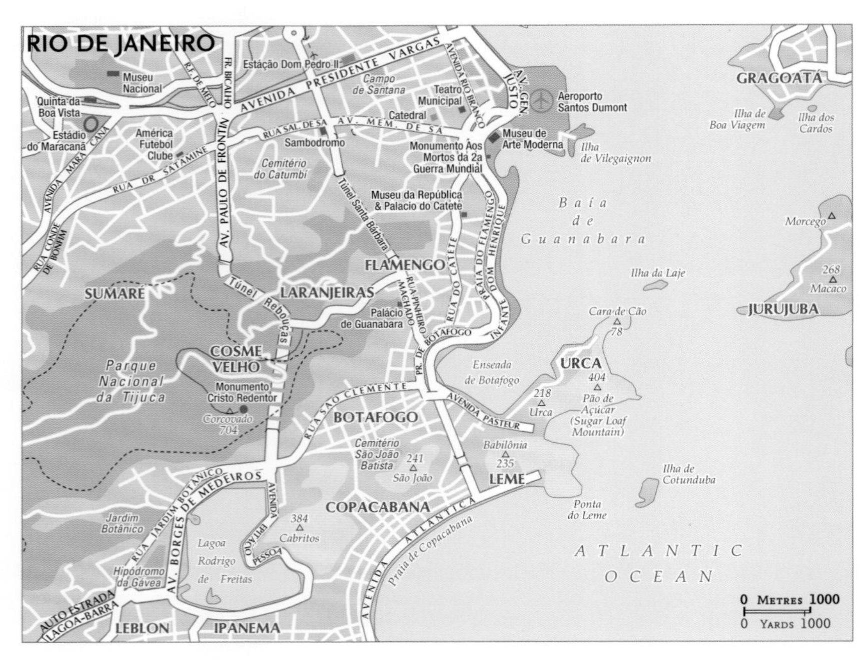
RIO DE JANEIRO
GRAGOATÁ
Aeroporto Santos Dumont
Museu Nacional
Estádio do Maracanã
Baía de Guanabara
FLAMENGO
LARANJEIRAS
SUMARE
COSME VELHO
Parque Nacional da Tijuca
BOTAFOGO
URCA
Pão de Açúcar (Sugar Loaf Mountain)
LEME
COPACABANA
Lagoa Rodrigo de Freitas
LEBLON
IPANEMA
JURUJUBA
ATLANTIC OCEAN
0 Metres 1000
0 Yards 1000

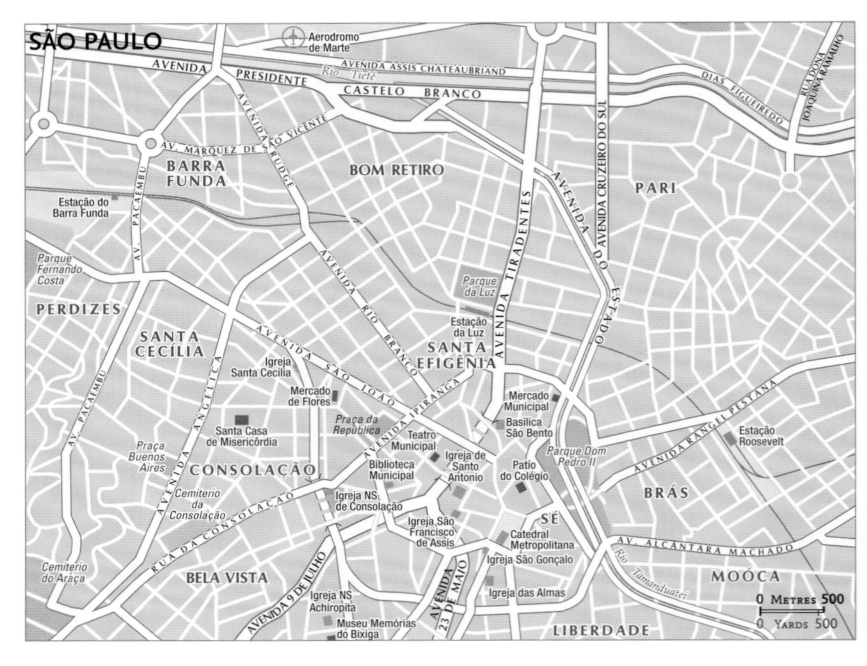
SÃO PAULO
Aerodromo de Marte
BARRA FUNDA
BOM RETIRO
PARI
PERDIZES
SANTA CECILIA
SANTA EFIGÊNIA
CONSOLAÇÃO
BRÁS
SÉ
BELA VISTA
MOOCA
LIBERDADE
Estação da Luz
Mercado Municipal
Catedral Metropolitana
Teatro Municipal
Estação Roosevelt
0 Metres 500
0 Yards 500

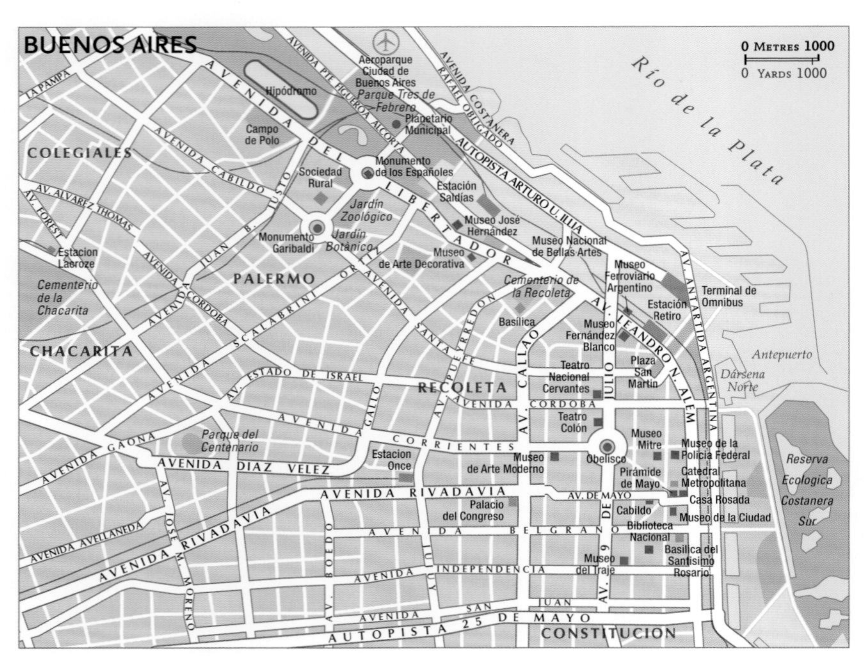
BUENOS AIRES
Aeroparque Ciudad de Buenos Aires
Río de la Plata
Hipódromo
COLEGIALES
PALERMO
CHACARITA
RECOLETA
Cementerio de la Recoleta
Cementerio de la Chacarita
Estación Retiro
Terminal de Omnibus
Teatro Colón
Obelisco
Casa Rosada
Cabildo
Palacio del Congreso
Reserva Ecologica Costanera Sur
Parque del Centenario
Avenida Rivadavia
Autopista 25 de Mayo
CONSTITUCION
0 Metres 1000
0 Yards 1000

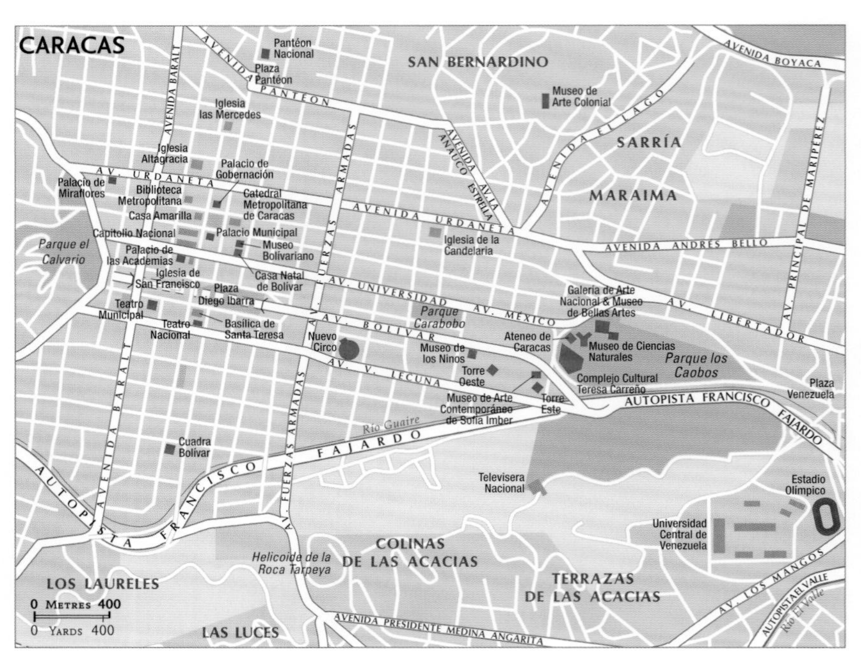
CARACAS
Panteón Nacional
SAN BERNARDINO
Museo de Arte Colonial
SARRÍA
MARAIMA
Palacio de Miraflores
Parque el Calvario
Catedral Metropolitana de Caracas
Capitolio Nacional
Teatro Municipal
Parque Carabobo
Nuevo Circo
Museo de Ciencias Naturales
Parque los Caobos
Plaza Venezuela
Autopista Francisco Fajardo
Universidad Central de Venezuela
Estadio Olimpico
COLINAS DE LAS ACACIAS
TERRAZAS DE LAS ACACIAS
LOS LAURELES
LAS LUCES
0 Metres 400
0 Yards 400

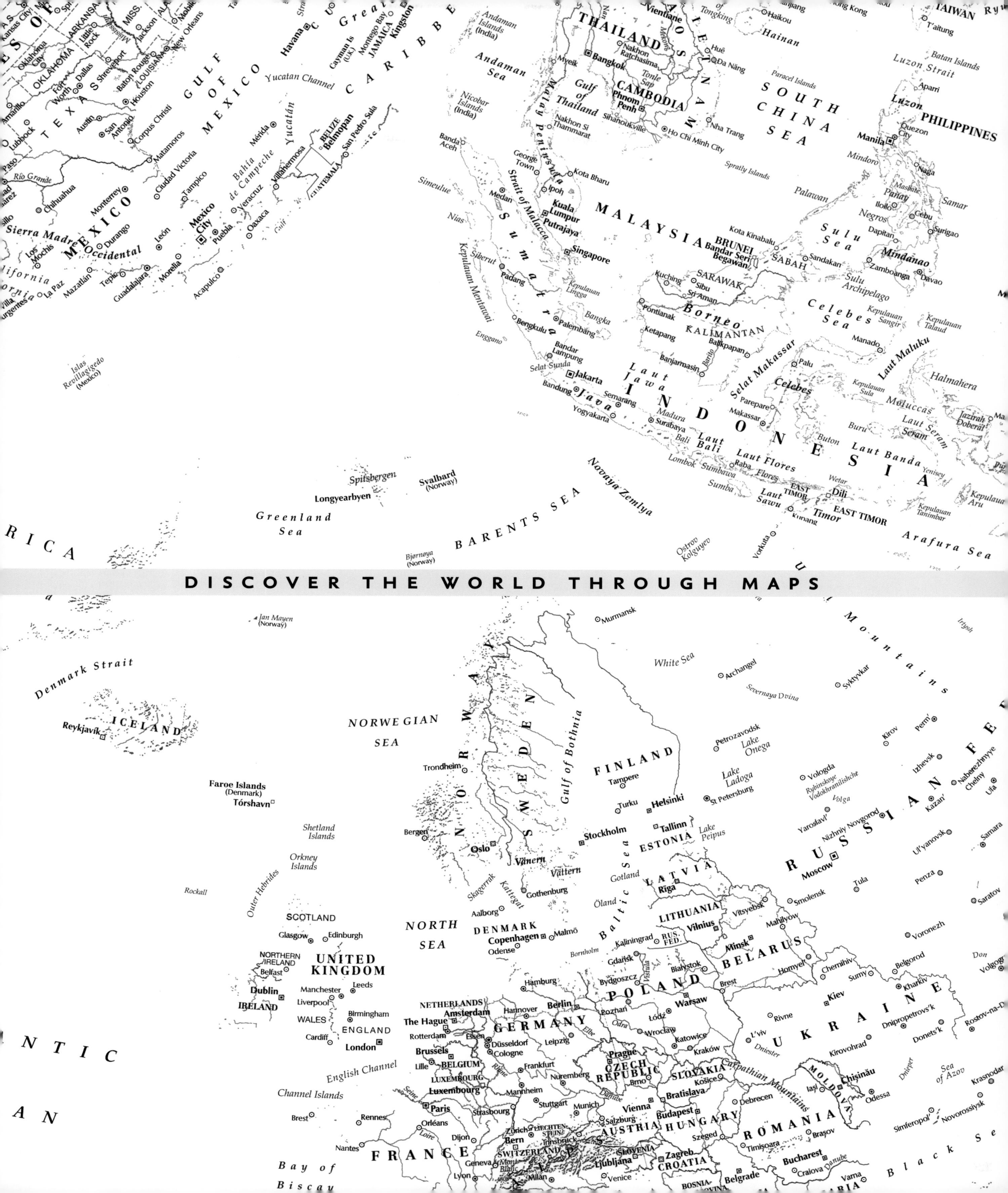
OKLAHOMA
ARKANSAS
MISS.
Oklahoma City
Little Rock
Jackson
Mobile
New Orleans
LOUISIANA
Baton Rouge
Shreveport
Dallas
Fort Worth
TEXAS
Houston
Austin
San Antonio
Corpus Christi
Lubbock
Amarillo
Río Grande
Matamoros
Ciudad Victoria
Tampico
Monterrey
Chihuahua
MEXICO
Sierra Madre Occidental
Durango
Los Mochis
León
Mexico City
Puebla
Veracruz
Oaxaca
Morelia
Guadalajara
Tepic
Mazatlán
La Paz
Acapulco
GULF OF MEXICO
Bahía de Campeche
Villahermosa
Mérida
Yucatán
Yucatan Channel
BELIZE
Belmopan
GUATEMALA
San Pedro Sula
Havana
Cayman Is (UK)
Montego Bay
JAMAICA
Kingston
CARIBBE
Islas Revillagigedo (Mexico)
Andaman Islands (India)
Andaman Sea
Nicobar Islands (India)
Banda Aceh
Myeik
THAILAND
Bangkok
Nakhon Ratchasima
Gulf of Thailand
Nakhon Si Thammarat
Vientiane
LAOS
VIETNAM
Hanoi
Haiphong
Gulf of Tongking
Hainan
Huê
Da Nang
CAMBODIA
Phnom Penh
Tonle Sap
Sihanoukville
Ho Chi Minh City
Nha Trang
Paracel Islands
SOUTH CHINA SEA
Spratly Islands
TAIWAN
T'aitung
Batan Islands
Luzon Strait
Aparri
Luzon
PHILIPPINES
Manila
Quezon City
Mindoro
Naga
Palawan
Panay
Masbate
Samar
Iloilo
Cebu
Negros
Surigao
Dapitan
Mindanao
Zamboanga
Davao
Sulu Sea
Sulu Archipelago
Malay Peninsula
George Town
Kota Bharu
Ipoh
Strait of Malacca
Medan
Kuala Lumpur
Putrajaya
Singapore
MALAYSIA
Kota Kinabalu
BRUNEI
Bandar Seri Begawan
SABAH
Sandakan
SARAWAK
Kuching
Sibu
Sri Aman
Simeulue
Nias
Siberut
Kepulauan Mentawai
Padang
Sumatra
Kepulauan Lingga
Bangka
Bengkulu
Palembang
Enggano
Bandar Lampung
Selat Sunda
Jakarta
Bandung
Java
Semarang
Yogyakarta
Surabaya
Madura
Bali
Lombok
Sumbawa
Sumba
Laut Jawa
Laut Bali
Laut Flores
Flores
Raba
Borneo
KALIMANTAN
Pontianak
Ketapang
Balikpapan
Banjarmasin
Barito
Selat Makassar
Celebes
Palu
Parepare
Makassar
Celebes Sea
Kepulauan Sangir
Kepulauan Talaud
Manado
Laut Maluku
Halmahera
Kepulauan Sula
Moluccas
Laut Seram
Seram
Buru
Buton
Laut Banda
INDONESIA
Wetar
Dili
EAST TIMOR
Timor
Laut Sawu
Kupang
Kepulauan Aru
Kepulauan Tanimbar
Arafura Sea
Spitsbergen
Svalbard (Norway)
Longyearbyen
Greenland Sea
BARENTS SEA
Novaya Zemlya
Bjørnøya (Norway)
Ostrov Kolguyev
Vorkuta
Jan Mayen (Norway)
Denmark Strait
ICELAND
Reykjavík
NORWEGIAN SEA
Faroe Islands (Denmark)
Tórshavn
Shetland Islands
Orkney Islands
Outer Hebrides
Rockall
SCOTLAND
Glasgow
Edinburgh
NORTHERN IRELAND
Belfast
UNITED KINGDOM
Dublin
IRELAND
Manchester
Leeds
Liverpool
Birmingham
WALES
ENGLAND
Cardiff
London
English Channel
Channel Islands
Brest
Rennes
Nantes
Bay of Biscay
NORTH SEA
NORWAY
Trondheim
Bergen
Oslo
SWEDEN
Vänern
Vättern
Gothenburg
Stockholm
Gulf of Bothnia
Skagerrak
Kattegat
Aalborg
DENMARK
Copenhagen
Malmö
Odense
Bornholm
Gotland
Öland
Baltic Sea
FINLAND
Tampere
Turku
Helsinki
Murmansk
White Sea
Archangel
Severnaya Dvina
Syktyvkar
Petrozavodsk
Lake Onega
Lake Ladoga
St Petersburg
Tallinn
ESTONIA
Lake Peipus
LATVIA
Riga
LITHUANIA
Vilnius
Kaliningrad
RUS. FED.
Gdańsk
Vistula
Bydgoszcz
Białystok
POLAND
Warsaw
Poznań
Łódź
Wrocław
Katowice
Kraków
Odra
Vitsyebsk
Mahilyow
Minsk
BELARUS
Brest
Homyel'
Smolensk
Moscow
RUSSIAN FE
Tula
Vologda
Rybinskoye Vodokhranilishche
Yaroslavl'
Nizhniy Novgorod
Volga
Kirov
Perm'
Izhevsk
Kazan'
Naberezhnyye Chelny
Ufa
Ul'yanovsk
Samara
Penza
Saratov
Voronezh
Don
Volgograd
Belgorod
Kharkiv
Sumy
Chernihiv
Kiev
UKRAINE
Rivne
L'viv
Dniester
Dnipropetrovs'k
Donets'k
Rostov-na-Donu
Kirovohrad
Dnieper
Sea of Azov
Krasnodar
Chişinău
MOLDOVA
Iaşi
Odessa
Simferopol'
Novorossiysk
Black Sea
ROMANIA
Braşov
Bucharest
Craiova
Danube
Timişoara
Varna
Carpathian Mountains
Ural Mountains
Irtysh
Hamburg
NETHERLANDS
Amsterdam
The Hague
Rotterdam
Hannover
Berlin
GERMANY
Elbe
Essen
Düsseldorf
Cologne
Leipzig
Brussels
Lille
BELGIUM
LUXEMBOURG
Luxembourg
Frankfurt
Rhine
Nuremberg
Mannheim
Stuttgart
Munich
Strasbourg
Seine
Paris
Orléans
Loire
Dijon
FRANCE
Lyon
Geneva
Zurich
Bern
SWITZERLAND
LIECHTENSTEIN
Innsbruck
Milan
Venice
Prague
CZECH REPUBLIC
Brno
Danube
SLOVAKIA
Košice
Bratislava
Vienna
Salzburg
AUSTRIA
Budapest
HUNGARY
Debrecen
Szeged
SLOVENIA
Ljubljana
Zagreb
CROATIA
BOSNIA-
Belgrade

Introduction to the Atlas and Map Symbols

These pages explain the editorial policies followed for map pages 110 to 240 and the map symbols used on the maps are also explained here. The map sequence starts at the International Date Line in the Pacific Ocean and broadly works westwards, moving from Oceania through Asia, Europe, Africa, North America and finally to South America. The alphanumeric reference system used in the index is based on latitude and longitude, and the number and letter for each graticule square are shown within each map frame. The numbers of adjoining or overlapping plates are shown by arrows in the frame and accompanying numbers in the margin.

Boundaries
The status of nations, their names and their boundaries, are shown in this atlas as they are at the time of going to press, as far as can be ascertained. The atlas includes any recent changes of status of nations and their boundaries. Where an international boundary symbol appears in the sea or ocean it does not necessarily infer a legal maritime boundary, but shows which islands belong to which country.

Where international boundaries are the subject of dispute it may be that no portrayal of them will meet with the approval of any of the countries involved. It is not seen as the function of this atlas to try to adjudicate between the rights and wrongs of political issues, and reference mapping at atlas scales is not the ideal medium for indicating the claims of many separatist and irredentist movements. However, every reasonable attempt is made to show where an active territorial dispute exists, and where there is an important difference between 'de facto' (existing in fact, on the ground) and 'de jure' (according to law) boundaries. This is done by the use of a different symbol where international boundaries are disputed, or where the alignment is unconfirmed, to that used for settled international boundaries. Ceasefire lines are also shown by a separate symbol. For clarity, disputed boundaries and areas are annotated where this is considered necessary. The atlas aims to take a strictly neutral viewpoint of all such cases, based on advice from expert consultants.

Scale
In order to directly compare areas throughout the world it would be necessary to maintain a single map scale throughout the atlas. However, the desirability of mapping more densely populated and more significant areas of the world at larger, and therefore more detailed, scales means that a range of scales have been used. Scales for continental maps range from 1:17 500 000 to 1:32 000 000, depending on the size of the continental land mass being covered. Scales for regional maps are typically in the range 1:12 000 000 to 1:20 000 000, although smaller scales are used for a few remoter areas such as northern Asia. Mapping for most countries is at scales between 1:5 000 000 and 1:7 000 000, although for the most densely populated areas of Europe the scale increases to 1:2 000 000.

Map Projections
The representation or 'projection' of the Earth into only two dimensions is a perennial problem for the cartographer. Distortions are inevitable and all map projections are compromises. Some projections seek to maintain correct area relationships (equal area projections), true distances and bearings from a point (equidistant projections) or correct angles and shapes (conformal projections). Others attempt to achieve a balance between these properties. The choice of projections used in this atlas has been made on an individual continental and regional basis. Projections used, and their individual parameters, have been defined to provide the best representation of the area mapped, to minimize distortion and to reduce scale errors as much as possible. The projection used is indicated at the bottom left of each map plate.

Place Names
The spelling of place names on maps has always been a matter of great complexity, because of the variety of the world's languages and the systems used to write them down. There is no standard way of spelling names or of converting them from one alphabet, or symbol set, to another. Instead, conventional ways of spelling have evolved in each of the world's major languages, and the results often differ significantly from the name as it is spelled in the original language. Familiar examples of English conventional names include Munich (München), Florence (Firenze) and Moscow (from the transliterated form, Moskva).

In this atlas, local name forms are used where these are in the Roman alphabet, though for major cities and main physical features, conventional English names are given first. The local forms are those which are officially recognized by the government of the country concerned, usually as represented by its official mapping agency. This is a basic principle laid down by the United Kingdom government's Permanent Committee on Geographical Names (PCGN) and the equivalent United States Board on Geographic Names (BGN). Prominent English-language and historic names are not neglected, however. These, and significant superseded names and alternate spellings, are included in brackets on the maps where space permits, and are cross-referenced in the index.

Country names are shown in conventional English form and include any recent changes promulgated by national governments and adopted by the United Nations. The names of continents, oceans, seas and under-water features in international waters also appear in English throughout the atlas, as do those of other international features where such an English form exists and is in common use. International features are defined as features crossing one or more international boundary.

For languages in non-Roman alphabets or symbol sets, names need to be 'Romanized' through a process of transliteration (the conversion of characters or symbols from one alphabet into another) or transcription (conversion of names based on pronunciation). Different systems often exist for this process, but PCGN and its United States counterpart, the Board on Geographic Names (BGN), usually follow the same Romanization principles, and the general policy for this atlas is to follow their lead.

Abbreviations

Arch.	Archipelago		
B.	Bay		
	Bahia, Baía	Portuguese	bay
	Bahía	Spanish	bay
	Baie	French	bay
C.	Cape		
	Cabo	Portuguese, Spanish	cape, headland
	Cap	French	cape, headland
Co	Cerro	Spanish	hill, peak, summit
E.	East, Eastern		
Est.	Estrecho	Spanish	strait
G.	Gebel	Arabic	hill, mountain
Gt	Great		
I.	Island, Isle		
	Ilha	Portuguese	island
	Islas	Spanish	island
Is	Islands, Isles		
	Islas	Spanish	islands
Kep.	Kepulauan	Indonesian	islands
Khr.	Khrebet	Russian	mountain range

L.	Lake		
	Loch	(Scotland)	lake
	Lough	(Ireland)	lake
	Lac	French	lake
	Lago	Portuguese, Spanish	lake
M.	Mys	Russian	cape, point
Mt	Mount		
	Mont	French	hill, mountain
Mt.	Mountain		
Mte	Monte	Portuguese, Spanish	hill, mountain
Mts	Mountains		
	Monts	French	hills, mountains
N.	North, Northern		
O.	Ostrov	Russian	island
Pk	Puncak	Indonesian, Malay	hill, mountain
Pt	Point		
Pta	Punta	Italian, Spanish	cape, point
R.	River		
	Rio	Portuguese	river
	Río	Spanish	river
	Rivière	French	river

Ra.	Range		mountain range
S.	South, Southern		
	Salar, Salina,		
	Salinas	Spanish	salt pan, salt pans
Sa	Serra	Portuguese,	mountain range
	Sierra	Spanish	mountain range
Sd	Sound		
S.E.	Southeast, Southeastern		
St	Saint		
	Sankt	German	Saint
	Sint	Dutch	Saint
Sta	Santa	Italian, Portuguese, Spanish	Saint
Ste	Sainte	French	Saint
Str.	Strait		
Tk	Teluk	Indonesian, Malay	bay, gulf
Tg	Tanjong, Tanjung	Indonesian, Malay	cape, point
Vdkhr.	Vodokhranilishche	Russian	reservoir
W.	West, Western		strait
	Wadi, Wâdi, Wādī	Arabic	watercourse

Travel Commentary and World Heritage Sites

Alongside the mapping pages a travel commentary is provided for the major destination countries of the world. Wherever possible the commentary appears alongside the most relevant map but occasionally the commentary has been moved to an overlapping map page to allow greater detail in areas where numerous countries are shown together. Smaller countries and those without as many tourist arrivals do not have a commentary. A simple statistical overview is provided for these countries alongside the ocean maps on pages 235 to 240.

World Heritage Sites are shown in one of two ways.

Where a site is located away from a major urban area the symbol is shown and the full official name for the heritage site is given:

☆ New Lanark

Due to the fact that many urban areas have numerous sites, whenever there is a site located in an urban area the symbol is shown, but the name of the specific site or sites is not:

Edinburgh ☆

Due to mapping scales, not every site is shown on each map, but every site can be located on at least one map, usually the largest scale map that it would appear on.

Land and Water Features

———	River	I	Dam/Barrage
- - - - -	Impermanent river/Wadi	˘	Oasis
⊥⊥⊥⊥	Canal		Lake
··········	Flood dyke		Salt lake/Lagoon
———	Coral reef		Dry salt lake/Salt pan
˄˄˄˄˄	Escarpment		Impermanent lake
1234 △	Summit Height in metres		Impermanent salt lake
⁔ 123	Pass Height in metres		Marsh
1234 ▲	Volcano Height in metres		Sandy desert/Dunes
123	Ocean deep Depth in metres		Rocky desert
‖	Waterfall		Lava field

Transport

═══	Motorway Shown on large-scale maps only
———	Main road
———	Other road
- - - -	Track
─┼┼┼─	Road tunnel
———	Main railway
———	Other railway
─┼┼┼─	Railway tunnel
✈	Main airport
✈	Regional airport

Cities and Towns

Population	National Capital	Administrative Capital Shown for selected countries only	Other City or Town
over 10 million	**Tōkyō** ▣	**Karachi** ◉	**New York** ◉
5 million to 10 million	**Santiago** ▣	**Tianjin** ◉	**Philadelphia** ◉
1 million to 5 million	**Damascus** ▣	**Douala** ◉	**Barranquilla** ◉
500 000 to 1 million	**Bangui** ▣	**Bulawayo** ◎	**El Paso** ◎
100 000 to 500 000	Wellington ▣	Mansa ◉	Mobile ○
50 000 to 100 000	Port of Spain ▢	Lubango ◉	Zaraza ○
10 000 to 50 000	Malabo ▫	Chinhoyi ◦	El Tigre ○
under 10 000	Roseau ▫	Ati ◦	Soledad ○

Boundaries

▬▬▬	International boundary
▬◼▬◼	Disputed international boundary/ alignment unconfirmed
●●●●●	Ceasefire line
▬▬▬	Administrative boundary

Styles of Lettering

Cities and towns are explained above	
Country	**FRANCE**
Overseas Territory/Dependency	**Guadeloupe**
Disputed Territory	AKSAI CHIN
Administrative name Shown for selected countries only	SCOTLAND
Area name	PATAGONIA

Island	*Gran Canaria*
Lake	*Lake Erie*
Mountain	*Mont Blanc*
River	*Thames*
Region	*LAPPLAND*

Miscellaneous Symbols

- - - - -	National park
·········	Reserve
⌣⌣⌣⌣	Ancient wall
∴	Site of specific interest
	Built-up area

World Physical

The shapes of the continents and oceans have evolved over millions of years. Movement of the tectonic plates which make up the Earth's crust has created some of the best known land features. From the highest point Mount Everest to the deepest in the Mariana Trench is a height of almost 20 000 m /over 65 000 ft. Earthquakes, volcanoes, erosion, climatic variations and man's intervention all continue to affect the Earth's landscapes. Different landscapes reflect great variations in climate from deserts such as the Sahara, to the frozen ice cap of Antarctica.

Facts

- The Pacific Ocean is larger than the continents' land areas combined.

- The average height of the Earth's land surface is 840 m (2755 ft) above sea level and 52 per cent of the land is below 500 m (1640 ft). Approximately 10 per cent of the surface is permanently covered by ice.

- The Ural Mountains define part of the boundary between Europe and Asia.

- The collision of two tectonic plates – the Indo-Australia and the Eurasian Plates – formed the Himalaya mountains. The mountains are still rising at a rate of approximately 5 mm (0.2 inch) a year.

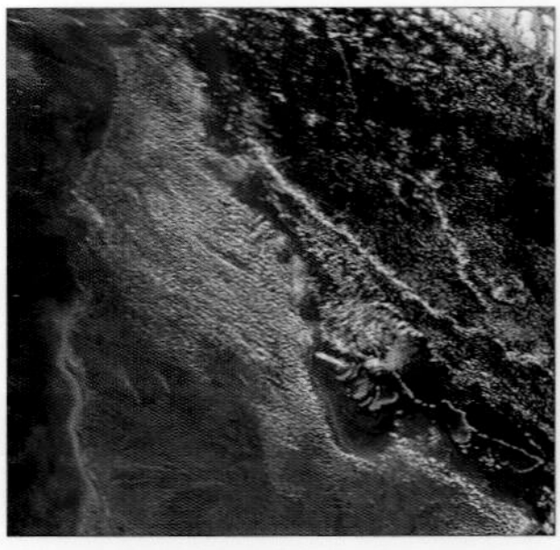

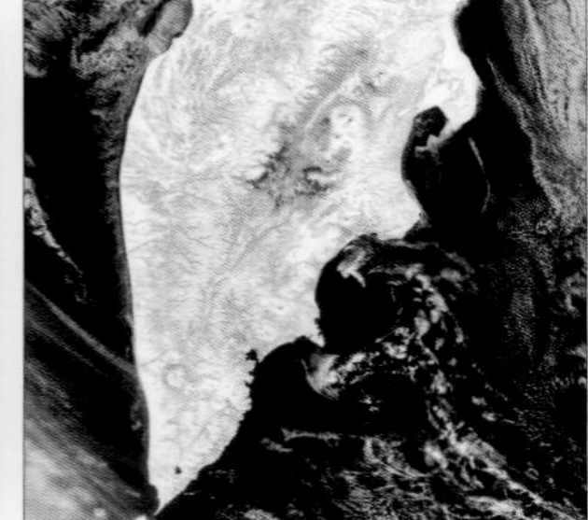

The Great Barrier Reef stretches for 2600 km (1616 miles) over an area of approximately 344 400 sq km (132 974 sq miles). The reef is located off the eastern coast of Queensland, Australia and can be seen from space.

The Kamchatka Peninsula in northeastern Asia is a mountainous landscape with numerous active volcanoes.

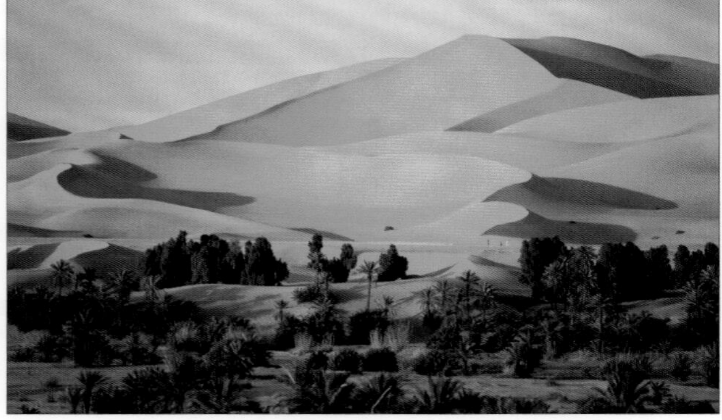

High sand dunes, sculpted by the wind, dwarf a desert oasis in the Sahara.

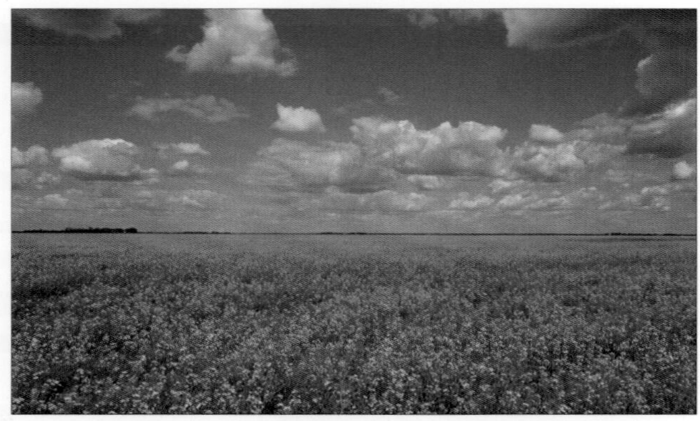

The flat featureless Great Plains of North America stretch from Saskatchewan, Canada in the north to Texas, USA in the south.

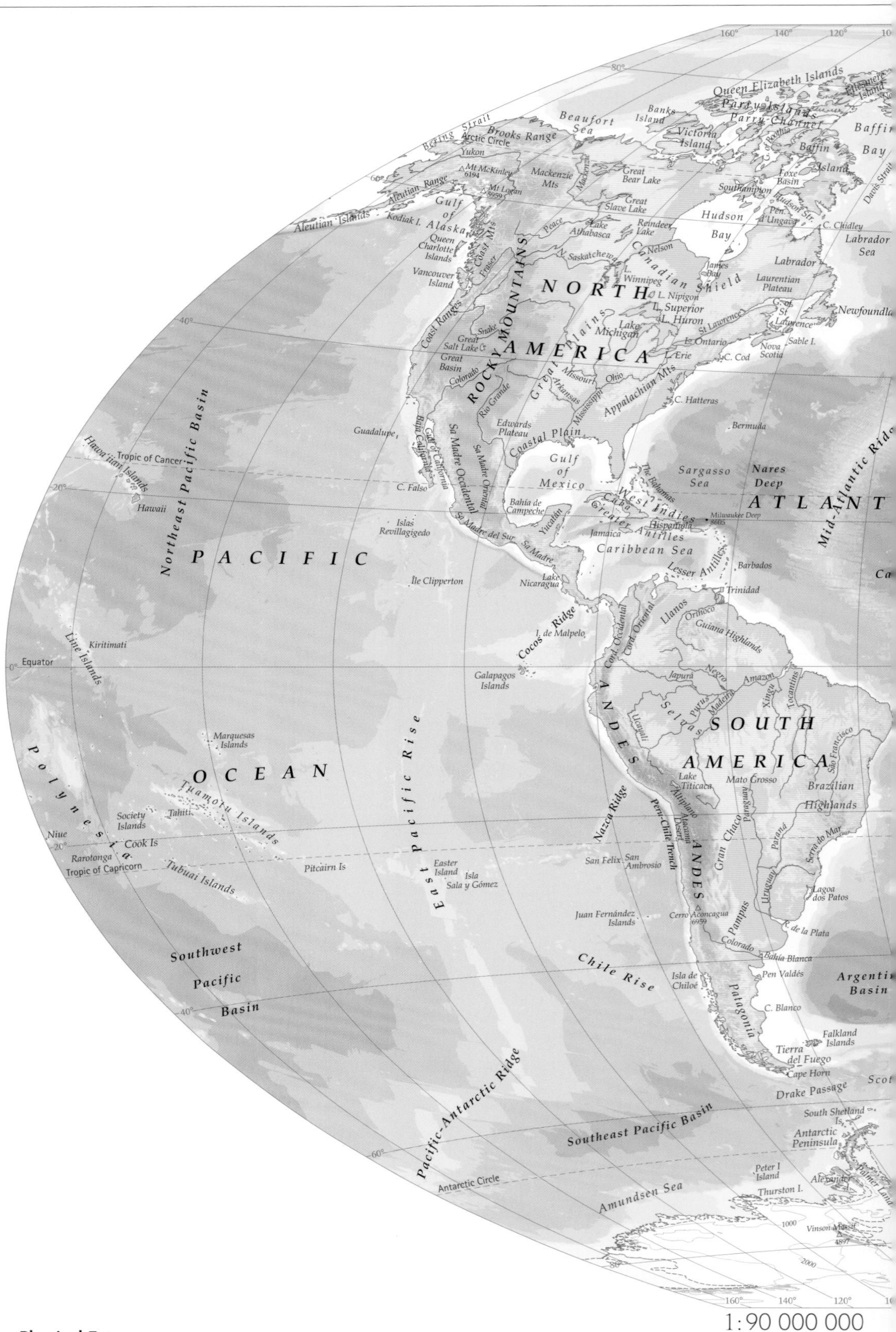

1 : 90 000 000

Physical Extremes

EARTH'S DIMENSIONS		HIGHEST MOUNTAINS	metres	feet
Mass	5.974 x 10²¹ tonnes	Mt Everest, China/Nepal	8 848	29 028
Volume	1 083 207 x 10⁶ cu km / 259 911 x 10⁶ cu miles	K2, China/Pakistan	8 611	28 251
Total area	509 450 000 sq km / 196 699 000 sq miles	Kangchenjunga, India/Nepal	8 586	28 169
Land area	149 450 000 sq km / 57 703 000 sq miles	Lhotse, China/Nepal	8 516	27 939
Water area	360 000 000 sq km / 138 996 000 sq miles	Makalu, China/Nepal	8 463	27 765
Water volume	1 389 500 x 10³ cu km / 333 405 x 10³ cu miles	Cho Oyu, China/Nepal	8 201	26 906
Equatorial diameter	12 756 km / 7 927 miles	Dhaulagiri, Nepal	8 167	26 794
Polar diameter	12 714 km / 7 901 miles	Manaslu, Nepal	8 163	26 781
Equatorial circumference	40 075 km / 24 903 miles	Nanga Parbat, Pakistan	8 126	26 660
Meridional circumference	40 008 km / 24 861 miles	Annapurna I, Nepal	8 091	26 545

Winkel Tripel Projection

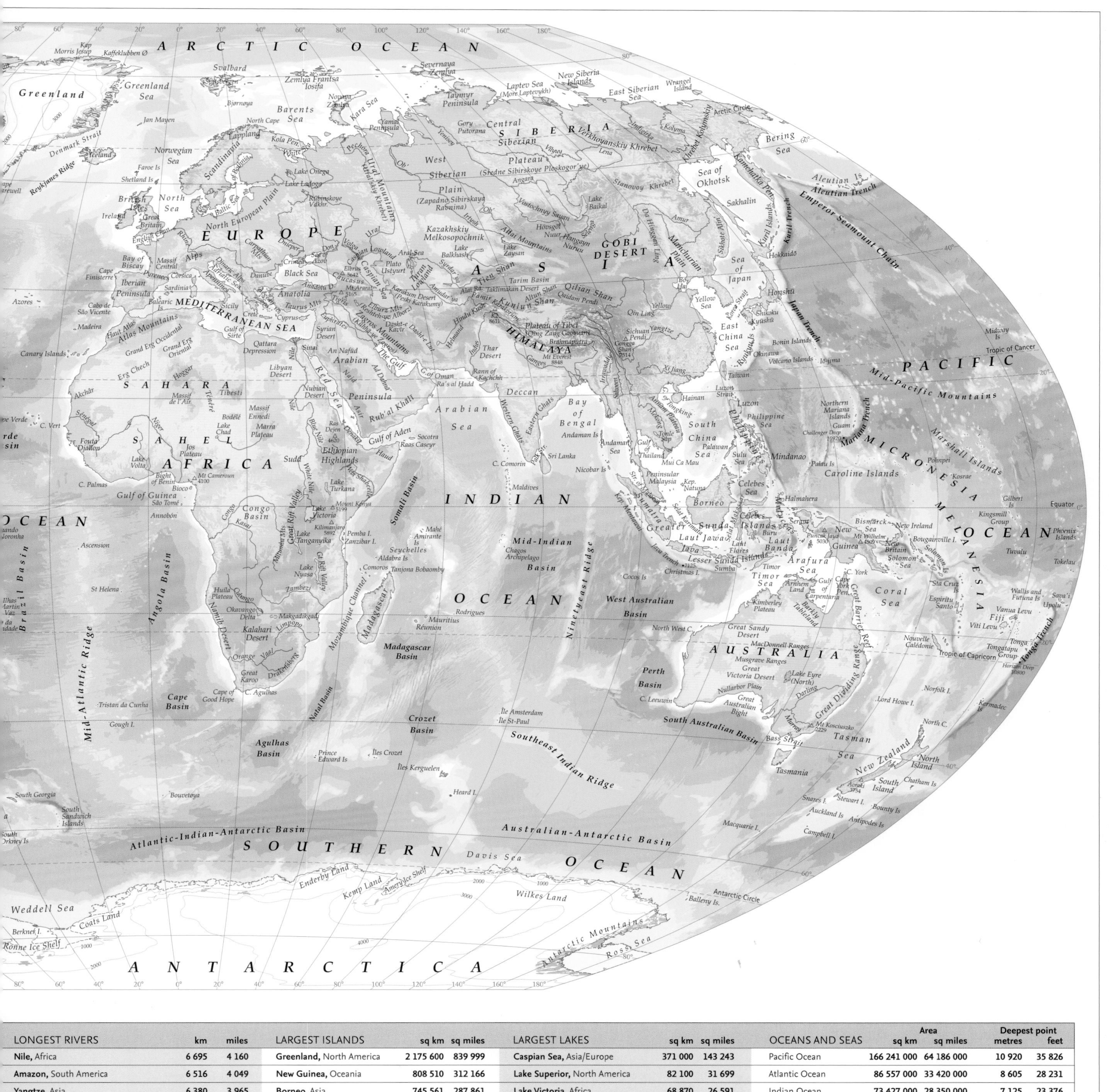

LONGEST RIVERS	km	miles	LARGEST ISLANDS	sq km	sq miles	LARGEST LAKES	sq km	sq miles	OCEANS AND SEAS	Area sq km	sq miles	Deepest point metres	feet
Nile, Africa	6 695	4 160	Greenland, North America	2 175 600	839 999	Caspian Sea, Asia/Europe	371 000	143 243	Pacific Ocean	166 241 000	64 186 000	10 920	35 826
Amazon, South America	6 516	4 049	New Guinea, Oceania	808 510	312 166	Lake Superior, North America	82 100	31 699	Atlantic Ocean	86 557 000	33 420 000	8 605	28 231
Yangtze, Asia	6 380	3 965	Borneo, Asia	745 561	287 861	Lake Victoria, Africa	68 870	26 591	Indian Ocean	73 427 000	28 350 000	7 125	23 376
Mississippi-Missouri, North America	5 969	3 709	Madagascar, Africa	587 040	266 656	Lake Huron, North America	59 600	23 012	Arctic Ocean	9 485 000	3 662 000	5 450	17 880
Ob'-Irtysh, Asia	5 568	3 460	Baffin Island, North America	507 451	195 927	Lake Michigan, North America	57 800	22 317	South China Sea	2 590 000	1 000 000	5 514	18 090
Yenisey-Angara-Selenga, Asia	5 550	3 449	Sumatra, Asia	473 606	182 859	Lake Tanganyika, Africa	32 600	12 587	Caribbean Sea	2 512 000	970 000	7 680	25 197
Yellow, Asia	5 464	3 395	Honshū, Asia	227 414	87 805	Great Bear Lake, North America	31 328	12 096	Mediterranean Sea	2 510 000	969 000	5 121	16 801
Congo, Africa	4 667	2 900	Great Britain, Europe	218 476	84 354	Lake Baikal, Asia	30 500	11 776	Bering Sea	2 261 000	873 000	4 150	13 615
Río de la Plata-Paraná, South America	4 500	2 796	Victoria Island, North America	217 291	83 896	Lake Nyasa, Africa	29 500	11 390	Bay of Bengal	2 172 000	839 000	4 500	14 764
Irtysh, Asia	4 440	2 759	Ellesmere Island, North America	196 236	75 767	Great Slave Lake, North America	28 568	11 030	Gulf of Mexico	1 544 000	596 000	3 504	11 496

World Political

The present picture of the political world is the result of a long history of exploration, colonialism, conflict and negotiation. In 1950 there were eighty-two independent countries. Since then there has been a significant trend away from colonial influences and although many dependent territories still exist there are now 195 independent countries. The newest country is Kosovo which gained independence from Serbia in February 2008. The shapes of countries reflect a combination of natural features, such as mountain ranges, and political agreements. There are still areas of the world where boundaries are disputed or only temporarily settled as ceasefire lines.

Facts

- The break up of the Soviet Union (or the U.S.S.R. – Union of Soviet Socialist Republics) in 1991 created fifteen new countries including the Russian Federation.

- The Maldives in the Indian Ocean consist of approximately 1200 low-lying islands, all under 2 m (6.5 ft) in height.

- The Commonwealth, first defined in 1926, has evolved from communities within the British Empire, to a free association of fifty-three member countries.

- Both China and the Russian Federation have borders with fourteen different countries.

The United Nations

The name "United Nations" was coined by United States President Franklin D. Roosevelt, and was first used in the "Declaration by United Nations" of 1 January 1942. The United Nations (UN) officially came into existence on 24 October 1945, when the United Nations Charter was ratified by China, France, the Soviet Union, the United Kingdom, the United States and a majority of other signatories. It was a successor to the League of Nations which had been unsuccessful in preventing the Second World War.

All *de facto* independent countries of the world, except Taiwan and Vatican City, are members – 192 in total. Kosovo is also not a member. The principal headquarters of the UN are in New York but other major agencies of the Organization are found in Geneva, The Hague, Vienna and other locations.

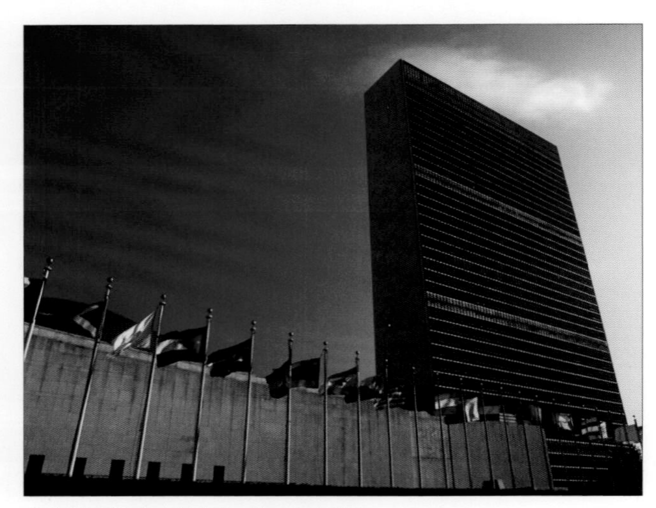

The United Nations building, New York, USA.

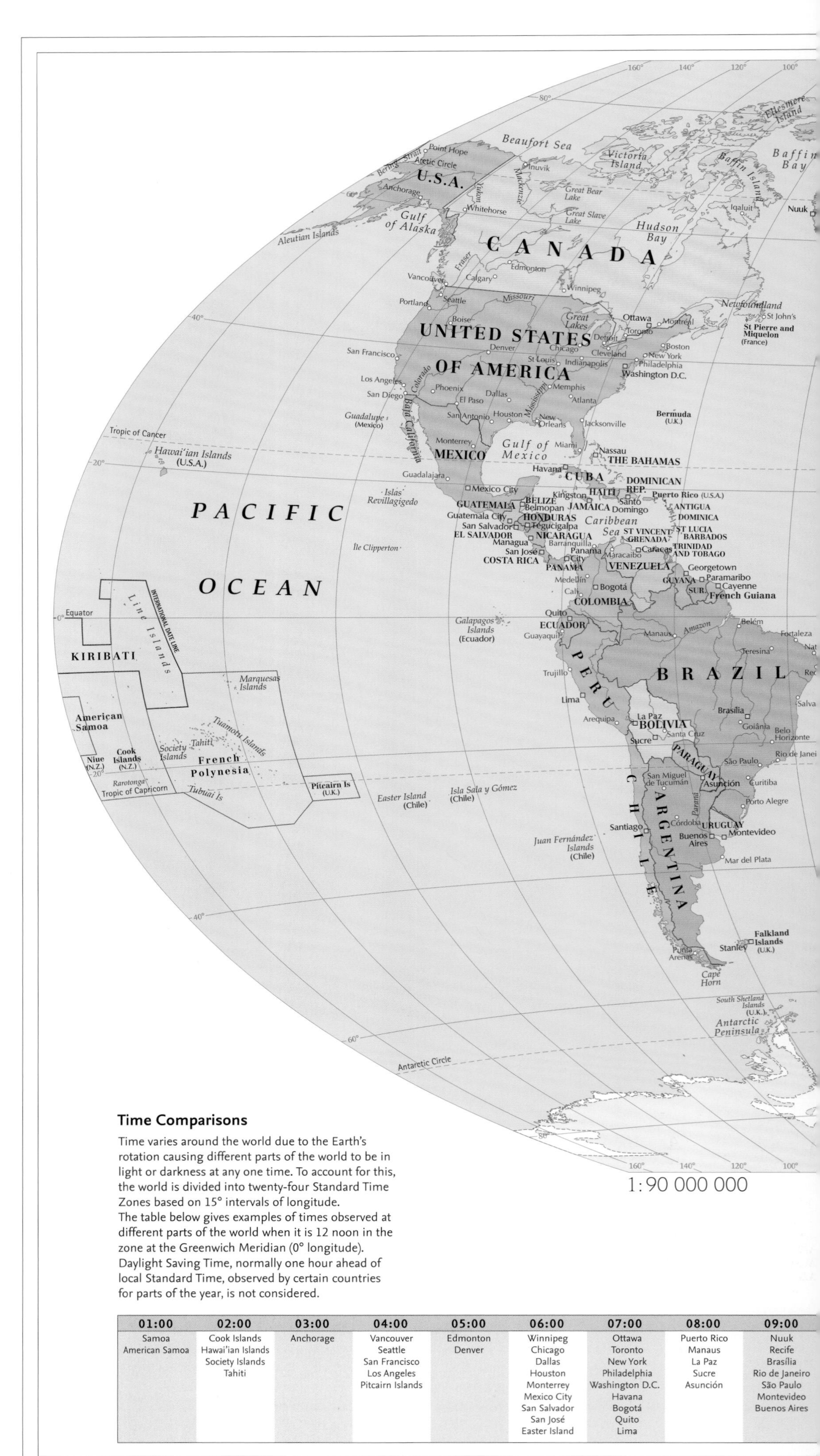

1 : 90 000 000

Winkel Tripel Projection

Time Comparisons

Time varies around the world due to the Earth's rotation causing different parts of the world to be in light or darkness at any one time. To account for this, the world is divided into twenty-four Standard Time Zones based on 15° intervals of longitude.
The table below gives examples of times observed at different parts of the world when it is 12 noon in the zone at the Greenwich Meridian (0° longitude). Daylight Saving Time, normally one hour ahead of local Standard Time, observed by certain countries for parts of the year, is not considered.

01:00	02:00	03:00	04:00	05:00	06:00	07:00	08:00	09:00
Samoa	Cook Islands	Anchorage	Vancouver	Edmonton	Winnipeg	Ottawa	Puerto Rico	Nuuk
American Samoa	Hawai'ian Islands		Seattle	Denver	Chicago	Toronto	Manaus	Recife
	Society Islands		San Francisco		Dallas	New York	La Paz	Brasília
	Tahiti		Los Angeles		Houston	Philadelphia	Sucre	Rio de Janeiro
			Pitcairn Islands		Monterrey	Washington D.C.	Asunción	São Paulo
					Mexico City	Havana		Montevideo
					San Salvador	Bogotá		Buenos Aires
					San José	Quito		
					Easter Island	Lima		

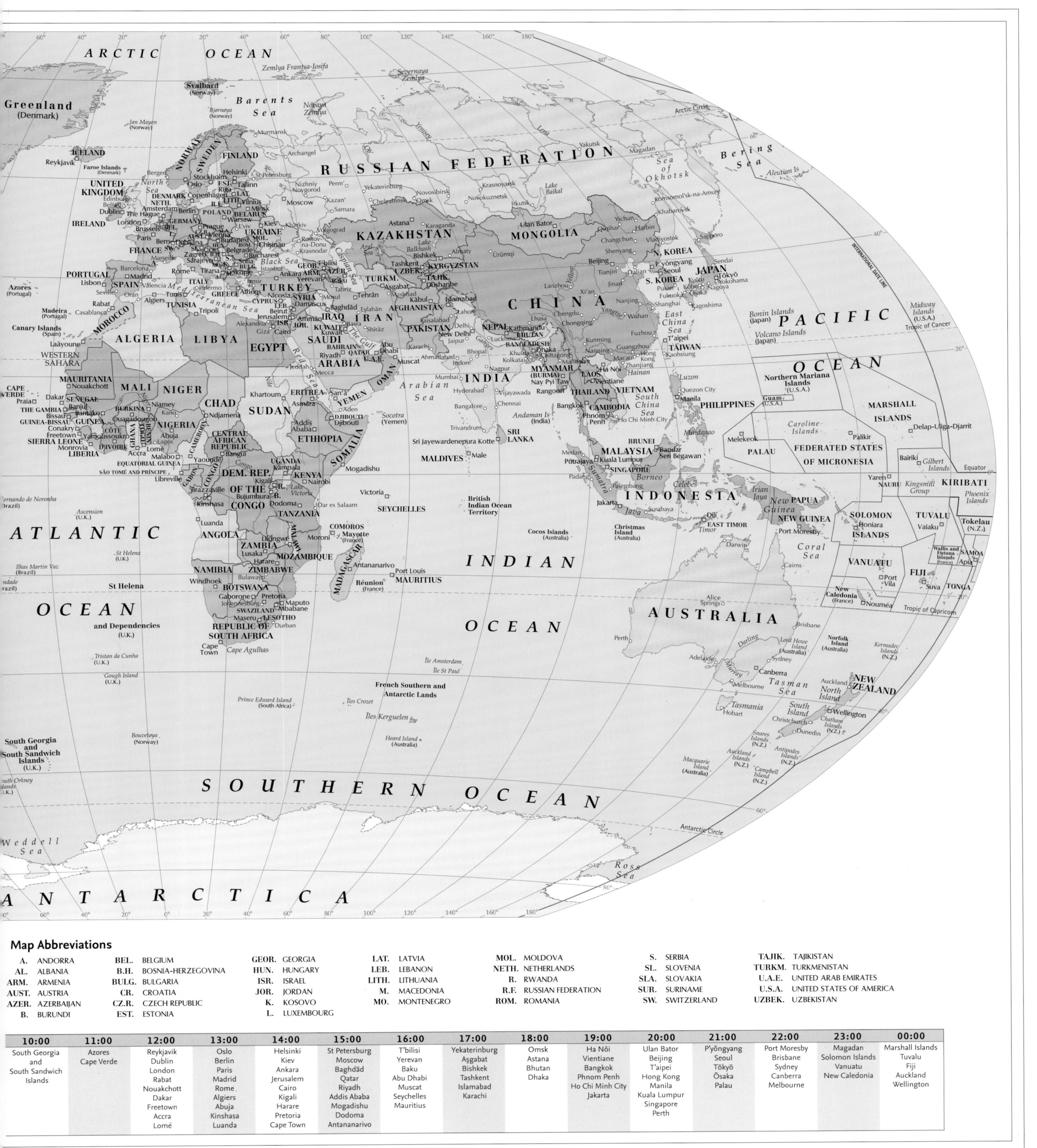

Map Abbreviations

A.	ANDORRA
AL.	ALBANIA
ARM.	ARMENIA
AUST.	AUSTRIA
AZER.	AZERBAIJAN
B.	BURUNDI
BEL.	BELGIUM
B.H.	BOSNIA-HERZEGOVINA
BULG.	BULGARIA
CR.	CROATIA
CZ.R.	CZECH REPUBLIC
EST.	ESTONIA
GEOR.	GEORGIA
HUN.	HUNGARY
ISR.	ISRAEL
JOR.	JORDAN
K.	KOSOVO
L.	LUXEMBOURG
LAT.	LATVIA
LEB.	LEBANON
LITH.	LITHUANIA
M.	MACEDONIA
MO.	MONTENEGRO
MOL.	MOLDOVA
NETH.	NETHERLANDS
R.	RWANDA
R.F.	RUSSIAN FEDERATION
ROM.	ROMANIA
S.	SERBIA
SL.	SLOVENIA
SLA.	SLOVAKIA
SUR.	SURINAME
SW.	SWITZERLAND
TAJIK.	TAJIKISTAN
TURKM.	TURKMENISTAN
U.A.E.	UNITED ARAB EMIRATES
U.S.A.	UNITED STATES OF AMERICA
UZBEK.	UZBEKISTAN

10:00	11:00	12:00	13:00	14:00	15:00	16:00	17:00	18:00	19:00	20:00	21:00	22:00	23:00	00:00
South Georgia and South Sandwich Islands	Azores Cape Verde	Reykjavik Dublin London Rabat Nouakchott Dakar Freetown Accra Lomé	Oslo Berlin Paris Madrid Rome Algiers Abuja Kinshasa Luanda	Helsinki Kiev Ankara Jerusalem Cairo Kigali Harare Pretoria Cape Town	St Petersburg Moscow Baghdād Qatar Addis Ababa Mogadishu Dodoma Antananarivo	T'bilisi Yerevan Baku Abu Dhabi Muscat Seychelles Mauritius	Yekaterinburg Aşgabat Bishkek Tashkent Islamabad Karachi	Omsk Astana Bhutan Dhaka	Ha Nôi Vientiane Bangkok Phnom Penh Ho Chi Minh City Jakarta	Ulan Bator Beijing T'aipei Hong Kong Kuala Lumpur Singapore Perth	P'yŏngyang Seoul Tōkyō Ōsaka Palau	Port Moresby Brisbane Sydney Canberra Melbourne	Magadan Solomon Islands Vanuatu New Caledonia	Marshall Islands Tuvalu Fiji Auckland Wellington

© Collins Bartholomew Ltd

113

Oceania Physical

The map highlights the three major island groupings traditionally used to categorise the enormously extensive Pacific island chains and their people: Micronesia ('small islands'), in the northwest, covering chiefly the North Mariana, Marshall and Caroline Islands; Melanesia ('black islands'), in the middle, mainly consisting of the Solomon Islands and Papua New Guinea; and Polynesia ('many islands'), encompassing all the rest across much of the Pacific. The Great Dividing Range, running down the eastern side of Australia, is prominent, as is the mountainous ridge forming the backbone of New Guinea. New Guinea in our definition is shared between Oceania and Asia.

Facts

- Tasmania, and the Tasman Sea to the east of it, are named after Abel Tasman, a 17th century Dutch explorer. Tasmania was originally named Van Diemen's Land (by Tasman himself). The Cook Islands, in the middle of Polynesia, are named after the 18th century British sea captain, James Cook.

- It has been proved by genetic research that the Pacific islands were originally populated over hundreds of years by adventurous seafarers from the Asian side, although the Norwegian Thor Heyerdahl's 'Kon-Tiki' expedition of the 1950s had strongly suggested that the people came from the Americas.

- Pitcairn Island, in the far east of Polynesia, was uninhabited until it was occupied by mutineers from the 18th century British ship 'Bounty'. The present-day inhabitants are descended from them.

HIGHEST MOUNTAINS	m	ft
Puncak Jaya, Indonesia	5 030	16 502
Puncak Trikora, Indonesia	4 730	15 518
Puncak Mandala, Indonesia	4 700	15 420
Puncak Yamin, Indonesia	4 595	15 075
Mt Wilhelm, Papua New Guinea	4 509	14 793
Mt Kubor, Papua New Guinea	4 359	14 301

LARGEST ISLANDS	sq km	sq miles
New Guinea	808 510	312 167
South Island, New Zealand	151 215	58 384
North Island, New Zealand	115 777	44 701
Tasmania	67 800	26 178

LONGEST RIVERS	km	miles
Murray-Darling	3 750	2 330
Darling	2 739	1 702
Murray	2 589	1 609
Murrumbidgee	1 690	1 050
Lachlan	1 480	920
Macquarie	950	590

LARGEST LAKES	sq km	sq miles
Lake Eyre	0–8 900	0–3 436
Lake Torrens	0–5 780	0–2 232

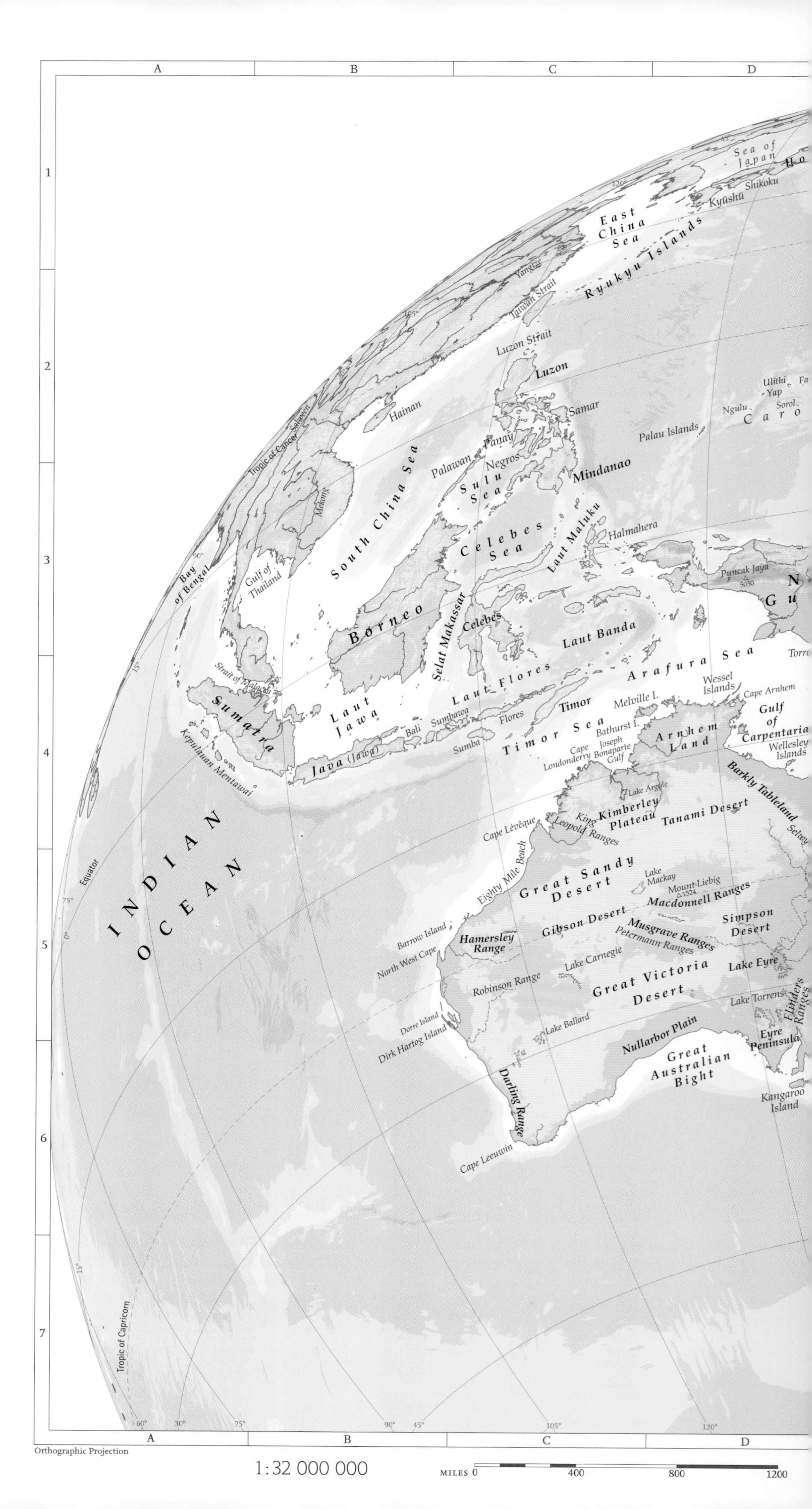

Orthographic Projection

1 : 32 000 000

MILES 0   400   800   1200

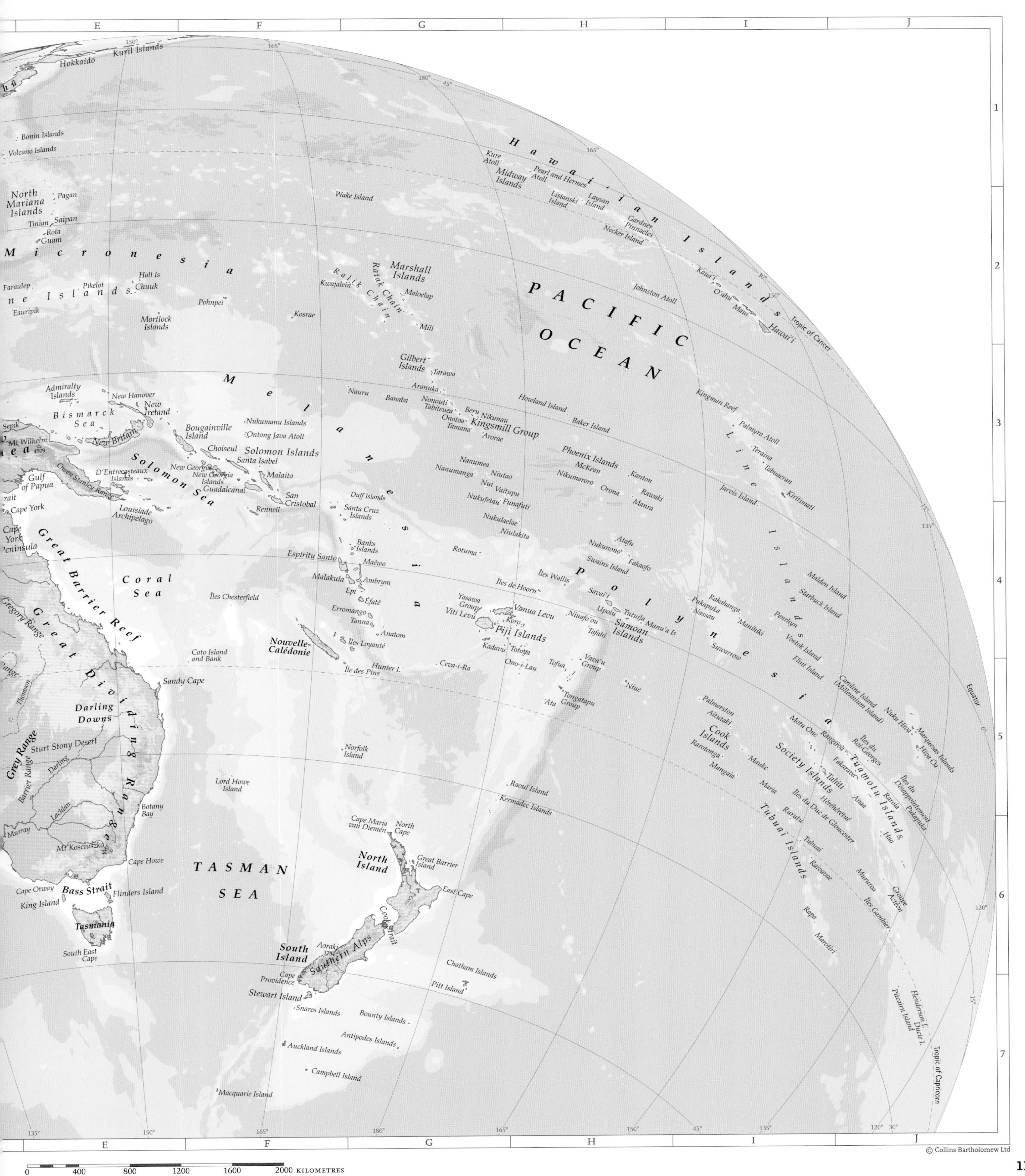

Hokkaido   Kuril Islands

Bonin Islands
Volcano Islands

North
Mariana
Islands   Pagan
Tinian Saipan
Rota
Guam

M i c r o n e s i a

Faraulep   Pikelot
ne I s l a n d s   Hall Is   Chuuk
Eauripik   Pohnpei
                Mortlock
                Islands

Sepik   Admiralty
            Islands   New Hanover
Mt Wilhelm   Bismarck   New   New
4509   Sea   Ireland
        New Britain

Gulf   Owen Stanley Range
of Papua   D'Entrecasteaux
        Islands   New Georgia
Cape York   Islands   New Georgia
        Louisiade   Guadalcanal
Cape   Archipelago
York
Peninsula

H a w a i i a n   I s l a n d s

Kure
Atoll   Pearl and Hermes
Midway   Atoll
Islands   Lisianski   Laysan
        Island   Island   Gardner
                Pinnacles   Kaua'i
                    Necker Island   O'ahu
                        Johnston Atoll   Maui
                                Hawai'i
                                    Tropic of Cancer

PACIFIC

OCEAN

Marshall
Islands
Ralik Chain   Maloelap
Rafak Chain   Kwajalein
        Mili
    Kosrae

M e l a n e s i a

Nauru   Banaba   Nonouti   Beru Nikunau   Howland Island   Baker Island
Gilbert   Tabiteuea   Onotoa   Tamana   Kingsmill Group
Islands   Tarawa   Aranuka   Arorae   Howland Island
        Phoenix Islands   Baker Island

Solomon Islands
Choiseul   Santa Isabel
Malaita
San
Cristobal
Rennell

Nukumanu Islands
Ontong Java Atoll

Duff Islands
Santa Cruz
Islands

Banks
Islands   Rotuma
Espíritu Santo   Maéwo
Malakula   Ambrym
Epi   Éfaté
Erromango
Tanna   Anatom
Îles Loyauté   Hunter I.

Nanumea   Niutao
Nanumanga   Nui Vaitupu
        Nukufetau Funafuti
        Nukulaelae
        Niulakita

McKean   Kanton
Nikumaroro   Orona   Rawaki
    Manra

Nukunono   Atafu
    Fakaofo
Swains Island.

P o l y n e s i a

Malden Island
Starbuck Island
Vostok Island
Flint Island

Line Islands

Kingman Reef
Palmyra Atoll   Teraina
    Tabuaeran

Kiritimati

Jarvis Island.

Caroline Island   Nuku Hiva
(Millennium Island)   Hiva Oa
    Marquesas Islands

Îles du
Roi-Georges   Eiao
    Rangiroa   Ranui   Anaa
    Tahiti   Fakarava
        Hérehérétué

Îles du Duc de Gloucester   Hao

 Îles de Hoorn
Îles Wallis
Savai'i   Upolu   Tutuila Manu'a Is
        Samoan
Niuafo'ou   Islands   Tafahi
Yasawa   Vanua Levu   Niutao
Group   Koro   Totoja
Viti Levu   Fiji Islands
    Kadavu   Totoya
    Ono-i-Lau
Ceva-i-Ra   Tofua
    Vava'u
    Group
    Tongatapu
Ata   Group

Rakahanga
Pukapuka   Manihiki
Nassau

Penrhyn

Suwarrow

Palmerston
Aitutaki
Cook
Islands   Mauke
Rarotonga   Mangaia

Society Islands   Tahaa
    Maria

Tubuai Islands

Rurutu   Tubuai
Raivavae

Îles du
Désappointement
Takapoto

Mururoa

Groupe
Actéon
Îles Gambier

Rapa   Marotiri

Henderson I.
Pitcairn Island

Tropic of Capricorn

ha

Coral
Sea
Îles Chesterfield

Cato Island
and Bank   Nouvelle-
Calédonie
Sandy Cape   Île des Pins

Great Barrier Reef

Gregory Range
Great Dividing Ra

Darling
Downs

Grey Range   Sturt Stony Desert
Barrier Range   Darling
Lachlan
Murray   Mt Kosciuszko
        2229

Cape Otway   Bass Strait
King Island   Flinders Island

Tasmania

South East
Cape

Norfolk
Island

Lord Howe
Island

Raoul Island
Kermadec Islands

Cape Maria   North
van Diemen   Cape

North
Island   Great Barrier
        Island

East Cape

TASMAN

SEA

Cook Strait

South
Island
Aoraki   Southern Alps
Cape
Providence
Stewart Island   Snares Islands

Chatham Islands

Pitt Island

Bounty Islands

Antipodes Islands
Auckland Islands

Campbell Island

Macquarie Island

© Collins Bartholomew Ltd

115

0   400   800   1200   1600   2000 KILOMETRES

Oceania Political

Oceania is defined here as covering Australia, New Zealand and all the independent nations of the Pacific Ocean, along with various islands in the southwestern Pacific which remain as dependent territories. We also count the whole of Papua New Guinea as being within Oceania, following a common convention – although this does result in dividing the large island of New Guinea arbitrarily into two along the political boundary. Such definitions are not regarded by geographers as hard and fast, however. The political boundaries shown on this map are intended to clarify the physical coverage of island countries and dependencies rather than actually defining strict territorial limits, which are very much more complex and sometimes as yet unsettled.

Facts

- The former UN Trust Territory of the Pacific Islands, administered by the USA, was divided during the 1980s to form the independent nations of Micronesia, the Marshall Islands, and Palau (see p.131) – plus Guam and the Northern Mariana Islands, which remain as US dependencies.

- Several small uninhabited islands and atolls scattered across the Pacific are also under US control: those shown on this map are Wake, Howland, Baker, Jarvis and Palmyra. Hawaii has been a state of the USA since the late 1950s.

- Kiribati (pronounced 'Kiribass') was formerly known as the Gilbert Islands. (The name Kiribati is a local phonetic variation on 'Gilbert'). Tuvalu used to be a UK dependency known as the Ellice Islands. Vanuatu was once a UK/French territory, the New Hebrides.

LARGEST COUNTRIES	Area sq km	sq miles
Australia	7 692 024	2 969 907
Papua New Guinea	462 840	178 704
New Zealand	270 534	104 454
Solomon Islands	28 370	10 954
Fiji	18 330	7 077
Vanuatu	12 190	4 707
Samoa	2 831	1 093
Tonga	748	289
Kiribati	717	277
Federated States of Micronesia	701	271

MOST POPULATED COUNTRIES	Population
Australia	20 743 000
Papua New Guinea	6 331 000
New Zealand	4 179 000
Fiji	839 000
Solomon Islands	496 000
Vanuatu	226 000
Samoa	187 000
Federated States of Micronesia	111 000
Tonga	100 000
Kiribati	95 000

CAPITALS		
Largest population	**Canberra,** Australia	378 000
Smallest population	**Kingston,** Norfolk Island	32
Most northerly	**Delap-Uliga-Djarrit,** Marshall Islands	7° 07' N
Most southerly	**Wellington,** New Zealand	41° 18' S
Highest	**Canberra,** Australia	581 m/1906 ft

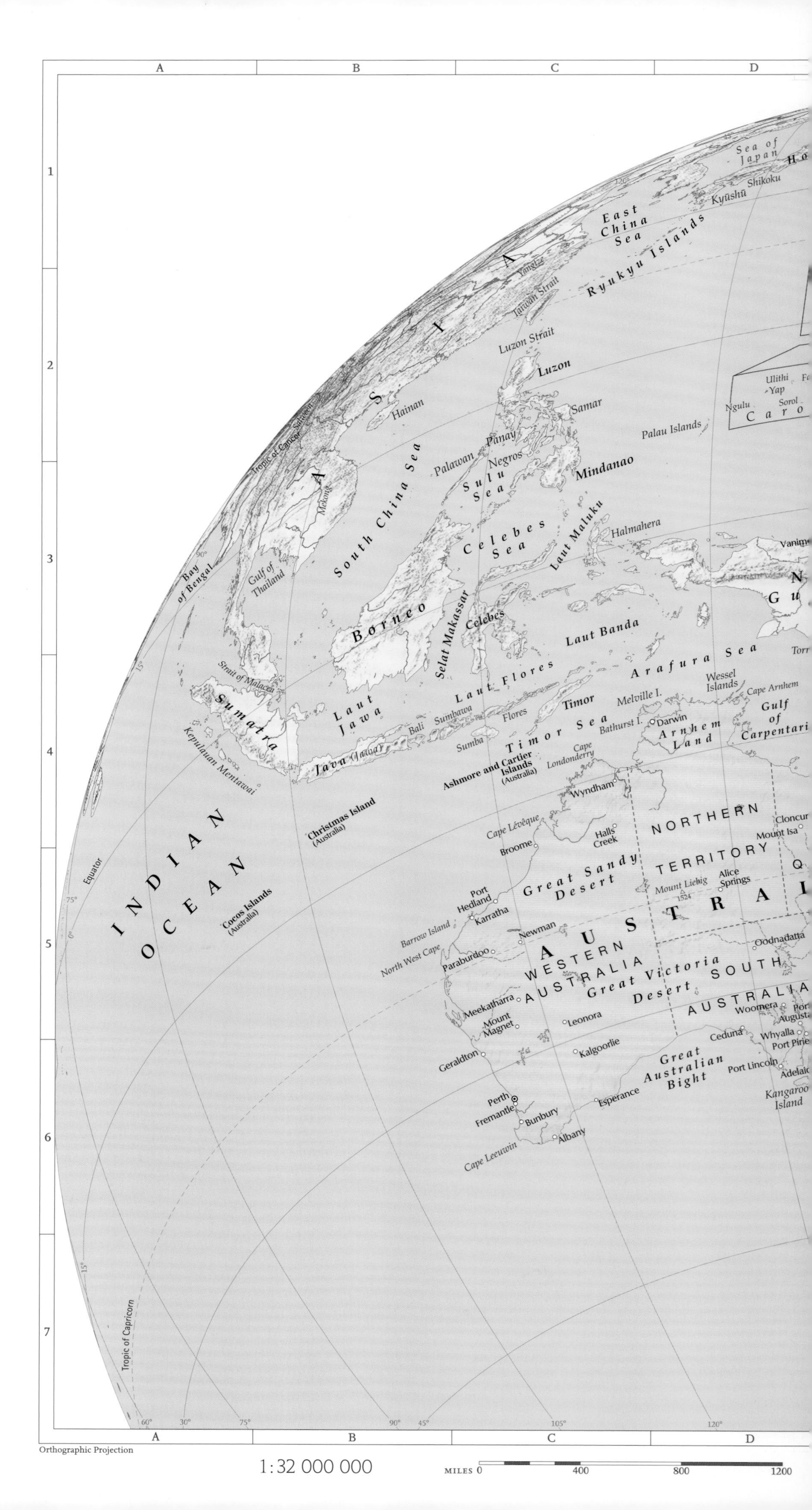

Orthographic Projection

1:32 000 000

MILES 0   400   800   1200

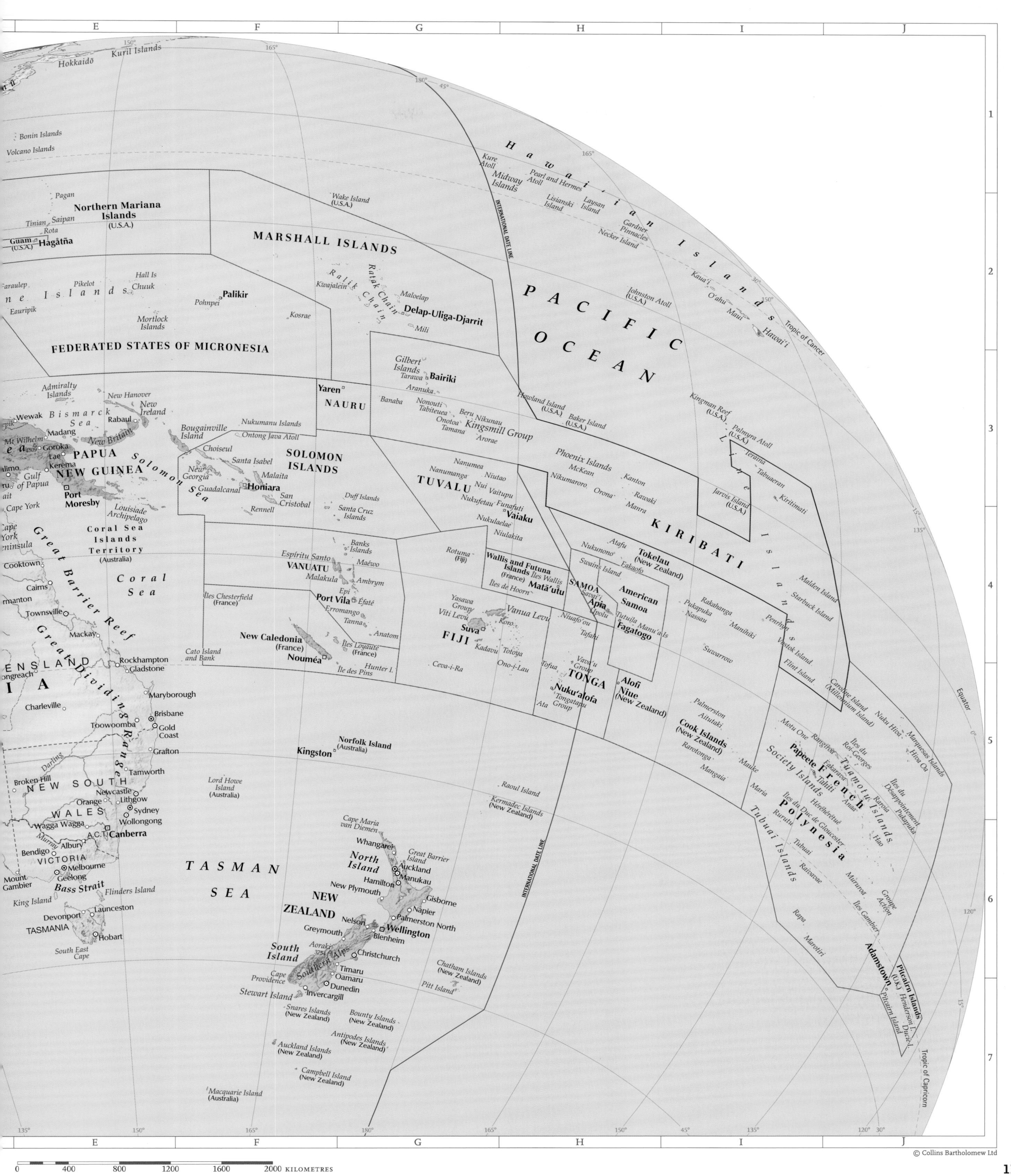

E
F
G
H
I
J
1
2
3
4
5
6
7
Hokkaidō
Kuril Islands
Bonin Islands
Volcano Islands
Pagan
Northern Mariana Islands (U.S.A.)
Saipan
Tinian
Rota
Guam (U.S.A.)
Hagåtña
Wake Island (U.S.A.)
MARSHALL ISLANDS
Ralik Chain
Ratak Chain
Kwajalein
Maloelap
Delap-Uliga-Djarrit
Mili
Hall Is
Pikelot
Chuuk
Palikir
Pohnpei
Kosrae
Mortlock Islands
Eauripik
FEDERATED STATES OF MICRONESIA
Kure Atoll
Midway Islands
Pearl and Hermes Atoll
Lisianski Island
Laysan Island
Gardner Pinnacles
Necker Island
Hawaiian Islands
Kaua'i
O'ahu
Maui
Hawai'i
Johnston Atoll (U.S.A.)
Tropic of Cancer
INTERNATIONAL DATE LINE
PACIFIC OCEAN
Gilbert Islands
Tarawa
Bairiki
Aranuka
Yaren
NAURU
Banaba
Nonouti
Tabiteuea
Beru
Nikunau
Onotoa
Tamana
Kingsmill Group
Arorae
Howland Island (U.S.A.)
Baker Island (U.S.A.)
Kingman Reef (U.S.A.)
Palmyra Atoll (U.S.A.)
Teraina
Tabuaeran
Kiritimati
Jarvis Island (U.S.A.)
Line Islands
Phoenix Islands
McKean
Nikumaroro
Orona
Kanton
Rawaki
Manra
KIRIBATI
Admiralty Islands
New Hanover
New Ireland
Wewak
Bismarck Sea
Madang
Rabaul
New Britain
Mt Wilhelm
Goroka
Lae
Kerema
PAPUA NEW GUINEA
Gulf of Papua
Port Moresby
Cape York
Cape York Peninsula
Bougainville Island
Nukumanu Islands
Ontong Java Atoll
Choiseul
Santa Isabel
New Georgia
Malaita
SOLOMON ISLANDS
Solomon Sea
Guadalcanal
Honiara
San Cristobal
Rennell
Louisiade Archipelago
Duff Islands
Santa Cruz Islands
Coral Sea Islands Territory (Australia)
Coral Sea
Great Barrier Reef
Nanumea
Nanumanga
Niutao
TUVALU
Nui
Vaitupu
Nukufetau
Funafuti
Vaiaku
Nukulaelae
Niulakita
Banks Islands
Espíritu Santo
Maéwo
VANUATU
Malakula
Ambrym
Epi
Port Vila
Éfaté
Erromango
Tanna
Anatom
Îles Chesterfield (France)
New Caledonia (France)
Îles Loyauté (France)
Nouméa
Île des Pins
Hunter I.
Cato Island and Bank
Rotuma (Fiji)
Wallis and Futuna Islands (France)
Îles Wallis
Matā'utu
Îles de Hoorn
Yasawa Group
Viti Levu
Vanua Levu
Suva
Koro
FIJI
Kadavu
Totoya
Ono-i-Lau
Ceva-i-Ra
Atafu
Nukunonu
Fakaofo
Tokelau (New Zealand)
Swains Island
SAMOA
Savai'i
Apia
Upolu
American Samoa
Tutuila
Manu'a Is
Fagatogo
Niuafo'ou
Tafahi
Vava'u Group
TONGA
Tofua
Nuku'alofa
Tongatapu Group
Ata
Alofi
Niue (New Zealand)
Pukapuka
Nassau
Rakahanga
Manihiki
Penrhyn
Suwarrow
Malden Island
Starbuck Island
Vostok Island
Flint Island
Caroline Island (Millennium Island)
Nuku Hiva
Marquesas Islands
Hiva Oa
Palmerston
Aitutaki
Cook Islands (New Zealand)
Rarotonga
Mangaia
Mauke
Motu One
Society Islands
Papeete
Tahiti
Rangiroa
Îles du Roi-Georges
Tuamotu Islands
French Polynesia
Raroia
Îles du Désappointement
Pukapuka
Anaa
Hao
Hereheretue
Îles du Duc de Gloucester
Maria
Rurutu
Tubuai
Tubuai Islands
Raivavae
Mururoa
Groupe Actéon
Îles Gambier
Rapa
Marotiri
Adamstown
Pitcairn Islands (U.K.)
Henderson I.
Ducie I.
Pitcairn Island
Equator
Tropic of Capricorn
Cooktown
Cairns
Townsville
Mackay
Rockhampton
Gladstone
Maryborough
Charleville
Brisbane
Toowoomba
Gold Coast
Great Dividing Range
Grafton
Darling
Tamworth
Broken Hill
NEW SOUTH WALES
Newcastle
Orange
Lithgow
Sydney
Wollongong
Wagga Wagga
A.C.T.
Canberra
Murray
Albury
Bendigo
VICTORIA
Melbourne
Geelong
Mount Gambier
Bass Strait
Flinders Island
King Island
Devonport
Launceston
TASMANIA
Hobart
South East Cape
Norfolk Island (Australia)
Kingston
Lord Howe Island (Australia)
Raoul Island
Kermadec Islands (New Zealand)
TASMAN SEA
Cape Maria van Diemen
Whangarei
Great Barrier Island
North Island
Auckland
Manukau
Hamilton
New Plymouth
NEW ZEALAND
Gisborne
Napier
Palmerston North
Nelson
Wellington
Greymouth
Blenheim
South Island
Aoraki
Southern Alps
Christchurch
Timaru
Oamaru
Cape Providence
Dunedin
Invercargill
Stewart Island
Chatham Islands (New Zealand)
Pitt Island
Snares Islands (New Zealand)
Bounty Islands (New Zealand)
Antipodes Islands (New Zealand)
Auckland Islands (New Zealand)
Campbell Island (New Zealand)
Macquarie Island (Australia)
0 400 800 1200 1600 2000 KILOMETRES

Australia and Southwest Pacific

PACIFIC ISLAND NATIONS

A warm tropical climate all year round, over 25 000 islands, and the lure of clear blue waters and white sandy beaches fringed with palm trees, means that the south Pacific is high on the wish list of destinations for people seeking a tropical island experience.

Pacific island travel packages feature the main destinations of Fiji, Samoa, Tonga, Vanuatu and the Cook Islands, promoting them as relaxing holiday destinations or romantic getaways in a truly exotic location. The islands are a tantalizing mix of forest-covered mountains and low-lying coral reef atolls with unlimited potential for customised island-hopping itineraries. Against this background of paradise there are some environmental threats. Some low-lying islands are gradually being submerged by the rising water levels of the Pacific Ocean and the Ring of Fire arcs across the region so active volcanoes and earthquakes are common.

The area covers an incredible diversity of ethnic cultures in a mix of independent nation states and overseas territories. Throughout the whole region there are strong musical and dance traditions, and the traveller can experience varied and colourful displays of movement and song.

Warm seas and turquoise lagoons mean that water sports feature strongly in many island holidays. With spectacular underwater scenery and shipwrecks to explore, the possibilities for scuba diving are particularly extensive and almost every resort has its own dive operator.

FIJI Capital: Suva
Area: 18 330 km²/7 077 miles² Population: 839 000
Languages: English, Fijian, Hindi Religions: Christian, Hindu, Sunni Muslim Currency: Fiji dollar

Originally an aircraft refuelling stop on the Sydney to Honolulu route, Fiji is now a booming tourist destination in its own right.

One attraction to visitors is the 'Bula' welcome which shows the renowned hospitality of the nation. A mix of indigenous customs, together with Indian, Chinese and European traditions, has created a colourful mosaic of culture immediately apparent in the food, music and dance. The international airport is at Nadi, on the main island of Viti Levu. Ferries also leave Nadi for the Mamanuca Group, heralded as Fiji's 'tourism gem'; there are day cruises and resort stays on these stunning small islands. Booking well ahead is recommended for a resort stay in the peak season between June and October. The Yasawa Group of islands is less accessible, except for Tavewa, which caters mainly for backpacking travellers.

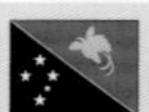

PAUA NEW GUINEA Capital: Port Moresby
Area: 462 840 km²/178 704 miles²
Population: 6 331 000 Languages: English, Tok Pisin (Creole), local languages Religions: Protestant, Roman Catholic, traditional beliefs Currency: Kina

An undeveloped infrastructure and rugged terrain makes Papua New Guinea a challenging place to visit. For many travellers it is this authentic travel experience that is the main attraction. Mainland Papua New Guinea is the mountainous eastern half of the island of New Guinea. Offshore are numerous outlying islands. The forested volcanic landscape is a paradise for wildlife enthusiasts, with an amazing diversity of plants and animals. Many undiscovered species are thought to exist in the interior of the country. The culture is also astoundingly diverse, with hundreds of ethnic groups and over 850 indigenous languages. Many remote villages can only be reached by light aircraft or on foot, meaning that this is one of the world's least explored countries.

Lambert Azimuthal Equal Area Projection

1 : 20 000 000

MILES 0   200   400   600

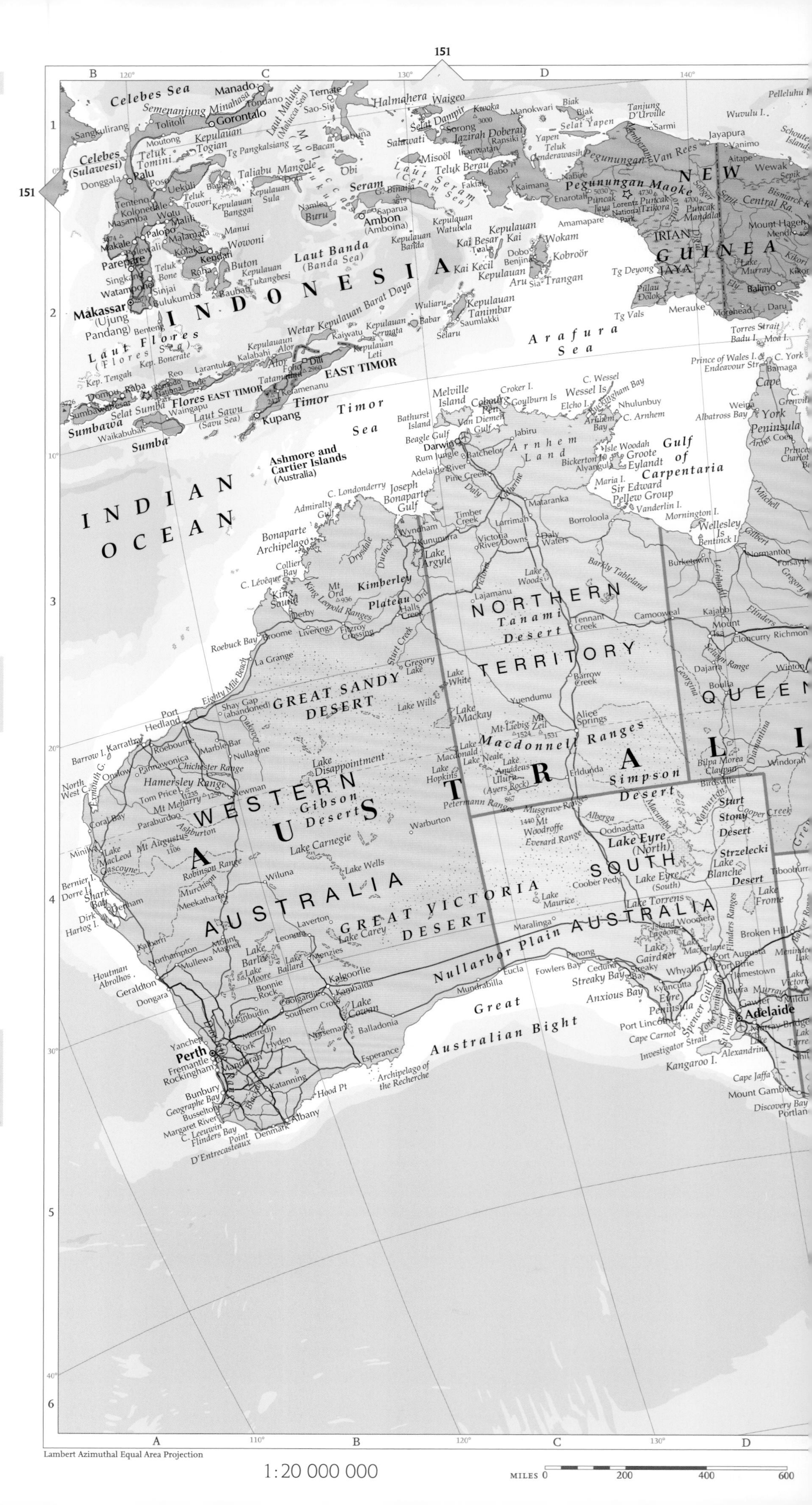

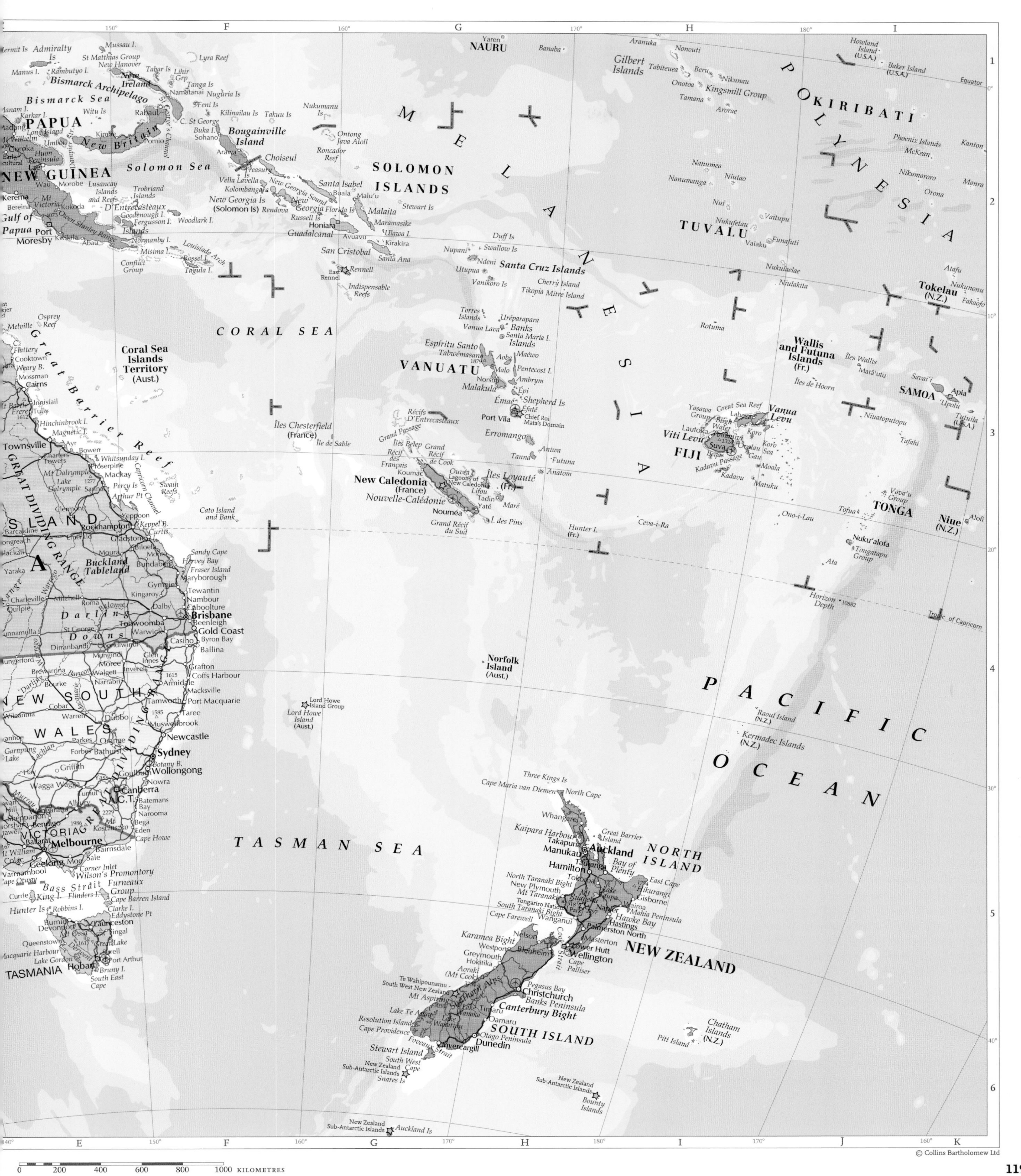

F · 150° · G · 160° · H · 170° · I · 180°

NAURU   Banaba   Aranuka   Nonouti   Howland   Baker Island (U.S.A.)

Admiralty Is   Mussau I.   Yaren   Tabiteuea   Beru   Nikunau   Island (U.S.A.)   Equator

Hermit Is   St Matthias Group   Gilbert   Tabiteuea   Kingsmill Group   Arorae

Manus I.   Rambutyo I.   New Hanover   Islands   Onotoa

Bismarck Archipelago   Tabar Is   Lihir   Nanumea   Niutao   Phoenix Islands   Kanton

Bismarck Sea   New Ireland   Grp   Nuguria Is   Nanumanga   McKean

Anam I.   Karkar I.   Witu Is   Tanga Is   Takuu Is   Nui   POLYNESIA   Nikumaroro   Manra

PAPUA   Long Island   Kimbe   Namatanai Is   Nukumanu Is   Nukufetau   Vaitupu   Orona

Madang   Mt Wilhelm   New Britain   Rabaul   Feni Is   MELANESIA   TUVALU   Vaiaku   Funafuti

Goroka   Umboi   Pomio   Buka I.   Kilinailau Is   Nukulaelae

Mt Victoria   Wau   Morobe   St George's Channel   Bougainville   Choiseul   SOLOMON   Nukunonu

NEW GUINEA   Huon Peninsula   Lusancay Islands and Reefs   Sohano   Island   Arawa   ISLANDS   Tokelau (N.Z.)   Atafu   Fakaofo

Kokoda   Trobriand Islands   Treasury   Santa Isabel   Malu'u   Stewart Is   Niulakita

Kerema   D'Entrecasteaux Islands   Vella Lavella   New Georgia Sound   Buala   Maramasike   Duff Is   Rotuma   Wallis and Futuna Islands (Fr.)

Gulf of Papua   Goodenough I.   Fergusson I.   New Georgia Is (Solomon Is)   New Georgia   Florida Is   Malaita   Swallow Is   Nupani   Îles Wallis   Matä'utu

Port Moresby   Woodlark I.   Rendova   Russell Is   Honiara   Ulawa I.   Santa Cruz Islands   Espíritu Santo   Vanua Lava   Üréparapara   Îles de Hoorn   SAMOA   Apia

Abau   Misima I.   Louisiade Arch.   San Cristobal   Kirakira   Ndeni   Torres Islands   Banks Islands   Savai'i   Upolu

Conflict Group   Rossel I.   Tagula I.   Santa Ana   Utupua   Cherry Island   Santa María I.   Tutuila (U.S.A.)

CORAL SEA   East Rennel   Rennell   Indispensable Reefs   Vanikoro Is   Tikopia Mitre Island   Niuatoputopu   Tafahi

Osprey Reef   Coral Sea Islands Territory (Aust.)   Espíritu Santo   Tabwémasana 1879   Aoba   Maëwo   Yasawa Group   Great Sea Reef   Labasa   Vanua Levu

Melville   Flattery   Îles Chesterfield (France)   VANUATU   Malo   Pentecost I.   Lautoka   Blight Water   Koro   Koro

Cooktown   Île de Sable   Norsup   Ambrym   Viti Levu   Ovalau   Sea   Gau

Cairns   Récifs D'Entrecasteaux   Malakula   Épi   Émaé   Shepherd Is   Nadi   Suva   FIJI   Moala

Innisfail   Îles Belep   Grand Passage   Efaté   Chief Roi   Kadavu Passage   Matuku

Tully   Hinchinbrook I.   Récif des Français   Grand Récif de Cook   Port Vila   Mata's Domain   Kadavu

Townsville   Magnetic I.   Koumac   Erromango   Anatom   Vava'u Group

Ayr   Bowen   New Caledonia (France)   Îles Loyauté (Fr.)   Aniwa   Futuna   Tofua   TONGA

Whitsunday I.   Nouvelle-Calédonie   Ouvéa   Tanna   Ceva-i-Ra   Niue (N.Z.)   Alofi

Proserpine   Lagoons of New Caledonia   Lifou   Ono-i-Lau

Mt Dalrymple   Mackay   Nouméa   Tadine   Maré

GREAT BARRIER REEF   Swain Reefs   Yaté   Nuku'alofa   Tongatapu Group

Percy Is   Cato Island and Bank   Grand Récif du Sud   I. des Pins   Hunter I. (Fr.)   Ata   Horizon Depth 10882

Rockhampton   Keppel B.   Curtis   Tropic of Capricorn

Gladstone   Buckland Tableland   NORFOLK ISLAND (Aust.)

Bundaberg   Sandy Cape   Harvey Bay   Fraser Island

Maryborough   Gympie   Nambour   Brisbane   Lord Howe Island Group   PACIFIC

Toowoomba   Caboolture   Gold Coast   Lord Howe Island (Aust.)

Warwick   Beenleigh   Byron Bay   Raoul Island (N.Z.)

Casino   Ballina   Kermadec Islands (N.Z.)   OCEAN

Grafton   Coffs Harbour

NEW SOUTH   Armidale   Macksville   Port Macquarie

WALES   Tamworth   Taree   Three Kings Is   Cape Maria van Diemen   North Cape

Dubbo   Muswellbrook   Lord Howe   Whangarei

Newcastle   Kaipara Harbour   Great Barrier Island   NORTH

Sydney   Takapuna   Auckland   ISLAND

Wollongong   Manukau   Bay of Plenty

Canberra   Hamilton   Tauranga   East Cape

A.C.T.   North Taranaki Bight   Tokoroa   Hikurangi   Gisborne

TASMAN SEA   New Plymouth   Mt Taranaki   Mahia Peninsula

Melbourne   South Taranaki Bight   Napier   Hawke Bay

VICTORIA   Cape Farewell   Wanganui   Hastings

Nelson   Palmerston North

Wilson's Promontory   Karamea Bight   Westport   Blenheim   Masterton   NEW ZEALAND

Furneaux Group   Greymouth   Lower Hutt   Wellington

Hunter Is   Hokitika   Cape Palliser

Launceston   Te Wahipounamu   Pegasus Bay   Banks Peninsula

TASMANIA   Hobart   Southern Alps   Christchurch   Chatham Islands (N.Z.)

Mt Aspiring   Canterbury Bight

Port Arthur   Bruny I.   Lake Te Anau   Oamaru   Pitt Island

Resolution Islands   Cape Providence   Foveaux Strait   SOUTH ISLAND

Stewart Island   Invercargill   Dunedin

New Zealand Sub-Antarctic Islands   Snares Is   New Zealand Sub-Antarctic Islands   Bounty Islands

New Zealand Sub-Antarctic Islands   Auckland Is

40° · 150° · 160° · 170° · 180° · 170° · 160°

0   200   400   600   800   1000 KILOMETRES

© Collins Bartholomew Ltd

119

West Australia

AUSTRALIA Capital: **Canberra**
Area: **7 692 024 km²/2 969 907 miles²**
Population: **20 743 000** Languages: **English, Italian, Greek**
Religions: **Roman Catholic, Orthodox**
Currency: **Australian dollar**

Australia is promoted as a laid-back country, with a reputation for informality. It is large and varied, offering many renowned attractions as well as opportunities for action-packed outdoor adventures. Several cosmopolitan cities offer world-class cultural attractions in arts and sport.

Major international sporting events such as the 2000 Sydney Olympics and 2003 Rugby World Cup have attracted large numbers of visitors to Australia. Backpackers make up a large proportion of visitors, working holiday visas enabling some to extend their stay and explore the country to a greater extent.

Visitors come not only to see the iconic sites of Ayers Rock, the Sydney Opera House and the Great Barrier Reef, but also to experience the 'outback' with its Aboriginal culture and wildlife. Some animals and birds such as kangaroos, koalas, dingoes and kookaburras have come to symbolize Australia.

Aboriginal culture is one of the world's longest surviving cultures, dating back at least 50,000 years. As semi-nomadic hunters and gatherers the indigenous peoples based their way of life on a spiritual relationship with the land. Colonization by settlers introduced many problems and heralded a declining native population. Civil and land rights have now been restored, but few Aborigines follow a truly traditional lifestyle, and those that do, live in remote Reserve areas often requiring permits. For the tourist, this a culture that is therefore difficult to experience, although opportunities on offer include bushland walks with Aboriginal guides, demonstrations of ancient bush skills and visits to Aboriginal art sites.

Most of Australia is desert, with only the southwest and south-east having a temperate climate. Summer months (November to March) can get very hot. Winters (June to August) get colder and wetter the further south you go.

WESTERN AUSTRALIA

Western Australia is characterized by the huge desert areas of the Great Sandy Desert, Gibson Desert and western part of the Great Victoria Desert. It is a sparsely populated region, where travel across the remote arid regions of 'outback' is not difficult on the main roads, although distances are long. Driving the more isolated tracks requires more advance planning and the use of a reliable four-wheel drive vehicle. Travel in the remote areas of northern Australia is not advised in the wet season (November to April) when heavy rain can make roads impassable. Most international visitors either hire cars or book organised tours.

In the Northern Territory a major tourist site is Uluṟu (Ayers Rock), one of Australia's most recognised icons. The gorges and waterfalls of the Karijini National Park, and further north, the wild and beautiful landscapes of the Kimberley region are also becoming more popular with visitors. Travelling this region gives an experience not only of the natural wonder of the landscape but also of Aboriginal culture and the historic townships built by gold rush pioneers.

Perth is one of the most isolated metropolitan areas in the world, yet it is a growing city. To the north is a long stretch of safe sandy beaches known as the Sunset Coast.

Connecting Western Australia to South Australia is the longest straight railway line in the world, crossing the flat and arid Nullarbor Plain.

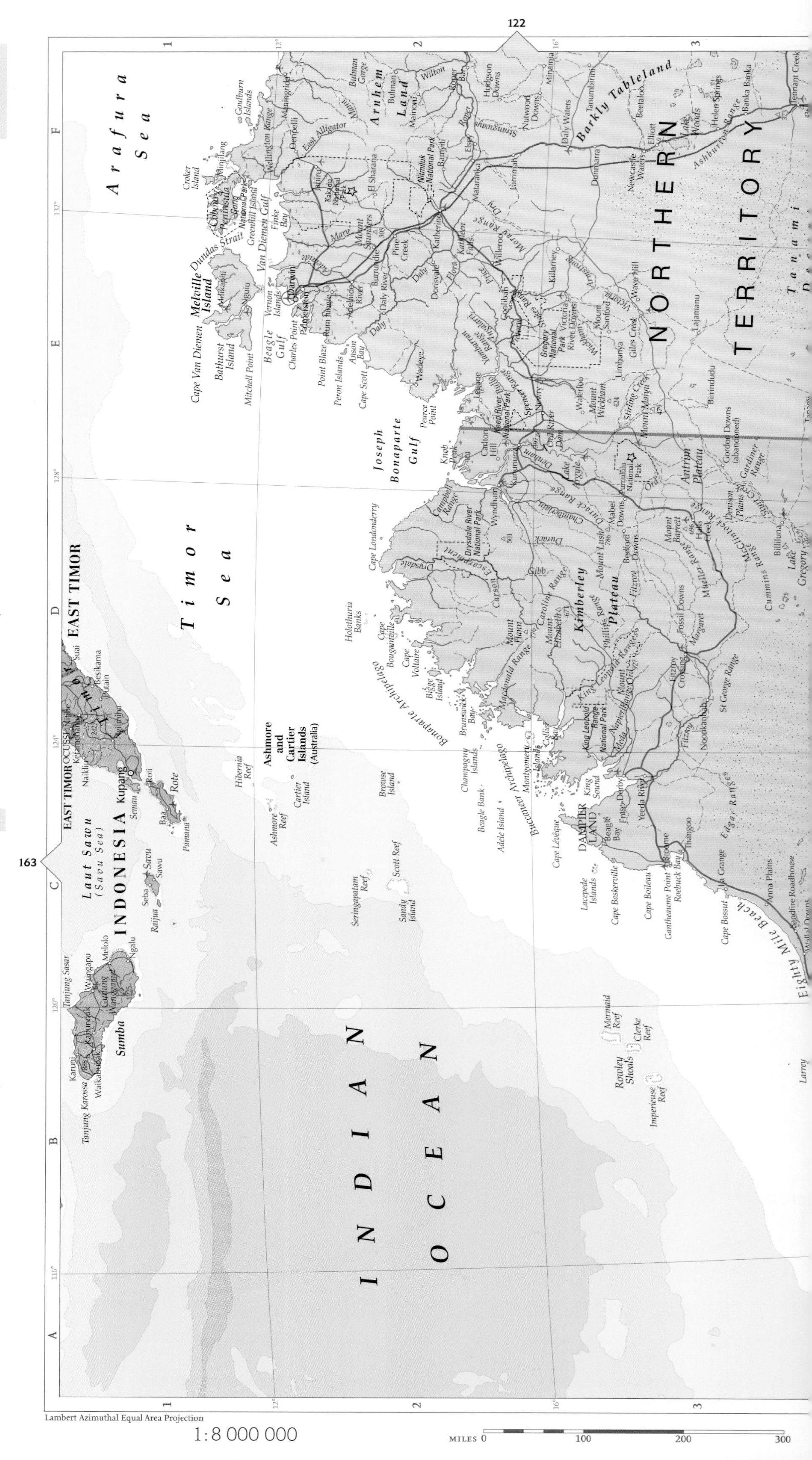

Lambert Azimuthal Equal Area Projection

1 : 8 000 000

MILES 0   100   200   300

WESTERN AUSTRALIA

SOUTH AUSTRALIA

Great Victoria Desert

Gibson Desert

Little Sandy Desert

Great Sandy Desert

Nullarbor Plain

Great Australian Bight

Hamersley Range

Macdonnell Ranges

James Ranges

Reynolds Range

Musgrave Ranges

Petermann Ranges

Robinson Range

Carnarvon Range

Chichester Range

Kennedy Range

Eyre Peninsula

Uluru (Ayers Rock)

Alice Springs

Perth

Fremantle

Kalgoorlie

Boulder

Esperance

Albany

Bunbury

Geraldton

Port Lincoln

Shark Bay

Tropic of Capricorn

Barrow Island

Montebello Islands

North West Cape

Exmouth Gulf

Cape Leeuwin

Archipelago of the Recherche

Houtman Abrolhos

Geelvink Channel

© Collins Bartholomew Ltd

0   100   200   300   400   500 KILOMETRES

East Australia

Eastern Australia

Stretching for over 2000 km (1249 miles) down the coast of eastern Australia is the Great Barrier Reef, the largest coral reef in the world and one of the country's greatest natural wonders. With over 3000 individual reef systems it has an amazingly prolific marine life, offering travel experiences ranging from exclusive tropical island retreats, 'live-aboard' scuba-diving and tours to see the magnitude of the reef from the air.

The main Barrier Reef coast towns and cities – Cairns, Townsville, Mackay and Rockhampton – are all good bases from which to explore the coastal region. Further south is Brisbane, Australia's third most popular city for international tourists, after Sydney and Melbourne.

The Great Dividing Range extends from the northern tip of Queensland down the length of the eastern coastline. It is an area of mountain ranges, plateaus and escarpments.

Inland, in the foothills of the MacDonnell Ranges, is Alice Springs where galleries showcase indigenous Australian art. East of Alice Springs are important cultural sites for Aboriginal people, several of which contain examples of rock art.

Further south, the Lake Eyre Basin is a vast, mainly flat and arid area of riverbeds straddling large parts of South Australia, the Northern Territory, Queensland and New South Wales. There are tours extending into some very remote destinations in this outback. Within the basin is Lake Eyre, the largest salt lake in Australia and the site of various land speed record attempts.

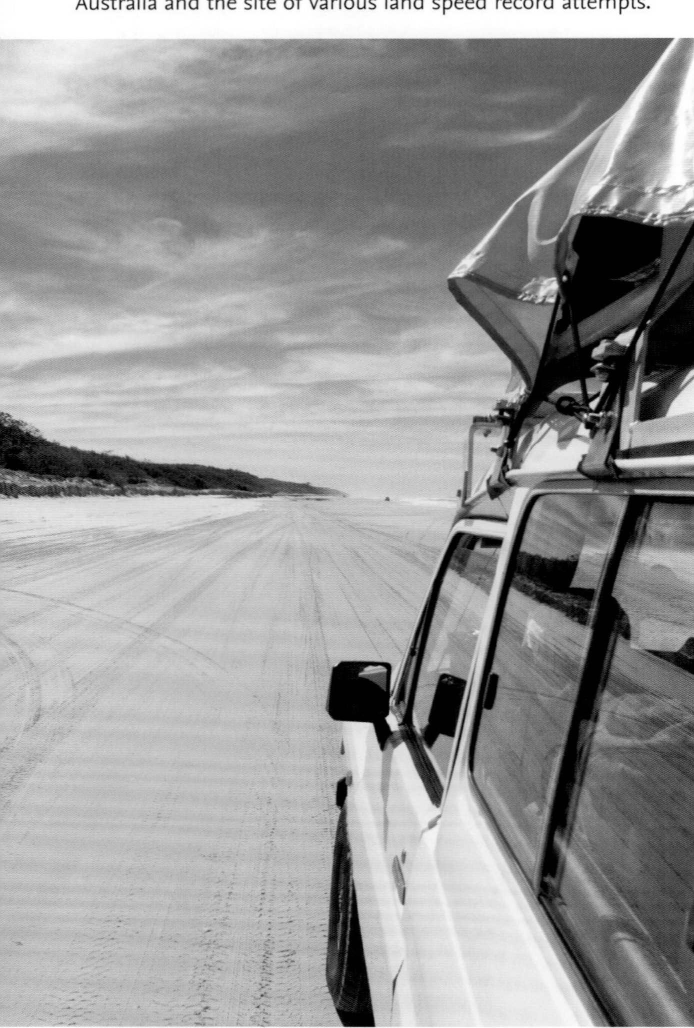

Enjoy a four-wheel drive beach ride on **Fraser Island**, Queensland, the largest sand island in the world

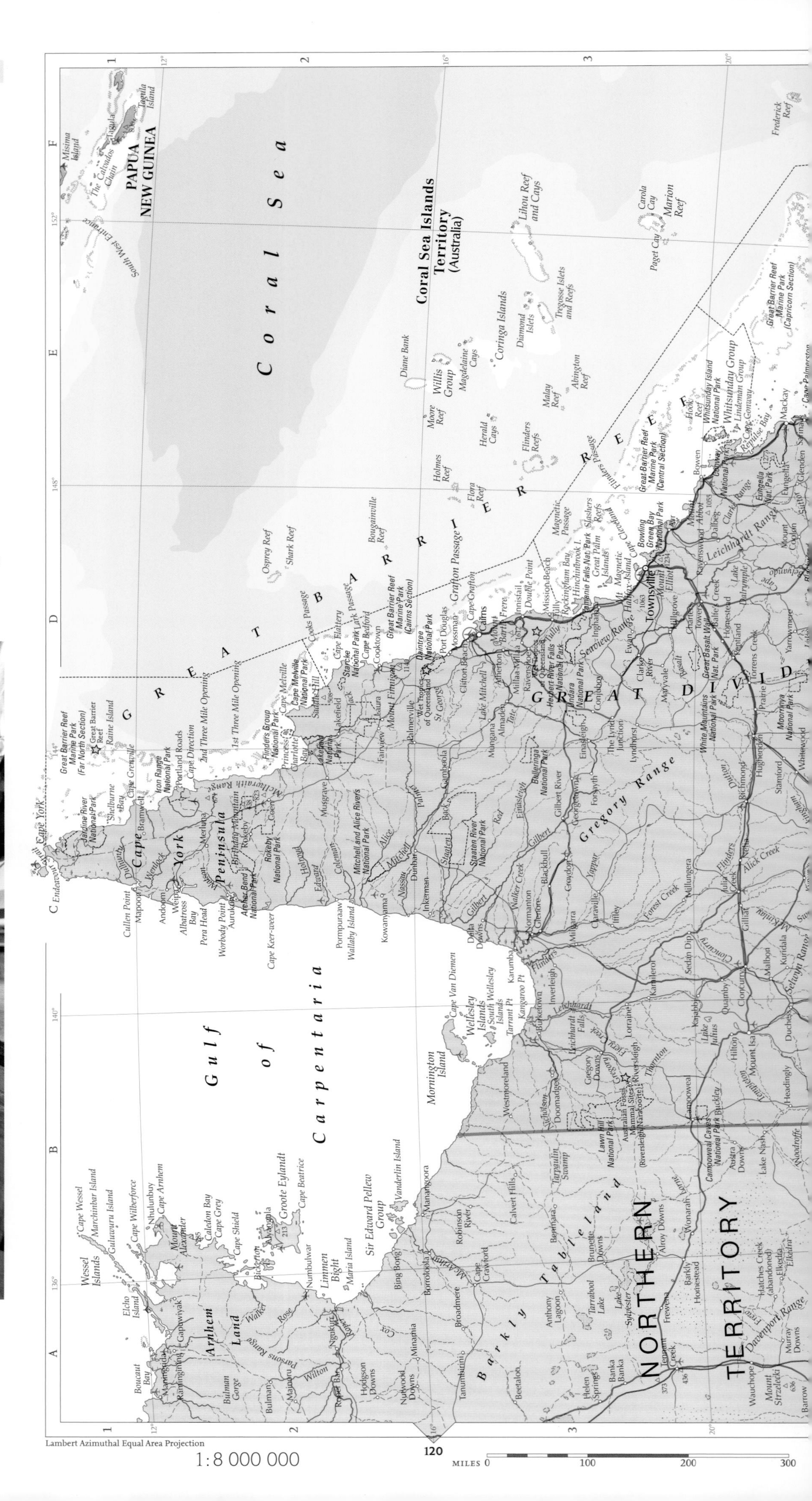

Lambert Azimuthal Equal Area Projection

1:8 000 000

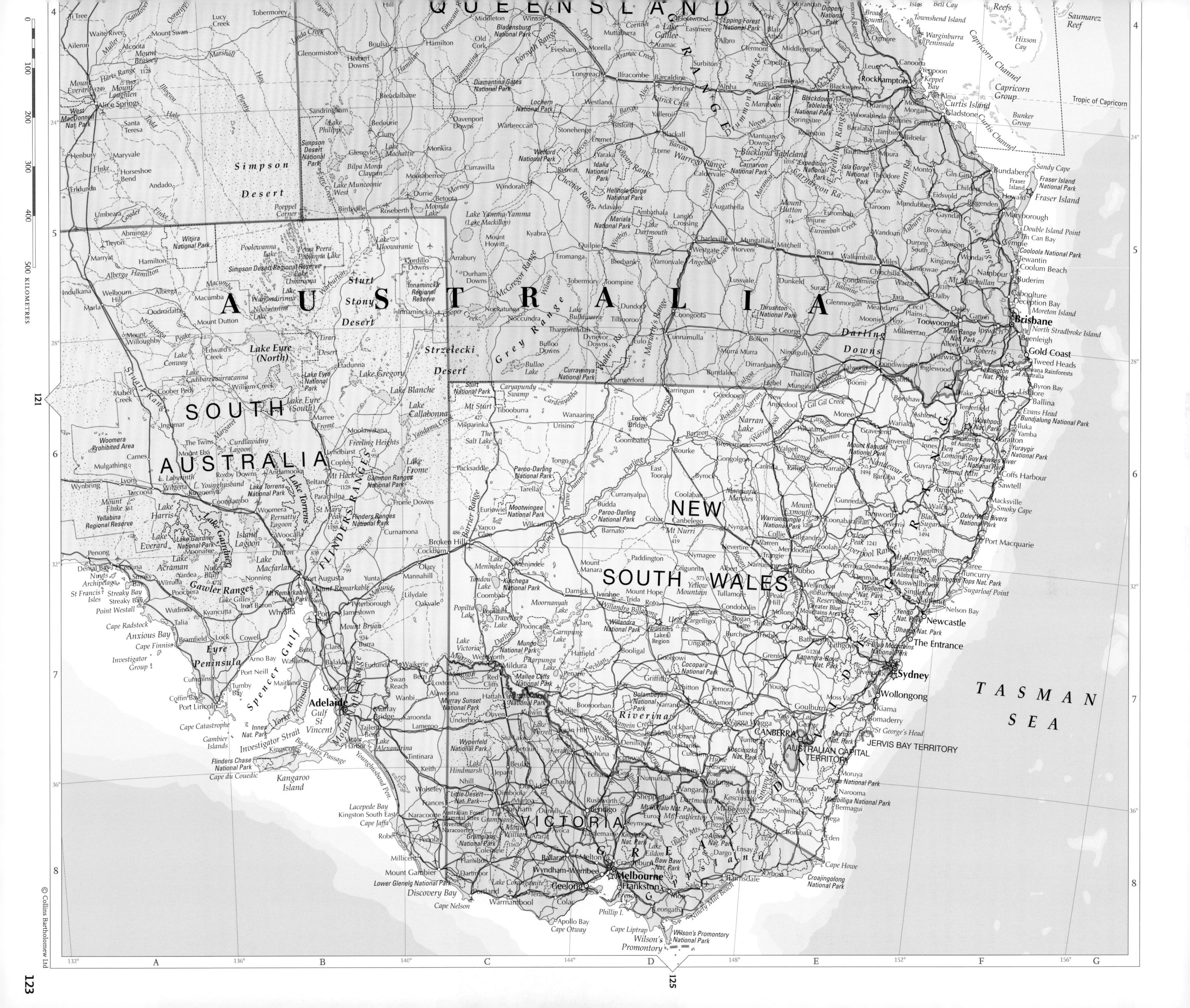

QUEENSLAND
AUSTRALIA
SOUTH AUSTRALIA
NEW SOUTH WALES
VICTORIA
AUSTRALIAN CAPITAL TERRITORY
JERVIS BAY TERRITORY
TASMAN SEA
Brisbane
Gold Coast
Toowoomba
Rockhampton
Newcastle
The Entrance
Sydney
Wollongong
CANBERRA
Melbourne
Frankston
Geelong
Adelaide
Simpson Desert
Sturt Stony Desert
Strzelecki Desert
Lake Eyre (North)
Lake Torrens
Lake Gairdner
Darling Downs
Spencer Gulf
Gulf St Vincent
Kangaroo Island
Eyre Peninsula
FLINDERS RANGES
Tropic of Capricorn
0 100 200 300 400 500 KILOMETRES
© Collins Bartholomew Ltd
121
125

Southeast Australia

SOUTHEAST AUSTRALIA

Southeast Australia is the most densely populated region of the country. The cities of Melbourne, Sydney and Canberra draw in visitors but surrounding these centres is a vast and accessible natural 'playground' for both the domestic city-dweller and the traveller.

Fishing, sailing, walking trails and winter sports are all available in the Snowy Mountains. A summer ascent of the gentle peak of Mt Kosciuszko, the highest mountain in Australia, is a very popular walk for both locals and visitors.

The most scenic route from Melbourne to Adelaide is the 250 km (155 miles) Great Ocean Road. It passes some magnificent cliffs and beaches, especially around Port Campbell.

MELBOURNE

On the shores of Port Philip Bay is Melbourne, Australia's most southerly city. The centre is neatly planned on a grid system with a mix of both ornate Victorian architecture and modern skyscrapers. Five out of Australia's six tallest buildings are found in Melbourne. Already widely regarded for shopping and dining, it is also enjoying growth as a popular destination for international conferences.

It is a lively city, leading the way for the country in culture and sport. The city was the birthplace of Australian film and cinema and is now the centre for contemporary Australian music. A year-round programme of festivals, exhibitions and performing arts means there is much on offer for the visitor.

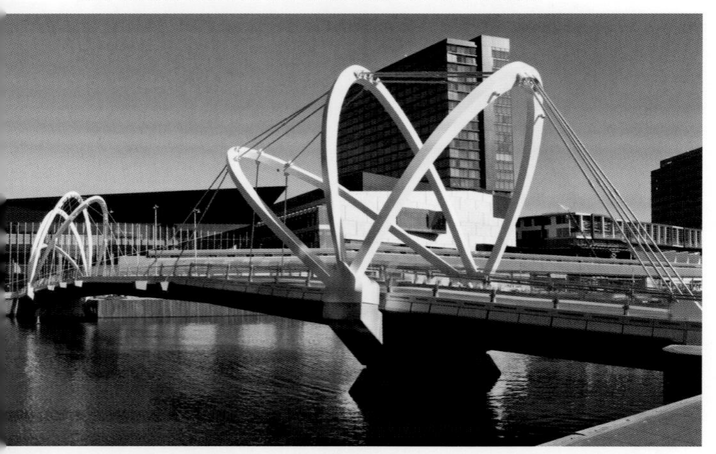

Footbridge at the Exhibition and Conference Centre, **Melbourne**

TASMANIA

There are regular ferry crossings from Melbourne across the Bass Strait to Tasmania, although flights from the mainland can sometime be the cheaper option. Once on the island, public transport is limited and the easiest way to travel is by car.

Tasmania is mountainous, with a landscape of lush forests and distinctive geological formations. The east coast is a land of long white beaches. The west encompasses the Tasmanian Wilderness World Heritage area, a region of mighty rivers, lakes and jagged peaks forming one of the last expanses of temperate wilderness in the world.

Many species of flora and fauna are unique to Tasmania, including several frog species and the marsupial Tasmanian Devil.

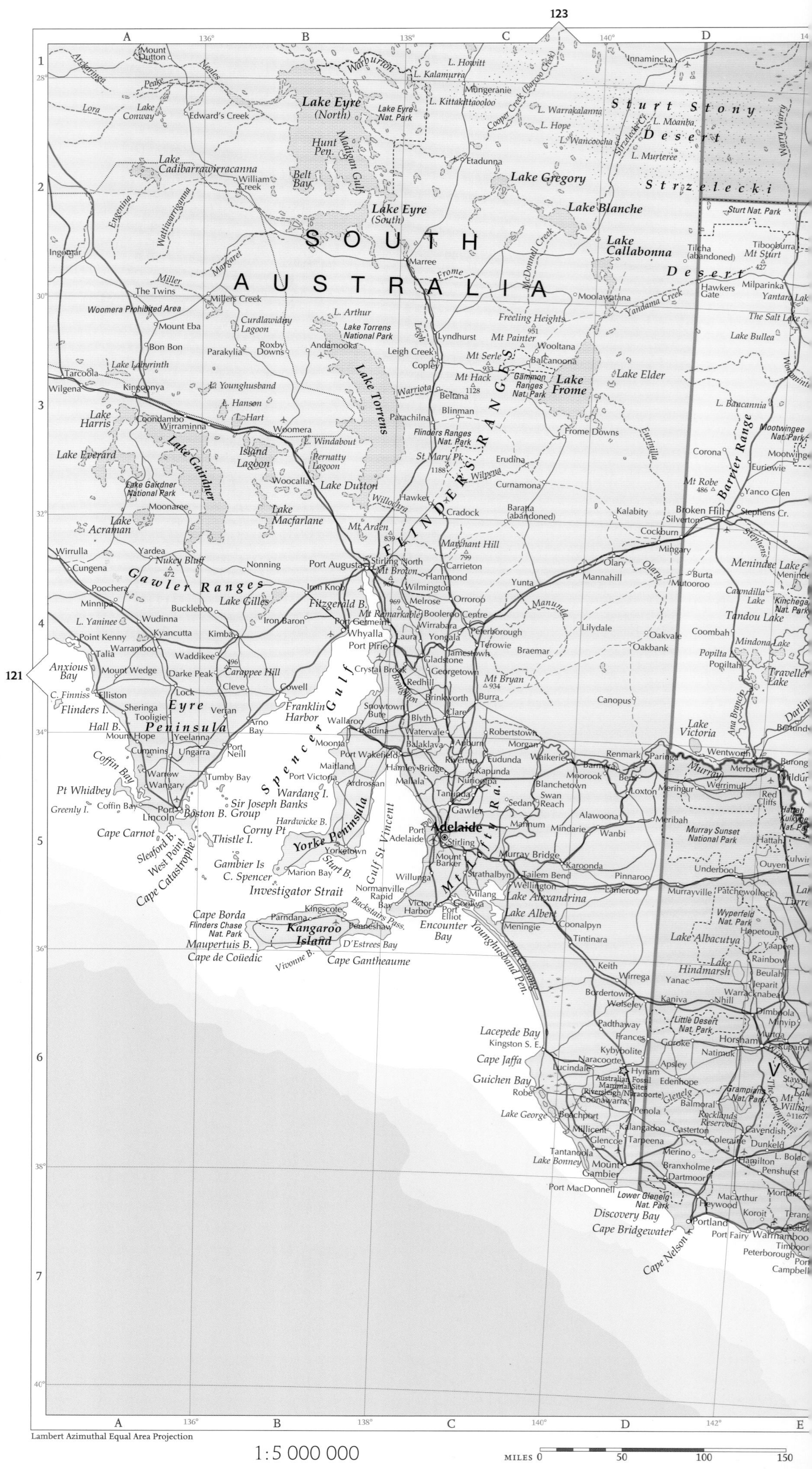

Lambert Azimuthal Equal Area Projection

1 : 5 000 000

MILES 0   50   100   150

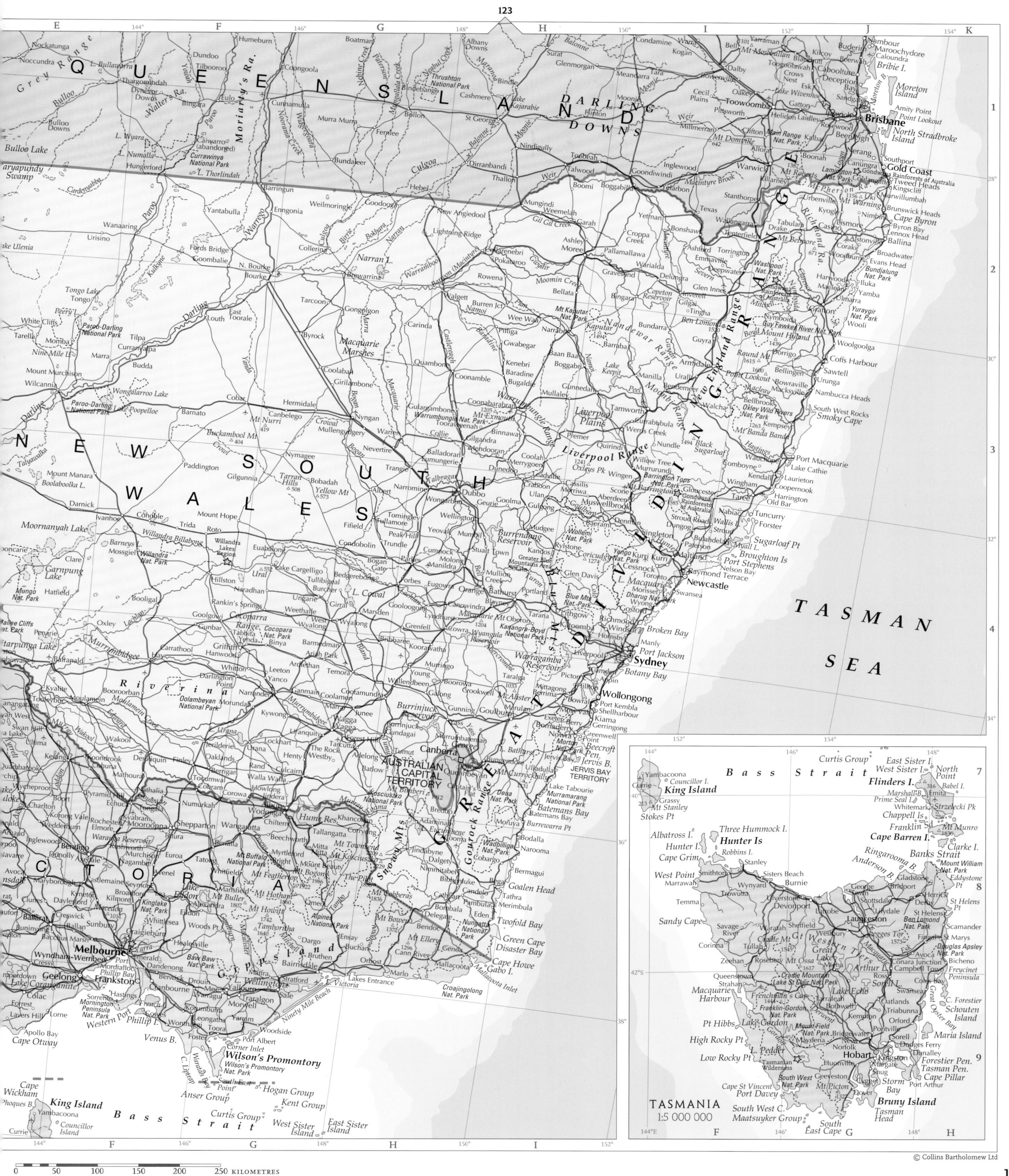

E 144° F 146° G 148° H 150° I 152° J 154° K

QUEENSLAND

Grey Range
Moriarty's Ra.

DARLING DOWNS

Brisbane
Gold Coast

NEW SOUTH WALES

GREAT DIVIDING RANGE

New England Range

Nandewar Range

Liverpool Plains

Liverpool Range

Dubbo

Newcastle

Sydney
Port Jackson
Botany Bay

Wollongong

TASMAN SEA

AUSTRALIAN CAPITAL TERRITORY
Canberra

JERVIS BAY TERRITORY

Snowy Mts.
Mt Kosciuszko

Kosciuszko National Park

VICTORIA

Melbourne
Geelong
Frankston

GIPPSLAND

Ninety Mile Beach

Wilson's Promontory

King Island

Bass Strait
Curtis Group
West Sister Island
East Sister Island

Cape Wickham
Currie

Bass Strait
King Island
Flinders I.
Hunter Is
Cape Barren I.

TASMANIA
1:5 000 000

Hobart
Bruny Island

F 144°E 146° G 148° H

© Collins Bartholomew Ltd

125

0 50 100 150 200 250 KILOMETRES

New Zealand

NEW ZEALAND Capital: **Wellington**
Area: **270 534 km²/104 454 miles²**
Population: **4 179 000** Languages: **English, Maori**
Religions: **Protestant, Roman Catholic**
Currency: **New Zealand dollar**

A country of amazing natural beauty, New Zealand is marketed as a 'clean, green' place to visit. Already one of the world's favourite destinations, responsible ecotourism is now an increasing attraction for visitors.

North Island is famed for its geysers and hot-springs, especially around Rotorua which is also an area of deep-rooted Māori culture.

South Island is more mountainous with the Southern Alps running the entire length of the island. The highest peak is Mt Cook. Further south is Queenstown, site of the world's first commercial jet boating and bungee jumping activities, and still New Zealand's capital of adventure tourism. The area is promoted as an exhilarating year-round 'adrenaline destination'. Further south again and the fjord of Milford Sound is a place of internationally recognised beauty. Despite its remote location it is one of the country's most visited places.

New Zealand's dramatic and diverse landscape made it the fitting location for filming J.R.R. Tolkien's 'Lord of the Rings' trilogy. Film locations are spread over both islands and although some are inaccessible, there are guided tours of many others.

The waters off New Zealand host a wealth of marine life. Kaikoura, on South Island, is one of the most accessible places in the world to see humpback and sperm whales in an award-winning whale watching experience.

Antarctica

ANTARCTICA

This is the coldest, driest and windiest continent and considered a desert, with annual precipitation of only 200 mm (8 inches) along the coast with less inland. The coldest recorded natural temperature on Earth was –89.2 °C (–128.6 °F) at the Russian Vostok Station in 1983. The ice averages 1.6 kms (1 mile) in thickness.

There are no permanent settlements, although up to 5000 people live at the various research stations. There is no overseeing government although forty-six countries have signed up to the 1959 Antarctic Treaty which does not allow military or mineral exploitation.

Some vegetation survives mainly around the coastal fringes, offshore islands and the western Antarctic peninsula which is warmer and wetter than elsewhere. Flora includes mosses, liverworts, lichens and fungi and only two species of flowering plants, Antarctic hair grass and pearlwort.

Penguins, seals and sea lions are year-round residents while albatross, petrels, fulmars, skuas and shearwaters are commonplace. The winters are too harsh for blue, humpback, minke and killer whales but they return to the rich Antarctic feeding grounds in the Spring.

'Expedition tourism' is increasing in popularity and focuses on specific scenic and wildlife locations, leaving the majority of the continent untouched. The industry is self-regulated by the International Association of Antarctica Tour Operators (IAATO).

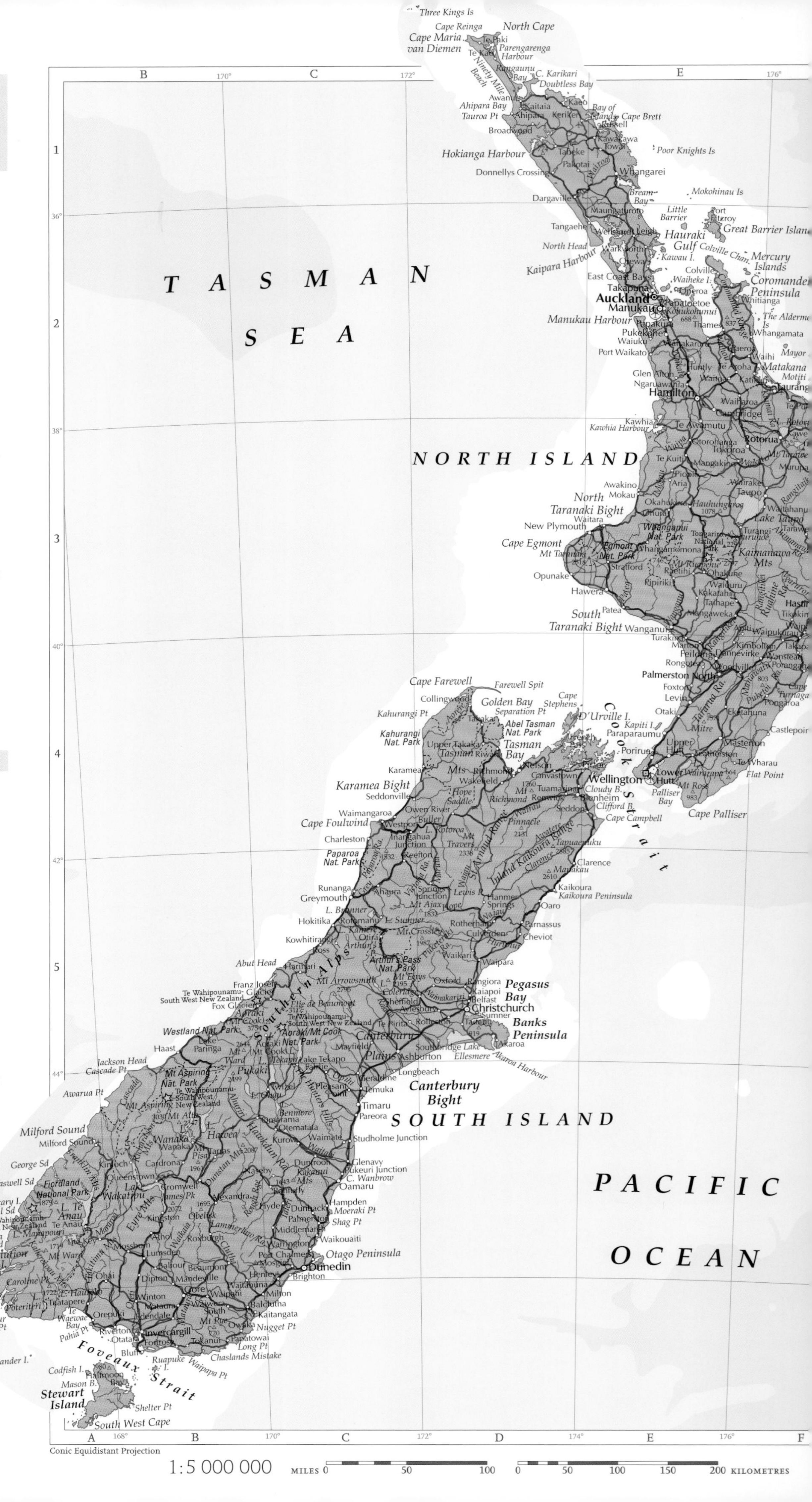

Conic Equidistant Projection

1:5 000 000

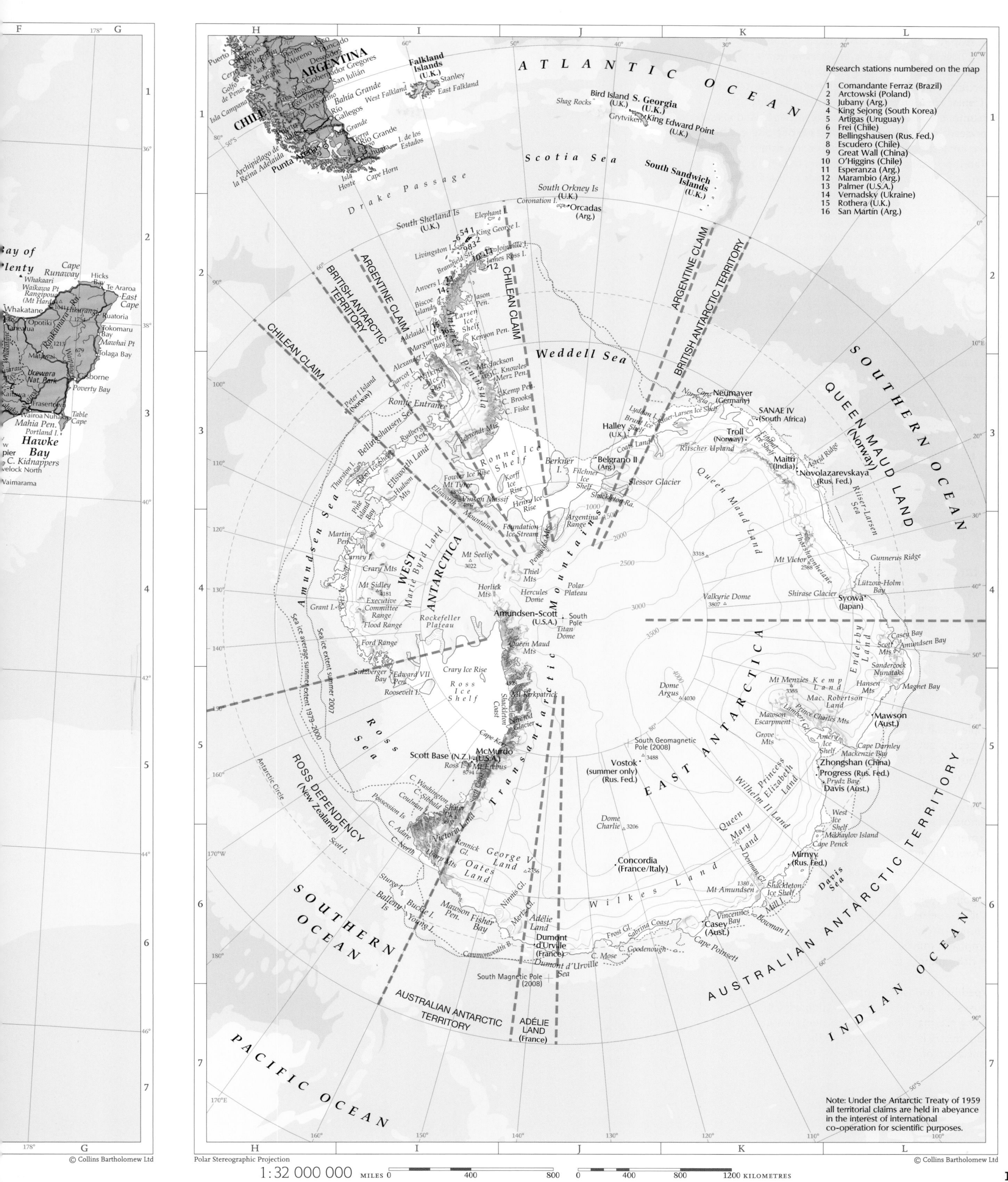

Research stations numbered on the map

1 Comandante Ferraz (Brazil)
2 Arctowski (Poland)
3 Jubany (Arg.)
4 King Sejong (South Korea)
5 Artigas (Uruguay)
6 Frei (Chile)
7 Bellingshausen (Rus. Fed.)
8 Escudero (Chile)
9 Great Wall (China)
10 O'Higgins (Chile)
11 Esperanza (Arg.)
12 Marambio (Arg.)
13 Palmer (U.S.A.)
14 Vernadsky (Ukraine)
15 Rothera (U.K.)
16 San Martin (Arg.)

Note: Under the Antarctic Treaty of 1959
all territorial claims are held in abeyance
in the interest of international
co-operation for scientific purposes.

1 : 32 000 000   MILES 0   400   800   0   400   800   1200 KILOMETRES

Asia Physical

The map highlights the many major mountain ranges – in particular the Himalaya – and plateaus which make up much of Asia. These contrast with enormous low-lying plains, especially in the far north (Siberia) and on the Yellow Sea coast of China. The Ganges and Indus rivers on the Indian subcontinent also occupy extensive lowlands. Indonesia represents by far the most complex archipelago, although there are also many other large and important islands, most notably, Sri Lanka (formerly Ceylon), the Philippines, Taiwan, Japan, and the various island groups in the Arctic Ocean.

Facts

• The outline of Asia is characterised by a number of major peninsulas, including Arabia, the Indian subcontinent, Indo-China and its offshoot the Malay Peninsula, Korea, and the highly volcanic Kamchatka Peninsula.

• Ninety of the world's 100 highest mountains are in Asia. Many lie in the Himalayan kingdom of Nepal where the height of the land ranges from 60 m to 8848 m (200 ft to 29 999 ft).

• The Indonesian archipelago is made up of over 13 000 islands.

• The deepest lake in the world is Lake Baikal in the Russian Federation which is over 1600 m (5250 ft) deep.

• The Gobi Desert, one of the world's biggest areas of desert and semi-desert, occupies a large zone of northern China and Mongolia.

HIGHEST MOUNTAINS	m	ft
Mt Everest (Sagarmatha/ Qomolangma Feng), China/Nepal	8 848	29 028
K2 (Qogir Feng), China/Pakistan	8 611	28 251
Kangchenjunga, India/Nepal	8 586	28 169
Lhotse, China/Nepal	8 516	27 939
Makalu, China/Nepal	8 463	27 765
Cho Oyu, China/Nepal	8 201	26 906

LARGEST ISLANDS	sq km	sq miles
Borneo	745 561	287 861
Sumatra (Sumatera)	473 606	182 859
Honshū	227 414	87 805
Celebes (Sulawesi)	189 216	73 056
Java (Jawa)	132 188	51 038
Luzon	104 690	40 421

LONGEST RIVERS	km	miles
Yangtze (Chang Jiang)	6 380	3 965
Ob'-Irtysh	5 568	3 460
Yenisey-Angara-Selenga	5 550	3 449
Yellow (Huang He)	5 464	3 395
Irtysh	4 440	2 759
Mekong	4 425	2 750

LARGEST LAKES	sq km	sq miles
Caspian Sea	371 000	143 243
Lake Baikal (Ozero Baykal)	30 500	11 776
Lake Balkhash (Ozero Balkhash)	17 400	6 718
Aral Sea (Aral'skoye More)	17 158	6 625
Ysyk-Köl	6 200	2 394

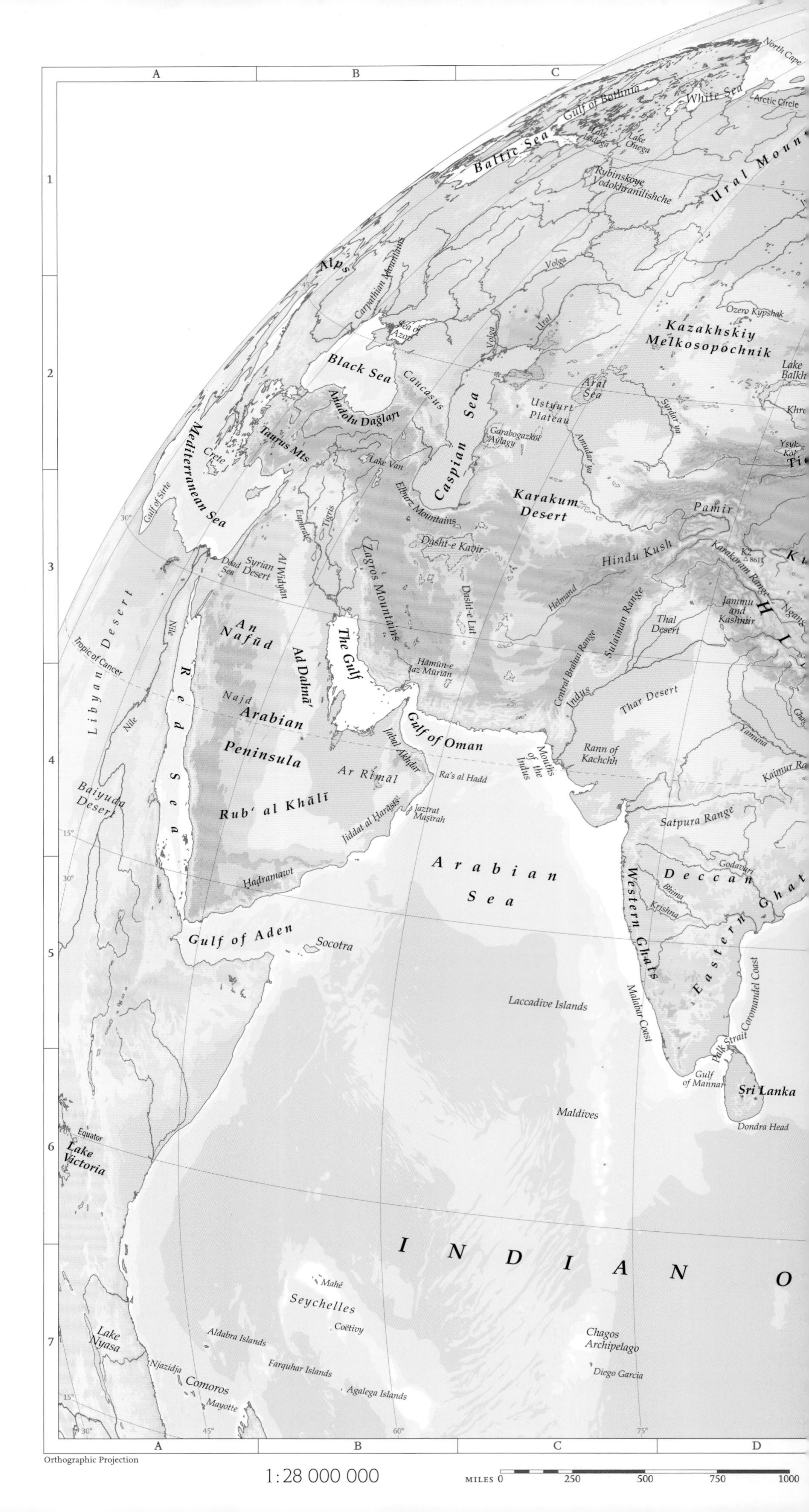

Orthographic Projection

1 : 28 000 000

MILES 0   250   500   750   1000

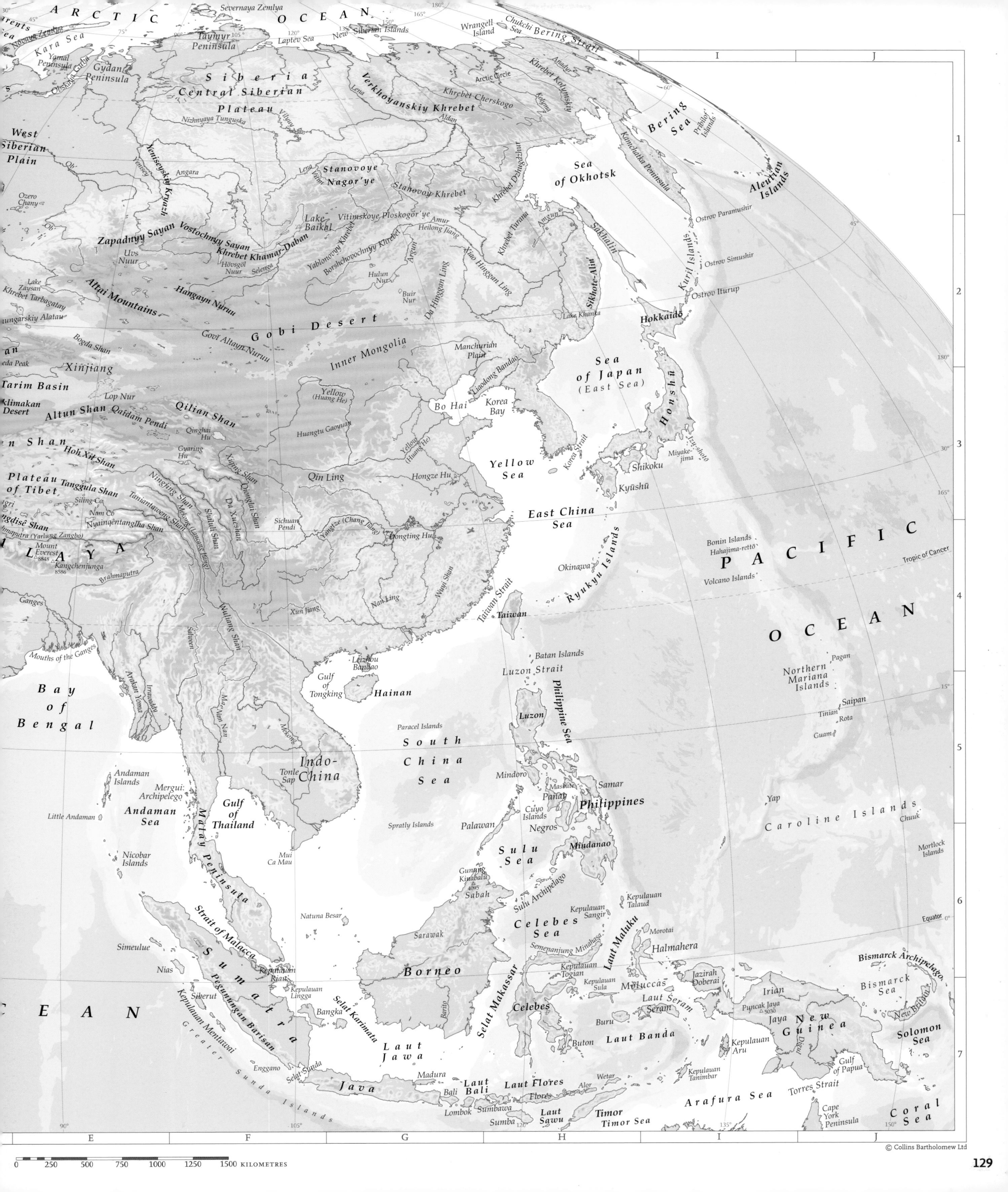

ARCTIC OCEAN
Severnaya Zemlya
Novaya Zemlya
Kara Sea
Yamal Peninsula
Gydan Peninsula
Obskaya Guba
Taymyr Peninsula
Laptev Sea
New Siberian Islands
Wrangell Island
Chukchi Sea
Bering Strait
Siberia
Central Siberian Plateau
Nizhnyaya Tunguska
Verkhoyanskiy Khrebet
Lena
Vilyuy
Aldan
Khrebet Cherskogo
Khrebet Kolymskiy
Kolyma
Anadyr
Arctic Circle
Bering Sea
Pribilof Islands
West Siberian Plain
Ob'
Yeniseyskiy Kryazh
Yenisey
Angara
Stanovoye Nagor'ye
Vitim
Stanovoy Khrebet
Khrebet Dzhugdzhur
Sea of Okhotsk
Kamchatka Peninsula
Aleutian Islands
Ozero Chany
Lake Baikal
Vitimskoye Ploskogor'ye
Amur
Heilong Jiang
Amgun'
Khrebet Turana
Sakhalin
Ostrov Paramushir
Zapadnyy Sayan
Vostochnyy Sayan
Khrebet Khamar-Daban
Yablonovyy Khrebet
Borshchovochnyy Khrebet
Argun'
Xiao Hinggan Ling
Kuril Islands
Ostrov Simushir
Uvs Nuur
Hövsgöl Nuur
Selenga
Hulun Nur
Buir Nur
Da Hinggan Ling
Sikhote-Alin'
Ostrov Iturup
Lake Zaysan
Khrebet Tarbagatay
Altai Mountains
Hangayn Nuruu
Dzhungarskiy Alatau
Gobi Desert
Lake Khanka
Hokkaidō
Bogda Shan
Govĭ Altayn Nuruu
Inner Mongolia
Manchurian Plain
Liaodong Bandao
Sea of Japan (East Sea)
Xinjiang
Tarim Basin
Lop Nur
Yellow (Huang He)
Bo Hai
Korea Bay
Honshū
Taklimakan Desert
Altun Shan
Qaidam Pendi
Qilian Shan
Qinghai Hu
Huangtu Gaoyuan
Gyaring Hu
Korea Strait
Izu-shotō
Miyake-jima
Hoh Xil Shan
Yellow Sea
Shikoku
Kyūshū
Plateau of Tibet
Tanggula Shan
Nyainqêntanglha Shan
Siling Co
Nam Co
Qin Ling
Hongze Hu
Gangdisê Shan
Sichuan Pendi
Yangtze (Chang Jiang)
Dongting Hu
East China Sea
Mount Everest 8848
Kangchenjunga 8586
Brahmaputra
Ganges
Wuyi Shan
Nan Ling
Xun Jiang
Okinawa
Ryukyu Islands
Taiwan Strait
Taiwan
Bonin Islands
Hahajima-rettō
Volcano Islands
PACIFIC OCEAN
Tropic of Cancer
Mouths of the Ganges
Salween
Irrawaddy
Arakan Yoma
Leizhou Bandao
Gulf of Tongking
Hainan
Batan Islands
Luzon Strait
Bay of Bengal
Paracel Islands
Luzon
Philippine Sea
Northern Mariana Islands
Pagan
Saipan
Tinian
Rota
Guam
Mekong
South China Sea
Indo-China
Tonle Sap
Andaman Islands
Mergui Archipelago
Mindoro
Samar
Masbate
Panay
Philippines
Yap
Gulf of Thailand
Andaman Sea
Little Andaman
Malay Peninsula
Cuyo Islands
Negros
Palawan
Spratly Islands
Caroline Islands
Chuuk
Mindanao
Sulu Sea
Nicobar Islands
Mui Ca Mau
Mortlock Islands
Gunung Kinabalu 4095
Sabah
Sulu Archipelago
Kepulauan Talaud
Kepulauan Sangir
Celebes Sea
Strait of Malacca
Natuna Besar
Sarawak
Morotai
Equator
Simeulue
Laut Maluku
Halmahera
Bismarck Archipelago
Nias
Sumatra
Kepulauan Riau
Borneo
Kepulauan Togian
Jazirah Doberai
Bismarck Sea
Kepulauan Sula
Moluccas
Irian
Siberut
Kepulauan Lingga
Pegunungan Barisan
Bangka
Selat Karimata
Selat Makassar
Celebes
Laut Seram
Seram
Puncak Jaya 5030
Jaya
New Guinea
New Britain
Kepulauan Mentawai
Buru
Laut Banda
Digul
Solomon Sea
Laut Jawa
Buton
Kepulauan Aru
Gulf of Papua
Greater Sunda Islands
Enggano
Selat Sunda
Java
Madura
Bali
Laut Bali
Laut Flores
Alor
Wetar
Kepulauan Tanimbar
Flores
Lombok
Sumbawa
Sumba
Laut Sawu
Timor
Timor Sea
Arafura Sea
Torres Strait
Cape York Peninsula
Coral Sea
0 250 500 750 1000 1250 1500 KILOMETRES

Asia Political

With approximately sixty per cent of the world's population, Asia is home to numerous cultures, people groups and lifestyles. It also has a great variety of physical regions which can be defined by the cultural, economic and political systems they support. The major regions are: the arid, oil-rich, mainly Islamic southwest; southern Asia, isolated from the rest of Asia by major mountain ranges; the Indian- and Chinese-influenced monsoon region of southeast Asia; the mainly Chinese-influenced industrialized areas of eastern Asia; and Soviet Asia, made up of most of the former Soviet Union.

Facts

- The line dividing Asia from Oceania is taken as the political boundary between Indonesia and Papua New Guinea. This results in the island of New Guinea being divided between the two continents.

- The break-up of the former Soviet Union in 1991 created two groups of countries in Asia: Kazakhstan, Uzbekistan, Turkmenistan, Tajikistan and Kyrgyzstan on the one hand and Georgia, Armenia and Azerbaijan on the other. This still left the Russian Federation as by far the largest country in the world.

- Cyprus, although now part of the European Union and having long-standing cultural links with Europe, is classed as being within Asia.

- Both China and the Russian Federation have borders with fourteen different countries.

LARGEST COUNTRIES	Area sq km	sq miles
Russian Federation	17 075 400	6 592 849
China	9 584 492	3 700 593
India	3 064 898	1 183 364
Kazakhstan	2 717 300	1 049 155
Saudi Arabia	2 200 000	849 425
Indonesia	1 919 445	741 102
Iran	1 648 000	636 296
Mongolia	1 565 000	604 250
Pakistan	803 940	310 403
Turkey	779 452	300 948

MOST POPULATED COUNTRIES	Population
China	1 313 437 000
India	1 169 016 000
Indonesia	231 627 000
Pakistan	163 902 000
Bangladesh	158 665 000
Russian Federation	142 499 000
Japan	127 967 000
Philippines	87 960 000
Vietnam	87 375 000
Turkey	74 877 000

CAPITALS		
Largest population	Tōkyō, Japan	35 467 000
Smallest population	Melekeok, Palau	391
Most northerly	Astana, Kazakhstan	51° 10' N
Most southerly	Dili, East Timor	8° 35' S
Highest	Thimphu, Bhutan	2 423 m/ 7 949 ft

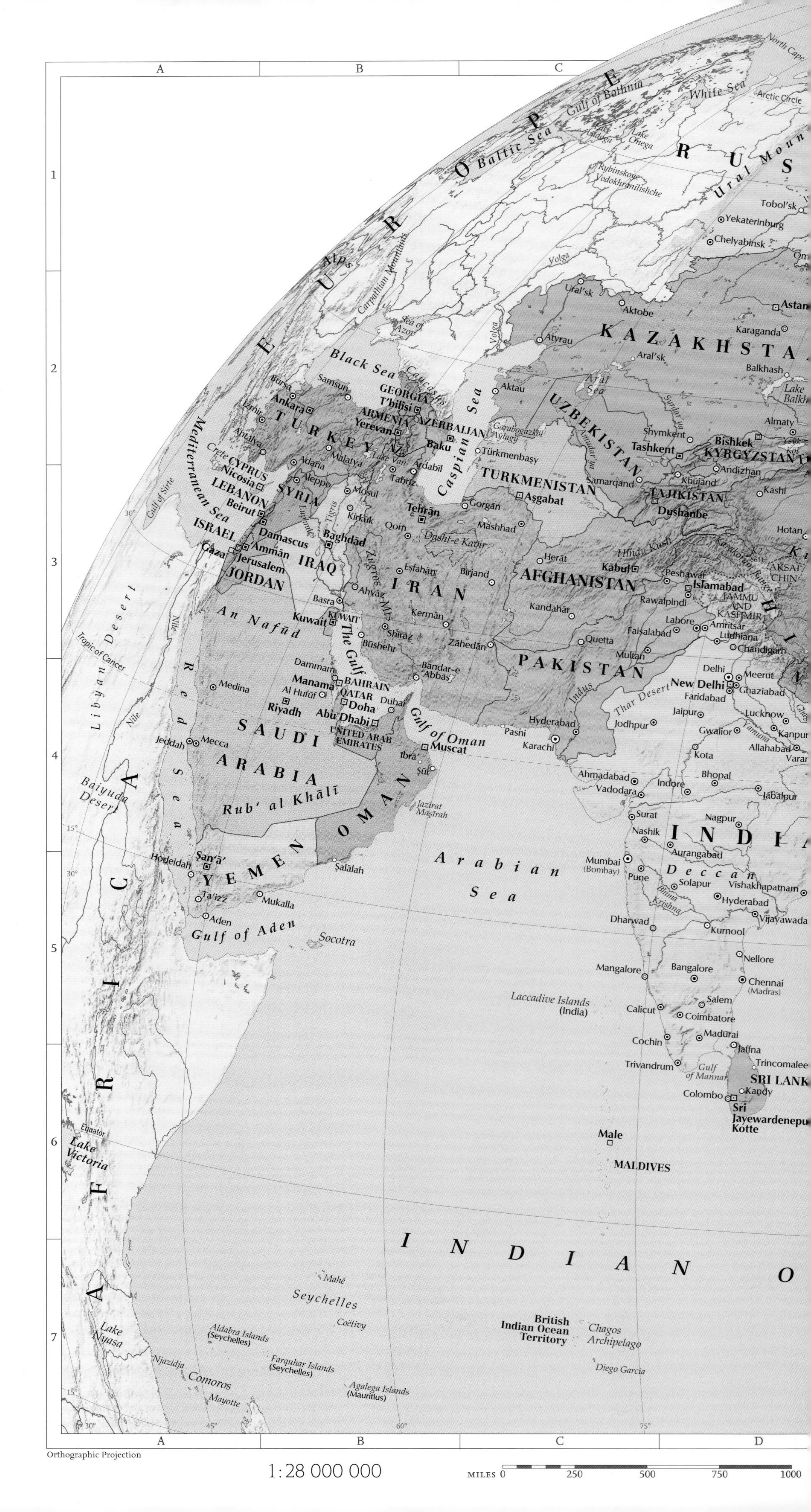

Orthographic Projection

1:28 000 000

MILES 0   250   500   750   1000

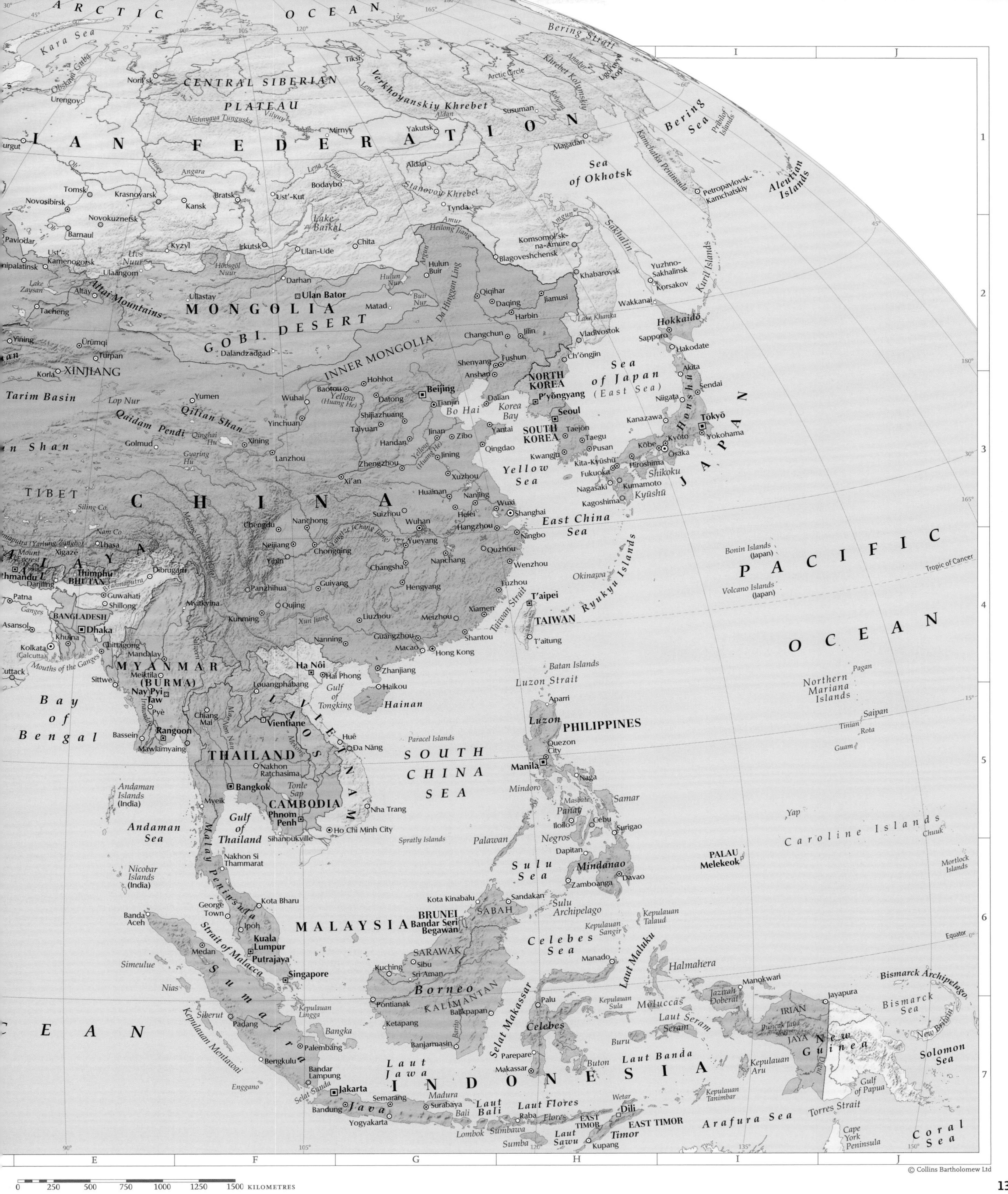

ARCTIC   OCEAN

Kara Sea

CENTRAL SIBERIAN
PLATEAU

IAN FEDERATION

Bering
Sea

Aleutian
Islands

MONGOLIA
GOBI DESERT
INNER MONGOLIA

Ulan Bator

Sea
of Okhotsk

Kamchatka Peninsula

Petropavlovsk-
Kamchatskiy

XINJIANG

Tarim Basin

TIBET

CHINA

NORTH
KOREA
P'yŏngyang
Beijing
Seoul
SOUTH
KOREA

Sea
of Japan
(East Sea)

Hokkaidō

JAPAN

Tōkyō
Yokohama

Yellow
Sea

Shanghai

East China
Sea

PACIFIC

OCEAN

Bay
of
Bengal

MYANMAR
(BURMA)
Nay Pyi
Taw

THAILAND

Bangkok

CAMBODIA
Phnom
Penh

Rangoon

VIETNAM

Vientiane

LAOS

Ha Nôi

Hainan

SOUTH

CHINA

SEA

TAIWAN
T'aipei

Luzon

PHILIPPINES

Manila

Quezon
City

Northern
Mariana
Islands

Saipan
Guam

Andaman
Sea

Andaman
Islands
(India)

Nicobar
Islands
(India)

Gulf
of
Thailand

Malay Peninsula

Strait of Malacca

Kuala
Lumpur
Putrajaya

MALAYSIA

Singapore

BRUNEI
Bandar Seri
Begawan

SABAH

SARAWAK

Borneo
KALIMANTAN

Sulu
Sea

Celebes
Sea

Mindanao

Davao

PALAU
Melekeok

Caroline Islands

Chuuk

Sumatra

INDONESIA

Java
Jakarta

Laut
Jawa

Celebes

New
Guinea

IRIAN
JAYA

Bismarck
Sea

Solomon
Sea

Arafura Sea

EAST
TIMOR

Timor

Coral
Sea

Cape
York
Peninsula

© Collins Bartholomew Ltd

0   250   500   750   1000   1250   1500 KILOMETRES

131

RUSSIAN FEDERATION Capital: **Moscow (Moskva)**
Area: **17 075 400 km²/6 592 849 miles²**
Population: **142 499 000** Languages: **Russian, Tatar, Ukrainian, local languages** Religions: **Russian Orthodox, Sunni Muslim, Protestant** Currency: **Russian rouble**

The vast scale of the country means that intercity travel is usually done by air or else by the Trans-Siberian railway which takes eight days to complete the whole route from Moscow to Vladivostok, crossing seven time zones.

The centre of Moscow has many sites of interest including Red Square, the Kremlin and the iconic St Basil's Cathedral. On the way to St Petersburg, visit Velikiy Novgorod, one of the oldest cities in Russia with many ancient churches and restored kremlin. St Petersburg has a more European feel than Moscow. The Nevsky Prospekt is lined with elegant buildings and the Hermitage museum has endless treasures to explore. The Winter Palace is adjacent but the Summer Palace (Peterhof) is on the outskirts and also has parklands to admire. Further east are the ancient wooden churches of Kizhi on an island in Lake Onega.

Volgograd was the site of a yearlong battle in the Second World War. The Caucasus Mountains are popular for hiking, and skiing in winter, with the Black Sea coastline known as the 'Russian Riviera' north from Sochi. Heading up the Volga river is Kazan, once a Tartar fortress. The Ural Mountains main centre is Yekaterinburg, the site of the murders of Tsar Nicholas II and his family. This rural border between Europe and Asia attracts walkers, hikers and fishermen.

The Altai region of southern Siberia is a mixture of pine forests and flower meadows in the spring, Tomsk being the most attractive city in the region with wooden mansions and the youthful outlook of an academic centre. Lake Baikal is the world's deepest freshwater lake and is best approached from Irkutsk.

Heading further east, Khabarovsk is a refreshing town after the vast plains of the Siberian taiga. Vladivostok on the Pacific coast is an impressive natural harbour.

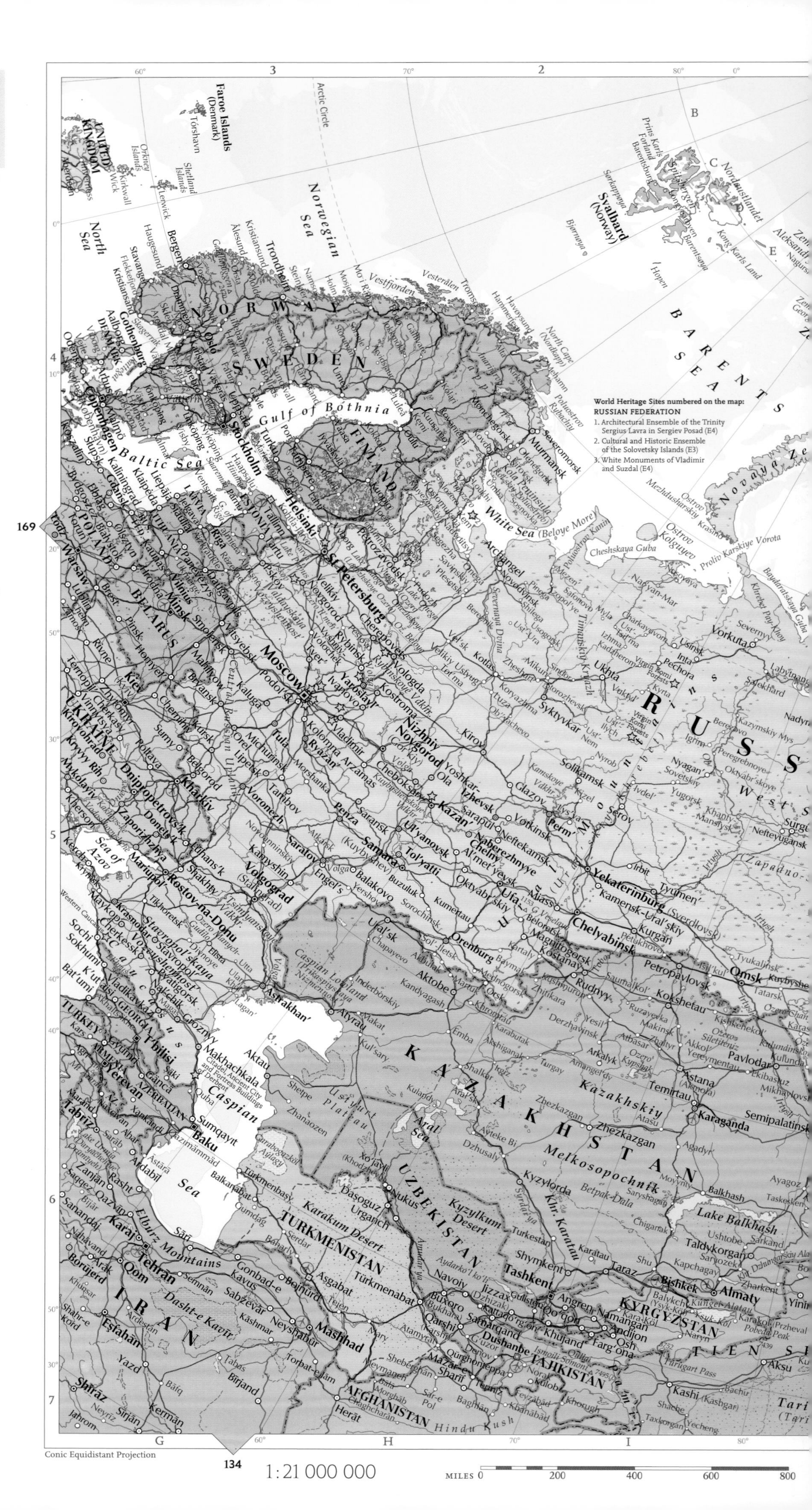

World Heritage Sites numbered on the map:
RUSSIAN FEDERATION
1. Architectural Ensemble of the Trinity Sergius Lavra in Sergiev Posad (E4)
2. Cultural and Historic Ensemble of the Solovetsky Islands (E3)
3. White Monuments of Vladimir and Suzdal (E4)

Conic Equidistant Projection

1 : 21 000 000   MILES 0   200   400   600   800

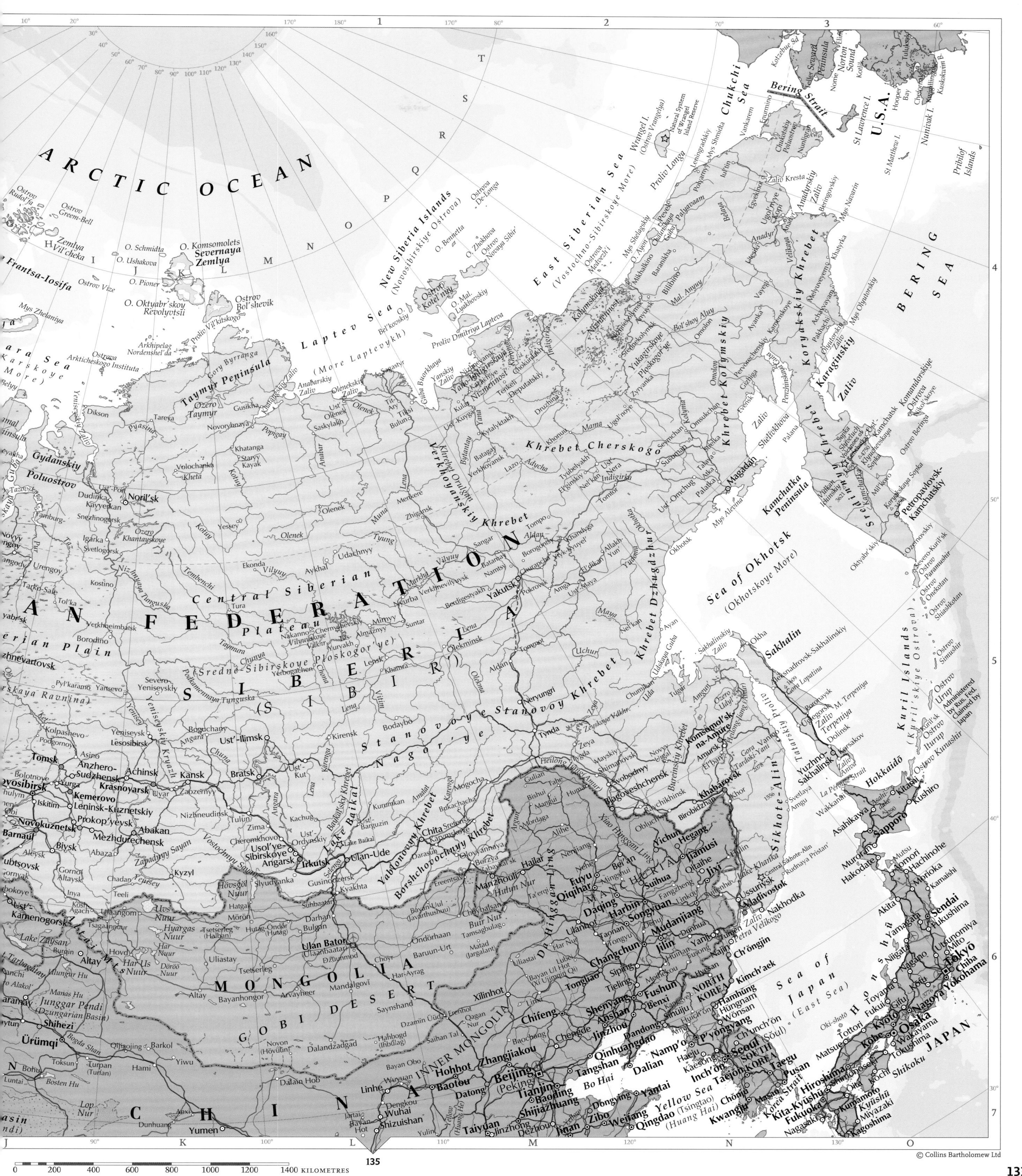

0   200   400   600   800   1000   1200   1400 KILOMETRES

ARCTIC OCEAN
Laptev Sea
(More Laptevykh)
East Siberian Sea
(Vostochno-Sibirskoye More)
Chukchi Sea
Bering Strait
BERING SEA
Sea of Okhotsk
(Okhotskoye More)
Sea of Japan
(East Sea)
Yellow Sea
(Huang Hai)
Bo Hai
Korea Strait
Kara Sea
(Karskoye More)
New Siberia Islands
(Novosibirskiye Ostrova)
Severnaya Zemlya
Zemlya Frantsa-Iosifa
Wrangel I.
(Ostrov Vrangelya)
Natural System of Wrangel Island Reserve
Taymyr Peninsula
Gydanskiy Poluostrov
Kamchatka Peninsula
Sakhalin
Kuril Islands
(Kuril'skiye Ostrova)
Administered by Rus. Fed., claimed by Japan
Hokkaidō
Honshū
Shikoku
Kyūshū
RUSSIAN FEDERATION
SIBERIA
(SIBIR')
Central Siberian Plateau
(Sredne-Sibirskoye Ploskogor'ye)
West Siberian Plain
Khrebet Cherskogo
Verkhoyanskiy Khrebet
Stanovoye Nagor'ye
Stanovoy Khrebet
Koryakskiy Khrebet
Khrebet Kolymskiy
Khrebet Dzhugdzhur
Sikhote-Alin
Yablonovyy Khrebet
Lake Baikal
MONGOLIA
GOBI DESERT
INNER MONGOLIA
CHINA
NORTH KOREA
SOUTH KOREA
JAPAN
U.S.A.
Noril'sk
Dudinka
Yakutsk
Magadan
Petropavlovsk-Kamchatskiy
Tiksi
Khatanga
Verkhoyansk
Neryungri
Tynda
Bratsk
Ust'-Ilimsk
Irkutsk
Ulan-Ude
Chita
Krasnoyarsk
Kemerovo
Novosibirsk
Tomsk
Novokuznetsk
Barnaul
Biysk
Abakan
Kyzyl
Khabarovsk
Komsomol'sk-na-Amure
Blagoveshchensk
Vladivostok
Nakhodka
Yuzhno-Sakhalinsk
Ulan Bator
(Ulaanbaatar)
Ürümqi
Shihezi
Harbin
Qiqihar
Changchun
Jilin
Shenyang
Anshan
Fushun
Dalian
Beijing
(Peking)
Tianjin
Baotou
Hohhot
Datong
Zhangjiakou
Chifeng
Tangshan
Qinhuangdao
Shijiazhuang
Taiyuan
Jinan
Zibo
Qingdao (Tsingtao)
Yantai
P'yŏngyang
Ch'ŏngjin
Hamhŭng
Seoul
(Sŏul)
Inch'ŏn
Taejŏn
Taegu
Pusan
Kwangju
Sapporo
Hakodate
Sendai
Tōkyō
Yokohama
Chiba
Nagoya
Kyōto
Ōsaka
Kōbe
Hiroshima
Kita-Kyūshū
Fukuoka
Kumamoto
Kagoshima
135

Central and Southern Asia

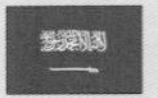

SAUDI ARABIA Capital: Riyadh (Ar Riyāḍ)
Area: 2 200 000 km²/849 425 miles²
Population: **24 735 000** Languages: **Arabic**
Religions: **Sunni Muslim, Shi'a Muslim**
Currency: **Saudi Arabian riyal**

Saudi Arabia is gradually letting visitors into the country. Previously, only those on the hajj pilgrimage would be welcomed to visit Mecca and Medina. Riyadh is a modern city with little evidence of its old town. Jeddah is a more open, cosmopolitan city with a mixture of old merchants' houses, Ottoman buildings and shopping malls. The coastline offers watersports as well as good diving sites to the pristine coral reefs. To the north is the ancient Nabataean city of Madain Saleh, while to the south is Aṭ Ṭā'if, the summer capital, at the start of a dramatic escarpment heading down to the Yemen border. There are cable cars to appreciate the scenery, and a road which follows the ridge through the wild vegetation of 'Asīr Najrān, close to the border, was an ancient caravan stop and has traditional mud brick buildings and an impressive fort.

OMAN Capital: Muscat (Masqaṭ)
Area: 309 500 km²/119 499 miles²
Population: **2 595 000** Languages: **Arabic, Baluchi, Indian languages** Religions: **Ibadhi Muslim, Sunni Muslim**
Currency: **Omani riyal**

Traditional Arabian values underpin the modern day Oman. Modernisation has been gradual with few high-rise buildings in the capital. Haggling is expected at the Muttrah Souk. Inland, the mountains can be explored from Nazwá, such as Jabal Shām which gives views into Wadi Ghul, a mini Grand Canyon. There are World Heritage sites at Bat with ancient burial mounds and Bahla which has a huge fort made of unbaked bricks. Şūr is where traditional dhow building continues and offers day trips to the Ras al-Jinz turtle reserve. The Dhofar region behind the lush coastal strip at Şalālah is where frankincense originates.

YEMEN Capital: Şan'ā'
Area: 527 968 km²/203 850 miles²
Population: **22 389 000** Languages: **Arabic**
Religions: **Sunni Muslim, Shi'a Muslim** Currency: **Yemeni riyal**

Travel to some parts of Yemen is unsafe at present which is unfortunate because there are some spectacular sites to see. Firstly, the capital Şan'ā', which has beautifully decorated buildings, ancient craft markets and over 100 mosques. Not far away are the ancient fortifications of Kawkabān and the remnants of Ma'rib, allegedly home of the Queen of Sheba. Further east in the Wadi Hadramawt, Shibām is a pre-Islamic high-rise settlement. The ancient port of Aden, which lies in an extinct volcanic crater, is the starting point for trips to the island of Socotra with its unique flora and fauna.

IRAQ Capital: Baghdād
Area: 438 317 km²/169 235 miles²
Population: **28 993 000** Languages: **Arabic, Kurdish, Turkmen**
Religions: **Shi'a Muslim, Sunni Muslim, Christian**
Currency: **Iraqi dinar**

Hopefully Iraq can slowly rebuild after the recent war but at present it is unwise to travel there. Since civilisation first developed here in the 6th millennium BC, there has been much unrest in the fertile lands of the Tigris and Euphrates rivers. From Nineveh, now Mosul, through Hatra and Ashur, the capital of the Assyrian Empire south to Samarra and Ctesiphon and on to Ur, there are some impressive archaeological sites but Babylon has undergone some unfortunate reconstruction work. Priceless treasures from these sites were taken from the museum in Baghdad. These important sites will encourage visitors back to this country in the future.

Albers Equal Area Conic Projection

1:20 000 000 MILES 0 200 400 600 800

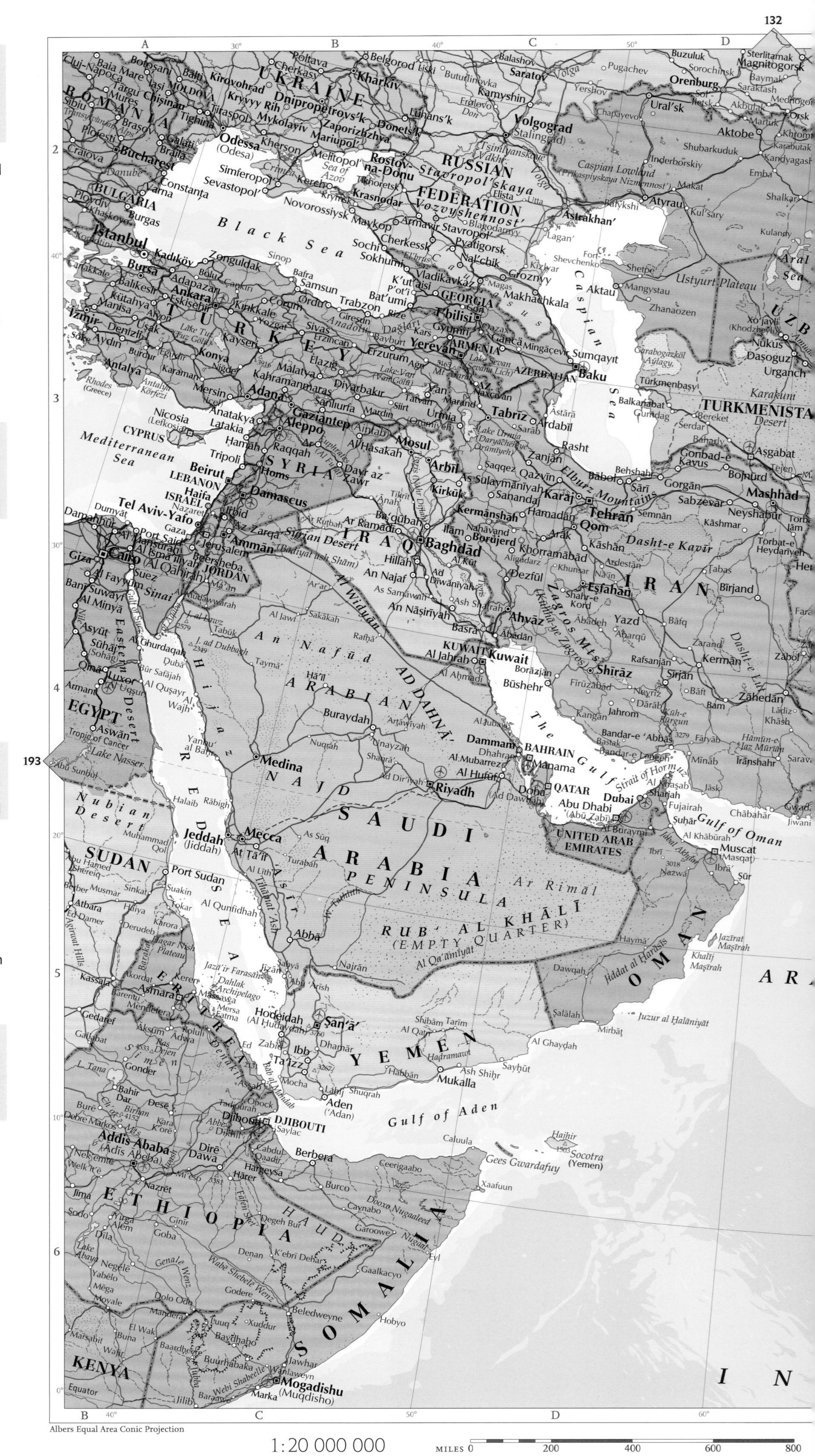

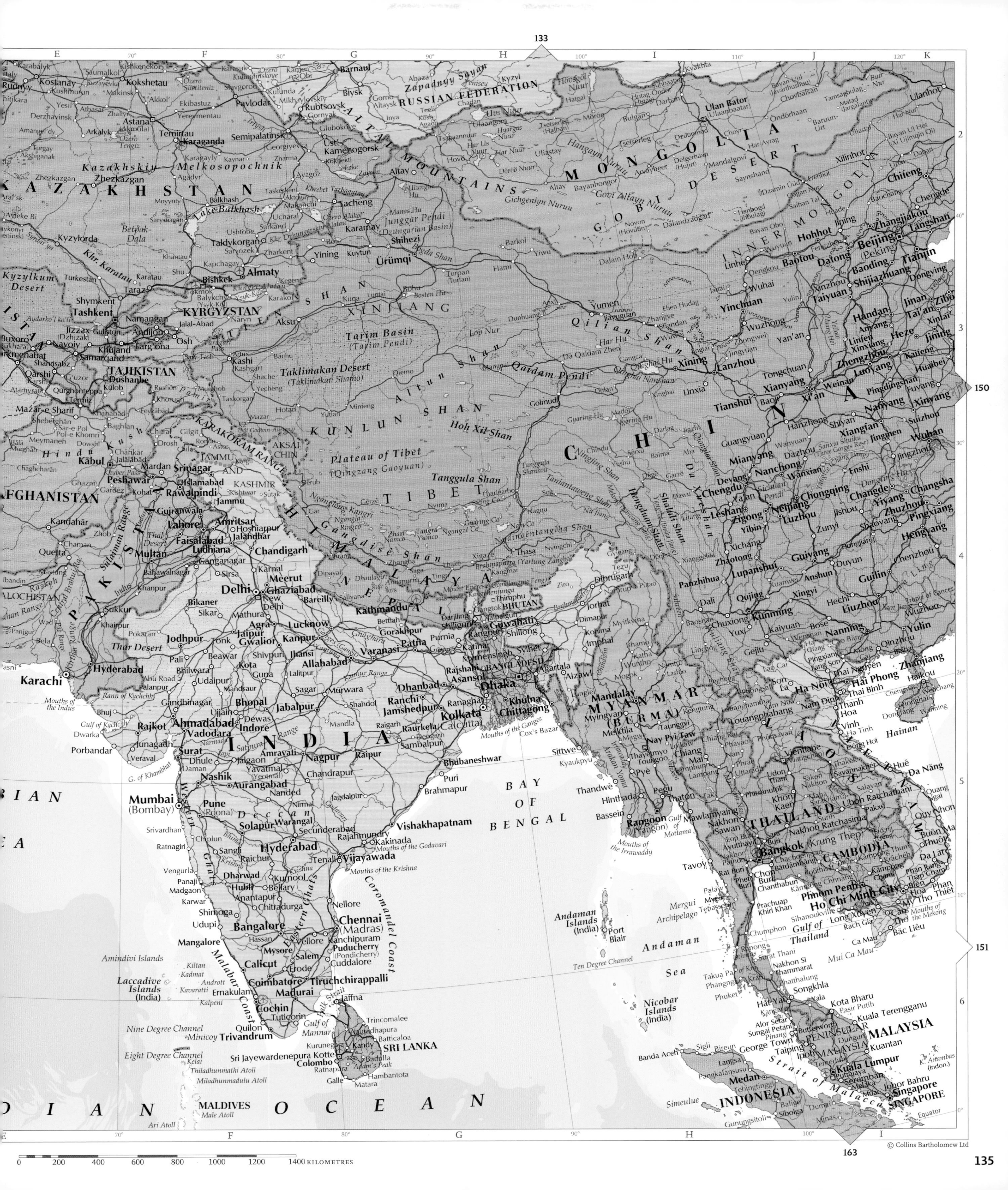

Eastern Mediterranean and The Caucasus

ARMENIA Capital: Yerevan (Erevan)
Area: 29 800 km²/11 506 miles²
Population: 3 002 000 Languages: Armenian, Azeri
Religions: Armenian Orthodox Currency: Dram

Beautiful natural scenery of mountains, verdant forests and lakes create a stunning backdrop for the many churches and monasteries scattered across Armenia. Haghpat and Sanahin monasteries are approached through a gorge in Debed. The capital Yerevan, has a thriving café culture and also houses ancient manuscripts in the National Gallery. The World Heritage site of Echmiadzin is the religious centre of the country. Although landlocked, there are beaches on the shores of Lake Sevan, famed for its pure waters. To the south, Jermuk, has hot mineral water springs.

AZERBAIJAN Capital: Baku
Area: 86 600 km²/33 436 miles² Population: 8 467 000
Languages: Azeri, Armenian, Russian, Lezgian
Religions: Shi'a Muslim, Sunni Muslim, Russian and Armenian Orthodox Currency: Azerbaijani manat

This is an oil-rich country with a fast-developing capital. Its situation made it an important stopping off point on the Silk Road. Baku has its old walled city, Içeri Seher surrounded by growing skyscrapers. Not far is Yanar Dag which produces a nonstop wall of flames due to natural gas underground. South is Qobustan which has strange mud volcanoes and caves with thousands of petroglyphs. Visitors are rare outside the capital but Şäki is a pretty town in the mountains and Xınalıq is a hill village which has kept its unique language and traditions. The enclave of Nagorno-Karabakh is disputed with Armenia.

GEORGIA Capital: T'bilisi
Area: 69 700 km²/26 911 miles² Population: 4 395 000
Languages: Georgian, Russian, Armenian, Azeri, Ossetian, Abkhaz
Religions: Georgian Orthodox, Russian Orthodox, Sunni Muslim
Currency: Lari

Georgia is steeped in history and is still battling with long disputes in Abkhazia and South Ossetia. However because of the stunning scenery, visitor numbers are growing. T'bilisi has some beautiful frescoed churches such as the fifth-century Sioni Cathedral. The best views can be seen from the Narikala Fortress. The Georgian Military Highway which heads to Vladikavkaz across the border, goes through the foothills of the Caucasus, ideal for winter sports, to the mountain town of Qazbegi. In contrast, Bat'umi, on the Black Sea has a semi-tropical feel and east of T'bilisi is the wine growing region.

TURKEY Capital: Ankara
Area: 779 452 km²/300 948 miles²
Population: 74 877 000 Languages: Turkish, Kurdish
Religions: Sunni Muslim, Shi'a Muslim Currency: Lira

Turkey is truly where east meets west. Although Istanbul is not the capital, it receives the most attention, with buildings such as the Blue Mosque, Topkapi Palace and the Grand Bazaar. It also is developing a thriving nightlife. Safranbolu, to the east, is a restored Ottoman town. More recent monuments are at Gallipoli which is strewn with battle sites. Further south are the classical cities of Ephesus and Pergamom (Bergama) and the ancient site of Troy. Inland are the mineral waters of Pamukkale creating a unique landscape. Walkers can tackle the Lycian Way from Fethiye to Antalya. Further east is the strange landscape of Cappadocia with its wind- and water-eroded rock formations.

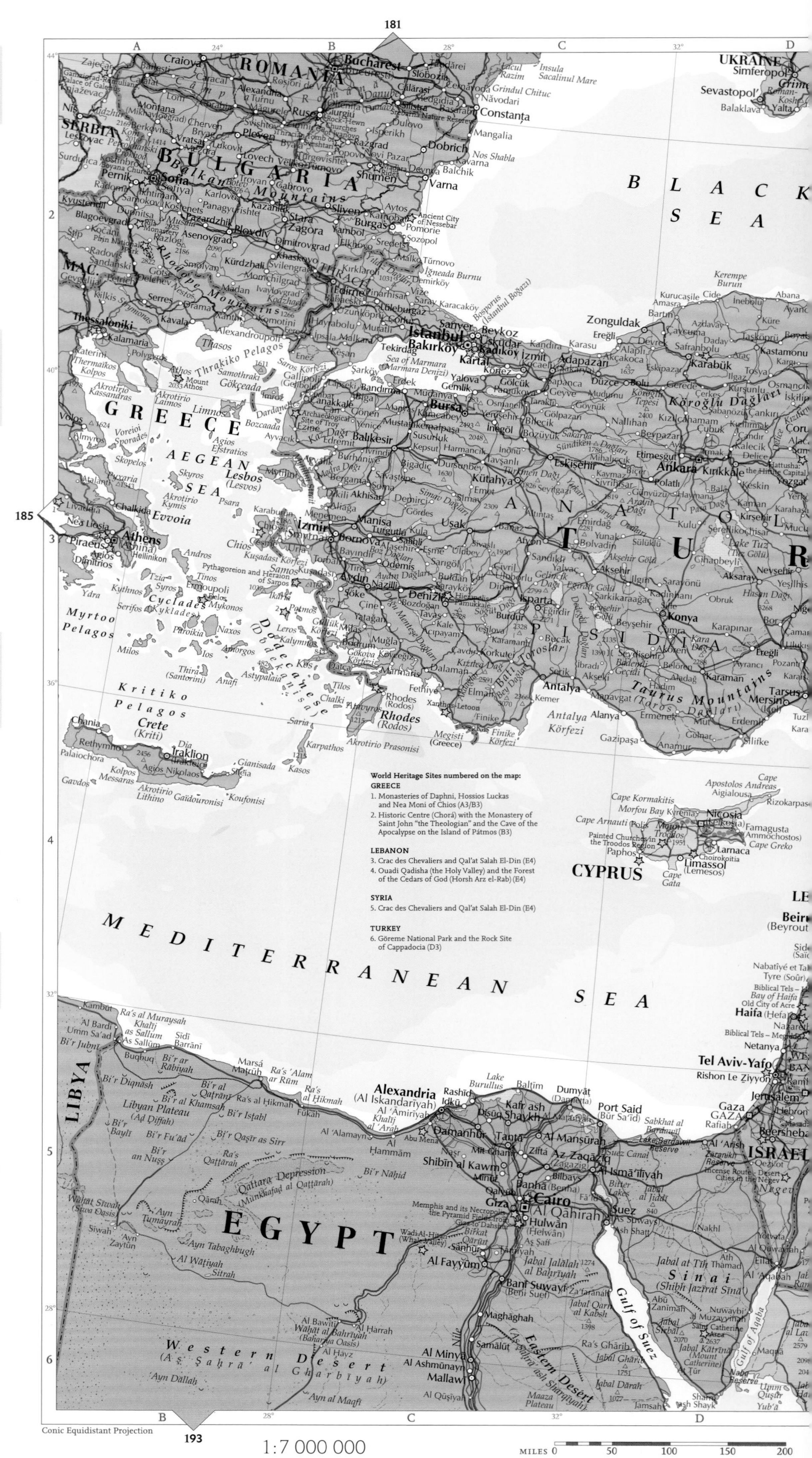

World Heritage Sites numbered on the map:
GREECE
1. Monasteries of Daphni, Hossios Luckas and Nea Moni of Chios (A3/B3)
2. Historic Centre (Chorá) with the Monastery of Saint John "the Theologian" and the Cave of the Apocalypse on the Island of Pátmos (B3)

LEBANON
3. Crac des Chevaliers and Qal'at Salah El-Din (E4)
4. Ouadi Qadisha (the Holy Valley) and the Forest of the Cedars of God (Horsh Arz el-Rab) (E4)

SYRIA
5. Crac des Chevaliers and Qal'at Salah El-Din (E4)

TURKEY
6. Göreme National Park and the Rock Site of Cappadocia (D3)

Conic Equidistant Projection

1:7 000 000

MILES 0   50   100   150   200

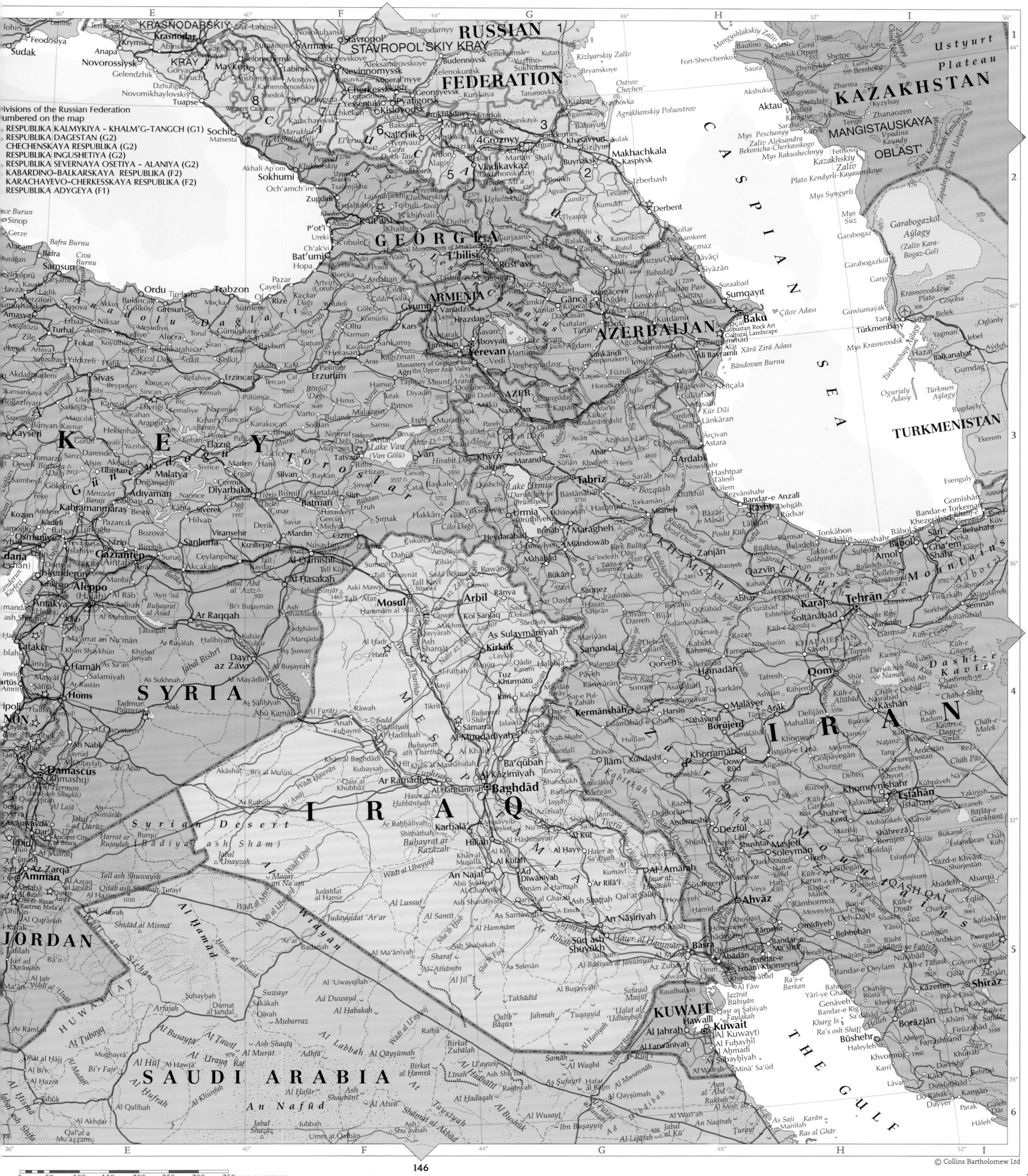

Divisions of the Russian Federation
numbered on the map

1 RESPUBLIKA KALMYKIYA – KHALM'G-TANGCH (G1)
2 RESPUBLIKA DAGESTAN (G2)
3 CHECHENSKAYA RESPUBLIKA (G2)
4 RESPUBLIKA INGUSHETIYA (G2)
5 RESPUBLIKA SEVERNAYA OSETIYA – ALANIYA (G2)
6 KABARDINO-BALKARSKAYA RESPUBLIKA (F2)
7 KARACHAYEVO-CHERKESSKAYA RESPUBLIKA (F2)
8 RESPUBLIKA ADYGEYA (F1)

RUSSIAN FEDERATION

KAZAKHSTAN

GEORGIA

ARMENIA

AZERBAIJAN

TURKMENISTAN

TURKEY

SYRIA

IRAQ

IRAN

JORDAN

SAUDI ARABIA

KUWAIT

CASPIAN SEA

THE GULF

© Collins Bartholomew Ltd

0 50 100 150 200 250 300 350 KILOMETRES

The Middle East

CYPRUS Capital: **Nicosia (Lefkosia)**
Area: **9 251 km²/3 572 miles²**
Population: **855 000** Languages: **Greek, Turkish, English**
Religions: **Greek Orthodox, Sunni Muslim** Currency: **Euro**

Nicosia is still a divided capital city but access from the southern Greek to northern Turkish part of the island is now possible. The island is a mix of Byzantine churches, Crusader castles, Roman mosaics and beach resorts. There are busy areas but escape to the Troödos Mountains for cooler temperatures, hilltop villages and Byzantine churches with beautiful frescoes. Evidence of Roman villas can be found amongst the all-year destination of Paphos. Kourion has a Greco-Roman theatre overlooking the sea and still stages plays. The wild Akamas peninsula is home to the protected loggerhead turtles during their breeding season.

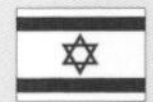

ISRAEL Capital: **Jerusalem (Yerushalayim) (El Quds)**
De facto capital. Disputed.
Area: **20 770 km²/8 019 miles²** Population: **6 928 000**
Languages: **Hebrew, Arabic** Religions: **Jewish, Sunni Muslim, Christian, Druze** Currency: **Shekel**

Israel is mixture of deserts, beaches, archaeology and spirituality. Jerusalem is the uneasy centre of the three main monotheistic faiths. Enter the old city through the Jaffa Gate, walk the Via Dolorosa, see the Western Wall and the Dome of the Rock. Relax in Tel Aviv, a vibrant coastal city. 'Akko is an atmospheric Crusader city further north. Inland is the picturesque Sea of Galilee, surrounded by Christian sites. View the world's lowest point, the Dead Sea, from Masada. Cross the Negev Desert stopping at Mitzpe Ramon to reach Eilat, a resort famed for its dive sites.

LEBANON Capital: **Beirut (Beyrouth)**
Area: **10 452 km²/4 036 miles²** Population: **4 099 000**
Languages: **Arabic, Armenian, French** Religions: **Shi'a Muslim, Sunni Muslim, Christian** Currency: **Lebanese pound**

Home to Byblos, possibly the oldest town in the world, and other ancient sites such as the Roman temple at Baalbek and hippodrome at Tyre. Contrast with the capital Beirut. With a backdrop of mountains, the Corniche seafront is being redeveloped. Caution is required if travelling to the south of the country.

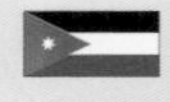

JORDAN Capital: **'Ammān**
Area: **89 206 km²/34 443 miles²**
Population: **5 924 000** Languages: **Arabic** Religions: **Sunni Muslim, Christian** Currency: **Jordanian dinar**

Jordan is a desert kingdom steeped in history. Petra is the main attraction; a hidden rock-hewn city which glows pink in sun. Jerash is one of the best-preserved Roman cities and Kerak is the dramatic setting for a Crusader castle. From the heights of Mount Nebo, survey Moses' 'promised land', and float in the salty waters of the Dead Sea. Madaba has some exceptional mosaics. Explore the wind-blown rock formations in the desert landscape of Wadi Rum on the way to Jordan's only coastal resort of Aqaba, a popular dive site on the Red Sea.

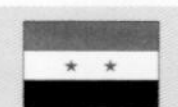

SYRIA Capital: **Damascus (Dimashq)**
Area: **185 180 km²/71 498 miles²**
Population: **19 929 000** Languages: **Arabic, Kurdish, Armenian**
Religions: **Sunni Muslim, Shi'a Muslim, Christian**
Currency: **Syrian pound**

Syria is a modern country becoming more outward-looking but is full of cultural riches from different civilisations. Damascus is an ancient city with an old centre of narrow alleyways around the Umayyad Mosque which started life as a Greek temple. Buṣrá ash Shām (Bosra) has an imposing citadel and well-preserved Roman theatre. Extensive Roman remains can be seen at Tadmur (Palmyra), set in a desert oasis. In the north Aleppo has an impressive citadel and the old city is being restored. From here visit the famous Crusader castle of Crac des Chevaliers, Apamea and the Dead Cities.

1:5 000 000

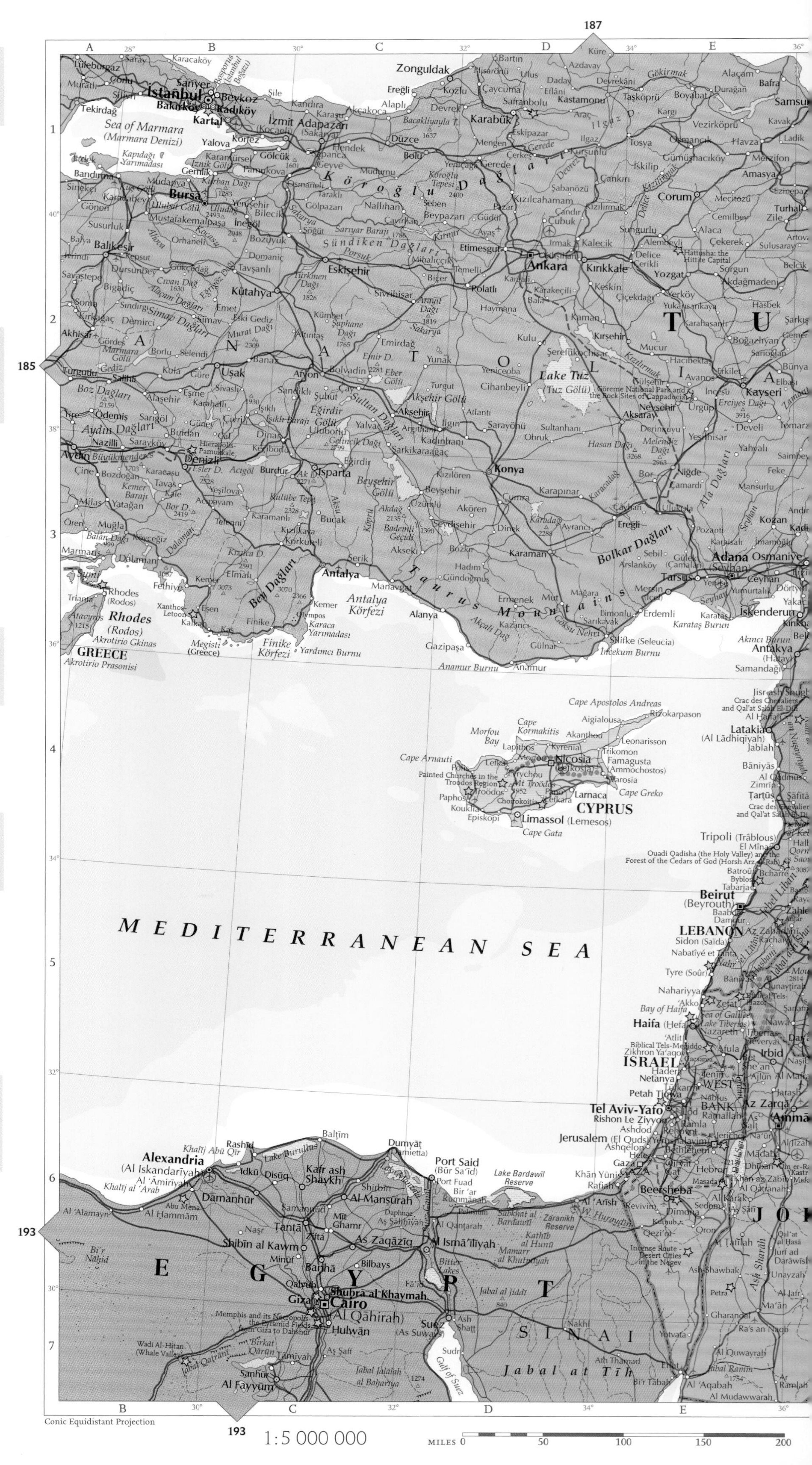

BLACK SEA

CASPIAN SEA

GEORGIA
ARMENIA
AZERBAIJAN
TURKEY
SYRIA
IRAQ
IRAN
SAUDI ARABIA
KUWAIT
JORDAN

Mesopotamia

Syrian Desert
(Bādiyat ash Shām)

Lake Van (Van Gölü)
Lake Sevan (Sevana Lich)
Lake Urmia

Key cities: Trabzon, Sivas, Malatya, Diyarbakır, Gaziantep (Antab), Aleppo (Halab), Ar Raqqah, Dayr az Zawr, Homs, Damascus, Hamāh, Erzurum, Yerevan, Tabrīz, Baku, Sumqayıt, Ganca, Mosul, Arbīl, Kirkūk, As Sulaymānīyah, Baghdād, Karbalā, Hillah, An Najaf, An Nāsirīyah, Basra, Ahvāz, Kuwait (Al Kuwayt), Hamadān, Kermānshāh, Tikrīt, Sāmarrā, Sanandaj

0 50 100 150 200 250 300 350 KILOMETRES

142

146

Central Asia

KAZAKHSTAN Capital: **Astana (Akmola)**
Area: **2 717 300 km²/1 049 155 miles²**
Population: **15 422 000** Languages: **Kazakh, Russian, Ukrainian, German, Uzbek, Tatar** Religions: **Sunni Muslim, Russian Orthodox, Protestant** Currency: **Tenge**

This huge country is dominated by the vast plains or steppes across which the local people led a nomadic life. Astana has only been the capital since 1998 and is growing fast. Before that Almaty (Alma-Ata), in the south, was the capital. It has a picturesque, mountainous backdrop and is still the commercial and social centre. Hiking and winter sports are popular in the foothills of the Tien Shan range. In the centre of the country is the Baykonur Cosmodrome from where Yuri Gagarin took off. Further north is Korgalzhyn, the most northerly home for flamingos.

KYRGYZSTAN Capital: **Bishkek (Frunze)**
Area: **198 500 km²/76 641 miles²** Population: **5 317 000**
Languages: **Kyrgyz, Russian, Uzbek** Religions: **Sunni Muslim, Russian Orthodox** Currency: **Kyrgyz som**

Tourism is starting to grow in this landlocked, mountainous country. Bishkek, the capital, is by far the largest town and is showing western influences. Osh, close to the Uzbek border, has a huge and busy market. The terrain is perfect for trekking to some of the hidden lakes and glaciers, but some areas are only for the experienced. Start from Karakol, close to the large lake of Ysyk-Köl, and head for the hot springs at Altyn Arashan. Further south is Tash Rabat, a welcome caravanserai on the Silk Road.

TAJIKISTAN Capital: **Dushanbe**
Area: **143 100 km²/55 251 miles²**
Population: **6 736 000** Languages: **Tajik, Uzbek, Russian**
Religions: **Sunni Muslim** Currency: **Somoni**

After the Soviet break-up there was civil unrest between the different peoples in Tajikistan, but at present the country is stable. The country is dominated by the Pamir and Altai Mountains and their inaccessibility helped protect the area from most invaders. Dushanbe is the capital and has a thriving Monday market. The road north to Khŭjand passes through spectacular scenery, as does the Pamir highway. The mountains and lakes are perfect for the adventure traveller. The Wakhan valley which crosses to Afghanistan has disused forts and Buddhist ruins, with views to the Hindu Kush.

TURKMENISTAN Capital: **Aşgabat (Ashkhabad)**
Area: **488 100 km²/188 456 miles²**
Population: **4 965 000** Languages: **Turkmen, Uzbek, Russian** Religions: **Sunni Muslim, Russian Orthodox** Currency: **Turkmen manat**

Until 2006 the country was dominated by its president, Niyazov (Turkmenbashi). In the capital, Aşgabat, there are gold statues to him. Independent travel was restricted and you will still need to hire a guide to accompany you. The Karakum desert covers the majority of the country, with sites of interest around the fringes. In the east, Merv was the second city of the Islamic world until destroyed by the sons of Ghenghis Khan. Nisa, west of the capital, was a major city of the Parthian kings in the 4th millennium BC. Close to Daşoguz (Tashauz) are the remains of Konye-Urgench, an ancient fortress town.

UZBEKISTAN Capital: **Tashkent**
Area: **447 400 km²/172 742 miles²** Population: **27 372 000**
Languages: **Uzbek, Russian, Tajik, Kazakh** Religions: **Sunni Muslim, Russian Orthodox** Currency: **Uzbek som**

Some of the finest gems of Central Asia fall within Uzbekistan. With profits from the Silk Road, the cities of Samarqand and Buxoro (Bukhara) thrived. Although Samarqand is surrounded by faceless Soviet-built buildings, the Registan, decorated with ornate mosaics and turquoise domes, dominates the old centre. Khiva, near Urganch, is a better example of the architecture because despite its brutal history, the whole city remains intact within the old walls. North is the Kyzylkum Desert and the vestiges of the Aral Sea. Little remains of the ancient city of Tashkent, the capital, after an earthquake in 1966. It was rebuilt in the Soviet style.

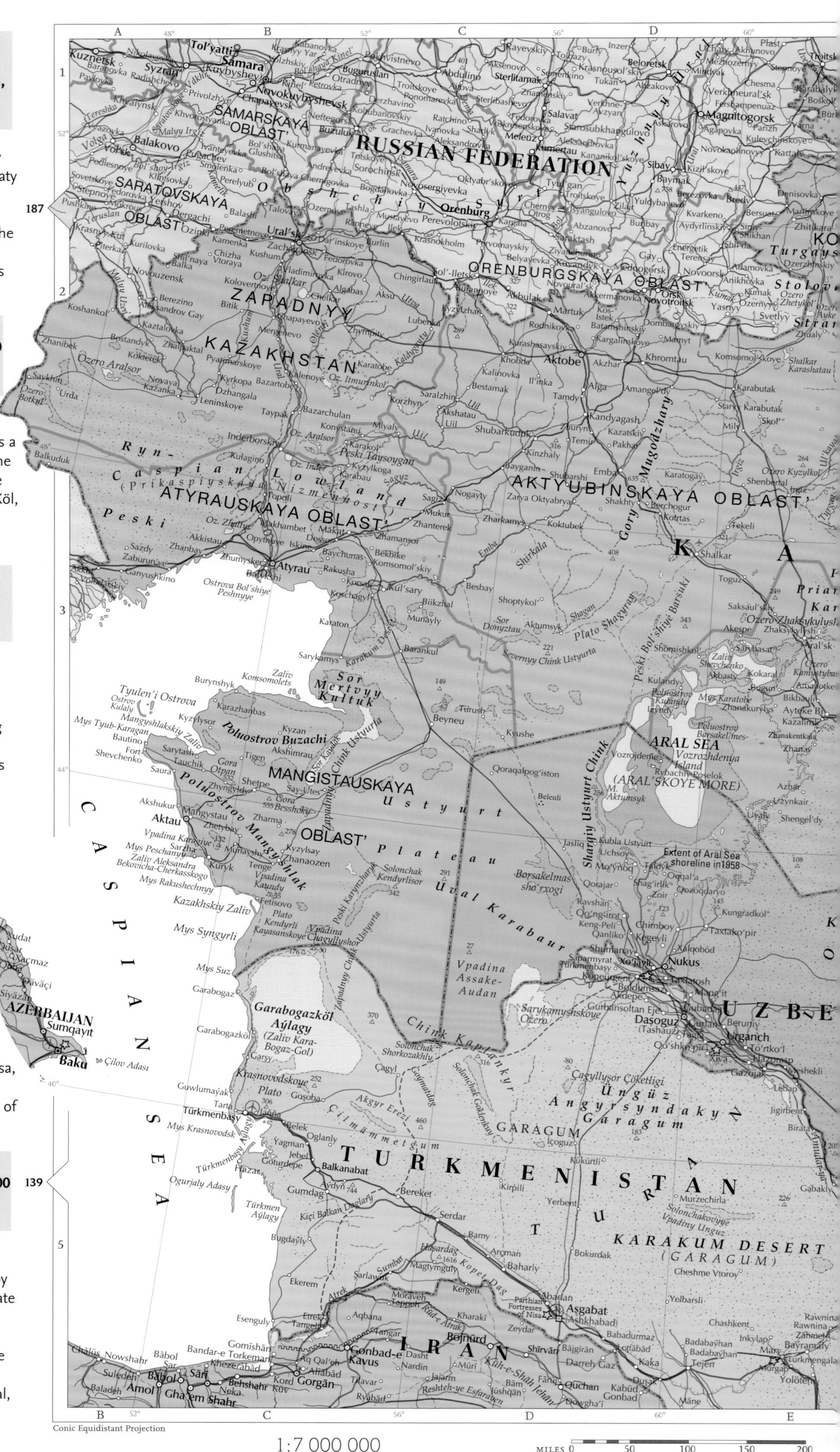

Conic Equidistant Projection

1:7 000 000

MILES 0   50   100   150   200

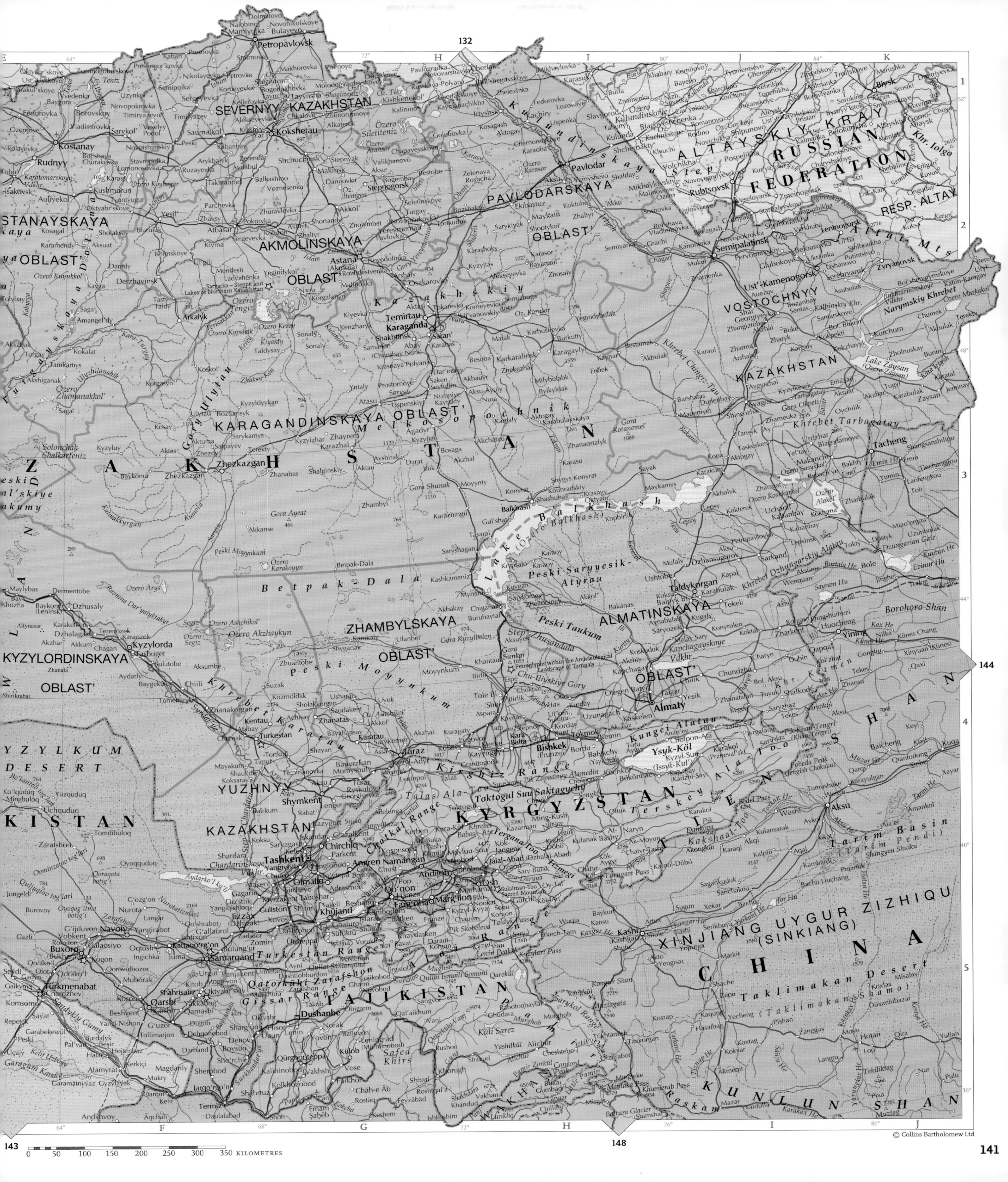

© Collins Bartholomew Ltd

0 50 100 150 200 250 300 350 KILOMETRES

The Gulf, Iran and Afghanistan

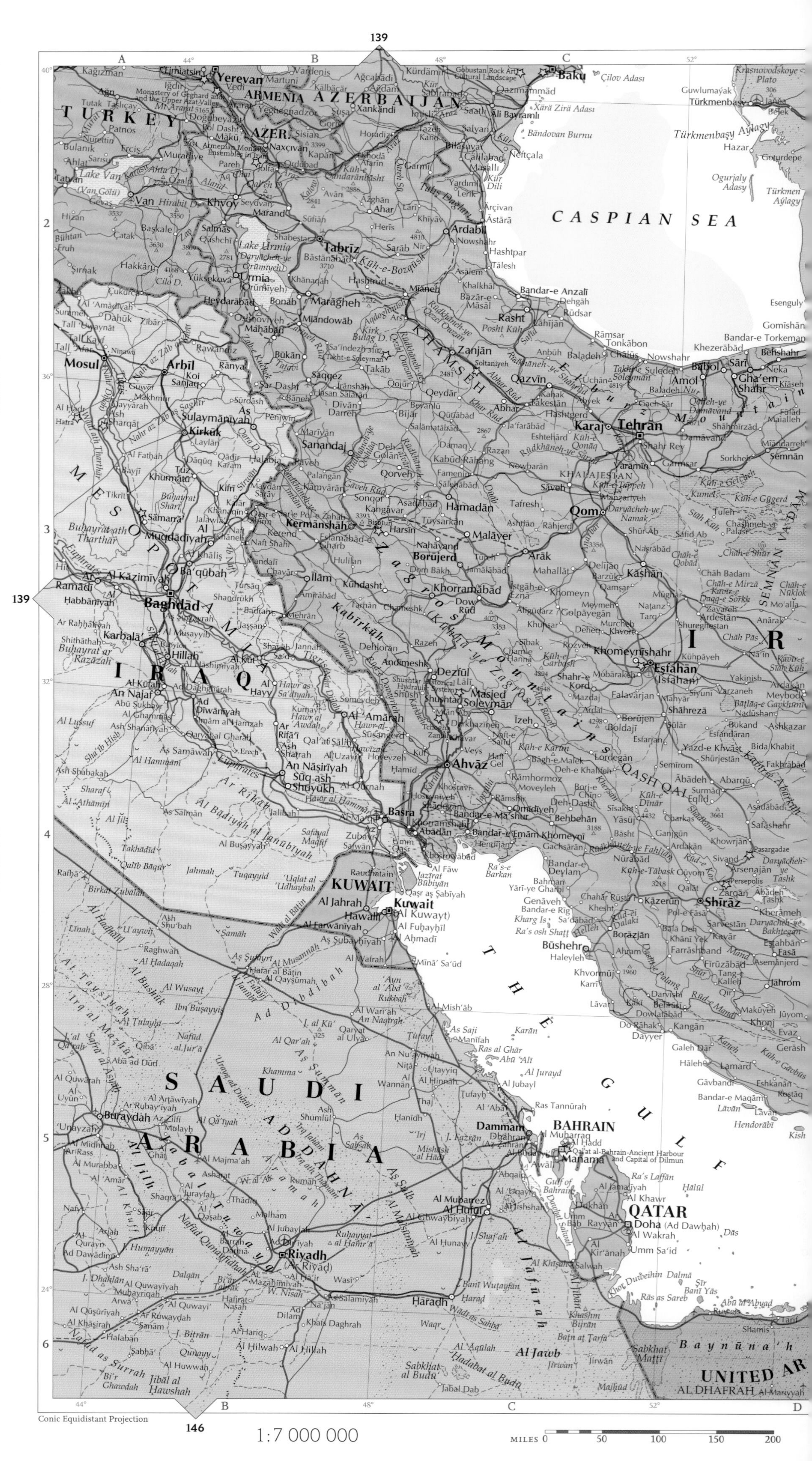

AFGHANISTAN Capital: Kābul
Area: 652 225 km²/251 825 miles²
Population: 27 145 000 Languages: **Dari, Pushtu, Uzbek, Turkmen**
Religions: **Sunni Muslim, Shi'a Muslim** Currency: **Afghani**

Travel to Afghanistan is strongly discouraged; some areas are still an active war zone, while there may be a risk of land mines in other parts. The draw of the country used to be the mountains, with the dramatic peaks of the Hindu Kush and the evocative Khyber Pass. Towns in the north grew in stature due to the Silk Road trade – such as Herāt, the first stop after Iran, and Balkh, which has been overtaken by Mazār-e Sharīf with its impressive Blue Mosque. Kābul is trying to rebuild itself after many years of unrest.

IRAN Capital: **Tehrān**
Area: **1 648 000 km²/636 296 miles²**
Population: **71 208 000** Languages: **Farsi, Azeri, Kurdish, regional languages** Religions: **Shi'a Muslim, Sunni Muslim**
Currency: **Iranian rial**

Rocky and salty deserts make up the centre of Iran, ringed with mountains. The border areas are unstable and caution should be taken. Entering the urban sprawl and smog of Tehrān gives the wrong impression of this modern and busy capital: there is a lively bazaar and many fascinating museums to visit. In the far northeast is the holiest city in Iran, Mashhad, with the beautiful Imam Reza shrine.

Heading south from Tehrān, Qom is another holy city and a centre for religious studies. Eşfahān (Isfahan) is one of the main destinations for travellers. Ignoring the industrial outskirts, this former Persian capital boasts stunning mosques decorated in intricate blue mosaic tiles, refreshing gardens and fascinating bazaars. Yazd, a desert city, was famed for its fabrics, especially silk. Enter Shīrāz through the Qor'an Gate to visit more restful gardens and beautiful mosques. From here visit the monumental ruins of Persepolis, dating back to 518 BC.

In The Gulf two islands show interesting contrasts: Kish, a free-trade zone full of shopping malls and stores, and Qeshm, a haven for migrating birds and an eco-tourist destination.

KUWAIT Capital: **Kuwait (Al Kuwayt)**
Area: **17 818 km²/6 880 miles²** Population: **2 851 000**
Languages: **Arabic** Religions: **Sunni Muslim, Shi'a Muslim, Christian, Hindu** Currency: **Kuwaiti dinar**

An oil-rich country eyed enviously by its neighbours, it is a mix of the strict Islamic world and westernisation. Kuwait City is full of high-rise buildings, wide boulevards, shopping malls and luxury hotels as well as grand mosques and the Seif Palace. Panoramic views of the city can be seen from one of the Kuwait Towers. Al Jahrah used to build traditional boats for fishing and trade, but now for pleasure. The island of Faylakah has Bronze Age and Greek remains, and dhows can be seen in the harbour.

Conic Equidistant Projection

1:7 000 000

MILES 0   50   100   150   200

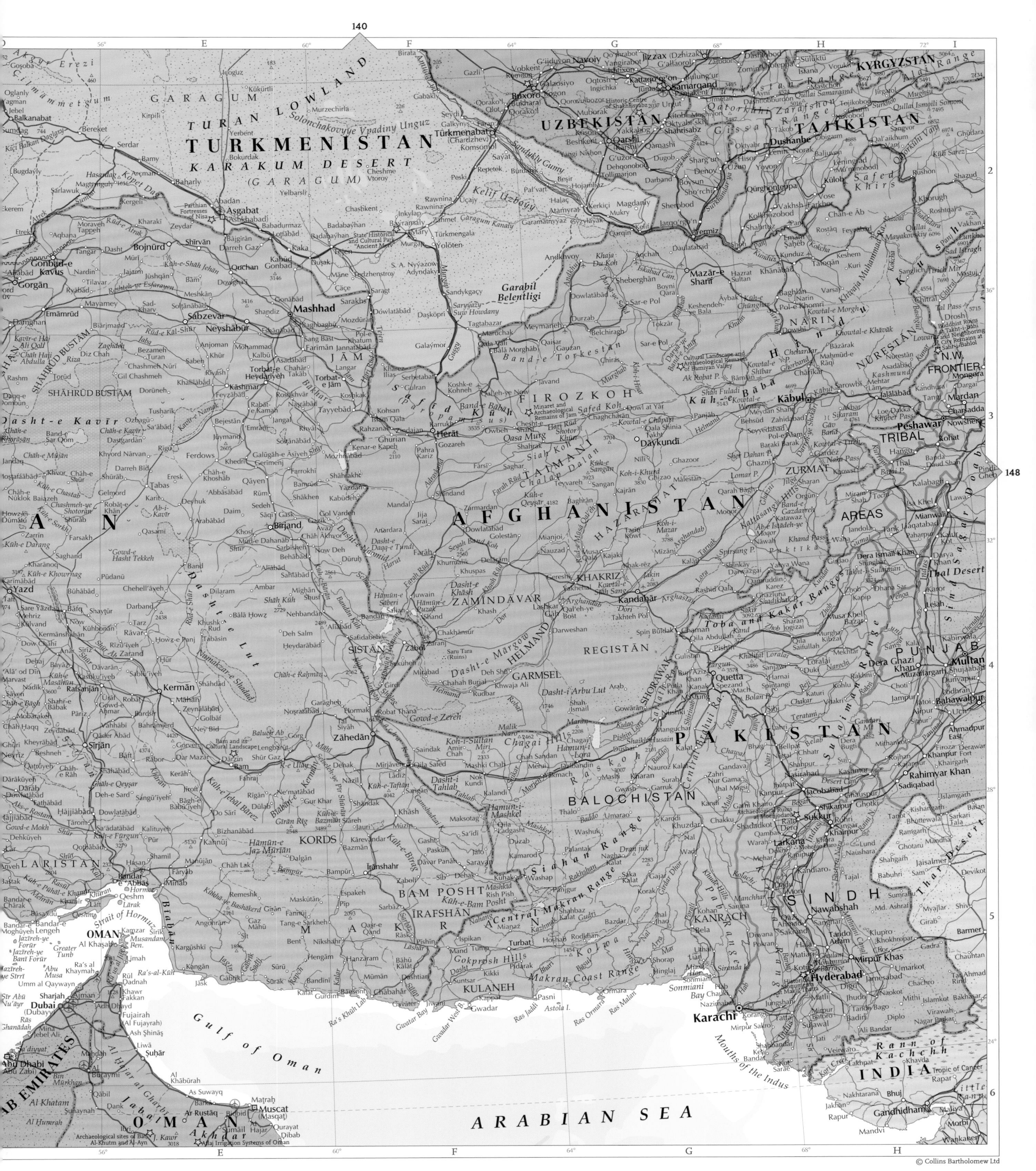

TURAN LOWLAND

GARAGUM

TURKMENISTAN

KARAKUM DESERT

(GARAGUM)

UZBEKISTAN

TAJIKISTAN

KYRGYZSTAN

Asgabat

Mashhad

AFGHANISTAN

Kābul

Peshawar

TRIBAL

N.W. FRONTIER

NŪRESTĀN

Herāt

Kandahar

PAKISTAN

BALOCHISTAN

SINDH

PUNJAB

Quetta

Karachi

Hyderabad

INDIA

Zāhedān

Kermān

OMAN

Muscat

Dubai

Abu Dhabi

AB EMIRATES

Gulf of Oman

Strait of Hormuz

ARABIAN SEA

Mouths of the Indus

Rann of Kachchh

Tropic of Cancer

© Collins Bartholomew Ltd

0 50 100 150 200 250 300 350 KILOMETRES

Southern Asia

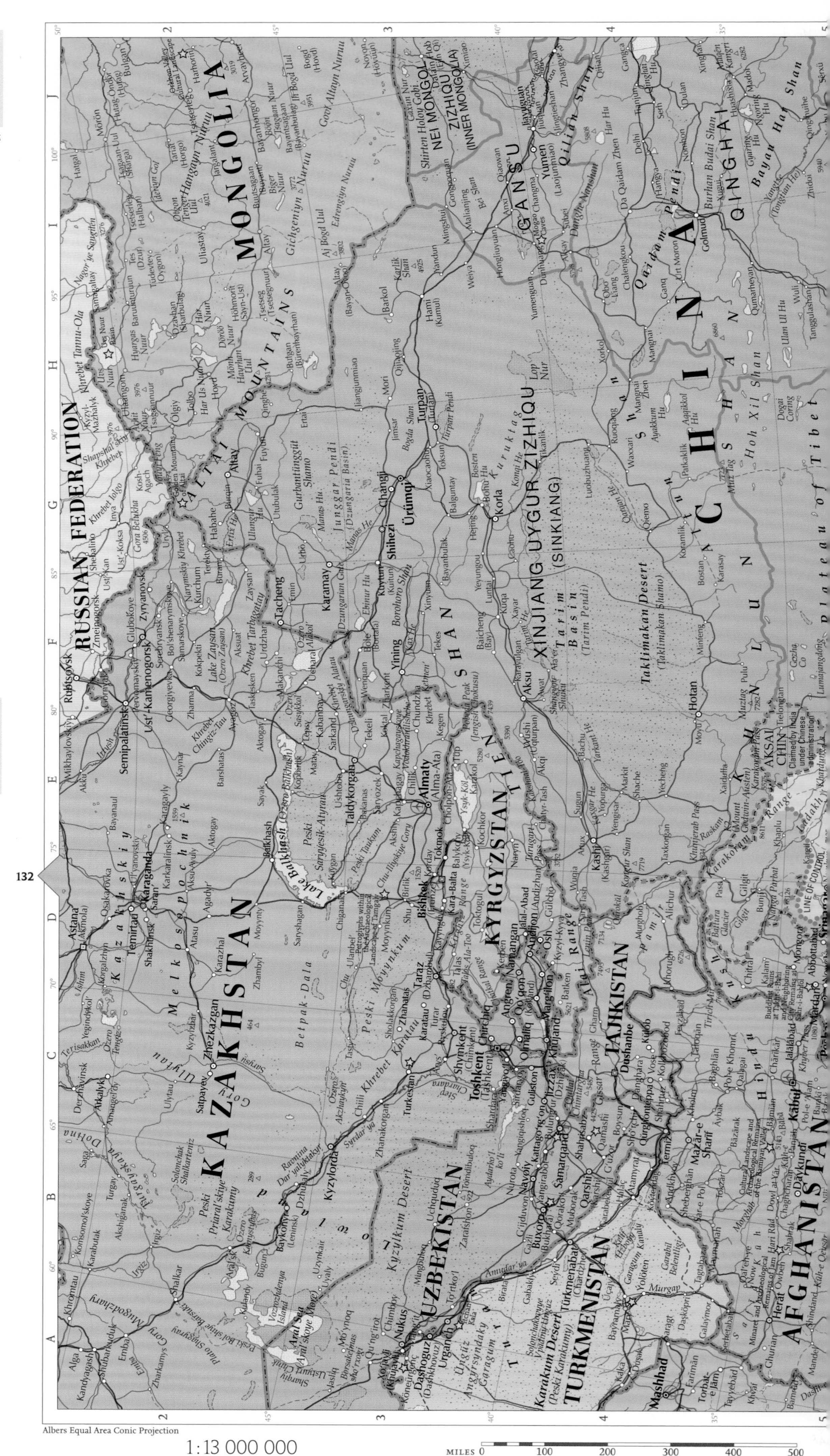

INDIA Capital: New Delhi
Area: 3 064 898 km²/1 183 364 miles²
Population: 1 169 016 000 Languages: Hindi, English, many regional languages Religions: Hindu, Sunni Muslim, Shi'a Muslim, Sikh, Christian Currency: Indian rupee

India is an assault on the senses. From densely populated cities such as Kolkata (Calcutta) and Mumbai (Bombay) to the clear air of the tea gardens of Darjiling and the palm-edged beaches of Goa, there is something everywhere to shock and amaze.

Starting in the north with the Himalayas and the contested North West Frontier; this area should be travelled with caution. Srinagar is the most northerly city, with beautiful Mughal gardens on the edge of the Dal Lake. Leh is closer to the Chinese border and a base for backpackers and climbers. Shimla, in the foothills, was the summer capital for the British. Close to the Pakistan border is Amritsar, with its Golden Temple, holy to the Sikh people. Brief visitors to the sub-continent usually start with Delhi, contrasting new with old, and then move onto Agra for the must-see visit to the Taj Mahal. Then to see the pink city of Jaipur with the Amber Fort. Worthwhile detours in this area include the fortified city of Fatehpur Sikri and the Hindu pilgrimage centre at Matthura. Visit the erotic carvings on the temples at Khajuraho on the way to the holy city of Varanasi (Benares) on the *ghats* (banks) of the sacred Ganges River. Close to Aurangabad are the caves and rock dwellings of Ellora and Ajanta. At Hampi in Karnataka are the extensive ruins of the fourteenth century city of the Vijayanagar Empire. Kerala and Goa provide their unique cuisines in relaxing coastal resorts. On the east coast, Chennai (Madras) is the main port, with a growing IT industry, and Puducherry (Pondicherry) has French influences from its past. Close to Myanmar are the Andaman and Nicobar Islands, ideal for beach lovers, snorkellers and divers.

PAKISTAN Capital: Islamabad
Area: 803 940 km²/310 403 miles²
Population: 163 902 000 Languages: Urdu, Punjabi, Sindhi, Pushtu, English Religions: Sunni Muslim, Shi'a Muslim, Christian, Hindu Currency: Pakistani rupee

The Karakoram Highway crosses the high mountain ranges into China, following the ancient Silk Road. The valleys in this northerly area, such as Chitral, Swat and Hunza, are blessed with fertile soil, in sharp contrast to their surroundings. The capital, Islamabad, is a relatively new city with parkland and gardens whereas the neighbouring city of Rawalpindi still shows its colonial background amongst the local architecture. Nearby is the ancient site of Taxila which has evidence of life from Neolithic to Buddhist. The mainly Pashtun city of Peshawar is close to the Afghan border and has refugee camps on its fringes.

Lahore was a Mughal city and has stunning pink and white marble buildings and the refreshing Shalimar gardens. Multan has beautiful Sufi tombs, well maintained by pilgrims. Moenjodaro, near Larkana, has 5000-year-old ruins across a huge area. Karachi is the business and commercial centre and has a cosmopolitan feel. Visit the ancient site of Thatta from here.

Pakistan is subject to unrest, especially in the Northern Areas, where care should be taken. Travel to some areas is restricted. This mountainous and desert land was home to several different civilisations and the evidence is easy to see.

Albers Equal Area Conic Projection

1:13 000 000

MILES 0   100   200   300   400   500

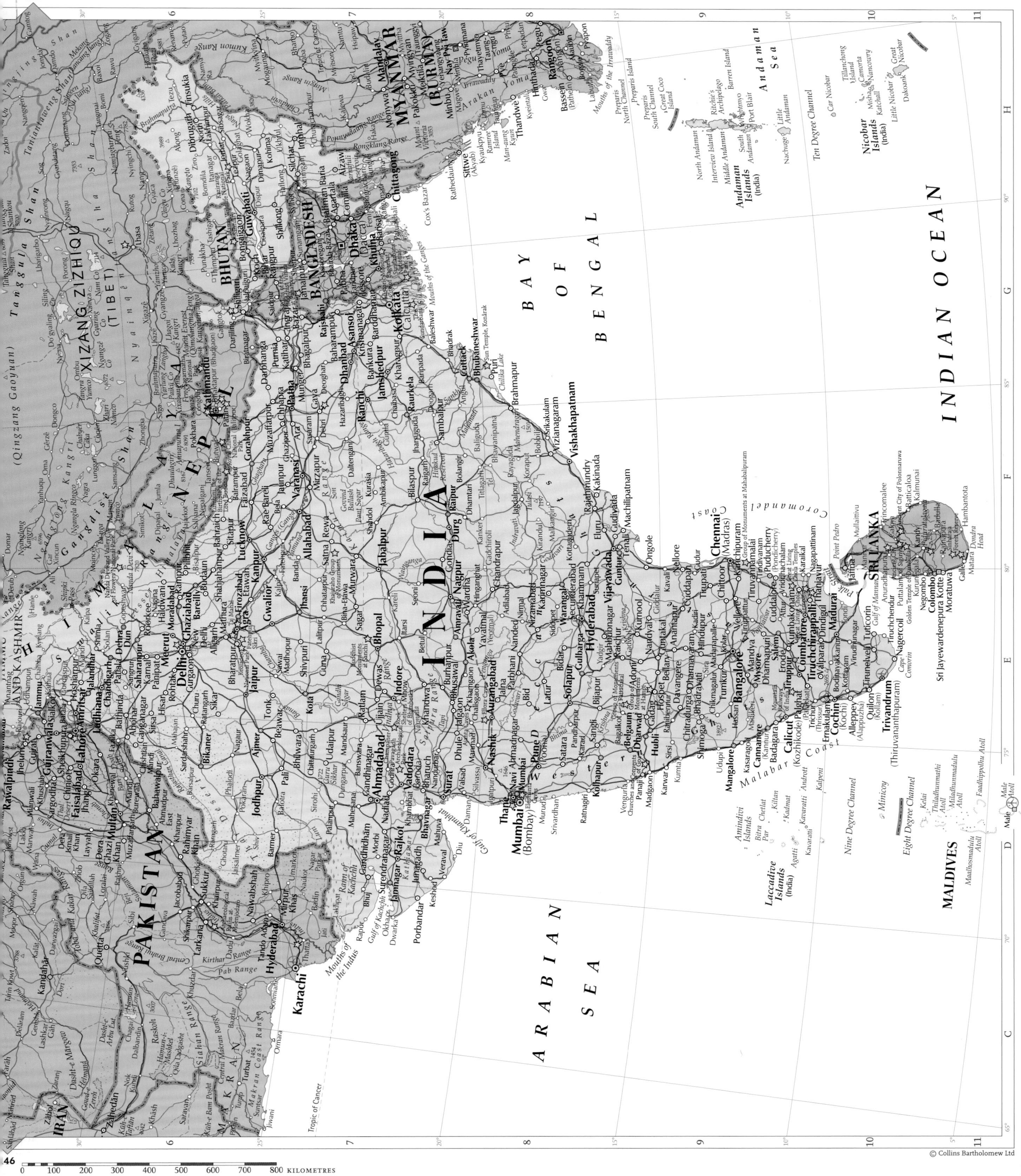

INDIA

PAKISTAN

IRAN

XIZANG ZIZHIQU (TIBET)

NEPAL

BHUTAN

BANGLADESH

MYANMAR (BURMA)

SRI LANKA

MALDIVES

JAMMU AND KASHMIR

ARABIAN SEA

BAY OF BENGAL

INDIAN OCEAN

Andaman Islands (India)

Nicobar Islands (India)

Andaman Sea

Laccadive Islands (India)

Mouths of the Ganges

Mouths of the Indus

Tropic of Cancer

0 100 200 300 400 500 600 700 800 KILOMETRES

© Collins Bartholomew Ltd

Arabian Peninsula

BAHRAIN
Capital: **Manama (Al Manāmah)**
Area: **691 km²/267 miles²** Population: **753 000**
Languages: **Arabic, English** Religions: **Shi'a Muslim,
Sunni Muslim, Christian** Currency: **Bahraini dinar**

Bahrain, with its liberal outlook, is attracting new visitors
through its Formula One racetrack as well as its shopping
malls and availability of alcohol. The islands are surrounded by
shallow waters, so land reclamation is extensive. The country's
wealth started from pearl diving in the clear waters. The
National Museum in the capital Manama explains the ancient
burial mounds at Sar, from the Dilmun civilisation. Visit the
sixteenth-century restored Portuguese fort and the ultra-
modern World Trade Centre. Al Muḥarraq has traditional
houses with a unique design to keep cool. For a taste of the
natural world, the Ḥuwār Islands are home to dolphins and
flamingos. South of the capital is the Tree of Life, sitting in
a desert landscape with no obvious source of fresh water.

QATAR
Capital: **Doha (Ad Dawḥah)**
Area: **11 437 km²/4 416 miles²** Population: **841 000**
Languages: **Arabic** Religions: **Sunni Muslim**
Currency: **Qatari riyal**

Qatar is one of the richest nations per capita with an elegant
capital city, Doha, which is expanding upwards and outwards.
A stroll along the Corniche will show off the city, including
the new Museum of Islamic Art. There are plenty of modern
shopping malls and the redeveloped Souq Waqif still retains an
authentic feel. The National Museum is situated in the Fariq
al-Salata Palace. Up the coast is Al Khawr, the former pearl
trading centre. Inland at Khorr al-Adaid are sand dunes to
explore or to experience a desert night.

UNITED ARAB EMIRATES
Capital: **Abu Dhabi (Abū Ẓabī)**
Area: **77 700 km²/30 000 miles²** Population: **4 380 000**
Languages: **Arabic, English** Religions: **Sunni Muslim,
Shi'a Muslim** Currency: **United Arab Emirates dirham**

The U.A.E. is a federation of seven Emirates. Dubai is the main
destination, with Abu Dhabi following closely. Ultra-modern
buildings abound and land reclamation projects such as Palm
Island are growing. Shop, dine and sunbathe in luxury but – to
see another side of the country head to the Bedouin camps in
the Liwā Oasis or to the hill town of Ḥattā.

Southern India and Sri Lanka

MALDIVES
Capital: **Male** Area: **298 km²/115 miles²**
Population: **306 000** Languages: **Divehi (Maldivian)**
Religions: **Sunni Muslim** Currency: **Rufiyaa**

This string of low-lying coral atolls conjures up thoughts of a
tropical paradise, with its white sandy beaches and crystal clear
waters perfect for snorkelling or scuba diving. But they are
susceptible to the effects of global warming and occasional
tsunami. El Niño weather effects have caused bleaching on
some of the coral reefs. The busy capital of Male has an interesting National Museum, Islamic Centre and Friday Mosque.
Hulhumale Island is manmade, reaching an exceptional two
metres above sea level. Island hopping is the best way to get
a taste of the islands.

SRI LANKA
Capital: **Sri Jayewardenepura Kotte**
Area: **65 610 km²/25 332 miles²**
Population: **19 299 000** Languages: **Sinhalese, Tamil, English**
Religions: **Buddhist, Hindu, Sunni Muslim, Roman Catholic**
Currency: **Sri Lankan rupee**

This island is slowly recovering from the tsunami of 2004 and the
more recent fighting in the north. Care should be taken when in
this area. The island has great ancient cities in Anuradhapura and
Polonnaruwa, and Sigiriya rock fortress rises from the plain. There
are cave temples at Dambulla. Tropical sandy beaches are a draw,
but there is also untouched rainforest to explore at Sinharaja and
leopards to spot in Yala National Park. Kandy set in the green hills
is an interesting city to visit for local crafts and customs.

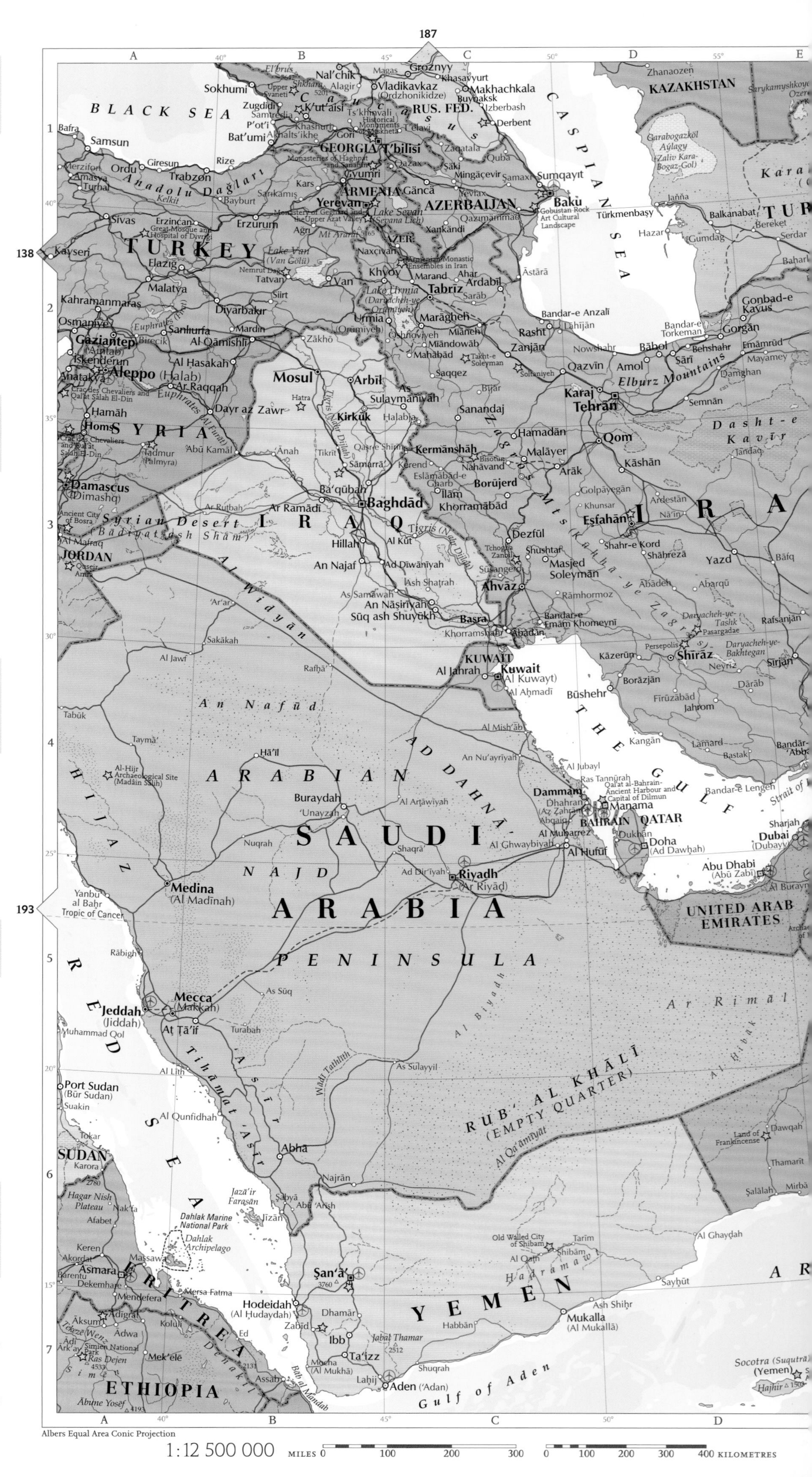

Albers Equal Area Conic Projection

1:12 500 000 MILES 0   100   200   300   0   100   200   300   400 KILOMETRES

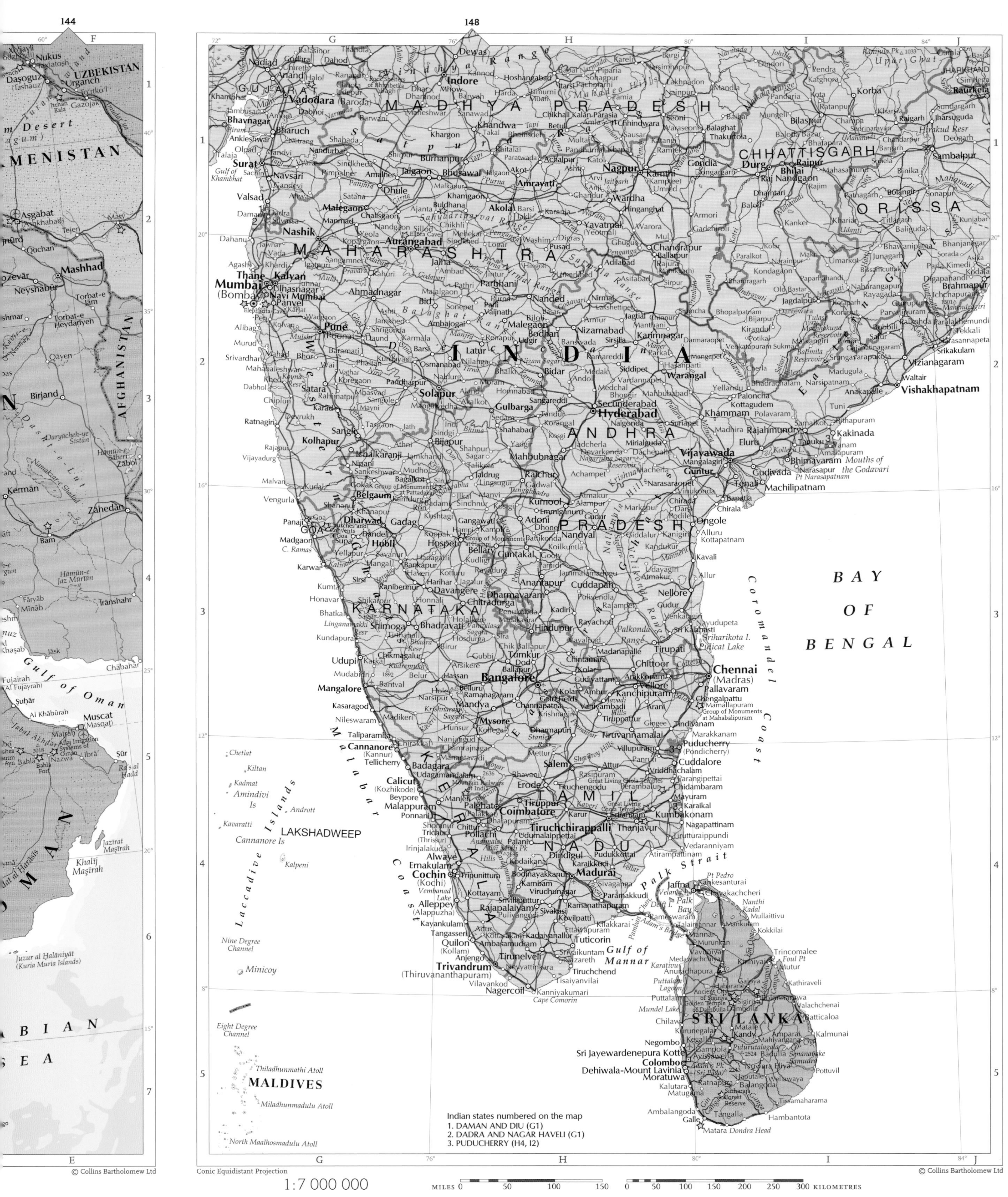

Indian states numbered on the map
1. DAMAN AND DIU (G1)
2. DADRA AND NAGAR HAVELI (G1)
3. PUDUCHERRY (H4, I2)

© Collins Bartholomew Ltd

Conic Equidistant Projection

© Collins Bartholomew Ltd

1:7 000 000

MILES 0   50   100   150

0   50   100   150   200   250   300 KILOMETRES

Northern India and the Himalaya

BANGLADESH Capital: **Dhaka (Dacca)**
Area: **143 998 km²/55 598 miles²**
Population: **158 665 000** Languages: **Bengali, English**
Religions: **Sunni Muslim, Hindu** Currency: **Taka**

The fertile plains created by the convergence of the Ganges and Brahmaputra rivers make up the majority of this country. Monsoon rains and flooding mean that the coastline is always changing shape. The Sundarbans, along the delta's coastline, are an impenetrable mangrove forest, home to the Royal Bengal tiger. Dhaka is the vast, hectic capital and a boat trip from here to Khulna is a good way to see the country. Cox's Bazar is the local holiday area, leading to the 100-mile-long Inani Beach. Sylhet , in the northeast, is the pilgrimage site of the fourteenth century Sufi, Hazret Shah Jalal.

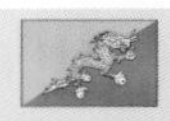

BHUTAN Capital: **Thimphu**
Area: **46 620 km²/18 000 miles²**
Population: **658 000** Languages: **Dzongkha, Nepali, Assamese**
Religions: **Buddhist, Hindu** Currency: **Ngultrum, Indian rupee**

Visiting Bhutan must be with a pre-planned, all inclusive guided tour, whether as an individual or in a group. This peaceful country is known for its strong traditional values, Buddhist culture, bio-diversity and mountain trekking. The temple of Changangkha Lhakhang at Thimphu gives a good view of the expanding capital. The valley around Paro has many sacred sites including the Taktsang monastery, built into the mountainside. The National Museum, in a *dzong* (fortress), includes ancient manuscripts. Trekking at this Himalayan altitude can be arranged for a day or, for the serious, the 'snowman' trek which could last twenty-five.

NEPAL Capital: **Kathmandu**
Area: **147 181 km²/56 827 miles²**
Population: **28 196 000** Languages: **Nepali, Maithili, Bhojpuri, English, local languages** Religions: **Hindu, Buddhist, Sunni Muslim** Currency: **Nepalese rupee**

Nepal is more than just a string of the world's highest mountain peaks. It plunges off the foothills into jungles and plains towards the Indian border. But most visitors come for mountain trekking, walking the ancient trails which link picturesque villages amongst a dramatic backdrop. Check whether you need a mountain permit for your destination.

Kathmandu is a sprawling, busy city but has interesting temples and shrines around Durbar Square. Day trips from here are recommended to the Buddhist temple of Swayambhu, with fine views over the Kathmandu valley, and to the Hindu temple of Pashputi. Also visit Patan, across the river from the capital, traffic-free Bhaktapur, and the world's largest stupa at Bauddhanath. Heading up to Pokhara, stop at Bandipur, a traditional Newari community – the indigenous valley people. Pokhara is the main starting point for trekking in the Annapurna range and sits beside a picturesque lake. For stunning panoramic views, continue further to Sarangkot. On the southern border, look for tiger and rhino in the Royal Chitwan National Park. The important religious site of Lumbini, the birthplace of Buddha, is surrounded by monasteries. Janakpur, further east, attracts Hindu pilgrims. For those heading to Everest, the starting point is Namche Bazar.

1:7 000 000

MILES 0   50   100   150   200

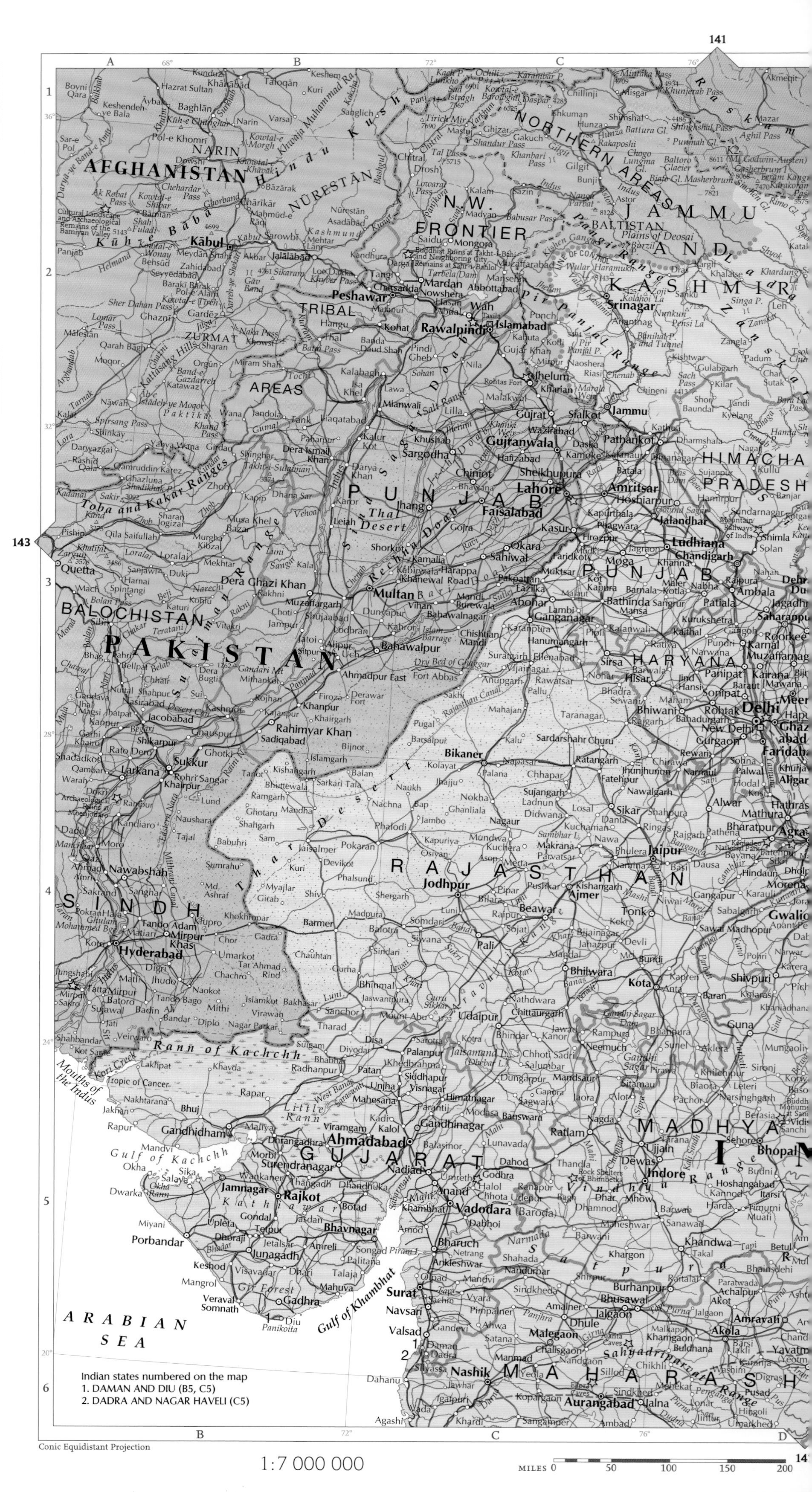

KUNLUN SHAN

XINJIANG UYGUR ZIZHIQU
(SINKIANG)

Karakax Shan

AKSAI CHIN

Claimed by India
under Chinese
administration

PLATEAU OF TIBET
(QINGZANG GAOYUAN) Dogai Coring

QINGHAI

C H I N A

XIZANG ZIZHIQU
(TIBET)

NYAINQÊNTANGLHA SHAN

Tanggula Shan

Taniantaweng Shan

Lhasa

H I M A L A Y A

Brahmaputra (Yarlung Zangbo)

ARUNACHAL
PRADESH

UTTARAKHAND

N E P A L

Kathmandu

Pokhara

SIKKIM

Thimphu

BHUTAN

ASSAM
(ASOM)

NAGALAND

U T T A R
P R A D E S H

Lucknow

Gorakhpur

Kanpur

B I H A R

Patna

Darbhanga

Muzaffarpur

WEST
BENGAL

Rangpur

MEGHALAYA

Shillong

Guwahati

MANIPUR

Imphal

Allahabad

Varanasi

Mirzapur

J H A R K H A N D

Dhanbad Asansol

Bokaro

Ranchi

Rajshahi

B A N G L A D E S H

Dhaka
Dacca

TRIPURA

Agartala

MIZORAM

Aizawl

Jabalpur

Jamshedpur

WEST
BENGAL

Durgapur

Khulna

Chittagong

CHHATTISGARH

Raurkela

Kharagpur

Kolkata
Calcutta

Haldia

Nagpur

Durg Bhilai

Raipur

Bilaspur

O R I S S A

Sambalpur

Baleshwar

Cuttack

Bhubaneswar
Puri

Mouths of the Ganges

B A Y

O F

B E N G A L

MYANMAR
(BURMA)

Sittwe
(Akyab)

Tropic of Cancer

I N D I A

M A D H Y A
P R A D E S H

0 50 100 150 200 250 300 350 KILOMETRES

© Collins Bartholomew Ltd

East and Southeast Asia

Indonesia is made up of over 17 000 islands, of which about
6000 are inhabited. Sitting on the edge of a tectonic plate,
active volcanoes and earthquakes are still shaping the country.
The islands cover a huge diversity of culture, language and ethnic peoples. Travelling about the country can be difficult,
requiring time and patience.

Sumatra is the most westerly island with large areas of wilderness, home to the Sumatran orangutan and tiger. As elsewhere
in the country, the rich biodiversity is under threat from log-
ging and palm oil production but it is easier to visit orangutan
conservation centres here than the remoter Kalimantan region
of Borneo. Java is the most densely populated island but from
the cultural centre of Yogyakarta the impressive Buddhist temple of Borobudur and the Hindu temple of Prambanan can be
reached. Heading east, Bali is the main destination for most
visitors with the quieter island of Lombok next in the chain of
islands. The islands of Flores and Sulawesi boast some spectacular dive sites while Komodo National Park covers three islands
and protects the Komodo dragon which is the world's largest
reptile. Maluku, the traditional 'spice islands' and Irian Jaya
remain remote and largely unexplored due to local unrest.

Travel to Myanmar is difficult due to a severe, strict military
regime. The local people however, are happy to see outside
visitors and the ethnically diverse population does not reflect
the strained relations with the West.

The Irrawaddy river stretches from the eastern fringes of the
Himalayan range down through dense forest to the coast. It
has attracted the majority of the population and the two main
cities of Mandalay and Rangoon are on its banks, as well as the
ancient city of Bagan with over 2000 pagodas and temples
dating from the eleventh century. The splendour of these
buildings contrast with the floating villages which can be found
on Inle Lake near Taunggyi, home to Intha people.

Thailand can offer a wide choice for the traveller, from white
beaches to mountain trekking to vibrant city life. Bangkok is no
longer just a stopover en route to Australia and the Far East. It
is a sprawling city which mixes sleek, modern shopping malls
with traditional market stalls. Shopping can be by boat at the
floating market or by the Skytrain to other areas of the city.
Possible excursions from the city include the ancient city of
Ayutthaya, the former capital of Thailand, which is a World
Heritage site and the site of the Bridge on the River Kwai,
while the Grand Palace in Bangkok is a complex of temples,
administrative and Royal court buildings.

For a relaxing break, the southern region of the Isthmus of Kra,
which becomes the Malay Peninsula, is edged with fine sandy
beaches. The eastern coast offers more relaxed coastal resorts
such as Ko Samui, whereas the Andaman Sea coast around
Phuket and Phang Nga Bay National Park has dramatic
limestone cliffs and islands. For the more adventurous, Chiang
Mai in the northwest is a good base to explore the forested
mountains, caves and waterfalls as well as the tribal hill villages.

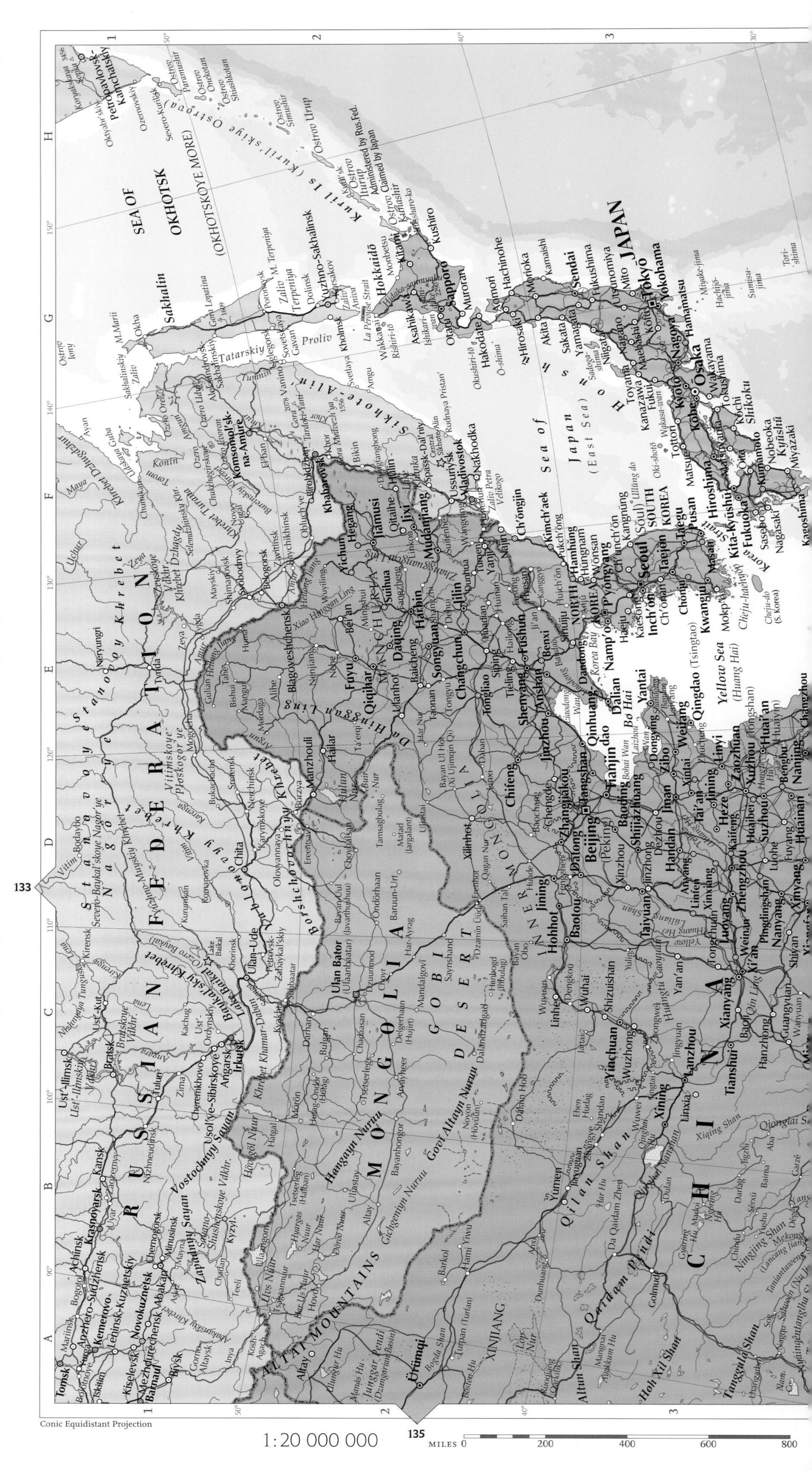

Conic Equidistant Projection

1:20 000 000

MILES 0   200   400   600   800

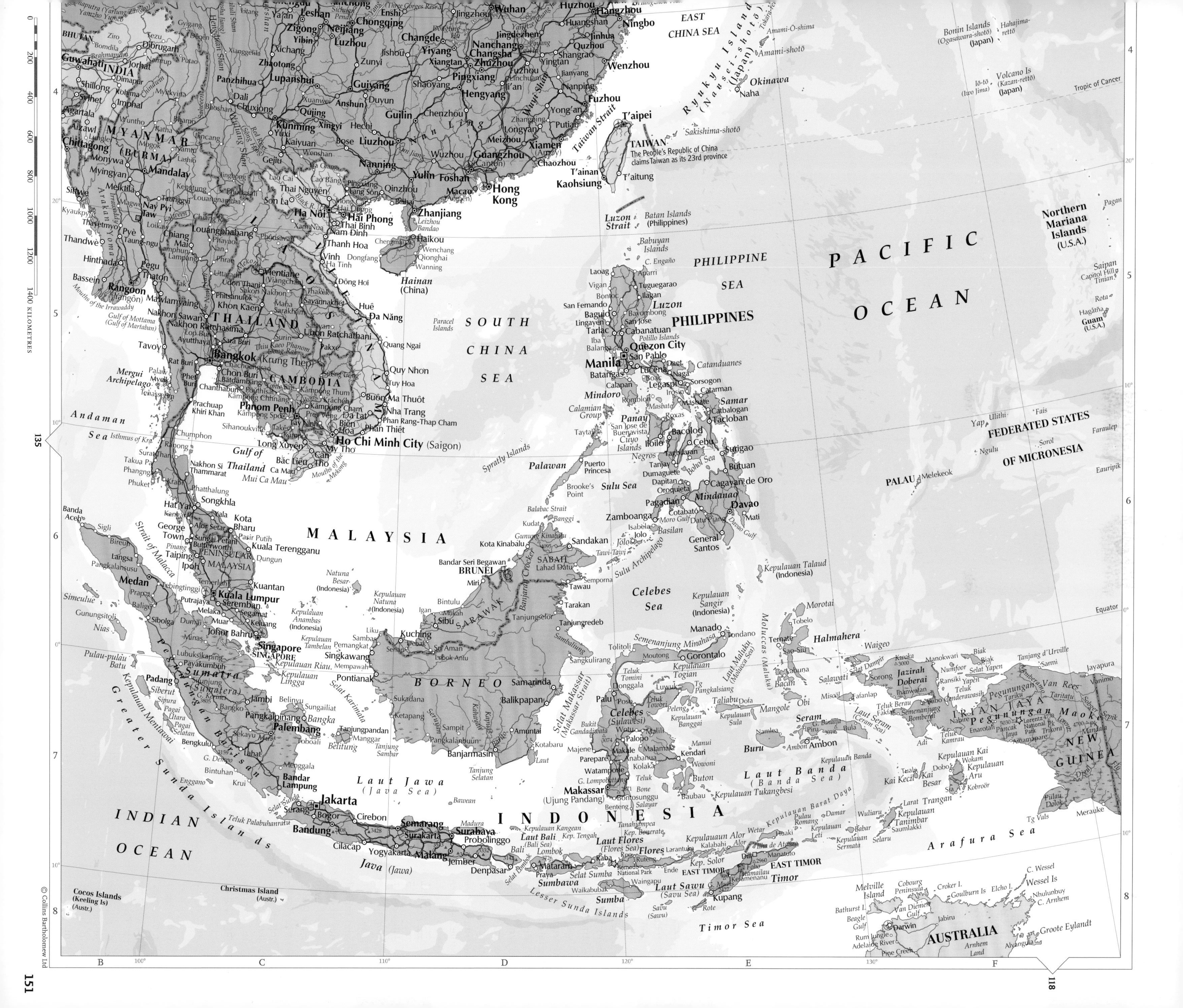

Eastern Asia

 MONGOLIA Capital: **Ulan Bator (Ulaanbaatar)**
Area: **1 565 000 km²/604 250 miles²**
Population: **2 629 000** Languages: **Khalka (Mongolian),
Kazakh, local languages** Religions: **Buddhist, Sunni Muslim**
Currency: **Tugrik (tögrög)**

This landlocked country known as the 'Land of Blue Skies' still
supports a nomadic lifestyle for its peoples living outside of
the towns and cities. Whereas Ulan Bator is developing fast,
the infrastructure outside the capital is still poor. The vast
empty landscape has few fences and is ideal for trekking, on
horses or camels, hiking and mountain biking but the travel
season is short. A popular starting point is the large freshwater
lake Hövsgöl Nuur in the northwest.

The highlight of the year is the two day sports festival of
Naadam, held in July in Ulan Bator, attracting competitors
nationwide in wrestling, archery and horseracing.

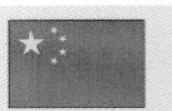

 CHINA Capital: **Beijing**
Area: **9 584 492 km²/3 700 593 miles²**
Population: **1 313 437 000** Languages: **Mandarin, Wu, Cantonese,
Hsiang, regional languages** Religions: **Confucian, Taoist,
Buddhist, Christian, Sunni Muslim** Currency: **Yuan,
Hong Kong dollar, Macao pataca**

The Olympic Games opened the door of China to many people,
tempting them with the great diversity in cultures and landscape
across such a huge country. Although it is one of the world's
oldest civilisations it continues to evolve and push towards the
future, evidenced by the futuristic cityscape of Shanghai.

China has over thirty World Heritage sites, one of the most
important being the Forbidden City in Beijing. It houses a
collection of the finest imperial architecture in the country.
Although the city is developing fast there is still a network of
the ancient *hutongs* or alleyways with traditional houses to
explore. One hour by train brings the Great Wall within reach.
The terracotta army of over 8000 soldiers with their chariots
and horses is another popular destination in the city of Xi'an
which was the eastern end of the Silk Road and has seen over
3000 years of history.

The limestone karst landscape provides a dramatic backdrop to
river cruises on the Yangtze through the Three Gorges despite
the current dam project. The scenic town of Guilin also has
trips on the Li river through a similar landscape and
excursions to the impressive rice terraces of Longsheng. Travel
about the country is especially busy during public holidays
when migrant workers and students return home.

The southern city of Kunming is a picturesque centre for
exploring the diverse Yunnan province which borders Tibet,
entry into which is strictly controlled. Further south, Hainan
Island is being developed as a beach holiday destination.
Shanghai is the most modern and dynamic city in China but
there is still evidence of its traditional past. It used to be one
of the few places where the West made contact with China and
these influences energise the city. Where Shanghai leads, other
cities are starting to follow.

Albers Conic Equal Area Projection

1 : 15 000 000

MILES 0   200   400

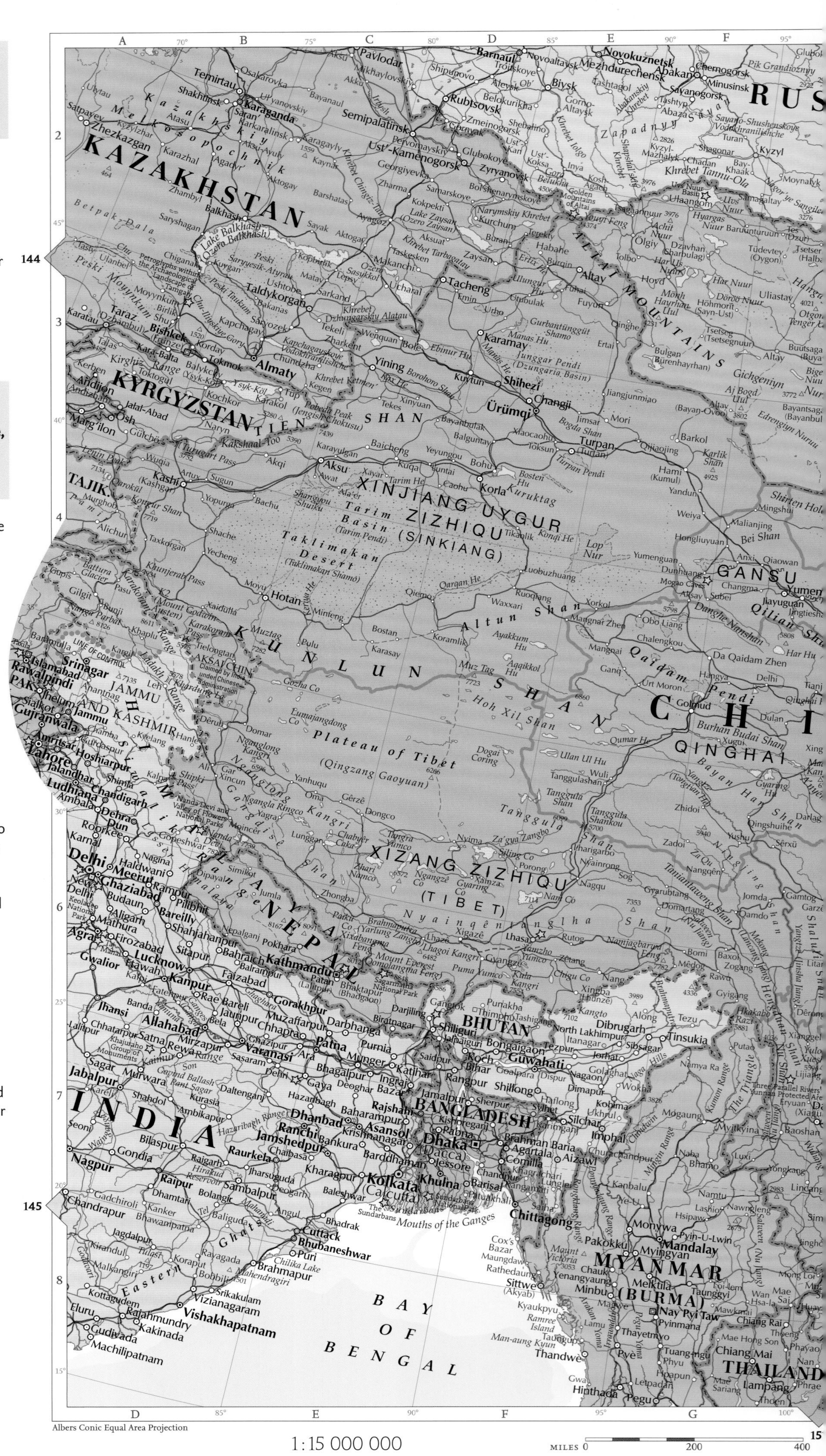

MAP LABELS

RUSSIAN FEDERATION

MONGOLIA

NEI MONGOL ZIZHIQU (INNER MONGOLIA)

GOBI DESERT

CHINA

Lake Baikal
Irkutsk
Ulan-Ude
Chita
Ulan Bator (Ulaanbaatar)
Darhan
Erdenet
Blagoveshchensk
Khabarovsk
Komsomol'sk-na-Amure
Yuzhno-Sakhalinsk
Sakhalin
Sea of Okhotsk (Okhotskoye More)

Harbin
HEILONGJIANG
Qiqihar
Daqing
Jiamusi
Mudanjiang
JILIN
Changchun
Jilin
Songyuan
Vladivostok
Nakhodka

Hokkaidō
Sapporo
Hakodate
Aomori
Akita
Sendai
JAPAN
Tokyo
Yokohama
Nagoya
Kyōto
Ōsaka
Kōbe
Hiroshima
Fukuoka
Kita-Kyūshū
Nagasaki
Kagoshima

NORTH KOREA
P'yŏngyang
Namp'o
Hamhŭng
Ch'ŏngjin

SOUTH KOREA
Seoul (Sŏul)
Inch'ŏn
Taejŏn
Taegu
Kwangju
Pusan
Ulsan
Cheju-do

Sea of Japan (East Sea)

Yellow Sea (Huang Hai)

Bo Hai

BEIJING (Pekin)
Tianjin
HEBEI
Shijiazhuang
Baoding
Tangshan
Qinhuangdao
Dalian
LIAONING
Shenyang
Anshan
Fushun
Jinzhou
Dandong

SHANXI
Taiyuan
Datong
NINGXIA HUIZU ZIZHIQU
Yinchuan
Hohhot
Baotou
Ordos (Dongsheng)

SHANDONG
Jinan
Qingdao (Tsingtao)
Yantai
Weifang
Zibo
Weihai
Shandong Bandao
Tai'an

SHAANXI
Xi'an
Xianyang
Baoji
Yan'an
Qin Ling

HENAN
Zhengzhou
Luoyang
Kaifeng
Xinxiang
Anyang
Pingdingshan
Nanyang

JIANGSU
Nanjing
Wuxi
Xuzhou
Yancheng
Lianyungang
Nantong

ANHUI
Hefei
Huainan
Bengbu
Wuhu

SHANGHAI

ZHEJIANG
Hangzhou
Ningbo
Wenzhou
Shaoxing
Jinhua

HUBEI
Wuhan
Yichang
Jingmen
Xiangfan

SICHUAN
Chengdu
Mianyang
Leshan
Nanchong

CHONGQING

HUNAN
Changsha
Hengyang
Zhuzhou
Xiangtan
Yueyang
Shaoyang

JIANGXI
Nanchang
Ji'an
Yichun
Jingdezhen

FUJIAN
Fuzhou
Xiamen (Amoy)
Quanzhou
Zhangzhou
Putian

TAIWAN
T'aipei
T'aichung
T'ainan
Kaohsiung
Chilung
Hualien

East China Sea (Dong Hai)

GUIZHOU
Guiyang
Zunyi
Anshun

YUNNAN
Kunming
Qujing
Gejiu

GUANGXI ZHUANGZU ZIZHIQU
Nanning
Guilin
Liuzhou
Yulin
Beihai

GUANGDONG
Guangzhou
Shenzhen
Hong Kong
Macao
Shantou
Zhanjiang
Zhaoqing
Foshan

HAINAN
Haikou
Sanya

VIETNAM
Hà Nôi
Hai Phong

LAOS

PHILIPPINES
Batan Islands
Babuyan Islands
Luzon Strait
Bashi Channel

SOUTH CHINA SEA

PACIFIC OCEAN

Ryukyu Islands (Nansei-shotō) (Japan)

Tropic of Cancer

The People's Republic of China claims Taiwan as its 23rd Province

0 200 400 600 800 KILOMETRES

Central and Eastern China

HONG KONG and MACAU (CHINA)

'One country, two systems' is the Chinese solution to these two former European colonies. They still operate their own currencies (the Hong Kong dollar and the pataca) and are interconnected by ferries. While Hong Kong is a major trading and financial centre, Macau has made its name as a centre for gambling.

Hong Kong includes over 250 islands but the population is concentrated on Kowloon and north Hong Kong Island. The views from Victoria Peak, reached by the tram, reveal a crowded city of skyscrapers towering over old colonial buildings and temples. A night time cruise around the busy and vibrant Victoria Harbour shows the mix of traditional and modern.

Macau peninsula is densely populated and has many casinos and visitor attractions but the Portuguese past is reflected in the colonial architecture of the old centre which is now a World Heritage site and is explained in the museum at the old fort. The two adjacent islands of Taipa and Coloane preserve old Macau, with colonial mansions and floating villages. The islands are connected now by the reclaimed land of Cotai which boasts a vast Venetian inspired casino, canals and shopping malls.

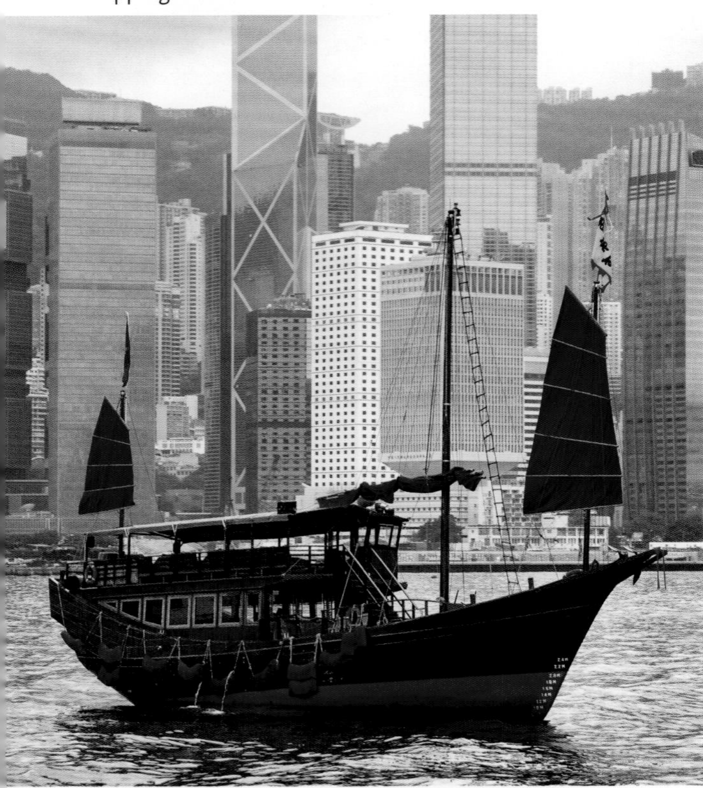

Hong Kong, a mix of traditional and modern China

TAIWAN Capital: T'aipei
Area: 36 179 km²/13 969 miles²
Population: **22 880 009** Languages: **Mandarin, Min, Hakka, local languages** Religions: **Buddhist, Taoist, Confucian, Christian** Currency: **Taiwan dollar**

Taiwan is not an obvious tourist destination but it is a tropical island of lush vegetation, secluded beaches and high mountains as well as the better known modern cities. The island is a mixture of traditional cultures and hi-tech businesses with a well-regarded cuisine, to suit all tastes. The plains of the west coast are edged with a string of cities linked by highways and railways but head eastwards and there are stunning marble canyons, steep cliffs, waterfalls and hot springs to explore. Taroko, near Hualien, is the most popular National Park.

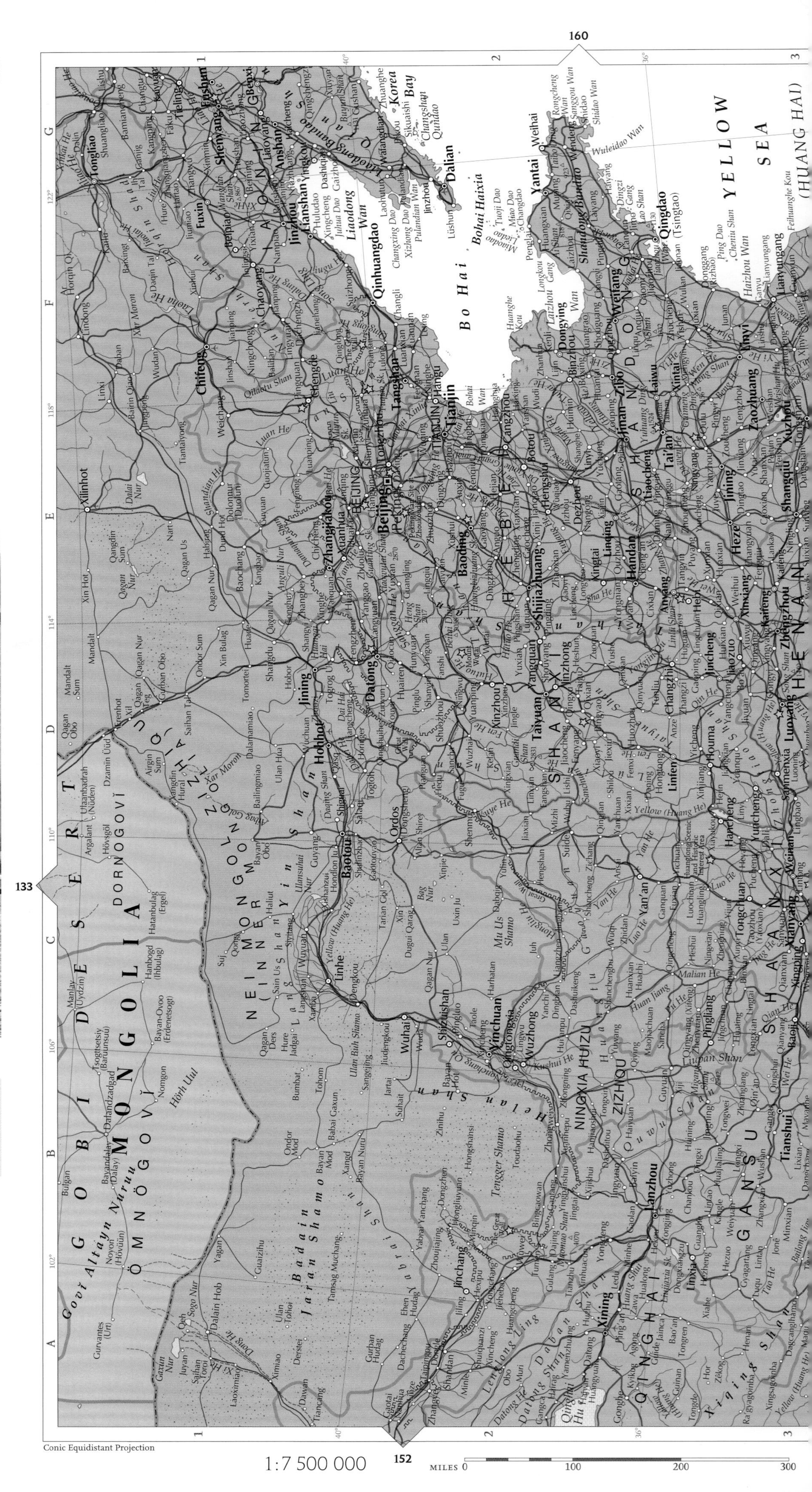

Conic Equidistant Projection

1:7 500 000

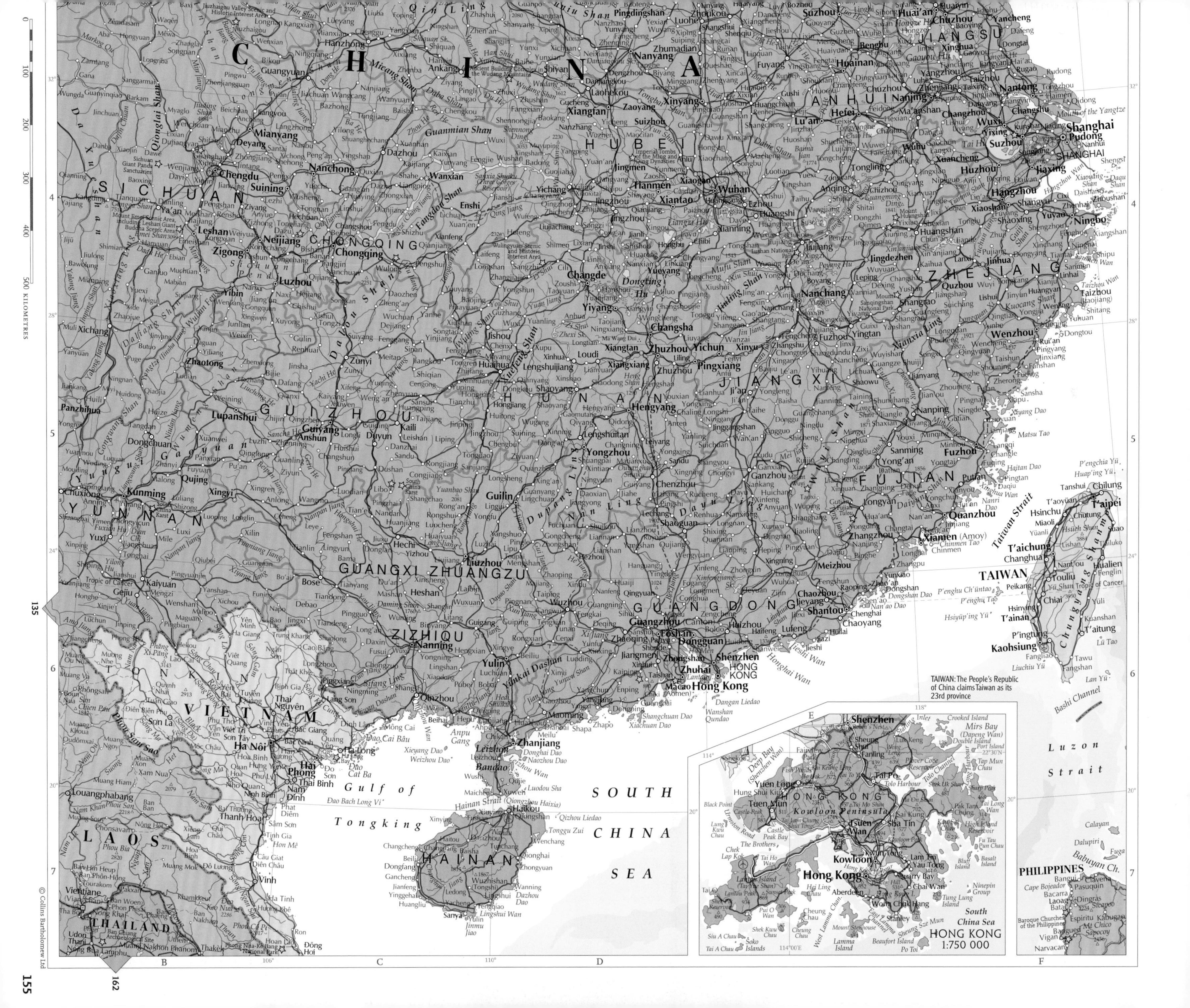

162

© Collins Bartholomew Ltd

0   100   200   300   400   500 KILOMETRES

Japan, North Korea and South Korea

The map shows Japan, North and South Korea, and neighbouring parts of China and the Russian Federation. The area has seen some significant territorial disputes over the years, most notably that between the two Koreas which led to the Korean War in the 1950s, the ownership of the small islets known as Liancourt Rocks (Tok-tō to the Koreans and Take-shima to the Japanese), and the status of the southern Kuril Islands – under Russian control but claimed by Japan. There is also an ongoing disagreement over the naming of the Sea of Japan (known to the Koreans as the East Sea).

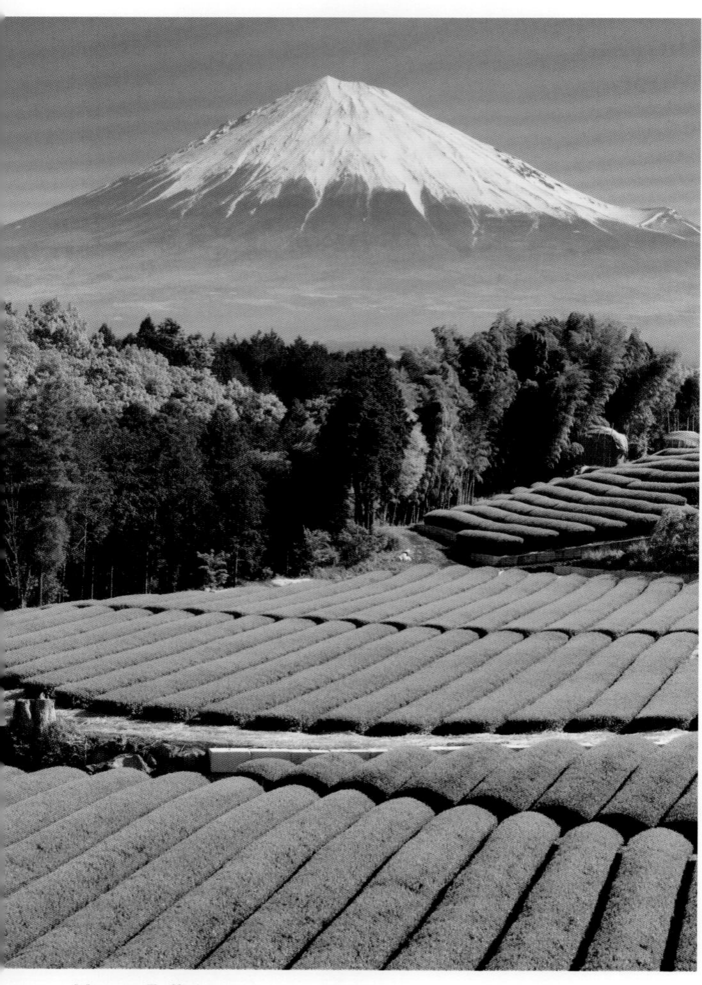

Mount Fuji, Japan

Japan lies directly on the boundary between the Eurasian, Philippine and Pacific tectonic plates. This boundary forms part of the 'Ring of Fire' – the zone around the edge of the Pacific Ocean marked by plate boundaries and therefore highly susceptible to earthquakes and volcanoes. Japan experiences approximately 1500 earthquakes each year and has suffered from numerous major events, the most deadly of which, in Tōkyō in 1923, killed more than 142 000 people. Japan also has 10 per cent of the earth's active volcanoes.

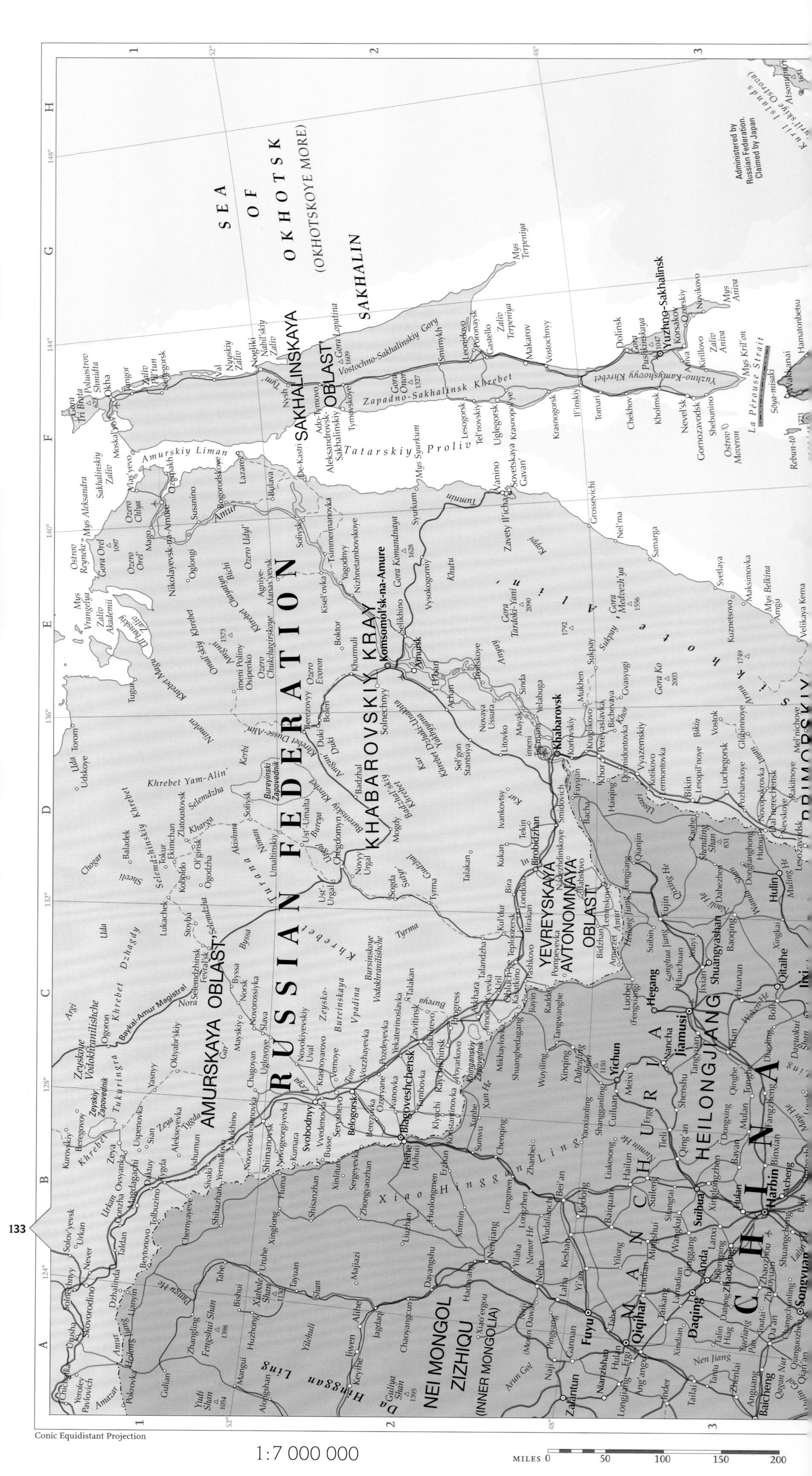

Conic Equidistant Projection

1 : 7 000 000

MILES 0   50   100   150   200

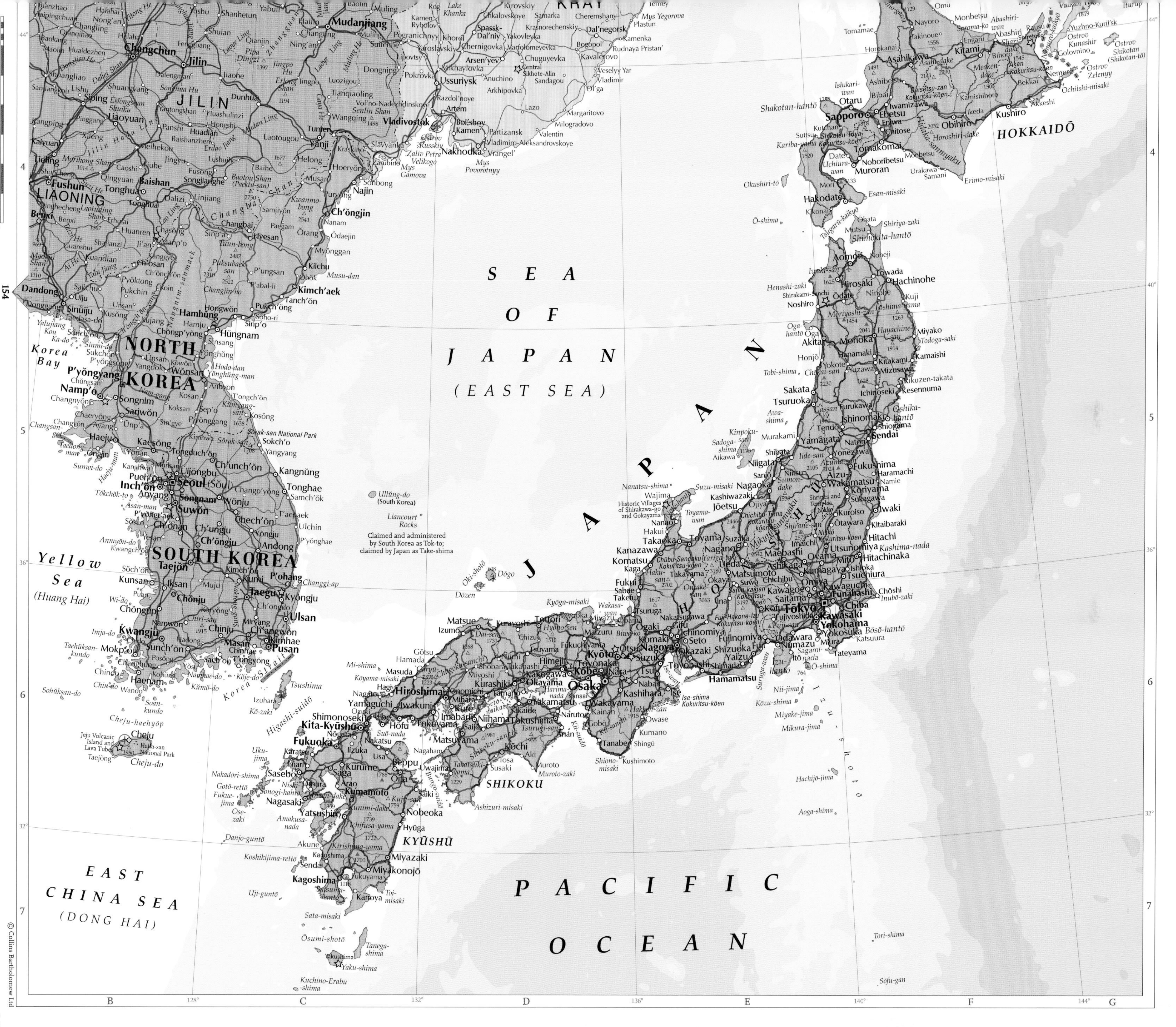

© Collins Bartholomew Ltd

SEA OF JAPAN
(EAST SEA)
PACIFIC OCEAN
EAST CHINA SEA
(DONG HAI)
Yellow Sea
(Huang Hai)
Korea Bay
JAPAN
NORTH KOREA
SOUTH KOREA
HOKKAIDŌ
SHIKOKU
KYŪSHŪ
JILIN
LIAONING
Claimed and administered by South Korea as Tok-to; claimed by Japan as Take-shima
0 50 100 150 200 250 300 350 KILOMETRES
154

Japan

JAPAN Capital: **Tōkyō**
Area: **377 727 km²/145 841 miles²**
Population: **127 967 000** Languages: **Japanese**
Religions: **Shintoist, Buddhist, Christian** Currency: **Yen**

The archipelago which makes up Japan stretches from Hokkaidō, with its ski resorts, in the north to the Ryuku Islands and the sub-tropical island of Okinawa, over 3000 km away in the south. Contrasts in culture are also wide with state-of-the-art technology next to the ancient traditions of geishas and tea ceremonies.

Tōkyō is an ultra-modern city with the emphasis on cutting-edge design, but with the temples at Asakusa and the Meiji Shrine and Imperial Palace still partly closed to the outside world, the traditional culture is still greatly respected. In the spring the parks of the city, such as Ueno Park, are busy with visitors partaking in *hanami* or cherry blossom viewing. The futuristic bullet train allows Mount Fuji to be visited in a day from Tōkyō but a longer stay allows time to climb to the top. The Izu islands continue the chain of volcanoes from Mount Fuji and can be reached by hydrofoil. The views from Ō-shima back across to Tōkyō are impressive. The National Park at Nikkō is another possible day trip with stone lanterns marking the way to a lavishly decorated shrine set in beautiful mountainous woodlands.

Kyōto was the capital for over 1000 years and is the cultural centre with many temples and shrines including the Kinkakuji which is covered in gold and the Ryoanji temple and Zen rock garden. Equidistant from Kyōto and Ōsaka is Nara, home to a World Heritage site containing eight significant sites of temples, shrines and ruins. Further south is Hiroshima, now a bustling modern city with the poignant Peace Memorial Park in the centre. The island of Miyajima is a favourite tourist site just off the coast of the city.

Hokkaidō, the most northerly island is less developed and has National Parks with hot springs and good hiking trails as well as winter ski resorts.

Conic Equidistant Projection

1:5 000 000

MILES 0   50   100   150   200

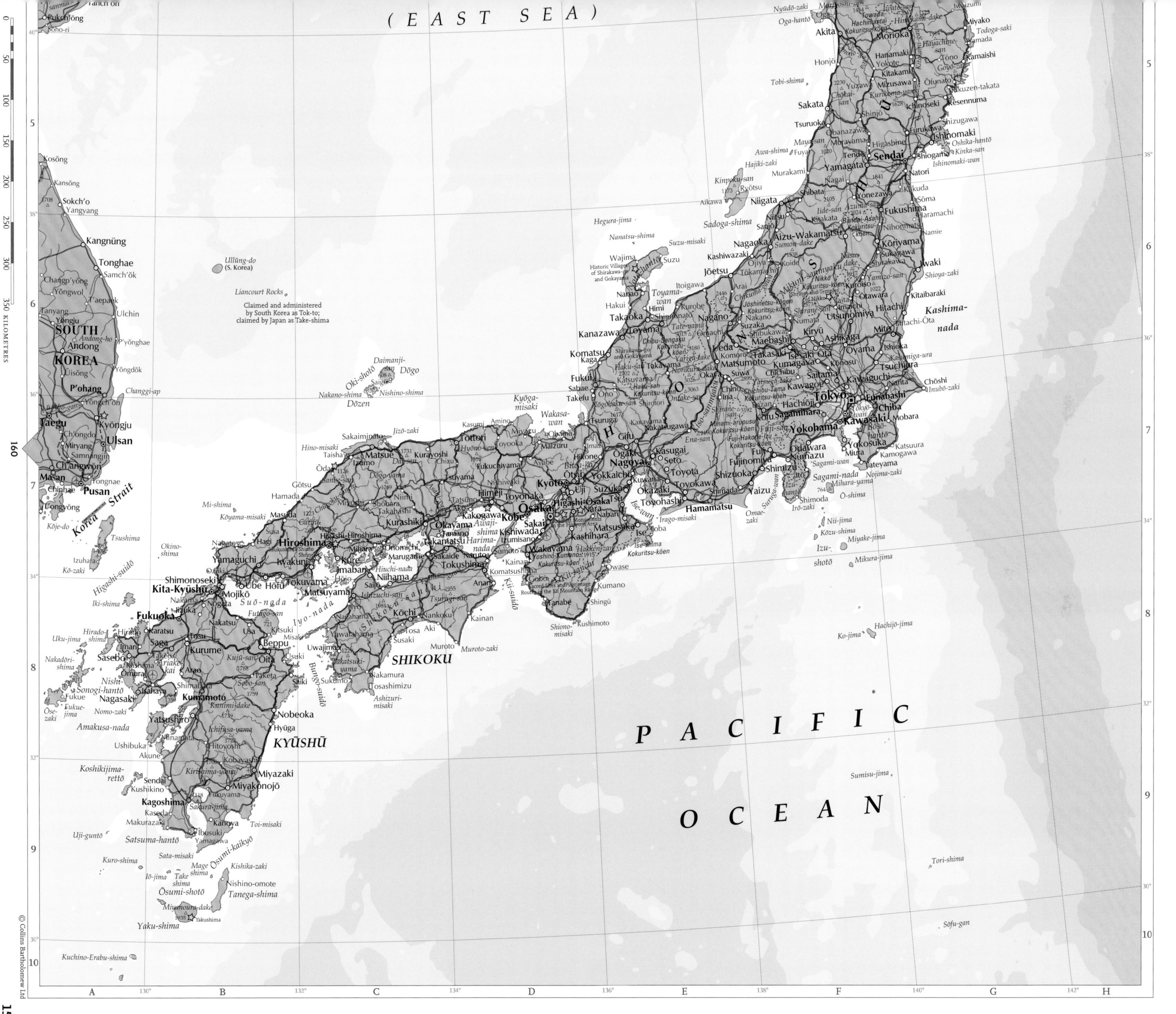

© Collins Bartholomew Ltd

0   50   100   150   200   250   300   350 KILOMETRES

North Korea and South Korea

NORTH KOREA Capital: P'yŏngyang
Area: 120 538 km²/46 540 miles² Population: 23 790 000
Languages: Korean Religions: Traditional beliefs, Chondoist, Buddhist Currency: North Korean won

Due to its isolation from the rest of the world, a visit to North Korea will be unique experience. No independent travel is permitted but tours are possible, with a government approved guide.

P'yŏngyang, the capital, has grand architectural buildings with huge statues of the country's former leader. The scenic Kŭmgung-san, known as the Diamond Mountains, fringe the east coast and is one area which can be accessed from South Korea. On the Chinese border Paekdu-san is considered sacred – it is the country's highest mountain with a huge crater lake.

SOUTH KOREA Capital: Seoul (Sŏul)
Area: 99 274 km²/38 330 miles² Population: 48 224 000
Languages: Korean Religions: Buddhist, Protestant, Roman Catholic Currency: South Korean won

South Korea has become more open to tourists in recent years and there is plenty to explore. The North Seoul Tower is perfect for viewing the capital city and the surrounding landscape. As well as a huge national museum to visit there are five royal palaces including Changdeok-gung with its secret gardens. South of Seoul is Suwŏn with the impressive Hwaseong Fortress.

The high speed KTX train takes you to Pusan, accessing the beautiful south coast of scattered islands, beaches and Hallyŏ Haesang Maritime National Park. Off the coast is Cheju-do, a holiday island in a volcanic landscape.

Philippines

PHILIPPINES Capital: Manila
Area: 300 000km²/115 831miles²
Population: 87 960 000 Languages: English, Filipino, Tagalog, Cebuano, local languages Religions: Roman Catholic, Protestant, Sunni Muslim, Aglipayan Currency: Philippine peso

The majority of the population live on only eleven of the 7000 islands which make up the country. While the land displays dramatic scenery such as the 2000-year-old rice terraces at Banaue, north of Baguio, it is the sea which is the major attraction. The tropical waters boast great marine life, coral gardens and shipwrecks for divers and snorkelers to explore. El Nido gives access to the superb seascapes of the Bacuit Archipelago and the shores of Palawan itself. The tiny island of Borocay, north of Panay is famous for its beaches and parties.

The Zamboango Peninsula on Mindanao and the Sulu Archipelago are subject to local political unrest.

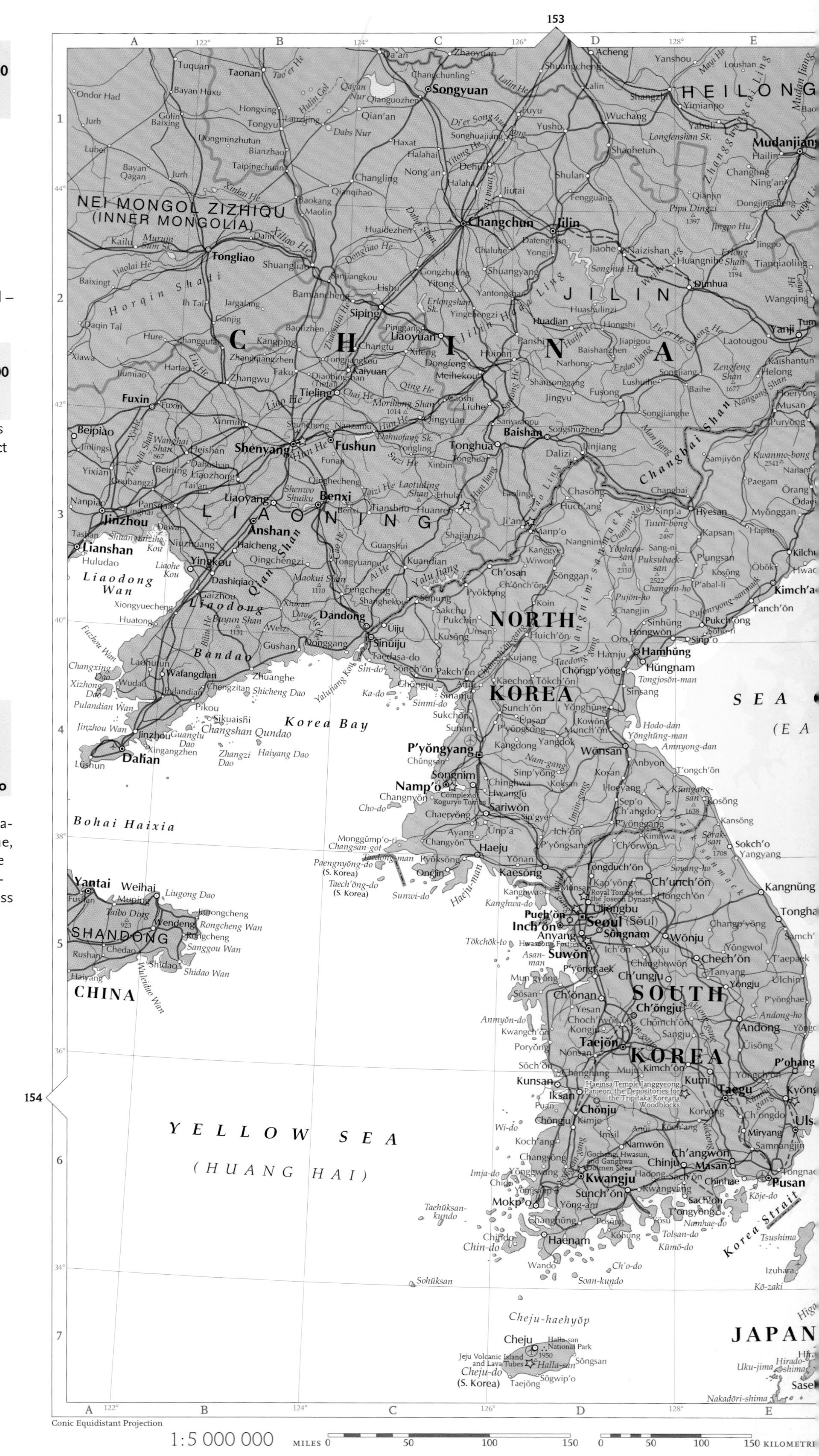

Conic Equidistant Projection

1:5 000 000 MILES 0   50   100   150   0   50   100   150 KILOMETRE

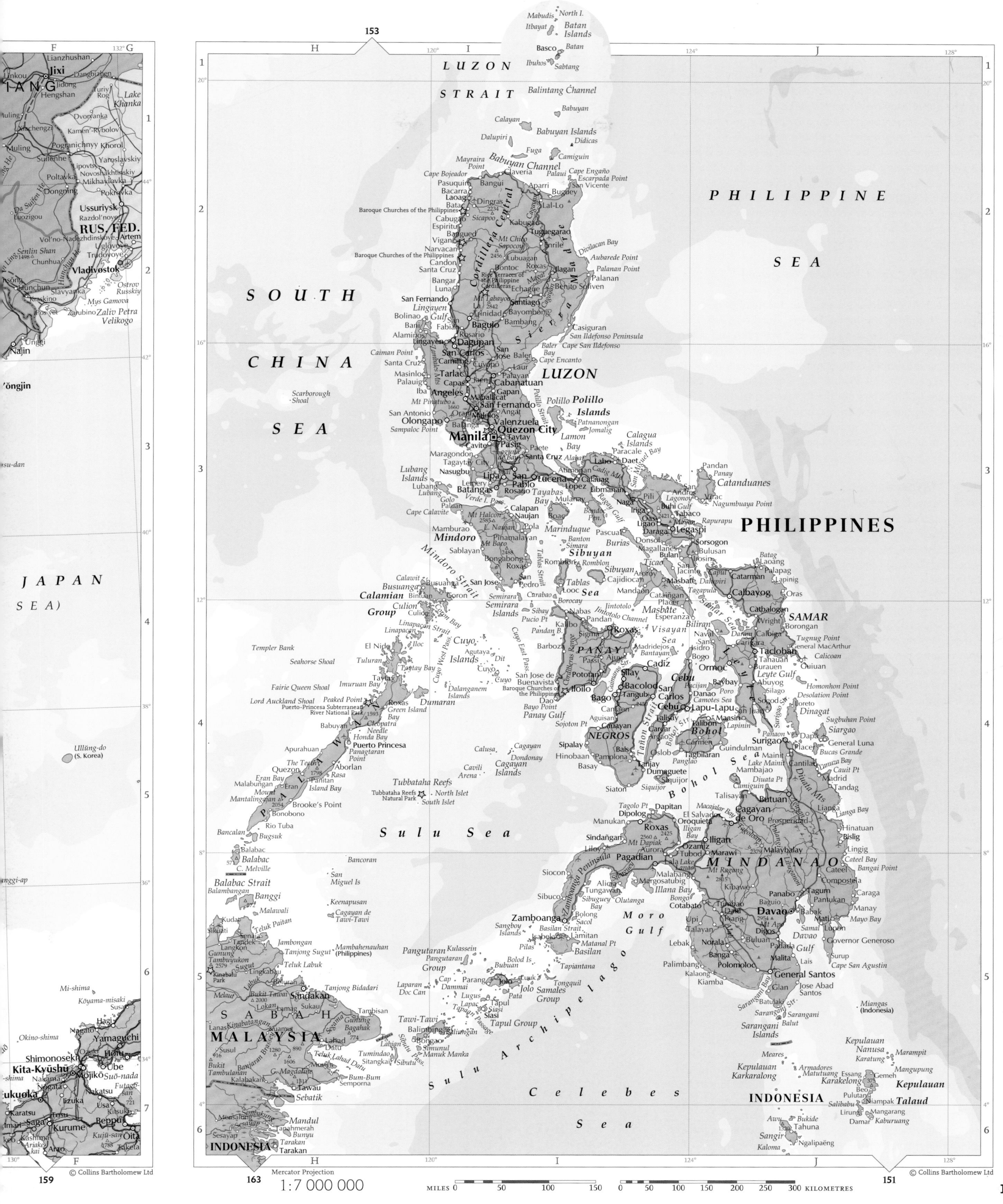

PHILIPPINES

LUZON STRAIT

SOUTH CHINA SEA

PHILIPPINE SEA

LUZON

Manila

JAPAN SEA)

Mindoro

Sibuyan Sea

Tablas Sea

PANAY

SAMAR

Visayan Sea

NEGROS

CEBU

Bohol Sea

Sulu Sea

PALAWAN

Puerto Princesa

MINDANAO

Davao

Moro Gulf

Zamboanga

General Santos

MALAYSIA

SABAH

Sulu Archipelago

Celebes Sea

INDONESIA

© Collins Bartholomew Ltd

Mercator Projection

1:7 000 000

MILES 0   50   100   150

0   50   100   150   200   250   300 KILOMETRES

© Collins Bartholomew Ltd

Indochina

 CAMBODIA Capital: **Phnom Penh**
Area: **181 000 km²/69 884 miles²** Population: **14 444 000**
Languages: **Khmer, Vietnamese** Religions: **Buddhist, Roman Catholic, Sunni Muslim** Currency: **Riel**

The country is developing as a popular destination and the land mine clearance programme is helping access inland. Phnom Penh has reminders of the Khmer Rouge past at the Genocide Museum, contrasting the stunning Silver Pagoda at the Royal Palace. Most visitors head to Siĕmréab (Siem Reap), adjacent to the floating villages on Tonle Sap to visit the impressive temples of Angkor. The temples at Koh Ker are lesser known and still being uncovered; they are a day's travel from Siĕmréab. On the Thai border is the hilltop temple of Preah Vihear.

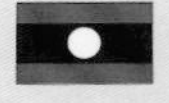

 LAOS Capital: **Vientiane (Viangchan)**
Area: **236 800 km²/91 429 miles²**
Population: **5 859 000** Languages: **Lao, local languages**
Religions: **Buddhist, traditional beliefs** Currency: **Kip**

Laos has only been accepting tourists since 1988 and still retains its traditions. Village life and the countryside are largely unaltered, and unspoilt national parks are becoming popular eco-tourist destinations. Vientiane is a relatively small town with French colonial buildings but the former capital, Luang Prabang is still the religious centre with over thirty-three temple complexes. The morning procession of saffron-robed monks receiving alms is timeless. From here trips to the Pak Ou caves and the mysterious Land of Jars are possible .

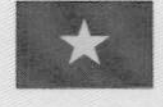

⭐ **VIETNAM** Capital: **Ha Nôi**
Area: **329 565 km²/127 246 miles²**
Population: **87 375 000** Languages: **Vietnamese, Thai, Khmer, Chinese, local languages** Religions: **Buddhist, Taoist, Roman Catholic, Cao Dai, Hoa Hao** Currency: **Dong**

The contrast between the buzzing city life and the tranquil countryside is startling. Ha Nôi, the capital, is a centre for the arts and the Old Quarter has a flavour of the former colonial influences. Ho Chi Minh City is the business centre and Huê is a fascinating past imperial capital. Away from the cities, there are river markets on the Mekong delta and great beaches at Nha Trang. Halong Bay, in the north, is full of weird shaped limestone outcrops and islands. In the mountains, the former colonial hill stations of Dalat and Sapa provide great views and relief from the heat.

West Indonesia and Malaysia

 BRUNEI Capital: **Bandar Seri Begawan**
Area: **5 765 km²/2 226 miles²** Population: **390 000**
Languages: **Malay, English, Chinese** Religions: **Sunni Muslim, Buddhist, Christian** Currency: **Brunei dollar**

Brunei is a tiny but very rich state due to underground oil and gas resources. The capital has the impressive Sultan Omar Ali Saifuddien Mosque as well as Istana Nurul Iman, the Sultan's home. Nearby is Kampong Ayer, a village built on stilts connected by wooden walkways. There are areas of virgin rainforest which can be explored by trails through the canopy in Ulu Temburong National Park, and boat trips to Bangar through dense mangroves to see the waterfalls, hot springs and traditional longhouses of the remote village communities.

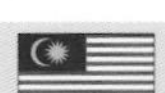

🇲🇾 **MALAYSIA** Capital: **Kuala Lumpur/Putrajaya**
Area: **332 965 km²/128 559 miles²**
Population: **26 572 000** Languages: **Malay, English, Chinese, Tamil, local languages** Religions: **Sunni Muslim, Buddhist, Hindu, Christian, traditional beliefs** Currency: **Ringgit**

Pure white sandy beaches, clear seas and a tropical jungle backdrop is the popular image of a Malaysian resort. Inland there are dense, stifling jungles to explore in the Taman Negara National Park and then the futuristic skyscrapers and historic temples of Kuala Lumpur. The Petronas Towers give a breathtaking view of the city. To escape the humidity, the Cameron Highlands offer relief.

Mercator Projection

1:7 500 000

MILES 0   100   150

0   100   200 KILOMETRES

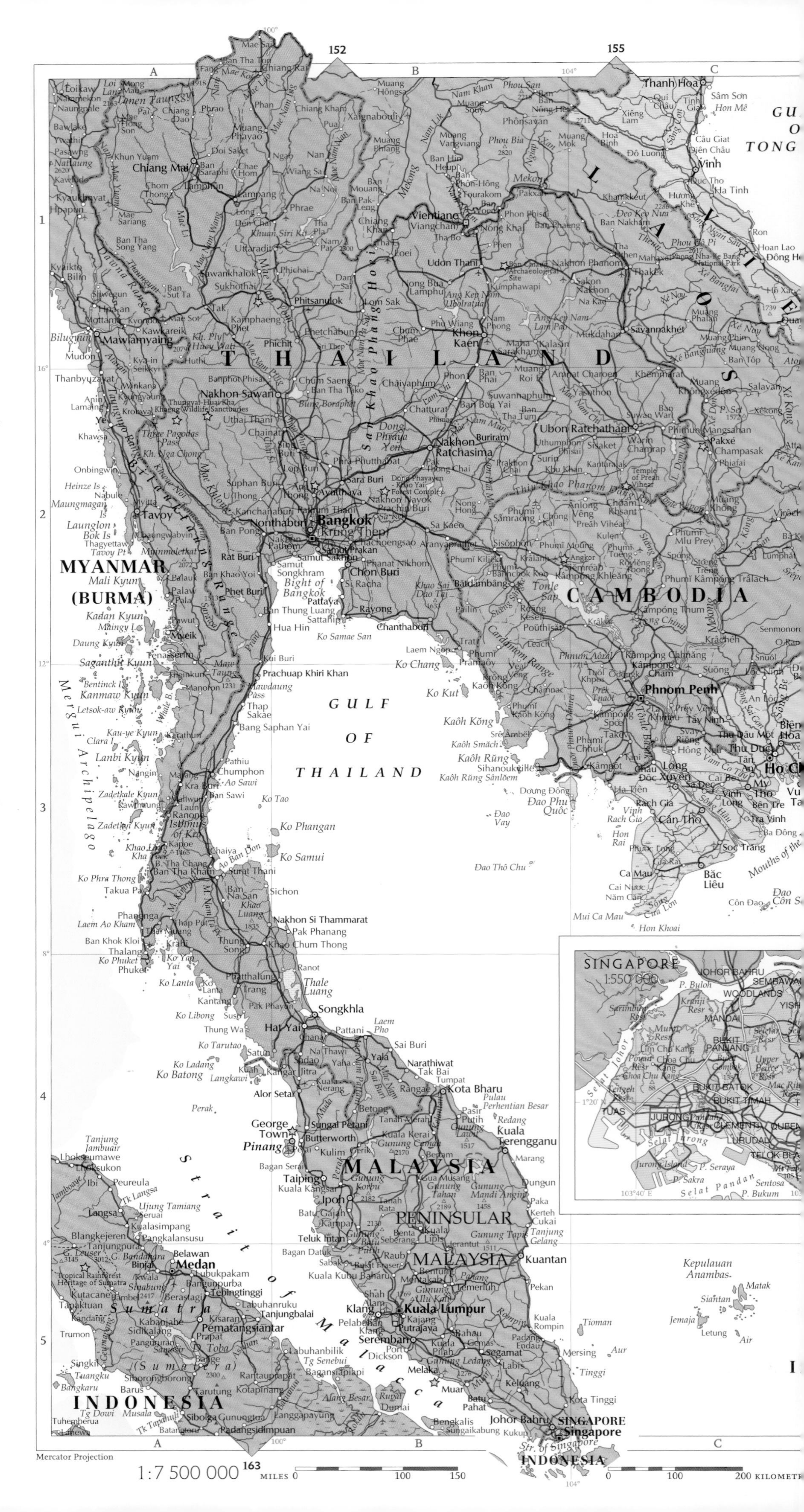

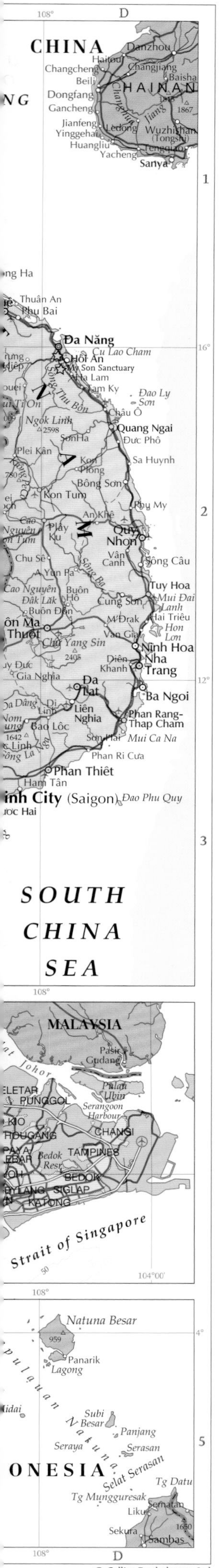

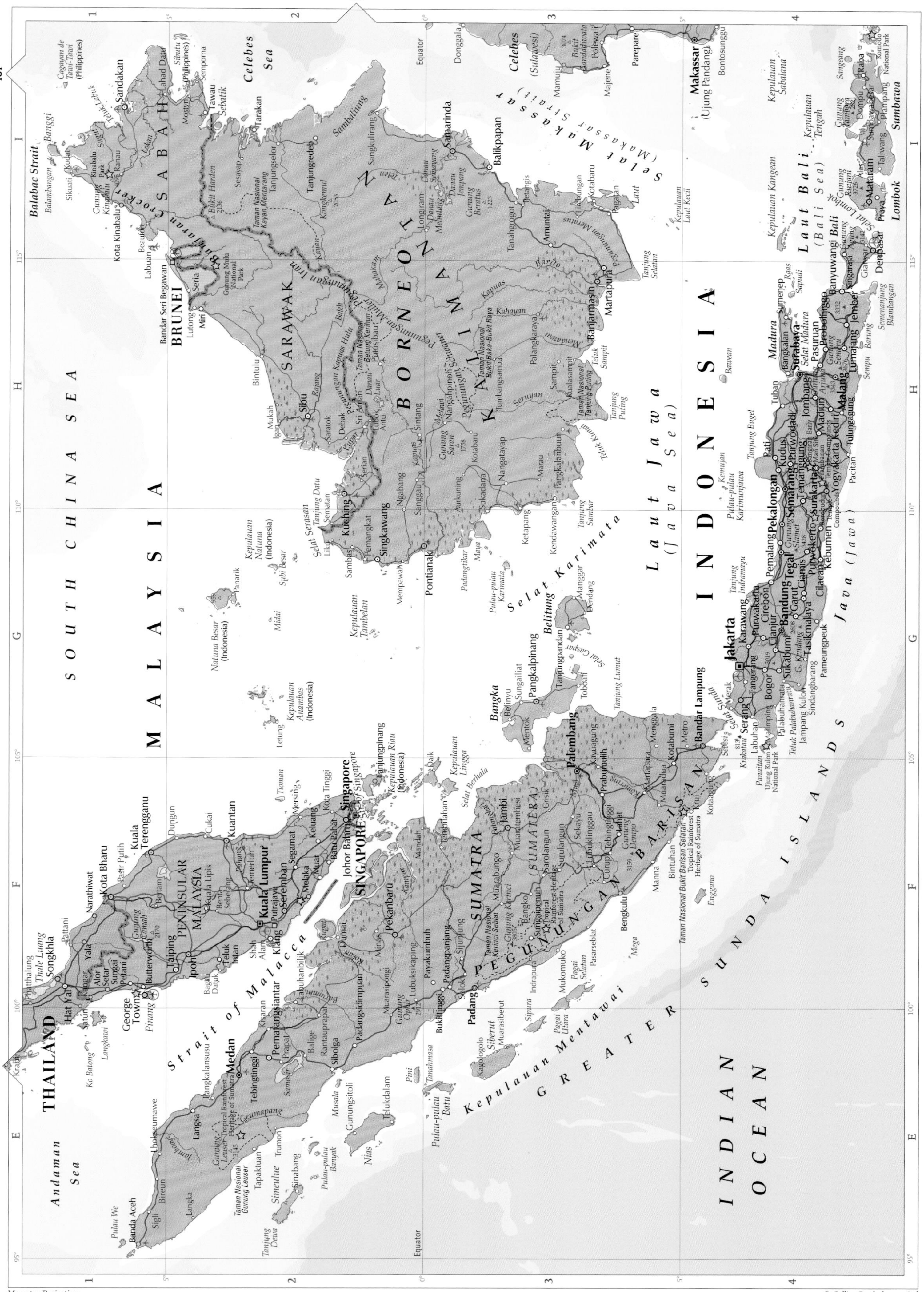

CHINA

HAINAN

Danzhou
Changcheng
Dongfang
Gancheng
Yinggehai
Huangliu
Yacheng
Sanya

SOUTH CHINA SEA

THAILAND

MALAYSIA

PENINSULAR MALAYSIA

SOUTH CHINA SEA

Balabac Strait

SABAH

Kota Kinabalu
Labuan

BRUNEI
Bandar Seri Begawan
Miri
Seria

SARAWAK

Kuching

BORNEO

KALIMANTAN

Celebes Sea

Celebes (Sulawesi)

Makassar (Ujung Pandang)

Samarinda
Balikpapan

Banjarmasin

Laut Bali (Bali Sea)

Bali
Denpasar
Mataram
Lombok
Sumbawa

Laut Jawa (Java Sea)

INDONESIA

Madura
Surabaya
Malang

Pontianak

Singkawang

Bangka
Pangkalpinang

Belitung

Palembang

SUMATERA

Jambi

Pekanbaru

Jakarta
Bandung
Semarang
Yogyakarta
Surakarta

JAVA (Jawa)

Bandar Lampung

Medan

George Town
Pinang

Kuala Lumpur
SINGAPORE

Strait of Malacca

Padang

PEGUNUNGAN BARISAN

GREATER SUNDA ISLANDS

Kepulauan Mentawai

INDIAN OCEAN

Banda Aceh

Andaman Sea

Strait of Singapore

Natuna Besar

1 : 10 000 000   MILES 0   100   200   0   100   200   300   400 KILOMETRES

Mercator Projection

© Collins Bartholomew Ltd

Europe Physical

The continent consists of a complex, irregular arrangement of extensive plains, plateaus, and mountain ranges. There are several significant island groups – notably the British Isles and Iceland in the Atlantic, and in the Mediterranean the Balearic Islands, Corsica and Sardinia, Sicily, and Crete. The general outline of the continent is complicated further by a number of prominent peninsulas, among which are the Balkan Peninsula (principally occupied by Greece), Italy, the Iberian Peninsula (Spain and Portugal), Denmark, and Scandinavia consisting of Norway and Sweden.

Facts

• The Danube flows through seven countries and has six different local names – Donau (Austria and Germany), Dunaj (Slovakia), Duna (Hungary), Dunav (Serbia), Dunarea (Romania) and Dunay (Ukraine). 'Danube' is the conventional English name.

• All the seas on this map (except the Caspian) are in effect branches of the Atlantic Ocean.

• Europe's four highest mountains – El'brus, Gora Dykh-Tau, Shkhara and Kazbek – are in the Caucasus. Mont Blanc, the highest mountain in the Alps, is fifth.

• By stretching north–south over more than 45 degrees of latitude, Europe has a greatly varied climate, from the hot Mediterranean to the frozen Arctic.

HIGHEST MOUNTAINS	m	ft
El'brus, Russian Federation	5 642	18 510
Gora Dykh-Tau, Russian Federation	5 204	17 073
Shkhara, Georgia/Russian Federation	5 201	17 063
Kazbek, Georgia/Russian Federation	5 047	16 558
Mont Blanc, France/Italy	4 808	15 774
Dufourspitze, Italy/Switzerland	4 634	15 203

LARGEST ISLANDS	sq km	sq miles
Great Britain	218 476	84 354
Iceland	102 820	39 699
Novaya Zemlya	90 650	35 000
Ireland	83 045	32 064
Spitsbergen	37 814	14 600
Sicily (Sicilia)	25 426	9 817

LONGEST RIVERS	km	miles
Volga	3 688	2 292
Danube	2 850	1 771
Dnieper	2 285	1 420
Kama	2 028	1 260
Don	1 931	1 200
Pechora	1 802	1 120

LARGEST LAKES	sq km	sq miles
Caspian Sea	371 000	143 243
Lake Ladoga (Ladozhskoye Ozero)	18 390	7 100
Lake Onega (Onezhskoye Ozero)	9 600	3 707
Vänern	5 585	2 156
Rybinskoye Vodokhranilishche	5 180	2 000

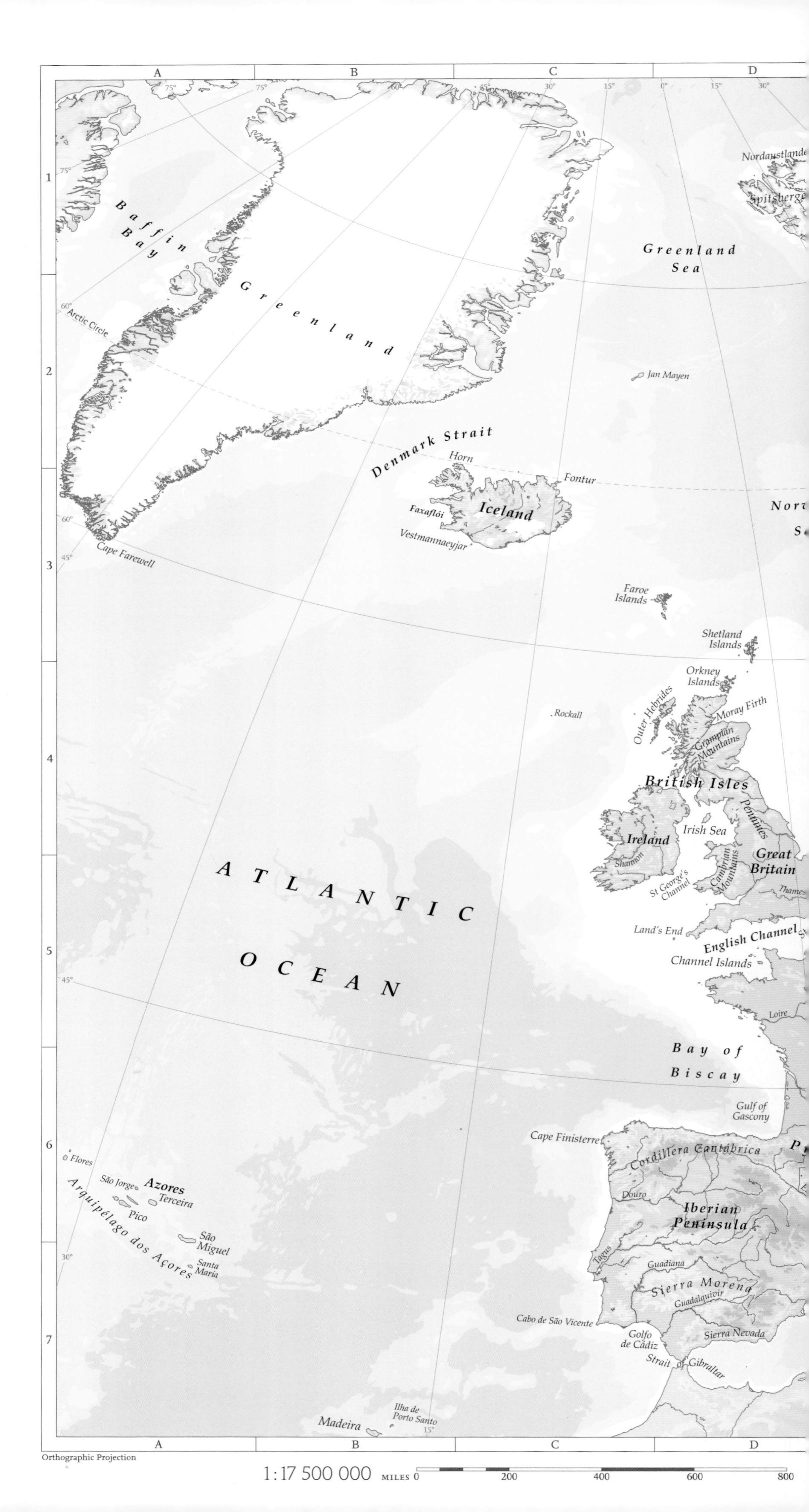

Orthographic Projection

1 : 17 500 000   MILES 0   200   400   600   800

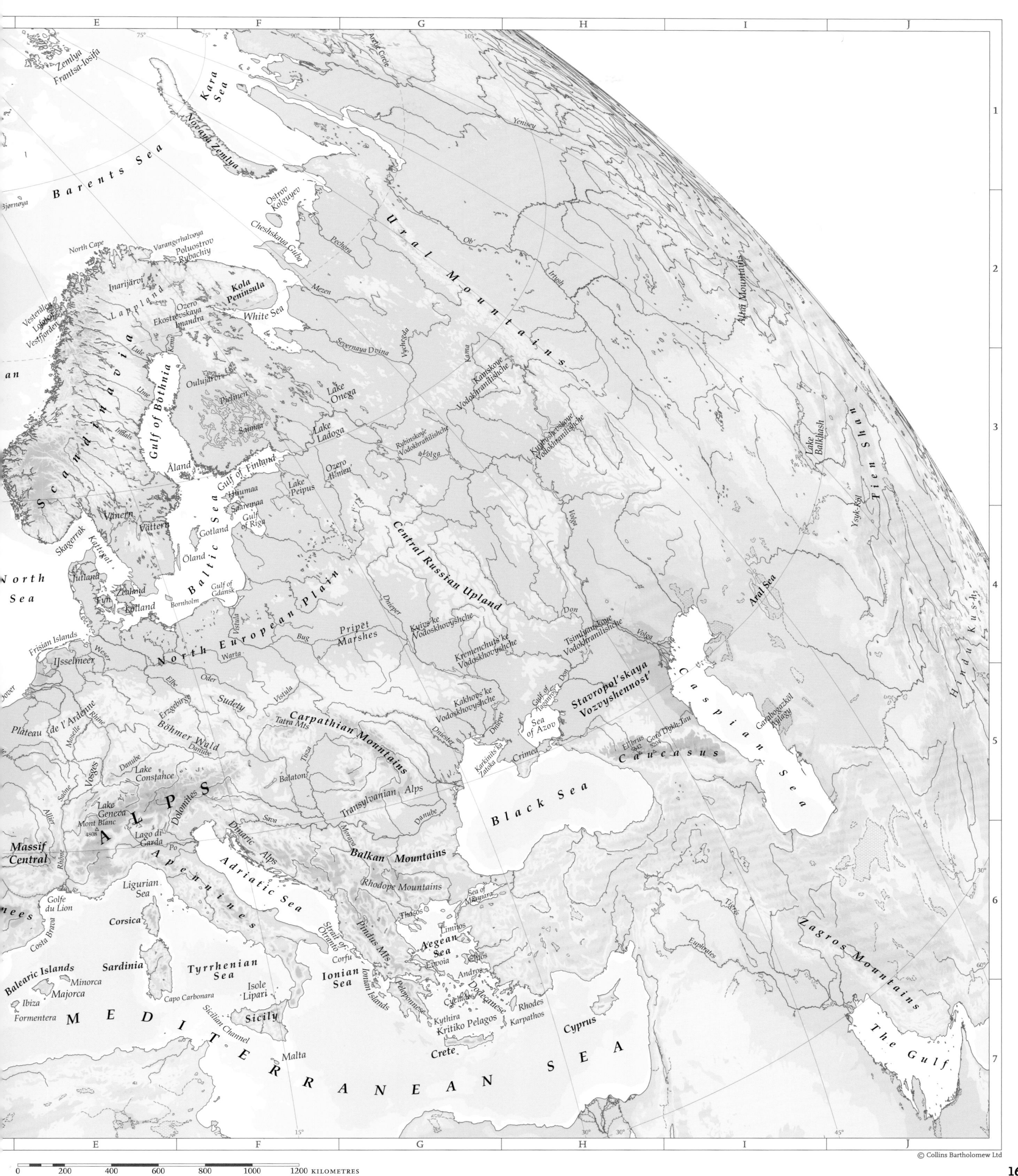

Zemlya
Frantsa-Iosifa

Kara
Sea

B a r e n t s   S e a

Bjørnøya

Novaya Zemlya

North Cape
Varangerhalvøya
Poluostrov
Rybachiy

Ostrov
Kolguyev

Cheshskaya Guba

Pechora

Kola
Peninsula

Inarijärvi

Vesterålen
Lofoten
Vestfjorden

L a p p l a n d

Ozero
Ekostrovskaya
Imandra

White Sea

Mezen

U r a l   M o u n t a i n s

Yenisey

Ob'

Irtysh

Altai Mountains

Lule
Kemi
Oulujärvi

Ume

Pielinen

Severnaya Dvina

Vychegda

Kama

Kamskoye
Vodokhranilishche

S c a n d i n a v i a

Gulf of Bothnia

Saimaa

Lake
Onega

Lake
Ladoga

Rybinskoye
Vodokhranilishche

Volga

Kuybyshevskoye
Vodokhranilishche

Volga

T i e n   S h a n

Lake
Balkhash

Ysyk-Köl

* Åland*

Hiiumaa
Gulf of Finland
Saaremaa
Gulf of
Riga

Lake
Peipus

Ozero
Il'men'

C e n t r a l   R u s s i a n   U p l a n d

Aral Sea

Vänern

Vättern

Gotland

Öland

B a l t i c   S e a

Gulf of Gdansk

N o r t h   E u r o p e a n   P l a i n

Dnieper

Don

Volga

C a s p i a n

Garabogazköl
Aylagy

N o r t h
S e a

Jutland

Zealand

Fyn

Lolland

Bornholm

Vistula

Bug

Pripet
Marshes

Warta

Kyïvs'ke
Vodoskhovyshche

Kremenchuts'ke
Vodoskhovyshche

Tsimlyanskoye
Vodokhranilishche

Volga

S t a v r o p o l' s k a y a
V o z v y s h e n n o s t'

C a s p i a n   S e a

Frisian Islands

Weser

IJsselmeer

Elbe

Oder

Vistula

Sudety

Dniester

Kakhovs'ke
Vodoskhovyshche

Dnieper

Gulf of
Taganrog

Don

Dover

Plateau de l'Ardenne

Moselle

Rhine

Erzgebirge

Böhmer Wald

Tatra Mts

C a r p a t h i a n   M o u n t a i n s

Tisza

Sea
of Azov

Elbrus
5642

Gora Dykh-Tau
5204

C a u c a s u s

Vosges

Danube

Lake
Constance

Balaton

Sava

Crimea

Kerch'
Strait

Karkinits'ka
Zatoka

Saône

Allier

Mont Blanc
4808

A L P S

Lake
Geneva

Dolomites

Lago di
Garda

Po

T r a n s y l v a n i a n   A l p s

Danube

B l a c k   S e a

Massif
Central

Rhône

D i n a r i c   A l p s

B a l k a n   M o u n t a i n s

A d r i a t i c   S e a

Ligurian
Sea

A p e n n i n e s

Maritsa

Rhodope Mountains

Danube

Sea of
Marmara

Golfe
du Lion

nees

Corsica

Costa Brava

Strait of
Otranto

P i n d u s   M t s

Thásos

Límnos

A e g e a n
S e a

Z a g r o s   M o u n t a i n s

Balearic Islands

Minorca

Sardinia

T y r r h e n i a n
S e a

Capo Carbonara

Isole
Lipari

I o n i a n
S e a

Corfu

Ionian Islands

Evvoia

Chíos

Andros

Euphrates

Majorca

Ibiza

Formentera

Peloponnese

Kýthira

C y c l a d e s

Dodecanese

Rhodes

Kárpathos

Cyprus

Tigris

Euphrates

T h e   G u l f

M E D I *Sicilian Channel*

Sicily

Malta

Kritiko Pelagos

Crete

T E R R A N E A N   S E A

0   200   400   600   800   1000   1200 KILOMETRES

© Collins Bartholomew Ltd

Europe Political

Europe's dense jigsaw of countries reflects the complex history of its many national groupings. The political map was redrawn significantly after the First and Second World Wars, and changes have continued since – Germany reunified in 1990, Yugoslavia and the former Soviet Union broke up in 1991, and Czechoslovakia was divided into two in 1993. Many European countries are small by world standards – some are among the world's smallest – but European Russia is part of the largest country in the world.

Facts

- The European Union increased its membership from fifteen to twenty-five members in 2004, with several other countries keen to join. It now includes Malta and Cyprus, and several eastern European countries, but not Norway, Switzerland or Iceland.

- Iceland and the Faroe Islands belong culturally and linguistically to Scandinavia.

- Europe has the two smallest independent countries in the world – Vatican City and Monaco.

- Since the Yugoslav civil war of 1991–1995 the country has been broken up. The most recent area to declare independence from Serbia is Kosovo, in February 2008.

LARGEST COUNTRIES	Area sq km	sq miles
Russian Federation	17 075 400	6 592 849
Ukraine	603 700	233 090
France	543 965	210 026
Spain	504 782	194 897
Sweden	449 964	173 732
Germany	357 022	137 849
Finland	338 145	130 559
Norway	323 878	125 050
Poland	312 683	120 728
Italy	301 245	116 311

MOST POPULATED COUNTRIES	Population
Russian Federation	142 499 000
Germany	82 599 000
France	61 647 000
United Kingdom	60 769 000
Italy	58 877 000
Ukraine	46 205 000
Spain	44 279 000
Poland	38 082 000
Romania	21 438 000
Netherlands	16 419 000

CAPITALS		
Largest population	Moscow, Russian Federation	10 967 000
Smallest population	Vatican City	921
Most northerly	Reykjavík, Iceland	64° 39' N
Most southerly	Valletta, Malta	35° 54' N
Highest	Andorra la Vella, Andorra	1 029 m/ 3 376 ft

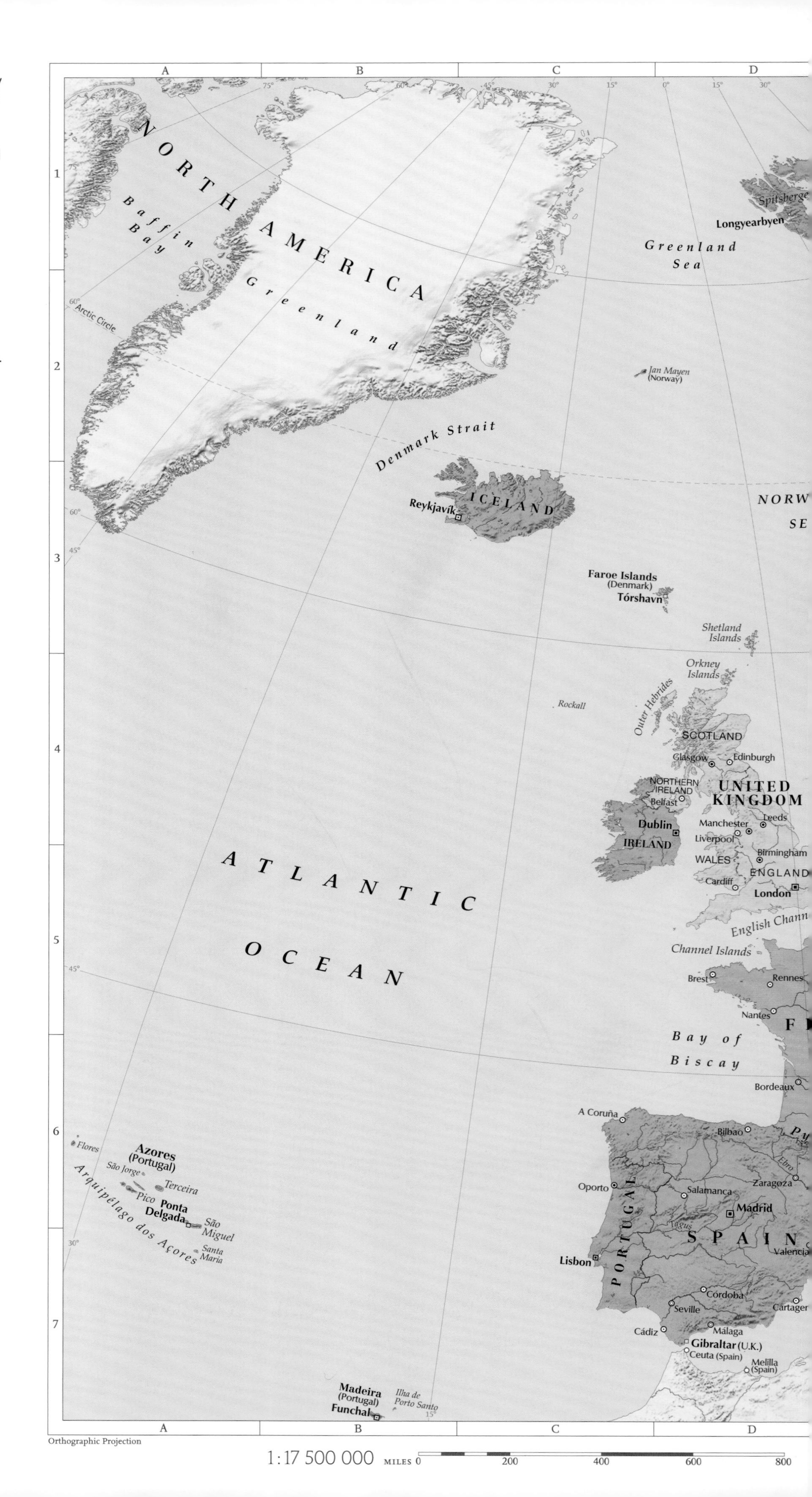

Orthographic Projection

1:17 500 000 MILES 0   200   400   600   800

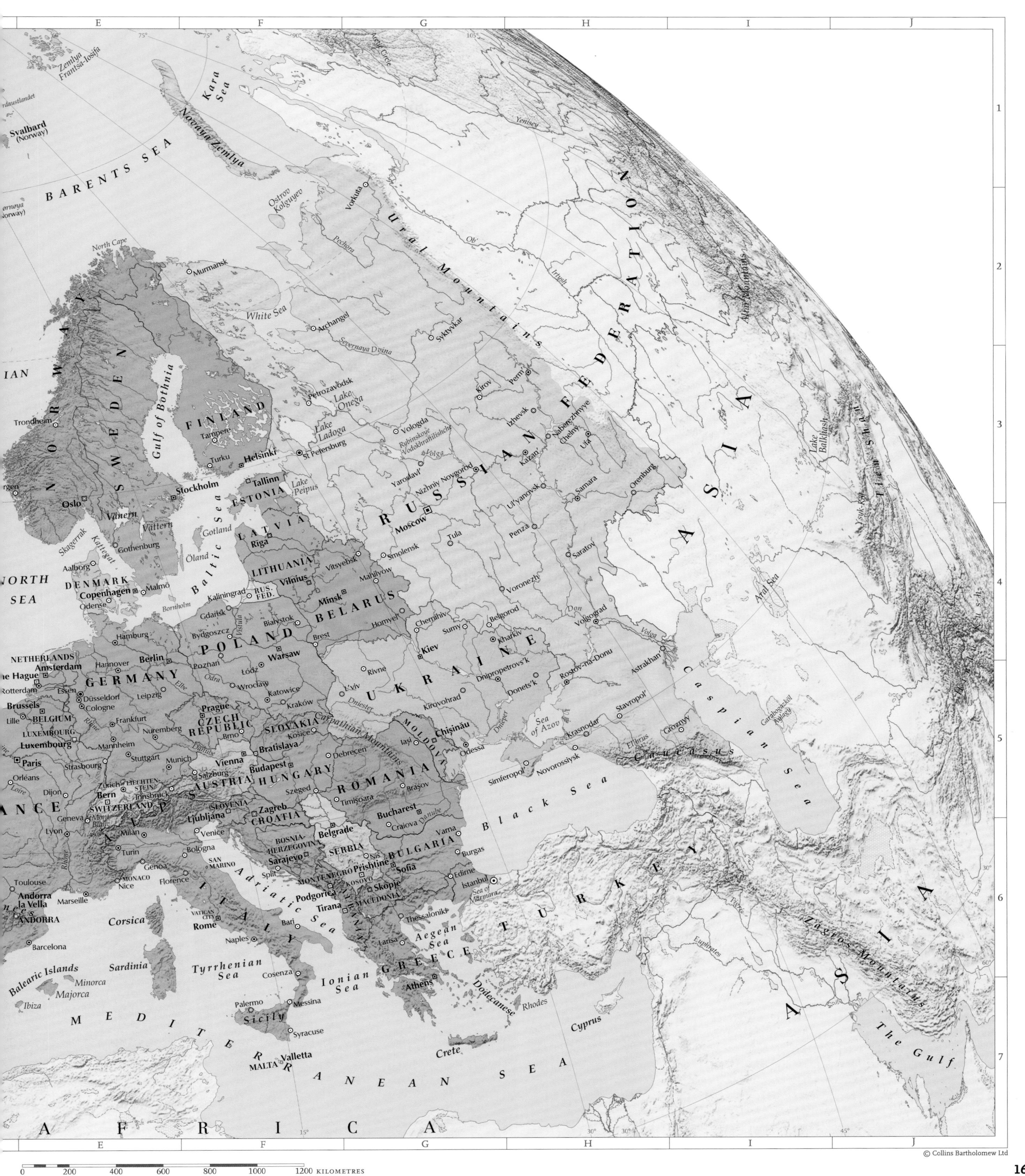

1

2

3

4

5

6

7

Zemlya
Frantsa-Iosfa

Svalbard
(Norway)

BARENTS SEA

Kara
Sea

Novaya Zemlya

Yenisey

Ostrov
Kolguyev

Vorkuta

Ob'

Pechora

North Cape

Ural Mountains

Altai Mountains

Murmansk

White Sea

Archangel

Severnaya Dvina

Syktyvkar

N O R W A Y

S W E D E N

FINLAND

Trondheim

Gulf of Bothnia

Tampere

Turku

Helsinki

St Petersburg

Lake
Onega

Petrozavodsk

Vologda

Kirov

Perm

Izhevsk

Naberezhnye
Chelny

Ufa

Lake
Ladoga

Rubinskoye
Vodokhranilishchi

Volga

Lake
Balkhash

R U S S I A N   F E D E R A T I O N

A S I A

Tien Shan

Lake
Ysyk-Köl

Oslo

Stockholm

Vänern

Vättern

Gothenburg

Tallinn

ESTONIA

Lake
Peipus

Gotland

Nizhniy Novgorod

Yaroslavl'

Kazan'

Ul'yanovsk

Samara

Orenburg

Moscow

Tula

Penza

Saratov

Aral Sea

Aalborg

Öland

Baltic Sea

LATVIA

Riga

LITHUANIA

Vilnius

Vitsyebsk

Mahilyow

Smolensk

Voronezh

Don

Belgorod

Volgograd

Volga

Astrakhan'

Caspian Sea

Karabogazköl Aylagy

DENMARK

Copenhagen

Odense

Malmö

Bornholm

Kaliningrad
RUS.
FED.

Gdańsk

Vistula

Białystok

Minsk

BELARUS

Homyel'

Chernihiv

Sumy

Kharkiv

Roztov-na-Donu

Krasnodar

Stavropol'

Groznyy

NORTH
SEA

Hamburg

Bydgoszcz

Poznań

POLAND

Brest

Warsaw

Odra

Łódź

Wrocław

Katowice

Kraków

Kiev

U K R A I N E

Dnieper

Dnipropetrovs'k

Donets'k

Sea
of Azov

Novorossiysk

Elbrus

Caucasus

NETHERLANDS

Amsterdam

he Hague

Rotterdam

Hannover

Berlin

Leipzig

GERMANY

Essen

Düsseldorf

Cologne

Frankfurt

Rivne

L'viv

Dniester

Kirovohrad

Odessa

Simferopol

Black Sea

Brussels

Lille

BELGIUM

Nuremberg

Prague

CZECH
REPUBLIC

Brno

SLOVAKIA

Košice

Carpathian Mountains

Iaşi

Chişinău

MOLDOVA

LUXEMBOURG

Luxembourg

Mannheim

Stuttgart

Munich

Danube

Vienna

Bratislava

Budapest

Debrecen

R O M A N I A

Paris

Strasbourg

Salzburg

Vienna

AUSTRIA

HUNGARY

Szeged

Timişoara

Braşov

Bucharest

Craiova

Danube

Varna

Burgas

Edirne

Istanbul

Sea of
Marmara

Orléans

Loire

Dijon

Zürich

Innsbruck

LIECHTEN-
STEIN

Bern

SWITZERLAND

A L P S

SLOVENIA

Ljubljana

Zagreb

CROATIA

Venice

Belgrade

SERBIA

BOSNIA-
HERZEGOVINA

Sarajevo

Niš

Sofia

BULGARIA

Soﬁa

T U R K E Y

FRANCE

Geneva

Lyon

Mont
Blanc

Milan

Turin

Bologna

Genoa

SAN
MARINO

Split

Podgorica

MONTENEGRO

Prishtinë

KOSOVO

Skopje

MACEDONIA

Thessaloniki

Toulouse

Andorra
la Vella

enees

ANDORRA

MONACO

Nice

Florence

I T A L Y

Adriatic Sea

Tirana

Larisa

Aegean
Sea

Euphrates

Marseille

Tigris

Zagros Mountains

Barcelona

Corsica

VATICAN
CITY

Rome

Bari

Naples

Tyrrhenian
Sea

G R E E C E

Athens

Dodecanese

Rhodes

Cyprus

The Gulf

Balearic Islands

Minorca

Majorca

Ibiza

Sardinia

Cosenza

Ionian
Sea

Palermo

Messina

Sicily

Syracuse

Crete

MALTA Valletta

A S I A

M E D I T E R R A N E A N   S E A

A F R I C A

Northern Europe

The Nordic lands of Iceland, Norway, Sweden, Finland and Denmark are distinct countries but have shared an interlinked history since the Viking age. They also share some common traits in culture and politics.

Northern Scandinavia is often referred to as 'Europe's last wilderness' and the main attractions for the visitor are the breathtaking natural scenery, clean air, abundant wildlife and year-round opportunities for outdoor pursuits. In summer the region is growing in popularity as a peaceful getaway and destination for boating, fishing and hiking. In winter there is skiing, skating, snowboarding, dog-sledding, snowmobile tours and ice climbing. Visitors travel to the far north to experience the Northern Lights (September to April), the Land of the Midnight Sun and to see the land of the Sami people, with their unique languages, culture and traditions. Further south are the capital cities of Oslo, Stockholm, Helsinki and Copenhagen. Easy access and a cosmopolitan blend of culture and nightlife has earned them a well-deserved reputation as appealing destinations for city breaks.

Separated from Scandinavia by the Baltic Sea are the Baltic states of Estonia, Latvia and Lithuania. Since achieving independence from the Soviet Union in 1990 and 1991 all three are countries in transition, largely free from mass tourism but keen to promote their unspoilt natural splendours and relaxed way of life.

ESTONIA Capital: **Tallinn**
Area: **45 200 km²/17 452 miles²** Population: **1 335 000**
Languages: **Estonian, Russian** Religions: **Protestant, Estonian and Russian Orthodox** Currency: **Kroon**

The emphasis of tourism to Estonia is on nature, with many specialised wildlife holiday itineraries available. About half the country is covered with forest, much of which is protected and crossed by a network of hiking trails. Fishing and boat trips on Lake Peipus, the fourth largest lake in Europe, are also popular. The medieval city of Tallinn is unusually well preserved with pastel coloured houses, winding cobble-stoned streets and impressive state and church buildings. The colourful Christmas market makes December a popular time to visit the city. With its sandy beaches, shallow waters and clapperboard houses, Pärnu is known as the 'summer capital' and has been a health resort since the 1930s.

LATVIA Capital: **Rīga**
Area: **63 700 km²/24 595 miles²** Population: **2 277 000**
Languages: **Latvian, Russian** Religions: **Protestant, Roman Catholic, Russian Orthodox** Currency: **Lats**

Rīga has a magnetic appeal to visitors who wish to combine the new with the old. The historic Old Town and Art Nouveau architecture are blended with a bustling nightlife and thriving restaurant scene. Stretching west from Rīga is the resort area of Jūrmala, a favourite holiday destination in Soviet times and still popular for its sandy beaches. Away from the cities, Latvia is a country of sandy coastline, forests, lakes and rivers with opportunities for boating, walking and fishing.

LITHUANIA Capital: **Vilnius**
Area: **65 200 km²/25 174 miles²**
Population: **3 390 000** Languages: **Lithuanian, Russian, Polish**
Religions: **Roman Catholic, Protestant, Russian Orthodox**
Currency: **Litas**

The southernmost of the Baltic states was the first Soviet republic to declare independence. Vilnius, with its baroque architecture and skyline of spires, is the main destination for most visitors. Further north, near Šiauliai, the Hill of Crosses is a unique place of national pilgrimage where over 100 000 crosses and crucifixes have been placed by Catholic pilgrims. Forest covers nearly a third of the country. The largest and most popular national park is Aukštaitija, a landscape of lakes and forest with boats and kayaks available for hire.

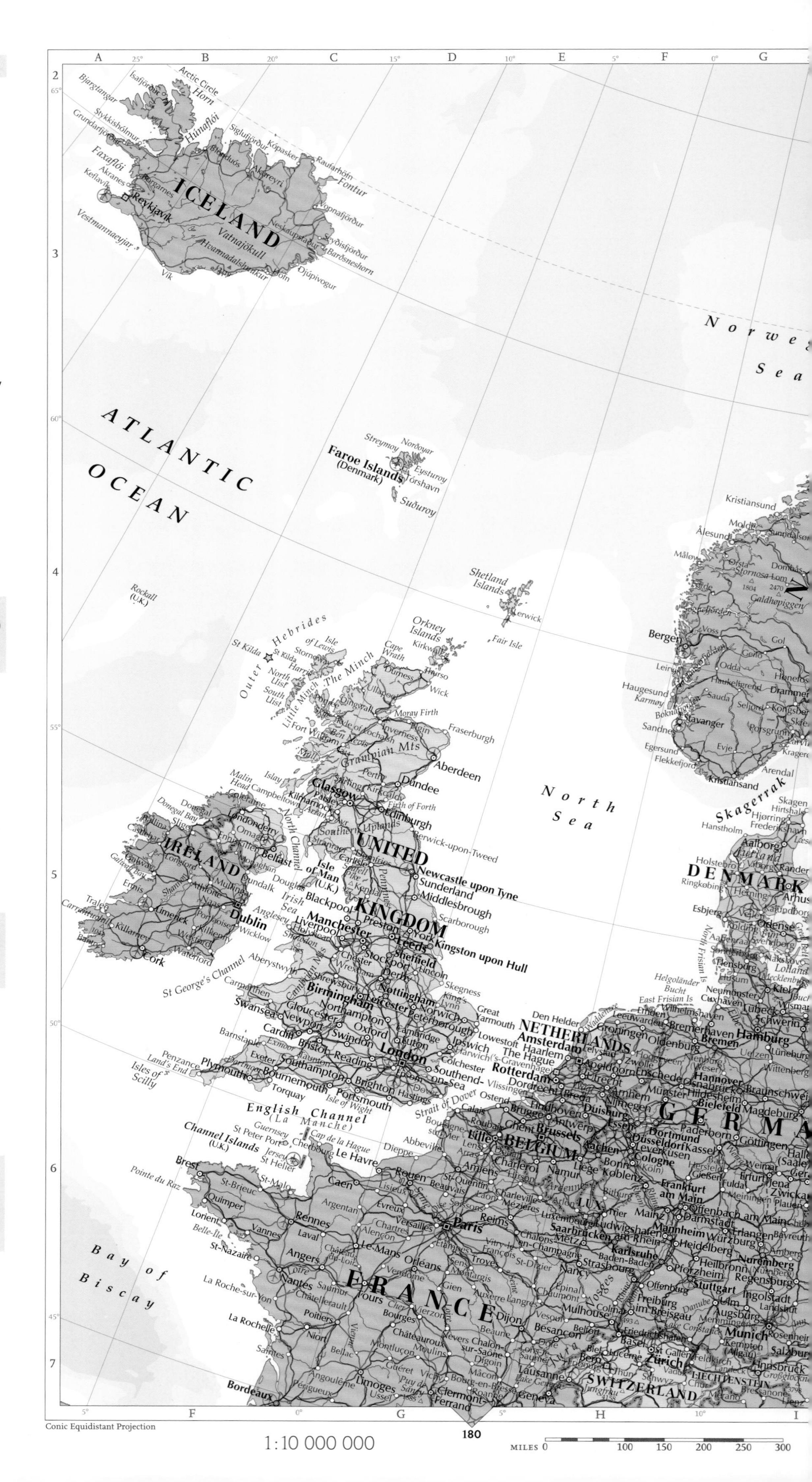

Conic Equidistant Projection

1:10 000 000

180

MILES 0   100   150   200   250   300

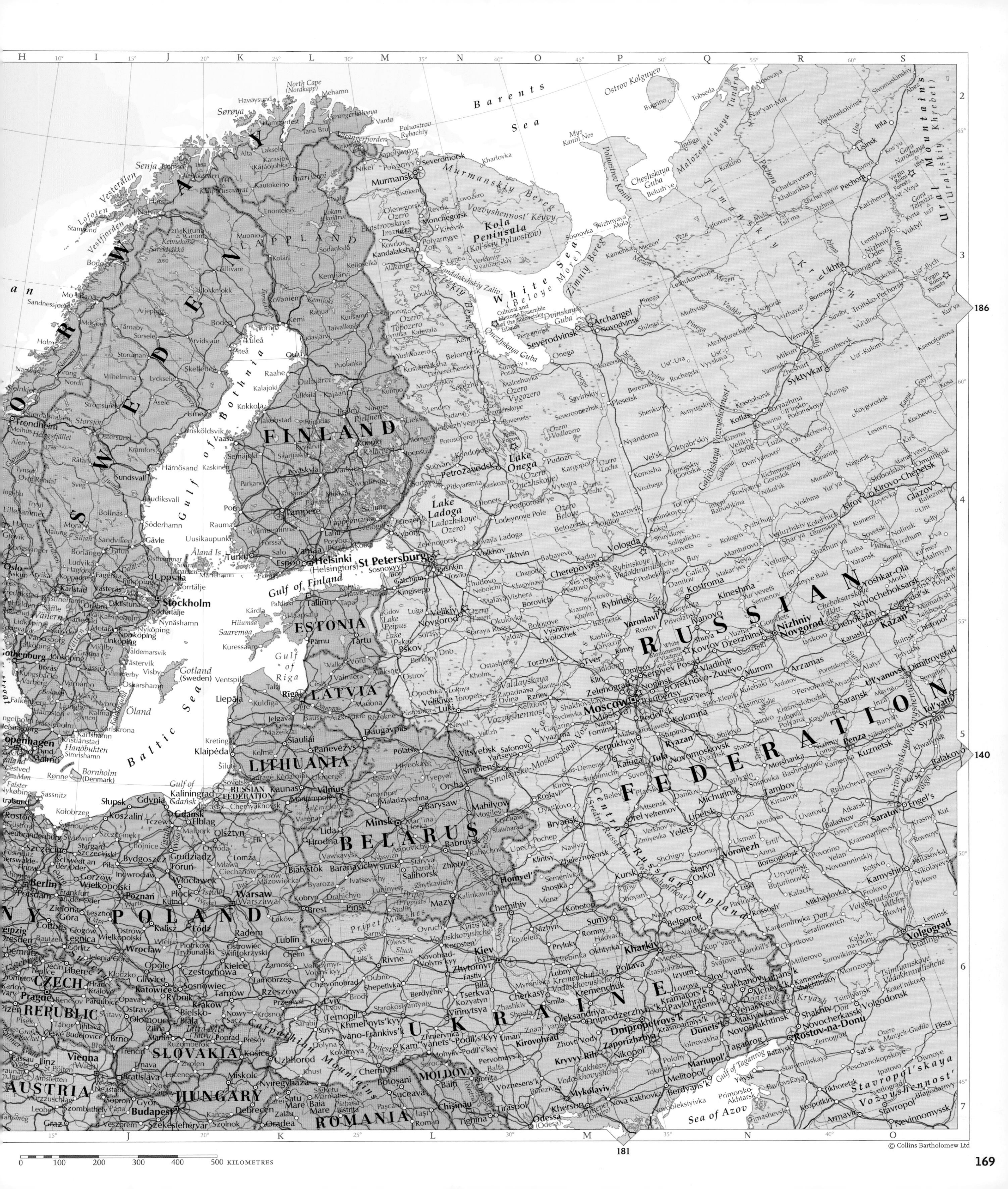

Barents Sea
White Sea (Beloye More)
Gulf of Bothnia
Gulf of Finland
Gulf of Riga
Baltic Sea
Sea of Azov
Gulf of Taganrog
NORWAY
SWEDEN
FINLAND
LAPPLAND
ESTONIA
LATVIA
LITHUANIA
RUSSIAN FEDERATION
BELARUS
POLAND
CZECH REPUBLIC
SLOVAKIA
AUSTRIA
HUNGARY
ROMANIA
MOLDOVA
UKRAINE
Kola Peninsula (Kol'skiy Poluostrov)
Lake Ladoga (Ladozhskoye Ozero)
Lake Onega (Onezhskoye Ozero)
Lake Peipus
Gotland (Sweden)
Åland Is.
Saaremaa
Hiiumaa
Öland
Bornholm (Denmark)
Carpathian Mountains
Pripet Marshes
Central Russian Upland
Ural Mountains (Ural'skiy Khrebet)
Timanskiy Kryazh
Stavropol'skaya Vozvyshennost'
North Cape (Nordkapp)
Murmansk
Archangel
Severodvinsk
Syktyvkar
Ukhta
Oulu
Helsinki (Helsingfors)
Tampere
Turku
Stockholm
Uppsala
Oslo
Trondheim
Gothenburg
Copenhagen
St Petersburg
Tallinn
Tartu
Riga
Vilnius
Kaunas
Kaliningrad
Minsk
Gdańsk
Warsaw (Warszawa)
Łódź
Kraków
Prague
Vienna (Wien)
Bratislava
Budapest
Berlin
Moscow (Moskva)
Tver
Yaroslavl'
Nizhniy Novgorod
Kazan'
Samara
Saratov
Volgograd
Voronezh
Kursk
Tula
Ryazan'
Penza
Kirov
Vologda
Novgorod
Pskov
Smolensk
Kiev (Kyiv)
Kharkiv
Dnipropetrovs'k
Zaporizhzhya
Donets'k
Luhans'k
Rostov-na-Donu
Odessa (Odesa)
Chişinău
L'viv
Mariupol'
Kryvyy Rih
Mykolayiv
Kherson
Stavropol'
© Collins Bartholomew Ltd
0 100 200 300 400 500 KILOMETRES
186
140
181

Scandinavia and the Baltic States

![Finland flag] **FINLAND** Capital: **Helsinki (Helsingfors)**
Area: **338 145 km²/130 559 miles²**
Population: **5 277 000** Languages: **Finnish, Swedish**
Religions: **Protestant, Greek Orthodox** Currency: **Euro**

Visitors to Finland appreciate the clean, unspoilt landscape. The country is mainly flat, a land of lakes and coniferous forest with thousands of tiny islands in the south. Nearly a third of the country is north of the Arctic Circle, where winters are long and cold. The main gateway into Finland is Helsinki. An efficient transport infrastructure, typical of Scandinavia, means that it is easy to travel around. With thick snow on the ground from November to May it is not surprising that snow-based activity holidays are well catered for. In the summer, bird watching, fishing and hunting are all popular whilst there is also a wide range of art and music festivals to enjoy.

![Iceland flag] **ICELAND** Capital: **Reykjavík**
Area: **102 820 km²/39 699 miles²**
Population: **301 000** Languages: **Icelandic**
Religions: **Protestant** Currency: **Icelandic króna**

Iceland is one of the most active volcanic regions in the world, with tourism growing as international visitors are drawn to the inspiring splendour of its scenery. Warmed by the Gulf Stream, the climate is more temperate than its northerly latitude would suggest. The city of Reykjavik, home to two-thirds of the population, is a favourite for short city break holidays. This means the interior is largely unspoilt wilderness. There are some unique experiences available to the traveller. Visits to the 'Golden Circle' attractions of the geysers, the majestic Gullfoss waterfall and historic parliament site of Þingvellir, feature on almost all tourist itineraries. Also popular with both organised tours and independent travellers are the colourful rhyolite mountains, lava fields of Landmannalaugar and Europe's largest glacier, Vatnajökull.

![Norway flag] **NORWAY** Capital: **Oslo**
Area: **323 878 km²/125 050 miles²**
Population: **4 698 000** Languages: **Norwegian**
Religions: **Protestant, Roman Catholic**
Currency: **Norwegian krone**

The landscape of fjords, mountains and glaciers is Norway's greatest attraction. The country is famous for its indented coastline and in the summer there are daily cruise ship departures to experience the magic of the fjords. Cruises can last anything from a few hours to a few weeks. Norway also specialises in providing relaxing retreats to mountain and lakeside cabins for fishing, hiking and wildlife. Skiing is a national sport and the ski season often lasts for six months. There are extensive facilities for telemark and alpine skiing, and many other winter sports. Popular resorts include Lillehammer, Hemsedal, Kvitfjell, Hemsedal, Trysil, Jotunheimen, Geilo and Høvringen-Rodane.

![Sweden flag] **SWEDEN** Capital: **Stockholm**
Area: **449 964 km²/173 732 miles²**
Population: **9 119 000** Languages: **Swedish**
Religions: **Protestant, Roman Catholic**
Currency: **Swedish krona**

Sweden is often described as being divided into two distinct regions. South of Stockholm are the woods, farmland, lakes and archipelagos of Götaland and southern Svealand. North of Stockholm is a more sparsely populated and mountainous wilderness, a land of forests, lakes, rivers, marshes and high mountains, making it popular hiking country. The major cities of the capital Stockholm, maritime Gothenburg (Göteborg), and multi-cultural Malmö, offer a wide variety of city breaks. Winter sports resorts provide a wide range of activities. Riksgränsen is the world's northernmost ski resort, 200 km (124 miles) north of the Arctic circle, where there is summer skiing in the light of the midnight sun in late May and June.

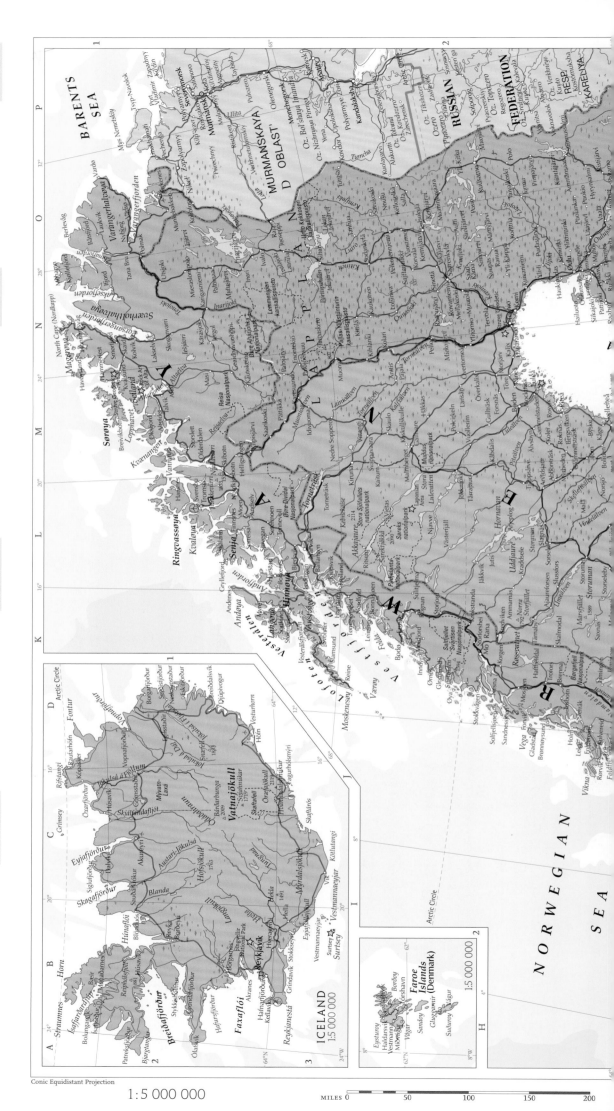

Conic Equidistant Projection

1:5 000 000

MILES 0   50   100   150   200

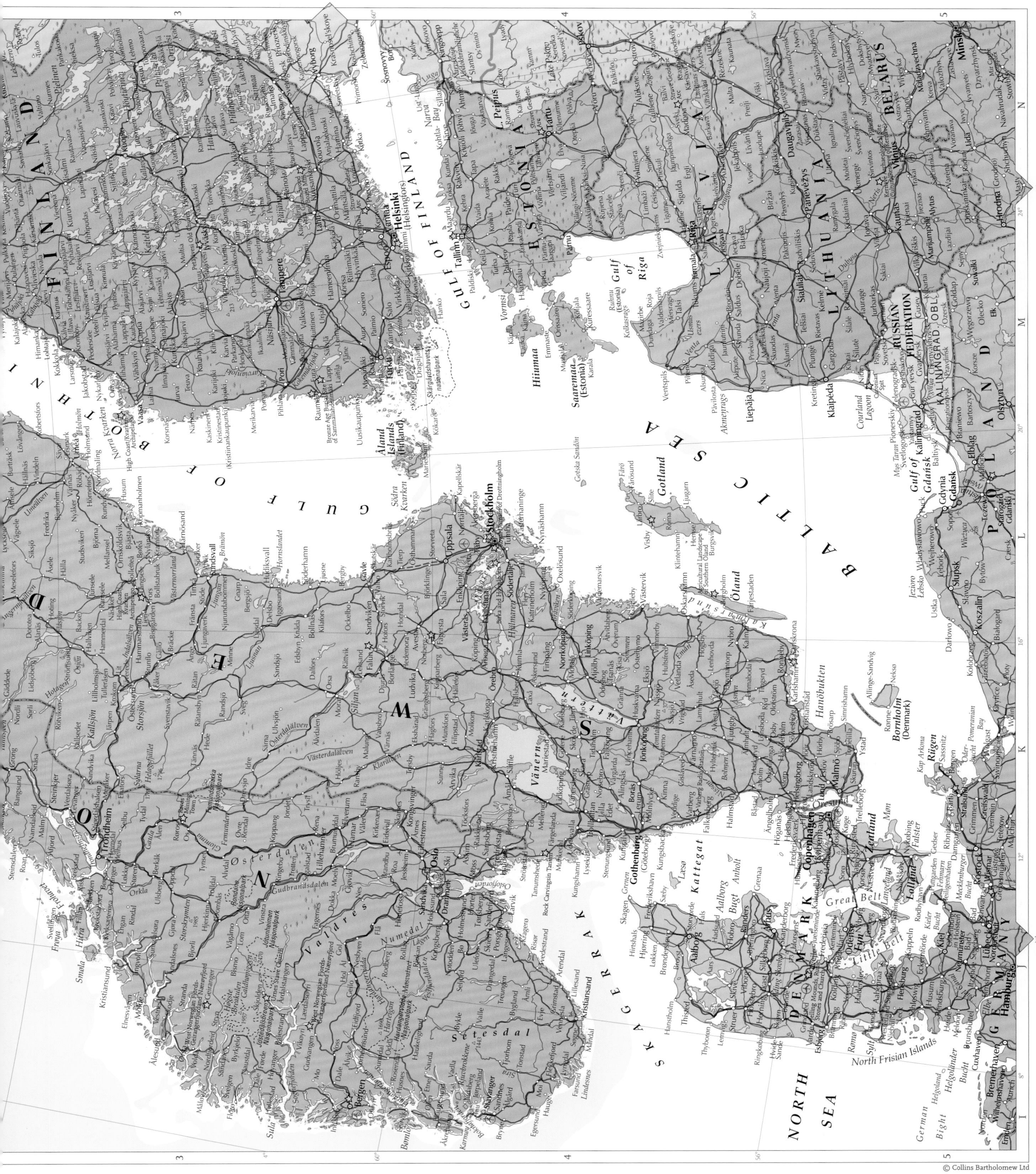

FINLAND

Helsinki (Helsingfors)

GULF OF FINLAND

ESTONIA

Tallinn

Tartu

Gulf of Riga

Hiiumaa

Saaremaa (Estonia)

LATVIA

Rīga

Daugavpils

LITHUANIA

Vilnius

Kaunas

Klaipėda

BELARUS

Minsk

RUSSIAN FEDERATION

KALININGRAD OBL.

Kaliningrad

GULF OF BOTHNIA

Vaasa

Tampere

Turku

Åland Islands (Finland)

Mariehamn

Södra Kvarken

Norra Kvarken

Umeå

SWEDEN

Sundsvall

Gävle

Uppsala

Stockholm

Södertälje

Örebro

Norrköping

Linköping

Jönköping

Gotland

Visby

BALTIC SEA

Vänern

Vättern

Öland

Bornholm (Denmark)

Gdynia

Gdańsk

POLAND

Koszalin

Słupsk

Gulf of Gdańsk

Elbląg

Trondheim

NORWAY

Oslo

Drammen

Valdres

Setesdal

Gudbrandsdalen

Østerdalen

Bergen

Stavanger

Kristiansand

SKAGERRAK

Gothenburg (Göteborg)

Malmö

Copenhagen

Helsingborg

DENMARK

Kattegat

Aalborg

Odense

Great Belt

Little Belt

Zealand

Fyn

Funen

Lolland

Falster

Rügen

Rostock

Lübeck

Hamburg

GERMANY

Bremerhaven

Wilhelmshaven

Cuxhaven

NORTH SEA

North Frisian Islands

German Bight

Helgoland

177

176

171

0 50 100 150 200 250 300 350 KILOMETRES

© Collins Bartholomew Ltd

England and Wales

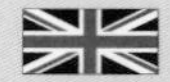

 UNITED KINGDOM Capital: **London**
Area: **243 609 km²/94 058 miles²**
Population: **60 769 000** Languages: **English, Welsh, Gaelic**
Religions: **Protestant, Roman Catholic, Muslim**
Currency: **Pound sterling**

ENGLAND

An image of the English countryside with patchwork fields, cottages and market towns, creates a conception of idealised rusticity of great appeal to many international visitors. This gentle landscape, together with the wilder areas of moor and mountain, gives England some varied scenery and provides a diversity of holiday experiences for the visitor.

The warm climate and magnificent coastline make the south-western counties of Cornwall and Devon one of the most visited regions. In contrast are the scenic uplands of the Pennines, from the Peak District in Derbyshire through the Yorkshire Dales to the Scottish border. West of the Pennines is the Lake District which remains a prime destination with both domestic and international visitors. It is a landscape with a rich literary and artistic heritage, marketed as Beatrix Potter and Wordsworth country and hence prone to over-crowding at popular sites, yet still retaining a peace and dignity in keeping with the stunning landscape of lakes and fells.

From the prehistoric site of Stonehenge to the grandeur of royal palaces, England also has a rich and varied heritage spanning many thousands of years. Stately homes and landscaped grounds such as Blenheim and Chatsworth are of great interest to international visitors, as are the 'dreaming spires' of Oxford and the architectural masterpieces of many churches and cathedrals.

Heathrow is the busiest airport in the world and London is a top world city destination, attracting over 15 million visitors a year. National museums and galleries such as the British Museum and National Gallery feature high on the list of most-visited attractions. Over hundreds of years the British royal family has also left its mark on the heritage of the capital and there are palaces, memorials and pageantry, all of appeal to visitors.

Maritime Greenwich, home to the Prime Meridian, is a reminder of England's strong nautical heritage. The National Maritime Museum is one of the greatest maritime museums in the world. The coastline of England boasts not only designated heritage coasts of natural beauty but also important archaeological sites.

WALES

A history of struggles against invasion has left a strong Welsh identity and a rich heritage of fortifications. In the 'land of castles' Beaumaris, Caernarfon and Conwy are the most impressive.

Including the islands of Anglesey and Holyhead, Wales has over 1680 miles (2704 km) of coastline. The diverse shoreline includes traditional seaside towns, the spectacular Pembrokeshire coast, the wide sweep of Cardigan Bay with its clean water and abundant marine life, and the sailing and surfing beaches of the Lleyn peninsula. Inland much of central and north Wales is mountainous, shaped by the last ice age. It is a place for walkers to explore, from the moors of the Brecon Beacons in the south to the rugged mountain ranges of Snowdonia in the north.

174

Conic Equidistant Projection

1 : 2 000 000

MILES 0   20   40   60   80

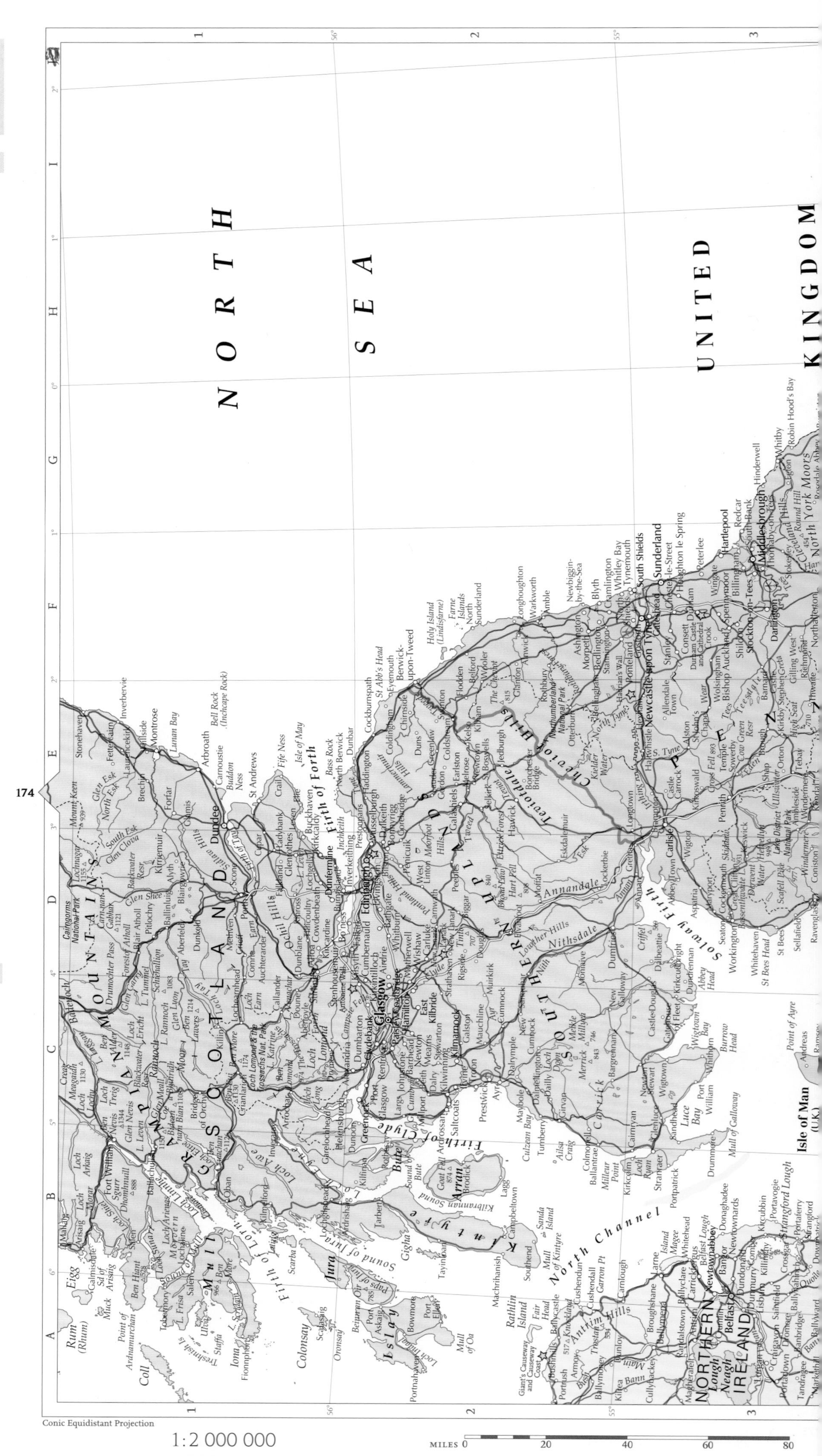

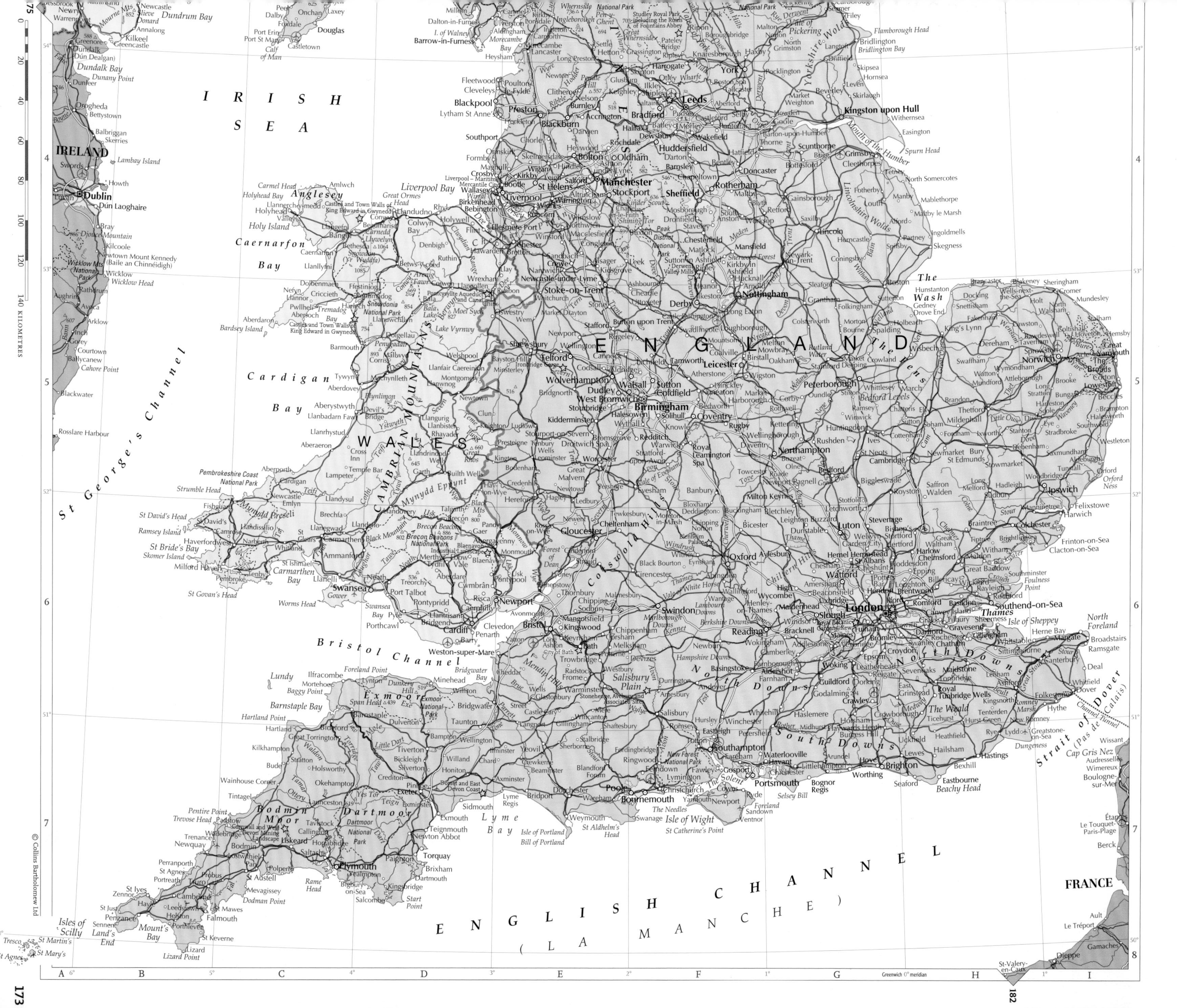

Scotland

SCOTLAND

Edinburgh is a vibrant cultural, shopping and business centre. The city is dominated by the medieval castle, perched high above the attractions of the Royal Mile and the Georgian elegance of the New Town. Edinburgh is home to many of Scotland's national arts and museum collections and its annual festivals are acclaimed worldwide. Glasgow is also one of Europe's great cultural destinations, with award winning museums and galleries, and a fine architectural heritage. Stirling Castle is famous as a focus point of Scottish history whilst many other castles, battlefields and forts remind the visitor of a turbulent past in Scotland's struggle for independence. The prehistoric landscape is equally well represented, with over 150 ancient sites in the western coast glens of Kilmartin, and the best preserved group of Stone Age houses in western Europe at Skara Brae on Orkney.

The western coast is indented with inlets and lochs formed by glaciers thousands of years ago. Oban is the 'gateway to the isles' with ferries to many of the islands whilst further north the island of Skye is accessible by road bridge. The remote outer islands of Shetland, Orkney and the Western Isles are for those looking for a totally different holiday experience. With its rugged crags, peaceful glens and clear blue lochs, the Highlands offer a diverse scenic splendour. Many walkers and climbers return again and again to the areas of Ben Nevis, Glen Coe, Cairn Gorm and the Cuillin Hills on Skye. In contrast is the soft, rolling countryside of the Scottish Borders.

Guided tours of many of the country's whisky distilleries are available, from the distinctive peaty single-malt of Laphhroaig on Islay to the world-famous distilleries of Glenfiddich and Glenlivet on the 112 km (70 mile) sign-posted Malt Whisky Trail in Speyside. For many, golf is a major attraction with over 550 courses in the country, including the prestigious championship courses of St Andrews, Troon and Turnberry.

NORTHERN IRELAND

Northern Ireland is part of the United Kingdom and contributes six of the nine counties of the historic province of Ulster. Although largely isolated to specific areas, the period of 'The Troubles' was a deterrent to many travellers. The 1998 Good Friday Agreement marked the beginning of the end of this turbulent period of Irish history. The rolling hills of the southern counties contrast with the upland areas of the Sperrin and Mourne Mountains. The amazing basalt columns of Giant's Causeway on the north coast is the most famous tourist destination in Ireland and is a World Heritage site.

Ireland

IRELAND Capital: **Dublin (Baile Átha Cliath)**
Area: **70 282 km²/27 136 miles²**
Population: **4 301 000** Languages: **English, Irish**
Religions: **Roman Catholic, Protestant** Currency: **Euro**

Ireland is known as the 'Emerald' Isle because of the abundance of greenery. Great Britain provides most of the visitors to Ireland and they are well served by the east and south coasts ports. Dublin is the main international airport although Shannon on the west coast is important for transatlantic flights. Internal travel is mainly by a road network which has improved substantially in recent years.

The 'Gaeltacht' are areas where the unique Irish culture and language is preserved. They are found along the west coast in Kerry, Galway, Mayo and Donegal with smaller areas in the counties of Cork, Waterford and Meath.

Dublin is the main centre for tourism. The Guinness Storehouse and Dublin Zoo are the two most visited attractions in Ireland. The most breathtaking scenery can be found along the west coast – the Burren, Connemara and the peninsulas of Dingle and Kerry. There are also many historical sites of interest including the World Heritage sites of The Bend of the Boyne and Skellig Michael.

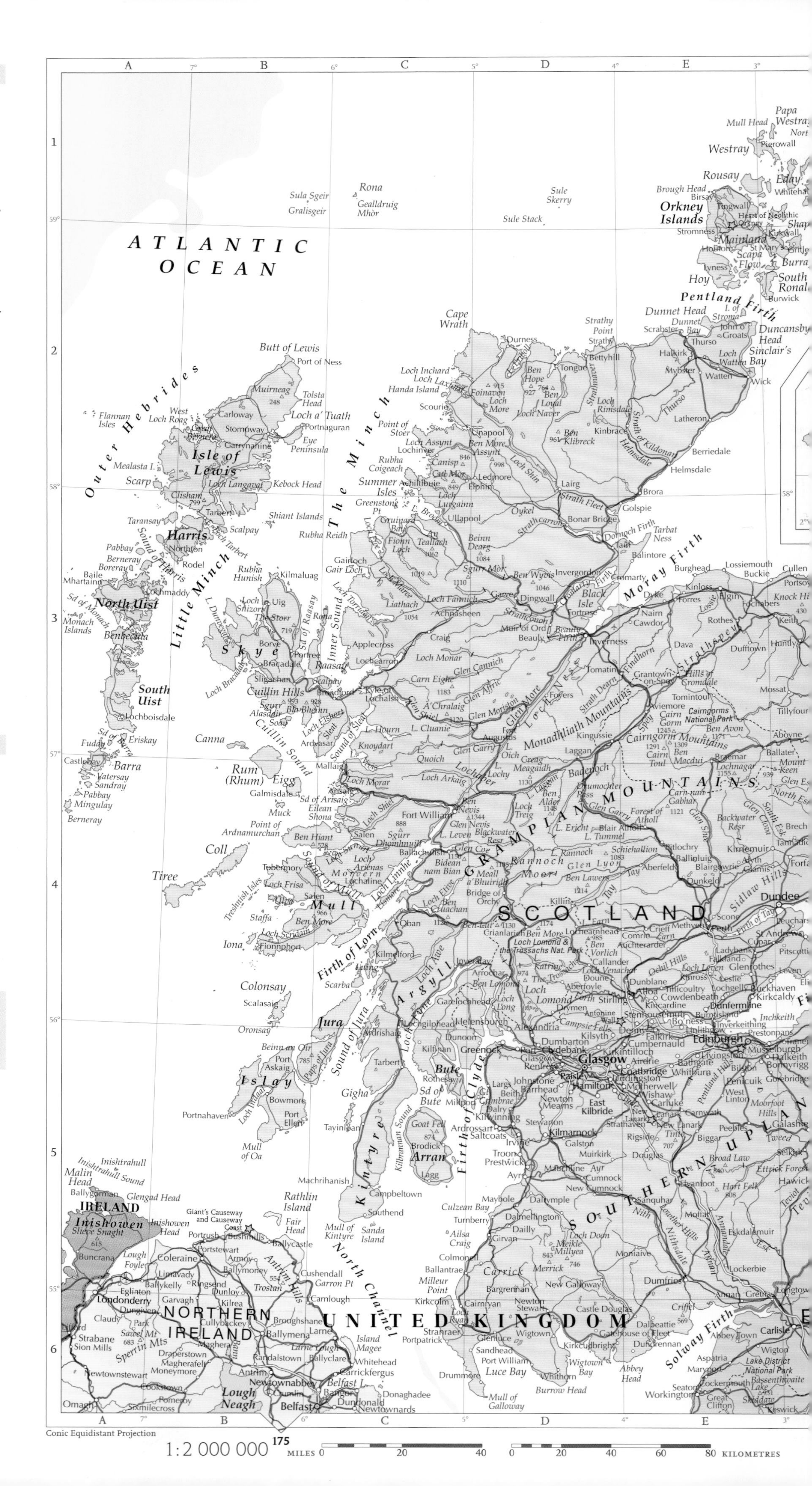

Conic Equidistant Projection

1 : 2 000 000
MILES 0   20   40
0   20   40   60   80 KILOMETRES

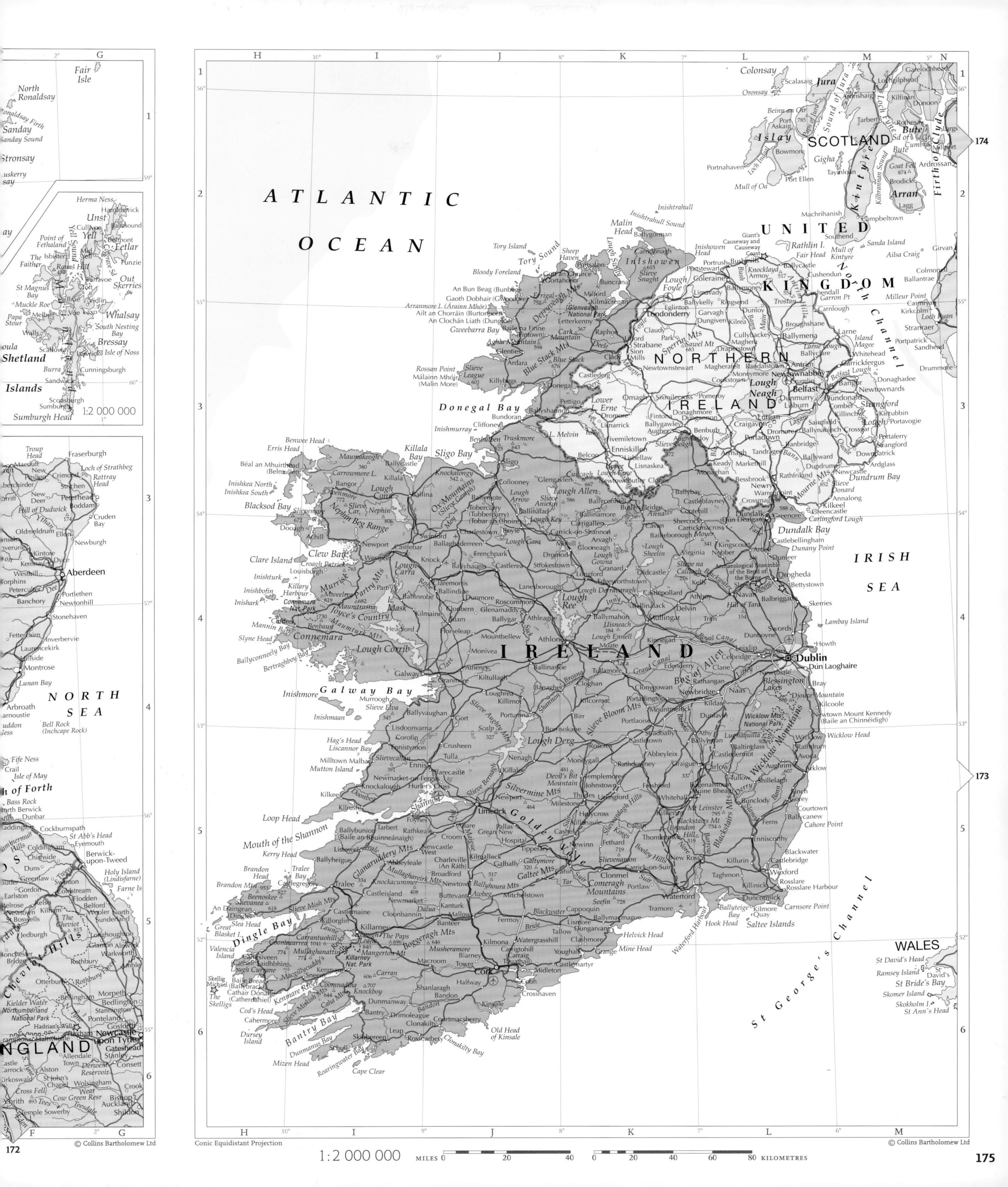
ATLANTIC OCEAN
IRELAND
NORTHERN IRELAND
UNITED KINGDOM
SCOTLAND
WALES
IRISH SEA
NORTH SEA
North Channel
St George's Channel
Shetland Islands
1:2 000 000
Fair Isle
North Ronaldsay
Sanday
Stronsay
Unst
Yell
Fetlar
Whalsay
Bressay
Sumburgh Head
Fraserburgh
Peterhead
Aberdeen
Stonehaven
Montrose
Arbroath
Bell Rock (Inchcape Rock)
Fife Ness
Isle of May
Bass Rock
Dunbar
Berwick-upon-Tweed
Holy Island (Lindisfarne)
Farne Is
Cheviot Hills
The Cheviot
Kielder Water
Northumberland National Park
Hadrian's Wall
Newcastle upon Tyne
Gateshead
ENGLAND
Cow Green Resr
Colonsay
Oronsay
Jura
Islay
Bowmore
Port Ellen
Mull of Oa
Portnahaven
Gigha
Kintyre
Campbeltown
Mull of Kintyre
Sanda Island
Ailsa Craig
Arran
Lagg
Goat Fell 874
Brodick
Ardrossan
Bute
Firth of Clyde
Dunoon
Girvan
Stranraer
Portpatrick
Mull of Galloway
Milleur Point
Inishtrahull
Malin Head
Inishowen
Slieve Snaght 615
Carndonagh
Buncrana
Lough Swilly
Lough Foyle
Tory Island
Bloody Foreland
Derryveagh Mts
Errigal 752
Glenveagh National Park
Letterkenny
Gweebarra Bay
Rossan Point
Slieve League 601
Killybegs
Donegal
Blue Stack Mts
Donegal Bay
Ballyshannon
Bundoran
Inishmurray
Londonderry
Limavady
Coleraine
Portrush
Portstewart
Giant's Causeway
Rathlin I.
Fair Head
Ballycastle
Ballymoney
Ballymena
Larne
Island Magee
Whitehead
Carrickfergus
Newtownabbey
Antrim
Belfast
Lough Neagh
Sperrin Mts
Sawel Mt 683
Strabane
Omagh
Cookstown
Dungannon
Lisburn
Bangor
Newtownards
Strangford Lough
Portaferry
Downpatrick
Ardglass
Dundrum Bay
Newcastle
Mourne Mts
Slieve Donard 852
Kilkeel
Newry
Armagh
Portadown
Craigavon
Banbridge
Enniskillen
Lower Erne
Upper Lough Erne
Lisnaskea
Carlingford Lough
Dundalk
Dundalk Bay
Drogheda
Navan
Hill of Tara
Trim
Skerries
Lambay Island
Swords
Howth
Dublin
Dún Laoghaire
Bray
Blessington Lakes
Djouce Mountain
Wicklow Mts National Park
Wicklow Mountains
Lugnaquilla 925
Wicklow
Wicklow Head
Arklow
Gorey
Courtown
Enniscorthy
Wexford
Rosslare
Rosslare Harbour
Carnsore Point
Saltee Islands
Hook Head
Waterford
Tramore
Dungarvan
Helvick Head
Mine Head
Youghal
Cork
Cobh
Midleton
Kinsale
Old Head of Kinsale
Clonakilty
Bandon
Skibbereen
Cape Clear
Mizen Head
Bantry
Bantry Bay
Dursey Island
Kenmare
Killarney
Killarney Nat. Park
Carrantuohill 1041
Macgillycuddy's Reeks
Mangerton Mt 840
The Paps 690
Boggeragh Mts
Valencia Island
The Skelligs
Dingle Bay
Dingle
Brandon Mt 953
Tralee
Tralee Bay
Kerry Head
Listowel
Mouth of the Shannon
Loop Head
Kilrush
Shannon
Limerick
Ennis
Clare
Mutton Island
Lahinch
Ennistymon
Lisdoonvarna
Hag's Head
Galway Bay
Inishmore
Inishmaan
Galway
Lough Corrib
Lough Mask
Connemara
Connemara Nat. Park
Twelve Bens
Maumturk Mts
Clifden
Slyne Head
Inishbofin
Inishturk
Clare Island
Clew Bay
Westport
Croagh Patrick 765
Achill
Blacksod Bay
Nephin Beg Range
Nephin 806
Ballina
Killala Bay
Sligo
Sligo Bay
Ox Mountains
Lough Allen
Carrick-on-Shannon
Roscommon
Castlerea
Boyle
Longford
Lough Ree
Athlone
Mullingar
Lough Ennell
Tullamore
Birr
Slieve Bloom Mts
Portlaoise
Kildare
Naas
Newbridge
Athy
Carlow
Kilkenny
Mt Leinster 795
Blackstairs Mts
New Ross
Clonmel
Cahir
Galtee Mts
Galtymore 920
Mitchelstown
Tipperary
Thurles
Roscrea
Nenagh
Lough Derg
Slieve Aughty Mts
Silvermine Mts
Mallow
Fermoy
Lismore
Conic Equidistant Projection
MILES
KILOMETRES
174
173
© Collins Bartholomew Ltd

North Central Europe

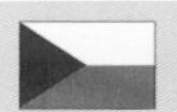

CZECH REPUBLIC
Capital: **Prague (Praha)**
Area: **78 864 km²/30 450 miles²**
Population: **10 186 000** Languages: **Czech, Moravian, Slovakian** Religions: **Roman Catholic, Protestant**
Currency: **Czech koruna**

The historic and beautiful city of Prague is the country's main tourist destination, luring visitors with a combination of ancient buildings, culture and nightlife. Prague Castle, including the landmark St Vitus Cathedral, is the largest medieval castle in Europe. Outside the capital there are a wealth of other castles, monuments and medieval towns to explore. The West Bohemian Spa Triangle reflects a long and prestigious history of spa treatment in the area. Karlovy Vary has been a spa resort since the Middle Ages and boasts numerous mineral water springs. Mariánské Lázně and Františkovy Lázně are more recent but both present well-preserved spa buildings in different styles. A dynamic arts and music scene is evident throughout the country with strong traditions in opera, classical music and puppetry.

DENMARK
Capital: **Copenhagen (København)**
Area: **43 075 km²/16 631 miles²**
Population: **5 442 000** Languages: **Danish** Religions: **Protestant**
Currency: **Danish krone**

With diverse cultural influences from the rest of Scandinavia and continental Europe, Denmark has evolved into a cosmopolitan nation. It has over 400 islands, some of which are linked by bridge to the mainland and others which can be explored by ferry. Most of Denmark is low and flat with a landscape dominated by small farms. An extensive network of clearly marked cycle routes makes the countryside a popular cycling holiday destination. Theme parks are another attraction for families and Tivoli Gardens in Copenhagen, with its rollercoaster rides and performing arts, is the most visited amusement park in Scandinavia. The largest tourist attraction outside Copenhagen is the world-famous Legoland at Billund.

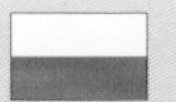

POLAND
Capital: **Warsaw (Warszawa)**
Area: **312 683 km²/120 728 miles²**
Population: **38 082 000** Languages: **Polish, German** Religions: **Roman Catholic, Polish Orthodox** Currency: **Złoty**

The number of visitors to Poland has increased since it joined the European Union in 2004, although in common with other Eastern European countries it has since suffered from an unfavourable exchange rate. The rocky peaks and valleys of the Tatry (Tatra) mountains, on the southern border, are considered to be the most spectacular scenery in the country. Most visitors stay in Zakopane, the 'winter capital of Poland'. In the north, the Mazury lake district and the primeval forest of Białowieża draw in visitors during the summer. Historic sites range from the Old Towns of Wrocław, Kraków and Toruń to the haunting atmosphere of Auschwitz-Birkenau, the largest and most notorious Nazi concentration camp and site of the mass extermination of over 1 million Jews between 1942 and 1944.

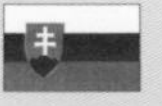

SLOVAKIA
Capital: **Bratislava**
Area: **49 035 km²/18 933 miles²**
Population: **5 390 000** Languages: **Slovakian, Hungarian, Czech** Religions: **Roman Catholic, Protestant, Orthodox**
Currency: **Slovakian koruna**

The hiking trails and ski resorts of the Tatry (Tatra) mountains have long been a popular destination but generally tourism to Slovakia has not been as pronounced as in other central European countries. Bratislava is the cultural hub of the country. It has a compact centre and the cobblestone streets of the Old Town are mostly pedestrianised so it is a pleasant place to explore. The old medieval mining centre of Banská Štiavnica is a World Heritage site. Elsewhere, Slovakia has over 600 castles, château and mansion houses, the best known of which are the castles of Bojnice and Spišský Hrad. Slovakia's karst areas have some impressive cave systems, many of which are open to visitors.

World Heritage Sites numbered on the map:
CZECH REPUBLIC
1. Kutná Hora: Historical Town Centre with the Church of St Barbara and the Cathedral of Our Lady at Sedlec (G5)

POLAND
2. Auschwitz Birkenau German Nazi Concentration and Extermination Camp (1940-1945) (I5)

SWITZERLAND
3. La Chaux-de-Fonds / Le Locle, watchmaking town planning (C7)
4. Swiss Tectonic Arena Sardona (D7)

Conic Equidistant Projection

1 : 5 000 000

MILES 0   50   100   150   200

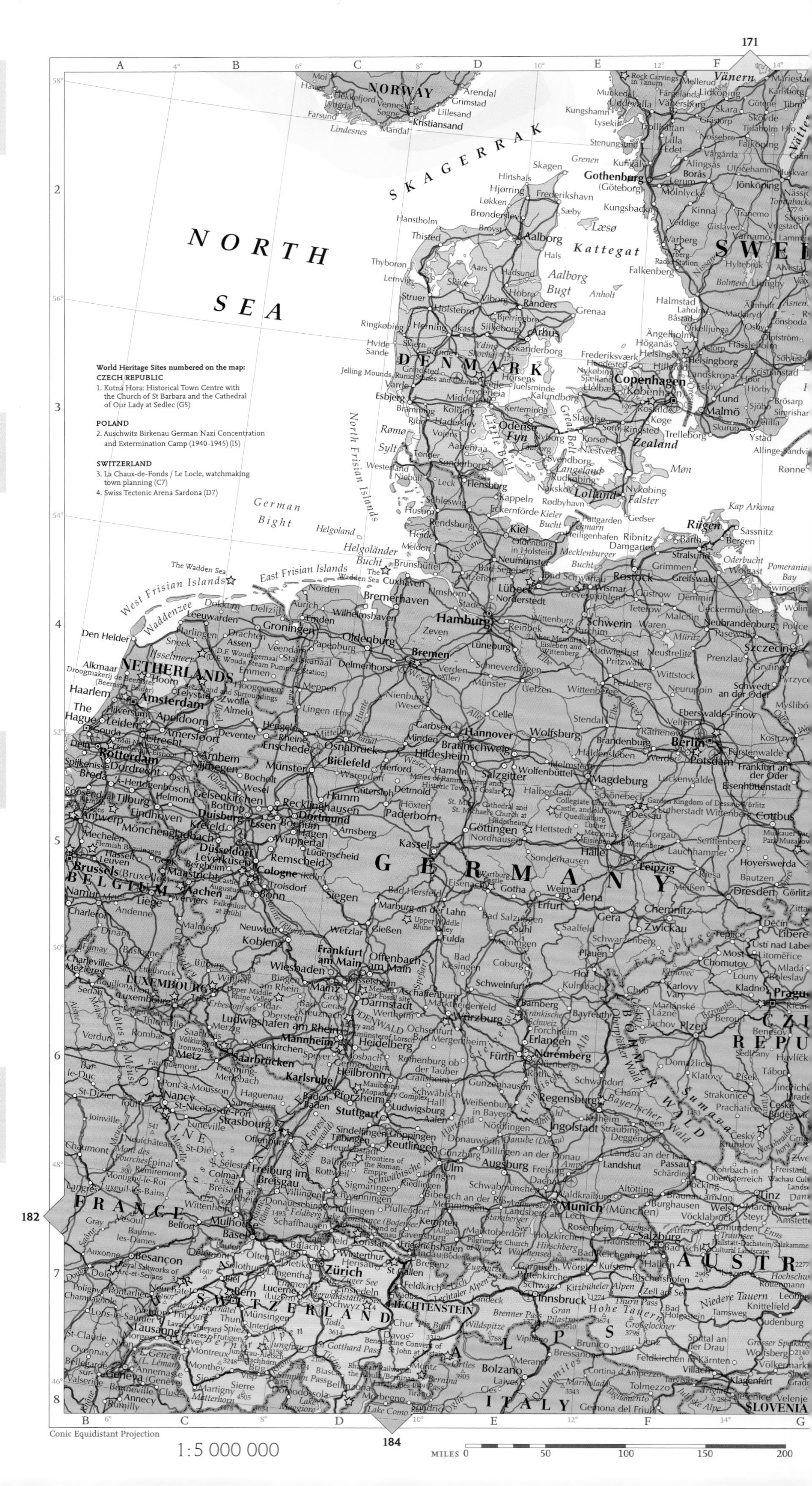

BALTIC SEA

Gulf of Riga

Gulf of Gdańsk

ESTONIA

LATVIA

LITHUANIA

RUSSIAN FEDERATION

PSKOV. OBL.

NOVGOROD. OBL.

TVERSKAYA OBL.

SMOLENSK. OBL.

SMOLENSK. OBL.

BELARUS

POLAND

RUS. FED.

KALININGRAD OBL.

UKRAINE

SLOVAKIA

HUNGARY

ROMANIA

MOLDOVA

Black Sea

Gotland

Öland

Bornholm (Denmark)

Saaremaa (Estonia)

BRYANSK. OBL.

Riga · Jūrmala · Liepāja · Ventspils · Šiauliai · Panevėžys · Klaipėda · Kaunas · Vilnius · Daugavpils · Minsk · Baranavichy · Babruysk · Homyel' · Pinsk · Brest · Warsaw (Warszawa) · Gdańsk · Gdynia · Kaliningrad · Szczecin · Bydgoszcz · Toruń · Poznań · Łódź · Wrocław · Lublin · Katowice · Kraków · Rzeszów · Lviv (L'viv) · Ternopil' · Rivne · Kiev (Kyiv) · Zhytomyr · Vinnytsya · Chernihiv · Ivano-Frankivs'k · Chernivtsi · Uzhhorod · Košice · Miskolc · Debrecen · Budapest · Odessa · Chisinau · Tiraspol · Vienna (Wien) · Bratislava · Brno

© Collins Bartholomew Ltd

0 50 100 150 200 250 300 350 KILOMETRES

Belgium, Netherlands and North Germany

BELGIUM Capital: Brussels (Bruxelles)
Area: **30 520 km²/11 784 miles²**
Population: **10 457 000** Languages: **Dutch (Flemish),
French (Walloon), German** Religions: **Roman Catholic,
Protestant** Currency: **Euro**

Belgium is famous not only for the children's characters Tin Tin
and the Smurfs but also for its chocolate and distinctive beers.
Six of the world's seven authentic Trappist beers are brewed in
Belgium. Festivals and parades play a large part in Belgian
culture. The Carnival of Binche dates back to the fourteenth
century and is held in the days before Ash Wednesday.

GERMANY Capital: Berlin
Area: **357 022 km²/137 847 miles²**
Population: **82 599 000** Languages: **German, Turkish**
Religions: **Protestant, Roman Catholic** Currency: **Euro**

Since 1990 Germany has presented a unified face to the visitor.
The extensive motorway (Autobahn) system and network of
high-speed trains means that it an easy and efficient country to
travel around in. Germany is a world leader in engineering,
science and financial services, sitting centre stage in the
globalised economy. Consequently many international trade
fairs are held in the major German cities of Berlin, Frankfurt and
Hannover, bringing publicity and visitors to these areas. The
cultural mix and reputation for tolerance, coupled with a unique
history, means that Berlin in particular has grown as a magnet
for visitors of all ages. Famous landmarks are the Reichstag
building, Brandenburg Gate and the remains of the Berlin Wall.

More traditional aspects of tourism in Germany have centred on
the Black Forest, scenic cruises on the river Rhine and the fairy-
tale castles of the Bavarian Alps. Most famous is the nineteenth
century Neuschwanstein Castle which was Walt Disney's
inspiration for Sleeping Beauty's castle at Disneyland. Germany's
most famous tourist route is the 350 km (217 mile) Romantic
Road, passing small historic towns and varied landscapes on its
way from Würzburg in the north to the Alps in the south. It gets
crowded in summer so is best off-season.

In Bavaria the Oberammergau Passion Play is held every ten
years and has been performed by villagers since 1634 as a
celebration of their faith. In contrast the annual Oktoberfest
festival held in Munich is a celebration of Bavarian beer and
cuisine, and is heralded as the world's largest fair.

LUXEMBOURG Capital: Luxembourg
Area: **2 586 km²/998 miles²** Population: **467 000**
Languages: **Letzeburgish, German, French**
Religions: **Roman Catholic** Currency: **Euro**

Measuring just 82 km (51 miles) by 57 km (35 miles),
Luxembourg is one of the smallest countries in the world. The
north, the 'Oesling', is dominated by the Ardennes hills while the
more densely populated south, the 'Gutland', has more diverse
landscapes of plateaus, thick forests and river valleys.

NETHERLANDS Capital: Amsterdam/The Hague
Area: **41 526 km²/16 033 miles²** Population: **16 419 000**
Languages: **Dutch, Frisian** Religions: **Roman Catholic,
Protestant, Sunni Muslim** Currency: **Euro**

Canals, windmills, flowers, clogs and the national dress are all
iconic images of the Netherlands. It is one of the most low-lying
countries in the world: half of the area is less than 1m above sea
level. Amsterdam is the capital with a rich culture and history,
well known for its many canals, historic buildings, red light
district and cannabis cafés. It also has popular attractions
relating to Van Gogh, Rembrandt and Anne Frank. Rotterdam is
the largest port in Europe stretching for a distance of 40 km
(25 miles) along the River Meuse (Maas). The famous, traditional
costume is still worn by residents of Volendam on the
IJsselmeer.

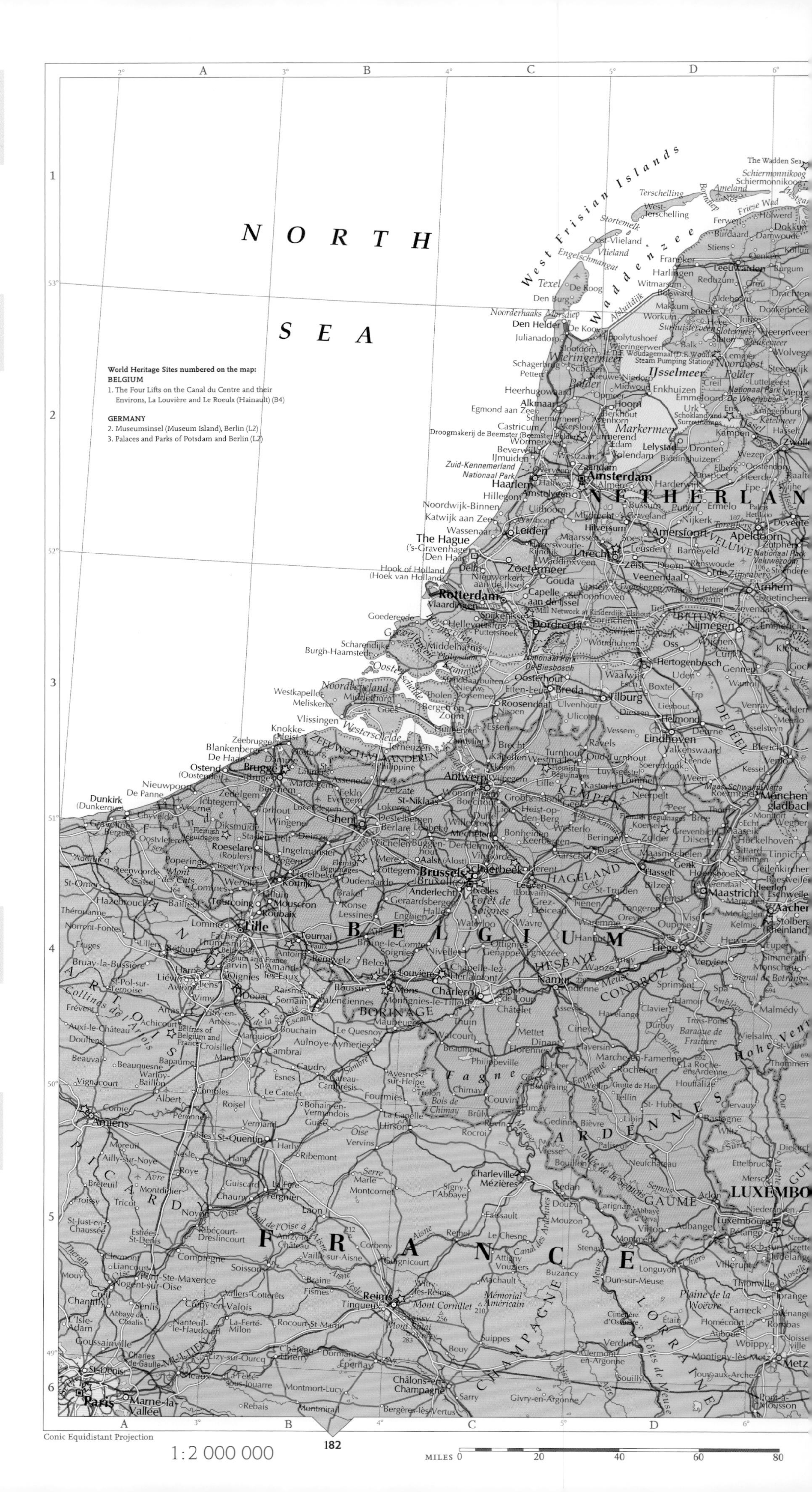

World Heritage Sites numbered on the map:
BELGIUM
1. The Four Lifts on the Canal du Centre and their
   Environs, La Louvière and Le Roeulx (Hainault) (B4)

GERMANY
2. Museumsinsel (Museum Island), Berlin (L2)
3. Palaces and Parks of Potsdam and Berlin (L2)

Conic Equidistant Projection

1:2 000 000

MILES 0   20   40   60   80

182

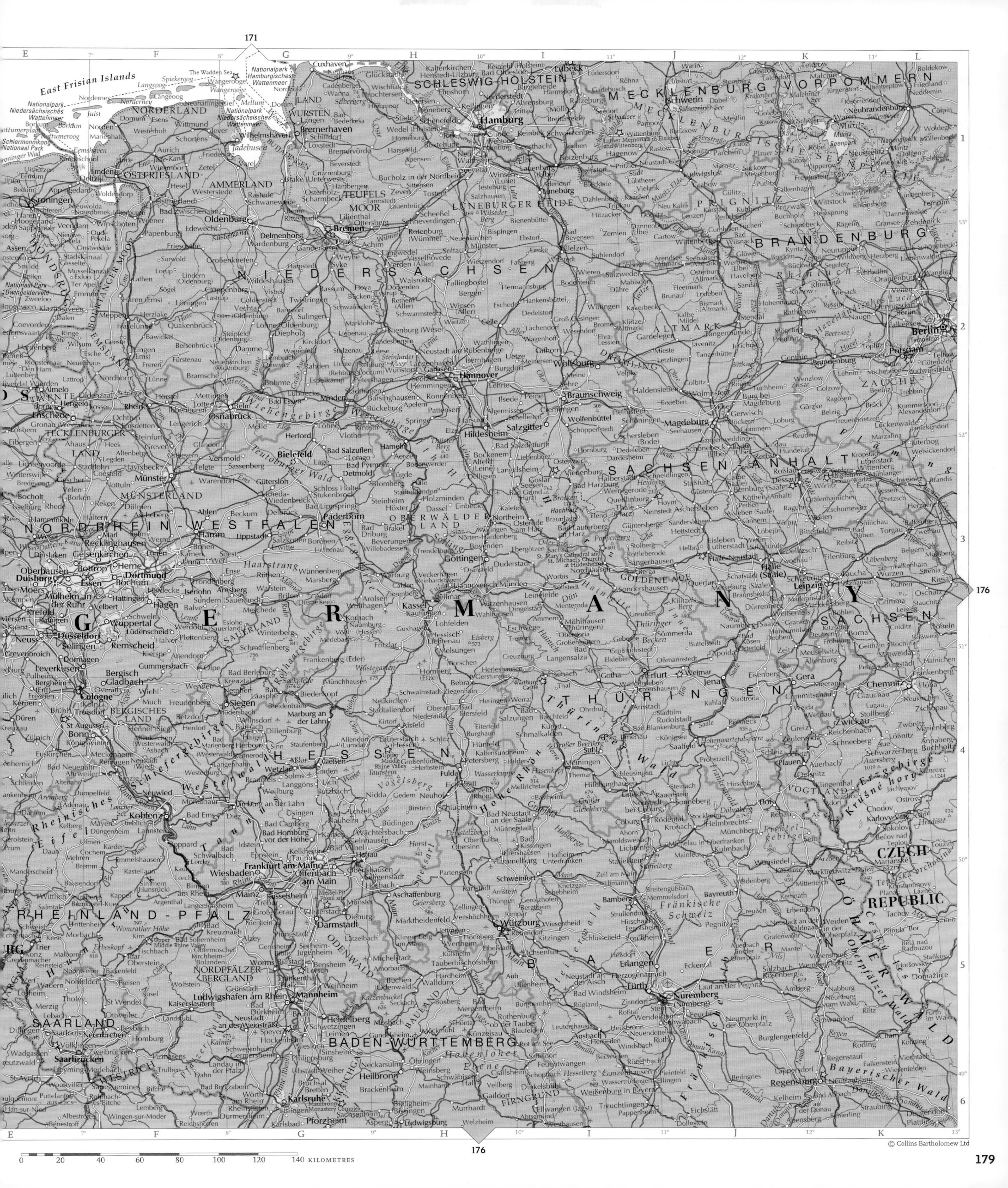
171
E F G H I J K L
East Frisian Islands
NORDERLAND
OSTFRIESLAND
AMMERLAND
LAND WURSTEN
TEUFELS MOOR
SCHLESWIG-HOLSTEIN
MECKLENBURG-VORPOMMERN
PRIGNITZ
LÜNEBURGER HEIDE
BRANDENBURG
NIEDERSACHSEN
ALTMARK
EMSLAND
Hamburg
Bremen
Bremerhaven
Oldenburg
Lübeck
Schwerin
Berlin
Potsdam
Hannover
Braunschweig
Magdeburg
Bielefeld
Münster
Osnabrück
Hildesheim
Salzgitter
Wolfsburg
TECKLENBURGER LAND
MÜNSTERLAND
NORDRHEIN-WESTFALEN
SACHSEN-ANHALT
ZAUCHE
Hamm
Dortmund
Essen
Duisburg
Düsseldorf
Cologne
Bonn
Kassel
Göttingen
Halle (Saale)
Leipzig
GOLDENE AUE
SAUERLAND
BERGISCHES LAND
G E R M A N Y
SACHSEN
THÜRINGEN
HESSEN
Erfurt
Weimar
Jena
Gera
Chemnitz
Zwickau
Plauen
Wiesbaden
Frankfurt am Main
Mainz
Darmstadt
Koblenz
RHEINLAND-PFALZ
SAARLAND
Saarbrücken
Mannheim
Heidelberg
Karlsruhe
Heilbronn
BADEN-WÜRTTEMBERG
Würzburg
Bamberg
Bayreuth
Nuremberg (Nürnberg)
Erlangen
Fürth
Regensburg
BAYERN
Fränkische Schweiz
Bayerischer Wald
BÖHMER WALD
CZECH REPUBLIC
VOGTLAND
Erzgebirge
Krušné hory
Thüringer Wald
Harz
Teutoburger Wald
Westerwald
Taunus
Eifel
Hunsrück
Spessart
Odenwald
Rhön
176
1 2 3 4 5 6
E F G H I J K
176
0 20 40 60 80 100 120 140 KILOMETRES

Southern Europe and the Mediterranean

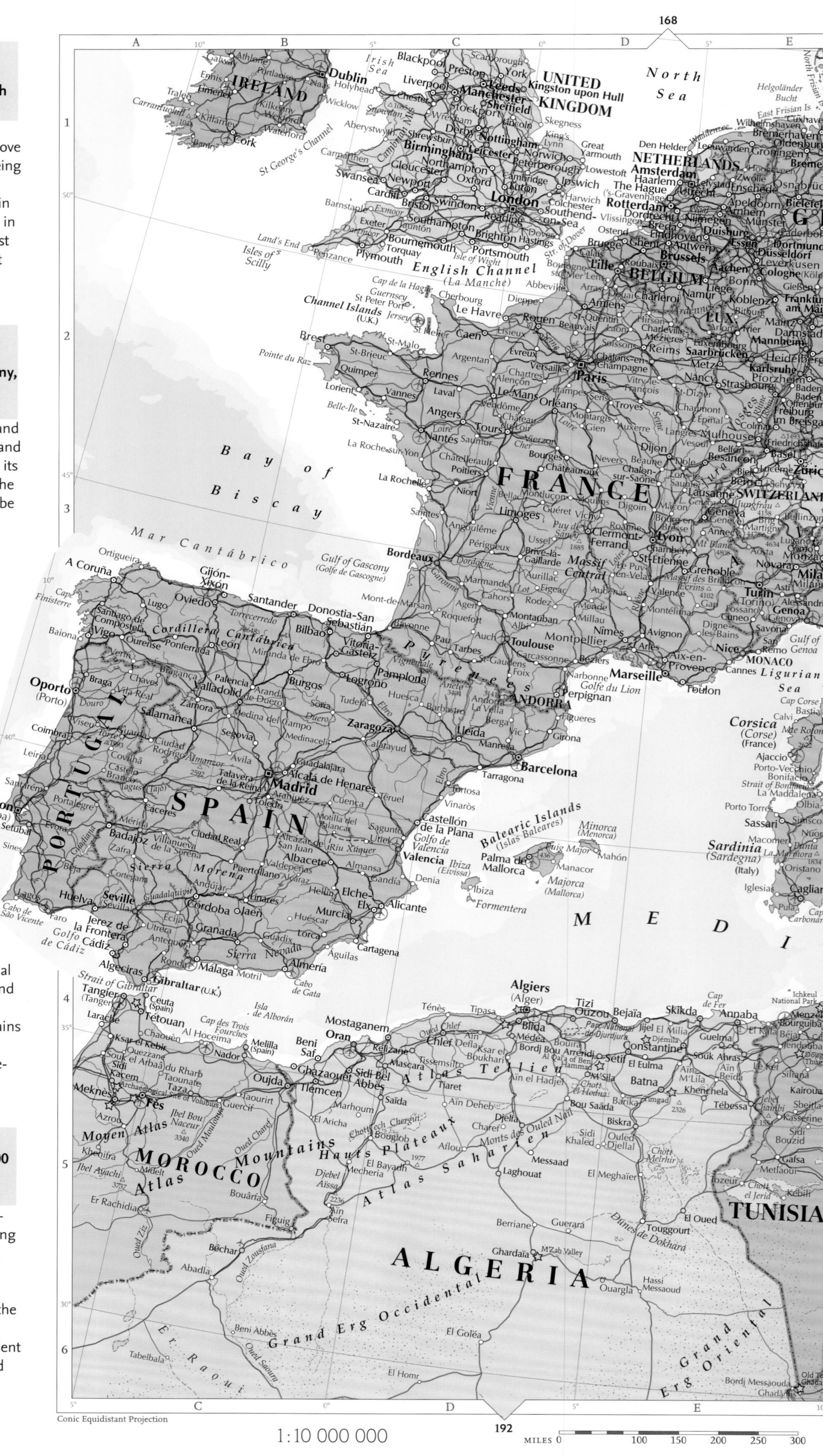

AUSTRIA Capital: Vienna (Wien)
Area: 83 855 km²/32 377 miles²
Population: 8 361 000 Languages: German, Croatian, Turkish
Religions: Roman Catholic, Protestant Currency: Euro

Towering Alpine peaks, clear blue skies and alpine meadows are images that Austria conjures up. Two thirds of the country are above 500 m (1650 ft) with the lowland areas of the Pannonian Plain being mainly in the east towards Vienna. These areas enjoy warmer summers and less rainfall than the alpine climate of the mountain areas. Many of the most famous composers in history were born in Austria – Haydn, Schubert, Mahler and Strauss Snr & Jnr amongst them. Mozart's birthplace in Salzburg is now a museum that first opened in 1880. Vienna is the most visited destination with its cathedral, 'Heurigen' (wine bars) and music events.

BULGARIA Capital: Sofia (Sofiya)
Area: 110 994 km²/42 855 miles²
Population: 7 639 000 Languages: Bulgarian, Turkish, Romany,
Macedonian Religions: Bulgarian Orthodox,
Sunni Muslim Currency: Lev

Bulgaria is situated in the remote southeast corner of Europe and has historically been a major crossroads between Europe, Asia and Africa. The Black Sea forms the eastern boundary and has seen its popularity as a tourist destination increasing since the end of the Cold War, while north of the Balkan mountain range the Danube forms the northern boundary with Romania. Prehistoric excavations in the centre of Sofia as well as its heritage and nightlife make it one of the prime destinations.

GREECE Capital: Athens (Athina)
Area: 131 957 km²/50 949 miles²
Population: 11 147 000 Languages: Greek
Religions: Greek Orthodox, Sunni Muslim Currency: Euro

Ancient Greece is considered the birthplace of Western civilisation with its origins in the Mycenaean and Minoan civilizations. 80 per cent of the country is mountainous or hilly – the Pindus range runs down the centre of the country while northeastern Greece features the Rhodope range, which is covered with thick, ancient forests. Greece has a huge number of islands, many of which are the peaks of the continuation of the mainland mountains – the Cyclades alone comprise 220 islands. The Dodecanese islands have many Byzantine churches and medieval castles.

HUNGARY Capital: Budapest
Area: 93 030 km²/35 919 miles²
Population: 10 030 000 Languages: Hungarian
Religions: Roman Catholic, Protestant Currency: Forint

Hungary has approximately 1500 thermal springs, about half of which are used for bathing – Lake Hévíz is the largest thermal lake in Europe. The climate is continental, with hot summers and cold winters – temperatures range from 42°C (108°F) to –29°C (–20°F). Most of Hungary's landscape consists of the rolling plains of the Pannonian Basin. To the west, Lake Balaton is a popular tourist destination with its shores becoming an important wine-growing area. Budapest sits on the banks of the Danube and cruises along the river are amongst its many attractions.

SWITZERLAND Capital: Bern
Area: 41 293 km²/15 943 miles² Population: 7 484 000
Languages: German, French, Italian, Romansch
Religions: Roman Catholic, Protestant Currency: Swiss franc

Any number of images are intrinsically linked with Switzerland – its financial institutions, fine cheeses and chocolate, watch making and the iconic peaks of the Eiger and the Matterhorn. However, for such a small nation there is a wide variety of landscapes on offer – the Swiss Alps in the south, the Central Plateau running through to the north of the country and the Jura mountains in the northwest. For connoisseurs of Swiss watches, 'Watch Valley' stretches across the Jura from Schaffhausen to Geneva. The ancient capital of Bern is a beautifully preserved medieval city and World Heritage site where Einstein discovered his theory of relativity.

Conic Equidistant Projection

1:10 000 000

MILES 0   100   150   200   250   300

169

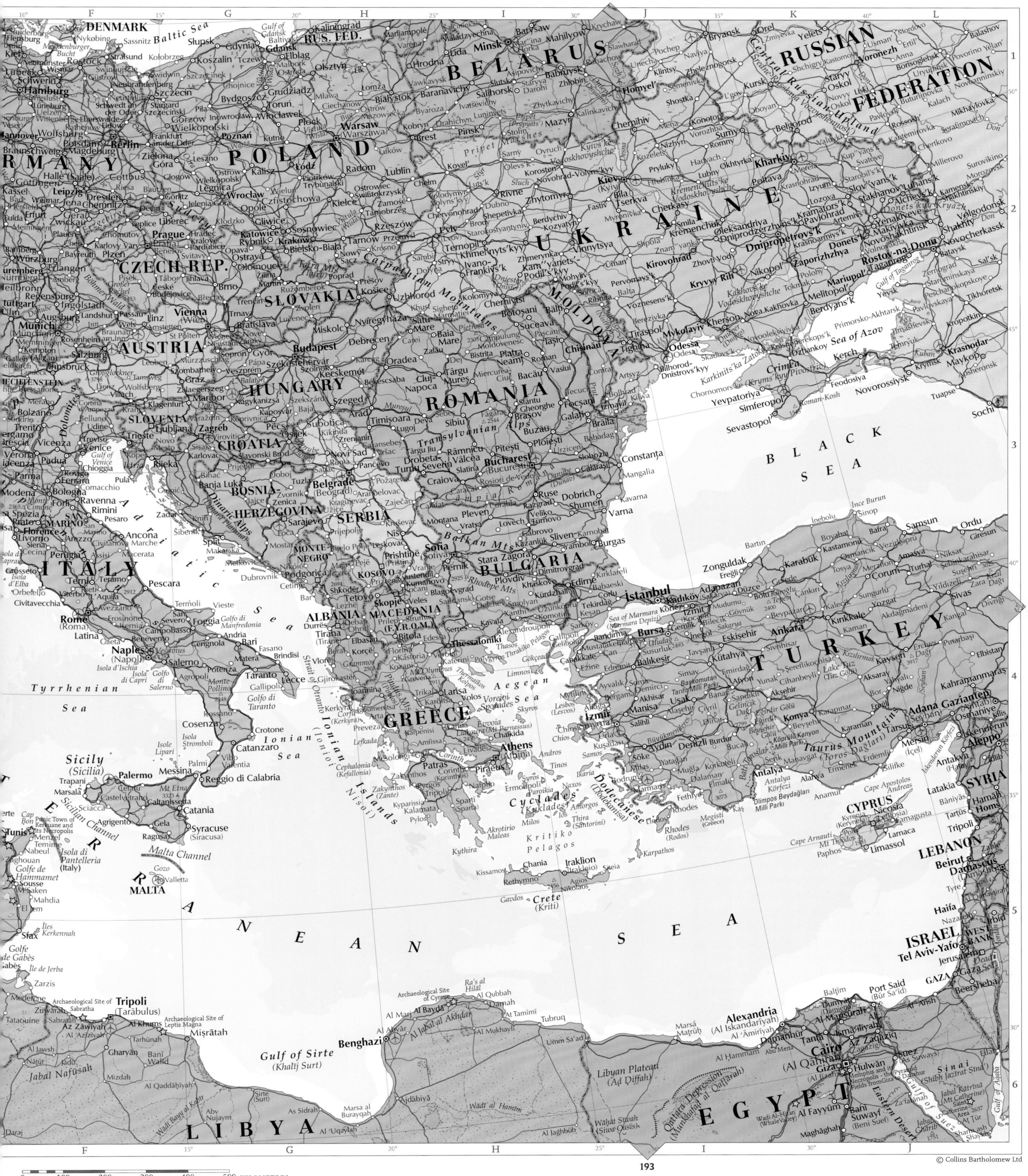
DENMARK
Baltic Sea
RUS. FED.
BELARUS
RUSSIAN FEDERATION
Central Russian Upland
POLAND
GERMANY
CZECH REP.
SLOVAKIA
AUSTRIA
HUNGARY
UKRAINE
MOLDOVA
ROMANIA
LIECHTENSTEIN
SLOVENIA
CROATIA
BOSNIA-HERZEGOVINA
SERBIA
MONTENEGRO
KOSOVO
ALBANIA
MACEDONIA (F.Y.R.O.M.)
BULGARIA
GREECE
TURKEY
CYPRUS
SYRIA
LEBANON
ISRAEL
WEST BANK
GAZA
EGYPT
LIBYA
MALTA
ITALY
SAN MARINO
Carpathian Mountains
Transylvanian Alps
Balkan Mts
Rhodope Mts
Dinaric Alps
Taurus Mountains (Toros Dağları)
Crimea
Sea of Azov
BLACK SEA
Sea of Marmara (Marmara Denizi)
Adriatic Sea
Tyrrhenian Sea
Ionian Sea
Aegean Sea
Cyclades (Kyklades)
Dodecanese (Dodekanisa)
Kritiko Pelagos
Crete (Kriti)
Sicily (Sicilia)
Sicilian Channel
Malta Channel
Gulf of Sirte (Khalīj Surt)
Libyan Plateau (Ad Diffah)
Qattara Depression (Munkhafaḍ al Qaţţārah)
MEDITERRANEAN SEA
Berlin
Warsaw (Warszawa)
Minsk
Kiev (Kyiv)
Prague
Vienna (Wien)
Bratislava
Budapest
Bucharest (Bucureşti)
Chişinău
Ljubljana
Zagreb
Sarajevo
Belgrade (Beograd)
Podgorica
Prishtinë (Priština)
Skopje
Tirana (Tiranë)
Sofia (Sofiya)
Athens (Athina)
Istanbul
Ankara
Nicosia (Lefkosia)
Beirut
Damascus (Dimashq)
Jerusalem
Tel Aviv-Yafo
Cairo (Al Qāhirah)
Alexandria (Al Iskandarīyah)
Tripoli (Ţarābulus)
Benghazi
Rome (Roma)
Naples (Napoli)
Valletta
Odesa (Odesa)
Kharkiv
Dnipropetrovs'k
Zaporizhzhya
Rostov-na-Donu
Krasnodar
Sevastopol'
Simferopol'
Constanţa
Varna
Burgas
Thessaloniki
İzmir
Bursa
Antalya
Adana
Aleppo
Limassol
Port Said (Būr Sa'īd)
Suez (As Suways)
Sinai
© Collins Bartholomew Ltd

136

193

0 100 200 300 400 500 KILOMETRES

France

ANDORRA
Capital: Andorra la Vella
Area: 465 km²/180 miles² Population: 75 000
Languages: Spanish, Catalan, French Religions: Roman Catholic Currency: Euro

Andorra is a mountainous country with an estimated 10.2 million annual visitors. Skiing, hiking and the night life in Europe's highest capital city, Andorra la Vella, are some of the attractions. There are no railways or airports although bus services cover most of the country.

FRANCE
Capital: Paris
Area: 543 965 km²/210 026 miles²
Population: 61 647 000 Languages: French, Arabic Religions: Roman Catholic, Protestant, Sunni Muslim Currency: Euro

France is one of the most visited tourist destinations in the world with many cities of cultural interest, ski resorts, beaches and historic attractions. The north is low-lying and similar to the Belgian landscape. Normandy is famous for the 1944 D-Day landings, the beaches having evocative codenames – Utah, Omaha, Gold, Juno and Sword. In the east, Alsace, Lorraine and Burgundy are well-known for their wines – pinot noirs, chardonnays and the 'Yellow wine' from the Jura. The Rhône and Saône flow southwards through the region while the Loire dominates the central region which is relatively untouched by tourism.

The southern Riviera coast is one of the most visited areas of France. Marseille and Toulon attract most visitors and pleasant villages dot the countryside. The Dordogne in the south-west has quintessentially French cuisine and towns. A replica of the famous caves of Lascaux, now closed to visitors, has exact copies of the prehistoric cave paintings. Languedoc has its own culture and language, Occitan which is now taught in many schools. The mountains of the Pyrenees and Alps are world renowned for skiing and mountaineering.

Spain and Portugal

PORTUGAL
Capital: Lisbon (Lisboa)
Area: 88 940 km²/34 340 miles²
Population: 10 623 000 Languages: Portuguese Religions: Roman Catholic, Protestant Currency: Euro

Portugal sits on the Iberian Peninsula and also includes the archipelagos of the Azores and Madeira. The northern landscape comprises mountains and plateaus whereas the south features mostly rolling plains and is warmer and drier. The Algarve on the south coast is popular for its beaches and also for golf. The capital, Lisbon, sits on the estuary of the Tagus river. Eduardo VII Park is a beautiful square and the Chiado district is noted for its cafes, restaurants, shops and street performers.

SPAIN
Capital: Madrid
Area: 504 782 km²/194 897 miles²
Population: 44 279 000 Languages: Spanish, Castilian, Catalan, Galician, Basque Religions: Roman Catholic Currency: Euro

The excellent climate and beaches are far from being the only attractions of Spain. Madrid is also ideal for family holidays with theme parks, zoos, historic buildings of interest and markets such as El Rastro, as well as its nightlife. The Pyrenees create a natural boundary between Spain and France while the smaller Sierra Nevada range in the south has the highest peak on the peninsula - Mulhacén at a height of 3482m (11 432ft). Many festivals take place throughout the year. The 'running of the bulls' has competitors chased by bulls through a town centre. Injuries both to participants and to the bulls are common.

The Canaries lie off the west coast of Africa, consisting of Gran Canaria, Tenerife and several smaller outliers including Lanzarote and Fuerteventura. The Balearics are off the east coast of Spain and comprise Majorca, Minorca, Ibiza and Formentera. They are renowned for the nightlife although Formentera is relatively untouched by tourism.

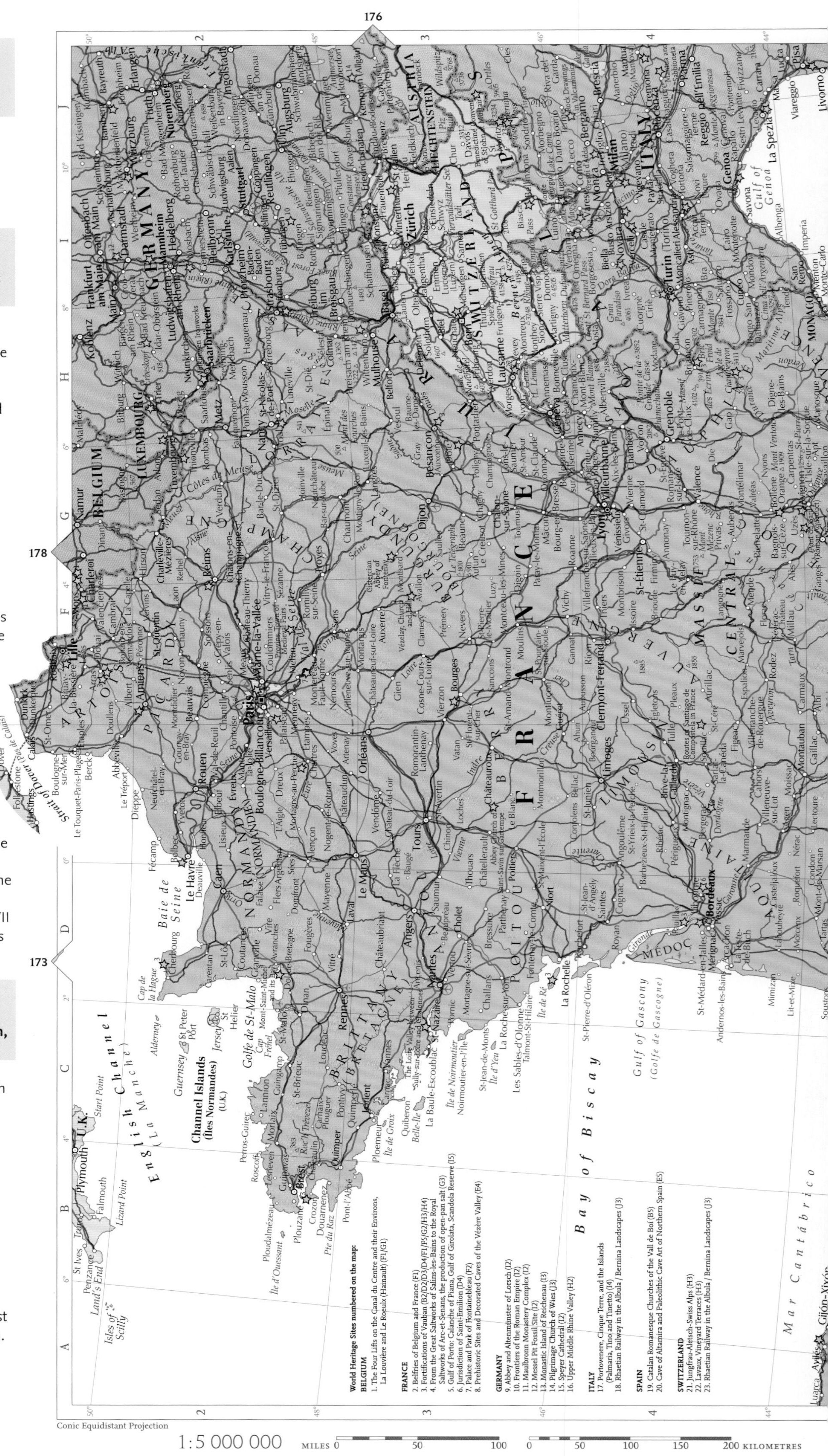

Conic Equidistant Projection

1:5 000 000

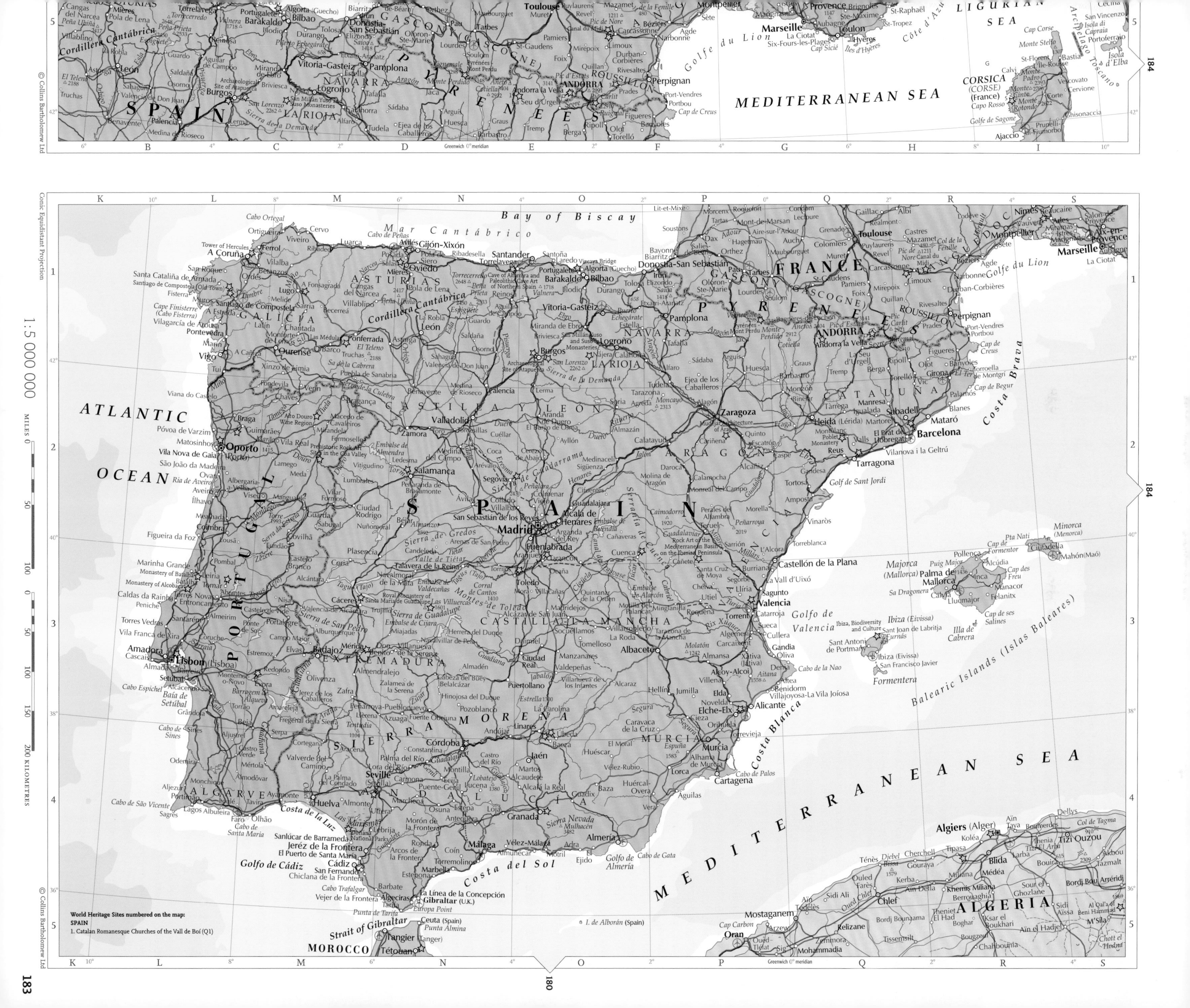

184
180
ATLANTIC OCEAN
Bay of Biscay
Mar Cantábrico
MEDITERRANEAN SEA
LIGURIAN SEA
Balearic Islands (Islas Baleares)
Golfe du Lion
Golfo de Valencia
Golfo de Cádiz
Strait of Gibraltar
Costa del Sol
Costa Blanca
Costa Brava
Costa de la Luz
SPAIN
PORTUGAL
FRANCE
ANDORRA
MOROCCO
ALGERIA
CORSICA (CORSE) (France)
PYRENEES
Madrid
Lisbon (Lisboa)
Barcelona
Valencia
Zaragoza
Bilbao
Seville (Sevilla)
Málaga
Granada
Córdoba
Murcia
Alicante
Valladolid
Salamanca
Toledo
Oporto (Porto)
Marseille
Toulouse
Perpignan
Algiers (Alger)
Oran
Tangier (Tanger)
Ceuta (Spain)
Gibraltar (U.K.)
Palma de Mallorca
Ibiza (Eivissa)
Minorca (Menorca)
Majorca (Mallorca)
Formentera
World Heritage Sites numbered on the map:
SPAIN
1. Catalan Romanesque Churches of the Vall de Boí (Q1)
Greenwich 0° meridian
Conic Equidistant Projection
1:5 000 000
MILES 0 50 100
0 50 100 150 200 KILOMETRES

Italy and the Balkans

176

CROATIA Capital: **Zagreb**
Area: **56 538 km²/21 829 miles²**
Population: **4 555 000** Languages: **Croatian, Serbian**
Religions: **Roman Catholic, Serbian Orthodox, Sunni Muslim**
Currency: **Kuna**

Croatia has a diverse landscape of lakes and rolling hills in the north, wooded mountains of the Dinaric Alps and a coastline that stretches for 5,835 km (3650 miles) which includes over a thousand islands. The sunny coastline attracts most visitors, although inland the capital Zagreb and the baroque architecture of Varaždin are popular destinations.

ITALY Capital: **Rome (Roma)**
Area: **301 245 km²/116 311 miles²**
Population: **58 877 000** Languages: **Italian**
Religions: **Roman Catholic** Currency: **Euro**

Italy is one of the most popular tourist destinations in Europe with some of the most famous attractions in the world – Pompeii, the Leaning Tower of Pisa, the Colosseum and Pantheon in Rome. The landscape varies from the Alpine mountains along its northern border to the plains in the valley of the Po of central Italy. The majestic Dolomites are a mecca for tourism – skiing, climbing, hiking and hang gliding. The 'Maratona dles Dolomites' is held in the first week in July – a gruelling cycle road race covering seven of the mountain passes.

Sicily and Sardinia are the largest islands in the Mediterranean and are autonomous regions of Italy. Sicily has one of the most active volcanoes in the world, Mount Etna, which along with its beaches and archaeology, make it an attractive destination for visitors. Sardinia has many reminders of its ancient past including the Phoenician town of Tharros on the west coast. Its coastline is largely rocky with deep bays and picturesque headlands.

There are two enclaves within Italy. Vatican City lies within Rome and is ruled by the Bishop of Rome, the Pope. San Marino in northern Italy is probably the oldest republic in the world, tourism is the main industry.

MACEDONIA Capital: **Skopje**
Area: **25 713 km²/9 928 miles²**
Population: **2 038 000** Languages: **Macedonian, Albanian, Turkish** Religions: **Macedonian Orthodox, Sunni Muslim**
Currency: **Macedonian denar**

Tourism plays a large part in the economy with the capital, Skopje and the picturesque city of Ohrid in the southwest, the most popular destination. The climate in the south is temperate Mediterranean while the north is more continental, with wider extremes in temperature.

MALTA Capital: **Valletta**
Area: **316 km²/122 miles²** Population: **407 000**
Languages: **Maltese, English** Religions: **Roman Catholic**
Currency: **Euro**

An archipelago of islands of which only three: Malta, Gozo and Comino, are inhabited. The many different occupations before independence from the UK in 1964 are reflected in the eclectic mix of cultures seen throughout the islands. The Islands are an open-air museum with some structures dating from 3600 – 3000 BC.

SLOVENIA Capital: **Ljubljana**
Area: **20 251 km²/7 819 miles²** Population: **2 002 000**
Languages: **Slovenian, Croatian, Serbian** Religions: **Roman Catholic, Protestant** Currency: **Euro**

Slovenia is the northernmost territory of the former Yugoslavia. It is heavily wooded and famous for its traditional foods, skiing and historic thermal baths dating from the twelfth century, many of which form the basis for modern health resorts. In the southwest is an area of karst limestone with many caves – Škocjan is a World Heritage site.

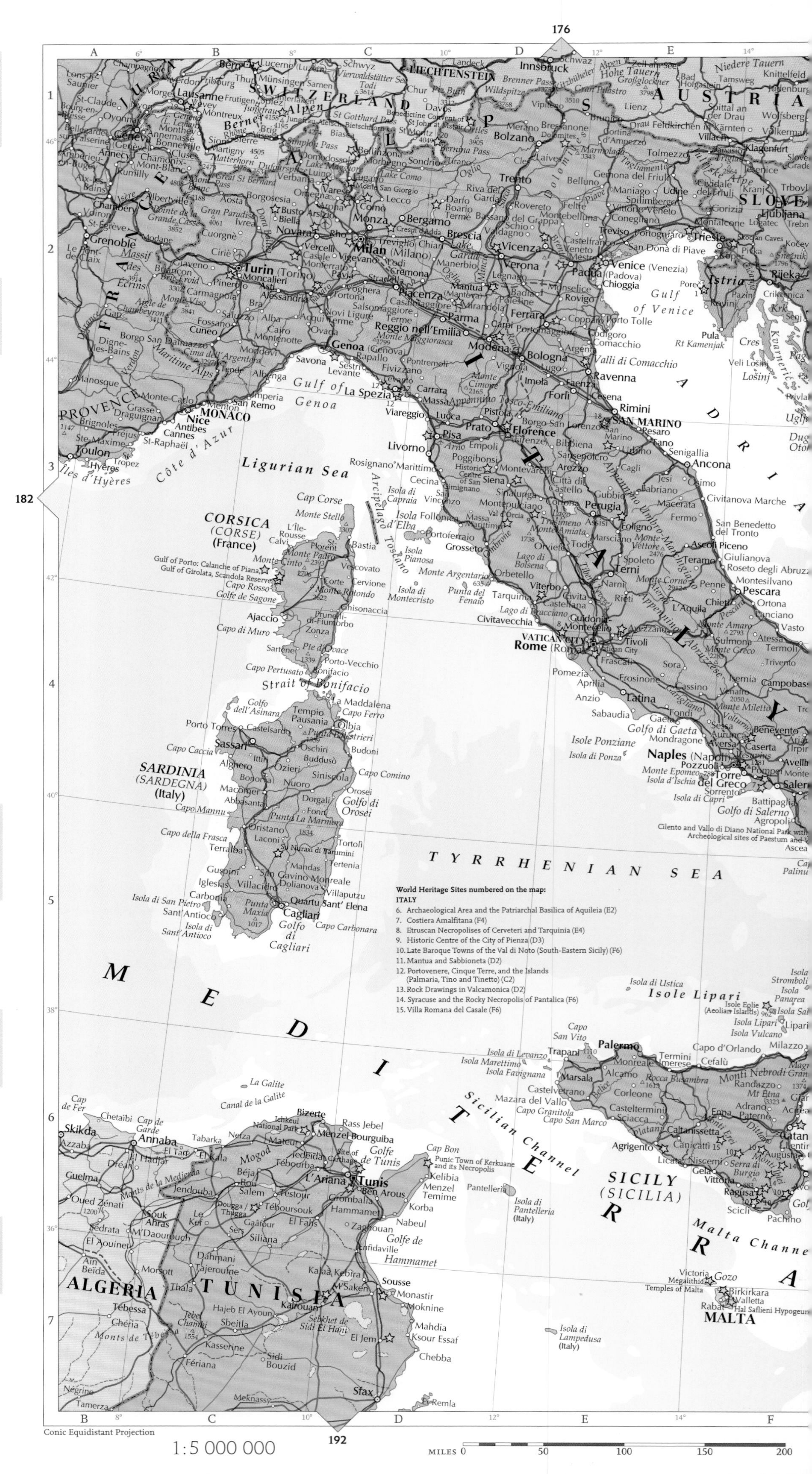

World Heritage Sites numbered on the map:
ITALY
6. Archaeological Area and the Patriarchal Basilica of Aquileia (E2)
7. Costiera Amalfitana (F4)
8. Etruscan Necropolises of Cerveteri and Tarquinia (E4)
9. Historic Centre of the City of Pienza (D3)
10. Late Baroque Towns of the Val di Noto (South-Eastern Sicily) (F6)
11. Mantua and Sabbioneta (D2)
12. Portovenere, Cinque Terre, and the Islands (Palmaria, Tino and Tinetto) (C2)
13. Rock Drawings in Valcamonica (D2)
14. Syracuse and the Rocky Necropolis of Pantalica (F6)
15. Villa Romana del Casale (F6)

Conic Equidistant Projection

1 : 5 000 000

MILES 0   50   100   150   200

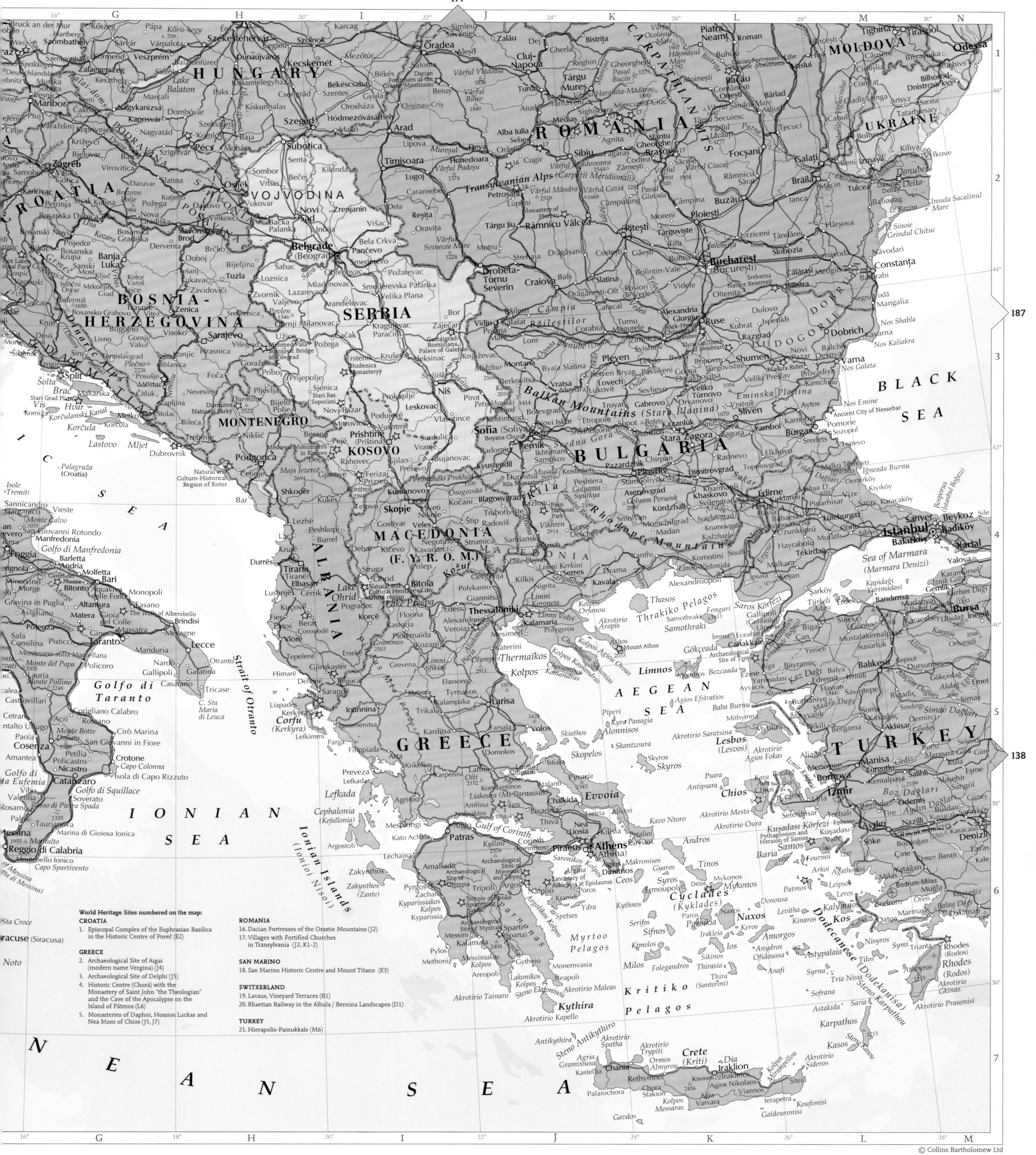

World Heritage Sites numbered on the map:

CROATIA
1. Episcopal Complex of the Euphrasian Basilica in the Historic Centre of Poreč (E2)

GREECE
2. Archaeological Site of Aigai (modern name Vergina) (J4)
3. Archaeological Site of Delphi (J5)
4. Historic Centre (Chorá) with the Monastery of Saint John "the Theologian" and the Cave of the Apocalypse on the Island of Pátmos (L6)
5. Monasteries of Daphni, Hossios Luckas and Nea Moni of Chios (J5, J7)

ROMANIA
16. Dacian Fortresses of the Orastie Mountains (J2)
17. Villages with Fortified Churches in Transylvania (J2, K1-2)

SAN MARINO
18. San Marino Historic Centre and Mount Titano (E3)

SWITZERLAND
19. Lavaux, Vineyard Terraces (B1)
20. Rhaetian Railway in the Albula / Bernina Landscapes (D1)

TURKEY
21. Hierapolis-Pamukkale (M6)

0 50 100 150 200 250 300 350 KILOMETRES

© Collins Bartholomew Ltd

West Russian Federation

BELARUS Capital: Minsk
Area: 207 600 km²/80 155 miles²

Population: 9 689 000 Languages: **Belorussian, Russian**
Religions: **Belorussian Orthodox, Roman Catholic**
Currency: **Belarus rouble**

Belarus (formerly Belorussia) declared independence from the Soviet Union in 1991. It has cold winters and moist summers, with average temperatures of around –6°C (21°F) and 18°C (64°F) respectively. Poor roads and lack of services make travelling by car difficult. The bus or train are probably the best means for getting around. The landscape of Belarus is characterised by expansive plains and an abundance of lakes and forest. A rich heritage dates back to the eleventh century with ancient castles, monasteries and picturesque villages dotting the landscape. Of particular interest is the Cathedral of St Francis Xavier in the ancient city of Hrodna (Grodno).

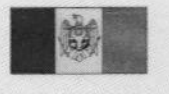

MOLDOVA Capital: Chişinău (Kishinev)
Area: 33 700 km²/13 012 miles²

Population: 3 794 000 Languages: **Romanian, Ukrainian, Gagauz, Russian** Religions: **Romanian Orthodox, Russian Orthodox** Currency: **Moldovan leu**

Moldova is one of the poorest nations in Europe, having no major mineral deposits, and as a consequence it has to import all of its petroleum, gas and coal. The climate is favourable to agriculture on which the economy largely depends. Most of the country lies between the Rivers Dniester and Prut. The area to the east of the Dniester, Trans-Dniester, declared its independence from Moldova in 1990. It has never been internationally recognised.

Easter is the most important religious holiday and the second Sunday after Easter is 'Paştele Blajinilor' – a day of mourning for departed family and friends. Chişinău has Moldova's only international airport.

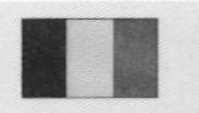

ROMANIA Capital: Bucharest (Bucureşti)
Area: 237 500 km²/91 699 miles²

Population: 21 438 000 Languages: **Romanian, Hungarian** Religions: **Romanian Orthodox, Protestant, Roman Catholic** Currency: **Romanian leu**

Romania borders the Black Sea into which the protected wetland of the Danube Delta is extending 20m (65ft) each year. Almost all of Romania's rivers source in the Carpathians and most join the Danube. The painted monasteries of Bucovina in northeastern Romania are masterpieces of Byzantine art and unique in Europe.

Surrounded by the arc of the Carpathians is Transylvania which has some of Europe's best-preserved medieval towns, most notably Brasov, featuring Old Saxon architecture and citadel ruins. Near Brasov is the Gothic Bran Castle which was used by Vlad Tepes (Vlad the Impaler), the inspiration for Bram Stoker's Dracula, during his raids into Transylvania.

UKRAINE Capital: Kiev (Kyiv)
Area: 603 700 km²/233 090 miles²

Population: 46 205 000 Languages: **Ukrainian, Russian** Religions: **Ukrainian Orthodox, Ukrainian Catholic, Roman Catholic** Currency: **Hryvnia**

Ukraine's capital, Kiev, has a history dating back to the sixth century and has many sites of interest reflecting its heritage. The peninsula of Crimea sits between between the Black Sea and the Sea of Azov and is popular for its beaches and mountains. The port of Odessa, 'The Black Sea Pearl', has one of the largest opera houses in the world. The 'Seven Wonders of Ukraine' are historic and cultural places of interest that were chosen by an internet vote in 2007. Ukrainians are among the foremost rail users in the world and the comfortable, affordable rail network connects most major cities.

Conic Equidistant Projection

1:7 000 000

MILES 0 50 100 150 200

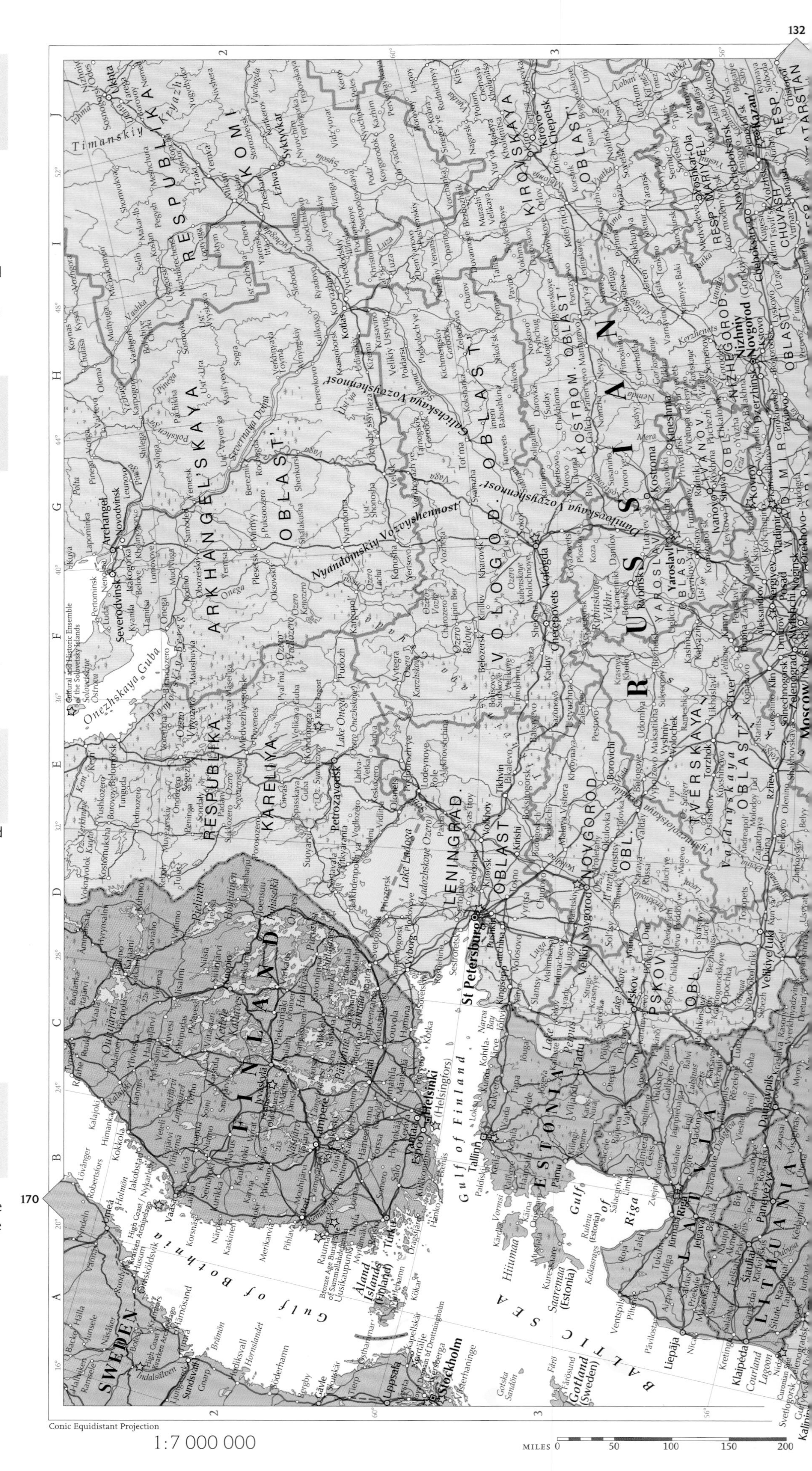

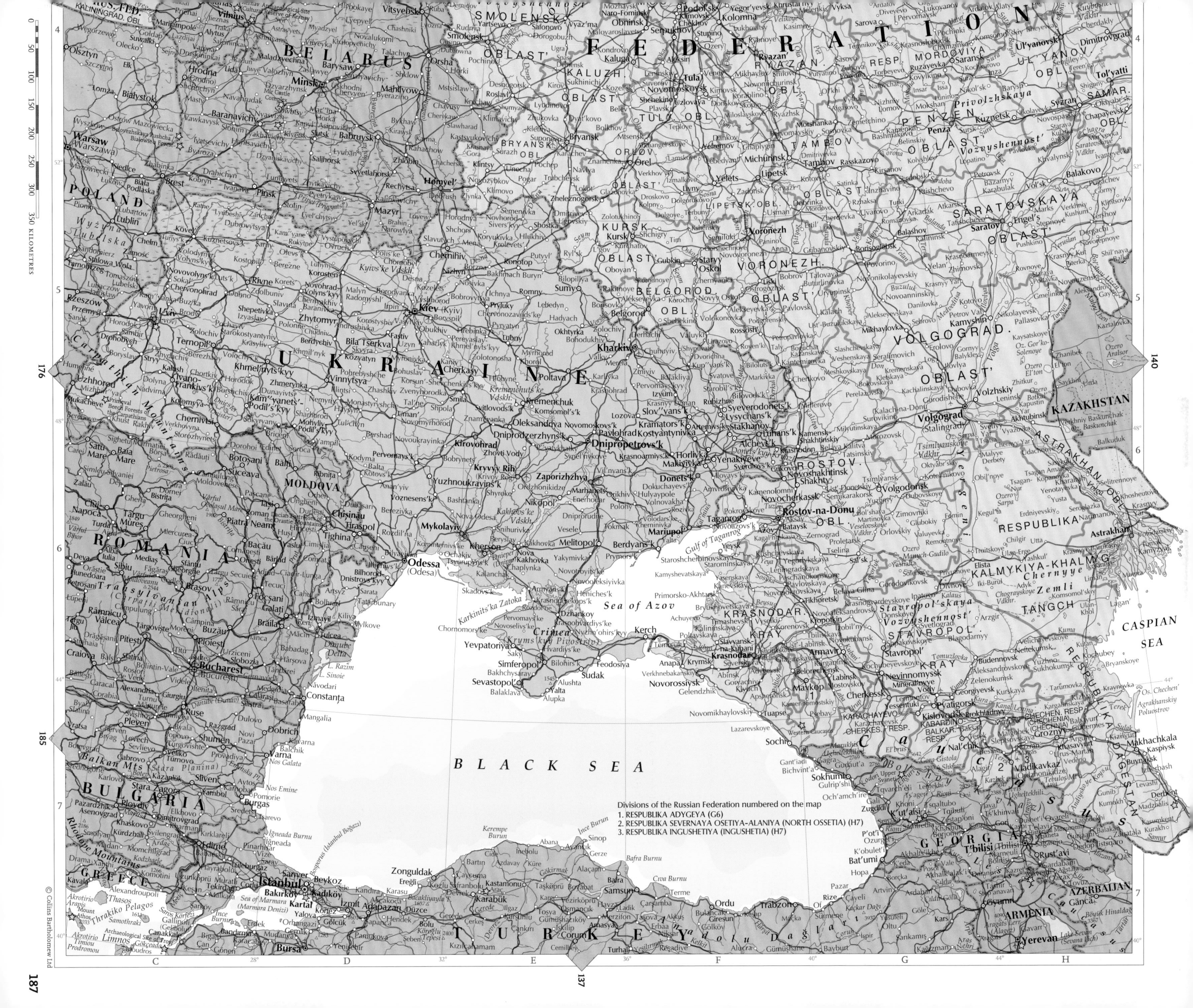

Divisions of the Russian Federation numbered on the map

1. RESPUBLIKA ADYGEYA (G6)
2. RESPUBLIKA SEVERNAYA OSETIYA-ALANIYA (NORTH OSSETIA) (H7)
3. RESPUBLIKA INGUSHETIYA (INGUSHETIA) (H7)

CASPIAN SEA

BLACK SEA

Sea of Azov

Gulf of Taganrog

© Collins Bartholomew Ltd

0 50 100 150 200 250 300 350 KILOMETRES

Africa Physical

Africa is connected to Asia at the narrow Sinai peninsula. It is also separated narrowly from Europe at the Strait of Gibraltar. It contains some of the world's greatest physical features. The north is dominated by the Sahara desert and the semi-arid Sahel region, while the mountainous zone of the Great Rift Valley runs down much of the east. The chief feature of central Africa is the vast Congo Basin, while the Kalahari and Namib deserts occupy large parts of the southwest.

Facts

- The Suez Canal, a crucial shipping route between the Atlantic and Indian Oceans, links the Mediterranean Sea to the Red Sea. It opened in 1869 and is 163 km (101 miles) long.

- The Sahara desert covers 9 million sq km (3.5 million sq miles), approximately 30 per cent of Africa's total land area.

- The floor of the Great Rift Valley varies from nearly 400 m (1300 ft) below sea level to over 1800 m (5900 ft) above sea level.

HIGHEST MOUNTAINS	m	ft
Kilimanjaro, Tanzania	5 892	19 330
Mt Kenya (Kirinyaga), Kenya	5 199	17 057
Margherita Peak, Dem. Rep. of the Congo/Uganda	5 110	16 765
Meru, Tanzania	4 565	14 977
Ras Dejen, Ethiopia	4 533	14 872
Mt Karisimbi, Rwanda	4 510	14 796

LARGEST ISLANDS	sq km	sq miles
Madagascar	587 040	226 656

LONGEST RIVERS	km	miles
Nile	6 695	4 160
Congo	4 667	2 900
Niger	4 184	2 600
Zambezi	2 736	1 700
Webi Shabeelle	2 490	1 547
Ubangi	2 250	1 398

LARGEST LAKES	sq km	sq miles
Lake Victoria	68 870	26 591
Lake Tanganyika	32 600	12 587
Lake Nyasa (Lake Malawi)	29 500	11 390
Lake Volta	8 482	3 275
Lake Turkana	6 500	2 510
Lake Albert	5 600	2 162

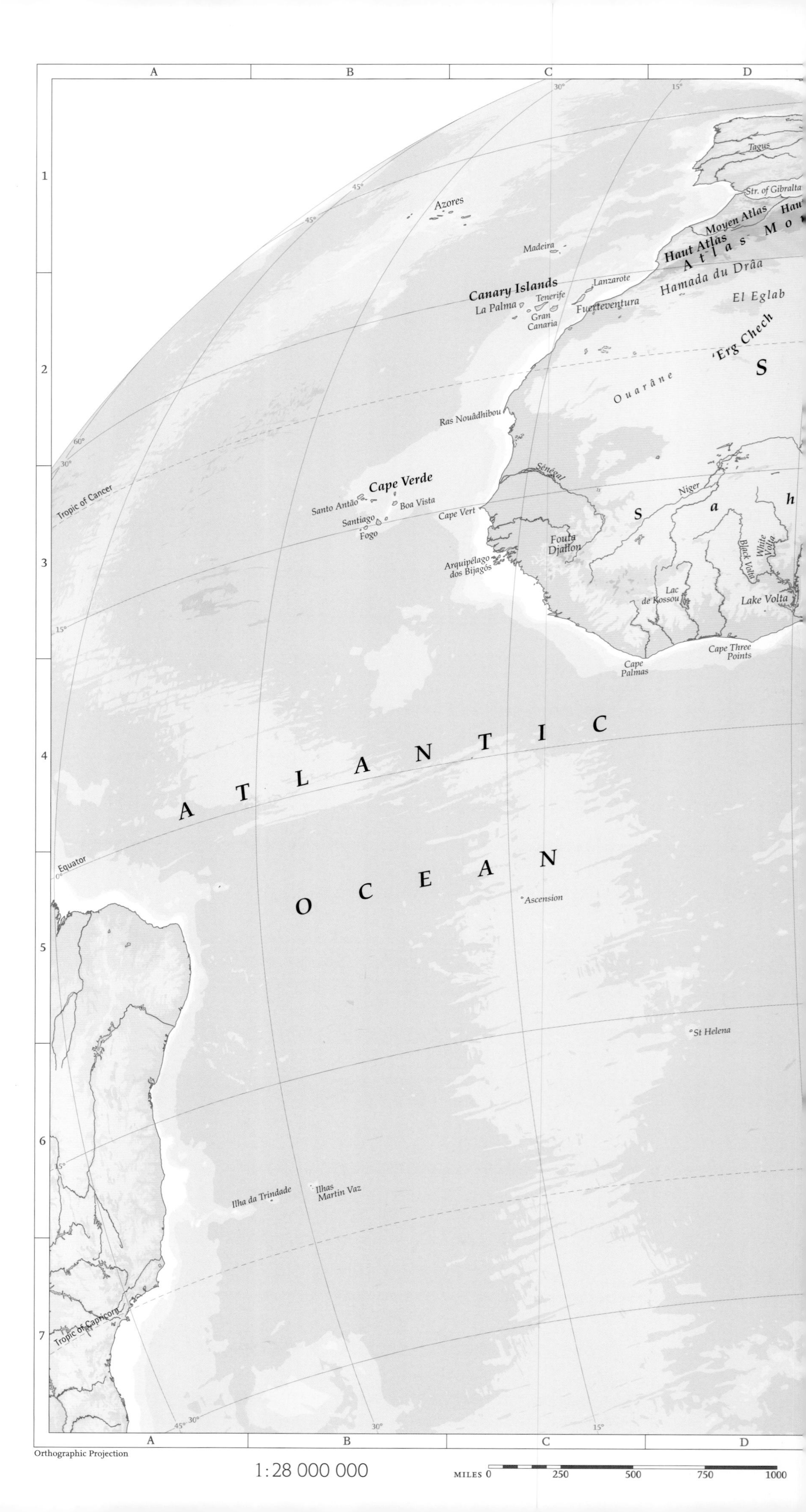

Orthographic Projection

1 : 28 000 000

MILES 0   250   500   750   1000

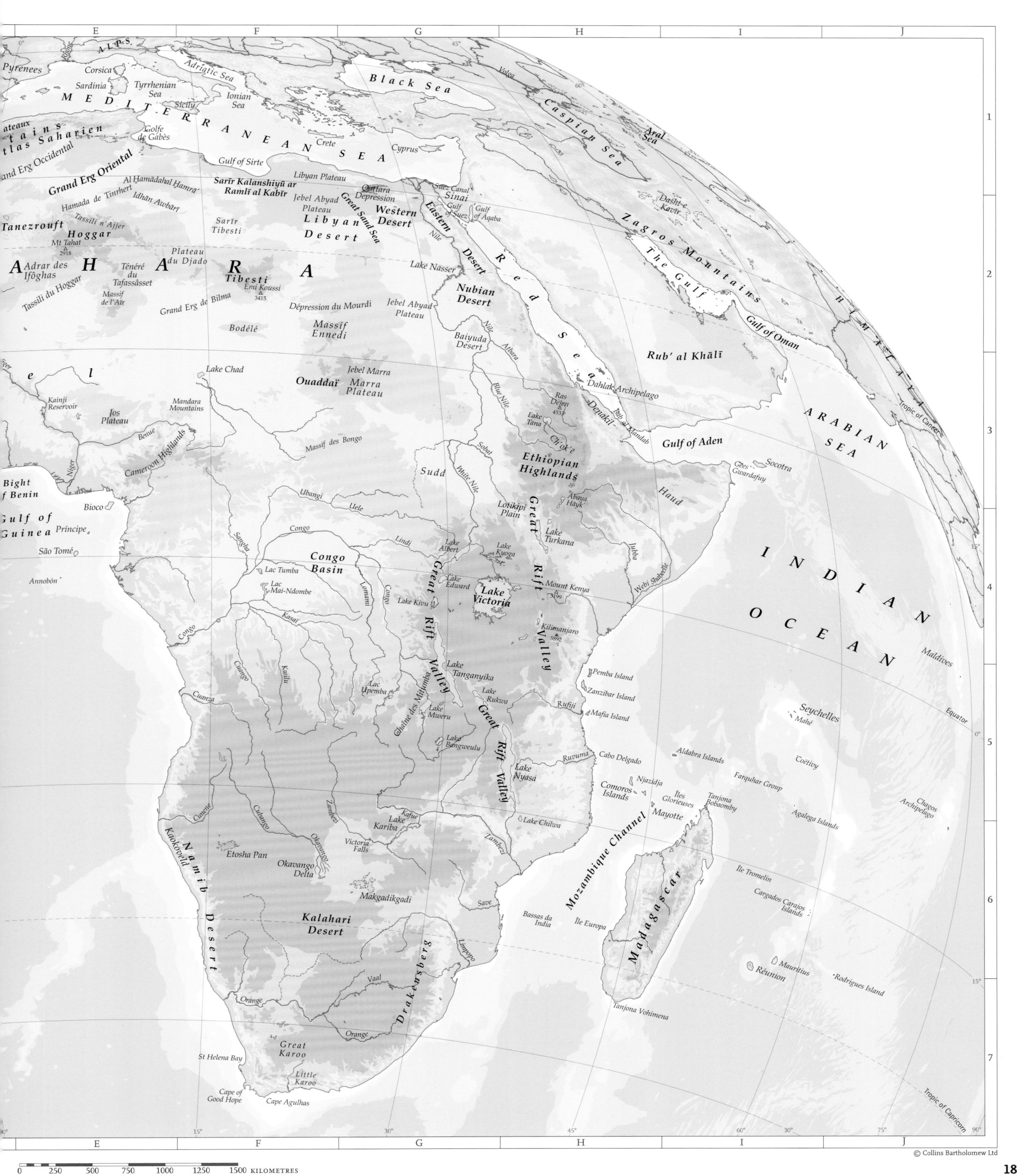

0   250   500   750   1000   1250   1500   KILOMETRES

Africa Political

The political patchwork of Africa is a result of a complex history and of boundaries formed largely during the colonial era, which saw European control of the majority of the continent from the 15th century until widespread moves to independence began in the 1950s. The colonial era effectively came to an end in the 1970s. The status of Western Sahara, formerly Spanish but now effectively under Moroccan control, remains to be agreed internationally. Today there are once again two countries called Congo, since Zaire reverted to the name Democratic Republic of the Congo in 1997.

Facts

- Many languages are spoken in different parts of Africa, although Arabic is the main native language all across the north. In most other areas, the languages of European powers (mainly English, French, Portuguese and Spanish, along with Afrikaans) remain in common use.

- Only Liberia and Ethiopia have remained free from colonial rule throughout their history.

- UN figures estimate that 258 million people throughout the African continent have no access to clean water.

- Of the ten countries in the world with children under-five mortality rates of more than 200 per 1000 live births, nine are in Africa.

LARGEST COUNTRIES	Area	
	sq km	sq miles
Sudan	2 505 813	967 500
Algeria	2 381 741	919 595
Democratic Republic of the Congo	2 345 410	905 568
Libya	1 759 540	679 362
Chad	1 284 000	495 755
Niger	1 267 000	489 191
Angola	1 246 700	481 354
Mali	1 240 140	478 821
Republic of South Africa	1 219 090	470 693
Ethiopia	1 133 880	437 794

MOST POPULATED COUNTRIES	Population
Nigeria	148 093 000
Ethiopia	83 099 000
Egypt	75 498 000
Democratic Republic of the Congo	62 636 000
Republic of South Africa	48 577 000
Tanzania	40 454 000
Sudan	38 560 000
Kenya	37 538 000
Algeria	33 858 000
Morocco	31 224 000

CAPITALS		
Largest population	**Cairo**, Egypt	12 041 000
Smallest population	**Jamestown**, St Helena	1 000
Most northerly	**Tunis**, Tunisia	36° 46' N
Most southerly	**Cape Town**, Republic of South Africa	33° 57' S
Highest	**Addis Ababa**, Ethiopia	2 408 m/ 7 900 ft

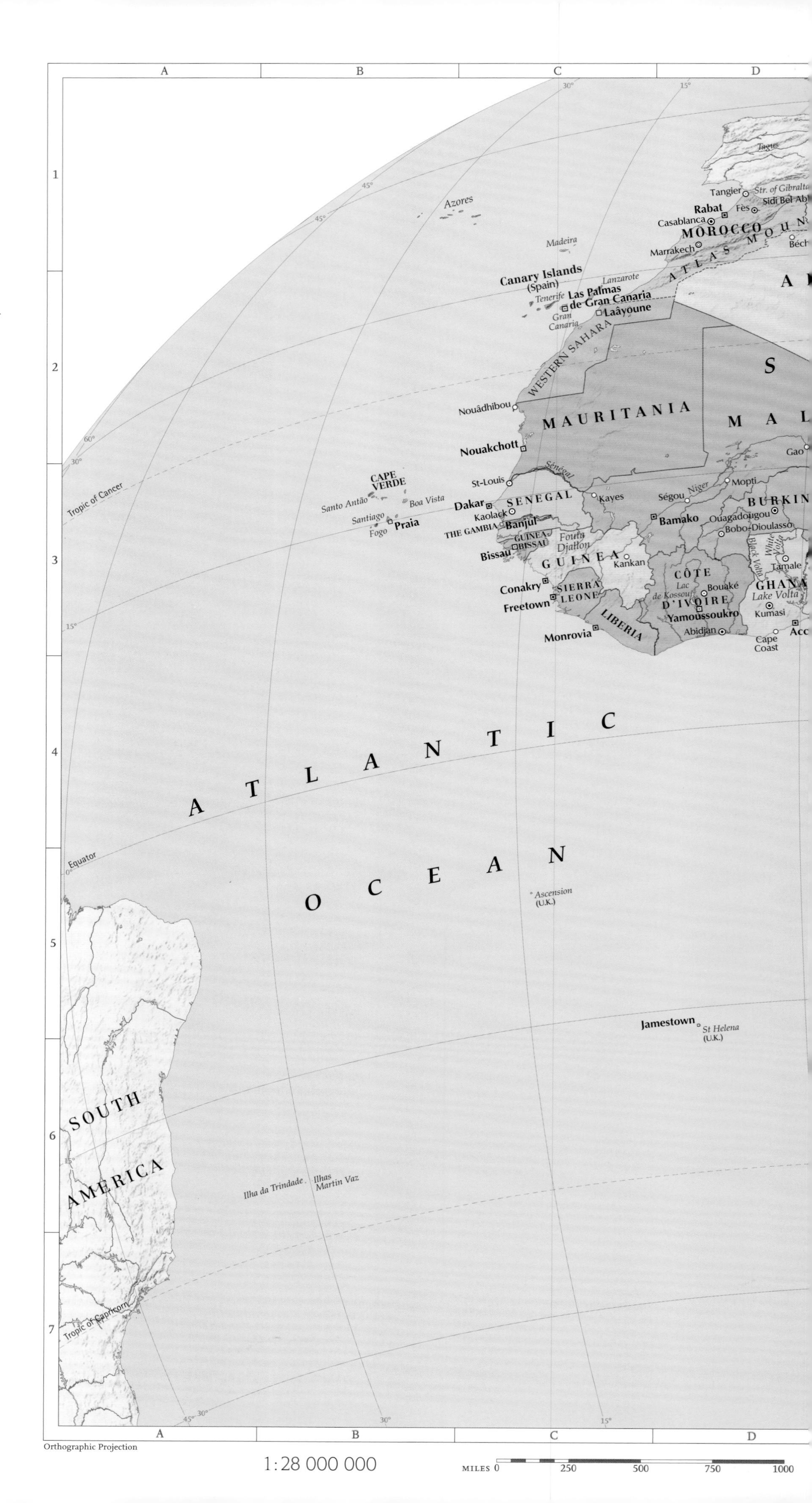

Orthographic Projection

1 : 28 000 000

MILES 0   250   500   750   1000

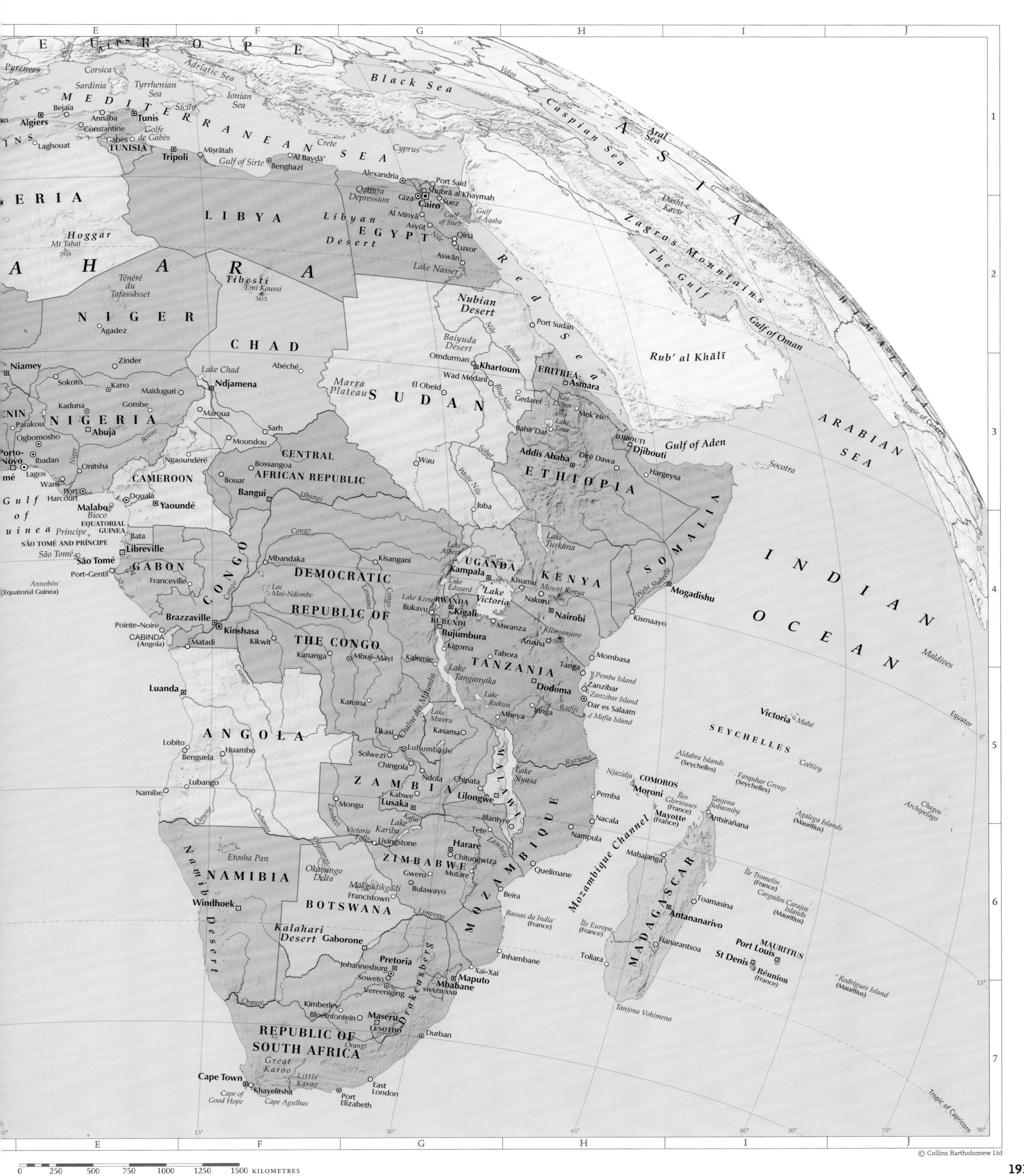

© Collins Bartholomew Ltd

0   250   500   750   1000   1250   1500 KILOMETRES

NORTHERN AFRICA

Northern Africa sits on Europe's doorstep, just 14.5 km/ 8 miles separating it from Europe across the Straits of Gibraltar. It is dominated by the world's largest desert, the Sahara. The area is an exciting blend of Arab culture, remote oases and modern cities, mountain landscapes and Mediterranean beaches, ancient ruins and atmospheric kasbahs, palaces and mosques. Established holiday locations in Morocco, Tunisia and Egypt have been welcoming tourists for many years, and Libya, slowly emerging from international isolation, now also welcomes visitors. Regional instability, and the threat of criminal and terrorist activity, make travel to areas bordering Sudan, Chad, Niger and Algeria highly dangerous.

EGYPT Capital: **Cairo (Al Qāhirah)**
Area: **1 000 250 km²/386 199 miles²**
Population: **75 498 000** Languages: **Arabic** Religions: **Sunni Muslim, Coptic Christian** Currency: **Egyptian pound**

Egypt, synonymous with the pyramids and fabulous monuments of the pharaohs, links the continents of Africa and Asia. The Nile, the world's longest river, offers water-borne tours on luxurious cruise ships or traditional *feluccas*. Cairo combines a modern city with the old; the Historic Cairo World Heritage site incorporates bazaars, mosques and palaces. World-class diving and snorkelling can be found along the Red Sea coast, with amazing sandy beaches and other water sports such as windsurfing and sailing. Visitors can experience the vast desert, one of the earth's most mysterious places, through organised treks, a camel ride or time with nomadic Bedouin tribes.

MOROCCO Capital: **Rabat**
Area: **446 550 km²/172 414 miles²**
Population: **31 224 000** Languages: **Arabic, Berber, French** Religions: **Sunni Muslim** Currency: **Moroccan dirham**

Morocco is a melting pot of cultures, with Roman, Arab and European influences visible throughout the country. The best-known traditional souks are in Fès and Marrakech, providing daytime shopping and night-time entertainment. World Heritage sites include medinas and the Roman ruins of Volubilis. The snow-capped Atlas Mountains are a draw for trekkers and the Atlantic and Mediterranean coasts offer popular seaside resorts and isolated beaches. To the north, in the Rif Mountains, is Chefchaouen, known for its distinctive blue-glazed houses (a tradition from the town's former Jewish inhabitants) and native crafts, many not found elsewhere in Morocco.

TUNISIA Capital: **Tunis**
Area: **164 150 km²/63 379 miles²**
Population: **10 327 000** Languages: **Arabic, French** Religions: **Sunni Muslim** Currency: **Tunisian dinar**

Tunisia is well known as a package-holiday destination, but its efficient public transport system makes it accessible for independent travellers. Often described as a microcosm of northern Africa, Tunisia has deserts, oases, mountains, beaches and ancient sites. The Bardo Museum in Tunis, contains one of the world's largest collections of mosaics. Carthage, founded by the Phoenician's and rebuilt by the Romans, lies to the north of Tunis. Sousse, further south, is the site of a remarkable collection of first-century catacombs. Sports enthusiasts are well catered for in all the tourist centres, with golf, tennis, diving, windsurfing and sailing some of the activities on offer.

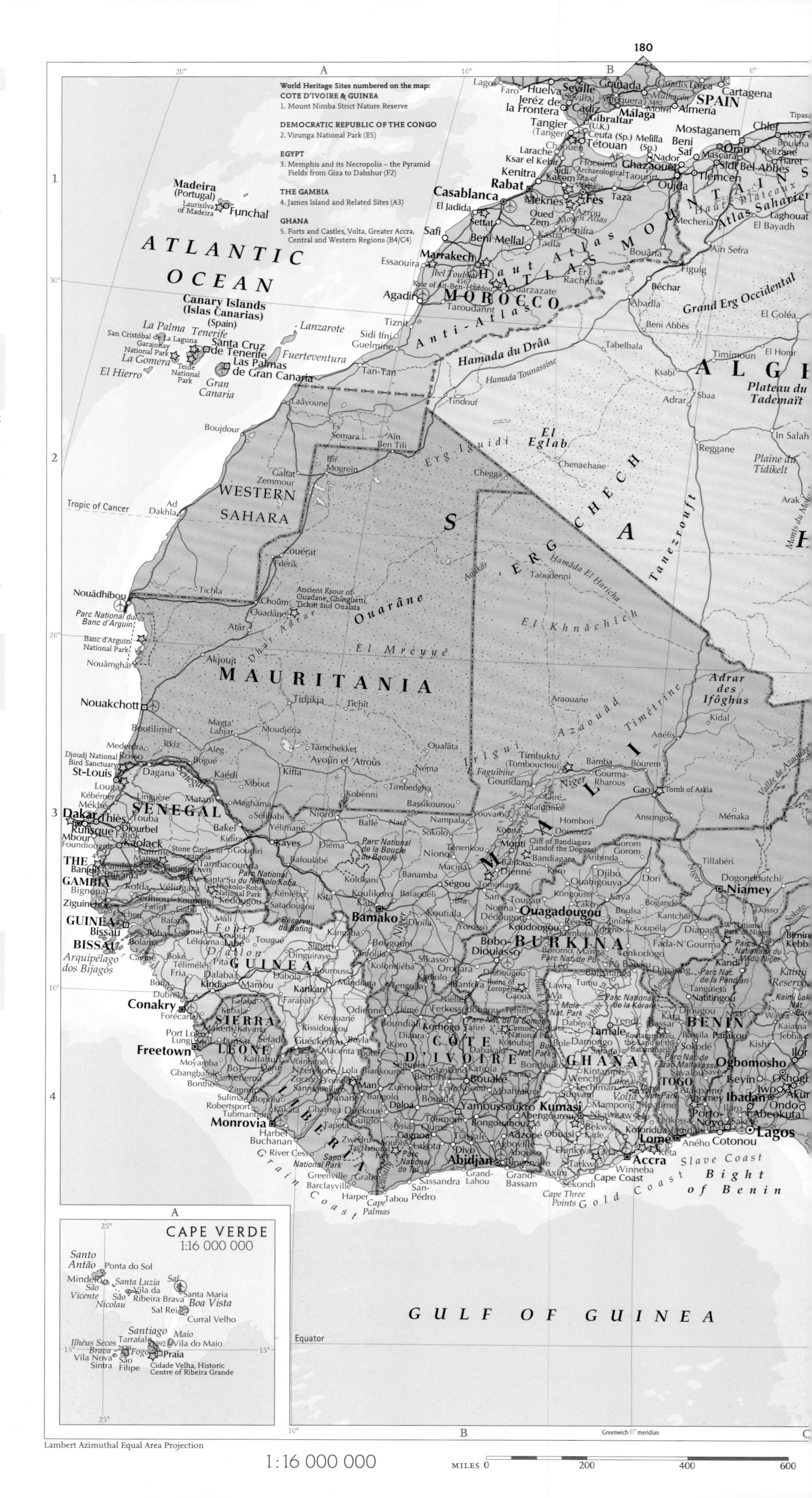

1:16 000 000

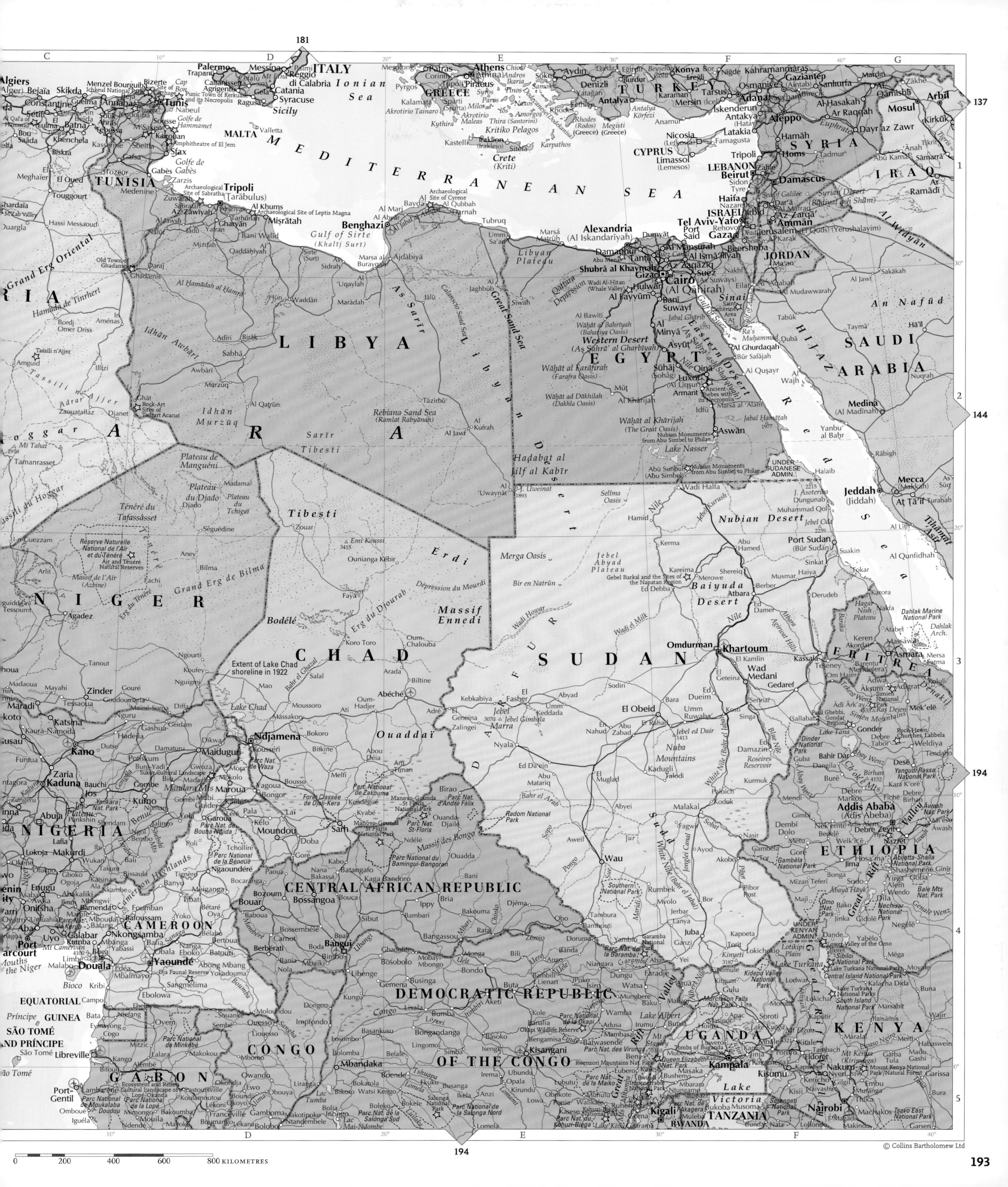
181
137
144
194
194
MEDITERRANEAN SEA
Ionian Sea
Gulf of Sirte (Khalīj Surt)
Red Sea
ITALY
Sicily
Palermo
Messina
Reggio di Calabria
Catania
Syracuse
MALTA
Valletta
GREECE
Athens (Athina)
Piraeus
Patras
Kalamata
Crete (Kriti)
Iraklion (Irakleio)
Karpathos
Rhodes (Rodos) (Greece)
TURKEY
Antalya
Adana
Konya
Denizli
Mersin (Içel)
Gaziantep (Antep)
Şanlıurfa
Iskenderun
Antakya (Hatay)
CYPRUS
Nicosia (Lefkosia)
Limassol (Lemesos)
Famagusta
SYRIA
Aleppo
Latakia
Ḥamāh
Homs
Damascus
Dayr az Zawr
Al Ḥasakah
Ar Raqqah
IRAQ
Mosul
Arbīl
Kirkūk
LEBANON
Beirut
Tripoli
Sidon
Tyre
ISRAEL
Haifa
Tel Aviv-Yafo
Jerusalem (Yerushalayim) (El Quds)
Gaza
JORDAN
'Ammān
Az Zarqā'
SAUDI ARABIA
Medina (Al Madīnah)
Mecca (Makkah)
Jeddah (Jiddah)
Tabūk
Yanbu' al Baḥr
Aṭ Ṭā'if
HIJAZ
An Nafūd
ALGERIA
Algiers (Alger)
Constantine
Annaba
Sétif
Batna
Biskra
Touggourt
Ouargla
Ghardaïa
Hassi Messaoud
Tamanrasset
Djanet
Grand Erg Oriental
Hamada de Tinrhert
Tassili n'Ajjer
Tassili du Hoggar
TUNISIA
Tunis
Bizerte
Sousse
Kairouan
Sfax
Gabès
Gafsa
Medenine
Zarzis
LIBYA
Tripoli (Ṭarābulus)
Az Zāwiyah
Al Khums
Mişrātah
Benghazi
Ajdābiyā
Sirte (Surt)
Ghadāmis
Sabhā
Murzuq
Al Kufrah
Ghāt
Idhān Awbārī
Idhān Murzūq
Rebiana Sand Sea (Ramlat Rabyānah)
Sarīr Tibesti
Libyan Desert
Great Sand Sea
Libyan Plateau
EGYPT
Alexandria (Al Iskandarīyah)
Cairo (Al Qāhirah)
Giza
Port Said
Suez
Ismailia (Al Ismā'īlīyah)
Ṭanṭā
Shubrā al Khaymah
Al Fayyūm
Asyūţ
Luxor (Al Uqşur)
Aswān
Siwah
Sinai
Western Desert (Aş Şaḥrā' al Gharbīyah)
Eastern Desert (Aş Şaḥrā' ash Sharqīyah)
Lake Nasser
Qattara Depression
Al Ghurdaqah
Ḥadabat al Jilf al Kabīr
UNDER SUDANESE ADMIN.
NIGER
Agadez
Zinder
Maradi
Tahoua
Diffa
Massif de l'Aïr (Azbine)
Ténéré du Tafassâsset
Grand Erg de Bilma
Bilma
Plateau du Djado
Réserve Naturelle Nationale de l'Aïr et du Ténéré
CHAD
Ndjamena
Abéché
Faya
Moundou
Sarh
Tibesti
Emi Koussi 3415
Erdi
Bodélé
Erg du Djourab
Massif Ennedi
Ouaddaï
Lake Chad
Extent of Lake Chad shoreline in 1922
SUDAN
Khartoum
Omdurman
Port Sudan (Bür Sūdān)
Kassala
Wad Medani
El Obeid
Atbara
Wadi Halfa
Nubian Desert
Bayuda Desert
Nuba Mountains
DARFUR
El Fasher
Nyala
Jebel Marra 3070
Wau
Juba
Malakal
Sudd
White Nile
Blue Nile
Nile
NIGERIA
Kano
Kaduna
Zaria
Maiduguri
Abuja
Jos
Port Harcourt
Enugu
Calabar
CAMEROON
Yaoundé
Douala
Garoua
Maroua
Ngaoundéré
Cameroon Highlands
Mt Cameroun 4100
CENTRAL AFRICAN REPUBLIC
Bangui
Bossangoa
Bambari
Bria
EQUATORIAL GUINEA
SÃO TOMÉ AND PRÍNCIPE
GABON
Libreville
Port-Gentil
CONGO
DEMOCRATIC REPUBLIC OF THE CONGO
Kisangani
Mbandaka
Lake Albert
UGANDA
Kampala
Lake Victoria
RWANDA
Kigali
TANZANIA
KENYA
Nairobi
Lake Turkana
ERITREA
Asmara
Massawa
Dahlak Archipelago
ETHIOPIA
Addis Ababa (Adis Abeba)
Gonder
Lake Tana
Dire Dawa
Great Rift Valley
UNDER KENYAN ADMIN.
0 200 400 600 800 KILOMETRES

Central and Southern Africa

SOUTH CENTRAL AFRICA

Although this part of the world is known for poverty and political unrest, there are wonderful experiences available for the adventurous and cautious traveller. Ethiopia has ancient ruins, medieval towns, castles and breathtaking scenery. Tanzania is the African tourist's dream, with the evocative destinations of Zanzibar, Kilimanjaro and Lake Victoria. Those wishing to see Victoria Falls should visit Zambia. Uganda is home to populations of endangered mountain gorillas and Botswana has extensive elephant herds. For tropical beaches and fantastic diving, Mozambique is a great destination, and to experience a unique beauty and sense of Africa's vastness, visit Namibia.

KENYA Capital: Nairobi
Area: 582 646 km²/224 961 miles²
Population: **37 538 000** Languages: **Swahili, English, local languages** Religions: **Christian, traditional beliefs**
Currency: **Kenyan shilling**

Kenya is a country of magnificent mountains, arid deserts, tropical coast and a spectacular stretch of the Great Rift Valley. It is a popular package safari destination. The southwest is the heartland of the Masai community and the Masai Mara Game Reserve is an area rich with zebra, giraffe, gazelle and topi, birds and monkeys, elephant and buffalo. Climb Mount Kenya, Africa's second highest mountain, or visit Lake Nakuru and its famed flamingos. The exotic beaches of the Indian Ocean, with their fragile and beautiful coral reefs, are bordered by rainforest, home to baboons and colobus monkeys.

MADAGASCAR Capital: Antananarivo
Area: 587 041 km²/226 658 miles²
Population: **19 683 000** Languages: **Malagasy, French**
Religions: **Traditional beliefs, Christian, Sunni Muslim**
Currency: **Malagasy franc**

Lying in the Indian Ocean, Madagascar is renowned for the great diversity of its unique flora and fauna – it is a special place to visit. In the east, the rainforests of the Atsinanana World Heritage site comprises six national parks. On the drier western coast is Tsingy de Bemaraha Strict Nature Reserve. Lemur are unique to Madagascar, the only location where they can be seen in their natural habitat. Beaches on the northern and western coasts are best for water sports. Whale watchers should visit the tourist destination of Nosy Boraha (Sainte Marie), an outstanding location for observing humpback whales.

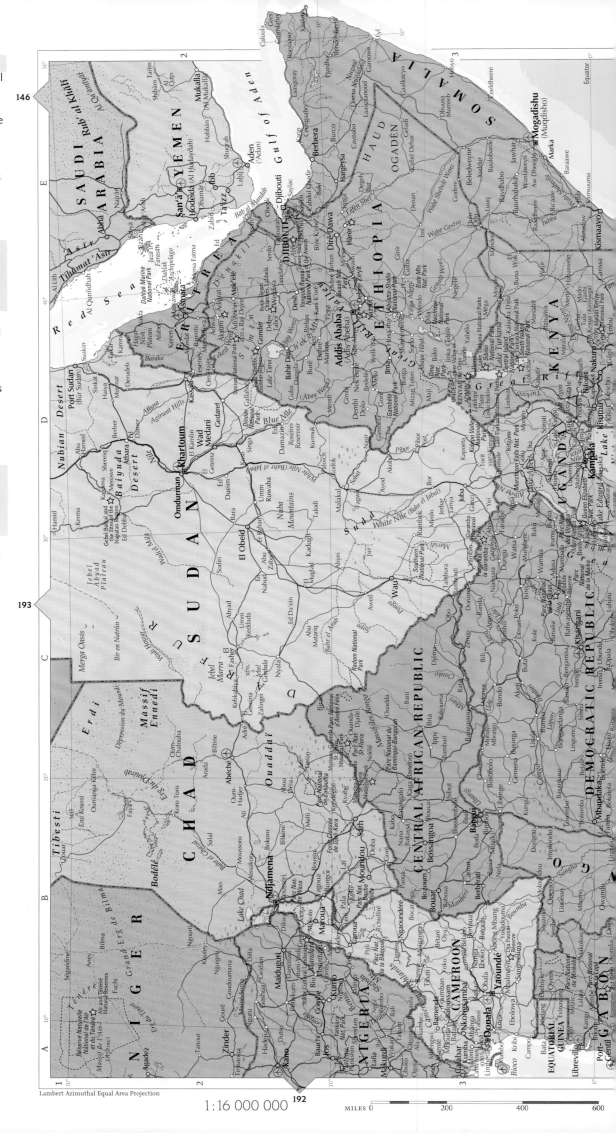

Lambert Azimuthal Equal Area Projection

1:16 000 000

MILES 0   200   400   600

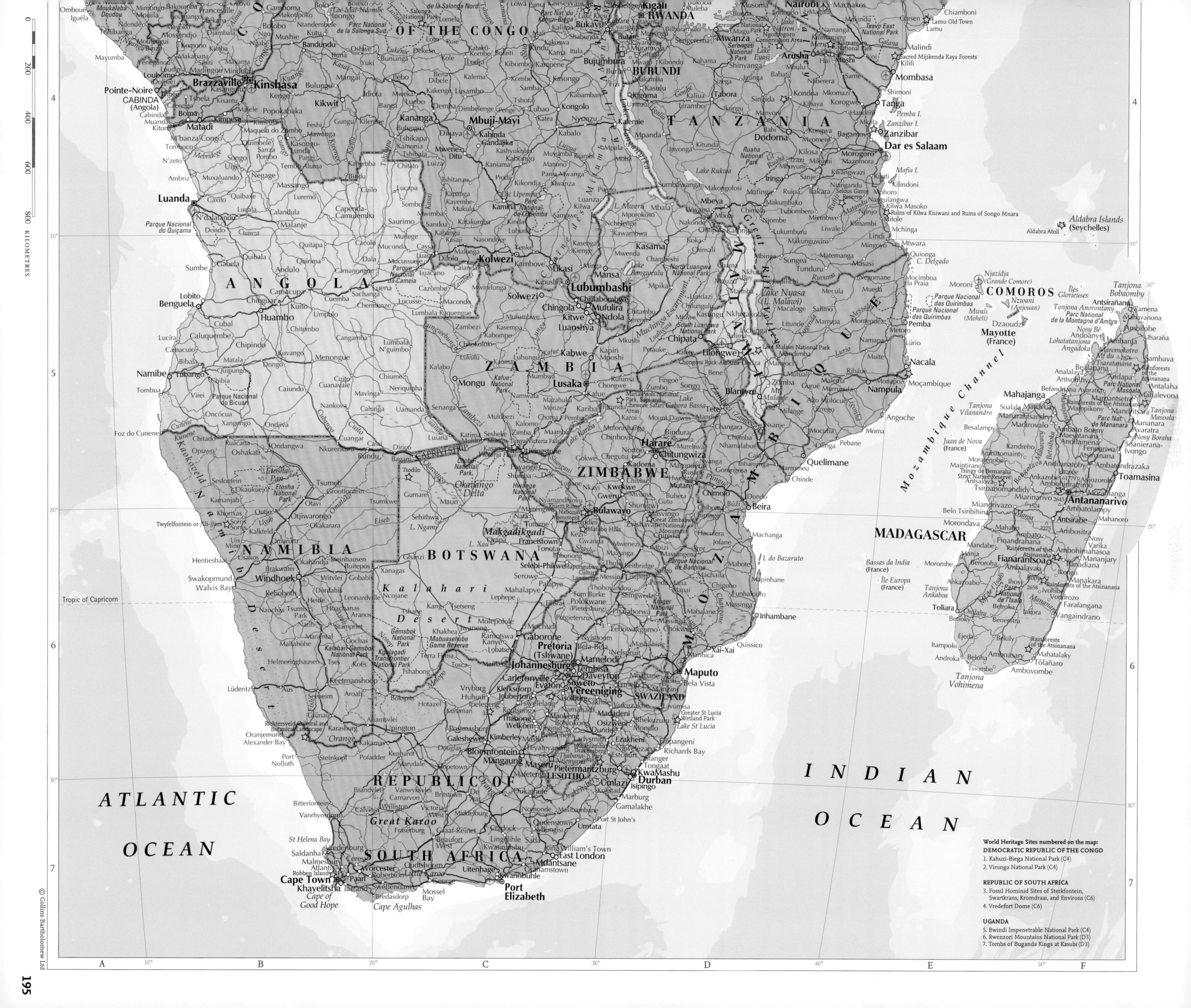

World Heritage Sites numbered on the map:

DEMOCRATIC REPUBLIC OF THE CONGO
1. Kahuzi-Biega National Park (C4)
2. Virunga National Park (C4)

REPUBLIC OF SOUTH AFRICA
3. Fossil Hominid Sites of Sterkfontein, Swartkrans, Kromdraai, and Environs (C6)
4. Vredefort Dome (C6)

UGANDA
5. Bwindi Impenetrable National Park (D3)
6. Rwenzori Mountains National Park (D3)
7. Tombs of Buganda Kings at Kasubi (D3)

ATLANTIC OCEAN

INDIAN OCEAN

DEMOCRATIC REPUBLIC OF THE CONGO

TANZANIA

ANGOLA

ZAMBIA

MALAWI

MOZAMBIQUE

ZIMBABWE

BOTSWANA

NAMIBIA

REPUBLIC OF SOUTH AFRICA

MADAGASCAR

COMOROS

RWANDA

BURUNDI

LESOTHO

SWAZILAND

Kalahari Desert

Namib Desert

0   200   400   600   800   KILOMETRES

Republic of South Africa

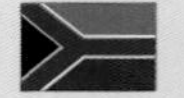

SOUTH AFRICA
Capital: **Pretoria (Tshwane)/Cape Town**
Area: **1 219 090 km²/470 693 miles²** Population: **48 577 000**
Languages: **Afrikaans, English, nine other official languages**
Religions: **Protestant, Roman Catholic, Sunni Muslim, Hindu**
Currency: **Rand**

South Africa has great natural beauty and vivid landscapes, mountains and deserts and the dramatic coastlines of both Atlantic and Indian Oceans. Famed for plentiful sunshine, it is becoming a favourite with those looking for extreme sports, as well as visitors wanting more sedate outdoor activities of all kinds.

The Eastern Cape is extremely beautiful, with a wild coast and surfing beaches, vast areas with game and Tiffindell ski resort (the only ski resort in South Africa).

Johannesburg has a number of museums documenting the country's historical and cultural heritage. Soweto, on the outskirts, is a lively area with the hugely popular attractions of Nelson Mandela's Soweto home and a memorial and museum named after Hector Pieterson, who was killed during the 1976 uprising. West of Johannesburg is the World Heritage site of Sterkfontein, Swarkrans, Kromdraai and Environs, where traces of humankind dating back 3.3 million years have been found.

Cape Town, a favoured tourist location, is overlooked by the famous Table Mountain. Tour the Cape Peninsula and visit Cape Point promontory with its lighthouse and far-reaching views. The vineyards of Stellenbosch are within an hour's drive of the city. Robben Island (a boat trip from Cape Town), infamous as the prison where anti-apartheid activists were held, is now a World Heritage site. Visit the sombre prison, now a museum; former political prisoners often lead tours.

The Garden Route, between Cape Town and Port Elizabeth is very attractive, bordered by forests, mountains, lakes and the fragrant bush of the *fynbos*. It is a floral kingdom unique to South Africa.

Kruger National Park in the northeast is one of the largest game reserves in Africa, offering classic opportunities for safaris.

KwaZulu-Natal has seaside resorts with whale and dolphin watching. Inland are game reserves and the Drakensberg mountains, as well as poignant memorials to the bloody wars fought between Zulu, British and Boer.

Lambert Azimuthal Equal Area Projection

1:5 000 000

MILES 0   50   100   150

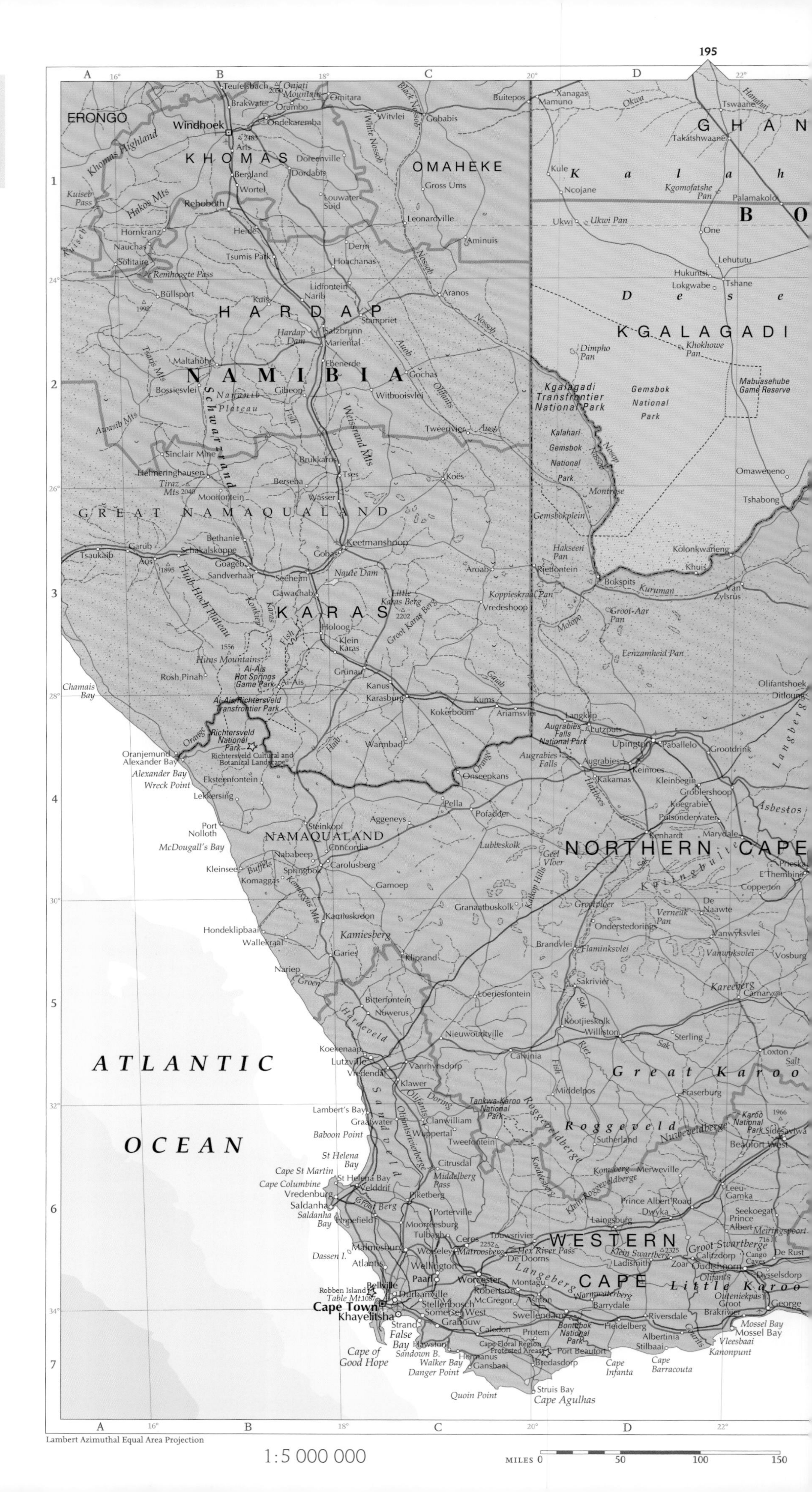

ZIMBABWE

INHAMBANE

TSWANA

CENTRAL

KWENENG

LIMPOPO

GAZA

MOZAMBIQUE

KGATLENG

SOUTHERN

SOUTH-EAST

Gaborone

Maputo

NORTH-WEST

GAUTENG

Pretoria (Tshwane)

Johannesburg

Soweto

MPUMALANGA

SWAZILAND

Mbabane

Manzini

Vereeniging

FREE STATE

GRIQUALAND WEST

REPUBLIC OF

Kimberley

Bloemfontein

Mangaung

Maseru

LESOTHO

KWAZULU-NATAL

Richards Bay

Pietermaritzburg

Durban

KwaMashu

Umlazi

SOUTH AFRICA

EASTERN CAPE

GRIQUALAND EAST

Port Edward

INDIAN OCEAN

Umtata

Wild Coast

East London

Mdantsane

Port Elizabeth

Cape Recife

Maputo

INHAMBANE

Tropic of Capricorn

KILOMETRES

0 50 100 150 200 250

© Collins Bartholomew Ltd

North America Physical

The continent of North America is taken to include Mexico, Central America and the Caribbean. Mexico is physically part of the continent, but since it is Spanish-speaking its cultural and linguistic links connect it closely with South and Central America. The mostly ice-covered island of Greenland – a dependency of Denmark – lies to the northeast. The continent contains a wide range of landscapes, from the Arctic north to sub-tropical Central America, and from the high mountains of the west, to the central Great Plains.

Facts

- The term Rocky Mountains is often applied to the whole mountain zone in the west. This area does, however, include many other significant mountain ranges and extensive plateaus.

- The Aleutian Islands, stretching in an arc across the northern Pacific, are part of Alaska.

- Lake Superior is the world's largest freshwater lake.

- Over 320 000 sq km (124 000 sq miles) of the USA is protected for conservation purposes.

- The inlet of the Pacific Ocean known as the Gulf of California is entirely within Mexico. The peninsula which defines it is known as Baja California, meaning Lower California.

HIGHEST MOUNTAINS	m	ft
Mt McKinley, USA	6 194	20 321
Mt Logan, Canada	5 959	19 550
Pico de Orizaba, Mexico	5 610	18 405
Mt St Elias, USA	5 489	18 008
Volcán Popocatépetl, Mexico	5 452	17 887
Mt Foraker, USA	5 303	17 398

LARGEST ISLANDS	sq km	sq miles
Greenland	2 175 600	839 999
Baffin Island	507 451	195 927
Victoria Island	217 291	83 896
Ellesmere Island	196 236	75 767
Cuba	110 860	42 803
Newfoundland	108 860	42 031
Hispaniola	76 192	29 418

LONGEST RIVERS	km	miles
Mississippi-Missouri	5 969	3 709
Mackenzie-Peace-Finlay	4 241	2 635
Missouri	4 086	2 539
Mississippi	3 765	2 340
Yukon	3 185	1 979
Rio Grande (Río Bravo del Norte)	3 057	1 900

LARGEST LAKES	sq km	sq miles
Lake Superior	82 100	31 699
Lake Huron	59 600	23 012
Lake Michigan	57 800	22 317
Great Bear Lake	31 328	12 096
Great Slave Lake	28 568	11 030
Lake Erie	25 700	9 923
Lake Winnipeg	24 387	9 416
Lake Ontario	18 960	7 320

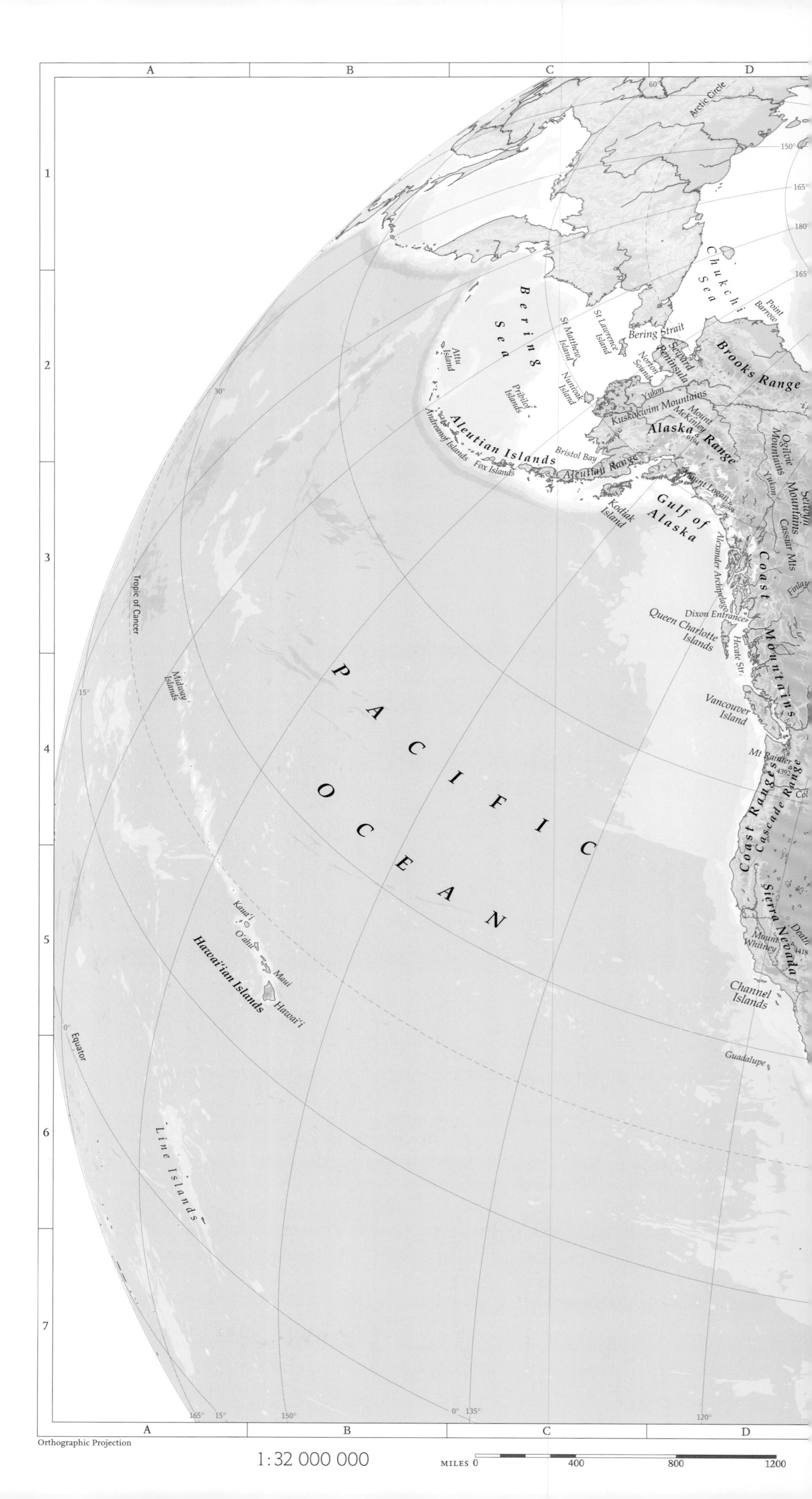

Orthographic Projection

1 : 32 000 000

MILES 0   400   800   1200

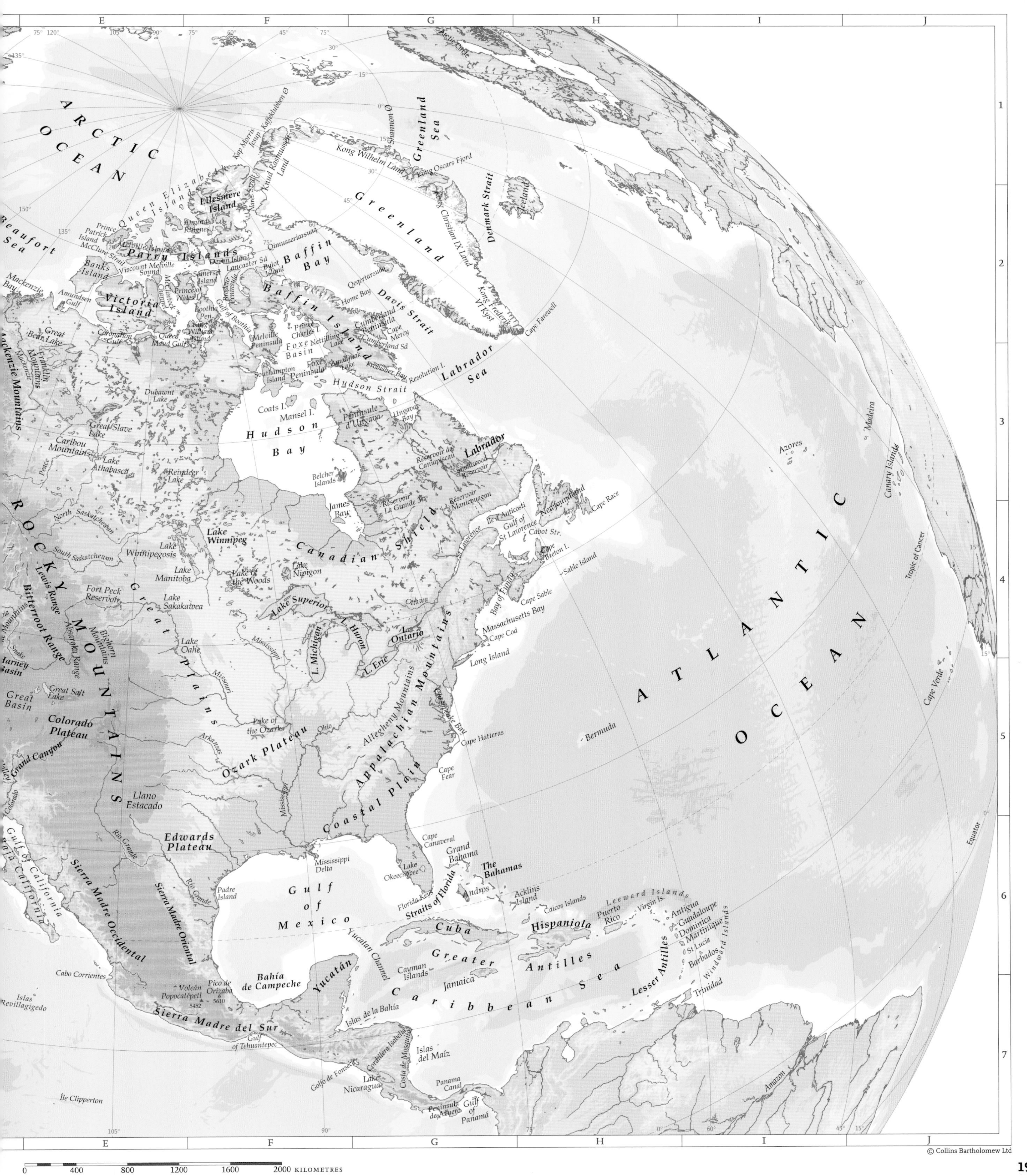

© Collins Bartholomew Ltd

0   400   800   1200   1600   2000 KILOMETRES

North America Political

The United States of America consists of the states south of the '49th Parallel', plus Hawaii, far out in the Pacific Ocean, and Alaska, the large peninsula in the northwest of the continent. Alaska lies partly within the Arctic Circle, and faces the Russian Federation across the narrow Bering Strait. Canada, formerly a dominion of the UK, occupies the north of the Continent. The region includes numerous overseas territories, from enormous Greenland to tiny islands in the Caribbean Sea.

Facts

- St Pierre and Miquelon is a small French dependent territory off the coast of Newfoundland and Labrador.

- The Caribbean Sea is defined as the area between the mainland of South America and the two major island arcs of the Greater Antilles (Cuba, Jamaica, Hispaniola, Puerto Rico) and the Lesser Antilles, which between them form the West Indies.

- Some islands of the West Indies remain as overseas dependencies of France, the Netherlands, the UK, and the USA.

- The world's longest single continuous land border stretches for 6416 km (3987 miles) between Canada and the USA.

LARGEST COUNTRIES	Area	
	sq km	sq miles
Canada	9 984 670	3 855 103
United States of America	9 826 635	3 794 085
Mexico	1 972 545	761 604
Nicaragua	130 000	50 193
Honduras	112 088	43 277
Cuba	110 860	42 803
Guatemala	108 890	42 043
Panama	77 082	29 762
Costa Rica	51 100	19 730
Dominican Republic	48 442	18 704

MOST POPULATED COUNTRIES	Population
United States of America	305 826 000
Mexico	106 535 000
Canada	32 876 000
Guatemala	13 354 000
Cuba	11 268 000
Dominican Republic	9 760 000
Haiti	9 598 000
Honduras	7 106 000
El Salvador	6 857 000
Nicaragua	5 603 000

CAPITALS		
Largest population	**Mexico City**, Mexico	20 688 000
Smallest population	**Brades**, Montserrat	1000
Most northerly	**Nuuk**, Greenland	64° 11' N
Most southerly	**Panama City**, Panama	8° 56' N
Highest	**Mexico City**, Mexico	2 300 m/ 7 546 ft

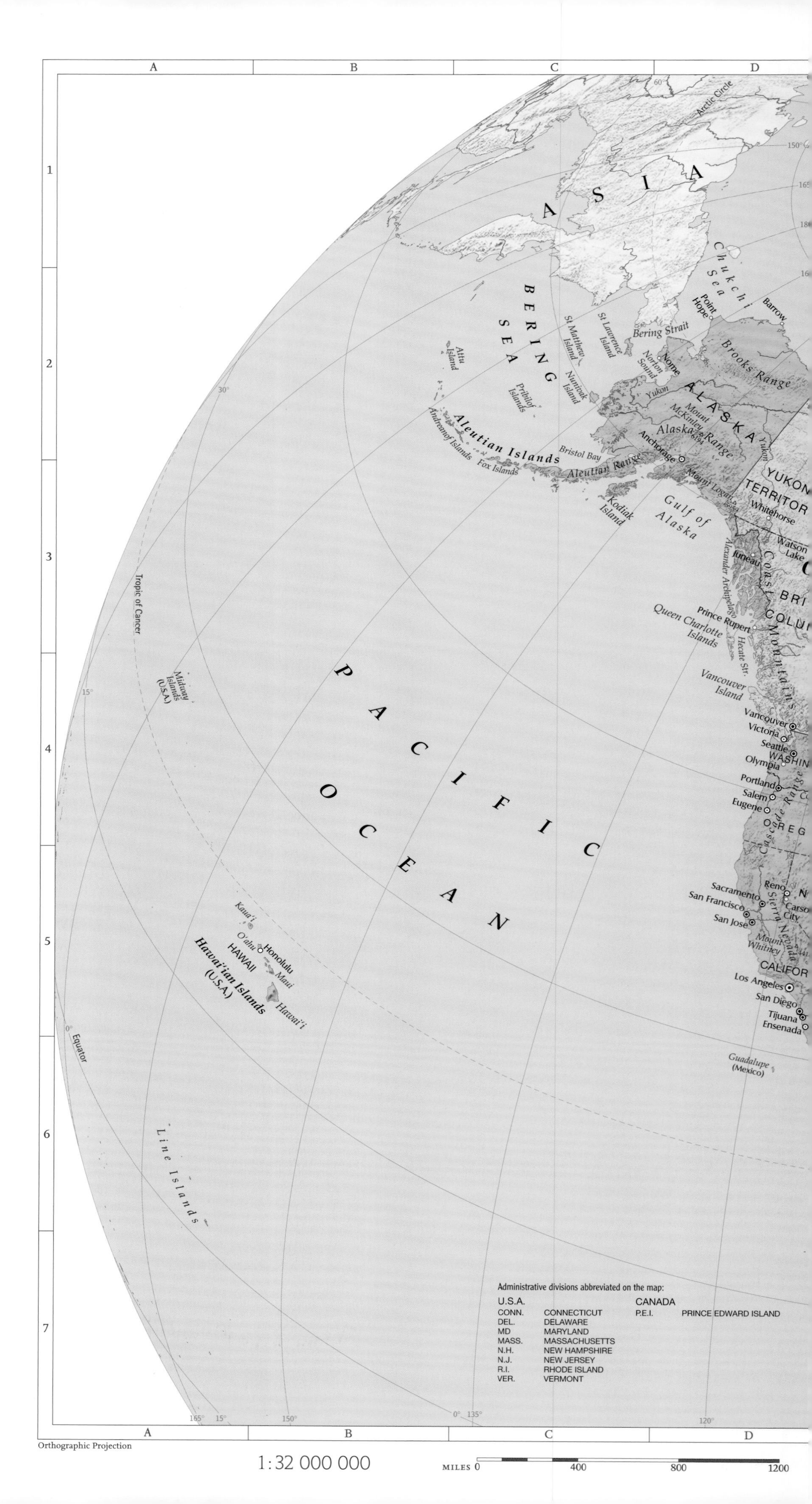

Administrative divisions abbreviated on the map:

U.S.A.		CANADA	
CONN.	CONNECTICUT	P.E.I.	PRINCE EDWARD ISLAND
DEL.	DELAWARE		
MD	MARYLAND		
MASS.	MASSACHUSETTS		
N.H.	NEW HAMPSHIRE		
N.J.	NEW JERSEY		
R.I.	RHODE ISLAND		
VER.	VERMONT		

Orthographic Projection

1 : 32 000 000

MILES 0   400   800   1200

ARCTIC OCEAN

EUROPE

Arctic Circle
Station Nord
Knud Rasmussen Land
Kong Wilhelm Land
Danebørg
Greenland Sea
Greenland
(Kalaallit Nunaat)
(Denmark)
Kong Christian IX Land
Kong Frederik VI Kyst
Denmark Strait
Iceland

Queen Elizabeth Islands
Ellesmere Island
Prince Patrick Island
Melville Island
McClure Strait
Banks Island
Viscount Melville Sound
Amund Ringnes I.
Devon Island
Lancaster Sd
Baffin Bay
Dundas
Nuussuaq
Clyde River
Ammassalik
Nuuk (Godthåb)

Beaufort Sea
Prince of Wales I.
Somerset Island
Baffin Island
Davis Strait
Cape Mercy
Labrador Sea
Nanortalik

Mackenzie Bay
Amundsen Gulf
Victoria Island
King William Island
Boothia Pen.
Gulf of Boothia
Prince Charles I.
Cumberland Sd
Iqaluit
Resolution I.

Sachs Harbour
Inuvik
Coronation Gulf
Melville Peninsula
Foxe Basin
Nain

Great Bear Lake
Déline
NUNAVUT
Bathurst Inlet
Repulse Bay
Southampton Island
Cape Dorset
Hudson Strait
Péninsule d'Ungava
Ungava Bay
NEWFOUNDLAND AND LABRADOR

NORTHWEST TERRITORIES
Yellowknife
Fort Simpson
Coral Harbour
Coats I.
Mansel I.
Arviat
HUDSON BAY
Chisasibi
Labrador
Smallwood Reservoir
Gander
St John's

Fort Nelson
Great Slave Lake
Uranium City
Lac Caniapiscau
Cape Race

Dawson Creek
McMurray
Lake Athabasca
Lynn Lake
Thompson
MANITOBA
Belcher Islands
James Bay
QUEBEC
Sept-Îles
Île d'Anticosti
Gulf of St Lawrence
St Pierre and Miquelon (France)

Grande Prairie
Jasper
ALBERTA
Lloydminster
Prince Albert
Saskatoon
SASKATCHEWAN
Lake Winnipeg
ONTARIO
Moosonee
Lac Nipigon
Timmins
Rouyn-Noranda
Chicoutimi
Québec
NEW BRUNSWICK
Charlottetown P.E.I.
Fredericton
NOVA SCOTIA
Cape Breton I.
Sable Island

Edmonton
Calgary
Medicine Hat
Regina
Winnipeg
Thunder Bay
Sault Ste Marie
North Bay
Montréal
Ottawa
MAINE
Halifax
Cape Sable

Lethbridge
Spokane
Great Falls
MONTANA
Helena
Billings
NORTH DAKOTA
Bismarck
Grand Forks
MINNESOTA
Duluth
Lake Superior
MICHIGAN
Toronto
L. Ontario
Montpelier VER.
NEW YORK
N.H.
Concord
MASS.
Boston
Providence
Cape Cod

IDAHO
Boise
WYOMING
Rapid City
SOUTH DAKOTA
Pierre
Sioux Falls
Minneapolis
St Paul
WISCONSIN
Rochester
Lansing
L. Michigan
Milwaukee
L. Huron
Detroit
Buffalo
Albany
Hartford CONN.
R.I.
New York

Twin Falls
Great Salt Lake
Salt Lake City
NEBRASKA
Cheyenne
North Platte
IOWA
Des Moines
Omaha
ILLINOIS
Chicago
Cleveland
L. Erie
Erie
PENNSYLVANIA
Pittsburgh
N.J.
Trenton
Philadelphia
DEL.

Las Vegas
UTAH
Denver
COLORADO
Lincoln
KANSAS
Kansas City
St Louis
MISSOURI
Springfield
Indianapolis
INDIANA
Cincinnati
OHIO
Columbus
Charleston
WEST VIRGINIA
Baltimore
Washington D.C.
Richmond
VIRGINIA

Albuquerque
Santa Fe
ARIZONA
Phoenix
Tucson
NEW MEXICO
Amarillo
Lubbock
OKLAHOMA
Oklahoma City
ARKANSAS
Little Rock
TENNESSEE
Nashville
Memphis
Knoxville
Charlotte
N.CAROLINA
Raleigh
Cape Hatteras
Columbia
S.CAROLINA

Mexicali
Tucson
El Paso
Ciudad Juárez
TEXAS
Fort Worth
Dallas
Shreveport
Jackson
MISS.
ALABAMA
Montgomery
GEORGIA
Savannah
UNITED STATES OF AMERICA
KENTUCKY
Atlanta

Hermosillo
Chihuahua
Rio Grande
Austin
San Antonio
Houston
Baton Rouge
LOUISIANA
New Orleans
Mobile
Tallahassee
Jacksonville

Gulf of California
Los Mochis
Monterrey
Matamoros
Corpus Christi
GULF OF MEXICO
Orlando
Tampa
FLORIDA
Cape Canaveral

Villa Insurgentes
La Paz
Mazatlán
MEXICO
Durango
Ciudad Victoria
Tampico
Monterrey
Miami
THE BAHAMAS
Nassau
Turks and Caicos Is (U.K.)

Tepic
Guadalajara
León
Morelia
Mexico City
Veracruz
Bahía de Campeche
Mérida
Yucatán
Yucatan Channel
Havana
Santa Clara
Holguín
CUBA
Hispaniola
DOMINICAN REPUBLIC
San Juan
Virgin Is (U.K.)
Anguilla (U.K.)
ANTIGUA AND BARBUDA
Guadeloupe (France)
DOMINICA

Islas Revillagigedo (Mexico)
Acapulco
Oaxaca
Puebla
Villahermosa
BELIZE
Belmopan
San Pedro Sula
Cayman Is (U.K.)
Montego Bay
JAMAICA
Kingston
Greater Antilles
HAITI
Port-au-Prince
Santo Domingo
Puerto Rico (U.S.A.)
ST KITTS AND NEVIS
Virgin Is (U.S.A.)
Montserrat (U.K.)
Martinique (France)
ST LUCIA
BARBADOS

Gulf of Tehuantepec
GUATEMALA
Guatemala City
San Salvador
EL SALVADOR
HONDURAS
Tegucigalpa
NICARAGUA
Lake Nicaragua
Managua
Colón
Panama City
PANAMA
San José
COSTA RICA
Gulf of Panama
CARIBBEAN SEA
Lesser Antilles
Netherlands Antilles
Aruba (Neth.)
ST VINCENT AND THE GRENADINES
GRENADA
TRINIDAD AND TOBAGO
Port of Spain

SOUTH AMERICA
Amazon

Île Clipperton (France)

ATLANTIC OCEAN
AFRICA
Madeira
Canary Islands
Azores
Tropic of Cancer
Cape Verde
Bermuda (U.K.)
Equator

© Collins Bartholomew Ltd

0   400   800   1200   1600   2000 KILOMETRES

201

Canada

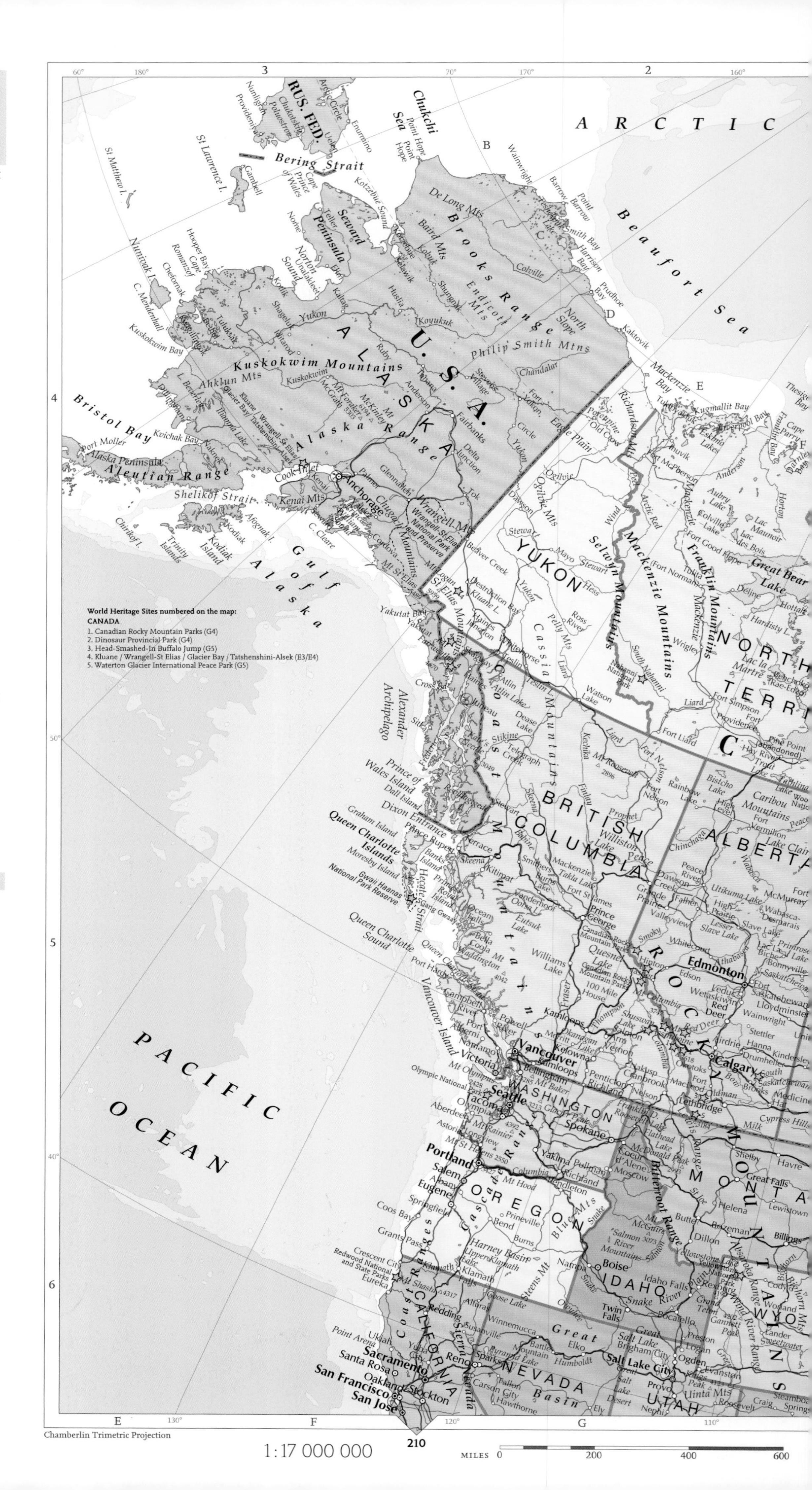

CANADA Capital: **Ottawa**
Area: **9 984 670 km²/3 855 103 miles²**
Population: **32 876 000** Languages: **English, French**
Religions: **Roman Catholic, Protestant, Eastern Orthodox,
Jewish** Currency: **Canadian dollar**

Canada is such a vast country that we have captured it over eight pages of mapping. These two pages show all of Canada and its border with the USA, together with Greenland, a self-governing Danish territory. Western Canada is shown on pages 204–5, eastern Canada on pages 206–7 and the Great Lakes area on pages 208–9.

Canada, the second largest country in the world by area after Russia, spans six time zones and borders three oceans. It is hugely varied, with thirteen provinces and immense natural beauty and sophisticated cities. Opportunities for winter sports, hiking, mountain biking and watersports, together with a vivid history, rich culture and multi-ethnic population mean that the choices for the traveller are endless.

Such an immense country invites journeying of all kinds. Make your own epic rail journey between Toronto and Vancouver, across the lakes of northern Ontario, the western prairies and the Rocky Mountains to the Pacific coast. Or, travel on a luxurious private rail car through the Montréal–Gaspé region of Québec visiting fabulous, award-winning gardens. There are railway museums too: Exporail in Montréal describes the vital role of the railways in Canada's development; the Canadian Museum of Rail Travel in Cranbrook, British Columbia, displays magnificently preserved railway passenger cars. Take the road trip of a lifetime along the Trans-Canada Highway, a route of 7 821 km (4 860 miles) between Victoria, British Columbia, and St John's, Newfoundland. Travel over mountains, through national parks, alongside lakes, and visit Canada's major cities on the way. Those with good sea legs can board a tall ship for a voyage through historic waterways, exploring Canada's amazing coastline (the longest of any country in the world); see glaciers and polar bears on an eco-cruise; or kayak through Saskatchewan's wilderness of 100 000 lakes and rivers. Hop on a plane to Inuvik, Yukon, Canada's largest community north of the Arctic Circle, land of the Midnight Sun and the Northern Lights (Aurora Borealis).

GREENLAND

Greenland, the largest island in the world, is visited for its breathtaking glaciers, ice sheets and fjords, the Aurora Borealis and the Midnight Sun. Snow and ice allow for exciting dog sled trips and snowmobiling; kayaking, sailing and hiking are also on offer. In the brief Arctic summer, mountain landscapes transform into colourful, flower-covered scenes. Fascinating birds and mammals can be seen all year round. Enjoy stunning vistas while bathing in hot springs, visit ancient Norse remains, or take *kaffemik* with a Greenlandic family. Greenland has a unique culture, and Nuuk, the capital, is an interesting combination of old and new.

World Heritage Sites numbered on the map:
CANADA
1. Canadian Rocky Mountain Parks (G4)
2. Dinosaur Provincial Park (G4)
3. Head-Smashed-In Buffalo Jump (G5)
4. Kluane / Wrangell-St Elias / Glacier Bay / Tatshenshini-Alsek (E3/E4)
5. Waterton Glacier International Peace Park (G5)

Chamberlin Trimetric Projection

1 : 17 000 000

MILES 0   200   400   600

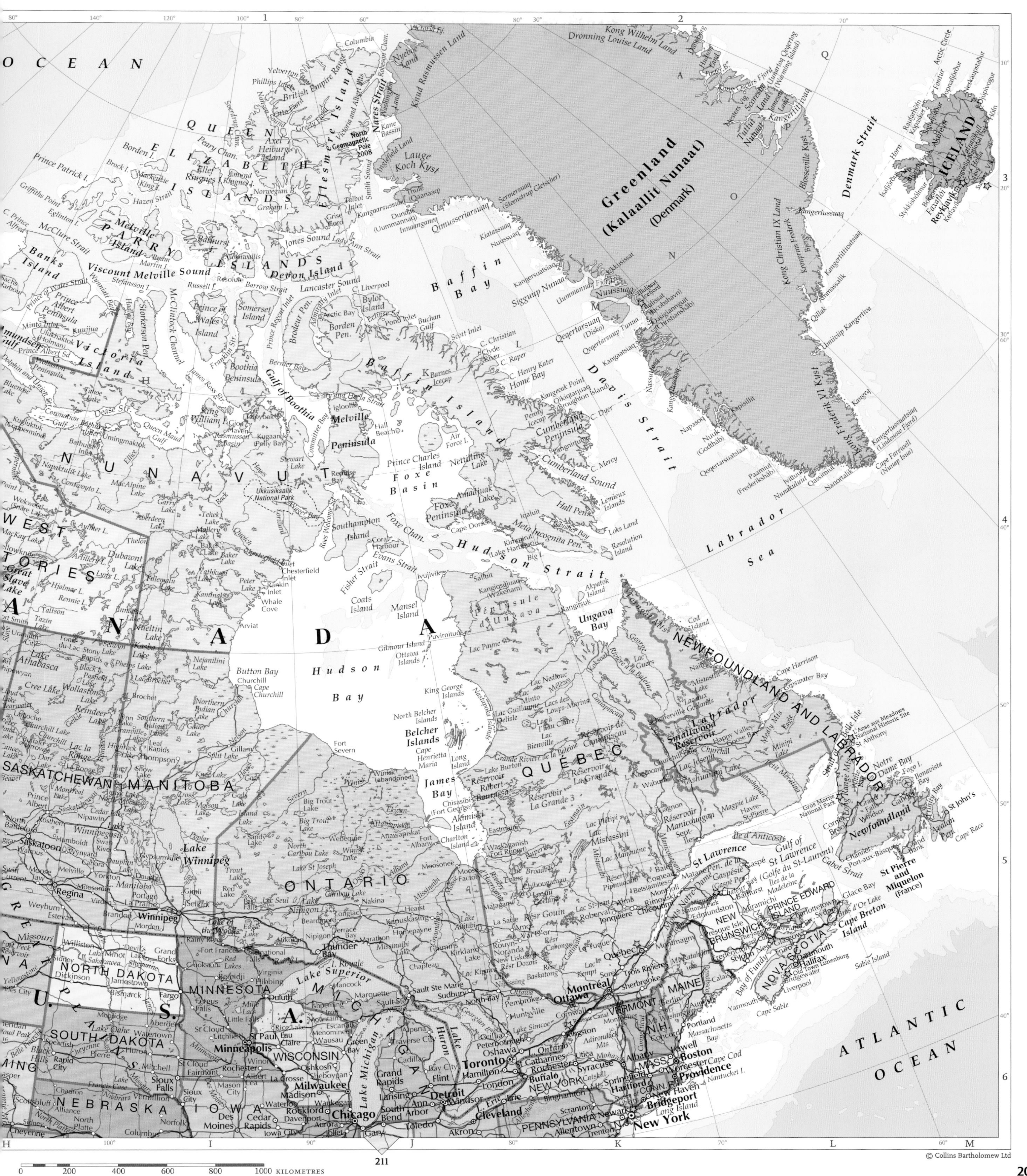
OCEAN
QUEEN ELIZABETH ISLANDS
PARRY ISLANDS
Ellesmere Island
Devon Island
Banks Island
Victoria Island
Viscount Melville Sound
Lancaster Sound
Baffin Bay
Baffin Island
Greenland (Kalaallit Nunaat) (Denmark)
Denmark Strait
ICELAND
Reykjavík
Davis Strait
Gulf of Boothia
Melville Peninsula
Foxe Basin
Southampton Island
Hudson Strait
Labrador Sea
Ungava Bay
Péninsule d'Ungava
NUNAVUT
NORTHWEST TERRITORIES
CANADA
Hudson Bay
James Bay
Belcher Islands
NEWFOUNDLAND AND LABRADOR
Labrador
Smallwood Reservoir
QUÉBEC
ONTARIO
MANITOBA
SASKATCHEWAN
Lake Winnipeg
Lake Athabasca
Winnipeg
Regina
Saskatoon
Gulf of St Lawrence
Newfoundland
St John's
St Pierre and Miquelon (France)
NEW BRUNSWICK
PRINCE EDWARD ISLAND
NOVA SCOTIA
Cape Breton Island
Halifax
Québec
Montréal
Ottawa
Toronto
Lake Superior
Lake Michigan
Lake Huron
Lake Ontario
L. Erie
NORTH DAKOTA
SOUTH DAKOTA
MINNESOTA
WISCONSIN
MICHIGAN
NEBRASKA
IOWA
NEW YORK
PENNSYLVANIA
VERMONT
MAINE
U.S.A.
Minneapolis
Milwaukee
Chicago
Detroit
Cleveland
Buffalo
Boston
Providence
New York
ATLANTIC OCEAN
0 200 400 600 800 1000 KILOMETRES

211

Western Canada

Canada's northwest comprises Yukon, the Northwest Territories and Nunavut, all home to arctic wildlife. Nunavut, with a largely Inuit population, has its capital in Iqaluit, where the museum houses large collections of Inuit sculpture, prints and artefacts. Nearby is a beautiful river and waterfalls.

The Rocky Mountains stretch from British Columbia through southwest Alberta, on into the United States. Ski, hike or rock climb, or take the Rocky Mountaineer train, past mountains, glaciers and wonderful wildlife. Visit Vancouver city for metropolitan sophistication; historic Victoria with glorious flower gardens; and Whistler's Olympic ski runs, winter trails and panoramic chairlifts. Calgary has great shopping and vibrant arts; Edmonton, over seventy museums and annual festivals.

Saskatchewan and Manitoba's wide open spaces present diverse contrasts – from golden wheat fields and prairie grass to sand dunes and Arctic tundra. Hike and camp in the forests; visit Lake Winnipeg to swim, sail or fish; raft or canoe the rivers and lakes. There are urban delights, too, with shopping and dining in Winnipeg, entertainment in Saskatoon's Broadway District, and museums and galleries in Regina.

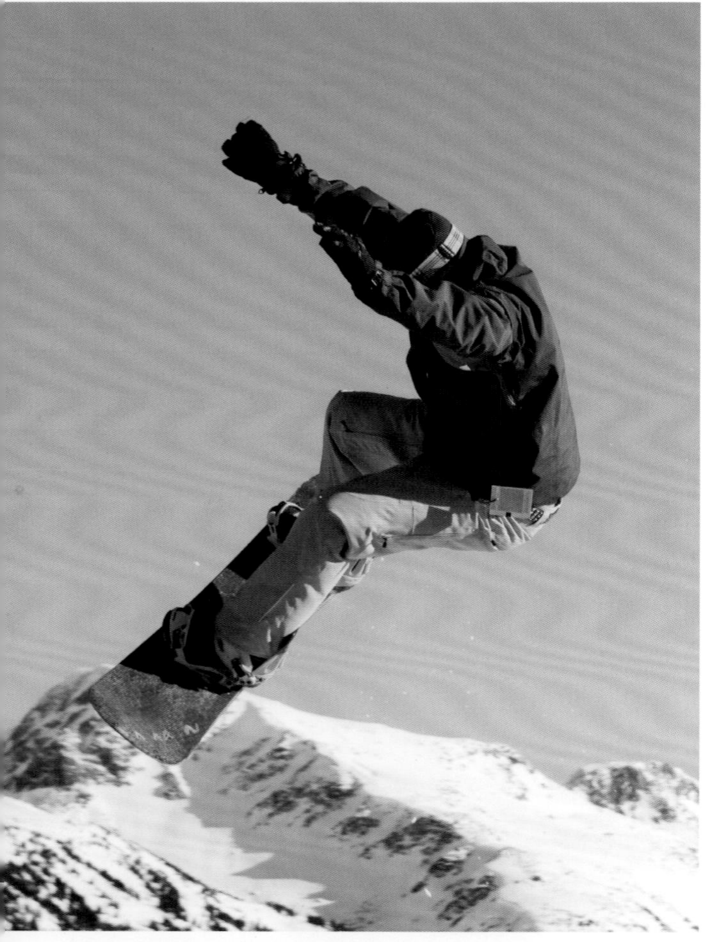

A snowboarder at the resort of **Whistler** in British Columbia, site of many of the events of the 2010 Winter Olympics.

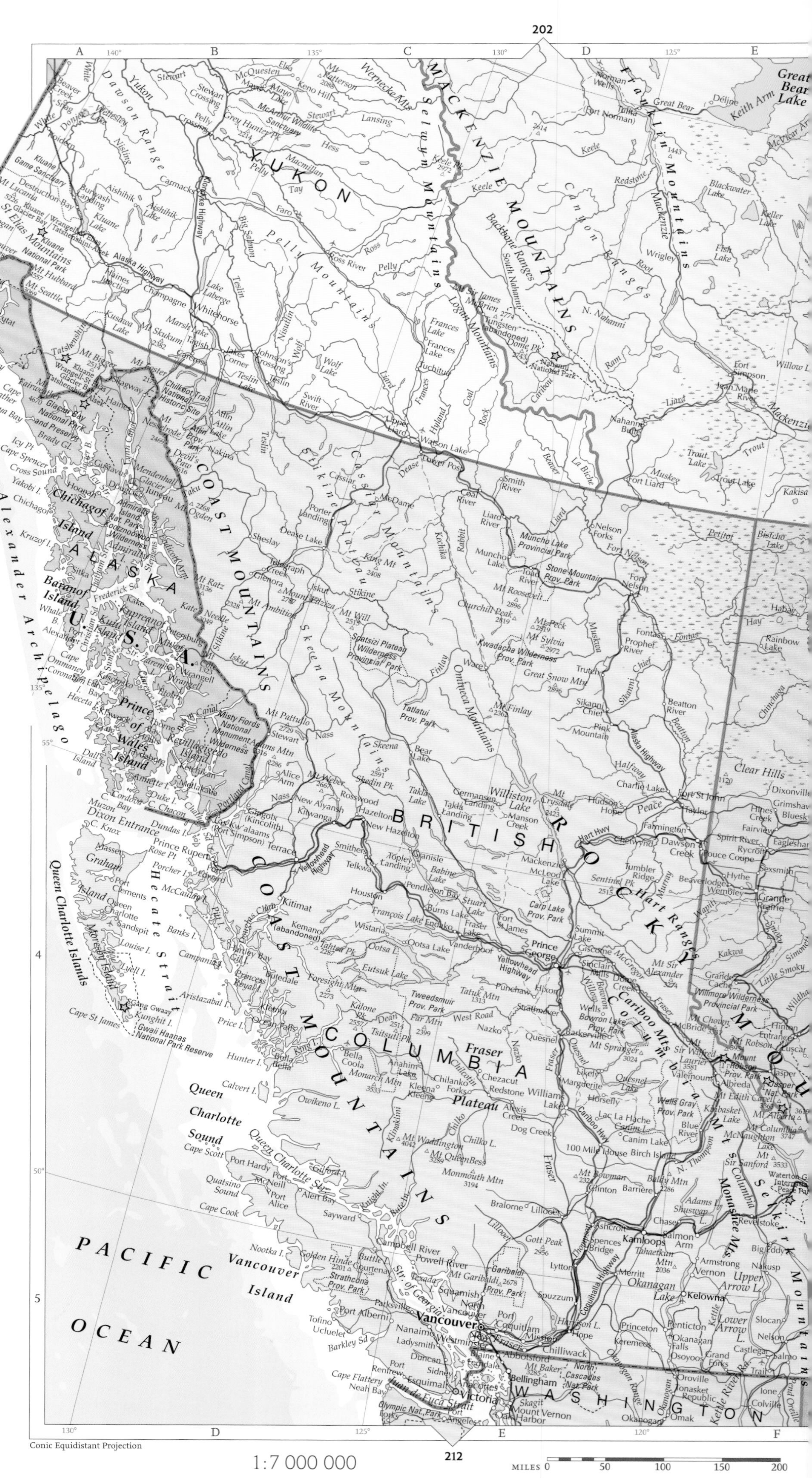

Conic Equidistant Projection

1:7 000 000

MILES 0   50   100   150   200

F G H I J K L M

120° 115° 110° 105° 100° 95° 90° 85°

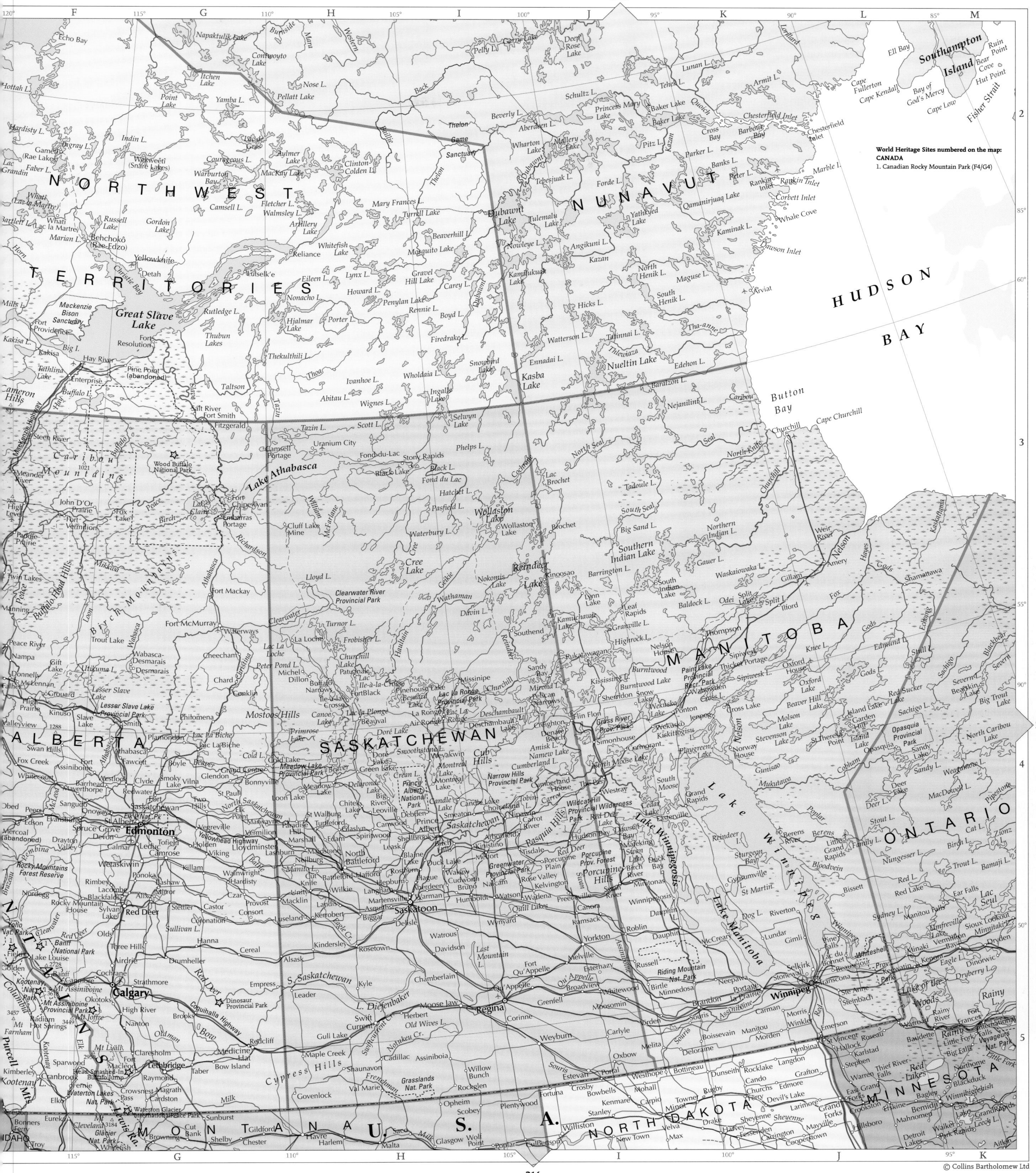

World Heritage Sites numbered on the map:
CANADA
1. Canadian Rocky Mountain Park (F4/G4)

N O R T H W E S T   T E R R I T O R I E S

N U N A V U T

HUDSON BAY

Southampton Island

Great Slave Lake

Lake Athabasca

Wood Buffalo National Park

A L B E R T A

S A S K A T C H E W A N

M A N I T O B A

O N T A R I O

Edmonton

Red Deer

Calgary

Saskatoon

Regina

Winnipeg

Lake Winnipeg

Lake Winnipegosis

Lake Manitoba

Reindeer Lake

Wollaston Lake

Cree Lake

Southern Indian Lake

Churchill

Prince Albert National Park

Riding Mountain Nat. Park

Grasslands Nat. Park

Banff National Park

Waterton Lakes Nat. Park

M O N T A N A   U. S. A.

N O R T H   D A K O T A

M I N N E S O T A

0 50 100 150 200 250 300 350 KILOMETRES

© Collins Bartholomew Ltd

Eastern Canada

The central provinces of Ontario and Québec offer cosmopolitan cities, magnificent rivers and lakes, and endless opportunities for great outdoor adventures, whether on foot, by bike or on the water. From the history and heritage of Québec City, Canada's capital Ottawa and its Parliament Hill, wineries and epicurean delights, rehabilitated polar bears in Cochrane and moose in Matane Wildlife Reserve, the art museums of Toronto, festivals and exhibitions in Montreal, St Lawrence River, the Rideau Canal and Niagara Falls, there is a huge choice of destinations and activities.

On the eastern edge of Canada, bordering the Atlantic Ocean, is a region of rugged coastline and islands: Newfoundland, Prince Edward Island (PEI), Cape Breton Island (all Canadian provinces except Cape Breton), and the provinces of New Brunswick, Nova Scotia, and Newfoundland and Labrador. There are routes and trails hugging the glorious beaches, winding through the national parks: discover a 1 000-year-old Norse settlement, and the house of Anne of Green Gables; explore the Bay of Fundy with the world's greatest tidal reach; the coloured sands of PEI's beaches and romantic 19th-century covered bridges; experience the lands of the Inuit people, and see black and polar bears and huge herds of caribou.

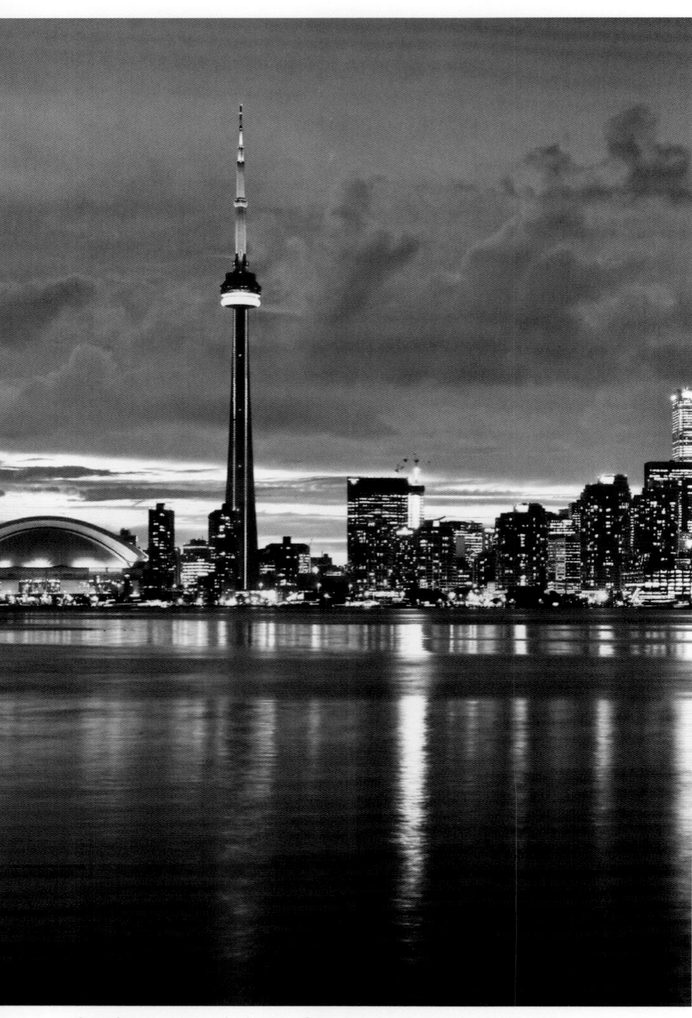

The distinctive skyline of **Toronto** Ontario, with the CN Tower in the middle and the Rogers Centre (formerly known as the SkyDome), home to the city's baseball team the Toronto Blue Jays, to the left.

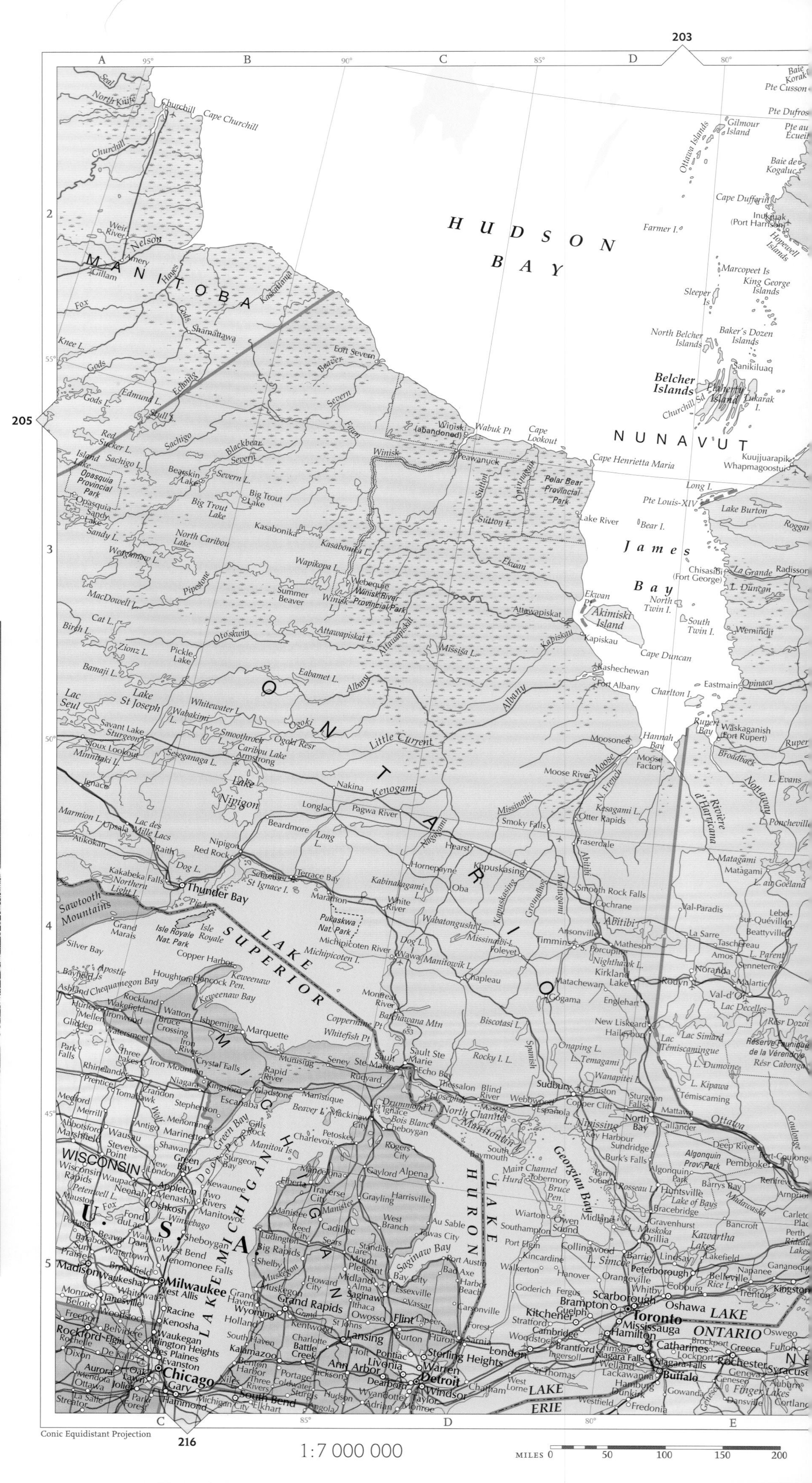

Conic Equidistant Projection

1:7 000 000

MILES 0   50   100   150   200

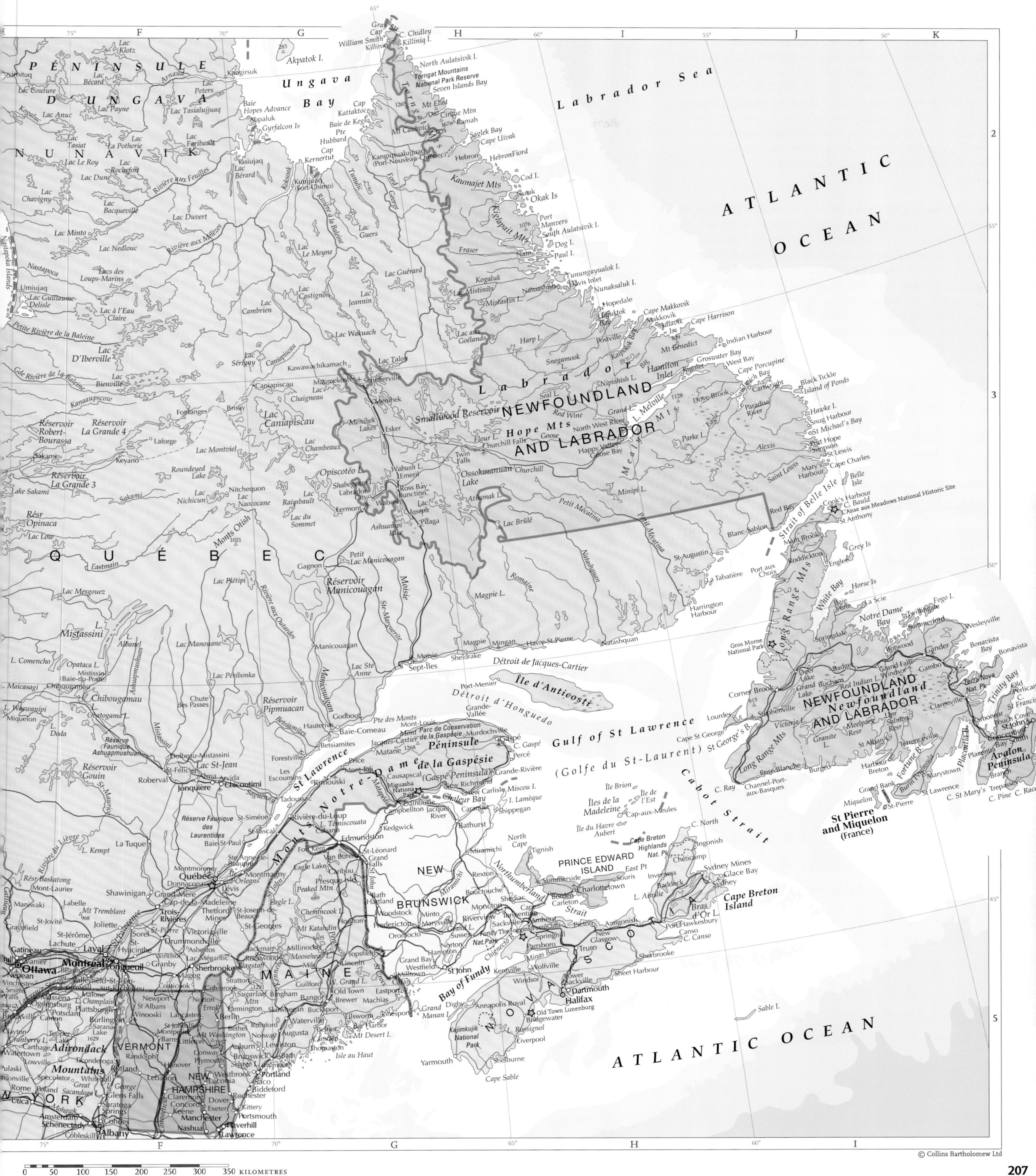

© Collins Bartholomew Ltd

PÉNINSULE D'UNGAVA
NUNAVIK
QUÉBEC
Ungava Bay
Labrador Sea
ATLANTIC OCEAN
Labrador
NEWFOUNDLAND AND LABRADOR
Newfoundland
Gulf of St Lawrence
(Golfe du St-Laurent)
Cabot Strait
Strait of Belle Isle
Détroit de Jacques-Cartier
Détroit d'Honguedo
Île d'Anticosti
Péninsule de la Gaspésie (Gaspé Peninsula)
Monts Notre-Dame
St Lawrence
Chaleur Bay
NEW BRUNSWICK
PRINCE EDWARD ISLAND
NOVA SCOTIA
Cape Breton Island
Northumberland Strait
Bay of Fundy
Îles de la Madeleine
St Pierre and Miquelon (France)
Avalon Peninsula
MAINE
VERMONT
NEW HAMPSHIRE
NEW YORK
Adirondack Mountains
Akpatok I.
Torngat Mountains National Park Reserve
Kaumajet Mts
Kiglapait Mts
Mealy Mts
Hope Mts
Long Range Mts
Smallwood Reservoir
Lac Caniapiscau
Réservoir Manicouagan
Réservoir Robert-Bourassa
Réservoir La Grande 4
Réservoir La Grande 3
Lac Mistassini
Lac St-Jean
Réservoir Gouin
Réservoir Pipmuacan
Lac Minto
Lac à l'Eau Claire
Lac Guillaume-Delisle
Lake Melville
Hamilton Inlet
Québec
Montréal
Ottawa
Sherbrooke
Trois-Rivières
Chicoutimi
Jonquière
Sept-Îles
Baie-Comeau
Gaspé
Rimouski
Rivière-du-Loup
Edmundston
Fredericton
Saint John
Moncton
Charlottetown
Halifax
Dartmouth
Sydney
Truro
Yarmouth
Bangor
Augusta
Portland
Burlington
Albany
Manchester
Concord
Kuujjuaq (Fort-Chimo)
Kangiqsualujjuaq (Port-Nouveau-Québec)
Nain
Hopedale
Happy Valley-Goose Bay
Labrador City
Wabush
Churchill Falls
Schefferville
Fermont
Blanc-Sablon
St Anthony
Corner Brook
Gander
Grand Falls-Windsor
St John's
Channel-Port-aux-Basques
Gros Morne National Park
L'Anse aux Meadows National Historic Site
Sable I.
Cape Sable
Cape Breton Highlands Nat. Pk
75° 70° 65° 60° 55° 50°
F G H I J K
2 3 4 5
0 50 100 150 200 250 300 350 KILOMETRES

The Great Lakes

The Great Lakes of North America – Superior, Huron, Erie and Ontario – are shared between the USA and Canada, with Lake Michigan lying entirely within the USA. The lakes are interconnected by channels and rivers. The Great Lakes Circle Tour is 10 500 km (6 500 miles) of scenic road tour circling each of the lakes and connecting them and the St Lawrence River. The route provides access to great wilderness areas and waterfront beaches in major cities. There are plentiful opportunities to camp and for all sorts of outdoor activities and sports.

Glorious Niagara Falls sits on the border between the Canadian province of Ontario and the US state of New York. The falls span two major sections separated by Goat Island: the Horseshoe Falls, the majority of which are in Canada; and the American Falls and Bridal Veil Falls, on the American side. Visitors can take a boat trip or travel deep into Niagara Gorge and follow a series of walkways to the famous Hurricane Deck, just 6 metres (20 feet) from the torrents of water. Rainbow Bridge offers great views of the falls, which are floodlight after dark. Close by there is a waterpark, an aviary and the Rainbow Tower.

The lakes have played a significant role in the economic development of North America and some of the continent's largest cities lie within the area.

Chicago is situated on the banks of Lake Michigan and is the USA's third-largest city. It offers miles of lakefront trails and peaceful gardens, as well as theatres and orchestras, restaurants and fantastic shopping. Millennium Park is a celebration of sculptures, fountains, landscaped gardens and architecture, with regular free concerts and events. The diversity of the city and its inhabitants is seen in museums such as the National Museum of Mexican Art, Polish Museum of America, DuSable Museum of African American History and the Oriental Institute. City Gallery is located in the Historic Water Tower, one of the few buildings to survive the Great Chicago Fire of 1871. Navy Pier is popular, with fairground rides, a landmark ferris wheel, boat cruises, theatre and the Smith Museum of Stained Glass. Skydeck Chicago and the Hancock Observatory offer stunning birds-eye views encompassing Chicago and four states – Indiana, Michigan, Wisconsin and Illinois.

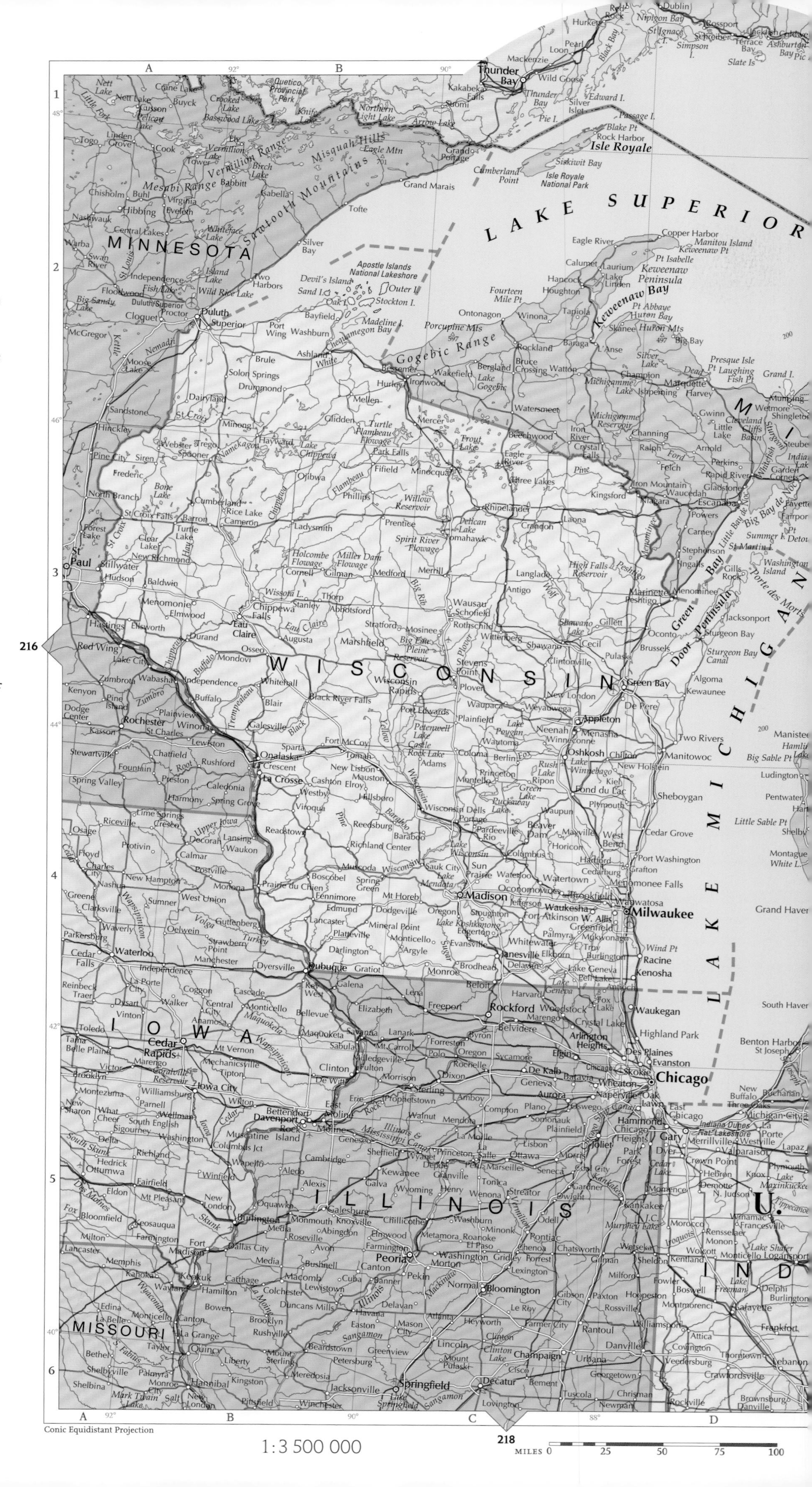

Conic Equidistant Projection

1:3 500 000

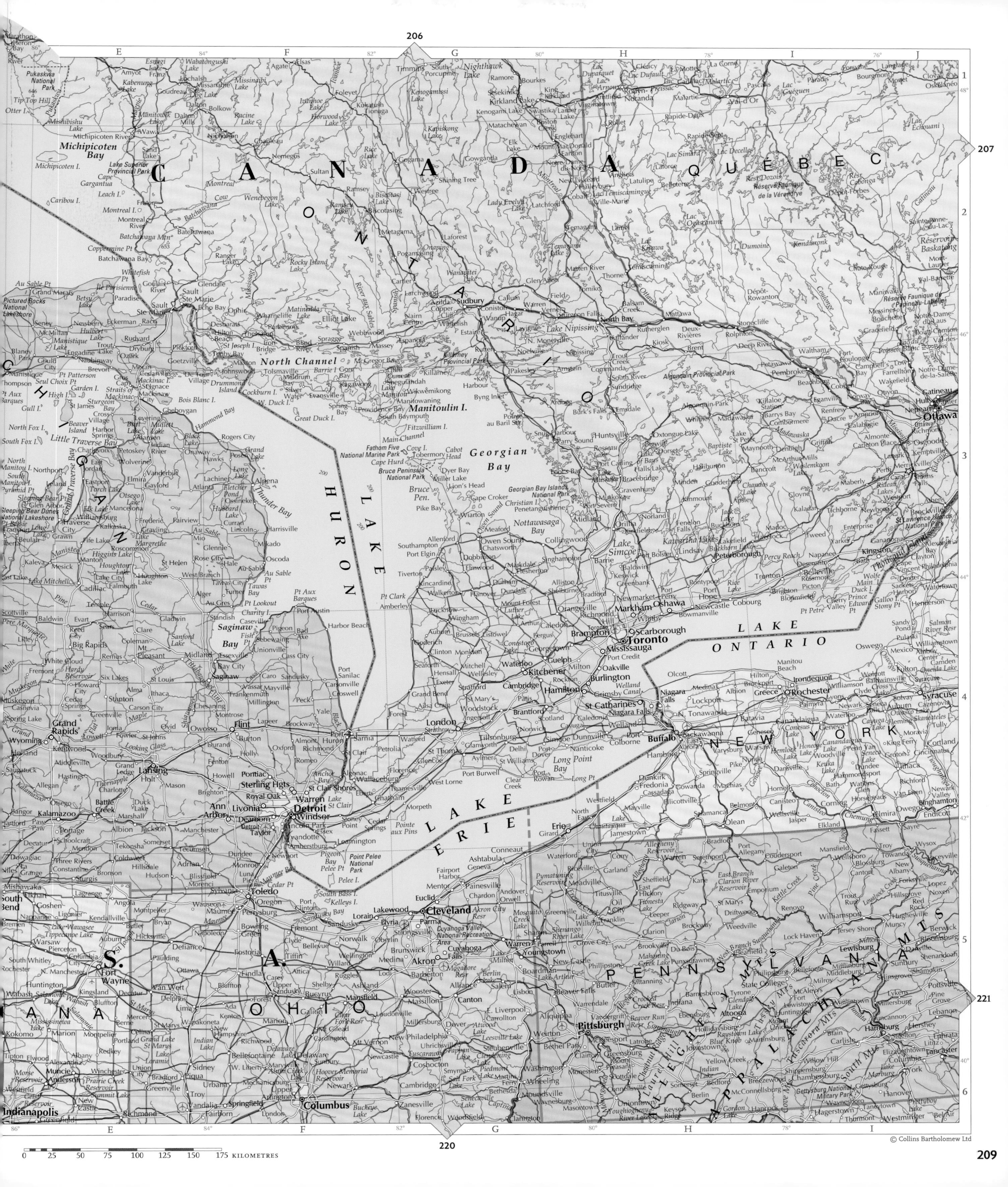

United States of America

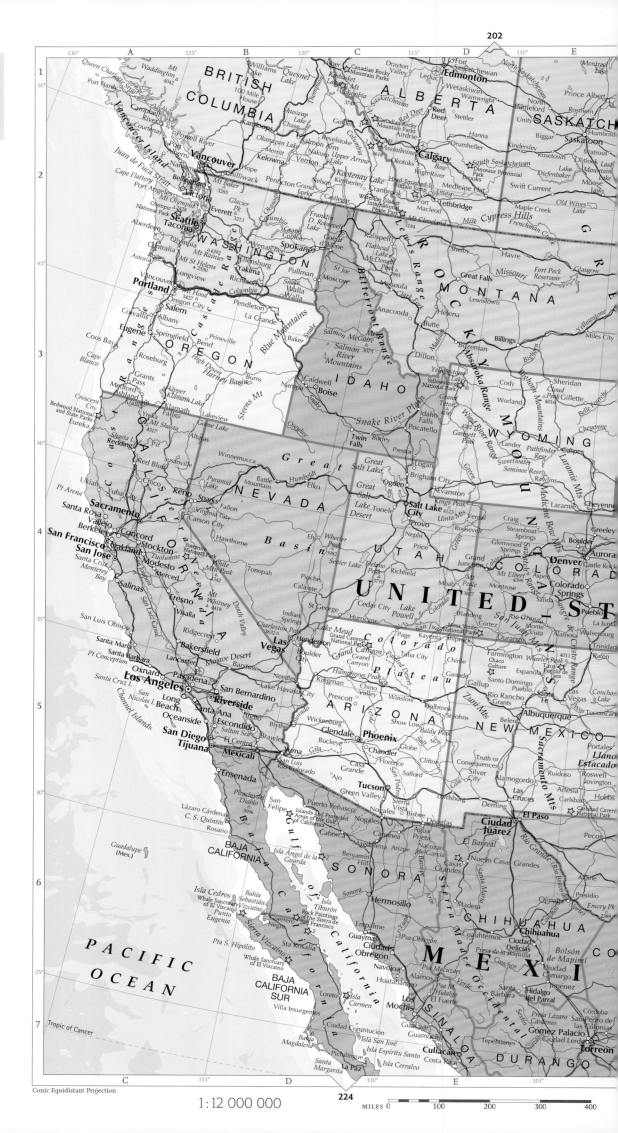

![US flag] **UNITED STATES OF AMERICA**
Capital: **Washington D.C.**
Area: **9 826 635 km²/3 794 085 miles²**
Population: **305 826 000** Languages: **English, Spanish**
Religions: **Protestant, Roman Catholic, Sunni Muslim, Jewish**
Currency: **United States dollar**

The USA, third-largest country of the world by area and population, is a melting pot of cultures – indigenous peoples inhabited the mainland for thousands of years and the modern country was founded on mass immigration from all parts of the world. It comprises fifty states (forty-eight are shown on this map, including the District of Columbia) plus Hawaii and Alaska.

It is a country of teeming cities and vast empty plains, art and culture, national parks and scenic byways (there are 151 distinct and diverse designated routes) and restaurants serving food from every part of the world. Leading destinations include Las Vegas, Los Angeles, San Francisco, Orlando, Miami, Walt Disney World® and New York City.

Flying is the quickest and often the most convenient way to travel this huge country. A coast-to-coast flight, from east to west, takes around six hours. The national rail system, Amtrak, provides services to many cities, traversing beautiful landscapes and offering views not seen from an aeroplane. Hire a car or motorbike for a classic American road trip following the interstate highways and freeways. Bus travel is the cheapest method of travel, but takes much longer, journeying cross-country taking several days.

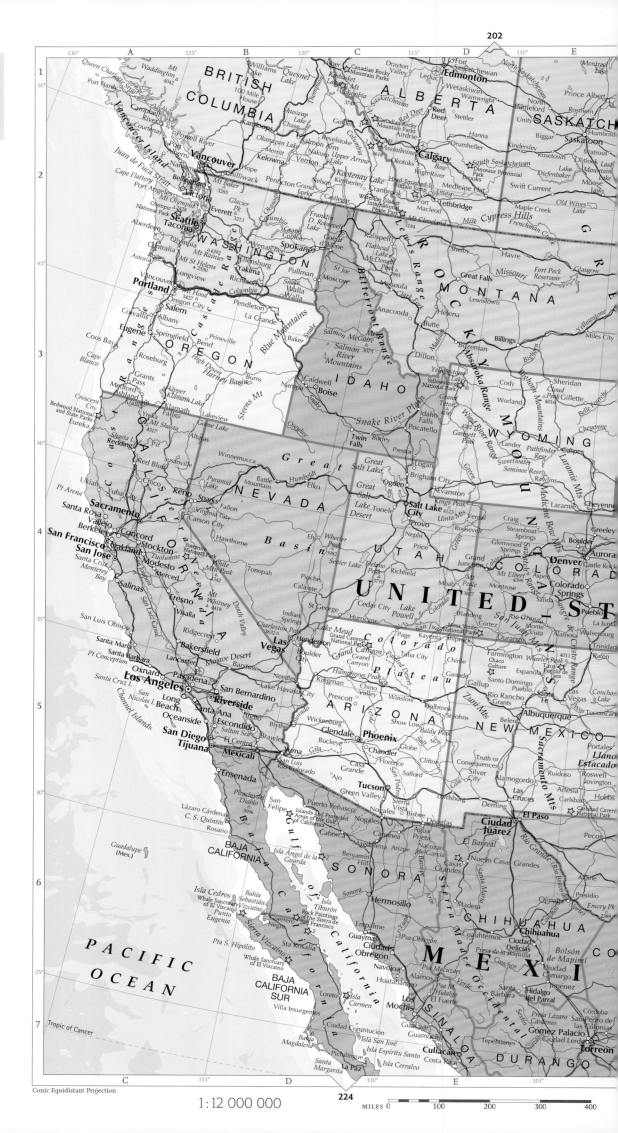

Conic Equidistant Projection

1 : 12 000 000

MILES 0   100   200   300   400

World Heritage Sites numbered on the map:
CANADA
1. Canadian Rocky Mountain Parks (C1)

MEXICO
2. Islands and Protected Areas of the Gulf of California (D6)

ATLANTIC OCEAN

GULF OF MEXICO

THE BAHAMAS

0   100   200   300   400   500   600   KILOMETRES

© Collins Bartholomew Ltd

Western USA

Mountains, deserts and the Pacific coast feature in this part of the USA. The Grand Canyon is a must-see for many visitors, an awe-inspiring natural spectacle of colourful ancient rock layers. Its sheer size is almost overwhelming, at 446 km (277 miles) long and around 1.8 km (over a mile) deep. Utah is a major tourist destination, particularly for outdoor sports, from mountain biking to skiing. The desert scenery is spectacular. Historic St George has museums, golf courses, a popular marathon and is the gateway to Zion and Bryce Canyon national parks. Las Vegas, in Nevada, is known the world over for its hotels and casinos, entertainment, restaurants and shopping. It also has many parks and outdoor spaces, and an arts district.

California, another must-do destination is home to the Redwood, Yosemite and Joshua Tree national parks, Lake Tahoe and the Big Sur, with a stunning coastline, waterfalls and panoramic views. It is also famed for its beaches, from windswept cliffs to expanses of smooth sand and rock pools. Anaheim in California is the location of the original Disneyland® and its Magic Kingdom, expanded in 2001 with the California Adventure Park, with shows, parades and attractions celebrating everything Californian.

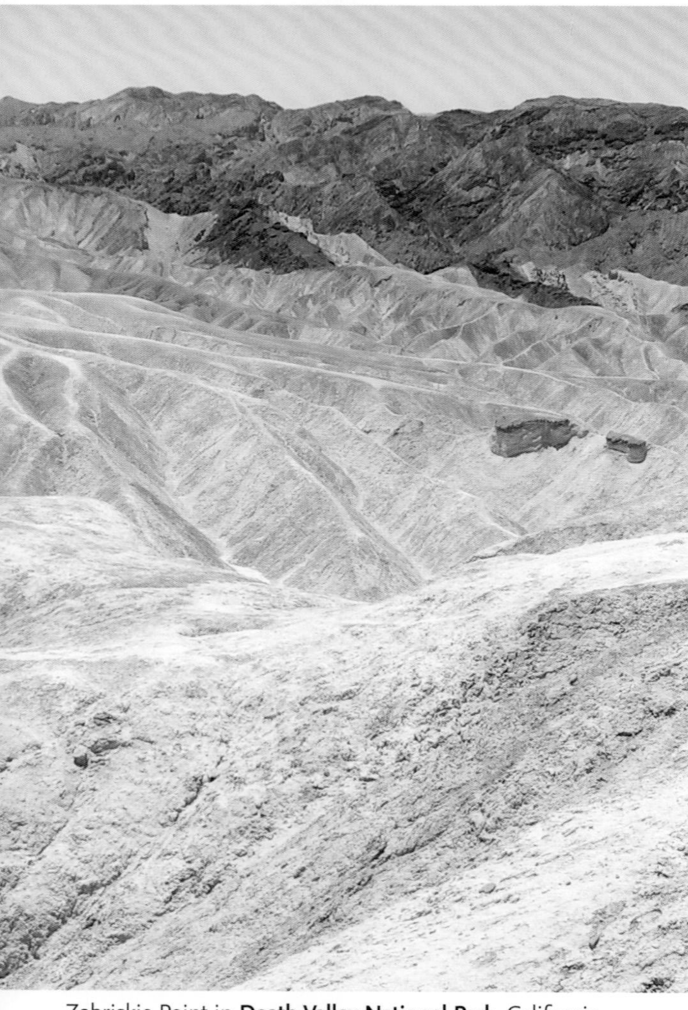

Zabriskie Point in **Death Valley National Park**, California.

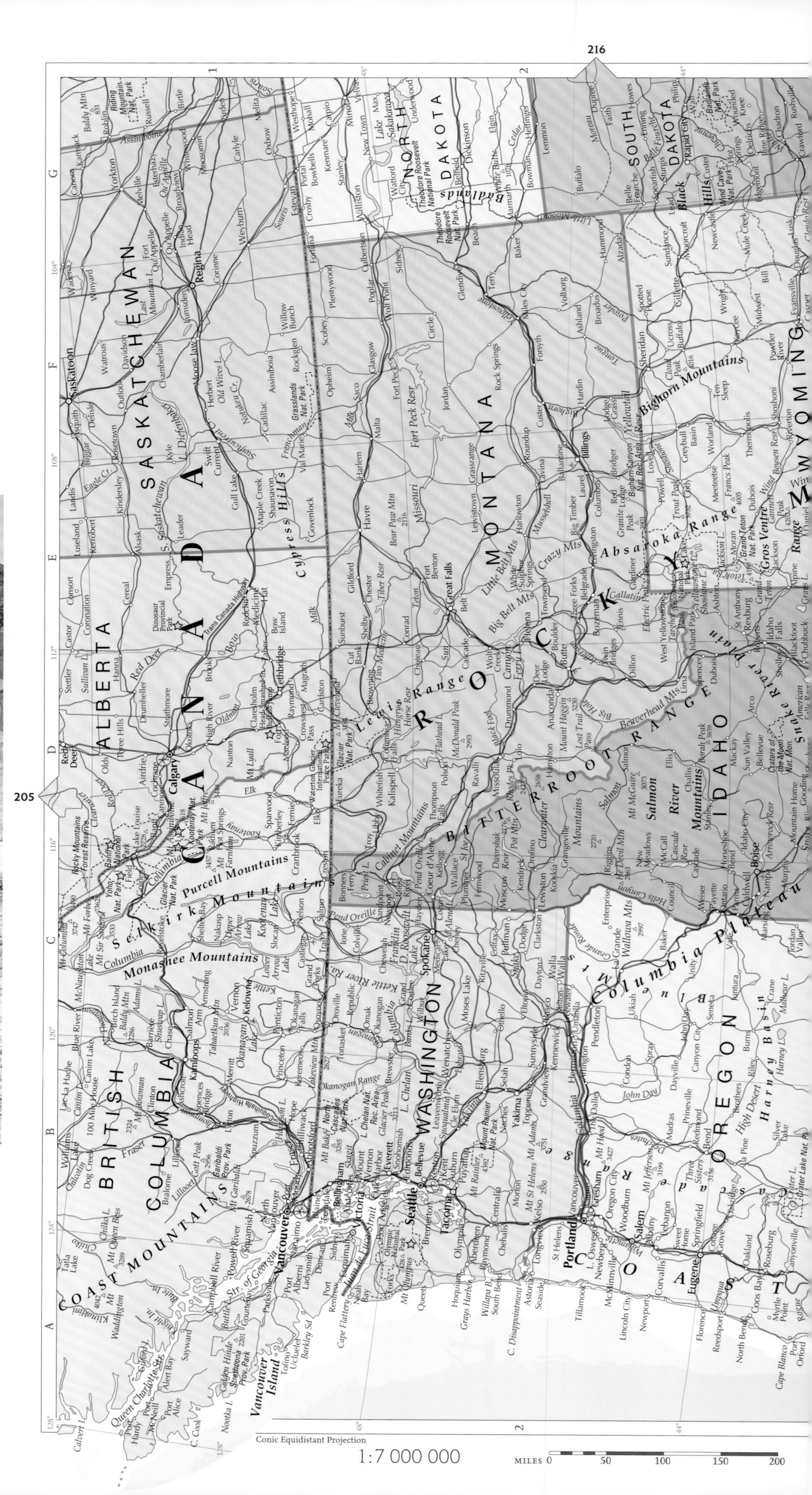

Conic Equidistant Projection

1:7 000 000

MILES 0   50   100   150   200

224

NEBRASKA
COLORADO
Denver
Aurora
Lakewood
Littleton
Colorado Springs
Pueblo
Sangre de Cristo Range
Medicine Bow Mts
Fort Collins
Boulder
Great Sand Dunes National Park and Preserve

WYOMING

M O U N T A I N S

Rock Springs
Green River

UTAH
Salt Lake City
Ogden
Provo
Orem
Murray
Great Salt Lake
Great Salt Lake Desert
Uinta Mts
Sawatch Range
Roan Plateau

NEW MEXICO
Santa Fe
Albuquerque
Los Alamos
Las Cruces
San Andres Mts
Sacramento Mountains
White Sands Nat. Mon.
Zuni Mts
Gallup

TEXAS
El Paso
Ciudad Juárez
Llano Estacado
Carlsbad
Roswell

CHIHUAHUA
Desierto de Chihuahua
Bolsón de Mapimí
Chihuahua

COLORADO

Grand Canyon
Grand Canyon National Park

ARIZONA
Flagstaff
Phoenix
Mesa
Scottsdale
Chandler
Glendale
Tucson
Yuma
P L A T E A U
Painted Desert
Organ Pipe Cactus National Monument

SONORA
Hermosillo
Guaymas

GREAT BASIN

NEVADA
Reno
Sparks
Carson City
Las Vegas
Henderson
Boulder City
Death Valley National Park
Mojave Desert
Panamint Range
Shoshone Mountains

CALIFORNIA
Sacramento
Stockton
Modesto
Fresno
Bakersfield
Los Angeles
Long Beach
Anaheim
Santa Ana
Riverside
San Bernardino
Oceanside
San Diego
Chula Vista
Pasadena
Glendale
Torrance
San Francisco
Oakland
San Jose
Sunnyvale
Hayward
Berkeley
Santa Rosa
Napa
Vallejo
Concord
Salinas
Santa Barbara
Oxnard
Ventura
Lancaster
Palmdale
Channel Islands
Santa Catalina I.
San Clemente I.
San Nicolas I.
Santa Cruz I.
S I E R R A   N E V A D A
San Joaquin Valley
Sacramento Valley
Klamath Mts
Warner Mountains
Mojave Desert
Joshua Tree National Park
Sacramento
Santa Lucia Range
Diablo Ra.

BAJA CALIFORNIA
Tijuana
Mexicali
Ensenada
Gulf of California

P A C I F I C   O C E A N

Guadalupe (Mexico)

World Heritage Sites numbered on the map:
CANADA
1. Canadian Rocky Mountain Parks (C1/D1)
MEXICO
2. Islands and Protected Areas of the Gulf of California (D6/D7)

0 50 100 150 200 250 300 350 KILOMETRES

© Collins Bartholomew Ltd

Southwest USA

HAWAII

The State of Hawaii comprises eight islands, six of which are generally visited. Kaua'i, the Garden Isle, is northernmost, with mountains and lush valleys, and a laid back atmosphere. There are towering cliffs and beautiful beaches, popular for swimming and snorkelling.

O'ahu has the capital Honolulu, Pearl Harbour and Waikīkī Beach – world famous for its surfing. Major surfing competitions are held on the north shore, where the pro surfers hang out.

Nearly half of Moloka'i's population are of native ancestry. The island is rural, with some of the largest beaches in the Hawai'ian islands. The world's highest sea cliffs are in Kalaupapa National Historical Park.

Lāna'i is a different destination altogether, with luxurious resorts, golfing and off-road driving. Keahiakawelo, the Garden of the Gods, is an area of rock towers and spires, most beautifully lit at sunset.

Maui, the second-largest island, has eighty-one beautiful beaches and sophisticated tourist facilities. Haleakalā Crater is a wonderful viewpoint, a popular place to watch the sun rise.

The island of Hawai'i is called the Big Island, to distinguish it from Hawaii State. It is has eleven different climatic zones, sandy beaches, snow-capped mountains, deserts, rainforests and Kilauea volcano, in the Volcanoes National Park.

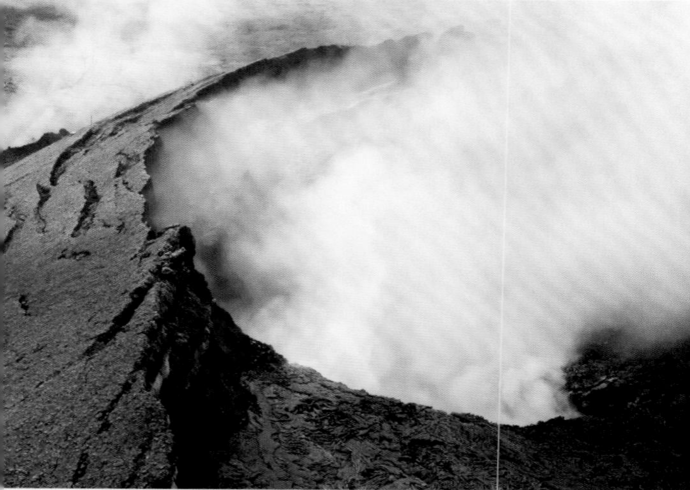

Kilauea volcano, **Volcanoes National Park**.

Los Angeles, the USA's second-largest city, is full of familiar landmarks including the Hollywood Bowl, Walt Disney Concert Hall and the Capitol Records Building. Hollywood features as a top destination, with Universal Studios and the Hollywood History Museum a film buff's dream. The city has a diverse collection of museums, from the Getty Centre and Museum of Contemporary Art to the Craft and Folk Museum and the Museum of Tolerance. For shoppers, there is exclusive Rodeo Drive or Venice Beach for souvenirs, the Farmers Market, The Grove and Chinatown. Beaches are a major draw for surfing, people-watching or sunbathing.

San Francisco is famous for its Golden Gate Bridge. It is a popular destination, known for steep hills, cable cars and Chinatown, the oldest in the country. Fisherman's Wharf is the place for seafood restaurants, nearby is Lombard Street, with its crazy hairpin turns. Much of the city's outdoor space is encompassed by the much-visited Golden Gate National Recreation Area, including Ocean Beach, Golden Gate Park, Candlestick Point and Alcatraz, infamous as a prison and now open to all, via ferry trips. The city is also well served by the performing arts, including Broadway shows, and museums.

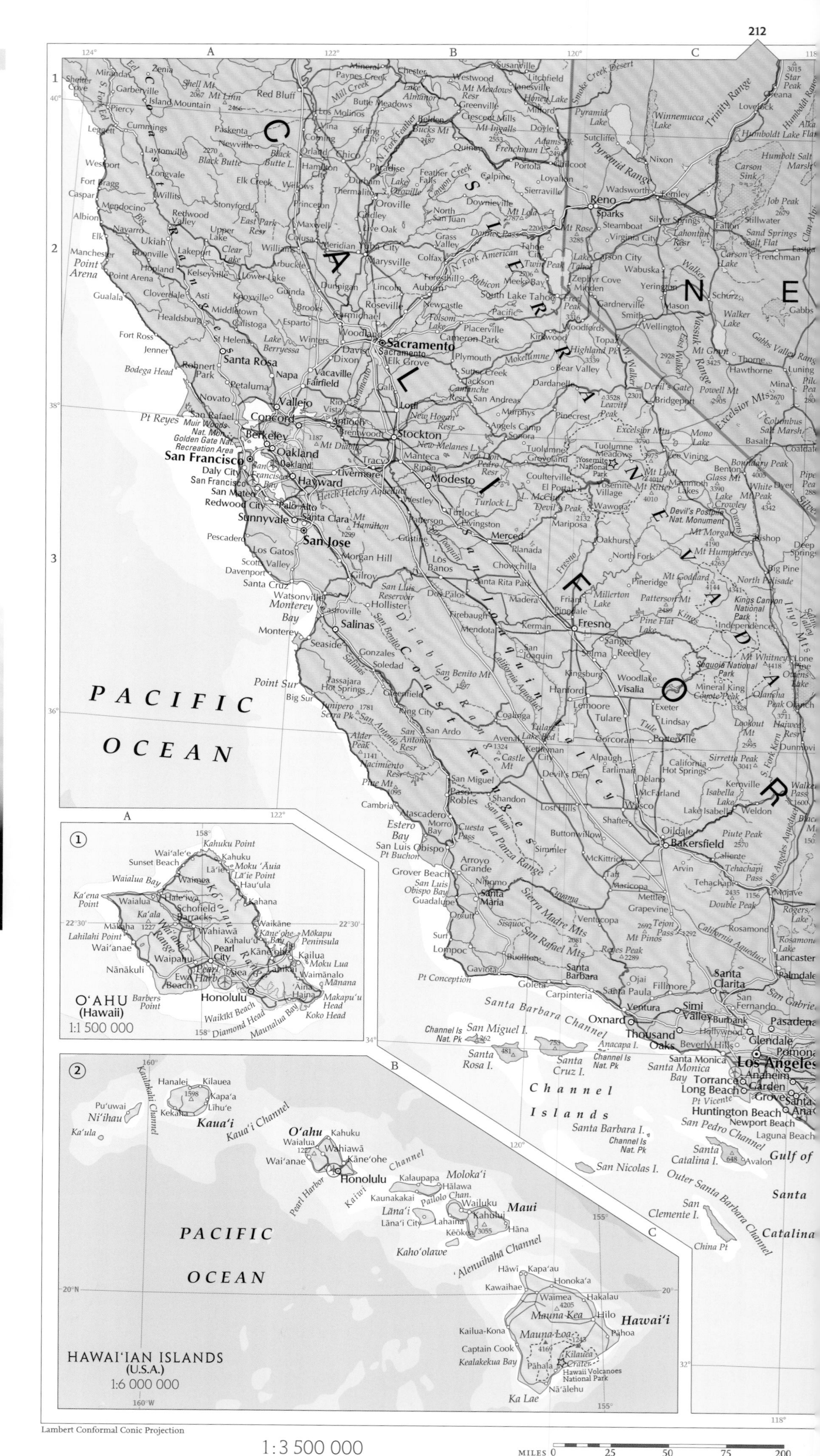

Lambert Conformal Conic Projection

1:3 500 000

MILES 0   25   50   75   200

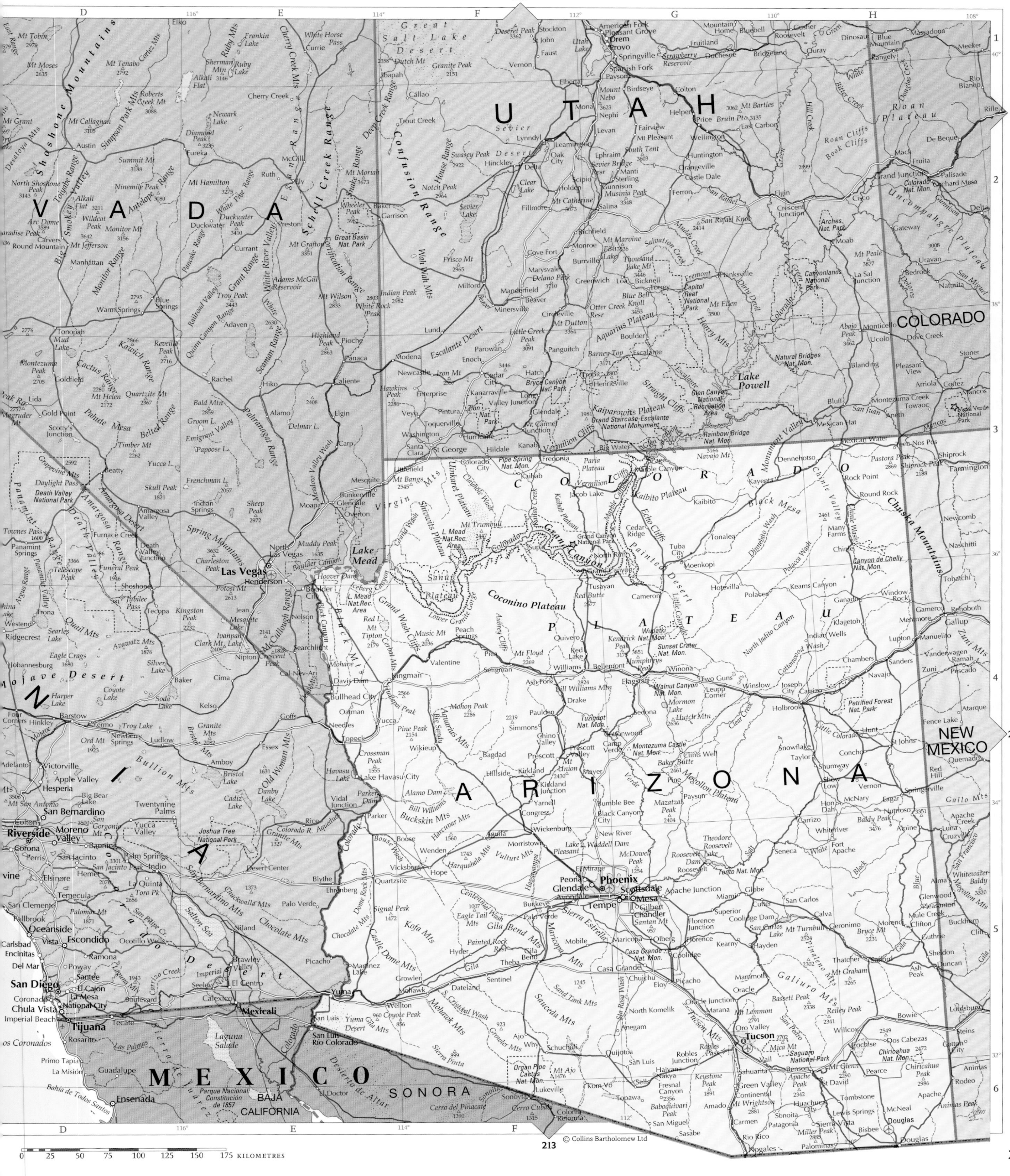

D 116° E 114° F 112° G 110° H 108°

U T A H

N E V A D A

COLORADO

C A L I F O R N I A

A R I Z O N A

NEW MEXICO

M E X I C O

SONORA

BAJA CALIFORNIA

C O L O R A D O   P L A T E A U

Coconino Plateau

Mojave Desert

Death Valley National Park

Great Salt Lake Desert

Sevier Desert

Lake Powell

Lake Mead

Las Vegas
North Las Vegas
Henderson
Boulder City

Phoenix
Glendale
Peoria
Scottsdale
Mesa
Tempe
Chandler
Gilbert
Avondale

Tucson

San Diego
Chula Vista
Coronado
La Mesa
El Cajon
Santee
National City
Imperial Beach

Tijuana
Mexicali

Riverside
Moreno Valley
San Bernardino
Colton

Oceanside
Carlsbad
Encinitas
Del Mar

Grand Canyon National Park

Joshua Tree National Park

Petrified Forest Nat. Park

Chuska Mountains

Spring Mountains

40°
38°
36°
34°

© Collins Bartholomew Ltd

0 25 50 75 100 125 150 175 KILOMETRES

Central USA

Central USA spans great plains and prairies. The eastern half of this map and the western part of the following map cover the American Midwest. South Dakota is home to Mount Rushmore and the immense sculptured heads of former US presidents.

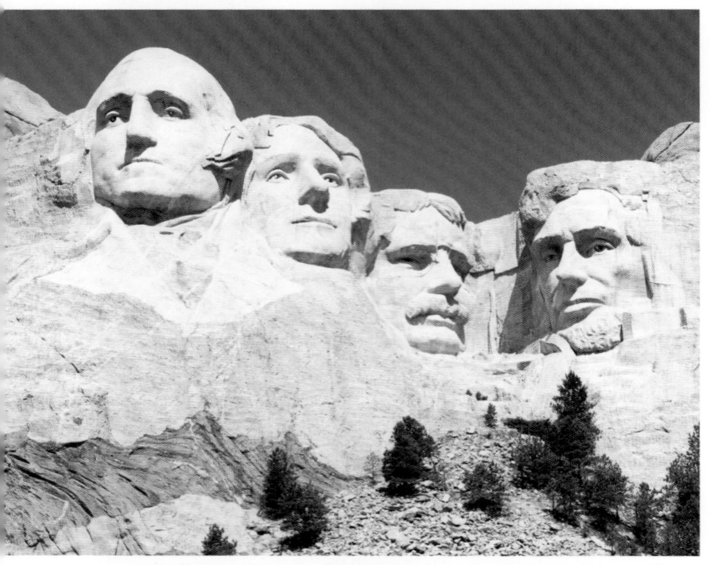

Mount Rushmore National Memorial, ten miles southwest of **Rapid City**, South Dakota.

Chicago is the area's largest city, known for its lively nightlife and performing arts. Des Moines, in Iowa, has wonderful historic buildings, museums and the State Capitol with a gold-leafed dome. Nearby is Madison Country and the historic covered bridges. Mississippi is famous for the Blues and its musicians. Densely forested, with lakes and miles of streams, the colours of the autumn foliage are breathtaking. The Mississippi–Missouri is North America's longest river and can be explored by road or river trip. Wisconsin Dells, named after the scenic rock formations on the Wisconsin River, is the home of water parks, both inside and outdoors. New Orleans is a popular tourist destination, with its French Quarter and jazz. Louisiana also features swamplands and special Cajun music and food. Texas, the second-largest state, is known for cities such as Dallas and Forth Worth, but also has famous heritage sites, such as the Alamo, and fabulous scenery to enjoy.

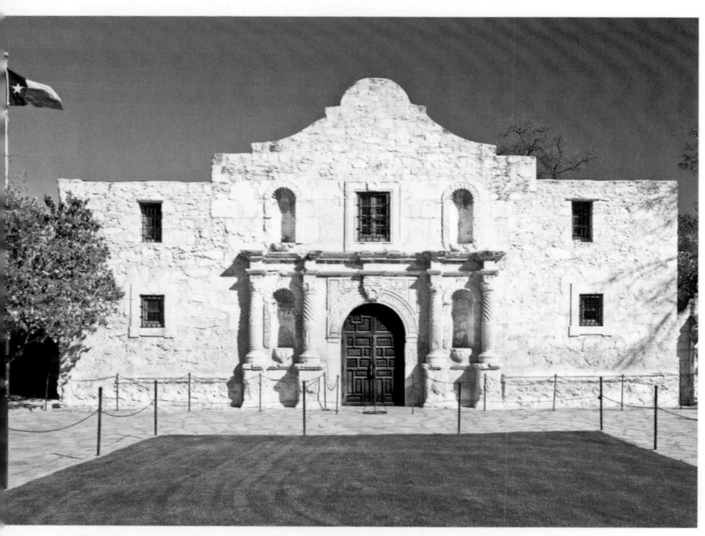

The entrance to the Alamo, **San Antonio**, Texas, site of the legendary battle.

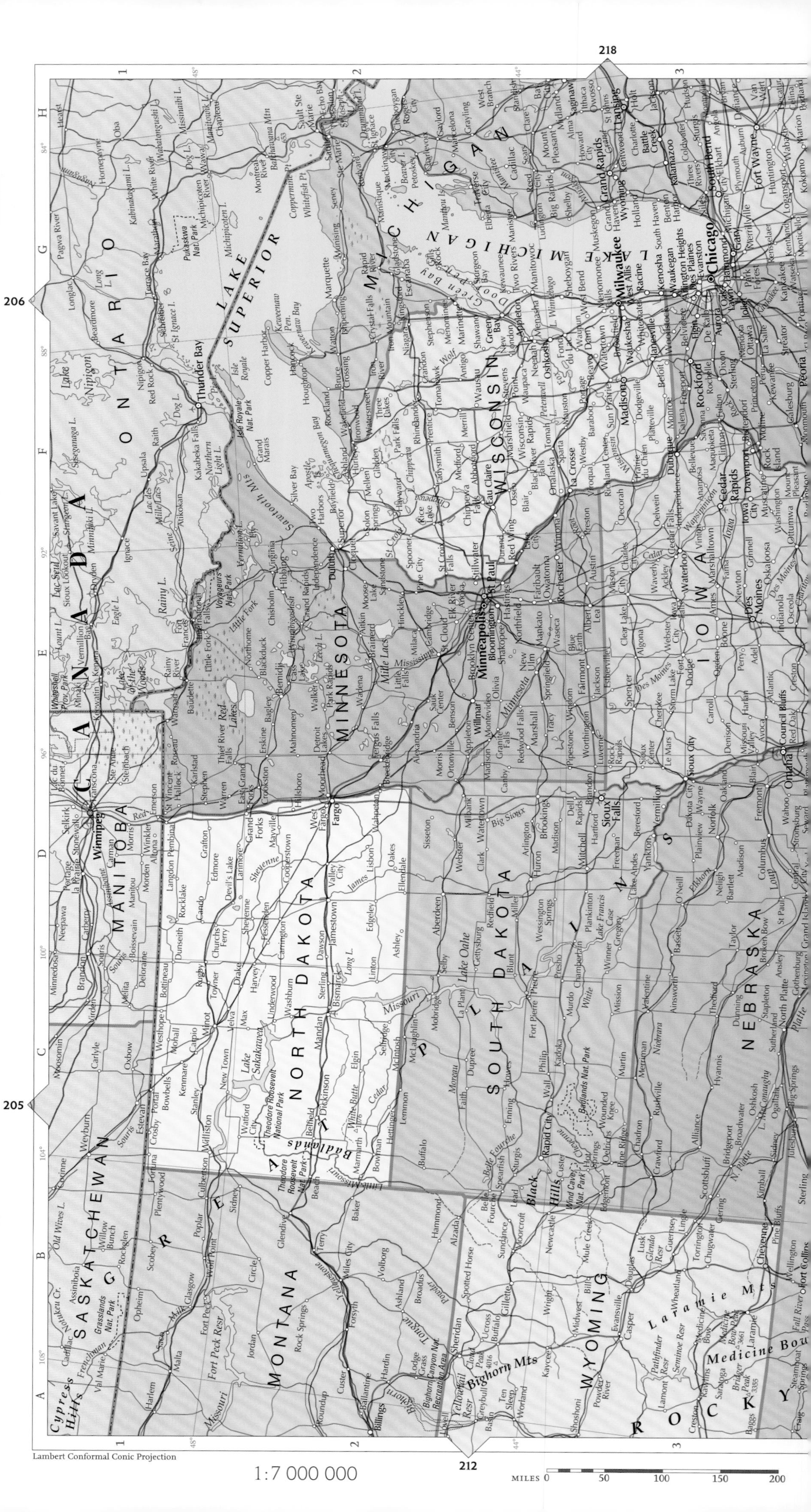

Lambert Conformal Conic Projection

1:7 000 000

MILES 0   50   100   150   200

GULF OF MEXICO

0 50 100 150 200 250 300 350 KILOMETRES

213
225

Eastern USA

Eastern USA was a centre of activity during American Independence and saw many Civil War battles. Organised tours are a fascinating way to gain insight into this period of American history. Maine is a great destination for outdoor activities and the agricultural fairs make for a fun day out. Springtime in Vermont is Maple Season, when the famous syrup is made. The state has beautiful landscapes and diverse wildlife. Philadelphia, at the centre of Independence, has interesting architecture and many sites of national historic importance. Those interested in the Civil Rights movement will want to follow Alabama's unique Civil Rights Trail. Both North and South Carolina feature wonderful landscapes, with Translyvania County in North Carolina known as Land of the Waterfalls. Grand Strand is almost 100 km (62 miles) of beach running northwards from Georgetown in South Carolina. Further south is the Sunshine State, Florida. As well as endless beaches, shore-front cities and pristine golf courses, Florida offers fascinating historic sites, from Indian burial mounds and pioneer settlements to Castillo de San Marco, a Spanish-built fort constructed in 1672. The state is notable for the Everglades, a national park and World Heritage site of fragile wetlands and mangrove forests.

THE BAHAMAS Capital: Nassau
Area: 13 939 635 km²/5 382 miles²
Population: 331 000 Languages: English, Creole
Religions: Protestant, Roman Catholic
Currency: Bahamian dollar

The Bahamas are a chain of 700 low-lying islands between the Atlantic Ocean and the Caribbean Sea. A place of vivid colours and warm, clear water. Paradise Island and New Providence Island, linked by bridge, are elegant resorts. The capital, Nassau, on New Providence can trace its history back to the pirate Blackbeard. Grand Bahama Island has one of the world's largest underwater cave systems and three national parks. Many of the settlements were founded by former slaves. The Out Islands are hidden gems of remote villages and a gentle way of life, boutique hotels and deserted beaches, with excellent dive and fishing sites.

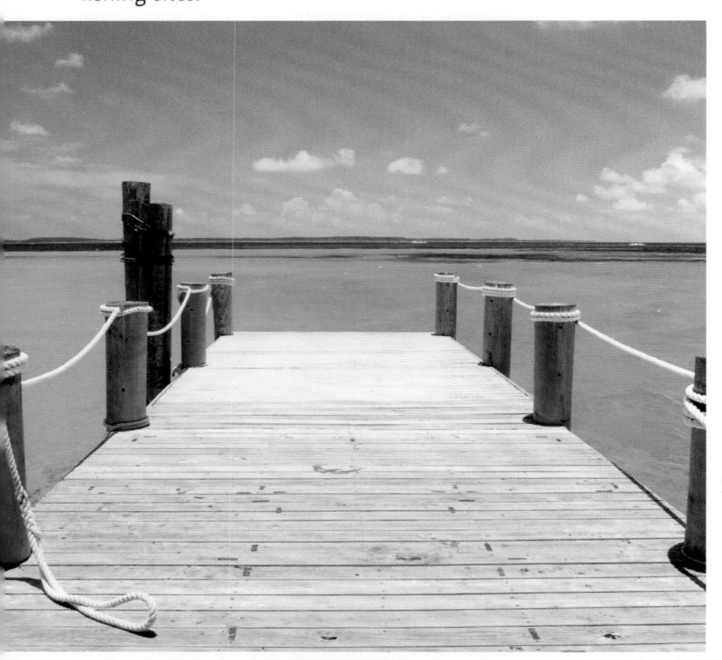

Jetty out over the Atlantic, near **Nassau,** New Providence Island, The Bahamas.

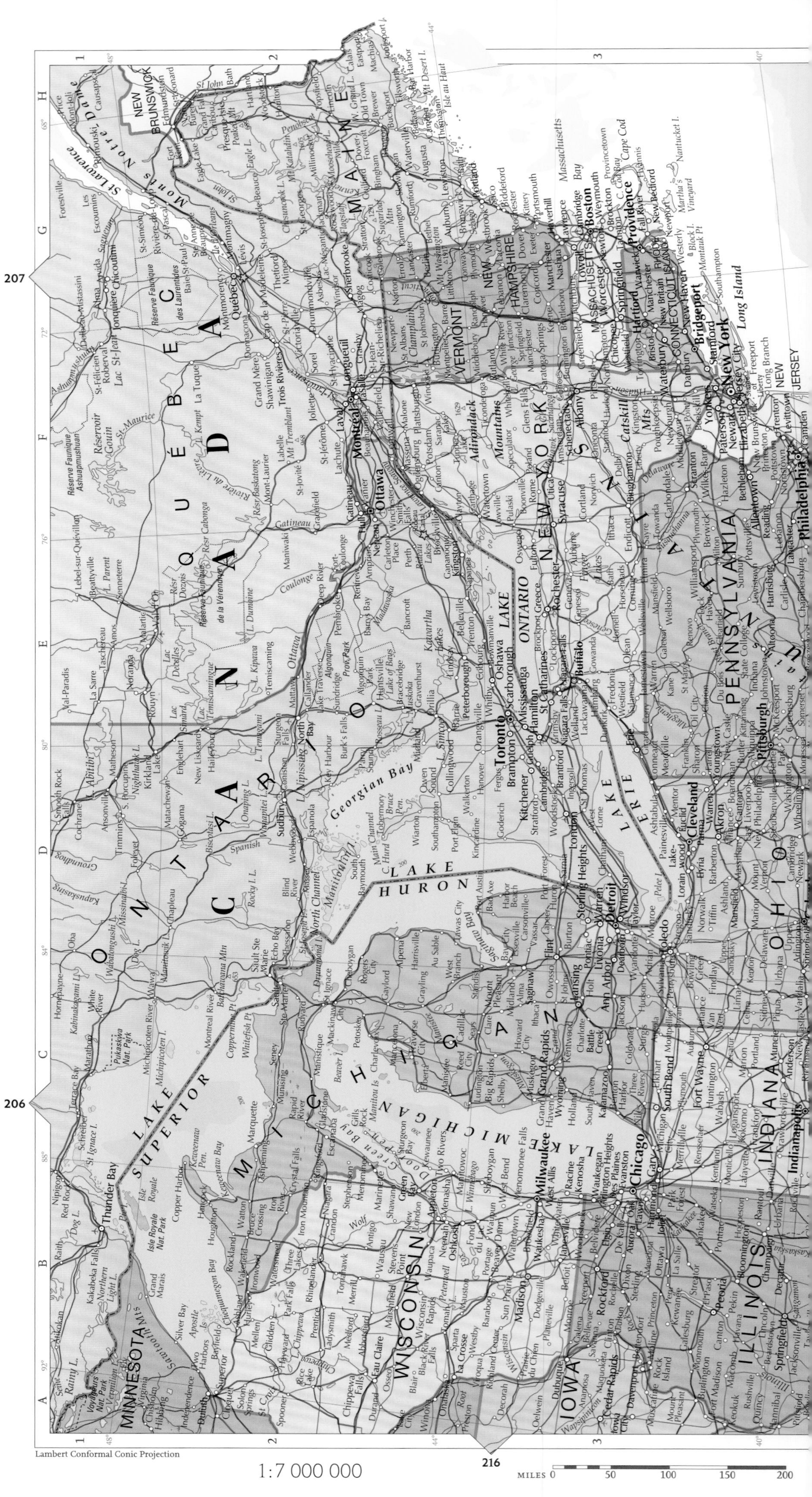

Lambert Conformal Conic Projection

1:7 000 000

MILES 0   50   100   150   200

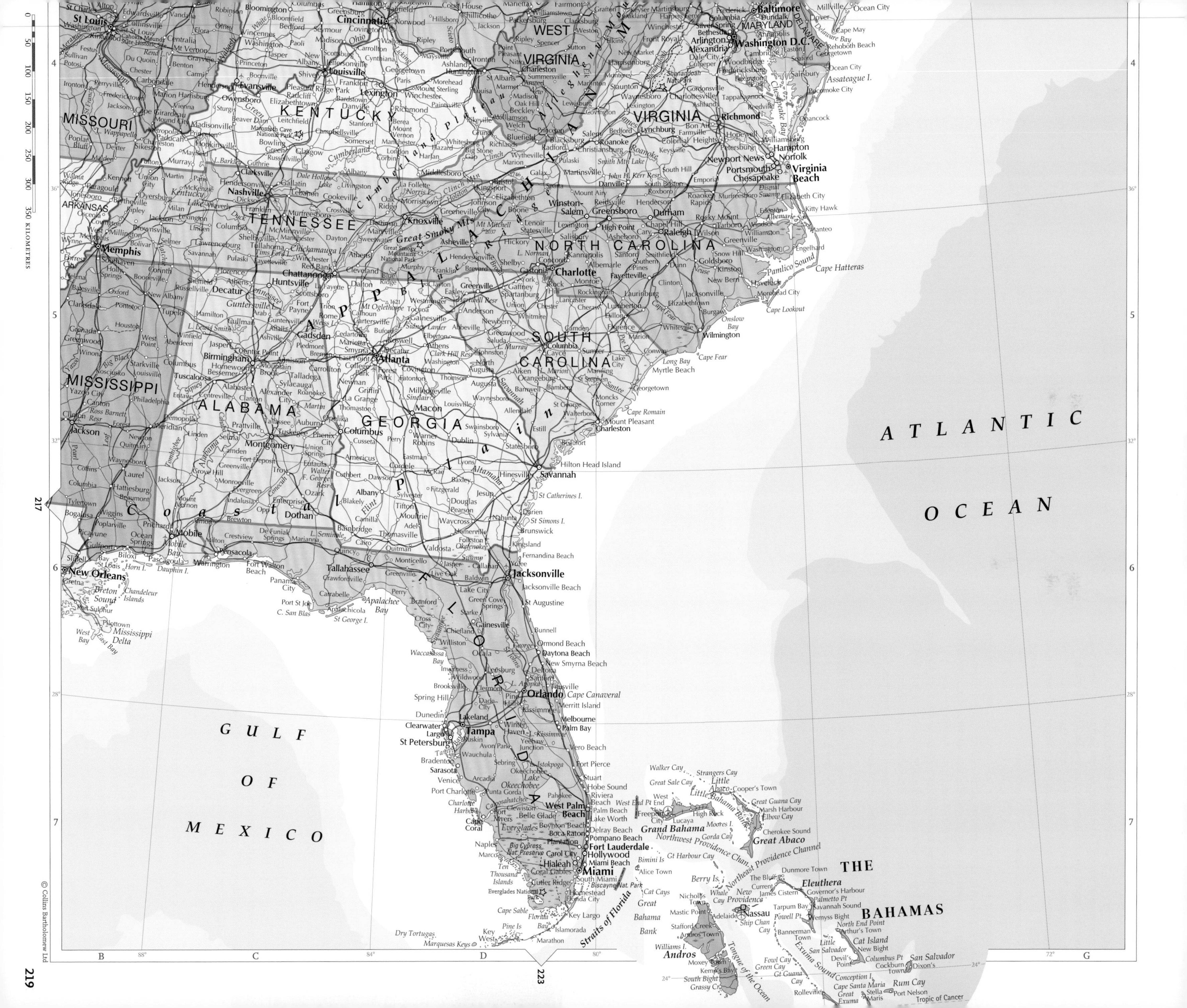
ATLANTIC OCEAN
GULF OF MEXICO
THE BAHAMAS
VIRGINIA
WEST VIRGINIA
KENTUCKY
TENNESSEE
NORTH CAROLINA
SOUTH CAROLINA
GEORGIA
ALABAMA
MISSISSIPPI
FLORIDA
MARYLAND
DELAWARE
MISSOURI
ARKANSAS
Washington D.C.
Baltimore
Richmond
Norfolk
Virginia Beach
Chesapeake
Louisville
Lexington
Cincinnati
Nashville
Memphis
Knoxville
Chattanooga
Charlotte
Greensboro
Durham
Raleigh
Columbia
Charleston
Savannah
Atlanta
Birmingham
Montgomery
Mobile
Jackson
New Orleans
Tallahassee
Jacksonville
Orlando
Tampa
St Petersburg
Miami
Fort Lauderdale
Nassau
Andros
Grand Bahama
Great Abaco
Eleuthera
Cat Island
Chesapeake Bay
Cape Hatteras
Cape Fear
Cape Canaveral
Straits of Florida
Tropic of Cancer
0 50 100 150 200 250 300 350 KILOMETRES

217

223

Northeastern USA

New York is a cosmopolitan city, location of the United Nations headquarters and Wall Street, an important centre for international affairs and a massive tourist destination. The city is known the world over for its iconic landmarks and celebrated attractions: the Statue of Liberty, the Empire State Building, Ellis Island, Times Square and Broadway. Magnificent architecture includes the Chrysler Building, the Rockfeller Centre and Grand Central Terminal (Station).

New York is a great centre for entertainment, the performing arts and as a place to shop, whether along Fifth or Madison Avenue, in Bloomingdales or in the many malls and markets. There are over 150 museums, including the Museum of Modern Art, the Guggenheim Museum and the Metropolitan Museum of Art; and hundreds of top restaurants and the ubiquituous hot dog stands. Central Park is a draw for both the New Yorker and visitors. Landscaped gardens, extensive trails and paths, public beaches and carriage rides are just a few of the amenities.

The events of 11 September 2001, when the city suffered its worst terrorist attack, are known worldwide. Many visitors travel to Ground Zero and to the Museum Workshop, filled with poignant images and remnants from the recovery.

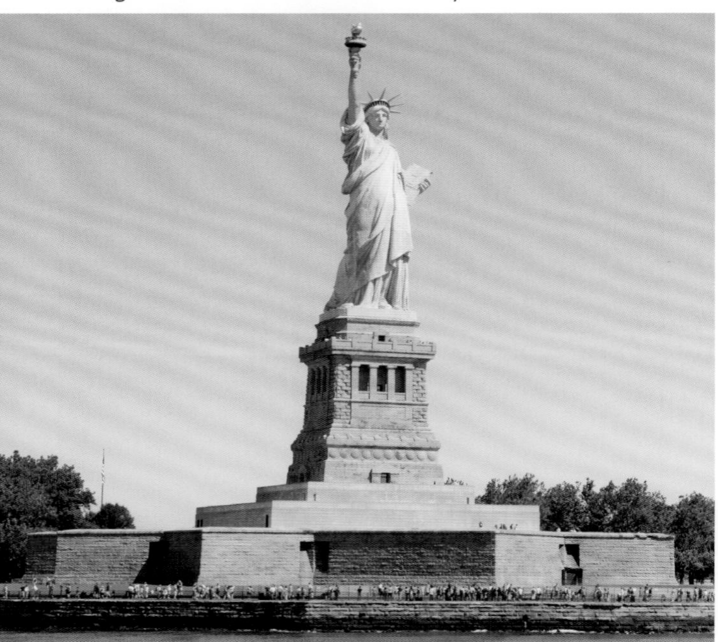

The famous statue, standing on **Liberty Island** in the Hudson River, one of New York's most popular visitor attractions.

Washington is the capital of the United States. Formally the District of Columbia, it is usually referred to as Washington DC. It is the home of the President at the White House, and the seat of government. Visitors can see the original Declaration of Independence, US Constitution, Bill of Rights and Emancipation Proclamation in the National Archives and enjoy the changing of the guard ceremony at the Arlington National Cemetery.

The numerous and remarkable museums and galleries are mostly free of charge. The National Gallery of Art houses the only Leonardo da Vinci in the western hemisphere, together with many old masters and contemporary artists. Other must-see locations include the Smithsonian and the National Portrait Gallery.

Riverboat cruises along the Potomac River are a popular way of viewing the city, its varied architecture and many parks and open spaces. The city is a thriving cultural capital with a wide range of performing arts, theatres, opera and ballet. The varied neighbourhoods include historic Georgetown and Capitol Hill. Downtown has a heritage trail, museums, theatres, hotels and restaurants; U Street and Shaw, birthplace of Duke Ellington, is home to exciting nightlife.

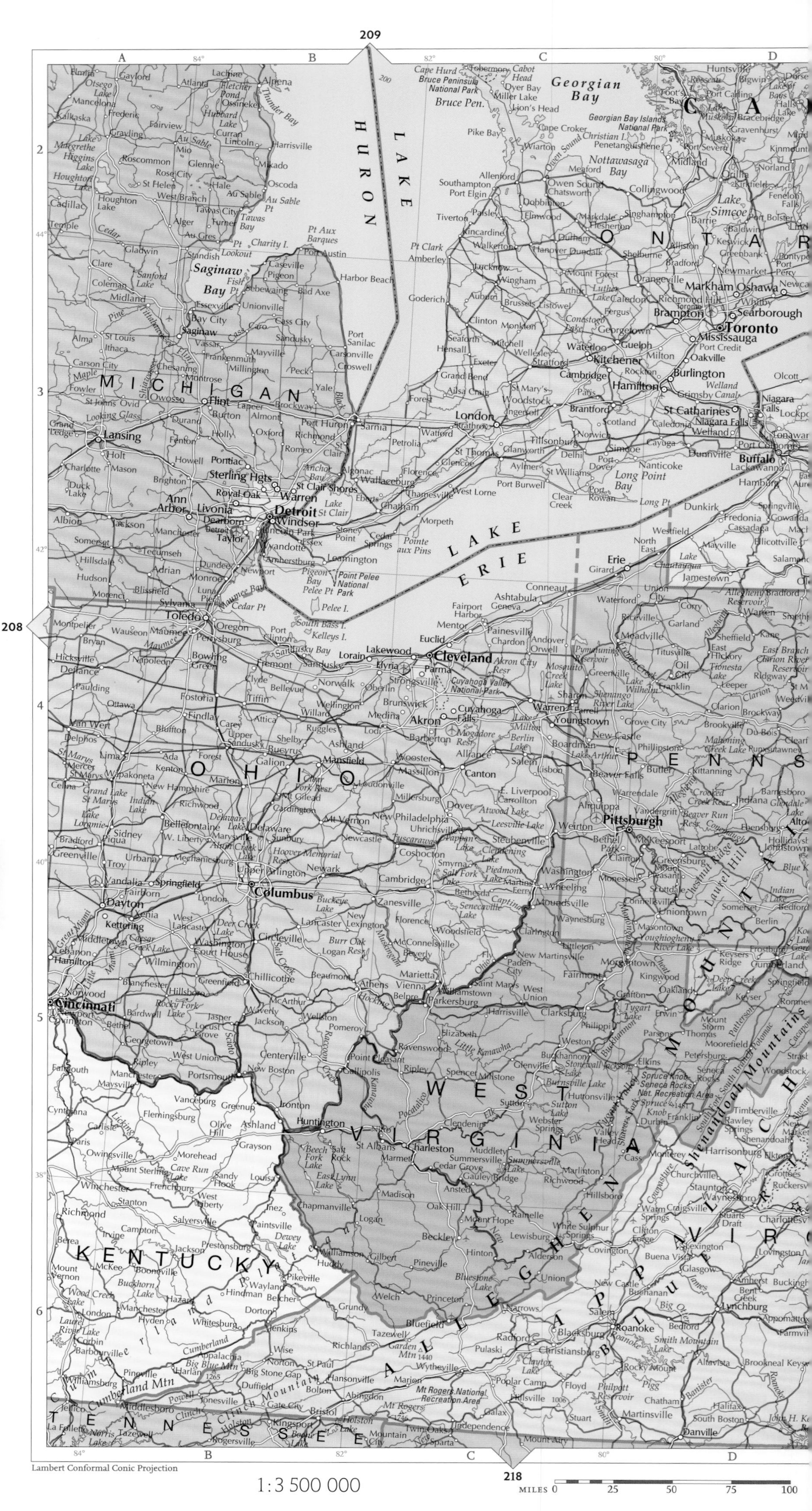

Lambert Conformal Conic Projection

1:3 500 000

MILES 0   25   50   75   100

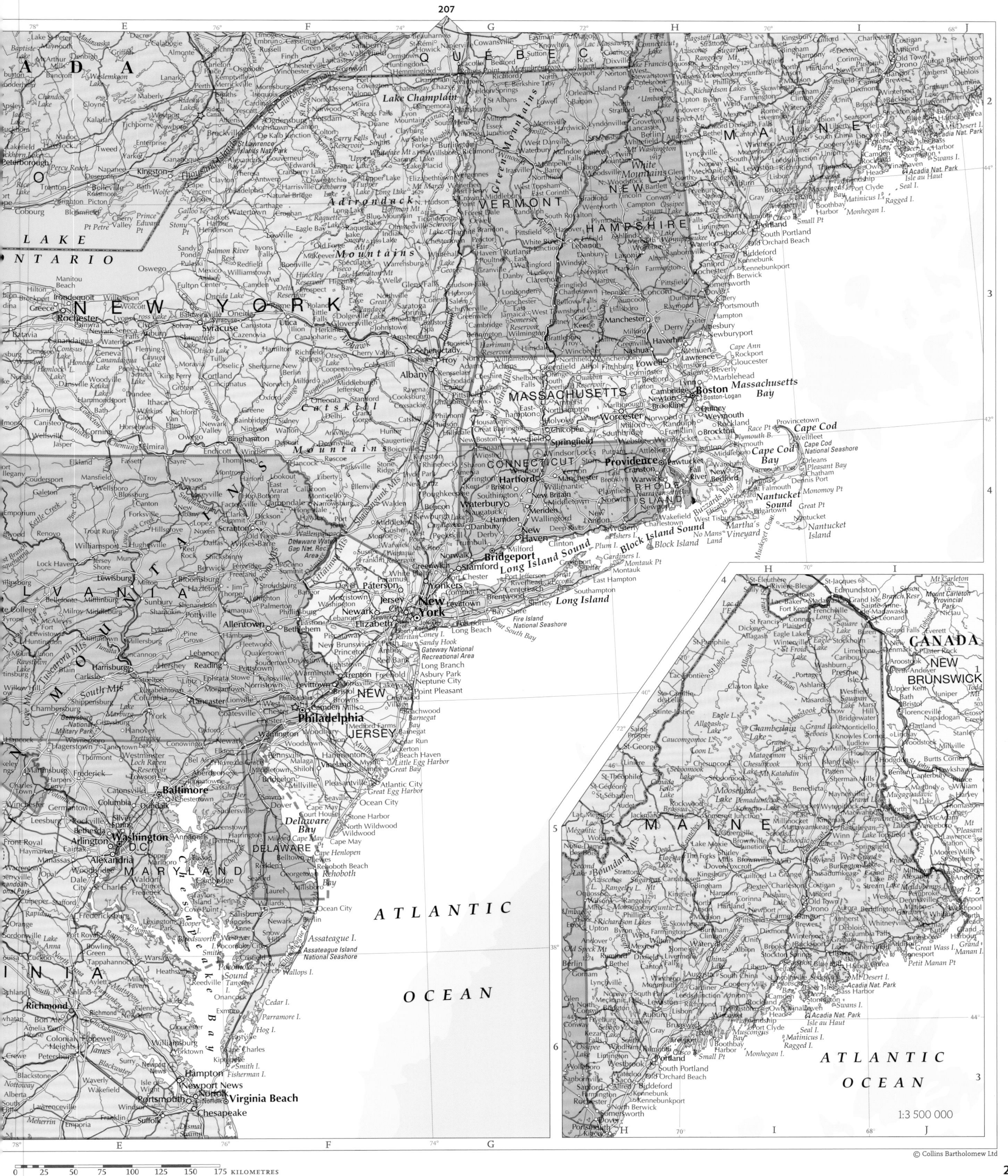

ATLANTIC

OCEAN

ATLANTIC
OCEAN

1:3 500 000

© Collins Bartholomew Ltd

0   25   50   75   100   125   150   175   KILOMETRES

Central America and The Caribbean

The Caribbean – sandwiched between the Atlantic and Pacific Oceans and encircled by a chain of over 7 000 islands, Central America and northern South America – is a popular holiday destination for tropical sun, sand, palm trees and warm, clear water. Diving is a favourite attraction, together with a wide choice of water sports.

BARBADOS Capital: **Bridgetown**
Area: 430 km²/166 miles² Population: 294 000
Languages: **English, Creole** Religions: **Protestant, Roman Catholic** Currency: **Barbados dollar**
Barbados is the most easterly Caribbean island, with strong links to the UK. It is the birthplace of rum and there are hundreds of rum shops. Crane Beach has been voted one of the world's best beaches.

CUBA Capital: **Havana (La Habana)**
Area: 110 860 km²/42 803 miles²
Population: **11 268 000** Languages: **Spanish**
Religions: **Roman Catholic, Protestant** Currency: **Cuban peso**
Cuba, known for revolution, Fidel Castro, ancient American cars and cigars, is visited for its climate and beaches, the colonial architecture and distinctive Cuban culture. Its music is a unique mix of European and African rhythm and sound. Parts of Havana are a World Heritage site and the old city stands much as it did 100 or so years ago – much has been done to restore its colonial character. Pinar del Rio is a popular area to visit, with attractive beaches, diving sites, hot springs and a beautiful landscape of mountains, valleys and hillside caves.

DOMINICAN REPUBLIC Capital: **Santo Domingo**
Area: 48 442 km²/18 704 miles²
Population: **9 760 000** Languages: **Spanish, Creole**
Religions: **Roman Catholic, Protestant** Currency: **Dominican peso**
Christopher Columbus described the Dominican Republic as 'a beautiful island paradise'. The island is home to gaming resorts and casinos, golf courses designed by world champion golfers, and many national parks and protected areas – much of its flora is endemic.

JAMAICA Capital: **Kingston**
Area: 10 991 km²/4 244 miles²
Population: **2 714 000** Languages: **English, Creole**
Religions: **Protestant, Roman Catholic**
Currency: **Jamaican dollar**
Jamaica is the third largest island in the Caribbean. Kingston is its capital, with the soaring Blue Mountains as a backdrop. Devon House, one of many preserved colonial mansions, is a national heritage site. Other attractions include the Bob Marley Museum, Jamaica's National Gallery, Hope Botanical Gardens, Spanish Town neighbourhood and Port Royal, once a haven for pirates. Montego Bay is home to a marine park, one of Jamaica's best coral reefs and offers stunning views from the town itself. Another popular destination is the resort of Ocho Rios, with restaurants and nightclubs, dolphin spotting, botanical gardens, horse riding, waterfalls and of course, the beaches.

MARTINIQUE
Volcanic Martinique offers an attractive French/Creole heritage that pervades the culture, cuisine, music and dance. Hiking and nature watching is available on the volcano slopes and through the tropical forest.

PUERTO RICO
Puerto Rico is distinctly Spanish in culture. It is a land of mountains, tropical rainforest, beaches, and Phosphorescent Bay – full of microscopic marine life that lights up when disturbed, best seen from an evening boat trip or snorkel.

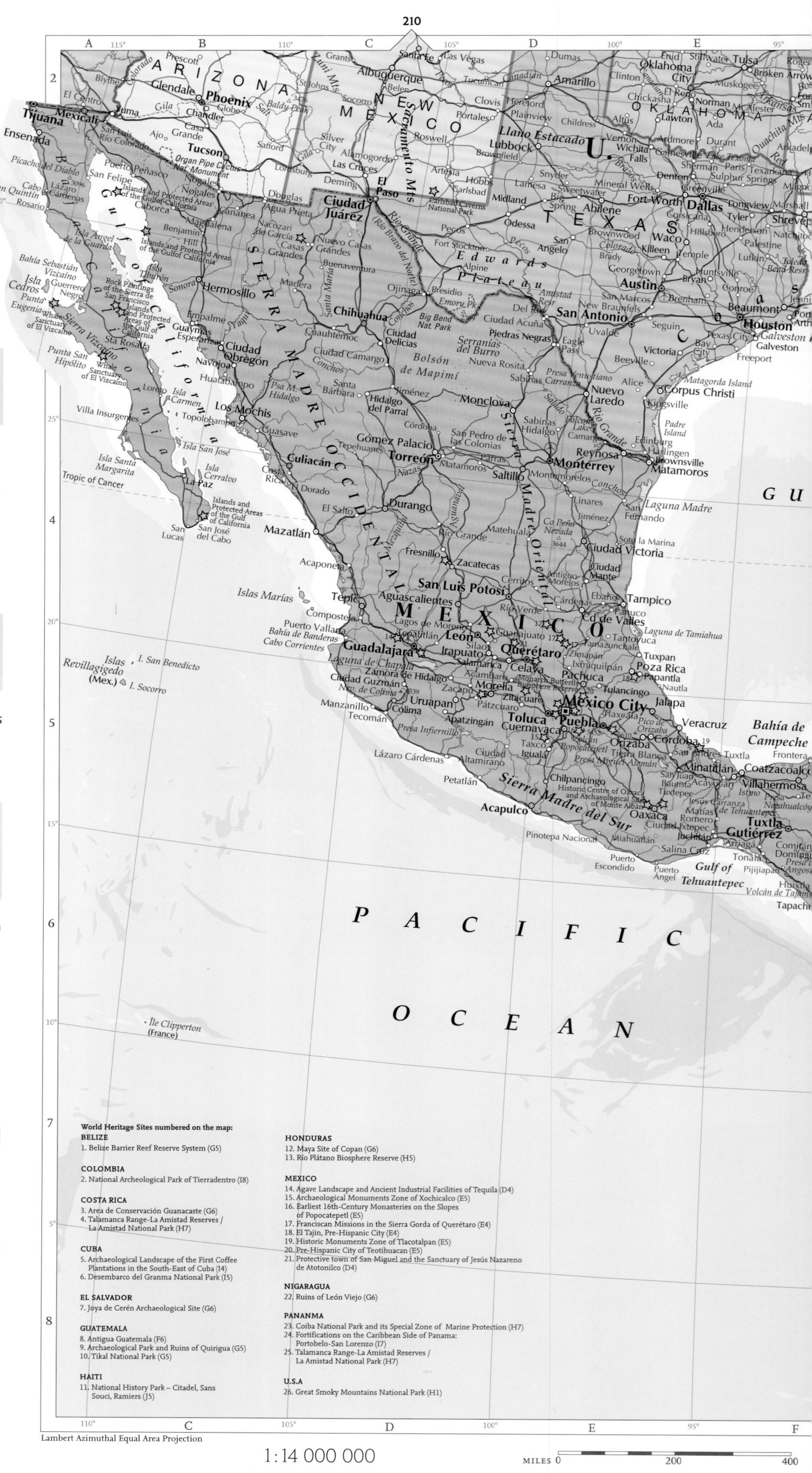

World Heritage Sites numbered on the map:

BELIZE
1. Belize Barrier Reef Reserve System (G5)

COLOMBIA
2. National Archeological Park of Tierradentro (I8)

COSTA RICA
3. Area de Conservación Guanacaste (G6)
4. Talamanca Range-La Amistad Reserves / La Amistad National Park (H7)

CUBA
5. Archaeological Landscape of the First Coffee Plantations in the South-East of Cuba (I4)
6. Desembarco del Granma National Park (I5)

EL SALVADOR
7. Joya de Cerén Archaeological Site (G6)

GUATEMALA
8. Antigua Guatemala (F6)
9. Archaeological Park and Ruins of Quirigua (G5)
10. Tikal National Park (G5)

HAITI
11. National History Park – Citadel, Sans Souci, Ramiers (J5)

HONDURAS
12. Maya Site of Copan (G6)
13. Río Plátano Biosphere Reserve (H5)

MEXICO
14. Agave Landscape and Ancient Industrial Facilities of Tequila (D4)
15. Archaeological Monuments Zone of Xochicalco (E5)
16. Earliest 16th-Century Monasteries on the Slopes of Popocatepetl (E5)
17. Franciscan Missions in the Sierra Gorda of Querétaro (E4)
18. El Tajin, Pre-Hispanic City (E4)
19. Historic Monuments Zone of Tlacotalpan (E5)
20. Pre-Hispanic City of Teotihuacan (E5)
21. Protective town of San Miguel and the Sanctuary of Jesús Nazareno de Atotonilco (D4)

NICARAGUA
22. Ruins of León Viejo (G6)

PANAMA
23. Coiba National Park and its Special Zone of Marine Protection (H7)
24. Fortifications on the Caribbean Side of Panama: Portobelo-San Lorenzo (I7)
25. Talamanca Range-La Amistad Reserves / La Amistad National Park (H7)

U.S.A
26. Great Smoky Mountains National Park (H1)

Lambert Azimuthal Equal Area Projection

1:14 000 000

MILES 0   200   400

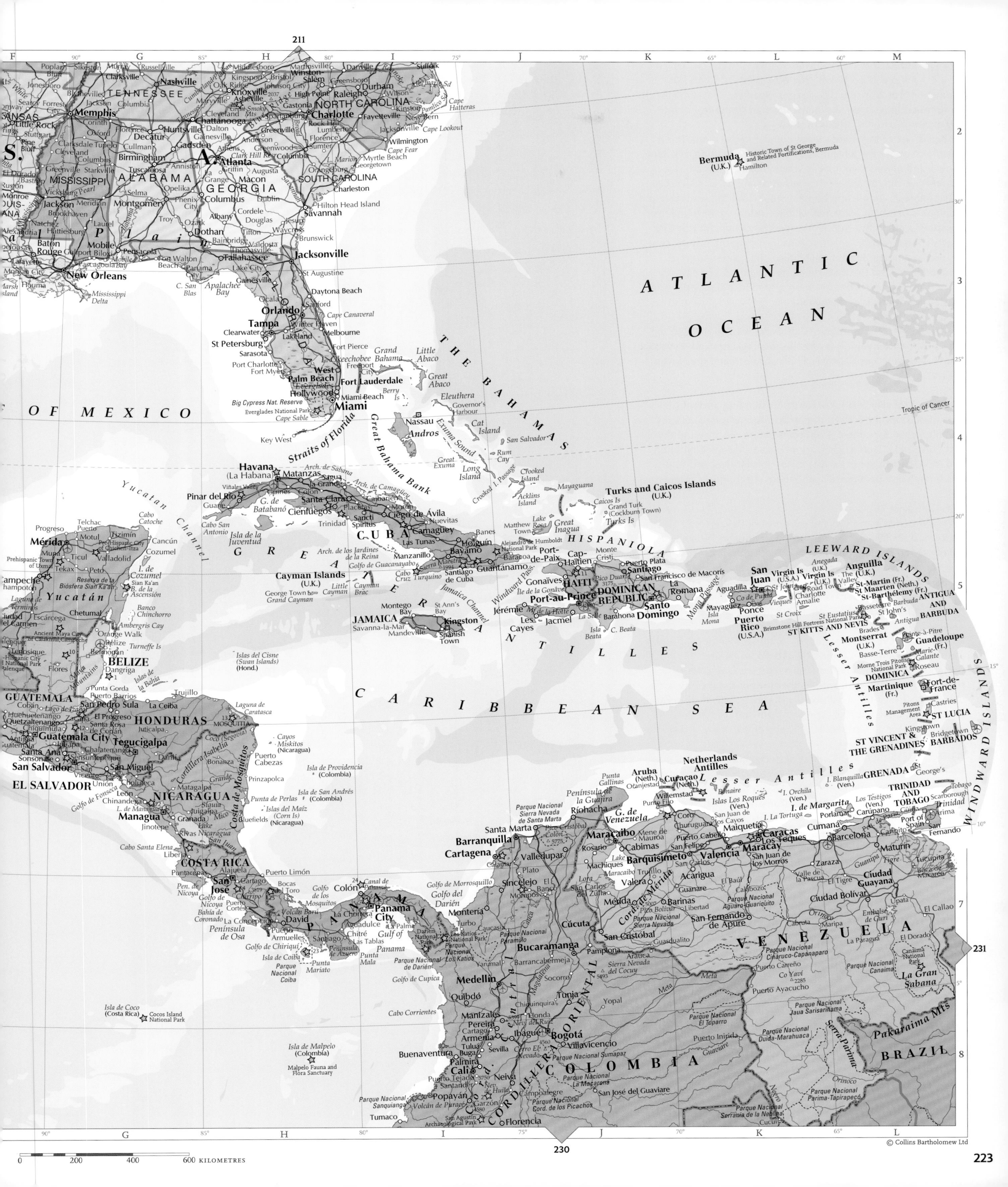

Mexico and Central America

MEXICO Capital: **Mexico City**
Area: **1 972 545 km²/761 604 miles²**
Population: **106 535 000** Languages: **Spanish, Amerindian languages** Religions: **Roman Catholic, Protestant** Currency: **Mexican peso**

Mexico is one of the world's most popular destinations. It is a great location for the adventurous, with diving, rafting, climbing, surfing and much more, readily accessible. Eco-tourism is a major draw, with biosphere reserves and national parks encompassing forests, jungle and deserts, mountains and waterfalls and a unique diversity of plant and wildlife, including the wonderful manatee found in the Gulf of Mexico. The capital, Mexico City, boasts a huge number of attractions including the historic centre, the floating gardens of Xochimilco, the golden Angel of Independence and the Plaza de las tres Culturas. The city has more than 150 fascinating museums, around 100 galleries and over 30 concert halls and theatres.

Bordered by the Pacific Ocean, Caribbean Sea and the Gulf of Mexico, the country offers a vast choice of beaches and distinctive resorts including Los Cabos, Acapulco, Cancún and the Mayan Riviera.

Mexico is probably best know for its outstanding ancient sites remaining from the many complex and sophisticated cultures that flourished for almost 4 000 years before the arrival of the first Europeans. Teotihuacán is northeast of Mexico City; Mitla and Monte Albán are in Oaxaca state; Chichén-Itzá and Tulum are on the Yucatán Peninsula; and there are countless more.

CENTRAL AMERICA

Central America comprises the countries of Belize, Costa Rica, Guatemala, El Salvador, Honduras, Nicaragu and Panama, linking North and South America via the Isthmus of Panama. An area with much political unrest towards the end of the last century, it is now becoming much more accessible to tourists.

COSTA RICA Capital: **San José**
Area: **51 100 km²/19 730 miles²**
Population: **4 468 000** Languages: **Spanish** Religions: **Roman Catholic, Protestant** Currency: **Costa Rican colón**

Costa Rica is Central America's most visited country. An early advocate of eco-tourism, around one-third of the country is protected. One of the most popular destinations is the limestone caves of Barra Honda. The variety of plant and wildlife is astonishing, the colourful quetzal is one of the many bird species.

HONDURAS Capital: **Tegucigalpa**
Area: **112 088 km²/43 277 miles²**
Population: **7 106 000** Languages: **Spanish, Amerindian languages** Religions: **Roman Catholic, Protestant** Currency: **Lempira**

Honduras has inviting beaches with vivid blue waters along its Caribbean coast. The magnificent Mayan ruins of Copán are a particular tourist draw. There are national parks across the country and the varied landscapes offer excellent hiking and bird watching.

NICARAGUA Capital: **Managua**
Area: **130 000 km²/50 193 miles²**
Population: **5 603 000** Languages: **Spanish, Amerindian languages** Religions: **Roman Catholic, Protestant** Currency: **Córdoba**

Nicaragua, shunned by tourists during its harsh dictatorship, is now encouraging visitors. Its tourist facilities are not as well developed as other Central American countries, however, this will add to its attraction for some visitors. The wonderful beaches are often deserted. Nicaragua's wildlife is enticing and exotic, including jaguars, manatees and turtles.

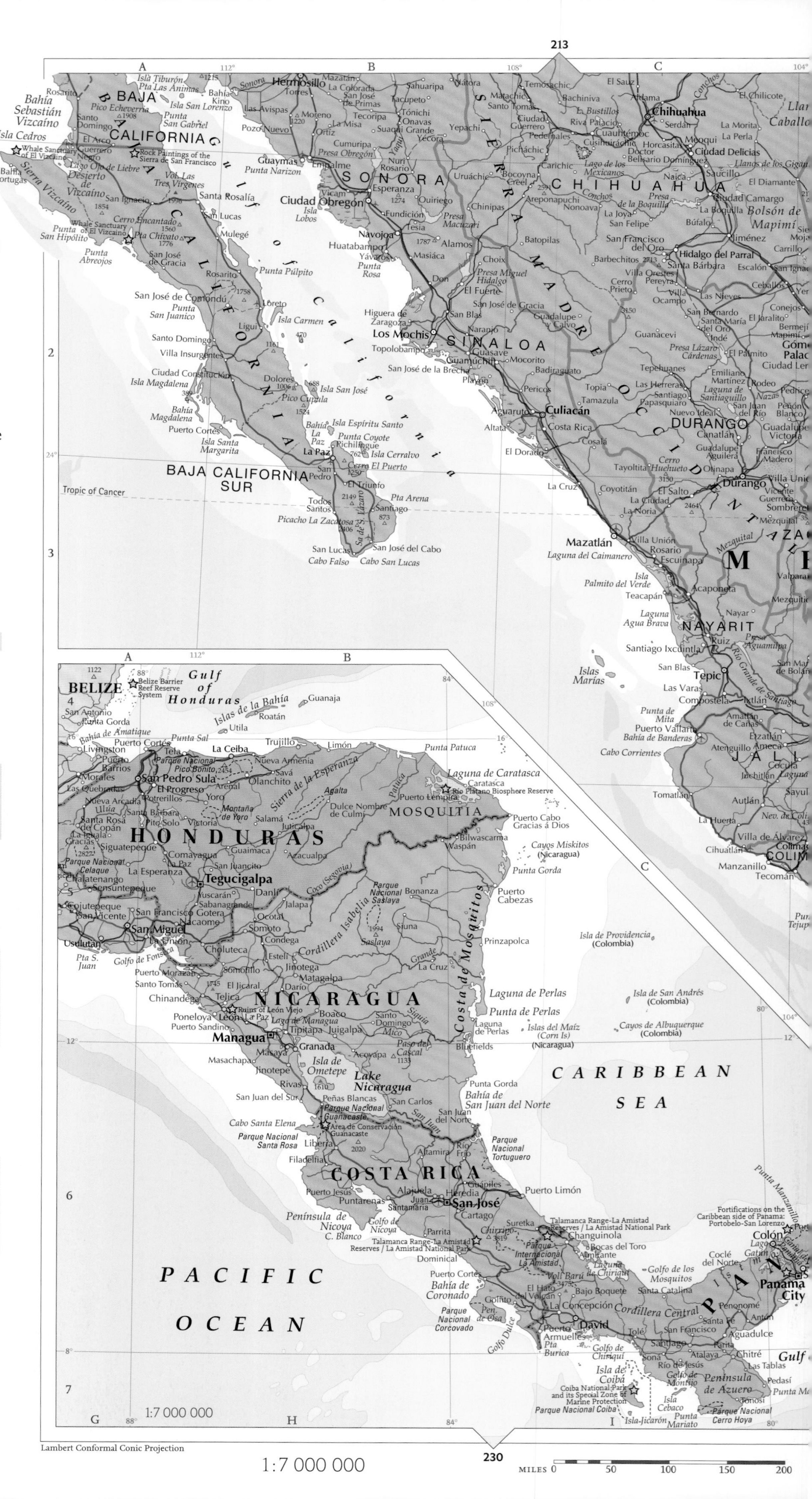

1:7 000 000

Lambert Conformal Conic Projection

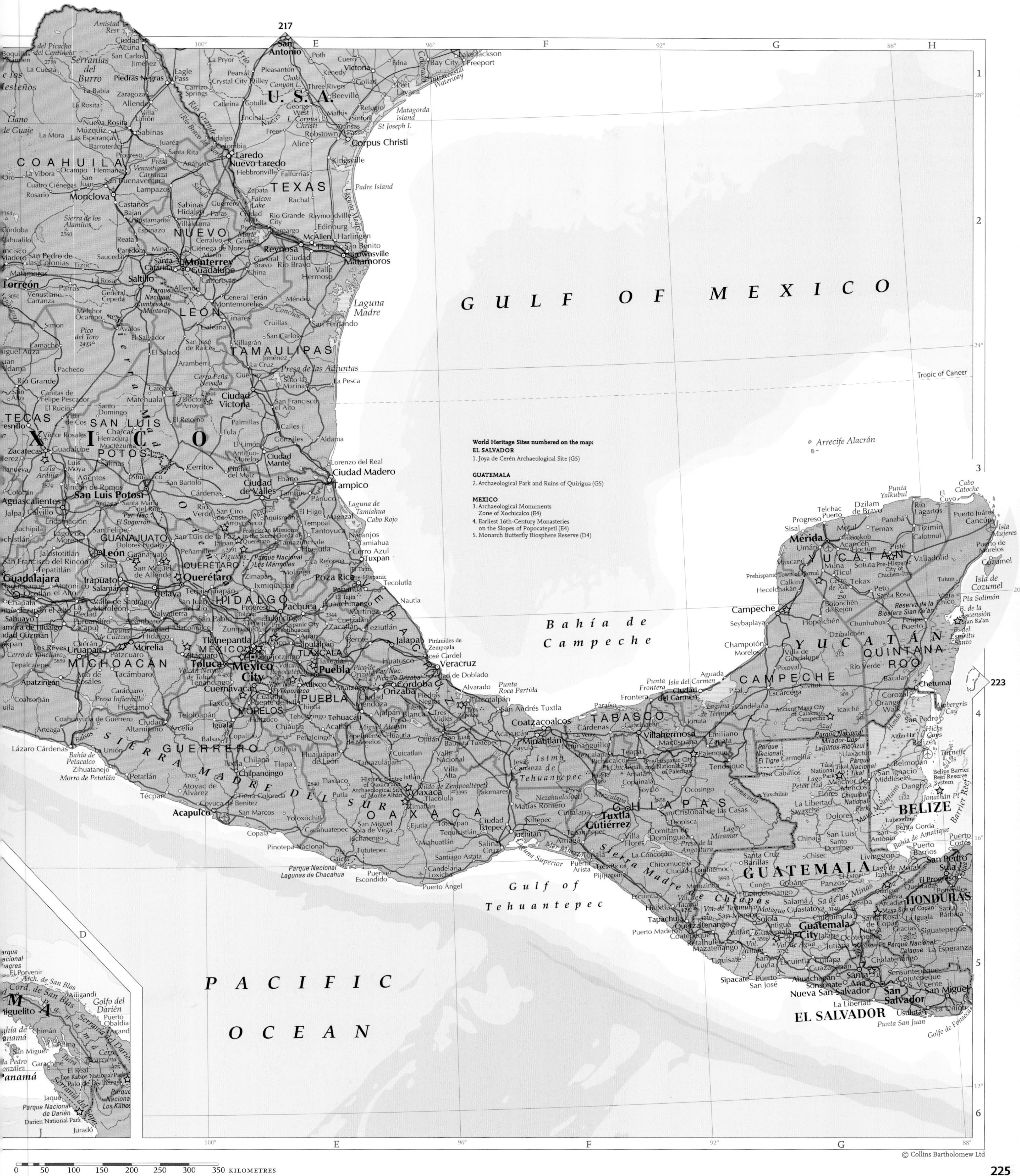

217
223
GULF OF MEXICO
PACIFIC OCEAN
Bahía de Campeche
Gulf of Tehuantepec
U.S.A.
TEXAS
COAHUILA
NUEVO LEÓN
TAMAULIPAS
SAN LUIS POTOSÍ
GUANAJUATO
QUERÉTARO
HIDALGO
MÉXICO
MICHOACÁN
TLAXCALA
PUEBLA
MORELOS
GUERRERO
OAXACA
VERACRUZ
TABASCO
CHIAPAS
CAMPECHE
YUCATÁN
QUINTANA ROO
BELIZE
GUATEMALA
HONDURAS
EL SALVADOR
Sierra Madre Oriental
Sierra Madre del Sur
Sierra Madre de Chiapas
Tropic of Cancer
Arrecife Alacrán
Laguna Madre
Padre Island
Corpus Christi
San Antonio
Laredo
Nuevo Laredo
Monterrey
Saltillo
Torreón
Reynosa
Matamoros
Brownsville
Ciudad Victoria
Tampico
Ciudad Madero
San Luis Potosí
Aguascalientes
Guadalajara
León
Querétaro
Pachuca
Mexico City
Toluca
Puebla
Veracruz
Jalapa
Cuernavaca
Acapulco
Oaxaca
Coatzacoalcos
Minatitlán
Villahermosa
Tuxtla Gutiérrez
Campeche
Mérida
Cancún
Chetumal
Guatemala City
San Salvador
Nueva San Salvador
Tapachula
Belmopan
Cozumel
World Heritage Sites numbered on the map:
EL SALVADOR
1. Joya de Cerén Archaeological Site (G5)
GUATEMALA
2. Archaeological Park and Ruins of Quiriguá (G5)
MEXICO
3. Archaeological Monuments Zone of Xochicalco (E4)
4. Earliest 16th-Century Monasteries on the Slopes of Popocatepetl (E4)
5. Monarch Butterfly Biosphere Reserve (D4)
0 50 100 150 200 250 300 350 KILOMETRES

South America Physical

South America stretches from north of the Equator to a point less than 1000 km (621 miles) away from Antarctica at Cape Horn. The most dominant physical features are the Andes, stretching down the western side, and the enormous Amazon Basin. Vast plains occupy much of the south and southeast – in the Pampas grasslands and the region of Patagonia in southern Argentina. Much of the rest of the continent consists of dissected plateaus, undulating lowlands, and lesser mountain ranges.

Facts

- The Galapagos Islands, made famous by research by Charles Darwin and renowned for its wildlife and biodiversity, are a far-flung part of Ecuador, situated about 750 km (466 miles) out in the Pacific Ocean.

- Cerro Aconcagua, at 6959 m (22 831 ft), is the highest point in the western hemisphere.

- South Georgia and the South Sandwich Islands, lying between South America and Antarctica, are collectively a UK dependency, with no permanent population.

- The world's driest desert is the Atacama, where only 1 mm of rain may fall as infrequently as once every five to twenty years.

HIGHEST MOUNTAINS	m	ft
Cerro Aconcagua, Argentina	6 959	22 831
Nevado Ojos del Salado, Argentina/Chile	6 908	22 664
Cerro Bonete, Argentina	6 872	22 546
Cerro Pissis, Argentina	6 858	22 500
Cerro Tupungato, Argentina/Chile	6 800	22 309
Cerro Mercedario, Argentina	6 770	22 211

LARGEST ISLANDS	sq km	sq miles
Isla Grande de Tierra del Fuego	47 000	18 147
Isla de Chiloé	8 394	3 241
East Falkland	6 760	2 610
West Falkland	5 413	2 090

LONGEST RIVERS	km	miles
Amazon (Amazonas)	6 516	4 049
Río de la Plata-Paraná	4 500	2 796
Purus	3 218	2 000
Madeira	3 200	1 988
São Francisco	2 900	1 802
Tocantins	2 750	1 709

LARGEST LAKES	sq km	sq miles
Lake Titicaca	8 340	3 220

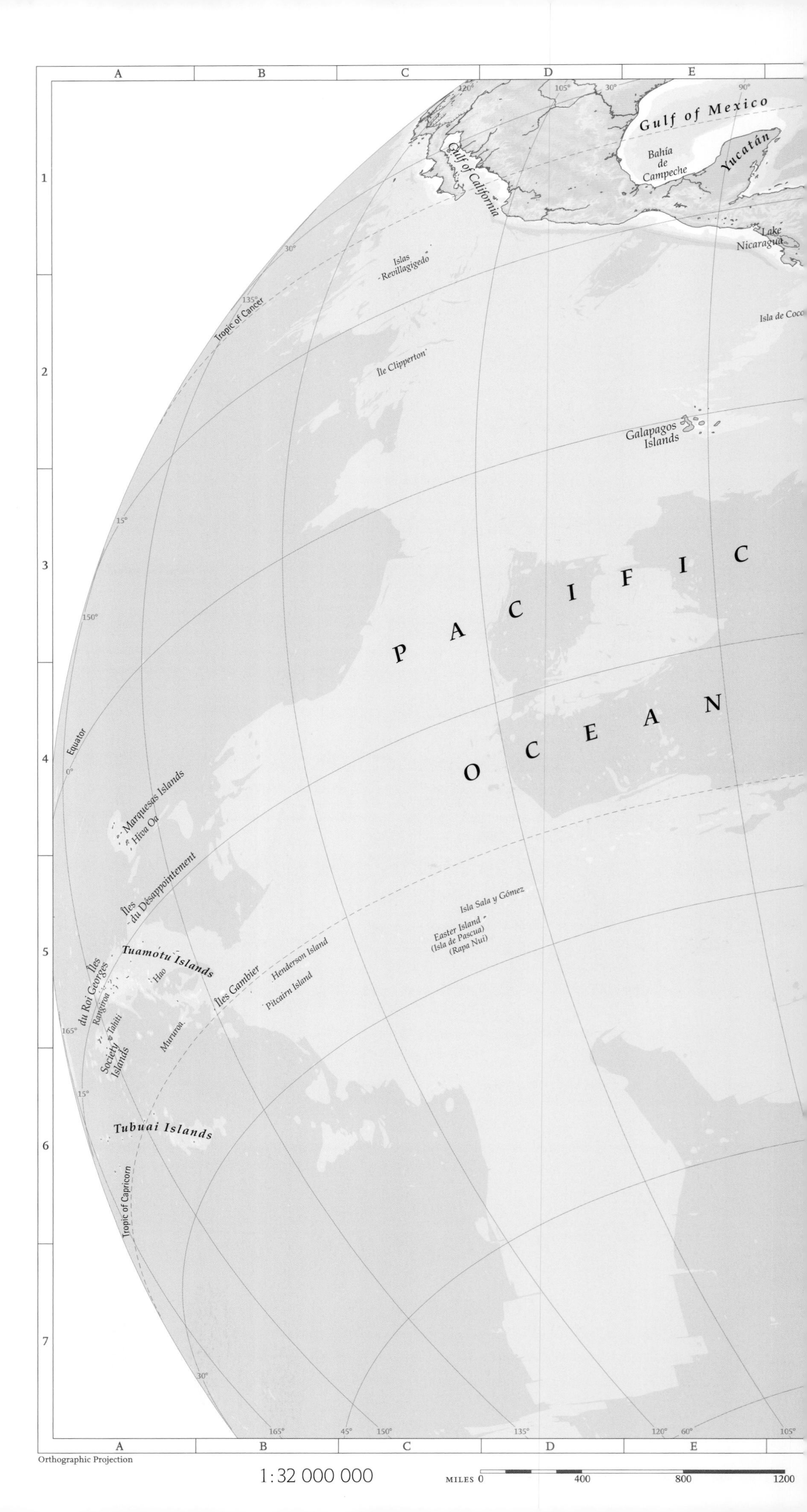

Orthographic Projection

1:32 000 000

MILES 0   400   800   1200

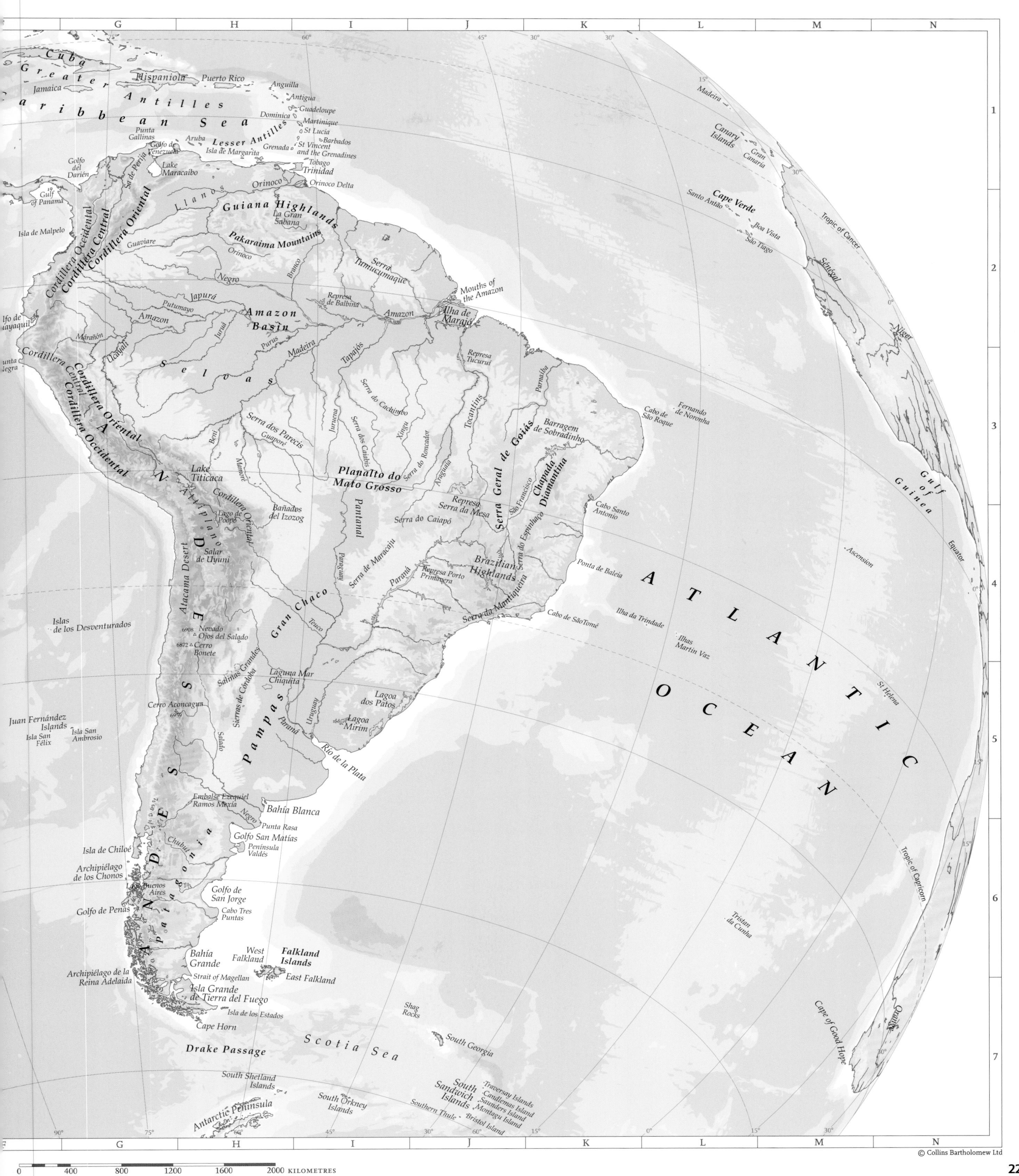

Cuba

Greater

Jamaica

Antilles

Caribbean Sea

Hispaniola · Puerto Rico · Anguilla

Antigua

Dominica · Guadeloupe

St Lucia · Martinique

Punta Gallinas

Golfo de Venezuela · Aruba · Isla de Margarita · Grenada · St Vincent and the Grenadines · Barbados

Lesser Antilles

Tobago

Trinidad

Gulf of Panama

Isla de Malpelo

Golfo del Darién

Sul de Perijá

Lake Maracaibo

Orinoco · Orinoco Delta

Cordillera Occidental
Cordillera Central
Cordillera Oriental

Llanos

Guiana Highlands

La Gran Sabana

Pakaraima Mountains

Guaviare

Orinoco

Serra Tumucumaque

Ifo de Guayaquil

Negro · Branco

Cordillera Occidental
Cordillera Central
Cordillera Oriental

Marañón

Putumayo · Japurá

Amazon

Represa de Balbina

Amazon

Mouths of the Amazon

Ilha de Marajó

Punta Negra

Huallaga · Ucayali

Amazon Basin

selvas

Juruá · Purus

Madeira · Tapajós

Represa Tucuruí

Parnaíba

Cordillera Occidental
Cordillera Central
Cordillera Oriental

Serra do Cachimbo

Serra dos Parecis

Branco

Guaporé

Xingu

Tocantins

Serra Geral de Goiás

Barragem de Sobradinho

Cabo de São Roque

Fernando de Noronha

A N D E S

Lake Titicaca

Cordillera Oriental

Bañados del Izozog

Planalto do Mato Grosso

Serra do Roncador

Araguaia

Represa Serra da Mesa

São Francisco

Chapada Diamantina

Cabo Santo Antônio

Altiplano

Lago de Poopó

Salar de Uyuni

Pantanal

Serra do Caiapó

Paraguai

Brazilian Highlands

Serra do Espinhaço

Ponta de Baleia

Atacama Desert

6908 Nevado Ojos del Salado
6872 Cerro Bonete

Gran Chaco

Serra de Maracaju

Paraná

Serra da Mantiqueira

Cabo de São Tomé

Ilha da Trindade

Salinas Grandes

Teuco

Pilcomayo

Represa Porto Primavera

Ilhas Martin Vaz

Islas de los Desventurados

Cerro Aconcagua 6959

Sierras de Córdoba

Salado

Pampas

Laguna Mar Chiquita

Uruguay

Lagoa dos Patos

Lagoa Mirim

Salado

Juan Fernández Islands

Isla San Félix · Isla San Ambrosio

Paraná

Río de la Plata

Embalse Ezequiel Ramos Mexía

Negro

Bahía Blanca

Punta Rasa

Golfo San Matías

Península Valdés

Isla de Chiloé

Archipiélago de los Chonos

Chubut

Patagonia

Lago Buenos Aires

Golfo de San Jorge

Cabo Tres Puntas

Golfo de Peñas

A N D E S

Bahía Grande

West Falkland

Falkland Islands

East Falkland

Archipiélago de la Reina Adelaida

Strait of Magellan

Isla Grande de Tierra del Fuego

Isla de los Estados

Cape Horn

Scotia Sea

Shag Rocks

South Georgia

Drake Passage

South Shetland Islands

South Orkney Islands

South Sandwich Islands

Traversay Islands
Candlemas Island
Saunders Island
Montagu Island
Southern Thule · Bristol Island

Antarctic Peninsula

ATLANTIC OCEAN

Madeira

Canary Islands · Gran Canaria

Cape Verde

Santo Antão · Boa Vista · São Tiago

Tropic of Cancer

Senegal

Niger

Gulf of Guinea

Ascension

Equator

St Helena

Tropic of Capricorn

Tristan da Cunha

Cape of Good Hope

Orange

© Collins Bartholomew Ltd

0 · 400 · 800 · 1200 · 1600 · 2000 KILOMETRES

South America Political

Brazil fills most of the north of the continent, while Argentina is the largest country in the narrower south. Chile consists of a long, narrow strip along the Pacific coast. French Guiana is the only remaining territory under overseas control, on a continent which has a long colonial history. Spanish is the language of the majority of the continent, although Brazil is largely Portuguese-speaking. There has been a steady process of urbanization and the majority of South America's population live in the major cities and close to the coast.

Facts

- South America is often referred to as Latin America, reflecting the historic influences of Spain and Portugal.

- Bolivia and Paraguay are the only landlocked countries on the continent.

- The Falkland Islands were first settled by the British, although Argentina retains a claim over them and calls them the Malvinas Islands (Islas Malvinas in Spanish). This claim resulted in a war in 1982 between Argentina and the UK.

- The Juan Fernández Islands (Archipiélago Juan Fernández), a group of Chilean islands in the Pacific, are known for having been the location of the famous 'castaway' novel, Robinson Crusoe.

LARGEST COUNTRIES	Area	
	sq km	sq miles
Brazil	8 514 879	3 287 613
Argentina	2 766 889	1 068 302
Peru	1 285 216	496 225
Colombia	1 141 748	440 831
Bolivia	1 098 581	424 164
Venezuela	912 050	352 144
Chile	756 945	292 258
Paraguay	406 752	157 048
Ecuador	272 045	105 037
Guyana	214 969	83 000

MOST POPULATED COUNTRIES	Population
Brazil	191 791 000
Colombia	46 156 000
Argentina	39 531 000
Peru	27 903 000
Venezuela	27 657 000
Chile	16 635 000
Ecuador	13 341 000
Bolivia	9 525 000
Paraguay	6 127 000
Uruguay	3 340 000

CAPITALS		
Largest population	**Buenos Aires**, Argentina	13 067 000
Smallest population	**Stanley**, Falkland Islands	2 115
Most northerly	**Caracas**, Venezuela	10° 28' N
Most southerly	**Stanley**, Falkland Islands	51° 43' S
Highest	**La Paz**, Bolivia	3 630 m/ 11 909 ft

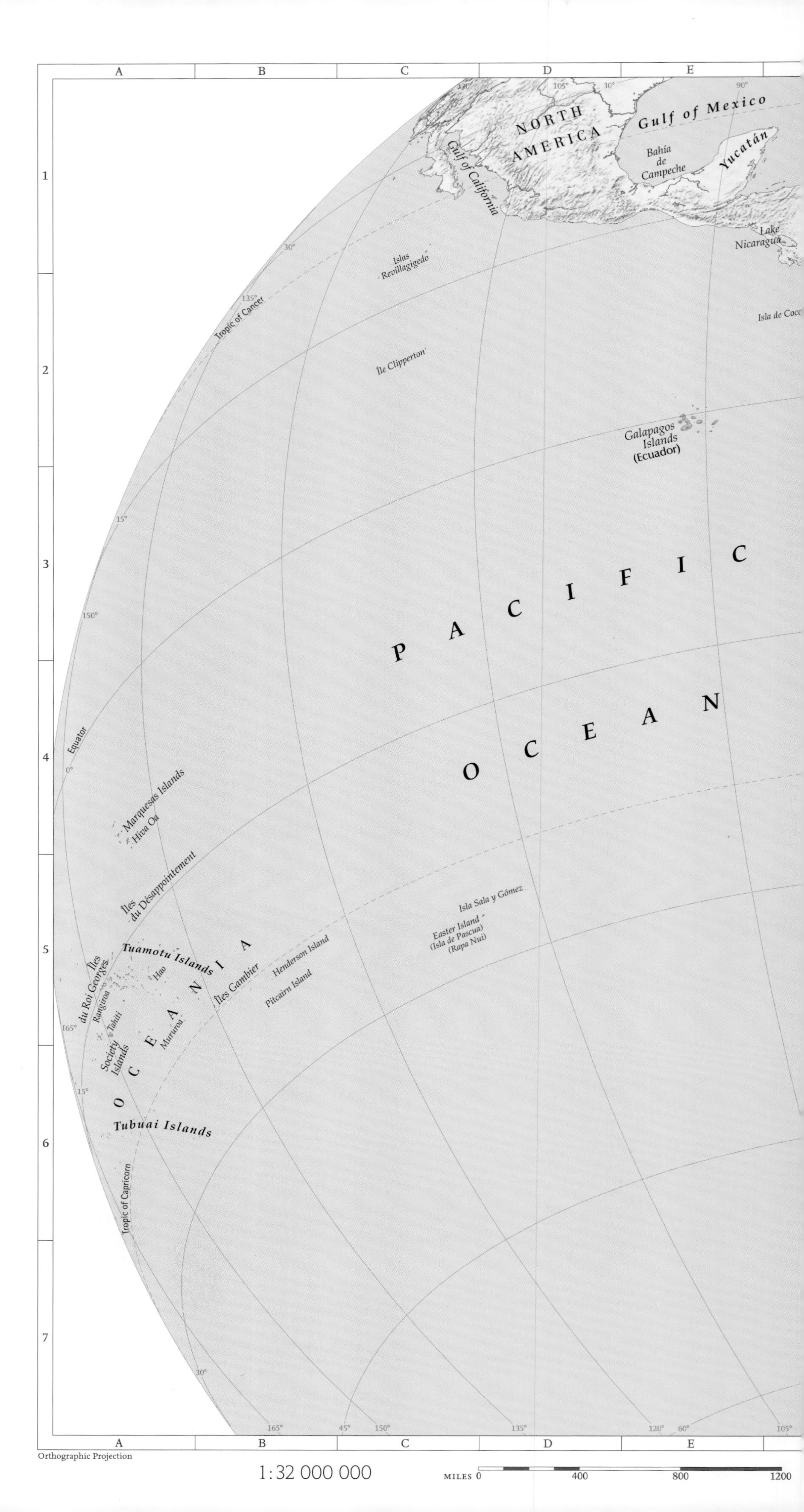

Orthographic Projection

1:32 000 000

MILES 0   400   800   1200

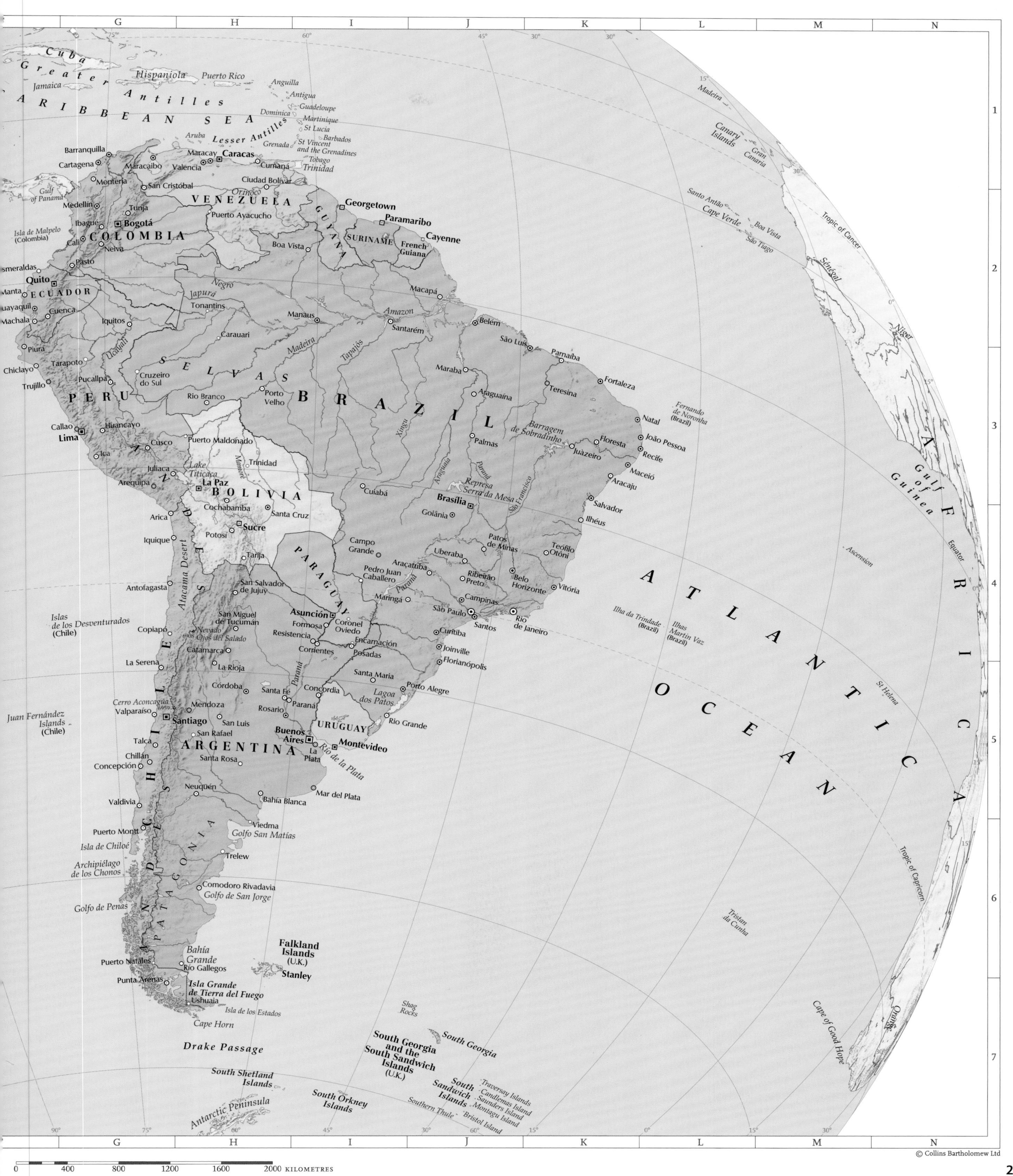

0   400   800   1200   1600   2000 KILOMETRES

© Collins Bartholomew Ltd

Northern South America

Rainforest and the Amazon dominate the greater part of this area. Major attractions are trips into the jungles and forests, to experience the unique atmosphere, plant life and wildlife. There is also much history, ancient and modern, and exciting culture to enjoy.

 BOLIVIA Capital: **La Paz/Sucre**
Area: **1 098 581 km²/424 164 miles²**
Population: **9 525 000** Languages: **Spanish, Quechua, Aymara**
Religions: **Roman Catholic, Protestant, Baha'i**
Currency: **Boliviano**

A landlocked country, Bolivia offers beautiful landscapes, river trips into the rainforest, bus rides along the mountain passes of the Andes and ancient sites such as those on Lake Titicaca. The large indigenous population is reflected in native cultures, dialects and music. The Spanish influence is visible in the colonial architecture, particularly in Sucre. Salar de Uyuni is the world's largest salt flat and, during November, a major breeding ground for pink flamingos. It is also the site of a train cemetery, the locomotives abandoned when the mining industry collapsed in the 1940s.

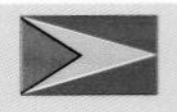

 GUYANA Capital: **Georgetown**
Area: **214 969 km²/83 000 miles²** Population: **738 000**
Languages: **English, Creole, Amerindian languages**
Religions: **Protestant, Hindu, Roman Catholic, Sunni Muslim**
Currency: **Guyana dollar**

Guyana's main attractions include the spectacular Kaieteur Falls on the Potaro River, Atlantic beaches, the Rupununi savanna, and river routes into the forests and jungles to see rare wildlife, including more than 700 indigenous bird species. The capital, Georgetown, has striking 19th-century stilted wooden buildings.

 SURINAME Capital: **Paramaribo**
Area: **163 820 km²/63 251 miles²** Population: **458 000**
Languages: **Dutch, Surinamese, English, Hindi**
Religions: **Hindu, Roman Catholic, Protestant, Sunni Muslim**
Currency: **Suriname guilder**

Rainforest covers 80 per cent of Suriname, which has eleven nature reserves and other special sites: the word's largest area of protected rainforest and a World Heritage site. Much of the interior, home to native tribes, is accessible only by canoeing the rivers and rapids.

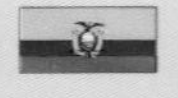

 ECUADOR Capital: **Quito**
Area: **272 045 km²/105 037 miles²**
Population: **13 341 000** Languages: **Spanish, Quechua and other Amerindian languages** Religions: **Roman Catholic**
Currency: **United States dollar**

Straddling the Equator, Ecuador is divided into three distinctive regions. The Andean highlands of La Sierra are known as the Avenue of Volcanoes, home to much of the population. El Oriente is covered in dense jungle and a network of rivers. La Costa is Ecuador's Pacific coast, with mangrove forests and attractive beaches. The capital, Quito, has a wonderfully preserved historic centre, the best in Latin America. The Galapagos Islands, far out into the Pacific, are famed for their unique wildlife.

PERU Capital: **Lima**
Area: **1 285 216 km²/496 225 miles²**
Population: **27 903 000** Languages: **Spanish, Quechua, Aymara** Religions: **Roman Catholic, Protestant** Currency: **Sol**

Peru is best known for the Inca trail from Cusco to Machu Picchu, the capital of the Inca Empire and a World Heritage site. It is also a country of snowy peaks, mountaintop lakes, deserts, beaches and jungle, and a popular destination for surfing, extreme mountain biking, adventurous river trips and trekking. The geoglyphs and lines (some stretching hundreds of kilometres) of Nasca and Pampas de Jumana, scratched onto the ground between 500 BC and AD 500 are one of the world's enigmas.

1:15 000 000

Lambert Azimuthal Equal Area Projection

MILES 0   100   200   300   400

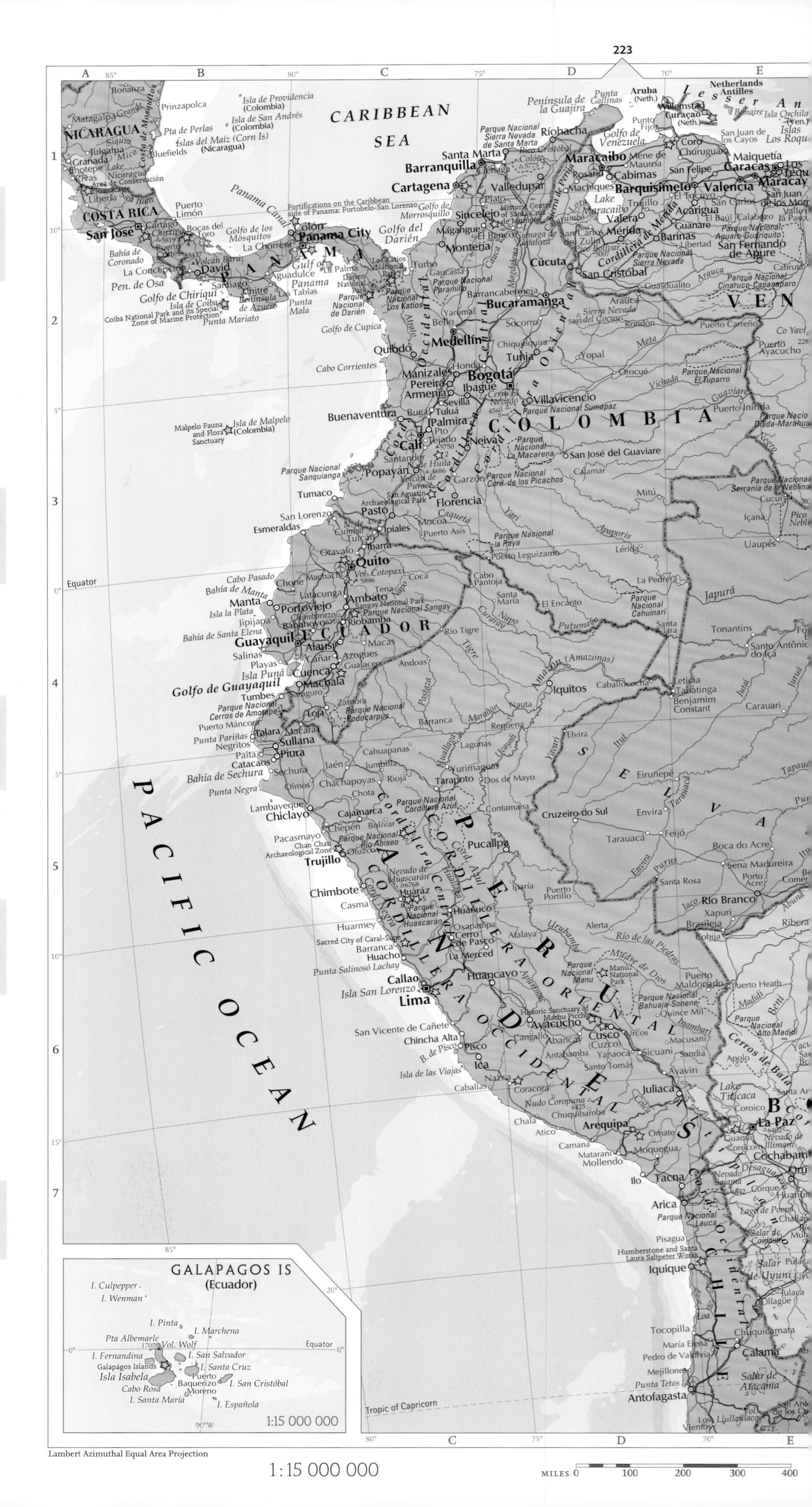

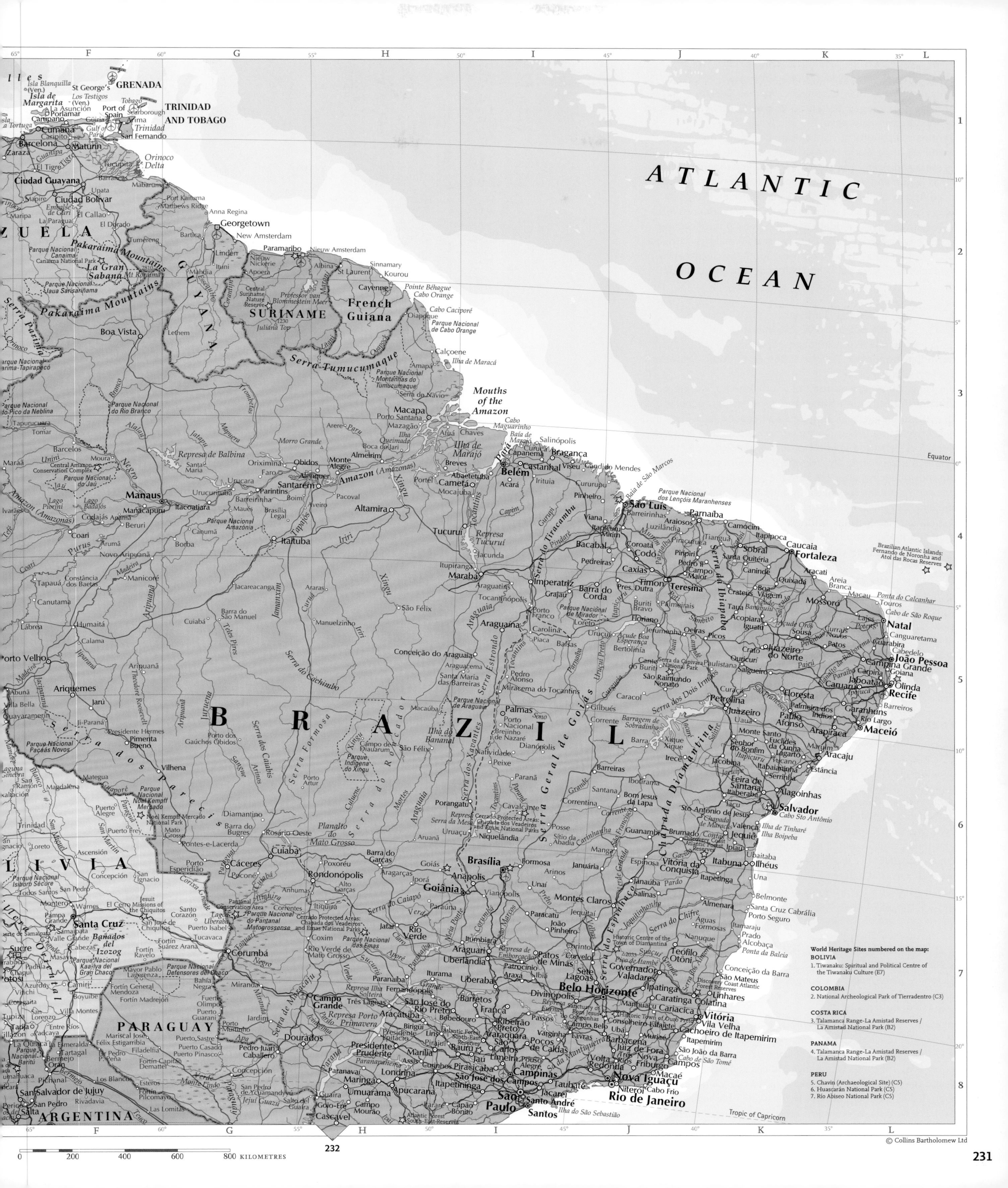

© Collins Bartholomew Ltd

0   200   400   600   800 KILOMETRES

ATLANTIC

OCEAN

World Heritage Sites numbered on the map:
BOLIVIA
1. Tiwanaku: Spiritual and Political Centre of
   the Tiwanaku Culture (E7)

COLOMBIA
2. National Archeological Park of Tierradentro (C3)

COSTA RICA
3. Talamanca Range-La Amistad Reserves /
   La Amistad National Park (B2)

PANAMA
4. Talamanca Range-La Amistad Reserves /
   La Amistad National Park (B2)

PERU
5. Chavin (Archaeological Site) (C5)
6. Huascarán National Park (C5)
7. Rio Abiseo National Park (C5)

Southern South America

ARGENTINA Capital: Buenos Aires
Area: **2 766 889 km²/1 068 302 miles²**
Population: **39 531 000** Languages: **Spanish, Italian, Amerindian languages** Religions: **Roman Catholic, Protestant**
Currency: **Argentinian peso**

Argentina is a country of vivid culture and stunning landscape. Iguazu Falls are a World Heritage site along the border of Argentina and Brazil. The area is home to endangered species such as jaguar and ocelot. To the south, Patagonia has snow-capped Andean peaks, the Perito Moreno Glacier, Península Valdés and the beautiful red mountains of Salta. Buenos Aires is a welcoming, lively, modern capital. Strong on performing arts, the city has around 100 cinemas and 90 theatres. Ushuaia is often described as the world's most southerly city, its attractions including Tierra del Fuego National Park and Lapataia Bay.

CHILE Capital: Santiago
Area: **756 945 km²/292 258 miles²**
Population: **16 635 000** Languages: **Spanish, Amerindian languages** Religions: **Roman Catholic, Protestant**
Currency: **Chilean peso**

Chile, lying along the west coast of South America, is a great destination for outdoor activities and is increasingly popular with adventure tourists looking for an adrenaline rush. The huge, dry Atacama Desert has the world's two highest active volcanoes: San Pedro and Volcan Llullaillaco. San Pedro de Atacama is home to a fascinating archaeological museum containing thousands of ancient artefacts from the Atacameno culture. In the centre, are the spectacular granite monoliths of the Cordillera del Paine. The lake district of Patagonia and Torres del Paine National Park, to the south, is an area of impressive mountains, glaciers and lakes.

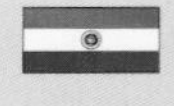

PARAGUAY Capital: Asunción
Area: **406 752 km²/157 048 miles²**
Population: **6 127 000** Languages: **Spanish, Guaraní**
Religions: **Roman Catholic, Protestant** Currency: **Guaraní**

Paraguay, landlocked and sandwiched between Brazil and Argentina on the great plain of Gran Chaco, has national parks, great areas of wilderness, jungles, forests and waterfalls. The capital, Asunción, sits on the banks of the Paraguay river and the Argentinian border and is one of the world's cheapest cities, popular for its parks, museums and boat tours.

Venezuela and Colombia

COLOMBIA Capital: Bogotá
Area: **1 141 748 km²/440 831 miles²**
Population: **46 156 000** Languages: **Spanish, Amerindian languages** Religions: **Roman Catholic, Protestant**
Currency: **Colombian peso**

Colombia has wonderful natural attractions of mountains, jungles and both Caribbean and Pacific coastlines. The variety of wildlife and plants is resulting in developing ecotourism and there are six UNESCO World Heritage sites. Birding is a tourist draw, with over 750 different bird species in the Colombian Amazon, accessible from the city of Leticia. Bogotá, high in the Andres, shows its colonial history in sharp contrast to the modern high-rise buildings.

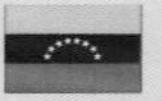

VENEZUELA Capital: Caracas
Area: **912 050 km²/352 144 miles²**
Population: **27 657 000** Languages: **Spanish, Amerindian languages** Religions: **Roman Catholic, Protestant**
Currency: **Bolívar fuerte**

Venezuela is known for oil but enthusiastically welcomes visitors to its tropical beaches, colonial towns, jungles and mountains. The Orinoco delta is a labyrinth of waterways with opportunities for river trips, meetings with native Indians and sightings of the rich and varied wildlife and extensive bird populations. Canaima lagoon, fed by waterfalls (including the world's highest, Angel Falls) has a fantastic backdrop of 'table' mountains, the *tepui*.

Lambert Azimuthal Equal Area Projection

1:15 000 000

MILES 0   100   200   300   0   200   400   600 KILOMETRES

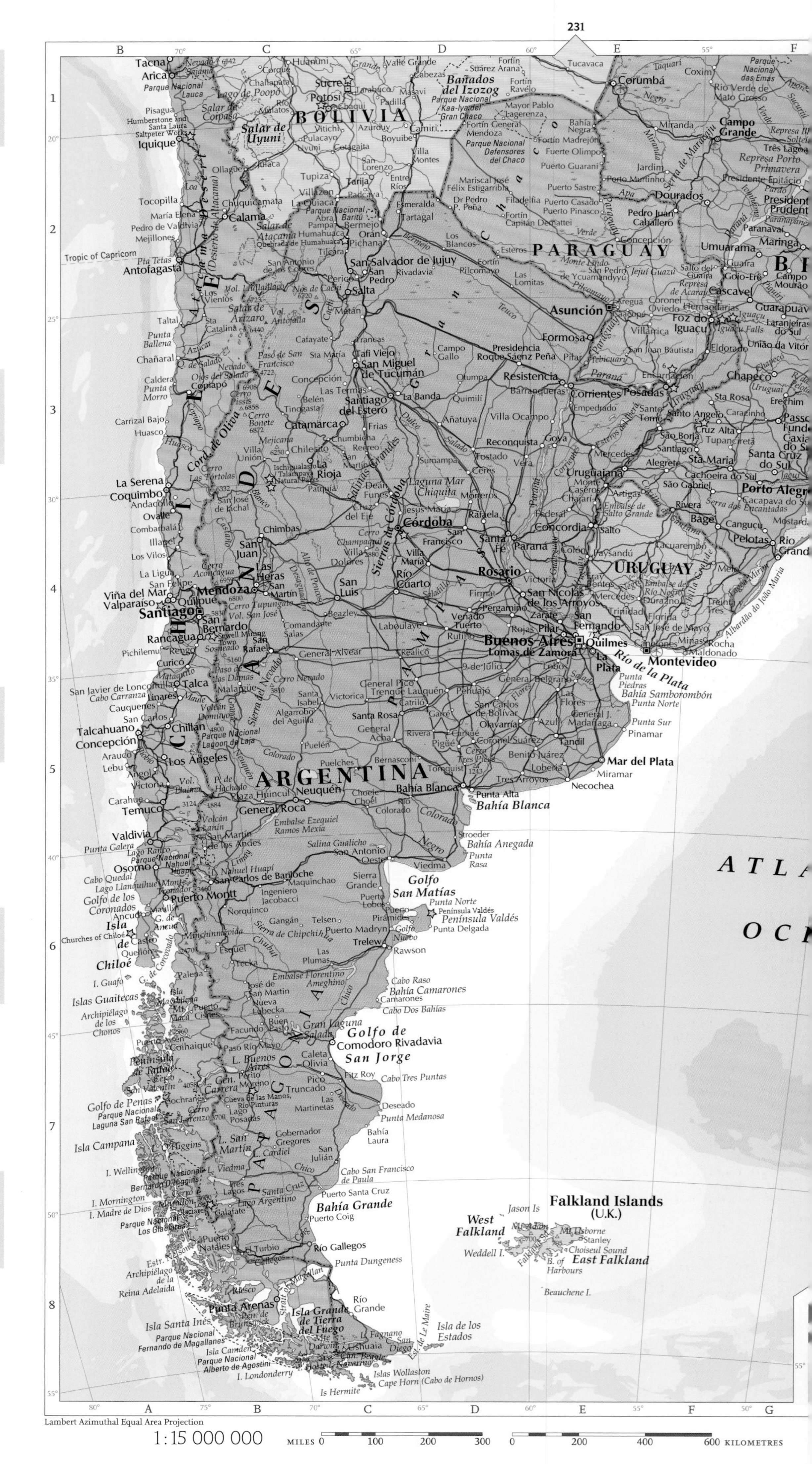

CARIBBEAN SEA

GRENADA

TRINIDAD AND TOBAGO

Netherlands Antilles (Neth.)

Aruba (Neth.)

V E N E Z U E L A

C O L O M B I A

B R A Z I L

RORAIMA

AMAZONAS

Lesser Antilles

ECUADOR

PANAMA

World Heritage Sites numbered on the map:

RGENTINA
. Iguazu National Park (F3)
. Jesuit Missions of the Guaranis: San Ignacio Miní, Santa Ana, Nuestra Señora de Loreto and Santa Maria Mayor (E3)

RAZIL
. Atlantic Forest South-East Reserves (F2/G2)
. Iguaçu National Park (F3)
. Jesuit Missions of the Guaranis: Ruins of Sao Miguel das Missoes (F3)

ARAGUAY
. Jesuit Missions of La Santísima Trinidad de Paraná and Jesús de Tavarangue (E3)

RUGUAY
. Historic Quarter of the City of Colonia del Sacramento (E4)

SOUTH GEORGIA (U.K.)

Cape Alexandra
Mt Paget
Grytviken
Cape Disappointment

1:15 000 000

© Collins Bartholomew Ltd

Lambert Azimuthal Equal Area Projection

1:7 500 000

MILES 0   50   100   150

0   50   100   150   200   250   300 KILOMETRES

© Collins Bartholomew Ltd

223

Southeast Brazil

BRAZIL Capital: Brasília
Area: 8 514 879 km²/3 287 613 miles²
Population: **191 791 000** Languages: **Portuguese**
Religions: **Roman Catholic, Protestant** Currency: **Real**

Portuguese-speaking Brazil is a good-time destination, known for football success and music, particularly the samba, ubiquitous in Brazil's carnivals. In Rio the focus of the carnival is in an open-air stadium, specially built to allow spectators to enjoy the samba dancing, costumes and floats. Salvador's carnival is the world's largest street party, according to the Guinness Book of Records. Celebrated for almost 300 years, thousands of visitors flock to the city for the party. Recife and Olinda are also great destinations to experience the exciting carnival atmosphere. Olinda, a charming town of Baroque churches and vividly painted houses, parades giant papier-mâché figures of folk heroes as part of its celebrations.

Brazil is not just a party destination. It has a beautiful coast and beaches, colonial towns and energetic cities, as well as the wild interior of Amazon rainforest, teeming with wildlife and plants. Over sixty national parks across the country provide plentiful opportunities for eco tourism. Brazil is also a great destination for fishing, trekking, surfing, rafting, diving, sailing and of course beach volleyball, synonymous with lively Brazilian beaches.

The Iguaçu Falls, located in the national park of the same name, is a popular draw, as is the Itaipu Dam on the Paraná River, between Brazil and Paraguay. Visitors are also drawn to the Triple Frontier, marking the borders of Brazil, Argentina and Paraguay.

Brasília, the capital, is a World Heritage site. It was a new city, developed in 1956 and designed with the intention that every element should be in harmony with the city's overall design.

Serra da Capivara Park is in the northeast of the country, a World Heritage site where rock shelters decorated with cave paintings, some more than 25 000 years old, have been discovered. There are over 300 important archaeological sites within the park.

Central Chile, Central Argentina and Uruguay

URUGUAY Capital: Montevideo
Area: 176 215 km²/68 037 miles²
Population: **3 340 000** Languages: **Spanish**
Religions: **Roman Catholic, Protestant, Jewish**
Currency: **Uruguayan peso**

Uruguay is growing in popularity as a destination in its own right, as well as an easy day trip from Buenos Aires, on the opposite bank of the Rio de la Plata. With around 650 km (400 miles) of marvellous coastline there are stretches of deserted beach and a variety of resorts offering water sports and trips to see whales, seals and turtles. Inland are the wide, open prairies – gaucho country where visitors can stay on estancias. Montevideo is a lively capital with its own carnival. Uruguay's oldest town, Colonia del Sacramento, is a World Heritage site of cobbled streets and historic buildings.

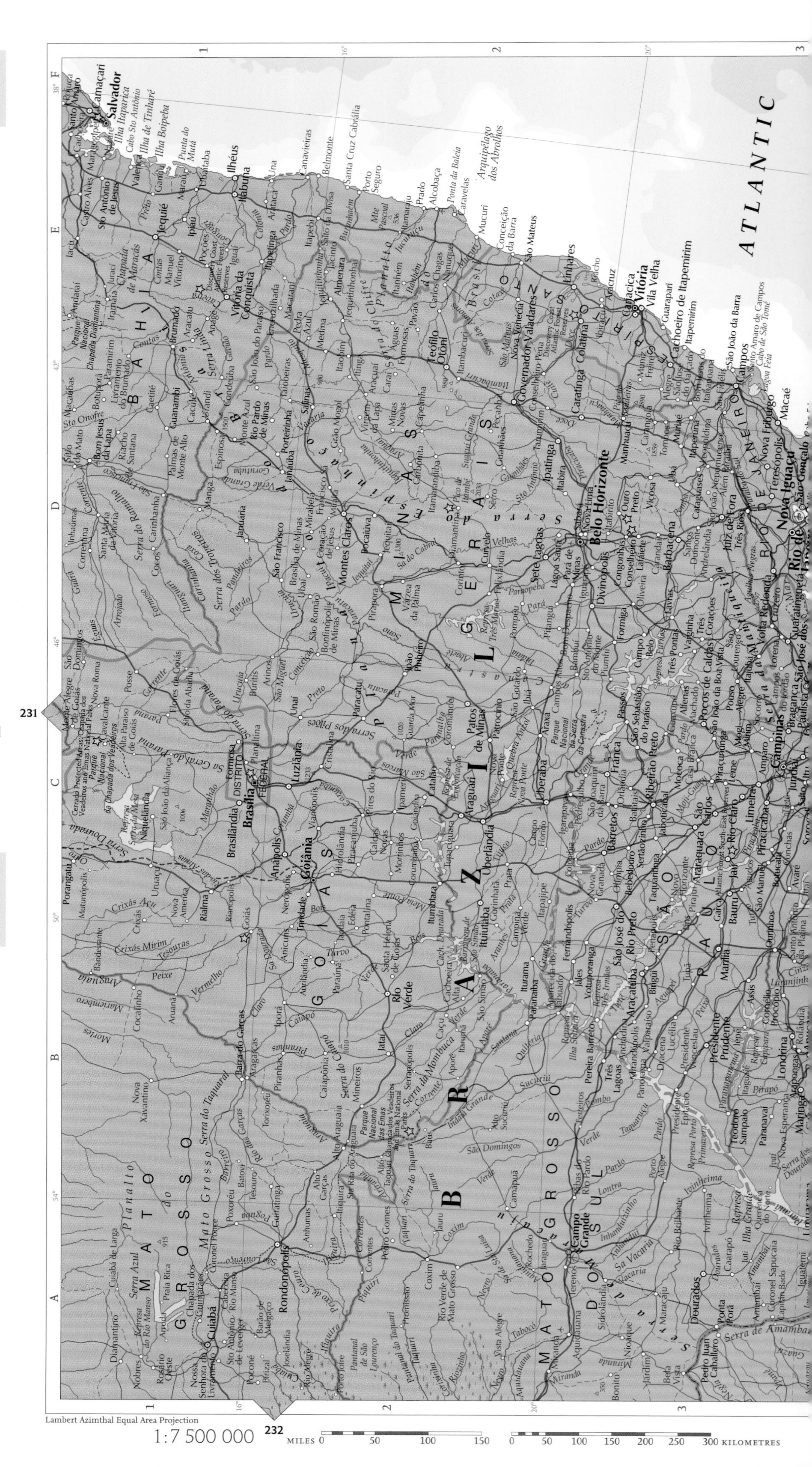

Lambert Azimuthal Equal Area Projection

1:7 500 000

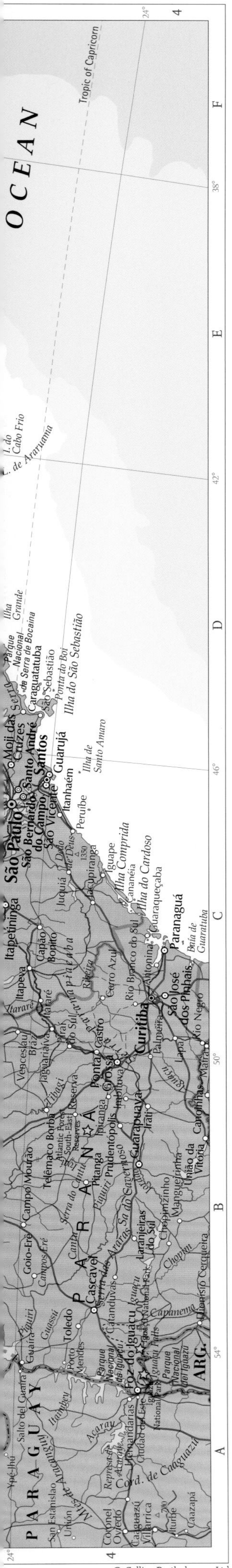

OCEAN

BRAZIL

URUGUAY

Montevideo
Río de la Plata

ATLANTIC OCEAN

PARAGUAY

São Paulo

ARGENTINA

BUENOS AIRES

Buenos Aires
Rosario
Córdoba
Mar del Plata
Bahía Blanca

SANTA FE
ENTRE RÍOS
CÓRDOBA
LA RIOJA
SAN JUAN
SAN LUIS
MENDOZA
LA PAMPA
RÍO NEGRO
NEUQUÉN
CHUBUT

Golfo San Matías

Mendoza
San Juan
Santiago
Valparaíso
Rancagua
Talcahuano
Concepción

CHILE
COQUIMBO
VALPARAISO
O'HIGGINS
MAULE
BIOBIO
ARAUCANIA
LOS LAGOS

La Serena
Coquimbo

Curitiba
Paranaguá

Lambert Azimuthal Equal Area Projection

1:7 500 000

MILES 0   50   100   150

0   50   100   150   200   250   300 KILOMETRES

© Collins Bartholomew Ltd

232

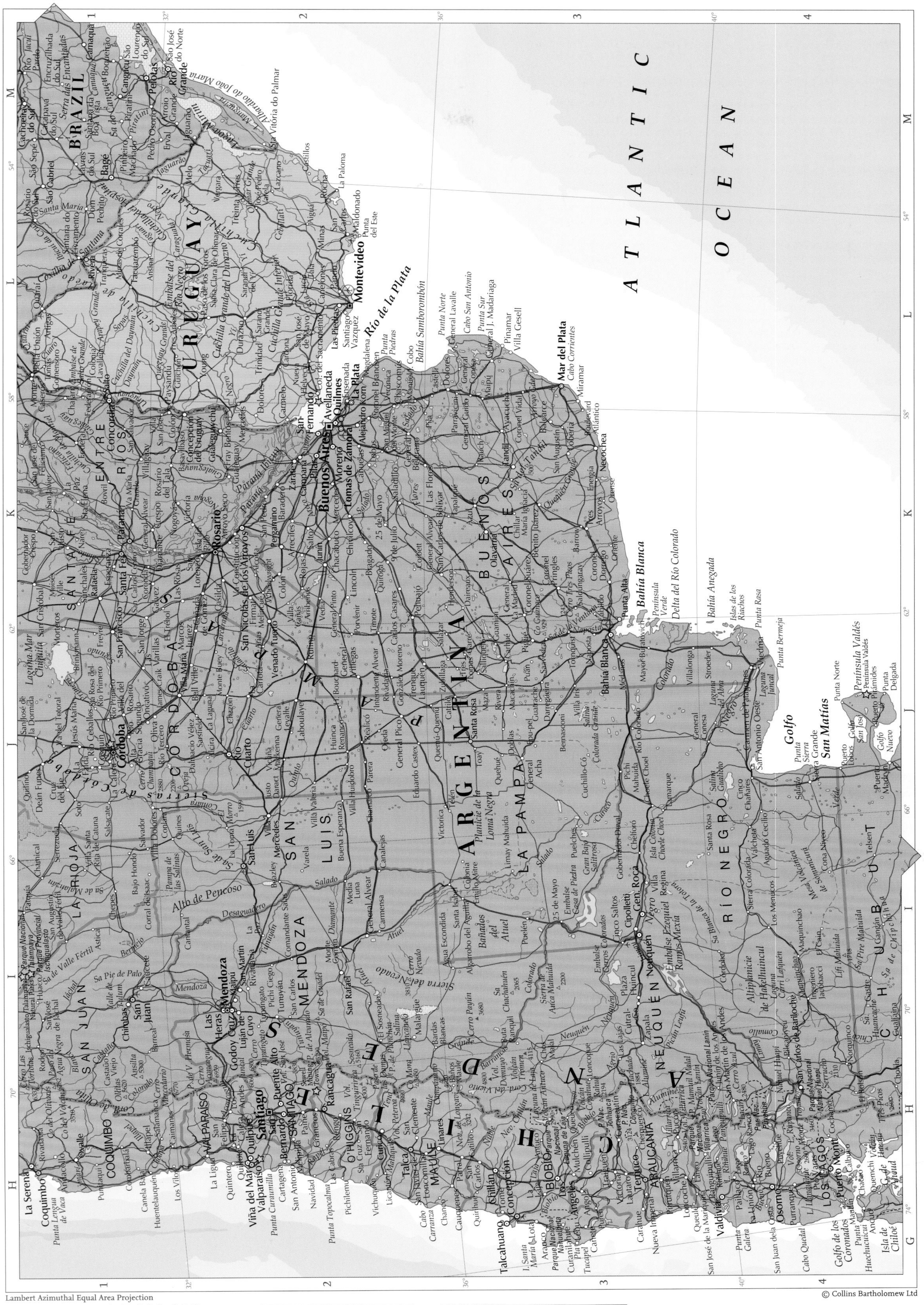

States and Territories (continued)

OCEANIA

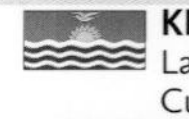

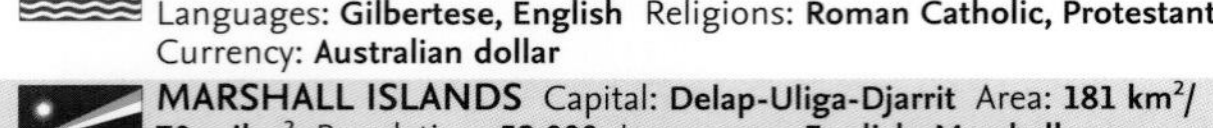

KIRIBATI Capital: **Bairiki** Population: **95 000** Area: **717 km²/277 miles²**
Languages: **Gilbertese, English** Religions: **Roman Catholic, Protestant**
Currency: **Australian dollar**

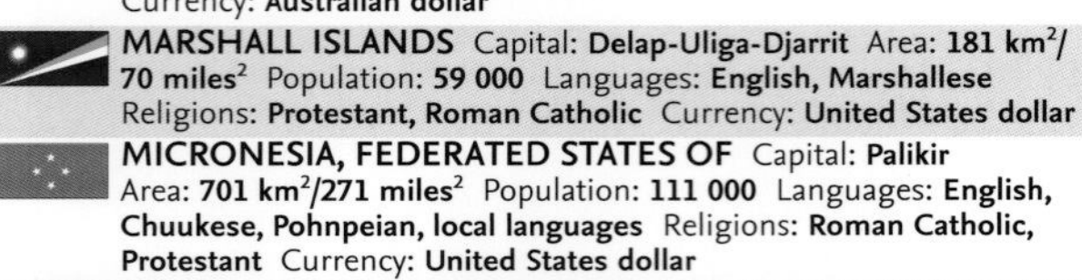

MARSHALL ISLANDS Capital: **Delap-Uliga-Djarrit** Area: **181 km²/**
70 miles² Population: **59 000** Languages: **English, Marshallese**
Religions: **Protestant, Roman Catholic** Currency: **United States dollar**

MICRONESIA, FEDERATED STATES OF Capital: **Palikir**
Area: **701 km²/271 miles²** Population: **111 000** Languages: **English,**
Chuukese, Pohnpeian, local languages Religions: **Roman Catholic,**
Protestant Currency: **United States dollar**

NAURU Capital **Yaren** Area: **21 km²/8 miles²** Population: **10 000**
Languages: **Nauruan, English** Religions: **Protestant, Roman Catholic**
Currency: **Australian dollar**

SAMOA Capital: **Apia** Area: **2 831 km²/1 093 km²** Population: **187 000**
Languages: **Samoan, English** Religions: **Protestant, Roman Catholic**
Currency: **Tala**

SOLOMON ISLANDS Capital: **Honiara** Area: **28 370 km²/**
10 954 miles² Population: **496 000** Languages: **English, Creole, local**
languages Religions: **Protestant, Roman Catholic** Currency: **Solomon**
Islands dollar

TONGA Capital: **Nuku'alofa** Area: **748 km²/289 miles²**
Population: **100 000** Languages: **Tongan, English** Religions: **Protestant,**
Roman Catholic Currency: **Pa'anga**

TUVALU Capital: **Vaiaku** Area: **25 km²/10 miles²** Population: **11 000**
Languages: **Tuvaluan, English** Religions: **Protestant**
Currency: **Australian dollar**

VANUATU Capital: **Port Vila** Area: **12 190 km²/4 707 miles²**
Population: **226 000** Languages: **English, Bislama (Creole), French**
Religions: **Protestant, Roman Catholic, traditional beliefs**
Currency: **Vatu**

ASIA

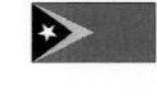

EAST TIMOR Capital: **Dili** Area **14 874 km²/5 743 miles²**
Population: **1 155 000** Languages: **Portuguese, Tetun, English**
Religions: **Roman Catholic** Currency: **United States dollar**

Gaza Capital: **Gaza** Area: **363 km²/140 miles²** Population: **1 586 008**
Languages: **Arabic** Religions: **Sunni Muslim, Shi'a Muslim**
Currency: **Israeli shekel**

Jammu amd Kashmir Capital: **Srinagar** Area: **222 236 km²/**
85 806 miles² Population: **13 000 000**

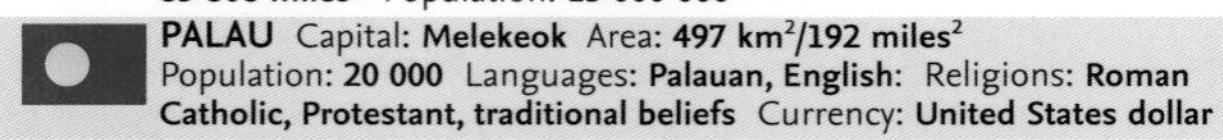

PALAU Capital: **Melekeok** Area: **497 km²/192 miles²**
Population: **20 000** Languages: **Palauan, English** Religions: **Roman**
Catholic, Protestant, traditional beliefs Currency: **United States dollar**

SINGAPORE Capital: **Singapore** Area: **639 km²/247 miles²**
Population: **4 436 000** Languages: **Chinese, English, Malay, Tamil**
Religions: **Buddhist, Taoist, Sunni Muslim, Christian, Hindu**
Currency: **Singapore dollar**

West Bank Area: **5 860 km²/2 263 miles²** Population: **2 676 284**
Languages: **Arabic, Hebrew** Religions: **Sunni Muslim, Jewish, Shi'a**
Muslim, Christian Currency: **Jordanian dinar, Isreali shekel**

EUROPE

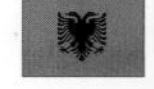

ALBANIA Capital: **Tirana (Tiranë)** Area: **28 748 km²/11 100 miles²**
Population: **3 190 000** Languages: **Albanian, Greek** Religions: **Sunni**
Muslim, Albanian Orthodox, Roman Catholic Currency: **Lek**

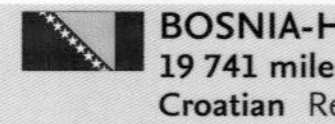

BOSNIA-HERZEGOVINA Capital: **Sarajevo** Area: **51 130 km²/**
19 741 miles² Population: **3 935 000** Languages: **Bosnian, Serbian,**
Croatian Religions: **Sunni Muslim, Serbian Orthodox, Roman Catholic,**
Protestant Currency: **Marka**

KOSOVO Capital: **Prishtinë (Priština)** Area: **10 908 km²/4 212 miles²**
Population: **2 069 989** Languages: **Albanian, Serbian** Religions: **Sunni**
Muslim, Serbian Orthodox Currency: **Euro**

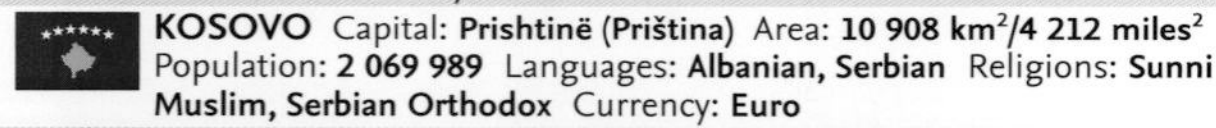

LIECHTENSTEIN Capital: **Vaduz** Area: **160 km²/62 miles²**
Population: **35 000** Languages: **German** Religions: **Roman Catholic,**
Protestant Currency: **Swiss franc**

MONACO Capital: **Monaco-Ville** Area: **2 km²/1 miles²**
Population: **33 000** Languages: **French, Monégasque, Italian**
Religions: **Roman Catholic** Currency: **Euro**

MONTENEGRO Capital: **Podgorica** Area: **13 812 km²/5 333 miles²**
Population: **598 000** Languages: **Serbian (Montenegrin), Albanian**
Religions: **Montenegrin Orthodox, Sunni Muslim** Currency: **Euro**

SAN MARINO Capital: **San Marino** Area: **61 km²/24 miles²**
Population: **31 000** Languages: **Italian** Religions: **Roman Catholic**
Currency: **Euro**

SERBIA Capital: **Belgrade (Beograd)** Area: **77 453 km²/29 904 miles²**
Population: **7 788 448** Languages: **Serbian, Hungarian**
Religions: **Serbian Orthodox, Roman Catholic, Sunni Muslim**
Currency: **Serbian dinar**

VATICAN CITY Capital: **Vatican City** Area: **0.5 km²/0.2 miles²**
Population: **557** Languages: **Italian** Religions: **Roman Catholic**
Currency: **Euro**

AFRICA

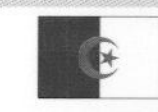

ALGERIA Capital: **Algiers (Alger)** Area: **2 381 741 km²/919 595 miles²**
Population: **33 858 000** Languages: **Arabic, French, Berber**
Religions: **Sunni Muslim** Currency: **Algerian dinar**

ANGOLA Capital: **Luanda** Area: **1 246 700 km²/481 354 miles²**
Population: **17 024 000** Languages: **Portuguese, Bantu, local languages**
Religions: **Roman Catholic, Protestant, traditional beliefs**
Currency:**y Kwanza**

BENIN Capital: **Porto-Novo** Area: **112 620 km²/43 483 miles²**
Population: **9 033 000** Languages: **French, Fon, Yoruba, Adja, local**
languages Religions: **Traditional beliefs, Roman Catholic, Sunni Muslim**
Currency: **CFA franc**

BOTSWANA Capital: **Gaborone** Area: **581 370 km²/224 468 miles²**
Population: **1 882 000** Languages: **English, Setswana, Shona, local**
languages Religions: **Traditional beliefs, Protestant, Roman Catholic**
Currency: **Pula**

BURKINA Capital: **Ouagadougou** Area: **274 200 km²/105 869 miles²**
Population: **14 784 000** Languages: **French, Moore (Mossi), Fulani, local**
languages Religions: **Sunni Muslim, traditional beliefs, Roman Catholic**
Currency: **CFA franc**

Pacific Ocean

Lambert Azimuthal Equal Area Projection

1:58 000 000   MILES 0   500   1000   1500   2000

10

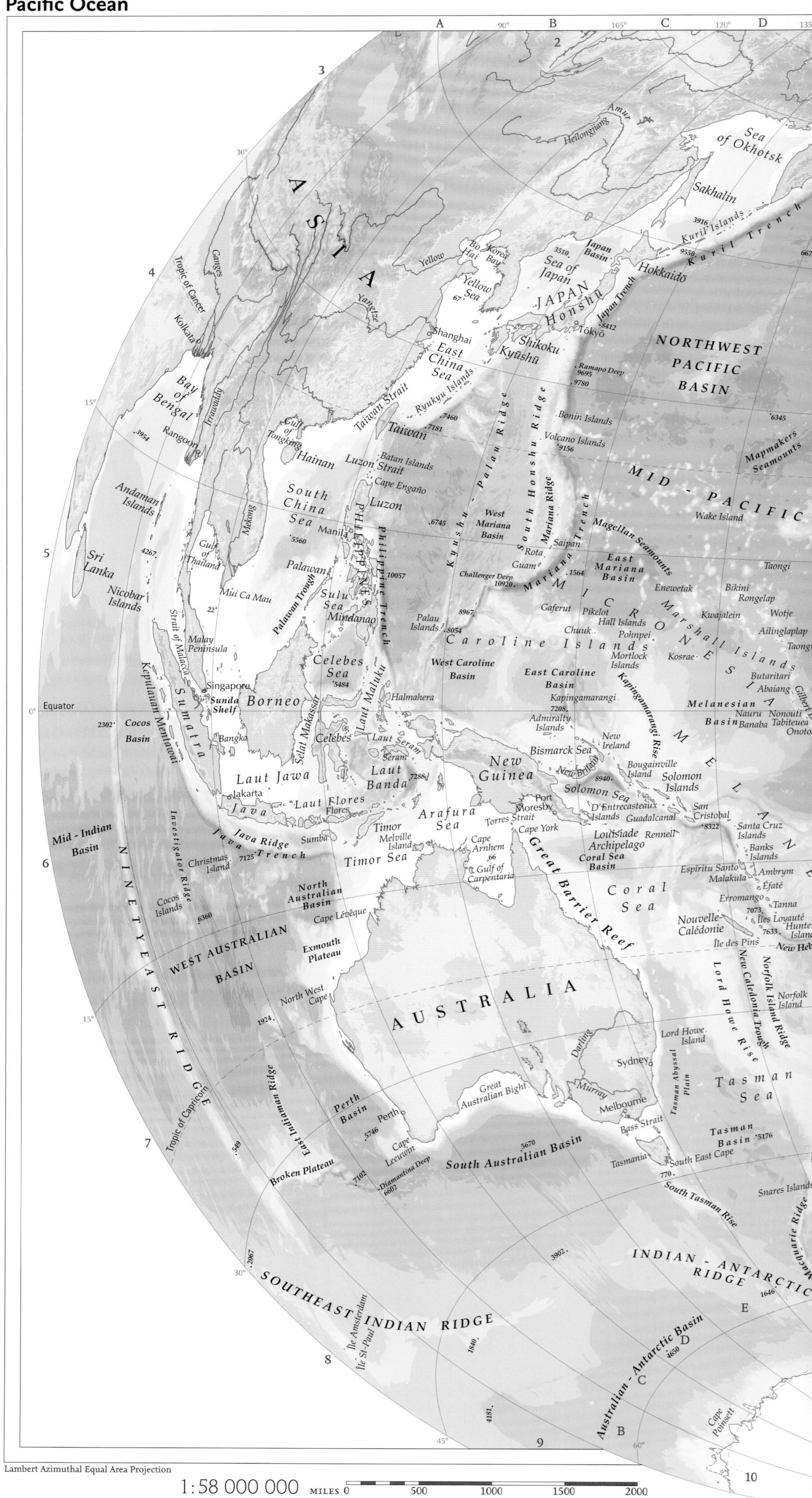

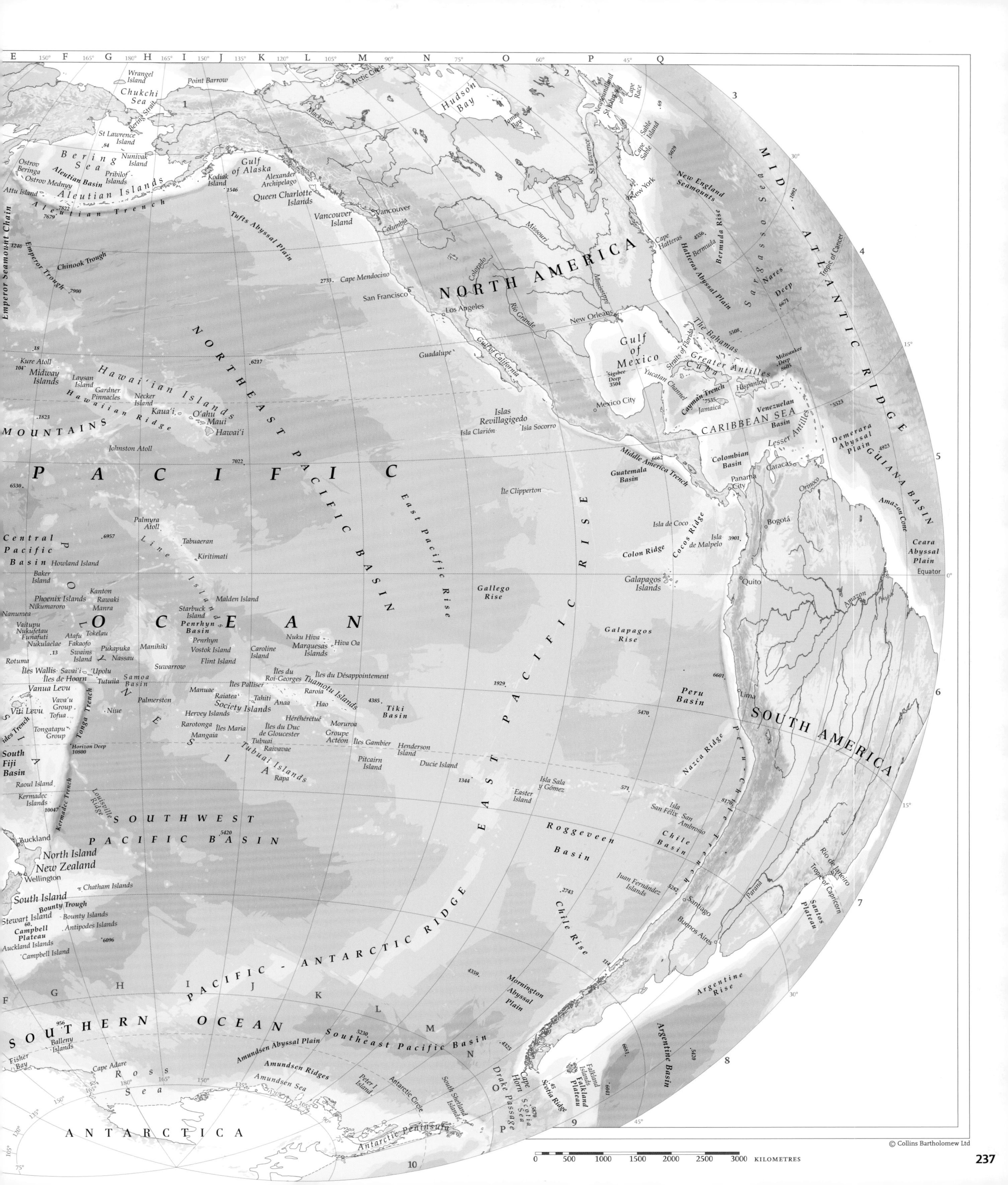

Wrangel Island
Chukchi Sea
Point Barrow
Bering Strait
St Lawrence Island
Bering Sea
Nunivak Island
Pribilof Islands
Ostrov Beringa
Ostrov Mednyy
Aleutian Basin
Aleutian Islands
Attu Island
Aleutian Trench
Kodiak Island
Gulf of Alaska
Alexander Archipelago
Queen Charlotte Islands
Vancouver Island
Vancouver
Columbia
Tufts Abyssal Plain
Arctic Circle
Mackenzie
Hudson Bay
James Bay
Newfoundland
St John's
Cape Race
Sable Island
Cape Sable
St Lawrence
New York
New England Seamounts
Cape Hatteras
Bermuda
Bermuda Rise
Hatteras Abyssal Plain
Sargasso Sea
Nares Deep
Tropic of Cancer
MID - ATLANTIC RIDGE
Missouri
NORTH AMERICA
Colorado
Mississippi
Rio Grande
New Orleans
Emperor Seamount Chain
Emperor Trough
Chinook Trough
Cape Mendocino
San Francisco
Los Angeles
Gulf of California
Guadalupe
Gulf of Mexico
Sigsbee Deep 3504
Straits of Florida
The Bahamas
Greater Antilles
Cuba
Yucatan Channel
Cayman Trench
Jamaica
Hispaniola
Milwaukee Deep 8605
Kure Atoll
Midway Islands
Laysan Island
Gardner Pinnacles
Hawai'ian Islands
Hawaiian Ridge
Necker Island
Kaua'i
O'ahu
Maui
Hawai'i
NORTHEAST PACIFIC BASIN
Mexico City
Islas Revillagigedo
Isla Clarión
Isla Socorro
CARIBBEAN SEA
Venezuelan Basin
Lesser Antilles
Demerara Abyssal Plain
MOUNTAINS
Johnston Atoll
Middle America Trench
Guatemala Basin
Colombian Basin
Caracas
Panama City
GUIANA BASIN
PACIFIC OCEAN
Île Clipperton
Orinoco
Amazon Cone
East Pacific Rise
Palmyra Atoll
Line Islands
Central Pacific Basin
Howland Island
Baker Island
Tabuaeran
Kiritimati
Isla de Coco
Cocos Ridge
Isla de Malpelo
Bogotá
Ceara Abyssal Plain
Colon Ridge
Equator
Galapagos Islands
Quito
Gallego Rise
Amazon
Phoenix Islands
Kanton
Rawaki
Nikumaroro
Manra
Nanumea
Malden Island
Starbuck Island
Penrhyn Basin
Vaitupu
Nukufetau
Funafuti
Nukulaelae
Atafu
Tokelau
Fakaofo
Swains Island
Pukapuka
Nassau
Manihiki
Penrhyn
Vostok Island
Flint Island
Caroline Island
Nuku Hiva
Marquesas Islands
Hiva Oa
Galapagos Rise
POLYNESIA
Rotuma
Îles Wallis
Savai'i
'Upolu
Îles de Hoorn
Tutuila
Samoa Basin
Suwarrow
Îles du Roi-Georges
Îles du Désappointement
Tuamotu Islands
Îles Palliser
Raroia
Vanua Levu
Viti Levu
Vava'u Group
Tofua
Tonga Trench
Niue
Palmerston
Manuae
Raiatea
Tahiti
Anaa
Hao
Society Islands
Hervey Islands
Rarotonga
Mangaia
Îles Maria
Hérěhérětué
Îles du Duc de Gloucester
Tubuai
Raivavae
Moruroa
Groupe Actéon
Tiki Basin
Îles Gambier
Henderson Island
Ducie Island
Pitcairn Island
Peru Basin
Lima
SOUTH AMERICA
Tongatapu Group
Horizon Deep 10800
South Fiji Basin
Tubuai Islands
Rapa
Raoul Island
Kermadec Islands
Kermadec Trench
Louisville Ridge
SOUTHWEST PACIFIC BASIN
Easter Island
Isla Sala y Gómez
Nazca Ridge
Peru-Chile Trench
Isla San Félix
San Ambrosio
Chile Basin
Roggeveen Basin
Auckland
North Island
New Zealand
Wellington
Chatham Islands
South Island
Bounty Trough
Bounty Islands
Antipodes Islands
Stewart Island
Campbell Plateau
Auckland Islands
Campbell Island
Juan Fernández Islands
Santiago
Buenos Aires
Paraná
Rio de Janeiro
Tropic of Capricorn
Santos Plateau
Chile Rise
PACIFIC - ANTARCTIC RIDGE
Argentine Rise
Mornington Abyssal Plain
SOUTHERN OCEAN
Balleny Islands
Southeast Pacific Basin
Amundsen Abyssal Plain
Amundsen Ridges
Amundsen Sea
Peter I Island
Antarctic Circle
South Shetland Islands
Drake Passage
Cape Horn
Scotia Sea
Scotia Ridge
Falkland Islands
Falkland Plateau
Argentine Basin
Fisher Bay
Cape Adare
Ross Sea
ANTARCTICA
Antarctic Peninsula
0 500 1000 1500 2000 2500 3000 KILOMETRES

States and Territories (continued)

AFRICA (continued)

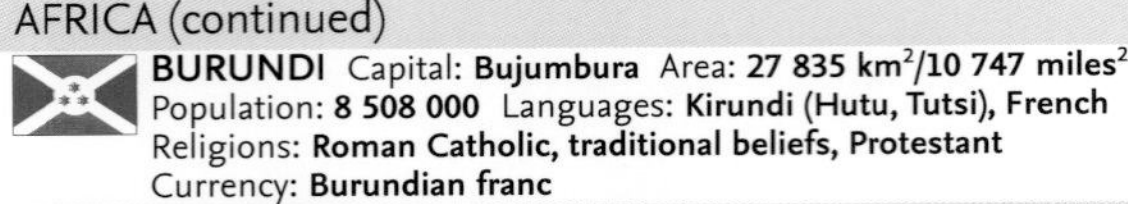

BURUNDI Capital: Bujumbura Area: 27 835 km²/10 747 miles²
Population: 8 508 000 Languages: Kirundi (Hutu, Tutsi), French
Religions: Roman Catholic, traditional beliefs, Protestant
Currency: Burundian franc

CAMEROON Capital: Yaoundé Area: 475 442 km²/183 569 miles²
Population: 18 549 000 Languages: French, English, Fang, Bamileke,
local languages Religions: Roman Catholic, traditional beliefs, Sunni
Muslim, Protestant Currency: CFA franc

CAPE VERDE Capital: Praia Area: 4 033 km²/1 557 miles²
Population: 530 000 Languages: Portuguese, Creole Religions: Roman
Catholic, Protestant Currency: Cape Verde escudo

CENTRAL AFRICAN REPUBLIC Capital: Bangui
Area: 622 436 km²/240 324 miles² Population: 4 343 000 Languages:
French, Sango, Banda, Baya, local languages Religions: Protestant,
Roman Catholic, traditional beliefs, Sunni Muslim Currency: CFA franc

CHAD Capital: Ndjamena Area: 1 284 000 km²/495 755 miles²
Population: 10 781 000 Languages: Arabic, French, Sara, local languages
Religions: Sunni Muslim, Roman Catholic, Protestant, traditional beliefs
Currency CFA franc

COMOROS Capital: Moroni Area: 1 862 km²/719 miles²
Population: 839 000 Languages: Comorian, French, Arabic
Religions: Sunni Muslim, Roman Catholic Currency: Comoros franc

CONGO Capital: Brazzaville Area: 342 000 km²/132 047 miles²
Population: 3 768 000 Languages: French, Kongo, Monokutuba, local
languages Religions: Roman Catholic, Protestant, traditional beliefs,
Sunni Muslim Currency: CFA franc

CONGO, DEMOCRATIC REPUBLIC OF THE Capital: Kinshasa
Area: 2 345 410 km²/905 568 miles² Population 62 636 000
Languages: French, Lingala, Swahili, Kongo, local languages
Religions: Christian, Sunni Muslim Currency: Congolese franc

CÔTE D'IVOIRE Capital :Yamoussoukro Area: 322 463 km²/
124 504 miles² Population: 19 262 000 Languages: French, Creole, Akan,
local languages Religions: Sunni Muslim, Roman Catholic, traditional
beliefs, Protestant Currency: CFA franc

DJIBOUTI Capital: Djibouti Area: 23 200 km²/8 958 miles²
Population 833 000 Languages: Somali, Afar, French, Arabic
Religions: Sunni Muslim, Christian Currency: Djibouti franc

EQUATORIAL GUINEA Capital: Malabo Area: 28 051 km²/
10 831 miles² Population: 507 000 Languages: Spanish, French, Fang
Religions: Roman Catholic, traditional beliefs Currency: CFA franc

ERITREA Capital: Asmara Area: 117 400 km²/45 328 miles²
Population: 4 851 000 Languages: Tigrinya, Tigre Religions: Sunni
Muslim, Coptic Christian Currency: Nakfa

ETHIOPIA Capital: Addis Ababa (Ādīs Ābeba) Area: 1 133 880 km²/
437 794 miles² Population: 83 099 000 Languages: Oromo, Amharic,
Tigrinya, local languages Religions: Ethiopian Orthodox, Sunni Muslim,
traditional beliefs Currency: Birr

GABON Capital: Libreville Area: 267 667 km²/103 347 miles²
Population: 1 331 000 Languages: French, Fang, local languages
Religions: Roman Catholic, Protestant, traditional beliefs
Currency: CFA franc

THE GAMBIA Capital: Banjul Area: 11 295 km²/4 361 miles²
Population: 1 709 000 Languages: English, Malinke, Fulani, Wolof
Religions: Sunni Muslim, Protestant Currency: Dalasi

GHANA Capital: Accra Area: 238 537 km²/92 100 miles²
Population: 23 478 000 Languages: English, Hausa, Akan, local languages
Religions: Christian, Sunni Muslim, traditional beliefs Currency: Cedi

GUINEA Capital: Conakry Area: 245 857 km²/94 926 miles² Population:
9 370 000 Languages: French, Fulani, Malinke, local languages
Religions: Sunni Muslim, traditional beliefs, Christian Currency: Guinea
franc

GUINEA-BISSAU Capital: Bissau Area: 36 125 km²/13 948 miles²
Population: 1 695 000 Languages: Portuguese, Crioulo, local languages
Religions: Traditional beliefs, Sunni Muslim, Christian
Currency: CFA franc

LESOTHO Capital: Maseru Area: 30 355 km²/11 720 miles²
Population: 2 008 000 Languages: Sesotho, English, Zulu
Religions: Christian, traditional beliefs Currency: Loti,
South African rand

LIBERIA Capital: Monrovia Area: 111 369 km²/43 000 miles²
Population: 3 750 000 Languages: English, Creole, local languages
Religions: Traditional beliefs, Christian, Sunni Muslim
Currency: Liberian dollar

LIBYA Capital: Tripoli (Ṭarābulus) Area: 1 759 540 km²/679 362 miles²
Population: 6 160 000 Languages: Arabic, Berber Religions: Sunni
Muslim Currency: Libyan dinar

MALAWI Capital: Lilongwe Area: 118 484 km²/45 747 miles²
Population: 13 925 000 Languages: Chichewa, English, local languages
Religions: Christian, traditional beliefs, Sunni Muslim
Currency: Malawian kwacha

MALI Capital: Bamako Area: 1 240 140 km²/478 821 miles² Population:
12 337 000 Languages: French, Bambara, local languages Religions:
Sunni Muslim, traditional beliefs, Christian
Currency: CFA franc

MAURITANIA Capital: Nouakchott Area: 1 030 700 km²/
397 955 miles² Population: 3 124 000 Languages: Arabic, French, local
languages Religions: Sunni Muslim Currency: Ouguiya

MAURITIUS Capital: Port Louis Area: 2 040 km²/788 miles²
Population: 1 262 000 Languages: English, Creole, Hindi, Bhojpurī,
French Religions: Hindu, Roman Catholic, Sunni Muslim
Currency: Mauritius rupee

MOZAMBIQUE Capital: Maputo Area: 799 380 km²/308 642 miles²
Population: 21 397 000 Languages: Portuguese, Makua, Tsonga, local
languages Religions: Traditional beliefs, Roman Catholic, Sunni Muslim
Currency: Metical

NAMIBIA Capital: Windhoek Area: 824 292 km²/318 261 miles²
Population: 2 074 000 Languages: English, Afrikaans, German, Ovambo,
local languages Religions: Protestant, Roman Catholic
Currency: Namibian dollar

Indian Ocean

Lambert Azimuthal Equal Area Projection

1 : 58 000 000 MILES 0   500   1000   1500   0   500   1000   1500   2000   2500 KILOMETRES

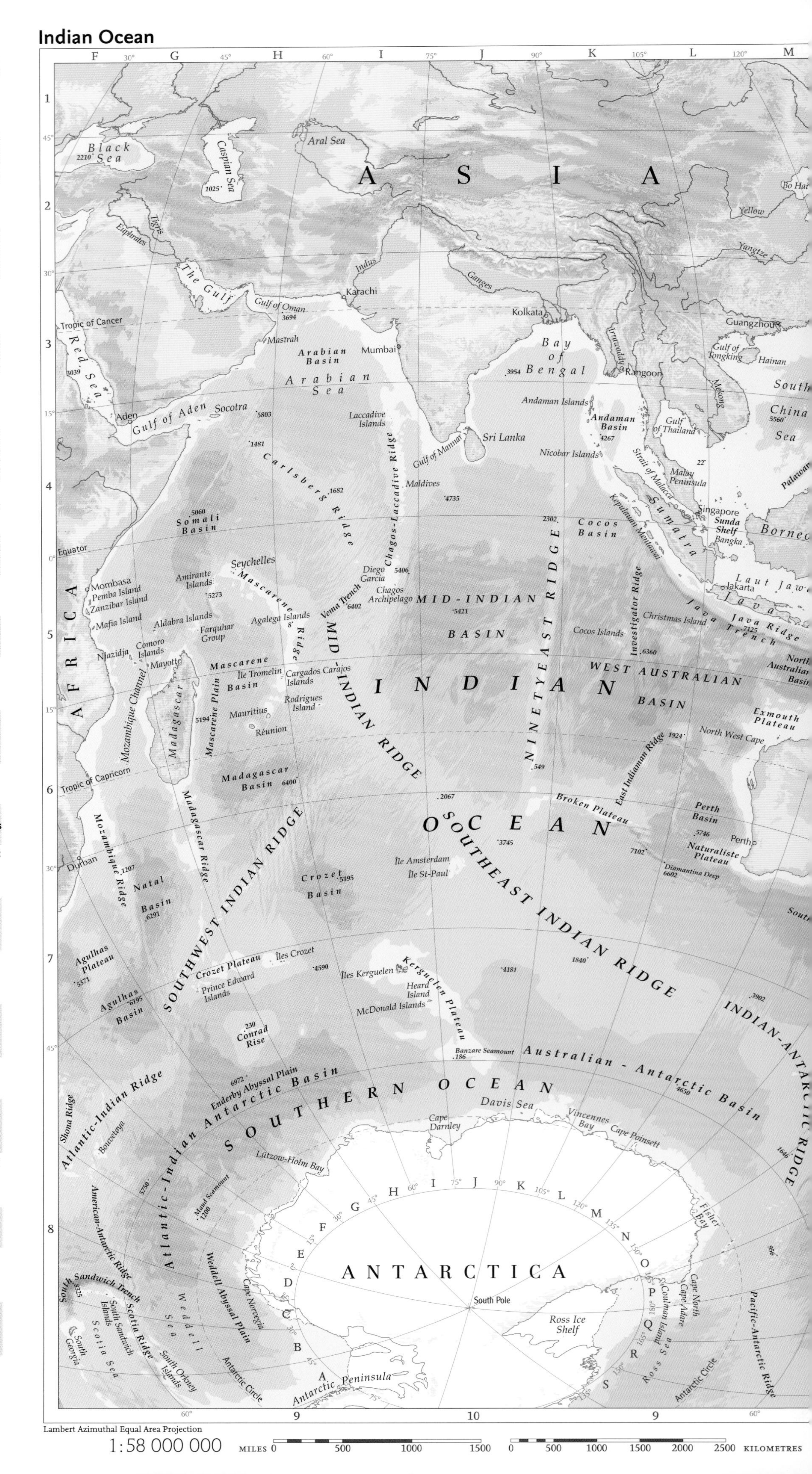

NORTH AMERICA
SOUTH AMERICA
EUROPE
AFRICA
AUSTRALIA

ATLANTIC OCEAN
MID-ATLANTIC RIDGE
MID-ATLANTIC RIDGE
ATLANTIC-INDIAN RIDGE
SOUTHERN OCEAN
CARIBBEAN SEA
MEDITERRANEAN SEA

Oceans, seas and basins

Japan Basin, Sea of Japan (East Sea), Korea Bay, Yellow Sea, East China Sea, Shanghai, Tokyo, Hokkaido, Honshu, Shikoku, Kyushu, Ryukyu Islands, Ryukyu Trench, Batan Islands, Luzon Strait, Cape Engaño, Luzon, Manila, Philippine Basin, Philippine Islands, Philippine Trench, Mindanao, Palau, Palawan, Sulu Sea, Celebes Sea, Halmahera, Celebes, Selat Makassar, Laut Seram, New Guinea, Laut Banda, Laut Flores, Sumba, Timor, Timor Sea, Arafura Sea, Cape Léveque, Gulf of Carpentaria, Great Australian Bight, Australian Basin, Darling, Murray, Sydney, Melbourne, Bass Strait, Tasmania, Tasman Sea, South East Cape, South Tasman Rise, Tasman Abyssal Plain, New Zealand, South Tasman Basin, Stewart Island, Macquarie Ridge, Macquarie Island, Auckland Islands, Campbell Plateau, Campbell Island, Antipodes Islands, Bounty Islands

Mackenzie, Baffin Bay, Lancaster Sd, Nares Strait, Greenland, Greenland Basin, Barents Sea, North Cape, Arctic Circle, Hudson Bay, Hudson Strait, Davis Strait, Jan Mayen, Icelandic Plateau, Norwegian Basin, Voring Plateau, Norwegian Sea, James Bay, Labrador Sea, Cape Farewell, Denmark Strait, Iceland, Faroe Islands, Faroe Rise, North Sea, Baltic Sea, British Isles, Rockall Bank, Celtic Shelf, London, English Chan, Rhine, Danube, St Lawrence, Newfoundland, St John's, Grand Banks of Newfoundland, Flemish Cap, Northwest Atlantic Mid-Ocean Channel, Reykjanes Ridge, Iceland Basin, Porcupine Abyssal Plain, Biscay Abyssal Plain, Adriatic Sea, New York, Cape Sable, Sable Island, Azores-Biscay Rise, Lisbon, Corsica, Sardinia, Balearic Is, MEDITERRANEAN SEA, Algiers, Str. of Gibraltar, Horseshoe Seamounts, Ampere Seamount, Cape Hatteras, Bermuda, Bermuda Rise, Corner Seamounts, New England Seamounts, Hatteras Abyssal Plain, Azores, Monaco Basin, Madeira, Great Meteor Tablemount, Canary Islands, New Orleans, Gulf of Mexico, Sigsbee Deep, Straits of Florida, Bahama Islands, Greater Antilles, Cuba, Sargasso Sea, Nares Deep, Nares Abyssal Plain, Cayman Trench, Jamaica, Hispaniola, Milwaukee Deep, Puerto Rico Trench, Venezuelan Basin, CARIBBEAN SEA, Colombian Basin, Lesser Antilles, Cape Verde Plateau, Krylov Seamount, Cape Verde, Cape Verde Basin, Dakar, Panama City, Caracas, Cocos Ridge, Panama, Orinoco, Demerara Abyssal Plain, GUIANA BASIN, Sierra Leone Rise, Sierra Leone Basin, Lagos, Niger, AFRICA, Isla de Malpelo, Quito, Amazon Cone, Ceara Abyssal Plain, São Pedro e São Paulo, Romanche Gap, Guinea Basin, Gulf of Guinea, Niger Cone, Príncipe, São Tomé, Equator, Annobón, Peru Basin, Lima, Amazon, SOUTH AMERICA, Recife, Fernando de Noronha, Pernambuco Plain, Ascension, Congo Cone, Luanda, Angola Basin, Stocks Seamount, Brazil Basin, St Helena, Abrolhos Bank, Vitória Seamount, Ilhas Martin Vaz, Ilha da Trindade, Nazca Ridge, Rio de Janeiro, Santos Plateau, Rio Grande Rise, Tristan da Cunha, Cape Basin, Tropic of Capricorn, Walvis Ridge, Namibia Abyssal Plain, Vema Seamount, Cape Town, Cape of Good Hope, Orange Cone, Isla San Félix, San Ambrosio, Chile Basin, Santiago, Buenos Aires, Gough Island, Discovery Seamounts, Agulhas Ridge, Agulhas Basin, Roggeveen Basin, Juan Fernández Islands, Peru-Chile Trench, Chile Rise, Argentine Rise, Argentine Basin, Chile Basin, Mornington Abyssal Plain, Argentine Abyssal Plain, Falkland Escarpment, Falkland Plateau, Falkland Islands, ATLANTIC-INDIAN RIDGE, Shona Ridge, Bouvetøya, Scotia Ridge, South Georgia, South Sandwich Islands, Yaghan Basin, Scotia Sea, South Orkney Islands, South Sandwich Trench, American-Antarctic Ridge, Cape Horn, Drake Passage, South Shetland Trough, South Shetland Islands, Enderby Abyssal Plain, Southeast Pacific Basin, Antarctic Peninsula, SOUTHERN OCEAN, Atlantic-Indian Antarctic Basin, Maud Seamount, Weddell Abyssal Plain, Weddell Sea, Antarctic Circle

Lambert Azimuthal Equal Area Projection
1:58 000 000   MILES 0   500   1000   1500
KILOMETRES 0   500   1000   1500   2000   2500

© Collins Bartholomew Ltd

239

AFRICA (continued)

NIGER Capital: Niamey Area: 1 267 000 km²/489 191 miles²
Population: 14 226 000 Languages: French, Hausa, Fulani, local languages Religions: Sunni Muslim, traditional beliefs
Currency: CFA franc

NIGERIA Capital: Abuja Area: 923 768 km²/356 669 miles²
Population: 148 093 000 Languages: English, Hausa, Yoruba, Ibo, Fulani, local languages Religions: Sunni Muslim, Christian, traditional beliefs
Currency: Naira

RWANDA Capital: Kigali Area: 26 338 km²/10 169 miles²
Population: 9 725 000 Languages: Kinyarwanda, French, English
Religions: Roman Catholic, traditional beliefs, Protestant
Currency: Rwandan franc

SÃO TOMÉ AND PRÍNCIPE Capital: São Tomé Area: 964 km²/
372 miles² Population: 158 000 Languages: Portuguese, Creole
Religions: Roman Catholic, Protestant Currency: Dobra

SENEGAL Capital: Dakar Area: 196 720 km²/75 954 miles²
Population: 12 379 000 Languages: French, Wolof, Fulani, local languages Religions Sunni Muslim, Roman Catholic, traditional beliefs
Currency: CFA franc

SEYCHELLES Capital: Victoria Area: 455 km²/176 miles²
Population: 87 000 Languages: English, French, Creole
Religions: Roman Catholic, Protestant Currency: Seychelles rupee

SIERRA LEONE Capital: Freetown Area: 71 740 km²/27 699 miles²
Population: 5 866 000 Languages: English, Creole, Mende, Temne, local languages Religions: Sunni Muslim, traditional beliefs
Currency: Leone

SOMALIA Capital: Mogadishu (Muqdisho) Area: 637 657 km²/
246 201 miles² Population: 8 699 000 Languages: Somali, Arabic
Religions: Sunni Muslim Currency: Somali shilling

SUDAN Capital: Khartoum Area: 2 505 813 km²/967 500 miles²
Population: 38 560 000 Languages: Arabic, Dinka, Nubian, Beja, Nuer, local languages Religions: Sunni Muslim, traditional beliefs, Christian
Currency: Sudanese pound (Sudani)

SWAZILAND Capital: Mbabane Area: 17 364 km²/6 704 miles²
Population: 1 141 000 Languages: Swazi, English Religions: Christian, traditional beliefs Currency: Emalangeni, South African rand

TANZANIA Capital: Dodoma Area: 945 087 km²/364 900 miles²
Population: 40 454 000 Languages: Swahili, English, Nyamwezi, local languages Religions: Shi'a Muslim, Sunni Muslim, traditional beliefs, Christian Currency: Tanzanian shilling

TOGO Capital: Lomé Area: 56 785 km²/21 925 miles²
Population: 6 585 000 Languages: French, Ewe, Kabre, local languages
Religions: Traditional beliefs, Christian, Sunni Muslim
Currency: CFA franc

UGANDA Capital: Kampala Area: 241 038 km²/93 065 miles²
Population: 30 884 000 Languages: English, Swahili, Luganda, local languages Religions: Roman Catholic, Protestant, Sunni Muslim, traditional beliefs Currency: Ugandan shilling

Western Sahara Capital: Laâyoune Area: 266 000 km²/102 703 miles²
Population: 480 000 Languages: Arabic Religions: Sunni Muslim
Currency: Moroccan dirham

ZAMBIA Capital: Lusaka Area: 752 614 km²/290 586 miles² Population:
11 922 000 Languages: English, Bemba, Nyanja, Tonga, local languages
Religions: Christian, traditional beliefs
Currency: Zambian kwacha

ZIMBABWE Capital: Harare Area: 390 759 km²/150 873 miles²
Population: 13 349 000 Languages: English, Shona, Ndebele
Religions: Christian, traditional beliefs Currency: Zimbabwean dollar

NORTH AMERICA

ANTIGUA AND BARBUDA Capital: St John's Area: 442 km²/
171 miles² Population: 85 000 Languages: English, Creole
Religions: Protestant, Roman Catholic Currency: East Caribbean dollar

BELIZE Capital: Belmopan Area: 22 965 km²/8 867 miles²
Population: 288 000 Languages: English, Spanish, Mayan, Creole
Religions: Roman Catholic, Protestant Currency: Belize dollar

DOMINICA Capital: Roseau Area: 750 km²/290 miles²
Population: 67 000 Languages: English, Creole Religions: Roman
Catholic, Protestant Currency: East Caribbean dollar

EL SALVADOR Capital: San Salvador Area: 21 041 km²/8 124 miles²
Population: 6 857 000 Languages: Spanish Religions: Roman Catholic, Protestant Currency: El Salvador colón, United States dollar

GRENADA Capital: St George's Area: 378 km²/146 miles²
Population: 106 000 Languages: English, Creole Religions: Roman
Catholic, Protestant Currency: East Caribbean dollar

GUATEMALA Capital: Guatemala City Area: 108 890 km²/
42 043 miles² Population: 13 354 000 Languages: Spanish, Mayan languages Religions: Roman Catholic, Protestant Currency: Quetzal, United States dollar

HAITI Capital: Port-au-Prince Area: 27 750 km²/10 714 miles²
Population: 9 598 000 Languages: French, Creole Religions: Roman
Catholic, Protestant, Voodoo Currency: Gourde

PANAMA Capital: Panama City Area: 77 082 km²/29 762 miles²
Population: 3 343 000 Languages: Spanish, English, Amerindian languages Religions: Roman Catholic, Protestant, Sunni Muslim
Currency: Balboa

ST KITTS AND NEVIS Capital: Basseterre Area: 261 km²/101 miles²
Population: 50 000 Languages: English, Creole Religions: Protestant, Roman Catholic Currency: East Caribbean dollar

ST LUCIA Capital: Castries Area: 616 km²/238 miles²
Population: 165 000 Languages: English, Creole Religions: Roman
Catholic, Protestant Currency: East Caribbean dollar

ST VINCENT AND THE GRENADINES Capital: Kingstown
Area: 389 km²/150 miles² Population: 120 000
Languages: English, Creole Religions: Protestant, Roman Catholic
Currency: East Caribbean dollar

TRINIDAD AND TOBAGO Capital: Port of Spain Area: 5 130 km²/
1 981 miles² Population: 1 333 000 Languages: English, Creole, Hindi
Religions: Roman Catholic, Hindu, Protestant, Sunni Muslim
Currency: Trinidad and Tobago dollar

Arctic Ocean

Polar Stereographic Projection

© Collins Bartholomew Ltd

1 : 38 500 000

MILES 0 200 400 600 800   0 400 800 1200 1600 KILOMETRES

INTRODUCTION TO THE INDEX

The index includes all names shown on the reference maps in the atlas, except for the UNESCO World Heritage sites which are listed on pages 56-90. Each entry includes the country or geographical area in which the feature is located, a page number and an alphanumeric reference. Additional entry details and aspects of the index are explained below.

REFERENCING

Names are referenced by page number and by grid reference. The grid reference relates to the alphanumeric values which appear in the margin of each map. These reflect the graticule on the map – the letter relates to longitude divisions, the number to latitude divisions.

Names are generally referenced to the largest scale map page on which they appear. For large geographical features, including countries, the reference is to the largest scale map on which the feature appears in its entirety, or on which the majority of it appears.

Rivers are referenced to their lowest downstream point – either their mouth or their confluence with another river. The river name will generally be positioned as close to this point as possible.

Entries relating to names appearing on insets are indicated by a small box symbol: □ followed by a grid reference if the inset has its own alphanumeric values.

ALTERNATIVE NAMES

Alternative names appear as cross-references and refer the user to the index entry for the form of the name used on the map.

For rivers with multiple names – for example those which flow through several countries – all alternative name forms are included within the main index entries, with details of the countries in which each form applies.

ADMINISTRATIVE QUALIFIERS

Administrative divisions are included in an entry to differentiate duplicate names – entries of exactly the same name and feature type within the one country – where these division names are shown on the maps. In such cases, duplicate names are alphabetized in the order of the administrative division names. Additional qualifiers are included for names within selected geographical areas, to indicate more clearly their location.

DESCRIPTORS

Entries, other than those for towns and cities, include a descriptor indicating the type of geographical feature. Descriptors are not included where the type of feature is implicit in the name itself, unless there is a town or city of exactly the same name.

NAME FORMS AND ALPHABETICAL ORDER

Name forms are as they appear on the maps, with additional alternative forms included as cross-references. Names appear in full in the index, although they may appear in abbreviated form on the maps.

The German character ß is alphabetized as 'ss'. Names beginning with Mac or Mc are alphabetized exactly as they appear. The terms Saint, Sainte, etc, are abbreviated to St, Ste, etc, but alphabetized as if in the full form.

NUMERICAL ENTRIES

Entries beginning with numerals appear at the beginning of the index, in numerical order. Elsewhere, numerals are alphabetized before 'a'.

PERMUTED TERMS

Names beginning with generic, geographical terms are permuted – the descriptive term is placed after, and the index alphabetized by, the main part of the name. For example, Lake Superior is indexed as Superior, Lake; Mount Everest as Everest, Mount. This policy is applied to all languages. Permuting has not been applied to names of towns, cities or administrative divisions beginning with such geographical terms. These remain in their full form, for example, Lake Isabella, USA.

INDEX ABBREVIATIONS

admin. dist.	administrative district	IN	Indiana	Phil.	Philippines
admin. div.	administrative division	Indon.	Indonesia	plat.	plateau
admin. reg.	administrative region	is	islands	P.N.G.	Papua New Guinea
Afgh.	Afghanistan	Kazakh.	Kazakhstan	Port.	Portugal
AK	Alaska	KS	Kansas	prov.	province
AL	Alabama	KY	Kentucky	pt	point
Alg.	Algeria	Kyrg.	Kyrgyzstan	Qld	Queensland
Alta	Alberta	l.	lake	Que.	Québec
AR	Arkansas	LA	Louisiana	r.	river
Arg.	Argentina	lag.	lagoon	reg.	region
aut. comm.	autonomous community	Lith.	Lithuania	res.	reserve
aut. reg.	autonomous region	Lux.	Luxembourg	resr	reservoir
aut. rep.	autonomous republic	MA	Massachusetts	RI	Rhode Island
AZ	Arizona	Madag.	Madagascar	r. mouth	river mouth
Azer.	Azerbaijan	Man.	Manitoba	Rus. Fed.	Russian Federation
b.	bay	MD	Maryland	S.	South
Bangl.	Bangladesh	ME	Maine	S.A.	South Australia
B.C.	British Columbia	Mex.	Mexico	S. Africa	Republic of South Africa
Bol.	Bolivia	MI	Michigan	salt l.	salt lake
Bos.-Herz.	Bosnia-Herzegovina	MN	Minnesota	Sask.	Saskatchewan
Bulg.	Bulgaria	MO	Missouri	SC	South Carolina
c.	cape	Mont.	Montenegro	SD	South Dakota
CA	California	Moz.	Mozambique	sea chan.	sea channel
Cent. Afr. Rep.	Central African Republic	MS	Mississippi	Sing.	Singapore
CO	Colorado	MT	Montana	Switz.	Switzerland
Col.	Colombia	mt.	mountain	Tajik.	Tajikistan
CT	Connecticut	mts	mountains	Tanz.	Tanzania
Czech Rep.	Czech Republic	N.	North, Northern	Tas.	Tasmania
DC	District of Columbia	nat. park	national park	terr.	territory
DE	Delaware	N.B.	New Brunswick	Thai.	Thailand
Dem. Rep. Congo	Democratic Republic of the Congo	NC	North Carolina	TN	Tennessee
depr.	depression	ND	North Dakota	Trin. and Tob.	Trinidad and Tobago
des.	desert	NE	Nebraska	Turkm.	Turkmenistan
Dom. Rep.	Dominican Republic	Neth.	Netherlands	TX	Texas
Equat. Guinea	Equatorial Guinea	Neth. Antilles	Netherlands Antilles	U.A.E.	United Arab Emirates
esc.	escarpment	Nfld.	Newfoundland	U.K.	United Kingdom
est.	estuary	NH	New Hampshire	Ukr.	Ukraine
Eth.	Ethiopia	NJ	New Jersey	U.S.A.	United States of America
Fin.	Finland	NM	New Mexico	UT	Utah
FL	Florida	N.S.	Nova Scotia	Uzbek.	Uzbekistan
for.	forest	N.S.W.	New South Wales	VA	Virginia
Fr. Guiana	French Guiana	N.W.T.	Northwest Territories	Venez.	Venezuela
Fr. Polynesia	French Polynesia	N.Z.	New Zealand	Vic.	Victoria
g.	gulf	NV	Nevada	vol.	volcano
GA	Georgia	NY	New York	vol. crater	volcanic crater
Guat.	Guatemala	OH	Ohio	VT	Vermont
h.	hill	OK	Oklahoma	W.	Western
hd	headland	Ont.	Ontario	WA	Washington
HI	Hawaii	OR	Oregon	W.A.	Western Australia
Hond.	Honduras	PA	Pennsylvania	WI	Wisconsin
i.	island	Pak.	Pakistan	WV	West Virginia
IA	Iowa	Para.	Paraguay	WY	Wyoming
ID	Idaho	P.E.I.	Prince Edward Island	Y.T.	Yukon Territory
IL	Illinois	pen.	peninsula		

Al Ḩumrah

225 E4 Ajalpán Mex.
147 G1 Ajanta India
170 K2 Ajaureforsen Sweden
126 D5 Ajax, Mount N.Z.
144 I3 Aj Bogd Uul mt. Mongolia
193 E1 Ajdābiyā Libya
158 G4 Ajigasawa Japan
138 E5 'Ajlūn Jordan
142 D5 'Ajman U.A.E.
148 C4 Ajmer India
215 F5 Ajo U.S.A.
215 F5 Ajo, Mount U.S.A.
161 I4 Ajuy Phil.
158 H3 Akabira Japan
156 E1 Akademii, Zaliv b. Rus. Fed.
147 H2 Akalkot India
158 I3 Akan Kokuritsu-kōen nat. park Japan
138 D4 Akanthou Cyprus
126 D5 Akaroa N.Z.
126 D5 Akaroa Harbour N.Z.
149 H4 Akas reg. India
137 E4 Akāshat Iraq
141 H3 Akbakay Kazakh.
141 G3 Akbalyk Kazakh.
143 H3 Akbar Afgh.
149 E4 Akbarpur India
140 E3 Akbasty Kazakh.
141 H2 Akbaur Kazakh.
141 G2 Akbeit Kazakh.
183 S4 Akbou Alg.
141 I2 Akbulak Vostochnyy Kazakhstan Kazakh.
141 K2 Akbulak Vostochnyy Kazakhstan Kazakh.
140 C2 Akbulak Rus. Fed.
139 F2 Akçadağ Turkey
139 G3 Akçakale Turkey
138 C1 Akçakoca Turkey
138 D3 Akçali Dağ mt. Turkey
141 H3 Akchatau Kazakh.
138 C3 Akdağ mt. Turkey
138 C3 Ak Dağı mt. Turkey
139 H2 Ak Dağı mts Turkey
136 C3 Akdağlar mts Turkey
138 E2 Akdağmadeni Turkey
140 D4 Akdepe Turkm.
171 L4 Åkersberga Sweden
178 C2 Akersloot Neth.
140 E3 Akespe Kazakh.
194 C3 Aketi Dem. Rep. Congo
140 C4 Akgyr Erezi hills Turkm.
Akhali-Afoni Georgia see Akhali Ap'oni
137 F2 Akhali Ap'oni Georgia
139 I1 Akhalk'alak'i Georgia
187 G7 Akhalts'ikhe Georgia
149 G5 Akhaura Bangl.
193 E1 Akhḑar, Al Jabal al mts Libya
147 E5 Akhḑar, Jabal mts Oman
138 A2 Akhisar Turkey
139 F3 Akhtarīn Syria
187 H5 Akhtubinsk Rus. Fed.
137 G2 Akhty Rus. Fed.
140 D1 Akhunovo Rus. Fed.
139 I1 Akhuryan Armenia
159 C8 Aki Japan
206 D3 Akimiski Island Canada
138 E3 Akıncı Burun pt Turkey
139 G1 Akıncılar Turkey
156 D1 Akishma r. Rus. Fed.
159 G5 Akita Japan
192 A3 Akjoujt Mauritania
140 E2 Akkabak Kazakh.
170 L2 Akkajaure l. Sweden
Akkala Uzbek. see Oqqal'a
141 G3 Akkanse Kazakh.
140 D2 Akkermanovka Rus. Fed.
158 I3 Akkeshi Japan
140 B3 Akkistau Kazakh.
138 E5 'Akko Israel
141 G2 Akkol' Akmolinskaya Oblast' Kazakh.
141 H3 Akkol' Almatinskaya Oblast' Kazakh.
140 B3 Akkol' Atyrauskaya Oblast' Kazakh.
141 G4 Akkol' Zhambylskaya Oblast' Kazakh.
141 I2 Akku Kazakh.
141 F3 Akkum Kazakh.
139 F1 Akkuş Turkey
Akkyr, Gory hills Turkm. see Akgyr Erezi
148 D4 Aklera India
171 M4 Akmeņrags pt Latvia
148 D1 Akmeqit China
Akmola Kazakh. see Astana
141 G2 Akmolinskaya Oblast' admin. div. Kazakh.
141 I4 Ak-Moyun Kyrg.
159 D7 Akō Japan
193 F4 Akobo Sudan
148 D5 Akola India
141 I4 Akongkür China
194 D2 Akordat Eritrea
138 D3 Akören Turkey
148 D5 Akot India
207 G1 Akpatok Island Canada
141 I4 Akqi China
170 B2 Akranes Iceland
171 I4 Åkrehamn Norway
143 G3 Ak Robat Pass Afgh.
213 G3 Akron CO U.S.A.
220 C4 Akron OH U.S.A.
220 C4 Akron City Reservoir U.S.A.
148 D2 Aksai Chin terr. Asia
138 E2 Aksaray Turkey
144 H4 Aksay China
141 H4 Ak-Say r. Kyrg.
187 F6 Aksay Rus. Fed.
148 D2 Aksayqin Hu l. China
138 C2 Akşehir Turkey
138 C2 Akşehir Gölü l. Turkey
138 C3 Akseki Turkey
140 C1 Aksenovo Rus. Fed.
142 D4 Aks-e Rostam r. Iran
153 J1 Aksha Rus. Fed.
140 C2 Akshatau Kazakh.
140 E2 Akshiganak Kazakh.
140 C3 Akshimrau Kazakh.
141 I4 Akshiy Kazakh.
140 B4 Akshukur Kazakh.
141 J3 Aksu Xinjiang China
141 J4 Aksu Xinjiang China
141 I3 Aksu Almatinskaya Oblast' Kazakh.
141 I1 Aksu Pavlodarskaya Oblast' Kazakh.
141 G1 Aksu Severnyy Kazakhstan Kazakh.
141 G4 Aksu Yuzhnyy Kazakhstan Kazakh.
140 C2 Aksu Zapadnyy Kazakhstan Kazakh.
141 I3 Aksu r. Kazakh.
138 C3 Aksu r. Turkey
141 F2 Aksuat Kustanayskaya Oblast' Kazakh.
141 J3 Aksuat Vostochnyy Kazakhstan Kazakh.
141 H2 Aksu-Ayuly Kazakh.
141 J4 Aksu He r. China
194 D2 Āksum Eth.
141 F3 Aksumbe Kazakh.
141 J3 Aksüme China
141 H3 Aksuyek Kazakh.
149 F1 Aktag mt. China
141 F2 Aktas Kazakh.
139 J2 Aktas Dağı mt. Turkey
139 I1 Aktaş Gölü l. Georgia
Aktash Uzbek. see Oqtosh
141 G3 Aktau Karagandinskaya Oblast' Kazakh.
141 H2 Aktau Karagandinskaya Oblast' Kazakh.
140 B4 Aktau Mangistauskaya Oblast' Kazakh.
141 I5 Akto China
140 D2 Aktobe Kazakh.
141 H2 Aktogay Karagandinskaya Oblast' Kazakh.
141 H1 Aktogay Pavlodarskaya Oblast' Kazakh.
141 I3 Aktogay Vostochnyy Kazakhstan Kazakh.
177 N4 Aktsyabrski Belarus
141 F2 Aktuma Kazakh.
140 D3 Aktumsyk Kazakh.
140 D3 Aktumsyk, Mys pt Uzbek.
141 H4 Ak-Tüz Kyrg.
140 D2 Aktyubinskaya Oblast' admin. div. Kazakh.
159 B8 Akune Japan
192 C4 Akure Nigeria
170 C2 Akureyri Iceland
149 G1 Akxokesay China
Akyab Myanmar see Sittwe
141 H3 Akzhal Karagandinskaya Oblast' Kazakh.
141 J2 Akzhal Vostochnyy Kazakhstan Kazakh.
140 D2 Akzhar Aktyubinskaya Oblast' Kazakh.
141 F3 Akzhar Kzyl-Ordinskaya Oblast' Kazakh.
141 J3 Akzhar Vostochnyy Kazakhstan Kazakh.
141 G4 Akzhar Zhambylskaya Oblast' Kazakh.
141 F3 Akzhaykyn, Ozero salt l. Kazakh.
139 G3 Akziyaret Turkey
171 J3 Ål Norway
142 C5 Al 'Abā Saudi Arabia
219 C6 Alabama r. U.S.A.
219 C5 Alabama state U.S.A.
219 C5 Alabaster U.S.A.
161 I3 Alabat i. Phil.
139 J7 Al 'Abţīyah well Iraq
141 G4 Ala-Buka Kyrg.
192 E1 Al Abyār Libya
138 E1 Alaca Turkey
139 F2 Alacahan Turkey
138 E1 Alaçam Turkey
138 B2 Alaçam Dağları mts Turkey
225 G3 Alacrán, Arrecife rf Mex.
136 D3 Aladağ Turkey
139 I2 Ala Dag mt. Turkey
139 I2 Ala Dağlar mts Turkey
138 E3 Ala Dağları mts Turkey
141 J4 Ala'er China
187 H7 Alagir Rus. Fed.
231 K6 Alagoinhas Brazil
183 P2 Alagón Spain
161 J5 Alah r. Phil.
171 M3 Alahärmä Fin.
139 K7 Al Aḩmadī Kuwait
141 G5 Alai Range mts Asia
171 M3 Alajärvi Fin.
224 H6 Alajuela Costa Rica
139 K2 Alajujeh Iran
137 E5 Al Akhḑar Saudi Arabia
148 D3 Alaknanda r. India
141 J3 Alakol', Ozero salt l. Kazakh.
170 O2 Alakurtti Rus. Fed.
138 B6 Al 'Alamayn Egypt
231 F4 Alalaú r. Brazil
139 I3 Al 'Amādīyah Iraq
142 B5 Al 'Amār Saudi Arabia
139 K6 Al 'Amārah Iraq
136 B5 'Alam ar Rūm, Ra's pt Egypt
Alamdo China see Alando
'Alam el Rûm, Râs pt Egypt see 'Alam ar Rūm, Ra's
139 J7 Al Amghar waterhole Iraq
161 H2 Alaminos Phil.
138 B6 Al 'Āmirīyah Egypt
225 D2 Alamítos, Sierra de los mt. Mex.
215 E3 Alamo U.S.A.
215 F4 Alamo Dam U.S.A.
213 F5 Alamogordo U.S.A.
217 D6 Alamo Heights U.S.A.
213 E6 Alamos Sonora Mex.
224 B2 Alamos Sonora Mex.
213 F4 Alamosa U.S.A.
147 H3 Alampur India
170 K2 Alanäs Sweden
Åland is Fin. see Åland Islands
179 J1 Aland r. Germany
147 H2 Aland India
142 B2 Aland r. Iran
171 L3 Åland Islands Fin.
149 H3 Alando China
162 B5 Alang Besar i. Indon.
Alaniya aut. rep. Rus. Fed. see Severnaya Osetiya-Alaniya, Respublika
209 E3 Alanson U.S.A.
138 D3 Alanya Turkey
142 D4 'Alā' od Dīn Iran
138 C1 Alaplı Turkey
Alappuzha India see Alleppey
138 E7 Al 'Aqabah Jordan
142 C6 Al 'Āqūlah well Saudi Arabia
183 O3 Alarcón, Embalse de resr Spain
138 D6 Al 'Arīsh Egypt
146 C4 Al Arţāwīyah Saudi Arabia
163 I4 Alas Indon.
138 B2 Alaşehir Turkey
136 C6 Al Ashmūnayn Egypt
139 I6 Al 'Āshūrīyah well Iraq
202 D3 Alaska state U.S.A.
202 D4 Alaska, Gulf of U.S.A.
204 E3 Alaska Highway Canada/U.S.A.
202 B4 Alaska Peninsula U.S.A.
202 D3 Alaska Range mts U.S.A.
139 L2 Älät Azer.
Alat Uzbek. see Olot
139 I6 Al 'Athāmīn hills Iraq
137 F5 Al Atwā' well Saudi Arabia
187 H4 Alatyr' Rus. Fed.
187 H4 Alatyr' r. Rus. Fed.
230 C4 Alausí Ecuador
139 J1 Alaverdi Armenia
170 N2 Alavieska Fin.
171 M3 Alavus Fin.
124 D5 Alawoona Australia
139 K1 Alazani r. Azer./Georgia
139 J5 Al 'Azīzīyah Iraq
193 D1 Al 'Azīzīyah Libya
137 E5 Al Azraq al Janūbī Jordan
184 C2 Alba Italy
139 F3 Al Bāb Syria
183 P3 Albacete Spain
124 D5 Albacutya, Lake dry lake Australia
139 J6 Al Bādiyah al Janūbīyah des. Iraq
185 J1 Alba Iulia Romania
207 F3 Albanel, Lac Canada
185 I4 Albania country Europe
118 B5 Albany Australia
206 C3 Albany r. Canada
219 C6 Albany GA U.S.A.
209 E5 Albany IN U.S.A.
219 C4 Albany KY U.S.A.
221 G3 Albany NY U.S.A.
212 B2 Albany OR U.S.A.
125 H1 Albany Downs Australia
235 M2 Albardão do João Maria coastal area Brazil
136 B5 Al Bardī Libya
142 B5 Al Barrah Saudi Arabia
Al Başrah Iraq see Basra
139 J6 Al Baţḩa' marsh Iraq
119 E3 Albatross Bay Australia
125 F8 Albatross Island Australia
193 E2 Al Bawītī Egypt
Al Bawiti Egypt see Al Bawītī
193 E1 Al Bayḑā' Libya
230 □ Albemarle, Punta pt Galapagos Is Ecuador
219 E5 Albemarle Sound sea chan. U.S.A.
184 C2 Albenga Italy
183 N3 Alberche r. Spain
123 A5 Alberga Australia
118 D4 Alberga watercourse Australia
183 L2 Albergaria-a-Velha Port.
125 G4 Albert Australia
182 F2 Albert France
124 C5 Albert, Lake Australia
194 D3 Albert, Lake Dem. Rep. Congo/Uganda
204 F4 Alberta prov. Canada
221 E6 Alberta U.S.A.
204 F4 Alberta, Mount Canada
196 D7 Albertinia S. Africa
178 D4 Albert Kanaal canal Belgium
216 E3 Albert Lea U.S.A.
194 D3 Albert Nile r. Sudan/Uganda
232 B8 Alberto de Agostini, Parque Nacional nat. park Chile
197 H3 Alberton S. Africa
182 H4 Albertville France
179 E6 Albestroff France
183 F5 Albi France
231 H2 Albina Suriname
214 A2 Albion CA U.S.A.
221 I2 Albion ME U.S.A.
209 E4 Albion MI U.S.A.
220 D3 Albion NY U.S.A.
137 E5 Al Bi'r Saudi Arabia
183 O5 Alborán, Isla de i. Spain
Ålborg Denmark see Aalborg
Ålborg Bugt b. Denmark see Aalborg Bugt
Alborz, Reshteh-ye mts Iran see Elburz Mountains
204 F4 Albreda Canada
123 D4 Albro Australia
Al Budayyi Bahrain see Al Budayyi'
142 C5 Al Budayyi' Bahrain
183 L4 Albufeira Port.
213 F5 Albuquerque U.S.A.
224 I5 Albuquerque, Cayos de is Col.
147 E5 Al Buraymī Oman
183 M3 Alburquerque Spain
125 G6 Albury Australia
139 H4 Al Buşayrah Syria
139 G7 Al Busayţā' plain Saudi Arabia
139 K6 Al Buşayyah Iraq
142 B4 Al Bushūk well Saudi Arabia
183 L3 Alcácer do Sal Port.
183 O2 Alcalá de Henares Spain
183 O4 Alcalá la Real Spain
184 E6 Alcamo Sicily Italy
183 P2 Alcañiz Spain
183 M3 Alcántara Spain
183 O3 Alcaraz Spain
183 N4 Alcaudete Spain
183 O3 Alcázar de San Juan Spain
187 F5 Alchevs'k Ukr.
235 J2 Alcira Arg.
234 E2 Alcobaça Brazil
121 F4 Alcoota Australia
235 K2 Alcorta Arg.
Alcoy Spain see Alcoy-Alcoi
183 P3 Alcoy-Alcoi Spain
183 R3 Alcúdia Spain
195 E4 Aldabra Islands Seychelles
224 C1 Aldama Chihuahua Mex.
225 E3 Aldama Tamaulipas Mex.
133 N4 Aldan Rus. Fed.
133 O3 Aldan r. Rus. Fed.
178 D1 Aldeboarn Neth.
173 I5 Aldeburgh U.K.
182 D2 Alderney i. U.K.
214 B4 Alder Peak U.S.A.
173 G6 Aldershot U.K.
220 C6 Alderson U.S.A.
142 D6 Al Dhafrah reg. U.A.E.
172 D3 Aldingham U.K.
173 F5 Aldridge U.K.
208 B5 Aledo U.S.A.
192 A3 Aleg Mauritania
234 E3 Alegre Brazil
232 E3 Alegrete Brazil
235 K2 Alejandro Korn Arg.
232 □ Alejandro Selkirk, Isla i. Atlantic Ocean
186 E2 Alekhovshchina Rus. Fed.
156 E1 Aleksandra, Mys hd Rus. Fed.
140 B4 Aleksandra Bekovicha-Cherkasskoga, Zaliv b. Kazakh.
186 F3 Aleksandrov Rus. Fed.
187 I5 Aleksandrov Gay Rus. Fed.
140 C1 Aleksandrovka Orenburgskaya Oblast' Rus. Fed.
140 D1 Aleksandrovka Respublika Bashkortostan Rus. Fed.
137 F1 Aleksandrovskoye Rus. Fed.
187 H6 Aleksandrovskoye Rus. Fed.
133 P4 Aleksandrovsk-Sakhalinskiy Rus. Fed.
132 F1 Aleksandry, Zemlya i. Rus. Fed.
141 G1 Alekseyevka Kokshetauskaya Oblast' Kazakh.
141 H2 Alekseyevka Pavlodarskaya Oblast' Kazakh.
156 B1 Alekseyevka Rus. Fed.
187 F5 Alekseyevka Belgorodskaya Oblast' Rus. Fed.
187 G5 Alekseyevskaya Rus. Fed.
187 F4 Aleksin Rus. Fed.
185 I3 Aleksinac Serbia
195 B4 Alèmbé Gabon
138 E1 Alembeyli Turkey
234 D3 Além Paraíba Brazil
171 J3 Ålen Norway
182 E2 Alençon France
231 H4 Alenquer Brazil
214 □² 'Alenuihāhā Channel U.S.A.
139 F3 Aleppo Syria
203 M1 Alert Canada
230 D6 Alerta Peru
204 D4 Alert Bay Canada
182 G4 Alès France
177 K7 Aleşd Romania
184 C2 Alessandria Italy
171 I3 Ålesund Norway
236 G2 Aleutian Basin sea feature Bering Sea
200 C2 Aleutian Islands AK U.S.A.
202 C4 Aleutian Range mts U.S.A.
237 H2 Aleutian Trench sea feature N. Pacific Ocean
133 Q4 Alevina, Mys c. Rus. Fed.
221 J2 Alexander U.S.A.
122 B2 Alexander, Mount h. Australia
204 B3 Alexander Archipelago is U.S.A.
196 B4 Alexander Bay b. Namibia/S. Africa
196 B4 Alexander Bay S. Africa
219 C5 Alexander City U.S.A.
127 I3 Alexander Island Antarctica
125 F6 Alexandra Australia
126 B6 Alexandra N.Z.
232 □ Alexandra, Cape Atlantic Ocean
185 J4 Alexandreia Greece
221 F2 Alexandria Canada
193 E1 Alexandria Egypt
185 K3 Alexandria Romania
197 G6 Alexandria S. Africa
174 D5 Alexandria U.K.
209 E5 Alexandria IN U.S.A.
217 E6 Alexandria LA U.S.A.
216 E2 Alexandria MN U.S.A.
221 E5 Alexandria VA U.S.A.
221 F2 Alexandria Bay U.S.A.
124 C5 Alexandrina, Lake Australia
185 K4 Alexandroupoli Greece
207 I3 Alexis r. Canada
208 B5 Alexis U.S.A.
204 E4 Alexis Creek Canada
141 J1 Aley r. Rus. Fed.
141 J1 Aleysk Rus. Fed.
179 F4 Alf Germany
183 P1 Alfaro Spain
139 K7 Al Farwānīyah Kuwait
139 I4 Al Fatḩah Iraq
139 L7 Al Fāw Iraq
193 F2 Al Fayyūm Egypt
179 H3 Alfeld (Leine) Germany
234 D3 Alfenas Brazil
139 L7 Al Finţās Kuwait
177 J7 Alföld plain Hungary
173 H4 Alford U.K.
221 F2 Alfred Canada
221 H3 Alfred U.S.A.
121 D5 Alfred and Marie Range hills Australia
139 L7 Al Fuḩayḩīl Kuwait
Al Fujayrah U.A.E. see Fujairah
139 J6 Al Furāt r. Iraq/Syria alt. Fırat (Turkey), conv. Euphrates
140 D2 Alga Kazakh.
140 C2 Algabas Kazakh.
171 I4 Ålgård Norway
235 I3 Algarrobo del Aguilla Arg.
183 L4 Algarve reg. Port.
187 G4 Algasovo Rus. Fed.
183 N4 Algeciras Spain
183 P3 Algemesí Spain
Alger Alg. see Algiers
209 E3 Alger U.S.A.
192 B2 Algeria country Africa
179 H2 Algermissen Germany
139 J6 Al Ghammās Iraq
142 B5 Al Ghāţ Saudi Arabia
146 D6 Al Ghayḑah Yemen
184 C4 Alghero Sardinia Italy
193 F2 Al Ghurdaqah Egypt
146 C4 Al Ghwaybiyah Saudi Arabia
192 C1 Algiers Alg.
197 F6 Algoa Bay S. Africa
208 D3 Algoma U.S.A.
216 E3 Algona U.S.A.
209 F4 Algonac U.S.A.
209 H3 Algonquin Park Canada
209 H3 Algonquin Provincial Park Canada
183 O1 Algorta Spain
139 I7 Al Habakah well Saudi Arabia
139 I5 Al Ḩabbānīyah Iraq
142 B4 Al Ḩadaqah well Saudi Arabia
142 C5 Al Ḩadd Bahrain
142 A4 Al Hadhālīl plat. Saudi Arabia
139 I4 Al Ḩadīthah Iraq
137 F4 Al Ḩaḑr Iraq
137 F5 Al Ḩafār well Saudi Arabia
139 F4 Al Ḩaffah Syria
142 B5 Al Ḩā'ir Saudi Arabia
143 E6 Al Hajar Oman
143 E5 Al Ḩajar al Gharbī mts Oman
139 G6 Al Ḩamād plain Jordan/Saudi Arabia
183 P4 Alhama de Murcia Spain
138 B6 Al Ḩammām Egypt
139 I6 Al Hammām well Iraq
139 J7 Al Haniyah esc. Iraq
142 B6 Al Hariq Saudi Arabia
136 C5 Al Ḩarrah Egypt
139 G6 Al Ḩarrah reg. Saudi Arabia
139 H3 Al Ḩasakah Syria
139 J5 Al Hāshimīyah Iraq
137 E5 Al Hawjā' Saudi Arabia
139 K5 Al Ḩayy Iraq
136 C5 Al Ḩayz Egypt
139 F6 Al Ḩazīm Jordan
137 E5 Al Ḩazm Saudi Arabia
142 B6 Al Ḩillah Saudi Arabia
142 B6 Al Ḩilwah Saudi Arabia
142 C5 Al Ḩinnāh Saudi Arabia
136 D5 Al Ḩismā plain Saudi Arabia
192 B1 Al Hoceima Morocco
Al Ḩudaydah Yemen see Hodeidah
137 E5 Al Ḩufrah reg. Saudi Arabia
146 C4 Al Hufūf Saudi Arabia
137 E5 Al Hūj hills Saudi Arabia
142 D6 Al Ḩumrah reg. U.A.E.

Bismarck

163 B3 Berhala, Selat *sea chan.* Indon.
133 R4 Beringa, Ostrov *i.* Rus. Fed.
178 D3 Beringen Belgium
133 S3 Beringovskiy Rus. Fed.
133 S4 Bering Sea Pacific Ocean
202 B3 Bering Strait Rus. Fed./U.S.A.
171 J3 Berkåk Norway
179 E2 Berkel *r.* Neth.
214 A3 Berkeley U.S.A.
220 D5 Berkeley Springs U.S.A.
178 D2 Berkhout Neth.
127 J3 Berkner Island Antarctica
185 J3 Berkovitsa Bulg.
173 F6 Berkshire Downs *hills* U.K.
178 C3 Berlare Belgium
170 O1 Berlevåg Norway
179 L2 Berlin Germany (City Plan 97)
221 F5 Berlin *MD* U.S.A.
221 H2 Berlin *NH* U.S.A.
220 D5 Berlin *PA* U.S.A.
208 C4 Berlin *WI* U.S.A.
203 J2 Berlinguet Inlet Canada
220 C4 Berlin Lake U.S.A.
125 I6 Bermagui Australia
235 J4 Bermeja, Punta *pt* Arg.
225 D2 Bermejíllo Mex.
235 I1 Bermejo *r.* Arg.
232 D2 Bermejo *r.* Arg./Bol.
231 F8 Bermejo Bol.
223 M2 Bermuda *terr.* Atlantic Ocean
239 E4 Bermuda Rise *sea feature* N. Atlantic Ocean
176 C7 Bern Switz.
213 F5 Bernalillo U.S.A.
232 A7 Bernardo O'Higgins, Parque Nacional *nat. park* Chile
235 J3 Bernasconi Arg.
179 J3 Bernburg (Saale) Germany
179 G1 Berne Germany
209 E5 Berne U.S.A.
176 C7 Berner Alpen *mts* Switz.
174 A3 Berneray *i. Scotland* U.K.
174 A4 Berneray *i. Scotland* U.K.
203 J2 Bernier Bay Canada
118 B4 Bernier Island Australia
176 E7 Bernina Pass Switz.
179 F5 Bernkastel-Kues Germany
195 E6 Beroroha Madag.
176 G6 Beroun Czech Rep.
176 F5 Berounka *r.* Czech Rep.
124 D5 Berri Australia
180 D5 Berriane Alg.
123 E8 Berridale Australia
174 E2 Berriedale U.K.
125 F5 Berrigan Australia
125 I5 Berrima Australia
183 R4 Berrouaghia Alg.
125 I5 Berry Australia
182 E3 Berry *reg.* France
214 A2 Berryessa, Lake U.S.A.
219 E7 Berry Islands Bahamas
196 B3 Berseba Namibia
179 F2 Bersenbrück Germany
187 D5 Bershad' Ukr.
140 E1 Bersuat Rus. Fed.
163 B1 Bertam Malaysia
231 J5 Bertolinía Brazil
193 D4 Bertoua Cameroon
175 I4 Bertraghboy Bay Ireland
119 H2 Beru *atoll* Kiribati
Beruni Uzbek. *see* Beruniy
140 E4 Beruniy Uzbek.
231 F4 Beruri Brazil
125 F7 Berwick Australia
221 E4 Berwick U.S.A.
172 E2 Berwick-upon-Tweed U.K.
173 D5 Berwyn *hills* U.K.
187 E6 Beryslav Ukr.
195 E5 Besalampy Madag.
182 H3 Besançon France
140 C3 Besbay Kazakh.
141 G4 Beshariq Uzbek.
Besharyk Uzbek. *see* Beshariq
Beshir Turkm. *see* Beşir
141 F5 Beshkent Uzbek.
142 D4 Beshneh Iran
120 D1 Besikama Indon.
141 F5 Beşir Turkm.
139 H3 Beşiri Turkey
187 H7 Beslan Rus. Fed.
205 H3 Besnard Lake Canada
139 F3 Besni Turkey
141 H2 Besoba Kazakh.
175 L3 Bessbrook U.K.
219 C5 Bessemer *AL* U.S.A.
208 B2 Bessemer *MI* U.S.A.
140 C3 Besshoky, Gora *h.* Kazakh.
140 C2 Bestamak *Aktyubinskaya Oblast'* Kazakh.
141 I2 Bestamak *Vostochnyy Kazakhstan* Kazakh.
141 H1 Bestobe Kazakh.
195 E6 Betanty Madag.
183 L1 Betanzos Spain
193 D4 Bétaré Oya Cameroon
197 H3 Bethal S. Africa
196 B3 Bethanie Namibia
216 E3 Bethany *MO* U.S.A.
217 D5 Bethany *OK* U.S.A.
202 B3 Bethel *AK* U.S.A.
221 H2 Bethel *ME* U.S.A.
208 A6 Bethel *MO* U.S.A.
220 A5 Bethel *OH* U.S.A.
220 D4 Bethel Park U.S.A.
173 C4 Bethesda U.K.
221 E5 Bethesda *MD* U.S.A.
220 C4 Bethesda *OH* U.S.A.
197 F5 Bethesdaweg S. Africa
197 H4 Bethlehem S. Africa
221 F4 Bethlehem U.S.A.
138 E6 Bethlehem West Bank
197 F5 Bethulie S. Africa
178 A4 Béthune France
233 J2 Betijoque Venez.
195 E6 Betioky Madag.
162 B4 Betong Thai.
123 C5 Betoota Australia
141 G3 Betpak-Dala Kazakh.
141 G3 Betpak-Dala *plain* Kazakh.
195 E6 Betroka Madag.
138 E5 Bet She'an Israel
207 G4 Betsiamites Canada
207 G4 Betsiamites *r.* Canada
195 E5 Betsiboka *r.* Madag.
208 D3 Betsie, Point U.S.A.
209 E2 Betsy Lake U.S.A.
208 B5 Bettendorf U.S.A.
149 F4 Bettiah India
174 D2 Bettyhill U.K.
175 L4 Bettystown Ireland
148 D5 Betul India
163 H2 Betung Kerihun, Taman Nasional *nat. park* Indon./Malaysia
178 D3 Betuwe *reg.* Neth.
148 D4 Betwa *r.* India
173 D4 Betws-y-coed U.K.
179 F4 Betzdorf Germany
125 E5 Beulah Australia
208 D3 Beulah U.S.A.
173 H6 Beult *r.* U.K.
173 G4 Beverley U.K.
202 C4 Beverley, Lake U.S.A.
221 H3 Beverly *MA* U.S.A.
220 C5 Beverly *OH* U.S.A.
214 C4 Beverly Hills U.S.A.
205 I2 Beverly Lake Canada
179 G1 Beverstedt Germany
179 H3 Beverungen Germany
178 C2 Beverwijk Neth.
179 F5 Bexbach Germany
173 H7 Bexhill U.K.
149 E3 Beyānlū Iran
138 C3 Bey Dağları *mts* Turkey
138 B1 Beykoz Turkey
192 B4 Beyla Guinea
139 K2 Beyläqan Azer.
140 C3 Beyneu Kazakh.
138 C1 Beypazarı Turkey
139 F2 Beypınarı Turkey
147 G4 Beypore India
Beyrouth Lebanon *see* Beirut
138 C3 Beyşehir Turkey
138 C3 Beyşehir Gölü *l.* Turkey
187 F6 Beysug *r.* Rus. Fed.
156 B1 Beytonovo Rus. Fed.
139 I3 Beytüşşebap Turkey
143 E3 Bezameh Iran
186 I3 Bezbozhnik Rus. Fed.
186 D3 Bezhanitsy Rus. Fed.
186 F3 Bezhetsk Rus. Fed.
183 F5 Béziers France
148 B4 Bhabhar India
149 E4 Bhabhua India
148 B5 Bhadar *r.* India
Bhadgaon Nepal *see* Bhaktapur
149 E4 Bhadohi India
149 F4 Bhadra India
147 I2 Bhadrachalam India
149 F5 Bhadrak India
147 G3 Bhadra Reservoir India
147 G3 Bhadravati India
148 A3 Bhag Pak.
148 D2 Bhaga *r.* India
149 F4 Bhagalpur India
149 G5 Bhagirathi *r.* India
148 D5 Bhainsdehi India
149 G4 Bhairab Bazar Bangl.
149 E4 Bhairawa Nepal
149 F4 Bhaktapur Nepal
147 H2 Bhalki India
151 B4 Bhamo Myanmar
147 I2 Bhamragarh India
148 D4 Bhander India
149 F6 Bhanjanagar India
148 C4 Bhanpura India
148 D5 Bhanrer Range *hills* India
148 D4 Bharatpur India
149 H4 Bhareli *r.* India
143 F5 Bhari *r.* Pak.
148 C5 Bharuch India
147 I1 Bhatapara India
147 G3 Bhatkal India
149 G5 Bhatpara India
147 H4 Bhavani India
147 H4 Bhavani *r.* India
148 C5 Bhavnagar India
148 C3 Bhawana Pak.
147 I2 Bhawanipatna India
197 I3 Bhekuzulu S. Africa
149 E3 Bheri *r.* Nepal
149 E5 Bhilai India
148 C4 Bhilwara India
147 H2 Bhima *r.* India
147 I2 Bhimavaram India
148 D4 Bhind India
148 C4 Bhindar India
149 E4 Bhinga India
148 C4 Bhinmal India
197 G6 Bhisho S. Africa
148 D3 Bhiwani India
149 F4 Bhojpur Nepal
147 H2 Bhongir India
197 H5 Bhongweni S. Africa
148 D5 Bhopal India
147 I2 Bhopalpatnam India
147 G2 Bhor India
149 F5 Bhuban India
149 F5 Bhubaneshwar India
148 B5 Bhuj India
148 C5 Bhusawal India
149 G4 Bhutan *country* Asia
148 B4 Bhuttewala India
162 B1 Bia, Phou *mt.* Laos
143 E5 Biābān *mts* Iran
148 C2 Biafo Glacier Pak.
151 F7 Biak Indon.
151 F7 Biak *i.* Indon.
177 K4 Biała Podlaska Poland
176 G4 Białogard Poland
177 K4 Białystok Poland
192 B4 Biankouma Côte d'Ivoire
150 B1 Bianzhao China
148 D5 Biaora India
142 D2 Biārjmand Iran
183 D5 Biarritz France
142 B5 Bi'ār Tabrāk *well* Saudi Arabia
176 D7 Biasca Switz.
158 G3 Bibai Japan
195 B5 Bibala Angola
125 H6 Bibbenluke Australia
184 D3 Bibbiena Italy
176 D6 Biberach an der Riß Germany
149 G4 Bibiyana *r.* Bangl.
179 G5 Biblis Germany
138 C2 Biçer Turkey
173 F6 Bicester U.K.
125 H8 Bicheno Australia
156 D3 Bichevaya Rus. Fed.
156 E1 Bichi *r.* Rus. Fed.
187 G7 Bichvint'a Georgia
118 D3 Bickerton Island Australia
173 D7 Bickleigh U.K.
215 G2 Bicknell U.S.A.
195 B5 Bicuari, Parque Nacional do *nat. park* Angola
147 G2 Bid India
192 C4 Bida Nigeria
161 H5 Bidadari, Tanjung *pt Sabah* Malaysia
142 D4 Bida Khabit Iran
147 H2 Bidar India
143 E6 Bidbid Oman
221 H3 Biddeford U.S.A.
178 D2 Biddinghuizen Neth.
174 C4 Bidean nam Bian *mt.* U.K.
173 C6 Bideford U.K.
Bideford Bay *b.* U.K. *see* Barnstaple Bay
156 C3 Bidzhan Rus. Fed.
177 K4 Biebrza *r.* Poland
179 G4 Biedenkopf Germany
176 C7 Biel Switz.
177 H5 Bielawa Poland
179 G2 Bielefeld Germany
184 C2 Biella Italy
177 I6 Bielsko-Biała Poland
177 K4 Bielsk Podlaski Poland
179 I1 Bienenbüttel Germany
162 C3 Biên Hoa Vietnam
207 F2 Bienville, Lac *l.* Canada
123 D5 Bierbank Australia
197 F3 Biesiesvlei S. Africa
179 H6 Bietigheim-Bissingen Germany
178 D5 Bièvre Belgium
195 B4 Bifoun Gabon
207 I3 Big *r.* Canada
214 A2 Big *r.* U.S.A.
187 C7 Biga Turkey
138 B2 Bigadiç Turkey
185 L5 Biga Yarımadası *pen.* Turkey
208 D2 Big Bay U.S.A.
208 D3 Big Bay de Noc U.S.A.
215 D4 Big Bear Lake U.S.A.
212 E2 Big Belt Mountains U.S.A.
197 I3 Big Bend Swaziland
217 C6 Big Bend National Park U.S.A.
217 F5 Big Black *r.* U.S.A.
173 D7 Bigbury-on-Sea U.K.
219 D7 Big Cypress National Preserve U.S.A.
208 C3 Big Eau Pleine Reservoir U.S.A.
204 F4 Big Eddy Canada
144 I2 Biger Nuur *salt l.* Mongolia
205 K5 Big Falls U.S.A.
205 H4 Biggar Canada
174 E5 Biggar U.K.
120 D2 Bigge Island Australia
123 F5 Biggenden Australia
204 B3 Bigger, Mount Canada
173 G5 Biggleswade U.K.
212 D2 Big Hole *r.* U.S.A.
212 F2 Bighorn *r.* U.S.A.
212 E2 Bighorn Canyon National Recreation Area *park* U.S.A.
212 F2 Bighorn Mountains U.S.A.
203 K3 Big Island *Nunavut* Canada
204 F2 Big Island *N.W.T.* Canada
221 J2 Big Lake U.S.A.
192 A3 Bignona Senegal
220 D6 Big Otter *r.* U.S.A.
214 C3 Big Pine U.S.A.
209 E4 Big Rapids U.S.A.
208 C3 Big Rib *r.* U.S.A.
205 H4 Big River Canada
208 D3 Big Sable Point U.S.A.
204 C2 Big Salmon *r.* Canada
205 J3 Big Sand Lake Canada
215 F4 Big Sandy *watercourse* U.S.A.
216 D2 Big Sioux *r.* U.S.A.
215 D2 Big Smokey Valley U.S.A.
217 C5 Big Spring U.S.A.
216 C3 Big Springs U.S.A.
220 B6 Big Stone Gap U.S.A.
214 B3 Big Sur U.S.A.
212 E2 Big Timber U.S.A.
206 C3 Big Trout Lake Canada
206 C3 Big Trout Lake *l.* Canada
215 G3 Big Water U.S.A.
209 H3 Bigwin Canada
184 F2 Bihać Bos.-Herz.
149 F4 Bihar *state* India
149 F4 Bihar Sharif India
177 K7 Bihor, Vârful *mt.* Romania
158 I3 Bihoro Japan
140 C3 Biikzhal Kazakh.
192 A3 Bijagós, Arquipélago dos *is* Guinea-Bissau
148 C4 Bijainagar India
147 G2 Bijapur India
142 B3 Bījār Iran
147 I2 Bijarpur India
185 H2 Bijeljina Bos.-Herz.
185 H3 Bijelo Polje Montenegro
155 B5 Bijie China
149 G4 Bijni India
148 D3 Bijnor India
148 B3 Bijnot Pak.
142 C5 Bijrān, Khashm *h.* Saudi Arabia
148 C3 Bikaner India
140 E3 Bikbauli Kazakh.
150 F2 Bikin Rus. Fed.
158 D1 Bikin *r.* Rus. Fed.
236 G5 Bikini *atoll* Marshall Is
195 B4 Bikoro Dem. Rep. Congo
154 B3 Bikou China
148 C4 Bilara India
147 I1 Bilaspur India
139 L2 Biläsuvar Azer.
187 D5 Bila Tserkva Ukr.
162 A2 Bilauktaung Range *mts* Myanmar/Thai.
183 O1 Bilbao Spain
138 C6 Bilbays Egypt
185 H3 Bileća Bos.-Herz.
138 B1 Bilecik Turkey
177 K5 Biłgoraj Poland
195 D4 Bilharamulo Tanz.
187 D6 Bilhorod-Dnistrovs'kyy Ukr.
194 C3 Bili Dem. Rep. Congo
133 R3 Bilibino Rus. Fed.
161 J4 Biliran *i.* Phil.
160 B4 Biliu He *r.* China
213 F3 Bill U.S.A.
121 A5 Billabalong Australia
173 H6 Billericay U.K.
120 D3 Billiluna Australia
239 J2 Billingford U.K.
172 F3 Billingham U.K.
212 E2 Billings U.S.A.
173 E7 Bill of Portland *hd* U.K.
215 F4 Bill Williams *r.* U.S.A.
215 F4 Bill Williams Mountain U.S.A.
193 D3 Bilma Niger
193 D3 Bilma, Grand Erg de *des.* Niger
119 F4 Biloela Australia
187 E6 Bilohirs'k Ukr.
177 M5 Bilohir"ya Ukr.
147 H2 Biloli India
187 F5 Biloluts'k Ukr.
187 E5 Bilopillya Ukr.
187 F5 Bilovods'k Ukr.
219 B6 Biloxi U.S.A.
118 D4 Bilpa Morea Claypan *salt flat* Australia
174 E5 Bilston U.K.
193 E3 Biltine Chad
162 A1 Bilugyun Island Myanmar
224 I5 Bilwascarma Nicaragua
187 I4 Bilyarsk Rus. Fed.
187 D6 Bilyayivka Ukr.
178 D4 Bilzen Belgium
125 H5 Bimberi, Mount Australia
194 B3 Bimbo C.A.R.
219 E7 Bimini Islands Bahamas
139 L3 Bināb Iran
148 D4 Bina-Etawa India
151 E7 Binaija, Gunung *mt.* Indon.
139 F2 Binboğa Daği *mt.* Turkey
125 G1 Bindebango Australia
149 E4 Bindki India
125 H1 Bindle Australia
195 B4 Bindu Dem. Rep. Congo
195 D5 Bindura Zimbabwe
183 Q2 Binefar Spain
125 I2 Bingara *N.S.W.* Australia
125 F2 Bingara *Qld* Australia
122 B2 Bing Bong Australia
154 B2 Bingcaowan China
179 F5 Bingen am Rhein Germany
192 B4 Bingerville Côte d'Ivoire
221 I2 Bingham U.S.A.
221 F3 Binghamton U.S.A.
139 H2 Bingöl Turkey
139 H2 Bingol Dağı *mt.* Turkey
155 C6 Binh Gia Vietnam
Binh Sơn Vietnam *see* Châu Ô
149 H4 Bini India
147 I1 Binika India
162 A5 Binjai Indon.
142 D5 Bin Mürkhan *well* U.A.E.
125 H3 Binnaway Australia
162 C5 Bintan *i.* Indon.
161 I3 Bintuan Phil.
163 B3 Bintuhan Indon.
163 H2 Bintulu *Sarawak* Malaysia
156 B3 Binxian China
154 C3 Binxian China
125 G5 Binya Australia
155 C6 Binyang China
154 F2 Binzhou China
235 H3 Bíobío *admin. reg.* Chile
235 H3 Bíobío *r.* Chile
192 C4 Bioco *i.* Equat. Guinea
184 F3 Biograd na Moru Croatia
185 G3 Biokovo *mts* Croatia
156 D2 Bira Rus. Fed.
143 F5 Bīrag, Kūh-e *mts* Iran
193 D2 Birāk Libya
156 C2 Birakan Rus. Fed.
136 B5 Bi'r al Khamsah *well* Egypt
139 H5 Bi'r al Mulūsi Iraq
136 B5 Bi'r al Qaṭrānī *well* Egypt
186 F2 Birandozero Rus. Fed.
Bi'r an Nuṣf *well* Egypt *see* Bi'r an Nuṣṣ
136 B5 Bi'r an Nuṣṣ *well* Egypt
194 C2 Birao Centr. Afr. Rep.
136 B5 Bi'r ar Rābiyah *well* Egypt
138 D6 Bi'r ar Rummānah Egypt
140 E4 Birata Turkm.
149 F4 Biratnagar Nepal
136 B5 Bi'r Baylī *well* Egypt
139 G3 Bi'r Buṭaymān Syria
205 G3 Birch *r.* Canada
205 H4 Birch Hills Canada
125 E5 Birchip Australia
204 F4 Birch Island Canada
205 K4 Birch Lake Canada
208 B2 Birch Lake U.S.A.
205 G3 Birch Mountains Canada
205 I4 Birch River Canada
Birdaard Neth. *see* Burdaard
Bîr Dignâsh *well* Egypt *see* Bi'r Diqnāsh
136 B5 Bi'r Diqnāsh *well* Egypt
127 J1 Bird Island S. Georgia
215 G2 Birdseye U.S.A.
118 D4 Birdsville Australia
139 F3 Birecik Turkey
Bîr el Isṭabl *well* Egypt *see* Bi'r Isṭabl
Bîr el Khamsa *well* Egypt *see* Bi'r al Khamsah
Bîr el Nuṣṣ *well* Egypt *see* Bi'r an Nuṣṣ
Bîr el Qaṭrâni *well* Egypt *see* Bi'r al Qaṭrānī
Bîr el Râbia *well* Egypt *see* Bi'r ar Rābiyah
193 E3 Bir en Natrûn *well* Sudan
163 E1 Bireun Indon.
137 E5 Bi'r Fajr *well* Saudi Arabia
136 B5 Bi'r Fu'ād *well* Egypt
142 B6 Bi'r Ghawdah *well* Saudi Arabia
194 D2 Birhan *mt.* Eth.
Bi'r Ibn Hirmās Saudi Arabia *see* Al Bi'r
234 B3 Birigüi Brazil
136 B5 Bi'r Isṭabl *well* Egypt
143 E3 Bīrjand Iran
136 B5 Bi'r Jubnī *well* Libya
139 J6 Birkát Hamad *well* Iraq
179 F5 Birkenfeld Germany
173 D4 Birkenhead U.K.
139 J3 Bīrkim Iraq
184 F7 Birkirkara Malta
121 E5 Birksgate Range *hills* Australia
141 H3 Birlik Kazakh.
141 H4 Birlik Kazakh.
173 F5 Birmingham U.K.
219 C5 Birmingham U.S.A.
192 A2 Bîr Mogreïn Mauritania
138 B6 Bi'r Nāḥid *oasis* Egypt
192 C3 Birnin-Kebbi Nigeria
192 C3 Birnin Konni Niger
150 F2 Birobidzhan Rus. Fed.
136 B5 Bi'r Qaṣīr as Sirr *well* Egypt
175 K4 Birr Ireland
125 G2 Birrie *r.* Australia
120 E3 Birrindudu Australia
139 I5 Bi'r Sābil Iraq
174 E1 Birsay U.K.
173 F5 Birstall U.K.
179 H4 Birstein Germany
138 E7 Bi'r Ṭābah Egypt
122 C2 Birthday Mountain *h.* Australia
205 I4 Birtle Canada
149 H3 Biru China
147 G3 Birur India
171 N4 Biržai Lith.
145 E6 Bisalpur India
215 H6 Bisbee U.S.A.
182 B4 Biscay, Bay of *sea* France/Spain
239 I3 Biscay Abyssal Plain *sea feature* N. Atlantic Ocean
219 D7 Biscayne National Park U.S.A.
176 F7 Bischofshofen Austria
127 I2 Biscoe Islands Antarctica
209 F2 Biscotasi Lake Canada
209 F2 Biscotasing Canada
155 C4 Bishan China
139 L5 Bīsheh Iran
141 H4 Bishkek Kyrg.
149 F5 Bishnupur India
214 C3 Bishop U.S.A.
172 F3 Bishop Auckland U.K.
173 H6 Bishop's Stortford U.K.
139 G4 Bishrī, Jabal *hills* Syria
150 E1 Bishui China
192 C1 Biskra Alg.
161 J4 Bislig Phil.
216 C2 Bismarck U.S.A.

Bismarck Archipelago

119 E2 **Bismarck Archipelago** *is* P.N.G.
119 E2 **Bismarck Range** *mts* P.N.G.
119 E2 **Bismarck Sea** P.N.G.
179 J2 **Bismark (Altmark)** Germany
139 H3 **Bismil** Turkey
171 J3 **Bismo** Norway
139 K4 **Bīsotūn** Iran
171 L3 **Bispgården** Sweden
179 I1 **Bispingen** Germany
183 Q4 **Bissa, Djebel** *mt.* Alg.
147 I2 **Bissamcuttak** India
192 A3 **Bissau** Guinea-Bissau
193 D4 **Bissaula** Nigeria
205 J4 **Bissett** Canada
204 F3 **Bistcho Lake** Canada
177 L7 **Bistrița** Romania
177 M7 **Bistrița** *r.* Romania
179 E5 **Bitburg** Germany
179 F5 **Bitche** France
140 B2 **Bitik** Kazakh.
193 D3 **Bitkine** Chad
139 I2 **Bitlis** Turkey
185 I4 **Bitola** Macedonia
185 G4 **Bitonto** Italy
142 B6 **Bitrān, Jabal** *h.* Saudi Arabia
145 D9 **Bitra Par** *reef* India
215 H2 **Bitter Creek** *r.* U.S.A.
179 K3 **Bitterfeld** Germany
196 C5 **Bitterfontein** S. Africa
138 D6 **Bitter Lakes** Egypt
212 D2 **Bitterroot Range** *mts* U.S.A.
179 J2 **Bittkau** Germany
187 G5 **Bityug** *r.* Rus. Fed.
193 D3 **Biu** Nigeria
159 D7 **Biwa-ko** *l.* Japan
141 K1 **Biya** *r.* Rus. Fed.
154 D3 **Biyang** China
194 E2 **Bīye K'obē** Eth.
141 K1 **Biysk** Rus. Fed.
197 H5 **Bizana** S. Africa
192 C1 **Bizerte** Tunisia
143 E5 **Bīzhanābād** Iran
170 A2 **Bjargtangar** *hd* Iceland
171 L3 **Bjästa** Sweden
185 G2 **Bjelovar** Croatia
170 L1 **Bjerkvik** Norway
171 J4 **Bjerringbro** Denmark
171 L3 **Björklinge** Sweden
171 J3 **Bjorli** Norway
171 L3 **Björna** Sweden
132 C2 **Bjørnøya** *i.* Svalbard
171 L3 **Bjurholm** Sweden
192 B3 **Bla** Mali
174 B3 **Bla Bheinn** *h.* U.K.
217 F5 **Black** *r.* *AR* U.S.A.
215 H5 **Black** *r.* *AZ* U.S.A.
209 F4 **Black** *r.* *MI* U.S.A.
208 B3 **Black** *r.* *WI* U.S.A.
155 B6 **Black** *r.* Vietnam
119 E4 **Blackall** Australia
208 C1 **Black Bay** Canada
206 B3 **Blackbear** *r.* Canada
173 F6 **Black Bourton** U.K.
122 C3 **Blackbull** Australia
173 E4 **Blackburn** U.K.
125 J1 **Blackbutt** Australia
214 A2 **Black Butte** *mt.* U.S.A.
214 A2 **Black Butte Lake** U.S.A.
215 E4 **Black Canyon** *gorge* U.S.A.
215 F4 **Black Canyon City** U.S.A.
123 E4 **Blackdown Tableland National Park** Australia
216 E2 **Blackduck** U.S.A.
205 G4 **Blackfalds** Canada
213 D3 **Blackfoot** U.S.A.
212 D2 **Black Foot** *r.* U.S.A.
176 D6 **Black Forest** *mts* Germany
216 C2 **Black Hills** U.S.A.
174 D3 **Black Isle** *pen.* U.K.
205 H3 **Black Lake** Canada
205 H3 **Black Lake** *l.* Canada
209 E3 **Black Lake** *l.* U.S.A.
215 G3 **Black Mesa** *ridge* U.S.A.
173 D6 **Black Mountain** *hills* U.K.
215 D4 **Black Mountain** U.S.A.
173 D6 **Black Mountains** U.K.
215 E4 **Black Mountains** U.S.A.
196 C1 **Black Nossob** *watercourse* Namibia
155 □ **Black Point** *Hong Kong* China
173 D4 **Blackpool** U.K.
208 B3 **Black River Falls** U.S.A.
213 C3 **Black Rock Desert** U.S.A.
220 C6 **Blacksburg** U.S.A.
187 E7 **Black Sea** Asia/Europe
175 H3 **Blacksod Bay** Ireland
175 L5 **Blackstairs Mountain** *h.* Ireland
175 L5 **Blackstairs Mountains** Ireland
221 E6 **Blackstone** U.S.A.
125 I3 **Black Sugarloaf** *mt.* Australia
207 I3 **Black Tickle** Canada
192 B4 **Black Volta** *r.* Africa
123 E4 **Blackwater** Australia
175 L5 **Blackwater** Ireland
175 K5 **Blackwater** *r.* Ireland
175 L4 **Blackwater** *r.* Ireland
175 J3 **Blackwater** *r.* Ireland/U.K.
173 H6 **Blackwater** *r.* U.K.
221 E6 **Blackwater** *r.* U.S.A.
204 E2 **Blackwater Lake** Canada
174 D4 **Blackwater Reservoir** U.K.
217 D4 **Blackwell** U.S.A.
118 B5 **Blackwood** *r.* Australia
123 D4 **Blackwood National Park** Australia
123 C4 **Bladensburg National Park** Australia
173 D6 **Blaenavon** U.K.
141 J3 **Blagodarnoye** Kazakh.
187 G6 **Blagodarnyy** Rus. Fed.
185 J3 **Blagoevgrad** Bulg.
141 I1 **Blagoveshchenka** Rus. Fed.
150 E1 **Blagoveshchensk** Rus. Fed.
221 E4 **Blain** U.S.A.
212 B1 **Blaine** U.S.A.
205 H4 **Blaine Lake** Canada
216 D3 **Blair** *NE* U.S.A.
208 B3 **Blair** *WI* U.S.A.
123 D4 **Blair Athol** Australia
174 E4 **Blair Atholl** U.K.
174 E4 **Blairgowrie** U.K.
219 C6 **Blakely** U.S.A.
173 I5 **Blakeney** U.K.
208 C1 **Blake Point** U.S.A.
163 H4 **Blambangan, Semenanjung** *pen.* Indon.
182 H4 **Blanc, Mont** *mt.* France/Italy
235 K3 **Blanca, Bahía** *b.* Arg.
235 I3 **Blanca de la Totora, Sierra** *hills* Arg.
213 F4 **Blanca Peak** U.S.A.
121 C4 **Blanche, Lake** *salt flat* Australia
124 C2 **Blanche, Lake** *salt flat* Australia
220 B5 **Blanchester** U.S.A.
124 C5 **Blanchetown** Australia
235 I1 **Blanco** *r.* Arg.
231 F6 **Blanco** *r.* Bol.
224 H6 **Blanco, Cabo** *c.* Costa Rica
212 A3 **Blanco, Cape** U.S.A.
207 I3 **Blanc-Sablon** Canada
125 G4 **Bland** *r.* Australia
170 B2 **Blanda** *r.* Iceland
173 E7 **Blandford Forum** U.K.
215 H3 **Blanding** U.S.A.
183 R2 **Blanes** Spain
209 E2 **Blaney Park** U.S.A.
162 □ **Blangah, Telok** Sing.
162 A5 **Blangkejeren** Indon.
178 B3 **Blankenberge** Belgium
179 E4 **Blankenheim** Germany
233 K2 **Blanquilla, Isla** *i.* Venez.
177 H6 **Blansko** Czech Rep.
195 D5 **Blantyre** Malawi
175 J6 **Blarney** Ireland
179 H5 **Blaufelden** Germany
170 L2 **Blåviksjön** Sweden
125 H4 **Blayney** Australia
120 E2 **Blaze, Point** Australia
179 I1 **Bleckede** Germany
126 D4 **Blenheim** N.Z.
173 F6 **Blenheim Palace** *tourist site* U.K.
179 E3 **Blerick** Neth.
175 L4 **Blessington Lakes** Ireland
173 G5 **Bletchley** U.K.
192 C1 **Blida** Alg.
179 F5 **Blies** *r.* Germany
119 H3 **Bligh Water** *b.* Fiji
209 F2 **Blind River** Canada
124 C3 **Blinman** Australia
213 D3 **Bliss** U.S.A.
209 F5 **Blissfield** U.S.A.
221 H4 **Block Island** U.S.A.
221 H4 **Block Island Sound** *sea chan.* U.S.A.
197 G4 **Bloemfontein** S. Africa
197 F3 **Bloemhof** S. Africa
197 F3 **Bloemhof Dam** S. Africa
179 H3 **Blomberg** Germany
170 B2 **Blönduós** Iceland
121 E5 **Bloods Range** *mts* Australia
221 E5 **Bloodsworth Island** U.S.A.
205 J4 **Bloodvein** *r.* Canada
175 J2 **Bloody Foreland** *pt* Ireland
209 I4 **Bloomfield** Canada
208 A5 **Bloomfield** *IA* U.S.A.
219 C4 **Bloomfield** *IN* U.S.A.
213 E4 **Bloomfield** *NM* U.S.A.
208 C5 **Bloomington** *IL* U.S.A.
219 C4 **Bloomington** *IN* U.S.A.
216 E2 **Bloomington** *MN* U.S.A.
221 E4 **Bloomsburg** U.S.A.
221 E4 **Blossburg** U.S.A.
203 P3 **Blosseville Kyst** *coastal area* Greenland
197 H1 **Blouberg** S. Africa
173 F5 **Bloxham** U.K.
215 H5 **Blue** *watercourse* U.S.A.
215 G1 **Bluebell** U.S.A.
215 G2 **Blue Bell Knoll** *mt.* U.S.A.
216 E3 **Blue Earth** U.S.A.
220 C6 **Bluefield** U.S.A.
224 I5 **Bluefields** Nicaragua
221 I2 **Blue Hill** U.S.A.
209 H5 **Blue Knob** *h.* U.S.A.
149 H5 **Blue Mountain** *mt.* India
215 H1 **Blue Mountain** U.S.A.
221 F3 **Blue Mountain Lake** U.S.A.
197 G4 **Blue Mountain Pass** Lesotho
125 I4 **Blue Mountains** Australia
212 C2 **Blue Mountains** U.S.A.
125 I4 **Blue Mountains National Park** Australia
193 F3 **Blue Nile** *r.* Sudan *alt.* **Ābay Wenz (Ethiopia),** *alt.* **Azraq, Bahr el (Sudan)**
202 G3 **Bluenose Lake** Canada
219 C5 **Blue Ridge** U.S.A.
220 D6 **Blue Ridge** *mts* U.S.A.
204 F4 **Blue River** Canada
204 F3 **Bluesky** Canada
215 D2 **Blue Springs** U.S.A.
175 J3 **Blue Stack** *h.* Ireland
175 J3 **Blue Stack Mountains** Ireland
220 C6 **Bluestone Lake** U.S.A.
126 B7 **Bluff** N.Z.
215 H3 **Bluff** U.S.A.
155 □ **Bluff Island** *Hong Kong* China
121 B7 **Bluff Knoll** *mt.* Australia
209 E5 **Bluffton** *IN* U.S.A.
220 B4 **Bluffton** *OH* U.S.A.
233 G3 **Blumenau** Brazil
216 C2 **Blunt** U.S.A.
213 B3 **Bly** U.S.A.
124 C4 **Blyth** Australia
172 F2 **Blyth** *England* U.K.
173 F4 **Blyth** *England* U.K.
215 E5 **Blythe** U.S.A.
217 F5 **Blytheville** U.S.A.
171 J4 **Bø** Norway
192 A4 **Bo** Sierra Leone
161 I3 **Boac** Phil.
224 H5 **Boaco** Nicaragua
231 J5 **Boa Esperança, Açude** *resr* Brazil
154 D3 **Bo'ai** *Henan* China
155 C6 **Bo'ai** *Yunnan* China
194 B3 **Boali** Centr. Afr. Rep.
197 J3 **Boane** Moz.
220 C4 **Boardman** U.S.A.
197 F1 **Boatlaname** Botswana
125 G1 **Boatman** Australia
231 K5 **Boa Viagem** Brazil
233 L4 **Boa Vista** Brazil
192 □ **Boa Vista** *i.* Cape Verde
125 G4 **Bobadah** Australia
155 D6 **Bobai** China
195 E5 **Bobaomby, Tanjona** *c.* Madag.
147 I2 **Bobbili** India
192 B3 **Bobo-Dioulasso** Burkina
195 C6 **Bobonong** Botswana
141 G4 **Boboyob, Gora** *mt.* Uzbek.
187 G5 **Bobrov** Rus. Fed.
187 D5 **Bobrovytsya** Ukr.
187 E5 **Bobrynets'** Ukr.
195 E6 **Boby** *mt.* Madag.
233 K2 **Boca del Pao** Venez.
223 L7 **Boca de Macareo** Venez.
230 E5 **Boca do Acre** Brazil
233 K4 **Boca do Jari** Brazil
233 L2 **Boca Grande** *r. mouth* Venez.
234 D2 **Bocaiúva** Brazil
233 J2 **Bocanó** *r.* Venez.
194 B3 **Bocaranga** Centr. Afr. Rep.
219 D7 **Boca Raton** U.S.A.
224 I6 **Bocas del Toro** Panama
177 J6 **Bochnia** Poland
179 E3 **Bocholt** Germany
179 F3 **Bochum** Germany
Bochum S. Africa *see* **Senwabarwana**
179 I2 **Bockenem** Germany
233 J2 **Boconó** Venez.
224 C2 **Bocoyna** Mex.
194 B3 **Boda** Centr. Afr. Rep.
125 I6 **Bodalla** Australia
121 B6 **Bodallin** Australia
150 D1 **Bodaybo** Rus. Fed.
217 E5 **Bodcau Reservoir** U.S.A.
175 G3 **Boddam** U.K.
179 J3 **Bode** *r.* Germany
214 A2 **Bodega Head** U.S.A.
193 D3 **Bodélé** *reg.* Chad
170 M2 **Boden** Sweden
173 E5 **Bodenham** U.K.
Bodensee *l.* Germany/Switz. *see* **Constance, Lake**
179 I2 **Bodenteich** Germany
179 H3 **Bodenwerder** Germany
147 H2 **Bodhan** India
149 F4 **Bodh Gaya** India
147 H4 **Bodinayakkanur** India
173 C7 **Bodmin** U.K.
173 C7 **Bodmin Moor** *moorland* U.K.
170 K2 **Bodø** Norway
185 L6 **Bodrum** Turkey
185 L6 **Bodrum-Milas** *airport* Turkey
178 C3 **Boechout** Belgium
195 C4 **Boende** Dem. Rep. Congo
192 A3 **Boffa** Guinea
149 H3 **Boga** India
Bogalay Myanmar *see* **Bogale**
145 I8 **Bogale** Myanmar
217 F6 **Bogalusa** U.S.A.
125 G3 **Bogan** *r.* Australia
192 B3 **Bogandé** Burkina
125 G4 **Bogan Gate** Australia
186 I3 **Bogatye Saby** Rus. Fed.
138 E2 **Boğazlıyan** Turkey
149 F3 **Bogcang Zangbo** *r.* China
144 J3 **Bogd** Mongolia
140 C1 **Bogdanovka** Rus. Fed.
150 A2 **Bogda Shan** *mts* China
141 H1 **Bogembay** Kazakh.
125 I2 **Boggabilla** Australia
125 I3 **Boggabri** Australia
175 I5 **Boggeragh Mountains** Ireland
183 R5 **Boghar** Alg.
173 G7 **Bognor Regis** U.K.
161 J4 **Bogo** Phil.
141 G1 **Bogodukhovka** Kazakh.
175 K4 **Bog of Allen** *reg.* Ireland
187 E4 **Bogolyubovo** Rus. Fed.
125 G6 **Bogong, Mount** Australia
158 D2 **Bogopol'** Rus. Fed.
163 G4 **Bogor** Indon.
186 G3 **Bogorodsk** Rus. Fed.
156 F1 **Bogorodskoye** Rus. Fed.
186 I3 **Bogorodskoye** Rus. Fed.
233 I3 **Bogotá** Col.
150 A1 **Bogotol** Rus. Fed.
149 G4 **Bogra** Bangl.
133 K4 **Boguchany** Rus. Fed.
187 G5 **Boguchar** Rus. Fed.
192 A3 **Bogué** Mauritania
154 F2 **Bo Hai** *g.* China
160 A4 **Bohai Haixia** *sea chan.* China
182 F2 **Bohain-en-Vermandois** France
154 E2 **Bohai Wan** *b.* China
179 K3 **Böhlen** Germany
197 H4 **Bohlokong** S. Africa
179 K5 **Böhmer Wald** *mts* Germany
179 G2 **Bohmte** Germany
187 E5 **Bohodukhiv** Ukr.
161 J4 **Bohol** *i.* Phil.
161 J4 **Bohol Sea** Phil.
161 I4 **Bohol Strait** Phil.
Böhöt Mongolia *see* **Öndörshil**
135 G2 **Bohu** China
187 D5 **Bohuslav** Ukr.
235 D4 **Boi, Ponta do** *pt* Brazil
221 F4 **Boiceville** U.S.A.
197 E4 **Boichoko** S. Africa
197 G3 **Boikhutso** S. Africa
120 C3 **Boileau, Cape** Australia
231 G4 **Boim** Brazil
149 H5 **Boinu** *r.* Myanmar
234 E1 **Boipeba, Ilha** *i.* Brazil
234 C2 **Bois** *r.* Brazil
202 F3 **Bois, Lac des** *l.* Canada
209 E3 **Bois Blanc Island** U.S.A.
213 C3 **Boise** U.S.A.
217 C4 **Boise City** U.S.A.
205 I5 **Boissevain** Canada
197 F3 **Boitumelong** S. Africa
179 I1 **Boizenburg** Germany
161 I2 **Bojeador, Cape** Phil.
143 E2 **Bojnūrd** Iran
149 H4 **Bokajan** India
140 E4 **Bo'kantov tog'lari** *hills* Uzbek.
149 F5 **Bokaro** India
195 B4 **Bokatola** Dem. Rep. Congo
192 A3 **Boké** Guinea
141 J2 **Boke** Kazakh.
195 C4 **Bokele** Dem. Rep. Congo
125 G2 **Bokhara** *r.* Australia
171 I4 **Boknafjorden** *sea chan.* Norway
141 I4 **Bökönbaev** Kyrg.
193 D3 **Bokoro** Chad
187 G5 **Bokovskaya** Rus. Fed.
186 E3 **Boksitogorsk** Rus. Fed.
196 D3 **Bokspits** Botswana
156 E2 **Boktor** Rus. Fed.
140 D5 **Bokurdak** Turkm.
195 C4 **Bolaiti** Dem. Rep. Congo
192 A3 **Bolama** Guinea-Bissau
148 A3 **Bolan** *r.* Pak.
147 I1 **Bolangir** India
148 A3 **Bolan Pass** Pak.
182 E2 **Bolbec** France
142 C4 **Boldajī** Iran
179 L1 **Boldekow** Germany
140 D4 **Boldumsaz** Turkm.
141 J3 **Bole** China
192 B4 **Bole** Ghana
195 B4 **Boleko** Dem. Rep. Congo
156 D2 **Bolen** Rus. Fed.
192 B3 **Bolgatanga** Ghana
187 D6 **Bolhrad** Ukr.
158 B2 **Boli** China
195 B4 **Bolia** Dem. Rep. Congo
170 M2 **Boliden** Sweden
161 H2 **Bolinao** Phil.
185 K2 **Bolintin-Vale** Romania
233 H3 **Bolívar** Col.
230 C5 **Bolívar** Peru
217 E4 **Bolivar** *MO* U.S.A.
219 B5 **Bolivar** *TN* U.S.A.
233 J2 **Bolívar, Pico** *mt.* Venez.
230 E7 **Bolivia** *country* S. America
138 E3 **Bolkar Dağları** *mts* Turkey
187 F4 **Bolkhov** Rus. Fed.
209 F1 **Bolkow** Canada
182 G4 **Bollène** France
171 L3 **Bollnäs** Sweden
125 G2 **Bollon** Australia
171 L3 **Bollstabruk** Sweden
171 K4 **Bolmen** *l.* Sweden
187 H7 **Bolnisi** Georgia
195 B4 **Bolobo** Dem. Rep. Congo
161 I5 **Bolod Islands** Phil.
184 D2 **Bologna** Italy
177 O2 **Bologovo** Rus. Fed.
186 E3 **Bologoye** Rus. Fed.
197 F4 **Bolokanang** S. Africa
194 B3 **Bolomba** Dem. Rep. Congo
Bolon' Rus. Fed. *see* **Achan**
225 G3 **Bolonchén de Rejón** Mex.
161 I5 **Bolong** Phil.
133 J4 **Bolotnoye** Rus. Fed.
149 F5 **Bolpur** India
184 D3 **Bolsena, Lago di** *l.* Italy
177 J3 **Bol'shakovo** Rus. Fed.
140 B1 **Bol'shaya Chernigovka** Rus. Fed.
Bol'shaya Churakova Kazakh. *see* **Bol'shaya Churakovka**
141 F1 **Bol'shaya Churakovka** Kazakh.
140 B1 **Bol'shaya Glushitsa** Rus. Fed.
170 P2 **Bol'shaya Imandra, Ozero** *l.* Rus. Fed.
140 B1 **Bol'shaya Kinel'** *r.* Rus. Fed.
187 G6 **Bol'shaya Martinovka** Rus. Fed.
141 I2 **Bol'shaya Vladimirovka** Kazakh.
141 H1 **Bol'shegrivskoye** Rus. Fed.
141 K2 **Bol'shenarymskoye** Kazakh.
133 L2 **Bol'shevik, Ostrov** *i.* Rus. Fed.
169 Q2 **Bol'shezemel'skaya Tundra** *lowland* Rus. Fed.
140 D3 **Bol'shiye Barsuki, Peski** *des.* Kazakh.
186 H2 **Bol'shiye Chirki** Rus. Fed.
140 B3 **Bol'shiye Peshnyye, Ostrova** *is* Kazakh.
141 I4 **Bol'shoy Aksu** Kazakh.
133 R3 **Bol'shoy Aluy** *r.* Rus. Fed.
141 J2 **Bol'shoy Bukon'** Kazakh.
140 D2 **Bol'shoy Ik** *r.* Rus. Fed.
140 B2 **Bol'shoy Irgiz** *r.* Rus. Fed.
158 C3 **Bol'shoy Kamen'** Rus. Fed.
Bol'shoy Kavkaz *mts* Asia/Europe *see* **Caucasus**
187 I5 **Bol'shoy Uzen'** *r.* Rus. Fed.
224 C2 **Bolsón de Mapimí** *des.* Mex.
178 D1 **Bolsward** Neth.
173 E4 **Bolton** U.K.
220 B6 **Bolton** U.S.A.
138 C1 **Bolu** Turkey
170 B1 **Bolungarvík** Iceland
155 E6 **Boluo** China
138 C2 **Bolvadin** Turkey
184 D1 **Bolzano** Italy
195 B4 **Boma** Dem. Rep. Congo
125 I5 **Bomaderry** Australia
125 H6 **Bombala** Australia
Bombay India *see* **Mumbai**
151 F7 **Bomberai, Semenanjung** *pen.* Indon.
230 E5 **Bom Comércio** Brazil
234 D2 **Bom Despacho** Brazil
149 H4 **Bomdila** India
149 H3 **Bomi** China
234 D1 **Bom Jesus da Lapa** Brazil
234 E3 **Bom Jesus do Itabapoana** Brazil
171 I4 **Bømlo** *i.* Norway
193 D1 **Bon, Cap** *c.* Tunisia
142 B2 **Bonāb** Iran
221 E6 **Bon Air** U.S.A.
223 K6 **Bonaire** *i.* Neth. Antilles
224 H5 **Bonanza** Nicaragua
118 C3 **Bonaparte Archipelago** *is* Australia
174 D3 **Bonar Bridge** U.K.
207 J4 **Bonavista** Canada
207 J4 **Bonavista Bay** Canada
124 A3 **Bon Bon** Australia
175 F5 **Bonchester Bridge** U.K.
194 C3 **Bondo** Dem. Rep. Congo
161 I3 **Bondoc Peninsula** Phil.
192 B4 **Bondoukou** Côte d'Ivoire
151 E7 **Bone, Teluk** *b.* Indon.
208 A3 **Bone Lake** U.S.A.
179 F3 **Bönen** Germany
151 E7 **Bonerate, Kepulauan** *is* Indon.
174 E4 **Bo'ness** U.K.
234 D2 **Bonfinópolis de Minas** Brazil
194 D3 **Bonga** Eth.
161 I3 **Bongabong** Phil.
149 G4 **Bongaigaon** India
194 C3 **Bongandanga** Dem. Rep. Congo
196 H3 **Bongani** S. Africa
161 H5 **Bongao** Phil.
149 G3 **Bong Co** *l.* China
161 J5 **Bongo** *i.* Phil.
194 C3 **Bongo, Massif des** *mts* Centr. Afr. Rep.
195 E5 **Bongolava** *mts* Madag.
193 D3 **Bongor** Chad
192 B4 **Bongouanou** Côte d'Ivoire
163 D2 **Bông Sơn** Vietnam
178 C3 **Bonheiden** Belgium
184 C4 **Bonifacio** *Corsica* France
184 C4 **Bonifacio, Strait of** France/Italy
151 G4 **Bonin Islands** Japan
234 A3 **Bonito** Brazil
179 F4 **Bonn** Germany
170 K2 **Bonnåsjøen** Norway
212 C1 **Bonners Ferry** U.S.A.
182 H3 **Bonneville** France
124 D6 **Bonney, Lake** Australia
118 B5 **Bonnie Rock** Australia
174 E5 **Bonnyrigg** U.K.
205 G4 **Bonnyville** Canada
161 H4 **Bonobono** Phil.
Bonom Mhai *mt.* Vietnam *see* **S'Lung, B'Nom**
184 C4 **Bonorva** *Sardinia* Italy
125 I2 **Bonshaw** Australia
196 D7 **Bontebok National Park** S. Africa
192 A4 **Bonthe** Sierra Leone
161 I2 **Bontoc** Phil.
163 I4 **Bontosunggu** Indon.
197 F6 **Bontrug** S. Africa
197 G1 **Bonwapitse** Botswana
215 H2 **Book Cliffs** *ridge* U.S.A.
125 E4 **Boolaboolka Lake** *imp. l.* Australia
124 C4 **Booleroo Centre** Australia
175 K5 **Booley Hills** Ireland
125 F4 **Booligal** Australia
125 H2 **Boomi** Australia

Broadford

125 F6 Broadford Australia
175 J5 Broadford Ireland
174 C3 Broadford U.K.
174 E5 Broad Law h. U.K.
122 A3 Broadmere Australia
123 E4 Broad Sound sea chan. Australia
173 I6 Broadstairs U.K.
212 F2 Broadus U.S.A.
205 I4 Broadview Canada
125 J2 Broadwater Australia
216 C3 Broadwater U.S.A.
126 D1 Broadwood N.Z.
171 M4 Brocēni Latvia
205 I3 Brochet Canada
205 I3 Brochet, Lac l. Canada
179 I3 Brocken mt. Germany
202 G2 Brock Island Canada
121 B4 Brockman, Mount Australia
221 E3 Brockport U.S.A.
221 H3 Brockton U.S.A.
209 J3 Brockville Canada
209 F4 Brockway MI U.S.A.
220 D4 Brockway PA U.S.A.
203 J2 Brodeur Peninsula Canada
208 C4 Brodhead U.S.A.
174 C5 Brodick U.K.
177 I4 Brodnica Poland
187 C5 Brody Ukr.
217 E4 Broken Arrow U.S.A.
125 I4 Broken Bay Australia
216 D3 Broken Bow NE U.S.A.
217 E5 Broken Bow OK U.S.A.
124 D3 Broken Hill Australia
238 K7 Broken Plateau sea feature Indian Ocean
179 I2 Brome Germany
173 G6 Bromley U.K.
173 E5 Bromsgrove U.K.
171 J4 Brønderslev Denmark
197 H2 Bronkhorstspruit S. Africa
170 K2 Brønnøysund Norway
209 E5 Bronson U.S.A.
173 I5 Brooke U.K.
161 H4 Brooke's Point Phil.
208 C4 Brookfield U.S.A.
217 F6 Brookhaven U.S.A.
213 A3 Brookings OR U.S.A.
216 D2 Brookings SD U.S.A.
221 H3 Brookline U.S.A.
208 A5 Brooklyn IA U.S.A.
208 B5 Brooklyn IL U.S.A.
216 E2 Brooklyn Center U.S.A.
220 D6 Brookneal U.S.A.
205 G4 Brooks Canada
214 A2 Brooks CA U.S.A.
221 I2 Brooks ME U.S.A.
127 J3 Brooks, Cape Antarctica
202 D3 Brooks Range mts U.S.A.
219 D6 Brooksville U.S.A.
121 B7 Brookton Australia
220 D4 Brookville U.S.A.
174 C3 Broom, Loch inlet U.K.
118 C3 Broome Australia
174 E2 Brora U.K.
171 K5 Brösarp Sweden
175 K4 Brosna r. Ireland
213 B3 Brothers U.S.A.
155 □ Brothers, The is Hong Kong China
172 E3 Brough U.K.
174 E1 Brough Head U.K.
175 L3 Broughshane U.K.
124 C4 Broughton r. Australia
Broughton Island Canada see Qikiqtarjuaq
125 J4 Broughton Islands Australia
177 O5 Brovary Ukr.
123 E5 Brovinia Australia
171 J4 Brovst Denmark
124 C4 Brown, Mount h. Australia
121 D5 Browne Range hills Australia
217 C5 Brownfield U.S.A.
212 D1 Browning U.S.A.
208 D6 Brownsburg U.S.A.
221 F5 Browns Mills U.S.A.
219 B5 Brownsville TN U.S.A.
217 D7 Brownsville TX U.S.A.
221 I2 Brownville U.S.A.
221 I2 Brownville Junction U.S.A.
217 D6 Brownwood U.S.A.
120 C2 Browse Island Australia
177 N4 Brozha Belarus
182 F1 Bruay-la-Bussière France
208 C2 Bruce Crossing U.S.A.
206 D4 Bruce Peninsula Canada
209 G3 Bruce Peninsula National Park Canada
121 B6 Bruce Rock Australia
179 G5 Bruchsal Germany
179 K2 Brück Germany
176 G7 Bruck an der Mur Austria
173 E6 Brue r. U.K.
Bruges Belgium see Brugge
178 B3 Brugge Belgium
179 G5 Brühl Baden-Württemberg Germany
179 E4 Brühl Nordrhein-Westfalen Germany
215 G2 Bruin Point mt. U.S.A.
149 I3 Bruint India
196 C2 Brukkaros Namibia
208 B2 Brule U.S.A.
207 H3 Brûlé, Lac l. Canada
178 C5 Brûly Belgium
234 E1 Brumado Brazil
171 J3 Brumunddal Norway
175 L4 Brú Na Bóinne tourist site Ireland
179 J2 Brunau Germany
213 D3 Bruneau U.S.A.
213 D3 Bruneau r. U.S.A.
163 H2 Brunei country Asia
122 A3 Brunette Downs Australia
171 K3 Brunflo Sweden
184 D1 Brunico Italy
126 C5 Brunner, Lake N.Z.
205 H4 Bruno Canada
176 D4 Brunsbüttel Germany
219 D6 Brunswick GA U.S.A.
221 I3 Brunswick ME U.S.A.
220 C4 Brunswick OH U.S.A.
232 B8 Brunswick, Península de pen. Chile
120 D2 Brunswick Bay Australia
Brunswick Head Australia see Brunswick Heads
125 J2 Brunswick Heads Australia
177 H6 Bruntál Czech Rep.
127 J3 Brunt Ice Shelf Antarctica
197 I4 Bruntville S. Africa
125 G9 Bruny Island Australia
213 G3 Brush U.S.A.
178 C4 Brussels Belgium (City Plan 97)
209 G4 Brussels Canada
208 D3 Brussels U.S.A.
177 N5 Brusyliv Ukr.
125 G6 Bruthen Australia
Bruxelles Belgium see Brussels
220 A4 Bryan OH U.S.A.
217 D6 Bryan TX U.S.A.
124 C4 Bryan, Mount h. Australia
187 E4 Bryansk Rus. Fed.
187 E4 Bryanskaya Oblast' admin. div. Rus. Fed.
187 H6 Bryanskoye Rus. Fed.
215 F3 Bryce Canyon National Park U.S.A.
215 H5 Bryce Mountain U.S.A.
171 I4 Bryne Norway
187 F6 Bryukhovetskaya Rus. Fed.
177 H5 Brzeg Poland
194 E3 Bu'aale Somalia
119 F2 Buala Solomon Is
192 A3 Buba Guinea-Bissau
139 L7 Būbiyān, Jazīrat Kuwait
161 I5 Bubuan i. Phil.
138 C3 Bucak Turkey
233 I3 Bucaramanga Col.
161 J4 Bucas Grande i. Phil.
120 C3 Buccaneer Archipelago is Australia
125 H6 Buchan Australia
192 A4 Buchanan Liberia
208 D5 Buchanan MI U.S.A.
220 D6 Buchanan VA U.S.A.
123 D4 Buchanan, Lake salt flat Australia
217 D6 Buchanan, Lake U.S.A.
203 K2 Buchan Gulf Canada
207 I4 Buchans Canada
185 L2 Bucharest Romania
179 I1 Büchen Germany
179 H5 Buchen (Odenwald) Germany
179 K1 Buchholz Germany
179 H1 Bucholz in der Nordheide Germany
214 B4 Buchon, Point U.S.A.
177 L7 Bucin, Pasul pass Romania
125 F3 Buckambool Mountain h. Australia
179 H2 Bückeburg Germany
179 H2 Bücken Germany
215 F5 Buckeye U.S.A.
220 B5 Buckeye Lake U.S.A.
220 C5 Buckhannon U.S.A.
220 C5 Buckhannon r. U.S.A.
174 E4 Buckhaven U.K.
209 H3 Buckhorn Canada
215 H5 Buckhorn U.S.A.
209 H3 Buckhorn Lake Canada
220 B6 Buckhorn Lake U.S.A.
175 F3 Buckie U.K.
209 J3 Buckingham Canada
173 G5 Buckingham U.K.
220 D6 Buckingham U.S.A.
118 D3 Buckingham Bay Australia
119 E4 Buckland Tableland reg. Australia
124 B4 Buckleboo Australia
127 I6 Buckle Island Antarctica
123 B4 Buckley watercourse Australia
215 F4 Buckskin Mountains U.S.A.
214 B2 Bucks Mountain U.S.A.
221 I2 Bucksport U.S.A.
179 K2 Bückwitz Germany
Bucureşti Romania see Bucharest
220 B4 Bucyrus U.S.A.
177 O4 Buda-Kashalyova Belarus
145 I7 Budalin Myanmar
177 I7 Budapest Hungary
148 D3 Budaun India
125 F3 Budda Australia
175 F4 Buddon Ness pt U.K.
184 C4 Buddusò Sardinia Italy
173 C7 Bude U.K.
217 F6 Bude U.S.A.
187 H6 Budennovsk Rus. Fed.
125 J1 Buderim Australia
179 H4 Büdingen Germany
148 D5 Budni India
186 E3 Budogoshch' Rus. Fed.
149 H2 Budongquan China
184 C4 Budoni Sardinia Italy
142 C6 Budū, Ḩadabat al plain Saudi Arabia
142 C6 Budū', Sabkhat al salt pan Saudi Arabia
192 C4 Buea Cameroon
214 B4 Buellton U.S.A.
235 J2 Buena Esperanza Arg.
233 H4 Buenaventura Col.
222 C3 Buenaventura Mex.
233 H4 Buenaventura, Bahía de b. Col.
213 F4 Buena Vista CO U.S.A.
220 D6 Buena Vista VA U.S.A.
183 O2 Buendia, Embalse de resr Spain
235 H4 Bueno r. Chile
235 K2 Buenos Aires Arg. (City Plan 106)
235 K3 Buenos Aires prov. Arg.
232 B7 Buenos Aires, Lago l. Arg./Chile
232 C7 Buen Pasto Arg.
224 C2 Búfalo Mex.
205 G3 Buffalo r. Canada
220 D3 Buffalo NY U.S.A.
217 D4 Buffalo OK U.S.A.
216 C2 Buffalo SD U.S.A.
217 D6 Buffalo TX U.S.A.
208 B3 Buffalo WI U.S.A.
212 F2 Buffalo WY U.S.A.
208 B3 Buffalo r. U.S.A.
125 G6 Buffalo, Mount h. Australia
204 F3 Buffalo Head Hills Canada
204 F2 Buffalo Lake Canada
205 H3 Buffalo Narrows Canada
196 B4 Buffels watercourse S. Africa
197 G1 Buffels Drift S. Africa
219 D5 Buford U.S.A.
185 K2 Buftea Romania
177 J4 Bug r. Poland
233 H4 Buga Col.
233 H3 Bugalagrande Col.
125 H3 Bugaldie Australia
Bugdayli Turkm. see Bugdaýly
140 C5 Bugdaýly Turkm.
163 H4 Bugel, Tanjung pt Indon.
178 C3 Buggenhout Belgium
185 G2 Bugojno Bos.-Herz.
169 P2 Bugrino Rus. Fed.
161 H4 Bugsuk i. Phil.
153 L2 Bugt China
161 I2 Bugueу Phil.
140 E3 Bugun' Kazakh.
140 C1 Buguruslan Rus. Fed.
142 D4 Būhābād Iran
195 D5 Buhera Zimbabwe
161 I3 Buhi Phil.
213 D3 Buhl ID U.S.A.
208 A2 Buhl MN U.S.A.
139 I3 Bühtan r. Turkey
177 M7 Buhuşi Romania
173 D5 Builth Wells U.K.
192 B4 Bui National Park Ghana
187 I4 Buinsk Rus. Fed.
139 K4 Bu'in Soflā Iran
150 D2 Buir Nur l. Mongolia
195 B6 Buitepos Namibia
185 I3 Bujanovac Serbia
195 C4 Bujumbura Burundi
150 D1 Bukachacha Rus. Fed.
149 G1 Buka Daban mt. China
119 F2 Buka Island P.N.G.
142 B2 Būkān Iran
142 D4 Būkand Iran
141 J1 Bukanskoye Rus. Fed.
Bukantau, Gory h. Uzbek. see Bo'kantov tog'lari
195 C4 Bukavu Dem. Rep. Congo
Bukhara Uzbek. see Buxoro
141 K2 Bukhtarminskoye Vodokhranilishche resr Kazakh.
161 J6 Bukide i. Indon.
163 H3 Bukit Baka-Bukit Raya, Taman Nasional nat. park Indon.
163 B4 Bukit Barisan Selatan, Taman Nasional nat. park Indon.
162 B5 Bukit Fraser Malaysia
162 □ Bukit Timah Sing.
163 B3 Bukittinggi Indon.
195 D4 Bukoba Tanz.
162 □ Bukum, Pulau i. Sing.
151 F7 Bula Indon.
187 I4 Bula r. Rus. Fed.
176 D7 Bülach Switz.
125 J4 Bulahdelah Australia
Bulahdelal Australia see Bulahdelah
161 I3 Bulan Phil.
139 G1 Bulancak Turkey
139 I2 Bulanık Turkey
156 F2 Bulava Rus. Fed.
195 C6 Bulawayo Zimbabwe
141 G1 Bulayevo Kazakh.
139 F3 Bulbul Syria
138 B2 Buldan Turkey
148 D5 Buldhana India
197 I2 Bulembu Swaziland
Bulgan Mongolia see Bürenhayrhan
150 C2 Bulgan Mongolia
154 B1 Bulgan Mongolia
185 K3 Bulgaria country Europe
125 E1 Bullawarra, Lake salt flat Australia
124 D3 Bullea, Lake salt flat Australia
126 D4 Buller r. N.Z.
125 G6 Buller, Mount Australia
122 C3 Bulleringa National Park Australia
121 B6 Bullfinch Australia
215 E4 Bullhead City U.S.A.
215 D4 Bullion Mountains U.S.A.
120 E2 Bullo r. Australia
125 E2 Bulloo watercourse Australia
125 E2 Bulloo Downs Australia
125 E2 Bulloo Lake salt flat Australia
196 B2 Büllsport Namibia
120 F2 Bulman Australia
120 F2 Bulman Gorge Australia
162 □ Buloh, Pulau i. Sing.
125 E6 Buloke, Lake dry lake Australia
197 G4 Bultfontein S. Africa
161 J5 Buluan Phil.
118 C2 Bulukumba Indon.
133 N2 Bulun Rus. Fed.
195 B4 Bulungu Bandundu Dem. Rep. Congo
195 C4 Bulungu Kasai-Occidental Dem. Rep. Congo
Bulungur Uzbek. see Bulung'ur
141 F5 Bulung'ur Uzbek.
161 J3 Bulusan Phil.
194 C3 Bumba Dem. Rep. Congo
154 B1 Bumbat China
214 F4 Bumble Bee U.S.A.
161 H5 Bum-Bum i. Malaysia
195 B4 Buna Dem. Rep. Congo
194 D3 Buna Kenya
195 D4 Bunazi Tanz.
Bunbeg Ireland see An Bun Beag
118 B5 Bunbury Australia
175 L5 Bunclody Ireland
175 K2 Buncrana Ireland
195 D4 Bunda Tanz.
119 F4 Bundaberg Australia
125 G2 Bundaleer Australia
125 I3 Bundarra Australia
148 C4 Bundi India
125 J2 Bundjalung National Park Australia
175 J3 Bundoran Ireland
149 F5 Bundu India
173 I5 Bungay U.K.
125 H5 Bungendore Australia
Bungle Bungle National Park nat. park Australia see Purnululu National Park
159 C8 Bungo-suidō sea chan. Japan
194 D3 Bunia Dem. Rep. Congo
195 C4 Bunianga Dem. Rep. Congo
121 C6 Buningonia well Australia
125 E6 Buninyong Australia
193 D3 Buni-Yadi Nigeria
148 C2 Bunji Pak.
123 F4 Bunker Group atolls Australia
215 E3 Bunkerville U.S.A.
217 E6 Bunkie U.S.A.
219 D6 Bunnell U.S.A.
138 E2 Bünyan Turkey
161 H6 Bunyu i. Indon.
162 C2 Buôn Đôn Vietnam
163 D2 Buôn Hô Vietnam
163 D2 Buôn Ma Thuôt Vietnam
Buôn Mê Thuôt Vietnam see Buôn Ma Thuôt
133 O2 Buorkhaya, Guba b. Rus. Fed.
136 B5 Buqbuq Egypt
195 D4 Bura Kenya
141 K2 Buran Kazakh.
Burang China see Jirang
234 E2 Buranhaém r. Brazil
140 C2 Burannoye Rus. Fed.
Burao Somalia see Burco
161 J4 Burauen Phil.
146 B4 Buraydah Saudi Arabia
179 G4 Burbach Germany
214 C4 Burbank U.S.A.
125 G4 Burcher Australia
194 E3 Burco Somalia
178 D1 Burdaard Neth.
141 F5 Burdalyk Turkm.
138 C3 Burdur Turkey
194 D2 Burē Eth.
173 I5 Bure r. U.K.
170 M2 Bureå Sweden
150 F1 Bureinskiy Khrebet mts Rus. Fed.
144 H2 Bürenhayrhan Mongolia
156 C2 Bureya r. Rus. Fed.
156 D2 Bureyinski Zapovednik nature res. Rus. Fed.
Bûr Fu'ad Egypt see Port Fuad
185 L3 Burgas Bulg.
219 E5 Burgaw U.S.A.
179 J2 Burg bei Magdeburg Germany
179 I5 Burgbernheim Germany
179 I2 Burgdorf Germany
207 I4 Burgeo Canada
197 G5 Burgersdorp S. Africa
197 I2 Burgersfort S. Africa
121 C6 Burges, Mount h. Australia
173 G7 Burgess Hill U.K.
179 H4 Burghaun Germany
176 F6 Burghausen Germany
174 E3 Burghead U.K.
178 B3 Burgh-Haamstede Neth.
184 F6 Burgio, Serra di h. Sicily Italy
179 K5 Burglengenfeld Germany
183 O1 Burgos Spain
179 K4 Burgstädt Germany
171 L4 Burgsvik Sweden
179 E1 Burgum Neth.
182 G3 Burgundy reg. France
150 B3 Burhan Budai Shan mts China
185 L5 Burhaniye Turkey
148 D5 Burhanpur India
149 E5 Burhar-Dhanpuri India
149 F4 Burhi Gandak r. India
161 I3 Burias i. Phil.
140 D2 Buribay Rus. Fed.
224 I6 Burica, Punta pt Costa Rica
149 H4 Buri Dihing r. India
149 E4 Buri Gandak r. Nepal
207 I4 Burin Peninsula Canada
162 B2 Buriram Thai.
231 J5 Buriti Bravo Brazil
234 C1 Buritis Brazil
143 G4 Burj Aziz Khan Pak.
118 D3 Burketown Australia
192 B3 Burkina country Africa
209 H3 Burk's Falls Canada
141 I2 Burkutty Kazakh.
141 I1 Burla Rus. Fed.
141 I1 Burla r. Rus. Fed.
213 D3 Burley U.S.A.
140 E1 Burli Kazakh.
140 C2 Burlin Kazakh.
209 H4 Burlington Canada
217 C4 Burlington CO U.S.A.
208 B5 Burlington IA U.S.A.
208 D5 Burlington IN U.S.A.
221 I2 Burlington ME U.S.A.
221 G2 Burlington VT U.S.A.
208 C4 Burlington WI U.S.A.
140 D1 Burly Rus. Fed.
Burma country Asia see Myanmar
217 D6 Burnet U.S.A.
213 B3 Burney U.S.A.
221 I2 Burnham U.S.A.
125 F8 Burnie Australia
172 G3 Burniston U.K.
173 E4 Burnley U.K.
213 C3 Burns U.S.A.
205 H1 Burnside r. Canada
121 C5 Burnside, Lake salt flat Australia
202 F4 Burns Lake Canada
220 C5 Burnsville Lake U.S.A.
174 E4 Burntisland U.K.
205 J3 Burntwood r. Canada
205 I3 Burntwood Lake Canada
125 E5 Buronga Australia
140 E4 Burovoy Uzbek.
133 J5 Burqin China
139 G5 Burqu' Jordan
124 C4 Burra Australia
174 □ Burra i. U.K.
174 □ Burravoe U.K.
175 F2 Burray i. U.K.
185 I4 Burrel Albania
125 H4 Burrendong, Lake Australia
125 H3 Burren Junction Australia
125 I5 Burrewarra Point Australia
183 P3 Burriana Spain
125 H5 Burrinjuck Australia
125 H5 Burrinjuck Reservoir Australia
225 D1 Burro, Serranías del mts Mex.
220 B5 Burr Oak Reservoir U.S.A.
174 D6 Burrow Head U.K.
120 E2 Burrundie Australia
215 G2 Burrville U.S.A.
138 B1 Bursa Turkey
193 F2 Būr Safājah Egypt
Būr Sa'īd Egypt see Port Said
156 C2 Bursinskoye Vodokhranilishche resr Rus. Fed.
179 G5 Bürstadt Germany
Būr Sudan Sudan see Port Sudan
124 D4 Burta Australia
209 E3 Burt Lake U.S.A.
209 F4 Burton U.S.A.
206 E3 Burton, Lac l. Canada
Burtonport Ireland see Ailt an Chorráin
173 F5 Burton upon Trent U.K.
170 M2 Burträsk Sweden
221 J1 Burtts Corner Canada
125 E4 Burtundy Australia
121 F4 Burt Well Australia
151 E7 Buru i. Indon.
141 H3 Burubaytal Kazakh.
138 C6 Burullus, Bahra el lag. Egypt
Burultokay China see Fuhai
195 D4 Burundi country Africa
195 C4 Bururi Burundi
204 B2 Burwash Landing Canada
175 F2 Burwick U.K.
187 E5 Buryn' Ukr.
140 B3 Burynshyk Kazakh.
173 H5 Bury St Edmunds U.K.
148 C2 Burzil Pass Pak.
195 C4 Busanga Dem. Rep. Congo
175 L2 Bush r. U.K.
142 C4 Būshehr Iran
149 E2 Bushêngcaka China
195 D4 Bushenyi Uganda
175 L2 Bushmills U.K.
208 B5 Bushnell U.S.A.
162 □ Busing, Pulau i. Sing.
194 C3 Businga Dem. Rep. Congo
139 F5 Buşrá ash Shām Syria
156 B2 Busse Rus. Fed.
118 B5 Busselton Australia
178 D2 Bussum Neth.
225 D2 Bustamante Mex.
224 C1 Bustillos, Lago Mex.

Cantábrica, Cordillera

184 C2 **Busto Arsizio** Italy
161 H3 **Busuanga** Phil.
161 H3 **Busuanga** *i.* Phil.
194 C3 **Buta** Dem. Rep. Congo
235 I3 **Buta Ranquil** Arg.
195 C4 **Butare** Rwanda
236 G6 **Butaritari** *atoll* Kiribati
124 B4 **Bute** Australia
174 C5 **Bute** *i.* U.K.
174 C5 **Bute, Sound of** *sea chan.* U.K.
204 D4 **Butedale** Canada
204 D4 **Bute Inlet** Canada
197 H4 **Butha-Buthe** Lesotho
Butha Qi China *see* **Zalantun**
179 G1 **Butjadingen** *reg.* Germany
209 E5 **Butler** *IN* U.S.A.
220 D4 **Butler** *PA* U.S.A.
175 K3 **Butlers Bridge** Ireland
151 E7 **Buton** *i.* Indon.
179 K1 **Bütow** Germany
212 D2 **Butte** U.S.A.
179 J3 **Buttelstedt** Germany
214 B1 **Butte Meadows** U.S.A.
163 B1 **Butterworth** Malaysia
197 H6 **Butterworth** S. Africa
175 J5 **Buttevant** Ireland
204 D5 **Buttle Lake** Canada
174 B2 **Butt of Lewis** *hd* U.K.
203 I4 **Button Bay** Canada
214 C4 **Buttonwillow** U.S.A.
161 J4 **Butuan** Phil.
155 B5 **Butuo** China
187 G5 **Buturlinovka** Rus. Fed.
149 E4 **Butwal** Nepal
179 G4 **Butzbach** Germany
194 E3 **Buulobarde** Somalia
195 E4 **Buur Gaabo** Somalia
194 E3 **Buurhabaka** Somalia
144 I2 **Buutsagaan** Mongolia
149 F4 **Buxar** India
141 F5 **Buxoro** Uzbek.
179 H1 **Buxtehude** Germany
173 F4 **Buxton** U.K.
186 G3 **Buy** Rus. Fed.
Buyant Mongolia *see* **Buutsagaan**
208 A1 **Buyck** U.S.A.
187 H7 **Buynaksk** Rus. Fed.
138 A3 **Büyükmenderes** *r.* Turkey
160 B3 **Buyun Shan** *mt.* China
140 B3 **Buzachi, Poluostrov** *pen.* Kazakh.
141 H5 **Buzai Gumbad** Afgh.
178 C5 **Buzancy** France
185 L2 **Buzău** Romania
195 D5 **Búzi** Moz.
141 F2 **Buzuluk** Kazakh.
140 C1 **Buzuluk** Rus. Fed.
187 G5 **Buzuluk** *r.* Rus. Fed.
221 H4 **Buzzards Bay** U.S.A.
185 K3 **Byala** Bulg.
185 J3 **Byala Slatina** Bulg.
177 N4 **Byalynichy** Belarus
203 H2 **Byam Martin Island** Canada
187 D4 **Byarezina** *r.* Belarus
187 C4 **Byaroza** Belarus
138 E4 **Byblos** *tourist site* Lebanon
177 I4 **Bydgoszcz** Poland
187 D4 **Byerazino** Belarus
213 F4 **Byers** U.S.A.
177 N3 **Byeshankovichy** Belarus
171 I4 **Bygland** Norway
187 D4 **Bykhaw** Belarus
171 I4 **Bykle** Norway
169 P6 **Bykovo** Rus. Fed.
141 H2 **Bylkyldak** Kazakh.
203 K2 **Bylot Island** Canada
209 G3 **Byng Inlet** Canada
171 I3 **Byrkjelo** Norway
125 G3 **Byrock** Australia
208 C4 **Byron** *IL* U.S.A.
221 H2 **Byron** *ME* U.S.A.
125 J2 **Byron, Cape** Australia
125 J2 **Byron Bay** Australia
133 L2 **Byrranga, Gory** *mts* Rus. Fed.
170 M2 **Byske** Sweden
156 C1 **Byssa** Rus. Fed.
156 C1 **Byssa** *r.* Rus. Fed.
141 K1 **Bystryy Istok** Rus. Fed.
133 O3 **Bytantay** *r.* Rus. Fed.
177 I5 **Bytom** Poland
177 H3 **Bytów** Poland

C

232 E3 **Caacupé** Para.
235 A4 **Caaguazú** Para.
235 A4 **Caaguazú, Cordillera de** *hills* Para.
234 A3 **Caarapó** Brazil
235 A4 **Caazapá** Para.
230 C6 **Caballas** Peru
230 D4 **Caballococha** Peru
225 D1 **Caballos Mesteños, Llano de los** *plain* Mex.
161 I3 **Cabanatuan** Phil.
207 G4 **Cabano** Canada
194 E2 **Cabdul Qaadir** Somalia
234 A1 **Cabeceira Rio Manso** Brazil
231 L5 **Cabedelo** Brazil
183 N3 **Cabeza del Buey** Spain
231 F7 **Cabezas** Bol.
235 K3 **Cabildo** Arg.
233 J2 **Cabimas** Venez.
195 B4 **Cabinda** Angola
195 B4 **Cabinda** *prov.* Angola
212 C1 **Cabinet Mountains** U.S.A.
233 I3 **Cable Way** *pass* Col.
234 D3 **Cabo Frio** Brazil
234 E3 **Cabo Frio, Ilha do** *i.* Brazil
206 E4 **Cabonga, Réservoir** *resr* Canada
217 E4 **Cabool** U.S.A.
125 J1 **Caboolture** Australia
231 H3 **Cabo Orange, Parque Nacional de** *nat. park* Brazil
230 C4 **Cabo Pantoja** Peru
195 D5 **Cabora Bassa, Lake** *resr* Moz.
222 B2 **Caborca** Mex.
209 G3 **Cabot Head** Canada
207 I4 **Cabot Strait** Canada
234 D2 **Cabral, Serra do** *mts* Brazil
139 K2 **Cäbrayıl** Azer.
183 R3 **Cabrera, Illa de** *i.* Spain
183 M1 **Cabrera, Sierra de la** *mts* Spain
183 P3 **Cabriel** *r.* Spain
233 K3 **Cabruta** Venez.
161 I2 **Cabugao** Phil.
232 F3 **Caçador** Brazil
225 E4 **Cacahuatepec** Mex.
185 I3 **Čačak** Serbia
235 M1 **Cacapava do Sul** Brazil
220 D5 **Cacapon** *r.* U.S.A.
233 I3 **Cácares** Col.
184 C4 **Caccia, Capo** *c.* *Sardinia* Italy
143 F2 **Çäçe** Turkm.
231 G7 **Cáceres** Brazil
183 M3 **Cáceres** Spain
213 D3 **Cache Peak** U.S.A.
192 A3 **Cacheu** Guinea-Bissau
232 C3 **Cachi** *r.* Arg.
232 C2 **Cachi, Nevados de** *mts* Arg.
231 H5 **Cachimbo, Serra do** *hills* Brazil
233 I3 **Cáchira** Col.
234 E1 **Cachoeira** Brazil
234 B2 **Cachoeira Alta** Brazil
235 M1 **Cachoeira do Sul** Brazil
234 E3 **Cachoeiro de Itapemirim** Brazil
192 A3 **Cacine** Guinea-Bissau
231 H3 **Caciporé, Cabo** *c.* Brazil
195 B5 **Cacolo** Angola
195 B4 **Cacongo** Angola
215 D3 **Cactus Range** *mts* U.S.A.
234 B2 **Caçu** Brazil
234 D1 **Caculé** Brazil
177 I6 **Čadca** Slovakia
179 H1 **Cadenberge** Germany
225 D2 **Cadereyta** Mex.
124 A2 **Cadibarrawirracanna, Lake** *salt flat* Australia
161 I3 **Cadig Mountains** Phil.
209 H1 **Cadillac** *Que.* Canada
205 H5 **Cadillac** *Sask.* Canada
209 E3 **Cadillac** U.S.A.
161 I4 **Cadiz** Phil.
183 M4 **Cádiz** Spain
183 M4 **Cádiz, Golfo de** *g.* Spain
215 E4 **Cadiz Lake** U.S.A.
182 D2 **Caen** France
173 C4 **Caernarfon** U.K.
173 C4 **Caernarfon Bay** U.K.
173 D6 **Caerphilly** U.K.
220 B5 **Caesar Creek Lake** U.S.A.
138 E5 **Caesarea** *tourist site* Israel
234 D1 **Caetité** Brazil
232 C3 **Cafayate** Arg.
161 I4 **Cagayan** *i.* Phil.
161 I2 **Cagayan** *r.* Phil.
161 J4 **Cagayan de Oro** Phil.
161 H5 **Cagayan de Tawi-Tawi** *i.* Phil.
161 I4 **Cagayan Islands** Phil.
184 E3 **Cagli** Italy
184 C5 **Cagliari** *Sardinia* Italy
184 C5 **Cagliari, Golfo di** *b.* *Sardinia* Italy
233 I4 **Caguán** *r.* Col.
140 C4 **Çagyl** Turkm.
140 D4 **Çagyllyşor Çöketligi** *depr.* Turkm.
219 C5 **Cahaba** *r.* U.S.A.
175 I6 **Caha Mountains** Ireland
175 H6 **Cahermore** Ireland
175 K5 **Cahir** Ireland
175 H6 **Cahirsiveen** Ireland
Cahora Bassa, Lago de *resr* Moz. *see* **Cabora Bassa, Lake**
175 L5 **Cahore Point** Ireland
182 E4 **Cahors** France
230 C5 **Cahuapanas** Peru
230 D4 **Cahuinarí, Parque Nacional** *nat. park* Col.
187 D6 **Cahul** Moldova
195 D5 **Caia** Moz.
231 G6 **Caiabis, Serra dos** *hills* Brazil
195 C5 **Caianda** Angola
234 B2 **Caiapó** *r.* Brazil
234 B2 **Caiapó, Serra do** *mts* Brazil
234 B2 **Caiapônia** Brazil
223 I4 **Caibarién** Cuba
155 C6 **Cai Bâu, Đao** *i.* Vietnam
162 C3 **Cai Be** Vietnam
233 K3 **Caicara** Venez.
223 J4 **Caicos Islands** Turks and Caicos Is
155 E4 **Caidian** China
121 D7 **Caiguna** Australia
224 C3 **Caimanero, Laguna del** *lag.* Mex.
235 H1 **Caimanes** Chile
161 H3 **Caiman Point** Phil.
183 P2 **Caimodorro** *mt.* Spain
162 C3 **Cai Nước** Vietnam
174 E3 **Cairn Gorm** *mt.* U.K.
174 E3 **Cairngorm Mountains** U.K.
174 D4 **Cairngorms National Park** U.K.
174 C6 **Cairnryan** U.K.
119 E3 **Cairns** Australia
174 E3 **Cairn Toul** *mt.* U.K.
193 F1 **Cairo** Egypt (City Plan **102**)
219 C6 **Cairo** U.S.A.
184 C2 **Cairo Montenotte** Italy
195 B5 **Caiundo** Angola
125 F2 **Caiwarro (abandoned)** Australia
230 C5 **Cajamarca** Peru
161 I3 **Cajidiocan** Phil.
185 G1 **Čakovec** Croatia
138 B2 **Çal** Turkey
197 G5 **Cala** S. Africa
192 C4 **Calabar** Nigeria
209 I3 **Calabogie** Canada
233 K2 **Calabozo** Venez.
185 J3 **Calafat** Romania
232 B8 **Calafate** Arg.
161 I3 **Calagua Islands** Phil.
183 P1 **Calahorra** Spain
195 B5 **Calai** Angola
182 E1 **Calais** France
221 J2 **Calais** U.S.A.
225 G4 **Calakmul** *tourist site* Mex.
231 F5 **Calama** Brazil
232 C2 **Calama** Chile
233 I2 **Calamar** *Bolívar* Col.
233 I4 **Calamar** *Guaviare* Col.
161 H4 **Calamian Group** *is* Phil.
183 P2 **Calamocha** Spain
195 B4 **Calandula** Angola
161 I3 **Calapan** Phil.
185 L2 **Călărași** Romania
183 P2 **Calatayud** Spain
161 I3 **Calauag** Phil.
161 I3 **Calavite, Cape** Phil.
161 H3 **Calawit** *i.* Phil.
161 I2 **Calayan** *i.* Phil.
161 J3 **Calbayog** Phil.
179 J3 **Calbe (Saale)** Germany
161 J4 **Calbiga** Phil.
235 H4 **Calbuco** Chile
231 K5 **Calcanhar, Ponta do** *pt* Brazil
217 E6 **Calcasieu Lake** U.S.A.
231 H3 **Calçoene** Brazil
Calcutta India *see* **Kolkata**
183 L3 **Caldas da Rainha** Port.
234 C2 **Caldas Novas** Brazil
179 H3 **Calden** Germany
232 B3 **Caldera** Chile
123 D5 **Caldervale** Australia
139 I2 **Çaldıran** Turkey
213 C3 **Caldwell** U.S.A.
220 D3 **Caledon** Canada
197 G5 **Caledon** *r.* Lesotho/S. Africa
196 C7 **Caledon** S. Africa
122 B2 **Caledon Bay** Australia
209 H4 **Caledonia** Canada
208 B4 **Caledonia** U.S.A.
232 C7 **Caleta Olivia** Arg.
215 E5 **Calexico** U.S.A.
172 C3 **Calf of Man** *i.* U.K.
205 G4 **Calgary** Canada
219 C5 **Calhoun** U.S.A.
233 H4 **Cali** Col.
161 J4 **Calicoan** *i.* Phil.
147 G4 **Calicut** India
214 C4 **Caliente** *CA* U.S.A.
215 E3 **Caliente** *NV* U.S.A.
214 B3 **California** *state* U.S.A.
California, Golfo de *g.* Mex. *see* **California, Gulf of**
224 B2 **California, Gulf of** Mex.
214 B3 **California Aqueduct** *canal* U.S.A.
214 C4 **California Hot Springs** U.S.A.
139 L2 **Cälilabad** Azer.
213 D5 **Calipatria** U.S.A.
214 A2 **Calistoga** U.S.A.
196 D6 **Calitzdorp** S. Africa
225 G3 **Calkiní** Mex.
124 D2 **Callabonna, Lake** *salt flat* Australia
215 D2 **Callaghan, Mount** U.S.A.
219 D6 **Callahan** U.S.A.
175 K5 **Callan** Ireland
209 H2 **Callander** Canada
174 D4 **Callander** U.K.
230 C6 **Callao** Peru
215 F2 **Callao** U.S.A.
225 E3 **Calles** Mex.
221 F4 **Callicoon** U.S.A.
173 C7 **Callington** U.K.
123 E5 **Calliope** Australia
209 G2 **Callum** Canada
205 G4 **Calmar** Canada
208 B4 **Calmar** U.S.A.
215 E4 **Cal-Nev-Ari** U.S.A.
219 D7 **Caloosahatchee** *r.* U.S.A.
225 G3 **Calotmul** Mex.
125 J1 **Caloundra** Australia
214 B2 **Calpine** U.S.A.
225 E4 **Calpulálpan** Mex.
184 F6 **Caltanissetta** *Sicily* Italy
208 C2 **Calumet** U.S.A.
195 B5 **Calunga** Angola
195 B5 **Caluquembe** Angola
161 I4 **Calusa** *i.* Phil.
194 F2 **Caluula** Somalia
215 G5 **Calva** U.S.A.
122 B3 **Calvert Hills** Australia
204 D4 **Calvert Island** Canada
184 C3 **Calvi** *Corsica* France
183 R3 **Calvià** Spain
225 D3 **Calvillo** Mex.
196 C5 **Calvinia** S. Africa
184 F4 **Calvo, Monte** *mt.* Italy
173 H5 **Cam** *r.* U.K.
234 E1 **Camaçari** Brazil
214 B2 **Camache Reservoir** U.S.A.
225 D2 **Camacho** Mex.
195 B5 **Camacuio** Angola
195 B5 **Camacupa** Angola
233 K2 **Camaguán** Venez.
223 I4 **Camagüey** Cuba
223 I4 **Camagüey, Archipiélago de** *is* Cuba
163 B1 **Camah, Gunung** *mt.* Malaysia
Çamalan Turkey *see* **Gülek**
230 D7 **Camana** Peru
195 C5 **Camanongue** Angola
234 B2 **Camapuã** Brazil
235 M1 **Camaquã** Brazil
235 M1 **Camaquã** *r.* Brazil
138 E3 **Çamardı** Turkey
225 E2 **Camargo** Mex.
232 C6 **Camarones** Arg.
232 C6 **Camarones, Bahía** *b.* Arg.
212 B2 **Camas** U.S.A.
162 C3 **Ca Mau** Vietnam
162 C3 **Ca Mau, Mui** *c.* Vietnam
173 G6 **Camberley** U.K.
162 C2 **Cambodia** *country* Asia
173 B7 **Camborne** U.K.
182 F1 **Cambrai** France
214 B4 **Cambria** U.S.A.
173 D5 **Cambrian Mountains** U.K.
209 G4 **Cambridge** Canada
126 E2 **Cambridge** N.Z.
173 H5 **Cambridge** U.K.
208 B5 **Cambridge** *IL* U.S.A.
221 H3 **Cambridge** *MA* U.S.A.
221 E5 **Cambridge** *MD* U.S.A.
216 E2 **Cambridge** *MN* U.S.A.
221 G3 **Cambridge** *NY* U.S.A.
220 C4 **Cambridge** *OH* U.S.A.
207 G2 **Cambrien, Lac** *l.* Canada
196 F6 **Camdeboo National Park** S. Africa
125 I5 **Camden** Australia
219 C5 **Camden** *AL* U.S.A.
217 E5 **Camden** *AR* U.S.A.
221 I2 **Camden** *ME* U.S.A.
221 F5 **Camden** *NJ* U.S.A.
221 F3 **Camden** *NY* U.S.A.
219 D5 **Camden** *SC* U.S.A.
232 B8 **Camden, Isla** *i.* Chile
195 C5 **Cameia, Parque Nacional da** *nat. park* Angola
215 G4 **Cameron** *AZ* U.S.A.
217 E6 **Cameron** *LA* U.S.A.
217 E4 **Cameron** *MO* U.S.A.
217 D6 **Cameron** *TX* U.S.A.
208 B3 **Cameron** *WI* U.S.A.
204 F3 **Cameron Hills** Canada
214 B2 **Cameron Park** U.S.A.
193 D4 **Cameroon** *country* Africa
193 D4 **Cameroon Highlands** *slope* Cameroon/Nigeria
192 C4 **Cameroun, Mont** *vol.* Cameroon
231 I4 **Cametá** Brazil
161 I2 **Camiguin** *i.* Phil.
161 J4 **Camiguin** *i.* Phil.
161 I3 **Camiling** Phil.
219 C6 **Camilla** U.S.A.
231 F8 **Camiri** Bol.
231 J4 **Camocim** Brazil
118 D3 **Camooweal** Australia
123 B4 **Camooweal Caves National Park** Australia
145 H10 **Camorta** *i.* India
161 J4 **Camotes Sea** *g.* Phil.
235 K2 **Campana** Arg.
233 I4 **Campana, Cerro** *h.* Col.
232 A7 **Campana, Isla** *i.* Chile
235 H2 **Campanario** *mt.* Arg./Chile
204 D4 **Campania Island** Canada
197 E4 **Campbell** S. Africa
126 E4 **Campbell, Cape** N.Z.
121 E4 **Campbell, Mount** *h.* Australia
117 F7 **Campbell Island** N.Z.
236 G9 **Campbell Plateau** *sea feature* S. Pacific Ocean
120 D2 **Campbell Range** *hills* Australia
204 D4 **Campbell River** Canada
209 I3 **Campbell's Bay** Canada
219 C4 **Campbellsville** U.S.A.
207 G4 **Campbellton** Canada
125 G8 **Campbell Town** Australia
174 C5 **Campbeltown** U.K.
225 G4 **Campeche** Mex.
225 G4 **Campeche** *state* Mex.
225 F4 **Campeche, Bahía de** *g.* Mex.
125 E7 **Camperdown** Australia
185 K2 **Câmpina** Romania
231 K5 **Campina Grande** Brazil
234 C3 **Campinas** Brazil
234 C2 **Campina Verde** Brazil
192 C4 **Campo** Cameroon
233 I4 **Campoalegre** Col.
184 F4 **Campobasso** Italy
234 D3 **Campo Belo** Brazil
231 H6 **Campo de Diauarum** Brazil
234 C2 **Campo Florido** Brazil
232 D3 **Campo Gallo** Arg.
234 A3 **Campo Grande** Brazil
231 J4 **Campo Maior** Brazil
183 M3 **Campo Maior** Port.
233 J2 **Campo Mara** Venez.
235 B4 **Campo Mourão** Brazil
234 E3 **Campos** Brazil
234 C2 **Campos Altos** Brazil
234 D3 **Campos do Jordão** Brazil
174 D4 **Campsie Fells** *hills* U.K.
220 B6 **Campton** *KY* U.S.A.
221 H3 **Campton** *NH* U.S.A.
185 K2 **Câmpulung** Romania
177 L7 **Câmpulung Moldovenesc** Romania
215 G4 **Camp Verde** U.S.A.
Cam Ranh Vietnam *see* **Ba Ngoi**
205 G4 **Camrose** Canada
173 B6 **Camrose** U.K.
205 G2 **Camsell Lake** Canada
205 H3 **Camsell Portage** Canada
187 C7 **Çan** Turkey
163 D3 **Ca Na, Mui** *hd* Vietnam
221 G3 **Canaan** U.S.A.
202 G3 **Canada** *country* N. America
240 O1 **Canada Basin** *sea feature* Arctic Ocean
235 K2 **Cañada de Gómez** Arg.
221 H2 **Canada Falls Lake** U.S.A.
217 C5 **Canadian** *r.* U.S.A.
233 L3 **Canaima, Parque Nacional** *nat. park* Venez.
221 F3 **Canajoharie** U.S.A.
187 C7 **Çanakkale** Turkey
Çanakkale Boğazı *str.* Turkey *see* **Dardanelles**
235 I2 **Canalejas** Arg.
221 E3 **Canandaigua** U.S.A.
221 E3 **Canandaigua Lake** U.S.A.
222 B2 **Cananea** Mex.
235 C4 **Cananéia** Brazil
233 J4 **Canapiare, Cerro** *h.* Col.
230 C4 **Cañar** Ecuador
Canarias, Islas *terr.* N. Atlantic Ocean *see* **Canary Islands**
192 A2 **Canary Islands** *terr.* N. Atlantic Ocean
221 F3 **Canastota** U.S.A.
234 C2 **Canastra, Serra da** *mts* Brazil
224 C2 **Canatlán** Mex.
219 D6 **Canaveral, Cape** U.S.A.
183 O2 **Cañaveras** Spain
234 E1 **Canavieiras** Brazil
125 G3 **Canbelego** Australia
125 H5 **Canberra** Australia
213 B3 **Canby** *CA* U.S.A.
216 D2 **Canby** *MN* U.S.A.
225 H3 **Cancún** Mex.
225 G4 **Candelaria** *Campeche* Mex.
213 F6 **Candelaria** *Chihuahua* Mex.
225 E5 **Candelaria Loxicha** Mex.
183 N2 **Candeleda** Spain
125 H6 **Candelo** Australia
231 I4 **Cândido Mendes** Brazil
138 D1 **Çandır** Turkey
205 H4 **Candle Lake** Canada
205 H4 **Candle Lake** *l.* Canada
229 G7 **Candlemas Island** S. Sandwich Is
221 G4 **Candlewood, Lake** U.S.A.
216 D1 **Cando** U.S.A.
161 I2 **Candon** Phil.
121 A4 **Cane** *r.* Australia
235 H1 **Canela Baja** Chile
235 L2 **Canelones** Uruguay
235 H3 **Cañete** Chile
183 P2 **Cañete** Spain
230 D6 **Cangallo** Peru
195 B5 **Cangamba** Angola
183 M1 **Cangas del Narcea** Spain
197 E6 **Cango Caves** S. Africa
231 K5 **Canguaretama** Brazil
235 M1 **Canguçu** Brazil
235 M1 **Canguçu, Serra do** *hills* Brazil
155 D6 **Cangwu** China
154 E2 **Cangzhou** China
207 G3 **Caniapiscau** Canada
207 G2 **Caniapiscau** *r.* Canada
207 G3 **Caniapiscau, Lac** Canada
203 K4 **Caniapiscau, Réservoir de** *l.* Canada
184 E6 **Canicattì** *Sicily* Italy
204 E4 **Canim Lake** Canada
204 E4 **Canim Lake** *l.* Canada
231 K4 **Canindé** Brazil
231 J5 **Canindé** *r.* Brazil
174 C2 **Canisp** *h.* U.K.
221 E3 **Canisteo** U.S.A.
221 E3 **Canisteo** *r.* U.S.A.
225 D3 **Cañitas de Felipe Pescador** Mex.
138 D1 **Çankırı** Turkey
161 I4 **Canlaon** Phil.
204 F4 **Canmore** Canada
121 A6 **Canna** Australia
174 B3 **Canna** *i.* U.K.
147 G4 **Cannanore** India
147 G4 **Cannanore Islands** India
183 H5 **Cannes** France
173 E5 **Cannock** U.K.
125 H6 **Cann River** Australia
232 F3 **Canoas** Brazil
205 H3 **Canoe Lake** Canada
235 B4 **Canoinhas** Brazil
213 F4 **Canon City** U.S.A.
123 E4 **Canoona** Australia
124 D4 **Canopus** Australia
205 I4 **Canora** Canada
125 H4 **Canowindra** Australia
207 H4 **Canso, Cape** Canada
183 N1 **Cantábrica, Cordillera** *mts* Spain

263

Dodecanese

185 L6 Dodecanese is Greece
Dodekanisa is Greece see Dodecanese
212 C2 Dodge U.S.A.
208 A3 Dodge Center U.S.A.
217 C4 Dodge City U.S.A.
125 G9 Dodges Ferry Australia
208 B4 Dodgeville U.S.A.
173 C7 Dodman Point U.K.
195 D4 Dodoma Tanz.
179 E3 Doetinchem Neth.
151 E7 Dofa Indon.
149 G2 Dogai Coring salt l. China
149 G2 Dogaicoring Qangco salt l. China
139 F2 Doğanşehir Turkey
204 E4 Dog Creek Canada
149 G3 Dogên Co l. China
207 H2 Dog Island Canada
205 J4 Dog Lake Canada
209 E1 Dog Lake Canada
159 C6 Dōgo i. Japan
192 C3 Dogondoutchi Niger
159 C7 Dōgo-yama mt. Japan
139 J2 Doğubeyazıt Turkey
136 C3 Doğu Menteşe Dağları mts Turkey
149 F3 Dogxung Zangbo r. China
149 G3 Do'gyaling China
142 C5 Doha Qatar
149 H5 Dohazari Bangl.
Doilungdêqên China see Namka
162 A1 Doi Saket Thai.
231 J5 Dois Irmãos, Serra dos hills Brazil
185 J4 Dojran, Lake Greece/Macedonia
139 J4 Dokan, Sadd Iraq
180 E5 Dokhara, Dunes de des. Alg.
171 J3 Dokka Norway
179 E1 Dokkum Neth.
148 B4 Dokri Pak.
Dokshukino Rus. Fed. see Nartkala
177 M3 Dokshytsy Belarus
156 G3 Dokuchayeva, Mys c. Rus. Fed.
187 F6 Dokuchayevs'k Ukr.
207 F4 Dolbeau-Mistassini Canada
173 C5 Dolbenmaen U.K.
182 D2 Dol-de-Bretagne France
182 G3 Dole France
173 D5 Dolgellau U.K.
179 L1 Dolgen Germany
221 F3 Dolgeville U.S.A.
187 F4 Dolgorukovo Rus. Fed.
187 F4 Dolgoye Rus. Fed.
184 C5 Dolianova Sardinia Italy
150 G2 Dolinsk Rus. Fed.
Dolisie Congo see Loubomo
179 J6 Dollnstein Germany
141 G1 Dolmatovo Kazakh.
151 F7 Dolok, Pulau i. Indon.
184 D1 Dolomites mts Italy
154 E1 Dolonnur China
194 E3 Dolo Odo Eth.
235 L3 Dolores Arg.
225 G4 Dolores Guat.
224 B2 Dolores Mex.
235 K2 Dolores Uruguay
215 H2 Dolores r. U.S.A.
225 D3 Dolores Hidalgo Mex.
202 G3 Dolphin and Union Strait Canada
155 B7 Đô Lương Vietnam
187 B5 Dolyna Ukr.
138 B2 Domaniç Turkey
149 E2 Domar China
149 H3 Domartang China
176 F6 Domažlice Czech Rep.
149 H2 Domba China
142 B3 Dom Bākh Iran
140 D2 Dombarovskiy Rus. Fed.
171 J3 Dombås Norway
177 I7 Dombóvár Hungary
Domda China see Qingshuihe
Dome Circe ice feature Antarctica see Charlie, Dome
204 E4 Dome Creek Canada
127 K4 Dome Fuji research stn Antarctica
204 D2 Dome Peak Canada
215 E5 Dome Rock Mountains U.S.A.
182 D2 Domfront France
223 L5 Dominica country Caribbean Sea
224 I6 Dominical Costa Rica
223 J5 Dominican Republic country Caribbean Sea
179 J1 Dömitz Germany
162 C2 Dom Noi, Lam r. Thai.
184 C1 Domodossola Italy
185 J5 Domokos Greece
235 L1 Dom Pedrito Brazil
163 I4 Dompu Indon.
235 H3 Domuyo, Volcán vol. Arg.
125 I2 Domville, Mount h. Australia
147 H2 Don r. India
224 B2 Don Mex.
187 G5 Don r. Rus. Fed.
175 F3 Don r. U.K.
162 C2 Don, Xé r. Laos
175 M3 Donaghadee U.K.
175 L3 Donaghmore U.K.
125 E6 Donald Australia
176 G6 Donau r. Austria/Germany alt. Duna (Hungary), alt. Dunaj (Slovakia), alt. Dunărea (Romania), alt. Dunav (Bulgaria/Serbia), conv. Danube
176 D7 Donaueschingen Germany
176 E6 Donauwörth Germany
183 N3 Don Benito Spain
173 F4 Doncaster U.K.
195 B4 Dondo Angola
195 D5 Dondo Moz.
161 I4 Dondonay i. Phil.
147 I5 Dondra Head Sri Lanka
175 J3 Donegal Ireland
175 J3 Donegal Bay Ireland
187 F6 Donets'k Ukr.
187 F5 Donets'kyy Kryazh hills Rus. Fed./Ukr.
155 D5 Dong'an China
118 B4 Dongara Australia
149 E5 Dongargarh India
150 E2 Dongbei reg. China
Dongbo China see Mêdog
155 B5 Dongchuan China
149 F2 Dongco China
155 C7 Dongfang China
158 C1 Dongfanghong China
160 C2 Dongfeng China
163 I3 Donggala Indon.
154 F3 Donggang China
160 C4 Donggang China
155 E5 Donggu China
155 D6 Dongguan China
162 C1 Đông Ha Vietnam
154 F3 Donghai China
155 D6 Donghai Dao i. China
154 C3 Dong He r. China
154 A1 Dong He watercourse China
162 C1 Đông Hơi Vietnam
160 E1 Dongjingcheng China
149 H3 Dongjug Xizang China
149 H3 Dongjug Xizang China
155 D5 Dongkou China
149 G4 Dongkya La pass India
155 C5 Donglan China
154 A2 Dongle China
160 C2 Dongliao He r. China
160 B1 Dongminzhutun China
161 F2 Dongning China
195 B5 Dongo Angola
194 B3 Dongou Congo
162 B2 Dong Phraya Yen esc. Thai.
155 D6 Dongping Guangdong China
Dongping China see Zhoucheng
149 G3 Dongqiao China
155 E6 Dongshan China
155 E6 Dongshan Dao i. China
Dongsheng China see Ordos
154 F3 Dongtai China
154 F3 Dongtai He r. China
155 D4 Dongting Hu l. China
155 F5 Dongtou China
155 E4 Dongxiang China
154 B3 Dongxiangzu China
156 B3 Dongxing China
155 F4 Dongyang China
154 F2 Dongying China
154 B2 Dongzhen China
155 E4 Dongzhi China
204 B2 Donjek r. Canada
179 E1 Donkerbroek Neth.
149 G5 Donmanick Islands Bangl.
207 F4 Donnacona Canada
204 F3 Donnelly Canada
126 D1 Donnellys Crossing N.Z.
214 B2 Donner Pass U.S.A.
183 P1 Donostia-San Sebastián Spain
185 K6 Donousa i. Greece
187 F4 Donskoy Rus. Fed.
187 G6 Donskoye Rus. Fed.
161 I3 Donsol Phil.
140 D3 Donyztau, Sor dry lake Kazakh.
175 H4 Dooagh Ireland
122 B3 Doomadgee Australia
174 D5 Doon, Loch l. U.K.
175 I5 Doonbeg r. Ireland
178 D2 Doorn Neth.
208 D3 Door Peninsula U.S.A.
178 D3 Doorwerth Neth.
194 E3 Dooxo Nugaaleed val. Somalia
143 F4 Dor watercourse Afgh.
217 C5 Dora U.S.A.
121 C4 Dora, Lake salt flat Australia
184 C2 Dora Baltea r. Italy
142 C5 Do Rāhak Iran
173 E7 Dorchester U.K.
195 B6 Dordabis Namibia
182 E4 Dordogne r. France
178 C3 Dordrecht Neth.
197 G5 Dordrecht S. Africa
196 C1 Doreenville Namibia
205 H4 Doré Lake Canada
205 H4 Doré Lake l. Canada
184 C4 Dorgali Sardinia Italy
149 H2 Dorgê Co l. China
143 G4 Dori r. Afgh.
192 B3 Dori Burkina
196 C5 Doring r. S. Africa
120 E2 Dorisvale Australia
173 G6 Dorking U.K.
179 E3 Dormagen Germany
178 B5 Dormans France
156 D3 Dormidontovka Rus. Fed.
174 D3 Dornoch Firth est. U.K.
154 C1 Dornogovĭ prov. Mongolia
179 F1 Dornum Germany
187 E4 Dorogobuzh Rus. Fed.
177 M7 Dorohoi Romania
150 B2 Döröö Nuur salt l. Mongolia
170 L2 Dorotea Sweden
118 B4 Dorre Island Australia
125 J3 Dorrigo Australia
213 B3 Dorris U.S.A.
209 H3 Dorset Canada
173 D7 Dorset and East Devon Coast tourist site U.K.
179 F3 Dortmund Germany
220 B6 Dorton U.S.A.
139 F3 Dörtyol Turkey
179 G1 Dorum Germany
194 C3 Doruma Dem. Rep. Congo
143 E3 Dorūneh Iran
179 H2 Dörverden Germany
143 E4 Do Sārī Iran
232 C6 Dos Bahías, Cabo c. Arg.
215 H5 Dos Cabezas U.S.A.
230 C5 Dos de Mayo Peru
Đo Son Vietnam see Đồ Sơn
155 C6 Đồ Sơn Vietnam
214 B3 Dos Palos U.S.A.
179 K2 Dosse r. Germany
192 C3 Dosso Niger
140 C3 Dossor Kazakh.
141 G4 Do'stlik Uzbek.
141 J3 Dostyk Kazakh.
219 C6 Dothan U.S.A.
182 F1 Douai France
192 C4 Douala Cameroon
182 B2 Douarnenez France
155 □ Double Island Hong Kong China
123 F5 Double Island Point Australia
214 C4 Double Peak U.S.A.
122 D3 Double Point Australia
182 H3 Doubs r. France
126 A6 Doubtful Sound inlet N.Z.
126 D1 Doubtless Bay N.Z.
192 B3 Douentza Mali
172 C3 Douglas Isle of Man
197 E4 Douglas S. Africa
175 F5 Douglas U.K.
204 C3 Douglas AK U.S.A.
215 H6 Douglas AZ U.S.A.
219 D6 Douglas GA U.S.A.
213 F3 Douglas WY U.S.A.
125 H8 Douglas Apsley National Park Australia
204 D4 Douglas Channel Canada
215 H2 Douglas Creek r. U.S.A.
182 F1 Doullens France
174 D4 Doune U.K.
234 C2 Dourada, Cachoeira waterfall Brazil
234 B2 Dourada, Serra hills Brazil
234 C1 Dourada, Serra mts Brazil
234 A3 Dourados Brazil
234 A3 Dourados r. Brazil
234 B3 Dourados, Serra dos hills Brazil
183 M2 Douro r. Port. alt. Duero (Spain)
178 D5 Douzy France
173 F4 Dove r. England U.K.
173 I5 Dove r. England U.K.
207 I3 Dove Brook Canada
215 H3 Dove Creek U.S.A.
125 G9 Dover Australia
173 I6 Dover U.K.
221 F5 Dover DE U.S.A.
221 H3 Dover NH U.S.A.
221 F4 Dover NJ U.S.A.
220 C4 Dover OH U.S.A.
173 I7 Dover, Strait of France/U.K.
221 I2 Dover-Foxcroft U.S.A.
173 D5 Dovey r. U.K.
142 B3 Doveyrīch, Rūd-e r. Iran/Iraq
208 D5 Dowagiac U.S.A.
142 D4 Dow Chāhī Iran
143 E3 Dowgha'ī Iran
162 A5 Dowi, Tanjung pt Indon.
143 F3 Dowlatābād Afgh.
143 G2 Dowlatābād Afgh.
142 D4 Dowlatābād Iran
142 D4 Dowlatābād Iran
143 E4 Dowlatābād Iran
143 F2 Dowlatābād Iran
143 G3 Dowl at Yār Afgh.
214 B2 Downieville U.S.A.
175 M3 Downpatrick U.K.
221 F3 Downsville U.S.A.
142 C3 Dow Rūd Iran
139 K4 Dow Sar Iran
143 H3 Dowshī Afgh.
214 B1 Doyle U.S.A.
221 F4 Doylestown U.S.A.
159 C6 Dōzen is Japan
209 I2 Dozois, Réservoir resr Canada
192 B2 Drâa, Hamada du plat. Alg.
234 B3 Dracena Brazil
179 E1 Drachten Neth.
185 K2 Drăgănești-Olt Romania
185 K2 Drăgășani Romania
233 L2 Dragon's Mouths str. Trin. and Tob./Venez.
171 M3 Dragsfjärd Fin.
184 B3 Draguignan France
187 C4 Drahichyn Belarus
125 J2 Drake Australia
215 F4 Drake AZ U.S.A.
205 I5 Drake ND U.S.A.
197 H5 Drakensberg mts Lesotho/S. Africa
197 I2 Drakensberg mts S. Africa
239 E9 Drake Passage sea chan. S. Atlantic Ocean
185 K4 Drama Greece
171 J4 Drammen Norway
171 J4 Drangedal Norway
143 G5 Dranjuk h. Pak.
179 H3 Dransfeld Germany
175 L3 Draperstown U.K.
148 C2 Dras India
176 F7 Drau r. Austria
185 H2 Drava r. Europe
Drave r. Europe see Drava
205 G4 Drayton Valley Canada
184 B6 Dréan Alg.
179 H4 Dreistelzberge h. Germany
176 F5 Dresden Germany
187 D4 Dretun' Belarus
182 E2 Dreux France
171 K3 Drevsjø Norway
172 G3 Driffield U.K.
220 D4 Driftwood U.S.A.
175 I6 Drimoleague Ireland
185 G3 Drniš Croatia
185 J2 Drobeta-Turnu Severin Romania
179 H1 Drochtersen Germany
175 L4 Drogheda Ireland
187 B5 Drohobych Ukr.
173 E5 Droitwich Spa U.K.
147 G4 Drokung India
179 I2 Drömling reg. Germany
175 K4 Dromod Ireland
175 K3 Dromore Northern Ireland U.K.
175 L3 Dromore Northern Ireland U.K.
173 F4 Dronfield U.K.
203 P2 Dronning Louise Land reg. Greenland
178 D2 Dronten Neth.
148 B2 Drosh Pak.
187 F4 Droskovo Rus. Fed.
125 F7 Drouin Australia
205 G4 Drumheller Canada
212 D2 Drummond MT U.S.A.
208 B2 Drummond WI U.S.A.
209 F3 Drummond Island U.S.A.
123 D5 Drummond Range hills Australia
207 F4 Drummondville Canada
174 D6 Drummore U.K.
174 D4 Drumochter, Pass of U.K.
171 N5 Druskininkai Lith.
133 P3 Druzhina Rus. Fed.
120 F2 Dry r. Australia
185 K3 Dryanovo Bulg.
204 B3 Dry Bay U.S.A.
205 K5 Dryberry Lake Canada
209 E2 Dryburg U.S.A.
205 K5 Dryden Canada
215 D2 Dry Lake U.S.A.
174 D4 Drymen U.K.
118 C3 Drysdale r. Australia
120 D2 Drysdale River National Park Australia
142 C3 Dūāb r. Iran
155 C6 Du'an China
221 F2 Duane U.S.A.
123 E4 Duaringa Australia
149 G4 Duars reg. India
223 J5 Duarte, Pico mt. Dom. Rep.
134 B4 Ḍubā Saudi Arabia
147 E4 Dubai U.A.E.
177 N7 Dubăsari Moldova
205 I2 Dubawnt r. Canada
205 I2 Dubawnt Lake Canada
Dubayy U.A.E. see Dubai
134 B4 Dubbagh, Jabal ad mt. Saudi Arabia
125 H4 Dubbo Australia
141 J4 Dubin Kazakh.
208 D1 Dublin Canada
175 L4 Dublin Ireland
219 D5 Dublin U.S.A.
186 F3 Dubna Rus. Fed.
187 C5 Dubno Ukr.
212 D2 Dubois ID U.S.A.
213 E3 Dubois WY U.S.A.
220 D4 Du Bois U.S.A.
187 H5 Dubovka Rus. Fed.
187 G6 Dubovskoye Rus. Fed.
192 A4 Dubréka Guinea
185 H3 Dubrovnik Croatia
187 C5 Dubrovytsya Ukr.
187 D4 Dubrowna Belarus
208 B4 Dubuque U.S.A.
171 M5 Dubysa r. Lith.
162 C3 Đưc Bôn Vietnam
117 J6 Duc de Gloucester, Îles du is Fr. Polynesia
155 E4 Duchang China
215 G1 Duchesne U.S.A.
123 B4 Duchess Australia
117 J7 Ducie Island atoll Pitcairn Is
219 C5 Duck r. U.S.A.
205 I4 Duck Bay Canada
121 B4 Duck Creek r. Australia
205 H4 Duck Lake Canada
209 E4 Duck Lake U.S.A.
215 E2 Duckwater U.S.A.
215 E2 Duckwater Peak U.S.A.
162 C3 Đưc Linh Vietnam
163 D2 Đưc Phô Vietnam
Đưc Pho Vietnam see Đưc Phô
162 C1 Đưc Tho Vietnam
Đưc Trong Vietnam see Liên Nghia
233 I4 Duda r. Col.
179 E5 Dudelange Lux.
179 I3 Duderstadt Germany
149 E4 Dudhi India
149 G4 Dudhnai India
133 J3 Dudinka Rus. Fed.
173 E5 Dudley U.K.
148 D6 Dudna r. India
175 F3 Dudwick, Hill of U.K.
192 B4 Duékoué Côte d'Ivoire
183 M2 Duero r. Spain alt. Douro (Portugal)
209 H1 Dufault, Lac l. Canada
178 C3 Duffel Belgium
206 E2 Dufferin, Cape Canada
220 B6 Duffield U.S.A.
119 G2 Duff Islands Solomon Is
174 E3 Dufftown U.K.
184 B2 Dufourspitze mt. Italy/Switz.
206 E1 Dufrost, Pointe Canada
Dugab Uzbek. see Dugob
184 F3 Dugi Otok i. Croatia
141 F5 Dugob Uzbek.
154 C2 Dugui Qarag China
154 D3 Du He r. China
233 K4 Duida, Cerro mt. Venez.
230 E3 Duida-Marahuaca, Parque Nacional Venez.
179 E3 Duisburg Germany
233 I3 Duitama Col.
197 I1 Duiwelskloof S. Africa
155 B4 Dujiangyan China
197 G5 Dukathole S. Africa
204 C4 Duke Island U.S.A.
142 C5 Dukhān Qatar
177 P3 Dukhovshchina Rus. Fed.
148 B3 Duki Pak.
156 D2 Duki Rus. Fed.
156 D2 Duki r. Rus. Fed.
171 N5 Dūkštas Lith.
143 E4 Dūlab Iran
150 B3 Dulan China
232 D3 Dulce r. Arg.
224 I6 Dulce, Golfo b. Costa Rica
224 H5 Dulce Nombre de Culmí Hond.
153 J1 Dul'durga Rus. Fed.
122 C1 Dulhunty r. Australia
149 E2 Dulishi Hu salt l. China
197 I2 Dullstroom S. Africa
179 F3 Dülmen Germany
185 L3 Dulovo Bulg.
208 A2 Duluth U.S.A.
208 A2 Duluth/Superior airport U.S.A.
173 D6 Dulverton U.K.
139 F5 Dūmā Syria
161 I4 Dumaguete Phil.
163 B2 Dumai Indon.
161 I4 Dumaran i. Phil.
217 F5 Dumas AR U.S.A.
217 C5 Dumas TX U.S.A.
139 F5 Ḍumayr Syria
174 D5 Dumbarton U.K.
197 I3 Dumbe S. Africa
177 I6 Ďumbier mt. Slovakia
148 D2 Dumchele India
149 G5 Dum-Dum India
149 H4 Dum Duma India
174 E5 Dumfries U.K.
149 F4 Dumka India
179 G2 Dümmer l. Germany
206 E4 Dumoine, Lac Canada
127 J6 Dumont d'Urville research stn Antarctica
127 J6 Dumont d'Urville Sea Antarctica
179 E4 Dümpelfeld Germany
193 F1 Dumyāṭ Egypt
179 I3 Dün ridge Germany
185 H1 Duna r. Hungary alt. Donau (Austria/Germany), alt. Dunaj (Slovakia), alt. Dunărea (Romania), alt. Dunav (Bulgaria/Serbia), conv. Danube
185 L3 Dunaj r. Slovakia alt. Donau (Austria/Germany), alt. Duna (Hungary), alt. Dunărea (Romania), alt. Dunav (Bulgaria/Serbia), conv. Danube
177 H7 Dunajská Streda Slovakia
177 I7 Dunakeszi Hungary
125 G9 Dunalley Australia
175 L4 Dunany Point Ireland
185 L3 Dunărea r. Romania alt. Donau (Austria/Germany), alt. Duna (Hungary), alt. Dunaj (Slovakia), alt. Dunav (Bulgaria/Serbia), conv. Danube
177 I7 Dunaújváros Hungary
185 L3 Dunav r. Bulgaria/Serbia alt. Donau (Austria/Germany), alt. Duna (Hungary), alt. Dunaj (Slovakia), alt. Dunărea (Romania), conv. Danube
187 C5 Dunayivtsi Ukr.
126 C6 Dunback N.Z.
122 C3 Dunbar Australia
175 F4 Dunbar U.K.
174 E4 Dunblane U.K.
175 L4 Dunboyne Ireland
204 E5 Duncan Canada
215 H5 Duncan AZ U.S.A.
217 D5 Duncan OK U.S.A.
206 D3 Duncan, Cape Canada
206 E3 Duncan, Lac l. Canada

Elbeuf

182 E2 Elbeuf France
139 F2 Elbistan Turkey
177 I3 Elbląg Poland
235 H4 El Bolsón Arg.
219 E7 Elbow Cay i. Bahamas
187 G7 El'brus mt. Rus. Fed.
178 D2 Elburg Neth.
183 O2 El Burgo de Osma Spain
142 C2 Elburz Mountains Iran
235 I4 El Cain Arg.
215 D5 El Cajon U.S.A.
233 L3 El Callao Venez.
217 D6 El Campo U.S.A.
213 F5 El Capitan Mountain U.S.A.
215 E5 El Centro U.S.A.
231 F7 El Cerro Bol.
233 K2 El Chaparro Venez.
Elche Spain see Elche-Elx
183 P3 Elche-Elx Spain
225 F4 El Chichónal vol. Mex.
224 C1 El Chilicote Mex.
118 D3 Elcho Island Australia
233 I3 El Cocuy Col.
233 I3 El Cocuy, Parque Nacional nat. park Col.
225 H3 El Cuyo Mex.
183 P3 Elda Spain
209 H2 Eldee Canada
124 D3 Elder, Lake Australia
225 D2 El Diamante Mex.
233 I2 El Difícil Col.
133 O3 El'dikan Rus. Fed.
233 H4 El Diviso Col.
215 E6 El Doctor Mex.
208 A5 Eldon IA U.S.A.
217 E4 Eldon MO U.S.A.
232 F3 Eldorado Arg.
224 C2 El Dorado Mex.
217 E5 El Dorado AR U.S.A.
217 D4 El Dorado KS U.S.A.
217 C6 Eldorado U.S.A.
233 L3 El Dorado Venez.
194 D3 Eldoret Kenya
212 E2 Electric Peak U.S.A.
192 B2 El Eglab plat. Alg.
183 O4 El Ejido Spain
230 D4 El Encanto Col.
179 I3 Elend Germany
147 G2 Elephanta Caves tourist site India
213 F5 Elephant Butte Reservoir U.S.A.
127 I2 Elephant Island Antarctica
149 H5 Elephant Point Bangl.
139 I2 Eleşkirt Turkey
225 G5 El Estor Guat.
192 C1 El Eulma Alg.
219 E7 Eleuthera i. Bahamas
184 C6 El Fahs Tunisia
193 E3 El Fasher Sudan
179 H4 Elfershausen Germany
224 B2 El Fuerte Mex.
El Gara Egypt see Qārah
193 E3 El Geneina Sudan
193 F3 El Geteina Sudan
174 E3 Elgin U.K.
208 C4 Elgin IL U.S.A.
216 C2 Elgin ND U.S.A.
215 E3 Elgin NV U.S.A.
215 G2 Elgin UT U.S.A.
133 P3 El'ginskiy Rus. Fed.
225 D3 El Gogorrón, Parque Nacional nat. park Mex.
192 C1 El Goléa Alg.
193 F4 Elgon, Mount Uganda
184 B6 El Hadjar Alg.
El Ḩarra Egypt see Al Ḩarrah
224 I6 El Hato del Volcán Panama
El Ḩeiz Egypt see Al Ḩayz
192 A2 El Hierro i. Canary Is
225 E3 El Higo Mex.
192 C2 El Homr Alg.
175 F4 Elie U.K.
126 C5 Elie de Beaumont mt. N.Z.
202 B3 Elim U.S.A.
207 H2 Eliot, Mount Canada
187 H6 Elista Rus. Fed.
208 B4 Elizabeth IL U.S.A.
221 F4 Elizabeth NJ U.S.A.
220 C5 Elizabeth WV U.S.A.
120 D3 Elizabeth, Mount h. Australia
219 E4 Elizabeth City U.S.A.
221 H4 Elizabeth Islands U.S.A.
219 D4 Elizabethton U.S.A.
219 C4 Elizabethtown KY U.S.A.
219 E5 Elizabethtown NC U.S.A.
221 G2 Elizabethtown NY U.S.A.
221 E4 Elizabethtown PA U.S.A.
183 P1 Elizondo Spain
192 B1 El Jadida Morocco
224 C2 El Jaralito Mex.
184 D7 El Jem Tunisia
224 H5 El Jicaral Nicaragua
205 G4 Elk r. Canada
177 K4 Ełk Poland
214 A2 Elk U.S.A.
220 C5 Elk r. U.S.A.
184 C6 El Kala Alg.
193 F3 El Kamlin Sudan
217 D5 Elk City U.S.A.
214 A2 Elk Creek U.S.A.
123 A4 Elkedra Australia
123 B4 Elkedra watercourse Australia
214 B2 Elk Grove U.S.A.
209 E5 Elkhart U.S.A.
192 B2 El Khnâchîch esc. Mali
208 C4 Elkhorn U.S.A.
216 D3 Elkhorn r. U.S.A.
185 L3 Elkhovo Bulg.
220 D5 Elkins U.S.A.
205 G4 Elk Island National Park Canada
209 G2 Elk Lake Canada
209 E3 Elk Lake l. U.S.A.
221 E4 Elkland U.S.A.
204 F5 Elko Canada
213 D3 Elko U.S.A.
205 G4 Elk Point Canada
216 E2 Elk River U.S.A.
221 F5 Elkton MD U.S.A.
220 D5 Elkton VA U.S.A.
205 L2 Ell Bay Canada
203 H2 Ellef Ringnes Island Canada
215 G2 Ellen, Mount U.S.A.
148 C3 Ellenabad India
216 D2 Ellendale U.S.A.
212 B2 Ellensburg U.S.A.
221 F4 Ellenville U.S.A.
125 H6 Ellery, Mount Australia
126 D5 Ellesmere, Lake N.Z.
203 J2 Ellesmere Island Canada
173 E4 Ellesmere Port U.K.
203 H3 Ellice r. Canada
220 D3 Ellicottville U.S.A.
225 E3 El Limón Mex.
179 I5 Ellingen Germany
197 G5 Elliot S. Africa
122 D3 Elliot, Mount Australia
197 H5 Elliotdale S. Africa
209 F2 Elliot Lake Canada
120 F3 Elliott Australia
212 D2 Ellis U.S.A.
Ellisras S. Africa see Lephalale
124 A4 Elliston Australia
175 F3 Ellon U.K.
148 C5 Ellora Caves tourist site India
221 I2 Ellsworth ME U.S.A.
208 A3 Ellsworth WI U.S.A.
127 I3 Ellsworth Land reg. Antarctica
127 I3 Ellsworth Mountains Antarctica
179 I6 Ellwangen (Jagst) Germany
138 B3 Elmalı Turkey
215 D6 El Maneadero Mex.
233 L3 El Manteco Venez.
El Maţarîya Egypt see Al Maţarīyah
192 C1 El Meghaïer Alg.
233 L3 El Miamo Venez.
180 E4 El Milia Alg.
El Mîna Lebanon see El Mina
138 E4 El Mîna Lebanon
209 E3 Elmira MI U.S.A.
221 E3 Elmira NY U.S.A.
215 F5 El Mirage U.S.A.
183 O4 El Moral Spain
125 F6 Elmore Australia
235 J2 El Morro mt. Arg.
192 B2 El Mreyyé reg. Mauritania
179 H1 Elmshorn Germany
193 E3 El Muglad Sudan
209 G3 Elmwood Canada
208 C5 Elmwood IL U.S.A.
208 A3 Elmwood WI U.S.A.
171 I3 Elnesvågen Norway
233 I3 El Nevado, Cerro mt. Col.
161 H4 El Nido Phil.
193 F3 El Obeid Sudan
225 D2 El Oro Mex.
233 J3 Elorza Venez.
192 C1 El Oued Alg.
215 G5 Eloy U.S.A.
224 C2 El Palmito Mex.
233 L2 El Pao Bolívar Venez.
233 J2 El Pao Cojedes Venez.
208 C5 El Paso IL U.S.A.
213 F6 El Paso TX U.S.A.
174 C2 Elphin U.K.
214 C3 El Portal U.S.A.
El Porvenír Panama see El Porvenir
224 J6 El Porvenir Panama
183 R2 El Prat de Llobregat Spain
El Progreso Guat. see Guastatoya
225 H5 El Progreso Hond.
224 B2 El Puerto, Cerro mt. Mex.
183 M4 El Puerto de Santa María Spain
El Quds Israel/West Bank see Jerusalem
El Qûsîya Egypt see Al Qūşīyah
224 J6 El Real Panama
217 D5 El Reno U.S.A.
225 D3 El Retorno Mex.
208 B4 Elroy U.S.A.
225 D3 El Rucio Mex.
204 B2 Elsa Canada
225 D2 El Salado Mex.
224 C3 El Salto Mex.
225 G5 El Salvador country Central America
225 D2 El Salvador Mex.
161 J4 El Salvador Phil.
233 J3 El Samán de Apure Venez.
209 F1 Elsas Canada
224 C1 El Sauz Mex.
179 G2 Else r. Germany
El Sellûm Egypt see As Sallūm
Elsen Nur l. China see Dorgê Co
120 F2 Elsey Australia
120 F2 El Sharana Australia
215 D5 Elsinore U.S.A.
233 K2 El Sombrero Venez.
235 I2 El Sosneado Arg.
225 E3 El Tajín tourist site Mex.
233 I3 El Tama, Parque Nacional nat. park Venez.
184 C6 El Tarf Alg.
183 M1 El Teleno mt. Spain
225 E4 El Tepozteco, Parque Nacional nat. park Mex.
183 R1 El Ter r. Spain
233 K2 El Tigre Venez.
225 G4 El Tigre, Parque Nacional nat. park Guat.
179 I5 Eltmann Germany
233 J2 El Tocuyo Venez.
187 H5 El'ton Rus. Fed.
187 H5 El'ton, Ozero l. Rus. Fed.
212 C2 Eltopia U.S.A.
233 L2 El Toro Venez.
235 K2 El Trébol Arg.
224 B3 El Triunfo Mex.
233 J3 El Tuparro, Parque Nacional nat. park Col.
232 B8 El Turbio Chile
147 I2 Eluru India
171 N4 Elva Estonia
233 H3 El Valle Col.
174 E5 Elvanfoot U.K.
183 M3 Elvas Port.
171 J3 Elverum Norway
233 I3 El Viejo mt. Col.
233 J2 El Vigía Venez.
230 D5 Elvira Brazil
194 E3 El Wak Kenya
El Wâtya well Egypt see Al Wāţiyah
209 E5 Elwood U.S.A.
179 I3 Elxleben Germany
173 H5 Ely U.K.
208 B2 Ely MN U.S.A.
215 E2 Ely NV U.S.A.
220 B4 Elyria U.S.A.
179 G4 Elz Germany
179 H2 Elze Germany
119 G3 Émaé i. Vanuatu
142 D2 Emāmrūd Iran
143 H2 Emām Şaḩēb Afgh.
Emām Şaḩēb Afgh. see Emām Şaḩēb
139 K5 Emāmzādeh Naşrod Dīn Iran
171 L4 Emån r. Sweden
234 B2 Emas, Parque Nacional das nat. park Brazil
141 J3 Emazar Kazakh.
140 D2 Emba Kazakh.
140 C3 Emba r. Kazakh.
197 H3 Embalenhle S. Africa
205 G3 Embarras Portage Canada
234 C2 Emborcação, Represa de resr Brazil
221 F2 Embrun Canada
195 D4 Embu Kenya
179 F1 Emden Germany
155 B4 Emeishan China
155 B4 Emei Shan mt. China
141 J3 Emel' r. Kazakh.
119 E4 Emerald Qld Australia
125 F6 Emerald Vic. Australia
207 G3 Emeril Canada
205 J5 Emerson Canada
138 B2 Emet Turkey
197 I2 eMgwenya S. Africa
215 E3 Emigrant Valley U.S.A.
eMijindini S. Africa see eMjindini
193 D3 Emi Koussi mt. Chad
224 C2 Emiliano Martínez Mex.
225 G4 Emiliano Zapata Mex.
141 J3 Emin China
185 L3 Emine, Nos pt Bulg.
141 J3 Emin He r. China
185 L3 Eminska Planina hills Bulg.
138 C2 Emirdağ Turkey
138 C2 Emir Dağı mt. Turkey
125 G8 Emita Australia
197 I2 eMjindini S. Africa
171 K4 Emmaboda Sweden
171 M4 Emmaste Estonia
125 I2 Emmaville Australia
178 D2 Emmeloord Neth.
179 F4 Emmelshausen Germany
179 E2 Emmen Neth.
176 D7 Emmen Switz.
179 E3 Emmerich Germany
123 D5 Emmet Australia
147 H3 Emmiganuru India
217 C6 Emory Peak U.S.A.
224 B2 Empalme Mex.
197 I4 Empangeni S. Africa
232 E3 Empedrado Arg.
236 G2 Emperor Seamount Chain sea feature N. Pacific Ocean
236 G2 Emperor Trough sea feature N. Pacific Ocean
184 D3 Empoli Italy
217 D4 Emporia KS U.S.A.
221 E6 Emporia VA U.S.A.
220 D4 Emporium U.S.A.
205 G4 Empress Canada
143 E3 'Emrānī Iran
179 F2 Ems r. Germany
209 H3 Emsdale Canada
179 F2 Emsdetten Germany
179 F1 Ems-Jade-Kanal canal Germany
179 F2 Emsland reg. Germany
197 H3 eMzinoni S. Africa
171 K3 Enafors Sweden
151 F7 Enarotali Indon.
159 E7 Ena-san mt. Japan
141 I2 Enbek Kazakh.
235 M1 Encantadas, Serra das hills Brazil
224 A2 Encantado, Cerro mt. Mex.
161 I3 Encanto, Cape Phil.
225 D3 Encarnación Mex.
232 E3 Encarnación Para.
217 D6 Encinal U.S.A.
215 D5 Encinitas U.S.A.
213 F5 Encino U.S.A.
124 C5 Encounter Bay Australia
234 E1 Encruzilhada Brazil
235 M1 Encruzilhada do Sul Brazil
204 D4 Endako Canada
151 E7 Ende Indon.
119 E3 Endeavour Strait Australia
Endeh Indon. see Ende
239 L9 Enderby Abyssal Plain sea feature Southern Ocean
127 L4 Enderby Land reg. Antarctica
221 E3 Endicott U.S.A.
204 C3 Endicott Arm est. U.S.A.
202 C3 Endicott Mountains U.S.A.
140 D2 Energetik Rus. Fed.
235 K3 Energía Arg.
187 E6 Enerhodar Ukr.
236 G6 Enewetak atoll Marshall Is
136 B2 Enez Turkey
184 D6 Enfidaville Tunisia
221 G3 Enfield U.S.A.
209 E2 Engadine U.S.A.
171 J3 Engan Norway
161 I2 Engaño, Cape Phil.
158 H2 Engaru Japan
197 G5 Engcobo S. Africa
219 F5 Engelhard U.S.A.
187 H5 Engel's Rus. Fed.
178 C1 Engelschmangat sea chan. Neth.
124 A2 Engenina watercourse Australia
163 B4 Enggano i. Indon.
178 C4 Enghien Belgium
173 E5 England admin. div. U.K.
207 I3 Englee Canada
209 H2 Englehart Canada
211 H1 English r. Canada
173 D7 English Channel France/U.K.
187 G7 Enguri r. Georgia
197 I4 Enhlalakahle S. Africa
217 D4 Enid U.S.A.
158 G3 Eniwa Japan
178 D2 Enkhuizen Neth.
171 L4 Enköping Sweden
184 F6 Enna Sicily Italy
205 I2 Ennadai Lake Canada
193 E3 En Nahud Sudan
193 E3 Ennedi, Massif mts Chad
175 K4 Ennell, Lough l. Ireland
125 F2 Enngonia Australia
216 C2 Enning U.S.A.
175 J5 Ennis Ireland
212 E2 Ennis MT U.S.A.
217 D5 Ennis TX U.S.A.
175 L5 Enniscorthy Ireland
175 K3 Enniskillen U.K.
175 I5 Ennistymon Ireland
176 G7 Enns r. Austria
171 O3 Eno Fin.
215 F3 Enoch U.S.A.
170 M1 Enontekiö Fin.
155 D6 Enping China
161 I2 Enrile Phil.
178 D2 Ens Neth.
125 G6 Ensay Australia
179 E2 Enschede Neth.
179 G3 Ense Germany
235 L2 Ensenada Arg.
222 A2 Ensenada Mex.
155 C4 Enshi China
204 F2 Enterprise N.W.T. Canada
209 I3 Enterprise Ont. Canada
219 C6 Enterprise AL U.S.A.
212 C2 Enterprise OR U.S.A.
215 F3 Enterprise UT U.S.A.
204 F4 Entrance Canada
235 K2 Entre Ríos prov. Arg.
231 F8 Entre Ríos Bol.
183 L3 Entroncamento Port.
192 C4 Enugu Nigeria
133 U3 Enurmino Rus. Fed.
230 D5 Envira Brazil
230 D5 Envira r. Brazil
126 C5 Enys, Mount N.Z.
159 F7 Enzan Japan
178 D2 Epe Neth.
178 B5 Épernay France
185 L6 Ephesus tourist site Turkey
215 G2 Ephraim U.S.A.
221 E4 Ephrata PA U.S.A.
212 C2 Ephrata WA U.S.A.
119 G3 Épi i. Vanuatu
182 H2 Épinal France
138 D4 Episkopi Cyprus
184 E4 Epomeo, Monte vol. Italy
173 H6 Epping U.K.
123 D4 Epping Forest National Park Australia
179 G4 Eppstein Germany
173 D5 Eppynt, Mynydd hills U.K.
173 G6 Epsom U.K.
235 J3 Epu-pel Arg.
142 D4 Eqlīd Iran
192 C4 Equatorial Guinea country Africa
233 L3 Equeipa Venez.
161 H4 Eran Phil.
161 H4 Eran Bay Phil.
139 F1 Erbaa Turkey
179 K5 Erbendorf Germany
179 F5 Erbeskopf h. Germany
139 I2 Erçek Turkey
139 I2 Erciş Turkey
138 E2 Erciyes Dağı mt. Turkey
177 I7 Érd Hungary
149 H2 Erdaogou China
160 D2 Erdao Jiang r. China
138 A1 Erdek Turkey
138 E3 Erdemli Turkey
Erdenedalay Mongolia see Sangiyn Dalay
153 H2 Erdenet Mongolia
153 K2 Erdenetsagaan Mongolia
Erdenetsogt Mongolia see Bayan-Ovoo
193 E3 Erdi reg. Chad
187 H6 Erdniyevskiy Rus. Fed.
235 B4 Eré, Campos hills Brazil
233 K3 Erebato r. Venez.
127 I5 Erebus, Mount vol. Antarctica
139 J6 Erech tourist site Iraq
232 F3 Erechim Brazil
150 D2 Ereentsav Mongolia
138 E3 Ereğli Konya Turkey
138 C1 Ereğli Zonguldak Turkey
184 F6 Erei, Monti mts Sicily Italy
Eréndira Mex. see Carácuaro
154 D1 Erenhot China
143 E3 Eresk Iran
183 N2 Eresma r. Spain
185 J5 Eretria Greece
179 J4 Erfurt Germany
139 G2 Ergani Turkey
192 B2 'Erg Chech des. Alg./Mali
Ergel Mongolia see Hatanbulag
185 L4 Ergene r. Turkey
171 N4 Ērgļi Latvia
158 A1 Ergu China
153 L1 Ergun China
Ergun Youqi China see Ergun
160 C3 Erhulai China
174 D2 Eriboll, Loch inlet U.K.
174 D4 Ericht, Loch l. U.K.
208 B5 Erie IL U.S.A.
217 E4 Erie KS U.S.A.
220 C3 Erie PA U.S.A.
209 G4 Erie, Lake Canada/U.S.A.
158 H3 Erimo Japan
158 H4 Erimo-misaki c. Japan
174 A3 Eriskay i. U.K.
194 D2 Eritrea country Africa
141 H5 Erkech-Tam Kyrg.
138 E2 Erkilet Turkey
179 J5 Erlangen Germany
118 D4 Erldunda Australia
121 C5 Erlistoun watercourse Australia
160 E2 Erlong Shan mt. China
160 C2 Erlongshan Shuiku resr China
178 D2 Ermelo Neth.
197 H3 Ermelo S. Africa
138 D3 Ermenek Turkey
185 K6 Ermoupoli Greece
147 H4 Ernakulam India
121 C5 Ernest Giles Range hills Australia
147 H4 Erode India
123 C5 Eromanga Australia
196 A1 Erongo admin. reg. Namibia
178 D3 Erp Neth.
121 A5 Errabiddy Hills Australia
192 B1 Er Rachidia Morocco
193 F3 Er Rahad Sudan
180 C6 Er Raoui des. Alg.
195 D5 Errego Moz.
184 D7 Er Remla Tunisia
175 J2 Errigal h. Ireland
175 H3 Erris Head Ireland
221 H2 Errol U.S.A.
119 G3 Erromango i. Vanuatu
185 I4 Ersekë Albania
216 D2 Erskine U.S.A.
171 M3 Ersmark Sweden
144 H2 Ertai China
187 G5 Ertil' Rus. Fed.
144 G2 Ertix He r. China/Kazakh.
124 C3 Erudina Australia
139 I3 Eruh Turkey
235 M2 Erval Brazil
220 D5 Erwin U.S.A.
179 G3 Erwitte Germany
179 J2 Erxleben Sachsen-Anhalt Germany
179 J2 Erxleben Sachsen-Anhalt Germany
152 G6 Eryuan China
179 K4 Erzgebirge mts Czech Rep./Germany
156 B2 Erzhan China
139 F3 Erzin Turkey
139 G2 Erzincan Turkey
139 H2 Erzurum Turkey
158 G4 Esan-misaki pt Japan
158 G4 Esashi Japan
158 H2 Esashi Japan
171 J5 Esbjerg Denmark
215 G3 Escalante U.S.A.
215 G3 Escalante r. U.S.A.
215 F3 Escalante Desert U.S.A.
224 C2 Escalón Mex.
208 D3 Escanaba U.S.A.
225 G4 Escárcega Mex.
161 I2 Escarpada Point Phil.
183 P2 Escatrón Spain

Fenaio, Punta del

178 B4 **Escaut** *r.* Belgium
178 D3 **Esch** Neth.
179 E2 **Esche** Germany
179 I2 **Eschede** Germany
178 D5 **Esch-sur-Alzette** Lux.
179 I3 **Eschwege** Germany
179 E4 **Eschweiler** Germany
215 D5 **Escondido** U.S.A.
224 C3 **Escuinapa** Mex.
225 G5 **Escuintla** Guat.
225 F5 **Escuintla** Mex.
233 J3 **Escutillas** Col.
138 B3 **Eşen** Turkey
140 C5 **Esenguly** Turkm.
179 F1 **Esens** Germany
142 C3 **Eşfahān** Iran
142 D4 **Esfandāran** Iran
143 E2 **Esfarayen, Reshteh-ye** *mts* Iran
142 C4 **Esfarjan** Iran
143 E3 **Eshāqābād** Iran
142 D5 **Eshkanān** Iran
197 I4 **Eshowe** S. Africa
142 C3 **Eshtehārd** Iran
195 C6 **Esigodini** Zimbabwe
197 J4 **Esikhawini** S. Africa
125 J1 **Esk** Australia
125 G8 **Esk** *r.* Australia
172 D2 **Esk** *r.* U.K.
174 E5 **Eskdalemuir** U.K.
207 G3 **Esker** Canada
170 D2 **Eskifjörður** Iceland
138 B2 **Eski Gediz** Turkey
171 L4 **Eskilstuna** Sweden
202 E3 **Eskimo Lakes** Canada
141 H4 **Eski-Nookat** Kyrg.
138 D1 **Eskipazar** Turkey
138 C2 **Eskişehir** Turkey
183 N1 **Esla** *r.* Spain
142 B3 **Eslāmābād-e Gharb** Iran
138 B3 **Esler Dağı** *mt.* Turkey
179 G3 **Eslohe (Sauerland)** Germany
171 K5 **Eslöv** Sweden
138 B2 **Eşme** Turkey
230 C3 **Esmeraldas** Ecuador
209 E1 **Esnagi Lake** Canada
178 B4 **Esnes** France
143 F5 **Espakeh** Iran
182 F4 **Espalion** France
209 G2 **Espanola** Canada
213 F4 **Espanola** U.S.A.
230 □ **Española, Isla** *i. Galapagos Is* Ecuador
214 A2 **Esparto** U.S.A.
141 H4 **Espe** Kazakh.
179 G2 **Espelkamp** Germany
118 C5 **Esperance** Australia
121 C7 **Esperance Bay** Australia
127 L2 **Esperanza** *research stn* Antarctica
235 K1 **Esperanza** Arg.
224 B2 **Esperanza** Mex.
161 J4 **Esperanza** Phil.
224 H5 **Esperanza, Sierra de la** *mts* Hond.
183 L3 **Espichel, Cabo** *c.* Port.
183 N1 **Espigüete** *mt.* Spain
225 D2 **Espinazo** Mex.
234 D2 **Espinhaço, Serra do** *mts* Brazil
234 D1 **Espinosa** Brazil
234 E2 **Espírito Santo** *state* Brazil
161 I2 **Espiritu** Phil.
119 G3 **Espíritu Santo** *i.* Vanuatu
225 H4 **Espíritu Santo, Bahía del** *b.* Mex.
224 B2 **Espíritu Santo, Isla** *i.* Mex.
171 N3 **Espoo** Fin.
183 P4 **Espuña** *mt.* Spain
232 B6 **Esquel** Arg.
204 E5 **Esquimalt** Canada
161 J5 **Essang** Indon.
192 B1 **Essaouira** Morocco
192 A2 **Es Semara** W. Sahara
178 C3 **Essen** Belgium
179 F3 **Essen** Germany
179 F2 **Essen (Oldenburg)** Germany
231 G3 **Essequibo** *r.* Guyana
209 F4 **Essex** Canada
215 E4 **Essex** U.S.A.
221 G2 **Essex Junction** U.S.A.
209 F4 **Essexville** U.S.A.
133 Q4 **Esso** Rus. Fed.
207 H4 **Est, Île de l'** *i.* Canada
221 I1 **Est, Lac de l'** *l.* Canada
232 D8 **Estados, Isla de los** *i.* Arg.
142 D4 **Eşţahbān** Iran
209 G2 **Estaire** Canada
231 K6 **Estância** Brazil
183 Q1 **Estats, Pic d'** *mt.* France/Spain
197 H4 **Estcourt** S. Africa
179 H1 **Este** *r.* Germany
224 H5 **Estelí** Nicaragua
183 O1 **Estella** Spain
183 N4 **Estepa** Spain
183 N4 **Estepona** Spain
205 I4 **Esterhazy** Canada
214 B4 **Estero Bay** U.S.A.
232 D2 **Esteros** Para.
205 I5 **Estevan** Canada
216 E3 **Estherville** U.S.A.
219 D5 **Estill** U.S.A.
171 N4 **Estonia** *country* Europe
178 A5 **Estrées-St-Denis** France
183 M2 **Estrela, Serra da** *mts* Port.
183 O3 **Estrella** *mt.* Spain
215 F5 **Estrella, Sierra** *mts* U.S.A.
183 M3 **Estremoz** Port.
231 I5 **Estrondo, Serra** *hills* Brazil
139 L4 **Estūh** Iran
124 C2 **Etadunna** Australia
148 D4 **Etah** India
178 D5 **Étain** France
182 F2 **Étampes** France
182 E1 **Étaples** France
148 D4 **Etawah** India
197 I3 **Ethandakukhanya** S. Africa
121 C4 **Ethel Creek** Australia
197 E4 **E'Thembini** S. Africa
194 D3 **Ethiopia** *country* Africa
138 D2 **Etimesğut** Turkey
174 C4 **Etive, Loch** *inlet* U.K.
184 F6 **Etna, Mount** *vol. Sicily* Italy
171 I4 **Etne** Norway
204 C3 **Etolin Island** U.S.A.
195 B5 **Etosha National Park** Namibia
195 B5 **Etosha Pan** *salt pan* Namibia
140 C5 **Etrek** Turkm.
185 K3 **Etropole** Bulg.
147 H4 **Ettaiyapuram** India
179 E5 **Ettelbruck** Lux.
178 C3 **Etten-Leur** Neth.
179 G6 **Ettlingen** Germany
174 E5 **Ettrick Forest** *reg.* U.K.
Etxarri Spain *see* **Etxarri-Aranatz**
183 O1 **Etxarri-Aranatz** Spain
224 C3 **Etzatlán** Mex.
125 G4 **Euabalong** Australia
118 C5 **Eucla** Australia
220 C4 **Euclid** U.S.A.
231 K6 **Euclides da Cunha** Brazil
125 H6 **Eucumbene, Lake** Australia
124 C5 **Eudunda** Australia
219 C5 **Eufaula** U.S.A.
217 E5 **Eufaula Lake** *resr* U.S.A.
212 B2 **Eugene** U.S.A.
213 D7 **Eugenia, Punta** *pt* Mex.
125 H4 **Eugowra** Australia
125 F2 **Eulo** Australia
125 H3 **Eumungerie** Australia
123 E4 **Eungella** Australia
123 E4 **Eungella National Park** Australia
217 E6 **Eunice** U.S.A.
179 E4 **Eupen** Belgium
139 J6 **Euphrates** *r.* Asia *alt.* **Al Furāt (Iraq/Syria),** *alt.* **Fırat (Turkey)**
171 M3 **Eura** Fin.
182 E2 **Eure** *r.* France
213 A3 **Eureka** *CA* U.S.A.
212 D1 **Eureka** *MT* U.S.A.
215 E2 **Eureka** *NV* U.S.A.
124 D3 **Eurinilla** *watercourse* Australia
124 D3 **Euriowie** Australia
125 F6 **Euroa** Australia
123 E5 **Eurombah** Australia
123 E5 **Eurombah Creek** *r.* Australia
195 E6 **Europa, Île** *i.* Indian Ocean
183 N4 **Europa Point** Gibraltar
166 **Europe**
179 E4 **Euskirchen** Germany
125 E5 **Euston** Australia
219 C5 **Eutaw** U.S.A.
204 D4 **Eutsuk Lake** Canada
179 K3 **Eutzsch** Germany
120 F3 **Eva Downs** Australia
197 H3 **Evander** S. Africa
206 E3 **Evans, Lac** *l.* Canada
213 F4 **Evans, Mount** U.S.A.
204 F4 **Evansburg** Canada
125 J2 **Evans Head** Australia
123 F6 **Evans Head** *hd* Australia
203 J3 **Evans Strait** Canada
208 D4 **Evanston** *IL* U.S.A.
213 E3 **Evanston** *WY* U.S.A.
209 F3 **Evansville** Canada
219 C4 **Evansville** *IN* U.S.A.
208 C4 **Evansville** *WI* U.S.A.
213 F3 **Evansville** *WY* U.S.A.
209 E4 **Evart** U.S.A.
197 G3 **Evaton** S. Africa
142 D5 **Evaz** Iran
208 A2 **Eveleth** U.S.A.
133 Q3 **Evensk** Rus. Fed.
124 A3 **Everard, Lake** *salt flat* Australia
121 F4 **Everard, Mount** Australia
118 D4 **Everard Range** *hills* Australia
178 D2 **Everdingen** Neth.
149 F4 **Everest, Mount** China/Nepal
221 J1 **Everett** Canada
212 B1 **Everett** U.S.A.
178 B3 **Evergem** Belgium
219 D7 **Everglades** *swamp* U.S.A.
219 D7 **Everglades National Park** U.S.A.
217 G6 **Evergreen** U.S.A.
123 C4 **Evesham** Australia
173 F5 **Evesham** U.K.
173 F5 **Evesham, Vale of** *val.* U.K.
171 M3 **Evijärvi** Fin.
193 D4 **Evinayong** Equat. Guinea
171 I4 **Evje** Norway
183 M3 **Évora** Port.
150 F1 **Evoron, Ozero** *l.* Rus. Fed.
139 J2 **Evowghlī** Iran
182 E2 **Évreux** France
185 J6 **Evrotas** *r.* Greece
138 D4 **Evrychou** Cyprus
185 K5 **Evvoia** *i.* Greece
214 □[1] **'Ewa Beach** U.S.A.
122 D3 **Ewan** Australia
194 D3 **Ewaso Ngiro** *r.* Kenya
174 C3 **Ewe, Loch** *b.* U.K.
195 B4 **Ewo** Congo
230 E6 **Exaltación** Bol.
197 G4 **Excelsior** S. Africa
214 C2 **Excelsior Mountain** U.S.A.
214 C2 **Excelsior Mountains** U.S.A.
217 E4 **Excelsior Springs** U.S.A.
173 D6 **Exe** *r.* U.K.
127 I4 **Executive Committee Range** *mts* Antarctica
125 I5 **Exeter** Australia
209 G4 **Exeter** Canada
173 D7 **Exeter** U.K.
214 C3 **Exeter** *CA* U.S.A.
221 H3 **Exeter** *NH* U.S.A.
179 E2 **Exloo** Neth.
173 D7 **Exminster** U.K.
173 D6 **Exmoor** *hills* U.K.
173 D6 **Exmoor National Park** U.K.
221 F6 **Exmore** U.S.A.
121 A4 **Exmouth** Australia
173 D7 **Exmouth** U.K.
125 H3 **Exmouth, Mount** Australia
118 B4 **Exmouth Gulf** Australia
238 L6 **Exmouth Plateau** *sea feature* Indian Ocean
123 E5 **Expedition National Park** Australia
123 E5 **Expedition Range** *mts* Australia
183 N3 **Extremadura** *aut. comm.* Spain
219 E7 **Exuma Sound** *sea chan.* Bahamas
195 D4 **Eyasi, Lake** *salt l.* Tanz.
173 I5 **Eye** U.K.
175 F5 **Eyemouth** U.K.
174 B2 **Eye Peninsula** U.K.
170 C3 **Eyjafjallajökull** *ice cap* Iceland
170 C1 **Eyjafjörður** *inlet* Iceland
194 E3 **Eyl** Somalia
173 F6 **Eynsham** U.K.
124 B2 **Eyre (North), Lake** *salt flat* Australia
124 B2 **Eyre (South), Lake** *salt flat* Australia
123 B6 **Eyre, Lake** Australia
123 B5 **Eyre Creek** *watercourse* Australia
126 B6 **Eyre Mountains** N.Z.
124 A4 **Eyre Peninsula** Australia
179 H2 **Eystrup** Germany
168 E3 **Eysturoy** *i.* Faroe Is
170 □ **Eysturoy** *i.* Faroe Is
197 I4 **Ezakheni** S. Africa
197 H3 **Ezenzeleni** S. Africa
235 I3 **Ezequiel Ramos Mexía, Embalse** *resr* Arg.
155 E4 **Ezhou** China
186 I2 **Ezhva** Rus. Fed.
185 L5 **Ezine** Turkey
139 F1 **Ezinepazar** Turkey

F

171 J5 **Faaborg** Denmark
217 B6 **Fabens** U.S.A.
162 □ **Faber, Mount** *h.* Sing.
204 F2 **Faber Lake** Canada
Fåborg Denmark *see* **Faaborg**
184 E3 **Fabriano** Italy
233 I3 **Facatativá** Col.
178 B4 **Faches-Thumesnil** France
193 D3 **Fachi** Niger
221 F4 **Factoryville** U.S.A.
232 B7 **Facundo** Arg.
192 C3 **Fada-N'Gourma** Burkina
139 H4 **Fadghāmī** Syria
184 D2 **Faenza** Italy
Faeroes *terr.* Atlantic Ocean *see* **Faroe Islands**
151 F7 **Fafanlap** Indon.
194 E3 **Fafen Shet'** *watercourse* Eth.
185 K2 **Făgăraş** Romania
171 J3 **Fagernes** Norway
171 K4 **Fagersta** Sweden
232 C8 **Fagnano, Lago** *l.* Arg./Chile
178 C4 **Fagne** *reg.* Belgium
192 B3 **Faguibine, Lac** *l.* Mali
170 C3 **Fagurhólsmýri** Iceland
193 F4 **Fagwir** Sudan
142 C4 **Fahlīān, Rūdkhāneh-ye** *watercourse* Iran
143 E4 **Fahraj** Iran
138 D6 **Fā'id** Egypt
202 D3 **Fairbanks** U.S.A.
220 B5 **Fairborn** U.S.A.
216 D3 **Fairbury** U.S.A.
221 E5 **Fairfax** U.S.A.
214 A2 **Fairfield** *CA* U.S.A.
208 B5 **Fairfield** *IA* U.S.A.
219 C4 **Fairfield** *OH* U.S.A.
217 D6 **Fairfield** *TX* U.S.A.
221 G3 **Fair Haven** U.S.A.
175 L2 **Fair Head** U.K.
161 H4 **Fairie Queen Shoal** *sea feature* Phil.
175 G1 **Fair Isle** *i.* U.K.
126 C7 **Fairlie** N.Z.
216 E3 **Fairmont** *MN* U.S.A.
220 C5 **Fairmont** *WV* U.S.A.
213 F4 **Fairplay** U.S.A.
208 D3 **Fairport** U.S.A.
220 C4 **Fairport Harbor** U.S.A.
122 D2 **Fairview** Australia
204 F3 **Fairview** Canada
209 E3 **Fairview** *MI* U.S.A.
217 D4 **Fairview** *OK* U.S.A.
215 G2 **Fairview** *UT* U.S.A.
155 □ **Fairview Park** *Hong Kong* China
204 B3 **Fairweather, Cape** U.S.A.
204 B3 **Fairweather, Mount** Canada/U.S.A.
151 G6 **Fais** *i.* Micronesia
148 C3 **Faisalabad** Pak.
178 C5 **Faissault** France
216 C2 **Faith** U.S.A.
149 E4 **Faizabad** India
119 I2 **Fakaofo** *atoll* Tokelau
173 H5 **Fakenham** U.K.
171 K3 **Fåker** Sweden
151 F7 **Fakfak** Indon.
142 D4 **Fakhrābād** Iran
160 B2 **Faku** China
173 C7 **Fal** *r.* U.K.
192 A4 **Falaba** Sierra Leone
182 D2 **Falaise** France
149 G4 **Falakata** India
149 H5 **Falam** Myanmar
142 C3 **Falavarjan** Iran
217 D7 **Falcon Lake** Mex./U.S.A.
217 D7 **Falfurrias** U.S.A.
204 F3 **Falher** Canada
179 L3 **Falkenberg** Germany
171 K4 **Falkenberg** Sweden
179 K1 **Falkenhagen** Germany
179 K3 **Falkenhain** Germany
179 L2 **Falkensee** Germany
179 K5 **Falkenstein** Germany
174 E5 **Falkirk** U.K.
174 E4 **Falkland** U.K.
239 F9 **Falkland Escarpment** *sea feature* S. Atlantic Ocean
232 E8 **Falkland Islands** *terr.* Atlantic Ocean
239 F9 **Falkland Plateau** *sea feature* S. Atlantic Ocean
232 D8 **Falkland Sound** *sea chan.* Falkland Is
171 K4 **Falköping** Sweden
215 D5 **Fallbrook** U.S.A.
179 H2 **Fallingbostel** Germany
214 C2 **Fallon** U.S.A.
221 H4 **Fall River** U.S.A.
213 F3 **Fall River Pass** U.S.A.
216 E3 **Falls City** U.S.A.
173 B7 **Falmouth** U.K.
220 A5 **Falmouth** *KY* U.S.A.
221 H3 **Falmouth** *ME* U.S.A.
209 E3 **Falmouth** *MI* U.S.A.
196 C7 **False Bay** S. Africa
224 B3 **Falso, Cabo** *c.* Mex.
171 J5 **Falster** *i.* Denmark
177 M7 **Fălticeni** Romania
171 K3 **Falun** Sweden
138 D4 **Famagusta** Cyprus
179 E5 **Fameck** France
142 C3 **Famenin** Iran
178 D4 **Famenne** *val.* Belgium
121 C5 **Fame Range** *hills* Australia
205 J4 **Family Lake** Canada
121 D4 **Family Well** Australia
155 F4 **Fanchang** China
175 L4 **Fane** *r.* Ireland
162 A1 **Fang** Thai.
154 D3 **Fangcheng** China
155 C4 **Fangdou Shan** *mts* China
155 F6 **Fangliao** Taiwan
154 E2 **Fangshan** *Beijing* China
154 D2 **Fangshan** *Shanxi* China
155 F6 **Fangshan** Taiwan
154 D3 **Fangxian** China
158 A2 **Fangzheng** China
155 □ **Fanling** *Hong Kong* China
174 C3 **Fannich, Loch** *l.* U.K.
143 E5 **Fannūj** Iran
184 E3 **Fano** Italy
155 F5 **Fanshan** China
154 D2 **Fanshi** China
Fan Si Pan *mt.* Vietnam *see* **Phăng Xi Păng**
194 C3 **Faradje** Dem. Rep. Congo
195 E6 **Farafangana** Madag.
193 E2 **Farāfirah, Wāḩāt al** *oasis* Egypt
Farafra Oasis *oasis* Egypt *see* **Farāfirah, Wāḩāt al**
143 F3 **Farāh** Afgh.
143 F4 **Farah Rūd** *watercourse* Afgh.
233 H4 **Farallones de Cali, Parque Nacional** *nat. park* Col.
192 A3 **Faranah** Guinea
143 F2 **Farap** Turkm.
146 B6 **Farasān, Jazā'ir** *is* Saudi Arabia
151 G6 **Faraulep** *atoll* Micronesia
173 F7 **Fareham** U.K.
203 N4 **Farewell, Cape** Greenland
126 D4 **Farewell, Cape** N.Z.
126 D4 **Farewell Spit** N.Z.
171 K4 **Färgelanda** Sweden
216 D2 **Fargo** U.S.A.
141 G4 **Farg'ona** Uzbek.
216 E2 **Faribault** U.S.A.
207 F2 **Faribault, Lac** *l.* Canada
148 D3 **Faridabad** India
148 C3 **Faridkot** India
149 G5 **Faridpur** Bangl.
192 A3 **Farim** Guinea-Bissau
143 E3 **Farīmān** Iran
171 L4 **Färjestaden** Sweden
141 G5 **Farkhor** Tajik.
139 L4 **Farmahin** Iran
208 C5 **Farmer City** U.S.A.
206 D2 **Farmer Island** Canada
204 E3 **Farmington** Canada
208 B5 **Farmington** *IA* U.S.A.
208 B5 **Farmington** *IL* U.S.A.
221 H2 **Farmington** *ME* U.S.A.
221 H3 **Farmington** *NH* U.S.A.
215 H3 **Farmington** *NM* U.S.A.
213 E3 **Farmington** *UT* U.S.A.
204 D4 **Far Mountain** Canada
220 D6 **Farmville** U.S.A.
173 G6 **Farnborough** U.K.
172 F2 **Farne Islands** U.K.
173 G6 **Farnham** U.K.
121 D5 **Farnham, Lake** *salt flat* Australia
204 F4 **Farnham, Mount** Canada
231 G4 **Faro** Brazil
204 C2 **Faro** Canada
183 M4 **Faro** Port.
171 L4 **Fårö** *i.* Sweden
170 □[2] **Faroe Islands** *terr.* N. Atlantic Ocean
171 L4 **Fårösund** Sweden
191 I5 **Farquhar Group** *is* Seychelles
Farquhar Islands Seychelles *see* **Farquhar Group**
121 C5 **Farquharson Tableland** *hills* Australia
142 D4 **Farrāshband** Iran
220 C4 **Farrell** U.S.A.
209 J3 **Farrellton** Canada
143 E3 **Farrokhī** Iran
142 D3 **Farsakh** Iran
185 J5 **Farsala** Greece
143 F3 **Fārsī** Afgh.
213 E3 **Farson** U.S.A.
171 I4 **Farsund** Norway
140 D5 **Fārūj** Iran
Farvel, Kap *c.* Greenland *see* **Farewell, Cape**
217 C5 **Farwell** U.S.A.
143 E5 **Fāryāb** Iran
142 D4 **Fasā** Iran
185 G4 **Fasano** Italy
179 I2 **Faßberg** Germany
221 E4 **Fassett** U.S.A.
187 D5 **Fastiv** Ukr.
148 D4 **Fatehgarh** India
148 C4 **Fatehpur** *Rajasthan* India
149 E4 **Fatehpur** *Uttar Pradesh* India
148 D4 **Fatehpur Sikri** India
142 D4 **Fatḩābād** Iran
209 G3 **Fathom Five National Marine Park** Canada
192 A3 **Fatick** Senegal
182 H2 **Faulquemont** France
197 F4 **Fauresmith** S. Africa
170 K2 **Fauske** Norway
215 F1 **Faust** U.S.A.
184 E6 **Favignana, Isola** *i. Sicily* Italy
205 G4 **Fawcett** Canada
173 F7 **Fawley** U.K.
206 C3 **Fawn** *r.* Canada
170 B2 **Faxaflói** *b.* Iceland
171 L3 **Faxälven** *r.* Sweden
193 D3 **Faya** Chad
208 D3 **Fayette** U.S.A.
217 E4 **Fayetteville** *AR* U.S.A.
219 E5 **Fayetteville** *NC* U.S.A.
219 C5 **Fayetteville** *TN* U.S.A.
139 L7 **Faylakah** *i.* Kuwait
192 C4 **Fazao Malfakassa, Parc National de** *nat. park* Togo
148 C3 **Fazilka** India
142 C5 **Fazrān, Jabal** *h.* Saudi Arabia
192 A2 **Fdérik** Mauritania
175 I5 **Feale** *r.* Ireland
219 E5 **Fear, Cape** U.S.A.
214 B2 **Feather, North Fork** *r.* U.S.A.
214 B2 **Feather Falls** U.S.A.
126 E4 **Featherston** N.Z.
125 G6 **Feathertop, Mount** Australia
182 E2 **Fécamp** France
235 L1 **Federación** Arg.
232 E4 **Federal** Arg.
140 E1 **Fedorovka** *Kustanayskaya Oblast'* Kazakh.
141 I1 **Fedorovka** *Pavlodarskaya Oblast'* Kazakh.
140 B2 **Fedorovka** *Zapadnyy Kazakhstan* Kazakh.
140 C1 **Fedorovka** Rus. Fed.
176 E3 **Fehmarn** *i.* Germany
179 K2 **Fehrbellin** Germany
234 E3 **Feia, Lagoa** *lag.* Brazil
155 E4 **Feidong** China
154 F3 **Feihuanghe Kou** *r. mouth* China
230 D5 **Feijó** Brazil
126 E4 **Feilding** N.Z.
231 K6 **Feira de Santana** Brazil
155 E4 **Feixi** China
138 E3 **Feke** Turkey
183 R3 **Felanitx** Spain
208 D3 **Felch** U.S.A.
179 L1 **Feldberg** Germany
176 D7 **Feldberg** *mt.* Germany
176 D7 **Feldkirch** Austria
176 G7 **Feldkirchen in Kärnten** Austria
235 K1 **Feliciano** *r.* Arg.
225 G4 **Felipe C. Puerto** Mex.
234 D2 **Felixlândia** Brazil
173 I6 **Felixstowe** U.K.
184 D1 **Feltre** Italy
171 J3 **Femunden** *l.* Norway
171 K3 **Femundsmarka Nasjonalpark** *nat. park* Norway
184 D3 **Fenaio, Punta del** *pt* Italy

215 H4 **Fence Lake** U.S.A.
209 H3 **Fenelon Falls** Canada
185 K4 **Fengari** *mt.* Greece
155 E4 **Fengcheng** *Jiangxi* China
160 C3 **Fengcheng** *Liaoning* China
155 C4 **Fengdu** China
155 C5 **Fenggang** China
160 D1 **Fengguang** China
155 F4 **Fenghua** China
155 C5 **Fenghuang** China
155 C4 **Fengjie** China
155 D6 **Fengkai** China
155 F6 **Fenglin** Taiwan
154 F2 **Fengnan** China
154 E1 **Fengning** China
154 E3 **Fengqiu** China
155 C5 **Fengshan** China
156 A1 **Fengshui Shan** *mt.* China
155 E6 **Fengshun** China
154 E3 **Fengtai** China
153 I5 **Fengxian** China
Fengxiang China *see* **Luobei**
155 E4 **Fengxin** China
154 E3 **Fengyang** China
154 D1 **Fengzhen** China
154 D2 **Fen He** *r.* China
149 G5 **Feni** Bangl.
119 F2 **Feni Islands** P.N.G.
183 F5 **Fenille, Col de la** *pass* France
208 B4 **Fennimore** U.S.A.
195 E5 **Fenoarivo Atsinanana** Madag.
209 F4 **Fenton** U.S.A.
154 D2 **Fenxi** China
154 D2 **Fenyang** China
155 E5 **Fenyi** China
187 E6 **Feodosiya** Ukr.
184 B6 **Fer, Cap de** *c.* Alg.
Férai Greece *see* **Feres**
143 E3 **Ferdows** Iran
136 B2 **Feres** Greece
Fergana Uzbek. *see* **Farg'ona**
141 H4 **Fergana Too Tizmegi** *mts* Kyrg.
209 G4 **Fergus** Canada
216 D2 **Fergus Falls** U.S.A.
119 F2 **Fergusson Island** P.N.G.
184 C7 **Fériana** Tunisia
185 I3 **Ferizaj** Kosovo
192 B4 **Ferkessédougou** Côte d'Ivoire
184 E3 **Fermo** Italy
207 G3 **Fermont** Canada
183 M2 **Fermoselle** Spain
175 J5 **Fermoy** Ireland
230 □ **Fernandina, Isla** *i.* *Galapagos Is* Ecuador
219 D6 **Fernandina Beach** U.S.A.
232 B8 **Fernando de Magallanes, Parque Nacional** *nat. park* Chile
239 G6 **Fernando de Noronha** *i.* Brazil
234 B3 **Fernandópolis** Brazil
212 B1 **Ferndale** U.S.A.
173 F7 **Ferndown** U.K.
204 F5 **Fernie** Canada
125 G2 **Fernlee** Australia
214 C2 **Fernley** U.S.A.
221 F4 **Fernridge** U.S.A.
175 L5 **Ferns** Ireland
212 C2 **Fernwood** U.S.A.
184 D2 **Ferrara** Italy
234 B3 **Ferreiros** Brazil
217 F6 **Ferriday** U.S.A.
184 C4 **Ferro, Capo** *c.* *Sardinia* Italy
183 L1 **Ferrol** Spain
215 G2 **Ferron** U.S.A.
140 D1 **Fershampenuaz** Rus. Fed.
Ferwerd Neth. *see* **Ferwert**
178 D1 **Ferwert** Neth.
192 B1 **Fès** Morocco
195 B4 **Feshi** Dem. Rep. Congo
205 J5 **Fessenden** U.S.A.
217 F4 **Festus** U.S.A.
174 □ **Fethaland, Point of** U.K.
175 K5 **Fethard** Ireland
138 B3 **Fethiye** Turkey
140 C4 **Fetisovo** Kazakh.
174 □ **Fetlar** *i.* U.K.
175 F4 **Fettercairn** U.K.
179 J5 **Feucht** Germany
179 I5 **Feuchtwangen** Germany
207 F2 **Feuilles, Rivière aux** *r.* Canada
156 C1 **Fevral'sk** Rus. Fed.
139 F3 **Fevzipaşa** Turkey
143 H2 **Feyzābād** Afgh.
143 E3 **Feyzābād** Iran
173 D5 **Ffestiniog** U.K.
195 E6 **Fianarantsoa** Madag.
194 D3 **Fichē** Eth.
179 K4 **Fichtelgebirge** *hills* Germany
197 G4 **Ficksburg** S. Africa
204 F4 **Field** *B.C.* Canada
209 G2 **Field** *Ont.* Canada
185 H4 **Fier** Albania
122 B3 **Fiery Creek** *r.* Australia
209 E3 **Fife Lake** U.S.A.
175 F4 **Fife Ness** *pt* U.K.
125 G4 **Fifield** Australia
208 B3 **Fifield** U.S.A.
182 F4 **Figeac** France
183 L2 **Figueira da Foz** Port.
183 R1 **Figueres** Spain
192 B1 **Figuig** Morocco
119 H3 **Fiji** *country* Pacific Ocean
224 H6 **Filadelfia** Costa Rica
232 D2 **Filadelfia** Para.
127 J3 **Filchner Ice Shelf** Antarctica
172 G3 **Filey** U.K.
185 I5 **Filippiada** Greece
171 K4 **Filipstad** Sweden
171 J3 **Fillan** Norway
214 C4 **Fillmore** *CA* U.S.A.
215 F2 **Fillmore** *UT* U.S.A.
127 K3 **Fimbull Ice Shelf** Antarctica
221 F2 **Finch** Canada
174 E3 **Findhorn** *r.* U.K.
139 H3 **Fındık** Turkey
220 B4 **Findlay** U.S.A.
125 H8 **Fingal** Australia
206 E5 **Finger Lakes** U.S.A.
195 D5 **Fingoè** Moz.
138 C3 **Finike** Turkey
138 C3 **Finike Körfezi** *b.* Turkey
183 L1 **Finisterre, Cape** Spain
123 A5 **Finke** *watercourse* Australia
121 F6 **Finke, Mount** *h.* Australia
120 E2 **Finke Bay** Australia
186 S5 **Finland** *country* Europe
171 M4 **Finland, Gulf of** Europe
204 D3 **Finlay** *r.* Canada
204 D3 **Finlay, Mount** Canada
125 F5 **Finley** Australia
179 J3 **Finne** *ridge* Germany
122 D2 **Finnigan, Mount** Australia
124 A4 **Finniss, Cape** Australia
170 L1 **Finnsnes** Norway
171 K4 **Finspång** Sweden
175 K3 **Fintona** U.K.
Fintown Ireland *see* **Baile na Finne**
123 C4 **Finucane Range** *hills* Australia
174 C3 **Fionn Loch** *l.* U.K.
174 B4 **Fionnphort** U.K.
126 A6 **Fiordland National Park** N.Z.
139 G2 **Firat** *r.* Turkey *alt.* **Al Furāt (Iraq/Syria),** *conv.* **Euphrates**
214 B3 **Firebaugh** U.S.A.
205 I2 **Firedrake Lake** Canada
221 G4 **Fire Island National Seashore** *nature res.* U.S.A.
Firenze Italy *see* **Florence**
139 J6 **Firk, Sha'īb** *watercourse* Iraq
235 K2 **Firmat** Arg.
182 G4 **Firminy** France
179 I6 **Firngrund** *reg.* Germany
177 P2 **Firovo** Rus. Fed.
148 B3 **Firoza** Pak.
148 D4 **Firozabad** India
143 G3 **Firozkoh** *reg.* Afgh.
148 C3 **Firozpur** India
221 H2 **First Connecticut Lake** U.S.A.
122 D2 **First Three Mile Opening** *sea chan.* Australia
142 D4 **Fīrūzābād** Iran
137 I4 **Fīrūzkūh** Iran
179 F5 **Fischbach** Germany
195 B6 **Fish** *watercourse* Namibia
196 D5 **Fish** *r.* S. Africa
121 E6 **Fisher (abandoned)** Australia
127 I6 **Fisher Bay** Antarctica
221 F6 **Fisherman Island** U.S.A.
221 H4 **Fishers Island** U.S.A.
205 M2 **Fisher Strait** Canada
173 C6 **Fishguard** U.K.
204 E2 **Fish Lake** Canada
208 A2 **Fish Lake** *MN* U.S.A.
215 G2 **Fish Lake** *UT* U.S.A.
209 F4 **Fish Point** U.S.A.
127 J3 **Fiske, Cape** Antarctica
178 B5 **Fismes** France
183 L1 **Fisterra** Spain
Fisterra, Cabo *c.* Spain *see* **Finisterre, Cape**
221 H3 **Fitchburg** U.S.A.
205 G3 **Fitzgerald** Canada
219 D6 **Fitzgerald** U.S.A.
124 B4 **Fitzgerald Bay** Australia
121 B7 **Fitzgerald River National Park** Australia
232 C7 **Fitz Roy** Arg.
120 C3 **Fitzroy** *r.* Australia
118 C3 **Fitzroy Crossing** Australia
209 G3 **Fitzwilliam Island** Canada
175 K3 **Fivemiletown** U.K.
184 D2 **Fivizzano** Italy
195 C4 **Fizi** Dem. Rep. Congo
171 J3 **Flå** Norway
197 H5 **Flagstaff** S. Africa
215 G4 **Flagstaff** U.S.A.
221 H2 **Flagstaff Lake** U.S.A.
206 E2 **Flaherty Island** Canada
208 B3 **Flambeau** *r.* U.S.A.
172 G3 **Flamborough Head** U.K.
179 K2 **Fläming** *hills* Germany
213 E3 **Flaming Gorge Reservoir** U.S.A.
196 D5 **Flaminksvlei** *salt pan* S. Africa
178 A3 **Flanders** *reg.* Europe
178 A4 **Flandre** *reg.* France
174 A2 **Flannan Isles** U.K.
170 K2 **Flåsjön** *l.* Sweden
209 E4 **Flat** *r.* U.S.A.
212 D2 **Flathead Lake** U.S.A.
126 E4 **Flat Point** N.Z.
119 E3 **Flattery, Cape** Australia
212 A1 **Flattery, Cape** U.S.A.
179 J2 **Fleetmark** Germany
123 D4 **Fleetwood** Australia
173 D4 **Fleetwood** U.K.
221 F4 **Fleetwood** U.S.A.
171 I4 **Flekkefjord** Norway
221 E3 **Fleming** U.S.A.
220 B5 **Flemingsburg** U.S.A.
239 G2 **Flemish Cap** *sea feature* N. Atlantic Ocean
171 L4 **Flen** Sweden
176 D3 **Flensburg** Germany
182 D2 **Flers** France
209 G3 **Flesherton** Canada
205 H2 **Fletcher Lake** Canada
209 F3 **Fletcher Pond** *l.* U.S.A.
119 E3 **Flinders** *r.* Australia
118 B5 **Flinders Bay** Australia
124 B5 **Flinders Chase National Park** Australia
122 D2 **Flinders Group National Park** Australia
124 A4 **Flinders Island** *S.A.* Australia
125 H7 **Flinders Island** *Tas.* Australia
122 E3 **Flinders Passage** Australia
124 C3 **Flinders Ranges** *mts* Australia
124 C3 **Flinders Ranges National Park** Australia
122 E3 **Flinders Reefs** Australia
205 I4 **Flin Flon** Canada
173 D4 **Flint** U.K.
209 F4 **Flint** U.S.A.
219 C6 **Flint** *r.* *GA* U.S.A.
209 F4 **Flint** *r.* *MI* U.S.A.
237 I5 **Flint Island** Kiribati
125 H1 **Flinton** Australia
171 K3 **Flisa** Norway
172 E2 **Flodden** U.K.
179 L4 **Flöha** Germany
179 L4 **Flöha** *r.* Germany
127 I4 **Flood Range** *mts* Antarctica
208 A2 **Floodwood** U.S.A.
120 E2 **Flora** *r.* Australia
218 B4 **Flora** U.S.A.
182 F4 **Florac** France
179 E5 **Florange** France
122 D3 **Flora Reef** Australia
209 F4 **Florence** Canada
184 D3 **Florence** Italy
219 C5 **Florence** *AL* U.S.A.
215 G5 **Florence** *AZ* U.S.A.
217 D4 **Florence** *KS* U.S.A.
220 C5 **Florence** *OH* U.S.A.
213 A3 **Florence** *OR* U.S.A.
219 E5 **Florence** *SC* U.S.A.
215 G5 **Florence Junction** U.S.A.
221 J1 **Florenceville** Canada
233 I4 **Florencia** Col.
178 C4 **Florennes** Belgium
232 C6 **Florentino Ameghino, Embalse** *resr* Arg.
235 K2 **Flores** *r.* Arg.
166 A6 **Flores** *i.* Azores
225 G4 **Flores** Guat.
151 E7 **Flores** *i.* Indon.
151 D7 **Flores, Laut** *sea* Indon.
234 C1 **Flores de Goiás** Brazil
Flores Sea *sea* Indon. *see* **Flores, Laut**
231 K5 **Floresta** Brazil
231 J5 **Floriano** Brazil
233 G3 **Florianópolis** Brazil
235 L2 **Florida** Uruguay
219 D6 **Florida** *state* U.S.A.
223 H4 **Florida, Straits of** Bahamas/U.S.A.
219 D7 **Florida Bay** U.S.A.
219 D7 **Florida City** U.S.A.
119 G2 **Florida Islands** Solomon Is
211 J7 **Florida Keys** *is* U.S.A.
185 I4 **Florina** Greece
171 I3 **Florø** Norway
207 H3 **Flour Lake** Canada
208 A4 **Floyd** *IA* U.S.A.
220 C6 **Floyd** *VA* U.S.A.
215 F4 **Floyd, Mount** U.S.A.
217 C5 **Floydada** U.S.A.
119 E2 **Fly** *r.* P.N.G.
220 C5 **Fly** U.S.A.
185 H3 **Foča** Bos.-Herz.
174 E3 **Fochabers** U.K.
197 G3 **Fochville** S. Africa
185 L2 **Focşani** Romania
155 D6 **Fogang** China
184 F4 **Foggia** Italy
192 □ **Fogo** *i.* Cape Verde
207 J4 **Fogo Island** Canada
174 D2 **Foinaven** *h.* U.K.
183 E5 **Foix** France
170 K2 **Folda** *sea chan.* Norway
170 K2 **Foldereid** Norway
170 J2 **Foldfjorden** *sea chan.* Norway
185 K6 **Folegandros** *i.* Greece
209 F1 **Foleyet** Canada
184 E3 **Foligno** Italy
173 I6 **Folkestone** U.K.
173 G5 **Folkingham** U.K.
219 D6 **Folkston** U.S.A.
171 J3 **Folldal** Norway
184 D3 **Follonica** Italy
214 B2 **Folsom Lake** U.S.A.
187 G6 **Fomin** Rus. Fed.
186 I2 **Fominskiy** Rus. Fed.
169 O4 **Fominskoye** Rus. Fed.
205 H3 **Fond-du-Lac** Canada
205 I3 **Fond du Lac** *r.* Canada
208 C4 **Fond du Lac** U.S.A.
183 L2 **Fondevila** Spain
184 E4 **Fondi** Italy
184 C4 **Fonni** *Sardinia* Italy
224 H5 **Fonseca, Golfo do** *b.* Central America
207 F3 **Fontanges** Canada
204 E3 **Fontas** Canada
204 E3 **Fontas** *r.* Canada
230 E4 **Fonte Boa** Brazil
182 D3 **Fontenay-le-Comte** France
170 D1 **Fontur** *pt* Iceland
209 H3 **Foot's Bay** Canada
154 C3 **Foping** China
125 H4 **Forbes** Australia
212 C1 **Forbes, Mount** Canada
179 J5 **Forchheim** Germany
207 G2 **Ford** *r.* Canada
208 D2 **Ford** *r.* U.S.A.
171 I3 **Førde** Norway
205 J2 **Forde Lake** Canada
173 H5 **Fordham** U.K.
173 F7 **Fordingbridge** U.K.
127 I4 **Ford Range** *mts* Antarctica
125 F2 **Fords Bridge** Australia
217 E5 **Fordyce** U.S.A.
192 A4 **Forécariah** Guinea
173 F7 **Foreland** *hd* U.K.
173 D6 **Foreland Point** U.K.
204 D4 **Foresight Mountain** Canada
209 G4 **Forest** Canada
217 F5 **Forest** *MS* U.S.A.
220 B4 **Forest** *OH* U.S.A.
122 C3 **Forest Creek** *r.* Australia
221 G3 **Forest Dale** U.S.A.
125 G5 **Forest Hill** Australia
214 B2 **Foresthill** U.S.A.
125 H9 **Forestier, Cape** Australia
125 H9 **Forestier Peninsula** Australia
208 A3 **Forest Lake** U.S.A.
219 C5 **Forest Park** U.S.A.
207 G4 **Forestville** Canada
175 F4 **Forfar** U.K.
212 A2 **Forks** U.S.A.
221 E4 **Forksville** U.S.A.
184 E2 **Forlì** Italy
173 D4 **Formby** U.K.
183 Q3 **Formentera** *i.* Spain
183 R3 **Formentor, Cap de** *c.* Spain
234 D3 **Formiga** Brazil
232 E3 **Formosa** Arg.
234 C1 **Formosa** Brazil
231 G6 **Formosa, Serra** *hills* Brazil
234 D1 **Formoso** *r.* Brazil
174 E3 **Forres** U.K.
125 E7 **Forrest** *Vic.* Australia
121 E6 **Forrest** *W.A.* Australia
208 C5 **Forrest** U.S.A.
217 F5 **Forrest City** U.S.A.
121 E6 **Forrest Lakes** *salt flat* Australia
208 C4 **Forreston** U.S.A.
171 L3 **Fors** Sweden
119 E3 **Forsayth** Australia
170 M2 **Forsnäs** Sweden
171 M3 **Forssa** Fin.
125 J4 **Forster** Australia
217 E4 **Forsyth** *MO* U.S.A.
212 F2 **Forsyth** *MT* U.S.A.
209 I1 **Forsythe** Canada
123 C4 **Forsyth Range** *hills* Australia
148 C3 **Fort Abbas** Pak.
206 D3 **Fort Albany** Canada
231 K4 **Fortaleza** Brazil
215 H5 **Fort Apache** U.S.A.
205 G4 **Fort Assiniboine** Canada
208 C4 **Fort Atkinson** U.S.A.
174 D3 **Fort Augustus** U.K.
197 G6 **Fort Beaufort** S. Africa
212 E2 **Fort Benton** U.S.A.
205 H3 **Fort Black** Canada
214 A2 **Fort Bragg** U.S.A.
Fort-Chimo Canada *see* **Kuujjuaq**
205 G3 **Fort Chipewyan** Canada
217 D5 **Fort Cobb Reservoir** U.S.A.
213 F3 **Fort Collins** U.S.A.
209 I3 **Fort-Coulonge** Canada
221 F2 **Fort Covington** U.S.A.
217 C6 **Fort Davis** U.S.A.
223 L6 **Fort-de-France** Martinique
219 C5 **Fort Deposit** U.S.A.
216 E3 **Fort Dodge** U.S.A.
121 B4 **Fortescue** *r.* Australia
216 E1 **Fort Frances** U.S.A.
Fort George Canada *see* **Chisasibi**
202 F3 **Fort Good Hope** Canada
174 D4 **Forth** *r.* U.K.
175 F4 **Forth, Firth of** *est.* U.K.
215 E2 **Fortification Range** *mts* U.S.A.
232 D2 **Fortín Capitán Demattei** Para.
232 D2 **Fortín General Mendoza** Para.
232 E2 **Fortín Madrejón** Para.
232 D2 **Fortín Pilcomayo** Arg.
231 F7 **Fortín Ravelo** Bol.
231 F7 **Fortín Suárez Arana** Bol.
221 I1 **Fort Kent** U.S.A.
219 D7 **Fort Lauderdale** U.S.A.
204 E2 **Fort Liard** Canada
205 G3 **Fort Mackay** Canada
205 G5 **Fort Macleod** Canada
208 B5 **Fort Madison** U.S.A.
208 B3 **Fort McCoy** U.S.A.
205 G3 **Fort McMurray** Canada
202 E3 **Fort McPherson** Canada
213 G3 **Fort Morgan** U.S.A.
219 D7 **Fort Myers** U.S.A.
204 E3 **Fort Nelson** Canada
204 E3 **Fort Nelson** *r.* Canada
Fort Norman Canada *see* **Tulita**
219 C5 **Fort Payne** U.S.A.
212 F1 **Fort Peck** U.S.A.
212 F2 **Fort Peck Reservoir** U.S.A.
219 D7 **Fort Pierce** U.S.A.
216 C2 **Fort Pierre** U.S.A.
204 F2 **Fort Providence** Canada
205 I4 **Fort Qu'Appelle** Canada
205 G2 **Fort Resolution** Canada
126 B7 **Fortrose** N.Z.
174 D3 **Fortrose** U.K.
214 A2 **Fort Ross** U.S.A.
Fort Rupert Canada *see* **Waskaganish**
204 E4 **Fort St James** Canada
204 E3 **Fort St John** Canada
205 G4 **Fort Saskatchewan** Canada
217 E4 **Fort Scott** U.S.A.
206 C2 **Fort Severn** Canada
140 B3 **Fort-Shevchenko** Kazakh.
204 E2 **Fort Simpson** Canada
205 G2 **Fort Smith** Canada
217 E5 **Fort Smith** U.S.A.
217 C6 **Fort Stockton** U.S.A.
213 F5 **Fort Sumner** U.S.A.
213 A3 **Fortuna** *CA* U.S.A.
216 C1 **Fortuna** *ND* U.S.A.
207 I4 **Fortune Bay** Canada
204 F3 **Fort Vermilion** Canada
219 C6 **Fort Walton Beach** U.S.A.
209 E5 **Fort Wayne** U.S.A.
174 C4 **Fort William** U.K.
217 D5 **Fort Worth** U.S.A.
202 D3 **Fort Yukon** U.S.A.
142 D5 **Forūr, Jazīreh-ye** *i.* Iran
170 K2 **Forvik** Norway
155 D6 **Foshan** China
184 B2 **Fossano** Italy
120 D3 **Fossil Downs** Australia
125 G7 **Foster** Australia
204 B3 **Foster, Mount** Canada/U.S.A.
203 P2 **Foster Bugt** *b.* Greenland
220 B4 **Fostoria** U.S.A.
173 G4 **Fotherby** U.K.
182 D2 **Fougères** France
174 □ **Foula** *i.* U.K.
173 H6 **Foulness Point** U.K.
147 I4 **Foul Point** Sri Lanka
126 C4 **Foulwind, Cape** N.Z.
193 D4 **Foumban** Cameroon
127 J4 **Foundation Ice Stream** *glacier* Antarctica
192 A3 **Foundiougne** Senegal
208 A4 **Fountain** U.S.A.
172 F3 **Fountains Abbey & Royal Water Garden (NT)** *tourist site* U.K.
182 G2 **Fourches, Mont des** *h.* France
215 D4 **Four Corners** U.S.A.
197 H4 **Fouriesburg** S. Africa
178 C4 **Fourmies** France
185 L6 **Fournoi** *i.* Greece
208 C2 **Fourteen Mile Point** U.S.A.
192 A3 **Fouta Djallon** *reg.* Guinea
126 A7 **Foveaux Strait** N.Z.
219 E7 **Fowl Cay** *i.* Bahamas
213 F4 **Fowler** *CO* U.S.A.
208 D5 **Fowler** *IN* U.S.A.
209 E4 **Fowler** *MI* U.S.A.
127 I3 **Fowler Ice Rise** Antarctica
118 D5 **Fowlers Bay** Australia
121 F7 **Fowlers Bay** *b.* Australia
139 L3 **Fowman** Iran
205 K3 **Fox** *r.* Canada
208 C4 **Fox** *r.* U.S.A.
204 F4 **Fox Creek** Canada
172 C3 **Foxdale** U.K.
203 J3 **Foxe Basin** *g.* Canada
203 J3 **Foxe Channel** Canada
203 K3 **Foxe Peninsula** Canada
126 C5 **Fox Glacier** N.Z.
205 G3 **Fox Lake** Canada
208 C4 **Fox Lake** U.S.A.
126 E4 **Foxton** N.Z.
174 D3 **Foyers** U.K.
175 K3 **Foyle** *r.* Ireland/U.K.
175 K2 **Foyle, Lough** *b.* Ireland/U.K.
175 I5 **Foynes** Ireland
195 B5 **Foz do Cunene** Angola
235 A4 **Foz do Iguaçu** Brazil
183 Q2 **Fraga** Spain
234 C3 **Franca** Brazil
119 G3 **Français, Récif des** *rf* New Caledonia
182 F3 **France** *country* Europe
124 D6 **Frances** Australia
204 D2 **Frances** *r.* Canada
204 D2 **Frances Lake** Canada
204 D2 **Frances Lake** *l.* Canada
208 D5 **Francesville** U.S.A.
195 B4 **Franceville** Gabon
221 H2 **Francis, Lake** U.S.A.
216 D3 **Francis Case, Lake** U.S.A.
225 D2 **Francisco I. Madero** *Coahuila* Mex.
224 C2 **Francisco I. Madero** *Durango* Mex.
234 D2 **Francisco Sá** Brazil
195 C6 **Francistown** Botswana
204 D4 **François Lake** Canada
121 A5 **Francois Peron National Park** Australia
213 E3 **Francs Peak** U.S.A.
178 D1 **Franeker** Neth.
179 L4 **Frankenberg** Germany
179 G3 **Frankenberg (Eder)** Germany
209 F4 **Frankenmuth** U.S.A.
179 G5 **Frankenthal (Pfalz)** Germany
179 J4 **Frankenwald** *mts* Germany
197 H3 **Frankfort** S. Africa

Garabekevyul

Garabekevyul Turkm. *see* **Garabekewül**
141 F5 **Garabekewül** Turkm.
143 F2 **Garabil Belentligi** *hills* Turkm.
140 C4 **Garabogaz** Turkm.
140 C4 **Garabogazköl** Turkm.
140 C4 **Garabogazköl Aýlagy** *b.* Turkm.
224 J6 **Garachiné** Panama
143 F4 **Garāgheh** Iran
140 D5 **Garagum** *des.* Turkm.
Garagum *des.* Turkm. *see* **Karakum Desert**
140 E5 **Garagum Kanaly** *canal* Turkm.
125 H2 **Garah** Australia
141 F5 **Garamätnyýaz** Turkm.
194 C3 **Garamba** *r.* Dem. Rep. Congo
194 C3 **Garamba, Parc National de la** *nat. park* Dem. Rep. Congo
231 K5 **Garanhuns** Brazil
197 G2 **Ga-Rankuwa** S. Africa
194 D3 **Garba Tula** Kenya
214 A1 **Garberville** U.S.A.
Garbo China *see* **Lhozhag**
142 C3 **Garbosh, Kūh-e** *mt.* Iran
179 H2 **Garbsen** Germany
234 C3 **Garça** Brazil
234 B1 **Garças, Rio das** *r.* Brazil
149 G2 **Garco** China
184 D2 **Garda, Lake** Italy
139 J1 **Gardabani** Georgia
184 B6 **Garde, Cap de** *c.* Alg.
179 J2 **Gardelegen** Germany
217 C4 **Garden City** U.S.A.
208 D3 **Garden Corners** U.S.A.
214 C5 **Garden Grove** U.S.A.
205 K4 **Garden Hill** Canada
209 E3 **Garden Island** U.S.A.
Gardez Afgh. *see* **Gardēz**
143 H3 **Gardēz** Afgh.
221 I2 **Gardiner** *ME* U.S.A.
212 E2 **Gardiner** *MT* U.S.A.
121 F4 **Gardiner, Mount** Australia
120 E3 **Gardiner Range** *hills* Australia
221 G4 **Gardiners Island** U.S.A.
208 C5 **Gardner** U.S.A.
221 J2 **Gardner Lake** U.S.A.
117 H2 **Gardner Pinnacles** *is* U.S.A.
214 C2 **Gardnerville** U.S.A.
174 D4 **Garelochhead** U.K.
209 E2 **Gargantua, Cape** Canada
139 L6 **Gargar** Iran
171 M5 **Gargždai** Lith.
148 D5 **Garhakota** India
148 A3 **Garhi Khairo** Pak.
148 D4 **Garhi Malehra** India
204 E5 **Garibaldi, Mount** Canada
204 E5 **Garibaldi Provincial Park** Canada
197 F5 **Gariep Dam** *resr* S. Africa
196 B5 **Garies** S. Africa
184 E4 **Garigliano** *r.* Italy
195 D4 **Garissa** Kenya
171 N4 **Garkalne** Latvia
220 D4 **Garland** *PA* U.S.A.
217 D5 **Garland** *TX* U.S.A.
142 C2 **Garmī** Iran
176 E7 **Garmisch-Partenkirchen** Germany
Garmo, Qullai *mt.* Tajik. *see* **Ismoili Somoní, Qullai**
142 D3 **Garmsar** Iran
143 F4 **Garmsel** *reg.* Afgh.
217 E4 **Garnett** U.S.A.
125 E4 **Garnpung Lake** *imp. l.* Australia
149 G4 **Garo Hills** India
182 D4 **Garonne** *r.* France
194 E3 **Garoowe** Somalia
233 G3 **Garopaba** Brazil
193 D4 **Garoua** Cameroon
235 J3 **Garré** Arg.
215 E2 **Garrison** U.S.A.
175 M2 **Garron Point** U.K.
143 G4 **Garruk** Pak.
174 D4 **Garry, Loch** *l.* U.K.
205 I1 **Garry Lake** Canada
174 B2 **Garrynahine** U.K.
195 E4 **Garsen** Kenya
140 C4 **Garşy** Turkm.
173 D5 **Garth** U.K.
179 J1 **Gartow** Germany
196 B3 **Garub** Namibia
163 G4 **Garut** Indon.
175 L3 **Garvagh** U.K.
174 D3 **Garve** U.K.
152 D5 **Gar Xincun** China
208 D5 **Gary** U.S.A.
149 E3 **Garyarsa** China
159 C7 **Garyū-zan** *mt.* Japan
148 D2 **Gar Zangbo** *r.* China
150 B3 **Garzê** China
233 I4 **Garzón** Col.
Gascogne, Golfe de *g.* France/Spain *see* **Gascony, Gulf of**
217 E4 **Gasconade** *r.* U.S.A.
183 D5 **Gascony** *reg.* France
182 C4 **Gascony, Gulf of** France/Spain
118 B4 **Gascoyne** *r.* Australia
121 A5 **Gascoyne Junction** Australia
148 D2 **Gasherbrum I** *mt.* China/Pakistan
143 F5 **Gasht** Iran
193 D3 **Gashua** Nigeria
143 E3 **Gask** Iran
163 G3 **Gaspar, Selat** *sea chan.* Indon.
207 H4 **Gaspé** Canada
207 H4 **Gaspé, Cap** *c.* Canada
207 G4 **Gaspésie, Parc de Conservation de la** *nature res.* Canada
207 G4 **Gaspésie, Péninsule de la** *pen.* Canada
157 F5 **Gassan** *vol.* Japan
179 E2 **Gasselte** Neth.
156 F2 **Gastello** Rus. Fed.
219 D5 **Gastonia** U.S.A.
235 I4 **Gastre** Arg.
183 O4 **Gata, Cabo de** *c.* Spain
138 D4 **Gata, Cape** Cyprus
186 D3 **Gatchina** Rus. Fed.
220 B6 **Gate City** U.S.A.
174 D6 **Gatehouse of Fleet** U.K.
172 F3 **Gateshead** U.K.
217 D6 **Gatesville** U.S.A.
215 H2 **Gateway** U.S.A.
221 F4 **Gateway National Recreational Area** *park* U.S.A.
209 J3 **Gatineau** Canada
209 J2 **Gatineau** *r.* Canada
Gatong China *see* **Jomda**
125 J1 **Gatton** Australia
224 I6 **Gatún, Lago** *l.* Panama
139 L5 **Gatvand** Iran
119 H3 **Gau** *i.* Fiji
205 J3 **Gauer Lake** Canada
171 J3 **Gaula** *r.* Norway
220 C5 **Gauley Bridge** U.S.A.
178 D5 **Gaume** *reg.* Belgium
149 F4 **Gauri Sankar** *mt.* China
197 G3 **Gauteng** *prov.* S. Africa
143 G3 **Gauzan** Afgh.
139 J1 **Gavarr** Armenia
143 F5 **Gavāter** Iran
143 H3 **Gāv Band** Afgh.
142 D5 **Gāvbandī** Iran
142 D5 **Gāvbūs, Kūh-e** *mts* Iran
185 K7 **Gavdos** *i.* Greece
142 B3 **Gāveh Rūd** *r.* Iran
234 E1 **Gavião** *r.* Brazil
139 K4 **Gavīleh** Iran
214 B4 **Gaviota** U.S.A.
171 L3 **Gävle** Sweden
186 F3 **Gavrilov-Yam** Rus. Fed.
196 B3 **Gawachab** Namibia
124 C5 **Gawler** Australia
124 A4 **Gawler Ranges** *hills* Australia
154 A1 **Gaxun Nur** *salt l.* China
140 D2 **Gay** Rus. Fed.
149 F4 **Gaya** India
192 C3 **Gaya** Niger
160 E2 **Gaya He** *r.* China
209 E3 **Gaylord** U.S.A.
123 E5 **Gayndah** Australia
169 Q3 **Gayny** Rus. Fed.
138 E6 **Gaza** *terr.* Asia
138 E6 **Gaza** Gaza
197 J1 **Gaza** *prov.* Moz.
Gaz-Achak Turkm. *see* **Gazojak**
141 G4 **G'azalkent** Uzbek.
Gazandzhyk Turkm. *see* **Bereket**
143 H3 **Gazdarreh, Band-e** Afgh.
Gazgan Uzbek. *see* **G'ozg'on**
139 F3 **Gazi Antep** Turkey
Gaziantep Turkey *see* **Gazi Antep**
143 F3 **Gazīk** Iran
153 K1 **Gazimurskiy Khrebet** *mts* Rus. Fed.
153 K1 **Gazimurskiy Zavod** Rus. Fed.
138 D3 **Gazipaşa** Turkey
140 E4 **Gazli** Uzbek.
143 E5 **Gaz Māhū** Iran
140 E4 **Gazojak** Turkm.
194 C3 **Gbadolite** Dem. Rep. Congo
192 A4 **Gbangbatok** Sierra Leone
192 B4 **Gbarnga** Liberia
192 C4 **Gboko** Nigeria
177 I3 **Gdańsk** Poland
177 I3 **Gdańsk, Gulf of** Poland/Rus. Fed.
186 C3 **Gdov** Rus. Fed.
177 I3 **Gdynia** Poland
170 M1 **Geaidnovuohppi** Norway
174 C1 **Gealldruig Mhòr** *i.* U.K.
179 I3 **Gebesee** Germany
193 F3 **Gedaref** Sudan
179 H4 **Gedern** Germany
178 C5 **Gedinne** Belgium
138 A2 **Gediz** *r.* Turkey
173 H5 **Gedney Drove End** U.K.
171 J5 **Gedser** Denmark
178 D3 **Geel** Belgium
125 F7 **Geelong** Australia
121 A6 **Geelvink Channel** Australia
196 D4 **Geel Vloer** *salt pan* S. Africa
179 F2 **Geeste** Germany
179 I1 **Geesthacht** Germany
125 G9 **Geeveston** Australia
193 D3 **Geidam** Nigeria
179 H5 **Geiersberg** *h.* Germany
205 I3 **Geikie** *r.* Canada
179 E4 **Geilenkirchen** Germany
171 J3 **Geilo** Norway
171 I3 **Geiranger** Norway
209 E3 **Geist Reservoir** U.S.A.
179 K3 **Geithain** Germany
155 B6 **Gejiu** China
184 F6 **Gela** *Sicily* Italy
194 E3 **Geladī** Eth.
162 B4 **Gelang, Tanjung** *pt* Malaysia
179 E3 **Geldern** Germany
187 F6 **Gelendzhik** Rus. Fed.
177 K3 **Gelgaudiškis** Lith.
Gelibolu Turkey *see* **Gallipoli**
138 C2 **Gelincik Dağı** *mt.* Turkey
143 E3 **Gelmord** Iran
179 H4 **Gelnhausen** Germany
179 F3 **Gelsenkirchen** Germany
162 B5 **Gemas** Malaysia
161 J5 **Gemeh** Indon.
194 B3 **Gemena** Dem. Rep. Congo
139 F2 **Gemerek** Turkey
138 B1 **Gemlik** Turkey
184 E1 **Gemona del Friuli** Italy
Gemsa Egypt *see* **Jamsah**
195 C6 **Gemsbok National Park** Botswana
196 D3 **Gemsbokplein** *well* S. Africa
194 E3 **Genalē Wenz** *r.* Eth.
178 C4 **Genappe** Belgium
142 C4 **Genāveh** Iran
235 J3 **General Acha** Arg.
235 K3 **General Alvear** *Buenos Aires* Arg.
235 K1 **General Alvear** *Entre Ríos* Arg.
235 I2 **General Alvear** *Mendoza* Arg.
235 K2 **General Belgrano** Arg.
225 E2 **General Bravo** Mex.
232 B7 **General Carrera, Lago** *l.* Chile
225 D2 **General Cepeda** Mex.
235 L3 **General Conesa** *Buenos Aires* Arg.
235 J4 **General Conesa** *Río Negro* Arg.
235 L3 **General Guido** Arg.
235 L3 **General Juan Madariaga** Arg.
235 K3 **General La Madrid** Arg.
235 L3 **General Lavalle** Arg.
235 J2 **General Levalle** Arg.
161 J4 **General Luna** Phil.
161 J4 **General MacArthur** Phil.
235 J2 **General Pico** Arg.
235 K2 **General Pinto** Arg.
235 L3 **General Roca** Arg.
161 J5 **General Santos** Phil.
225 E2 **General Terán** Mex.
235 J2 **General Villegas** Arg.
220 D3 **Genesee** *r.* U.S.A.
208 B5 **Geneseo** *IL* U.S.A.
221 E3 **Geneseo** *NY* U.S.A.
197 G3 **Geneva** S. Africa
176 C7 **Geneva** Switz.
208 C5 **Geneva** *IL* U.S.A.
216 D3 **Geneva** *NE* U.S.A.
221 E3 **Geneva** *NY* U.S.A.
220 C4 **Geneva** *OH* U.S.A.
182 H3 **Geneva, Lake** France/Switz.
208 C4 **Geneva, Lake** U.S.A.
Genève Switz. *see* **Geneva**
183 N4 **Genil** *r.* Spain
178 D4 **Genk** Belgium
178 D3 **Gennep** Neth.
125 H6 **Genoa** Australia
184 C2 **Genoa** Italy
184 C2 **Genoa, Gulf of** Italy
Genova Italy *see* **Genoa**
Gent Belgium *see* **Ghent**
179 K2 **Genthin** Germany
118 B5 **Geographe Bay** Australia
132 F2 **Georga, Zemlya** *i.* Rus. Fed.
207 G2 **George** *r.* Canada
197 E6 **George** S. Africa
125 H5 **George, Lake** *N.S.W.* Australia
124 C6 **George, Lake** *S.A.* Australia
219 D6 **George, Lake** *FL* U.S.A.
221 G3 **George, Lake** *NY* U.S.A.
126 A6 **George Sound** *inlet* N.Z.
122 C3 **Georgetown** *Qld* Australia
124 C4 **Georgetown** *S.A.* Australia
125 G8 **George Town** Australia
209 H4 **Georgetown** Canada
192 A3 **Georgetown** Gambia
231 G2 **Georgetown** Guyana
163 B1 **George Town** Malaysia
221 F5 **Georgetown** *DE* U.S.A.
208 D6 **Georgetown** *IL* U.S.A.
219 C4 **Georgetown** *KY* U.S.A.
220 B5 **Georgetown** *OH* U.S.A.
219 E5 **Georgetown** *SC* U.S.A.
217 D6 **Georgetown** *TX* U.S.A.
127 J6 **George V Land** *reg.* Antarctica
217 D6 **George West** U.S.A.
187 G7 **Georgia** *country* Asia
219 D5 **Georgia** *state* U.S.A.
204 E5 **Georgia, Strait of** Canada
209 G3 **Georgian Bay** Canada
209 H3 **Georgian Bay Islands National Park** Canada
118 D4 **Georgina** *watercourse* Australia
141 J2 **Georgiyevka** *Vostochnyy Kazakhstan* Kazakh.
141 G4 **Georgiyevka** *Yuzhnyy Kazakhstan* Kazakh.
187 G6 **Georgiyevsk** Rus. Fed.
186 H3 **Georgiyevskoye** Rus. Fed.
179 K4 **Gera** Germany
178 B4 **Geraardsbergen** Belgium
231 I6 **Geral de Goiás, Serra** *hills* Brazil
126 C6 **Geraldine** N.Z.
234 C1 **Geral do Paraná, Serra** *hills* Brazil
118 B4 **Geraldton** Australia
142 D5 **Gerāsh** Iran
139 H3 **Gercüş** Turkey
138 D1 **Gerede** Turkey
138 D1 **Gerede** *r.* Turkey
143 G4 **Gereshk** Afgh.
162 B4 **Gerik** Malaysia
143 E3 **Gerīmenj** Iran
216 C3 **Gering** U.S.A.
213 C3 **Gerlach** U.S.A.
177 C3 **German Bight** *g.* Denmark/Ger.
204 E3 **Germansen Landing** Canada
221 E5 **Germantown** U.S.A.
176 E5 **Germany** *country* Europe
179 G5 **Germersheim** Germany
197 H3 **Germiston** S. Africa
179 G5 **Gernsheim** Germany
179 E4 **Gerolstein** Germany
179 I5 **Gerolzhofen** Germany
215 G5 **Geronimo** U.S.A.
125 I5 **Gerringong** Australia
179 H4 **Gersfeld (Rhön)** Germany
179 I4 **Gerstungen** Germany
179 J2 **Gerwisch** Germany
149 F2 **Gêrzê** China
187 E7 **Gerze** Turkey
179 F3 **Gescher** Germany
194 E3 **Gestro, Wabē** *r.* Eth.
142 D3 **Getcheh, Kūh-e** *hills* Iran
178 D4 **Gete** *r.* Belgium
221 E5 **Gettysburg** *PA* U.S.A.
216 D2 **Gettysburg** *SD* U.S.A.
221 E5 **Gettysburg National Military Park** *nat. park* U.S.A.
155 C5 **Getu He** *r.* China
127 I4 **Getz Ice Shelf** Antarctica
163 E2 **Geumapang** *r.* Indon.
125 H4 **Geurie** Australia
139 I2 **Gevaş** Turkey
185 J4 **Gevgelija** Macedonia
162 □ **Geylang** Sing.
197 F3 **Geysdorp** S. Africa
138 C1 **Geyve** Turkey
197 F2 **Ghaap Plateau** S. Africa
139 I5 **Ghadaf, Wādī al** *watercourse* Iraq
192 C1 **Ghadāmis** Libya
142 D2 **Gha'em Shahr** Iran
141 G4 **Ghafurov** Tajik.
148 C3 **Ghaggar, Dry Bed of** *watercourse* Pak.
149 E4 **Ghaghara** *r.* India
149 F5 **Ghaghra** India
192 B4 **Ghana** *country* Africa
142 D5 **Ghanādah, Rās** *pt* U.A.E.
148 C4 **Ghanliala** India
195 C6 **Ghanzi** Botswana
197 E1 **Ghanzi** *admin. dist.* Botswana
142 C5 **Ghār, Ras al** *pt* Saudi Arabia
138 E6 **Gharandal** Jordan
192 C1 **Ghardaïa** Alg.
193 F2 **Ghārib, Jabal** *mt.* Egypt
Ghārib, Jabal *mt.* Egypt *see* **Ḩamāţah, Jabal**
141 G5 **Gharm** Tajik.
193 D1 **Gharyān** Libya
139 F5 **Gharz, Wādī al** *watercourse* Syria
193 D2 **Ghāt** Libya
148 B3 **Ghauspur** Pak.
193 D3 **Ghazal, Bahr el** *watercourse* Chad
192 B1 **Ghazaouet** Alg.
148 D3 **Ghaziabad** India
149 E4 **Ghazipur** India
148 A3 **Ghazluna** Pak.
143 H3 **Ghaznī** Afgh.
143 H3 **Ghazni** *r.* Afgh.
143 G3 **Ghazoor** Afgh.
178 B3 **Ghent** Belgium
177 L7 **Gheorgheni** Romania
177 K7 **Gherla** Romania
184 C3 **Ghisonaccia** *Corsica* France
143 G3 **Ghizao** Afgh.
148 C1 **Ghizar** Pak.
147 G2 **Ghod** *r.* India
149 G4 **Ghoraghat** Bangl.
143 H3 **Ghorband** *r.* Afgh.
148 B4 **Ghotaru** India
148 B4 **Ghotki** Pak.
Ghuari *r.* India *see* **Ghugri**
141 H5 **Ghūdara** Tajik.
149 F4 **Ghugri** *r.* India
148 D6 **Ghugus** India
148 B4 **Ghulam Mohammed Barrage** Pak.
142 D4 **Ghūrī** Iran
143 F3 **Ghurian** Afgh.
178 A3 **Ghyvelde** France
Gia Đinh Vietnam *see* **Thu Đuc**
187 G6 **Giaginskaya** Rus. Fed.
162 C2 **Gia Nghia** Vietnam
136 B4 **Gianisada** *i.* Greece
185 J4 **Giannitsa** Greece
197 H4 **Giant's Castle** *mt.* S. Africa
175 L2 **Giant's Causeway** *lava field* U.K.
163 I4 **Gianyar** Indon.
162 C3 **Gia Rai** Vietnam
184 F6 **Giarre** *Sicily* Italy
184 B2 **Giaveno** Italy
120 D2 **Gibb** *r.* Australia
196 B2 **Gibeon** Namibia
183 N4 **Gibraltar** Europe
183 M5 **Gibraltar, Strait of** Morocco/Spain
121 C7 **Gibson** Australia
208 C5 **Gibson City** U.S.A.
118 C4 **Gibson Desert** Australia
150 B2 **Gichgeniyn Nuruu** *mts* Mongolia
147 H3 **Giddalur** India
194 D3 **Gīdolē** Eth.
182 F3 **Gien** France
179 G4 **Gießen** Germany
179 I2 **Gifhorn** Germany
204 F3 **Gift Lake** Canada
159 E7 **Gifu** Japan
233 I4 **Gigante** Col.
174 C5 **Gigha** *i.* U.K.
141 F4 **G'ijduvon** Uzbek.
Gijón Spain *see* **Gijón-Xixón**
183 N1 **Gijón-Xixón** Spain
215 F5 **Gila** *r.* U.S.A.
215 F5 **Gila Bend** U.S.A.
215 F5 **Gila Bend Mountains** U.S.A.
215 E5 **Gila Mountains** U.S.A.
139 J4 **Gīlān-e Gharb** Iran
139 L1 **Giläzi** Azer.
119 E3 **Gilbert** *r.* Australia
215 G5 **Gilbert** *AZ* U.S.A.
220 C6 **Gilbert** *WV* U.S.A.
119 H2 **Gilbert Islands** Kiribati
236 G6 **Gilbert Ridge** *sea feature* Pacific Ocean
122 C3 **Gilbert River** Australia
231 I5 **Gilbués** Brazil
143 E3 **Gil Chashmeh** Iran
212 E1 **Gildford** U.S.A.
120 E3 **Giles Creek** *r.* Australia
204 D4 **Gilford Island** Canada
125 I2 **Gilgai** Australia
125 H3 **Gilgandra** Australia
195 D4 **Gilgil** Kenya
125 H2 **Gil Gil Creek** *r.* Australia
148 C2 **Gilgit** Pak.
148 C2 **Gilgit** *r.* Pak.
125 G4 **Gilgunnia** Australia
204 D4 **Gil Island** Canada
205 K3 **Gillam** Canada
124 B4 **Gilles, Lake** *salt flat* Australia
208 C3 **Gillett** U.S.A.
212 F2 **Gillette** U.S.A.
123 C4 **Gilliat** Australia
173 E6 **Gillingham** *England* U.K.
173 H6 **Gillingham** *England* U.K.
172 F3 **Gilling West** U.K.
208 D3 **Gills Rock** U.S.A.
208 D5 **Gilman** *IL* U.S.A.
208 B3 **Gilman** *WI* U.S.A.
206 E2 **Gilmour Island** Canada
214 B3 **Gilroy** U.S.A.
221 G3 **Gilsum** U.S.A.
193 E3 **Gimbala, Jebel** *mt.* Sudan
194 D3 **Gīmbī** Eth.
Gimhae S. Korea *see* **Kimhae**
205 J4 **Gimli** Canada
230 E6 **Ginebra, Laguna** *l.* Bol.
147 I5 **Gin Ganga** *r.* Sri Lanka
147 H3 **Gingee** India
123 E5 **Gin Gin** Australia
121 A6 **Gingin** Australia
204 D3 **Gingolx** Canada
194 E3 **Gīnīr** Eth.
185 G4 **Ginosa** Italy
185 G4 **Gioia del Colle** Italy
125 G6 **Gippsland** *reg.* Australia
148 B4 **Girab** India
143 E5 **Gīrān** Iran
143 E4 **Gīrān Rīg** *mt.* Iran
220 C3 **Girard** U.S.A.
148 B3 **Girdao** Pak.
143 G5 **Girdar Dhor** *r.* Pak.
143 F4 **Girdi** Iran
139 G1 **Giresun** Turkey
148 B5 **Gir Forest** India
149 F4 **Giridih** India
125 G3 **Girilambone** Australia
148 C5 **Girna** *r.* India
183 R2 **Girona** Spain
182 D4 **Gironde** *est.* France
125 G4 **Girral** Australia
174 D5 **Girvan** U.K.
186 E2 **Girvas** Rus. Fed.
149 E4 **Girwan** India
127 G3 **Gisborne** N.Z.
204 E4 **Giscome** Canada
171 K4 **Gislaved** Sweden
141 F5 **Gissar Range** *mts* Tajik./Uzbek.
187 G7 **Gistola, Gora** *mt.* Georgia/Rus. Fed.
195 C4 **Gitarama** Rwanda
195 C4 **Gitega** Burundi
184 E3 **Giulianova** Italy
185 K3 **Giurgiu** Romania
185 K2 **Giuvala, Pasul** *pass* Romania
178 C4 **Givet** France
182 G4 **Givors** France
178 C6 **Givry-en-Argonne** France
197 I1 **Giyani** S. Africa
193 F2 **Giza** Egypt
139 K4 **Gīzeh Rūd** *r.* Iran
Gizhduvan Uzbek. *see* **G'ijduvon**
133 R3 **Gizhiga** Rus. Fed.
185 I3 **Gjakovë** Kosovo
185 I3 **Gjilan** Kosovo
185 I4 **Gjirokastër** Albania
203 I3 **Gjoa Haven** Canada
171 J3 **Gjøra** Norway
171 J3 **Gjøvik** Norway
185 M6 **Gkinas, Akrotirio** *pt* Greece
207 I4 **Glace Bay** Canada
204 B3 **Glacier Bay** U.S.A.

204 B3 Glacier Bay National Park and Preserve U.S.A.
204 F4 Glacier National Park Canada
212 D1 Glacier National Park U.S.A.
212 B1 Glacier Peak vol. U.S.A.
170 J2 Gladstad Norway
119 F4 Gladstone Qld Australia
124 C4 Gladstone S.A. Australia
125 H8 Gladstone Tas. Australia
208 D3 Gladstone U.S.A.
209 E4 Gladwin U.S.A.
174 E4 Glamis U.K.
179 F5 Glan r. Germany
161 J5 Glan Phil.
175 I5 Glanaruddery Mountains Ireland
179 G2 Glandorf Germany
172 F2 Glanton U.K.
209 G4 Glanworth Canada
174 D5 Glasgow U.K.
219 C4 Glasgow KY U.S.A.
212 F1 Glasgow MT U.S.A.
220 D6 Glasgow VA U.S.A.
205 H4 Glaslyn Canada
214 C3 Glass Mountain U.S.A.
173 E6 Glastonbury U.K.
179 K4 Glauchau Germany
132 G4 Glazov Rus. Fed.
187 F4 Glazunovka Rus. Fed.
177 O3 Glazunovo Rus. Fed.
221 H2 Glen U.S.A.
174 C3 Glen Affric val. U.K.
209 G2 Glen Afton Canada
126 E2 Glen Afton N.Z.
197 H1 Glen Alpine Dam S. Africa
175 J4 Glenamaddy Ireland
209 E3 Glen Arbor U.S.A.
126 C6 Glenavy N.Z.
174 C3 Glen Cannich val. U.K.
213 E4 Glen Canyon gorge U.S.A.
215 G3 Glen Canyon National Recreation Area park U.S.A.
174 E4 Glen Clova val. U.K.
124 D6 Glencoe Australia
209 G4 Glencoe Canada
197 I4 Glencoe S. Africa
174 C4 Glen Coe val. U.K.
209 E2 Glendale Canada
215 F5 Glendale AZ U.S.A.
214 C4 Glendale CA U.S.A.
215 E3 Glendale NV U.S.A.
215 F3 Glendale UT U.S.A.
220 D4 Glendale Lake U.S.A.
125 I4 Glen Davis Australia
123 E4 Glenden Australia
212 F2 Glendive U.S.A.
205 G4 Glendon Canada
213 F3 Glendo Reservoir U.S.A.
124 D6 Glenelg r. Australia
175 F4 Glen Esk val. U.K.
174 A5 Glengad Head Ireland
174 C3 Glen Garry val. Scotland U.K.
174 D4 Glen Garry val. Scotland U.K.
175 K3 Glengavlen Ireland
123 B5 Glengyle Australia
125 I2 Glen Innes Australia
174 D6 Glenluce U.K.
174 D4 Glen Lyon val. U.K.
174 D3 Glen More val. U.K.
125 H1 Glenmorgan Australia
174 D3 Glen Moriston val. U.K.
215 G6 Glenn, Mount U.S.A.
202 D3 Glennallen U.S.A.
174 C4 Glen Nevis val. U.K.
209 F3 Glennie U.S.A.
221 E6 Glenns U.S.A.
204 C3 Glenora Canada
122 C3 Glenore Australia
123 B4 Glenormiston Australia
221 F2 Glen Robertson Canada
174 E4 Glenrothes U.K.
221 G3 Glens Falls U.S.A.
174 E4 Glen Shee val. U.K.
174 C3 Glen Shiel val. U.K.
175 J3 Glenties Ireland
175 K2 Glenveagh National Park Ireland
220 C5 Glenville U.S.A.
217 E5 Glenwood AR U.S.A.
215 H5 Glenwood NM U.S.A.
213 F4 Glenwood Springs U.S.A.
208 B2 Glidden U.S.A.
179 I1 Glinde Germany
177 I5 Gliwice Poland
215 G5 Globe U.S.A.
177 H5 Głogów Poland
170 K2 Glomfjord Norway
171 J4 Glomma r. Norway
195 E5 Glorieuses, Îles is Indian Ocean
125 I3 Gloucester Australia
173 E6 Gloucester U.K.
221 H3 Gloucester MA U.S.A.
221 E6 Gloucester VA U.S.A.
221 F3 Gloversville U.S.A.
179 K2 Glöwen Germany
158 D1 Glubinnoye Rus. Fed.
152 G1 Glubokiy Rus. Fed.
187 G6 Glubokiy Rus. Fed.
141 J2 Glubokoye Kazakh.
179 H1 Glückstadt Germany
170 □ Gluggarnir h. Faroe Is
173 F4 Glusburn U.K.
187 H5 Gmelinka Rus. Fed.
176 G6 Gmünd Austria
176 F7 Gmunden Austria
171 L3 Gnarp Sweden
179 H1 Gnarrenburg Germany
177 H4 Gniezno Poland
121 B7 Gnowangerup Australia
121 B6 Gnows Nest Range hills Australia
147 G3 Goa India
147 G3 Goa state India
196 B3 Goageb Namibia
125 I6 Goalen Head Australia
149 G4 Goalpara India
174 C5 Goat Fell h. U.K.
194 E3 Goba Eth.
195 B6 Gobabis Namibia
196 C3 Gobas Namibia
235 K1 Gobernador Crespo Arg.
235 I3 Gobernador Duval Arg.
232 B7 Gobernador Gregores Arg.
150 C2 Gobi Desert Mongolia
159 D8 Gobō Japan
179 E3 Goch Germany
195 B6 Gochas Namibia
173 G6 Godalming U.K.
147 I2 Godavari r. India
147 I2 Godavari, Mouths of the India
207 G4 Godbout Canada
214 C3 Goddard, Mount U.S.A.
194 E3 Godere Eth.
209 G4 Goderich Canada
148 C5 Godhra India
235 I2 Godoy Cruz Arg.
205 K3 Gods r. Canada
205 K3 Gods Lake Canada
205 L2 God's Mercy, Bay of Canada
Godthåb Greenland see Nuuk
Godwin-Austen, Mount mt. China/Pakistan see K2
178 B3 Goedereede Neth.
206 E4 Goéland, Lac au l. Canada
207 H2 Goëlands, Lac aux l. Canada
178 B3 Goes Neth.
209 E2 Goetzville U.S.A.
215 E4 Goffs U.S.A.
209 G2 Gogama Canada
208 C2 Gogebic, Lake U.S.A.
208 C2 Gogebic Range hills U.S.A.
148 D4 Gohad India
231 L5 Goiana Brazil
234 C2 Goiandira Brazil
234 C2 Goiânia Brazil
234 B1 Goiás Brazil
234 B2 Goiás state Brazil
235 B4 Goio-Erê Brazil
148 C3 Gojra Pak.
147 G2 Gokak India
187 C7 Gökçeada i. Turkey
138 B2 Gökçedağ Turkey
148 G3 Gokhar La pass China
139 E1 Gökirmak r. Turkey
140 D4 Goklenkuy, Solonchak salt l. Turkm.
136 B3 Gökova Körfezi b. Turkey
143 F5 Gokprosh Hills Pak.
139 F2 Göksun Turkey
138 E3 Göksu Nehri r. Turkey
195 C5 Gokwe Zimbabwe
171 J3 Gol Norway
149 E3 Gola India
149 H4 Golaghat India
143 E4 Golbāf Iran
139 F3 Gölbaşı Turkey
138 B1 Gölcük Turkey
177 K3 Gołdap Poland
179 K1 Goldberg Germany
125 J2 Gold Coast Australia
192 B4 Gold Coast coastal area Ghana
204 F4 Golden Canada
126 D4 Golden Bay N.Z.
179 I3 Goldene Aue reg. Germany
214 A3 Golden Gate National Recreation Area park U.S.A.
204 D5 Golden Hinde mt. Canada
179 G2 Goldenstedt Germany
175 J5 Golden Vale lowland Ireland
215 D3 Goldfield U.S.A.
215 D3 Gold Point U.S.A.
219 E5 Goldsboro U.S.A.
121 B4 Goldsworthy (abandoned) Australia
217 D6 Goldthwaite U.S.A.
139 I1 Göle Turkey
143 F3 Golestān Afgh.
214 C4 Goleta U.S.A.
153 I1 Golets-Davydov, Gora mt. Rus. Fed.
224 I6 Golfito Costa Rica
217 D6 Goliad U.S.A.
160 A1 Golin Baixing China
139 F1 Gölköy Turkey
179 K2 Golm Germany
139 J3 Golmānkhāneh Iran
150 B3 Golmud China
149 H1 Golmud He r. China
161 I3 Golo i. Phil.
158 I3 Golovnino Rus. Fed.
142 C3 Golpāyegān Iran
138 C1 Gölpazarı Turkey
174 E3 Golspie U.K.
141 H1 Golubovka Kazakh.
143 F3 Gol Vardeh Iran
185 K4 Golyama Syutkya mt. Bulg.
185 K4 Golyam Persenk mt. Bulg.
Golyshi Rus. Fed. see Vetluzhskiy
179 K2 Golzow Germany
149 G3 Gomang Co salt l. China
149 E4 Gomati r. India
162 □ Gombak, Bukit h. Sing.
193 D3 Gombe Nigeria
195 D4 Gombe r. Tanz.
193 D3 Gombi Nigeria
225 D2 Gómez Palacio Mex.
142 D2 Gomīshān Iran
179 J2 Gommern Germany
149 F2 Gomo Co salt l. China
143 E2 Gonābād Iran
223 J5 Gonaïves Haiti
197 I1 Gonarezhou National Park Zimbabwe
223 J5 Gonâve, Île de la i. Haiti
142 D2 Gonbad-e Kavus Iran
149 E4 Gonda India
148 B5 Gondal India
194 D2 Gonder Eth.
149 E5 Gondia India
138 A1 Gönen Turkey
155 D4 Gong'an China
149 G3 Gongbalou China
155 D5 Gongcheng China
149 G3 Gongga Shan mt. China
154 A2 Gonghe China
154 E1 Gonghui China
141 J4 Gongliu China
234 E1 Gongogi r. Brazil
193 D3 Gongola r. Nigeria
125 G3 Gongolgon Australia
144 I3 Gongpoquan China
155 B4 Gongquan China
155 B5 Gongwang Shan mts China
Gongxian China see Gongquan
154 D3 Gongyi China
160 C2 Gongzhuling China
197 H6 Gonubie S. Africa
225 E3 Gonzáles Mex.
214 B3 Gonzales CA U.S.A.
217 D6 Gonzales TX U.S.A.
235 J2 González Moreno Arg.
156 B1 Gonzha Rus. Fed.
221 E6 Goochland U.S.A.
127 J6 Goodenough, Cape Antarctica
119 F2 Goodenough Island P.N.G.
209 H3 Gooderham Canada
196 C7 Good Hope, Cape of S. Africa
213 D3 Gooding U.S.A.
217 C4 Goodland U.S.A.
125 G2 Goodooga Australia
173 G4 Goole U.K.
125 F5 Goolgowi Australia
125 H4 Goolma Australia
125 H4 Gooloogong Australia
124 C5 Goolwa Australia
121 B6 Goomalling Australia
125 F2 Goombalie Australia
125 I2 Goondiwindi Australia
121 C6 Goongarrie, Lake salt flat Australia
121 C6 Goongarrie National Park Australia
123 D4 Goonyella Australia
121 B6 Goorly, Lake salt flat Australia
207 H3 Goose r. Canada
213 B3 Goose Lake U.S.A.
147 H3 Gooty India
152 C5 Gopeshwar India
176 D6 Göppingen Germany
149 E4 Gorakhpur India
185 H3 Goražde Bos.-Herz.
186 G3 Gorchukha Rus. Fed.
224 I5 Gorda, Punta pt Nicaragua
219 E7 Gorda Cay i. Bahamas
138 B2 Gördes Turkey
177 O4 Gordeyevka Rus. Fed.
125 F9 Gordon r. Australia
175 F5 Gordon U.K.
125 G9 Gordon, Lake Australia
120 E3 Gordon Downs (abandoned) Australia
205 G2 Gordon Lake Canada
220 D5 Gordon Lake U.S.A.
220 D5 Gordonsville U.S.A.
193 D4 Goré Chad
194 D3 Gorē Eth.
126 B7 Gore N.Z.
209 F3 Gore Bay Canada
174 E5 Gorebridge U.K.
138 E2 Göreme Milli Parkı nat. park Turkey
175 L5 Gorey Ireland
143 E4 Gorg Iran
142 D2 Gorgān Iran
137 I3 Gorgān, Khalīj-e Iran
121 B4 Gorge Range hills Australia
233 H4 Gorgona, Isla i. Col.
221 H2 Gorham U.S.A.
187 H7 Gori Georgia
178 C3 Gorinchem Neth.
139 K2 Goris Armenia
184 E2 Gorizia Italy
Gor'kiy Rus. Fed. see Nizhniy Novgorod
187 H5 Gor'ko-Solenoye, Ozero l. Rus. Fed.
186 G3 Gor'kovskoye Vodokhranilishche resr Rus. Fed.
141 J1 Gor'koye, Ozero salt l. Rus. Fed.
177 J6 Gorlice Poland
176 G5 Görlitz Germany
148 D4 Gormi India
185 K3 Gorna Oryakhovitsa Bulg.
185 I2 Gornji Milanovac Serbia
185 G3 Gornji Vakuf Bos.-Herz.
141 K2 Gorno-Altaysk Rus. Fed.
158 G1 Gornozavodsk Rus. Fed.
141 J2 Gornyak Rus. Fed.
158 C2 Gornyy Primorskiy Kray Rus. Fed.
187 I5 Gornyy Saratovskaya Oblast' Rus. Fed.
187 H5 Gornyy Balykley Rus. Fed.
158 C2 Gornyye Klyuchi Rus. Fed.
186 G3 Gorodets Rus. Fed.
187 H5 Gorodishche Rus. Fed.
Gorodok Rus. Fed. see Zakamensk
187 G6 Gorodovikovsk Rus. Fed.
119 E2 Goroka P.N.G.
124 D6 Goroke Australia
186 G3 Gorokhovets Rus. Fed.
192 B3 Gorom Gorom Burkina
195 D5 Gorongosa Moz.
151 E6 Gorontalo Indon.
187 F5 Gorshechnoye Rus. Fed.
175 J4 Gort Ireland
Gortahork Ireland see Gort an Choirce
175 J2 Gort an Choirce Ireland
234 D1 Gorutuba r. Brazil
143 E4 Gorveh Iran
187 F6 Goryachiy Klyuch Rus. Fed.
179 K2 Görzke Germany
176 G4 Gorzów Wielkopolski Poland
125 I4 Gosford Australia
172 F2 Gosforth U.K.
209 E5 Goshen IN U.S.A.
221 F4 Goshen NY U.S.A.
158 G4 Goshogawara Japan
179 I3 Goslar Germany
140 C4 Goşoba Turkm.
184 F2 Gospić Croatia
173 F7 Gosport U.K.
185 I4 Gostivar Macedonia
Göteborg Sweden see Gothenburg
171 K4 Götene Sweden
179 I4 Gotha Germany
171 J4 Gothenburg Sweden
216 C3 Gothenburg U.S.A.
171 L4 Gotland i. Sweden
157 C6 Gotō-rettō is Japan
185 J4 Gotse Delchev Bulg.
171 L4 Gotska Sandön i. Sweden
159 C7 Gōtsu Japan
179 H3 Göttingen Germany
204 E4 Gott Peak Canada
140 C5 Goturdepe Turkm.
160 A3 Goubangzi China
178 C2 Gouda Neth.
192 A3 Goudiri Senegal
193 D3 Goudoumaria Niger
209 E1 Goudreau Canada
239 I8 Gough Island S. Atlantic Ocean
207 F4 Gouin, Réservoir resr Canada
209 E2 Goulais River Canada
125 H5 Goulburn Australia
125 I4 Goulburn r. N.S.W. Australia
125 F6 Goulburn r. Vic. Australia
118 D3 Goulburn Islands Australia
209 E2 Gould City U.S.A.
192 B3 Goundam Mali
183 Q4 Gouraya Alg.
193 D3 Gouré Niger
196 D7 Gourits r. S. Africa
192 B3 Gourma-Rharous Mali
182 E2 Gournay-en-Bray France
125 H6 Gourock Range mts Australia
178 A5 Goussainville France
221 F2 Gouverneur U.S.A.
205 H5 Govenlock Canada
234 E2 Governador Valadares Brazil
161 J5 Governor Generoso Phil.
219 E7 Governor's Harbour Bahamas
150 B2 Govĭ Altayn Nuruu mts Mongolia
149 E4 Govind Ballash Pant Sagar resr India
148 D3 Govind Sagar resr India
Govurdak Turkm. see Magdanly
220 D3 Gowanda U.S.A.
123 D5 Gowan Range hills Australia
143 G4 Gowārān Afgh.
142 D4 Gowd-e Aḥmar Iran
173 C6 Gower pen. U.K.
209 G2 Gowganda Canada
175 K4 Gowna, Lough l. Ireland
232 E3 Goya Arg.
139 K1 Göyçay Azer.
121 F5 Goyder watercourse Australia
140 C4 Goymatdag hills Turkm.
181 J3 Göynük Turkey
139 H2 Göynük Turkey
159 G5 Goyō-zan mt. Japan
139 L2 Göytäpä Azer.
143 F3 Gozareh Afgh.
Gōzareh Afgh. see Gozareh
139 G2 Gözene Turkey
141 F4 G'ozg'on Uzbek.
149 E2 Gozha Co salt l. China
184 F6 Gozo i. Malta
197 F6 Graaff-Reinet S. Africa
Graaf-Reinet S. Africa see Graaff-Reinet
196 C6 Graafwater S. Africa
179 I4 Grabfeld plain Germany
192 B4 Grabo Côte d'Ivoire
196 C7 Grabouw S. Africa
179 J1 Grabow Germany
184 F2 Gračac Croatia
209 I2 Gracefield Canada
140 C1 Grachevka Rus. Fed.
141 I2 Grachi Kazakh.
224 G5 Gracias Hond.
179 K3 Gräfenhainichen Germany
179 J5 Grafenwöhr Germany
125 J2 Grafton Australia
216 D1 Grafton ND U.S.A.
208 D4 Grafton WI U.S.A.
220 C5 Grafton WV U.S.A.
122 D3 Grafton, Cape Australia
215 E2 Grafton, Mount U.S.A.
122 D3 Grafton Passage Australia
217 D5 Graham U.S.A.
215 H5 Graham, Mount U.S.A.
Graham Bell Island i. Rus. Fed. see Greem-Bell, Ostrov
204 C4 Graham Island B.C. Canada
203 I2 Graham Island Nunavut Canada
221 I2 Graham Lake U.S.A.
197 G6 Grahamstown S. Africa
175 L5 Graigue Ireland
192 A4 Grain Coast Liberia
231 I5 Grajaú Brazil
174 B1 Gralisgeir i. U.K.
185 I4 Grammos mt. Greece
174 D4 Grampian Mountains U.K.
125 E6 Grampians National Park Australia
196 C5 Granaatboskolk S. Africa
233 I4 Granada Col.
224 H6 Granada Nicaragua
183 O4 Granada Spain
217 C4 Granada U.S.A.
175 K4 Granard Ireland
235 I3 Gran Bajo Salitroso salt flat Arg.
207 F4 Granby Canada
192 A2 Gran Canaria i. Canary Is
232 D3 Gran Chaco reg. Arg./Para.
208 D4 Grand MI U.S.A.
216 E3 Grand r. MO U.S.A.
219 E7 Grand Bahama i. Bahamas
207 I4 Grand Bank Canada
239 F3 Grand Banks of Newfoundland sea feature N. Atlantic Ocean
192 B4 Grand-Bassam Côte d'Ivoire
Grand Bay Canada see Grand Bay-Westfield
207 G4 Grand Bay-Westfield Canada
209 G4 Grand Bend Canada
Grand Canal canal China see Da Yunhe
175 K4 Grand Canal Ireland
215 F3 Grand Canyon U.S.A.
215 F3 Grand Canyon gorge U.S.A.
215 F3 Grand Canyon National Park U.S.A.
223 H5 Grand Cayman i. Cayman Is
205 G4 Grand Centre Canada
212 C2 Grand Coulee U.S.A.
235 I3 Grande r. Arg.
231 F7 Grande r. Bol.
231 I6 Grande r. Bahia Brazil
234 B2 Grande r. São Paulo Brazil
235 L3 Grande, Arroyo r. Arg.
232 C8 Grande, Bahía b. Arg.
234 D3 Grande, Ilha i. Brazil
233 L4 Grande, Serra mt. Brazil
204 F4 Grande Cache Canada
182 H4 Grande Casse, Pointe de la mt. France
Grande Comore i. Comoros see Njazidja
204 F3 Grande Prairie Canada
192 B1 Grand Erg Occidental des. Alg.
192 C2 Grand Erg Oriental des. Alg.
207 H4 Grande-Rivière Canada
212 C2 Grande Ronde r. U.S.A.
232 C4 Grandes, Salinas salt flat Arg.
207 G4 Grande-Vallée Canada
207 G4 Grand Falls N.B. Canada
207 I4 Grand Falls-Windsor Nfld Canada
204 F5 Grand Forks Canada
216 D2 Grand Forks U.S.A.
221 F3 Grand Gorge U.S.A.
221 J2 Grand Harbour Canada
208 D4 Grand Haven U.S.A.
204 F2 Grandin, Lac l. Canada
152 G1 Grandioznyy, Pik mt. Rus. Fed.
216 D3 Grand Island NE U.S.A.
208 D2 Grand Island i. MI U.S.A.
217 F6 Grand Isle LA U.S.A.
221 I1 Grand Isle ME U.S.A.
215 H2 Grand Junction U.S.A.
192 B4 Grand-Lahou Côte d'Ivoire
207 H3 Grand Lake Nfld Canada
207 I4 Grand Lake Nfld Canada
217 E6 Grand Lake LA U.S.A.
221 J2 Grand Lake ME U.S.A.
209 F3 Grand Lake MI U.S.A.
221 I1 Grand Lake Matagamon U.S.A.
220 A4 Grand Lake St Marys U.S.A.
221 I1 Grand Lake Seboeis U.S.A.
221 J2 Grand Lake Stream U.S.A.
209 E4 Grand Ledge U.S.A.
207 G5 Grand Manan Island Canada
209 E2 Grand Marais MI U.S.A.
208 B2 Grand Marais MN U.S.A.
207 F4 Grand-Mère Canada
183 L3 Grândola Port.
119 G3 Grand Passage New Caledonia
208 C2 Grand Portage U.S.A.
205 J4 Grand Rapids Canada
209 E4 Grand Rapids MI U.S.A.

Hammerdal

194 D2 Guba Eth.
140 D4 Gubadag Turkm.
147 H3 Gubbi India
184 E3 Gubbio Italy
187 F5 Gubkin Rus. Fed.
154 D3 Gucheng China
187 G7 Gudaut'a Georgia
171 J3 Gudbrandsdalen val. Norway
187 H7 Gudermes Rus. Fed.
147 I2 Gudivada India
147 H3 Gudiyattam India
160 E2 Gudong He r. China
143 G5 Gudri r. Pak.
138 D1 Güdül Turkey
147 H3 Gudur Andhra Pradesh India
147 H3 Gudur Andhra Pradesh India
171 I3 Gudvangen Norway
156 D2 Gudzhal r. Rus. Fed.
Guecho Spain see Algorta
192 A4 Guéckédou Guinea
209 I1 Guéguen, Lac l. Canada
233 I4 Güejar r. Col.
192 C1 Guelma Alg.
192 A2 Guelmine Morocco
209 G4 Guelph Canada
225 E3 Guémez Mex.
179 E5 Guénange France
233 K2 Güera r. Venez.
180 D5 Guerara Alg.
207 G2 Guérard, Lac l. Canada
180 C5 Guercif Morocco
182 E3 Guéret France
182 C2 Guernsey i. U.K.
213 F3 Guernsey U.S.A.
225 E2 Guerrero Mex.
225 D4 Guerrero state Mex.
224 A2 Guerrero Negro Mex.
203 L4 Guers, Lac l. Canada
142 D3 Gügerd, Kūh-e mts Iran
239 F5 Guiana Basin sea feature N. Atlantic Ocean
124 C6 Guichen Bay Australia
Guichi China see Chizhou
235 L2 Guichón Uruguay
154 A3 Guide China
193 D4 Guider Cameroon
155 C5 Guiding China
184 E4 Guidonia-Montecelio Italy
155 C6 Guigang China
192 B4 Guiglo Côte d'Ivoire
178 B5 Guignicourt France
197 J2 Guija Moz.
155 D6 Gui Jiang r. China
155 F4 Guiji Shan mts China
173 G6 Guildford U.K.
221 I2 Guilford U.S.A.
155 D5 Guilin China
206 E2 Guillaume-Delisle, Lac l. Canada
183 L2 Guimarães Port.
161 I4 Guimaras Strait Phil.
154 E3 Guimeng Ding mt. China
154 A3 Guinan China
214 A2 Guinda U.S.A.
161 J4 Guindulman Phil.
192 A3 Guinea country Africa
192 B4 Guinea, Gulf of Africa
239 I5 Guinea Basin sea feature N. Atlantic Ocean
192 A3 Guinea-Bissau country Africa
223 H4 Güines Cuba
182 C2 Guingamp France
182 B2 Guipavas France
155 D6 Guiping China
234 B2 Guiratinga Brazil
233 L2 Güiria Venez.
178 B5 Guiscard France
178 B5 Guise France
161 J4 Guiuan Phil.
155 E4 Guixi China
155 C5 Guiyang Guizhou China
155 D5 Guiyang Hunan China
155 C5 Guizhou prov. China
148 B5 Gujarat state India
148 C2 Gujar Khan Pak.
148 C2 Gujranwala Pak.
148 C2 Gujrat Pak.
187 F5 Gukovo Rus. Fed.
139 J3 Gük Tappeh Iran
148 D2 Gulabgarh India
Gulabie Uzbek. see Taxiatosh
154 B2 Gulang China
125 H3 Gulargambone Australia
147 H2 Gulbarga India
171 N4 Gulbene Latvia
141 H4 Gülchö Kyrg.
138 E3 Gülek Turkey
146 D4 Gulf, The Asia
Gulf of Martaban g. Myanmar see Mottama, Gulf of
217 F6 Gulfport U.S.A.
125 H4 Gulgong Australia
150 E1 Gulian China
155 B5 Gulin China
143 G4 Gulistan Pak.
Gulistan Uzbek. see Guliston
141 G4 Guliston Uzbek.
179 J1 Gülitz Germany
156 A2 Guliya Shan mt. China
209 E3 Gull Island U.S.A.
205 H4 Gull Lake Canada
170 M2 Gullträsk Sweden
136 B3 Güllük Körfezi b. Turkey
138 D3 Gülnar Turkey
143 F3 Gulran Afgh.
187 G7 Gulrip'shi Georgia
138 E2 Gülşehir Turkey
141 H3 Gul'shat Kazakh.
194 D3 Gulu Uganda
122 B1 Guluwuru Island Australia
148 B3 Gumal r. Pak.
195 C5 Gumare Botswana
140 C5 Gumdag Turkm.
149 F5 Gumia India
147 J1 Gumla India
179 F3 Gummersbach Germany
138 E1 Gümüşhacıköy Turkey
139 G1 Gümüşhane Turkey
148 D4 Guna India
125 F5 Gunbar Australia
125 H5 Gundagai Australia
179 H5 Gundelsheim Germany
138 D3 Gündoğmuş Turkey
138 B2 Güney Turkey
136 F3 Güneydoğu Toroslar plat. Turkey
195 B4 Gungu Dem. Rep. Congo
187 H7 Gunib Rus. Fed.
205 J4 Gunisao r. Canada
125 I3 Gunnedah Australia
127 L4 Gunnerus Ridge sea feature Southern Ocean
125 H5 Gunning Australia
213 F4 Gunnison CO U.S.A.
215 G2 Gunnison UT U.S.A.
213 E4 Gunnison r. U.S.A.
141 G5 Gunt r. Tajik.
147 H3 Guntakal India
179 I3 Güntersberge Germany
219 C5 Guntersville U.S.A.
219 C5 Guntersville Lake U.S.A.
147 I2 Guntur India
163 E2 Gunung Leuser, Taman Nasional nat. park Indon.
163 E2 Gunungsitoli Indon.
162 A5 Gunungtua Indon.
147 I2 Gunupur India
136 C3 Günyüzü Turkey
176 E6 Günzburg Germany
179 I5 Gunzenhausen Germany
155 D4 Guojiaba China
154 E1 Guojiatun China
154 E3 Guoyang China
152 B4 Gupis Jammu and Kashmir
154 A2 Gurban Hudag China
154 D1 Gurban Obo China
140 D4 Gurbansoltan Eje Turkm.
144 G3 Gurbantünggüt Shamo des. China
152 C5 Gurdaspur India
143 F5 Gurdim Iran
138 B3 Güre Turkey
148 D3 Gurgaon India
231 J5 Gurgueia r. Brazil
148 B4 Gurha India
233 L3 Guri, Embalse de resr Venez.
120 F1 Gurig National Park Australia
234 C2 Gurinhatã Brazil
187 H7 Gurjaani Georgia
142 E4 Gur Khar Iran
140 E4 Gurlan Uzbek.
Gurlen Uzbek. see Gurlan
139 I2 Gürpınar Turkey
149 G3 Guru China
195 D5 Guruè Moz.
139 F2 Gürün Turkey
231 I4 Gurupi r. Brazil
148 C4 Guru Sikhar mt. India
154 A1 Gurvantes Mongolia
187 B4 Gur'yevsk Rus. Fed.
192 C3 Gusau Nigeria
179 J2 Güsen Germany
177 K3 Gusev Rus. Fed.
143 F3 Guşgy r. Turkm.
160 B4 Gushan China
215 H1 Gusher U.S.A.
154 E3 Gushi China
133 L2 Gusikha Rus. Fed.
187 D4 Gusino Rus. Fed.
133 L4 Gusinoozersk Rus. Fed.
149 F5 Guskara India
187 G4 Gus'-Khrustal'nyy Rus. Fed.
184 C5 Guspini Sardinia Italy
204 B3 Gustavus U.S.A.
179 J3 Güsten Germany
214 B3 Gustine U.S.A.
179 K1 Güstrow Germany
149 H3 Gutang China
179 L2 Güterfelde Germany
179 G3 Gütersloh Germany
215 H5 Guthrie AZ U.S.A.
219 C4 Guthrie KY U.S.A.
217 D5 Guthrie OK U.S.A.
217 C5 Guthrie TX U.S.A.
155 E5 Gutian Fujian China
155 F5 Gutian Fujian China
179 E5 Gutland reg. Germany/Lux.
155 F5 Gutsuo China
208 B4 Guttenberg U.S.A.
195 D5 Gutu Zimbabwe
149 G4 Guwahati India
139 I3 Guwēr Iraq
140 C4 Guwlumaýak Turkm.
179 H3 Guxhagen Germany
231 G2 Guyana country S. America
154 D1 Guyang China
123 F6 Guy Fawkes River National Park Australia
217 C4 Guymon U.S.A.
142 D4 Güyom Iran
125 I3 Guyra Australia
154 E1 Guyuan Hebei China
154 C3 Guyuan Ningxia China
Guzar Uzbek. see G'uzor
155 C4 Guzhang China
154 E3 Guzhen China
141 F5 G'uzor Uzbek.
177 J3 Gvardeysk Rus. Fed.
156 E3 Gvasyugi Rus. Fed.
152 F8 Gwa Myanmar
125 H3 Gwabegar Australia
143 F5 Gwadar Pak.
143 F5 Gwadar West Bay Pak.
202 E4 Gwaii Haanas National Park Reserve Canada
148 D4 Gwalior India
195 C6 Gwanda Zimbabwe
194 F2 Gwardafuy, Gees c. Somalia
143 G4 Gwash Pak.
143 F5 Gwatar Bay Pak.
175 J3 Gweebarra Bay Ireland
Gweedore Ireland see Gaoth Dobhair
195 C5 Gweru Zimbabwe
208 D2 Gwinn U.S.A.
193 D3 Gwoza Nigeria
125 H2 Gwydir r. Australia
149 H3 Gyaca China
154 B3 Gyagartang China
149 F2 Gyangnyi Caka salt l. China
149 F3 Gyangrang China
149 G3 Gyangzê China
149 G3 Gyaring Co l. China
150 B3 Gyaring Hu l. China
185 K6 Gyaros i. Greece
149 H3 Gyarubtang China
132 I2 Gydan Peninsula Rus. Fed.
Gydanskiy Poluostrov pen. Rus. Fed. see Gydan Peninsula
151 B4 Gyigang China
149 H3 Gyimda China
149 F3 Gyirong Xizang China
149 F3 Gyirong Xizang China
149 H2 Gyiza China
119 F4 Gympie Australia
177 I7 Gyöngyös Hungary
177 H7 Győr Hungary
205 J4 Gypsumville Canada
207 G2 Gyrfalcon Islands Canada
185 J6 Gytheio Greece
177 J7 Gyula Hungary
139 I1 Gyumri Armenia
Gyzylarbat Turkm. see Serdar
141 F5 Gyzylaýak Turkm.
Gyzyletrek Turkm. see Etrek

H

171 N3 Haapajärvi Fin.
170 N2 Haapavesi Fin.
171 M4 Haapsalu Estonia
178 C2 Haarlem Neth.
197 E6 Haarlem S. Africa
179 G3 Haarstrang ridge Germany
126 B5 Haast N.Z.
143 G5 Hab r. Pak.
144 G2 Habahe China
147 I4 Habarane Sri Lanka
194 D3 Habaswein Kenya
204 F3 Habay Canada
146 C7 Habbān Yemen
139 I5 Ḩabbānīyah, Hawr al l. Iraq
143 G5 Hab Chauki Pak.
149 G4 Habiganj Bangl.
154 E1 Habirag China
149 G5 Habra India
233 I5 Hacha Col.
235 H3 Hachado, Paso de pass Arg./Chile
159 F8 Hachijō-jima i. Japan
158 G4 Hachinohe Japan
159 F7 Hachiōji Japan
138 E2 Hacıbektaş Turkey
139 H2 Hacıömer Turkey
124 C3 Hack, Mount Australia
195 D6 Hacufera Moz.
147 G3 Hadagalli India
156 B2 Hadayang China
147 E5 Ḩadd, Ra's al pt Oman
175 F5 Haddington U.K.
193 D3 Hadejia Nigeria
138 E5 Ḩadera Israel
171 J5 Haderslev Denmark
138 D3 Hadım Turkey
173 H5 Hadleigh U.K.
203 H2 Hadley Bay Canada
160 D6 Hadong S. Korea
162 Ha Đông Vietnam
139 F6 Ḩadraj, Wādī watercourse Saudi Arabia
146 C6 Ḩaḑramawt reg. Yemen
172 E3 Hadrian's Wall tourist site U.K.
171 J4 Hadsund Denmark
187 E5 Hadyach Ukr.
235 L1 Haedo, Cuchilla de hills Uruguay
160 C4 Haeju N. Korea
160 C5 Haeju-man b. N. Korea
160 D6 Haenam S. Korea
197 H1 Haenertsburg S. Africa
142 B4 Ḩafar al Bāţin Saudi Arabia
205 H4 Hafford Canada
139 F2 Hafik Turkey
142 B5 Hafirat Nasah Saudi Arabia
148 C2 Hafizabad Pak.
149 H4 Haflong India
170 B2 Hafnarfjörður Iceland
142 C4 Haft Gel Iran
170 B2 Hafursfjörður b. Iceland
209 G2 Hagar Canada
147 H3 Hagari r. India
194 D2 Hagar Nish Plateau Eritrea
151 G5 Hagåtña Guam
178 C4 Hageland reg. Belgium
179 F3 Hagen Germany
179 J1 Hagenow Germany
221 E5 Hagerstown U.S.A.
183 D5 Hagetmau France
171 K3 Hagfors Sweden
212 D2 Haggin, Mount U.S.A.
159 B7 Hagi Japan
155 B6 Ha Giang Vietnam
173 E5 Hagley U.K.
175 I5 Hag's Head Ireland
205 H4 Hague Canada
182 D2 Hague, Cap de la c. France
182 H2 Haguenau France
151 G4 Hahajima-rettō is Japan
195 D4 Hai Tanz.
154 F3 Hai'an China
196 B4 Haib watercourse Namibia
160 B3 Haicheng China
179 J5 Haidenaab r. Germany
155 C6 Hai Dương Vietnam
138 E5 Haifa Israel
138 E5 Haifa, Bay of Israel
155 E6 Haifeng China
121 D6 Haig Australia
179 G4 Haiger Germany
154 E2 Hai He r. China
155 D6 Haikou China
146 B4 Ḩā'il Saudi Arabia
209 H2 Haileybury Canada
160 E1 Hailin China
173 H7 Hailsham U.K.
156 B3 Hailun China
170 N2 Hailuoto Fin.
155 F4 Haimen China
155 D7 Hainan i. China
155 C7 Hainan prov. China
155 C6 Hainan Strait China
204 B3 Haines U.S.A.
204 B2 Haines Junction Canada
179 I3 Hainich ridge Germany
179 L4 Hainichen Germany
179 I3 Hainleite ridge Germany
155 C6 Hai Phong Vietnam
156 D3 Haiqing China
154 A2 Hairag China
Hairhan Namag China see Guaizihu
155 F5 Haitan Dao i. China
223 J5 Haiti country Caribbean Sea
155 C7 Haitou China
163 D2 Hai Triêu Vietnam
215 G5 Haivana Nakya U.S.A.
215 D3 Haiwee Reservoir U.S.A.
154 E2 Haixing China
193 F3 Haiya Sudan
154 A2 Haiyan Qinghai China
155 F4 Haiyan Zhejiang China
160 A5 Haiyang China
160 B4 Haiyang Dao i. China
154 B2 Haiyuan China
154 F3 Haizhou Wan b. China
142 D3 Ḩāj Ali Qoli, Kavīr-e salt l. Iran
177 J7 Hajdúböszörmény Hungary
184 C7 Hajeb El Ayoun Tunisia
146 D7 Ḩajhir mt. Yemen
142 D3 Haji Abdulla, Chāh well Iran
159 F5 Hajiki-zaki pt Japan
149 F4 Hajipur India
142 D4 Ḩājjīābād Iran
142 D4 Ḩājjīābād Iran
149 H5 Haka Myanmar
214 □2 Hakalau U.S.A.
235 I4 Hakelhuincul, Altiplanicie de plat. Arg.
139 I3 Hakkâri Turkey
170 M2 Hakkas Sweden
159 D7 Hakken-zan mt. Japan
158 H2 Hako-dake mt. Japan
158 G4 Hakodate Japan
196 B1 Hakos Mountains Namibia
196 D3 Hakseen Pan salt pan S. Africa
159 E6 Hakui Japan
159 E6 Haku-san vol. Japan
159 E6 Haku-san Kokuritsu-kōen nat. park Japan
148 B4 Hala Pak.
Ḩalab Syria see Aleppo
142 B6 Halabān Saudi Arabia
139 J4 Ḩalabja Iraq
141 F5 Halaç Turkm.
160 C1 Halaha China
160 C1 Halahai China
193 F2 Halaib Sudan
163 D2 Ha Lam Vietnam
147 E6 Ḩalāniyāt, Juzur al is Oman
214 □2 Hālawa U.S.A.
Halawa U.S.A. see Hālawa
139 F4 Halba Lebanon
Halban Mongolia see Tsetserleg
179 J3 Halberstadt Germany
161 I3 Halcon, Mount Phil.
170 □ Haldarsvik Faroe Is
171 J4 Halden Norway
179 J2 Haldensleben Germany
149 G5 Haldi r. India
149 G5 Haldia India
149 G4 Haldibari India
148 D3 Haldwani India
123 A5 Hale watercourse Australia
209 F3 Hale U.S.A.
142 D5 Hāleh Iran
Haleiwa U.S.A. see Hale'iwa
214 □1 Hale'iwa U.S.A.
173 E5 Halesowen U.K.
173 I5 Halesworth U.K.
142 C4 Haleyleh Iran
139 F3 Halfeti Turkey
126 B7 Halfmoon Bay N.Z.
204 E3 Halfway r. Canada
175 J6 Halfway Ireland
178 C2 Halfweg Neth.
153 K2 Halhgol Mongolia
149 E4 Halia India
139 G4 Ḩalībīyah Syria
209 H3 Haliburton Canada
207 H5 Halifax Canada
173 F4 Halifax U.K.
220 D6 Halifax U.S.A.
122 D3 Halifax, Mount Australia
154 C1 Haliut China
174 E2 Halkirk U.K.
171 L3 Hälla Sweden
160 D7 Halla-san mt. S. Korea
160 D7 Halla-san National Park S. Korea
124 A5 Hall Bay Australia
203 J3 Hall Beach Canada
178 C4 Halle Belgium
179 E3 Halle Neth.
179 J3 Halle (Saale) Germany
171 K4 Hällefors Sweden
176 F7 Hallein Austria
179 J3 Halle-Neustadt Germany
127 J3 Halley research stn Antarctica
117 E2 Hall Islands Micronesia
170 L2 Hällnäs Sweden
216 D1 Hallock U.S.A.
203 L3 Hall Peninsula Canada
171 K4 Hallsberg Sweden
118 C3 Halls Creek Australia
209 H3 Halls Lake Canada
178 B4 Halluin France
171 K3 Hallviken Sweden
151 E6 Halmahera i. Indon.
171 K4 Halmstad Sweden
148 C5 Halol India
155 C6 Ha Long Vietnam
171 J4 Hals Denmark
171 N3 Halsua Fin.
179 F3 Haltern Germany
172 E3 Haltwhistle U.K.
142 D5 Ḩālūl i. Qatar
179 F3 Halver Germany
178 B5 Ham France
159 C7 Hamada Japan
142 C3 Hamadān Iran
139 F4 Ḩamāh Syria
158 G3 Hamamasu Japan
159 E7 Hamamatsu Japan
171 J3 Hamar Norway
170 K1 Hamarøy Norway
193 F2 Ḩamāţah, Jabal mt. Egypt
Ḩamāţah, Jabal mt. Egypt see Ghārib, Jabal
158 H2 Hamatonbetsu Japan
147 I5 Hambantota Sri Lanka
179 G1 Hambergen Germany
172 F3 Hambleton Hills U.K.
179 H1 Hamburg Germany
197 G6 Hamburg S. Africa
217 F5 Hamburg AR U.S.A.
220 D3 Hamburg NY U.S.A.
221 F4 Hamburg PA U.S.A.
179 G1 Hamburgisches Wattenmeer, Nationalpark nat. park Germany
221 G4 Hamden U.S.A.
171 N3 Hämeenlinna Fin.
121 A5 Hamelin Australia
179 H2 Hameln Germany
121 B6 Hamersley Lakes salt flat Australia
118 B4 Hamersley Range mts Australia
160 D4 Hamhŭng N. Korea
150 B2 Hami China
142 C4 Ḩamīd Iran
193 F2 Hamid Sudan
123 C4 Hamilton Qld Australia
123 A5 Hamilton S.A. Australia
125 E6 Hamilton Australia
123 B4 Hamilton watercourse Qld Australia
123 A5 Hamilton watercourse S.A. Australia
223 L2 Hamilton Bermuda
209 H4 Hamilton Canada
126 E2 Hamilton N.Z.
174 D5 Hamilton U.K.
219 C5 Hamilton AL U.S.A.
208 B5 Hamilton IL U.S.A.
212 D2 Hamilton MT U.S.A.
221 F3 Hamilton NY U.S.A.
220 A5 Hamilton OH U.S.A.
214 B3 Hamilton, Mount CA U.S.A.
215 E2 Hamilton, Mount NV U.S.A.
214 A2 Hamilton City U.S.A.
181 H5 Hamīm, Wādī al watercourse Libya
171 N3 Hamina Fin.
139 H6 Ḩāmir, Wādī al watercourse Saudi Arabia
148 D3 Hamirpur India
160 D4 Hamju N. Korea
124 C5 Hamley Bridge Australia
208 D3 Hamlin Lake U.S.A.
179 F3 Hamm Germany
139 I3 Ḩammām al 'Alīl Iraq
184 D6 Hammamet Tunisia
193 D1 Hammamet, Golfe de g. Tunisia
139 K6 Ḩammār, Hawr al imp. l. Iraq
171 L3 Hammarstrand Sweden
179 H4 Hammelburg Germany
171 K3 Hammerdal Sweden

Hopefield

173 G6 Hemel Hempstead U.K.
215 D5 Hemet U.S.A.
221 E3 Hemlock Lake U.S.A.
179 H2 Hemmingen Germany
221 G2 Hemmingford Canada
179 H1 Hemmoor Germany
217 D6 Hempstead U.S.A.
173 I5 Hemsby U.K.
171 L4 Hemse Sweden
154 A3 Henan China
154 D3 Henan prov. China
183 O2 Henares r. Spain
158 F4 Henashi-zaki pt Japan
121 F5 Henbury Australia
138 C1 Hendek Turkey
235 K3 Henderson Arg.
219 C4 Henderson KY U.S.A.
219 E4 Henderson NC U.S.A.
215 E3 Henderson NV U.S.A.
221 E3 Henderson NY U.S.A.
217 E5 Henderson TX U.S.A.
117 J7 Henderson Island Pitcairn Is
219 D5 Hendersonville NC U.S.A.
219 C4 Hendersonville TN U.S.A.
142 C4 Hendījān Iran
173 G6 Hendon U.K.
142 D5 Hendorābī i. Iran
143 E5 Hengām Iran
151 B4 Hengduan Shan mts China
179 E2 Hengelo Neth.
161 F1 Hengshan Heilong. China
155 D5 Hengshan Hunan China
154 C2 Hengshan Shaanxi China
155 D5 Heng Shan mt. Hunan China
154 D2 Heng Shan mts Shanxi China
154 E2 Hengshui China
155 C6 Hengxian China
155 D5 Hengyang Hunan China
155 D5 Hengyang Hunan China
187 E6 Heniches'k Ukr.
126 C6 Henley N.Z.
173 G6 Henley-on-Thames U.K.
221 F5 Henlopen, Cape U.S.A.
179 F4 Hennef (Sieg) Germany
197 G3 Hennenman S. Africa
179 L2 Hennigsdorf Berlin Germany
221 H3 Henniker U.S.A.
217 D5 Henrietta U.S.A.
206 D2 Henrietta Maria, Cape Canada
215 G3 Henrieville U.S.A.
208 C5 Henry U.S.A.
127 J3 Henry Ice Rise Antarctica
203 L3 Henry Kater, Cape Canada
215 G2 Henry Mountains U.S.A.
209 G4 Hensall Canada
179 H1 Henstedt-Ulzburg Germany
195 B6 Hentiesbaai Namibia
125 G5 Henty Australia
Henzada Myanmar see Hinthada
205 H4 Hepburn Canada
155 E5 Heping China
155 C6 Hepu China
154 D2 Hequ China
122 E3 Herald Cays atolls Australia
143 F3 Herāt Afgh.
183 F5 Hérault r. France
205 H4 Herbert Canada
123 B4 Herbert Downs Australia
122 D3 Herbert River Falls National Park Australia
121 D5 Herbert Wash salt flat Australia
179 G4 Herborn Germany
179 H4 Herbstein Germany
127 J4 Hercules Dome ice feature Antarctica
179 F3 Herdecke Germany
179 F4 Herdorf Germany
224 H6 Heredia Costa Rica
173 E5 Hereford U.K.
217 C5 Hereford U.S.A.
117 J6 Héréhérétué atoll Fr. Polynesia
178 C4 Herent Belgium
179 G2 Herford Germany
179 I4 Heringen (Werra) Germany
217 D4 Herington U.S.A.
142 B2 Herīs Iran
176 D7 Herisau Switz.
221 F3 Herkimer U.S.A.
153 K2 Herlen Gol r. China/Mongolia
Herlen He r. China/Mongolia see Herlen Gol
179 I3 Herleshausen Germany
225 D2 Hermanas Mex.
174 □ Herma Ness hd U.K.
179 I2 Hermannsburg Germany
196 C7 Hermanus S. Africa
137 E4 Hermel Lebanon
197 H5 Hermes, Cape S. Africa
125 G3 Hermidale Australia
212 C2 Hermiston U.S.A.
232 C9 Hermite, Islas Chile
119 E2 Hermit Islands P.N.G.
138 E5 Hermon, Mount Lebanon/Syria
Hermopolis Magna Egypt see Al Ashmūnayn
224 B1 Hermosillo Mex.
232 F3 Hernandarias Para.
179 F3 Herne Germany
173 I6 Herne Bay U.K.
171 J4 Herning Denmark
208 D1 Heron Bay Canada
225 D3 Herradura Mex.
183 N3 Herrera del Duque Spain
125 G8 Herrick Australia
179 I5 Herrieden Germany
221 E4 Hershey U.S.A.
173 G6 Hertford U.K.
197 F4 Hertzogville S. Africa
178 D4 Herve Belgium
119 F4 Hervey Bay Australia
237 I7 Hervey Islands Cook Is
179 K2 Herzberg Brandenburg Germany
179 L3 Herzberg Brandenburg Germany
179 F2 Herzlake Germany
179 I5 Herzogenaurach Germany
179 K1 Herzsprung Germany
139 L4 Ḩeşar Iran
178 C4 Hesbaye reg. Belgium
179 F1 Hesel Germany
155 C6 Heshan China
154 C3 Heshui China
154 D2 Heshun China
215 D4 Hesperia U.S.A.
204 C2 Hess r. Canada
179 I5 Heßdorf Germany
179 I5 Hesselberg h. Germany
179 H4 Hessen land Germany
179 H3 Hessisch Lichtenau Germany
155 B6 Het r. Laos
214 B3 Hetch Hetchy Aqueduct canal U.S.A.
178 D3 Heteren Neth.
216 C2 Hettinger U.S.A.
172 E3 Hetton U.K.
179 J3 Hettstedt Germany
172 E3 Hexham U.K.
155 F4 Hexian China
154 B2 Hexipu China
196 C6 Hex River Pass S. Africa
154 C3 Heyang China
142 B2 Ḩeydarābād Iran
143 F4 Ḩeydarābād Iran
172 E3 Heysham U.K.
155 E6 Heyuan China
124 D7 Heywood Australia
173 E4 Heywood U.K.
208 C5 Heyworth U.S.A.
154 E3 Heze China
155 B5 Hezhang China
154 B3 Hezheng China
155 D5 Hezhou China
154 B3 Hezuo China
219 D7 Hialeah U.S.A.
217 E4 Hiawatha U.S.A.
208 A2 Hibbing U.S.A.
125 F9 Hibbs, Point Australia
120 C2 Hibernia Reef Australia
219 D5 Hickory U.S.A.
127 G2 Hicks Bay N.Z.
225 G4 Hicks Cays is Belize
205 J2 Hicks Lake Canada
220 A4 Hicksville U.S.A.
217 D5 Hico U.S.A.
158 H3 Hidaka-sanmyaku mts Japan
225 E2 Hidalgo Mex.
225 E3 Hidalgo state Mex.
224 C2 Hidalgo del Parral Mex.
234 C2 Hidrolândia Brazil
159 C7 Higashi-Hiroshima Japan
159 G5 Higashine Japan
159 D7 Higashi-Ōsaka Japan
159 A8 Higashi-suidō sea chan. Japan
221 F3 Higgins Bay U.S.A.
209 E3 Higgins Lake U.S.A.
213 B3 High Desert U.S.A.
208 C3 High Falls Reservoir U.S.A.
209 E3 High Island U.S.A.
155 □ High Island Reservoir Hong Kong China
208 D4 Highland Park U.S.A.
214 C2 Highland Peak CA U.S.A.
215 E3 Highland Peak NV U.S.A.
204 F3 High Level Canada
149 F5 High Level Canal India
219 E5 High Point U.S.A.
204 F3 High Prairie Canada
205 G4 High River Canada
219 E7 High Rock Bahamas
205 I3 Highrock Lake Canada
125 F9 High Rocky Point Australia
172 E3 High Seat h. U.K.
High Tatras mts Poland/Slovakia see Tatra Mountains
221 F4 Hightstown U.S.A.
173 G6 High Wycombe U.K.
224 B2 Higuera de Zaragoza Mex.
233 K2 Higuerote Venez.
171 M4 Hiiumaa i. Estonia
146 A4 Hijaz reg. Saudi Arabia
136 B5 Ḩikmah, Ra's al pt Egypt
215 E3 Hiko U.S.A.
159 E7 Hikone Japan
127 G2 Hikurangi mt. N.Z.
181 H5 Hilāl, Ra's al pt Libya
215 F3 Hildale U.S.A.
179 I4 Hildburghausen Germany
179 I4 Hilders Germany
179 H2 Hildesheim Germany
149 G4 Hili Bangl.
139 J5 Hillah Iraq
217 D4 Hill City U.S.A.
215 H2 Hill Creek r. U.S.A.
178 C2 Hillegom Neth.
171 K5 Hillerød Denmark
122 D3 Hillgrove Australia
216 D2 Hillsboro ND U.S.A.
221 H3 Hillsboro NH U.S.A.
220 B5 Hillsboro OH U.S.A.
217 D5 Hillsboro TX U.S.A.
208 B4 Hillsboro WI U.S.A.
220 C5 Hillsboro WV U.S.A.
209 E5 Hillsdale MI U.S.A.
221 G3 Hillsdale NY U.S.A.
221 E4 Hillsgrove U.S.A.
121 B4 Hillside Australia
175 F4 Hillside U.K.
215 F4 Hillside U.S.A.
125 F4 Hillston Australia
220 C6 Hillsville U.S.A.
125 I5 Hilltop Australia
214 □[2] Hilo U.S.A.
123 B4 Hilton Australia
197 I4 Hilton S. Africa
221 E3 Hilton U.S.A.
209 F2 Hilton Beach Canada
219 D5 Hilton Head Island U.S.A.
139 G3 Hilvan Turkey
178 D2 Hilversum Neth.
148 D3 Himachal Pradesh state India
148 D2 Himalaya mts Asia
149 F3 Himalchul mt. Nepal
170 M2 Himanka Fin.
185 H4 Himarë Albania
148 C5 Himatnagar India
159 D7 Himeji Japan
159 G5 Himekami-dake mt. Japan
197 H4 Himeville S. Africa
159 E6 Himi Japan
Ḩimş Syria see Homs
161 J4 Hinatuan Phil.
177 N7 Hînceşti Moldova
119 E3 Hinchinbrook Island Australia
173 F5 Hinckley U.K.
208 A2 Hinckley MN U.S.A.
215 F2 Hinckley UT U.S.A.
221 F3 Hinckley Reservoir U.S.A.
148 D4 Hindaun India
172 G3 Hinderwell U.K.
173 E4 Hindley U.K.
220 B6 Hindman U.S.A.
124 D6 Hindmarsh, Lake dry lake Australia
147 J1 Hindola India
143 G3 Hindu Kush mts Afgh./Pak.
147 H3 Hindupur India
204 F3 Hines Creek Canada
219 D6 Hinesville U.S.A.
148 D5 Hinganghat India
143 G5 Hinglaj Pak.
143 G5 Hingol r. Pak.
148 D6 Hingoli India
139 H2 Hınıs Turkey
215 D4 Hinkley U.S.A.
170 K1 Hinnøya i. Norway
161 I4 Hinobaan Phil.
183 N3 Hinojosa del Duque Spain
159 C7 Hino-misaki pt Japan
221 G3 Hinsdale U.S.A.
179 F1 Hinte Germany
151 B5 Hinthada Myanmar
204 F4 Hinton Canada
220 C6 Hinton U.S.A.
Hiort i. U.K. see St Kilda
178 C2 Hippolytushoef Neth.
139 J2 Hirabit Dağ mt. Turkey
159 A8 Hirado Japan
159 A8 Hirado-shima i. Japan
147 I1 Hirakud Reservoir India
158 H3 Hiroo Japan
158 G4 Hirosaki Japan
159 C7 Hiroshima Japan
179 J5 Hirschaid Germany
179 J4 Hirschberg Germany
176 E7 Hirschberg mt. Germany
182 G2 Hirson France
171 J4 Hirtshals Denmark
148 C3 Hisar India
139 L3 Hisar Iran
143 G3 Hisar, Koh-i- mts Afgh.
138 D1 Hisarönü Turkey
139 J6 Ḩisb, Sha'īb watercourse Iraq
141 G5 Hisor Tajik.
223 J4 Hispaniola i. Caribbean Sea
149 F4 Hisua India
139 I5 Hīt Iraq
159 G6 Hitachi Japan
157 F5 Hitachinaka Japan
159 G6 Hitachi-Ōta Japan
159 B8 Hitoyoshi Japan
171 J3 Hitra i. Norway
179 J1 Hitzacker Germany
159 C7 Hiuchi-nada b. Japan
117 J5 Hiva Oa i. Fr. Polynesia
204 E4 Hixon Canada
123 F4 Hixson Cay reef Australia
139 I2 Hizan Turkey
171 K4 Hjälmaren l. Sweden
205 H2 Hjalmar Lake Canada
171 J3 Hjerkinn Norway
171 K4 Hjo Sweden
171 J4 Hjørring Denmark
152 G6 Hkakabo Razi mt. China/Myanmar
197 I4 Hlabisa S. Africa
197 I3 Hlatikulu Swaziland
187 E5 Hlobyne Ukr.
197 G4 Hlohlowane S. Africa
197 H4 Hlotse Lesotho
197 J4 Hluhluwe S. Africa
187 E5 Hlukhiv Ukr.
177 N4 Hlusha Belarus
187 C4 Hlybokaye Belarus
192 C4 Ho Ghana
155 B6 Hoa Binh Vietnam
162 C1 Hoa Binh Vietnam
195 B6 Hoachanas Namibia
162 C1 Hoan Lao Vietnam
125 G9 Hobart Australia
217 D5 Hobart U.S.A.
217 C5 Hobbs U.S.A.
219 D7 Hobe Sound U.S.A.
154 D1 Hobor China
171 J4 Hobro Denmark
194 E3 Hobyo Somalia
179 H5 Höchberg Germany
179 I3 Hochharz nat. park Germany
162 C3 Ho Chi Minh City Vietnam
176 G7 Hochschwab mt. Austria
179 G5 Hockenheim Germany
220 B5 Hocking r. U.S.A.
225 G3 Hoctún Mex.
148 D4 Hodal India
173 E4 Hodder r. U.K.
173 G6 Hoddesdon U.K.
146 B7 Hodeidah Yemen
221 J1 Hodgdon U.S.A.
120 F2 Hodgson Downs Australia
177 J7 Hódmezővásárhely Hungary
183 S5 Hodna, Chott el salt l. Alg.
160 D4 Hodo-dan pt N. Korea
Hoek van Holland Neth. see Hook of Holland
178 D4 Hoensbroek Neth.
160 E2 Hoeryŏng N. Korea
160 D4 Hoeyang N. Korea
179 J4 Hof Germany
179 I4 Hofheim in Unterfranken Germany
197 F5 Hofmeyr S. Africa
170 D2 Höfn Iceland
171 L3 Hofors Sweden
170 C2 Hofsjökull ice cap Iceland
159 B7 Hōfu Japan
171 K4 Höganäs Sweden
125 G7 Hogan Group is Australia
192 C2 Hoggar plat. Alg.
221 F6 Hog Island U.S.A.
171 L4 Högsby Sweden
171 I3 Høgste Breakulen mt. Norway
179 H5 Hohenloher Ebene plain Germany
179 K3 Hohenmölsen Germany
179 K2 Hohennauen Germany
179 J4 Hohenwartetalsperre resr Germany
179 H4 Hohe Rhön mts Germany
176 F7 Hohe Tauern mts Austria
179 E4 Hohe Venn moorland Belgium
154 D1 Hohhot China
144 H2 Höhmorït Mongolia
149 H2 Hoh Sai Hu l. China
149 G2 Hoh Xil Hu salt l. China
149 G2 Hoh Xil Shan mts China
163 D2 Hôi An Vietnam
194 D3 Hoima Uganda
Hôi Xuân Vietnam see Quan Hoa
149 H4 Hojai India
141 F5 Hojambaz Turkm.
159 C8 Hōjo Japan
126 D1 Hokianga Harbour N.Z.
126 C5 Hokitika N.Z.
158 H3 Hokkaidō i. Japan
171 J4 Hokksund Norway
Hoktemberyan Armenia see Armavir
171 J3 Hol Norway
147 H3 Holalkere India
171 J5 Holbæk Denmark
173 H5 Holbeach U.K.
215 G4 Holbrook U.S.A.
208 B3 Holcombe Flowage resr U.S.A.
205 G4 Holden Canada
215 F2 Holden U.S.A.
217 D5 Holdenville U.S.A.
216 D3 Holdrege U.S.A.
147 H3 Hole Narsipur India
223 I4 Holguín Cuba
171 K3 Höljes Sweden
Holland country Europe see Netherlands
208 D4 Holland U.S.A.
220 D4 Hollidaysburg U.S.A.
204 C3 Hollis AK U.S.A.
217 D5 Hollis OK U.S.A.
214 B3 Hollister U.S.A.
209 F4 Holly U.S.A.
217 F5 Holly Springs U.S.A.
214 C4 Hollywood U.S.A.
219 D7 Hollywood U.S.A.
170 K2 Holm Norway
Holman Canada see Ulukhaktok
122 D3 Holmes Reef Australia
171 J4 Holmestrand Norway
171 M3 Holmön i. Sweden
171 M3 Holmsund Sweden
196 B3 Holoog Namibia
120 D2 Holothuria Banks reef Australia
122 C2 Holroyd r. Australia
171 J4 Holstebro Denmark
219 D4 Holston r. U.S.A.
220 C6 Holston Lake U.S.A.
173 C7 Holsworthy U.K.
173 I5 Holt U.K.
209 E4 Holt U.S.A.
217 E4 Holton U.S.A.
178 D1 Holwerd Neth.
175 K5 Holycross Ireland
173 C4 Holyhead U.K.
173 C4 Holyhead Bay U.K.
172 F2 Holy Island England U.K.
173 C4 Holy Island Wales U.K.
221 G3 Holyoke U.S.A.
173 D4 Holywell U.K.
179 K3 Holzhausen Germany
176 E7 Holzkirchen Germany
179 H3 Holzminden Germany
179 H3 Homberg (Efze) Germany
192 B3 Hombori Mali
179 F5 Homburg Germany
203 L3 Home Bay Canada
178 D5 Homécourt France
217 E5 Homer U.S.A.
219 D6 Homerville U.S.A.
123 D4 Homestead Australia
219 D7 Homestead U.S.A.
219 C5 Homewood U.S.A.
147 H2 Homnabad India
161 J4 Homonhon Point Phil.
139 F4 Homs Syria
187 D4 Homyel' Belarus
147 G3 Honavar India
233 I3 Honda Col.
161 H4 Honda Bay Phil.
215 H4 Hon Dah U.S.A.
196 B5 Hondeklipbaai S. Africa
154 C1 Hondlon Ju China
225 G4 Hondo r. Belize/Mex.
217 D6 Hondo U.S.A.
179 E1 Hondsrug reg. Neth.
224 H5 Honduras country Central America
224 H4 Honduras, Gulf of Belize/Hond.
171 J3 Hønefoss Norway
221 F4 Honesdale U.S.A.
214 B1 Honey Lake salt l. U.S.A.
221 E3 Honeyoye Lake U.S.A.
182 E2 Honfleur France
Hông, Sông r. Vietnam see Red
155 E4 Hong'an China
160 D5 Hongch'ŏn S. Korea
Hông Gai Vietnam see Ha Long
155 E6 Honghai Wan b. China
155 B6 Honghe China
154 E3 Hong He r. China
155 D4 Honghu China
155 C5 Hongjiang Hunan China
155 C5 Hongjiang Hunan China
155 E6 Hong Kong China (City Plan 93)
155 □ Hong Kong aut. reg. China
155 □ Hong Kong Island Hong Kong China
154 C2 Hongliu He r. China
Hongliuwan China see Aksay
144 I3 Hongliuyuan China
154 B2 Hongliuyuan China
162 C3 Hông Ngư Vietnam
154 B2 Hongshansi China
160 D2 Hongshi China
155 D6 Hongshui He r. China
154 D2 Hongtong China
207 G4 Honguedo, Détroit d' sea chan. Canada
160 D3 Hongwŏn N. Korea
160 B1 Hongxing China
154 B3 Hongyuan China
154 F3 Hongze China
154 F3 Hongze Hu l. China
119 F2 Honiara Solomon Is
173 D7 Honiton U.K.
159 G5 Honjō Japan
171 M3 Honkajoki Fin.
147 G3 Honnali India
170 N1 Honningsvåg Norway
Honokaa U.S.A. see Honoka'a
214 □[2] Honoka'a U.S.A.
214 □[1] Honolulu U.S.A.
159 D6 Honshū i. Japan
212 B2 Hood, Mount vol. U.S.A.
118 B5 Hood Point Australia
179 E2 Hoogeveen Neth.
179 E1 Hoogezand-Sappemeer Neth.
217 C4 Hooker U.S.A.
175 L5 Hook Head Ireland
178 C3 Hook of Holland Neth.
122 E3 Hook Reef Australia
204 B3 Hoonah U.S.A.
202 B3 Hooper Bay U.S.A.
221 E5 Hooper Island U.S.A.
208 D5 Hoopeston U.S.A.
197 F3 Hoopstad S. Africa
171 K5 Höör Sweden
178 D2 Hoorn Neth.
119 I3 Hoorn, Îles de is Wallis and Futuna Is
221 G3 Hoosick U.S.A.
215 E3 Hoover Dam U.S.A.
220 B4 Hoover Memorial Reservoir U.S.A.
139 H1 Hopa Turkey
221 F4 Hop Bottom U.S.A.
204 E5 Hope Canada
126 D5 Hope r. N.Z.
217 E5 Hope AR U.S.A.
215 F5 Hope AZ U.S.A.
121 C7 Hope, Lake salt flat Australia
124 C2 Hope, Lake salt flat Australia
202 B3 Hope, Point U.S.A.
207 I2 Hopedale Canada
196 C6 Hopefield S. Africa

Kadzhi-Say

183 M3 Jerez de los Caballeros Spain
Jerggul Norway *see* Jergol
170 N1 Jergol Norway
185 I5 Jergucat Albania
123 D4 Jericho Australia
138 E6 Jericho West Bank
179 K2 Jerichow Germany
180 E5 Jerid, Chott el *salt l.* Tunisia
125 F5 Jerilderie Australia
139 J2 Jermuk Armenia
213 D3 Jerome U.S.A.
182 C2 Jersey *i.* U.K.
221 F4 Jersey City U.S.A.
221 E4 Jersey Shore U.S.A.
219 B4 Jerseyville U.S.A.
231 J5 Jerumenha Brazil
138 E6 Jerusalem Israel/West Bank (City Plan 96)
125 I5 Jervis Bay Australia
125 I5 Jervis Bay *b.* Australia
125 I5 Jervis Bay Territory *admin. div.* Australia
184 F1 Jesenice Slovenia
184 E3 Jesi Italy
179 K3 Jessen Germany
171 J3 Jessheim Norway
149 G5 Jessore Bangl.
179 H1 Jesteburg Germany
219 D6 Jesup U.S.A.
225 F4 Jesús Carranza Mex.
235 J1 Jesús María Arg.
148 B5 Jetalsar India
217 D4 Jetmore U.S.A.
179 F1 Jever Germany
Jewish Autonomous Oblast *admin. div.* Rus. Fed. *see* Yevreyskaya Avtonomnaya Oblast'
149 F4 Jha Jha India
148 C4 Jhajju India
149 G5 Jhalakati Bangl.
143 G5 Jhal Jhao Pak.
148 A3 Jhal Magsi Pak.
148 C3 Jhang Pak.
148 D4 Jhansi India
149 F5 Jharia India
149 F4 Jharkhand *state* India
147 J1 Jharsuguda India
148 B3 Jhatpat Pak.
148 C2 Jhelum Pak.
148 C2 Jhelum *r.* Pak.
149 G5 Jhenaidah Bangl.
148 B4 Jhudo Pak.
149 F4 Jhumritilaiya India
148 C3 Jhunjhunun India
154 C3 Jiachuan China
155 F4 Jiading China
155 D5 Jiahe China
155 B4 Jiajiang China
154 B3 Jialing Jiang *r.* China
158 B1 Jiamusi China
155 E5 Ji'an *Jiangxi* China
155 E5 Ji'an *Jiangxi* China
160 D3 Ji'an China
154 F1 Jianchang China
155 F4 Jiande China
155 C7 Jianfeng China
155 B4 Jiang'an China
155 A6 Jiangcheng China
155 B5 Jiangchuan China
Jiange China *see* Pu'an
155 C4 Jiangjin China
144 G3 Jiangjunmiao China
155 C5 Jiangkou China
155 E5 Jiangle China
155 D6 Jiangmen China
155 F4 Jiangshan China
154 F3 Jiangsu *prov.* China
155 E5 Jiangxi *prov.* China
155 E4 Jiangxia China
154 D3 Jiangxian China
154 F3 Jiangyan China
155 F4 Jiangyin China
155 D5 Jiangyong China
155 B4 Jiangyou China
154 F3 Jianhu China
155 D6 Jian Jiang *r.* China
155 A5 Jiankang China
155 D4 Jianli China
155 E5 Jianning China
155 F5 Jian'ou China
154 F1 Jianping *Liaoning* China
154 F1 Jianping *Liaoning* China
154 E2 Jianqiao China
155 C4 Jianshi China
155 B6 Jianshui China
155 F5 Jianyang *Fujian* China
155 B4 Jianyang *Sichuan* China
154 D2 Jiaocheng China
160 D2 Jiaohe China
Jiaojiang China *see* Taizhou
160 A2 Jiaolai He *r. Nei Mongol* China
154 F2 Jiaolai He *r. Shandong* China
155 E5 Jiaoling China
154 F3 Jiaonan China
154 F2 Jiaozhou China
154 F2 Jiaozhou Wan *b.* China
154 D3 Jiaozuo China
160 D2 Jiapigou China
141 I5 Jiashi China
154 D2 Jiaxian China
155 F4 Jiaxing China
156 C2 Jiayin China
155 D4 Jiayu China
150 B3 Jiayuguan China
155 E6 Jiazi China
224 I7 Jicarón, Isla *i.* Panama
Jiddah Saudi Arabia *see* Jeddah
138 D6 Jiddī, Jabal al *h.* Egypt
161 F1 Jidong China
154 B2 Jieheba China
Jiehkkevarri *mt.* Norway *see* Jiehkkevárri
170 L1 Jiehkkevárri *mt.* Norway
155 E6 Jieshi China
155 E6 Jieshi Wan *b.* China
154 E3 Jieshou China
Iešjávri *l.* Norway *see* Iešjávri
155 E6 Jiexi China
154 D2 Jiexiu China
155 E6 Jieyang China
171 N5 Jieznas Lith.
140 E4 Jigerbent Turkm.
154 A3 Jigzhi China
176 G6 Jihlava Czech Rep.
143 F3 Jija Sarai Afgh.
180 E4 Jijel Alg.
194 E3 Jijiga Eth.
155 A4 Jijü China
193 E2 Jilf al Kabīr, Haḍabat al *plat.* Egypt
143 H3 Jilga *r.* Afgh.
194 E3 Jilib Somalia
160 D2 Jilin China
160 C2 Jilin *prov.* China
154 A2 Jiling China
160 C2 Jilin Hada Ling *mts* China
194 D3 Jīma Eth.
224 C2 Jiménez *Chihuahua* Mex.
225 D1 Jiménez *Coahuila* Mex.
225 E2 Jiménez *Tamaulipas* Mex.
154 F2 Jimo China
144 G3 Jimsar China
221 F4 Jim Thorpe U.S.A.
154 E2 Jinan China
Jinbi China *see* Dayao
154 B2 Jinchang China
154 D3 Jincheng China
155 B4 Jinchuan China
148 D3 Jind India
125 H6 Jindabyne Australia
125 G5 Jindera Australia
176 G6 Jindřichův Hradec Czech Rep.
155 E4 Jing'an China
154 C2 Jingbian China
154 C3 Jingchuan China
155 F4 Jingde China
155 E4 Jingdezhen China
155 E5 Jinggangshan China
155 E4 Jinggongqiao China
154 E2 Jinghai China
141 J3 Jinghe China
154 C3 Jing He *r.* China
151 C4 Jinghong China
154 F3 Jingjiang China
154 D2 Jingle China
155 D4 Jingmen China
154 B3 Jingning China
154 E1 Jingpeng China
160 E2 Jingpo China
160 E2 Jingpo Hu *l.* China
154 B2 Jingtai China
144 I4 Jingtieshan China
155 C6 Jingxi China
155 F4 Jingxian China
160 D2 Jingyu China
154 B2 Jingyuan China
155 D4 Jingzhou *Hubei* China
155 D4 Jingzhou *Hubei* China
155 C5 Jingzhou *Hunan* China
154 F3 Jinhu China
155 F4 Jinhua China
154 D1 Jining *Nei Mongol* China
154 E3 Jining *Shandong* China
194 D3 Jinja Uganda
155 F5 Jinjiang China
155 E4 Jin Jiang *r.* China
194 D3 Jinka Eth.
160 A3 Jinlingsi China
155 C7 Jinmu Jiao *pt* China
224 H5 Jinotega Nicaragua
224 H6 Jinotepe Nicaragua
155 C5 Jinping *Guizhou* China
155 B6 Jinping *Yunnan* China
155 A5 Jinping Shan *mts* China
155 C5 Jinsha China
155 B4 Jinsha Jiang *r.* China *alt.* Chang Jiang, *alt.* Tongtian He, *alt.* Zhi Qu, *conv.* Yangtze, *long* Yangtze Kiang
154 F1 Jinshan *Nei Mongol* China
Jinshan China *see* Zhujing
155 D4 Jinshi China
155 B4 Jintang China
161 I4 Jintotolo *i.* Phil.
161 I4 Jintotolo Channel Phil.
148 D6 Jintur India
155 E5 Jinxi China
155 E4 Jinxian China
154 E3 Jinxiang *Shandong* China
155 F5 Jinxiang *Zhejiang* China
155 B5 Jinyang China
155 F4 Jinyun China
155 E4 Jinzhai China
154 D2 Jinzhong China
160 A3 Jinzhou *Liaoning* China
160 A4 Jinzhou *Liaoning* China
160 A4 Jinzhou Wan *b.* China
231 F6 Ji-Paraná Brazil
231 F5 Jiparaná *r.* Brazil
230 B4 Jipijapa Ecuador
149 H2 Ji Qu *r.* China
149 E3 Jirang China
141 G5 Jirgatol Tajik.
143 E4 Jīroft Iran
142 C6 Jirwān Saudi Arabia
142 C6 Jirwan *well* Saudi Arabia
155 C4 Jishou China
139 F4 Jisr ash Shughūr Syria
162 B4 Jitra Malaysia
154 C2 Jiudengkou China
155 B4 Jiuding Shan *mt.* China
154 C3 Jiufoping China
155 E4 Jiujiang *Jiangxi* China
155 E4 Jiujiang *Jiangxi* China
Jiulian China *see* Mojiang
155 E4 Jiuling Shan *mts* China
155 A4 Jiulong China
160 A2 Jiumiao China
144 I4 Jiuquan China
160 B5 Jiurongcheng China
160 C1 Jiutai China
155 C5 Jiuxu China
154 B3 Jiuzhaigou China
143 F5 Jiwani Pak.
156 A2 Jiwen China
155 F4 Jixi *Anhui* China
161 F1 Jixi *Heilong.* China
158 B1 Jixian China
154 D3 Jiyuan China
146 B6 Jīzān Saudi Arabia
154 E2 Jizhou China
159 C7 Jizō-zaki *pt* Japan
141 F4 Jizzax Uzbek.
231 L5 João Pessoa Brazil
234 C2 João Pinheiro Brazil
214 C2 Job Peak U.S.A.
179 K4 Jocketa Germany
147 J1 Joda India
148 C4 Jodhpur India
171 O3 Joensuu Fin.
159 F6 Jōetsu Japan
195 D6 Jofane Moz.
204 F4 Joffre, Mount Canada
171 N4 Jõgeva Estonia
197 G3 Johannesburg S. Africa
215 D4 Johannesburg U.S.A.
149 E5 Johilla *r.* India
212 C2 John Day U.S.A.
212 B2 John Day *r.* U.S.A.
204 F3 John D'Or Prairie Canada
221 G4 John F. Kennedy *airport* U.S.A.
220 D6 John H. Kerr Reservoir U.S.A.
174 E2 John o'Groats U.K.
219 D4 Johnson City U.S.A.
204 C2 Johnson's Crossing Canada
219 D5 Johnston U.S.A.
121 C7 Johnston, Lake *salt flat* Australia
117 H2 Johnston Atoll *terr.* N. Pacific Ocean
174 D5 Johnstone U.K.
121 B6 Johnston Range *hills* Australia
175 K5 Johnstown Ireland
221 F3 Johnstown *NY* U.S.A.
220 D4 Johnstown *PA* U.S.A.
209 F3 Johnswood U.S.A.
162 □ Johor, Selat *str.* Malaysia/Sing.
163 B2 Johor Bahru Malaysia
171 N4 Jõhvi Estonia
233 G3 Joinville Brazil
182 G2 Joinville France
127 I2 Joinville Island Antarctica
170 L2 Jokkmokk Sweden
170 D2 Jökulsá á Dál *r.* Iceland
170 C1 Jökulsá á Fjöllum *r.* Iceland
170 D2 Jökulsá í Fljótsdal *r.* Iceland
142 B2 Jolfa Iran
208 C5 Joliet U.S.A.
207 F4 Joliette Canada
161 I5 Jolo Phil.
161 I5 Jolo *i.* Phil.
161 I3 Jomalig *i.* Phil.
163 H4 Jombang Indon.
152 G5 Jomda China
225 G4 Jonathan Point Belize
171 N5 Jonava Lith.
154 B3 Jonê China
217 F5 Jonesboro *AR* U.S.A.
221 J2 Jonesboro *ME* U.S.A.
221 J2 Jonesport U.S.A.
203 J2 Jones Sound *sea chan.* Canada
220 B6 Jonesville U.S.A.
140 E4 Jongeldi Uzbek.
193 F4 Jonglei Canal Sudan
147 I1 Jonk *r.* India
171 K4 Jönköping Sweden
207 F4 Jonquière Canada
225 F4 Jonuta Mex.
217 E4 Joplin U.S.A.
221 E5 Joppatowne U.S.A.
148 D4 Jora India
139 F6 Jordan *country* Asia
138 E6 Jordan *r.* Asia
212 F2 Jordan U.S.A.
213 E3 Jordan *r.* U.S.A.
213 C3 Jordan Valley U.S.A.
235 B4 Jordão *r.* Brazil
171 K3 Jordet Norway
149 H4 Jorhat India
141 I5 Jor Hu *l.* China
179 H1 Jork Germany
170 M2 Jörn Sweden
171 N3 Joroinen Fin.
171 I4 Jørpeland Norway
192 C4 Jos Nigeria
161 J5 Jose Abad Santos Phil.
225 E4 José Cardel Mex.
232 B6 José de San Martin Arg.
234 A2 Joselândia Brazil
235 L2 José Pedro Varela Uruguay
207 G3 Joseph, Lac *l.* Canada
118 C3 Joseph Bonaparte Gulf Australia
215 G4 Joseph City U.S.A.
159 F6 Jōshinetsu-kōgen Kokuritsu-kōen *nat. park* Japan
215 E5 Joshua Tree National Park U.S.A.
192 C4 Jos Plateau Nigeria
171 I3 Jostedalsbreen Nasjonalpark *nat. park* Norway
171 J3 Jotunheimen Nasjonalpark *nat. park* Norway
197 E6 Joubertina S. Africa
197 G3 Jouberton S. Africa
171 N4 Jõuga Estonia
136 D4 Joûnié Lebanon
178 D2 Joure Neth.
171 N3 Joutsa Fin.
171 O3 Joutseno Fin.
179 E5 Jouy-aux-Arches France
149 H4 Jowai India
175 I4 Joyce's Country *reg.* Ireland
225 D2 Juan Aldama Mex.
212 A1 Juan de Fuca Strait U.S.A.
195 E5 Juan de Nova *i.* Indian Ocean
228 E5 Juan Fernández, Archipiélago *is* S. Pacific Ocean
171 O3 Juankoski Fin.
224 H6 Juan Santamaria *airport* Costa Rica
225 D2 Juaréz Mex.
231 J5 Juàzeiro Brazil
231 K5 Juàzeiro do Norte Brazil
193 F4 Juba Sudan
127 L2 Jubany *research stn* Antarctica
194 E3 Jubba *r.* Somalia
137 F5 Jubbah Saudi Arabia
121 D6 Jubilee Lake *salt flat* Australia
215 D4 Jubilee Pass U.S.A.
225 E4 Juchatengo Mex.
225 D3 Juchipila Mex.
225 F4 Juchitán Mex.
224 C3 Juchitlán Mex.
234 E2 Jucuruçu *r.* Brazil
171 I4 Judaberg Norway
139 H6 Judaidat al Hamir Iraq
139 G4 Judaydah Syria
139 H6 Judayyidat 'Ar'ar *well* Iraq
176 G7 Judenburg Austria
171 J5 Juelsminde Denmark
154 C2 Juh China
154 F1 Juhua Dao *i.* China
224 H5 Juigalpa Nicaragua
179 F1 Juist *i.* Germany
234 D3 Juiz de Fora Brazil
230 E8 Julaca Bol.
216 C3 Julesburg U.S.A.
230 D7 Juliaca Peru
123 C4 Julia Creek Australia
178 C2 Julianadorp Neth.
231 G3 Juliana Top *mt.* Suriname
179 E4 Jülich Germany
184 E1 Julijske Alpe *mts* Slovenia
123 B4 Julius, Lake Australia
141 F5 Juma Uzbek.
230 C5 Jumbilla Peru
183 P3 Jumilla Spain
149 E3 Jumla Nepal
Jumna *r.* India *see* Yamuna
148 B5 Junagadh India
147 I2 Junagarh India
154 F3 Junan China
235 H2 Juncal *mt.* Chile
Juncal, Lago *l.* Arg. *see* Juncal, Laguna
235 J4 Juncal, Laguna *l.* Arg.
217 D6 Junction *TX* U.S.A.
213 D4 Junction *UT* U.S.A.
217 D4 Junction City U.S.A.
234 C3 Jundiaí Brazil
204 C3 Juneau U.S.A.
125 G5 Junee Australia
Jungar Qi China *see* Shagedu
176 D7 Jungfrau *mt.* Switz.
135 G2 Junggar Pendi *basin* China
148 A4 Jungshahi Pak.
221 E4 Juniata *r.* U.S.A.
235 K2 Junín Arg.
235 H3 Junín de los Andes Arg.
221 J1 Juniper Canada
214 B3 Junipero Serro Peak U.S.A.
155 B4 Junlian China
147 G2 Junnar India
171 L3 Junsele Sweden
213 C3 Juntura U.S.A.
171 N4 Juodupė Lith.
235 C4 Juquiá Brazil
193 E4 Jur *r.* Sudan
182 H3 Jura *mts* France/Switz.
174 C4 Jura *i.* U.K.
142 B5 Jur'ā, Nafūd al *des.* Saudi Arabia
174 C5 Jura, Sound of *sea chan.* U.K.
234 E1 Jurací Brazil
233 H3 Juradó Col.
171 M5 Jurbarkas Lith.
138 E6 Jurf ad Darāwīsh Jordan
179 K1 Jürgenstorf Germany
160 A1 Jurh *Nei Mongol* China
160 A1 Jurh *Nei Mongol* China
Jurhen Ul Shan *mts* China *see* Zurhen Ul Shan
171 M4 Jūrmala Latvia
170 N2 Jurmu Fin.
155 F4 Jurong China
162 □ Jurong Sing.
162 □ Jurong, Selat *str.* Sing.
230 E4 Juruá *r.* Brazil
231 G6 Juruena *r.* Brazil
171 M3 Jurva Fin.
143 E2 Jūshqān Iran
235 J2 Justo Daract Arg.
230 E4 Jutaí *r.* Brazil
179 L3 Jüterbog Germany
234 A3 Juti Brazil
225 G5 Jutiapa Guat.
224 H5 Juticalpa Hond.
170 L2 Jutis Sweden
168 H4 Jutland *pen.* Denmark
171 O3 Juuka Fin.
171 N3 Juva Fin.
223 H4 Juventud, Isla de la *i.* Cuba
143 F4 Juwain Afgh.
154 F3 Juxian China
154 A1 Juyan China
154 E3 Juye China
143 E3 Jūymand Iran
142 D4 Jūyom Iran
195 C6 Jwaneng Botswana
Jylland *pen.* Denmark *see* Jutland
141 I4 Jyrgalang Kyrg.
171 N3 Jyväskylä Fin.

K

148 D2 K2 *mt.* China/Pakistan
231 F7 Kaa-Iya del Gran Chaco, Parque Nacional *nat. park* Bol.
Kaala *mt.* U.S.A. *see* Ka'ala
214 □1 Ka'ala *mt.* U.S.A.
171 M3 Kaarina Fin.
179 J1 Kaarßen Germany
179 E3 Kaarst Germany
171 O3 Kaavi Fin.
Kaba China *see* Habahe
118 C2 Kabaena *i.* Indon.
Kabakly Turkm. *see* Gabakly
192 A4 Kabala Sierra Leone
195 C4 Kabale Uganda
195 C4 Kabalo Dem. Rep. Congo
195 C4 Kabambare Dem. Rep. Congo
141 F1 Kaban' Kazakh.
141 J3 Kabanbay Kazakh.
141 J3 Kabanbay *Almatinskaya Oblast'* Kazakh.
141 F1 Kabanbay *Severnyy Kazakhstan* Kazakh.
195 C5 Kabangu Dem. Rep. Congo
162 A5 Kabanjahe Indon.
140 B1 Kabanovka Rus. Fed.
187 G7 Kabardino-Balkarskaya Respublika *aut. rep.* Rus. Fed.
195 C4 Kabare Dem. Rep. Congo
170 M2 Kåbdalis Sweden
209 E1 Kabenung Lake Canada
206 D4 Kabinakagami Lake Canada
195 C4 Kabinda Dem. Rep. Congo
142 B3 Kabīrkūh *mts* Iran
148 B3 Kabirwala Pak.
194 B3 Kabo Centr. Afr. Rep.
195 C5 Kabompo Zambia
195 C4 Kabongo Dem. Rep. Congo
143 F3 Kabūdeh Iran
143 E2 Kabūd Gonbad Iran
142 C3 Kabūd Rāhang Iran
161 I2 Kabugao Phil.
143 H3 Kābul Afgh.
143 H3 Kābul *r.* Afgh.
Kabūl *r.* Afgh. *see* Kābul
120 B1 Kabunduk Indon.
161 J6 Kaburuang *i.* Indon.
195 C5 Kabwe Zambia
140 E2 Kabyrga *r.* Kazakh.
Kabzn' Kazakh. *see* Kaban'
143 F4 Kacha Kuh *mts* Iran/Pak.
187 H5 Kachalinskaya Rus. Fed.
148 B5 Kachchh, Gulf of India
148 B4 Kachchh, Rann of *marsh* India
141 I1 Kachiry Kazakh.
148 C1 Kach Pass Afgh.
137 G2 Kachret'i Georgia
150 C1 Kachug Rus. Fed.
139 H1 Kaçkar Dağı *mt.* Turkey
147 H4 Kadaiyanallur India
148 A3 Kadanai *r.* Afgh./Pak.
162 A2 Kadan Kyun *i.* Myanmar
119 H3 Kadavu *i.* Fiji
119 H3 Kadavu Passage Fiji
192 B4 Kade Ghana
148 C5 Kadi India
138 B1 Kadıköy Turkey
124 B4 Kadina Australia
138 D2 Kadınhanı Turkey
192 B3 Kadiolo Mali
147 H3 Kadiri India
139 F3 Kadirli Turkey
147 G4 Kadmat *atoll* India
160 C4 Ka-do *i.* N. Korea
216 C3 Kadoka U.S.A.
195 C5 Kadoma Zimbabwe
193 E3 Kadugli Sudan
192 C3 Kaduna Nigeria
192 C3 Kaduna *state* Nigeria
149 I3 Kadusam *mt.* China
186 F3 Kaduy Rus. Fed.
186 G3 Kadyy Rus. Fed.
132 G3 Kadzherom Rus. Fed.
Kadzhi-Say Kyrg. *see* Kajy-Say

Kealakekua Bay

194 D3 **Kaputir** Kenya
177 H7 **Kapuvár** Hungary
187 C4 **Kapyl'** Belarus
160 D5 **Kap'yŏng** S. Korea
141 I5 **Kaqung** China
192 C4 **Kara** Togo
139 H2 **Kara** *r.* Turkey
185 L5 **Kara Ada** *i.* Turkey
138 D2 **Karaali** Turkey
141 H4 **Kara-Balta** Kyrg.
140 E1 **Karabalyk** Kazakh.
141 H2 **Karabas** Kazakh.
140 C2 **Karabau** Kazakh.
140 C4 **Karabaur, Uval** *hills* Uzbek.
Karabil', Vozvyshennost' *hills* Turkm. *see* **Garabil Belentligi**
Kara-Bogaz-Gol, Zaliv *b.* Turkm. *see* **Garabogazköl Aýlagy**
Karabogazkel' Turkm. *see* **Garabogazköl**
138 D1 **Karabük** Turkey
141 I3 **Karabulak** *Almatinskaya Oblast'* Kazakh.
141 K3 **Karabulak** *Vostochnyy Kazakhstan* Kazakh.
141 H2 **Karabulakskaya** Kazakh.
136 B3 **Karaburun** Turkey
140 E2 **Karabutak** Kazakh.
138 B1 **Karacabey** Turkey
139 G3 **Karacadağ** Turkey
138 D3 **Karacadağ** *mts* Turkey
138 B1 **Karacaköy** Turkey
139 G3 **Karacalı Dağ** *mt.* Turkey
138 B3 **Karacasu** Turkey
138 C3 **Karaca Yarımadası** *pen.* Turkey
187 G7 **Karachayevo-Cherkesskaya Respublika** *aut. rep.* Rus. Fed.
187 G7 **Karachayevsk** Rus. Fed.
187 E4 **Karachev** Rus. Fed.
143 G5 **Karachi** Pak. (City Plan **93**)
139 I2 **Karaçoban** Turkey
147 G2 **Karad** India
138 D3 **Kara Dağ** *mt.* Turkey
139 I3 **Kara Dağ** *mt.* Turkey
141 H4 **Kara-Daryya** *r.* Kyrg.
141 H2 **Karaganda** Kazakh.
141 G2 **Karagandinskaya Oblast'** *admin. div.* Kazakh.
141 H2 **Karagayly** Kazakh.
133 R4 **Karaginskiy Zaliv** *b.* Rus. Fed.
140 B4 **Karagiye, Vpadina** *depr.* Kazakh.
141 J2 **Karaguzhikha** Kazakh.
138 B2 **Karahallı** Turkey
138 E2 **Karahasanlı** Turkey
147 H4 **Karaikal** India
147 H4 **Karaikkudi** India
141 K3 **Kara Irtysh** *r.* Kazakh.
138 E3 **Karaisalı** Turkey
142 C3 **Karaj** Iran
142 C3 **Karaj** *r.* Iran
Karakalpakiya Uzbek. *see* **Qoraqalpog'iston**
Karakatinskaya, Vpadina *depr.* Uzbek. *see* **Qoraqata botig'i**
149 E1 **Karakax He** *r.* China
149 E2 **Karakax Shan** *mts* China
139 G3 **Karakeçi** Turkey
138 D2 **Karakeçili** Turkey
151 E6 **Karakelong** *i.* Indon.
141 F3 **Karaketken** Kazakh.
139 H2 **Karakoçan** Turkey
140 C2 **Karakol'** Kazakh.
141 H4 **Kara-Köl** Kyrg.
141 I4 **Karakol** Kyrg.
141 I4 **Karakol** Kyrg.
148 D2 **Karakoram Pass** China/India
135 F3 **Karakoram Range** *mts* Asia
194 D2 **Kara K'orē** Eth.
Karakorum Range *mts* Asia *see* **Karakoram Range**
141 G3 **Karakoyyn, Ozero** *salt l.* Kazakh.
Karakul' Uzbek. *see* **Qorako'l**
140 E1 **Karakul'skoye** Rus. Fed.
141 I3 **Karakum** Kazakh.
Karakum, Peski *des.* Kazakh. *see* **Karakum Desert**
140 C3 **Karakum Desert** Kazakh.
143 F2 **Karakum Desert** Turkm.
Karakumskiy Kanal *canal* Turkm. *see* **Garagum Kanaly**
Kara Kumy *des.* Turkm. *see* **Garagum**
Karakumy, Peski *des.* Turkm. *see* **Karakum Desert**
139 I1 **Karakurt** Turkey
171 M4 **Karala** Estonia
121 B5 **Karalundi** Australia
138 D3 **Karaman** Turkey
138 B3 **Karamanlı** Turkey
135 G2 **Karamay** China
148 C1 **Karambar Pass** Afgh./Pak.
126 D4 **Karamea** N.Z.
126 C4 **Karamea Bight** *b.* N.Z.
141 F2 **Karamendy** Kazakh.
Karamet-Niyaz Turkm. *see* **Garamätnyýaz**
149 F1 **Karamiran** China
149 F1 **Karamiran Shankou** *pass* China
138 B1 **Karamürsel** Turkey
186 D3 **Karamyshevo** Rus. Fed.
142 C5 **Karān** *i.* Saudi Arabia
148 D5 **Karanja** India
147 H2 **Karanja** *r.* India
149 F5 **Karanjia** India
148 C3 **Karanpura** India
141 I1 **Karaoba** Kazakh.
141 H3 **Karaoy** *Almatinskaya Oblast'* Kazakh.
141 H3 **Karaoy** *Almatinskaya Oblast'* Kazakh.
141 F3 **Karaozek** Kazakh.
138 D3 **Karapınar** Turkey
141 I4 **Karaqi** China
196 B3 **Karas** *admin. reg.* Namibia
196 B3 **Karas** *watercourse* Namibia
152 D4 **Karasay** China
141 I4 **Kara-Say** Kyrg.
195 B6 **Karasburg** Namibia
132 I2 **Kara Sea** Rus. Fed.
141 H2 **Karashoky** Kazakh.
Kárášjohka Norway *see* **Karasjok**
170 N1 **Karasjok** Norway
141 H2 **Karasor** Kazakh.
141 H2 **Karasor, Ozero** *salt l. Karagandinskaya Oblast'* Kazakh.
141 H1 **Karasor, Ozero** *salt l. Pavlodarskaya Oblast'* Kazakh.
141 H3 **Karasu** *Karagandinskaya Oblast'* Kazakh.
141 F1 **Karasu** *Kustanayskaya Oblast'* Kazakh.
141 H1 **Karasu** *r.* Kazakh.
138 C1 **Karasu** Turkey
139 I2 **Karasu** *r.* Turkey
141 I1 **Karasuk** Rus. Fed.
141 H4 **Kara-Suu** Kyrg.
141 K3 **Karatal** Kazakh.
138 E3 **Karataş** Turkey
138 E3 **Karataş Burun** *pt* Turkey
141 G4 **Karatau** Kazakh.
141 F3 **Karatau, Khrebet** *mts* Kazakh.
Karatax Shan *mts* China *see* **Karakax Shan**
162 A3 **Karathuri** Myanmar
147 H4 **Karativu** *i.* Sri Lanka
140 C2 **Karatobe** Kazakh.
140 D3 **Karatobe, Mys** *pt* Kazakh.
140 D2 **Karatogay** Kazakh.
141 I3 **Karatol** *r.* Kazakh.
140 E1 **Karatomarskoye Vodokhranilishche** *resr* Kazakh.
140 C3 **Karaton** Kazakh.
149 G4 **Karatoya** *r.* Bangl.
159 A8 **Karatsu** Japan
161 J5 **Karatung** *i.* Indon.
141 F2 **Kara-Turgay** *r.* Kazakh.
141 I2 **Karaul** Kazakh.
Karaulbazar Uzbek. *see* **Qorovulbozor**
148 D4 **Karauli** India
139 I1 **Karaurgan** Turkey
163 G4 **Karawang** Indon.
141 J4 **Karayulgan** China
141 G2 **Karazhal** Kazakh.
140 B3 **Karazhanbas** Kazakh.
Karazhar Uzbek. *see* **Qorajar**
141 H3 **Karazhingil** Kazakh.
139 J5 **Karbalā'** Iraq
179 G4 **Karben** Germany
141 H2 **Karbushevka** Kazakh.
177 J7 **Karcag** Hungary
179 F4 **Karden** Germany
185 I5 **Karditsa** Greece
171 M4 **Kärdla** Estonia
197 G4 **Karee** S. Africa
196 D5 **Kareeberge** *mts* S. Africa
193 F3 **Kareima** Sudan
187 G7 **K'areli** Georgia
148 D5 **Kareli** India
186 E2 **Kareliya, Respublika** *aut. rep.* Rus. Fed.
169 M2 **Karel'skiy Bereg** *coastal area* Rus. Fed.
150 D1 **Karenga** *r.* Rus. Fed.
148 D4 **Karera** India
170 M1 **Karesuando** Sweden
143 F5 **Kārevāndar** Iran
140 C2 **Kargala** Rus. Fed.
187 H7 **Kargalinskaya** Rus. Fed.
140 D2 **Kargalinskoye** Kazakh.
141 H2 **Kargaly** *Karagandinskaya Oblast'* Kazakh.
141 J2 **Kargaly** *Vostochnyy Kazakhstan* Kazakh.
139 H2 **Kargapazarı Dağları** *mts* Turkey
138 E1 **Kargı** Turkey
148 D2 **Kargil** India
186 F2 **Kargopol'** Rus. Fed.
143 E5 **Kargūshkī** Iran
Karholmsbruk Sweden *see* **Karlholmsbruk**
195 C5 **Kariba** Zimbabwe
195 C5 **Kariba, Lake** *resr* Zambia/Zimbabwe
158 F3 **Kariba-yama** *vol.* Japan
197 E6 **Kariega** *r.* S. Africa
170 N1 **Karigasniemi** Fin.
121 B4 **Karijini National Park** Australia
171 M3 **Karijoki** Fin.
157 F4 **Karikachi-tōge** *pass* Japan
126 D1 **Karikari, Cape** N.Z.
142 D3 **Karīmābād** Iran
163 G3 **Karimata, Pulau-pulau** *is* Indon.
163 G3 **Karimata, Selat** *str.* Indon.
152 F7 **Karimganj** India
147 H2 **Karimnagar** India
163 H4 **Karimunjawa, Pulau-pulau** *is* Indon.
194 E2 **Karin** Somalia
143 E3 **Karit** Iran
147 G2 **Karjat** India
149 F5 **Karkai** *r.* India
147 G3 **Karkal** India
141 H2 **Karkaralinsk** Kazakh.
161 J5 **Karkaralong, Kepulauan** *is* Indon.
119 E2 **Karkar Island** P.N.G.
142 C4 **Karkheh, Rūdkhāneh-ye** *r.* Iran
187 E6 **Karkinits'ka Zatoka** *g.* Ukr.
171 N3 **Kärkölä** Fin.
171 N4 **Karksi-Nuia** Estonia
171 L3 **Karlholmsbruk** Sweden
144 H3 **Karlik Shan** *mt.* China
139 H2 **Karlıova** Turkey
187 E5 **Karlivka** Ukr.
Karl-Marx-Stadt Germany *see* **Chemnitz**
184 F2 **Karlovac** Croatia
185 K3 **Karlovo** Bulg.
176 F5 **Karlovy Vary** Czech Rep.
179 G6 **Karlsbad** Germany
171 K4 **Karlsborg** Sweden
171 K4 **Karlshamn** Sweden
171 K4 **Karlskoga** Sweden
171 K4 **Karlskrona** Sweden
179 G5 **Karlsruhe** Germany
171 K4 **Karlstad** Sweden
216 D1 **Karlstad** U.S.A.
179 H5 **Karlstadt** Germany
187 D4 **Karma** Belarus
147 G2 **Karmala** India
Karmanovka Kazakh. *see* **Kyrkopa**
171 I4 **Karmøy** *i.* Norway
149 H5 **Karnafuli Reservoir** Bangl.
148 D3 **Karnal** India
149 E3 **Karnali** *r.* Nepal
147 G3 **Karnataka** *state* India
185 L3 **Karnobat** Bulg.
143 G5 **Karodi** Pak.
195 C5 **Karoi** Zimbabwe
149 G3 **Karo La** *pass* China
149 H4 **Karong** India
195 D4 **Karonga** Malawi
121 C6 **Karonie** Australia
141 I4 **Karool-Döbö** Kyrg.
197 E6 **Karoo National Park** S. Africa
124 C5 **Karoonda** Australia
148 B3 **Karor** Pak.
194 D2 **Karora** Eritrea
120 B1 **Karossa, Tanjung** *pt* Indon.
179 K1 **Karow** Germany
185 L7 **Karpathos** *i.* Greece
185 L6 **Karpathou, Steno** *sea chan.* Greece
185 I5 **Karpenisi** Greece
186 H1 **Karpogory** Rus. Fed.
118 B4 **Karratha** Australia
142 C4 **Karrī** Iran
143 F3 **Karrukh** Afgh.
139 I1 **Kars** Turkey
171 N3 **Kärsämäki** Fin.
171 N4 **Kārsava** Latvia
Karshi Turkm. *see* **Garşy**
Karshi Uzbek. *see* **Qarshi**
149 G4 **Karsiyang** India
132 G3 **Karskiye Vorota, Proliv** *str.* Rus. Fed.
Karskoye More *sea* Rus. Fed. *see* **Kara Sea**
179 J1 **Karstädt** Germany
171 N3 **Karstula** Fin.
138 B1 **Kartal** Turkey
140 E1 **Kartaly** Rus. Fed.
171 N3 **Karttula** Fin.
122 C3 **Karumba** Australia
142 C4 **Karun, Kūh-e** *h.* Iran
142 C4 **Kārūn, Rūd-e** *r.* Iran
120 B1 **Karuni** Indon.
147 H4 **Karur** India
171 M3 **Karvia** Fin.
171 M3 **Karvianjoki** *r.* Fin.
147 G3 **Karwar** India
150 D1 **Karymskoye** Rus. Fed.
140 C4 **Karynzharyk, Peski** *des.* Kazakh.
185 K5 **Karystos** Greece
138 B3 **Kaş** Turkey
206 C3 **Kasabonika** Canada
206 C3 **Kasabonika Lake** Canada
195 B4 **Kasaï** *r.* Dem. Rep. Congo
195 C5 **Kasaji** Dem. Rep. Congo
195 D5 **Kasama** Zambia
Kasan Uzbek. *see* **Koson**
195 C5 **Kasane** Botswana
195 B4 **Kasangulu** Dem. Rep. Congo
Kasansay Uzbek. *see* **Kosonsoy**
147 G3 **Kasaragod** India
156 C2 **Kasatkino** Rus. Fed.
205 I2 **Kasba Lake** Canada
192 B1 **Kasba Tadla** Morocco
159 B9 **Kaseda** Japan
139 K4 **Kāseh Garān** Iran
195 C5 **Kasempa** Zambia
195 C5 **Kasenga** Dem. Rep. Congo
195 C4 **Kasese** Dem. Rep. Congo
194 D3 **Kasese** Uganda
148 D4 **Kasganj** India
142 C3 **Kāshān** Iran
206 D3 **Kashechewan** Canada
Kashgar China *see* **Kashi**
141 I5 **Kashi** China
159 D7 **Kashihara** Japan
159 B8 **Kashima** Japan
159 G6 **Kashima-nada** *b.* Japan
186 F3 **Kashin** Rus. Fed.
148 D3 **Kashipur** India
159 F6 **Kashiwazaki** Japan
139 K5 **Kashkan** *r.* Iran
141 H3 **Kashkanteniz** Kazakh.
142 D4 **Kashku'iyeh** Iran
143 E3 **Kāshmar** Iran
148 C2 **Kashmir, Vale of** *reg.* India
148 B3 **Kashmor** Pak.
143 H3 **Kashmund** *reg.* Afgh.
195 C4 **Kashyukulu** Dem. Rep. Congo
187 G4 **Kasimov** Rus. Fed.
219 B4 **Kaskaskia** *r.* U.S.A.
205 K3 **Kaskattama** *r.* Canada
141 I4 **Kaskelen** Kazakh.
171 M3 **Kaskinen** Fin.
195 C4 **Kasongo** Dem. Rep. Congo
195 B4 **Kasongo-Lunda** Dem. Rep. Congo
185 L7 **Kasos** *i.* Greece
185 L7 **Kasou, Steno** *sea chan.* Greece
187 H7 **Kaspi** Georgia
187 H7 **Kaspiysk** Rus. Fed.
177 O3 **Kasplya** Rus. Fed.
193 F3 **Kassala** Sudan
136 A3 **Kassandras, Akrotirio** *pt* Greece
185 J4 **Kassandras, Chersonisos** *pen.* Greece
185 J4 **Kassandras, Kolpos** *b.* Greece
179 H3 **Kassel** Germany
192 C1 **Kasserine** Tunisia
208 A3 **Kasson** U.S.A.
138 D1 **Kastamonu** Turkey
179 F4 **Kastellaun** Germany
185 J7 **Kastellia** Greece
Kastéllion Greece *see* **Kissamos**
178 C3 **Kasterlee** Belgium
185 I4 **Kastoria** Greece
181 K1 **Kastornoye** Rus. Fed.
187 E4 **Kastsyukovichy** Belarus
159 E7 **Kasugai** Japan
195 D4 **Kasulu** Tanz.
159 D7 **Kasumi** Japan
159 G6 **Kasumiga-ura** *l.* Japan
187 I7 **Kasumkent** Rus. Fed.
195 D5 **Kasungu** Malawi
148 C3 **Kasur** Pak.
221 I2 **Katahdin, Mount** U.S.A.
148 D2 **Kataklik** India
195 C4 **Katako-Kombe** Dem. Rep. Congo
148 D5 **Katangi** India
118 B5 **Katanning** Australia
143 H3 **Katawaz** Afgh.
145 H10 **Katchall** *i.* India
195 C4 **Katea** Dem. Rep. Congo
185 J4 **Katerini** Greece
204 C3 **Kate's Needle** *mt.* Canada/U.S.A.
195 D5 **Katete** Zambia
147 I1 **Katghora** India
151 B4 **Katha** Myanmar
Katherîna, Gebel *mt.* Egypt *see* **Kātrīnā, Jabal**
120 F2 **Katherine** Australia
118 D3 **Katherine** *r.* Australia
Katherine Gorge National Park *nat. park* Australia *see* **Nitmiluk National Park**
148 B5 **Kathiawar** *pen.* India
147 I4 **Kathiraveli** Sri Lanka
120 E2 **Kathleen Falls** Australia
Kathlehong S. Africa *see* **Katlehong**
149 F4 **Kathmandu** Nepal
197 E3 **Kathu** S. Africa
148 C2 **Kathua** India
192 B3 **Kati** Mali
149 F4 **Katihar** India
126 E2 **Katikati** N.Z.
197 G6 **Katikati** S. Africa
195 C5 **Katima Mulilo** Namibia
192 B4 **Katiola** Côte d'Ivoire
196 D4 **Katkop Hills** S. Africa
197 H3 **Katlehong** S. Africa
185 I5 **Kato Achaïa** Greece
148 D5 **Katol** India
162 □ **Katong** Sing.
141 K2 **Katon-Karagay** Kazakh.
125 I4 **Katoomba** Australia
177 I5 **Katowice** Poland
149 G5 **Katoya** India
136 D5 **Kātrīnā, Jabal** *mt.* Egypt
174 D4 **Katrine, Loch** *l.* U.K.
171 L4 **Katrineholm** Sweden
192 C3 **Katsina** Nigeria
192 C4 **Katsina-Ala** Nigeria
159 G7 **Katsuura** Japan
159 E6 **Katsuyama** Japan
207 G2 **Kattaktoc, Cap** *c.* Canada
Kattakurgan Uzbek. *see* **Kattaqo'rg'on**
121 D4 **Kattamudda Well** Australia
141 F5 **Kattaqo'rg'on** Uzbek.
143 G3 **Kattasang Hills** Afgh.
171 J4 **Kattegat** *str.* Denmark/Sweden
141 K1 **Katun'** *r.* Rus. Fed.
148 B3 **Katuri** Pak.
178 C2 **Katwijk aan Zee** Neth.
179 H5 **Katzenbuckel** *h.* Germany
Kauai *i.* U.S.A. *see* **Kaua'i**
214 □[2] **Kaua'i** *i.* U.S.A.
214 □[2] **Kaua'i Channel** U.S.A.
179 F4 **Kaub** Germany
179 H3 **Kaufungen** Germany
171 M3 **Kauhajoki** Fin.
171 M3 **Kauhava** Fin.
170 N2 **Kaukonen** Fin.
214 □[2] **Ka'ula** *i.* U.S.A.
214 □[2] **Kaulakahi Channel** U.S.A.
207 H2 **Kaumajet Mountains** Canada
214 □[2] **Kaunakakai** U.S.A.
171 M5 **Kaunas** Lith.
171 N4 **Kaunata** Latvia
140 C4 **Kaundy, Vpadina** *depr.* Kazakh.
192 C3 **Kaura-Namoda** Nigeria
155 □ **Kau Sai Chau** *i. Hong Kong* China
171 M3 **Kaustinen** Fin.
170 M1 **Kautokeino** Norway
162 A3 **Kau-ye Kyun** *i.* Myanmar
185 J4 **Kavadarci** Macedonia
139 F1 **Kavak** Turkey
185 K4 **Kavala** Greece
158 D2 **Kavalerovo** Rus. Fed.
147 I3 **Kavali** India
142 D4 **Kavār** Iran
145 D9 **Kavaratti** India
147 G4 **Kavaratti** *atoll* India
185 M3 **Kavarna** Bulg.
147 H4 **Kaveri** *r.* India
Kavīr *salt flat* Iran *see* **Daqq-e Sorkh, Kavīr-e**
Kavīr *salt flat* Iran *see* **Sīāh Kūh, Kavīr-e**
143 E3 **Kavīr, Chāh-e** *well* Iran
142 D3 **Kavīr, Dasht-e** *des.* Iran
159 F7 **Kawagoe** Japan
159 F7 **Kawaguchi** Japan
214 □[2] **Kawaihae** U.S.A.
126 E1 **Kawakawa** N.Z.
195 C4 **Kawambwa** Zambia
206 E5 **Kawartha Lakes** Canada
159 F7 **Kawasaki** Japan
126 E2 **Kawau Island** N.Z.
207 G2 **Kawawachikamach** Canada
126 F3 **Kawerau** N.Z.
126 E3 **Kawhia** N.Z.
126 E3 **Kawhia Harbour** N.Z.
215 D3 **Kawich Range** *mts* U.S.A.
162 A1 **Kawkareik** Myanmar
162 A1 **Kawludo** Myanmar
142 E6 **Kawr, Jabal** *mt.* Oman
162 A3 **Kawthaung** Myanmar
141 I5 **Kaxgar He** *r.* China
141 J4 **Kax He** *r.* China
192 B3 **Kaya** Burkina
139 F2 **Kayadibi** Turkey
163 I2 **Kayan** *r.* Indon.
195 C4 **Kayanaza** Burundi
147 H4 **Kayankulam** India
163 I2 **Kayan Mentarang, Taman Nasional** *nat. park* Indon.
213 F3 **Kaycee** U.S.A.
140 C3 **Kaydak, Sor** *dry lake* Kazakh.
195 C4 **Kayembe-Mukulu** Dem. Rep. Congo
215 G3 **Kayenta** U.S.A.
192 A3 **Kayes** Mali
141 F2 **Kayga** Kazakh.
192 A4 **Kayima** Sierra Leone
141 H1 **Kaymanachikha** Kazakh.
136 C3 **Kaymaz** Turkey
141 I2 **Kaynar** *Vostochnyy Kazakhstan* Kazakh.
141 H4 **Kaynar** *Zhambylskaya Oblast'* Kazakh.
139 F2 **Kaynar** Turkey
139 F3 **Kaypak** Turkey
187 H5 **Kaysatskoye** Rus. Fed.
138 E2 **Kayseri** Turkey
163 B3 **Kayuagung** Indon.
133 J3 **Kayyerkan** Rus. Fed.
141 H4 **Kayyngdy** Kyrg.
133 O2 **Kazach'ye** Rus. Fed.
Kazakhdar'ya Uzbek. *see* **Qozoqdaryo**
141 G2 **Kazakhskiy Melkosopochnik** *plain* Kazakh.
140 C4 **Kazakhskiy Zaliv** *b.* Kazakh.
140 D3 **Kazakhstan** *country* Asia
140 E3 **Kazalinsk** Kazakh.
205 J2 **Kazan** *r.* Canada
187 I4 **Kazan'** Rus. Fed.
138 D3 **Kazancı** Turkey
187 I4 **Kazanka** *r.* Rus. Fed.
185 K3 **Kazanlŭk** Bulg.
Kazan-rettō *is* Japan *see* **Volcano Islands**
187 G5 **Kazanskaya** Rus. Fed.
141 H4 **Kazarman** Kyrg.
140 D2 **Kazatskiy** Kazakh.
187 H7 **Kazbek** *mt.* Georgia/Rus. Fed.
185 L5 **Kaz Dağı** *mts* Turkey
142 C4 **Kāzerūn** Iran
186 I2 **Kazhim** Rus. Fed.
143 F5 **Kazhmak** *r.* Pak.
177 J6 **Kazincbarcika** Hungary
149 H4 **Kaziranga National Park** India
187 H7 **Kazret'i** Georgia
140 B2 **Kaztalovka** Kazakh.
158 G4 **Kazuno** Japan
141 G4 **Kazygurt** Kazakh.
132 H3 **Kazymskiy Mys** Rus. Fed.
175 L3 **Keady** U.K.
214 □[2] **Kealakekua Bay** U.S.A.

197 F1 **Khudumelapye** Botswana
142 B5 **Khuff** Saudi Arabia
143 F5 **Khūh Lab, Ra's** *pt* Iran
196 D3 **Khuis** Botswana
141 G4 **Khŭjand** Tajik.
162 C2 **Khu Khan** Thai.
143 G3 **Khulm** *r.* Afgh.
149 G5 **Khulna** Bangl.
139 I1 **Khulo** Georgia
197 G3 **Khuma** S. Africa
148 C2 **Khunjerab Pass** China/Pakistan
142 C3 **Khunsar** Iran
149 F5 **Khunti** India
162 A1 **Khun Yuam** Thai.
143 E3 **Khūr** Iran
148 D4 **Khurai** India
142 D5 **Khūran** *sea chan.* Iran
143 G3 **Khurd, Koh-i-** *mt.* Afgh.
149 F5 **Khurda** India
148 D3 **Khurja** India
143 F3 **Khurmalik** Afgh.
156 E2 **Khurmuli** Rus. Fed.
139 I6 **Khurr, Wādī al** *watercourse* Saudi Arabia
137 I5 **Khūrrāb** Iran
148 C2 **Khushab** Pak.
139 L3 **Khūshāvar** Iran
143 E4 **Khushk Rud** Iran
143 F3 **Khuspas** Afgh.
187 B5 **Khust** Ukr.
138 D6 **Khutmīyah, Mamarr al** *pass* Egypt
197 G3 **Khutsong** S. Africa
156 E2 **Khutu** *r.* Rus. Fed.
143 G5 **Khuzdar** Pak.
143 F3 **Khvāf** Iran
143 F3 **Khvājeh** Iran
187 I4 **Khvalynsk** Rus. Fed.
142 D3 **Khvor** Iran
143 E3 **Khvord Nārvan** Iran
142 C4 **Khvormūj** Iran
140 B1 **Khvorostyanka** Rus. Fed.
139 K3 **Khvosh Maqām** Iran
142 B2 **Khvoy** Iran
186 E3 **Khvoynaya** Rus. Fed.
162 A2 **Khwae Noi** *r.* Thai.
143 F4 **Khwaja Ali** Afgh.
143 H2 **Khwaja Muhammad Range** *mts* Afgh.
148 B2 **Khyber Pass** Afgh./Pak.
125 I5 **Kiama** Australia
161 J5 **Kiamba** Phil.
195 C4 **Kiambi** Dem. Rep. Congo
217 E5 **Kiamichi** *r.* U.S.A.
170 O2 **Kiantajärvi** *l.* Fin.
142 D2 **Kīāseh** Iran
203 L2 **Kiatassuaq** *i.* Greenland
161 J5 **Kibawe** Phil.
195 D4 **Kibaya** Tanz.
195 D4 **Kibiti** Tanz.
195 C4 **Kibombo** Dem. Rep. Congo
195 D4 **Kibondo** Tanz.
185 I4 **Kičevo** Macedonia
186 H3 **Kichmengskiy Gorodok** Rus. Fed.
140 C5 **Kiçi Balkan Daglary** *h.* Turkm.
192 C3 **Kidal** Mali
173 E5 **Kidderminster** U.K.
194 D3 **Kidepo Valley National Park** Uganda
192 A3 **Kidira** Senegal
148 D2 **Kidmang** India
126 F3 **Kidnappers, Cape** N.Z.
173 E4 **Kidsgrove** U.K.
176 E3 **Kiel** Germany
208 C4 **Kiel** U.S.A.
176 D3 **Kiel Canal** Germany
177 J5 **Kielce** Poland
172 E2 **Kielder Water** *resr* U.K.
176 E3 **Kieler Bucht** *b.* Germany
195 C5 **Kienge** Dem. Rep. Congo
179 F3 **Kierspe** Germany
187 D5 **Kiev** Ukr.
192 A3 **Kiffa** Mauritania
185 J5 **Kifisia** Greece
139 J4 **Kifrī** Iraq
195 D4 **Kigali** Rwanda
139 H2 **Kiğı** Turkey
207 H2 **Kiglapait Mountains** Canada
195 C4 **Kigoma** Tanz.
170 M2 **Kihlanki** Fin.
171 M3 **Kihniö** Fin.
141 H3 **Kiik** Kazakh.
170 N2 **Kiiminki** Fin.
159 D8 **Kii-sanchi** *mts* Japan
159 D8 **Kii-suidō** *sea chan.* Japan
185 I2 **Kikinda** Serbia
143 F5 **Kikki** Pak.
186 H3 **Kiknur** Rus. Fed.
158 G4 **Kikonai** Japan
195 C4 **Kikondja** Dem. Rep. Congo
119 E2 **Kikori** P.N.G.
119 E2 **Kikori** *r.* P.N.G.
195 B4 **Kikwit** Dem. Rep. Congo
171 L3 **Kilafors** Sweden
147 H4 **Kilakkarai** India
148 D2 **Kilar** India
214 □[2] **Kilauea** U.S.A.
214 □[2] **Kilauea Crater** U.S.A.
174 C5 **Kilbrannan Sound** *sea chan.* U.K.
160 E3 **Kilchu** N. Korea
175 L4 **Kilcoole** Ireland
175 K4 **Kilcormac** Ireland
125 J1 **Kilcoy** Australia
175 L4 **Kildare** Ireland
170 P1 **Kil'dinstroy** Rus. Fed.
195 B4 **Kilembe** Dem. Rep. Congo
174 C5 **Kilfinan** U.K.
217 E5 **Kilgore** U.S.A.
172 E2 **Kilham** U.K.
195 D4 **Kilifi** Kenya
195 D4 **Kilimanjaro** *vol.* Tanz.
195 D4 **Kilimanjaro National Park** Tanz.
119 F2 **Kilinailau Islands** P.N.G.
195 D4 **Kilindoni** Tanz.
171 N4 **Kilingi-Nõmme** Estonia
139 F3 **Kilis** Turkey
187 D6 **Kiliya** Ukr.
175 I5 **Kilkee** Ireland
175 M3 **Kilkeel** U.K.
175 K5 **Kilkenny** Ireland
173 C7 **Kilkhampton** U.K.
185 J4 **Kilkis** Greece
175 I3 **Killala** Ireland
175 I3 **Killala Bay** Ireland
175 J5 **Killaloe** Ireland
209 I3 **Killaloe Station** Canada
205 G4 **Killam** Canada
120 E3 **Killarney** Australia
125 J2 **Killarney** Australia
209 G3 **Killarney** Canada
175 I5 **Killarney** Ireland
175 I6 **Killarney National Park** Ireland
209 G2 **Killarney Provincial Park** Canada
175 I4 **Killary Harbour** *b.* Ireland
217 D6 **Killeen** U.S.A.
175 K5 **Killenaule** Ireland
175 J4 **Killimor** Ireland
174 D4 **Killin** U.K.
175 M3 **Killinchy** U.K.
175 L5 **Killinick** Ireland
207 H1 **Killiniq** Canada
207 H1 **Killiniq Island** Canada
175 I5 **Killorglin** Ireland
175 I5 **Killurin** Ireland
175 J3 **Killybegs** Ireland
175 K2 **Kilmacrenan** Ireland
175 I4 **Kilmaine** Ireland
175 J5 **Kilmallock** Ireland
174 B3 **Kilmaluag** U.K.
174 D5 **Kilmarnock** U.K.
174 C4 **Kilmelford** U.K.
186 I3 **Kil'mez'** Rus. Fed.
186 I3 **Kil'mez'** *r.* Rus. Fed.
175 J6 **Kilmona** Ireland
125 F6 **Kilmore** Australia
175 L5 **Kilmore Quay** Ireland
195 D4 **Kilosa** Tanz.
170 M1 **Kilpisjärvi** Fin.
170 P1 **Kilp"yavr** Rus. Fed.
175 L3 **Kilrea** U.K.
175 I5 **Kilrush** Ireland
174 D5 **Kilsyth** U.K.
147 G4 **Kiltan** *atoll* India
175 J4 **Kiltullagh** Ireland
195 C4 **Kilwa** Dem. Rep. Congo
195 D4 **Kilwa Masoko** Tanz.
174 D5 **Kilwinning** U.K.
195 D4 **Kimambi** Tanz.
124 B4 **Kimba** Australia
195 B4 **Kimba** Congo
216 C3 **Kimball** U.S.A.
119 F2 **Kimbe** P.N.G.
204 F5 **Kimberley** Canada
197 F4 **Kimberley** S. Africa
118 C3 **Kimberley Plateau** Australia
121 B5 **Kimberley Range** *hills* Australia
126 E4 **Kimbolton** N.Z.
160 E3 **Kimch'aek** N. Korea
160 E5 **Kimch'ŏn** S. Korea
157 C6 **Kimhae** S. Korea
160 D4 **Kimhwa** S. Korea
171 M3 **Kimito** Fin.
160 D6 **Kimje** S. Korea
203 L3 **Kimmirut** Canada
185 K6 **Kimolos** *i.* Greece
187 F4 **Kimovsk** Rus. Fed.
195 B4 **Kimpese** Dem. Rep. Congo
186 F3 **Kimry** Rus. Fed.
195 B4 **Kimvula** Dem. Rep. Congo
163 I1 **Kinabalu, Gunung** *mt. Sabah* Malaysia
161 H5 **Kinabatangan** *r. Sabah* Malaysia
185 L6 **Kinaros** *i.* Greece
204 F4 **Kinbasket Lake** Canada
174 E2 **Kinbrace** U.K.
209 G3 **Kincardine** Canada
174 E4 **Kincardine** U.K.
125 E4 **Kinchega National Park** Australia
Kincolith Canada *see* **Gingolx**
195 C4 **Kinda** Dem. Rep. Congo
149 H5 **Kindat** Myanmar
217 E6 **Kinder** U.S.A.
173 F4 **Kinder Scout** *h.* U.K.
205 H4 **Kindersley** Canada
192 A3 **Kindia** Guinea
195 C4 **Kindu** Dem. Rep. Congo
140 B1 **Kinel'** Rus. Fed.
186 G3 **Kineshma** Rus. Fed.
119 F4 **Kingaroy** Australia
214 B3 **King City** U.S.A.
127 J1 **King Edward Point** *research stn* Antarctica
221 E3 **King Ferry** U.S.A.
221 H2 **Kingfield** U.S.A.
217 D5 **Kingfisher** U.S.A.
127 I2 **King George Island** Antarctica
206 E2 **King George Islands** Canada
121 C4 **King Hill** Australia
186 D3 **Kingisepp** Rus. Fed.
125 F8 **King Island** Australia
204 D4 **King Island** Canada
209 H1 **King Kirkland** Canada
125 F6 **Kinglake National Park** Australia
120 D3 **King Leopold Range National Park** Australia
118 C3 **King Leopold Ranges** *hills* Australia
215 E4 **Kingman** *AZ* U.S.A.
217 D4 **Kingman** *KS* U.S.A.
221 I2 **Kingman** *ME* U.S.A.
117 I3 **Kingman Reef** *terr.* N. Pacific Ocean
204 D3 **King Mountain** Canada
124 A3 **Kingoonya** Australia
175 K5 **Kings** *r.* Ireland
214 C3 **Kings** *r.* U.S.A.
173 D7 **Kingsbridge** U.K.
214 C3 **Kingsburg** U.S.A.
221 I2 **Kingsbury** U.S.A.
214 C3 **Kings Canyon National Park** U.S.A.
125 J2 **Kingscliff** Australia
124 B5 **Kingscote** Australia
175 L4 **Kingscourt** Ireland
127 L2 **King Sejong** *research stn* Antarctica
208 C3 **Kingsford** U.S.A.
219 D6 **Kingsland** *GA* U.S.A.
209 E5 **Kingsland** *IN* U.S.A.
173 H5 **King's Lynn** U.K.
119 H2 **Kingsmill Group** *is* Kiribati
173 H6 **Kingsnorth** U.K.
118 C3 **King Sound** *b.* Australia
213 E3 **Kings Peak** U.S.A.
220 B6 **Kingsport** U.S.A.
209 I3 **Kingston** Canada
223 I5 **Kingston** Jamaica
126 B6 **Kingston** N.Z.
208 B6 **Kingston** *IL* U.S.A.
221 F4 **Kingston** *NY* U.S.A.
125 G9 **Kingston**
215 E4 **Kingston Peak** U.S.A.
124 C6 **Kingston South East** Australia
173 G4 **Kingston upon Hull** U.K.
223 L6 **Kingstown** St Vincent
217 D7 **Kingsville** U.S.A.
173 E6 **Kingswood** U.K.
173 D5 **Kington** U.K.
174 D3 **Kingussie** U.K.
203 I3 **King William Island** Canada
197 G6 **King William's Town** S. Africa
217 E6 **Kingwood** *TX* U.S.A.
220 D5 **Kingwood** *WV* U.S.A.
205 I4 **Kinistino** Canada
159 G5 **Kinka-san** *i.* Japan
126 B6 **Kinloch** N.Z.
174 E3 **Kinloss** U.K.
209 H3 **Kinmount** Canada
171 K4 **Kinna** Sweden
175 K4 **Kinnegad** Ireland
Kinneret, Yam *l.* Israel *see* **Galilee, Sea of**
147 I4 **Kinniyai** Sri Lanka
171 N3 **Kinnula** Fin.
205 I3 **Kinoosao** Canada
159 F5 **Kinpoku-san** *mt.* Japan
174 E4 **Kinross** U.K.
175 J6 **Kinsale** Ireland
195 B4 **Kinshasa** Dem. Rep. Congo
217 D4 **Kinsley** U.S.A.
219 E5 **Kinston** U.S.A.
171 M5 **Kintai** Lith.
192 B4 **Kintampo** Ghana
175 F3 **Kintore** U.K.
174 C5 **Kintyre** *pen.* U.K.
204 F3 **Kinuso** Canada
193 F4 **Kinyeti** *mt.* Sudan
140 D2 **Kinzhaly** Kazakh.
179 H4 **Kinzig** *r.* Germany
209 H2 **Kiosk** Canada
206 E4 **Kipawa, Lac** *l.* Canada
221 F6 **Kiptopeke** U.S.A.
195 C5 **Kipushi** Dem. Rep. Congo
119 G3 **Kirakira** Solomon Is
147 I2 **Kirandul** India
187 D4 **Kirawsk** Belarus
179 G2 **Kirchdorf** Germany
179 G5 **Kirchheim-Bolanden** Germany
175 M3 **Kircubbin** U.K.
151 C1 **Kirenga** *r.* Rus. Fed.
150 C1 **Kirensk** Rus. Fed.
141 H4 **Kirghiz Range** *mts* Asia
117 H4 **Kiribati** *country* Pacific Ocean
139 H1 **Kırık** Turkey
139 F3 **Kırıkhan** Turkey
138 D2 **Kırıkkale** Turkey
186 F3 **Kirillov** Rus. Fed.
156 F3 **Kirillovo** Rus. Fed.
Kirinyaga *mt.* Kenya *see* **Kenya, Mount**
186 E3 **Kirishi** Rus. Fed.
159 B9 **Kirishima-yama** *vol.* Japan
117 I4 **Kiritimati** *atoll* Kiribati
138 A2 **Kırkağaç** Turkey
142 B2 **Kirk Bulāg Dāgi** *mt.* Iran
173 E4 **Kirkby** U.K.
173 F4 **Kirkby in Ashfield** U.K.
172 E3 **Kirkby Lonsdale** U.K.
172 E3 **Kirkby Stephen** U.K.
174 E4 **Kirkcaldy** U.K.
174 C6 **Kirkcolm** U.K.
174 D6 **Kirkcudbright** U.K.
171 K3 **Kirkenær** Norway
170 O1 **Kirkenes** Norway
209 H3 **Kirkfield** Canada
174 D5 **Kirkintilloch** U.K.
171 N3 **Kirkkonummi** Fin.
215 F4 **Kirkland** U.S.A.
215 F4 **Kirkland Junction** U.S.A.
209 G1 **Kirkland Lake** Canada
187 C7 **Kırklareli** Turkey
172 C3 **Kirk Michael** U.K.
172 E3 **Kirkoswald** U.K.
127 J5 **Kirkpatrick, Mount** Antarctica
216 E3 **Kirksville** U.S.A.
139 J4 **Kirkūk** Iraq
175 F2 **Kirkwall** U.K.
197 F6 **Kirkwood** S. Africa
214 B2 **Kirkwood** *CA* U.S.A.
217 F4 **Kirkwood** *MO* U.S.A.
138 C1 **Kırmır** *r.* Turkey
179 F5 **Kirn** Germany
187 E4 **Kirov** *Kaluzhskaya Oblast'* Rus. Fed.
186 I3 **Kirov** *Kirovskaya Oblast'* Rus. Fed.
Kirovabad Azer. *see* **Gäncä**
140 C2 **Kirovo** Kazakh.
186 I3 **Kirovo-Chepetsk** Rus. Fed.
187 E5 **Kirovohrad** Ukr.
139 L2 **Kirovsk** Azer.
186 D3 **Kirovsk** *Leningradskaya Oblast'* Rus. Fed.
170 P2 **Kirovsk** *Murmanskaya Oblast'* Rus. Fed.
186 I3 **Kirovskaya Oblast'** *admin. div.* Rus. Fed.
158 C2 **Kirovskiy** Rus. Fed.
140 D5 **Kirpili** Turkm.
174 E4 **Kirriemuir** U.K.
186 J3 **Kirs** Rus. Fed.
187 G4 **Kirsanov** Rus. Fed.
138 E2 **Kırşehir** Turkey
143 G5 **Kirthar Range** *mts* Pak.
179 H4 **Kirtorf** Germany
170 M2 **Kiruna** Sweden
195 C4 **Kirundu** Dem. Rep. Congo
187 H4 **Kirya** Rus. Fed.
159 F6 **Kiryū** Japan
171 K4 **Kisa** Sweden
194 C3 **Kisangani** Dem. Rep. Congo
195 B4 **Kisantu** Dem. Rep. Congo
163 E2 **Kisaran** Indon.
150 A1 **Kiselevsk** Rus. Fed.
156 E2 **Kisel'ovka** Rus. Fed.
142 D5 **Kish** *i.* Iran
149 F4 **Kishanganj** India
148 B4 **Kishangarh** *Rajasthan* India
148 C4 **Kishangarh** *Rajasthan* India
148 C2 **Kishen Ganga** *r.* India/Pak.
192 C4 **Kishi** Nigeria
159 B9 **Kishika-zaki** *pt* Japan
Kishinev Moldova *see* **Chişinău**
159 D7 **Kishiwada** Japan
141 H1 **Kishkenekol'** Kazakh.
149 G4 **Kishoreganj** Bangl.
Kishorganj Bangl. *see* **Kishoreganj**
148 C2 **Kishtwar** India
Kisi Nigeria *see* **Kishi**
195 D4 **Kisii** Kenya
205 J4 **Kiskittogisu Lake** Canada
177 I7 **Kiskunfélegyháza** Hungary
177 I7 **Kiskunhalas** Hungary
187 G7 **Kislovodsk** Rus. Fed.
195 E4 **Kismaayo** Somalia
159 E7 **Kiso-sanmyaku** *mts* Japan
181 H4 **Kissamos** Greece
192 A4 **Kissidougou** Guinea
219 D6 **Kissimmee** U.S.A.
219 D7 **Kissimmee, Lake** U.S.A.
195 D4 **Kisumu** Kenya
192 B3 **Kita** Mali
Kitab Uzbek. *see* **Kitob**
153 N6 **Kita-Daitō-jima** *i.* Japan
159 G6 **Kitaibaraki** Japan
159 G5 **Kitakami** Japan
159 G5 **Kitakami-gawa** *r.* Japan
159 F6 **Kitakata** Japan
159 B8 **Kita-Kyūshū** Japan
194 D3 **Kitale** Kenya
133 P5 **Kitami** Japan
213 G4 **Kit Carson** U.S.A.
209 G4 **Kitchener** Canada
171 O3 **Kitee** Fin.
194 D3 **Kitgum** Uganda
204 D4 **Kitimat** Canada
170 N2 **Kitinen** *r.* Fin.
141 F5 **Kitob** Uzbek.
195 B4 **Kitona** Dem. Rep. Congo
159 B8 **Kitsuki** Japan
124 C2 **Kittakittaooloo, Lake** *salt flat* Australia
220 D4 **Kittanning** U.S.A.
221 F4 **Kittatinny Mountains** U.S.A.
221 H3 **Kittery** U.S.A.
170 N2 **Kittilä** Fin.
219 F4 **Kitty Hawk** U.S.A.
195 D4 **Kitunda** Tanz.
204 D3 **Kitwanga** Canada
195 C5 **Kitwe** Zambia
176 F7 **Kitzbüheler Alpen** *mts* Austria
179 I5 **Kitzingen** Germany
179 K3 **Kitzscher** Germany
171 N3 **Kiuruvesi** Fin.
171 N3 **Kivijärvi** Fin.
171 N4 **Kiviõli** Estonia
195 C4 **Kivu, Lake** Dem. Rep. Congo/Rwanda
141 G2 **Kiyakty, Ozero** *salt l.* Kazakh.
141 G2 **Kiyevka** Kazakh.
158 C3 **Kiyevka** Rus. Fed.
185 M4 **Kıyıköy** Turkey
141 F2 **Kiyma** Kazakh.
132 G4 **Kizel** Rus. Fed.
186 H2 **Kizema** Rus. Fed.
141 J4 **Kizil** China
138 B3 **Kızılca Dağ** *mt.* Turkey
138 D1 **Kızılcahamam** Turkey
139 G2 **Kızıl Dağı** *mt.* Turkey
138 D1 **Kızılırmak** Turkey
138 D2 **Kızılırmak** *r.* Turkey
138 C3 **Kızılkaya** Turkey
138 D3 **Kızılören** Turkey
140 D1 **Kizil'skoye** Rus. Fed.
139 H3 **Kızıltepe** Turkey
187 H7 **Kizilyurt** Rus. Fed.
Kizil"yurt Rus. Fed. *see* **Kizilyurt**
187 H7 **Kizlyar** Rus. Fed.
137 G1 **Kizlyarskiy Zaliv** *b.* Rus. Fed.
Kizylayak Turkm. *see* **Gyzylaýak**
170 N1 **Kjøllefjord** Norway
170 L1 **Kjøpsvik** Norway
176 G5 **Kladno** Czech Rep.
176 G7 **Klagenfurt** Austria
215 H4 **Klagetoh** U.S.A.
171 M5 **Klaipėda** Lith.
170 □ **Klaksvík** Faroe Is
213 B3 **Klamath** *r.* U.S.A.
213 B3 **Klamath Falls** U.S.A.
213 B3 **Klamath Mountains** U.S.A.
163 B2 **Klang** Malaysia
171 K4 **Klarälven** *r.* Sweden
176 F6 **Klatovy** Czech Rep.
196 C5 **Klawer** S. Africa
204 C3 **Klawock** U.S.A.
179 E2 **Klazienaveen** Neth.
204 E4 **Kleena Kleene** Canada
196 D4 **Kleinbegin** S. Africa
196 C3 **Klein Karas** Namibia
197 F6 **Kleinpoort** S. Africa
196 D6 **Klein Roggeveldberge** *mts* S. Africa
196 B4 **Kleinsee** S. Africa
196 D6 **Klein Swartberg** *mt.* S. Africa
204 D4 **Klemtu** Canada
197 G3 **Klerksdorp** S. Africa
187 E4 **Kletnya** Rus. Fed.
187 G5 **Kletskaya** Rus. Fed.
179 E3 **Kleve** Germany
187 D4 **Klimavichy** Belarus
187 E4 **Klimovo** Rus. Fed.
187 F4 **Klimovsk** Rus. Fed.
186 F3 **Klin** Rus. Fed.
204 D4 **Klinaklini** *r.* Canada
179 H5 **Klingenberg am Main** Germany
179 K4 **Klingenthal** Germany
179 K1 **Klink** Germany
176 F5 **Klínovec** *mt.* Czech Rep.
171 L4 **Klintehamn** Sweden
187 I5 **Klintsovka** Rus. Fed.
187 E4 **Klintsy** Rus. Fed.
196 C5 **Kliprand** S. Africa
185 G2 **Ključ** Bos.-Herz.
177 H5 **Kłodzko** Poland
179 E2 **Kloosterhaar** Neth.
177 H6 **Klosterneuburg** Austria
207 F1 **Klotz, Lac** *l.* Canada
179 J2 **Klötze (Altmark)** Germany
204 A2 **Kluane Game Sanctuary** *nature res.* Canada
204 B2 **Kluane Lake** Canada
204 B2 **Kluane National Park** Canada
177 I5 **Kluczbork** Poland
137 F2 **Klukhorskiy, Pereval** Georgia/Rus. Fed.
148 B4 **Klupro** Pak.
187 C4 **Klyetsk** Belarus
133 R4 **Klyuchevskaya, Sopka** *vol.* Rus. Fed.
156 B2 **Klyuchi** Rus. Fed.
141 I1 **Klyuchi** Rus. Fed.
171 K3 **Knåda** Sweden
172 F3 **Knaresborough** U.K.
205 K3 **Knee Lake** Canada
179 I5 **Knetzgau** Germany
208 B1 **Knife Lake** Canada/U.S.A.
204 D4 **Knight Inlet** Canada
173 D5 **Knighton** U.K.
185 G2 **Knin** Croatia
176 G7 **Knittelfeld** Austria
185 J3 **Knjaževac** Serbia
120 E2 **Knob Peak** *h.* Australia
175 J4 **Knock** Ireland
175 I5 **Knockacummer** *h.* Ireland
175 J3 **Knockalongy** *h.* Ireland
175 I5 **Knockalough** Ireland
175 I6 **Knockboy** *h.* Ireland
175 F3 **Knock Hill** U.K.
175 L2 **Knocklayd** *h.* U.K.
178 B3 **Knokke-Heist** Belgium
179 L1 **Knorrendorf** Germany
185 K7 **Knossos** *tourist site* Greece
173 F5 **Knowle** U.K.
127 I3 **Knowles, Cape** Antarctica
221 I1 **Knowles Corner** U.S.A.
221 G2 **Knowlton** Canada
208 D5 **Knox** U.S.A.
204 C4 **Knox, Cape** Canada
214 A2 **Knoxville** *CA* U.S.A.
208 B5 **Knoxville** *IL* U.S.A.
219 D4 **Knoxville** *TN* U.S.A.
174 C3 **Knoydart** *mts* U.K.
203 M1 **Knud Rasmussen Land** *reg.* Greenland
197 E7 **Knysna** S. Africa
156 E3 **Ko, Gora** *mt.* Rus. Fed.

185 G2 Kozara mts Bos.-Herz.
187 D5 Kozelets' Ukr.
187 E4 Kozel'sk Rus. Fed.
Kozhikode India see Calicut
138 C1 Kozlu Turkey
186 H3 Koz'modem'yansk Rus. Fed.
141 G4 Kozmoldak Kazakh.
185 J4 Kožuf mts Greece/Macedonia
159 F7 Kōzu-shima i. Japan
187 D5 Kozyatyn Ukr.
192 C4 Kpalimé Togo
162 A3 Kra, Isthmus of Thai.
162 A3 Krabi Thai.
162 A3 Kra Buri Thai.
162 C2 Krâchéh Cambodia
170 L2 Kraddsele Sweden
171 J4 Kragerø Norway
178 D2 Kraggenburg Neth.
185 I2 Kragujevac Serbia
179 G5 Kraichgau reg. Germany
163 G4 Krakatau i. Indon.
162 C2 Krâkôr Cambodia
177 I5 Kraków Poland
179 K1 Krakower See l. Germany
162 B2 Krâlănh Cambodia
233 J1 Kralendijk Neth. Antilles
187 F5 Kramators'k Ukr.
171 L3 Kramfors Sweden
178 C3 Krammer est. Neth.
185 J6 Kranidi Greece
184 F1 Kranj Slovenia
162 □ Kranji Reservoir Sing.
197 I4 Kranskop S. Africa
186 H2 Krasavino Rus. Fed.
132 G2 Krasino Rus. Fed.
158 B3 Kraskino Rus. Fed.
171 N5 Krāslava Latvia
179 K4 Kraslice Czech Rep.
177 O4 Krasnapollye Belarus
187 D4 Krasnaya Gora Rus. Fed.
141 H2 Krasnaya Polyana Kazakh.
187 H5 Krasnoarmeysk Rus. Fed.
187 F5 Krasnoarmiys'k Ukr.
186 H2 Krasnoborsk Rus. Fed.
187 F6 Krasnodar Rus. Fed.
187 F6 Krasnodarskiy Kray admin. div. Rus. Fed.
187 F5 Krasnodon Ukr.
186 D3 Krasnogorodskoye Rus. Fed.
156 F2 Krasnogorsk Rus. Fed.
187 G6 Krasnogvardeyskoye Rus. Fed.
187 E5 Krasnohrad Ukr.
187 E6 Krasnohvardiys'ke Ukr.
140 C2 Krasnokholm Rus. Fed.
177 Q2 Krasnomayskiy Rus. Fed.
187 E6 Krasnoperekops'k Ukr.
156 F2 Krasnopol'ye Rus. Fed.
158 D2 Krasnorechenskiy Rus. Fed.
171 O3 Krasnosel'skoye Rus. Fed.
187 G4 Krasnoslobodsk Rus. Fed.
140 D1 Krasnousol'skiy Rus. Fed.
140 C5 Krasnovodsk, Mys pt Turkm.
Krasnovodskiy Zaliv b. Turkm. see Türkmenbaşy Aýlagy
140 C4 Krasnovodskoye Plato plat. Turkm.
156 C2 Krasnoyarovo Rus. Fed.
150 B1 Krasnoyarsk Rus. Fed.
177 O3 Krasnyy Rus. Fed.
153 I1 Krasnyy Chikoy Rus. Fed.
186 H3 Krasnyye Baki Rus. Fed.
187 H6 Krasnyye Barrikady Rus. Fed.
186 F3 Krasnyy Kholm Rus. Fed.
187 H5 Krasnyy Kut Rus. Fed.
186 D3 Krasnyy Luch Rus. Fed.
187 F5 Krasnyy Lyman Ukr.
141 I3 Krasnyy Oktyabr' Kazakh.
141 G1 Krasnyy Yar Kazakh.
187 I6 Krasnyy Yar Astrakhanskaya Oblast' Rus. Fed.
140 B1 Krasnyy Yar Samarskaya Oblast' Rus. Fed.
187 H5 Krasnyy Yar Volgogradskaya Oblast' Rus. Fed.
187 C5 Krasyliv Ukr.
187 H7 Kraynovka Rus. Fed.
179 E3 Krefeld Germany
187 E5 Kremenchuk Ukr.
187 E5 Kremenchuts'ke Vodoskhovyshche resr Ukr.
187 G5 Kremenskaya Rus. Fed.
176 G6 Křemešník h. Czech Rep.
213 F3 Kremmling U.S.A.
176 G6 Krems an der Donau Austria
133 T3 Kresta, Zaliv g. Rus. Fed.
186 E3 Kresttsy Rus. Fed.
171 M5 Kretinga Lith.
179 E4 Kreuzau Germany
179 F4 Kreuztal Germany
177 M3 Kreva Belarus
192 C4 Kribi Cameroon
197 H3 Kriel S. Africa
185 I5 Krikellos Greece
158 H2 Kril'on, Mys c. Rus. Fed.
135 F5 Krishna r. India
135 G5 Krishna, Mouths of the India
147 H3 Krishnagiri India
149 G5 Krishnanagar India
147 H3 Krishnaraja Sagara l. India
171 I4 Kristiansand Norway
171 K4 Kristianstad Sweden
171 I3 Kristiansund Norway
Kristiinankaupunki Fin. see Kristinestad
171 K4 Kristinehamn Sweden
171 M3 Kristinestad Fin.
Kriti i. Greece see Crete
185 K6 Kritiko Pelagos sea Greece
Krivoy Rog Ukr. see Kryvyy Rih
185 G1 Križevci Croatia
184 F2 Krk i. Croatia
171 K3 Krokom Sweden
171 J3 Krokstadøra Norway
170 K2 Krokstranda Norway
187 E5 Krolevets' Ukr.
179 J4 Kronach Germany
162 B3 Krŏng Kaôh Kŏng Cambodia
171 M3 Kronoby Fin.
203 O3 Kronprins Frederik Bjerge nunataks Greenland
162 A2 Kronwa Myanmar
197 G3 Kroonstad S. Africa
187 G6 Kropotkin Rus. Fed.
179 K3 Kropstädt Germany
177 J6 Krosno Poland
177 H5 Krotoszyn Poland
197 I2 Kruger National Park S. Africa
156 D2 Kruglikovo Rus. Fed.
177 N3 Kruhlaye Belarus
163 B4 Krui Indon.
197 F7 Kruisfontein S. Africa
185 H4 Krujë Albania
185 K4 Krumovgrad Bulg.
Krung Thep Thai. see Bangkok
177 N3 Krupki Belarus
185 I3 Kruševac Serbia
179 K4 Krušné hory mts Czech Rep.
204 B3 Kruzof Island U.S.A.
187 D4 Krychaw Belarus
239 H4 Krylov Seamount sea feature N. Atlantic Ocean
187 F6 Krymsk Rus. Fed.
Kryms'kyy Pivostriv pen. Ukr. see Crimea
141 H3 Krypsalo Kazakh.
187 E6 Kryvyy Rih Ukr.
192 B2 Ksabi Alg.
192 C1 Ksar el Boukhari Alg.
192 B1 Ksar el Kebir Morocco
169 R3 Ksenofontova Rus. Fed.
187 F5 Kshenskiy Rus. Fed.
184 D7 Ksour Essaf Tunisia
186 H3 Kstovo Rus. Fed.
142 B5 Kū', Jabal al h. Saudi Arabia
162 A4 Kuah Malaysia
162 B4 Kuala Kangsar Malaysia
162 B4 Kuala Kerai Malaysia
162 B5 Kuala Kubu Baharu Malaysia
163 B2 Kuala Lipis Malaysia
163 B2 Kuala Lumpur Malaysia
162 B4 Kuala Nerang Malaysia
162 B5 Kuala Pilah Malaysia
162 B5 Kuala Rompin Malaysia
163 H3 Kualasampit Indon.
162 A4 Kualasimpang Indon.
163 B1 Kuala Terengganu Malaysia
161 H5 Kuamut Sabah Malaysia
160 C3 Kuandian China
155 F6 Kuanshan Taiwan
163 B2 Kuantan Malaysia
187 G6 Kuban' r. Rus. Fed.
139 G4 Kubār Syria
139 I5 Kubaysah Iraq
186 F3 Kubenskoye, Ozero l. Rus. Fed.
140 D4 Kubla Ustyurt Uzbek.
187 H4 Kubnya r. Rus. Fed.
185 L3 Kubrat Bulg.
148 C4 Kuchaman India
148 C4 Kuchera India
163 H2 Kuching Sarawak Malaysia
159 A10 Kuchino-Erabu-shima i. Japan
141 I1 Kuchukskoye, Ozero salt l. Rus. Fed.
185 H4 Kuçovë Albania
147 G3 Kudal India
163 I1 Kudat Sabah Malaysia
147 H3 Kudligi India
147 G3 Kudremukh mt. India
163 H4 Kudus Indon.
176 F7 Kufstein Austria
203 J3 Kugaaruk Canada
141 I3 Kugaly Kazakh.
186 H3 Kugesi Rus. Fed.
202 G3 Kugluktuk Canada
202 E3 Kugmallit Bay Canada
143 E5 Kūh, Ra's-al- pt Iran
143 F5 Kūhak Iran
149 E3 Kuhanbokano mt. China
179 K1 Kuhbier Germany
143 E4 Kūhbonān Iran
142 B3 Kūhdasht Iran
139 L3 Kūhīn Iran
170 O2 Kuhmo Fin.
171 N3 Kuhmoinen Fin.
142 D3 Kūhpāyeh Iran
179 K3 Kühren Germany
162 A2 Kui Buri Thai.
196 B2 Kuis Namibia
196 A1 Kuiseb Pass Namibia
195 B5 Kuito Angola
204 C3 Kuiu Island U.S.A.
170 N2 Kuivaniemi Fin.
149 F5 Kujang India
160 C4 Kujang N. Korea
158 G4 Kuji Japan
159 B8 Kujū-san vol. Japan
156 D2 Kukan Rus. Fed.
209 F1 Kukatush Canada
185 I3 Kukës Albania
186 I3 Kukmor Rus. Fed.
162 B5 Kukup Malaysia
140 D5 Kükürtli Turkm.
142 D5 Kūl r. Iran
138 B2 Kula Turkey
140 B2 Kulagino Kazakh.
149 G3 Kula Kangri mt. Bhutan
140 B3 Kulaly, Ostrov i. Kazakh.
141 H4 Kulan Kazakh.
141 H4 Kulanak Kyrg.
140 D3 Kulandy Kazakh.
140 D3 Kulandy, Poluostrov pen. Kazakh.
143 F5 Kulaneh reg. Pak.
141 G2 Kulanotpes watercourse Kazakh.
141 I4 Kulansarak China
143 G4 Kulao r. Pak.
133 O2 Kular Rus. Fed.
161 I5 Kulassein i. Phil.
149 H4 Kulaura Bangl.
171 M4 Kuldīga Latvia
156 C2 Kul'dur Rus. Fed.
Kul'dzhuktau, Gory h. Uzbek. see Quljuqtov tog'lari
196 D1 Kule Botswana
187 G4 Kulebaki Rus. Fed.
162 C2 Kulen Cambodia
140 E1 Kulevchinskoye Rus. Fed.
121 F5 Kulgera Australia
186 H2 Kulikovo Rus. Fed.
162 B4 Kulim Malaysia
121 B7 Kulin Australia
121 B6 Kulja Australia
Kulkuduk Uzbek. see Ko'lquduq
125 F3 Kulkyne watercourse Australia
148 D3 Kullu India
179 J4 Kulmbach Germany
141 G5 Kŭlob Tajik.
139 H2 Kulp Turkey
148 D4 Kulpahar India
221 F4 Kulpsville U.S.A.
140 C3 Kul'sary Kazakh.
179 H5 Külsheim Germany
138 D2 Kulu Turkey
138 C3 Kulübe Tepe mt. Turkey
141 I1 Kulunda Rus. Fed.
141 J1 Kulunda r. Rus. Fed.
141 H1 Kulundinskaya Step' plain Kazakh./Rus. Fed.
141 I1 Kulundinskoye, Ozero salt l. Rus. Fed.
142 D4 Kūlvand Iran
125 E5 Kulwin Australia
187 H6 Kuma r. Rus. Fed.
159 F6 Kumagaya Japan
163 H3 Kumai, Teluk b. Indon.
158 F3 Kumaishi Japan
140 E2 Kumak Rus. Fed.
140 D2 Kumak r. Rus. Fed.
159 B8 Kumamoto Japan
159 E8 Kumano Japan
185 I3 Kumanovo Macedonia
156 B2 Kumara Rus. Fed.
192 B4 Kumasi Ghana
192 C4 Kumba Cameroon
147 H4 Kumbakonam India
138 C2 Kümbet Turkey
197 E1 Kumchuru Botswana
142 D3 Kumel well Iran
169 P4 Kumeny Rus. Fed.
140 C1 Kumertau Rus. Fed.
160 D5 Kŭm-gang r. S. Korea
160 E4 Kŭmgang-san mt. N. Korea
160 E6 Kŭmho-gang r. S. Korea
160 E5 Kumi S. Korea
171 K4 Kumla Sweden
179 L2 Kummersdorf-Alexanderdorf Germany
193 D3 Kumo Nigeria
160 D6 Kŭmŏ-do i. S. Korea
141 F3 Kumola watercourse Kazakh.
152 G6 Kumon Range mts Myanmar
162 B1 Kumphawapi Thai.
196 C4 Kums Namibia
147 G3 Kumta India
187 H7 Kumukh Rus. Fed.
143 H3 Kunar r. Afgh.
150 G2 Kunashir, Ostrov i. Rus. Fed.
149 E2 Kunchuk Tso salt l. China
171 N4 Kunda Estonia
149 E4 Kunda India
147 G3 Kundapura India
148 B2 Kundar r. Afgh./Pak.
143 H2 Kunduz Afgh.
143 H2 Kunduz r. Afgh.
195 B5 Kunene r. Angola/Namibia alt. Cunene
Künes China see Xinyuan
141 J4 Künes Chang China
141 J4 Künes He r. China
171 J4 Kungälv Sweden
141 I4 Kungei Alatau mts Kazakh./Kyrg.
204 C4 Kunghit Island Canada
Kungrad Uzbek. see Qo'ng'irot
140 E4 Kungradkol' Uzbek.
171 K4 Kungsbacka Sweden
171 J4 Kungshamn Sweden
194 B3 Kungu Dem. Rep. Congo
148 D6 Kuni r. India
159 B8 Kunimi-dake mt. Japan
149 F5 Kunjabar India
149 G4 Kunlui r. India/Nepal
135 F3 Kunlun Shan mts China
149 H2 Kunlun Shankou pass China
155 B5 Kunming China
148 D4 Kuno r. India
160 D6 Kunsan S. Korea
155 F4 Kunshan China
118 C3 Kununurra Australia
148 D4 Kunwari r. India
186 D3 Kun'ya Rus. Fed.
Kunyu Shan h. China see Taibo Ding
179 H5 Künzelsau Germany
179 J3 Künzels-Berg h. Germany
155 F4 Kuocang Shan mts China
171 N3 Kuohijärvi l. Fin.
170 O2 Kuolayarvi Rus. Fed.
171 N3 Kuopio Fin.
171 M3 Kuortane Fin.
184 2 Kupa r. Croatia/Slovenia
151 E8 Kupang Indon.
171 N5 Kupiškis Lith.
204 C3 Kupreanof Island U.S.A.
187 F5 Kup"yans'k Ukr.
141 J4 Kuqa China
139 L2 Kür r. Azer.
156 D2 Kur r. Rus. Fed.
139 J1 Kura r. Azer./Georgia
137 G2 Kura r. Georgia
187 G7 Kura r. Georgia/Rus. Fed.
141 H4 Kuragaty Kazakh.
187 H7 Kurakh Rus. Fed.
140 D2 Kurashasayskiy Kazakh.
159 C7 Kurashiki Japan
187 E5 Kurasia India
159 C7 Kurayoshi Japan
138 B1 Kurban Dağı mt. Turkey
187 E5 Kurchatov Rus. Fed.
141 J2 Kurchum Kazakh.
139 L1 Kürdämir Azer.
141 H4 Kurday Kazakh.
139 L2 Kür Dili pt Azer.
147 G2 Kurduvadi India
185 K4 Kŭrdzhali Bulg.
159 C7 Kure Japan
138 D1 Küre Turkey
117 G1 Kure Atoll U.S.A.
171 M4 Kuressaare Estonia
132 H4 Kurgan Rus. Fed.
187 G6 Kurganinsk Rus. Fed.
143 H2 Kuri Afgh.
148 B4 Kuri India
Kuria Muria Islands is Oman see Ḥalāniyāt, Juzur al
149 G4 Kuri Chhu r. Bhutan
123 C4 Kuridala Australia
171 M3 Kurikka Fin.
159 G5 Kurikoma-yama vol. Japan
236 E2 Kuril Basin sea feature Sea of Okhotsk
150 G2 Kuril Islands Rus. Fed.
140 B2 Kurilovka Rus. Fed.
150 G2 Kuril'sk Rus. Fed.
Kuril'skiye Ostrova is Rus. Fed. see Kuril Islands
236 E3 Kuril Trench sea feature N. Pacific Ocean
140 B1 Kurmanayevka Rus. Fed.
193 F3 Kurmuk Sudan
147 H3 Kurnool India
138 E6 Kurnub tourist site Israel
159 E6 Kurobe Japan
158 G4 Kuroishi Japan
159 G6 Kuroiso Japan
159 A9 Kuro-shima i. Japan
156 B1 Kurovskiy Rus. Fed.
126 C6 Kurow N.Z.
148 B2 Kurram r. Afgh./Pak.
125 I4 Kurri Kurri Australia
137 F1 Kursavka Rus. Fed.
187 F5 Kursk Rus. Fed.
187 H6 Kurskaya Rus. Fed.
187 F5 Kurskaya Oblast' admin. div. Rus. Fed.
138 D1 Kurşunlu Turkey
139 H3 Kurtalan Turkey
141 I3 Kurtty r. Kazakh.
136 D2 Kurucaşile Turkey
139 G2 Kuruçay Turkey
148 D3 Kurukshetra India
150 A2 Kuruktag mts China
197 E3 Kuruman S. Africa
196 D3 Kuruman watercourse S. Africa
159 B8 Kurume Japan
150 D1 Kurumkan Rus. Fed.
147 I5 Kurunegala Sri Lanka
193 F2 Kurush, Jebel hills Sudan
169 R3 Kur'ya Rus. Fed.
141 J2 Kur'ya Rus. Fed.
140 B4 Kuryk Kazakh.
185 L6 Kuşadası Turkey
185 L6 Kuşadası Körfezi b. Turkey
204 B2 Kusawa Lake Canada
179 F5 Kusel Germany
138 A1 Kuş Gölü l. Turkey
187 F6 Kushchevskaya Rus. Fed.
159 B9 Kushikino Japan
159 D8 Kushimoto Japan
158 I3 Kushiro Japan
158 I3 Kushiro-Shitsugen Kokuritsu-kōen nat. park Japan
139 L5 Kūshkak Iran
141 F1 Kushmurun Kazakh.
147 H3 Kushtagi India
149 G5 Kushtia Bangl.
154 C2 Kushui He r. China
140 B2 Kushum Kazakh.
140 B2 Kushum r. Kazakh.
202 C3 Kuskokwim r. U.S.A.
202 B4 Kuskokwim Bay U.S.A.
202 C3 Kuskokwim Mountains U.S.A.
160 C4 Kusŏng N. Korea
158 I3 Kussharo-ko l. Japan
179 F1 Küstenkanal canal Germany
142 C4 Kut Iran
162 B3 Kut, Ko i. Thai.
139 L6 Kūt 'Abdollāh Iran
162 A5 Kutacane Indon.
138 B2 Kütahya Turkey
187 G7 K'ut'aisi Georgia
187 H6 Kutan Rus. Fed.
158 G3 Kutchan Japan
139 L5 Kūt-e Gapu tourist site Iran
185 G2 Kutina Croatia
185 G2 Kutjevo Croatia
177 I4 Kutno Poland
195 B4 Kutu Dem. Rep. Congo
149 G5 Kutubdia Island Bangl.
202 G2 Kuujjua r. Canada
207 G2 Kuujjuaq Canada
206 E2 Kuujjuarapik Canada
Kuuli-Mayak Turkm. see Guwlumaýak
170 O2 Kuusamo Fin.
171 N3 Kuusankoski Fin.
140 D2 Kuvandyk Rus. Fed.
195 B5 Kuvango Angola
186 E3 Kuvshinovo Rus. Fed.
139 K7 Kuwait country Asia
139 K7 Kuwait Kuwait
139 K7 Kuwait Jun b. Kuwait
159 E7 Kuwana Japan
186 G1 Kuya Rus. Fed.
132 I4 Kuybyshev Novosibirskaya Oblast' Rus. Fed.
Kuybyshev Samarskaya Oblast' Rus. Fed. see Samara
187 I4 Kuybyshevskoye Vodokhranilishche resr Rus. Fed.
154 D2 Kuye He r. China
141 H3 Kuygan Kazakh.
135 G2 Kuytun China
153 H1 Kuytun Rus. Fed.
141 J3 Kuytun He r. China
185 M6 Kuyucak Turkey
141 F2 Kuyukkol', Ozero salt l. Kazakh.
141 K2 Kuyus Rus. Fed.
171 O3 Kuznechnoye Rus. Fed.
187 H4 Kuznetsk Rus. Fed.
158 F1 Kuznetsovo Rus. Fed.
187 C5 Kuznetsovs'k Ukr.
170 M1 Kvænangen sea chan. Norway
170 L1 Kvaløya i. Norway
170 M1 Kvalsund Norway
140 D1 Kvarkeno Rus. Fed.
184 F2 Kvarnerić sea chan. Croatia
202 C4 Kvichak Bay U.S.A.
204 D3 Kwadacha Wilderness Provincial Park Canada
155 □ Kwai Tau Leng h. Hong Kong China
236 G6 Kwajalein atoll Marshall Is
162 A5 Kwala Indon.
197 I4 KwaMashu S. Africa
197 H2 KwaMhlanga S. Africa
160 D5 Kwangch'ŏn S. Korea
160 D6 Kwangju S. Korea
195 B4 Kwango r. Dem. Rep. Congo
195 D4 Kwangwazi Tanz.
160 D6 Kwangyang S. Korea
160 E3 Kwanmo-bong mt. N. Korea
197 F6 Kwanobuhle S. Africa
197 F6 KwaNojoli S. Africa
197 G6 Kwanonqubela S. Africa
197 F5 KwaNonzame S. Africa
197 G6 Kwatinidubu S. Africa
197 H3 KwaZamokuhle S. Africa
197 F6 KwaZamukucinga S. Africa
197 F5 Kwazamuxolo S. Africa
197 H3 KwaZanele S. Africa
197 I4 KwaZulu-Natal prov. S. Africa
195 C5 Kwekwe Zimbabwe
197 F1 Kweneng admin. dist. Botswana
195 B4 Kwenge r. Dem. Rep. Congo
197 G5 Kwezi-Naledi S. Africa
177 I4 Kwidzyn Poland
202 B4 Kwigillingok U.S.A.
119 E2 Kwikila P.N.G.
195 B4 Kwilu r. Angola/Dem. Rep. Congo
151 F7 Kwoka mt. Indon.
155 □ Kwun Tong Hong Kong China
193 D4 Kyabé Chad
123 C5 Kyabra Australia
125 F6 Kyabram Australia
162 A1 Kya-in Seikkyi Myanmar
150 C1 Kyakhta Rus. Fed.
125 E5 Kyalite Australia
124 A4 Kyancutta Australia
186 F1 Kyanda Rus. Fed.
162 A1 Kyaukhnyat Myanmar
149 H6 Kyaukpyu Myanmar
149 H5 Kyauktaw Myanmar
171 M5 Kybartai Lith.
124 D6 Kybybolite Australia
155 C6 Ky Cung, Sông r. Vietnam
145 H8 Kyeintali Myanmar
148 D2 Kyelang India
154 A2 Kyikug China
Kyiv Ukr. see Kiev
187 D5 Kyivs'ke Vodoskhovyshche resr Ukr.
Kyklades is Greece see Cyclades
205 H4 Kyle Canada

Kyle of Lochalsh

174 C3 **Kyle of Lochalsh** U.K.
179 E5 **Kyll** *r.* Germany
185 J6 **Kyllini** *mt.* Greece
136 B3 **Kymis, Akrotirio** *pt* Greece
125 F6 **Kyneton** Australia
123 C4 **Kynuna** Australia
194 D3 **Kyoga, Lake** Uganda
159 D7 **Kyōga-misaki** *pt* Japan
125 J2 **Kyogle** Australia
162 A1 **Kyondo** Myanmar
160 E6 **Kyŏngju** S. Korea
159 D7 **Kyōto** Japan
185 I6 **Kyparissia** Greece
185 I6 **Kyparissiakos Kolpos** *b.* Greece
141 G2 **Kypshak, Ozero** *salt l.* Kazakh.
153 J2 **Kyra** Rus. Fed.
185 K5 **Kyra Panagia** *i.* Greece
138 D4 **Kyrenia** Cyprus
141 H4 **Kyrgyzstan** *country* Asia
179 K2 **Kyritz** Germany
140 B2 **Kyrkopa** Kazakh.
171 J3 **Kyrksæterøra** Norway
132 G3 **Kyrta** Rus. Fed.
186 H1 **Kyssa** Rus. Fed.
133 O3 **Kytalyktakh** Rus. Fed.
185 J6 **Kythira** *i.* Greece
185 K6 **Kythnos** *i.* Greece
162 A2 **Kyungyaung** Myanmar
140 D3 **Kyushe** Kazakh.
159 B8 **Kyūshū** *i.* Japan
236 E4 **Kyushu-Palau Ridge** *sea feature* N. Pacific Ocean
185 J3 **Kyustendil** Bulg.
125 G5 **Kywong** Australia
171 N3 **Kyyjärvi** Fin.
140 C3 **Kyzan** Kazakh.
150 B1 **Kyzyl** Rus. Fed.
141 G4 **Kyzyl-Adyr** Kyrg.
141 H5 **Kyzylart Pass** Kyrg.
141 H3 **Kyzylbelen, Gora** *h.* Kazakh.
141 G2 **Kyzyldyykan** Kazakh.
141 J3 **Kyzylkesek** Kazakh.
140 C2 **Kyzylkoga** Kazakh.
140 E2 **Kyzylkol', Ozero** *l.* Kazakh.
140 E4 **Kyzylkum Desert** Uzbek.
141 H4 **Kyzyl-Kyya** Kyrg.
144 H1 **Kyzyl-Mazhalyk** Rus. Fed.
141 F3 **Kyzylorda** Kazakh.
140 E3 **Kyzylordinskaya Oblast'** *admin. div.* Kazakh.
140 C4 **Kyzylsay** Kazakh.
141 I4 **Kyzyl-Suu** Kyrg.
141 H5 **Kyzyl-Suu** *r.* Kyrg.
141 H2 **Kyzyltas** Kazakh.
141 H3 **Kyzyltau** Kazakh.
141 F2 **Kyzyluy** Kazakh.
140 B3 **Kyzylysor** Kazakh.
140 C2 **Kyzylzhar** *Aktyubinskaya Oblast'* Kazakh.
141 G2 **Kyzylzhar** *Karagandinskaya Oblast'* Kazakh.

L

179 F4 **Laacher See** *l.* Germany
171 N4 **Laagri** Estonia
224 I6 **La Amistad, Parque Internacional** *nat. park* Costa Rica/Panama
225 F5 **La Angostura, Presa de** *resr* Mex.
170 N1 **Laanila** Fin.
225 D3 **La Ardilla, Cerro** *mt.* Mex.
194 E3 **Laascaanood** Somalia
194 E2 **Laasgoray** Somalia
233 L2 **La Asunción** Venez.
192 A2 **Laâyoune** W. Sahara
187 G6 **Laba** *r.* Rus. Fed.
225 D1 **La Babia** Mex.
232 D3 **La Banda** Arg.
213 E3 **La Barge** U.S.A.
119 H3 **Labasa** Fiji
182 C3 **La Baule-Escoublac** France
192 A3 **Labé** Guinea
207 F4 **Labelle** Canada
208 B5 **La Belle** U.S.A.
204 B2 **Laberge, Lake** Canada
161 H5 **Labian, Tanjung** *pt Sabah* Malaysia
204 E2 **La Biche** *r.* Canada
205 G4 **La Biche, Lac** *l.* Canada
187 G6 **Labinsk** Rus. Fed.
162 B5 **Labis** Malaysia
161 I3 **Labo** Phil.
224 C2 **La Boquilla** Mex.
139 F4 **Laboué** Lebanon
182 D4 **Labouheyre** France
235 J2 **Laboulaye** Arg.
207 H3 **Labrador** *reg.* Canada
207 G3 **Labrador City** Canada
203 M3 **Labrador Sea** Canada/Greenland
231 F5 **Lábrea** Brazil
163 I1 **Labuan** Malaysia
Labudalin China *see* **Ergun**
163 G4 **Labuhan** Indon.
163 B2 **Labuhanbilik** Indon.
162 A5 **Labuhanruku** Indon.
161 H5 **Labuk** *r. Sabah* Malaysia
163 I1 **Labuk, Teluk** *b. Sabah* Malaysia
151 E7 **Labuna** Indon.
145 H8 **Labutta** Myanmar
124 A3 **Labyrinth, Lake** *salt flat* Australia
132 H3 **Labytnangi** Rus. Fed.
185 H4 **Laç** Albania
235 J1 **La Calera** Arg.
235 H2 **La Calera** Chile
182 F2 **La Capelle** France
235 H4 **Lácar, Lago** *l.* Arg.
235 J2 **La Carlota** Arg.
183 O3 **La Carolina** Spain
185 L2 **Lăcăuţi, Vârful** *mt.* Romania
221 I1 **Lac-Baker** Canada
135 F5 **Laccadive Islands** India
205 J4 **Lac du Bonnet** Canada
224 H5 **La Ceiba** Hond.
233 J2 **La Ceiba** Venez.
124 C6 **Lacepede Bay** Australia
120 C3 **Lacepede Islands** Australia
221 E4 **Laceyville** U.S.A.
221 H1 **Lac-Frontière** Canada
186 F2 **Lacha, Ozero** *l.* Rus. Fed.
179 I2 **Lachendorf** Germany
209 F3 **Lachine** U.S.A.
125 F5 **Lachlan** *r.* Australia
230 C2 **La Chorrera** Panama
207 F4 **Lachute** Canada
139 K2 **Laçın** Azer.
183 G5 **La Ciotat** France
224 C3 **La Ciudad** Mex.
220 D3 **Lackawanna** U.S.A.
205 G4 **Lac La Biche** Canada
204 E4 **Lac La Hache** Canada
Lac la Martre Canada *see* **Whatì**
205 H3 **Lac La Ronge Provincial Park** Canada
207 F4 **Lac-Mégantic** Canada
221 G2 **Lacolle** Canada
224 B1 **La Colorada** Mex.
205 G4 **Lacombe** Canada
224 I6 **La Concepción** Panama
225 F4 **La Concordia** Mex.
184 C5 **Laconi** *Sardinia* Italy
221 H3 **Laconia** U.S.A.
209 I1 **La Corne** Canada
208 B4 **La Crescent** U.S.A.
208 B4 **La Crosse** U.S.A.
233 H4 **La Cruz** Col.
224 C3 **La Cruz** *Sinaloa* Mex.
225 E2 **La Cruz** *Tamaulipas* Mex.
224 H5 **La Cruz** Nicaragua
225 D1 **La Cuesta** Mex.
217 E4 **La Cygne** U.S.A.
148 D2 **Ladakh Range** *mts* India
162 A4 **Ladang, Ko** *i.* Thai.
138 E1 **Ladik** Turkey
196 D6 **Ladismith** S. Africa
143 F4 **Lādīz** Iran
148 C4 **Ladnun** India
186 D2 **Ladoga, Lake** Rus. Fed.
233 I3 **La Dorada** Col.
Ladozhskoye Ozero *l.* Rus. Fed. *see* **Ladoga, Lake**
149 H4 **Ladu** *mt.* India
186 E2 **Ladva** Rus. Fed.
186 E2 **Ladva-Vetka** Rus. Fed.
203 J2 **Lady Ann Strait** Canada
174 E4 **Ladybank** U.K.
197 G4 **Ladybrand** S. Africa
209 G2 **Lady Evelyn Lake** Canada
197 G5 **Lady Frere** S. Africa
197 G5 **Lady Grey** S. Africa
204 E5 **Ladysmith** Canada
197 H4 **Ladysmith** S. Africa
208 B3 **Ladysmith** U.S.A.
141 G2 **Ladyzhenka** Kazakh.
Ladzhanurges Georgia *see* **Lajanurpekhi**
119 E2 **Lae** P.N.G.
162 B2 **Laem Ngop** Thai.
171 I3 **Lærdalsøyri** Norway
231 F8 **La Esmeralda** Bol.
233 K4 **La Esmeralda** Venez.
171 J4 **Læsø** *i.* Denmark
224 G5 **La Esperanza** Hond.
235 J1 **La Falda** Arg.
213 F4 **Lafayette** *CO* U.S.A.
208 D5 **Lafayette** *IN* U.S.A.
217 E6 **Lafayette** *LA* U.S.A.
219 C5 **La Fayette** U.S.A.
178 B5 **La Fère** France
178 B5 **La-Ferté-Milon** France
178 B6 **La Ferté-sous-Jouarre** France
142 C5 **Laffān, Ra's** *pt* Qatar
192 C4 **Lafia** Nigeria
182 D3 **La Flèche** France
220 A6 **La Follette** U.S.A.
209 H2 **Laforce** Canada
209 G2 **Laforest** Canada
207 F3 **Laforge** Canada
233 I2 **La Fría** Venez.
142 D5 **Lāft** Iran
184 C6 **La Galite** *i.* Tunisia
187 H6 **Lagan'** Rus. Fed.
132 C4 **Lagan** Sweden
175 L3 **Lagan** *r.* U.K.
231 K6 **Lagarto** Brazil
179 G3 **Lage** Germany
171 J4 **Lågen** *r.* Norway
174 C5 **Lagg** U.K.
174 D3 **Laggan** U.K.
174 D4 **Laggan, Loch** *l.* U.K.
192 C1 **Laghouat** Alg.
149 F2 **Lagkor Co** *salt l.* China
233 I2 **La Gloria** Col.
233 H4 **Lago Agrio** Ecuador
234 D2 **Lagoa Santa** Brazil
139 K1 **Lagodekhi** Georgia
192 A2 **La Gomera** *i.* Canary Is
163 D5 **Lagong** *i.* Indon.
161 I3 **Lagonoy Gulf** Phil.
232 B7 **Lago Posadas** Arg.
235 H4 **Lago Ranco** Chile
192 C4 **Lagos** Nigeria
183 L4 **Lagos** Port.
225 D3 **Lagos de Moreno** Mex.
206 E3 **La Grande** *r.* Canada
212 C2 **La Grande** U.S.A.
206 E3 **La Grande 3, Réservoir** *resr* Canada
207 F3 **La Grande 4, Réservoir** *resr* Canada
Lagrange Australia *see* **La Grange**
118 C3 **La Grange** Australia
219 C5 **La Grange** *GA* U.S.A.
221 I2 **La Grange** *ME* U.S.A.
208 D5 **La Grange** *MI* U.S.A.
208 B5 **La Grange** *MO* U.S.A.
217 D6 **La Grange** *TX* U.S.A.
209 E5 **Lagrange** U.S.A.
233 L3 **La Gran Sabana** *plat.* Venez.
233 G3 **Laguna** Brazil
215 D5 **Laguna Beach** U.S.A.
235 H3 **Laguna de Laja, Parque Nacional** *nat. park* Chile
224 I5 **Laguna de Perlas** Nicaragua
215 D5 **Laguna Mountains** U.S.A.
230 C5 **Lagunas** Peru
232 A7 **Laguna San Rafael, Parque Nacional** *nat. park* Chile
225 E5 **Lagunas de Chacahua, Parque Nacional** *nat. park* Mex.
233 J2 **Lagunillas** Venez.
156 B2 **Laha** China
La Habana Cuba *see* **Havana**
163 I1 **Lahad Datu** *Sabah* Malaysia
161 H5 **Lahad Datu, Teluk** *b. Sabah* Malaysia
214 □[2] **Lahaina** U.S.A.
163 B3 **Lahat** Indon.
162 A5 **Lahewa** Indon.
146 B7 **Laḥij** Yemen
142 C2 **Lāhījān** Iran
214 □[1] **Lahilahi Point** U.S.A.
179 F4 **Lahn** *r.* Germany
179 F4 **Lahnstein** Germany
171 K4 **Laholm** Sweden
214 C2 **Lahontan Reservoir** U.S.A.
148 C3 **Lahore** Pak.
233 L3 **La Horqueta** Venez.
148 B3 **Lahri** Pak.
171 N3 **Lahti** Fin.
224 C4 **La Huerta** Mex.
193 D4 **Laï** Chad
154 F3 **Lai'an** China
155 C6 **Laibin** China
125 J1 **Laidley** Australia
214 □[1] **Lā'ie** U.S.A.
214 □[1] **Lā'ie Point** U.S.A.
155 C4 **Laifeng** China
182 E2 **L'Aigle** France
224 G5 **La Iguala** Hond.
171 M3 **Laihia** Fin.
149 H4 **Laimakuri** India
136 A3 **Laimos, Akrotirio** *pt* Greece
196 D6 **Laingsburg** S. Africa
170 M2 **Lainioälven** *r.* Sweden
174 D2 **Lairg** U.K.
161 J5 **Lais** Phil.
169 P4 **Laishevo** Rus. Fed.
171 M3 **Laitila** Fin.
184 D1 **Laives** Italy
154 E2 **Laiwu** China
154 F2 **Laiyang** China
154 E2 **Laiyuan** China
154 F2 **Laizhou** China
154 F2 **Laizhou Wan** *b.* China
235 H3 **Laja** *r.* Chile
235 H3 **Laja, Laguna de** *l.* Chile
118 D3 **Lajamanu** Australia
137 F2 **Lajanurpekhi** Georgia
231 K5 **Lajes** *Rio Grande do Norte* Brazil
232 F3 **Lajes** *Santa Catarina* Brazil
224 C2 **La Joya** Mex.
213 G4 **La Junta** U.S.A.
212 E2 **Lake** U.S.A.
216 D3 **Lake Andes** U.S.A.
138 D6 **Lake Bardawil Reserve** *nature res.* Egypt
125 E6 **Lake Bolac** Australia
125 G4 **Lake Cargelligo** Australia
125 J3 **Lake Cathie** Australia
217 E6 **Lake Charles** U.S.A.
212 B1 **Lake Chelan National Recreation Area** *park* U.S.A.
219 D6 **Lake City** *FL* U.S.A.
209 E3 **Lake City** *MI* U.S.A.
208 A3 **Lake City** *MN* U.S.A.
219 E5 **Lake City** *SC* U.S.A.
172 D3 **Lake District National Park** U.K.
124 B2 **Lake Eyre National Park** Australia
122 D2 **Lakefield** Australia
209 H3 **Lakefield** Canada
122 D2 **Lakefield National Park** Australia
123 B7 **Lake Gairdner National Park** Australia
208 C4 **Lake Geneva** U.S.A.
121 B7 **Lake Grace** Australia
Lake Harbour Canada *see* **Kimmirut**
215 E4 **Lake Havasu City** U.S.A.
214 C4 **Lake Isabella** U.S.A.
217 E6 **Lake Jackson** U.S.A.
121 B7 **Lake King** Australia
219 D6 **Lakeland** U.S.A.
208 C2 **Lake Linden** U.S.A.
204 F4 **Lake Louise** Canada
215 E4 **Lake Mead National Recreation Area** *park* U.S.A.
217 C5 **Lake Meredith National Recreation Area** *park* U.S.A.
221 I2 **Lake Moxie** U.S.A.
123 B4 **Lake Nash** Australia
212 B2 **Lake Oswego** U.S.A.
126 B5 **Lake Paringa** N.Z.
221 G2 **Lake Placid** U.S.A.
214 A2 **Lakeport** U.S.A.
217 F5 **Lake Providence** U.S.A.
206 D3 **Lake River** Canada
209 H3 **Lake St Peter** Canada
125 H6 **Lakes Entrance** Australia
209 E2 **Lake Superior Provincial Park** Canada
125 I5 **Lake Tabourie** Australia
126 C6 **Lake Tekapo** N.Z.
123 B6 **Lake Torrens National Park** Australia
213 B3 **Lakeview** U.S.A.
217 F5 **Lake Village** U.S.A.
213 F4 **Lakewood** *CO* U.S.A.
221 F4 **Lakewood** *NJ* U.S.A.
220 C4 **Lakewood** *OH* U.S.A.
219 D7 **Lake Worth** U.S.A.
186 D2 **Lakhdenpokh'ya** Rus. Fed.
149 E4 **Lakhimpur** India
149 F4 **Lakhisarai** India
148 D5 **Lakhnadon** India
148 B5 **Lakhpat** India
145 D5 **Lakki Marwat** Pak.
185 J6 **Lakonikos Kolpos** *b.* Greece
192 B4 **Lakota** Côte d'Ivoire
170 N1 **Laksefjorden** *sea chan.* Norway
170 N1 **Lakselv** Norway
135 F5 **Lakshadweep** *union terr.* India
149 G5 **Laksham** Bangl.
147 H2 **Lakshettipet** India
149 G5 **Lakshmikantapur** India
161 I5 **Lala** Phil.
235 J2 **La Laguna** Arg.
235 H3 **La Laja** Chile
194 B3 **Lalara** Gabon
183 P2 **L'Alcora** Spain
179 K1 **Lalendorf** Germany
142 C3 **Lālī** Iran
225 G5 **La Libertad** El Salvador
225 G4 **La Libertad** Guat.
235 H2 **La Ligua** Chile
160 D1 **Lalin** China
183 L1 **Lalín** Spain
183 N4 **La Línea de la Concepción** Spain
160 C1 **Lalin He** *r.* China
148 D4 **Lalitpur** India
161 I2 **La-Lo** Phil.
205 H3 **La Loche** Canada
205 H3 **La Loche, Lac** *l.* Canada
178 C4 **La Louvière** Belgium
186 H2 **Lal'sk** Rus. Fed.
149 H5 **Lama** Bangl.
233 I4 **La Macarena, Parque Nacional** *nat. park* Col.
184 C4 **La Maddalena** *Sardinia* Italy
156 B3 **Lamadian** China
Lamadianzi China *see* **Lamadian**
161 H5 **Lamag** *Sabah* Malaysia
162 A2 **Lamaing** Myanmar
La Manche *str.* France/U.K. *see* **English Channel**
217 C4 **Lamar** *CO* U.S.A.
217 E4 **Lamar** *MO* U.S.A.
142 D5 **Lamard** Iran
184 C5 **La Marmora, Punta** *mt. Sardinia* Italy
235 J3 **Lamarque** Arg.
217 E6 **La Marque** U.S.A.
204 F2 **La Martre, Lac** *l.* Canada
195 B4 **Lambaréné** Gabon
230 C5 **Lambayeque** Peru
175 M4 **Lambay Island** Ireland
127 K5 **Lambert Glacier** Antarctica
196 C6 **Lambert's Bay** S. Africa
148 C3 **Lambi** India
173 F6 **Lambourn Downs** *hills* U.K.
183 M2 **Lamego** Port.
207 H4 **Lamèque, Île** *i.* Canada
230 C6 **La Merced** Peru
124 D5 **Lameroo** Australia
215 D5 **La Mesa** U.S.A.
217 C5 **Lamesa** U.S.A.
185 J5 **Lamia** Greece
125 J2 **Lamington National Park** Australia
224 B1 **La Misa** Mex.
215 D5 **La Misión** Mex.
161 I5 **Lamitan** Phil.
155 □ **Lamma Island** *Hong Kong* China
126 B6 **Lammerlaw Range** *mts* N.Z.
175 F5 **Lammermuir Hills** U.K.
171 K4 **Lammhult** Sweden
171 N3 **Lammi** Fin.
208 C5 **La Moille** U.S.A.
221 G2 **Lamoille** *r.* U.S.A.
208 B5 **La Moine** *r.* U.S.A.
161 I3 **Lamon Bay** Phil.
216 E3 **Lamoni** U.S.A.
213 F3 **Lamont** U.S.A.
225 D2 **La Mora** Mex.
224 C1 **La Morita** Mex.
209 H1 **La Motte** Canada
162 A1 **Lampang** Thai.
162 B1 **Lam Pao, Ang Kep Nam** Thai.
217 D6 **Lampasas** U.S.A.
225 D2 **Lampazos** Mex.
184 E7 **Lampedusa, Isola di** *i. Sicily* Italy
173 C5 **Lampeter** U.K.
162 A1 **Lamphun** Thai.
187 F4 **Lamskoye** Rus. Fed.
155 □ **Lam Tin** *Hong Kong* China
195 E4 **Lamu** Kenya
149 H6 **Lamu** Myanmar
214 □[2] **Lāna'i** *i.* U.S.A.
Lanai *i.* U.S.A. *see* **Lāna'i**
Lanai City U.S.A. *see* **Lāna'i City**
214 □[2] **Lāna'i City** U.S.A.
161 J5 **Lanao, Lake** Phil.
209 I3 **Lanark** Canada
174 E5 **Lanark** U.K.
208 C4 **Lanark** U.S.A.
161 H5 **Lanas** *Sabah* Malaysia
162 A3 **Lanbi Kyun** *i.* Myanmar
150 B3 **Lancang Jiang** *r.* China *conv.* **Mekong**
221 F2 **Lancaster** Canada
172 E3 **Lancaster** U.K.
214 C4 **Lancaster** *CA* U.S.A.
208 A5 **Lancaster** *MO* U.S.A.
221 H2 **Lancaster** *NH* U.S.A.
220 B5 **Lancaster** *OH* U.S.A.
221 E4 **Lancaster** *PA* U.S.A.
208 B4 **Lancaster** *WI* U.S.A.
173 E4 **Lancaster Canal** U.K.
203 J2 **Lancaster Sound** *str.* Canada
184 F3 **Lanciano** Italy
235 H3 **Lanco** Chile
154 F2 **Lancun** China
176 F6 **Landau an der Isar** Germany
179 G5 **Landau in der Pfalz** Germany
176 E7 **Landeck** Austria
121 E4 **Lander** *watercourse* Australia
213 E3 **Lander** U.S.A.
179 H2 **Landesbergen** Germany
205 H4 **Landis** Canada
121 B5 **Landor** Australia
176 E6 **Landsberg am Lech** Germany
173 B7 **Land's End** *pt* U.K.
176 F6 **Landshut** Germany
171 K5 **Landskrona** Sweden
179 F5 **Landstuhl** Germany
179 G1 **Land Wursten** *reg.* Germany
175 K4 **Lanesborough** Ireland
La Nga *r.* Vietnam *see* **La Nga, Sông**
162 C3 **La Nga, Sông** *r.* Vietnam
149 E3 **La'nga Co** *l.* China
154 C3 **Langao** China
141 H5 **Langar** Afgh.
143 F3 **Langar** Iran
141 F4 **Langar** Uzbek.
174 B2 **Langavat, Loch** *l.* U.K.
197 E4 **Langberg** *mts* S. Africa
216 D1 **Langdon** U.S.A.
196 C6 **Langeberg** *mts* S. Africa
171 J5 **Langeland** *i.* Denmark
171 N3 **Längelmäki** Fin.
171 N3 **Längelmävesi** *l.* Fin.
179 I3 **Langelsheim** Germany
179 G1 **Langen** Germany
179 H2 **Langenhagen** Germany
179 F4 **Langenhahn** Germany
179 F5 **Langenlonsheim** Germany
176 C7 **Langenthal** Switz.
179 J2 **Langenweddingen** Germany
179 F1 **Langeoog** Germany
179 F1 **Langeoog** *i.* Germany
171 J4 **Langesund** Norway
153 K4 **Langfang** China
162 B5 **Langgapayung** Indon.
179 G4 **Langgöns** Germany
205 H4 **Langham** Canada
170 B2 **Langjökull** *ice cap* Iceland
163 E2 **Langka** Indon.
163 E1 **Langkawi** *i.* Malaysia
162 A3 **Lang Kha Toek, Khao** *mt.* Thai.
196 D4 **Langklip** S. Africa
161 H5 **Langkon** *Sabah* Malaysia
209 J1 **Langlade** Canada
208 C3 **Langlade** U.S.A.
123 D5 **Langlo Crossing** Australia
182 F4 **Langogne** France
170 K1 **Langøya** *i.* Norway
149 F3 **Langphu** *mt.* China
173 E6 **Langport** U.K.
148 D3 **Langqên Zangbo** *r.* China
155 F5 **Langqi** China
182 G3 **Langres** France
148 D1 **Langru** China
163 E2 **Langsa** Indon.
162 A4 **Langsa, Teluk** *b.* Indon.
171 L3 **Långsele** Sweden
154 C1 **Langshan** China
154 C1 **Lang Shan** *mts* China
155 C6 **Lang Sơn** Vietnam
172 G3 **Langtoft** U.K.
217 C6 **Langtry** U.S.A.
183 F5 **Languedoc** *reg.* France
170 M2 **Långvattnet** Sweden
179 H2 **Langwedel** Germany
155 F4 **Langxi** China
155 C4 **Langzhong** China
209 H2 **Laniel** Canada
205 H4 **Lanigan** Canada
214 □[1] **Lanikai** U.S.A.
235 H3 **Lanín, Parque Nacional** *nat. park* Arg.
235 H3 **Lanín, Volcán** *vol.* Arg.
154 E3 **Lankao** China
139 L2 **Länkäran** Azer.
182 C2 **Lannion** France
224 C3 **La Noria** Mex.
170 M2 **Lansån** Sweden

118 C4 Leonora Australia
234 D3 Leopoldina Brazil
205 H4 Leoville Canada
197 G1 Lephalala r. S. Africa
197 G1 Lephalale S. Africa
195 C6 Lephepe Botswana
197 F5 Lephoi S. Africa
155 E4 Leping China
182 G4 Le Pont-de-Claix France
171 N3 Leppävirta Fin.
141 J3 Lepsinsk Kazakh.
141 I3 Lepsy Kazakh.
141 I3 Lepsy r. Kazakh.
182 F4 Le Puy-en-Velay France
178 B4 Le Quesnoy France
197 G1 Lerala Botswana
197 G4 Leratswana S. Africa
193 D4 Léré Chad
233 J5 Lérida Col.
Lérida Spain see Lleida
139 L2 Lerik Azer.
183 O1 Lerma Spain
187 G6 Lermontov Rus. Fed.
158 D1 Lermontovka Rus. Fed.
185 L6 Leros i. Greece
208 C5 Le Roy U.S.A.
206 E2 Le Roy, Lac l. Canada
171 K4 Lerum Sweden
174 □ Lerwick U.K.
185 K5 Lesbos i. Greece
223 J5 Les Cayes Haiti
207 G4 Les Escoumins Canada
221 I1 Les Étroits Canada
155 B4 Leshan China
169 P3 Leshukonskoye Rus. Fed.
185 I3 Leskovac Serbia
174 E4 Leslie U.K.
182 B2 Lesneven France
186 J3 Lesnoy Rus. Fed.
156 F2 Lesogorsk Rus. Fed.
158 D1 Lesopil'noye Rus. Fed.
133 K4 Lesosibirsk Rus. Fed.
197 H4 Lesotho country Africa
158 C2 Lesozavodsk Rus. Fed.
182 D3 Les Sables-d'Olonne France
178 D4 Lesse r. Belgium
223 K6 Lesser Antilles is Caribbean Sea
139 I1 Lesser Caucasus mts Asia
152 C5 Lesser Himalaya mts India/Nepal
205 G3 Lesser Slave Lake Canada
205 G3 Lesser Slave Lake Provincial Park Canada
151 D7 Lesser Sunda Islands Indon.
178 B4 Lessines Belgium
171 N3 Lestijärvi Fin.
171 N3 Lestijärvi l. Fin.
Lesvos i. Greece see Lesbos
177 H5 Leszno Poland
197 I1 Letaba S. Africa
173 G6 Letchworth Garden City U.K.
182 G3 Le Télégraphe h. France
148 D4 Leteri India
149 H5 Letha Range mts Myanmar
205 G5 Lethbridge Canada
231 G3 Lethem Guyana
151 E7 Leti, Kepulauan is Indon.
230 E4 Leticia Col.
154 F2 Leting China
197 F2 Letlhakeng Botswana
169 M3 Letnerechenskiy Rus. Fed.
173 I7 Le Touquet-Paris-Plage France
152 G8 Letpadan Myanmar
182 E1 Le Tréport France
197 I1 Letsitele S. Africa
162 A3 Letsok-aw Kyun i. Myanmar
197 F3 Letsopa S. Africa
175 K3 Letterkenny Ireland
163 G2 Letung Indon.
179 J2 Letzlingen Germany
175 F4 Leuchars U.K.
186 G1 Leunovo Rus. Fed.
215 G4 Leupp Corner U.S.A.
123 E4 Leura Australia
178 D2 Leusden Neth.
163 E2 Leuser, Gunung mt. Indon.
179 I5 Leutershausen Germany
178 C4 Leuven Belgium
215 G2 Levan U.S.A.
171 J3 Levanger Norway
184 C2 Levanto Italy
184 E5 Levanzo, Isola di i. Sicily Italy
187 H7 Levashi Rus. Fed.
217 C5 Levelland U.S.A.
173 G4 Leven England U.K.
175 F4 Leven Scotland U.K.
174 C4 Leven, Loch inlet U.K.
174 E4 Leven, Loch l. U.K.
118 C3 Lévêque, Cape Australia
209 E3 Levering U.S.A.
179 E3 Leverkusen Germany
177 I6 Levice Slovakia
126 E4 Levin N.Z.
207 F4 Lévis Canada
185 L6 Levitha i. Greece
221 G4 Levittown NY U.S.A.
221 F4 Levittown PA U.S.A.
185 K3 Levski Bulg.
173 H7 Lewes U.K.
221 F5 Lewes U.S.A.
174 B2 Lewis, Isle of i. U.K.
121 F4 Lewis, Lake salt flat Australia
221 E4 Lewisburg PA U.S.A.
220 C6 Lewisburg WV U.S.A.
126 D5 Lewis Pass N.Z.
121 E4 Lewis Range hills Australia
212 D1 Lewis Range mts U.S.A.
219 C5 Lewis Smith, Lake U.S.A.
215 G6 Lewis Springs U.S.A.
212 C2 Lewiston ID U.S.A.
221 H2 Lewiston ME U.S.A.
208 B4 Lewiston MN U.S.A.
208 B5 Lewistown IL U.S.A.
212 E2 Lewistown MT U.S.A.
221 E4 Lewistown PA U.S.A.
217 E5 Lewisville U.S.A.
217 D5 Lewisville, Lake U.S.A.
208 C5 Lexington IL U.S.A.
219 C4 Lexington KY U.S.A.
217 E4 Lexington MO U.S.A.
219 D5 Lexington NC U.S.A.
216 D3 Lexington NE U.S.A.
219 B5 Lexington TN U.S.A.
220 D6 Lexington VA U.S.A.
221 E5 Lexington Park U.S.A.
197 I1 Leydsdorp S. Africa
155 C5 Leye China
139 K3 Leyla Dāgh mt. Iran
161 J4 Leyte i. Phil.
161 J4 Leyte Gulf Phil.
185 H4 Lezhë Albania
155 B4 Lezhi China
187 E5 L'gov Rus. Fed.
149 F3 Lhagoi Kangri mt. China
Lhari China see Si'erdingka
149 G2 Lharigarbo China
149 G3 Lhasa China
149 G3 Lhasa He r. China
149 F3 Lhazê China
149 F3 Lhazhong China
163 E1 Lhokseumawe Indon.
162 A4 Lhoksukon Indon.
149 H3 Lhorong China
145 H6 Lhozhag China
Lhünzê China see Xingba
Lhünzhub China see Gaindainqoinkor
162 A1 Li, Mae r. Thai.
185 J5 Liakoura mt. Greece
155 E5 Liancheng China
178 A5 Liancourt France
159 B6 Liancourt Rocks i. Japan
161 J4 Lianga Phil.
161 J4 Lianga Bay Phil.
154 D1 Liangcheng China
154 C3 Liangdang China
154 B3 Lianghekou China
155 C4 Liangping China
155 B5 Liangwang Shan mts China
154 C2 Liangzhen China
155 E4 Liangzi Hu l. China
155 D5 Lianhua China
155 E6 Lianhua Shan mts China
155 F5 Lianjiang Fujian China
155 D6 Lianjiang Guangdong China
155 D5 Liannan China
155 E5 Lianping China
155 D5 Lianshan Guangdong China
160 A3 Lianshan Liaoning China
154 F3 Lianshui China
156 A1 Lianyin China
155 D5 Lianyuan China
154 F3 Lianyungang Jiangsu China
155 D5 Lianzhou China
161 F1 Lianzhushan China
154 E2 Liaocheng China
160 B3 Liaodong Bandao pen. China
160 A3 Liaodong Wan b. China
160 B2 Liao He r. China
160 B3 Liaohe Kou r. mouth China
160 B3 Liaoning prov. China
160 B3 Liaoyang China
160 C2 Liaoyuan China
160 B3 Liaozhong China
185 H5 Liapades Greece
148 B2 Liaqatabad Pak.
204 E2 Liard r. Canada
204 D3 Liard River Canada
143 G5 Liari Pak.
174 C3 Liathach mt. U.K.
139 F4 Liban, Jebel mts Lebanon
233 I3 Libano Col.
212 D1 Libby U.S.A.
194 B3 Libenge Dem. Rep. Congo
217 C4 Liberal U.S.A.
176 G5 Liberec Czech Rep.
192 B4 Liberia country Africa
224 H6 Liberia Costa Rica
233 J2 Libertad Barinas Venez.
233 J2 Libertad Cojedes Venez.
208 B6 Liberty IL U.S.A.
221 I2 Liberty ME U.S.A.
217 E4 Liberty MO U.S.A.
221 F4 Liberty NY U.S.A.
217 E6 Liberty TX U.S.A.
178 D5 Libin Belgium
161 I3 Libmanan Phil.
155 C5 Libo China
197 H5 Libode S. Africa
162 A4 Libong, Ko i. Thai.
182 D4 Libourne France
121 D4 Libral Well Australia
194 A3 Libreville Gabon
161 J5 Libuganon r. Phil.
193 D2 Libya country Africa
193 E2 Libyan Desert Egypt/Libya
193 E1 Libyan Plateau Egypt
235 H2 Licantén Chile
184 E6 Licata Sicily Italy
139 H2 Lice Turkey
179 G4 Lich Germany
173 F5 Lichfield U.K.
195 D5 Lichinga Moz.
179 J4 Lichte Germany
179 G3 Lichtenau Germany
197 G3 Lichtenburg S. Africa
179 J4 Lichtenfels Germany
179 E3 Lichtenvoorde Neth.
155 C4 Lichuan Hubei China
155 E5 Lichuan Jiangxi China
220 B5 Licking r. U.S.A.
187 C4 Lida Belarus
215 D3 Lida U.S.A.
196 C2 Lidfontein Namibia
171 K4 Lidköping Sweden
170 K2 Lidsjöberg Sweden
179 H2 Liebenau Germany
179 I2 Liebenburg Germany
179 L2 Liebenwalde Germany
118 D4 Liebig, Mount Australia
182 I3 Liechtenstein country Europe
178 D4 Liège Belgium
171 O3 Lieksa Fin.
177 L2 Lielupe r. Latvia
171 N4 Lielvārde Latvia
171 L3 Lien Sweden
194 C3 Lienart Dem. Rep. Congo
163 D3 Liên Nghia Vietnam
176 F7 Lienz Austria
171 M4 Liepāja Latvia
178 C3 Lier Belgium
178 D3 Lieshout Neth.
178 A4 Liévin France
209 J2 Lièvre, Rivière du r. Canada
176 G7 Liezen Austria
175 L4 Liffey r. Ireland
175 K3 Lifford Ireland
235 I4 Lifi Mahuida mt. Arg.
119 G4 Lifou i. New Caledonia
161 I3 Ligao Phil.
171 N4 Līgatne Latvia
125 G2 Lightning Ridge Australia
195 D5 Ligonha r. Moz.
209 E5 Ligonier U.S.A.
224 B2 Ligui Mex.
183 I5 Ligurian Sea France/Italy
119 F2 Lihir Group is P.N.G.
122 E3 Lihou Reef and Cays Australia
Lihue U.S.A. see Līhu'e
214 □[2] Līhu'e U.S.A.
153 H6 Lijiang China
155 D5 Li Jiang r. China
154 F2 Lijin China
162 B1 Lik, Nam r. Laos
195 C5 Likasi Dem. Rep. Congo
204 E4 Likely Canada
186 E3 Likhoslavl' Rus. Fed.
163 G2 Liku Indon.
186 G3 Likurga Rus. Fed.
184 C3 L'Île-Rousse Corsica France
179 G1 Lilienthal Germany
155 D5 Liling China
148 C2 Lilla Pak.
171 K4 Lilla Edet Sweden
178 C3 Lille Belgium
182 F1 Lille France
Lille Bælt sea chan. Denmark see Little Belt
171 J3 Lillehammer Norway
178 A4 Lillers France
171 J4 Lillesand Norway
171 J4 Lillestrøm Norway
209 E4 Lilley U.S.A.
171 K3 Lillholmsjö Sweden
121 D5 Lillian, Point h. Australia
204 E4 Lillooet Canada
204 E4 Lillooet r. Canada
149 H4 Lilong India
195 D5 Lilongwe Malawi
161 I4 Liloy Phil.
124 C4 Lilydale S.A. Australia
125 G8 Lilydale Tas. Australia
230 C6 Lima Peru (City Plan 106)
212 D2 Lima MT U.S.A.
220 A4 Lima OH U.S.A.
143 E5 Līmah Oman
187 H6 Liman Rus. Fed.
235 H1 Limarí r. Chile
149 E2 Lima Ringma Tso salt l. China
138 D4 Limassol Cyprus
175 L2 Limavady U.K.
235 I3 Limay r. Arg.
235 I3 Limay Mahuida Arg.
171 N4 Limbaži Latvia
192 C4 Limbe Cameroon
163 I3 Limbungan Indon.
120 E3 Limbunya Australia
179 G4 Limburg an der Lahn Germany
162 □ Lim Chu Kang Sing.
162 □ Lim Chu Kang h. Sing.
197 E4 Lime Acres S. Africa
234 C3 Limeira Brazil
175 J5 Limerick Ireland
208 A4 Lime Springs U.S.A.
221 J1 Limestone U.S.A.
170 K2 Limingen Norway
170 K2 Limingen l. Norway
221 H3 Limington U.S.A.
170 N2 Liminka Fin.
122 B2 Limmen Bight b. Australia
185 K5 Limnos i. Greece
221 F2 Limoges Canada
182 E4 Limoges France
Limón Costa Rica see Puerto Limón
224 H5 Limón Hond.
213 G4 Limon U.S.A.
138 E3 Limonlu Turkey
182 E4 Limousin reg. France
182 F5 Limoux France
197 J1 Limpopo r. Africa
197 H1 Limpopo prov. S. Africa
197 I1 Limpopo National Park S. Africa
142 A4 Līnah well Saudi Arabia
170 O1 Linakhamari Rus. Fed.
155 F4 Lin'an China
161 H4 Linapacan i. Phil.
161 H4 Linapacan Strait Phil.
235 H2 Linares Chile
225 E2 Linares Mex.
183 O3 Linares Spain
151 C4 Lincang China
154 E2 Lincheng China
Linchuan China see Fuzhou
235 K2 Lincoln Arg.
173 G4 Lincoln U.K.
214 B2 Lincoln CA U.S.A.
208 C5 Lincoln IL U.S.A.
221 I2 Lincoln ME U.S.A.
209 F3 Lincoln MI U.S.A.
216 D3 Lincoln NE U.S.A.
221 H2 Lincoln NH U.S.A.
212 A2 Lincoln City U.S.A.
209 F4 Lincoln Park U.S.A.
173 G4 Lincolnshire Wolds hills U.K.
221 I2 Lincolnville U.S.A.
234 E1 Linda, Serra hills Brazil
123 B4 Linda Creek watercourse Australia
179 K2 Lindau Germany
176 D7 Lindau (Bodensee) Germany
123 E4 Lindeman Group is Australia
179 G4 Linden Germany
231 G2 Linden Guyana
219 C5 Linden AL U.S.A.
219 C5 Linden TN U.S.A.
208 A2 Linden Grove U.S.A.
Lindenow Fjord inlet Greenland see Kangerlussuatsiaq
179 F2 Lindern (Oldenburg) Germany
171 I4 Lindesnes c. Norway
Líndhos Greece see Lindos
194 C3 Lindi r. Dem. Rep. Congo
195 D4 Lindi Tanz.
156 B3 Lindian China
Lindisfarne i. U.K. see Holy Island
197 G3 Lindley S. Africa
154 F1 Lindong China
181 I4 Lindos Greece
221 J1 Lindsay N.B. Canada
209 H3 Lindsay Ont. Canada
214 C3 Lindsay U.S.A.
117 I3 Line Islands S. Pacific Ocean
154 D2 Linfen China
147 G3 Linganamakki Reservoir India
161 I2 Lingayen Phil.
161 I2 Lingayen Gulf Phil.
154 D3 Lingbao China
154 E3 Lingbi China
155 D5 Lingchuan Guangxi China
154 D3 Lingchuan Shanxi China
197 G6 Lingelethu S. Africa
197 F6 Lingelihle S. Africa
179 F2 Lingen (Ems) Germany
163 B3 Lingga, Kepulauan is Indon.
160 A3 Linghai China
161 J5 Lingig Phil.
161 H5 Lingkabau Sabah Malaysia
213 F3 Lingle U.S.A.
194 C3 Lingomo Dem. Rep. Congo
154 E2 Lingqiu China
155 C6 Lingshan China
155 C7 Lingshui China
155 C7 Lingshui Wan b. China
147 H2 Lingsugur India
154 C3 Lingtai China
192 A3 Linguère Senegal
155 D5 Lingui China
154 C2 Lingwu China
154 F1 Lingyuan China
155 C5 Lingyun China
148 D2 Lingzi Tang reg. Aksai Chin
155 F4 Linhai China
234 E2 Linhares Brazil
Linh Cam Vietnam see Duc Tho
154 C1 Linhe China
221 H1 Linière Canada
139 I3 Līnik, Chiyā-ē mt. Iraq
160 D3 Linjiang China
171 K4 Linköping Sweden
161 F1 Linkou China
155 D4 Linli China
174 E5 Linlithgow U.K.
154 D2 Linlü Shan mt. China
214 I1 Linn, Mount U.S.A.
174 C4 Linnhe, Loch inlet U.K.
179 E4 Linnich Germany
154 E2 Linqing China
154 F2 Linqu China
154 E3 Linquan China
234 C3 Lins Brazil
154 C3 Linshu China
155 C4 Linshui China
154 B3 Lintan China
154 B3 Lintao China
216 C2 Linton U.S.A.
154 C3 Lintong China
154 F1 Linxi China
154 B3 Linxia China
155 D4 Linxian China
155 D4 Linxiang China
154 E2 Linyi Shandong China
154 F3 Linyi Shandong China
154 D3 Linyi Shanxi China
154 E3 Linying China
176 G6 Linz Austria
154 A2 Linze China
183 F5 Lion, Golfe du g. France
209 G3 Lion's Head Canada
221 F4 Lionville U.S.A.
194 B3 Liouesso Congo
161 I3 Lipa Phil.
184 F5 Lipari Isole Lipari Italy
184 F5 Lipari, Isola i. Isole Lipari Italy
184 F5 Lipari, Isole is Italy
187 F4 Lipetsk Rus. Fed.
187 F4 Lipetskaya Oblast' admin. div. Rus. Fed.
186 F2 Lipin Bor Rus. Fed.
155 C5 Liping China
185 I1 Lipova Romania
158 B2 Lipovtsy Rus. Fed.
179 E3 Lippe r. Germany
179 G3 Lippstadt Germany
149 E3 Lipti Lekh pass Nepal
125 F7 Liptrap, Cape Australia
155 D5 Lipu China
194 D3 Lira Uganda
195 B4 Liranga Congo
161 J6 Lirung Indon.
140 E1 Lisakovsk Kazakh.
194 C3 Lisala Dem. Rep. Congo
175 K3 Lisbellaw U.K.
Lisboa Port. see Lisbon
183 L3 Lisbon Port.
208 C5 Lisbon IL U.S.A.
221 H2 Lisbon ME U.S.A.
216 D2 Lisbon ND U.S.A.
221 H2 Lisbon NH U.S.A.
220 C4 Lisbon OH U.S.A.
175 L3 Lisburn U.K.
175 I5 Liscannor Bay Ireland
175 I4 Lisdoonvarna Ireland
155 F5 Lishan Taiwan
154 D2 Lishi China
160 C2 Lishu China
155 F4 Lishui Jiangsu China
155 F4 Lishui Zhejiang China
155 D4 Li Shui r. China
117 H2 Lisianski Island U.S.A.
182 E2 Lisieux France
173 C7 Liskeard U.K.
187 F5 Liski Rus. Fed.
178 A5 L'Isle-Adam France
183 G5 L'Isle-sur-la-Sorgue France
125 J2 Lismore Australia
175 K5 Lismore Ireland
174 C4 Lismore i. U.K.
175 K3 Lisnarrick U.K.
175 K3 Lisnaskea U.K.
209 G4 Listowel Canada
175 I5 Listowel Ireland
171 K3 Lit Sweden
155 C6 Litang Guangxi China
150 C3 Litang Sichuan China
231 H3 Litani r. Fr. Guiana/Suriname
Līṭānī r. Lebanon see Līṭānī, Nahr el
138 E5 Līṭānī, Nahr el r. Lebanon
214 B1 Litchfield CA U.S.A.
219 B4 Litchfield IL U.S.A.
211 H2 Litchfield MN U.S.A.
182 D4 Lit-et-Mixe France
125 I4 Lithgow Australia
136 B4 Lithino, Akrotirio pt Greece
171 M5 Lithuania country Europe
221 E4 Lititz U.S.A.
176 G5 Litoměřice Czech Rep.
156 D2 Litovko Rus. Fed.
219 E7 Little Abaco i. Bahamas
145 H9 Little Andaman i. India
219 E7 Little Bahama Bank sea feature Bahamas
126 E2 Little Barrier i. N.Z.
208 D3 Little Bay de Noc U.S.A.
171 J5 Little Belt sea chan. Denmark
212 E2 Little Belt Mountains U.S.A.
223 H5 Little Cayman i. Cayman Is
215 H4 Little Colorado r. U.S.A.
215 F3 Little Creek Peak U.S.A.
209 G3 Little Current Canada
206 C3 Little Current r. Canada
173 D7 Little Dart r. U.K.
124 D6 Little Desert National Park Australia
221 F5 Little Egg Harbor inlet U.S.A.
216 E2 Little Falls MN U.S.A.
221 F3 Little Falls NY U.S.A.
215 F3 Littlefield AZ U.S.A.
217 C5 Littlefield TX U.S.A.
216 E1 Little Fork U.S.A.
208 A1 Little Fork r. U.S.A.
149 F4 Little Gandak r. India
205 J4 Little Grand Rapids Canada
173 G7 Littlehampton U.K.
220 C5 Little Kanawha r. U.S.A.
196 C3 Little Karas Berg plat. Namibia
196 D6 Little Karoo plat. S. Africa
208 D2 Little Lake U.S.A.
220 A5 Little Miami r. U.S.A.
174 B3 Little Minch sea chan. U.K.
216 C2 Little Missouri r. U.S.A.
145 H10 Little Nicobar i. India
173 H5 Little Ouse r. U.K.
141 H5 Little Pamir mts Afgh.
208 D1 Little Pic r. Canada
148 B5 Little Rann marsh India
217 E5 Little Rock U.S.A.

Mangai

195 B4 **Mangai** Dem. Rep. Congo
117 I5 **Mangaia** *i.* Cook Is
126 E3 **Mangakino** N.Z.
147 I2 **Mangalagiri** India
149 H4 **Mangaldai** India
185 M3 **Mangalia** Romania
147 G3 **Mangalore** India
147 G2 **Mangalvedha** India
149 G4 **Mangan** India
147 I2 **Mangapet** India
161 J6 **Mangarang** Indon.
197 G4 **Mangaung** S. Africa
126 E3 **Mangaweka** N.Z.
149 G4 **Mangde Chhu** *r.* Bhutan
175 I6 **Mangerton Mountain** *h.* Ireland
163 G3 **Manggar** Indon.
Mangin Range *mts* Myanmar *see* **Mingin Range**
140 C3 **Mangistauskaya Oblast'** *admin. div.* Kazakh.
140 E4 **Mang'it** Uzbek.
Mangit Uzbek. *see* **Mang'it**
150 B3 **Mangnai** China
144 H4 **Mangnai Zhen** China
195 D5 **Mangochi** Malawi
151 E7 **Mangole** *i.* Indon.
173 E6 **Mangotsfield** U.K.
148 B5 **Mangrol** India
Mangshi China *see* **Luxi**
183 M2 **Mangualde** Port.
143 G4 **Manguchar** Pak.
235 M2 **Mangueira, Lago** *l.* Brazil
235 B4 **Mangueirinha** Brazil
193 D2 **Manguéni, Plateau du** Niger
150 E1 **Mangui** China
161 J5 **Mangupung** *i.* Indon.
140 B3 **Mangyshlak, Poluostrov** *pen.* Kazakh.
140 B3 **Mangyshlakskiy Zaliv** *b.* Kazakh.
140 B4 **Mangystau** Kazakh.
217 D4 **Manhattan** *KS* U.S.A.
215 D2 **Manhattan** *NV* U.S.A.
195 D6 **Manhica** Moz.
197 J3 **Manhoca** Moz.
234 D3 **Manhuaçu** Brazil
234 E2 **Manhuaçu** *r.* Brazil
233 I3 **Mani** Col.
195 E5 **Mania** *r.* Madag.
184 E1 **Maniago** Italy
231 F5 **Manicoré** Brazil
207 G3 **Manicouagan** Canada
207 G3 **Manicouagan** *r.* Canada
207 G3 **Manicouagan, Petit Lac** *l.* Canada
207 G3 **Manicouagan, Réservoir** *resr* Canada
142 C5 **Manīfah** Saudi Arabia
117 I4 **Manihiki** *atoll* Cook Is
Manikgarh India *see* **Rajura**
149 E4 **Manikpur** India
161 I3 **Manila** Phil.
213 E3 **Manila** U.S.A. (City Plan **92**)
12 H4 **Manildra** Australia
125 I3 **Manilla** Australia
120 F2 **Maningrida** Australia
149 H4 **Manipur** *state* India
185 L5 **Manisa** Turkey
208 D3 **Manistee** U.S.A.
209 E3 **Manistee** *r.* U.S.A.
208 D3 **Manistique** U.S.A.
209 E2 **Manistique Lake** U.S.A.
205 J3 **Manitoba** *prov.* Canada
205 J4 **Manitoba, Lake** Canada
205 H4 **Manito Lake** Canada
205 J5 **Manitou** Canada
209 G3 **Manitou, Lake** Canada
221 E3 **Manitou Beach** U.S.A.
205 K4 **Manitou Falls** Canada
208 D2 **Manitou Island** U.S.A.
218 C2 **Manitou Islands** U.S.A.
209 F3 **Manitoulin Island** Canada
209 G3 **Manitowaning** Canada
209 E1 **Manitowik Lake** Canada
208 D3 **Manitowoc** U.S.A.
209 J2 **Maniwaki** Canada
233 I3 **Manizales** Col.
195 E6 **Manja** Madag.
197 J2 **Manjacaze** Moz.
147 H4 **Manjeri** India
160 D3 **Man Jiang** *r.* China
139 L3 **Manjil** Iran
147 H2 **Manjra** *r.* India
216 E2 **Mankato** U.S.A.
197 I3 **Mankayane** Swaziland
192 B4 **Mankono** Côte d'Ivoire
147 I4 **Mankulam** Sri Lanka
154 C1 **Manlay** Mongolia
125 I4 **Manly** Australia
148 C5 **Manmad** India
120 F2 **Mann** *r.* Australia
121 E5 **Mann, Mount** Australia
163 B3 **Manna** Indon.
124 C4 **Mannahill** Australia
147 H4 **Mannar** Sri Lanka
147 H4 **Mannar, Gulf of** India/Sri Lanka
147 H3 **Manneru** *r.* India
179 G5 **Mannheim** Germany
175 H4 **Mannin Bay** Ireland
123 F6 **Manning** *r.* Australia
204 F3 **Manning** Canada
219 D5 **Manning** U.S.A.
173 I6 **Manningtree** U.K.
121 E5 **Mann Ranges** *mts* Australia
184 C4 **Mannu, Capo** *c. Sardinia* Italy
124 C5 **Mannum** Australia
151 F7 **Manokwari** Indon.
195 C4 **Manono** Dem. Rep. Congo
162 A3 **Manoron** Myanmar
183 G5 **Manosque** France
203 K4 **Manouane, Lac** *l.* Canada
160 D3 **Manp'o** N. Korea
119 I2 **Manra** *i.* Kiribati
183 Q2 **Manresa** Spain
148 C3 **Mansa** India
195 C5 **Mansa** Zambia
192 A3 **Mansa Konko** Gambia
148 C2 **Mansehra** Pak.
203 K3 **Mansel Island** Canada
125 G6 **Mansfield** Australia
173 F4 **Mansfield** U.K.
217 E5 **Mansfield** *LA* U.S.A.
220 B4 **Mansfield** *OH* U.S.A.
221 E4 **Mansfield** *PA* U.S.A.
204 E3 **Manson Creek** Canada
139 L6 **Manṣūrī** Iran
138 E3 **Mansurlu** Turkey
230 B4 **Manta** Ecuador
230 B4 **Manta, Bahía de** *b.* Ecuador
161 H4 **Mantalingajan, Mount** Phil.
214 B3 **Manteca** U.S.A.
233 J3 **Mantecal** Venez.
179 K5 **Mantel** Germany
219 F5 **Manteo** U.S.A.
182 E2 **Mantes-la-Jolie** France
147 H2 **Manthani** India
215 G2 **Manti** U.S.A.
234 D3 **Mantiqueira, Serra da** *mts* Brazil
209 E3 **Manton** U.S.A.
Mantova Italy *see* **Mantua**
171 N3 **Mäntsälä** Fin.
171 N3 **Mänttä** Fin.
184 D2 **Mantua** Italy
123 D5 **Mantuan Downs** Australia
186 H3 **Manturovo** Rus. Fed.
171 N3 **Mäntyharju** Fin.
170 N2 **Mäntyjärvi** Fin.
230 D6 **Manu, Parque Nacional** *nat. park* Peru
237 I7 **Manuae** *atoll* Fr. Polynesia
Manua Islands American Samoa *see* **Manu'a Islands**
117 H4 **Manu'a Islands** American Samoa
215 H4 **Manuelito** U.S.A.
235 L2 **Manuel J. Cobo** Arg.
234 E1 **Manuel Vitorino** Brazil
231 H5 **Manuelzinho** Brazil
151 E7 **Manui** *i.* Indon.
143 E5 **Manūjān** Iran
161 I4 **Manukan** Phil.
126 E2 **Manukau** N.Z.
126 E2 **Manukau Harbour** N.Z.
161 H5 **Manuk Manka** *i.* Phil.
124 C4 **Manunda** *watercourse* Australia
119 E2 **Manus Island** P.N.G.
147 H3 **Manvi** India
197 F2 **Manyana** Botswana
136 B2 **Manyas** Turkey
187 G6 **Manych-Gudilo, Ozero** *l.* Rus. Fed.
215 H3 **Many Farms** U.S.A.
195 D4 **Manyoni** Tanz.
138 D6 **Manzala, Lake** *lag.* Egypt
183 O3 **Manzanares** Spain
223 I4 **Manzanillo** Cuba
224 C4 **Manzanillo** Mex.
224 J6 **Manzanillo, Punta** *pt* Panama
142 C3 **Manẓarīyeh** Iran
150 D2 **Manzhouli** China
197 I3 **Manzini** Swaziland
193 D3 **Mao** Chad
Maó Spain *see* **Mahón**
155 D4 **Maocifan** China
154 C2 **Maojiachuan** China
151 F7 **Maoke, Pegunungan** *mts* Indon.
197 G3 **Maokeng** S. Africa
160 B3 **Maokui Shan** *mt.* China
160 B2 **Maolin** China
154 B2 **Maomao Shan** *mt.* China
155 D6 **Maoming** China
155 □ **Ma On Shan** *h. Hong Kong* China
195 D6 **Mapai** Moz.
149 E3 **Mapam Yumco** *l.* China
118 C2 **Mapane** Indon.
197 F5 **Maphodi** S. Africa
225 D2 **Mapimí** Mex.
195 D6 **Mapinhane** Moz.
233 K3 **Mapire** Venez.
209 E4 **Maple** *r.* U.S.A.
205 H5 **Maple Creek** Canada
236 G4 **Mapmakers Seamounts** *sea feature* N. Pacific Ocean
122 C1 **Mapoon** Australia
197 G4 **Mapoteng** Lesotho
231 G4 **Mapuera** *r.* Brazil
197 J2 **Mapulanguene** Moz.
197 H1 **Mapungubwe National Park** S. Africa
195 D6 **Maputo** Moz.
197 J2 **Maputo** *prov.* Moz.
197 J3 **Maputo** *r.* Moz.
197 G4 **Maputsoe** Lesotho
139 H6 **Maqar an Na'am** *well* Iraq
153 H5 **Maqên** China
152 G5 **Maqên Kangri** *mt.* China
136 D5 **Maqnā** Saudi Arabia
154 B3 **Maqu** China
149 H3 **Maquan He** *r.* China
195 B4 **Maquela do Zombo** Angola
235 I4 **Maquinchao** Arg.
235 I4 **Maquinchao** *r.* Arg.
208 B4 **Maquoketa** U.S.A.
208 B4 **Maquoketa** *r.* U.S.A.
143 G5 **Mar** *r.* Pak.
234 D3 **Mar, Serra do** *mts* Brazil
205 H1 **Mara** *r.* Canada
149 E5 **Mara** India
197 H1 **Mara** S. Africa
230 E4 **Maraã** Brazil
231 I5 **Marabá** Brazil
123 E4 **Maraboon, Lake** *resr* Australia
231 H3 **Maracá, Ilha de** *i.* Brazil
233 J2 **Maracaibo** Venez.
233 J2 **Maracaibo, Lake** *inlet* Venez.
234 A3 **Maracaju** Brazil
234 A3 **Maracaju, Serra de** *hills* Brazil
234 E1 **Maracás, Chapada de** *hills* Brazil
233 K2 **Maracay** Venez.
193 D2 **Marādah** Libya
192 C3 **Maradi** Niger
142 B2 **Marāgheh** Iran
234 E1 **Maragogipe** Brazil
161 I3 **Maragondon** Phil.
233 K4 **Marahuaca, Cerro** *mt.* Venez.
231 I4 **Marajó, Baía de** *est.* Brazil
231 H4 **Marajó, Ilha de** *i.* Brazil
197 G2 **Marakele National Park** S. Africa
147 H3 **Marakkanam** India
194 D3 **Maralal** Kenya
148 C2 **Marala Weir** Pak.
139 I1 **Maralik** Armenia
118 D5 **Maralinga** Australia
119 G2 **Maramasike** *i.* Solomon Is
127 L2 **Marambio** *research stn* Antarctica
161 J5 **Marampit** *i.* Indon.
143 G4 **Maran** *mt.* Pak.
139 J4 **Marāna** Iraq
215 G5 **Marana** U.S.A.
142 B2 **Marand** Iran
162 B4 **Marang** Malaysia
162 A3 **Marang** Myanmar
234 C1 **Maranhão** *r.* Brazil
123 E5 **Maranoa** *r.* Australia
230 D4 **Marañón** *r.* Peru
197 K2 **Marão** Moz.
183 M2 **Marão** *mt.* Port.
233 K4 **Marari** *r.* Brazil
126 A6 **Mararoa** *r.* N.Z.
208 D1 **Marathon** Canada
219 D7 **Marathon** *FL* U.S.A.
217 C6 **Marathon** *TX* U.S.A.
234 E1 **Maraú** Brazil
163 H3 **Marau** Indon.
233 K4 **Marauiá** *r.* Brazil
161 J4 **Marawi** Phil.
139 L1 **Märäzä** Azer.
183 N4 **Marbella** Spain
118 B4 **Marble Bar** Australia
215 G3 **Marble Canyon** U.S.A.
215 G3 **Marble Canyon** *gorge* U.S.A.
197 H2 **Marble Hall** S. Africa
221 H3 **Marblehead** U.S.A.
205 K2 **Marble Island** Canada
197 I5 **Marburg** S. Africa
221 E5 **Marburg, Lake** U.S.A.
179 G4 **Marburg an der Lahn** Germany
177 H7 **Marcali** Hungary
173 H5 **March** U.K.
124 C4 **Marchant Hill** Australia
178 D4 **Marche-en-Famenne** Belgium
183 N4 **Marchena** Spain
230 □ **Marchena, Isla** *i. Galapagos Is* Ecuador
122 B1 **Marchinbar Island** Australia
Mar Chiquita, Lago *l.* Arg. *see* **Mar Chiquita, Laguna**
235 J1 **Mar Chiquita, Laguna** *l.* Arg.
176 G6 **Marchtrenk** Austria
219 D7 **Marco** U.S.A.
178 B4 **Marcoing** France
206 E2 **Marcopeet Islands** Canada
235 J2 **Marcos Juárez** Arg.
221 G2 **Marcy, Mount** U.S.A.
148 C2 **Mardan** Pak.
235 L3 **Mar del Plata** Arg.
139 H3 **Mardın** Turkey
119 G4 **Maré** *i.* New Caledonia
174 C3 **Maree, Loch** *l.* U.K.
208 A5 **Marengo** *IA* U.S.A.
208 C4 **Marengo** *IL* U.S.A.
184 E6 **Marettimo, Isola** *i. Sicily* Italy
186 E3 **Marevo** Rus. Fed.
217 B6 **Marfa** U.S.A.
120 D3 **Margaret** *r.* Australia
124 B2 **Margaret** *watercourse* Australia
121 B4 **Margaret, Mount** *h.* Australia
118 B5 **Margaret River** Australia
233 L2 **Margarita, Isla de** *i.* Venez.
158 D3 **Margaritovo** Rus. Fed.
125 G9 **Margate** Australia
197 I5 **Margate** S. Africa
173 I6 **Margate** U.K.
194 C3 **Margherita Peak** Dem. Rep. Congo/Uganda
Margilan Uzbek. *see* **Marg'ilon**
141 G4 **Marg'ilon** Uzbek.
Margo, Dasht-i *des.* Afgh. *see* **Mārgow, Dasht-e**
161 I5 **Margosatubig** Phil.
143 F4 **Mārgow, Dasht-e** *des.* Afgh.
178 D4 **Margraten** Neth.
209 E3 **Margrethe, Lake** U.S.A.
204 E4 **Marguerite** Canada
127 I2 **Marguerite Bay** Antarctica
149 G3 **Margyang** China
139 K5 **Marhaj Khalīl** Iraq
141 H4 **Marhamat** Uzbek.
139 I3 **Marhan Dāgh** *h.* Iraq
187 E6 **Marhanets'** Ukr.
180 C5 **Marhoum** Alg.
237 I7 **Maria** *atoll* Fr. Polynesia
232 C2 **María Elena** Chile
235 K3 **María Ignacia** Arg.
125 H9 **Maria Island** Australia
118 D3 **Maria Island** Australia
123 D5 **Mariala National Park** Australia
236 E4 **Mariana Ridge** *sea feature* N. Pacific Ocean
236 E5 **Mariana Trench** *sea feature* N. Pacific Ocean
149 H4 **Mariani** India
204 F2 **Marian Lake** Canada
217 F5 **Marianna** *AR* U.S.A.
219 C6 **Marianna** *FL* U.S.A.
176 F6 **Mariánské Lázně** Czech Rep.
224 C3 **Marías, Islas** Mex.
224 I7 **Mariato, Punta** *pt* Panama
126 D1 **Maria van Diemen, Cape** N.Z.
184 F1 **Maribor** Slovenia
215 F5 **Maricopa** *AZ* U.S.A.
214 C4 **Maricopa** *CA* U.S.A.
215 F5 **Maricopa Mountains** U.S.A.
193 E4 **Maridi** *watercourse* Sudan
127 I4 **Marie Byrd Land** *reg.* Antarctica
223 L5 **Marie-Galante** *i.* Guadeloupe
171 L3 **Mariehamn** Fin.
234 B1 **Mariembero** *r.* Brazil
179 L4 **Marienberg** Germany
179 F1 **Marienhafe** Germany
195 B6 **Mariental** Namibia
171 K4 **Mariestad** Sweden
219 C5 **Marietta** *GA* U.S.A.
220 C5 **Marietta** *OH* U.S.A.
183 G5 **Marignane** France
150 G1 **Marii, Mys** *pt* Rus. Fed.
150 A1 **Mariinsk** Rus. Fed.
140 E1 **Mariinskoye** Rus. Fed.
171 M5 **Marijampolė** Lith.
234 C3 **Marília** Brazil
121 B4 **Marillana** Australia
225 D2 **Marín** Mex.
183 L1 **Marín** Spain
185 G5 **Marina di Gioiosa Ionica** Italy
187 D4 **Mar"ina Horka** Belarus
161 I3 **Marinduque** *i.* Phil.
208 D3 **Marinette** U.S.A.
234 B3 **Maringá** Brazil
183 L3 **Marinha Grande** Port.
219 B4 **Marion** *IL* U.S.A.
209 E5 **Marion** *IN* U.S.A.
221 J2 **Marion** *ME* U.S.A.
220 B4 **Marion** *OH* U.S.A.
219 E5 **Marion** *SC* U.S.A.
220 C6 **Marion** *VA* U.S.A.
219 D5 **Marion, Lake** U.S.A.
124 B5 **Marion Bay** Australia
122 F3 **Marion Reef** Australia
233 K3 **Maripa** Venez.
214 C3 **Mariposa** U.S.A.
Mariscal Estigarribia Para. *see* **Mariscal José Félix Estigarribia**
232 D2 **Mariscal José Félix Estigarribia** Para.
182 H4 **Maritime Alps** *mts* France/Italy
185 K3 **Maritsa** *r.* Bulg.
186 I3 **Mari-Turek** Rus. Fed.
187 F6 **Mariupol'** Ukr.
233 L2 **Mariusa, Caño** *r.* Venez.
142 B3 **Marīvān** Iran
186 I3 **Mariy El, Respublika** *aut. rep.* Rus. Fed.
194 E3 **Marka** Somalia
141 K2 **Markakol', Ozero** *l.* Kazakh.
139 J2 **Mārkān** Iran
147 H3 **Markapur** India
171 K4 **Markaryd** Sweden
209 G3 **Markdale** Canada
197 H1 **Marken** S. Africa
178 D2 **Markermeer** *l.* Neth.
173 G5 **Market Deeping** U.K.
173 E5 **Market Drayton** U.K.
173 G5 **Market Harborough** U.K.
175 L3 **Markethill** U.K.
173 G4 **Market Weighton** U.K.
133 M3 **Markha** *r.* Rus. Fed.
209 H4 **Markham** Canada
Markhamet Uzbek. *see* **Marhamat**
141 I5 **Markit** China
187 F5 **Markivka** Ukr.
179 K3 **Markkleeberg** Germany
179 H2 **Marklohe** Germany
154 A3 **Markog Qu** *r.* China
179 K3 **Markranstädt** Germany
187 H5 **Marks** Rus. Fed.
179 H5 **Marktheidenfeld** Germany
176 E7 **Marktoberdorf** Germany
179 K4 **Marktredwitz** Germany
208 B6 **Mark Twain Lake** U.S.A.
179 F3 **Marl** Germany
121 F5 **Marla** Australia
221 H3 **Marlborough** U.S.A.
173 F6 **Marlborough Downs** *hills* U.K.
178 B5 **Marle** France
217 D6 **Marlin** U.S.A.
220 C5 **Marlinton** U.S.A.
125 H6 **Marlo** Australia
182 E4 **Marmande** France
138 B1 **Marmara, Sea of** *g.* Turkey
Marmara Denizi *g.* Turkey *see* **Marmara, Sea of**
138 B2 **Marmara Gölü** *l.* Turkey
138 B3 **Marmaris** Turkey
216 C2 **Marmarth** U.S.A.
220 C5 **Marmet** U.S.A.
121 C6 **Marmion, Lake** *salt l.* Australia
206 B4 **Marmion Lake** Canada
184 D1 **Marmolada** *mt.* Italy
182 F2 **Marne-la-Vallée** France
139 J1 **Marneuli** Georgia
179 J1 **Marnitz** Germany
125 E6 **Marnoo** Australia
195 E5 **Maroantsetra** Madag.
179 I4 **Maroldsweisach** Germany
195 E5 **Maromokotro** *mt.* Madag.
195 D5 **Marondera** Zimbabwe
231 H2 **Maroni** *r.* Fr. Guiana
125 J1 **Maroochydore** Australia
121 A4 **Maroonah** Australia
117 I6 **Marotiri** *is* Fr. Polynesia
193 D3 **Maroua** Cameroon
195 E5 **Marovoay** Madag.
139 H4 **Marqādah** Syria
197 G4 **Marquard** S. Africa
117 J5 **Marquesas Islands** Fr. Polynesia
219 D7 **Marquesas Keys** *is* U.S.A.
208 D2 **Marquette** U.S.A.
178 B4 **Marquion** France
Marquises, Îles *is* Fr. Polynesia *see* **Marquesas Islands**
125 E3 **Marra** Australia
125 G3 **Marra** *r.* Australia
193 E3 **Marra, Jebel** Sudan
197 J2 **Marracuene** Moz.
192 B1 **Marrakech** Morocco
197 K2 **Marrangua, Lagoa** *l.* Moz.
125 G5 **Marrar** Australia
125 F8 **Marrawah** Australia
124 C2 **Marree** Australia
217 F6 **Marrero** U.S.A.
195 D5 **Marromeu** Moz.
195 D5 **Marrupa** Moz.
121 F5 **Marryat** Australia
193 F2 **Marsá al 'Alam** Egypt
193 D1 **Marsa al Burayqah** Libya
194 D3 **Marsabit** Kenya
184 E6 **Marsala** *Sicily* Italy
193 E1 **Marsá Maṭrūḥ** Egypt
179 G3 **Marsberg** Germany
184 E3 **Marsciano** Italy
125 G4 **Marsden** Australia
178 C2 **Marsdiep** *sea chan.* Neth.
183 G5 **Marseille** France
208 C5 **Marseilles** U.S.A.
170 K2 **Marsfjället** *mt.* Sweden
123 B4 **Marshall** *watercourse* Australia
205 H4 **Marshall** Canada
217 E5 **Marshall** *AR* U.S.A.
219 C4 **Marshall** *IL* U.S.A.
209 E4 **Marshall** *MI* U.S.A.
216 E2 **Marshall** *MN* U.S.A.
217 E4 **Marshall** *MO* U.S.A.
217 E5 **Marshall** *TX* U.S.A.
125 G7 **Marshall Bay** Australia
117 F2 **Marshall Islands** *country* N. Pacific Ocean
216 E3 **Marshalltown** U.S.A.
208 B3 **Marshfield** U.S.A.
219 E7 **Marsh Harbour** Bahamas
221 J1 **Mars Hill** U.S.A.
217 F6 **Marsh Island** U.S.A.
204 C2 **Marsh Lake** Canada
139 L3 **Marshūn** Iran
213 C3 **Marsing** U.S.A.
171 L4 **Märsta** Sweden
149 F4 **Marsyangdi** *r.* Nepal
Martaban Myanmar *see* **Mottama**
163 H3 **Martapura** *Kalimantan* Indon.
163 B3 **Martapura** *Sumatera* Indon.
209 H2 **Marten River** Canada
205 H4 **Martensville** Canada
225 E2 **Marte R. Gómez, Presa** *resr* Mex.
221 H4 **Martha's Vineyard** *i.* U.S.A.
176 C7 **Martigny** Switz.
177 I6 **Martin** Slovakia
216 C3 **Martin** *SD* U.S.A.
219 B4 **Martin** *TN* U.S.A.
219 C5 **Martin, Lake** U.S.A.
225 E3 **Martínez** Mex.
215 E5 **Martinez Lake** U.S.A.
223 L6 **Martinique** *terr.* Caribbean Sea
127 I4 **Martin Peninsula** Antarctica
220 D4 **Martinsburg** *PA* U.S.A.
221 E5 **Martinsburg** *WV* U.S.A.
220 C4 **Martins Ferry** U.S.A.
220 D6 **Martinsville** U.S.A.
239 H7 **Martin Vaz, Ilhas** *is* S. Atlantic Ocean
126 E4 **Marton** N.Z.
183 Q2 **Martorell** Spain
183 O4 **Martos** Spain
140 D2 **Martuk** Kazakh.
139 J1 **Martuni** Armenia
143 F3 **Maruchak** Afgh.
159 C7 **Marugame** Japan

Meghri

126 D5 **Maruia** *r.* N.Z.
231 K6 **Maruim** Brazil
187 G7 **Marukhis Ugheltekhili** *pass* Georgia/Rus. Fed.
125 H5 **Marulan** Australia
141 K1 **Marushka** Rus. Fed.
142 D4 **Marvast** Iran
182 F4 **Marvejols** France
215 G2 **Marvine, Mount** U.S.A.
205 G4 **Marwayne** Canada
120 E2 **Mary** *r.* Australia
143 F2 **Mary** Turkm.
119 F4 **Maryborough** *Qld* Australia
125 E6 **Maryborough** *Vic.* Australia
196 H3 **Marydale** S. Africa
187 I4 **Mar'yevka** Rus. Fed.
205 H2 **Mary Frances Lake** Canada
221 E5 **Maryland** *state* U.S.A.
172 D3 **Maryport** U.K.
207 I3 **Mary's Harbour** Canada
207 J4 **Marystown** Canada
215 F2 **Marysvale** U.S.A.
207 G4 **Marysville** Canada
214 B2 **Marysville** *CA* U.S.A.
217 D4 **Marysville** *KS* U.S.A.
220 B4 **Marysville** *OH* U.S.A.
121 F5 **Maryvale** *N.T.* Australia
122 D3 **Maryvale** *Qld* Australia
216 E3 **Maryville** *MO* U.S.A.
219 C5 **Maryville** *TN* U.S.A.
179 K2 **Marzahna** Germany
224 H6 **Masachapa** Nicaragua
138 E6 **Masada** *tourist site* Israel
142 D4 **Masāhūn, Kūh-e** *mt.* Iran
195 D4 **Masaka** Uganda
197 G5 **Masakhane** S. Africa
139 L2 **Masallı** Azer.
118 C2 **Masamba** Indon.
160 E6 **Masan** S. Korea
221 I1 **Masardis** U.S.A.
195 D5 **Masasi** Tanz.
231 F7 **Masavi** Bol.
224 H6 **Masaya** Nicaragua
161 I3 **Masbate** Phil.
161 I4 **Masbate** *i.* Phil.
192 C1 **Mascara** Alg.
238 H6 **Mascarene Basin** *sea feature* Indian Ocean
238 H6 **Mascarene Plain** *sea feature* Indian Ocean
238 H5 **Mascarene Ridge** *sea feature* Indian Ocean
221 G2 **Mascouche** Canada
197 G4 **Maseru** Lesotho
197 H4 **Mashai** Lesotho
155 C6 **Mashan** China
142 D2 **Masherbrum** *mt.* Pak.
143 E2 **Mashhad** Iran
148 C4 **Mashi** *r.* India
139 K2 **Mashīrān** Iran
197 I2 **Mashishing** S. Africa
143 F4 **Mashkel, Hamun-i-** *salt flat* Pak.
143 F5 **Mashket** *r.* Pak.
143 F4 **Mashki Chah** Pak.
143 F5 **Māshkīd** *r.* Iran
170 M1 **Masi** Norway
224 B2 **Masiáca** Mex.
197 G5 **Masibambane** S. Africa
197 G4 **Masilo** S. Africa
195 D3 **Masindi** Uganda
161 H3 **Masinloc** Phil.
197 E5 **Masinyusane** S. Africa
Masīrah *i.* Oman *see* **Maşīrah, Jazīrat**
147 E5 **Maşīrah, Jazīrat** *i.* Oman
139 J1 **Masis** Armenia
142 C4 **Masjed Soleymān** Iran
175 I4 **Mask, Lough** *l.* Ireland
139 G3 **Maskanah** Syria
143 E5 **Maskūtān** Iran
143 G4 **Maslti** Pak.
195 E5 **Masoala, Parc National** Madag.
195 F5 **Masoala, Tanjona** *c.* Madag.
209 E4 **Mason** *MI* U.S.A.
214 C2 **Mason** *NV* U.S.A.
217 D6 **Mason** *TX* U.S.A.
121 B5 **Mason, Lake** *salt flat* Australia
126 A7 **Mason Bay** N.Z.
216 E3 **Mason City** *IA* U.S.A.
208 C5 **Mason City** *IL* U.S.A.
220 D5 **Masontown** U.S.A.
Masqaţ Oman *see* **Muscat**
184 D2 **Massa** Italy
221 G3 **Massachusetts** *state* U.S.A.
221 H3 **Massachusetts Bay** U.S.A.
215 H1 **Massadona** U.S.A.
185 G4 **Massafra** Italy
193 D3 **Massakory** Chad
184 D3 **Massa Marittimo** Italy
195 D6 **Massangena** Moz.
195 B4 **Massango** Angola
194 D2 **Massawa** Eritrea
221 G2 **Massawippi, Lac** *l.* Canada
221 F2 **Massena** U.S.A.
204 C4 **Masset** Canada
209 F2 **Massey** Canada
182 F4 **Massif Central** *mts* France
220 C4 **Massillon** U.S.A.
195 D6 **Massinga** Moz.
195 D6 **Massingir** Moz.
197 J1 **Massingir, Barragem de** *resr* Moz.
197 J2 **Massintonto** *r.* Moz./S. Africa
209 J3 **Masson-Angers** Canada
139 L1 **Maştağa** Azer.
141 G5 **Mastchoh** Tajik.
126 E4 **Masterton** N.Z.
219 E7 **Mastic Point** Bahamas
148 C1 **Mastuj** Pak.
143 G4 **Mastung** Pak.
187 C4 **Masty** Belarus
159 B7 **Masuda** Japan
139 L3 **Masuleh** Iran
195 D6 **Masvingo** Zimbabwe
139 F4 **Maşyāf** Syria
209 G2 **Matachewan** Canada
224 C1 **Matachic** Mex.
233 K4 **Matacuni** *r.* Venez.
150 D2 **Matad** Mongolia
195 B4 **Matadi** Dem. Rep. Congo
224 H5 **Matagalpa** Nicaragua
206 E4 **Matagami** Canada
206 E4 **Matagami, Lac** *l.* Canada
217 D6 **Matagorda Island** U.S.A.
162 C5 **Matak** *i.* Indon.
141 H2 **Matak** Kazakh.
126 F2 **Matakana Island** N.Z.
195 B5 **Matala** Angola
147 I5 **Matale** Sri Lanka
192 A3 **Matam** Senegal
225 D2 **Matamoros** *Coahuila* Mex.
225 E2 **Matamoros** *Tamaulipas* Mex.
161 I5 **Matanal Point** Phil.
195 D4 **Matandu** *r.* Tanz.
207 G4 **Matane** Canada
148 B2 **Matanui** Pak.
223 H4 **Matanzas** Cuba
207 G4 **Matapédia** *r.* Canada
235 H2 **Mataquito** *r.* Chile
147 I5 **Matara** Sri Lanka
163 H4 **Mataram** Indon.
230 D7 **Matarani** Peru
118 D3 **Mataranka** Australia
183 R2 **Mataró** Spain
197 H5 **Matatiele** S. Africa
126 B7 **Mataura** N.Z.
126 B7 **Mataura** *r.* N.Z.
119 J3 **Matā'utu** Wallis and Futuna Is
233 J3 **Mataveni** *r.* Col.
126 F3 **Matawai** N.Z.
144 E2 **Matay** Kazakh.
231 F6 **Mategua** Bol.
225 D3 **Matehuala** Mex.
195 D5 **Matemanga** Tanz.
185 G4 **Matera** Italy
184 C6 **Mateur** Tunisia
206 D4 **Matheson** Canada
217 D6 **Mathis** U.S.A.
125 F5 **Mathoura** Australia
148 D4 **Mathura** India
161 J5 **Mati** Phil.
149 G4 **Matiali** India
155 D5 **Matianxu** China
148 B4 **Matiari** Pak.
225 F4 **Matías Romero** Mex.
207 G3 **Matimekosh** Canada
209 F2 **Matinenda Lake** Canada
221 I3 **Matinicus Island** U.S.A.
149 G5 **Matla** *r.* India
197 G2 **Matlabas** S. Africa
197 G2 **Matlabas** *r.* S. Africa
148 B4 **Matli** Pak.
173 F4 **Matlock** U.K.
233 K3 **Mato** *r.* Venez.
233 K3 **Mato, Cerro** *mt.* Venez.
231 G7 **Mato Grosso** Brazil
234 A1 **Mato Grosso** *state* Brazil
234 A1 **Mato Grosso, Planalto do** *plat.* Brazil
234 A3 **Mato Grosso do Sul** *state* Brazil
197 J2 **Matola** Moz.
183 L2 **Matosinhos** Port.
147 E5 **Maţraḩ** Oman
196 C6 **Matroosberg** *mt.* S. Africa
137 E2 **Matsesta** Rus. Fed.
159 C7 **Matsue** Japan
158 G4 **Matsumae** Japan
159 E6 **Matsumoto** Japan
159 E7 **Matsusaka** Japan
155 F5 **Matsu Tao** *i.* Taiwan
159 C8 **Matsuyama** Japan
206 D4 **Mattagami** *r.* Canada
209 H2 **Mattawa** Canada
221 I2 **Mattawamkeag** U.S.A.
176 C7 **Matterhorn** *mt.* Italy/Switz.
213 D3 **Matterhorn** *mt.* U.S.A.
117 G2 **Matthew Island** S. Pacific Ocean
233 L3 **Matthews Ridge** Guyana
223 J4 **Matthew Town** Bahamas
142 D6 **Maţţī, Sabkhat** *salt pan* Saudi Arabia
219 B4 **Mattoon** U.S.A.
147 I5 **Matugama** Sri Lanka
119 H3 **Matuku** *i.* Fiji
233 L2 **Maturín** Venez.
161 J5 **Matutuang** *i.* Indon.
197 G4 **Matwabeng** S. Africa
149 E4 **Mau** India
149 E4 **Mau Aimma** India
178 B4 **Maubeuge** France
145 I8 **Maubin** Myanmar
183 E5 **Maubourguet** France
174 D5 **Mauchline** U.K.
239 J10 **Maud Seamount** *sea feature* S. Atlantic Ocean
231 G4 **Maués** Brazil
149 E4 **Mauganj** India
214 □2 **Maui** *i.* U.S.A.
179 G6 **Maulbronn** Germany
235 H2 **Maule** *admin. reg.* Chile
235 H2 **Maule** *r.* Chile
235 H4 **Maullín** Chile
175 I3 **Maumakeogh** *h.* Ireland
220 B4 **Maumee** U.S.A.
220 B4 **Maumee** *r.* U.S.A.
209 F5 **Maumee Bay** U.S.A.
175 I4 **Maumtrasna** *h.* Ireland
175 I4 **Maumturk Mountains** Ireland
195 C5 **Maun** Botswana
214 □2 **Mauna Kea** *vol.* U.S.A.
214 □2 **Mauna Loa** *vol.* U.S.A.
Maunalua B. U.S.A. *see* **Maunalua Bay**
214 □1 **Maunalua Bay** U.S.A.
149 E4 **Maunath Bhanjan** India
197 G1 **Maunatlala** Botswana
126 E2 **Maungaturoto** N.Z.
149 H5 **Maungdaw** Myanmar
162 A2 **Maungmagan Islands** Myanmar
202 F3 **Maunoir, Lac** *l.* Canada
124 B5 **Maupertuis Bay** Australia
118 D4 **Maurice, Lake** *salt flat* Australia
178 D3 **Maurik** Neth.
192 A3 **Mauritania** *country* Africa
191 I6 **Mauritius** *country* Indian Ocean
208 B4 **Mauston** U.S.A.
233 K4 **Mavaca** *r.* Venez.
195 C5 **Mavinga** Angola
197 G5 **Mavuya** S. Africa
148 D3 **Mawana** India
195 B4 **Mawanga** Dem. Rep. Congo
155 D4 **Ma Wang Dui** *tourist site* China
162 A3 **Mawdaung Pass** Myanmar/Thai.
127 G3 **Mawhai Point** N.Z.
152 G7 **Mawkmai** Myanmar
162 A1 **Mawlamyaing** Myanmar
127 L5 **Mawson** *research stn* Antarctica
127 K5 **Mawson Escarpment** Antarctica
127 I6 **Mawson Peninsula** Antarctica
162 A3 **Maw Taung** *mt.* Myanmar
216 C2 **Max** U.S.A.
225 G3 **Maxcanú** Mex.
184 C5 **Maxia, Punta** *mt. Sardinia* Italy
208 D5 **Maxinkuckee, Lake** U.S.A.
171 M3 **Maxmo** Fin.
209 F2 **Maxton** U.S.A.
214 A2 **Maxwell** U.S.A.
175 F4 **May, Isle of** *i.* U.K.
163 G3 **Maya** *i.* Indon.
150 F1 **Maya** *r.* Rus. Fed.
223 J4 **Mayaguana** *i.* Bahamas
223 K5 **Mayagüez** Puerto Rico
192 C3 **Mayahi** Niger
156 E2 **Mayak** Rus. Fed.
143 H2 **Mayakovskiy, Qullai** *mt.* Tajik.
141 G4 **Mayakum** Kazakh.
195 B4 **Mayama** Congo
142 D2 **Mayamey** Iran
225 G4 **Maya Mountains** Belize
155 C5 **Mayang** China
154 B3 **Mayanhe** China
159 F5 **Maya-san** *mt.* Japan
174 D5 **Maybole** U.K.
139 J4 **Maydān Sarāy** Iraq
Maydā Shahr Afgh. *see* **Meydān Shahr**
125 G9 **Maydena** Australia
179 F4 **Mayen** Germany
182 D2 **Mayenne** France
182 D2 **Mayenne** *r.* France
215 F4 **Mayer** U.S.A.
204 F4 **Mayerthorpe** Canada
126 C5 **Mayfield** N.Z.
219 B4 **Mayfield** U.S.A.
213 F5 **Mayhill** U.S.A.
160 E1 **Mayi He** *r.* China
141 H2 **Maykain** Kazakh.
141 I3 **Maykamys** Kazakh.
141 G5 **Maykhura** Tajik.
187 G6 **Maykop** Rus. Fed.
141 H4 **Mayluu-Suu** Kyrg.
140 E3 **Maylybas** Kazakh.
141 K1 **Mayma** Rus. Fed.
141 G4 **Maymak** Kazakh.
143 G3 **Maymanah** Afgh.
Maymyo Myanmar *see* **Pyin-U-Lwin**
169 P5 **Mayna** Rus. Fed.
150 B1 **Mayna** Rus. Fed.
147 G2 **Mayni** India
209 I3 **Maynooth** Canada
204 B2 **Mayo** Canada
161 J5 **Mayo Bay** Phil.
195 B4 **Mayoko** Congo
204 B2 **Mayo Lake** Canada
161 I3 **Mayon** *vol.* Phil.
235 J3 **Mayor Buratovich** Arg.
126 F2 **Mayor Island** N.Z.
232 D1 **Mayor Pablo Lagerenza** Para.
195 E5 **Mayotte** *terr.* Africa
161 I2 **Mayraira Point** Phil.
137 G2 **Mayskiy** Rus. Fed.
150 E1 **Mayskiy** Rus. Fed.
220 B5 **Maysville** U.S.A.
195 B4 **Mayumba** Gabon
149 E3 **Mayum La** *pass* China
147 H4 **Mayuram** India
209 F4 **Mayville** *MI* U.S.A.
216 D2 **Mayville** *ND* U.S.A.
220 D3 **Mayville** *NY* U.S.A.
208 C4 **Mayville** *WI* U.S.A.
216 C3 **Maywood** U.S.A.
235 J3 **Maza** Arg.
186 F3 **Maza** Rus. Fed.
195 C5 **Mazabuka** Zambia
231 H4 **Mazagão** Brazil
183 F5 **Mazamet** France
148 D1 **Mazar** China
143 G3 **Mazar, Koh-i-** *mt.* Afgh.
184 E6 **Mazara del Vallo** *Sicily* Italy
143 G2 **Mazār-e Sharīf** Afgh.
233 L3 **Mazaruni** *r.* Guyana
224 B1 **Mazatán** Mex.
225 G5 **Mazatenango** Guat.
224 C3 **Mazatlán** Mex.
215 G4 **Mazatzal Peak** U.S.A.
142 C3 **Mazdaj** Iran
171 M4 **Mažeikiai** Lith.
139 G2 **Mazgirt** Turkey
142 A5 **Maẕhūr, 'Irq al** *des.* Saudi Arabia
171 M4 **Mazirbe** Latvia
195 D4 **Mazomora** Tanz.
177 J4 **Mazowiecka, Nizina** *lowland* Poland
139 L3 **Mazr'eh** Iran
139 L5 **Māzū** Iran
195 C6 **Mazunga** Zimbabwe
187 D4 **Mazyr** Belarus
197 I3 **Mbabane** Swaziland
192 B4 **Mbahiakro** Côte d'Ivoire
194 B3 **Mbaïki** Centr. Afr. Rep.
195 D4 **Mbala** Zambia
194 D3 **Mbale** Uganda
193 D4 **Mbalmayo** Cameroon
195 B4 **Mbandaka** Dem. Rep. Congo
192 C4 **Mbanga** Cameroon
195 B4 **M'banza Congo** Angola
195 D4 **Mbarara** Uganda
194 C3 **Mbari** *r.* Centr. Afr. Rep.
197 J3 **Mbaswana** S. Africa
193 D4 **Mbengwi** Cameroon
195 D4 **Mbeya** Tanz.
195 D5 **Mbinga** Tanz.
195 D6 **Mbizi** Zimbabwe
194 B3 **Mbomo** Congo
193 D4 **Mbouda** Cameroon
192 A3 **Mbour** Senegal
192 A3 **Mbout** Mauritania
195 D4 **Mbozi** Tanz.
195 C4 **Mbuji-Mayi** Dem. Rep. Congo
195 D4 **Mbulu** Tanz.
195 D4 **Mbuyuni** Tanz.
221 J2 **McAdam** Canada
217 E5 **McAlester** U.S.A.
221 E4 **McAlevys Fort** U.S.A.
125 H5 **McAlister** *mt.* Australia
217 D7 **McAllen** U.S.A.
122 B2 **McArthur** *r.* Australia
220 B5 **McArthur** U.S.A.
209 I3 **McArthur Mills** Canada
204 B2 **McArthur Wildlife Sanctuary** *nature res.* Canada
204 E4 **McBride** Canada
212 C2 **McCall** U.S.A.
217 C6 **McCamey** U.S.A.
213 D3 **McCammon** U.S.A.
204 C4 **McCauley Island** Canada
203 H2 **McClintock Channel** Canada
120 D3 **McClintock Range** *hills* Australia
214 B3 **McClure, Lake** U.S.A.
202 F2 **McClure Strait** Canada
217 F6 **McComb** U.S.A.
216 C3 **McConaughy, Lake** U.S.A.
220 C5 **McConnelsville** U.S.A.
216 C3 **McCook** U.S.A.
205 J4 **McCreary** Canada
215 E4 **McCullough Range** *mts* U.S.A.
204 D3 **McDame** Canada
213 C3 **McDermitt** U.S.A.
238 I8 **McDonald Islands** Indian Ocean
212 D2 **McDonald Peak** U.S.A.
124 C2 **McDonnell Creek** *watercourse* Australia
196 B4 **McDougall's Bay** S. Africa
215 G5 **McDowell Peak** U.S.A.
214 C4 **McFarland** U.S.A.
205 H3 **McFarlane** *r.* Canada
215 E2 **McGill** U.S.A.
202 C3 **McGrath** U.S.A.
204 E4 **McGregor** *r.* Canada
196 C6 **McGregor** S. Africa
208 A2 **McGregor** U.S.A.
209 G2 **McGregor Bay** Canada
123 C5 **McGregor Range** *hills* Australia
212 D2 **McGuire, Mount** U.S.A.
195 D4 **Mchinga** Tanz.
122 C2 **McIlwraith Range** *hills* Australia
221 G2 **McIndoe Falls** U.S.A.
216 C2 **McIntosh** U.S.A.
121 C4 **McKay Range** *hills* Australia
119 I2 **McKean** *i.* Kiribati
220 A6 **McKee** U.S.A.
220 D4 **McKeesport** U.S.A.
221 F3 **McKeever** U.S.A.
219 B4 **McKenzie** U.S.A.
123 C4 **McKinlay** *r.* Australia
202 C3 **McKinley, Mount** U.S.A.
217 D5 **McKinney** U.S.A.
214 C4 **McKittrick** U.S.A.
216 C2 **McLaughlin** U.S.A.
204 F3 **McLennan** Canada
204 F4 **McLeod** *r.* Canada
204 E3 **McLeod Lake** Canada
213 B3 **McLoughlin, Mount** U.S.A.
209 E2 **McMillan** U.S.A.
212 B2 **McMinnville** *OR* U.S.A.
219 C5 **McMinnville** *TN* U.S.A.
127 I5 **McMurdo** *research stn* Antarctica
215 H4 **McNary** U.S.A.
204 F4 **McNaughton Lake** Canada
215 H6 **McNeal** U.S.A.
217 D4 **McPherson** U.S.A.
125 J2 **McPherson Range** *mts* Australia
204 B2 **McQuesten** *r.* Canada
219 D5 **McRae** U.S.A.
204 E1 **McVicar Arm** *b.* Canada
197 G6 **Mdantsane** S. Africa
184 B6 **M'Daourouch** Alg.
163 D2 **M'Đrak** Vietnam
162 C1 **Mê, Hon** *i.* Vietnam
215 E3 **Mead, Lake** *resr* U.S.A.
217 C4 **Meade** U.S.A.
121 A5 **Meadow** Australia
205 H4 **Meadow Lake** Canada
205 H4 **Meadow Lake Provincial Park** Canada
215 E3 **Meadow Valley Wash** *r.* U.S.A.
220 C4 **Meadville** U.S.A.
209 G3 **Meaford** Canada
158 I3 **Meaken-dake** *vol.* Japan
174 A2 **Mealasta Island** U.K.
183 L2 **Mealhada** Port.
174 D4 **Meall a' Bhuiridh** *mt.* U.K.
207 I3 **Mealy Mountains** Canada
125 H1 **Meandarra** Australia
204 F3 **Meander River** Canada
161 J5 **Meares** *i.* Indon.
182 F2 **Meaux** France
195 B4 **Mebridege** *r.* Angola
146 A5 **Mecca** Saudi Arabia (City Plan **96**)
221 H2 **Mechanic Falls** U.S.A.
220 B4 **Mechanicsburg** U.S.A.
208 B5 **Mechanicsville** U.S.A.
178 C3 **Mechelen** Belgium
178 D4 **Mechelen** Neth.
192 B1 **Mecheria** Alg.
179 E4 **Mechernich** Germany
138 E1 **Mecitözü** Turkey
179 F4 **Meckenheim** Germany
176 E3 **Mecklenburger Bucht** *b.* Germany
179 J1 **Mecklenburgische Seenplatte** *reg.* Germany
179 K1 **Mecklenburg-Vorpommern** *land* Germany
195 D5 **Mecula** Moz.
120 C3 **Meda** *r.* Australia
183 M2 **Meda** Port.
147 H2 **Medak** India
163 E2 **Medan** Indon.
235 J3 **Médanos** Arg.
232 C7 **Medanosa, Punta** *pt* Arg.
147 I4 **Medawachchiya** Sri Lanka
147 H2 **Medchal** India
221 J2 **Meddybemps Lake** U.S.A.
183 R4 **Médéa** Alg.
179 G3 **Medebach** Germany
233 I3 **Medellín** Col.
173 F4 **Meden** *r.* U.K.
193 D1 **Medenine** Tunisia
192 A3 **Mederdra** Mauritania
213 B3 **Medford** *OR* U.S.A.
208 B3 **Medford** *WI* U.S.A.
221 F5 **Medford Farms** U.S.A.
185 M2 **Medgidia** Romania
208 B5 **Media** U.S.A.
235 I2 **Media Luna** Arg.
177 L7 **Mediaş** Romania
212 C2 **Medical Lake** U.S.A.
213 F3 **Medicine Bow** U.S.A.
213 F3 **Medicine Bow Mountains** U.S.A.
213 F3 **Medicine Bow Peak** U.S.A.
205 G4 **Medicine Hat** Canada
217 D4 **Medicine Lodge** U.S.A.
234 E2 **Medina** Brazil
146 A5 **Medina** Saudi Arabia
220 D3 **Medina** *NY* U.S.A.
220 C4 **Medina** *OH* U.S.A.
183 O2 **Medinaceli** Spain
183 N2 **Medina del Campo** Spain
183 N2 **Medina de Rioseco** Spain
149 F5 **Medinipur** India
166 F5 **Mediterranean Sea** Africa/Europe
184 B6 **Medjerda, Monts de la** *mts* Alg.
140 D2 **Mednogorsk** Rus. Fed.
182 D4 **Médoc** *reg.* France
152 G6 **Mêdog** China
186 H3 **Medvedevo** Rus. Fed.
187 H5 **Medveditsa** *r.* Rus. Fed.
184 F2 **Medvednica** *mts* Croatia
133 R2 **Medvezh'i, Ostrova** *is* Rus. Fed.
150 F2 **Medvezh'ya, Gora** *mt.* China/Rus. Fed.
186 E2 **Medvezh'yegorsk** Rus. Fed.
173 H6 **Medway** *r.* U.K.
118 B4 **Meekatharra** Australia
215 H1 **Meeker** U.S.A.
214 B2 **Meeks Bay** U.S.A.
207 I4 **Meelpaeg Reservoir** Canada
179 K4 **Meerane** Germany
179 E3 **Meerlo** Neth.
148 D3 **Meerut** India
212 E2 **Meeteetse** U.S.A.
194 D3 **Mēga** Eth.
163 B3 **Mega** *i.* Indon.
149 G4 **Meghalaya** *state* India
149 F5 **Meghasani** *mt.* India
149 G5 **Meghna** *r.* Bangl.
139 K2 **Meghri** Armenia

Mytilini

185 L5 **Mytilini** Greece
136 B3 **Mytilini Strait** Greece/Turkey
187 F4 **Mytishchi** Rus. Fed.
170 C2 **Mývatn-Laxá** *nature res.* Iceland
197 G5 **Mzamomhle** S. Africa
179 K5 **Mže** *r.* Czech Rep.
195 D5 **Mzimba** Malawi
195 D5 **Mzuzu** Malawi

N

155 B6 **Na, Nam** *r.* China/Vietnam
179 J5 **Naab** *r.* Germany
Naalehu U.S.A. *see* **Nā'ālehu**
214 □2 **Nā'ālehu** U.S.A.
171 M3 **Naantali** Fin.
175 L4 **Naas** Ireland
152 G7 **Naba** Myanmar
196 B4 **Nababeep** S. Africa
147 I2 **Nabarangapur** India
159 E7 **Nabari** Japan
161 I4 **Nabas** Phil.
138 E5 **Nabatîyé et Tahta** Lebanon
Nabatiyet et Tahta Lebanon *see* **Nabatîyé et Tahta**
121 C5 **Nabberu, Lake** *salt flat* Australia
179 K5 **Nabburg** Germany
195 D4 **Naberera** Tanz.
132 G4 **Naberezhnyye Chelny** Rus. Fed.
193 D1 **Nabeul** Tunisia
148 D3 **Nabha** India
125 J4 **Nabiac** Australia
156 F2 **Nabil'skiy Zaliv** *lag.* Rus. Fed.
151 F7 **Nabire** Indon.
138 E5 **Nāblus** West Bank
197 H2 **Naboomspruit** S. Africa
136 D5 **Nabq Reserve** *nature res.* Egypt
162 A2 **Nabule** Myanmar
195 E5 **Nacala** Moz.
224 H5 **Nacaome** Hond.
212 B2 **Naches** U.S.A.
148 B4 **Nachna** India
145 H9 **Nachuge** India
214 B4 **Nacimiento Reservoir** U.S.A.
217 E6 **Nacogdoches** U.S.A.
222 C2 **Nacozari de García** Mex.
156 D2 **Nadezhdinskoye** Rus. Fed.
148 C5 **Nadiad** India
142 D4 **Nadīk** Iran
192 B1 **Nador** Morocco
142 D3 **Nadūshan** Iran
187 C5 **Nadvirna** Ukr.
132 E3 **Nadvoitsy** Rus. Fed.
132 I3 **Nadym** Rus. Fed.
171 J5 **Næstved** Denmark
185 I5 **Nafpaktos** Greece
185 J6 **Nafplio** Greece
139 J5 **Naft, Āb** *r.* Iraq
137 G2 **Naftalan** Azer.
142 C4 **Naft-e Safīd** Iran
139 J5 **Naft Khāneh** Iraq
142 B3 **Naft Shahr** Iran
181 F5 **Nafūsah, Jabal** *hills* Libya
142 A5 **Nafy** Saudi Arabia
149 G2 **Nag, Co** *l.* China
161 I3 **Naga** Phil.
206 D4 **Nagagami** *r.* Canada
159 C8 **Nagahama** Japan
149 H4 **Naga Hills** India
159 G5 **Nagai** Japan
149 H4 **Nagaland** *state* India
125 F6 **Nagambie** Australia
159 F6 **Nagano** Japan
159 F6 **Nagaoka** Japan
149 H4 **Nagaon** India
147 H4 **Nagapattinam** India
148 D2 **Nagar** India
147 H2 **Nagarjuna Sagar Reservoir** India
148 B4 **Nagar Parkar** Pak.
149 G3 **Nagarzê** China
159 A8 **Nagasaki** Japan
159 B7 **Nagato** Japan
148 C4 **Nagaur** India
147 I2 **Nagavali** *r.* India
148 C5 **Nagda** India
147 H4 **Nagercoil** India
143 G5 **Nagha Kalat** Pak.
148 D3 **Nagina** India
149 E3 **Nagma** Nepal
186 I3 **Nagorsk** Rus. Fed.
159 E7 **Nagoya** Japan
148 D5 **Nagpur** India
149 H3 **Nagqu** China
161 J3 **Nagumbuaya Point** Phil.
132 F1 **Nagurskoye** Rus. Fed.
185 G1 **Nagyatád** Hungary
177 H7 **Nagykanizsa** Hungary
151 E4 **Naha** Japan
148 D3 **Nahan** India
143 F5 **Nahang** *r.* Iran/Pak.
204 E2 **Nahanni Butte** Canada
Nahanni National Park Canada *see* **Nahanni National Park Reserve**
204 D2 **Nahanni National Park Reserve** Canada
138 E5 **Nahariyya** Israel
142 C3 **Nahāvand** Iran
179 F5 **Nahe** *r.* Germany
235 H3 **Nahuelbuta, Parque Nacional** *nat. park* Chile
235 H4 **Nahuel Huapí, Lago** *l.* Arg.
235 H4 **Nahuel Huapí, Parque Nacional** *nat. park* Arg.
219 D6 **Nahunta** U.S.A.
224 C2 **Naica** Mex.
149 H2 **Naij Tal** China
120 C1 **Naikliu** Indon.
207 H2 **Nain** Canada
142 D3 **Nā'īn** Iran
148 D3 **Nainital** India
149 E5 **Nainpur** India
174 E3 **Nairn** U.K.
209 G2 **Nairn Centre** Canada
195 D4 **Nairobi** Kenya
195 D4 **Naivasha** Kenya
160 D2 **Naizishan** China
142 B5 **Na'jān** Saudi Arabia
146 B4 **Najd** *reg.* Saudi Arabia
183 O1 **Nájera** Spain
156 A2 **Naji** China
148 D3 **Najibabad** India
161 F2 **Najin** N. Korea
Najitun China *see* **Naji**
146 B6 **Najrān** Saudi Arabia
159 A8 **Nakadōri-shima** *i.* Japan
162 C1 **Na Kae** Thai.
159 B8 **Nakama** Japan
159 C8 **Nakamura** Japan
133 L3 **Nakanno** Rus. Fed.
159 F6 **Nakano** Japan
159 C6 **Nakano-shima** *i.* Japan
143 H3 **Naka Pass** Afgh.
159 B8 **Nakatsu** Japan
159 E7 **Nakatsugawa** Japan
194 D2 **Nakfa** Eritrea
193 F1 **Nakhl** Egypt
150 F2 **Nakhodka** Rus. Fed.
162 B2 **Nakhon Nayok** Thai.
162 B2 **Nakhon Pathom** Thai.
162 C1 **Nakhon Phanom** Thai.
162 B2 **Nakhon Ratchasima** Thai.
162 B2 **Nakhon Sawan** Thai.
162 A3 **Nakhon Si Thammarat** Thai.
148 B5 **Nakhtarana** India
204 C3 **Nakina** *B.C.* Canada
206 C3 **Nakina** *Ont.* Canada
202 C4 **Naknek** U.S.A.
195 D4 **Nakonde** Zambia
171 J5 **Nakskov** Denmark
160 E6 **Naktong-gang** *r.* S. Korea
195 D4 **Nakuru** Kenya
204 F4 **Nakusp** Canada
143 G5 **Nal** Pak.
143 G5 **Nal** *r.* Pak.
197 J2 **Nalázi** Moz.
149 G4 **Nalbari** India
187 G7 **Nal'chik** Rus. Fed.
147 H2 **Naldurg** India
147 H2 **Nalgonda** India
147 H3 **Nallamala Hills** India
138 C1 **Nallıhan** Turkey
141 G1 **Nalobino** Kazakh.
193 D1 **Nālūt** Libya
197 J2 **Namaacha** Moz.
197 H3 **Namahadi** S. Africa
142 C3 **Namak, Daryācheh-ye** *salt flat* Iran
143 E3 **Namak, Kavīr-e** *salt flat* Iran
143 E4 **Namakzar-e Shadad** *salt flat* Iran
195 D4 **Namanga** Kenya
141 G4 **Namangan** Uzbek.
195 D5 **Namapa** Moz.
196 B4 **Namaqualand** *reg.* S. Africa
139 J3 **Namashīr** Iran
119 F2 **Namatanai** P.N.G.
125 J1 **Nambour** Australia
125 J3 **Nambucca Heads** Australia
121 A6 **Nambung National Park** Australia
162 C3 **Năm Căn** Vietnam
Namch'ŏn N. Korea *see* **P'yŏngsan**
150 B3 **Nam Co** *salt l.* China
170 K2 **Namdalen** *val.* Norway
170 J2 **Namdalseid** Norway
155 C6 **Nam Đinh** Vietnam
208 B3 **Namekagon** *r.* U.S.A.
160 D4 **Nam-gang** *r.* N. Korea
160 E6 **Namhae-do** *i.* S. Korea
195 B6 **Namib Desert** Namibia
195 B5 **Namibe** Angola
195 B6 **Namibia** *country* Africa
239 J8 **Namibia Abyssal Plain** *sea feature* N. Atlantic Ocean
159 G6 **Namie** Japan
137 H3 **Namīn** Iran
149 H3 **Namjagbarwa Feng** *mt.* China
149 G3 **Namka** China
151 E7 **Namlea** Indon.
162 A1 **Nammekon** Myanmar
125 H3 **Namoi** *r.* Australia
204 F3 **Nampa** Canada
149 E3 **Nampa** *mt.* Nepal
213 C3 **Nampa** U.S.A.
192 B3 **Nampala** Mali
162 B1 **Nam Pat** Thai.
162 B1 **Nam Phong** Thai.
160 C4 **Namp'o** N. Korea
195 D5 **Nampula** Moz.
135 H4 **Namrup** India
149 H4 **Namsai** India
149 E3 **Namsê La** *pass* Nepal
170 J2 **Namsen** *r.* Norway
149 G3 **Namsi La** *pass* Bhutan
170 J2 **Namsos** Norway
133 N3 **Namtsy** Rus. Fed.
151 B4 **Namtu** Myanmar
178 C4 **Namur** Belgium
195 C5 **Namwala** Zambia
160 D6 **Namwŏn** S. Korea
152 G6 **Namya Ra** Myanmar
162 B1 **Nan** Thai.
162 B1 **Nan, Mae Nam** *r.* Thai.
194 B3 **Nana Bakassa** Centr. Afr. Rep.
204 E5 **Nanaimo** Canada
214 □1 **Nānākuli** U.S.A.
Nanakuli U.S.A. *see* **Nānākuli**
160 E3 **Nanam** N. Korea
155 F5 **Nan'an** China
196 B2 **Nananib Plateau** Namibia
159 E6 **Nanao** Japan
155 E6 **Nan'ao Dao** *i.* China
159 E6 **Nanatsu-shima** *i.* Japan
155 C4 **Nanbu** China
158 A1 **Nancha** China
155 E4 **Nanchang** *Jiangxi* China
155 E4 **Nanchang** *Jiangxi* China
155 E5 **Nancheng** China
155 C4 **Nanchong** China
155 C4 **Nanchuan** China
145 H10 **Nancowry** *i.* India
182 H2 **Nancy** France
149 E3 **Nanda Devi** *mt.* India
149 E3 **Nanda Kot** *mt.* India
155 C5 **Nandan** China
147 H2 **Nanded** India
125 I3 **Nandewar Range** *mts* Australia
148 C5 **Nandgaon** India
155 D6 **Nandu Jiang** *r.* China
148 C5 **Nandurbar** India
147 H3 **Nandyal** India
155 D6 **Nanfeng** *Guangdong* China
155 E5 **Nanfeng** *Jiangxi* China
149 H3 **Nang** China
193 D4 **Nanga Eboko** Cameroon
163 H3 **Nangahpinoh** Indon.
160 E2 **Nangang Shan** *mts* China/N. Korea
148 C2 **Nanga Parbat** *mt.* Pak.
163 H3 **Nangatayap** Indon.
162 A2 **Nangin** Myanmar
160 D3 **Nangnim** N. Korea
160 D3 **Nangnim-sanmaek** *mts* N. Korea
154 E2 **Nangong** China
152 G5 **Nangqên** China
195 D4 **Nangulangwa** Tanz.
154 A2 **Nanhua** China
155 F4 **Nanhui** China
147 H3 **Nanjangud** India
154 C3 **Nanjiang** China
155 E5 **Nanjing** *Fujian* China
154 F3 **Nanjing** *Jiangsu* China
155 E5 **Nankang** China
Nanking *Jiangsu* China *see* **Nanjing**
159 C8 **Nankoku** Japan
195 B5 **Nankova** Angola
154 E2 **Nanle** China
155 F4 **Nanling** China
155 D5 **Nan Ling** *mts* China
155 C6 **Nanliu Jiang** *r.* China
121 B5 **Nannine** Australia
155 C6 **Nanning** China
121 A7 **Nannup** Australia
162 B1 **Na Noi** Thai.
203 N3 **Nanortalik** Greenland
155 C5 **Nanpan Jiang** *r.* China
160 A3 **Nanpiao** China
155 F5 **Nanping** China
155 F5 **Nanri Dao** *i.* China
Nansei-shotō *is* Japan *see* **Ryukyu Islands**
240 B1 **Nansen Basin** *sea feature* Arctic Ocean
203 I1 **Nansen Sound** *sea chan.* Canada
182 D3 **Nantes** France
178 A5 **Nanteuil-le-Haudouin** France
147 I4 **Nanthi Kadal** *lag.* Sri Lanka
209 G4 **Nanticoke** Canada
215 F5 **Nanticoke** *r.* U.S.A.
205 G4 **Nanton** Canada
155 F4 **Nantong** China
155 F6 **Nant'ou** Taiwan
221 H4 **Nantucket** U.S.A.
221 H4 **Nantucket Island** U.S.A.
221 H4 **Nantucket Sound** *g.* U.S.A.
173 E4 **Nantwich** U.K.
119 H2 **Nanumanga** *i.* Tuvalu
119 H2 **Nanumea** *atoll* Tuvalu
234 E2 **Nanuque** Brazil
161 J5 **Nanusa, Kepulauan** *is* Indon.
155 B4 **Nanxi** China
155 D4 **Nanxian** China
155 E5 **Nanxiong** China
154 D3 **Nanyang** China
160 C3 **Nanzamu** China
155 D4 **Nanzhang** China
154 D3 **Nanzhao** China
183 Q3 **Nao, Cabo de la** *c.* Spain
207 F3 **Naococane, Lac** *l.* Canada
149 G4 **Naogaon** Bangl.
158 C1 **Naoli He** *r.* China
143 F3 **Naomid, Dasht-e** *des.* Afgh./Iran
148 C2 **Naoshera** India
155 D6 **Naozhou Dao** *i.* China
214 A2 **Napa** U.S.A.
221 J1 **Napadogan** Canada
205 G1 **Napaktulik Lake** Canada
209 I3 **Napanee** Canada
148 C4 **Napasar** India
203 M3 **Napasoq** Greenland
208 C5 **Naperville** U.S.A.
126 F3 **Napier** N.Z.
120 D3 **Napier Range** *hills* Australia
221 G2 **Napierville** Canada
184 F4 **Naples** Italy
219 D7 **Naples** *FL* U.S.A.
221 H3 **Naples** *ME* U.S.A.
155 B6 **Napo** China
230 D4 **Napo** *r.* Ecuador/Peru
220 A4 **Napoleon** U.S.A.
Napoli Italy *see* **Naples**
235 J3 **Naposta** Arg.
235 J3 **Naposta** *r.* Arg.
209 E5 **Nappanee** U.S.A.
139 J3 **Naqadeh** Iran
139 L4 **Naqqash** Iran
159 D7 **Nara** Japan
192 B3 **Nara** Mali
177 M3 **Narach** Belarus
124 D6 **Naracoorte** Australia
125 G4 **Naradhan** Australia
148 C4 **Naraina** India
149 E6 **Narainpur** India
224 B2 **Naranjo** Mex.
225 E3 **Naranjos** Mex.
147 J2 **Narasannapeta** India
147 I2 **Narasapatnam, Point** India
147 I2 **Narasapur** India
147 I2 **Narasaraopet** India
149 F5 **Narasinghapur** India
162 B4 **Narathiwat** Thai.
149 G4 **Narayangaon** India
173 C6 **Narberth** U.K.
183 F5 **Narbonne** France
183 M1 **Narcea** *r.* Spain
142 D2 **Nardin** Iran
184 H4 **Nardò** Italy
235 K1 **Nare** Arg.
148 B3 **Narechi** *r.* Pak.
121 B7 **Narembeen** Australia
239 E4 **Nares Abyssal Plain** *sea feature* S. Atlantic Ocean
239 E4 **Nares Deep** *sea feature* N. Atlantic Ocean
203 L1 **Nares Strait** Canada/Greenland
121 D6 **Naretha** Australia
177 J4 **Narew** *r.* Poland
160 D2 **Narhong** China
148 A3 **Nari** *r.* Pak.
195 B6 **Narib** Namibia
196 B5 **Nariep** S. Africa
187 H6 **Narimanov** Rus. Fed.
143 H2 **Narin** Afgh.
143 H3 **Narin** *reg.* Afgh.
139 G3 **Narince** Turkey
149 H1 **Narin Gol** *watercourse* China
159 G7 **Narita** Japan
224 B2 **Narizon, Punta** *pt* Mex.
148 C5 **Narmada** *r.* India
139 H1 **Narman** Turkey
148 D3 **Narnaul** India
184 E3 **Narni** Italy
169 S3 **Narodnaya, Gora** *mt.* Rus. Fed.
177 N5 **Narodychi** Ukr.
187 F4 **Naro-Fominsk** Rus. Fed.
125 I6 **Narooma** Australia
187 G4 **Narovchat** Rus. Fed.
187 D5 **Narowlya** Belarus
171 M3 **Närpes** Fin.
125 H3 **Narrabri** Australia
221 H4 **Narragansett Bay** U.S.A.
125 G2 **Narran** *r.* Australia
125 G5 **Narrandera** Australia
125 G2 **Narran Lake** Australia
121 B7 **Narrogin** Australia
125 H4 **Narromine** Australia
205 I4 **Narrow Hills Provincial Park** Canada
220 C6 **Narrows** U.S.A.
221 F4 **Narrowsburg** U.S.A.
Narsimhapur India *see* **Narsinghpur**
149 G5 **Narsingdi** Bangl.
148 D5 **Narsinghgarh** India
148 D5 **Narsinghpur** India
147 I2 **Narsipatnam** India
154 E1 **Nart** China
137 F2 **Nartkala** Rus. Fed.
159 D7 **Naruto** Japan
171 O4 **Narva** Estonia
171 N4 **Narva Bay** Estonia/Rus. Fed.
161 I2 **Narvacan** Phil.
Narva Reservoir Estonia/Rus. Fed. *see* **Narvskoye Vodokhranilische**
170 L1 **Narvik** Norway
171 O4 **Narvskoye Vodokhranilishche** *resr* Estonia/Rus. Fed.
148 D3 **Narwana** India
148 D4 **Narwar** India
132 G3 **Nar'yan-Mar** Rus. Fed.
141 K2 **Narymskiy Khrebet** *mts* Kazakh.
141 H4 **Naryn** Kyrg.
141 H4 **Naryn** *r.* Kyrg.
141 J4 **Narynkol** Kazakh.
171 L3 **Näsåker** Sweden
Na Scealagae Skelligs *is* Ireland *see* **The Skelligs**
215 H3 **Naschitti** U.S.A.
126 C6 **Naseby** N.Z.
148 C5 **Nashik** India
208 A4 **Nashua** *IA* U.S.A.
221 H3 **Nashua** *NH* U.S.A.
219 C4 **Nashville** U.S.A.
139 F5 **Naṣīb** Syria
171 M3 **Näsijärvi** *l.* Fin.
193 F4 **Nasir** Sudan
193 F2 **Nāṣir, Buḥayrat** *resr* Egypt
148 B3 **Nasirabad** Pak.
195 C5 **Nasondoye** Dem. Rep. Congo
138 C6 **Naṣr** Egypt
142 C3 **Naṣrābād** Iran
143 E3 **Naṣrābād** Iran
139 K5 **Naṣrīān-e Pā'īn** Iran
204 D3 **Nass** *r.* Canada
122 C2 **Nassau** *r.* Australia
219 E7 **Nassau** Bahamas
237 H6 **Nassau** *i.* Cook Is
171 K4 **Nässjö** Sweden
203 M3 **Nassuttooq** *inlet* Greenland
206 E2 **Nastapoca** *r.* Canada
206 E2 **Nastapoka Islands** Canada
159 F6 **Nasu-dake** *vol.* Japan
161 I3 **Nasugbu** Phil.
177 O2 **Nasva** Rus. Fed.
195 C6 **Nata** Botswana
195 D4 **Nata** Tanz.
233 I4 **Natagaima** Col.
231 K5 **Natal** Brazil
Natal *prov.* S. Africa *see* **KwaZulu-Natal**
238 G7 **Natal Basin** *sea feature* Indian Ocean
142 C3 **Naṭanz** Iran
207 H3 **Natashquan** Canada
207 H3 **Natashquan** *r.* Canada
217 F6 **Natchez** U.S.A.
217 E6 **Natchitoches** U.S.A.
176 G4 **Natecka, Puszcza** *for.* Poland
125 F6 **Nathalia** Australia
162 B4 **Na Thawi** Thai.
148 C4 **Nathdwara** India
183 R2 **Nati, Punta** *pt* Spain
124 D6 **Natimuk** Australia
215 D5 **National City** U.S.A.
192 C3 **Natitingou** Benin
231 I6 **Natividade** Brazil
224 B1 **Nátora** Mex.
159 G5 **Natori** Japan
195 D4 **Natron, Lake** *salt l.* Tanz.
162 A1 **Nattaung** *mt.* Myanmar
207 H2 **Natuashish** Canada
163 G2 **Natuna, Kepulauan** *is* Indon.
163 G2 **Natuna Besar** *i.* Indon.
221 F2 **Natural Bridge** U.S.A.
215 G3 **Natural Bridges National Monument** *nat. park* U.S.A.
121 A7 **Naturaliste, Cape** Australia
238 L7 **Naturaliste Plateau** *sea feature* Indian Ocean
215 H2 **Naturita** U.S.A.
209 E2 **Naubinway** U.S.A.
195 B6 **Nauchas** Namibia
179 K2 **Nauen** Germany
221 G4 **Naugatuck** U.S.A.
161 I3 **Naujan** Phil.
161 I3 **Naujan, Lake** Phil.
171 M4 **Naujoji Akmenė** Lith.
148 C4 **Naukh** India
148 B4 **Naukot** Pak.
179 H3 **Naumburg (Hessen)** Germany
179 J3 **Naumburg (Saale)** Germany
162 A1 **Naungpale** Myanmar
138 E6 **Na'ūr** Jordan
143 G4 **Nauroz Kalat** Pak.
137 G2 **Naurskaya** Rus. Fed.
119 G2 **Nauru** *country* Pacific Ocean
148 B4 **Naushara** Pak.
171 I3 **Naustdal** Norway
230 D4 **Nauta** Peru
196 C3 **Naute Dam** Namibia
225 E3 **Nautla** Mex.
143 G3 **Nauzad** Afgh.
149 G5 **Navadwip** India
187 C4 **Navahrudak** Belarus
215 H4 **Navajo** U.S.A.
213 F4 **Navajo Lake** U.S.A.
215 G3 **Navajo Mountain** U.S.A.
161 J4 **Naval** Phil.
183 N3 **Navalmoral de la Mata** Spain
183 N3 **Navalvillar de Pela** Spain
175 L4 **Navan** Ireland
187 D4 **Navapolatsk** Belarus
133 S3 **Navarin, Mys** *c.* Rus. Fed.
232 C9 **Navarino, Isla** *i.* Chile
183 P1 **Navarra** *aut. comm.* Spain
125 E6 **Navarre** Australia
214 A2 **Navarro** U.S.A.
187 G4 **Navashino** Rus. Fed.
217 D6 **Navasota** U.S.A.
174 D2 **Naver, Loch** *l.* U.K.
171 K3 **Näverede** Sweden
235 H2 **Navidad** Chile
147 G2 **Navi Mumbai** India
187 E4 **Navlya** Rus. Fed.
185 M2 **Năvodari** Romania
Navoi Uzbek. *see* **Navoiy**
141 F4 **Navoiy** Uzbek.
224 B2 **Navojoa** Mex.
186 G3 **Navoloki** Rus. Fed.
148 C5 **Navsari** India
148 C4 **Nawa** India
139 F5 **Nawá** Syria
149 G4 **Nawabganj** Bangl.
148 B4 **Nawabshah** Pak.
149 F4 **Nawada** India
143 G3 **Nāwah** Afgh.
148 C4 **Nawalgarh** India
152 G7 **Nawngleng** Myanmar
139 J2 **Naxçıvan** Azer.
155 B4 **Naxi** China
185 K6 **Naxos** Greece
185 K6 **Naxos** *i.* Greece

Nierstein

Nây, Mui *pt* Vietnam *see* **Đai Lanh, Mui**
233 H4 **Naya** Col.
147 J1 **Nayagarh** India
224 C3 **Nayar** Mex.
224 C3 **Nayarit** *state* Mex.
158 H2 **Nayoro** Japan
135 H5 **Nay Pyi Taw** Myanmar
147 H3 **Nayudupeta** India
234 E1 **Nazaré** Brazil
147 H4 **Nazareth** India
138 E5 **Nazareth** Israel
217 B7 **Nazas** Mex.
224 C2 **Nazas** *r.* Mex.
230 D6 **Nazca** Peru
237 N7 **Nazca Ridge** *sea feature* S. Pacific Ocean
Nazerat Israel *see* **Nazareth**
139 J2 **Nāzīk** Iran
139 I2 **Nazik Gölü** *l.* Turkey
143 F4 **Nāzīl** Iran
138 B3 **Nazilli** Turkey
143 G5 **Nazimabad** Pak.
139 G2 **Nazımiye** Turkey
149 H4 **Nazira** India
204 E4 **Nazko** Canada
204 E4 **Nazko** *r.* Canada
139 J3 **Nāzlū** *r.* Iran
187 H7 **Nazran'** Rus. Fed.
194 D3 **Nazrēt** Eth.
147 E5 **Nazwá** Oman
195 C4 **Nchelenge** Zambia
195 C6 **Ncojane** Botswana
195 B4 **N'dalatando** Angola
194 C3 **Ndélé** Centr. Afr. Rep.
195 B4 **Ndendé** Gabon
119 G3 **Ndeni** *i.* Solomon Is
193 D3 **Ndjamena** Chad
195 C5 **Ndola** Zambia
197 I4 **Ndwedwe** S. Africa
125 G1 **Neabul Creek** *r.* Australia
175 L3 **Neagh, Lough** *l.* U.K.
212 A1 **Neah Bay** U.S.A.
118 D4 **Neale, Lake** *salt flat* Australia
124 B2 **Neales** *watercourse* Australia
185 J5 **Nea Liosia** Greece
185 J6 **Neapoli** Greece
173 D6 **Neath** U.K.
173 D6 **Neath** *r.* U.K.
125 G1 **Nebine Creek** *r.* Australia
Nebitdag Turkm. *see* **Balkanabat**
233 K4 **Neblina, Pico da** *mt.* Brazil
123 E4 **Nebo** Australia
215 G2 **Nebo, Mount** U.S.A.
186 E3 **Nebolchi** Rus. Fed.
216 C3 **Nebraska** *state* U.S.A.
216 E3 **Nebraska City** U.S.A.
184 F6 **Nebrodi, Monti** *mts Sicily* Italy
217 E6 **Neches** *r.* U.S.A.
233 I3 **Nechí** *r.* Col.
194 D3 **Nechisar National Park** Eth.
179 G5 **Neckar** *r.* Germany
179 H5 **Neckarsulm** Germany
117 H2 **Necker Island** U.S.A.
235 K3 **Necochea** Arg.
179 L1 **Neddemin** Germany
207 F2 **Nedlouc, Lac** *l.* Canada
Nêdong China *see* **Zêtang**
170 M1 **Nedre Soppero** Sweden
215 E4 **Needles** U.S.A.
148 C4 **Neemuch** India
208 C3 **Neenah** U.S.A.
205 J4 **Neepawa** Canada
203 J2 **Neergaard Lake** Canada
178 D3 **Neerijnen** Neth.
178 D3 **Neerpelt** Belgium
139 L2 **Neftçala** Azer.
156 F1 **Neftegorsk** Rus. Fed.
140 B1 **Neftegorsk** Rus. Fed.
132 G4 **Neftekamsk** Rus. Fed.
187 H6 **Neftekumsk** Rus. Fed.
132 I3 **Nefteyugansk** Rus. Fed.
173 C5 **Nefyn** U.K.
184 C6 **Nefza** Tunisia
195 B4 **Negage** Angola
194 D3 **Negēlē** Eth.
136 D5 **Negev** *des.* Israel
234 A3 **Negla** *r.* Para.
195 D5 **Negomane** Moz.
147 H5 **Negombo** Sri Lanka
185 J4 **Negotino** Macedonia
230 C5 **Negra, Cordillera** *mts* Peru
230 B5 **Negra, Punta** *pt* Peru
184 B7 **Négrine** Alg.
230 B4 **Negritos** Peru
235 J4 **Negro** *r.* Arg.
234 A2 **Negro** *r.* Brazil
231 F4 **Negro** *r.* S. America
235 L2 **Negro** *r.* Uruguay
161 I4 **Negros** *i.* Phil.
185 M3 **Negru Vodă** Romania
139 L4 **Nehavand** Iran
143 F4 **Nehbandān** Iran
150 E2 **Nehe** China
155 B4 **Neijiang** China
205 H4 **Neilburg** Canada
179 J3 **Neinstedt** Germany
176 G5 **Neiße** *r.* Germany/Poland
233 I4 **Neiva** Col.
154 D3 **Neixiang** China
205 J3 **Nejanilini Lake** Canada
142 D2 **Neka** Iran
194 D3 **Nek'emtē** Eth.
171 K5 **Neksø** Denmark
148 D3 **Nelang** India
123 C4 **Nelia** Australia
186 E3 **Nelidovo** Rus. Fed.
216 D3 **Neligh** U.S.A.
133 P3 **Nel'kan** Rus. Fed.
150 F1 **Nel'kan** Rus. Fed.
147 H3 **Nellore** India
156 E3 **Nel'ma** Rus. Fed.
204 F5 **Nelson** Canada
205 K3 **Nelson** *r.* Canada
126 D4 **Nelson** N.Z.
173 E4 **Nelson** U.K.
215 E4 **Nelson** U.S.A.
124 D7 **Nelson, Cape** Australia
232 B8 **Nelson, Estrecho** *str.* Chile
125 J4 **Nelson Bay** Australia
204 E3 **Nelson Forks** Canada
205 J3 **Nelson House** Canada
197 I2 **Nelspruit** S. Africa
192 B3 **Néma** Mauritania
186 I3 **Nema** Rus. Fed.
208 A2 **Nemadji** *r.* U.S.A.
187 B4 **Neman** Rus. Fed.
143 E4 **Ne'matābād** Iran
186 G3 **Nemda** *r.* Rus. Fed.
186 J2 **Nemed** Rus. Fed.
209 F2 **Nemegos** Canada
170 O1 **Nemetskiy, Mys** *c.* Rus. Fed.
156 B2 **Nemor He** *r.* China
182 F2 **Nemours** France
139 I2 **Nemrut Dağı** *mt.* Turkey
158 I3 **Nemuro** Japan
158 I3 **Nemuro-kaikyō** *sea chan.* Japan
187 D5 **Nemyriv** Ukr.
175 J5 **Nenagh** Ireland
173 H5 **Nene** *r.* U.K.
150 E2 **Nenjiang** China
156 B3 **Nen Jiang** *r.* China
179 E5 **Nennig** *tourist site* Germany
186 F1 **Nenoksa** Rus. Fed.
174 E1 **Neolithic Orkney** *tourist site* U.K.
217 E4 **Neosho** U.S.A.
217 E4 **Neosho** *r.* U.S.A.
149 E3 **Nepal** *country* Asia
152 D6 **Nepalganj** Nepal
209 J3 **Nepean** Canada
215 G2 **Nephi** U.S.A.
175 I3 **Nephin** *h.* Ireland
175 I3 **Nephin Beg Range** *hills* Ireland
194 C3 **Nepoko** *r.* Dem. Rep. Congo
Neptune U.S.A. *see* **Neptune City**
221 F4 **Neptune City** U.S.A.
182 E4 **Nérac** France
125 J1 **Nerang** Australia
150 D1 **Nerchinsk** Rus. Fed.
186 G3 **Nerekhta** Rus. Fed.
185 G3 **Neretva** *r.* Bos.-Herz./Croatia
195 C5 **Neriquinha** Angola
171 M5 **Neris** *r.* Lith.
186 F3 **Nerl'** *r.* Rus. Fed.
234 C2 **Nerópolis** Brazil
150 E1 **Neryungri** Rus. Fed.
178 D1 **Nes** Neth.
171 J3 **Nes** Norway
171 J3 **Nesbyen** Norway
170 D2 **Neskaupstaður** Iceland
178 A5 **Nesle** France
170 K2 **Nesna** Norway
174 D3 **Ness, Loch** *l.* U.K.
217 D4 **Ness City** U.S.A.
179 I4 **Nesse** *r.* Germany
204 C3 **Nesselrode, Mount** Canada/U.S.A.
185 K4 **Nestos** *r.* Greece
138 E5 **Netanya** Israel
205 M2 **Netchek, Cape** Canada
178 D2 **Netherlands** *country* Europe
233 J1 **Netherlands Antilles** *terr.* Caribbean Sea
179 G4 **Netphen** Germany
149 G4 **Netrakona** Bangl.
148 C5 **Netrang** India
203 K3 **Nettilling Lake** Canada
208 A1 **Nett Lake** U.S.A.
208 A1 **Nett Lake** *l.* U.S.A.
179 L1 **Neubrandenburg** Germany
176 C7 **Neuchâtel** Switz.
176 C7 **Neuchâtel, Lac de** *l.* Switz.
179 I5 **Neuendettelsau** Germany
179 E2 **Neuenhaus** Germany
179 H1 **Neuenkirchen** Germany
179 G2 **Neuenkirchen (Oldenburg)** Germany
178 D5 **Neufchâteau** Belgium
182 G2 **Neufchâteau** France
182 E2 **Neufchâtel-en-Bray** France
179 F1 **Neuharlingersiel** Germany
179 H1 **Neuhaus (Oste)** Germany
179 H4 **Neuhof** Germany
179 J1 **Neu Kaliß** Germany
179 H4 **Neukirchen** *Hessen* Germany
179 K4 **Neukirchen** *Sachsen* Germany
179 J5 **Neumarkt in der Oberpfalz** Germany
127 K3 **Neumayer** *research stn* Antarctica
176 D3 **Neumünster** Germany
179 K5 **Neunburg vorm Wald** Germany
177 H7 **Neunkirchen** Austria
179 F5 **Neunkirchen** Germany
235 I3 **Neuquén** Arg.
235 I3 **Neuquén** *prov.* Arg.
235 I3 **Neuquén** *r.* Arg.
179 K2 **Neuruppin** Germany
219 E5 **Neuse** *r.* U.S.A.
177 H7 **Neusiedler See** *l.* Austria/Hungary
179 E3 **Neuss** Germany
179 F4 **Neustadt (Wied)** Germany
179 H2 **Neustadt am Rübenberge** Germany
179 I5 **Neustadt an der Aisch** Germany
179 K5 **Neustadt an der Waldnaab** Germany
179 G5 **Neustadt an der Weinstraße** Germany
179 J4 **Neustadt bei Coburg** Germany
179 J1 **Neustadt-Glewe** Germany
179 L1 **Neustrelitz** Germany
179 K6 **Neutraubling** Germany
179 F4 **Neuwied** Germany
179 H1 **Neu Wulmstorf** Germany
217 E4 **Nevada** U.S.A.
215 D2 **Nevada** *state* U.S.A.
183 O4 **Nevada, Sierra** *mts* Spain
214 B1 **Nevada, Sierra** *mts* U.S.A.
235 I2 **Nevado, Cerro** *mt.* Arg.
235 I3 **Nevado, Sierra del** *mts* Arg.
225 E4 **Nevado de Toluca, Volcán** *vol.* Mex.
186 D3 **Nevel'** Rus. Fed.
156 F3 **Nevel'sk** Rus. Fed.
156 B1 **Never** Rus. Fed.
182 F3 **Nevers** France
125 G3 **Nevertire** Australia
185 H3 **Nevesinje** Bos.-Herz.
187 G6 **Nevinnomyssk** Rus. Fed.
174 C3 **Nevis, Loch** *inlet* U.K.
138 E2 **Nevşehir** Turkey
158 C2 **Nevskoye** Rus. Fed.
215 E5 **New** *r.* *CA* U.S.A.
220 C6 **New** *r.* *WV* U.S.A.
204 D3 **New Aiyansh** Canada
219 C4 **New Albany** *IN* U.S.A.
217 F5 **New Albany** *MS* U.S.A.
221 E4 **New Albany** *PA* U.S.A.
231 G2 **New Amsterdam** Guyana
125 G2 **New Angledool** Australia
221 F5 **Newark** *DE* U.S.A.
221 F5 **Newark** *MD* U.S.A.
221 F4 **Newark** *NJ* U.S.A.
221 E3 **Newark** *NY* U.S.A.
220 B4 **Newark** *OH* U.S.A.
221 F4 **Newark** *airport* U.S.A.
215 E2 **Newark Lake** U.S.A.
173 G4 **Newark-on-Trent** U.K.
221 E3 **Newark Valley** U.S.A.
221 H4 **New Bedford** U.S.A.
212 B2 **Newberg** U.S.A.
221 F3 **New Berlin** U.S.A.
219 E5 **New Bern** U.S.A.
209 E2 **Newberry** *MI* U.S.A.
219 D5 **Newberry** *SC* U.S.A.
215 D4 **Newberry Springs** U.S.A.
172 F2 **Newbiggin-by-the-Sea** U.K.
219 F7 **New Bight** Bahamas
209 I3 **Newboro** Canada
221 G3 **New Boston** *MA* U.S.A.
220 B5 **New Boston** *OH* U.S.A.
217 D6 **New Braunfels** U.S.A.
175 L4 **Newbridge** Ireland
119 E2 **New Britain** *i.* P.N.G.
221 G4 **New Britain** U.S.A.
236 F6 **New Britain Trench** *sea feature* Pacific Ocean
207 G4 **New Brunswick** *prov.* Canada
221 F4 **New Brunswick** U.S.A.
208 D5 **New Buffalo** U.S.A.
175 F3 **Newburgh** U.K.
221 F4 **Newburgh** U.S.A.
173 F6 **Newbury** U.K.
221 H3 **Newburyport** U.S.A.
172 E3 **Newby Bridge** U.K.
119 G4 **New Caledonia** *terr.* S. Pacific Ocean
236 F7 **New Caledonia Trough** *sea feature* Tasman Sea
207 G4 **New Carlisle** Canada
125 I4 **Newcastle** Australia
209 H4 **Newcastle** Canada
175 L4 **Newcastle** Ireland
197 H3 **Newcastle** S. Africa
175 M3 **Newcastle** U.K.
214 B2 **Newcastle** *CA* U.S.A.
209 E6 **New Castle** *IN* U.S.A.
220 B4 **Newcastle** *OH* U.S.A.
220 C4 **New Castle** *PA* U.S.A.
215 F3 **Newcastle** *UT* U.S.A.
220 C6 **New Castle** *VA* U.S.A.
213 F3 **Newcastle** *WY* U.S.A.
173 C5 **Newcastle Emlyn** U.K.
173 E4 **Newcastle-under-Lyme** U.K.
172 F3 **Newcastle upon Tyne** U.K.
120 F3 **Newcastle Waters** Australia
175 I5 **Newcastle West** Ireland
221 F6 **New Church** U.S.A.
215 H3 **Newcomb** U.S.A.
174 D5 **New Cumnock** U.K.
175 F3 **New Deer** U.K.
148 D3 **New Delhi** India
221 J1 **New Denmark** Canada
214 B3 **New Don Pedro Reservoir** U.S.A.
121 D5 **Newell, Lake** *salt flat* Australia
125 I3 **New England Range** *mts* Australia
239 F3 **New England Seamounts** *sea feature* N. Atlantic Ocean
173 E6 **Newent** U.K.
173 F7 **New Forest National Park** U.K.
203 M5 **Newfoundland** *i.* Canada
Newfoundland *prov.* Canada *see* **Newfoundland and Labrador**
207 I4 **Newfoundland and Labrador** *prov.* Canada
213 D3 **Newfoundland Evaporation Basin** *salt l.* U.S.A.
174 D5 **New Galloway** U.K.
119 F2 **New Georgia** *i.* Solomon Is
119 F2 **New Georgia Islands** Solomon Is
119 F2 **New Georgia Sound** *sea chan.* Solomon Is
207 H4 **New Glasgow** Canada
119 E2 **New Guinea** *i.* Asia
220 B4 **New Hampshire** U.S.A.
221 G3 **New Hampshire** *state* U.S.A.
208 A4 **New Hampton** U.S.A.
119 F2 **New Hanover** *i.* P.N.G.
197 I4 **New Hanover** S. Africa
221 G4 **New Haven** U.S.A.
204 D3 **New Hazelton** Canada
236 G7 **New Hebrides Trench** *sea feature* Pacific Ocean
214 B2 **New Hogan Reservoir** U.S.A.
208 C4 **New Holstein** U.S.A.
217 F6 **New Iberia** U.S.A.
197 I2 **Newington** S. Africa
175 K5 **Newinn** Ireland
119 F2 **New Ireland** *i.* P.N.G.
221 F5 **New Jersey** *state* U.S.A.
221 E6 **New Kent** U.S.A.
174 E5 **New Lanark** U.K.
121 C6 **Newland Range** *hills* Australia
220 B5 **New Lexington** U.S.A.
208 B4 **New Lisbon** U.S.A.
209 H2 **New Liskeard** Canada
221 G4 **New London** *CT* U.S.A.
208 B5 **New London** *IA* U.S.A.
208 B6 **New London** *MO* U.S.A.
208 C3 **New London** *WI* U.S.A.
118 B4 **Newman** Australia
208 D6 **Newman** U.S.A.
209 H3 **Newmarket** Canada
175 I5 **Newmarket** Ireland
173 H5 **Newmarket** U.K.
220 D5 **New Market** U.S.A.
175 J5 **Newmarket-on-Fergus** Ireland
220 C5 **New Martinsville** U.S.A.
212 C2 **New Meadows** U.S.A.
214 B3 **New Melones Lake** U.S.A.
213 F5 **New Mexico** *state* U.S.A.
219 C5 **Newnan** U.S.A.
125 G9 **New Norfolk** Australia
217 F6 **New Orleans** U.S.A.
221 F4 **New Paltz** U.S.A.
220 C4 **New Philadelphia** U.S.A.
175 F3 **New Pitsligo** U.K.
126 E3 **New Plymouth** N.Z.
175 I4 **Newport** *Mayo* Ireland
175 J5 **Newport** *Tipperary* Ireland
173 E5 **Newport** *England* U.K.
173 F7 **Newport** *England* U.K.
173 D6 **Newport** *Wales* U.K.
217 F5 **Newport** *AR* U.S.A.
220 A5 **Newport** *KY* U.S.A.
221 I2 **Newport** *ME* U.S.A.
209 F5 **Newport** *MI* U.S.A.
221 G3 **Newport** *NH* U.S.A.
212 A2 **Newport** *OR* U.S.A.
221 H4 **Newport** *RI* U.S.A.
221 G2 **Newport** *VT* U.S.A.
212 C1 **Newport** *WA* U.S.A.
215 D5 **Newport Beach** U.S.A.
211 K4 **Newport News** U.S.A.
221 E6 **Newport News** *airport* U.S.A.
173 G5 **Newport Pagnell** U.K.
219 E7 **New Providence** *i.* Bahamas
173 B7 **Newquay** U.K.
207 G4 **New Richmond** Canada
208 A3 **New Richmond** U.S.A.
215 F5 **New River** U.S.A.
217 F6 **New Roads** U.S.A.
173 H7 **New Romney** U.K.
175 L5 **New Ross** Ireland
120 E3 **Newry** Australia
175 L3 **Newry** U.K.
208 A5 **New Sharon** U.S.A.
133 P2 **New Siberia Islands** Rus. Fed.
219 D6 **New Smyrna Beach** U.S.A.
125 G4 **New South Wales** *state* Australia
155 □ **New Territories** *reg.* *Hong Kong* China
173 E4 **Newton** U.K.
216 E3 **Newton** *IA* U.S.A.
217 D4 **Newton** *KS* U.S.A.
221 H3 **Newton** *MA* U.S.A.
217 F5 **Newton** *MS* U.S.A.
221 F4 **Newton** *NJ* U.S.A.
173 D7 **Newton Abbot** U.K.
175 F3 **Newtonhill** U.K.
174 D5 **Newton Mearns** U.K.
174 D6 **Newton Stewart** U.K.
175 J5 **Newtown** Ireland
173 E5 **Newtown** *England* U.K.
173 D5 **Newtown** *Wales* U.K.
216 C1 **New Town** U.S.A.
175 M3 **Newtownabbey** U.K.
175 M3 **Newtownards** U.K.
175 K3 **Newtownbutler** U.K.
175 L4 **Newtown Mount Kennedy** Ireland
175 F5 **Newtown St Boswells** U.K.
175 K3 **Newtownstewart** U.K.
216 E2 **New Ulm** U.S.A.
214 A2 **Newville** U.S.A.
204 E5 **New Westminster** Canada
221 G4 **New York** U.S.A. (City Plan **104**)
221 E3 **New York** *state* U.S.A.
126 **New Zealand** *country* Oceania
186 G3 **Neya** Rus. Fed.
143 E4 **Ney Bīd** Iran
142 D4 **Neyrīz** Iran
143 E2 **Neyshābūr** Iran
147 H4 **Neyyattinkara** India
225 F4 **Nezahualcóyotl, Presa** *resr* Mex.
163 H2 **Ngabang** Indon.
195 B4 **Ngabé** Congo
162 A2 **Nga Chong, Khao** *mt.* Myanmar/Thai.
161 J6 **Ngalipaëng** Indon.
120 C1 **Ngalu** Indon.
195 C6 **Ngami, Lake** Botswana
149 F3 **Ngamring** China
149 E3 **Ngangla Ringco** *salt l.* China
149 E2 **Nganglong Kangri** *mt.* China
149 E2 **Nganglong Kangri** *mts* China
149 F3 **Ngangzê Co** *salt l.* China
162 C1 **Ngan Sâu, Sông** *r.* Vietnam
Ngan Sau, Sông *r.* Vietnam *see* **Ngan Sâu, Sông**
155 B6 **Ngân Sơn** Vietnam
162 A1 **Ngao** Thai.
193 D4 **Ngaoundéré** Cameroon
126 E2 **Ngaruawahia** N.Z.
126 F3 **Ngaruroro** *r.* N.Z.
126 E3 **Ngauruhoe** *vol.* N.Z.
162 B1 **Ngiap** *r.* Laos
120 D1 **Ngilmina** Indon.
195 B4 **Ngo** Congo
Ngoc Linh *mt.* Vietnam *see* **Ngok Linh**
149 F3 **Ngoin, Co** *salt l.* China
162 C2 **Ngok Linh** *mt.* Vietnam
193 D4 **Ngol Bembo** Nigeria
149 F2 **Ngoqumaima** China
150 B3 **Ngoring Hu** *l.* China
195 D4 **Ngorongoro Conservation Area** *nature res.* Tanz.
193 D3 **Ngourti** Niger
193 D3 **Nguigmi** Niger
120 E1 **Nguiu** Australia
122 A2 **Ngukurr** Australia
151 F6 **Ngulu** *atoll* Micronesia
162 B1 **Ngum, Nam** *r.* Laos
193 D3 **Nguru** Nigeria
Nguyên Binh Vietnam *see* **Ngân Sơn**
Ngwaketse *admin. dist.* Botswana *see* **Southern**
197 G3 **Ngwathe** S. Africa
197 I3 **Ngwavuma** *r.* Swaziland
197 I4 **Ngwelezana** S. Africa
195 D5 **Nhamalabué** Moz.
163 D2 **Nha Trang** Vietnam
124 D6 **Nhill** Australia
197 I3 **Nhlangano** Swaziland
155 B6 **Nho Quan** Vietnam
118 D3 **Nhulunbuy** Australia
205 I4 **Niacam** Canada
192 B3 **Niafounké** Mali
209 H4 **Niagara** *r.* Canada/U.S.A.
208 D3 **Niagara** U.S.A.
209 H4 **Niagara Falls** Canada
220 D3 **Niagara Falls** U.S.A.
192 C3 **Niamey** Niger
161 J5 **Niampak** Indon.
195 D4 **Niangandu** Tanz.
194 C3 **Niangara** Dem. Rep. Congo
156 A3 **Nianzishan** China
163 E2 **Nias** *i.* Indon.
121 D4 **Nibil Well** Australia
171 M4 **Nīca** Latvia
224 H5 **Nicaragua** *country* Central America
224 H6 **Nicaragua, Lake** Nicaragua
185 G5 **Nicastro** Italy
183 H5 **Nice** France
207 F3 **Nichicun, Lac** *l.* Canada
149 E4 **Nichlaul** India
219 E7 **Nicholl's Town** Bahamas
122 B3 **Nicholson** *r.* Australia
209 F2 **Nicholson** Canada
121 B5 **Nicholson Range** *hills* Australia
135 H6 **Nicobar Islands** India
138 D4 **Nicosia** Cyprus
224 H6 **Nicoya, Golfo de** *b.* Costa Rica
224 H6 **Nicoya, Península de** *pen.* Costa Rica
221 J1 **Nictau** Canada
171 M5 **Nida** Lith.
173 F4 **Nidd** *r.* U.K.
179 H4 **Nidda** Germany
179 H4 **Nidder** *r.* Germany
177 J4 **Nidzica** Poland
176 D3 **Niebüll** Germany
179 E5 **Niederanven** Lux.
179 H4 **Niederaula** Germany
176 F7 **Niedere Tauern** *mts* Austria
179 G2 **Niedersachsen** *Land* Germany
179 E1 **Niedersächsisches Wattenmeer, Nationalpark** Germany
193 D4 **Niefang** Equat. Guinea
192 B3 **Niellé** Côte d'Ivoire
179 H2 **Nienburg (Weser)** Germany
179 E3 **Niers** *r.* Germany
179 G5 **Nierstein** Germany

234 A1 **Nossa Senhora do Livramento** Brazil
171 K4 **Nossebro** Sweden
196 C2 **Nossob** *watercourse* Africa *alt.* **Nosop**
195 E6 **Nosy Varika** Madag.
215 F2 **Notch Peak** U.S.A.
177 H4 **Noteć** *r.* Poland
184 F6 **Noto, Golfo di** *g. Sicily* Italy
171 J4 **Notodden** Norway
159 E6 **Noto-hantō** *pen.* Japan
207 G4 **Notre-Dame, Monts** *mts* Canada
207 J4 **Notre Dame Bay** Canada
209 J3 **Notre-Dame-de-la-Salette** Canada
221 H2 **Notre-Dame-des-Bois** Canada
209 J2 **Notre-Dame-du-Laus** Canada
209 H2 **Notre-Dame-du-Nord** Canada
209 G3 **Nottawasaga Bay** Canada
206 E3 **Nottaway** *r.* Canada
173 F5 **Nottingham** U.K.
221 E6 **Nottoway** *r.* U.S.A.
179 F3 **Nottuln** Germany
205 H5 **Notukeu Creek** *r.* Canada
192 A2 **Nouâdhibou** Mauritania
192 A3 **Nouakchott** Mauritania
192 A3 **Nouâmghâr** Mauritania
162 C2 **Nouei** Vietnam
119 G4 **Nouméa** New Caledonia
192 B3 **Nouna** Burkina
197 F5 **Noupoort** S. Africa
170 O2 **Nousu** Fin.
119 G4 **Nouvelle-Calédonie** *i.* S. Pacific Ocean
141 G4 **Nov** Tajik.
234 C1 **Nova América** Brazil
234 B3 **Nova Esperança** Brazil
234 D3 **Nova Friburgo** Brazil
185 G2 **Nova Gradiška** Croatia
234 C3 **Nova Granada** Brazil
234 D3 **Nova Iguaçu** Brazil
187 E6 **Nova Kakhovka** Ukr.
234 D2 **Nova Lima** Brazil
187 D4 **Novalukoml'** Belarus
187 D6 **Nova Odesa** Ukr.
234 C2 **Nova Ponte** Brazil
234 C2 **Nova Ponte, Represa** *resr* Brazil
184 C2 **Novara** Italy
234 C1 **Nova Roma** Brazil
207 H5 **Nova Scotia** *prov.* Canada
214 A2 **Novato** U.S.A.
234 E2 **Nova Venécia** Brazil
234 B1 **Nova Xavantino** Brazil
140 B2 **Novaya Kazanka** Kazakh.
169 M3 **Novaya Ladoga** Rus. Fed.
133 Q2 **Novaya Sibir', Ostrov** *i.* Rus. Fed.
156 E2 **Novaya Ussura** Rus. Fed.
132 G2 **Novaya Zemlya** *is* Rus. Fed.
185 L3 **Nova Zagora** Bulg.
183 P3 **Novelda** Spain
177 I7 **Nové Zámky** Slovakia
186 E3 **Novgorodskaya Oblast'** *admin. div.* Rus. Fed.
187 E5 **Novhorod-Sivers'kyy** Ukr.
141 J1 **Novichikha** Rus. Fed.
185 J3 **Novi Iskŭr** Bulg.
158 H1 **Novikovo** Rus. Fed.
184 C2 **Novi Ligure** Italy
185 L3 **Novi Pazar** Bulg.
185 I3 **Novi Pazar** Serbia
185 H2 **Novi Sad** Serbia
187 G6 **Novoaleksandrovsk** Rus. Fed.
152 D1 **Novoaltaysk** Rus. Fed.
187 G5 **Novoanninskiy** Rus. Fed.
231 F5 **Novo Aripuanã** Brazil
187 F6 **Novoazovs'k** Ukr.
141 G5 **Novobod** Tajik.
186 H3 **Novocheboksarsk** Rus. Fed.
187 G6 **Novocherkassk** Rus. Fed.
141 H2 **Novodolinka** Kazakh.
186 G1 **Novodvinsk** Rus. Fed.
156 B2 **Novogeorgiyevka** Rus. Fed.
232 F3 **Novo Hamburgo** Brazil
234 C3 **Novo Horizonte** Brazil
176 G6 **Novohradské hory** *mts* Czech Rep.
187 C5 **Novohrad-Volyns'kyy** Ukr.
141 F1 **Novoishimskiy** Kazakh.
140 D1 **Novokaolinovyy** Rus. Fed.
156 C2 **Novokiyevskiy Uval** Rus. Fed.
187 G6 **Novokubansk** Rus. Fed.
140 B1 **Novokuybyshevsk** Rus. Fed.
150 A1 **Novokuznetsk** Rus. Fed.
127 K3 **Novolazarevskaya** *research stn* Antarctica
141 H2 **Novomarkovka** Kazakh.
184 F2 **Novo Mesto** Slovenia
187 F4 **Novomichurinsk** Rus. Fed.
187 F6 **Novomikhaylovskiy** Rus. Fed.
187 F4 **Novomoskovsk** Rus. Fed.
187 E5 **Novomoskovs'k** Ukr.
187 D5 **Novomyrhorod** Ukr.
187 G5 **Novonikolayevskiy** Rus. Fed.
141 G1 **Novonikolskoye** Kazakh.
187 E6 **Novooleksiyivka** Ukr.
140 D2 **Novoorsk** Rus. Fed.
141 F1 **Novopokrovka** *Kustanayskaya Oblast'* Kazakh.
141 F1 **Novopokrovka** *Severnyy Kazakhstan* Kazakh.
141 J2 **Novopokrovka** *Vostochnyy Kazakhstan* Kazakh.
158 D2 **Novopokrovka** Rus. Fed.
187 G6 **Novopokrovskaya** Rus. Fed.
187 I5 **Novorepnoye** Rus. Fed.
156 C1 **Novorossiyka** Rus. Fed.
187 F6 **Novorossiysk** Rus. Fed.
133 L2 **Novorybnaya** Rus. Fed.
177 N2 **Novorzhev** Rus. Fed.
187 E6 **Novoselivs'ke** Ukr.
Novoselskoye Rus. Fed. *see* **Achkhoy-Martan**
177 N1 **Novosel'ye** Rus. Fed.
140 C1 **Novosergiyevka** Rus. Fed.
187 F6 **Novoshakhtinsk** Rus. Fed.
158 C2 **Novoshakhtinskiy** Rus. Fed.
133 J4 **Novosibirsk** Rus. Fed.
Novosibirskiye Ostrova *is* Rus. Fed. *see* **New Siberia Islands**
186 D3 **Novosokol'niki** Rus. Fed.
187 H4 **Novospasskoye** Rus. Fed.
140 D2 **Novotroitsk** Rus. Fed.
187 E6 **Novotroyits'ke** Ukr.
187 D5 **Novoukrayinka** Ukr.
140 D2 **Novoural'sk** Rus. Fed.
187 I5 **Novouzensk** Rus. Fed.
141 H1 **Novovarshavka** Rus. Fed.
187 C5 **Novovolyns'k** Ukr.
187 F5 **Novovoronezh** Rus. Fed.
156 B1 **Novovoskresenovka** Rus. Fed.
141 J2 **Novoyegor'yevskoye** Rus. Fed.
187 D4 **Novozybkov** Rus. Fed.
177 H6 **Nový Jičín** Czech Rep.
Novyy Afon Georgia *see* **Akhali Ap'oni**
187 F5 **Novyy Oskol** Rus. Fed.
132 I3 **Novyy Port** Rus. Fed.
186 I3 **Novyy Tor'yal** Rus. Fed.
132 I3 **Novyy Urengoy** Rus. Fed.
150 F1 **Novyy Urgal** Rus. Fed.
142 D4 **Now** Iran
217 E4 **Nowata** U.S.A.
142 C3 **Nowbarān** Iran
143 E3 **Now Deh** Iran
139 L3 **Nowdī** Iran
148 D4 **Nowgong** India
205 I2 **Nowleye Lake** Canada
176 G4 **Nowogard** Poland
125 I5 **Nowra** Australia
142 C2 **Nowshahr** Iran
142 C2 **Nowshahr** Iran
148 C2 **Nowshera** Pak.
177 J6 **Nowy Sącz** Poland
177 J6 **Nowy Targ** Poland
221 E4 **Noxen** U.S.A.
162 C1 **Noy, Xé** *r.* Laos
162 C1 **Noy, Xé** *r.* Laos
132 I3 **Noyabr'sk** Rus. Fed.
204 C3 **Noyes Island** U.S.A.
182 F2 **Noyon** France
150 C2 **Noyon** Mongolia
197 F5 **Nozizwe** S. Africa
197 G6 **Nqamakwe** S. Africa
197 I4 **Nqutu** S. Africa
195 D5 **Nsanje** Malawi
195 B4 **Ntandembele** Dem. Rep. Congo
197 G3 **Ntha** S. Africa
185 K5 **Ntoro, Kavo** *pt* Greece
195 D4 **Ntungamo** Uganda
193 F3 **Nuba Mountains** Sudan
139 J1 **Nubarashen** Armenia
193 F2 **Nubian Desert** Sudan
235 H3 **Ñuble** *r.* Chile
Nüden Mongolia *see* **Ulaanbadrah**
230 D7 **Nudo Coropuna** *mt.* Peru
217 D6 **Nueces** *r.* U.S.A.
205 J2 **Nueltin Lake** Canada
224 G5 **Nueva Arcadia** Hond.
224 H5 **Nueva Armenia** Hond.
233 J2 **Nueva Florida** Venez.
235 L2 **Nueva Helvecia** Uruguay
235 H3 **Nueva Imperial** Chile
Nueva Loja Ecuador *see* **Lago Agrio**
232 B6 **Nueva Lubecka** Arg.
225 G5 **Nueva Ocotepeque** Hond.
225 D2 **Nueva Rosita** Mex.
225 G5 **Nueva San Salvador** El Salvador
223 I4 **Nuevitas** Cuba
235 J4 **Nuevo, Golfo** *g.* Arg.
222 C2 **Nuevo Casas Grandes** Mex.
224 C2 **Nuevo Ideal** Mex.
225 E2 **Nuevo Laredo** Mex.
225 E2 **Nuevo León** *state* Mex.
194 E3 **Nugaal** *watercourse* Somalia
126 B7 **Nugget Point** N.Z.
119 F2 **Nuguria Islands** P.N.G.
126 F3 **Nuhaka** N.Z.
119 H2 **Nui** *atoll* Tuvalu
162 C2 **Nui Ti On** *mt.* Vietnam
Nu Jiang *r.* China *see* **Salween**
124 A4 **Nukey Bluff** *h.* Australia
142 D3 **Nūklok, Chāh-e** *well* Iran
Nuku'alofa Tonga *see* **Nuku'alofa**
119 I4 **Nuku'alofa** Tonga
119 H2 **Nukufetau** *atoll* Tuvalu
117 J5 **Nuku Hiva** *i.* Fr. Polynesia
119 H2 **Nukulaelae** *atoll* Tuvalu
119 F2 **Nukumanu Islands** P.N.G.
Nukunono *i.* Pacific Ocean *see* **Nukunonu**
119 I2 **Nukunonu** *atoll* Pacific Ocean
140 D4 **Nukus** Uzbek.
118 C4 **Nullagine** Australia
121 E6 **Nullarbor** Australia
121 E6 **Nullarbor National Park** Australia
118 C5 **Nullarbor Plain** Australia
121 E6 **Nullarbor Regional Reserve** *park* Australia
154 F1 **Nulu'erhu Shan** *mts* China
125 F2 **Numalla, Lake** *salt flat* Australia
193 D4 **Numan** Nigeria
159 F6 **Numata** Japan
159 F7 **Numazu** Japan
122 A2 **Numbulwar** Australia
171 J3 **Numedal** *val.* Norway
151 F7 **Numfoor** *i.* Indon.
156 B3 **Numin He** *r.* China
125 F6 **Numurkah** Australia
207 H2 **Nunaksaluk Island** Canada
203 N3 **Nunakuluut** *i.* Greenland
Nunap Isua *c.* Greenland *see* **Farewell, Cape**
206 E2 **Nunavik** *reg.* U.S.A.
203 H3 **Nunavut** *admin. div.* Canada
221 E3 **Nunda** U.S.A.
125 I3 **Nundle** Australia
173 F5 **Nuneaton** U.K.
125 H6 **Nungatta National Park** Australia
205 K4 **Nungesser Lake** Canada
153 K2 **Nungnain Sum** China
202 B4 **Nunivak Island** U.S.A.
148 D2 **Nunkun** *mt.* India
133 T3 **Nunligran** Rus. Fed.
183 M2 **Nuñomoral** Spain
178 D2 **Nunspeet** Neth.
184 C4 **Nuoro** *Sardinia* Italy
119 G3 **Nupani** *i.* Solomon Is
146 B4 **Nuqrah** Saudi Arabia
233 H3 **Nuquí** Col.
149 E1 **Nur** China
142 D2 **Nur** *r.* Iran
141 H2 **Nura** Kazakh.
141 G2 **Nura** *r.* Kazakh.
142 C4 **Nūrābād** Iran
Nurata Uzbek. *see* **Nurota**
Nuratau, Khrebet *mts* Uzbek. *see* **Nurota tizmasi**
136 D3 **Nur Dağları** *mts* Turkey
179 J5 **Nuremberg** Germany
143 H3 **Nūrestān** Afgh.
143 H3 **Nūrestān** *reg.* Afgh.
139 I2 **Nurettin** Turkey
224 B1 **Nuri** Mex.
124 C5 **Nuriootpa** Australia
187 I4 **Nurlaty** Rus. Fed.
171 O3 **Nurmes** Fin.
171 M3 **Nurmo** Fin.
Nürnberg Germany *see* **Nuremberg**
141 F4 **Nurota** Uzbek.
141 F4 **Nurota tizmasi** *mts* Uzbek.
125 G3 **Nurri, Mount** *h.* Australia
149 H1 **Nur Turu** China
139 H3 **Nusaybin** Turkey
139 F4 **Nuşayrīyah, Jabal an** *mts* Syria
152 G6 **Nu Shan** *mts* China
143 G4 **Nushki** Pak.
207 H2 **Nutak** Canada
215 H5 **Nutrioso** U.S.A.
148 B3 **Nuttal** Pak.
120 F2 **Nutwood Downs** Australia
240 U2 **Nuuk** Greenland
170 N2 **Nuupas** Fin.
203 M2 **Nuussuaq** Greenland
203 M2 **Nuussuaq** *pen.* Greenland
147 I5 **Nuwara Eliya** Sri Lanka
136 D5 **Nuwaybi' al Muzayyinah** Egypt
Nuweiba el Muzeina Egypt *see* **Nuwaybi' al Muzayyinah**
196 C5 **Nuwerus** S. Africa
196 D6 **Nuweveldberge** *mts* S. Africa
121 B7 **Nuyts, Point** Australia
121 F7 **Nuyts Archipelago** *is* Australia
139 J4 **Nuzi** *tourist site* Iraq
197 I1 **Nwanedi Nature Reserve** S. Africa
132 H3 **Nyagan'** Rus. Fed.
125 E5 **Nyah West** Australia
149 G3 **Nyainqêntanglha Feng** *mt.* China
149 G3 **Nyainqêntanglha Shan** *mts* China
149 H2 **Nyainrong** China
171 L3 **Nyåker** Sweden
193 E3 **Nyala** Sudan
Nyalam China *see* **Congdü**
195 C5 **Nyamandhiovu** Zimbabwe
186 G2 **Nyandoma** Rus. Fed.
186 F2 **Nyandomskiy Vozvyshennost'** *hills* Rus. Fed.
195 B4 **Nyanga** *r.* Gabon
195 D5 **Nyanga** Zimbabwe
149 G3 **Nyang Qu** *r. Xizang* China
149 H3 **Nyang Qu** *r. Xizang* China
148 D3 **Nyar** *r.* India
195 D5 **Nyasa, Lake** Africa
187 C4 **Nyasvizh** Belarus
171 J5 **Nyborg** Denmark
170 O1 **Nyborg** Norway
171 K4 **Nybro** Sweden
203 M1 **Nyeboe Land** *reg.* Greenland
149 G3 **Nyêmo** China
195 D4 **Nyeri** Kenya
149 F3 **Nyima** China
151 B4 **Nyingchi** China
177 J7 **Nyíregyháza** Hungary
171 M3 **Nykarleby** Fin.
171 J5 **Nykøbing** Denmark
171 J5 **Nykøbing Sjælland** Denmark
171 L4 **Nyköping** Sweden
171 L3 **Nyland** Sweden
Nylstroom S. Africa *see* **Modimolle**
125 G4 **Nymagee** Australia
125 J2 **Nymboida** Australia
125 J2 **Nymboida** *r.* Australia
171 L4 **Nynäshamn** Sweden
125 G3 **Nyngan** Australia
177 K4 **Nyoman** *r.* Belarus/Lith.
176 C7 **Nyon** Switz.
149 F3 **Nyonni Ri** *mt.* China
182 G4 **Nyons** France
132 G3 **Nyrob** Rus. Fed.
177 H5 **Nysa** Poland
156 F2 **Nysh** Rus. Fed.
186 I2 **Nyuchpas** Rus. Fed.
159 F5 **Nyūdō-zaki** *pt* Japan
195 C4 **Nyunzu** Dem. Rep. Congo
133 M3 **Nyurba** Rus. Fed.
186 I2 **Nyuvchim** Rus. Fed.
156 F1 **Nyyskiy Zaliv** *lag.* Rus. Fed.
187 E6 **Nyzhn'ohirs'kyy** Ukr.
195 D4 **Nzega** Tanz.
192 B4 **Nzérékoré** Guinea
195 B4 **N'zeto** Angola
197 I1 **Nzhelele Dam** S. Africa
195 E5 **Nzwani** *i.* Comoros

O

216 C2 **Oahe, Lake** U.S.A.
Oahu *i.* U.S.A. *see* **O'ahu**
214 □1 **O'ahu** *i.* U.S.A.
124 D4 **Oakbank** Australia
215 F2 **Oak City** U.S.A.
217 E6 **Oakdale** U.S.A.
216 D2 **Oakes** U.S.A.
125 I1 **Oakey** Australia
173 G5 **Oakham** U.K.
212 B1 **Oak Harbor** U.S.A.
220 C6 **Oak Hill** U.S.A.
214 C3 **Oakhurst** U.S.A.
208 B2 **Oak Island** U.S.A.
214 A3 **Oakland** *CA* U.S.A.
220 D5 **Oakland** *MD* U.S.A.
216 D3 **Oakland** *NE* U.S.A.
213 B3 **Oakland** *OR* U.S.A.
125 G5 **Oaklands** Australia
208 D5 **Oak Lawn** U.S.A.
217 C4 **Oakley** U.S.A.
118 C4 **Oakover** *r.* Australia
213 B3 **Oakridge** U.S.A.
219 C4 **Oak Ridge** U.S.A.
124 D4 **Oakvale** Australia
209 H4 **Oakville** Canada
126 C6 **Oamaru** N.Z.
126 D5 **Oaro** N.Z.
161 I3 **Oas** Phil.
213 D3 **Oasis** U.S.A.
127 I6 **Oates Land** *reg.* Antarctica
125 G9 **Oatlands** Australia
215 E4 **Oatman** U.S.A.
225 E4 **Oaxaca** Mex.
225 E4 **Oaxaca** *state* Mex.
132 H3 **Ob'** *r.* Rus. Fed.
193 D4 **Obala** Cameroon
159 D7 **Obama** Japan
174 C4 **Oban** U.K.
159 G5 **Obanazawa** Japan
183 M1 **O Barco** Spain
207 F4 **Obatogamau, Lac** Canada
204 F4 **Obed** Canada
126 B6 **Obelisk** *mt.* N.Z.
179 H4 **Oberaula** Germany
179 I3 **Oberdorla** Germany
179 E3 **Oberhausen** Germany
217 C4 **Oberlin** *KS* U.S.A.
220 B4 **Oberlin** *OH* U.S.A.
179 F5 **Obermoschel** Germany
125 H4 **Oberon** Australia
179 K5 **Oberpfälzer Wald** *mts* Germany
179 H4 **Obersinn** Germany
179 H4 **Oberthulba** Germany
179 G4 **Obertshausen** Germany
179 H3 **Oberwälder Land** *reg.* Germany
151 E7 **Obi** *i.* Indon.
231 G4 **Óbidos** Brazil
141 G5 **Obigarm** Tajik.
158 H3 **Obihiro** Japan
187 H6 **Obil'noye** Rus. Fed.
233 J2 **Obispos** Venez.
150 F2 **Obluch'ye** Rus. Fed.
187 F4 **Obninsk** Rus. Fed.
194 C3 **Obo** Centr. Afr. Rep.
154 A2 **Obo** China
194 E2 **Obock** Djibouti
160 E3 **Ŏbŏk** N. Korea
195 C4 **Obokote** Dem. Rep. Congo
144 H4 **Obo Liang** China
187 E5 **Oboyan'** Rus. Fed.
186 G2 **Obozerskiy** Rus. Fed.
149 E4 **Obra** India
149 E4 **Obra Dam** India
224 B1 **Obregón, Presa** *resr* Mex.
185 I2 **Obrenovac** Serbia
138 D2 **Obruk** Turkey
221 F6 **Observatory Hill** Australia
140 B2 **Obshchiy Syrt** *hills* Rus. Fed.
132 I2 **Obskaya Guba** *sea chan.* Rus. Fed.
192 B4 **Obuasi** Ghana
187 D5 **Obukhiv** Ukr.
186 I2 **Ob"yachevo** Rus. Fed.
219 D6 **Ocala** U.S.A.
233 K4 **Ocamo** *r.* Venez.
225 D2 **Ocampo** Mex.
233 I2 **Ocaña** Col.
183 O3 **Ocaña** Spain
230 E7 **Occidental, Cordillera** *mts* Chile
233 H4 **Occidental, Cordillera** *mts* Col.
230 C6 **Occidental, Cordillera** *mts* Peru
204 B3 **Ocean Cape** U.S.A.
221 F5 **Ocean City** *MD* U.S.A.
221 F5 **Ocean City** *NJ* U.S.A.
204 D4 **Ocean Falls** Canada
215 D5 **Oceanside** U.S.A.
217 F6 **Ocean Springs** U.S.A.
187 D6 **Ochakiv** Ukr.
187 G7 **Och'amch'ire** Georgia
157 G4 **Ochiishi-misaki** *pt* Japan
174 E4 **Ochil Hills** U.K.
148 C1 **Ochili Pass** Afgh.
179 I5 **Ochsenfurt** Germany
179 F2 **Ochtrup** Germany
171 L3 **Ockelbo** Sweden
177 L7 **Ocolaşul Mare, Vârful** *mt.* Romania
211 J5 **Oconee** *r.* U.S.A.
208 C4 **Oconomowoc** U.S.A.
208 D3 **Oconto** U.S.A.
225 F4 **Ocosingo** Mex.
224 H5 **Ocotal** Nicaragua
215 D5 **Ocotillo Wells** U.S.A.
225 D3 **Ocotlán** Mex.
120 D1 **Ocussi** *enclave* East Timor
192 B4 **Oda** Ghana
159 C7 **Ōda** Japan
170 C2 **Ódáðahraun** *lava field* Iceland
160 E3 **Ŏdaejin** N. Korea
158 G4 **Ōdate** Japan
159 F7 **Odawara** Japan
171 I3 **Odda** Norway
205 J3 **Odei** *r.* Canada
208 C5 **Odell** U.S.A.
183 L4 **Odemira** Port.
138 A2 **Ödemiş** Turkey
197 G3 **Odendaalsrus** S. Africa
171 J5 **Odense** Denmark
179 G5 **Odenwald** *reg.* Germany
179 I3 **Oder** *r.* Germany *alt.* **Odra (Poland)**
176 G3 **Oderbucht** *b.* Germany
Odesa Ukr. *see* **Odessa**
187 D6 **Odessa** Ukr.
171 K4 **Ödeshog** Sweden
217 C6 **Odessa** U.S.A.
141 H1 **Odesskoye** Rus. Fed.
183 M4 **Odiel** *r.* Spain
192 B4 **Odienné** Côte d'Ivoire
187 F4 **Odintsovo** Rus. Fed.
162 C3 **Ôdôngk** Cambodia
176 G4 **Odra** *r.* Poland *alt.* **Oder (Germany)**
231 J5 **Oeiras** Brazil
216 C3 **Oelrichs** U.S.A.
179 K4 **Oelsnitz** Germany
208 B4 **Oelwein** U.S.A.
178 D1 **Oenkerk** Neth.
120 F2 **Oenpelli** Australia
139 H1 **Of** Turkey
185 G4 **Ofanto** *r.* Italy
179 G4 **Offenbach am Main** Germany
179 F6 **Offenburg** Germany
185 L6 **Ofidoussa** *i.* Greece
159 G5 **Ōfunato** Japan
159 F5 **Oga** Japan
194 E3 **Ogadēn** *reg.* Eth.
159 F5 **Oga-hantō** *pen.* Japan
159 E7 **Ōgaki** Japan
216 C3 **Ogallala** U.S.A.
Ogasawara-shotō *is* Japan *see* **Bonin Islands**
209 H2 **Ogascanane, Lac** *l.* Canada
192 C4 **Ogbomosho** Nigeria
Ogbomoso Nigeria *see* **Ogbomosho**
216 E3 **Ogden** *IA* U.S.A.
213 E3 **Ogden** *UT* U.S.A.
204 C3 **Ogden, Mount** Canada
221 F2 **Ogdensburg** U.S.A.
202 E3 **Ogilvie** *r.* Canada
202 E3 **Ogilvie Mountains** Canada
140 C5 **Oglanly** Turkm.
219 C5 **Oglethorpe, Mount** U.S.A.
184 D1 **Oglio** *r.* Italy
156 E1 **Oglongi** Rus. Fed.
123 E4 **Ogmore** Australia
156 D1 **Ogodzha** Rus. Fed.
192 C4 **Ogoja** Nigeria
206 C3 **Ogoki** *r.* Canada
206 C3 **Ogoki Reservoir** Canada
156 C1 **Ogoron** Rus. Fed.
185 J3 **Ogosta** *r.* Bulg.
171 N4 **Ogre** Latvia
Ogurchinskiy, Ostrov *i.* Turkm. *see* **Ogurjaly Adasy**
140 C5 **Ogurjaly Adasy** *i.* Turkm.
139 K1 **Oğuz** Azer.
126 A6 **Ohai** N.Z.
126 E3 **Ohakune** N.Z.
158 G4 **Ōhata** Japan
126 B6 **Ohau, Lake** N.Z.
235 H2 **O'Higgins** *admin. reg.* Chile
127 L2 **O'Higgins (Chile)** *research stn* Antarctica
232 B7 **O'Higgins, Lago** *l.* Chile
219 C4 **Ohio** *r.* U.S.A.

220 B4 Ohio state U.S.A.
179 G4 Ohm r. Germany
179 I4 Ohrdruf Germany
179 K4 Ohře r. Czech Rep.
179 J2 Ohre r. Germany
185 I4 Ohrid Macedonia
185 I4 Ohrid, Lake Albania/Macedonia
197 I2 Ohrigstad S. Africa
179 H5 Öhringen Germany
126 E3 Ohura N.Z.
231 H3 Oiapoque Brazil
174 D3 Oich, Loch l. U.K.
149 H3 Oiga China
178 A4 Oignies France
220 D4 Oil City U.S.A.
214 C4 Oildale U.S.A.
182 F2 Oise r. France
178 B5 Oise à l'Aisne, Canal de l' France
159 B8 Ōita Japan
185 J5 Oiti mt. Greece
214 C4 Ojai U.S.A.
235 J2 Ojeda Arg.
208 B3 Ojibwa U.S.A.
222 D3 Ojinaga Mex.
225 E4 Ojitlán Mex.
159 F6 Ojiya Japan
224 A2 Ojo de Liebre, Lago b. Mex.
232 C3 Ojos del Salado, Nevado mt. Arg.
153 H1 Oka r. Rus. Fed.
187 G4 Oka r. Rus. Fed.
195 B6 Okahandja Namibia
126 E3 Okahukura N.Z.
195 B6 Okakarara Namibia
207 H2 Okak Islands Canada
204 F5 Okanagan Falls Canada
204 F4 Okanagan Lake Canada
212 C1 Okanogan r. Canada/U.S.A.
204 F5 Okanogan U.S.A.
212 B1 Okanogan Range mts U.S.A.
194 C3 Okapi, Parc National de la nat. park Dem. Rep. Congo
148 C3 Okara Pak.
Okarem Turkm. see Ekerem
195 B5 Okaukuejo Namibia
195 C5 Okavango r. Botswana/Namibia
195 C5 Okavango Delta swamp Botswana
159 F6 Okaya Japan
159 C7 Okayama Japan
159 E7 Okazaki Japan
219 D7 Okeechobee U.S.A.
219 D7 Okeechobee, Lake U.S.A.
219 D6 Okefenokee Swamp U.S.A.
173 C7 Okehampton U.K.
192 C4 Okene Nigeria
179 I2 Oker r. Germany
148 B5 Okha India
150 G1 Okha Rus. Fed.
149 F4 Okhaldhunga Nepal
148 B5 Okha Rann marsh India
133 P3 Okhotka r. Rus. Fed.
133 P4 Okhotsk Rus. Fed.
133 P4 Okhotsk, Sea of Rus. Fed.
Okhotskoye More sea Rus. Fed. see Okhotsk, Sea of
187 E5 Okhtyrka Ukr.
151 E4 Okinawa i. Japan
Okinawa-guntō is Japan see Okinawa-shotō
151 E4 Okinawa-shotō is Japan
153 N7 Okino-Daitō-jima i. Japan
159 B7 Okino-shima i. Japan
153 N4 Oki-shotō is Japan
159 C6 Oki-shotō is Japan
217 D5 Oklahoma state U.S.A.
217 D5 Oklahoma City U.S.A.
217 D5 Okmulgee U.S.A.
195 B4 Okondja Gabon
205 G4 Okotoks Canada
187 E4 Okovskiy Les for. Rus. Fed.
195 B4 Okoyo Congo
141 J3 Okpeti, Gora mt. Kazakh.
170 M1 Øksfjord Norway
186 F2 Oksovskiy Rus. Fed.
141 G5 Oktyabr Tajik.
187 I4 Oktyabr'sk Rus. Fed.
156 C1 Oktyabr'skiy Amurskaya Oblast' Rus. Fed.
186 G2 Oktyabr'skiy Arkhangel'skaya Oblast' Rus. Fed.
150 H1 Oktyabr'skiy Kamchatskiy Kray Rus. Fed.
132 G4 Oktyabr'skiy Respublika Bashkortostan Rus. Fed.
187 G6 Oktyabr'skiy Volgogradskaya Oblast' Rus. Fed.
141 F5 Oktyabr'skiy Uzbek.
141 F1 Oktyabr'skoye Kazakh.
140 E1 Oktyabr'skoye Chelyabinskaya Oblast' Rus. Fed.
140 C1 Oktyabr'skoye Orenburgskaya Oblast' Rus. Fed.
132 H3 Oktyabr'skoye Rus. Fed.
133 K2 Oktyabr'skoy Revolyutsii, Ostrov i. Rus. Fed.
Oktyah'sk Turkm. see Saparmyrat Türkmenbaşy
186 E3 Okulovka Rus. Fed.
158 F3 Okushiri-tō i. Japan
197 E1 Okwa watercourse Botswana
170 B2 Ólafsvík Iceland
214 C3 Olancha U.S.A.
214 C3 Olancha Peak U.S.A.
224 H5 Olanchito Hond.
171 L4 Öland i. Sweden
170 O2 Olanga Rus. Fed.
124 D4 Olary Australia
124 D4 Olary watercourse Australia
217 E4 Olathe U.S.A.
235 K3 Olavarría Arg.
177 H5 Oława Poland
215 G5 Olberg U.S.A.
184 C4 Olbia Sardinia Italy
220 D3 Olcott U.S.A.
125 J3 Old Bar Australia
147 I2 Old Bastar India
175 K4 Oldcastle Ireland
123 C4 Old Cork Australia
202 E3 Old Crow Canada
Oldeboorn Neth. see Aldeboarn
179 G1 Oldenburg Germany
176 E3 Oldenburg in Holstein Germany
179 E2 Oldenzaal Neth.
170 M1 Olderdalen Norway
221 F3 Old Forge NY U.S.A.
221 F4 Old Forge PA U.S.A.
121 B5 Old Gidgee Australia
173 E4 Oldham U.K.
175 J6 Old Head of Kinsale Ireland
205 G4 Oldman r. Canada
175 F3 Oldmeldrum U.K.
221 H3 Old Orchard Beach U.S.A.
207 J4 Old Perlican Canada
205 G4 Olds Canada
221 I2 Old Town U.S.A.
185 I6 Olduvai Gorge tourist site Tanz.
205 H4 Old Wives Lake Canada
215 E4 Old Woman Mountains U.S.A.
220 D3 Olean U.S.A.
177 K3 Olecko Poland
133 N4 Olekma r. Rus. Fed.
133 N3 Olekminsk Rus. Fed.
187 E5 Oleksandriya Ukr.
186 H1 Olema Rus. Fed.
171 I4 Ølen Norway
170 P1 Olenegorsk Rus. Fed.
133 M3 Olenek Rus. Fed.
133 N2 Olenek r. Rus. Fed.
133 N2 Olenekskiy Zaliv b. Rus. Fed.
186 E3 Olenino Rus. Fed.
141 H1 Olenti r. Pavlodarskaya Oblast' Kazakh.
140 C2 Olenti r. Zapadnyy Kazakhstan Kazakh.
187 C5 Olevs'k Ukr.
158 D3 Ol'ga Rus. Fed.
121 E5 Olga, Mount Australia
156 D1 Ol'ginsk Rus. Fed.
144 G2 Ölgiy Mongolia
183 M4 Olhão Port.
121 E5 Olia Chain mts Australia
196 C2 Olifants watercourse Namibia
197 I1 Olifants S. Africa
196 C5 Olifants r. W. Cape S. Africa
196 D6 Olifants r. W. Cape S. Africa
197 E3 Olifantshoek S. Africa
196 C6 Olifantsrivierberge mts S. Africa
235 L2 Olimar Grande r. Uruguay
234 C3 Olímpia Brazil
181 J4 Olimpos Beydağları Milli Parkı nat. park Turkey
225 E4 Olinalá Mex.
231 L5 Olinda Brazil
195 D5 Olinga Moz.
123 C4 Olio Australia
197 G2 Oliphants Drift Botswana
235 J2 Oliva Arg.
183 P3 Oliva Spain
232 C3 Oliva, Cordillera de mts Arg./Chile
235 I1 Olivares, Cerro de mt. Chile
220 B5 Olive Hill U.S.A.
234 D3 Oliveira Brazil
183 M3 Olivenza Spain
216 E2 Olivia U.S.A.
187 G4 Ol'khi Rus. Fed.
232 C2 Ollagüe Chile
235 H1 Ollita, Cordillera de mts Arg./Chile
235 H1 Ollitas mt. Arg.
141 G4 Olmaliq Uzbek.
230 C5 Olmos Peru
221 G3 Olmstedville U.S.A.
173 G5 Olney U.K.
219 C4 Olney U.S.A.
171 K4 Olofström Sweden
177 H6 Olomouc Czech Rep.
186 E2 Olonets Rus. Fed.
161 I3 Olongapo Phil.
183 D5 Oloron-Ste-Marie France
183 R1 Olot Spain
140 E5 Olot Uzbek.
150 D1 Olovyannaya Rus. Fed.
148 C5 Olpad India
179 F3 Olpe Germany
177 J4 Olsztyn Poland
176 C7 Olten Switz.
185 L2 Oltenița Romania
139 H1 Oltu Turkey
161 I5 Olutanga i. Phil.
185 I6 Olympia tourist site Greece
212 B2 Olympia U.S.A.
212 A2 Olympic National Park U.S.A.
138 C4 Olympos tourist site Turkey
185 J4 Olympus, Mount Greece
212 B2 Olympus, Mount U.S.A.
133 S4 Olyutorskiy, Mys c. Rus. Fed.
133 R4 Olyutorskiy Zaliv b. Rus. Fed.
149 E2 Oma China
158 G4 Ōma Japan
159 E6 Ōmachi Japan
159 F7 Omae-zaki pt Japan
175 K3 Omagh U.K.
216 E3 Omaha U.S.A.
196 C1 Omaheke admin. reg. Namibia
212 C1 Omak U.S.A.
156 E1 Omal'skiy Khrebet mts Rus. Fed.
147 E6 Oman country Asia
143 E5 Oman, Gulf of Asia
126 B6 Omarama N.Z.
195 B6 Omaruru Namibia
195 B5 Omatako watercourse Namibia
230 D7 Omate Peru
197 E2 Omaweneno Botswana
158 G4 Ōma-zaki c. Japan
195 A4 Omboué Gabon
184 D3 Ombrone r. Italy
149 F3 Ombu China
197 E5 Omdraaisvlei S. Africa
193 F3 Omdurman Sudan
184 C2 Omegna Italy
125 G6 Omeo Australia
224 H6 Ometepe, Isla de i. Nicaragua
194 D2 Om Hajēr Eritrea
142 C4 Omīdīyeh Iran
204 D3 Omineca Mountains Canada
196 C1 Omitara Namibia
157 E6 Ōmiya Japan
204 C3 Ommaney, Cape U.S.A.
179 E2 Ommen Neth.
154 B1 Ömnögovĭ prov. Mongolia
133 R3 Omolon Rus. Fed.
133 Q3 Omolon r. Rus. Fed.
194 D3 Omo National Park Eth.
159 G5 Omono-gawa r. Japan
132 I4 Omsk Rus. Fed.
133 Q3 Omsukchan Rus. Fed.
158 H2 Ōmū Japan
185 K2 Omu, Vârful mt. Romania
159 A8 Ōmura Japan
169 Q4 Omutninsk Rus. Fed.
208 B4 Onalaska U.S.A.
221 F6 Onancock U.S.A.
206 D4 Onaping Lake Canada
224 B1 Onavas Mex.
209 E3 Onaway U.S.A.
162 A2 Onbingwin Myanmar
235 J1 Oncativo Arg.
172 C3 Onchan U.K.
195 B5 Oncócua Angola
195 B5 Ondangwa Namibia
196 B1 Ondekaremba Namibia
196 D5 Onderstedorings S. Africa
195 B5 Ondjiva Angola
192 C4 Ondo Nigeria
150 D2 Öndörhaan Mongolia
160 A1 Ondor Had China
154 B1 Ondor Mod China
153 I2 Öndörshil Mongolia
154 D1 Ondor Sum China
186 E2 Ondozero Rus. Fed.
196 D1 One Botswana
186 F2 Onega Rus. Fed.
186 F2 Onega r. Rus. Fed.
186 E2 Onega, Lake Rus. Fed.
221 F3 Oneida U.S.A.
221 F3 Oneida Lake U.S.A.
216 D3 O'Neill U.S.A.
150 H2 Onekotan, Ostrov i. Rus. Fed.
221 F3 Oneonta U.S.A.
126 E2 Oneroa N.Z.
177 M7 Onești Romania
186 E1 Onezhskaya Guba g. Rus. Fed.
132 E3 Onezhskoye Ozero Rus. Fed.
Onezhskoye Ozero l. Rus. Fed. see Onega, Lake
147 I1 Ong r. India
195 B4 Onga Gabon
197 E4 Ongers watercourse S. Africa
Ongi Mongolia see Sayhan-Ovoo
144 J3 Ongiyn Gol r. Mongolia
160 C5 Ongjin N. Korea
147 I3 Ongole India
141 K2 Onguday Rus. Fed.
187 G7 Oni Georgia
195 E6 Onilahy r. Madag.
192 C4 Onitsha Nigeria
196 B1 Onjati Mountain Namibia
159 E7 Ōno Japan
119 I4 Ono-i-Lau i. Fiji
159 C7 Onomichi Japan
156 F2 Onor, Gora mt. Rus. Fed.
119 H2 Onotoa atoll Kiribati
205 G4 Onoway Canada
196 C4 Onseepkans S. Africa
118 B4 Onslow Australia
219 E5 Onslow Bay U.S.A.
161 F2 Onsŏng N. Korea
179 F1 Onstwedde Neth.
159 E7 Ontake-san vol. Japan
206 C3 Ontario prov. Canada
212 C2 Ontario U.S.A.
209 H4 Ontario, Lake Canada/U.S.A.
208 C2 Ontonagon U.S.A.
119 F2 Ontong Java Atoll Solomon Is
118 D4 Oodnadatta Australia
125 F5 Oolambeyan National Park Australia
121 E6 Ooldea Australia
121 E6 Ooldea Range hills Australia
217 E4 Oologah Lake resr U.S.A.
123 B4 Ooratippra r. Australia
178 B3 Oostburg Neth.
Oostende Belgium see Ostend
178 D2 Oostendorp Neth.
178 C3 Oosterhout Neth.
178 B3 Oosterschelde est. Neth.
179 E2 Oosterwolde Neth.
178 A4 Oostvleteren Belgium
178 D1 Oost-Vlieland Neth.
204 D4 Ootsa Lake Canada
204 D4 Ootsa Lake l. Canada
221 E5 Opal U.S.A.
195 C4 Opala Dem. Rep. Congo
186 I3 Oparino Rus. Fed.
206 B3 Opasquia Canada
206 B3 Opasquia Provincial Park Canada
207 F3 Opataca, Lac l. Canada
177 H6 Opava Czech Rep.
219 C5 Opelika U.S.A.
217 E6 Opelousas U.S.A.
212 F1 Opheim U.S.A.
209 F2 Ophir Canada
163 B2 Ophir, Gunung vol. Indon.
126 C6 Opihi r. N.Z.
206 E3 Opinaca r. Canada
206 E3 Opinaca, Réservoir resr Canada
206 D3 Opinnagau r. Canada
139 J5 Opis tourist site Iraq
207 G3 Opiscotéo, Lac l. Canada
178 C2 Opmeer Neth.
186 D3 Opochka Rus. Fed.
177 H5 Opole Poland
183 L2 Oporto Port.
126 F3 Opotiki N.Z.
219 C6 Opp U.S.A.
171 J3 Oppdal Norway
126 D3 Opunake N.Z.
195 B5 Opuwo Namibia
140 B3 Opytnoye Kazakh.
140 D4 Oqqal'a Uzbek.
141 H5 Oqsu r. Tajik.
141 F5 Oqtosh Uzbek.
208 B5 Oquawka U.S.A.
221 H2 Oquossoc U.S.A.
140 D2 Or' r. Rus. Fed.
215 G5 Oracle U.S.A.
215 G5 Oracle Junction U.S.A.
177 J7 Oradea Romania
170 C2 Öræfajökull glacier Iceland
148 D4 Orai India
192 B1 Oran Alg.
232 D2 Orán Arg.
162 C2 O Rang Cambodia
160 E3 Ŏrang N. Korea
125 H4 Orange Australia
182 G4 Orange France
196 B4 Orange r. Namibia/S. Africa
221 G3 Orange MA U.S.A.
217 E6 Orange TX U.S.A.
220 D5 Orange VA U.S.A.
231 H3 Orange, Cabo c. Brazil
219 D5 Orangeburg U.S.A.
239 J8 Orange Cone sea feature S. Atlantic Ocean
Orange Free State prov. S. Africa see Free State
209 G3 Orangeville Canada
215 G2 Orangeville U.S.A.
225 G4 Orange Walk Belize
161 I3 Orani Phil.
179 L2 Oranienburg Germany
195 B6 Oranjemund Namibia
233 J1 Oranjestad Aruba
175 J4 Oranmore Ireland
195 C6 Orapa Botswana
161 J3 Oras Phil.
185 J2 Orăștie Romania
171 M3 Oravais Fin.
185 I2 Oravița Romania
149 E2 Orba Co l. China
184 D3 Orbetello Italy
183 N1 Orbigo r. Spain
125 H6 Orbost Australia
127 J2 Orcadas research stn S. Atlantic Ocean
215 H2 Orchard Mesa U.S.A.
233 K2 Orchila, Isla i. Venez.
214 B4 Orcutt U.S.A.
118 C3 Ord r. Australia
118 C3 Ord, Mount h. Australia
213 D4 Orderville U.S.A.
183 L1 Ordes Spain
215 D4 Ord Mountain U.S.A.
154 D2 Ordos China
120 E3 Ord River Dam Australia
139 F1 Ordu Turkey
139 K2 Ordubad Azer.
213 G4 Ordway U.S.A.
Ordzhonikidze Rus. Fed. see Vladikavkaz
187 E6 Ordzhonikidze Ukr.
214 C1 Oreana U.S.A.
171 K4 Örebro Sweden
208 C4 Oregon IL U.S.A.
220 B4 Oregon OH U.S.A.
208 C4 Oregon WI U.S.A.
213 B3 Oregon state U.S.A.
212 B2 Oregon City U.S.A.
187 F4 Orekhovo-Zuyevo Rus. Fed.
187 F4 Orel Rus. Fed.
156 E1 Orel, Gora mt. Rus. Fed.
150 F1 Orel', Ozero l. Rus. Fed.
215 G1 Orem U.S.A.
138 A2 Ören Turkey
185 L6 Ören Turkey
140 C2 Orenburg Rus. Fed.
140 C2 Orenburgskaya Oblast' admin. div. Rus. Fed.
235 K3 Orense Arg.
126 A7 Orepuki N.Z.
171 K5 Öresund str. Denmark
126 B7 Oreti r. N.Z.
126 E2 Orewa N.Z.
178 D4 Oreye Belgium
185 J4 Orfanou, Kolpos b. Greece
125 G9 Orford Australia
173 I5 Orford U.K.
173 I5 Orford Ness hd U.K.
215 F5 Organ Pipe Cactus National Monument nat. park U.S.A.
143 H3 Orgūn Afgh.
138 B2 Orhaneli Turkey
187 D7 Orhangazi Turkey
177 N7 Orhei Moldova
153 I1 Orhon Gol r. Mongolia
186 I3 Orichi Rus. Fed.
221 J2 Orient U.S.A.
230 E7 Oriental, Cordillera mts Bol.
233 I3 Oriental, Cordillera mts Col.
230 D6 Oriental, Cordillera mts Peru
235 K3 Oriente Arg.
183 P3 Orihuela Spain
187 E6 Orikhiv Ukr.
209 H3 Orillia Canada
171 N3 Orimattila Fin.
233 L2 Orinoco r. Col./Venez.
233 L2 Orinoco Delta Venez.
147 J1 Orissa state India
171 M4 Orissaare Estonia
184 C5 Oristano Sardinia Italy
171 N3 Orivesi Fin.
171 O3 Orivesi l. Fin.
231 G4 Oriximiná Brazil
225 E4 Orizaba Mex.
225 E4 Orizaba, Pico de vol. Mex.
171 J3 Orkanger Norway
171 K4 Örkelljunga Sweden
171 J3 Orkla r. Norway
197 G3 Orkney S. Africa
174 E1 Orkney Islands U.K.
217 C6 Orla U.S.A.
214 A2 Orland U.S.A.
234 C3 Orlândia Brazil
219 D6 Orlando U.S.A.
182 E3 Orléans France
221 I4 Orleans MA U.S.A.
221 G2 Orleans VT U.S.A.
152 G1 Orlik Rus. Fed.
186 I3 Orlov Rus. Fed.
187 F4 Orlovskaya Oblast' admin. div. Rus. Fed.
187 G6 Orlovskiy Rus. Fed.
143 G5 Ormara Pak.
143 G5 Ormara, Ras hd Pak.
161 J4 Ormoc Phil.
219 D6 Ormond Beach U.S.A.
173 E4 Ormskirk U.K.
221 G2 Ormstown Canada
182 D2 Orne r. France
170 K2 Ørnes Norway
171 L3 Örnsköldsvik Sweden
160 D4 Oro N. Korea
233 J3 Orocué Col.
192 B3 Orodara Burkina
212 C2 Orofino U.S.A.
213 F5 Orogrande U.S.A.
207 G4 Oromocto Canada
138 E6 Oron Israel
119 I2 Orona atoll Kiribati
221 I2 Orono U.S.A.
174 B4 Oronsay i. U.K.
161 I4 Oroquieta Phil.
231 K5 Orós, Açude resr Brazil
184 C4 Orosei Sardinia Italy
184 C4 Orosei, Golfo di b. Sardinia Italy
177 J7 Orosháza Hungary
215 G5 Oro Valley U.S.A.
214 B2 Oroville CA U.S.A.
212 C1 Oroville WA U.S.A.
214 B2 Oroville, Lake resr U.S.A.
124 C4 Orroroo Australia
171 K3 Orsa Sweden
187 D4 Orsha Belarus
140 D2 Orsk Rus. Fed.
171 I3 Ørsta Norway
183 M1 Ortegal, Cabo c. Spain
183 D5 Orthez France
183 M1 Ortigueira Spain
224 B1 Ortíz Mex.
233 K2 Ortíz Venez.
184 D1 Ortles mt. Italy
172 E3 Orton U.K.
184 F3 Ortona Italy
216 D2 Ortonville U.S.A.
133 N3 Orulgan, Khrebet mts Rus. Fed.
196 B1 Orumbo Namibia
Orūmīyeh Iran see Urmia
Orūmīyeh, Daryācheh-ye salt l. Iran see Urmia, Lake
230 E7 Oruro Bol.
184 E3 Orvieto Italy
220 C4 Orwell OH U.S.A.
221 G3 Orwell VT U.S.A.
171 J3 Os Norway
224 I6 Osa, Península de Costa Rica
208 A4 Osage U.S.A.
217 E4 Osage r. U.S.A.
159 D7 Ōsaka Japan

Palmeira dos Índios

223 K5 Ponce Puerto Rico
213 F4 Poncha Springs U.S.A.
206 E3 Poncheville, Lac l. Canada
Pondicherry India see Puducherry
203 K2 Pond Inlet Canada
207 I3 Ponds, Island of Canada
224 H5 Poneloya Nicaragua
183 M1 Ponferrada Spain
126 F4 Pongaroa N.Z.
193 E4 Pongo watercourse Sudan
197 I3 Pongola r. S. Africa
197 I3 Pongolapoort Dam l. S. Africa
177 O3 Ponizov'ye Rus. Fed.
147 H3 Ponnaivar r. India
147 G4 Ponnani India
149 H5 Ponnyadaung Range mts Myanmar
205 G4 Ponoka Canada
140 C1 Ponomarevka Rus. Fed.
166 A6 Ponta Delgada Azores
192 □ Ponta do Sol Cape Verde
235 B4 Ponta Grossa Brazil
234 C2 Pontalina Brazil
182 H2 Pont-à-Mousson France
234 A3 Ponta Porã Brazil
182 H3 Pontarlier France
217 F6 Pontchartrain, Lake U.S.A.
178 C4 Pont-de-Loup Belgium
183 L3 Ponte de Sor Port.
173 F4 Pontefract U.K.
172 F2 Ponteland U.K.
231 G7 Pontes-e-Lacerda Brazil
183 L1 Pontevedra Spain
208 C5 Pontiac IL U.S.A.
209 F4 Pontiac MI U.S.A.
163 G3 Pontianak Indon.
182 C2 Pontivy France
182 B3 Pont-l'Abbé France
182 F2 Pontoise France
121 C6 Ponton watercourse Australia
205 J4 Ponton Canada
217 F5 Pontotoc U.S.A.
184 C2 Pontremoli Italy
178 A5 Pont-Ste-Maxence France
125 G9 Pontville Australia
209 H3 Pontypool Canada
173 D6 Pontypool U.K.
173 D6 Pontypridd U.K.
184 E4 Ponza, Isola di i. Italy
184 E4 Ponziane, Isole Italy
124 A4 Poochera Australia
173 F7 Poole U.K.
123 B5 Poolowanna Lake salt flat Australia
Poona India see Pune
125 E4 Pooncarie Australia
125 F3 Poopelloe Lake salt l. Australia
230 E7 Poopó, Lago de l. Bol.
126 E1 Poor Knights Islands N.Z.
141 G4 Pop Uzbek.
233 H4 Popayán Col.
178 A4 Poperinge Belgium
133 L2 Popigay r. Rus. Fed.
124 D4 Popiltah Australia
124 D4 Popilta Lake imp. l. Australia
205 J4 Poplar r. Canada
212 F1 Poplar U.S.A.
217 F4 Poplar Bluff U.S.A.
220 C6 Poplar Camp U.S.A.
217 F6 Poplarville U.S.A.
225 E4 Popocatépetl, Volcán vol. Mex.
195 B4 Popokabaka Dem. Rep. Congo
185 L3 Popovo Bulg.
179 I3 Poppenberg h. Germany
177 J6 Poprad Slovakia
143 G5 Porali r. Pak.
126 F4 Porangahau N.Z.
234 C1 Porangatu Brazil
148 B5 Porbandar India
233 I3 Porce r. Col.
204 C4 Porcher Island Canada
202 E3 Porcupine r. Canada/U.S.A.
207 I3 Porcupine, Cape Canada
239 H2 Porcupine Abyssal Plain sea feature N. Atlantic Ocean
205 I4 Porcupine Hills Canada
208 C2 Porcupine Mountains U.S.A.
205 I4 Porcupine Plain Canada
205 I4 Porcupine Provincial Forest nature res. Canada
233 J3 Pore Col.
184 E2 Poreč Croatia
187 H4 Poretskoye Rus. Fed.
171 M3 Pori Fin.
126 E4 Porirua N.Z.
186 D3 Porkhov Rus. Fed.
233 L2 Porlamar Venez.
122 C2 Pormpuraaw Australia
182 C3 Pornic France
161 J4 Poro i. Phil.
150 G2 Poronaysk Rus. Fed.
149 G3 Porong China
185 J6 Poros Greece
186 E2 Porosozero Rus. Fed.
Porsangen sea chan. Norway see Porsangerfjorden
170 N1 Porsangerfjorden sea chan. Norway
171 J4 Porsgrunn Norway
138 C2 Porsuk r. Turkey
124 C5 Port Adelaide Australia
175 L3 Portadown U.K.
175 M3 Portaferry U.K.
221 I1 Portage ME U.S.A.
209 E4 Portage MI U.S.A.
208 C4 Portage WI U.S.A.
205 J5 Portage la Prairie Canada
216 C1 Portal U.S.A.
204 E5 Port Alberni Canada
125 G7 Port Albert Australia
183 M3 Portalegre Port.
217 C5 Portales U.S.A.
204 C3 Port Alexander U.S.A.
197 G6 Port Alfred S. Africa
204 D4 Port Alice Canada
220 D4 Port Allegany U.S.A.
217 F6 Port Allen U.S.A.
123 E4 Port Alma Australia
212 B1 Port Angeles U.S.A.
175 K4 Portarlington Ireland
125 G9 Port Arthur Australia
217 E6 Port Arthur U.S.A.
174 B5 Port Askaig U.K.
124 B4 Port Augusta Australia
223 J5 Port-au-Prince Haiti
209 F3 Port Austin U.S.A.
207 I3 Port aux Choix Canada
175 M3 Portavogie U.K.
196 D7 Port Beaufort S. Africa
135 H5 Port Blair India
209 H3 Port Bolster Canada
183 R1 Portbou Spain
209 G4 Port Burwell Canada
125 E7 Port Campbell Australia
209 H3 Port Carling Canada
126 C6 Port Chalmers N.Z.
219 D7 Port Charlotte U.S.A.
221 G4 Port Chester U.S.A.
204 C4 Port Clements Canada
220 B4 Port Clinton U.S.A.
221 I3 Port Clyde U.S.A.
209 H4 Port Colborne Canada
204 E5 Port Coquitlam Canada
209 H4 Port Credit Canada
125 F9 Port Davey b. Australia
223 J5 Port-de-Paix Haiti
162 B5 Port Dickson Malaysia
122 D3 Port Douglas Australia
220 C3 Port Dover Canada
208 D3 Porte des Morts lake channel U.S.A.
204 C4 Port Edward Canada
197 I5 Port Edward S. Africa
208 C3 Port Edwards U.S.A.
234 D1 Porteirinha Brazil
231 H4 Portel Brazil
209 G3 Port Elgin Canada
197 F6 Port Elizabeth S. Africa
174 B5 Port Ellen U.K.
124 C5 Port Elliot Australia
172 C3 Port Erin U.K.
205 H2 Porter Lake Canada
204 C3 Porter Landing Canada
196 C6 Porterville S. Africa
214 C3 Porterville U.S.A.
125 E7 Port Fairy Australia
126 E2 Port Fitzroy N.Z.
138 D6 Port Fuad Egypt
195 A4 Port-Gentil Gabon
124 C4 Port Germein Australia
217 F6 Port Gibson U.S.A.
174 D5 Port Glasgow U.K.
192 C4 Port Harcourt Nigeria
204 D4 Port Hardy Canada
Port Harrison Canada see Inukjuak
207 H4 Port Hawkesbury Canada
173 D6 Porthcawl U.K.
118 B4 Port Hedland Australia
221 G2 Port Henry U.S.A.
173 B7 Porthleven U.K.
173 C5 Porthmadog U.K.
209 H4 Port Hope Canada
207 I3 Port Hope Simpson Canada
209 F4 Port Huron U.S.A.
139 L2 Port-İliç Azer.
183 L4 Portimão Port.
155 □ Port Island Hong Kong China
125 I4 Port Jackson inlet Australia
221 G4 Port Jefferson U.S.A.
221 F4 Port Jervis U.S.A.
231 G2 Port Kaituma Guyana
Port Keats Australia see Wadeye
125 I5 Port Kembla Australia
125 H4 Portland N.S.W. Australia
124 D7 Portland Vic. Australia
209 E5 Portland IN U.S.A.
221 H3 Portland ME U.S.A.
212 B2 Portland OR U.S.A.
173 E7 Portland, Isle of pen. U.K.
204 C3 Portland Canal inlet Canada
126 F3 Portland Island N.Z.
122 C2 Portland Roads Australia
175 K4 Portlaoise Ireland
217 D6 Port Lavaca U.S.A.
175 K5 Portlaw Ireland
175 F3 Portlethen U.K.
124 A5 Port Lincoln Australia
192 A4 Port Loko Sierra Leone
124 D7 Port MacDonnell Australia
125 J3 Port Macquarie Australia
207 H2 Port Manvers inlet Canada
204 D4 Port McNeill Canada
207 H4 Port-Menier Canada
202 B4 Port Moller b. U.S.A.
212 B1 Port Moody Canada
119 E2 Port Moresby P.N.G.
174 B2 Portnaguran U.K.
174 B5 Portnahaven U.K.
124 B5 Port Neill Australia
219 F7 Port Nelson Bahamas
Port Nis U.K. see Port of Ness
196 B4 Port Nolloth S. Africa
Port-Nouveau-Québec Canada see Kangiqsualujjuaq
Porto Port. see Oporto
230 E5 Porto Acre Brazil
234 B3 Porto Alegre Mato Grosso do Sul Brazil
232 F4 Porto Alegre Brazil
231 G6 Porto Artur Brazil
224 J6 Portobelo Panama
231 G6 Porto dos Gaúchos Óbidos Brazil
231 G7 Porto Esperidião Brazil
184 D3 Portoferraio Italy
174 B2 Port of Ness U.K.
231 I5 Porto Franco Brazil
233 L2 Port of Spain Trin. and Tob.
184 E2 Portogruaro Italy
234 A2 Porto Jofre Brazil
214 B2 Portola U.S.A.
184 D2 Portomaggiore Italy
235 A4 Porto Mendes Para.
231 G8 Porto Murtinho Brazil
231 I6 Porto Nacional Brazil
192 C4 Porto-Novo Benin
234 B3 Porto Primavera, Represa resr Brazil
213 A3 Port Orford U.S.A.
231 H4 Porto Santana Brazil
234 E2 Porto Seguro Brazil
184 E2 Porto Tolle Italy
184 C4 Porto Torres Sardinia Italy
184 C4 Porto-Vecchio Corsica France
231 F5 Porto Velho Brazil
230 B4 Portoviejo Ecuador
174 C6 Portpatrick U.K.
209 H3 Port Perry Canada
125 F7 Port Phillip Bay Australia
124 C4 Port Pirie Australia
173 B7 Portreath U.K.
174 B3 Portree U.K.
204 E5 Port Renfrew Canada
209 G4 Port Rowan Canada
221 E5 Port Royal U.S.A.
175 L2 Portrush U.K.
193 F1 Port Said Egypt
219 C6 Port St Joe U.S.A.
197 H5 Port St Johns S. Africa
172 C3 Port St Mary U.K.
175 K2 Portsalon Ireland
209 F4 Port Sanilac U.S.A.
209 H3 Port Severn Canada
155 □ Port Shelter b. Hong Kong China
197 I5 Port Shepstone S. Africa
Port Simpson Canada see Lax Kw'alaams
173 F7 Portsmouth U.K.
221 H3 Portsmouth NH U.S.A.
220 B5 Portsmouth OH U.S.A.
221 E6 Portsmouth VA U.S.A.
175 F3 Portsoy U.K.
125 J4 Port Stephens b. Australia
175 L2 Portstewart U.K.
193 F3 Port Sudan Sudan
219 B6 Port Sulphur U.S.A.
173 D6 Port Talbot U.K.
170 N1 Porttipahdan tekojärvi resr Fin.
183 L3 Portugal country Europe
183 E1 Portugalete Spain
233 J2 Portuguesa r. Venez.
175 J4 Portumna Ireland
183 F5 Port-Vendres France
124 B5 Port Victoria Australia
119 G3 Port Vila Vanuatu
170 P1 Port Vladimir Rus. Fed.
126 E2 Port Waikato N.Z.
124 C5 Port Wakefield Australia
208 D4 Port Washington U.S.A.
174 D6 Port William U.K.
208 B2 Port Wing U.S.A.
235 J2 Porvenir Arg.
171 N3 Porvoo Fin.
160 D5 Poryŏng S. Korea
183 N1 Posada Spain
232 E3 Posadas Arg.
185 H2 Posavina reg. Bos.-Herz./Croatia
209 F3 Posen U.S.A.
169 N4 Poshekhon'ye Rus. Fed.
Poshekon'ye-Volodarsk Rus. Fed. see Poshekhon'ye
139 K5 Posht-e Kūh mts Iran
142 C2 Posht Kūh h. Iran
170 O2 Posio Fin.
151 E7 Poso Indon.
139 I1 Posof Turkey
160 D6 Posŏng S. Korea
141 J1 Pospelikha Rus. Fed.
234 C1 Posse Brazil
127 I5 Possession Islands Antarctica
179 J4 Pößneck Germany
217 C5 Post U.S.A.
Poste-de-la-Baleine Canada see Kuujjuarapik
197 E4 Postmasburg S. Africa
207 I3 Postville Canada
208 B4 Postville U.S.A.
185 G3 Posušje Bos.-Herz.
158 B3 Pos'yet Rus. Fed.
197 G3 Potchefstroom S. Africa
217 E5 Poteau U.S.A.
231 K5 Potengi r. Brazil
184 F4 Potenza Italy
126 A7 Poteriteri, Lake N.Z.
197 F5 Potfontein S. Africa
Potgietersrus S. Africa see Mokopane
217 D6 Poth U.S.A.
231 J5 Poti r. Brazil
187 G7 P'ot'i Georgia
147 I2 Potikal India
193 D3 Potiskum Nigeria
212 D2 Pot Mountain U.S.A.
155 □ Po Toi i. Hong Kong China
221 E5 Potomac r. U.S.A.
220 D5 Potomac, South Branch r. U.S.A.
220 D5 Potomac, South Fork South Branch r. U.S.A.
230 E7 Potosí Bol.
217 F4 Potosi U.S.A.
215 E4 Potosi Mountain U.S.A.
161 I4 Pototan Phil.
225 H5 Potrerillos Hond.
179 L2 Potsdam Germany
221 F2 Potsdam U.S.A.
173 E6 Potterne U.K.
173 G6 Potters Bar U.K.
221 F4 Pottstown U.S.A.
221 E4 Pottsville U.S.A.
147 I5 Pottuvil Sri Lanka
204 E3 Pouce Coupe Canada
207 J4 Pouch Cove Canada
221 G4 Poughkeepsie U.S.A.
221 G3 Poultney U.S.A.
173 E4 Poulton-le-Fylde U.K.
234 D3 Pouso Alegre Brazil
162 B2 Poŭthĭsăt Cambodia
177 I6 Považská Bystrica Slovakia
186 E2 Povenets Rus. Fed.
126 F3 Poverty Bay N.Z.
185 H2 Povlen mt. Serbia
183 L2 Póvoa de Varzim Port.
187 G5 Povorino Rus. Fed.
158 C3 Povorotnyy, Mys hd Rus. Fed.
215 D5 Poway U.S.A.
212 F2 Powder r. U.S.A.
213 F3 Powder River U.S.A.
212 E2 Powell U.S.A.
220 B6 Powell r. U.S.A.
215 G3 Powell, Lake resr U.S.A.
214 C2 Powell Mountain U.S.A.
219 E7 Powell Point Bahamas
204 E5 Powell River Canada
208 D3 Powers U.S.A.
221 E6 Powhatan U.S.A.
234 A1 Poxoréu Brazil
155 E4 Poyang Hu l. China
162 □ Poyan Reservoir Sing.
156 C2 Poyarkovo Rus. Fed.
208 C3 Poygan, Lake U.S.A.
138 E3 Pozantı Turkey
185 I2 Požarevac Serbia
225 E3 Poza Rica Mex.
156 C2 Pozdeyevka Rus. Fed.
185 G2 Požega Croatia
185 I3 Požega Serbia
158 D1 Pozharskoye Rus. Fed.
177 H4 Poznań Poland
183 N3 Pozoblanco Spain
224 B1 Pozo Nuevo Mex.
184 F4 Pozzuoli Italy
163 B3 Prabumulih Indon.
176 G6 Prachatice Czech Rep.
149 F6 Prachi r. India
162 B2 Prachin Buri Thai.
162 A3 Prachuap Khiri Khan Thai.
183 F5 Prades France
234 E2 Prado Brazil
176 G5 Prague Czech Rep.
Praha Czech Rep. see Prague
192 □ Praia Cape Verde
197 J2 Praia do Bilene Moz.
234 A1 Praia Rica Brazil
123 D4 Prairie Australia
209 E5 Prairie Creek Reservoir U.S.A.
217 C5 Prairie Dog Town Fork r. U.S.A.
208 B4 Prairie du Chien U.S.A.
162 B2 Prakhon Chai Thai.
162 B2 Pran r. Thai.
147 H2 Pranhita r. India
163 E2 Prapat Indon.
185 L7 Prasonisi, Akrotirio pt Greece
234 C2 Prata Brazil
234 C2 Prata r. Brazil
184 D3 Prato Italy
217 D4 Pratt U.S.A.
217 G5 Prattville U.S.A.
147 G2 Pravara r. India
177 J3 Pravdinsk Rus. Fed.
163 I4 Praya Indon.
Preăh Vihear Cambodia see Preăh Vihéar
162 C2 Preăh Vihéar Cambodia
177 P3 Prechistoye Rus. Fed.
205 I4 Preeceville Canada
187 B4 Pregolya r. Rus. Fed.
171 N4 Preiļi Latvia
209 H1 Preissac, Lac l. Canada
125 H3 Premer Australia
182 F3 Prémery France
179 K2 Premnitz Germany
208 B3 Prentice U.S.A.
176 F4 Prenzlau Germany
158 C3 Preobrazheniye Rus. Fed.
145 H9 Preparis Island Cocos Is
145 H9 Preparis North Channel Cocos Is
145 H9 Preparis South Channel Cocos Is
177 H6 Přerov Czech Rep.
221 F2 Prescott Canada
215 F4 Prescott U.S.A.
215 F4 Prescott Valley U.S.A.
173 C6 Preseli, Mynydd hills U.K.
185 I3 Preševo Serbia
216 C3 Presho U.S.A.
232 D3 Presidencia Roque Sáenz Peña Arg.
231 J5 Presidente Dutra Brazil
234 B3 Presidente Epitácio Brazil
231 F6 Presidente Hermes Brazil
234 B3 Presidente Prudente Brazil
234 B3 Presidente Venceslau Brazil
217 B6 Presidio U.S.A.
141 F1 Presnogor'kovka Kazakh.
141 F1 Presnovka Kazakh.
177 J6 Prešov Slovakia
185 I4 Prespa, Lake Europe
221 J1 Presque Isle U.S.A.
208 D2 Presque Isle Point U.S.A.
173 D5 Presteigne U.K.
173 E4 Preston U.K.
213 E3 Preston ID U.S.A.
208 A4 Preston MN U.S.A.
217 E4 Preston MO U.S.A.
215 E2 Preston NV U.S.A.
121 B4 Preston, Cape Australia
175 F5 Prestonpans U.K.
220 B6 Prestonsburg U.S.A.
174 D5 Prestwick U.K.
234 E1 Preto r. Bahia Brazil
234 C2 Preto r. Minas Gerais Brazil
197 H2 Pretoria S. Africa
221 E5 Prettyboy Lake U.S.A.
179 K3 Pretzsch Germany
185 I5 Preveza Greece
162 C3 Prey Vêng Cambodia
140 E3 Priaral'skiye Karakumy, Peski des. Kazakh.
153 K1 Priargunsk Rus. Fed.
133 U4 Pribilof Islands U.S.A.
185 H3 Priboj Serbia
120 E2 Price r. Australia
207 G4 Price Canada
215 G2 Price U.S.A.
204 D4 Price Island Canada
219 B6 Prichard U.S.A.
171 M4 Priekule Latvia
171 N4 Priekuļi Latvia
171 M5 Prienai Lith.
197 E4 Prieska S. Africa
212 C1 Priest Lake U.S.A.
212 C1 Priest River U.S.A.
183 N1 Prieta, Peña mt. Spain
177 I6 Prievidza Slovakia
179 K1 Prignitz reg. Germany
185 G2 Prijedor Bos.-Herz.
185 H3 Prijepolje Serbia
Prikaspiyskaya Nizmennost' lowland Kazakh./Rus. Fed. see Caspian Lowland
185 I4 Prilep Macedonia
179 K5 Přimda Czech Rep.
235 J1 Primero r. Arg.
125 G8 Prime Seal Island Australia
171 O3 Primorsk Rus. Fed.
158 C2 Primorskiy Kray admin. div. Rus. Fed.
187 F6 Primorsko-Akhtarsk Rus. Fed.
215 D5 Primo Tapia Mex.
205 H4 Primrose Lake Canada
205 H4 Prince Albert Canada
197 E6 Prince Albert S. Africa
205 H4 Prince Albert National Park Canada
202 G2 Prince Albert Peninsula Canada
196 D6 Prince Albert Road S. Africa
202 G2 Prince Albert Sound sea chan. Canada
202 F2 Prince Alfred, Cape Canada
203 K3 Prince Charles Island Canada
127 K5 Prince Charles Mountains Antarctica
207 H4 Prince Edward Island prov. Canada
238 G8 Prince Edward Islands Indian Ocean
209 I4 Prince Edward Point Canada
221 E5 Prince Frederick U.S.A.
204 E4 Prince George Canada
202 B3 Prince of Wales, Cape U.S.A.
119 E3 Prince of Wales Island Australia
203 I2 Prince of Wales Island Canada
204 C3 Prince of Wales Island U.S.A.
202 G2 Prince of Wales Strait Canada
202 F2 Prince Patrick Island Canada
203 I2 Prince Regent Inlet sea chan. Canada
204 C4 Prince Rupert Canada
221 F5 Princess Anne U.S.A.
119 E3 Princess Charlotte Bay Australia
127 K5 Princess Elizabeth Land reg. Antarctica
205 J2 Princess Mary Lake Canada
204 D4 Princess Royal Island Canada
204 E5 Princeton Canada
214 A2 Princeton CA U.S.A.
208 C5 Princeton IL U.S.A.
219 C4 Princeton IN U.S.A.
219 C4 Princeton KY U.S.A.
221 J2 Princeton ME U.S.A.
216 E3 Princeton MO U.S.A.
221 F4 Princeton NJ U.S.A.

Seaman Range

Sibuguey

154 E2 Shanghe China
160 C3 Shanghekou China
154 D3 Shangjin China
155 C6 Shanglin China
154 C3 Shangluo China
154 D3 Shangnan China
154 E3 Shangqiu China
155 E4 Shangrao *Jiangxi* China
155 E4 Shangrao *Jiangxi* China
141 J3 Shangsanshilipu China
154 E3 Shangshui China
155 C6 Shangsi China
155 E4 Shangtang China
154 D1 Shangyi China
155 E5 Shangyou China
141 J4 Shangyou Shuiku *resr* China
Shangyou Sk. *salt flat* China *see* Shangyou Shuiku
155 F4 Shangyu China
160 D1 Shangzhi China
Shangzhou China *see* Shangluo
160 D1 Shanhetun China
175 I6 Shanlaragh Ireland
175 J5 Shannon *est.* Ireland
175 J4 Shannon *r.* Ireland
175 I5 Shannon, Mouth of the Ireland
121 B7 Shannon National Park Australia
160 D2 Shansonggang China
149 G5 Shantipur India
155 E6 Shantou China
155 E6 Shanwei China
154 D2 Shanxi *prov.* China
154 E3 Shanxian China
154 C3 Shanyang China
154 D2 Shanyin China
155 D5 Shaodong China
155 D5 Shaoguan China
155 E5 Shaowu China
155 F4 Shaoxing China
155 D5 Shaoyang *Hunan* China
155 D5 Shaoyang *Hunan* China
172 E3 Shap U.K.
155 D6 Shapa China
175 F1 Shapinsay *i.* U.K.
144 G1 Shapshal'skiy Khrebet *mts* Rus. Fed.
146 C4 Shaqrā' Saudi Arabia
141 J2 Shar Kazakh.
139 I6 Sharaf *well* Iraq
143 H3 Sharan Afgh.
148 B3 Sharan Jogizai Pak.
Sharbulag Mongolia *see* Dzavhan
141 J1 Sharchino Rus. Fed.
141 F4 Shardara Kazakh.
Sharga Mongolia *see* Tsagaan-Uul
Shargun' Uzbek. *see* Sharg'un
141 F5 Sharg'un Uzbek.
187 D5 Sharhorod Ukr.
Sharhulsan Mongolia *see* Mandal-Ovoo
139 J4 Shārī, Buḩayrat *imp. l.* Iraq
158 I3 Shari-dake *vol.* Japan
147 E4 Sharjah U.A.E.
177 M3 Sharkawshchyna Belarus
118 B4 Shark Bay Australia
122 D2 Shark Reef Australia
Sharlouk Turkm. *see* Şarlawuk
140 C1 Sharlyk Rus. Fed.
136 D6 Sharm ash Shaykh Egypt
Sharm el Sheikh Egypt *see* Sharm ash Shaykh
221 G4 Sharon *CT* U.S.A.
220 C4 Sharon *PA* U.S.A.
155 □ Sharp Peak Hong Kong China
138 E5 Sharqī, Jabal ash *mts* Lebanon/Syria
140 D4 Sharqiy Ustyurt Chink *esc.* Uzbek.
186 H3 Shar'ya Rus. Fed.
195 C6 Shashe *r.* Botswana/Zimbabwe
194 D3 Shashemenē Eth.
141 H3 Shashubay Kazakh.
213 B3 Shasta, Mount *vol.* U.S.A.
213 B3 Shasta Lake U.S.A.
155 □ Sha Tin Hong Kong China
187 H4 Shatki Rus. Fed.
169 O5 Shatsk Rus. Fed.
142 C4 Shaṭṭ, Ra's osh *pt* Iran
139 L7 Shaṭṭ al 'Arab *r.* Iran/Iraq
139 J6 Shaṭṭ al Hillah *r.* Iraq
187 F4 Shatura Rus. Fed.
141 G4 Shaul'der Kazakh.
205 H5 Shaunavon Canada
220 D5 Shavers Fork *r.* U.S.A.
121 B4 Shaw *r.* Australia
221 F4 Shawangunk Mountains U.S.A.
208 C3 Shawano U.S.A.
208 C3 Shawano Lake U.S.A.
207 F4 Shawinigan Canada
139 F4 Shawmarīyah, Jabal ash *mts* Syria
217 D5 Shawnee U.S.A.
155 F5 Sha Xi *r.* China
155 E5 Shaxian China
141 G4 Shayan Kazakh.
155 D4 Shayang China
118 C4 Shay Gap (abandoned) Australia
139 K5 Shaykh Jūwī Iraq
139 K5 Shaykh Sa'd Iraq
142 D4 Shaytūr Iran
137 F6 Shaẓāẓ, Jabal *mt.* Saudi Arabia
141 H5 Shazud Tajik.
187 F4 Shchekino Rus. Fed.
169 Q2 Shchel'yayur Rus. Fed.
141 I1 Shcherbakty Kazakh.
187 F5 Shchigry Rus. Fed.
187 D5 Shchors Ukr.
141 G1 Shchuchinsk Kazakh.
187 C4 Shchuchyn Belarus
141 K2 Shebalino Rus. Fed.
187 F5 Shebekino Rus. Fed.
Shebelē Wenz, Wabē *r.* Ethiopia/Somalia *see* Shabeelle, Webi
194 E3 Shebelē Wenz, Wabē *r.* Somalia
143 G2 Sheberghān Afgh.
208 D4 Sheboygan U.S.A.
193 D4 Shebshi Mountains Nigeria
156 F3 Shebunino Rus. Fed.
207 H4 Shediac Canada
204 D3 Shedin Peak Canada
137 F1 Shedok Rus. Fed.
175 K4 Sheelin, Lough *l.* Ireland
175 K2 Sheep Haven *b.* Ireland
197 I3 Sheepmoor S. Africa
215 E3 Sheep Peak U.S.A.
173 H6 Sheerness U.K.
207 H5 Sheet Harbour Canada
125 G8 Sheffield Australia
126 D5 Sheffield N.Z.
173 F4 Sheffield U.K.
219 C5 Sheffield *AL* U.S.A.
208 C5 Sheffield *IL* U.S.A.
220 D4 Sheffield *PA* U.S.A.
217 C6 Sheffield *TX* U.S.A.
209 G3 Sheguiandah Canada
155 B4 Shehong China
Sheikh, Jebel esh *mt.* Lebanon/Syria *see* Hermon, Mount
148 C3 Sheikhupura Pak.
143 H3 Shekārī, Darreh-ye *r.* Afgh.
155 □ Shek Kwu Chau *i.* Hong Kong China
155 □ Shek Pik Reservoir Hong Kong China
186 F3 Sheksna Rus. Fed.
155 □ Shek Uk Shan *mt.* Hong Kong China
143 F4 Shelag *watercourse* Afgh./Iran
133 S2 Shelagskiy, Mys *pt* Rus. Fed.
208 A6 Shelbina U.S.A.
207 G5 Shelburne *N.S.* Canada
209 G3 Shelburne *Ont.* Canada
122 C1 Shelburne Bay Australia
221 G3 Shelburne Falls U.S.A.
208 D4 Shelby *MI* U.S.A.
212 E1 Shelby *MT* U.S.A.
219 D5 Shelby *NC* U.S.A.
220 B4 Shelby *OH* U.S.A.
219 C4 Shelbyville *IN* U.S.A.
208 A6 Shelbyville *MO* U.S.A.
219 C5 Shelbyville *TN* U.S.A.
215 H5 Sheldon *AZ* U.S.A.
208 D5 Sheldon *IL* U.S.A.
221 G2 Sheldon Springs U.S.A.
207 H3 Sheldrake Canada
133 Q3 Shelikhova, Zaliv *g.* Rus. Fed.
202 C4 Shelikof Strait U.S.A.
205 H4 Shellbrook Canada
213 D3 Shelley U.S.A.
125 I5 Shellharbour Australia
214 A1 Shell Mountain U.S.A.
214 A1 Shelter Cove U.S.A.
155 □ Shelter Island Hong Kong China
221 G4 Shelter Island U.S.A.
126 B7 Shelter Point N.Z.
141 J2 Shemonaikha Kazakh.
216 E3 Shenandoah *IA* U.S.A.
221 E4 Shenandoah *PA* U.S.A.
220 D5 Shenandoah *VA* U.S.A.
220 D5 Shenandoah *r.* U.S.A.
220 D5 Shenandoah Mountains U.S.A.
220 D5 Shenandoah National Park U.S.A.
220 C4 Shenango River Lake U.S.A.
155 E6 Shen'ao China
140 E2 Shenbertal Kazakh.
192 C4 Shendam Nigeria
158 C1 Shending Shan *h.* China
140 E3 Shengel'dy Kazakh.
156 B3 Shengping China
155 G4 Shengsi China
155 F4 Shengzhou China
186 G2 Shenkursk Rus. Fed.
154 D2 Shenmu China
155 D4 Shennong Ding *mt.* China
155 D4 Shennongjia China
154 E3 Shenqiu China
158 A1 Shenshu China
121 C6 Shenton, Mount *h.* Australia
160 B3 Shenwo Shuiku *resr* China
160 B3 Shenyang China
155 E6 Shenzhen China
Shenzhen Wan *b.* Hong Kong China *see* Deep Bay
187 C5 Shepetivka Ukr.
119 G3 Shepherd Islands Vanuatu
125 F6 Shepparton Australia
173 H6 Sheppey, Isle of *i.* U.K.
Sherabad Uzbek. *see* Sherobod
173 E7 Sherborne U.K.
207 H4 Sherbrooke *N.S.* Canada
207 F4 Sherbrooke *Que.* Canada
221 F3 Sherburne U.S.A.
175 L4 Shercock Ireland
143 H3 Sher Dahan Pass Afgh.
193 F3 Shereiq Sudan
148 C4 Shergarh India
217 E5 Sheridan *AR* U.S.A.
212 F2 Sheridan *WY* U.S.A.
124 A4 Sheringa Australia
173 I5 Sheringham U.K.
217 D5 Sherman U.S.A.
221 I2 Sherman Mills U.S.A.
215 E1 Sherman Mountain U.S.A.
141 F5 Sherobod Uzbek.
149 G4 Sherpur Bangl.
205 I3 Sherridon Canada
178 D3 's-Hertogenbosch Neth.
173 F4 Sherwood Forest *reg.* U.K.
156 C2 Sheryshevo Rus. Fed.
204 C3 Sheslay Canada
132 A3 Shetland Islands U.K.
140 C3 Shetpe Kazakh.
155 □ Sheung Shui Hong Kong China
155 □ Sheung Sze Mun *sea chan.* Hong Kong China
147 H4 Shevaroy Hills India
140 E3 Shevchenko, Zaliv *l.* Kazakh.
156 D1 Shevli *r.* Rus. Fed.
155 F4 Shexian China
154 F3 Sheyang China
216 D2 Sheyenne U.S.A.
216 D2 Sheyenne *r.* U.S.A.
174 B3 Shiant Islands U.K.
150 H2 Shiashkotan, Ostrov *i.* Rus. Fed.
209 E4 Shiawassee *r.* U.S.A.
146 C6 Shibām Yemen
143 H3 Shībar, Kowtal-e Afgh.
159 F6 Shibata Japan
156 B1 Shibazhan China
158 H2 Shibetsu Japan
158 I3 Shibetsu Japan
138 C6 Shibīn al Kawm Egypt
Shibotsu-jima *i.* Rus. Fed. *see* Zelenyy, Ostrov
159 F6 Shibukawa Japan
155 E5 Shicheng China
160 B4 Shicheng Dao *i.* China
221 E4 Shickshinny U.S.A.
139 G6 Shidād al Mismā' *h.* Saudi Arabia
160 B5 Shidao China
160 B5 Shidao Wan *b.* China
141 H2 Shiderti *r.* Kazakh.
174 C4 Shiel, Loch *l.* U.K.
122 B2 Shield, Cape Australia
136 D5 Shifa, Jabal ash *mts* Saudi Arabia
155 B4 Shifang China
187 I4 Shigony Rus. Fed.
154 D1 Shiguai China
135 G2 Shihezi China
154 E2 Shijiazhuang China
143 F4 Shikar *r.* Pak.
147 G3 Shikarpur India
148 B4 Shikarpur Pak.
159 C8 Shikoku *i.* Japan
159 C8 Shikoku-sanchi *mts* Japan
157 G4 Shikotan, Ostrov *i.* Rus. Fed.
Shikotan-tō *i.* Rus. Fed. *see* Shikotan, Ostrov
158 G3 Shikotsu-Tōya Kokuritsu-kōen *nat. park* Japan
140 D2 Shil'da Rus. Fed.
172 F3 Shildon U.K.
186 H1 Shilega Rus. Fed.
149 G4 Shiliguri India
155 D4 Shilipu China
148 D2 Shilla *mt.* India
175 L5 Shillelagh Ireland
209 G1 Shillington Canada
149 G4 Shillong India
140 B2 Shil'naya Balka Kazakh.
221 F5 Shiloh U.S.A.
154 D2 Shilou China
187 G4 Shilovo Rus. Fed.
159 B8 Shimabara Japan
159 F7 Shimada Japan
150 E1 Shimanovsk Rus. Fed.
155 D4 Shimen China
155 B4 Shimian China
159 F7 Shimizu Japan
148 D3 Shimla India
159 F7 Shimoda Japan
147 G3 Shimoga India
157 F4 Shimokita-hantō *pen.* Japan
195 D4 Shimoni Kenya
159 B8 Shimonoseki Japan
148 C1 Shimshal Pak.
186 D3 Shimsk Rus. Fed.
174 D2 Shin, Loch *l.* U.K.
143 F3 Shīndand Afgh.
148 B3 Shinghar Pak.
148 C1 Shinghshal Pass Pak.
208 D2 Shingleton U.S.A.
141 J3 Shingozha Kazakh.
159 E8 Shingū Japan
197 I1 Shingwedzi S. Africa
197 I1 Shingwedzi *r.* S. Africa
173 E4 Shining Tor *h.* U.K.
209 G2 Shining Tree Canada
159 G5 Shinjō Japan
143 G4 Shīnkay Afgh.
159 E6 Shinminato Japan
221 I1 Shin Pond U.S.A.
195 D4 Shinyanga Tanz.
159 G5 Shiogama Japan
159 D8 Shiono-misaki *c.* Japan
159 G6 Shioya-zaki *pt* Japan
155 E4 Shipai China
219 E7 Ship Chan Cay *i.* Bahamas
155 B6 Shiping China
148 D3 Shipki Pass China/India
173 F4 Shipley U.K.
207 H4 Shippegan Canada
221 E4 Shippensburg U.S.A.
215 H3 Shiprock U.S.A.
215 H3 Shiprock Peak U.S.A.
155 F4 Shipu China
141 J1 Shipunovo Rus. Fed.
155 C5 Shiqian China
154 C3 Shiquan China
Shiquanhe China *see* Ali
149 E2 Shiquan He *r.* China *conv.* Indus
154 C3 Shiquan Shuiku *resr* China
139 L2 Shīrābād Iran
158 G4 Shirakami-sanchi *tourist site* Japan
159 G6 Shirakawa Japan
159 E6 Shirakawa-go and Gokayama *tourist site* Japan
150 F3 Shirane-san *mt.* Japan
159 F6 Shirane-san *vol.* Japan
127 L4 Shirase Glacier Antarctica
142 D4 Shīrāz Iran
138 C6 Shirbīn Egypt
158 I2 Shiretoko-misaki *c.* Japan
140 E3 Shirikrabat *tourist site* Kazakh.
141 G4 Shirin Uzbek.
143 G4 Shirinab *r.* Pak.
158 G4 Shiriya-zaki *c.* Japan
140 D3 Shirkala *reg.* Kazakh.
221 G4 Shirley U.S.A.
221 I2 Shirley Mills U.S.A.
159 E7 Shirotori Japan
148 C5 Shirpur India
144 I3 Shirten Holoy Gobi *des.* China
143 E2 Shīrvān Iran
156 B2 Shisanzhan China
155 D4 Shishou China
155 E4 Shitai China
155 F4 Shitang China
139 I5 Shithāthah Iraq
148 B4 Shiv India
133 R4 Shiveluch, Sopka *vol.* Rus. Fed.
219 C4 Shively U.S.A.
148 D4 Shivpuri India
215 F3 Shivwits Plateau U.S.A.
143 H2 Shiwal *l.* Afgh.
155 C6 Shiwan Dashan *mts* China
155 E5 Shixing China
154 D3 Shiyan China
155 C4 Shizhu China
155 B5 Shizong China
159 G5 Shizugawa Japan
154 C2 Shizuishan China
159 F7 Shizuoka Japan
146 B1 Shkhara *mt.* Georgia/Rus. Fed.
187 D4 Shklow Belarus
185 H3 Shkodër Albania
133 J1 Shmidta, Ostrov *i.* Rus. Fed.
156 F1 Shmidta, Poluostrov *pen.* Rus. Fed.
159 C7 Shōbara Japan
141 G5 Shoh Tajik.
158 G3 Shokanbetsu-dake *mt.* Japan
141 G4 Sholakkorgan Kazakh.
141 F2 Sholaksay Kazakh.
140 D3 Shomishkol' Kazakh.
186 I2 Shomvukva Rus. Fed.
174 C4 Shona, Eilean *i.* U.K.
239 J9 Shona Ridge *sea feature* S. Atlantic Ocean
140 D3 Shoptykol' *Aktyubinskaya Oblast'* Kazakh.
141 H2 Shoptykol' *Pavlodarskaya Oblast'* Kazakh.
148 D2 Shor India
147 H4 Shoranur India
143 G5 Shorap Pak.
143 G4 Shorawak *reg.* Afgh.
Shor Barsa-Kel'mes *salt marsh* Uzbek. *see* Borsakelmas sho'rxogi
141 F5 Sho'rchi Uzbek.
139 J3 Shor Gol Iran
148 C3 Shorkot Pak.
140 C4 Shorkozakhly, Solonchak *salt flat* Turkm.
141 G2 Shortandy Kazakh.
158 G2 Shosanbetsu Japan
215 D4 Shoshone *CA* U.S.A.
213 D3 Shoshone *ID* U.S.A.
212 E2 Shoshone *r.* U.S.A.
212 E2 Shoshone Lake U.S.A.
213 C4 Shoshone Mountains U.S.A.
197 G1 Shoshong Botswana
213 E3 Shoshoni U.S.A.
187 E5 Shostka Ukr.
142 D3 Shotoran, Chashmeh-ye *well* Iran
143 G3 Shotor Khūn Afgh.
154 F2 Shouguang China
155 F5 Shouning China
154 E3 Shouxian China
154 D2 Shouyang China
154 C3 Shouyang Shan *mt.* China
215 G4 Show Low U.S.A.
187 G6 Shpakovskoye Rus. Fed.
187 D5 Shpola Ukr.
217 E5 Shreveport U.S.A.
173 E5 Shrewsbury U.K.
147 G2 Shrigonda India
149 G5 Shrirampur India
141 H4 Shu Kazakh.
139 K6 Shu'aiba Iraq
155 A5 Shuangbai China
160 D1 Shuangcheng China
155 C4 Shuanghechang China
156 C2 Shuanghedagang China
160 B2 Shuangliao China
155 D5 Shuangpai China
Shuangshipu China *see* Fengxian
160 A3 Shuangtaizihe Kou *r. mouth* China
160 C2 Shuangyang China
158 B1 Shuangyashan China
140 D2 Shubarkuduk Kazakh.
140 D2 Shubarshi Kazakh.
139 C6 Shubrā al Khaymah Egypt
155 E4 Shucheng China
141 H5 Shufu China
154 F3 Shu He *r.* China
155 F5 Shuiji China
155 D5 Shuikou China
154 A2 Shuiquanzi China
148 B3 Shujaabad Pak.
160 D1 Shulan China
141 I5 Shule China
154 D1 Shulinzhao China
140 D4 Shumanay Uzbek.
158 H2 Shumarinai-ko *l.* Japan
195 C5 Shumba Zimbabwe
185 L3 Shumen Bulg.
187 H4 Shumerlya Rus. Fed.
177 N3 Shumilina Belarus
215 G4 Shumway U.S.A.
187 E4 Shumyachi Rus. Fed.
141 H3 Shunak, Gora *mt.* Kazakh.
155 E5 Shunchang China
160 B3 Shuncheng China
155 D6 Shunde China
202 C3 Shungnak U.S.A.
154 E1 Shunyi China
155 C6 Shuolong China
154 D2 Shuozhou China
146 C7 Shuqrah Yemen
142 D4 Shūr *r.* Iran
142 D4 Shūr *r.* Iran
143 F3 Shūr *r.* Iran
142 D4 Shūr *watercourse* Iran
142 D5 Shūr *watercourse* Iran
143 E3 Shur *watercourse* Iran
142 D3 Shūr, Chāh-e *well* Iran
143 E4 Shūr, Rūd-e *watercourse* Iran
142 C3 Shūr Āb Iran
142 D3 Shūrāb Iran
143 E3 Shūrāb Iran
143 E4 Shūr Āb *watercourse* Iran
Shurchi Uzbek. *see* Sho'rchi
142 D3 Shureghestan Iran
143 E4 Shūr Gaz Iran
142 D4 Shūrjestān Iran
141 G4 Shūrob Tajik.
195 D5 Shurugwi Zimbabwe
139 J6 Shuruppak *tourist site* Iraq
143 F4 Shusf Iran
142 C3 Shūsh Iran
142 C3 Shushtar Iran
204 F4 Shuswap Lake Canada
139 F6 Shuwaysh, Tall ash *h.* Jordan
186 G3 Shuya Rus. Fed.
154 F3 Shuyang China
169 O4 Shuyskoye Rus. Fed.
162 A1 Shwegun Myanmar
141 G3 Shyganak Kazakh.
141 H3 Shygys Konyrat Kazakh.
141 G4 Shymkent Kazakh.
148 D2 Shyok India
148 D2 Shyok *r.* India
187 F5 Shypuvate Ukr.
187 E6 Shyroke Ukr.
151 F7 Sia Indon.
148 D2 Siachen Glacier India
143 F5 Siahan Range *mts* Pak.
139 J2 Sīāh Chashmeh Iran
143 G3 Siah Koh *mts* Afgh.
142 D3 Sīāh Kūh *mts* Iran
142 D3 Sīāh Kūh, Kavīr-e *salt flat* Iran
143 G4 Sīāh Sang, Kowtal-e Afgh.
148 C2 Sialkot Pak.
156 B1 Sian Rus. Fed.
225 H4 Sian Ka'an, Reserva de la Biósfera *nature res.* Mex.
162 C5 Siantan *i.* Indon.
233 K4 Siapa *r.* Venez.
143 F4 Sīāreh Iran
161 J4 Siargao *i.* Phil.
161 I5 Siasi Phil.
161 I5 Siasi *i.* Phil.
161 I4 Siaton Phil.
171 M5 Šiauliai Lith.
143 F5 Sib Iran
142 C3 Sībak Iran
197 I1 Sibasa S. Africa
161 I4 Sibay *i.* Phil.
140 D1 Sibay Rus. Fed.
197 J3 Sibayi, Lake S. Africa
127 I5 Sibbald, Cape Antarctica
184 F3 Šibenik Croatia
133 M3 Siberia *reg.* Rus. Fed.
163 E3 Siberut *i.* Indon.
148 A3 Sibi Pak.
194 D3 Sibiloi National Park Kenya
Sibir' *reg.* Rus. Fed. *see* Siberia
158 C2 Sibirtsevo Rus. Fed.
195 B4 Sibiti Congo
185 K2 Sibiu Romania
162 A2 Sibolga Indon.
162 A5 Siborongborong Indon.
149 H4 Sibsagar India
163 H2 Sibu *Sarawak* Malaysia
161 I5 Sibuco Phil.
161 I5 Sibuguey *r.* Phil.

South Seal

185 L3 **Sliven** Bulg.
186 H2 **Sloboda** Rus. Fed.
186 I2 **Slobodchikovo** Rus. Fed.
169 Q4 **Slobodskoy** Rus. Fed.
185 L2 **Slobozia** Romania
204 F5 **Slocan** Canada
179 E1 **Slochteren** Neth.
187 C4 **Slonim** Belarus
178 C2 **Slootdorp** Neth.
178 D2 **Sloten** Neth.
178 D2 **Slotermeer** *l.* Neth.
173 G6 **Slough** U.K.
177 I6 **Slovakia** *country* Europe
184 F1 **Slovenia** *country* Europe
184 F1 **Slovenj Gradec** Slovenia
187 F5 **Slov"yans'k** Ukr.
181 I1 **Sluch** *r.* Ukr.
162 C3 **S'Lung, B'Nom** *mt.* Vietnam
177 H3 **Słupsk** Poland
170 L2 **Slussfors** Sweden
187 C4 **Slutsk** Belarus
175 H4 **Slyne Head** Ireland
133 L4 **Slyudyanka** Rus. Fed.
221 I3 **Small Point** U.S.A.
207 H3 **Smallwood Reservoir** Canada
187 D4 **Smalyavichy** Belarus
Smalyenskaya Wzwyshsha *hills* Belarus/Rus. Fed. *see* **Smolensko-Moskovskaya Vozvyshennost'**
177 M3 **Smarhon'** Belarus
197 E5 **Smartt Syndicate Dam** *resr* S. Africa
205 I4 **Smeaton** Canada
185 I2 **Smederevo** Serbia
185 I2 **Smederevska Palanka** Serbia
220 D4 **Smethport** U.S.A.
156 D2 **Smidovich** Rus. Fed.
187 D5 **Smila** Ukr.
179 E2 **Smilde** Neth.
171 N4 **Smiltene** Latvia
141 G1 **Smirnovo** Kazakh.
156 F2 **Smirnykh** Rus. Fed.
205 G3 **Smith** Canada
214 C2 **Smith** U.S.A.
220 C6 **Smith** *r.* U.S.A.
202 C2 **Smith Bay** U.S.A.
204 D4 **Smithers** Canada
197 G5 **Smithfield** S. Africa
219 E5 **Smithfield** *NC* U.S.A.
213 E3 **Smithfield** *UT* U.S.A.
221 E5 **Smith Island** *MD* U.S.A.
221 F6 **Smith Island** *VA* U.S.A.
220 D6 **Smith Mountain Lake** U.S.A.
204 D3 **Smith River** Canada
209 I3 **Smiths Falls** Canada
203 K2 **Smith Sound** *sea chan.* Canada/Greenland
125 F8 **Smithton** Australia
214 C1 **Smoke Creek Desert** U.S.A.
204 F4 **Smoky** *r.* Canada
121 F7 **Smoky Bay** Australia
125 J3 **Smoky Cape** Australia
206 D3 **Smoky Falls** Canada
217 C4 **Smoky Hill** *r.* U.S.A.
217 D4 **Smoky Hills** U.S.A.
205 G4 **Smoky Lake** Canada
171 I3 **Smøla** *i.* Norway
140 B2 **Smolenka** Rus. Fed.
187 E4 **Smolensk** Rus. Fed.
187 E4 **Smolenskaya Oblast'** *admin. div.* Rus. Fed.
Smolensk-Moscow Upland *hills* Belarus/Rus. Fed. *see* **Smolensko-Moskovskaya Vozvyshennost'**
169 M5 **Smolensko-Moskovskaya Vozvyshennost'** *hills* Belarus/Rus. Fed.
141 K1 **Smolenskoye** Rus. Fed.
185 K4 **Smolyan** Bulg.
158 C3 **Smolyoninovo** Rus. Fed.
206 D4 **Smooth Rock Falls** Canada
206 C3 **Smoothrock Lake** Canada
205 H4 **Smoothstone Lake** Canada
170 N1 **Smørfjord** Norway
221 F5 **Smyrna** *DE* U.S.A.
219 C5 **Smyrna** *GA* U.S.A.
220 C4 **Smyrna** *OH* U.S.A.
221 I1 **Smyrna Mills** U.S.A.
170 D2 **Snæfell** *mt.* Iceland
172 C3 **Snaefell** *h.* U.K.
204 A2 **Snag** Canada
213 D3 **Snake** *r.* U.S.A.
215 E2 **Snake Range** *mts* U.S.A.
213 D3 **Snake River Plain** U.S.A.
Snare Lakes Canada *see* **Wekweêtì**
119 G6 **Snares Islands** N.Z.
170 K2 **Snåsa** Norway
178 D1 **Sneek** Neth.
175 I6 **Sneem** Ireland
197 F6 **Sneeuberge** *mts* S. Africa
207 H3 **Snegamook Lake** Canada
173 H5 **Snettisham** U.K.
133 J3 **Snezhnogorsk** Rus. Fed.
184 F2 **Snežnik** *mt.* Slovenia
177 J4 **Śniardwy, Jezioro** *l.* Poland
187 E6 **Snihurivka** Ukr.
174 B3 **Snizort, Loch** *b.* U.K.
212 B2 **Snohomish** U.S.A.
212 B2 **Snoqualmie Pass** U.S.A.
170 K2 **Snøtinden** *mt.* Norway
205 I2 **Snowbird Lake** Canada
173 C4 **Snowdon** *mt.* U.K.
173 D5 **Snowdonia National Park** U.K.
215 G4 **Snowflake** U.S.A.
221 F5 **Snow Hill** *MD* U.S.A.
219 E5 **Snow Hill** *NC* U.S.A.
205 I4 **Snow Lake** Canada
124 C4 **Snowtown** Australia
213 D3 **Snowville** U.S.A.
125 H6 **Snowy** *r.* Australia
125 H6 **Snowy Mountains** Australia
125 G9 **Snug** Australia
207 I3 **Snug Harbour** *Nfld* Canada
209 G3 **Snug Harbour** *Ont.* Canada
162 C2 **Snuŏl** Cambodia
217 D5 **Snyder** *OK* U.S.A.
217 C5 **Snyder** *TX* U.S.A.
195 E5 **Soalala** Madag.
195 E5 **Soanierana-Ivongo** Madag.
160 D6 **Soan-kundo** *is* S. Korea
233 I3 **Soata** Col.
174 B3 **Soay** *i.* U.K.
160 D6 **Sobaek-sanmaek** *mts* S. Korea
193 F4 **Sobat** *r.* Sudan
151 G7 **Sobger** *r.* Indon.
159 B8 **Sobo-san** *mt.* Japan
231 J6 **Sobradinho, Barragem de** *resr* Brazil
231 J4 **Sobral** Brazil
187 F7 **Sochi** Rus. Fed.
160 D5 **Sŏch'ŏn** S. Korea
117 I5 **Society Islands** Fr. Polynesia
234 C3 **Socorro** Brazil
233 I3 **Socorro** Col.
213 F5 **Socorro** U.S.A.
222 B5 **Socorro, Isla** *i.* Mex.
146 D7 **Socotra** *i.* Yemen
162 C3 **Soc Trăng** Vietnam
183 O3 **Socuéllamos** Spain
215 D4 **Soda Lake** U.S.A.
170 N2 **Sodankylä** Fin.
148 D2 **Soda Plains** Aksai Chin
213 E3 **Soda Springs** U.S.A.
171 L3 **Söderhamn** Sweden
171 L4 **Söderköping** Sweden
171 L4 **Södertälje** Sweden
193 E3 **Sodiri** Sudan
194 D3 **Sodo** Eth.
171 L3 **Södra Kvarken** *str.* Fin./Sweden
197 H1 **Soekmekaar** S. Africa
178 D3 **Soerendonk** Neth.
179 G3 **Soest** Germany
178 D2 **Soest** Neth.
125 H4 **Sofala** Australia
185 J3 **Sofia** Bulg.
Sofiya Bulg. *see* **Sofia**
156 D1 **Sofiysk** *Khabarovskiy Kray* Rus. Fed.
156 E2 **Sofiysk** *Khabarovskiy Kray* Rus. Fed.
170 O2 **Sofporog** Rus. Fed.
185 L6 **Sofrana** *i.* Greece
159 G10 **Sōfu-gan** *i.* Japan
149 H3 **Sog** China
233 I3 **Sogamoso** Col.
139 G1 **Soğanlı Dağları** *mts* Turkey
156 D2 **Sogda** Rus. Fed.
179 F2 **Sögel** Germany
171 I4 **Søgne** Norway
171 I3 **Sognefjorden** *inlet* Norway
161 J4 **Sogod** Phil.
154 A1 **Sogo Nur** *l.* China
186 H2 **Sogra** Rus. Fed.
154 A3 **Sogruma** China
138 C1 **Söğüt** Turkey
136 C3 **Söğüt Dağı** *mts* Turkey
160 D7 **Sŏgwip'o** S. Korea
Sohâg Egypt *see* **Sūhāj**
148 D5 **Sohagpur** India
173 H5 **Soham** U.K.
148 B2 **Sohan** *r.* Pak.
119 F2 **Sohano** P.N.G.
147 I1 **Sohela** India
148 D3 **Sohna** India
160 E3 **Sŏho-ri** N. Korea
160 C6 **Sohŭksan** S. Korea
157 B6 **Sohŭksan-do** *i.* S. Korea
178 C4 **Soignes, Forêt de** *for.* Belgium
178 C4 **Soignies** Belgium
171 N3 **Soini** Fin.
182 F2 **Soissons** France
148 C4 **Sojat** India
161 I4 **Sojoton Point** Phil.
187 C5 **Sokal'** Ukr.
160 E4 **Sokch'o** S. Korea
185 L6 **Söke** Turkey
153 I1 **Sokhor, Gora** *mt.* Rus. Fed.
187 G7 **Sokhumi** Georgia
192 C4 **Sokodé** Togo
155 □ **Soko Islands** *Hong Kong* China
186 G3 **Sokol** Rus. Fed.
177 K4 **Sokółka** Poland
192 B3 **Sokolo** Mali
179 K4 **Sokolov** Czech Rep.
158 C3 **Sokolovka** Rus. Fed.
177 K4 **Sokołów Podlaski** Poland
192 C3 **Sokoto** Nigeria
192 C3 **Sokoto** *r.* Nigeria
187 C5 **Sokyryany** Ukr.
148 D3 **Solan** India
126 A7 **Solander Island** N.Z.
147 G2 **Solapur** India
233 I2 **Soledad** Col.
214 B3 **Soledad** U.S.A.
233 L2 **Soledad** Venez.
225 E4 **Soledad de Doblado** Mex.
187 G6 **Solenoye** Rus. Fed.
170 K2 **Solfjellsjøen** Norway
139 H2 **Solhan** Turkey
186 G3 **Soligalich** Rus. Fed.
173 F5 **Solihull** U.K.
132 G4 **Solikamsk** Rus. Fed.
140 C2 **Sol'-Iletsk** Rus. Fed.
225 H4 **Solimón, Punta** *pt* Mex.
179 F3 **Solingen** Germany
196 A1 **Solitaire** Namibia
139 L1 **Şollar** Azer.
171 L3 **Sollefteå** Sweden
179 K3 **Söllichau** Germany
179 H3 **Solling** *hills* Germany
179 I3 **Sollstedt** Germany
Sollum, Gulf of *b.* Egypt *see* **Sallum, Khalīj as**
179 G4 **Solms** Germany
186 F3 **Solnechnogorsk** Rus. Fed.
156 A1 **Solnechnyy** *Amurskaya Oblast'* Rus. Fed.
156 E2 **Solnechnyy** *Khabarovskiy Kray* Rus. Fed.
163 B3 **Solok** Indon.
225 G5 **Sololá** Guat.
119 G2 **Solomon Islands** *country* Pacific Ocean
119 F2 **Solomon Sea** P.N.G./Solomon Is
141 K2 **Soloneshnoye** Rus. Fed.
208 B2 **Solon Springs** U.S.A.
151 E7 **Solor, Kepulauan** *is* Indon.
176 C7 **Solothurn** Switz.
186 E1 **Solovetskiye Ostrova** *is* Rus. Fed.
186 H3 **Solovetskoye** Rus. Fed.
156 B1 **Solov'yevsk** Rus. Fed.
185 G3 **Šolta** *i.* Croatia
137 H4 **Solṭānābād** Iran
143 E2 **Solṭānābād** Iran
143 E3 **Solṭānābād** Iran
179 H2 **Soltau** Germany
186 D3 **Sol'tsy** Rus. Fed.
221 E3 **Solvay** U.S.A.
171 K4 **Sölvesborg** Sweden
174 E6 **Solway Firth** *est.* U.K.
195 C5 **Solwezi** Zambia
159 G6 **Sōma** Japan
138 A2 **Soma** Turkey
178 B4 **Somain** France
194 E3 **Somalia** *country* Africa
238 H5 **Somali Basin** *sea feature* Indian Ocean
195 C4 **Sombo** Angola
185 H2 **Sombor** Serbia
225 D3 **Sombrerete** Mex.
148 C4 **Somdari** India
221 I2 **Somerest Junction** U.S.A.
171 M3 **Somero** Fin.
219 C4 **Somerset** *KY* U.S.A.
209 E4 **Somerset** *MI* U.S.A.
220 D5 **Somerset** *PA* U.S.A.
197 F6 **Somerset East** S. Africa
203 I2 **Somerset Island** Canada
221 G3 **Somerset Reservoir** U.S.A.
196 C7 **Somerset West** S. Africa
221 H3 **Somersworth** U.S.A.
217 D6 **Somerville Reservoir** U.S.A.
142 B3 **Someydeh** Iran
171 K4 **Sommen** *l.* Sweden
179 J3 **Sömmerda** Germany
207 G3 **Sommet, Lac du** *l.* Canada
148 B5 **Somnath** India
208 C5 **Somonauk** U.S.A.
224 H5 **Somotillo** Nicaragua
224 H5 **Somoto** Nicaragua
235 I4 **Somuncurá, Mesa Volcánica de** *plat.* Arg.
149 F4 **Son** *r.* India
224 I7 **Soná** Panama
141 G2 **Sonaly** *Karagandinskaya Oblast'* Kazakh.
141 G2 **Sonaly** *Karagandinskaya Oblast'* Kazakh.
149 F5 **Sonamukhi** India
149 G5 **Sonamura** India
147 I1 **Sonapur** India
148 D4 **Sonar** *r.* India
149 H4 **Sonari** India
161 F2 **Sŏnbong** N. Korea
160 C4 **Sŏnch'ŏn** N. Korea
186 E2 **Sondaly** Rus. Fed.
171 J5 **Sønderborg** Denmark
179 I3 **Sondershausen** Germany
184 C1 **Sondrio** Italy
147 H2 **Sonepet** India
148 B5 **Songad** India
155 E4 **Songbu** China
163 D2 **Sông Câu** Vietnam
Sông Cau Vietnam *see* **Sông Câu**
195 D5 **Songea** Tanz.
160 D3 **Sŏnggan** N. Korea
160 D2 **Songhua Hu** *resr* China
160 C1 **Songhuajiang** China
158 B1 **Songhua Jiang** *r.* China
160 E2 **Songjiang** *Jilin* China
155 F4 **Songjiang** *Shanghai* China
160 D2 **Songjianghe** China
155 C4 **Songkan** China
162 B4 **Songkhla** Thai.
141 H4 **Songköl** *l.* Kyrg.
154 F1 **Song Ling** *mts* China
160 D5 **Sŏngnam** S. Korea
160 C4 **Songnim** N. Korea
195 B4 **Songo** Angola
195 D5 **Songo** Moz.
154 B3 **Songpan** China
149 G4 **Songsak** India
160 D7 **Sŏngsan** S. Korea
154 D3 **Song Shan** *mt.* China
160 D3 **Songshuzhen** China
155 C4 **Songtao** China
155 F5 **Songxi** China
154 D3 **Songxian** China
160 C1 **Songyuan** China
155 D4 **Songzi** China
163 D2 **Sơn Ha** Vietnam
163 D3 **Sơn Hai** Vietnam
148 D3 **Sonipat** India
171 N3 **Sonkajärvi** Fin.
155 B6 **Sơn La** Vietnam
143 G5 **Sonmiani** Pak.
143 G5 **Sonmiani Bay** Pak.
179 J4 **Sonneberg** Germany
234 D2 **Sono** *r. Minas Gerais* Brazil
231 I6 **Sono** *r.* Brazil
215 F6 **Sonoita** Mex.
215 F6 **Sonoita** *watercourse* Mex.
215 G6 **Sonoita** U.S.A.
224 B1 **Sonora** *r.* Mex.
224 B2 **Sonora** *state* Mex.
214 B3 **Sonora** *CA* U.S.A.
217 C6 **Sonora** *TX* U.S.A.
142 B3 **Sonqor** Iran
233 I3 **Sonsón** Col.
225 G5 **Sonsonate** El Salvador
155 B6 **Sơn Tây** Vietnam
197 H5 **Sonwabile** S. Africa
235 L1 **Sopas** *r.* Uruguay
193 E4 **Sopo** *watercourse* Sudan
185 K3 **Sopot** Bulg.
177 I3 **Sopot** Poland
177 H7 **Sopron** Hungary
141 H4 **Sopu-Korgon** Kyrg.
184 E4 **Sora** Italy
147 J2 **Sorada** India
171 L3 **Söråker** Sweden
160 E4 **Sŏrak-san** *mt.* S. Korea
157 C5 **Sŏrak-san National Park** S. Korea
207 F4 **Sorel** Canada
125 G9 **Sorell** Australia
125 G9 **Sorell Lake** Australia
138 E2 **Sorgun** Turkey
183 O2 **Soria** Spain
132 C2 **Sørkappøya** *i.* Svalbard
142 D3 **Sorkh, Kūh-e** *mts* Iran
142 D3 **Sorkheh** Iran
170 K2 **Sørli** Norway
171 J5 **Sorø** Denmark
149 F5 **Soro** India
187 D5 **Soroca** Moldova
234 C3 **Sorocaba** Brazil
140 C1 **Sorochinsk** Rus. Fed.
141 K1 **Sorokino** Rus. Fed.
151 G6 **Sorol** *atoll* Micronesia
151 F7 **Sorong** Indon.
194 D3 **Soroti** Uganda
170 M1 **Sørøya** *i.* Norway
183 L3 **Sorraia** *r.* Port.
170 L1 **Sørreisa** Norway
125 F7 **Sorrento** Australia
184 F4 **Sorrento** Italy
195 B6 **Sorris Sorris** Namibia
170 L2 **Sorsele** Sweden
161 J3 **Sorsogon** Phil.
186 D2 **Sortavala** Rus. Fed.
170 K1 **Sortland** Norway
186 I2 **Sortopolovskaya** Rus. Fed.
186 I3 **Sorvizhi** Rus. Fed.
160 D5 **Sŏsan** S. Korea
197 H2 **Soshanguve** S. Africa
187 F4 **Sosna** *r.* Rus. Fed.
235 I2 **Sosneado** *mt.* Arg.
186 J2 **Sosnogorsk** Rus. Fed.
141 I2 **Sosnovka** Kazakh.
186 H2 **Sosnovka** *Arkhangel'skaya Oblast'* Rus. Fed.
169 K5 **Sosnovka** Rus. Fed.
132 F3 **Sosnovka** *Murmanskaya Oblast'* Rus. Fed.
187 G4 **Sosnovka** *Tambovskaya Oblast'* Rus. Fed.
153 J1 **Sosnovo-Ozerskoye** Rus. Fed.
170 P2 **Sosnovyy** Rus. Fed.
171 O4 **Sosnovyy Bor** Rus. Fed.
177 I5 **Sosnowiec** Poland
187 F6 **Sosyka** *r.* Rus. Fed.
233 H4 **Sotara, Volcán** *vol.* Col.
170 O2 **Sotkamo** Fin.
235 J1 **Soto** Arg.
225 E3 **Soto la Marina** Mex.
225 G3 **Sotuta** Mex.
194 B3 **Souanké** Congo
192 B4 **Soubré** Côte d'Ivoire
221 F4 **Souderton** U.S.A.
185 L4 **Soufli** Greece
182 E4 **Souillac** France
178 D5 **Souilly** France
192 C1 **Souk Ahras** Alg.
180 B5 **Souk el Arbaâ du Rharb** Morocco
Sŏul S. Korea *see* **Seoul**
183 D5 **Soulom** France
Soûr Lebanon *see* **Tyre**
183 R4 **Sour el Ghozlane** Alg.
205 I5 **Souris** *Man.* Canada
207 H4 **Souris** *P.E.I.* Canada
205 I5 **Souris** *r.* Canada/U.S.A.
231 K5 **Sousa** Brazil
193 D1 **Sousse** Tunisia
183 D5 **Soustons** France
197 E4 **South Africa, Republic of** *country* Africa
228 **South America**
209 G3 **Southampton** Canada
173 F7 **Southampton** U.K.
221 G4 **Southampton** U.S.A.
205 L2 **Southampton Island** Canada
145 H9 **South Andaman** *i.* India
221 E6 **South Anna** *r.* U.S.A.
173 F4 **South Anston** U.K.
207 H2 **South Aulatsivik Island** Canada
118 D5 **South Australia** *state* Australia
238 L7 **South Australian Basin** *sea feature* Indian Ocean
217 F5 **Southaven** U.S.A.
213 F5 **South Baldy** *mt.* U.S.A.
172 F3 **South Bank** U.K.
220 B4 **South Bass Island** U.S.A.
209 F3 **South Baymouth** Canada
208 D5 **South Bend** *IN* U.S.A.
212 B2 **South Bend** *WA* U.S.A.
219 E7 **South Bight** *sea chan.* Bahamas
220 D6 **South Boston** U.S.A.
126 D5 **Southbridge** N.Z.
221 G3 **Southbridge** U.S.A.
South Cape *pt* U.S.A. *see* **Ka Lae**
219 D5 **South Carolina** *state* U.S.A.
221 I2 **South China** U.S.A.
163 G1 **South China Sea** Pacific Ocean
216 C2 **South Dakota** *state* U.S.A.
221 G3 **South Deerfield** U.S.A.
173 G7 **South Downs** *hills* U.K.
197 F2 **South-East** *admin. dist.* Botswana
125 G9 **South East Cape** Australia
238 J7 **Southeast Indian Ridge** *sea feature* Indian Ocean
121 C7 **South East Isles** Australia
237 L10 **Southeast Pacific Basin** *sea feature* S. Pacific Ocean
205 I3 **Southend** Canada
174 C5 **Southend** U.K.
173 H6 **Southend-on-Sea** U.K.
208 A5 **South English** U.S.A.
197 E2 **Southern** *admin. dist.* Botswana
126 C5 **Southern Alps** *mts* N.Z.
118 B5 **Southern Cross** Australia
205 J3 **Southern Indian Lake** Canada
193 E4 **Southern National Park** Sudan
236 E10 **Southern Ocean** World
219 E5 **Southern Pines** U.S.A.
229 G7 **Southern Thule** S. Sandwich Is
174 D5 **Southern Uplands** *hills* U.K.
175 F4 **South Esk** *r.* U.K.
120 D3 **South Esk Tableland** *reg.* Australia
208 B6 **South Fabius** *r.* U.S.A.
236 G7 **South Fiji Basin** *sea feature* S. Pacific Ocean
213 F4 **South Fork** U.S.A.
South Fork South Branch *r.* U.S.A. *see* **Potomac, South Fork South Branch**
209 E3 **South Fox Island** U.S.A.
127 J5 **South Geomagnetic Pole** Antarctica
232 □ **South Georgia** *terr.* S. Atlantic Ocean
229 G7 **South Georgia and the South Sandwich Islands** *terr.* Atlantic Ocean
174 A3 **South Harris** *pen.* U.K.
149 G5 **South Hatia Island** Bangl.
208 D4 **South Haven** U.S.A.
205 J2 **South Henik Lake** Canada
221 G2 **South Hero** U.S.A.
220 D6 **South Hill** U.S.A.
236 E3 **South Honshu Ridge** *sea feature* N. Pacific Ocean
205 J3 **South Indian Lake** Canada
221 G4 **Southington** U.S.A.
126 C6 **South Island** N.Z.
194 D3 **South Island National Park** Kenya
161 H4 **South Islet** *rf* Phil.
147 J1 **South Koel** *r.* India
160 D5 **South Korea** *country* Asia
214 B2 **South Lake Tahoe** U.S.A.
195 D5 **South Luangwa National Park** Zambia
127 J6 **South Magnetic Pole** Antarctica
208 D3 **South Manitou Island** U.S.A.
219 D7 **South Miami** U.S.A.
173 H6 **Southminster** U.K.
205 I4 **South Moose Lake** Canada
221 E5 **South Mountains** U.S.A.
202 F3 **South Nahanni** *r.* Can.
174 □ **South Nesting Bay** U.K.
239 G10 **South Orkney Islands** S. Atlantic Ocean
119 H5 **South Pacific Ocean**
221 H2 **South Paris** U.S.A.
213 G3 **South Platte** *r.* U.S.A.
127 J4 **South Pole** Antarctica
209 G1 **South Porcupine** Canada
125 J1 **Southport** Australia
173 D4 **Southport** U.K.
221 H3 **South Portland** U.S.A.
209 H3 **South River** Canada
175 F2 **South Ronaldsay** *i.* U.K.
221 G3 **South Royalton** U.S.A.
197 I5 **South Sand Bluff** *pt* S. Africa
239 H9 **South Sandwich Islands** S. Atlantic Ocean
239 H9 **South Sandwich Trench** *sea feature* S. Atlantic Ocean
205 H4 **South Saskatchewan** *r.* Canada
205 J3 **South Seal** *r.* Canada

South Shetland Islands

127 I2 South Shetland Islands Antarctica
239 E10 South Shetland Trough sea feature S. Atlantic Ocean
172 F2 South Shields U.K.
208 A5 South Skunk r. U.S.A.
236 F6 South Solomon Trench sea feature Pacific Ocean
126 E3 South Taranaki Bight b. N.Z.
238 N8 South Tasman Rise sea feature Southern Ocean
215 G2 South Tent mt. U.S.A.
149 E4 South Tons r. India
206 E3 South Twin Island Canada
172 E3 South Tyne r. U.K.
174 A3 South Uist i. U.K.
122 B3 South Wellesley Islands Australia
125 G9 South West Cape Australia
126 A7 South West Cape N.Z.
122 E1 South West Entrance sea chan. P.N.G.
238 G7 Southwest Indian Ridge sea feature Indian Ocean
207 G4 Southwest Miramichi r. Canada
125 G9 South West National Park Australia
237 I8 Southwest Pacific Basin sea feature S. Pacific Ocean
South-West Peru Ridge sea feature S. Pacific Ocean see Nazca Ridge
125 J3 South West Rocks Australia
209 E5 South Whitley U.S.A.
221 H3 South Windham U.S.A.
173 I5 Southwold U.K.
197 H1 Soutpansberg mts S. Africa
185 G5 Soverato Italy
187 B4 Sovetsk Kaliningradskaya Oblast' Rus. Fed.
186 I3 Sovetsk Kirovskaya Oblast' Rus. Fed.
150 G2 Sovetskaya Gavan' Rus. Fed.
132 H3 Sovetskiy Rus. Fed.
186 D2 Sovetskiy Leningradskaya Oblast' Rus. Fed.
186 I3 Sovetskiy Respublika Mariy El Rus. Fed.
197 G3 Soweto S. Africa
141 G5 So'x Tajik.
225 F4 Soyaló Mex.
158 G2 Sōya-misaki c. Japan
160 D4 Soyang-ho l. S. Korea
177 O4 Sozh r. Belarus
185 L3 Sozopol Bulg.
178 D4 Spa Belgium
183 N2 Spain country Europe
173 G5 Spalding U.K.
173 D6 Span Head h. U.K.
209 F2 Spanish Canada
209 G2 Spanish r. Canada
215 G1 Spanish Fork U.S.A.
223 I5 Spanish Town Jamaica
214 C2 Sparks U.S.A.
Sparta Greece see Sparti
220 C6 Sparta NC U.S.A.
208 B4 Sparta WI U.S.A.
219 D5 Spartanburg U.S.A.
185 J6 Sparti Greece
185 G6 Spartivento, Capo c. Italy
205 G5 Sparwood Canada
187 E4 Spas-Demensk Rus. Fed.
169 O4 Spas-Klepiki Rus. Fed.
150 E2 Spasskaya Guba Rus. Fed.
150 F2 Spassk-Dal'niy Rus. Fed.
185 J7 Spatha, Akrotirio pt Greece
204 D3 Spatsizi Plateau Wilderness Provincial Park Canada
216 C2 Spearfish U.S.A.
217 C5 Spearman U.S.A.
221 F3 Speculator U.S.A.
216 E3 Spencer IA U.S.A.
212 D2 Spencer ID U.S.A.
220 C5 Spencer WV U.S.A.
124 B5 Spencer, Cape Australia
204 B3 Spencer, Cape U.S.A.
124 B5 Spencer Gulf est. Australia
120 E2 Spencer Range hills Australia
204 E4 Spences Bridge Canada
172 F3 Spennymoor U.K.
175 K3 Sperrin Mountains U.K.
220 D5 Sperryville U.S.A.
179 H5 Spessart reg. Germany
185 J6 Spetses i. Greece
174 E3 Spey r. U.K.
179 G5 Speyer Germany
143 G4 Spezand Pak.
179 F1 Spiekeroog i. Germany
176 C7 Spiez Switz.
179 E1 Spijk Neth.
178 C3 Spijkenisse Neth.
184 E1 Spilimbergo Italy
173 H4 Spilsby U.K.
143 G4 Spīn Būldak Afgh.
148 B3 Spintangi Pak.
204 F3 Spirit River Canada
208 C3 Spirit River Flowage resr U.S.A.
205 H4 Spiritwood Canada
143 G3 Spirsang Pass Afgh.
177 J6 Spišská Nová Ves Slovakia
139 J1 Spitak Armenia
148 D3 Spiti r. India
132 C2 Spitsbergen i. Svalbard
176 F7 Spittal an der Drau Austria
185 G3 Split Croatia
205 J3 Split Lake Canada
205 J3 Split Lake l. Canada
212 C2 Spokane U.S.A.
184 E3 Spoleto Italy
Spong Cambodia see Spóng
162 C2 Spóng Cambodia
208 B3 Spooner U.S.A.
179 J1 Spornitz Germany
212 F2 Spotted Horse U.S.A.
209 F2 Spragge Canada
204 E4 Spranger, Mount Canada
151 D6 Spratly Islands S. China Sea
212 C2 Spray U.S.A.
176 G5 Spree r. Germany
178 D4 Sprimont Belgium
209 F3 Spring Bay Canada
196 B4 Springbok S. Africa
207 I4 Springdale Canada
217 E4 Springdale U.S.A.
179 H2 Springe Germany
213 F4 Springer U.S.A.
215 H4 Springerville U.S.A.
217 C4 Springfield CO U.S.A.
208 C6 Springfield IL U.S.A.
221 G3 Springfield MA U.S.A.
221 I2 Springfield ME U.S.A.
216 E2 Springfield MN U.S.A.
217 E4 Springfield MO U.S.A.
220 B5 Springfield OH U.S.A.
212 B2 Springfield OR U.S.A.
221 G3 Springfield VT U.S.A.
220 D5 Springfield WV U.S.A.
208 C6 Springfield, Lake U.S.A.
197 F5 Springfontein S. Africa
208 B4 Spring Green U.S.A.
208 B4 Spring Grove U.S.A.
207 H4 Springhill Canada
219 D6 Spring Hill U.S.A.
208 B4 Spring Lake U.S.A.
215 E3 Spring Mountains U.S.A.
126 D5 Springs Junction N.Z.
123 E5 Springsure Australia
208 A4 Spring Valley U.S.A.
220 D3 Springville NY U.S.A.
215 G1 Springville UT U.S.A.
173 I5 Sprowston U.K.
205 G4 Spruce Grove Canada
220 D5 Spruce Knob-Seneca Rocks National Recreation Area park U.S.A.
213 D3 Spruce Mountain U.S.A.
173 H4 Spurn Head U.K.
204 E5 Spuzzum Canada
204 E5 Squamish Canada
221 H3 Squam Lake U.S.A.
221 I1 Squapan Lake U.S.A.
221 I1 Square Lake U.S.A.
185 G5 Squillace, Golfo di g. Italy
121 D5 Squires, Mount h. Australia
Srbija country Europe see Serbia
162 B3 Srê Âmbĕl Cambodia
185 H2 Srebrenica Bos.-Herz.
185 L3 Sredets Bulg.
133 Q4 Sredinnyy Khrebet mts Rus. Fed.
185 J3 Sredna Gora mts Bulg.
133 Q3 Srednekolymsk Rus. Fed.
Sredne-Russkaya Vozvyshennost' hills Rus. Fed. see Central Russian Upland
Sredne-Sibirskoye Ploskogor'ye plat. Rus. Fed. see Central Siberian Plateau
170 O2 Sredneye Kuyto, Ozero l. Rus. Fed.
185 K3 Srednogorie Bulg.
162 C2 Srêpok, Tônlé r. Cambodia
150 D1 Sretensk Rus. Fed.
163 H2 Sri Aman Sarawak Malaysia
147 I3 Sriharikota Island India
147 H5 Sri Jayewardenepura Kotte Sri Lanka
147 J2 Srikakulam India
147 H3 Sri Kalahasti India
148 D3 Srikanta mt. India
147 I5 Sri Lanka country Asia
148 C2 Srinagar Jammu & Kashmir India
148 D3 Srinagar Uttaranchal India
Sri Pada mt. Sri Lanka see Adam's Pk
147 H4 Srirangam India
162 B1 Sri Thep tourist site Thai.
147 H4 Srivaikuntam India
147 G2 Srivardhan India
147 H4 Srivilliputtur India
141 K1 Srostki Rus. Fed.
147 I2 Srungavarapukota India
122 C3 Staaten r. Australia
122 C3 Staaten River National Park Australia
179 H1 Stade Germany
178 B4 Staden Belgium
179 E2 Stadskanaal Neth.
179 H4 Stadtallendorf Germany
179 H2 Stadthagen Germany
179 J4 Stadtilm Germany
179 E3 Stadtlohn Germany
179 H3 Stadtoldendorf Germany
179 J4 Stadtroda Germany
174 B4 Staffa i. U.K.
179 J4 Staffelberg h. Germany
179 I4 Staffelstein Germany
173 E5 Stafford U.K.
221 E5 Stafford U.S.A.
219 E7 Stafford Creek Bahamas
171 N4 Staicele Latvia
173 G6 Staines U.K.
187 F5 Stakhanov Ukr.
173 E7 Stalbridge U.K.
173 I5 Stalham U.K.
Stalingrad Rus. Fed. see Volgograd
177 K5 Stalowa Wola Poland
185 K3 Stamboliyski Bulg.
123 C4 Stamford Australia
173 G5 Stamford U.K.
221 G4 Stamford CT U.S.A.
221 F3 Stamford NY U.S.A.
195 B6 Stampriet Namibia
170 K1 Stamsund Norway
216 E3 Stanberry U.S.A.
178 C3 Standdaarbuiten Neth.
197 H3 Standerton S. Africa
209 F4 Standish U.S.A.
219 C4 Stanford U.S.A.
197 I4 Stanger S. Africa
179 L5 Staňkov Czech Rep.
125 F8 Stanley Australia
221 J1 Stanley Canada
155 □ Stanley Hong Kong China
232 E8 Stanley Falkland Is
172 F3 Stanley U.K.
212 D2 Stanley ID U.S.A.
216 C1 Stanley ND U.S.A.
208 B3 Stanley WI U.S.A.
121 E4 Stanley, Mount h. Australia
125 F8 Stanley, Mount h. Australia
147 H4 Stanley Reservoir India
172 F2 Stannington U.K.
150 D1 Stanovoye Nagor'ye mts Rus. Fed.
150 E1 Stanovoy Khrebet mts Rus. Fed.
121 E4 Stansmore Range hills Australia
125 I2 Stanthorpe Australia
173 H5 Stanton U.K.
220 B6 Stanton KY U.S.A.
209 E4 Stanton MI U.S.A.
216 C3 Stapleton U.S.A.
177 J5 Starachowice Poland
Stara Planina mts Bulg./Serbia see Balkan Mountains
187 H4 Staraya Kulatka Rus. Fed.
187 H5 Staraya Poltavka Rus. Fed.
186 D3 Staraya Russa Rus. Fed.
177 O2 Staraya Toropa Rus. Fed.
185 K3 Stara Zagora Bulg.
117 I4 Starbuck Island Kiribati
122 D2 Starcke National Park Australia
176 G4 Stargard Szczeciński Poland
186 E3 Staritsa Rus. Fed.
219 D6 Starke U.S.A.
217 F5 Starkville U.S.A.
176 E7 Starnberger See l. Germany
141 J2 Staroaleyskoye Rus. Fed.
187 F5 Starobil's'k Ukr.
177 P4 Starodub Rus. Fed.
177 I4 Starogard Gdański Poland
187 C5 Starokostyantyniv Ukr.
187 F6 Starominskaya Rus. Fed.
187 F6 Staroshcherbinovskaya Rus. Fed.
140 D1 Starosubkhangulovo Rus. Fed.
214 C1 Star Peak U.S.A.
173 D7 Start Point U.K.
177 N4 Staryya Darohi Belarus
140 D2 Staryy Karabutak Kazakh.
133 L2 Staryy Kayak Rus. Fed.
187 F5 Staryy Oskol Rus. Fed.
179 J3 Staßfurt Germany
221 E4 State College U.S.A.
219 D5 Statesboro U.S.A.
219 D5 Statesville U.S.A.
240 W1 Station Nord Greenland
179 L3 Stauchitz Germany
179 G4 Staufenberg Germany
220 D5 Staunton U.S.A.
171 I4 Stavanger Norway
173 F4 Staveley U.K.
179 K1 Stavenhagen, Reuterstadt Germany
187 G6 Stavropol' Rus. Fed.
141 F1 Stavropolka Kazakh.
187 G6 Stavropol'skaya Vozvyshennost' hills Rus. Fed.
187 G6 Stavropol'skiy Kray admin. div. Rus. Fed.
125 E6 Stawell Australia
197 H4 Steadville S. Africa
214 C2 Steamboat U.S.A.
213 F3 Steamboat Springs U.S.A.
221 E4 Steelton U.S.A.
179 E2 Steenderen Neth.
197 I2 Steenkampsberge mts S. Africa
204 F3 Steen River Canada
213 C3 Steens Mountain U.S.A.
Steenstrup Gletscher glacier Greenland see Sermersuaq
178 A4 Steenvoorde France
179 E2 Steenwijk Neth.
203 H2 Stefansson Island Canada
179 I5 Steigerwald mts Germany
179 J5 Stein Germany
179 J4 Steinach Germany
205 J5 Steinbach Canada
179 G2 Steinfeld (Oldenburg) Germany
179 F2 Steinfurt Germany
195 B6 Steinhausen Namibia
179 H3 Steinheim Germany
179 H2 Steinhuder Meer l. Germany
170 J2 Steinkjer Norway
196 B4 Steinkopf S. Africa
215 H5 Steins U.S.A.
170 J2 Steinsdalen Norway
197 F3 Stella S. Africa
219 F7 Stella Maris Bahamas
196 C6 Stellenbosch S. Africa
184 C3 Stello, Monte mt. Corsica France
178 D5 Stenay France
179 J2 Stendal Germany
155 □ Stenhouse, Mount h. Hong Kong China
174 E4 Stenhousemuir U.K.
171 J4 Stenungsund Sweden
Stepanakert Azer. see Xankändi
187 H7 Step'anavan Armenia
205 J5 Stephen U.S.A.
124 D4 Stephens watercourse Australia
126 D4 Stephens, Cape N.Z.
124 D3 Stephens Creek Australia
208 D3 Stephenson U.S.A.
204 C3 Stephens Passage U.S.A.
207 I4 Stephenville Canada
217 D5 Stephenville U.S.A.
141 G1 Stepnogorsk Kazakh.
141 H4 Stepnoy Kyrg.
140 E1 Stepnoye Chelyabinskaya Oblast' Rus. Fed.
187 H5 Stepnoye Saratovskaya Oblast' Rus. Fed.
141 G1 Stepnyak Kazakh.
197 H4 Sterkfontein Dam resr S. Africa
197 G5 Sterkstroom S. Africa
140 C1 Sterlibashevo Rus. Fed.
196 D5 Sterling S. Africa
213 G3 Sterling CO U.S.A.
208 C5 Sterling IL U.S.A.
216 C2 Sterling ND U.S.A.
215 G2 Sterling UT U.S.A.
217 C6 Sterling City U.S.A.
209 F4 Sterling Heights U.S.A.
140 C1 Sterlitamak Rus. Fed.
179 J1 Sternberg Germany
205 G4 Stettler Canada
208 D2 Steuben U.S.A.
220 C4 Steubenville U.S.A.
173 G6 Stevenage U.K.
205 J4 Stevenson Lake Canada
208 C3 Stevens Point U.S.A.
202 D3 Stevens Village U.S.A.
204 D3 Stewart Canada
204 B2 Stewart r. Canada
204 B2 Stewart Crossing Canada
126 A7 Stewart Island N.Z.
119 G2 Stewart Islands Solomon Is
203 J3 Stewart Lake Canada
174 D5 Stewarton U.K.
208 A4 Stewartville U.S.A.
197 F5 Steynsburg S. Africa
176 G6 Steyr Austria
197 F6 Steytlerville S. Africa
178 D1 Stiens Neth.
204 C3 Stikine r. Canada/U.S.A.
204 C3 Stikine Plateau Canada
196 D7 Stilbaai S. Africa
208 A3 Stillwater MN U.S.A.
214 C2 Stillwater NV U.S.A.
217 D4 Stillwater OK U.S.A.
213 C4 Stillwater Range mts U.S.A.
173 G5 Stilton U.K.
185 J4 Štip Macedonia
121 F4 Stirling Australia
124 C5 Stirling Australia
174 E4 Stirling U.K.
214 B2 Stirling City U.S.A.
120 E3 Stirling Creek r. Australia
124 B4 Stirling North Australia
121 B7 Stirling Range National Park Australia
171 J3 Stjørdalshalsen Norway
177 H6 Stockerau Austria
179 J4 Stockheim Germany
171 L4 Stockholm Sweden
221 I1 Stockholm U.S.A.
173 E4 Stockport U.K.
239 G6 Stocks Seamount sea feature S. Atlantic Ocean
214 B3 Stockton CA U.S.A.
217 D4 Stockton KS U.S.A.
215 F1 Stockton UT U.S.A.
208 B2 Stockton Island U.S.A.
217 E4 Stockton Lake U.S.A.
172 F3 Stockton-on-Tees U.K.
221 I2 Stockton Springs U.S.A.
171 L3 Stöde Sweden
162 C2 Stœng Trêng Cambodia
174 C2 Stoer, Point of U.K.
173 E4 Stoke-on-Trent U.K.
172 F3 Stokesley U.K.
125 E8 Stokes Point Australia
120 E3 Stokes Range hills Australia
170 B3 Stokkseyri Iceland
170 K2 Stokkvågen Norway
170 K1 Stokmarknes Norway
185 G3 Stolac Bos.-Herz.
179 E4 Stolberg (Rheinland) Germany
141 K2 Stolboukha Kazakh.
187 C5 Stolin Belarus
179 K4 Stollberg Germany
179 H2 Stolzenau Germany
173 E5 Stone U.K.
209 I2 Stonecliffe Canada
221 F5 Stone Harbor U.S.A.
175 F4 Stonehaven U.K.
123 C5 Stonehenge Australia
173 F6 Stonehenge tourist site U.K.
204 E3 Stone Mountain Provincial Park Canada
215 H3 Stoner U.S.A.
221 F4 Stone Ridge U.S.A.
205 J4 Stonewall Canada
220 C5 Stonewall Jackson Lake U.S.A.
209 F4 Stoney Point Canada
221 I2 Stonington U.S.A.
214 A2 Stonyford U.S.A.
221 E3 Stony Point U.S.A.
205 H3 Stony Rapids Canada
170 L2 Stora Lulevatten l. Sweden
170 L2 Stora Sjöfallets nationalpark nat. park Sweden
170 L2 Storavan l. Sweden
Store Bælt sea chan. Denmark see Great Belt
171 J3 Støren Norway
170 K2 Storforshei Norway
170 K2 Storjord Norway
203 H2 Storkerson Peninsula Canada
125 G9 Storm Bay Australia
197 G5 Stormberg S. Africa
197 G5 Stormberge mts S. Africa
216 E3 Storm Lake U.S.A.
168 H3 Stornosa mt. Norway
174 B2 Stornoway U.K.
186 J2 Storozhevsk Rus. Fed.
187 C5 Storozhynets' Ukr.
221 G4 Storrs U.S.A.
170 L2 Storseleby Sweden
171 K3 Storsjön l. Sweden
171 J3 Storskrymten mt. Norway
170 M1 Storslett Norway
178 D1 Stortemelk sea chan. Neth.
170 L2 Storuman Sweden
170 L2 Storuman l. Sweden
171 L3 Storvik Sweden
171 J4 Storvorde Denmark
171 L4 Storvreta Sweden
173 G5 Stotfold U.K.
208 C4 Stoughton U.S.A.
173 E7 Stour r. England U.K.
173 F5 Stour r. England U.K.
173 H6 Stour r. England U.K.
173 I6 Stour r. England U.K.
173 E5 Stourbridge U.K.
173 E5 Stourport-on-Severn U.K.
205 K4 Stout Lake Canada
187 C4 Stowbtsy Belarus
221 F4 Stowe U.S.A.
173 H5 Stowmarket U.K.
156 C1 Stoyba Rus. Fed.
175 K3 Strabane U.K.
175 K4 Stradbally Ireland
173 I5 Stradbroke U.K.
184 C2 Stradella Italy
125 F9 Strahan Australia
215 G3 Straight Cliffs ridge U.S.A.
232 B8 Strait of Magellan Chile
176 F6 Strakonice Czech Rep.
176 F3 Stralsund Germany
196 C7 Strand S. Africa
171 I3 Stranda Norway
219 E7 Strangers Cay i. Bahamas
175 M3 Strangford U.K.
175 M3 Strangford Lough inlet U.K.
120 F2 Strangways r. Australia
174 C6 Stranraer U.K.
182 H2 Strasbourg France
220 D5 Strasburg U.S.A.
125 G6 Stratford Australia
209 G4 Stratford Canada
126 E3 Stratford N.Z.
217 C4 Stratford TX U.S.A.
208 B3 Stratford WI U.S.A.
173 F5 Stratford-upon-Avon U.K.
124 C5 Strathalbyn Australia
174 D5 Strathaven U.K.
175 G3 Strathbeg, Loch of l. U.K.
174 D3 Strathcarron val. U.K.
204 D5 Strathcona Provincial Park Canada
174 D3 Strathconon val. U.K.
174 D3 Strath Dearn val. U.K.
174 D2 Strath Fleet val. U.K.
205 G4 Strathmore Canada
204 E4 Strathnaver Canada
174 D2 Strathnaver val. U.K.
174 E2 Strath of Kildonan val. U.K.
209 G4 Strathroy Canada
174 E3 Strathspey val. U.K.
174 E2 Strathy U.K.
174 D2 Strathy Point U.K.
173 C7 Stratton U.K.
221 H2 Stratton U.S.A.
179 K6 Straubing Germany
170 B1 Straumnes pt Iceland
208 B4 Strawberry Point U.S.A.
215 G1 Strawberry Reservoir U.S.A.
118 D5 Streaky Bay Australia
118 D5 Streaky Bay b. Australia
208 C5 Streator U.S.A.
173 E6 Street U.K.
185 J2 Strehaia Romania
179 L3 Strehla Germany
121 C6 Streich Mound h. Australia
133 Q3 Strelka Rus. Fed.
171 N4 Strenči Latvia
168 E3 Streymoy i. Faroe Is
179 K5 Stříbro Czech Rep.
175 F3 Strichen U.K.
235 J4 Stroeder Arg.
175 J4 Strokestown Ireland
174 E2 Stroma, Island of U.K.
184 F5 Stromboli, Isola i. Isole Lipari Italy
174 E2 Stromness U.K.
216 D3 Stromsburg U.S.A.
171 J4 Strömstad Sweden
171 K3 Strömsund Sweden
220 C4 Strongsville U.S.A.

Tres Picos, Cerro

235 K3 Tres Picos, Cerro *mt.* Arg.
213 F4 Tres Piedras U.S.A.
234 D3 Três Pontas Brazil
232 C7 Tres Puntas, Cabo *c.* Arg.
234 D3 Três Rios Brazil
225 E4 Tres Valles Mex.
225 F4 Tres Zapotes *tourist site* Mex.
171 J3 Tretten Norway
179 I6 Treuchtlingen Germany
179 K2 Treuenbrietzen Germany
171 J4 Treungen Norway
184 C2 Treviglio Italy
184 E2 Treviso Italy
173 B7 Trevose Head U.K.
125 G9 Triabunna Australia
185 L6 Tria Nisia *i.* Greece
185 M6 Trianta Greece
148 B2 Tribal Areas *admin. div.* Pak.
156 F1 Tri Brata, Gora *h.* Rus. Fed.
185 H5 Tricase Italy
147 H4 Trichur India
178 A5 Tricot France
125 F4 Trida Australia
179 E5 Trier Germany
184 E2 Trieste Italy
184 E1 Triglav *mt.* Slovenia
185 I5 Trikala Greece
138 D4 Trikomon Cyprus
151 F7 Trikora, Puncak *mt.* Indon.
175 L4 Trim Ireland
147 I4 Trincomalee Sri Lanka
234 C2 Trindade Brazil
239 H7 Trindade, Ilha da *i.* S. Atlantic Ocean
231 F6 Trinidad Bol.
233 J3 Trinidad Col.
223 I4 Trinidad Cuba
231 F1 Trinidad *i.* Trin. and Tob.
235 L2 Trinidad Uruguay
213 F4 Trinidad U.S.A.
233 L2 Trinidad and Tobago *country* Caribbean Sea
207 J4 Trinity Bay Canada
202 C4 Trinity Islands U.S.A.
214 C1 Trinity Range *mts* U.S.A.
219 C5 Trion U.S.A.
179 J1 Tripkau Germany
185 J6 Tripoli Greece
138 E4 Tripoli Lebanon
193 D1 Tripoli Libya
147 H4 Tripunittura India
149 G5 Tripura *state* India
239 I8 Tristan da Cunha *i.* S. Atlantic Ocean
148 D3 Trisul *mt.* India
149 F4 Trisul Dam Nepal
179 I1 Trittau Germany
179 E5 Trittenheim Germany
147 H4 Trivandrum India
184 F4 Trivento Italy
177 H6 Trnava Slovakia
119 F2 Trobriand Islands P.N.G.
170 K2 Trofors Norway
185 G3 Trogir Croatia
184 F4 Troia Italy
179 F4 Troisdorf Germany
180 C4 Trois Fourches, Cap des *c.* Morocco
178 D4 Trois-Ponts Belgium
207 F4 Trois-Rivières Canada
140 E1 Troitsk Rus. Fed.
169 R3 Troitsko-Pechorsk Rus. Fed.
141 K1 Troitskoye *Altayskiy Kray* Rus. Fed.
156 E2 Troitskoye Rus. Fed.
140 C1 Troitskoye *Orenburgskaya Oblast'* Rus. Fed.
140 D1 Troitskoye *Respublika Bashkortostan* Rus. Fed.
187 H6 Troitskoye *Respublika Kalmykiya - Khalm'g-Tangch* Rus. Fed.
127 K3 Troll *research stn* Antarctica
171 K4 Trollhättan Sweden
231 G3 Trombetas *r.* Brazil
191 I6 Tromelin, Île *i.* Indian Ocean
235 H3 Tromen, Volcán *vol.* Arg.
197 F5 Trompsburg S. Africa
170 L1 Tromsø Norway
215 D4 Trona U.S.A.
235 H4 Tronador, Monte *mt.* Arg.
171 J3 Trondheim Norway
171 J3 Trondheimsfjorden *sea chan.* Norway
149 G4 Trongsa Chhu *r.* Bhutan
138 D4 Troödos Cyprus
138 D4 Troödos, Mount Cyprus
174 D5 Troon U.K.
234 D1 Tropeiros, Serra dos *hills* Brazil
215 F3 Tropic U.S.A.
122 G4 Tropic of Capricorn
175 L2 Trostan *h.* U.K.
175 F3 Troup Head U.K.
204 E2 Trout *r.* Canada
209 H3 Trout Creek Canada
215 F2 Trout Creek U.S.A.
205 G3 Trout Lake *Alta* Canada
204 E2 Trout Lake Canada
204 E2 Trout Lake *l. N.W.T.* Canada
205 K4 Trout Lake *l. Ont.* Canada
209 E2 Trout Lake U.S.A.
208 C2 Trout Lake *l.* U.S.A.
212 E2 Trout Peak U.S.A.
221 E4 Trout Run U.S.A.
173 E6 Trowbridge U.K.
125 F8 Trowutta Australia
185 L5 Troy *tourist site* Turkey
219 C6 Troy *AL* U.S.A.
212 D2 Troy *MT* U.S.A.
221 G3 Troy *NH* U.S.A.
221 G3 Troy *NY* U.S.A.
220 A4 Troy *OH* U.S.A.
221 E4 Troy *PA* U.S.A.
185 K3 Troyan Bulg.
182 G2 Troyes France
215 D4 Troy Lake U.S.A.
215 E2 Troy Peak U.S.A.
185 I3 Trstenik Serbia
187 E4 Trubchevsk Rus. Fed.
183 M1 Truchas Spain
186 E3 Trud Rus. Fed.
158 C3 Trudovoye Rus. Fed.
224 H5 Trujillo Hond.
230 C5 Trujillo Peru
183 N3 Trujillo Spain
233 J2 Trujillo Venez.
179 F5 Trulben Germany
221 G4 Trumbull U.S.A.
215 F3 Trumbull, Mount U.S.A.
163 E2 Trumon Indon.
125 G4 Trundle Australia
162 C2 Trưng Hiệp Vietnam
155 C6 Trung Khanh Vietnam
207 H4 Truro Canada
173 B7 Truro U.K.
175 J3 Truskmore *h.* Ireland
204 E3 Trutch Canada
213 F5 Truth or Consequences U.S.A.
176 G5 Trutnov Czech Rep.
Truva *tourist site* Turkey *see* Troy
185 K7 Trypiti, Akrotirio *pt* Greece
171 K3 Trysil Norway
176 G3 Trzebiatów Poland
150 A2 Tsagaannuur Mongolia
144 I2 Tsagaan-Uul Mongolia
187 H6 Tsagan Aman Rus. Fed.
187 H6 Tsagan-Nur Rus. Fed.
187 G7 Ts'ageri Georgia
137 F2 Tsalenjikha Georgia
139 J1 Tsalka Georgia
195 E5 Tsaratanana, Massif du *mts* Madag.
185 L3 Tsarevo Bulg.
196 B2 Tsaris Mountains Namibia
187 H5 Tsatsa Rus. Fed.
196 A3 Tsaukaib Namibia
195 D4 Tsavo East National Park Kenya
187 G6 Tselina Rus. Fed.
153 I2 Tsenhermandal Mongolia
195 B6 Tses Namibia
144 H2 Tsetseg Mongolia
Tsetsegnuur Mongolia *see* Tsetseg
195 C6 Tsetseng Botswana
144 I2 Tsetserleg Mongolia
150 C2 Tsetserleg Mongolia
195 C6 Tshabong Botswana
195 C6 Tshane Botswana
187 F6 Tshchikskoye Vodokhranilishche *resr* Rus. Fed.
195 B4 Tshela Dem. Rep. Congo
195 C4 Tshibala Dem. Rep. Congo
195 C4 Tshikapa Dem. Rep. Congo
195 C4 Tshikapa *r.* Dem. Rep. Congo
197 G3 Tshing S. Africa
197 I1 Tshipise S. Africa
195 C4 Tshitanzu Dem. Rep. Congo
195 C4 Tshofa Dem. Rep. Congo
197 I2 Tshokwane S. Africa
195 C4 Tshuapa *r.* Dem. Rep. Congo
Tshwane S. Africa *see* Pretoria
187 G6 Tsimlyansk Rus. Fed.
187 G6 Tsimlyanskoye Vodokhranilishche *resr* Rus. Fed.
156 E2 Tsimmermanovka Rus. Fed.
197 E3 Tsineng S. Africa
Tsing Shan Wan *b.* China *see* Castle Peak Bay
Tsing Shui Wan *b.* China *see* Clear Water Bay
Tsingtao China *see* Qingdao
155 □ Tsing Yi *i. Hong Kong* China
195 E6 Tsiombe Madag.
195 E5 Tsiroanomandidy Madag.
197 E6 Tsitsikamma Forest and Coastal National Park S. Africa
204 D4 Tsitsutl Peak Canada
187 H4 Tsivil'sk Rus. Fed.
187 G7 Ts'khinvali Georgia
187 G4 Tsna *r.* Rus. Fed.
137 G2 Tsnori Georgia
154 B1 Tsogttsetsiy Mongolia
148 D2 Tsokar Chumo *l.* India
Tsokr Chumo *l.* India *see* Tsokar Chumo
197 H5 Tsolo S. Africa
197 G6 Tsomo S. Africa
Tso Morari Lake India *see* Morari, Tso
187 G7 Tsqaltubo Georgia
159 E7 Tsu Japan
159 G6 Tsuchiura Japan
155 □ Tsuen Wan *Hong Kong* China
158 G4 Tsugarū-kaikyō *str.* Japan
195 B5 Tsumeb Namibia
195 B6 Tsumis Park Namibia
195 C5 Tsumkwe Namibia
149 G4 Tsunthang India
159 E7 Tsuruga Japan
159 D8 Tsurugi-san *mt.* Japan
Tsurukhaytuy Rus. Fed. *see* Priargunsk
159 F5 Tsuruoka Japan
159 A7 Tsushima *is* Japan
159 D7 Tsuyama Japan
196 D1 Tswaane Botswana
197 F4 Tswaraganang S. Africa
197 F3 Tswelelang S. Africa
177 L4 Tsyelyakhany Belarus
170 P1 Tsyp-Navolok Rus. Fed.
187 E6 Tsyurupyns'k Ukr.
151 F7 Tual Indon.
175 J4 Tuam Ireland
126 D4 Tuamarina N.Z.
Tuamotu, Archipel des *is* Fr. Polynesia *see* Tuamotu Islands
117 J5 Tuamotu Islands Fr. Polynesia
155 B6 Tuân Giao Vietnam
162 A5 Tuangku *i.* Indon.
187 F6 Tuapse Rus. Fed.
162 □ Tuas Sing.
126 A7 Tuatapere N.Z.
174 B2 Tuath, Loch a' *b.* U.K.
215 G3 Tuba City U.S.A.
163 H4 Tuban Indon.
233 G3 Tubarão Brazil
161 H4 Tubbataha Reefs Phil.
Tubbercurry Ireland *see* Tobercurry
176 D6 Tübingen Germany
192 A4 Tubmanburg Liberia
161 I4 Tubod Phil.
193 E1 Tubruq Libya
237 J7 Tubuai *i.* Fr. Polynesia
117 I6 Tubuai Islands Fr. Polynesia
231 K6 Tucano Brazil
235 H3 Tucapel, Punta *pt* Chile
231 G7 Tucavaca Bol.
179 K1 Tüchen Germany
179 K2 Tuchheim Germany
204 D2 Tuchitua Canada
221 F5 Tuckerton U.S.A.
215 G5 Tucson U.S.A.
215 G5 Tucson Mountains U.S.A.
233 I2 Tucuco *r.* Venez.
213 G5 Tucumcari U.S.A.
233 L2 Tucupita Venez.
231 I4 Tucuruí Brazil
231 I4 Tucuruí, Represa *resr* Brazil
139 L5 Tū Dār Iran
183 P1 Tudela Spain
144 I2 Tüdevtey Mongolia
183 M2 Tuela *r.* Port.
155 □ Tuen Mun *Hong Kong* China
149 H4 Tuensang India
142 C5 Ţufayḩ Saudi Arabia
237 J2 Tufts Abyssal Plain *sea feature* N. Pacific Ocean
197 I4 Tugela *r.* S. Africa
161 J4 Tugnug Point Phil.
161 I2 Tuguegarao Phil.
133 O4 Tugur Rus. Fed.
141 K3 Tugyl Kazakh.
154 F2 Tuhai He *r.* China
162 A5 Tuhemberua Indon.
183 L1 Tui Spain
224 J6 Tuira *r.* Panama
140 D1 Tukan Rus. Fed.
151 E7 Tukangbesi, Kepulauan *is* Indon.
206 E2 Tukarak Island Canada
141 H5 Tŭkhtamish Tajik.
202 E3 Tuktoyaktuk Canada
171 M4 Tukums Latvia
156 B1 Tukuringra, Khrebet *mts* Rus. Fed.
225 E3 Tula Mex.
187 F4 Tula Rus. Fed.
149 H1 Tulagt Ar Gol *r.* China
225 E3 Tulancingo Mex.
214 C3 Tulare U.S.A.
214 C4 Tulare Lake Bed U.S.A.
213 F5 Tularosa U.S.A.
147 I2 Tulasi *mt.* India
196 C6 Tulbagh S. Africa
230 C3 Tulcán Ecuador
185 M2 Tulcea Romania
187 D5 Tul'chyn Ukr.
214 C3 Tule *r.* U.S.A.
142 D3 Tuleh Iran
149 G4 Tule La *pass* Bhutan
Tule-la Pass Bhutan *see* Tule La
205 I2 Tulemalu Lake Canada
217 C5 Tulia U.S.A.
204 D2 Tulita Canada
138 E5 Ţūlkarm West Bank
175 J5 Tulla Ireland
125 F8 Tullah Australia
219 C5 Tullahoma U.S.A.
125 G4 Tullamore Australia
175 K4 Tullamore Ireland
182 E4 Tulle France
171 K3 Tulleråsen Sweden
125 G4 Tullibigeal Australia
217 E6 Tullos U.S.A.
175 L5 Tullow Ireland
119 E3 Tully Australia
122 D3 Tully *r.* Australia
175 K3 Tully U.K.
221 E3 Tully U.S.A.
186 D2 Tulos Rus. Fed.
217 D4 Tulsa U.S.A.
187 F4 Tul'skaya Oblast' *admin. div.* Rus. Fed.
233 H3 Tuluá Col.
202 B3 Tuluksak U.S.A.
225 H3 Tulum *tourist site* Mex.
235 I1 Tulum, Valle de *val.* Arg.
150 C1 Tulun Rus. Fed.
163 H4 Tulungagung Indon.
149 H4 Tulung La *pass* China
161 H4 Tuluran *i.* Phil.
233 H4 Tumaco Col.
197 G3 Tumahole S. Africa
187 I6 Tumak Rus. Fed.
171 L4 Tumba Sweden
195 B4 Tumba, Lac *l.* Dem. Rep. Congo
163 H3 Tumbangsamba Indon.
161 J5 Tumbao Phil.
230 B4 Tumbes Peru
204 E3 Tumbler Ridge Canada
124 B5 Tumby Bay Australia
170 O2 Tumcha *r.* Fin./Rus. Fed.
154 B2 Tumen China
160 E2 Tumen China
160 E2 Tumen *r.* China/N. Korea
231 F2 Tumereng Guyana
161 H5 Tumindao *i.* Phil.
147 H3 Tumkur India
149 G3 Tum La *pass* China
174 E4 Tummel, Loch *l.* U.K.
150 G2 Tumnin *r.* Rus. Fed.
143 F5 Tump Pak.
162 B4 Tumpat Malaysia
192 B3 Tumu Ghana
231 G3 Tumucumaque, Serra *hills* Brazil
141 J4 Tumushuke China
125 H5 Tumut Australia
125 H5 Tumut *r.* Australia
173 H6 Tunbridge Wells, Royal U.K.
139 G2 Tunceli Turkey
155 D7 Tunchang China
125 J4 Tuncurry Australia
195 D5 Tunduru Tanz.
185 L3 Tundzha *r.* Bulg.
147 H3 Tungabhadra *r.* India
147 G3 Tungabhadra Reservoir India
149 H3 Tunga Pass China/India
161 I5 Tungawan Phil.
155 □ Tung Chung Wan *b. Hong Kong* China
170 C2 Tungnaá *r.* Iceland
156 F1 Tungor Rus. Fed.
Tung Pok Liu Hoi Hap China *see* East Lamma Channel
204 D2 Tungsten (abandoned) Canada
186 E1 Tunguda Rus. Fed.
155 □ Tung Wan *b. Hong Kong* China
147 I2 Tuni India
193 D1 Tunis Tunisia
184 D6 Tunis, Golfe de *g.* Tunisia
192 C1 Tunisia *country* Africa
233 I3 Tunja Col.
154 D2 Tunliu China
170 K2 Tunnsjøen *l.* Norway
173 I5 Tunstall U.K.
170 O2 Tuntsa Fin.
207 G2 Tunulic *r.* Canada
207 H2 Tunungayualok Island Canada
235 I2 Tunuyán Arg.
235 I2 Tunuyán *r.* Arg.
154 E3 Tuo He *r.* China
154 F2 Tuoji Dao *i.* China
162 C3 Tuŏl Khpos Cambodia
214 B3 Tuolumne U.S.A.
210 B4 Tuolumne *r.* U.S.A.
214 C3 Tuolumne Meadows U.S.A.
155 B5 Tuoniang Jiang *r.* China
Tuotuo He *r.* China *see* Togton He
141 I4 Tüp Kyrg.
234 B3 Tupã Brazil
234 C2 Tupaciguara Brazil
139 K3 Tūp Āghāj Iran
232 F3 Tupanciretã Brazil
233 J3 Tuparro *r.* Col.
217 F5 Tupelo U.S.A.
153 K1 Tupik Rus. Fed.
230 E8 Tupiza Bol.
221 F2 Tupper Lake U.S.A.
221 F2 Tupper Lake *l.* U.S.A.
235 I2 Tupungato Arg.
235 I2 Tupungato, Cerro *mt.* Arg./Chile
139 J7 Tuqayyid *well* Iraq
160 A1 Tuquan China
233 H4 Túquerres Col.
149 G4 Tura India
133 L3 Tura Rus. Fed.
146 B5 Turabah Saudi Arabia
233 K3 Turagua, Serranía *mt.* Venez.
126 E4 Turakina N.Z.
143 E3 Turan Iran
152 F1 Turan Rus. Fed.
150 F1 Turana, Khrebet *mts* Rus. Fed.
126 E3 Turangi N.Z.
143 E2 Turan Lowland Asia
141 G4 Turar Ryskulov Kazakh.
Turayf Saudi Arabia *see* Ţurayf
139 G6 Ţurayf Saudi Arabia
Turayf *well* Saudi Arabia *see* Ţurayf
142 C5 Ţurayf *well* Saudi Arabia
171 N4 Turba Estonia
233 I2 Turbaco Col.
143 F5 Turbat Pak.
233 H2 Turbo Col.
177 K7 Turda Romania
142 C3 Tūreh Iran
Turfan China *see* Turpan
141 H2 Turgay *Akmolinskaya Oblast'* Kazakh.
140 E2 Turgay *Kostanayskaya Oblast'* Kazakh.
140 E3 Turgay *r.* Kazakh.
140 E2 Turgayskaya Dolina *val.* Kazakh.
141 F2 Turgayskaya Oblast' Kazakh.
140 E2 Turgayskaya Stolovaya Strana *reg.* Kazakh.
185 L3 Türgovishte Bulg.
138 C2 Turgut Turkey
138 A2 Turgutlu Turkey
139 F1 Turhal Turkey
171 N4 Türi Estonia
183 P3 Turia *r.* Spain
233 K2 Turiamo Venez.
184 B2 Turin Italy
158 B2 Turiy Rog Rus. Fed.
187 C5 Turiys'k Ukr.
194 D3 Turkana, Lake *salt l.* Eth./Kenya
185 L4 Türkeli Adası *i.* Turkey
141 G4 Turkestan Kazakh.
141 G5 Turkestan Range *mts* Asia
138 E2 Turkey *country* Asia
208 B4 Turkey *r.* U.S.A.
187 G5 Turki Rus. Fed.
Turkmenabat Turkm. *see* Türkmenabat
140 E5 Türkmenabat Turkm.
140 C5 Türkmen Aýlagy *b.* Turkm.
Turkmenbashi Turkm. *see* Türkmenbaşy
140 C4 Türkmenbaşy Turkm.
140 C5 Türkmenbaşy Aýlagy *b.* Turkm.
138 C2 Türkmen Dağı *mt.* Turkey
Turkmengala Turkm. *see* Türkmengala
140 E5 Türkmengala Turkm.
140 C5 Turkmenistan *country* Asia
Turkmenskiy Zaliv *b.* Turkm. *see* Türkmen Aýlagy
139 F3 Türkoğlu Turkey
223 J4 Turks and Caicos Islands *terr.* Caribbean Sea
223 J4 Turks Islands Turks and Caicos Is
171 M3 Turku Fin.
194 D3 Turkwel *watercourse* Kenya
214 B3 Turlock U.S.A.
214 B3 Turlock Lake U.S.A.
126 F4 Turnagain, Cape N.Z.
174 D5 Turnberry U.K.
215 G5 Turnbull, Mount U.S.A.
225 H4 Turneffe Islands *atoll* Belize
209 F3 Turner U.S.A.
178 C3 Turnhout Belgium
205 H3 Turnor Lake Canada
185 K3 Turnu Măgurele Romania
Turnu Severin Romania *see* Drobeta-Turnu Severin
125 H4 Turon *r.* Australia
186 G3 Turovets Rus. Fed.
150 A2 Turpan China
150 A2 Turpan Pendi *depr.* China
223 I4 Turquino, Pico *mt.* Cuba
175 F3 Turriff U.K.
139 J5 Tursāq Iraq
Turtkul' Uzbek. *see* To'rtko'l
208 B2 Turtle Flambeau Flowage *resr* U.S.A.
205 H4 Turtleford Canada
208 A3 Turtle Lake U.S.A.
141 H4 Turugart Pass China/Kyrg.
140 D3 Turush Kazakh.
234 B2 Turvo *r. Goiás* Brazil
234 C3 Turvo *r. São Paulo* Brazil
215 F4 Tusayan U.S.A.
219 C5 Tuscaloosa U.S.A.
220 C4 Tuscarawas *r.* U.S.A.
221 E4 Tuscarora Mountains U.S.A.
208 C6 Tuscola *IL* U.S.A.
217 D5 Tuscola *TX* U.S.A.
143 E3 Tusharīk Iran
219 C5 Tuskegee U.S.A.
220 D4 Tussey Mountains U.S.A.
139 I2 Tutak Turkey
186 F3 Tutayev Rus. Fed.
147 H4 Tuticorin India
217 D4 Tuttle Creek Reservoir U.S.A.
176 D7 Tuttlingen Germany
203 P2 Tuttut Nunaat *reg.* Greenland
119 I3 Tutuila *i.* Pacific Ocean
195 C6 Tutume Botswana
225 E4 Tututepec Mex.
160 D3 Tuun-bong *mt.* N. Korea
171 O3 Tuupovaara Fin.
171 O3 Tuusniemi Fin.
119 H2 Tuvalu *country* Pacific Ocean
142 B5 Tuwayq, Jabal *hills* Saudi Arabia
225 D4 Tuxpan *Jalisco* Mex.
225 E3 Tuxpan *Veracruz* Mex.
225 F4 Tuxtla Gutiérrez Mex.
233 K2 Tuy *r.* Venez.
162 C2 Tuy Đức Vietnam
155 B6 Tuyên Quang Vietnam
163 D2 Tuy Hoa Vietnam
142 C3 Tüysarkān Iran
141 I4 Tuyuk Kazakh.
138 D2 Tuz, Lake *salt l.* Turkey

Tuz Gölü *salt l.* Turkey *see* **Tuz, Lake**
169 P4 **Tuzha** Rus. Fed.
215 F4 **Tuzigoot National Monument** *nat. park* U.S.A.
139 J4 **Tuz Khurmātū** Iraq
185 H2 **Tuzla** Bos.-Herz.
136 D3 **Tuzla** Turkey
139 H2 **Tuzla** *r.* Turkey
187 F6 **Tuzlov** *r.* Rus. Fed.
171 J4 **Tvedestrand** Norway
186 E3 **Tver'** Rus. Fed.
186 E3 **Tverskaya Oblast'** *admin. div.* Rus. Fed.
209 I3 **Tweed** Canada
175 F5 **Tweed** *r.* U.K.
125 J2 **Tweed Heads** Australia
204 D4 **Tweedsmuir Provincial Park** Canada
196 C6 **Tweefontein** S. Africa
196 C2 **Twee Rivier** Namibia
179 E2 **Twente** *reg.* Neth.
215 D4 **Twentynine Palms** U.S.A.
207 J4 **Twillingate** Canada
212 D2 **Twin Bridges** U.S.A.
217 C6 **Twin Buttes Reservoir** U.S.A.
207 H3 **Twin Falls** Canada
213 D3 **Twin Falls** U.S.A.
121 D4 **Twin Heads** *h.* Australia
204 F3 **Twin Lakes** Canada
221 H2 **Twin Mountain** U.S.A.
220 C6 **Twin Oaks** U.S.A.
214 B2 **Twin Peak** U.S.A.
179 G2 **Twistringen** Germany
126 C6 **Twizel** N.Z.
125 H6 **Twofold Bay** Australia
215 G4 **Two Guns** U.S.A.
208 B2 **Two Harbors** U.S.A.
205 G4 **Two Hills** Canada
212 D1 **Two Medicine** *r.* U.S.A.
208 D3 **Two Rivers** U.S.A.
149 H5 **Tyao** *r.* India/Myanmar
156 G3 **Tyatya, Vulkan** *vol.* Rus. Fed.
171 J3 **Tydal** Norway
220 D5 **Tygart Lake** U.S.A.
220 D5 **Tygart Valley** U.S.A.
150 E1 **Tygda** Rus. Fed.
156 B1 **Tygda** *r.* Rus. Fed.
217 E5 **Tyler** U.S.A.
217 F6 **Tylertown** U.S.A.
156 F2 **Tym'** *r.* Rus. Fed.
156 F2 **Tymovskoye** Rus. Fed.
150 E1 **Tynda** Rus. Fed.
204 A2 **Tyndall Glacier** U.S.A.
175 F4 **Tyne** *r.* U.K.
172 F2 **Tynemouth** U.K.
171 J3 **Tynset** Norway
Tyoploozyorsk Rus. Fed. *see* **Teploozersk**
Tyoploye Ozero Rus. Fed. *see* **Teploozersk**
138 E5 **Tyre** Lebanon
127 I3 **Tyree, Mount** Antarctica
156 D2 **Tyrma** Rus. Fed.
156 C2 **Tyrma** *r.* Rus. Fed.
170 N2 **Tyrnävä** Fin.
185 J5 **Tyrnavos** Greece
137 F2 **Tyrnyauz** Rus. Fed.
220 D4 **Tyrone** U.S.A.
125 E5 **Tyrrell** *r.* Australia
125 E5 **Tyrrell, Lake** *dry lake* Australia
205 H2 **Tyrrell Lake** Canada
184 D4 **Tyrrhenian Sea** France/Italy
133 P3 **Tyubelyakh** Rus. Fed.
140 B3 **Tyub-Karagan, Mys** *pt* Kazakh.
132 I4 **Tyukalinsk** Rus. Fed.
140 B3 **Tyulen'i Ostrova** *is* Kazakh.
140 D1 **Tyul'gan** Rus. Fed.
132 H4 **Tyumen'** Rus. Fed.
141 J1 **Tyumentsevo** Rus. Fed.
133 M3 **Tyung** *r.* Rus. Fed.
141 F1 **Tyuntyugur** Kazakh.
173 C6 **Tywi** *r.* U.K.
173 C5 **Tywyn** U.K.
197 I1 **Tzaneen** S. Africa

U

195 C5 **Uamanda** Angola
Uarc, Ras *c.* Morocco *see* **Trois Fourches, Cap des**
121 A4 **Uaroo** Australia
233 L4 **Uatatás** *r.* Brazil
231 K5 **Uauá** Brazil
233 K5 **Uaupés** Brazil
233 J4 **Uaupés** *r.* Brazil
225 G4 **Uaxactún** Guat.
142 B4 **U'aywij** *well* Saudi Arabia
139 I7 **U'aywij, Wādī al** *watercourse* Saudi Arabia
234 D3 **Ubá** Brazil
141 J2 **Uba** *r.* Kazakh.
141 F1 **Ubagan** *r.* Kazakh.
234 D2 **Ubaí** Brazil
234 E1 **Ubaitaba** Brazil
194 B3 **Ubangi** *r.* Centr. Afr. Rep./Dem. Rep. Congo
233 I3 **Ubate** Col.
139 I5 **Ubayyiḍ, Wādī al** *watercourse* Iraq/Saudi Arabia
159 B8 **Ube** Japan
183 O3 **Úbeda** Spain
234 C2 **Uberaba** Brazil
231 G7 **Uberaba, Lagoa** *l.* Bol./Brazil
234 C2 **Uberlândia** Brazil
162 □ **Ubin, Pulau** *i.* Sing.
183 N1 **Ubiña, Peña** *mt.* Spain
162 B1 **Ubolratna, Ang Kep Nam** Thai.
197 J3 **Ubombo** S. Africa
Ubonrat, Angkep Nam *resr* Thai. *see* **Ubolratna, Ang Kep Nam**
162 C2 **Ubon Ratchathani** Thai.
179 G5 **Ubstadt-Weiher** Germany
195 C4 **Ubundu** Dem. Rep. Congo
140 E5 **Üçajy** Turkm.
139 K1 **Ucar** Azer.
230 D5 **Ucayali** *r.* Peru
148 B3 **Uch** Pak.
Uch-Adzhi Turkm. *see* **Üçajy**
140 D1 **Uchaly** Rus. Fed.
142 C2 **Ūchān** Iran
141 J3 **Ucharal** Kazakh.
158 G3 **Uchiura-wan** *b.* Japan
137 F2 **Uchkeken** Rus. Fed.
Uchkuduk Uzbek. *see* **Uchquduq**
140 E4 **Uchquduq** Uzbek.
Uchsay Uzbek. *see* **Uchsoy**
140 D4 **Uchsoy** Uzbek.
179 G2 **Uchte** Germany
179 J2 **Uchte** *r.* Germany
150 F1 **Uchur** *r.* Rus. Fed.
173 H7 **Uckfield** U.K.
204 D5 **Ucluelet** Canada
215 H3 **Ucolo** U.S.A.
212 F2 **Ucross** U.S.A.
153 I1 **Uda** *r.* Rus. Fed.
133 O4 **Uda** *r.* Rus. Fed.
187 H6 **Udachnoye** Rus. Fed.
133 M3 **Udachnyy** Rus. Fed.
147 H4 **Udagamandalam** India
148 C4 **Udaipur** *Rajasthan* India
149 G5 **Udaipur** *Tripura* India
149 E5 **Udanti** *r.* India/Myanmar
147 H3 **Udayagiri** India
171 J4 **Uddevalla** Sweden
174 D5 **Uddingston** U.K.
170 L2 **Uddjaure** *l.* Sweden
178 D3 **Uden** Neth.
147 H2 **Udgir** India
145 E5 **Udhampur** India
186 H2 **Udimskiy** Rus. Fed.
184 E1 **Udine** Italy
207 I2 **Udjuktok Bay** Canada
186 E3 **Udomlya** Rus. Fed.
162 B1 **Udon Thani** Thai.
150 F1 **Udskaya Guba** *b.* Rus. Fed.
156 D1 **Udskoye** Rus. Fed.
147 H4 **Udumalaippettai** India
147 G3 **Udupi** India
150 F1 **Udyl', Ozero** *l.* Rus. Fed.
176 G4 **Ueckermünde** Germany
159 F6 **Ueda** Japan
118 C2 **Uekuli** Indon.
194 C3 **Uele** *r.* Dem. Rep. Congo
202 B3 **Uelen** Rus. Fed.
179 I2 **Uelzen** Germany
194 C3 **Uere** *r.* Dem. Rep. Congo
179 H1 **Uetersen** Germany
179 H5 **Uettingen** Germany
179 I2 **Uetze** Germany
132 G4 **Ufa** Rus. Fed.
179 I5 **Uffenheim** Germany
195 B6 **Ugab** *watercourse* Namibia
195 D4 **Ugalla** *r.* Tanz.
194 D3 **Uganda** *country* Africa
197 H5 **Ugie** S. Africa
150 G2 **Uglegorsk** Rus. Fed.
158 C3 **Uglekamensk** Rus. Fed.
186 F3 **Uglich** Rus. Fed.
184 F2 **Ugljan** *i.* Croatia
186 E3 **Uglovka** Rus. Fed.
156 C2 **Uglovoye** Rus. Fed.
158 C3 **Uglovoye** Rus. Fed.
141 J2 **Uglovskoye** Rus. Fed.
133 P3 **Ugol'noye** Rus. Fed.
133 S3 **Ugol'nyye Kopi** Rus. Fed.
187 E4 **Ugra** Rus. Fed.
141 H4 **Ügüt** Kyrg.
177 H6 **Uherské Hradiště** Czech Rep.
220 C4 **Uhrichsville** U.S.A.
174 B3 **Uig** U.K.
195 B4 **Uíge** Angola
160 D5 **Ŭijŏngbu** S. Korea
160 C3 **Ŭiju** N. Korea
140 C2 **Uil** Kazakh.
140 C2 **Uil** *r.* Kazakh.
171 O3 **Uimaharju** Fin.
215 F3 **Uinkaret Plateau** U.S.A.
213 E3 **Uinta Mountains** U.S.A.
195 B6 **Uis Mine** Namibia
175 K4 **Uisneach** *h.* Ireland
160 E5 **Ŭisŏng** S. Korea
197 F6 **Uitenhage** S. Africa
178 C2 **Uithoorn** Neth.
179 E1 **Uithuizen** Neth.
207 H2 **Uivak, Cape** Canada
159 D7 **Uji** Japan
159 A9 **Uji-guntō** *is* Japan
148 C5 **Ujjain** India
Ujung Pandang Indon. *see* **Makassar**
197 H4 **uKhahlamba-Drakensberg Park** *nat. park* S. Africa
139 I5 **Ukhaydir** *tourist site* Iraq
149 H4 **Ukhrul** India
186 J2 **Ukhta** Rus. Fed.
186 J2 **Ukhta** *r.* Rus. Fed.
125 J2 **Uki** Australia
214 A2 **Ukiah** *CA* U.S.A.
212 C2 **Ukiah** *OR* U.S.A.
203 J3 **Ukkusiksalik National Park** Canada
203 M2 **Ukkusissat** Greenland
171 N5 **Ukmergė** Lith.
187 D5 **Ukraine** *country* Europe
141 J2 **Ukrainka** Kazakh.
186 I2 **Uktym** Rus. Fed.
159 A8 **Uku-jima** *i.* Japan
196 D1 **Ukwi** Botswana
196 D1 **Ukwi Pan** *salt pan* Botswana
Ulaanbaatar Mongolia *see* **Ulan Bator**
154 D1 **Ulaanbadrah** Mongolia
150 B2 **Ulaangom** Mongolia
125 H4 **Ulan** Australia
154 A2 **Ulan** China
150 C2 **Ulan Bator** Mongolia
141 G3 **Ulanbel'** Kazakh.
154 C1 **Ulan Buh Shamo** *des.* China
187 H6 **Ulan-Erge** Rus. Fed.
150 E2 **Ulanhot** China
154 D1 **Ulan Hua** China
187 H6 **Ulan-Khol** Rus. Fed.
154 C1 **Ulansuhai Nur** *l.* China
154 A1 **Ulan Tohoi** China
150 C1 **Ulan-Ude** Rus. Fed.
149 G2 **Ulan Ul Hu** *l.* China
139 F2 **Ulaş** Turkey
119 G2 **Ulawa Island** Solomon Is
143 E4 **Ulāy, Kūh-e** *h.* Iran
141 J2 **Ul'ba** Kazakh.
156 E1 **Ul'banskiy Zaliv** *b.* Rus. Fed.
160 E5 **Ulchin** S. Korea
153 K2 **Uldz** *r.* Mongolia
171 J4 **Ulefoss** Norway
125 E2 **Ulenia, Lake** *salt flat* Australia
171 N4 **Ülenurme** Estonia
153 J1 **Ulety** Rus. Fed.
141 F2 **Ul'gili** Kazakh.
147 G2 **Ulhasnagar** India
150 D2 **Uliastai** China
150 B2 **Uliastay** Mongolia
178 C3 **Ulicoten** Neth.
170 P1 **Ulita** *r.* Rus. Fed.
151 F6 **Ulithi** *atoll* Micronesia
140 E2 **Ul'kayak** *r.* Kazakh.
141 H4 **Ul'ken Sulutor** Kazakh.
125 I5 **Ulladulla** Australia
174 C3 **Ullapool** U.K.
171 M3 **Ullava** Fin.
172 E3 **Ullswater** *l.* U.K.
151 F5 **Ullŭng-do** *i.* S. Korea
176 D6 **Ulm** Germany
125 J2 **Ulmarra** Australia
179 E4 **Ulmen** Germany
123 B5 **Uloowaranie, Lake** *salt flat* Australia
171 K4 **Ulricehamn** Sweden
179 E1 **Ulrum** Neth.
160 E6 **Ulsan** S. Korea
171 J3 **Ulsberg** Norway
175 K3 **Ulster Canal** Ireland/U.K.
125 E5 **Ultima** Australia
225 G5 **Ulúa** *r.* Hond.
138 B1 **Ulubat Gölü** *l.* Turkey
136 C3 **Ulubey** Turkey
138 C2 **Uluborlu** Turkey
138 B1 **Uludağ** *mt.* Turkey
162 B5 **Ulu Kali, Gunung** *mt.* Malaysia
202 G2 **Ulukhaktok** Canada
138 E3 **Ulukışla** Turkey
197 I4 **Ulundi** S. Africa
150 A2 **Ulungur Hu** *l.* China
153 J1 **Ulunkhan** Rus. Fed.
162 □ **Ulu Pandan** Sing.
118 D4 **Uluru** *h.* Australia
121 E5 **Uluru-Kata Tjuta National Park** Australia
Uluru National Park *nat. park* Australia *see* **Uluru-Kata Tjuta National Park**
138 D1 **Ulus** Turkey
174 B4 **Ulva** *i.* U.K.
178 C3 **Ulvenhout** Neth.
172 D3 **Ulverston** U.K.
125 G8 **Ulverstone** Australia
171 K3 **Ulvsjön** Sweden
Ul'yanovo Uzbek. *see* **Dashtobod**
187 I4 **Ul'yanovsk** Rus. Fed.
187 H4 **Ul'yanovskaya Oblast'** *admin. div.* Rus. Fed.
141 H2 **Ul'yanovskiy** Kazakh.
217 C4 **Ulysses** U.S.A.
141 F2 **Ulytau** Kazakh.
141 F3 **Ulytau, Gory** *mts* Kazakh.
156 D2 **Umaltinskiy** Rus. Fed.
225 G3 **Umán** Mex.
187 D5 **Uman'** Ukr.
143 G4 **Umarao** Pak.
149 E5 **Umaria** India
148 D6 **Umarkhed** India
147 I2 **Umarkot** India
148 B4 **Umarkot** Pak.
123 B5 **Umaroona, Lake** *salt flat* Australia
212 C2 **Umatilla** U.S.A.
132 E3 **Umba** Rus. Fed.
221 H2 **Umbagog Lake** U.S.A.
121 F5 **Umbeara** Australia
119 E2 **Umboi** *i.* P.N.G.
171 M3 **Umeå** Sweden
170 L2 **Umeälven** *r.* Sweden
197 I4 **Umfolozi** *r.* S. Africa
205 K4 **Umfreville Lake** Canada
139 K7 **Umgharah** Kuwait
Umhlanga S. Africa *see* **Umhlanga Rocks**
197 I4 **Umhlanga Rocks** S. Africa
203 N3 **Umiiviip Kangertiva** *inlet* Greenland
203 H3 **Umingmaktok** Canada
206 E2 **Umiujaq** Canada
197 I5 **Umkomaas** S. Africa
197 I4 **Umlazi** S. Africa
139 J6 **Umma** *tourist site* Iraq
142 D5 **Umm al Qaywayn** U.A.E.
137 F6 **Umm at Qalbān** Saudi Arabia
142 C5 **Umm Bāb** Qatar
193 E3 **Umm Keddada** Sudan
139 K6 **Umm Qaṣr** Iraq
136 D6 **Umm Quṣūr** *i.* Saudi Arabia
193 F3 **Umm Ruwaba** Sudan
193 E1 **Umm Sa'ad** Libya
142 C5 **Umm Sa'id** Qatar
213 A3 **Umpqua** *r.* U.S.A.
195 B5 **Umpulo** Angola
148 D5 **Umred** India
148 C5 **Umreth** India
197 H5 **Umtata** S. Africa
197 I5 **Umtentweni** S. Africa
192 C4 **Umuahia** Nigeria
234 B3 **Umuarama** Brazil
197 H5 **Umzimkulu** S. Africa
197 I5 **Umzinto** S. Africa
185 G2 **Una** *r.* Bos.-Herz./Croatia
234 E1 **Una** Brazil
139 F6 **'Unāb, Wādī al** *watercourse* Jordan
234 C2 **Unaí** Brazil
202 B3 **Unalakleet** U.S.A.
174 C2 **Unapool** U.K.
233 K2 **Unare** *r.* Venez.
138 E6 **'Unayzah** Jordan
146 B4 **'Unayzah** Saudi Arabia
139 G5 **'Unayzah, Jabal** *h.* Iraq
213 E4 **Uncompahgre Plateau** U.S.A.
122 D3 **Undara National Park** Australia
197 H4 **Underberg** S. Africa
124 D5 **Underbool** Australia
216 C2 **Underwood** U.S.A.
187 E4 **Unecha** Rus. Fed.
125 G4 **Ungarie** Australia
124 B5 **Ungarra** Australia
207 F1 **Ungava, Péninsule d'** *pen.* Canada
207 G2 **Ungava Bay** Canada
187 C6 **Ungheni** Moldova
140 E5 **Unguz, Solonchakovyye Vpadiny** *salt flat* Turkm.
140 D4 **Üngüz Angyrsyndaky Garagum** *des.* Turkm.
186 I3 **Uni** Rus. Fed.
235 B4 **União da Vitória** Brazil
233 I4 **Unilla** *r.* Col.
231 F4 **Unini** *r.* Brazil
235 A4 **Unión** Para.
221 I2 **Union** *ME* U.S.A.
219 D5 **Union** *SC* U.S.A.
220 C6 **Union** *WV* U.S.A.
215 F4 **Union, Mount** U.S.A.
209 E5 **Union City** *OH* U.S.A.
220 D4 **Union City** *PA* U.S.A.
219 B4 **Union City** *TN* U.S.A.
197 E6 **Uniondale** S. Africa
219 C5 **Union Springs** U.S.A.
220 D5 **Uniontown** U.S.A.
209 F4 **Unionville** U.S.A.
142 D6 **United Arab Emirates** *country* Asia
132 E3 **United Kingdom** *country* Europe
210 D4 **United States of America** *country* N. America
205 H4 **Unity** Canada
221 I2 **Unity** *ME* U.S.A.
212 C2 **Unity** *OR* U.S.A.
148 C5 **Unjha** India
179 F3 **Unna** Germany
149 E4 **Unnao** India
160 C4 **Ŭnp'a** N. Korea
160 C3 **Unsan** N. Korea
160 D4 **Ŭnsan** N. Korea
174 □ **Unst** *i.* U.K.
179 J3 **Unstrut** *r.* Germany
149 G2 **Unuli Horog** China
157 C6 **Unzen-dake** *vol.* Japan
147 J1 **Upar Ghat** *reg.* India
233 L2 **Upata** Venez.
195 C4 **Upemba, Lac** *l.* Dem. Rep. Congo
195 C4 **Upemba, Parc National de l'** *nat. park* Dem. Rep. Congo
161 J5 **Upi** Phil.
233 I3 **Upía** *r.* Col.
196 D4 **Upington** S. Africa
148 B5 **Upleta** India
170 O2 **Upoloksha** Rus. Fed.
119 I3 **'Upolu** *i.* Samoa
213 B3 **Upper Alkali Lake** U.S.A.
220 B4 **Upper Arlington** U.S.A.
204 F4 **Upper Arrow Lake** Canada
126 E4 **Upper Hutt** N.Z.
208 B4 **Upper Iowa** *r.* U.S.A.
221 J1 **Upper Kent** Canada
213 B3 **Upper Klamath Lake** U.S.A.
214 A2 **Upper Lake** U.S.A.
204 D2 **Upper Liard** Canada
175 K3 **Upper Lough Erne** *l.* U.K.
221 E5 **Upper Marlboro** U.S.A.
162 □ **Upper Peirce Reservoir** Sing.
207 I4 **Upper Salmon Reservoir** Canada
220 B4 **Upper Sandusky** U.S.A.
221 F2 **Upper Saranac Lake** U.S.A.
126 D4 **Upper Takaka** N.Z.
171 L4 **Uppsala** Sweden
206 B4 **Upsala** Canada
221 H2 **Upton** U.S.A.
139 K7 **'Uqlat al 'Udhaybah** *well* Iraq
139 K6 **Ur** *tourist site* Iraq
233 H2 **Urabá, Golfo de** *b.* Col.
143 E4 **Ūrāf** Iran
158 H3 **Urakawa** Japan
125 G4 **Ural** *h.* Australia
140 B3 **Ural** *r.* Kazakh./Rus. Fed.
125 I3 **Uralla** Australia
132 G4 **Ural Mountains** Rus. Fed.
140 B2 **Ural'sk** Kazakh.
Ural'skiy Khrebet *mts* Rus. Fed. *see* **Ural Mountains**
195 D4 **Urambo** Tanz.
125 G5 **Urana** Australia
125 G5 **Urana, Lake** Australia
123 B4 **Urandangi** Australia
234 D1 **Urandi** Brazil
205 H3 **Uranium City** Canada
125 G5 **Uranquinty** Australia
233 L4 **Uraricoera** Brazil
233 L4 **Uraricoera** *r.* Brazil
233 L4 **Uraricoera** *r.* Brazil
233 L3 **Uraucaima, Serra** *mt.* Brazil
215 H2 **Uravan** U.S.A.
157 E6 **Urawa** Japan
142 B5 **'Urayq ad Duḥūl** *des.* Saudi Arabia
187 F5 **Urazovo** Rus. Fed.
208 C5 **Urbana** *IL* U.S.A.
220 B4 **Urbana** *OH* U.S.A.
125 J2 **Urbenville** Australia
184 E3 **Urbino** Italy
230 D6 **Urcos** Peru
140 A2 **Urda** Kazakh.
186 I2 **Urdoma** Rus. Fed.
141 J3 **Urdzhar** Kazakh.
172 F3 **Ure** *r.* U.K.
137 F2 **Ureki** Georgia
186 H3 **Uren'** Rus. Fed.
132 I3 **Urengoy** Rus. Fed.
119 G3 **Uréparapara** *i.* Vanuatu
126 F3 **Urewera National Park** N.Z.
187 H4 **Urga** *r.* Rus. Fed.
156 D2 **Urgal** *r.* Rus. Fed.
140 E4 **Urganch** Uzbek.
Urgench Uzbek. *see* **Urganch**
138 E2 **Ürgüp** Turkey
141 F5 **Urgut** Uzbek.
144 G2 **Urho** China
170 N1 **Urho Kekkosen kansallispuisto** *nat. park* Fin.
233 I2 **Uribia** Col.
156 C2 **Uril** Rus. Fed.
125 E2 **Urisino** Australia
171 M3 **Urjala** Fin.
178 D2 **Urk** Neth.
156 B1 **Urkan** Rus. Fed.
156 B1 **Urkan** *r.* Rus. Fed.
187 H7 **Urkarakh** Rus. Fed.
185 L5 **Urla** Turkey
175 K5 **Urlingford** Ireland
153 I1 **Urluk** Rus. Fed.
141 G5 **Urmetan** Tajik.
142 B2 **Urmia** Iran
142 B2 **Urmia, Lake** *salt l.* Iran
155 □ **Urmston Road** *sea chan.* Hong Kong China
141 G5 **Ŭroteppa** Tajik.
149 F3 **Urru Co** *salt l.* China
Urt Mongolia *see* **Gurvantes**
144 H4 **Urt Moron** China
224 B2 **Uruáchic** Mex.
234 C1 **Uruaçu** Brazil
225 D4 **Uruapan** Mex.
230 D6 **Urubamba** *r.* Peru
231 G4 **Urucara** Brazil
231 J5 **Uruçuí** Brazil
234 D2 **Urucuia** *r.* Brazil
231 J5 **Uruçui Preto** *r.* Brazil
231 G4 **Urucurituba** Brazil
232 E3 **Uruguaiana** Brazil
232 E4 **Uruguay** *r.* Arg./Uruguay
235 L2 **Uruguay** *country* S. America
156 B2 **Uruhe** China
150 A2 **Ürümqi** China
125 J3 **Urunga** Australia
187 G6 **Urup** *r.* Rus. Fed.
150 H2 **Urup, Ostrov** *i.* Rus. Fed.
156 A1 **Urusha** Rus. Fed.
187 H7 **Urus-Martan** Rus. Fed.
141 K2 **Uryl'** Kazakh.
153 L1 **Uryupino** Rus. Fed.
187 G5 **Uryupinsk** Rus. Fed.
186 I3 **Urzhum** Rus. Fed.
185 L2 **Urziceni** Romania
159 B8 **Usa** Japan
169 R2 **Usa** *r.* Rus. Fed.
187 I4 **Usa** *r.* Rus. Fed.
138 B2 **Uşak** Turkey
195 B6 **Usakos** Namibia
127 I6 **Usarp Mountains** Antarctica
232 E8 **Usborne, Mount** *h.* Falkland Is
132 I1 **Ushakova, Ostrov** *i.* Rus. Fed.
141 J2 **Ushanovo** Kazakh.
141 G4 **Usharal** Kazakh.
152 G1 **Ush-Bel'dyr** Rus. Fed.
159 B8 **Ushibuka** Japan
141 I3 **Ushtobe** Kazakh.
232 C8 **Ushuaia** Arg.
156 B1 **Ushumun** Rus. Fed.
179 G4 **Usingen** Germany
132 G3 **Usinsk** Rus. Fed.

V

Vpadina Chagyllyshor

Vpadina Chagyllyshor *depr.* Turkm. *see* Chagyllyshor, Vpadina
158 C3 Vrangel' Rus. Fed.
156 E1 Vrangelya, Mys *pt* Rus. Fed.
Vrangelya, Ostrov *i.* Rus. Fed. *see* Wrangel Island
185 I3 Vranje Serbia
185 L3 Vratnik *pass* Bulg.
185 J3 Vratsa Bulg.
185 G2 Vrbas *r.* Bos.-Herz.
185 H2 Vrbas Serbia
197 H3 Vrede S. Africa
197 G3 Vredefort S. Africa
196 B6 Vredenburg S. Africa
196 C5 Vredendal S. Africa
178 C5 Vresse Belgium
147 H4 Vriddhachalam India
179 E1 Vries Neth.
171 K4 Vrigstad Sweden
185 I2 Vršac Serbia
197 F3 Vryburg S. Africa
197 I3 Vryheid S. Africa
186 D2 Vsevolozhsk Rus. Fed.
185 H2 Vukovar Croatia
132 G3 Vuktyl' Rus. Fed.
197 H3 Vukuzakhe S. Africa
184 F5 Vulcano, Isola *i. Isole Lipari* Italy
215 F5 Vulture Mountains U.S.A.
162 C3 Vung Tau Vietnam
171 N3 Vuohijärvi Fin.
170 N2 Vuolijoki Fin.
170 M2 Vuollerim Sweden
170 N2 Vuostimo Fin.
187 H4 Vurnary Rus. Fed.
185 I3 Vushtrri Kosovo
140 E1 Vvedenka Kazakh.
156 C2 Vvedenovka Rus. Fed.
195 D4 Vwawa Tanz.
148 C5 Vyara India
Vyatka Rus. Fed. *see* Kirov
186 I3 Vyatka *r.* Rus. Fed.
169 Q4 Vyatskiye Polyany Rus. Fed.
156 D3 Vyazemskiy Rus. Fed.
187 E4 Vyaz'ma Rus. Fed.
186 G3 Vyazniki Rus. Fed.
187 H5 Vyazovka *Astrakhanskaya Oblast'* Rus. Fed.
140 A1 Vyazovka *Saratovskaya Oblast'* Rus. Fed.
186 D2 Vyborg Rus. Fed.
186 I2 Vychegda *r.* Rus. Fed.
186 H2 Vychegodskiy Rus. Fed.
187 C4 Vyerkhnyadzvinsk Belarus
187 D4 Vyetryna Belarus
186 E2 Vygozero, Ozero *l.* Rus. Fed.
187 G4 Vyksa Rus. Fed.
187 D6 Vylkove Ukr.
169 Q3 Vym' *r.* Rus. Fed.
177 K6 Vynohradiv Ukr.
186 E3 Vypolzovo Rus. Fed.
186 D3 Vyritsa Rus. Fed.
173 D5 Vyrnwy, Lake U.K.
187 F6 Vyselki Rus. Fed.
187 G4 Vysha Rus. Fed.
187 D5 Vyshhorod Ukr.
186 E3 Vyshnevolotskaya Gryada *ridge* Rus. Fed.
186 E3 Vyshniy-Volochek Rus. Fed.
177 H6 Vyškov Czech Rep.
156 E2 Vysokogorniy Rus. Fed.
187 D5 Vystupovychi Ukr.
186 F2 Vytegra Rus. Fed.

W

192 B3 Wa Ghana
178 D3 Waal *r.* Neth.
178 D3 Waalwijk Neth.
206 B3 Wabakimi Lake Canada
205 G3 Wabasca *r.* Canada
205 G3 Wabasca-Desmarais Canada
209 E5 Wabash U.S.A.
209 E5 Wabash *r.* U.S.A.
208 A3 Wabasha U.S.A.
209 E1 Wabatongushi Lake Canada
205 J4 Wabowden Canada
206 C2 Wabuk Point Canada
207 G3 Wabush Canada
207 G3 Wabush Lake Canada
214 C2 Wabuska U.S.A.
219 D6 Waccasassa Bay U.S.A.
179 H4 Wächtersbach Germany
217 D6 Waco U.S.A.
143 G5 Wad Pak.
125 H6 Wadbilliga National Park Australia
193 D2 Waddān Libya
215 F5 Waddell Dam U.S.A.
178 C2 Waddenzee *sea chan.* Neth.
124 B4 Waddikee Australia
204 D4 Waddington, Mount Canada
178 C2 Waddinxveen Neth.
173 C7 Wadebridge U.K.
205 I4 Wadena Canada
216 E2 Wadena U.S.A.
179 E5 Wadern Germany
120 E2 Wadeye Australia
147 G2 Wadgaon India
179 E5 Wadgassen Germany
193 F2 Wadi Halfa Sudan
193 F3 Wad Medani Sudan
214 C2 Wadsworth U.S.A.
160 B4 Wafangdian China
179 G2 Wagenfeld Germany
179 I2 Wagenhoff Germany
203 J3 Wager Bay Canada
125 G5 Wagga Wagga Australia
148 C2 Wah Pak.
214 □[1] Wahiawā U.S.A.
179 H3 Wahlhausen Germany
216 D3 Wahoo U.S.A.
216 D2 Wahpeton U.S.A.
215 F2 Wah Wah Mountains U.S.A.
147 G2 Wai India
214 □[1] Wai'ale'e U.S.A.
214 □[1] Waialua *reg.* U.S.A.
214 □[1] Waialua Bay U.S.A.
214 □[1] Wai'anae U.S.A.
Waianae Ra. *mts* U.S.A. *see* Wai'anae Range
214 □[1] Wai'anae Range *mts* U.S.A.
126 D5 Waiau *r.* N.Z.
176 G7 Waidhofen an der Ybbs Austria
151 F7 Waigeo *i.* Indon.
126 E2 Waiharoa N.Z.
126 E2 Waiheke Island N.Z.
126 E2 Waihi N.Z.
126 E2 Waihou *r.* N.Z.
151 D7 Waikabubak Indon.
126 B6 Waikaia *r.* N.Z.
214 □[1] Waikāne U.S.A.
126 D5 Waikari N.Z.
126 E2 Waikato *r.* N.Z.
126 F2 Waikawa Point N.Z.
124 C5 Waikerie Australia
214 □[1] Waikīkī Beach U.S.A.
126 C6 Waikouaiti N.Z.
214 □[2] Wailuku U.S.A.
126 D5 Waimakariri *r.* N.Z.
214 □[1] Waimānalo U.S.A.
126 C4 Waimangaroa N.Z.
126 F3 Waimarama N.Z.
126 C6 Waimate N.Z.
214 □[2] Waimea *HI* U.S.A.
214 □[1] Waimea *HI* U.S.A.
148 D5 Wainganga *r.* India
151 E7 Waingapu Indon.
173 C7 Wainhouse Corner U.K.
205 G4 Wainwright Canada
202 C2 Wainwright U.S.A.
126 E3 Waiouru N.Z.
126 E3 Waipa *r.* N.Z.
126 B7 Waipahi N.Z.
214 □[1] Waipahu U.S.A.
126 F3 Waipaoa *r.* N.Z.
126 B7 Waipapa Point N.Z.
126 D5 Waipara N.Z.
126 F3 Waipawa N.Z.
126 F3 Waipukurau N.Z.
126 F3 Wairakei N.Z.
126 E4 Wairarapa, Lake N.Z.
126 D4 Wairau *r.* N.Z.
126 F3 Wairoa N.Z.
126 F3 Wairoa *r. Hawke's Bay* N.Z.
126 E1 Wairoa *r. Northland* N.Z.
126 F3 Waitahanui N.Z.
126 B6 Waitahuna N.Z.
126 E2 Waitakaruru N.Z.
126 C6 Waitaki *r.* N.Z.
126 E3 Waitara N.Z.
121 F4 Waite River Australia
126 E2 Waitoa N.Z.
126 E2 Waiuku N.Z.
126 B7 Waiwera South N.Z.
155 F5 Waiyang China
159 E6 Wajima Japan
194 E3 Wajir Kenya
159 D7 Wakasa-wan *b.* Japan
126 B6 Wakatipu, Lake N.Z.
205 H4 Wakaw Canada
159 D7 Wakayama Japan
217 D4 WaKeeney U.S.A.
209 J3 Wakefield Canada
126 D4 Wakefield N.Z.
173 F4 Wakefield U.K.
208 C2 Wakefield *MI* U.S.A.
221 H4 Wakefield *RI* U.S.A.
221 E6 Wakefield *VA* U.S.A.
Wakeham Canada *see* Kangiqsujuaq
117 F2 Wake Island *terr.* N. Pacific Ocean
141 H5 Wakhan *reg.* Afgh.
158 G4 Wakinosawa Japan
158 G3 Wakkanai Japan
197 I3 Wakkerstroom S. Africa
125 F5 Wakool Australia
125 E5 Wakool *r.* Australia
207 G2 Wakuach, Lac *l.* Canada
177 H5 Wałbrzych Poland
125 I3 Walcha Australia
176 E7 Walchensee *l.* Germany
178 C4 Walcourt Belgium
177 H4 Wałcz Poland
121 B5 Waldburg Range *mts* Australia
221 F4 Walden U.S.A.
176 F6 Waldkraiburg Germany
173 C7 Waldon *r.* U.K.
221 E5 Waldorf U.S.A.
121 B6 Walebing Australia
173 D5 Wales *admin. div.* U.K.
125 H3 Walgett Australia
195 C4 Walikale Dem. Rep. Congo
122 A2 Walker *r.* Australia
121 F5 Walker *watercourse* Australia
208 B4 Walker *IA* U.S.A.
216 E2 Walker *MN* U.S.A.
214 C2 Walker *r.* U.S.A.
196 C7 Walker Bay S. Africa
219 E7 Walker Cay *i.* Bahamas
122 C3 Walker Creek *r.* Australia
214 C2 Walker Lake U.S.A.
214 C4 Walker Pass U.S.A.
209 G3 Walkerton Canada
216 C2 Wall U.S.A.
121 B4 Wall, Mount *h.* Australia
122 C2 Wallaby Island Australia
212 C2 Wallace U.S.A.
209 F4 Wallaceburg Canada
120 C3 Wallal Downs Australia
125 I2 Wallangarra Australia
124 B4 Wallaroo Australia
173 D4 Wallasey U.K.
125 G5 Walla Walla Australia
212 C2 Walla Walla U.S.A.
179 H5 Walldürn Germany
196 B5 Wallekraal S. Africa
125 H5 Wallendbeen Australia
221 F4 Wallenpaupack, Lake U.S.A.
173 F6 Wallingford U.K.
221 G4 Wallingford U.S.A.
119 I3 Wallis, Îles *is* Pacific Ocean
119 I3 Wallis and Futuna Islands *terr.* Pacific Ocean
125 J4 Wallis Lake *inlet* Australia
221 F6 Wallops Island U.S.A.
212 C2 Wallowa Mountains U.S.A.
174 □ Walls U.K.
123 E5 Wallumbilla Australia
205 H2 Walmsley Lake Canada
172 D3 Walney, Isle of *i.* U.K.
208 C5 Walnut U.S.A.
215 G4 Walnut Canyon National Monument *nat. park* U.S.A.
217 F4 Walnut Ridge U.S.A.
149 I3 Walong India
173 F5 Walsall U.K.
213 F4 Walsenburg U.S.A.
179 H2 Walsrode Germany
147 I2 Waltair India
219 D5 Walterboro U.S.A.
219 C6 Walter F. George Reservoir U.S.A.
125 F2 Walter's Range *hills* Australia
209 I3 Waltham Canada
219 C4 Walton *KY* U.S.A.
221 F3 Walton *NY* U.S.A.
195 B6 Walvis Bay Namibia
239 I8 Walvis Ridge *sea feature* S. Atlantic Ocean
194 C3 Wamba Dem. Rep. Congo
148 B2 Wana Pak.
125 F2 Wanaaring Australia
126 B6 Wanaka N.Z.
126 B6 Wanaka, Lake N.Z.
155 E5 Wan'an China
209 G2 Wanapitei Lake Canada
221 F4 Wanaque Reservoir U.S.A.
124 D5 Wanbi Australia
126 C6 Wanbrow, Cape N.Z.
124 D2 Wancoocha, Lake *salt flat* Australia
158 C2 Wanda Shan *mts* China
179 I4 Wandersleben Germany
179 L2 Wandlitz Germany
160 D6 Wando S. Korea
123 E5 Wandoan Australia
162 A1 Wang, Mae Nam *r.* Thai.
126 E3 Wanganui N.Z.
126 E3 Wanganui *r.* N.Z.
125 G6 Wangaratta Australia
124 A5 Wangary Australia
154 C3 Wangcang China
155 D4 Wangcheng China
Wangda China *see* Zogang
179 F1 Wangerooge Germany
179 F1 Wangerooge *i.* Germany
120 C1 Wanggamet, Gunung *mt.* Indon.
160 A3 Wanghai Shan *h.* China
155 E4 Wangjiang China
156 B3 Wangkui China
155 C5 Wangmo China
160 E2 Wangqing China
152 G7 Wan Hsa-la Myanmar
148 B5 Wankaner India
194 E3 Wanlaweyn Somalia
179 G1 Wanna Germany
121 E6 Wanna Lakes *salt flat* Australia
155 F4 Wannian China
155 D7 Wanning China
154 E1 Wanquan China
178 D3 Wanroij Neth.
155 D6 Wanshan Qundao *is* China
126 F4 Wanstead N.Z.
173 F6 Wantage U.K.
209 G2 Wanup Canada
155 C4 Wanxian China
154 C3 Wanyuan China
155 E4 Wanzai China
178 D4 Wanze Belgium
220 A4 Wapakoneta U.S.A.
208 B5 Wapello U.S.A.
206 C3 Wapikopa Lake Canada
204 F4 Wapiti *r.* Canada
217 F4 Wappapello Lake *resr* U.S.A.
208 A5 Wapsipinicon *r.* U.S.A.
154 B3 Waqên China
142 C6 Waqr *well* Saudi Arabia
148 A4 Warah Pak.
147 H2 Warangal India
125 F6 Waranga Reservoir Australia
149 E5 Waraseoni India
125 F8 Waratah Australia
125 F7 Waratah Bay Australia
123 C5 Warbreccan Australia
179 H3 Warburg Germany
118 C4 Warburton Australia
124 B1 Warburton *watercourse* Australia
205 G2 Warburton Bay Canada
126 A6 Ward, Mount *Southland* N.Z.
126 B5 Ward, Mount *West Coast* N.Z.
124 B5 Wardang Island Australia
197 H3 Warden S. Africa
179 G1 Wardenburg Germany
148 D5 Wardha India
148 D6 Wardha *r.* India
204 D3 Ware Canada
221 G3 Ware U.S.A.
173 E7 Wareham U.K.
221 H4 Wareham U.S.A.
178 D4 Waremme Belgium
179 K1 Waren Germany
179 F3 Warendorf Germany
123 E4 Warginburra Peninsula Australia
125 I2 Warialda Australia
179 J1 Warin Germany
162 C2 Warin Chamrap Thai.
126 E2 Warkworth N.Z.
172 F2 Warkworth U.K.
178 A4 Warloy-Baillon France
205 H4 Warman Canada
196 C4 Warmbad Namibia
197 H2 Warmbad S. Africa
Warming Island *i.* Greenland *see* Uunartoq Qeqertoq
173 E6 Warminster U.K.
221 F4 Warminster U.S.A.
178 C2 Warmond Neth.
215 D2 Warm Springs *NV* U.S.A.
220 D5 Warm Springs *VA* U.S.A.
196 D6 Warmwaterberg *mts* S. Africa
221 H3 Warner U.S.A.
213 B3 Warner Mountains U.S.A.
219 D5 Warner Robins U.S.A.
231 F7 Warnes Bol.
125 J2 Warning, Mount Australia
148 D5 Warora India
125 I1 Warra Australia
125 E6 Warracknabeal Australia
125 I5 Warragamba Reservoir Australia
125 F7 Warragul Australia
124 C2 Warrakalanna, Lake *salt flat* Australia
124 A4 Warramboo Australia
125 G2 Warrambool *r.* Australia
123 B5 Warrandirinna, Lake *salt flat* Australia
121 C4 Warrawagine Australia
119 E4 Warrego *r.* Australia
123 D5 Warrego Range *hills* Australia
125 G3 Warren Australia
209 G2 Warren Canada
217 E5 Warren *AR* U.S.A.
209 F4 Warren *MI* U.S.A.
216 D1 Warren *MN* U.S.A.
220 C4 Warren *OH* U.S.A.
220 D4 Warren *PA* U.S.A.
220 C4 Warrendale U.S.A.
175 L3 Warrenpoint U.K.
217 E4 Warrensburg *MO* U.S.A.
221 G3 Warrensburg *NY* U.S.A.
197 F4 Warrenton S. Africa
221 E5 Warrenton U.S.A.
192 C4 Warri Nigeria
126 C6 Warrington N.Z.
173 E4 Warrington U.K.
219 C6 Warrington U.S.A.
124 C3 Warriota *watercourse* Australia
125 E7 Warrnambool Australia
216 E1 Warroad U.S.A.
124 A5 Warrow Australia
123 E6 Warrumbungle National Park Australia
125 H3 Warrumbungle Range *mts* Australia
124 D2 Warry Warry *watercourse* Australia
177 J4 Warsaw Poland
209 E5 Warsaw *IN* U.S.A.
217 E4 Warsaw *MO* U.S.A.
220 D3 Warsaw *NY* U.S.A.
221 E6 Warsaw *VA* U.S.A.
179 G3 Warstein Germany
Warszawa Poland *see* Warsaw
176 G4 Warta *r.* Poland
179 I4 Wartburg, Schloss *tourist site* Germany
125 J2 Warwick Australia
173 F5 Warwick U.K.
221 F4 Warwick *NY* U.S.A.
221 H4 Warwick *RI* U.S.A.
213 E4 Wasatch Range *mts* U.S.A.
197 I4 Wasbank S. Africa
214 C4 Wasco U.S.A.
216 E2 Waseca U.S.A.
143 F5 Washap Pak.
208 C5 Washburn *IL* U.S.A.
221 I1 Washburn *ME* U.S.A.
216 C2 Washburn *ND* U.S.A.
208 B2 Washburn *WI* U.S.A.
148 D5 Washim India
221 E5 Washington *DC* U.S.A. (City Plan 103)
219 D5 Washington *GA* U.S.A.
208 B5 Washington *IA* U.S.A.
208 C5 Washington *IL* U.S.A.
219 C4 Washington *IN* U.S.A.
217 F4 Washington *MO* U.S.A.
219 E5 Washington *NC* U.S.A.
221 F4 Washington *NJ* U.S.A.
220 C4 Washington *PA* U.S.A.
215 F3 Washington *UT* U.S.A.
212 B2 Washington *state* U.S.A.
127 I5 Washington, Cape Antarctica
221 H2 Washington, Mount U.S.A.
220 B5 Washington Court House U.S.A.
208 D3 Washington Island U.S.A.
203 L1 Washington Land *reg.* Greenland
217 D5 Washita *r.* U.S.A.
123 F6 Washpool National Park Australia
143 G5 Washuk Pak.
142 B5 Wasī' Saudi Arabia
139 K5 Wasit *tourist site* Iraq
206 E3 Waskaganish Canada
205 J3 Waskaiowaka Lake Canada
224 H5 Waspán Nicaragua
178 C2 Wassenaar Neth.
196 C3 Wasser Namibia
179 H4 Wasserkuppe *h.* Germany
179 I5 Wassertrüdingen Germany
214 C2 Wassuk Range *mts* U.S.A.
206 E4 Waswanipi, Lac *l.* Canada
151 E7 Watampone Indon.
121 E5 Watarrka National Park Australia
221 G4 Waterbury *CT* U.S.A.
221 G2 Waterbury *VT* U.S.A.
205 H3 Waterbury Lake Canada
175 K5 Waterford Ireland
220 D4 Waterford U.S.A.
175 L5 Waterford Harbour Ireland
175 J5 Watergrasshill Ireland
120 E3 Waterloo Australia
178 C4 Waterloo Belgium
209 G4 Waterloo Canada
208 A4 Waterloo *IA* U.S.A.
221 H3 Waterloo *ME* U.S.A.
221 E3 Waterloo *NY* U.S.A.
208 C4 Waterloo *WI* U.S.A.
173 F7 Waterlooville U.K.
197 H1 Waterpoort S. Africa
208 C2 Watersmeet U.S.A.
205 G5 Waterton Lakes National Park Canada
221 E3 Watertown *NY* U.S.A.
216 D2 Watertown *SD* U.S.A.
208 C4 Watertown *WI* U.S.A.
197 I2 Waterval Boven S. Africa
124 C4 Watervale Australia
221 I2 Waterville U.S.A.
205 G3 Waterways Canada
209 G4 Watford Canada
173 G6 Watford U.K.
216 C2 Watford City U.S.A.
205 I3 Wathaman *r.* Canada
121 A6 Watheroo National Park Australia
179 I2 Wathlingen Germany
221 E3 Watkins Glen U.S.A.
217 D5 Watonga U.S.A.
205 H4 Watrous Canada
194 C3 Watsa Dem. Rep. Congo
208 D5 Watseka U.S.A.
195 C4 Watsi Kengo Dem. Rep. Congo
122 C2 Watson *r.* Australia
205 I4 Watson Canada
204 D2 Watson Lake Canada
214 B3 Watsonville U.S.A.
174 E2 Watten U.K.
174 E2 Watten, Loch *l.* U.K.
205 I2 Watterson Lake Canada
124 A2 Wattiwarriganna *watercourse* Australia
173 H5 Watton U.K.
208 C2 Watton U.S.A.
118 D2 Watubela, Kepulauan *is* Indon.
119 E2 Wau P.N.G.
193 E4 Wau Sudan
208 D3 Waucedah U.S.A.
121 F4 Wauchope Australia
125 J3 Wauchope Australia
219 D7 Wauchula U.S.A.
121 C4 Waukarlycarly, Lake *salt flat* Australia
208 D4 Waukegan U.S.A.
208 C4 Waukesha U.S.A.
208 B4 Waukon U.S.A.
208 C3 Waupaca U.S.A.
208 C4 Waupun U.S.A.
217 D5 Waurika U.S.A.
208 C3 Wausau U.S.A.
220 A4 Wauseon U.S.A.
208 C3 Wautoma U.S.A.
208 C4 Wauwatosa U.S.A.
120 E3 Wave Hill Australia
173 I5 Waveney *r.* U.K.
208 A4 Waverly *IA* U.S.A.
220 B5 Waverly *OH* U.S.A.
219 C4 Waverly *TN* U.S.A.
221 E6 Waverly *VA* U.S.A.
178 C4 Wavre Belgium
209 E1 Wawa Canada
192 C4 Wawa Nigeria
209 E5 Wawasee, Lake U.S.A.
214 C3 Wawona U.S.A.
217 D5 Waxahachie U.S.A.
144 G4 Waxxari China
121 C5 Way, Lake *salt flat* Australia
219 D6 Waycross U.S.A.
220 B6 Wayland *KY* U.S.A.
208 B5 Wayland *MO* U.S.A.
216 D3 Wayne U.S.A.
219 D5 Waynesboro *GA* U.S.A.
217 F6 Waynesboro *MS* U.S.A.
221 E5 Waynesboro *PA* U.S.A.
220 D5 Waynesboro *VA* U.S.A.
220 C5 Waynesburg U.S.A.
217 E4 Waynesville U.S.A.
217 D4 Waynoka U.S.A.

151 B4 Ye-U Myanmar
182 C3 Yeu, Île d' i. France
139 K1 Yevlax Azer.
187 E6 Yevpatoriya Ukr.
156 D2 Yevreyskaya Avtonomnaya Oblast' admin. div. Rus. Fed.
154 D3 Yexian China
187 F6 Yeya r. Rus. Fed.
149 E1 Yeyik China
187 F6 Yeysk Rus. Fed.
144 G3 Yeyungou China
186 H1 Yezhuga r. Rus. Fed.
187 D4 Yezyaryshcha Belarus
235 L2 Yí r. Uruguay
156 B3 Yi'an China
Yianisádha i. Greece see Gianisada
155 B4 Yibin China
149 F2 Yibug Caka salt l. China
155 D4 Yichang Hubei China
155 D4 Yicheng Hubei China
154 D3 Yicheng Shanxi China
154 D3 Yichuan China
150 E2 Yichun Heilong. China
155 E5 Yichun Jiangxi China
155 E4 Yifeng China
154 D3 Yi He r. Henan China
154 D3 Yi He r. Shandong China
155 E5 Yihuang China
154 C3 Yijun China
156 B2 Yilaha China
158 A1 Yilan China
Yilan Taiwan see Ilan
185 L4 Yıldız Dağları mts Turkey
139 F2 Yıldızeli Turkey
156 A2 Yilehuli Shan mts China
155 B5 Yiliang Yunnan China
155 B5 Yiliang Yunnan China
155 D4 Yiling Hubei China
156 B3 Yilong China
155 C4 Yilong China
155 B6 Yilong Hu l. China
155 B5 Yimen China
160 C1 Yimianpo China
154 F3 Yinan China
154 C2 Yinchuan China
121 C6 Yindarlgooda, Lake salt flat Australia
160 C2 Yingchengzi China
155 D5 Yingde China
155 C7 Yinggehai China
154 E3 Ying He r. China
160 B3 Yingkou China
154 B2 Yingpanshui China
155 E4 Yingshan Hubei China
155 C4 Yingshan Sichuan China
154 E3 Yingshang China
155 E4 Yingtan China
154 D2 Yingxian China
141 J4 Yining China
155 C5 Yinjiang China
149 H5 Yinmabin Myanmar
160 C1 Yinma He r. China
154 C1 Yin Shan mts China
149 H3 Yi'ong Zangbo r. China
155 A5 Yipinglang China
194 D3 Yirga Alem Eth.
154 F2 Yi Shan mt. China
154 F3 Yishui China
162 □ Yishun Sing.
160 C2 Yitong China
160 C1 Yitong He r. China
153 L1 Yitulihe China
150 B2 Yiwu China
160 A3 Yiwulü Shan mts China
155 E4 Yixian Anhui China
160 A3 Yixian Liaoning China
155 F4 Yixing China
155 D4 Yiyang Hunan China
155 E5 Yiyang Jiangxi China
155 D5 Yizhang China
155 C5 Yizhou China
171 M3 Yläne Fin.
171 M3 Ylihärmä Fin.
170 N2 Yli-Ii Fin.
170 N2 Yli-Kärppä Fin.
170 N2 Ylikiiminki Fin.
170 O2 Yli-Kitka l. Fin.
171 M3 Ylistaro Fin.
170 M2 Ylitornio Fin.
170 N2 Ylivieska Fin.
171 M3 Ylöjärvi Fin.
141 G2 Yntaly Kazakh.
217 D6 Yoakum U.S.A.
158 G3 Yobetsu-dake vol. Japan
163 H4 Yogyakarta Indon.
204 F4 Yoho National Park Canada
160 D5 Yŏju S. Korea
193 D4 Yokadouma Cameroon
159 E7 Yokkaichi Japan
193 D4 Yoko Cameroon

159 F7 Yokohama Japan
159 F7 Yokosuka Japan
159 G5 Yokote Japan
158 G4 Yokotsu-dake mt. Japan
193 D4 Yola Nigeria
140 E5 Yŏlöten Turkm.
225 E4 Yoloxóchitl Mex.
162 B2 Yom, Mae Nam r. Thai.
192 B4 Yomou Guinea
160 D5 Yŏnan N. Korea
159 G6 Yonezawa Japan
124 C4 Yongala Australia
160 D6 Yŏng-am S. Korea
155 E5 Yong'an China
154 A2 Yongchang China
160 E6 Yŏngch'ŏn S. Korea
155 F5 Yongchun China
154 B2 Yongdeng China
155 E5 Yongding China
154 E2 Yongding He r. China
155 E5 Yŏngdŏk S. Korea
160 E5 Yongfeng China
155 C5 Yongfu China
160 D6 Yŏnggwang S. Korea
149 H3 Yonggyap pass India
160 D4 Yŏnghŭng N. Korea
160 D4 Yŏnghŭng-man b. N. Korea
160 D2 Yongji China
155 F4 Yongjia China
154 B3 Yongjing China
154 D2 Yongjin Qu r. China
160 E5 Yŏngju S. Korea
152 G7 Yongkang China
155 F4 Yongkang China
160 C3 Yongling China
154 E2 Yongnian China
155 C6 Yongning China
155 A5 Yongren China
160 E5 Yŏngsan-gang r. S. Korea
160 D6 Yŏngsanp'o S. Korea
155 C4 Yongshun China
155 F5 Yongtai China
160 E5 Yŏngwol S. Korea
155 D5 Yongxing Hunan China
155 E5 Yongxing Jiangxi China
155 E4 Yongxiu China
155 D5 Yongzhou China
160 D3 Yŏnhwa-san mt. N. Korea
221 G4 Yonkers U.S.A.
182 F2 Yonne r. France
233 I3 Yopal Col.
141 I5 Yopurga China
118 B5 York Australia
173 F4 York U.K.
216 D3 York NE U.S.A.
221 E5 York PA U.S.A.
219 D5 York SC U.S.A.
119 E3 York, Cape Australia
172 F3 York, Vale of val. U.K.
124 B5 Yorke Peninsula Australia
124 B5 Yorketown Australia
172 E3 Yorkshire Dales National Park U.K.
173 G4 Yorkshire Wolds hills U.K.
205 I4 Yorkton Canada
221 E6 Yorktown U.S.A.
224 H5 Yoro Hond.
192 B3 Yorosso Mali
214 C3 Yosemite National Park U.S.A.
214 C3 Yosemite Village U.S.A.
159 C8 Yoshino-gawa r. Japan
159 D7 Yoshino-Kumano Kokuritsu-kōen nat. park Japan
186 H3 Yoshkar-Ola Rus. Fed.
160 D6 Yŏsu S. Korea
138 E7 Yotvata Israel
175 K6 Youghal Ireland
220 D5 Youghiogheny River Lake U.S.A.
155 C6 Yu Jiang r. China
125 H5 Young Australia
235 L2 Young Uruguay
124 B3 Younghusband, Lake salt flat Australia
124 C5 Younghusband Peninsula Australia
127 I6 Young Island Antarctica
220 C4 Youngstown U.S.A.
192 B3 Youvarou Mali
155 F5 Youxi China
155 C4 Youxian China
155 C4 Youyang China
158 B1 Youyi China
144 G2 Youyi Feng mt. China/Rus. Fed.
141 G5 Yovon Tajik.
125 F1 Yowah watercourse Australia

138 E2 Yozgat Turkey
234 A3 Ypané r. Para.
234 A3 Ypé-Jhú Para.
Ypres Belgium see Ieper
213 B3 Yreka U.S.A.
Yr Wyddfa mt. U.K. see Snowdon
178 A4 Yser r. France
178 D3 Ysselsteyn Neth.
171 K5 Ystad Sweden
173 D5 Ystwyth r. U.K.
Ysyk-Köl Kyrg. see Balykchy
141 I4 Ysyk-Köl salt l. Kyrg.
175 F3 Ythan r. U.K.
133 O3 Ytyk-Kyuyel' Rus. Fed.
162 A1 Yuam, Nam Mae r. Myanmar/Thai.
155 D4 Yuan'an China
155 D4 Yuanbao Shan mt. China
155 D4 Yuanjiang Hunan China
155 A6 Yuanjiang Yunnan China
155 D4 Yuan Jiang r. Hunan China
155 B6 Yuan Jiang r. Yunnan China
155 F5 Yüanli Taiwan
155 D4 Yuanling China
155 A5 Yuanmou China
154 D2 Yuanping China
154 D3 Yuanqu China
136 D6 Yub'ä i. Saudi Arabia
214 B2 Yuba City U.S.A.
158 G3 Yūbari Japan
155 G4 Yubei China
225 G3 Yucatán pen. Mex.
225 G3 Yucatán state Mex.
223 G4 Yucatan Channel Cuba/Mex.
215 E5 Yucca U.S.A.
215 D3 Yucca Lake U.S.A.
215 C4 Yucca Valley U.S.A.
154 E2 Yucheng China
156 A1 Yudi Shan mt. China
133 O4 Yudoma r. Rus. Fed.
155 C4 Yudu China
155 C4 Yuechi China
156 A3 Yueliang Pao l. China
118 D4 Yuendumu Australia
155 □ Yuen Long Hong Kong China
155 F4 Yueqing China
155 E4 Yuexi Anhui China
155 B4 Yuexi Sichuan China
155 D4 Yueyang China
155 E4 Yugan China
132 H3 Yugorsk Rus. Fed.
186 J2 Yugydtydor Rus. Fed.
Yuhu China see Eryuan
155 F4 Yuhuan China
154 E2 Yuhuang Ding mt. China
121 B5 Yuin Australia
155 E4 Yujiang China
155 D6 Yu Jiang r. China
133 Q3 Yukagirskoye Ploskogor'ye plat. Rus. Fed.
136 C3 Yukarı Sakarya Ovaları plain Turkey
138 E2 Yukarısarıkaya Turkey
195 B4 Yuki Dem. Rep. Congo
202 C3 Yukon r. Canada/U.S.A.
204 B2 Yukon Territory admin. div. Canada
139 J3 Yüksekova Turkey
121 E5 Yulara Australia
140 D1 Yuldybayevo Rus. Fed.
121 B4 Yule r. Australia
219 D5 Yulee U.S.A.
155 F6 Yüli Taiwan
155 D6 Yulin Guangxi China
155 C7 Yulin Hainan China
154 C2 Yulin Shaanxi China
153 H6 Yulong Xueshan mt. China
215 E5 Yuma U.S.A.
215 E5 Yuma Desert U.S.A.
233 H4 Yumbo Col.
150 B3 Yumen China
144 H3 Yumenguan China
141 J3 Yumin China
138 E2 Yumurtalık Turkey
121 A6 Yuna Australia
138 C2 Yunak Turkey
155 D6 Yunan China
154 E3 Yuncheng Shandong China
154 D3 Yuncheng Shanxi China
121 C6 Yundamindera Australia
155 D6 Yunfu China
155 B5 Yungui Gaoyuan plat. China
155 F4 Yunhe China
155 D6 Yunkai Dashan mts China
155 D5 Yunmeng China
155 A5 Yunnan prov. China
155 D6 Yun Shui r. China
124 C5 Yunta Australia
155 D6 Yunwu Shan mts China

154 D3 Yunxi China
154 D3 Yunxian China
154 E6 Yunxiao China
155 C4 Yunyang Henan China
155 C4 Yunyang Sichuan China
155 C5 Yuping China
155 C5 Yuqian China
154 E1 Yuqiao Shuiku resr China
155 C5 Yuqing China
125 J2 Yuraygir National Park Australia
150 A1 Yurga Rus. Fed.
230 C5 Yurimaguas Peru
233 L3 Yuruán r. Venez.
233 L3 Yuruari r. Venez.
233 J2 Yurubi, Parque Nacional nat. park Venez.
149 E1 Yurungkax He r. China
186 I3 Yur'ya Rus. Fed.
186 G3 Yur'yevets Rus. Fed.
186 F3 Yur'yev-Pol'skiy Rus. Fed.
224 H5 Yuscarán Hond.
155 F4 Yushan China
155 F5 Yü Shan mt. Taiwan
154 D2 Yushe China
186 E1 Yushkozero Rus. Fed.
160 D1 Yushu Jilin China
150 B3 Yushu Qinghai China
186 I3 Yushut r. Rus. Fed.
187 H6 Yusta Rus. Fed.
139 H1 Yusufeli Turkey
169 Q4 Yus'va Rus. Fed.
154 E1 Yutai China
149 E1 Yutian China
154 C2 Yuwang China
155 B5 Yuxi China
154 E2 Yuxian Hebei China
154 D2 Yuxian Shanxi China
155 F4 Yuyao China
159 G5 Yuzawa Japan
186 G3 Yuzha Rus. Fed.
156 F3 Yuzhno-Kamyshovyy Khrebet ridge Rus. Fed.
156 F3 Yuzhno-Kuril'sk Rus. Fed.
150 D1 Yuzhno-Muyskiy Khrebet mts Rus. Fed.
150 G2 Yuzhno-Sakhalinsk Rus. Fed.
187 H6 Yuzhno-Sukhokumsk Rus. Fed.
187 D6 Yuzhnoukrayins'k Ukr.
187 G6 Yuzhnyy Rus. Fed.
141 G4 Yuzhnyy Kazakhstan admin. div. Kazakh.
140 D1 Yuzhnyy Ural mts Rus. Fed.
154 B3 Yuzhong China
154 D3 Yuzhou China
155 D4 Yuzuduk Uzbek. see Yuzquduq
140 E4 Yuzquduq Uzbek.
176 C7 Yverdon Switz.
182 E2 Yvetot France
162 A1 Ywathit Myanmar
162 A1 Ylanly Turkm. see Gurbansoltan Eje

Z

Zaamin Uzbek. see Zomin
178 C2 Zaandam Neth.
139 I3 Zāb al Kabīr, Nahr az r. Iraq
139 I4 Zāb aş Şaghīr, Nahr az r. Iraq
150 D2 Zabaykal'sk Rus. Fed.
142 B2 Zab-e Kuchek r. Iran
146 B7 Zabīd Yemen
143 F4 Zābol Iran
143 F5 Zābolī Iran
140 B3 Zaburun'ye Kazakh.
225 G5 Zacapa Guat.
225 D4 Zacapu Mex.
225 D3 Zacatecas Mex.
225 D3 Zacatecas state Mex.
225 E4 Zacatlán Mex.
140 B2 Zachagansk Kazakh.
185 I6 Zacharo Greece
184 F2 Zadar Croatia
162 A3 Zadetkale Kyun i. Myanmar
162 A3 Zadetkyi Kyun i. Myanmar
149 H2 Zadoi China
155 D6 Zadonsk Rus. Fed.
139 K4 Ẓafarābād Iran
Za'farâna Egypt see Za'farānah
136 D5 Za'farānah Egypt
183 M3 Zafra Spain
143 E3 Zaghdeh well Iran
139 L5 Zāgheh Iran

184 D6 Zaghouan Tunisia
184 F2 Zagreb Croatia
Zagros, Kūhhā-ye mts Iran see Zagros Mountains
142 B3 Zagros Mountains Iran
149 G3 Za'gya Zangbo r. China
143 F4 Zāhedān Iran
143 H3 Zahidabad Afgh.
138 E5 Zahlé Lebanon
140 E5 Zähmet Turkm.
143 G4 Zahri Nur Gama Pak.
Zair Uzbek. see Zoir
Zaïre country Africa see Congo, Democratic Republic of the
185 J3 Zaječar Serbia
153 H1 Zakamensk Rus. Fed.
Zakhmet Turkm. see Zähmet
139 I3 Zākhō Iraq
Zakhodnyaya Dzvina r. Europe see Zapadnaya Dvina
193 D3 Zakouma, Parc National de nat. park Chad
185 I6 Zakynthos Greece
185 I6 Zakynthos i. Greece
177 H7 Zalaegerszeg Hungary
177 H7 Zalai-domsag hills Hungary
183 N3 Zalamea de la Serena Spain
156 A3 Zalantun China
153 H1 Zalari Rus. Fed.
177 K7 Zalău Romania
186 F3 Zales'ye Rus. Fed.
193 E3 Zalingei Sudan
177 L6 Zalishchyky Ukr.
186 D3 Zaluch'ye Rus. Fed.
138 E2 Zamanti r. Turkey
161 I3 Zambales Mountains Phil.
195 C5 Zambeze r. Angola alt. Zambezi
195 D5 Zambezi r. Africa alt. Zambeze (Angola)
195 C5 Zambezi Zambia
195 C5 Zambia country Africa
161 I5 Zamboanga Phil.
161 I5 Zamboanga Peninsula Phil.
143 F4 Zamīndāvar reg. Afgh.
230 C4 Zamora Ecuador
183 N2 Zamora Spain
225 D4 Zamora de Hidalgo Mex.
177 K5 Zamość Poland
154 A3 Zamtang China
233 J2 Zamuro, Punta pt Venez.
233 L3 Zamuro, Sierra del mts Venez.
148 D3 Zanda China
197 K2 Zandamela Moz.
178 C3 Zandvliet Belgium
220 C5 Zanesville U.S.A.
141 I5 Zangguy China
148 D2 Zangla India
142 C2 Zanjān Iran
139 K3 Zanjān Rūd r. Iran
148 D2 Zanskar r. India
148 D2 Zanskar Mountains India
Zante i. Greece see Zakynthos
121 C6 Zanthus Australia
195 D4 Zanzibar Tanz.
195 D4 Zanzibar Island Tanz.
155 D4 Zaoshi China
192 C2 Zaouatallaz Alg.
155 D4 Zaoyang China
150 B1 Zaozernyy Rus. Fed.
154 E3 Zaozhuang China
193 I3 Zap r. Turkey
186 E3 Zapadnaya Dvina Rus. Fed.
187 D4 Zapadnaya Dvina r. Rus. Fed. alt. Daugava (Belarus/Latvia), alt. Zakhodnyaya Dzvina, conv. Western Dvina
185 J4 Zapadni Rodopi mts Bulg.
156 F2 Zapadno-Sakhalinskiy Khrebet mts Rus. Fed.
Zapadno-Sibirskaya Ravnina Rus. Fed. see West Siberian Plain
141 H4 Zapadnyy Alamedin, Pik mt. Kyrg.
140 C3 Zapadnyy Chink Ustyurta esc. Kazakh.
140 C4 Zapadnyy Chink Ustyurta esc. Kazakh.
140 B2 Zapadnyy Kazakhstan admin. div. Kazakh.
170 P1 Zapadnyy Kil'din Rus. Fed.
135 G1 Zapadnyy Sayan reg. Rus. Fed.
235 H3 Zapala Arg.

217 D7 Zapata U.S.A.
233 I3 Zapatoca Col.
233 I2 Zapatoza, Ciénaga de l. Col.
170 O1 Zapolyarnyy Rus. Fed.
187 E6 Zaporizhzhya Ukr.
149 E2 Zapug China
139 K1 Zaqatala Azer.
149 H2 Zaqên China
149 H2 Za Qu r. China
139 F2 Zara Turkey
Zarafshan Uzbek. see Zarafshon
141 G5 Zarafshon Tajik.
141 F4 Zarafshon Uzbek.
141 F5 Zarafshon r. Uzbek.
141 F5 Zarafshon, Qatorkŭhi mts Tajik.
233 I3 Zaragoza Col.
213 F6 Zaragoza Chihuahua Mex.
225 D1 Zaragoza Coahuila Mex.
183 P2 Zaragoza Spain
143 E4 Zarand Iran
138 E6 Zaranikh Reserve nature res. Egypt
143 F4 Zaranj Afgh.
171 N5 Zarasai Lith.
235 K2 Zárate Arg.
233 K2 Zaraza Venez.
Zarbdar Uzbek. see Zarbdor
141 G4 Zarbdor Uzbek.
139 K1 Zärdab Azer.
170 O2 Zarechensk Rus. Fed.
139 L4 Zāreh Iran
204 C3 Zarembo Island U.S.A.
148 A3 Zargun mt. Pak.
192 C3 Zaria Nigeria
187 C5 Zarichne Ukr.
142 B2 Zarīneh Rūd r. Iran
143 F3 Zarmardan Afgh.
139 K5 Zarneh Iran
185 K2 Zărneşti Romania
142 D4 Zarqān Iran
142 D3 Zarrīn Iran
158 B3 Zarubino Rus. Fed.
176 G5 Żary Poland
140 D2 Zarya Oktyabrya Kazakh.
233 H3 Zarzal Col.
193 D1 Zarzis Tunisia
170 O2 Zasheyek Rus. Fed.
Zaskar r. India see Zanskar
Zaskar Mountains India see Zanskar Mountains
187 C4 Zaslawye Belarus
197 G5 Zastron S. Africa
179 K2 Zauche reg. Germany
Zaunguzskiye Karakumy des. Turkm. see Üngüz Angyrsyndaky Garagum
142 D3 Zavareh Iran
156 F2 Zavety Il'icha Rus. Fed.
185 H2 Zavidovići Bos.-Herz.
150 E1 Zavitinsk Rus. Fed.
141 K1 Zavodskoy Rus. Fed.
141 J1 Zav'yalovo Rus. Fed.
154 A2 Zawa China
177 I5 Zawiercie Poland
141 K3 Zaysan Kazakh.
141 J2 Zaysan, Lake Kazakh.
Zayü China see Gyigang
176 G6 Žďár nad Sázavou Czech Rep.
187 C5 Zdolbuniv Ukr.
171 J5 Zealand i. Denmark
139 J3 Zēbār Iraq
197 H2 Zebediela S. Africa
178 B3 Zedelgem Belgium
178 B3 Zeebrugge Belgium
125 F8 Zeehan Australia
197 G2 Zeerust S. Africa
178 B3 Zeeuwsch-Vlaanderen reg. Neth.
138 E5 Zefat Israel
179 L2 Zehdenick Germany
118 D4 Zeil, Mount Australia
179 I4 Zeil am Main Germany
178 D2 Zeist Neth.
179 K3 Zeitz Germany
154 A3 Zêkog China
141 H1 Zelenaya Roshcha Kazakh.
170 P2 Zelenoborskiy Rus. Fed.
187 I4 Zelenodol'sk Rus. Fed.
171 O3 Zelenogorsk Rus. Fed.
186 F3 Zelenograd Rus. Fed.
187 B4 Zelenogradsk Rus. Fed.
187 G6 Zelenokumsk Rus. Fed.
186 H3 Zelentsovo Rus. Fed.
157 G4 Zelenyy, Ostrov i. Rus. Fed.
141 G2 Zelenyy Gay Kazakh.
176 F7 Zell am See Austria
179 H5 Zellingen Germany

Acknowledgements

Atlas of the World

Maps, design and origination by Collins Geo, HarperCollins Reference, Glasgow

Illustrations created by HarperCollins Publishers unless otherwise stated.

6–17
Blue Marble: Next Generation. NASA's Earth Observatory
18–19
NRSC/Science Photo Library and Blue Marble: Next Generation.
NASA's Earth Observatory
20–21
MODIS/NASA
22–23
Earthquake data: United States Geological Survey (USGS) National
Earthquakes Information Center, Denver, USA
Sumatra: IKONOS image © CRISP 2004
Mount Bromo: Michael Pitts/naturepl.com
24–25
Maryland: Image courtesy Lawrence Ong, EO-1 Mission Science
Office, NASA GSFC
Cyclone Nargis: MODIS/NASA
26–27
Climate Change 2007: Impacts, Adaptation and Vulnerability, Summary
for Policymakers. Intergovernmental Panel on Climate Change (IPCC)
McCarty Glacier. top: NSIDC/Ulysses S. Grant; bottom: NSIDC/
Bruce F. Molina
Male: Shahee Ilyas
28–29
Land cover map: Center for Remote Sensing,
Boston University, USA
Living Planet Index: WWF and ZSL, 2006 Living Planet
Report 2006
Protected Area of the World: UNEP-WCMC and World Database on
Protected Areas for terrestrial ecoregions as identified by the World
Wide Fund for Nature (WWF). www.unep-wcmc.org/wdpa
Sea Around Us Project (L. Wood, 2007), University of British
Columbia Fisheries Centre, in collaboration with UNEP-WCMC and
WWF, for large marine ecosystems. www.mpaglobal.org
Hamoun Wetlands. left: NASA Earth Observatory; right: Image
courtesy of UNEP

30–31
Population statistics: UN Department of Economic and Social Affairs
Population Division
Population map: 2005. Gridded Population of the World Version 3
(GPWv3).Palisades, NY: Socioeconomic Data and Applications Center
(SEDAC), Columbia University.
Available at: http://sedac.ciesin.columbia.edu/gpw
http://www.ciesin.columbia.edu
Hong Kong: Justin Guariglia/Getty Images
32–33
USGS EROS DATA CENTER
34–35
Edgar Cleijne/Still Pictures
36–37
David Vaughan/Science Photo Library
Internet capacity and telecommunications traffic
© Telegeography Research
38–39
Lake Eyre: MODIS/NASA
New Guinea: NASA/Goddard Space Flight Center/USGS
Borneo: NASA/Goddard Space Flight Center/USGS
Mt Everest: Alison Wright/CORBIS
Volga: CNES, 1996 Distribution SPOT Image/Science
Photo Library
Caspian Sea: MODIS/NASA
Madagascar: MODIS/NASA
Kilimanjaro: Tony Stone Images Ltd
40–41
Mississippi: ASTER/NASA
Greenland: MODIS/NASA
Mt McKinley: Tony Stone Images Ltd
Lake Titicaca: NASA
Cerro Aconcagua: Andes Press Agency
Amazon: MODIS/NASA
Vinson Massif: B. Storey/British Antarctic Survey
42–43
Top 50 Tourist Attractions: Reprinted by Permission of
Forbes Media LLC © 2010

Images on pages **44 to 220** supplied by www.shutterstock.com
unless noted with an asterisk.
All photographs credited unless unknown.

44 iofoto
45 A. Vogler
46 sunxuejun
47 Dmitry Rukhlenko
48 Zoran Karapancev
49 govicinity
50 Brian K.
51 javarman
52 gary718
53 Peter Dankov
54 gary yim
55 Johnathan Esper
56 (i) lexan; (ii) OPIS; (iii) Andrzej Gibasiewicz
57 (iv) ostill; (v)* Mark Steward; (vi) Wiktor Bubniak; (vii) enote;
(viii) Mariusz S. Jurgielewicz; (ix) John A. Anderson;
(x)* Africa Conservation Fund/www.gorilla.cd
60 Pete Niesen
61 pandeqiang
64–65 Mikhail Nekrasov
66 Jason Maehl
67 dibrova
72–73 Markus Gann
74 Marek Slusarczyk
75 Michael Avory
78–79 Vladimir Wrangel
82–83* Keith Moore
84 Kenneth V. Pilon
85 Katrina Leigh
88 javarman
89 urosr
90 Jarno Gonzalez Zarraonandia
110* Great Barrier Reef: Provided by the SeaWiFS Project,
NASA/Goddard Space Flight Center, and OrbImage
Kamchatka Peninsula: NASA/MODIS
Desert Oasis: Jose Fuste Raga/CORBIS
Great Plains: Robert Holmes/CORBIS
112* Joseph Sohm/Visions of America/CORBIS
122 Holger Mette
124 Neale Cousland
154 claudio zaccherini
156 Craig Hanson
204 Matt Ragen
206 Elena Elisseeva
212* Keith Moore
214 Bryan Busovicki
216 Mount Rushmore: iofoto; Alamo: BenC
218 Ariel Bravy
220 gracious_tiger

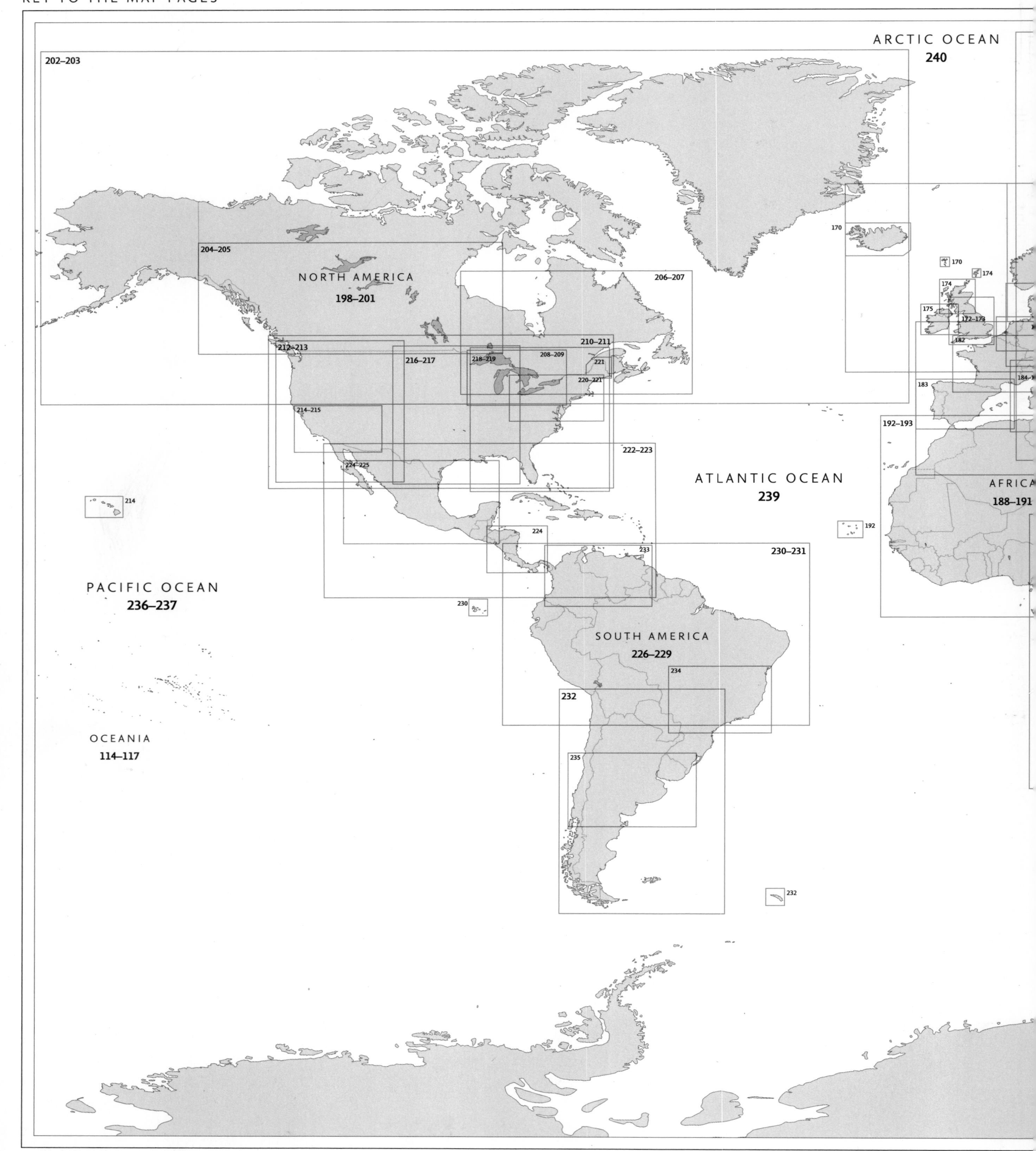

ARCTIC OCEAN
240

202–203

204–205

NORTH AMERICA
198–201

206–207

170

170

174
174

175

172–173

182

183

212–213

216–217

210–211

208–209

218–219

221

220–221

184–

214–215

192–193

222–223

AFRICA
188–191

224–225

214

224

233

230–231

PACIFIC OCEAN
236–237

ATLANTIC OCEAN
239

192

230

SOUTH AMERICA
226–229

234

OCEANIA
114–117

232

235

232